FAMILY STUDIES
Review Yearbook

The most comprehensive survey of the family studies field to date, **Family Studies Review Yearbook** is designed to offer an annual selection of the best and most relevant published and unpublished works. A distinguished Board of Editors ensures that articles communicate timely theoretical, empirical, and practical advances, as well as important insights into major issues. An essential reference for researchers, scholars, practitioners, policymakers, and students concerned with developments in contemporary knowledge of the family.

FAMILY STUDIES
Review Yearbook

Volume 1

1983

**David H. Olson
Brent C. Miller
Editors**

SAGE PUBLICATIONS
Beverly Hills / London / New Delhi

For information address:

SAGE Publications, Inc.
275 South Beverly Drive
Beverly Hills, California 90212

SAGE Publications India Pvt. Ltd.
C-236 Defence Colony
New Delhi 110 024, India

SAGE Publications Ltd
28 Banner Street
London EC1Y 8QE, England

Printed in the United States of America

International Standard Book Number 0-8039-1924-7

International Standard Series Number 0734-2926

FIRST PRINTING

Contents

About the Editors

DAVID H. OLSON, Ph.D., is Professor, Family Social Science, at the University of Minnesota. He is a licensed consulting psychologist and Fellow in the American Association of Marriage and Family Therapists (AAMFT). He is Associate Editor or on the Advisory Board of the *Journal of Marriage and the Family, Family Process, International Journal of Family Therapy, Journal of Marriage and Family Therapy, Family Therapy Quarterly, American Journal of Family Therapy,* and *Family System Medicine.* His books include *Treating Relationships, Power in Families,* and five volumes of the *Inventory of Marriage and Family Literature.*

BRENT C. MILLER, Ph.D., is Associate Professor, Family and Human Development, at Utah State University. He currently chairs the Research and Theory Section and is a member of the Board of Directors of the National Council on Family Relations. He is Associate Editor of the *Journal of Marriage and the Family* and *Family Relations,* and is a guest reviewer for *Family Process, Social Psychology Quarterly,* and *Demography.* He has recently co-authored *Marriage and Family Development* (6th edition) with Evelyn Duvall.

Preface

Sampling the best the family field has produced in the last couple of years is like going to a first-class smorgasbord. To stimulate one's intellectual appetite, there is a feast of tantalizing topics and a rich variety of enticing articles. The 53 articles included in Volume I of the *Family Studies Review Yearbook* provide a well-balanced picture of ten important topic areas in the family field.

In this first volume we have highlighted applied topics that are timely and relevant. The articles selected are not only salient, but they also provide useful theoretical and empirical integration and insights. In addition, they are illustrative of the systematic and innovative approaches that have been used to investigate these topical areas.

We anticipated that the process of selecting the topics and the articles for this introductory volume would be very difficult and demanding. However, the process was made much easier by the excellent work of the Editorial Board. First of all, we were very pleased that such a distinguished group of colleagues was willing to join the Editorial Board and to take time to select articles for this volume. They made the process still easier by completing their selections on a very tight schedule. It also helped that there was such a high level of agreement between them on the specific articles they recommended. Often the same article was selected by all three reviewers in a given content area.

Not only was the process made easier than we anticipated, but the outcome has also exceeded our expectations. Our thanks therefore go to the scholars who have chosen the family field as one worthy of study. Most importantly, they are the individuals ultimately responsible for the high quality of the articles included in this volume.

We wish to thank our department heads and secretarial staff at both the University of Minnesota and Utah State University for their cooperative spirit. We also greatly appreciate the understanding and support provided by our partners and families.

D.H.O. & B.C.M.

INTRODUCTION AND OVERVIEW

David H. Olson and Brent C. Miller

In this first volume of the *Family Studies Review Yearbook*, we have included what can be considered the *crème de la crème* of the family field. These 53 articles were selected from a potential group of over 5000 published and unpublished manuscripts. Selections were made by 29 experts in specialized areas of the family profession who served on the Editorial Board of the Yearbook. The peer review process greatly facilitated the selection of such high-quality articles.

We think that the articles included are on the cutting edge of the field both conceptually and empirically and that they will also serve as benchmarks of the field for years to come. Criteria for selecting the articles were content excellence, relevance to the content area, and significance to the field.

The ten topic areas selected in Volume I are among the most visible, applied, and sometimes controversial issues facing marriages and families today. The ten topic areas include the following: *family policy, family stress and coping, divorce and child custody, marital and family violence, alcoholism and drug abuse, work and the family, family economics, marital enrichment* and *premarital preparation, marital therapy,* and *family therapy.* Future volumes will provide reviews of other content areas, with each volume providing a variety of timely and significant topics.

The broad, multidisciplinary scope of the volume is also demonstrated by the fact that the 53 articles were selected from 18 professional journals. The journals represent not only the traditional family journals, but also those in applied speciality areas and from a range of other disciplines. A complete listing of the journals from which articles were taken is provided in Table 1.

PART I: FAMILY POLICY

Policymakers, scholars, and the average citizen all have in common a great interest in the relationships between families and public policies. During the Carter administration, an Office of Families was created amid controversy about government involvement in family life. In 1980, the White House Conferences on Families were held for the first time to try and better understand the needs of

TABLE 1   Sources of Articles for Yearbook, Volume I

Source of Article	Number of Articles
1. American Journal of Drug and Alcohol Abuse	2
2. American Journal of Family Therapy	3
3. Annals of the American Academy of Political and Social Science	1
4. Behavior Therapy	2
5. Family Economics Review	1
6. Family Process	5
7. Family Relations	10
8. Journal of Agricultural Economics	1
9. Journal of Applied Behavior Analysis	1
10. Journal of Consulting and Clinical Psychology	1
11. Journal of Divorce	2
12. Journal of Family Issues	1
13. Journal of Human Resources	1
14. Journal of Marital and Family Therapy	7
15. Journal of Marriage and the Family	7
16. Marriage and Family Review	1
17. Monthly Labor Review	2
18. Policy Studies Journal	1
19. Unpublished Articles	1
20. Book Chapters	3
Total Articles	53

families and how they are affected by government. Increasingly, "family" has come to be recognized on Capitol Hill as a volatile issue loaded with potential misunderstandings. What are the effects of public policies on family dynamics and well-being? Does a given policy or proposed legislation enhance or undermine the integrity of marriage or the family? In the past few years, marriage and family professionals have become increasingly involved in raising and addressing these questions.

Family Impact Analysis (FIA) is a specific tool for assessing how public policies impact on various aspects of marriage and family life. Recognizing that policymakers and program planners frequently fail to examine carefully both intended an unintended consequences of their programs and services, Marcia Ory and Robert Leik describe a six-step framework for developing and implementing Family Impact Analysis. The technique they describe is a very general one that could be useful in the assessment of a variety of policies and programs and their consequences for families.

The Federal Income Tax Reforms of 1981 will affect the tax liability of two-earner couples beginning in 1982 and 1983. As increasing numbers of married women enter the labor force, the significance of the so-called "marriage penalty" tax becomes more problematic. The background of family-related tax issues is described by Colien Hefferan, focusing on how marriage penalty taxes for dual-earner couples evolved and how 1981 tax reforms will reduce the differences between two-earner married couples and two single taxpayers filing as individuals. Marriage neutrality in income taxation will be more nearly achieved, although tax liability is still influenced by marital status in some cases.

Some investigators studying the marital and family consequences of welfare payments have reported that public assistance contributes to marital instability. Thomas Draper's article reviews recent evidence in this area and more thoroughly analyzes national longitudinal data bearing on this issue. Draper's research suggests that public assistance programs (AFDC, food stamps, and so forth) do not influence marital stability in any substantial way.

Based on data from the Denver and Seattle Income maintenance Experiments, Groeneveld, Tuma, and Hannan also address the issue of marital dissolution in relation to government income maintenance programs. Their findings show that marital dissolution rates are higher for couples in the experimental negative income tax programs than for control couples. Higher marital dissolution in the negative income tax programs was most clearly evident among whites and blacks (not Chicanos), and the least generous plans were most clearly related to marital dissolution.

PART II: FAMILY STRESS AND COPING

The study of family stress has a long-standing history, dating back to studies of families encountering the Great Depression and war separation and reunion. Early efforts at delineating types of stressors and family responses to these events have continued to play an important role in guiding thought and research in this area. However, in recent years significant advances have been made in understanding family adaptation and capacities for coping with stressors that emerge inside and outside the family unit.

The Double ABCX model developed by Hamilton McCubbin and Joan Patterson is an extension of Hill's seminal efforts to conceptualize family stress. In addition to the stressor event, the family resources for dealing with it, and the family's definition of the event before the crisis occurs, McCubbin and Patterson find that assessing postcrisis variables makes an important contribution to understanding family adaptation. They demonstrate the added value of assessing pile-up, coping, and member-to-family adaptation among 217 families as they cope over time with a child diagnosed as having cerebral palsy.

Normative stress that arises when family boundaries change with the addition and departure of family members is described by Pauline Boss. The perception of a family's boundaries (that is, who is perceived as inside and outside the family system) affects not only the interaction in the family but also between the family and the outside world. Family members are gained and lost not only through the social and biological events that have always been considered normative or inevitable (birth, marriage, death, and so on), but also in other increasingly frequent ways (divorce, remarriage, acquisition of children who are not biologically related, prolonged work absence, and so on). Stress can be expected whenever family boundaries become ambiguous through such changes.

The range and variety of family coping strategies and attempts to describe how these strategies are related to fundamental adaptive capacities within families is the focus of David Reiss and Mary Oliveri's article. Carefully controlled laboratory observations reveal that families develop a distinctive family paradigm, reflected by their orienting approach or perspective to problem solving in daily life. Major elements in their family paradigm include configuration, coordination, and closure. These shared beliefs about the social world shape the family's actions, reactions, and interactions.

An overview of the literature about stressors encountered by dual-career families and the strategies they use to deal with stress is provided by Denise Skinner. Internal stressors include overload, identity issues, and role cycling. External stress arises from normative pre- and proscriptions and the occupational structure. Skinner reviews the effects of these stressors on spouses and children and the coping strategies on which dual-career families rely both within and outside the home.

The focus of Voydanoff's article is on family-related stress associated with the corporate executive work role. Corporate work stressors are often chronic, including job insecurity, frequent and/or prolonged work absences from the family, upward mobility aspirations, frequent transfers, and the tendency for a divergence of interests to develop between husband and wife. The role of the corporate wife and typical coping strategies are also described by Voydanoff, along with management approaches for dealing with stress in corporate families.

Prolonged stress in families with mentally retarded children is the focus of the paper by Lynn Wikler. Rather than viewing the diagnosis of retardation as a specific and temporary stressor event to which families routinely adjust, Wikler argues that families with mentally retarded children frequently experience prolonged and recurring stress throughout the child's lifetime. Chronic stress and sorrow are hypothesized by Wikler to be most intense at normative developmental milestones for age mates. These are the times when clinical interventions are most likely to be needed and helpful.

PART III: DIVORCE AND CHILD CUSTODY

Changes in the frequency and acceptability of divorce have resulted in some of the most significant alterations of marriage and family life in this century. Public concern and professional studies have paralleled these remarkable changes. Divorce studies have resulted in a greater awareness of the complexity of the divorce experience, including psychological, social, parental, financial, practical, and other elements. There is also greater awareness of the importance and difficulty of co-parenting after the legal termination of a marriage. The issues surrounding child custody, how custody is decided, and the services for child(ren) and parents are continuing to expand.

A thorough overview of research on the antecedents and consequences of divorce is provided by Gay Kitson and Helen Raschke. Their review is exemplary in its systematic organization, historical awareness, and comprehensive perspective. The authors have synthesized the literature to provide a picture of who divorces, why, and with what consequences.

Jean Goldsmith's study documents the extent of continuing relationships among 129 former spouses who continue to share childrearing. In-depth interviews with former spouses in mother-custody families reveal considerable interaction between ex-spouses and the involvement of both parents in rearing their child(ren). The extent of interaction and involvement calls into question the concept of "single parents" in describing these families who might more accurately be referred to as "co-parents."

William Berman and Dennis Turk's multivariate analyses reveal that both problems and coping strategies need to be considered concurrently to more fully understand postdivorce adjustment. In support of Goldsmith's findings, these authors report that the factor of "former spouse contacts" accounted for the greatest percentage of variance in a checklist of problems and concerns, followed next by parent-child interactions. Nonfamily interpersonal relations and social activities were the coping experiences most strongly related to favorable mood states and life satisfaction following divorce.

Ahrons integrates family stress and system theories and provides a conceptual clarification of five transition points that are identified as normative. Rather than dissolving the family, Ahrons argues that divorce often redefines a nuclear family into a binuclear system. This is because contacts and interactions with former spouses and children are likely to persist along with remarriage and new family experiences. She hypothesizes that developing a stable and supportive binuclear family system can reduce stress and facilitate adjustment of all members.

The legal custody of children in divorce continues to be an area of great concern to everyone involved, and Franklin and Hibbs's article focuses on four major areas of child custody in transition. These include past eras of parental preference (both paternal and maternal), child preference, the right and responsibilities of custodial and noncustodial parents, and joint custody. Child custody laws and practices are evolving toward what is considered to be in the best interests of the children.

PART IV: MARITAL AND FAMILY VIOLENCE

From the beginning of this century through the 1950s, the family was generally viewed as a refuge from violence. Recognition of the battered-child syndrome in the early 1960s and studies of violence in marriage and family life during the 1970s have radically transformed the previous image of domestic tranquility. Widespread child abuse, spouse abuse, and abuse of the elderly have been increasingly documented. Indeed, it has been said that one is more likely to be hit or beaten by a family member than by someone who is not related. This section is devoted to articles that help us understand the incidence, causes, and consequences of violence in marriages and families.

In contrast to the lack of research and attention focused on family violence before the 1970s, the field mushroomed in the 1970s. Richard Gelles provides a comprehensive review of the recent research, documents the extent of family violence of all types, and identifies factors associated with its occurrence. Gelles's article also includes an unusually detailed and thorough analysis of theoretical perspectives and methodological issues in the study of family violence.

Child abuse has been the focus of considerable research in the last decade. Audrey Berger provides two reviews of this topic. Written as companion articles, both reviews take the approach that child abuse is a family problem, not usually an individual pathology. The first article focuses on methodological issues and parental characteristics of abusing families, including their own childhood experiences, marital relations, and perceptions and expectations of their children. The second article reviews characteristics of children and childrearing, environmental conditions, and typologies of child-abusing families. Taken together, Berger's two articles provide a comprehensive picture of child abuse as a complex phenomenon and a specific form of family violence.

One type of training program with demonstrated effectiveness for child-abusing parents who were referred for family therapy by the court is described by Wolfe, Sandler, and Kaufman. The eight-week intervention program designed by the authors included group family training and competency-based training with rehearsal in the home. Posttest results showed that child-abusing parents in the experimental group exhibited increased child management skills, lower problem occurrences, and lower treatment needs. A one-year follow-up indicated no incidents of child abuse, and improvements in family functioning persisted over a year's time. This project indicates one positive approach for ameliorating the violence found in child-abusing families.

Situational or contextual characteristics were often considered to be minor elements related to spouse abuse, but Hornung, McCullough, and Sugimoto present a theoretical rationale and empirical evidence supporting the importance of status relationships in marriage as factors in spouse abuse. Status inconsistency of either partner (in terms of educational and occupational attainment) and status incompatibility between partners are related to increased risk of psychological abuse, greater increased risk of physical aggression, and even greater risk of life-threatening violence. Some types of status inconsistency (underachievement in occupation by husbands) and status incompatibility (wife's higher occupational status) are related to the highest risks of spouse abuse and violence.

Cohabiting couples were studied by Yllo and Straus based on the premise that physical aggression would be lower than in married couples. They reasoned that since cohabitors are not legally bound to remain together, they would separate if violence occurred. However, based on analyses of a national sample, they found that cohabiting couples were considerably more violent than married couples. Certain control variables were found to be very important in the incidence of violence reported in cohabiting couples, with those over 30, previously married, with higher incomes, and having been together longer significantly less likely to report violence.

PART V: ALCOHOLISM, DRUG ABUSE, AND THE FAMILY

Alcoholism and drug abuse are increasingly viewed as a "family affair," with all family members involved in the addiction process. Family-based treatment of chemical dependency is increasingly becoming the treatment of choice. Family-based research is also beginning to answer some basic questions about etiology and the relative effectiveness of various types of treatment programs. To what extent are spouses, children, and parents instrumental in perpetuating substance abuse or its resolution? And how are intergenerational, cultural, and life history effects manifested in the families of alcoholics? These are some of the complex and important questions currently being addressed by scholars and therapists in this field.

Many myths have evolved about family patterns associated with substance abuse and with family therapy as a treatment modality for drug and alcohol patients. Edward Kaufman lists ten myths about family patterns and eleven myths about family therapy as related to substance abuse. These myths are followed by the realities as indicated from research and clinical experience. Kaufman's general position is that family therapy is at least helpful, and perhaps essential, in the treatment of substance abuse.

No critic can be immune from criticism, and Kaufman is no exception. Stanton's critique of Kaufman's myths and realities of family patterns and therapy is generally supportive, but Stanton thinks that several of the realities asserted by Kaufman are overstated or subject to alternative explanations. Taking issue with some of Kaufman's views while supporting others creates the kind of scholarly interchange that will result in clarifying the role of families in causing and treating substance abuse.

Home treatment is a regular pattern that wives attempt with their husbands before professional help is sought. This is a finding that emerged from in-depth interviews with 76 wives of alcoholic husbands by Jacqueline Wiseman. The wife's home treatment usually begins based on the belief that her husband will yield to her logical arguments and quit, or at least drink less. Often wives turn next to emotional pleading, threats, and indirect strategies aimed at reducing the husband's perceived reasons for drinking. Wiseman's position is that such home treatment attempts are doomed to failure and that wives might be spared months and years of stress, pain, and disappointment if they are reached early in the process by educators or counselors.

The cultural and ethnic impacts of alcoholic family systems are carefully documented in a long-term study by Joan Ablon. The study is based on four years of repeated interviews with 30 Catholic wives in Irish-, German-, and Italian-American families. Ablon uses a qualitative methodology and quotes frequently from her sources in developing a holistic perspective that shows a culturally defined set of family roles as a likely culprit in causing problem defined, especially among families with a strong Irish background.

While research on and clinical interest in alcoholic families has been accelerating, a developmental perspective on alcoholism has been almost totally absent. Drawing from the conceptual and research literature in family development, Peter Steinglass offers a life history model for the families of alcoholics. Rather than focusing on family composition and roles, however, the model emphasizes transition points that are likely to reveal chronic alcohol-related family problems. Steinglass suggests that in the alcoholic family, development does not occur in a series of progressive stages. The alcoholic family becomes bogged down by cycling repeatedly between sober and intoxicated states rather than dealing with a stepwise series of normative tasks.

PART VI: WORK AND THE FAMILY

Work and the family are, perhaps, the two most central organizing themes of human life. Yet the dynamic relationship between what one does for a living and one's marriage and family life have been relatively ignored by family specialists and those concerned with the business world alike. There have been dramatic increases in the percentage of married women and mothers who are employed, resulting in what is becoming the normative pattern of dual-earner households. This raises questions about how marital roles are affected by increasing female employment and the responses of employers in considering employees' families.

Setting the stage for this series of articles, Phyllis Moen presents a broad picture of work-family linkages, focusing specifically on the two-provider family. She describes the diversity of two-earner families, from both spouses being invested in high-level careers to one or both spouses being involuntarily employed in a marginal job. Two central aspects of work—money and time—are highlighted as having important implications for family well-being. Conflicts between work and family obligations are more often juggled than resolved. Moen emphasizes that employers have historically viewed employees as individuals, with little regard for their family situations.

How spouses' work roles are related to their marital solidarity was the focus of research by Ida Simpson and Paula England. In contrast to widely held theoretical notions that marriage would be viewed less positively when wives were employed, the authors' analyses of a national sample found just the opposite. Wives' employment is positively related to several indicators of favorable marital qualities as perceived by both husbands and wives. The results of this study are especially noteworthy because of good sample quality, multiple indicators of the variables, and appropriate statistical controls.

Flexible work schedules are being advocated and attempted in a variety of settings. Time allocated to family life as a result of implementing a flexible work schedule in federal agencies is the topic of research by Richard Winett and Michael Neale. Data on how family time was spent were collected by detailed logs completed by employees an average of twice a week for 35 weeks. Those changing their work schedules to arrive at and leave work earlier than the regular schedule spent significantly less time commuting and more evening time with family members. These results suggest some favorable family outcomes of flexitime based on very detailed and reliable microbehavioral analyses.

While farm women have traditionally been dedicated workers, they have seldom been given credit or recognition. Ruth Gasson has not only given the farm wife more visibility but has clarified the diversity and significance of her roles. Based on in-depth interviews with 44 (mostly married) farm women in the south of England, Gasson described three role types that seemed to be most common. Classifications were based on frequency of manual farm labor, responsibility for farm enterprises, division of labor between spouses, and participation in formal organizations. The three major roles of women on farms are "farm housewife," with limited responsibilities and work outside the home; the "working farmwife," who spends part of each day working manually on the farm; and "women farmers," who are engaged in a more complete farming partnership with their husbands or who farm alone because they are single or widowed. Gasson's article helps to illuminate the various tasks that women often do on farms and for which they are only rarely credited.

Children's work in the family is seldom considered of much value or significance. White and Brinkerhoff have made a rare contribution to overcoming this lack of knowledge by asking Nebraska parents about children's work around the house and yard. The data clearly show that children's work is related to age. The percentage of children with household chores and the hours they work increase as they grow older. By 10 years of age, over 90% of boys and girls have regular jobs around the house. About three-quarters of parents say that the reason for giving children work to do is for them to learn responsibility and to develop character. A minority of parents feel that children are obligated to work for the family, and some parents simply say that they need the children to help.

PART VII: FAMILY ECONOMICS

At first glance, this topic and "Work and the Family" seem to be almost synonymous. However, the concerns included under Family Economics are different from those of the family and work. Included in this section are articles dealing with inflation and recession, material well-being, earnings and net worth, budgets, and home and market production. This domain bridges the interests of professionals concerned with economic issues and family life.

How families cope with inflation and recession is described in a major survey of families by David Caplovitz. Surveys were done with 2000 families in four large cities in different regions of the country. The families most adversely affected are the less privileged. Cutting back on consumption was the most common response to inflation across all groups studied, but some families tried to raise family income by working overtime, taking a second job, or having additional family members get jobs. Caplovitz reports that about one-third of those interviewed indicated that the difficult economic times were causing problems in their marriage.

The assessment of family material well-being has been an elusive and confusing process. An innovative approach was developed by Fergusson, Harwood, and Beautrais that separates family economic well-being based on income from family material well-being that refers to the goods, commodities, and services the family actually has access to. The investigators make the case that two distinct kinds of material well-being should be taken into account, namely family ownership and economizing behaviors. The data analyses are based on interviews of over 1000 New Zealand families and clearly show the empirical utility of assessing standard of living through measures of family ownership and consumption.

What does a wife's employment mean in terms of the family's pattern of consumption and savings? Ann Foster's research addresses the question of how net worth accumulation in families where the wife works compares with the net worth of families where the same amount of money is earned by the husband alone. In national employment data, Foster found that the absolute level of family income was more important than its sources in determining net worth accumulation. However, families in which wives earned part of the income had lower net worth accumulation than families at the same income level in which wives earned no income. These differences could be due to increased job-related expenditures, the use of market goods and services in place of home production, or the preference for consumption over savings among families with employed wives. The working wife's income does raise the family income appreciably above what it would be without it, making both improved standard of living or net worth accumulation possible.

The cost-of-living index for various types of families is an important indicator of inflation and payments to families on government programs. Recently, a committee chaired by Harold Watts proposed four budget levels (rather than the current three) and made it applicable to six different types of families. The assessment was based on median expenditures rather than the detailed commodity lists currently used. This recommended methodology for constructing the budgets is a radical departure from previous procedures but yields similar results. The rationale for developing the new standards includes broader coverage of family types and areas, and making the budgets meaningful to a wider range of users.

There are dramatic differences and inconsistencies between the rewards for work at home versus work outside the home. The two economies have different values and reward structures, making movement between them difficult. Historically, the home economy functions have declined in relative terms as women have been drawn into paid employment of the market economy. Brown includes some feminist reflections on how participation in the home economy has subordinated women in society while at the same time providing critically important services such as childrearing. She concludes her essay by suggesting future scenarios of how home and market economics will continue to coexist with unequal status and rewards.

PART VIII: MARITAL ENRICHMENT AND PREMARITAL PREPARATION

The work of professionals active in this area is based on the premise that individuals and relationships have strengths they can build on to improve their relationship. Efforts aimed at marital enrichment have, for the most part, been directed at stable ongoing marriages that can be enhanced or enriched by a systematic program experience. Marital enrichment programs vary from brief intensive weekend retreats and encounters to several-week skill training programs. Premarital preparation sessions are often offered by clergy and are generally not well defined. All of the enrichment programs are in need of more rigorous evaluation research to document their effectiveness over time.

A comprehensive overview of marriage enrichment programs is provided by Larry Hof and William Miller. They survey these and describe various programs, provide the philosophical background to the movement, and characterize the processes underlying specific approaches. They recommend greater cooperation among professionals in the field in order to evaluate objectively the effectiveness of alternative programs and approaches.

An "E-R-A model" for classifying couple and family skill training programs according to their emotional (E), rational (R), or action (A) orientations was developed by Ulrici, L'Abate, and Wagner. Skill training programs emphasize different communication skills, and these authors maintain that knowing basic program orientations should be helpful to researchers concerned with the evaluation of outcomes and to clinicians in selecting training programs which are most appropriate for clients. The authors offer the E-R-A model as a heuristic device for furthering these purposes.

A three-stage model of marital enrichment designed to integrate participants' attitudinal and behavioral changes was designed by Larry Hof, Norman Epstein, and William Miller. The three-stage enrichment experience would include an initial intensive retreat to increase positive feelings and attitudes, and to heighten motivation. The second stage would be a highly structured training program lasting several weeks during which specific skills would be taught. The third stage would be an ongoing support group to help maintain and increase positive changes. The authors suggest that such a program is likely to be maximally effective in integrating and maintaining attitudinal and behavioral marital enrichment.

Premarital counseling and programs have traditionally been offered by clergy to couples before marriage, but they have seldom been systematically described or evaluated. Thirteen programs were described by Dennis Bagarozzi and Paul Rauen which had systematically followed some standardized procedures and had included some type of outcome measure to assess treatment effectiveness.

The authors critically appraise methods of evaluation that have (and have not) been employed to assess program effectiveness and conclude that much remains to be accomplished in this area.

One of the most carefully designed studies of an effective premarital program was conducted by Bader, Microys, Sinclair, Willett, and Conway. This Canadian marriage preparation program provided experiential training in a group setting of communication and conflict resolution in five premarital group sessions and three postmarital sessions. Measures of conflict resolution and help-seeking behavior were obtained before the treatment sessions and at six-month and one-year followups. Couples who participated in the preparation program were more likely to seek help when needed and were better able to resolve their conflicts constructively.

PART IX: MARITAL THERAPY

Marital therapy is coming of age conceptually, clinically, and empirically. A variety of conceptual frameworks have emerged and are being linked more carefully with clinical techniques and programs. Also, inventories for assessing aspects of relationships are being developed, and systematic research on the effectiveness of various approaches is being conducted.

In couple interaction, there are many levels of communication and meaning, and sometimes these various levels are expressed simultaneously (such as object, individual, transactional, and relational). Bernal and Baker have proposed a conceptual framework for marital therapy which takes multiple relationship levels into account. Their article illustrates the usefulness of a multilevel framework for understanding couple interaction and developing therapeutic goals and strategies. The framework is illustrated with excerpts from an actual couple therapy case.

Behavioral therapy and communication approaches to marital therapy have both been demonstrated empirically to benefit couples, but seldom have they been systematically compared. Turkewitz and O'Leary's study experimentally compared behavioral therapy, communication therapy, and controls over a ten-week period. Couples in both treatment programs reported significantly more therapeutic gains than control couples, but there was a differential effect of age on outcome. Younger couples changed more favorably in Behavioral Marital Therapy, and older couples tended to improve more with Communication Therapy. If this finding is replicated, it could have major implications for the kind of treatment program selected by clinicians and counselors.

Largely as a consequence of divorce, remarried family systems are increasingly common. Sager and his colleagues have spent several years trying to better understand and develop a therapeutic approach for working with those in remarried family systems. Remarried families are different and more complex, structurally and dynamically, from their once-married counterparts. In this article the authors describe their techniques for gaining valuable insights into remarried family systems and deciding on goals and directions for therapy.

While intimacy is considered a vital component of marriage and family life, it has been an elusive concept to define and measure. Also, few instruments have been developed so that marital therapists could assess the couple's current relationship and provide directions for improving the relationship. Mark Schaefer and David Olson have developed the PAIR (Personal Assessment of Intimacy in Relationships) with which couples can describe their present (perceived) intimacy and how they would like it to be (ideal). The 36-item PAIR inventory provides scores on emotional, social, sexual, intellectual, and recreational aspects of intimacy. The PAIR has undergone extensive development and includes scoring and interpretation information that makes this a valuable tool for marital therapists.

With tongue in cheek, Haley gives advice to marriage and family therapists about how to conceal or excuse their ignorance, ineffectiveness, and failures from colleagues and clients alike. In the process of his exposition, however, he mercilessly ridicules some techniques that are still widely used by therapists.

PART X: FAMILY THERAPY

While both marital and family therapy are concerned with the marital unit, family therapy has emerged as the treatment of choice for a wide range of symptoms. This section contains articles that reflect the diversity of theoretical and therapeutic approaches in the field. Beginning with an overview of the field, popular therapeutic approaches (structural and strategic) and techniques (paradox) are described. Two articles also demonstrate how communication and problem-solving skills are used with families. The last article demonstrates how schools and families can work together in a more integrative and effective manner with high-risk children.

Reviewing the fields of marital and family therapy demonstrates how these fields have developed integrative models, expanded their therapeutic repertoire, and conducted more systematic outcome research. David Olson, Candyce Russell, and Doug Sprenkle set the stage for the rest of the articles in this section.

Structural and strategic modes are among the most prominent and popular approaches to family therapy. Duncan Stanton's article describes how these two approaches can be creatively integrated. Stanton also illustrates how and when to use structural and strategic approaches in combination or sequentially in the same case.

Although becoming more popular, paradoxical interventions are controversial, and therapists need to be aware of both the indicators and contraindications of their use. Fisher, Anderson, and Jones are concerned that these powerful techniques need to be well understood and thoughtfully applied rather than used as quick and easy substitutes for more complex treatment approaches. In their experience, paradoxical techniques are most effective with certain kinds of problems but are contraindicated for several types of families. These authors are convinced of the value of paradoxical techniques, but they caution therapists against bandwagon adoption of these procedures without careful consideration in each specific case.

Cloe Madanes describes the use of paradox as one strategy for dealing with child psychopathology. She suggests that in some cases children adopt a problem that puts them in a position superior to their parents in order to protect the parents from their own difficulties, often including an incongruity in the family hierarchical organization. Madanes illustrates three techniques which put the parents more in control of the family and thereby minimize the symptomatic behaviors in the child.

Adolescence is a time of frequent parent-child conflict when families come in or are referred for treatment. Arthur Robin describes a comparison of skill training in problem solving and family therapy with a wait-list control group. Families who participated in the problem-solving communication program and family therapy both showed significantly reduced parent-adolescent conflict. However, only the problem-solving group demonstrated improved problem solving during family discussions.

One of the most systematically researched approaches to relationship enhancement has been developed by Bernard G. Guerney and colleagues. One of the programs they developed was the PARD (Parent-Adolescent Relationship Development). In this article, they describe the effectiveness of PARD compared with a traditional discussion group and a no-treatment group. Mothers and daughters participating in a traditional discussion-oriented treatment and the no-treatment control group showed no gain on the communication variables or the general quality of their relationship, whereas participants in PARD showed significant gains in specific and general communication variables and the overall quality of their relationship. Relationship enhancement effects of PARD were increased still further among those assigned to a "booster" condition to receive periodic phone reminders and group sessions.

Family therapists have seldom attempted to get parents and teachers to work together to deal with children who do poorly at school. Yet it is known that children who do poorly at school make up a majority of childhood clinic referrals, and school performance is related to many other measures of child and adult adjustment. Blechman, Kotanchik, and Taylor's article describes an effective early intervention designed to improve the school performance of inconsistent elementary school children. The experiment began by identifying "inconsistent" and "stable" student performance according to a scatter index of how consistently they performed during a baseline period. Inconsistent students were then assigned to control or treatment groups. The intervention involved collaboration between teachers who notified parents of child performance and parents who provided reinforcement when the child's performance was at or above their average level. This intervention produced significant reductions in scatter among the children who had been identified as inconsistent students.

PART I

FAMILY POLICY

Policymakers and program planners often fail to examine the intended or unintended consequences of health policies and social problems on family life. Family Impact Analysis has been developed as a specific tool for examining, and thus anticipating, how alternative policies, programs, and services impact on different aspects of family life. The purpose of this article is to present a six-step framework for developing and implementing Family Impact Analysis. The major steps of this model are briefly discussed and illustrated in a series of worksheet tables.

1

A GENERAL FRAMEWORK FOR FAMILY IMPACT ANALYSIS

Marcia G. Ory and Robert L. Leik

INTRODUCTION

While the implicit goal of public policies and social programs is to improve the quality of life, policymakers and program administrators often fail to anticipate the consequences of such policies on family life. Whether recognized or not, much public health and social legislation has a direct impact on family structure and functioning (Family Impact Seminar, Note 1). With a growing awareness of the rapidly changing structure of the American family and the interdependence of the family with other social institutions, policymakers, program administrators, and health practitioners alike are beginning to realize the importance of learning how health and social policies affect American families. (Although other definitions are sometimes used to specify

Dr. Ory is currently a Health Scientist Administrator, Social and Behavioral Research, National Institute on Aging, National Institutes of Health, Building 31, Room 5 CO5, Bethesda, MD 20205. At the time the research was conducted she was a postdoctoral fellow at the Minnesota Family Study Center, University of Minnesota in Minneapolis. Dr. Robert Leik is currently Director and Professor, Family Study Center and Department of Sociology, University of Minnesota in Minneapolis. Address reprint requests to Dr. Ory. Research for this paper was supported, in part, by NIMH Training Grant No. 5 T32 MH 14619.

more traditional or alternative family life styles, this article will utilize the general U.S. Census Bureau definition of family as: "two or more persons living in the same household who are related by blood, marriage or adoption.")

The purpose of this article is to present a general model for planning and implementing family impact analysis (FIA).As an aid to helping health services researchers assess the effects of policies on family life, a step-by-step framework for engaging in family impact analysis is described. Checklist tables are included to illustrate the categorization of different policy components, the nature of potential family impacts, and the variety of methodological strategies applicable to family impact analysis.

MAJOR STEPS

The step-by-step procedure to be presented represents a meshing of existing methodologies drawn from evaluation research (Guttentag & Struening, 1975; Rossi & Wright, 1977; Suchman, 1967; Weiss, 1972), social impact assessment literature, (Ukeles, 1977; Weiss, 1972; Wolf, 1976; Vlachos, et al., Note 2), and earlier attempts at specifying the process of family impact assessment (Family Impact Seminar, Note 3; Mattessich, Note 4; McDonald, Note 5; Wilson & McDonald, Note 6).

Step 1. Identify Policy or Program for Analysis

It is likely that family impact analysis will be initiated because a policymaker, administrator, or practitioner needs to know the familial impact of an existing or proposed policy/program. While it is certainly important to understand the socio-political factors that influence the adoption of policies and programs, it is the family impact analyst's role to start by asking how a certain policy (or policies) already affects, or will probably affect, families.

Step 1 entails two main substeps:

1.   selecting a policy or program for family impact analysis, and
2.   specifying relevant components of that policy or program.

As indicated in Table 1(top half), the following factors should be considered in deciding whether to select a particular policy or program for family impact analysis: (1) whether the policy will have a probable impact on a sufficient number of families, (2) the

TABLE 1   POLICY/PROGRAM CHARACTERISTICS

I. SELECTION OF POLICY FOR FAMILY IMPACT ANALYSIS			
Likeliness of Family Impact	Directness of Family Impact	Explicitness of Family Orientation	Standard of Comparison
High Medium Low	Direct impact Indirect impact Remote impact	Explicitly Family oriented Implicitly Family oriented Not Family oriented at all	Policy/program compared to its absence Alternative policies compared

II. SPECIFICATION OF POLICY COMPONENTS			
Policy Area	Domain	Current Status	Implementation Components
Health Education Income Maintenance Manpower and Social Services Employment Housing Other	Sector: Public Private Level: Local Intrastate regional State Interstate regional National	Already in existence To be proposed	Legal or judicial Regulatory Fiscal Delivery characteristics: Auspices Accessibility Coordination Sensitivity to Family

number of families to be affected, (3) how direct the family impact will be, and (4) whether the policy has explicit family goals.

While almost any policy or program could be considered to have some impact on families, it will be most profitable to evaluate those policies that are more likely to have an explicitly, or at least implicitly, stated impact on families. A final consideration is whether the presence of a single policy or program will be compared against its absence or whether the basis of comparison will be the relative impact of alternative policies.

Secondly, in order to examine the relationship between the selected policy/program and family variables, it is necessary to specify what particular aspects of the policy will be considered in the family impact analysis. Table 1 (bottom half) illustrates a framework for categorizing different policies by: (1) interest area, (2) domain, (3) current status, and (4) implementation components.

By asking whether the study addresses legal, regulatory, fiscal, or delivery characteristics of the policy under question, this last category identifies whether the impact analysis will focus on the policy, program, or service level (Family Impact Seminar, Note 3). On the level of service delivery, program influences can be further categorized in terms of program auspicies, convenience and accessibility, degree of coordination, and sensitivity to families' needs.

Thus, the first step involves: (1) a selection of a general policy or program, and (2) a review of the policy's goals, regulations, and actual implementation procedures in order to specify particular components for family impact analysis.

Step 2. Identify Impacts to be Examined

Just as it was important to identify specific policy components for analysis, it is necessary to specify expected family outcomes in terms of family structure and/or functioning. Both intended and unintended consequences should be examined.

The identification of family impacts is composed of two related processes:

1. the identification of target populations that will be affected by the policy, and
2. the specification of the ways in which target families will be affected.

Target populations can be defined: (1) by the general policy focus (whether the policy is oriented toward individuals, two-person family relationships, or the total family unit), or (2) by the specific type of family population which is affected. Table 2 shows a framework for identifying target populations by their: (1) family composition (the number and type of both internal and external family relationships); (2) family life stage (young, middle age, and aging families); and (3) physical, social, and cultural contexts

TABLE 2   FAMILY CHARACTERISTICS

FAMILY STRUCTURE	FAMILY FUNCTIONS & FUNCTIONING
FAMILY COMPOSITION AND RELATIONSHIPS	**FAMILY FUNCTIONS**

Number of people in the family
Age composition
Marital/parental status of adults
Extended kin relationships
Informal social support from non-kin
Formal institutional social support
	Provider function
	Socialization and nurturant function
	Initiation, maintenance, and dissolution
	  of family membership function
	Resource manipulation of informal
	  and formal services function

FAMILY LIFE STAGE	
Childless couples < 45 years Childbearing families--oldest child <2 yrs Families w/preschoolers--oldest child 2-6 Families w/schoolchildren--oldest child 7-13 Families w/teenagers--oldest child >14 Families in middle years--no child at home Aging families--retirement until death	**FAMILY FUNCTIONING**
PHYSICAL, SOCIAL AND CULTURAL STATUSES	Family decision making and division of labor Family cohesion Family conflict resolution Family adaptability
Health status of family members Socio-economic status (income, education and employment status) Racial-ethnic-religious identifications	

(physical health conditions, socio-economic status, and cultural identifications).

In addition to identifying target populations, it is important to specify what family characteristics are to be examined for possible impacts. Both the previously described family composition and context variables, as well as the family functioning categorizations (provider, socialization, membership, and resource manipulation functions), serve as family impact indicators. Definitions for family functions have been adapted from those used by the Family Impact Seminar: provider functions refer to the families' ability to provide for basic material needs of the family; socialization functions refer to the families' nurturance and care of young members as well as support and encouragement for family members' physical, cognitive, psychological, and social development; membership functions refer to families' determination of which, and how many, members are to be added, maintained, or dropped from the primary family household unit; resource utilization functions refer to families' ability to obtain and coordinate informal and formal institutional support for their members (Family Impact Seminar, Note 3).

For example, one can ask if, and how, a selected policy/program will affect: (1) family composition variables such as marital status, parental preferences and behaviors, or relationships with sources of support outside the household; (2) the family's employment and financial status; or (3) the family's ability to take care of and nurture its members. Other family outcomes of interest include how the policy affects the nature and quality of the internal family functioning. That is, does the policy change family decision making and division of labor among its members or affect the level of family cohesion? It is also useful to examine how policies/programs affect families at different life cycle stages.

Finally, family-related outcomes are measured by family indicators at any one of the following three levels: (1) the societal level (i.e., marriage or divorce rate); (2) the group level (i.e., family cohesion or conflict scores); and (3) the individual level (i.e., rates of satisfaction with marital or parental roles).

To summarize, the family structure and functioning variables listed in Table 2 are meant: (1) to identify major categories of target families, and (2) to indicate areas of potential family impact (intended or unintended).

The family composition variables are especially useful for identifying families lacking an informal and/or formal social support network. In turn, the level of social support available to families is important for tailoring social services to existing family resources. It should also be noted that family structure affects how families function. For example, single parents, and particularly young mothers, have a harder time providing for the needs of their families.

Most research, especially that using available large scale data sources, has focused only on aggregate demographic statistics such as health, marriage, or divorce rates. While it is admittedly harder to assess impacts on internal family dynamics, more systematic effort needs to be given to the construction, refinement, and distribution of reliable and valid family functioning measures that are easily administered and interpreted.

Step 3. Diagram the Relationship Between the Policy/Program and the Hypothesized Family Impacts

Steps 1 and 2 presented a framework for categorizing policy components and family variables of interest. It is now desirable to specify the connections between the policy and the predicted family outcome. A useful way to help conceptualize these connections is to draw a diagram.

Table 3 illustrates three sub-steps involved in developing a diagram:

1. define the basic relationship between the policy and family factors,
2. specify the intervening factors linking the policy inputs to family outcomes, and
3. consider external factors that might affect the basic relationships.

The first sub-step involves hypothesizing whether there is a direct relationship between the specified policy factors and predicted family impacts. The hypothesis can take two basic forms: (1) a simple descriptive statement that the policy will or will not have an impact on some aspect of family structure and/or functioning; and (2) a statement that indicates the direction of the family impact (i.e., a prediction whether policy will be associated with an increase or decrease in an indicator such as fertility, marriage, or divorce rates). When information is available it is desirable to indicate the direction of the hypothesized relationship.

TABLE 3. SPECIFICATION OF THE MODEL

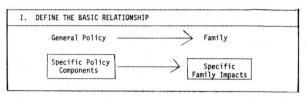

I. DEFINE THE BASIC RELATIONSHIP

General Policy ──────────────> Family

Specific Policy Components ──────────> Specific Family Impacts

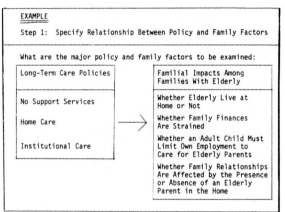

EXAMPLE

Step 1: Specify Relationship Between Policy and Family Factors

What are the major policy and family factors to be examined:

Long-Term Care Policies	Familial Impacts Among Families With Elderly
No Support Services	Whether Elderly Live at Home or Not
Home Care	Whether Family Finances Are Strained
Institutional Care	Whether an Adult Child Must Limit Own Employment to Care for Elderly Parents
	Whether Family Relationships Are Affected by the Presence or Absence of an Elderly Parent in the Home

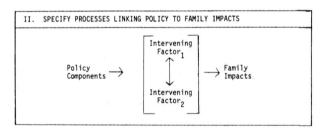

II. SPECIFY PROCESSES LINKING POLICY TO FAMILY IMPACTS

Policy Components →

Intervening Factor$_1$

Intervening Factor$_2$

→ Family Impacts

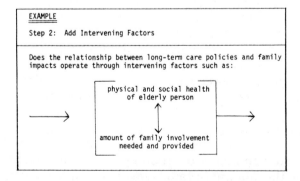

EXAMPLE

Step 2: Add Intervening Factors

Does the relationship between long-term care policies and family impacts operate through intervening factors such as:

physical and social health of elderly person

amount of family involvement needed and provided

TABLE 3 (Cont'd)

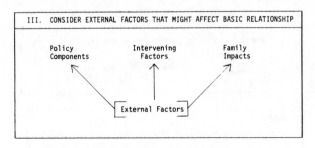

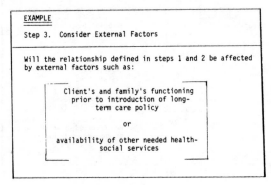

Predicting the direction of the relationship can come from several sources: (1) one's own personal or professional experience, (2) an informal poll of informed professionals from relevant disciplines, and (3) systematic review of the literature. To help illustrate these general comments, a specific example of steps taken for modeling the impact of alternative long-term care policies (no support; supplemental home care; or institutional care) on family composition and/or functioning is included (see Table 3, right-hand side).

Secondly, specifying intervening factors involves thinking through the causal sequences which links the policy to the family outcome. Although the policy may be intended to affect health and economic well-being of individuals, the latter factor may affect family membership patterns and activity levels (i.e., who lives with whom and provides what care) which, in turn, have a secondary effect on the nature and the quality of family functioning. In our family impact analysis of long-term care policies, intervening factors such as the physical health of elderly persons or the amount of family involvement needed and provided should be considered.

It is important to be aware of the social, economic, and political environment in which the policy and family factors are interacting. In order to distinguish real policy effects from spurious ones, the family impact analyst needs to try to identify and control for effects of relevant external factors (such as the general state of the economy, the ideological climate, and/or technological innovations) which might be falsely exaggerating or masking the hypothesized relationship between policy components and family outcomes.

There are two general methodological techniques for controlling the impact of external factors: (1) a field experiment approach in which a treatment is randomly assigned to one group and not the other so that the influence of external factors are equalized in both groups; and (2) a statistical control method in which external factors are controlled by statistical manipulations which "hold them constant" in order to eliminate the influence on the hypothesized policy family outcome relationship.

In our current example, external factors, such as the family's functioning prior to the introduction of the long-term care or the availability of other health/social services, should be considered.

Step 4. Design and Implement Family Impact Research

Having diagrammed the relationship between specific policy components and family outcomes, the analyst must test that relationship to the extent that resources and time permit. The fourth step is to select a research strategy for determining whether the policy actually impacts on the family in the predicted way. The selection of the research design and analysis should be based on: (1) the primary purpose of the study, (2) availability of personnel time and financial resources for research, (3) knowledge of advanced statistical techniques, and (4) access to family level data.

There are two basic parts in Step 4:

1. identification of possible kinds of research strategies and information needed to determine familial impacts, and
2. implementation of the selected research strategy.

In Steps 1, 2, and 3, the policy and family factors of interest were identified and the relationship between the factors specified. The first part of Step 4 involves developing indicators of and planning strategies for getting information on all policy, familial, intervening, and external variables specified in the model.

TABLE 4   RESEARCH STRATEGIES

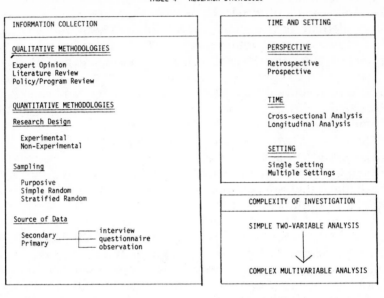

As discussed previously, the indicators for most of the structural variables (i.e., family size, composition, and presence of informal and formal relationships) are relatively straightforward and often obtainable in existing records and studies. However, for the more qualitative indicators of family functioning, the family impact analyst will need to designate how the different familial impacts are to be measured before planning other aspects of the research design.

In addition to developing indicators for all major variables, the family impact analyst needs to decide about the types and sources of possible information and how to sample those sources. As indicated in the first column of Table 4, information collection techniques are of two basic kinds: nondata or data-based.

In situations where data are unavailable or there are no resources for collection and analysis, the family impact analyst might adopt any of the following qualitative methodologies: (1) a review of existing literature, (2) reliance on judgement by experts, or (3) an examination of policy components and regulations to assess the probable family impacts. However, when accessible, quantitative, data-based sudies are advantageous because they allow for the collection of standardized information that can be analyzed in multiple ways depending on the purpose and resources of the researcher.

Quantitative, data-based studies are of two basic types: (1) secondary analyses that utilize previously collected data, and (2) primary analyses that obtain information first-hand by interview, questionnaire, or direct observation. In a primary analysis, the researcher will need to determine the appropriate research design (experimental with a planned intervention(s) vs. non-experimental with no intervention to test), and sampling strategy (e.g., purposive or random); and then design or borrow existing instruments for standardized data measurement.

Other factors to consider in research design are time and setting factors. Will the study be retrospective or prospective, cross-sectional or longitudinal, and involve single vs. multiple settings? Finally, the complexity of possible research designs varies from (1) the examination of a simple two-variable relationship between one policy factor and family factor to (2) the analysis of complex interactions between multiple policy components and family indicators.

Once the research strategy has been chosen, the second sub-step is to implement the selected design. A few general comments on the implementation process will be offered. First a common rule of thumb is that the research study will probably cost more and take longer to finish than originally expected. To facilitate implementation of primary data-based research in field settings, it is important to have planning and training sessions to foster open communication between the service and research staff so that each knows and respects the needs of the other.

In this section, measurement of family indicators and the selection of different research strategies for family impact analysis have been briefly discussed. These research strategies represent the beginning efforts toward family impact analysis. To address the key impact questions of how different policies/programs affect both family structure and functioning over time, more resources need to be channeled into the development and systematic collection of standardized family impact indicators.

Step 5. Analyze the Data

To a large extent, the particular data analysis technique will be "dictated" by the family impact questions that have motivated the study, the specification and measurement of policy components and family variables representing both intended and unintended effects, and the data collection and preparation methods.

The variety of techniques for analyzing existing data or projecting future trends can range from the presentation of simple frequency distributions and graphs to cross-tabulations of two or three variables, to multivariate statistical analyses such as multiple regression, log linear analysis and path analyses, to modeling techniques for forecasting time-series data. The different analyses may be easily computed by the use of packaged computer programs.

There are advantages and disadvantages to each type of analysis. In addition to reflecting the nature of the research problem, research design and availability of data, the selection of a particular analysis· and display of findings from the analysis should consider the research skills of the intended audience (i.e., are the findings being prepared for the general public, policymakers, practitioners, or academic professionals?).

No matter what particular techniques are selected for examining the relationship between policy factors and family outcomes, the analysis should address two basic questions:

1. how many and what kinds of families are affected by the policy or program(s) of interest; and
2. what policy or program components affect which family structures and/or functions in what manner?

A checklist format such as the one shown in Table 5 is useful for identifying the types of families affected by different policies. The extent of impact across families can be assessed by estimating (from census reports or other records) the proportion of families that fall into any one affected family composition category, life cycle stage, or physical, social, and cultural context.

It should be noted, however, that Table 5 illustrates a model checklist for categorizing and identifying different family types. For some policy analyses, the investigator may not find all the categories listed in Table 5 relevant. To supplement the checklist, space has been provided at the bottom of the table for a summary description of the different family types affected.

Findings pertaining to the specific impacts of different policy components on family structures and/or functioning can be summarized in worksheet fashion. Table 6 illustrates a sample format for assessing family impacts. However, as with Table 5, the investigator may want to modify this table for his/her own purposes.

As indicated in the Step 5 column of Table 6, the relationship between a particular policy component and family factors can be

TABLE 5   IDENTIFICATION OF FAMILY TYPES AFFECTED BY POLICY(S)

Policy 1. Briefly Describe:

Policy Component(s):

FAMILY TYPES

FAMILY COMPOSITION & RELATIONSHIPS

ALL FAMILIES:
☐
SIZE:
☐ small
☐ medium
☐ large

MARITAL STATUS:
☐ married
☐ unmarried

PARENTAL STATUS:
☐ childless
☐ children present
☐ single parent
☐ two-parent

EXTENDED KIN RELATIONSHIPS:
☐ those with
☐ those without

INFORMAL SOCIAL SUPPORT FROM NON-KIN:
☐ those with
☐ those without

FORMAL INSTITUTIONAL SUPPORT:
☐ those with
☐ those without

FAMILY LIFE STAGE

☐ childless
☐ childbearing
☐ with preschool children
☐ with school-age children
☐ with young adults
☐ in middle years
☐ aging families

HEALTH, SOCIAL, CULTURAL

HEALTH:
☐ no problems
☐ some problems
☐ multiple problems

ECONOMIC STATUS:
☐ low income
☐ middle income
☐ upper income

EMPLOYMENT STATUS:
☐ unemployed
☐ employed
☐ single wage earner
☐ dual wage earners
Indicate special cultural
    identifications:

SUMMARY: THIS POLICY MOST DIRECTLY AFFECTS THE FOLLOWING KINDS OF FAMILIES:

*Check family types which are affected. For each family type that is affected, estimate the number or proportion of families affected. Repeat process for each alternative policy or component examined.

categorized in terms of the likelihood that there will be an impact, how strong the impact will be and what family factors will be affected, such as the families' ability to perform provider, socialization-nurturant, membership, and resource manipulation functions or the families' general level of functioning. Separate worksheets will be necessary for assessing impacts across different policy components and family types.

An overview of the variety of analysis techniques that can be used in family impact analysis has been presented in this section. The use of a checklist worksheet was recommended as a good format for systematically assessing and summarizing the impacts of specific policies/programs on different aspects of family life.

Throughout the article, the research steps have been described separately and sequentially (identification and measurement of both policy and family factors, specification of hypotheses, selection of the research design, and data analysis techniques). It is important to recognize, however, that the different steps are mutually interdependent and cannot be formulated in isolation from one another. The choice for analysis techniques, for example, is largely predetermined by earlier research decisions.

Step 6. Evaluate the Findings and Prepare Policy Recommendations

Family impact analysis involves two distinct processes: (1) the identification of impacts, and (2) an evaluation of the impacts. Whereas the previous steps have concentrated on presenting the reader with alternative methodologies for identifying and obtaining information to answer the questions of "how many, what kinds of, and in what ways are families affected by a particular policy or program?", the sixth step will address issues involved in:

1. the evaluation of validity of the findings,
2. the evaluation of the desirability of the findings,
3. the presentation of policy recommendations.

In the first kind of evaluation, theoretical and methodological deficiencies of the study are reviewed to determine whether the family impacts found (or not found) can really be attributed to the policy under study or if they might actually be caused by some external factors not considered in the analysis. All research methodologies have some limitations, but, in general, results found in more carefully designed and executed studies (i.e., statistically manipulated or experimentally designed studies considering multiple interactions between policy components and family outcome over time) can be more readily accepted as representative of the true impact.

The second kind of evaluation involves an assessment of the desirability of the outcomes. In order to evaluate impacts on this dimension, it is necessary to identify criteria for assessing the desirability of policy-related, family impacts (i.e., what impacts are considered positive, neutral, or negative).

For those impacts which have explicitly stated criteria of desirability, the next sub-step is to compare the advantages and disadvantages of alternative policies and programs in terms of

TABLE 6   ASSESSMENT AND EVALUATION OF POLICY IMPACT ON FAMILIES

Policy (Briefly describe):
Implementation Component(s)*:

FAMILY IMPACTS**	STEP 5: ASSESSMENT OF IMPACTS			STEP 6: EVALUATION
	IS IMPACT LIKELY	MAGNITUDE OF IMPACT	DIRECTION OF IMPACT	DESIRABILITY
	Yes No	Strong Weak	(indicate)	+ 0 -
I. STRUCTURE health-social statuses				
II. FUNCTIONS provider socialization family membership resource manipulation				
III. FUNCTIONING family division of labor quality of interaction				
IV. OTHER IMPACTS				

SUMMARY: This policy affects families' ability to
These impacts are considered

*Indicate general policy and policy component(s) under analysis. Individual worksheets can be used for each policy or policy component.

**Assess and evaluate familial impacts by filling in proper response in space provided. Individual worksheets can be used for different family types.

those criteria. In addition to assessing impacts, the worksheet illustrated in Table 6 (Step 6, column 4) provides a framework for summarizing the desirability of different impacts in terms of whether policy effects on families are judged as positive, neutral, or negative.

Establishing a criterion of desirability is not always a clearcut process. It is important to recognize the values and assumptions implicit in designating one impact as more desirable than the other. Clearly some impacts such as those which put a stress on the family's ability to maintain provider, socialization, and resource manipulation functions are desirable.

However, there is less consensus on the meaning attributed to certain family types and functioning styles. For example, there can be some disagreement over whether a new baby, a marriage or divorce, or the displacement of young children and elderly to institutional care is actually beneficial or detrimental to the functioning of the family unit.

If there is no consensus on the desirability of the impacts, it will be difficult to evaluate the policy/program. In such cases, it is especially important to specify particular impacts on affected populations vis-à-vis other population groups. The family impact analyst should present the policymaker with a catalogue of conflicting impacts on different family types or for different members within the same family.

Having assessed policy impacts and, when possible, evaluated their desirability for different population groups, the analyst must summarize the findings and prepare policy recommendations for consideration. The kinds of policy recommendations the family impact analyst will make depend on:

1. the type and magnitude of policy impacts,
2. an assessment of the validity and reliability of the findings,
3. the family impact analyst's own values and assumptions about "desirable" family outcomes, and
4. a recognition of the constraints of the socio-political environment in which the policy is operating.

SUMMARY

A six-step, general framework for engaging in family impact analysis was presented in this paper. Sample checklists of policy and family factors were included to help the reader systematically identify, assess and evaluate familial impacts of alternative policies and programs (Table 1-6). A final worksheet (Table 7) is suggested for summarizing the results from the family impact analysis. For easy comparison and evaluation of findings from different impact studies, this sheet includes space for identifying the major policy components and family impacts of concern, as well as reporting the major research strategies employed. The results of the family impact analysis can be nicely summarized by coupling this final worksheet with a cross-matrix checklist of family impacts such as the models illustrated in Table 6.

Recently there has been much debate about the role of family impact analysis as a mandatory vs. voluntary tool for assessing policy impacts (Nye & McDonald, 1979). While this framework has been successfully utilized to report family impact studies in the area of child welfare service, the criminal justice system and economic and labor policies (Ory & Leik, Note 7), it is felt that, given the conceptual and methodological state of the art of FIA, it would be premature to mandate FIA as a necessary prerequisite to all policies and programs such as environmental impact analysis. The utility of FIA should be the sensitization of policymakers and administrators to the intended and unintended consequences of health policies and social programs on family life.

TABLE 7   STEP-BY-STEP SUMMARY WORKSHEET

I.   DESCRIBE POLICY UNDER STUDY

Policy Area

Sector/level:
Target population:
Current status:
Implementation components:

II.   LIST FAMILY IMPACTS EXAMINED

Family structure:
Family functioning:

III. MODEL THE RELATIONSHIP, CONSIDERING INTERVENING AND EXTERNAL FACTORS
      WHERE APPLICABLE

IV.   REPORT RESEARCH STRATEGY UTILIZED

Data collection: Sampling:
Research design: Source of data:
Analysis techniques:

V.   ASSESS AND EVALUATE FAMILY IMPACTS OF EACH POLICY/POLICY COMPONENT(S)

Likelihood of impact:
Type of impact:
Strength of impact:
Desirability of impacts:

VI.   PRESENT SUMMARY CONCLUSIONS AND RECOMMENDATIONS

REFERENCE NOTES

1. Family Impact Seminar. *Toward an inventory of federal programs with direct impact on families* (Mimeographed). Washington, D.C.: George Washington University, 1978.
2. Vlachos, E. et al. *Social impact assessment: An Overview.* Report submitted to the U.S. Army Engineer Institute for Water Resources, Fort Belvoir, Virginia, 1975.
3. Family Impact Seminar. *Interim report* (Mimeographed). Washington, D.C.: George Washington University, 1978.
4. Mattessich, P. *Family impact analysis.* St. Paul, Minnesota: State Planning Agency, Spring, 1977.
5. McDonald, G. *Family policy research and family impact analysis: Implications for public policy.* Paper presented in the Family Session of the Annual Meeting of the Society for the Study of Social Problems in San Francisco, California, September, 1978.
6. Wilson, L., & McDonald, G. Family impact analysis and the family policy advocate: The process of analysis. *Family impact series No. 4.* Minneapolis, Minnesota: Minnesota Family Study Center, University of Minnesota, 1977.
7. Ory, M.G., & Leik, R.K. Policy and the American family: A manual for family impact analysis. *Family impact series No. 14.* Minneapolis, Minnesota: Minnesota Family Study Center, University of Minnesota, 1977.

REFERENCES

Guttentag, M., & Struening, E. (Eds.). *Handbook of evaluation research* (Vols. 1 & 2). Beverly
    Hills: Sage Publications, 1975.
Nye, F.I., & McDonald, G. Family policy research: Emergent models and some theoretical
    issues. *Journal of Marriage and the Family* (Special issue), 1979, *41*(3), 473-485.
Rossi, P., & Wright, S. Evaluation research: An asessment of theory, practice, and politics.
    Evaluation Quarterly, 1977, 1(1), 5-52.
Suchman, E. *Evaluative research: Principles and practice in public service and social action
    programs.* New York: Russell Sage Foundation, 1967.
Ukeles, J. Policy analysis: Myth or reality. *Public Administration Review,* May-June 1977, *3,*
    223-227.
Weiss, C. *Evaluating action programs.* Boston: Allyn & Bacon, 1972.
Wolf, C. Social impact assessment: The state of the art restated. *Sociological Practice,* 1976,
    1, 56-68.

Federal income taxes have been higher for two-earner married couples than for unmarried individuals, giving rise to the popular term "marriage penalty tax." In 1981 federal legislation was passed to reduce the tax liability of two-earner married couples as part of a larger tax reform package. This article provides a background for the federal income tax laws of the past and describes how the new tax laws, taking effect in 1982 and 1983, will more nearly achieve marriage neutrality by reducing the tax liability difference between two-earner married couples and two single individuals filing separately.

2

FEDERAL INCOME TAXATION AND THE TWO-EARNER COUPLE

Colien Hefferan[1]

Legislation to reduce the Federal income tax liability of two-earner couples was enacted in 1981 as part of a larger tax reform package (see insert on p. 5). Under the provisions of P.L. 97-34, married couples with two earners can deduct from family income 10 percent of the lower paid spouse's earnings up to a maximum income of $30,000 per year. For two-earner married couples claiming the maximum deduction and paying the maximum rate of tax on earned income, 50 percent, the law will reduce their tax liability by $1,500. The deduction will be phased in over 2 years, with a 5-percent deduction available in 1982 and the full 10 percent in 1983.

The legislation is designed to improve the equity and efficiency of the Federal income tax system as it applies to two-earner married couples. This segment of the population is expected to comprise 60 percent of all married couples and 32 percent of all households by 1990 (9, 10). As women gain in education and labor force experience, women's earnings are expected to approach the level of men's. Rising labor force participation rates of married women, as well as increasing earnings, have made the tax treatment of two-earner families an issue of growing importance.

[1] Economist, Family Economics Research Group, Agricultural Research Service, U.S. Department of Agriculture.

Background

Since the introduction of the Federal income tax nearly 70 years ago, three concerns regarding the tax treatment of families have arisen: (1) The tax burden of single persons relative to that of married couples, (2) treatment of the costs of children and other dependents in assessing tax burdens, and (3) the tax burden of married couples with one earner relative to that of equal-income married couples with two earners (4). Most recently, attention has focused on issues 2 and 3 as the labor force participation rate of married women increased to just under 50 percent in 1979, up 9 percentage points since 1970 (11).

Family-related tax issues are difficult to resolve because the U.S. tax system is built on three broadly supported, but mutually conflicting, goals (8). Goal 1 is maintenance of progressivity, which means that the proportion of income paid in taxes should increase with income. This goal is based on the concept of declining marginal value of income and its corollary that taxpaying ability increases more than proportionately with income. Goal 2 is equal taxation of married couples with equal income. This is based on the premise that income and economic well-being are shared by husbands and wives regardless of who earns the income. Goal 3 is marriage neutrality, which implies that an indi-

From Colien Hefferan, "Federal Income Taxation and the Two-Earner Couple," *Family Economics Review*, Winter 1982, pp. 3-10. Reprinted by permission of the publisher and author.

vidual's tax liability should not be dependent on marital status. This is based on both economic efficiency and equity considerations.

Goal 1 of maintaining progressivity cannot be met when both goal 2 of equal taxation and goal 3 of marriage neutrality are accommodated. An example illustrates this conflict (see Fig. 1 on p. 4). The four units (unit D contains two single taxpayers who must each file a single return) in the example have the same total income, $20,000, but different composition and sources of earnings. For the tax system to meet the goal of married couples with equal income paying equal tax (goal 2), units A and B must pay the same tax. To meet the goal of marriage neutrality (goal 3), the tax liability of a single worker (unit C) must be the same as that of a married couple with the same income (unit A), and the tax of two single workers (unit D_1 and D_2) must be the same as that of two equal earning married workers (unit B). When these conditions are met, then the tax paid by a single taxpayer earning $20,000 (unit C) must equal that of two single taxpayers earning $10,000 each (unit D_1 and D_2). However, this violates the goal of progressivity (goal 1), which demands that tax rates rise with level of income. To meet this goal, the tax paid by unit C should be more than the combined tax of unit D_1 and unit D_2.

The family-related tax issues could be resolved only if one of the underlying goals were abandoned. Reduction of one inequity often creates another, generating the need for further tax reform. The history of the U.S. income tax system contains several examples of attempts to reduce the inequity of tax burdens for families of different types by abandoning one of those goals. In each case, reform itself created the need for further changes in the tax system.

1913-48. Prior to 1948, the individual rather than the family was the primary unit of taxation. One rate schedule was used for all taxpayers, regardless of marital status; exemptions were used to adjust tax for family size. The tax system was marriage neutral; however, couples with equal income did not necessarily pay equal tax. Residents of community property States could divide income between the husband and wife and thereby reduce their tax liability relative to that of married couples living in noncommunity property States. This inequity was resolved in 1948, when the tax system was changed to allow all married couples to split their income.

1948-69. Income splitting for married couples was effected by instituting separate rate schedules in which the tax brackets were twice as wide as they were for single taxpayers. This system assured that married couples with equal income, regardless of number of workers, would pay equal tax, but the system was not marriage neutral. In a progressive tax structure, income splitting between husband and wife has the effect of creating a tax bonus for marrying and a penalty on remain-

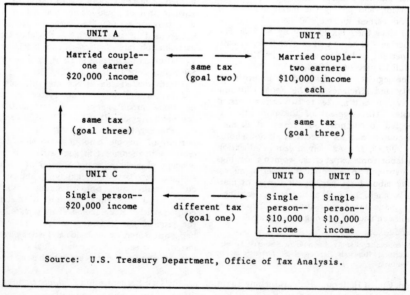

Source: U.S. Treasury Department, Office of Tax Analysis.

Figure 1

ECONOMIC RECOVERY TAX ACT OF 1981

The Economic Recovery Tax Act of 1981 (P.L. 97-34), signed into law on August 13, 1981, is purported to be the largest tax-cutting bill in U.S. history. It is estimated that the bill will save taxpayers more than $700 billion over the next 6 years.

The law contains eight titles including Individual Income Tax Provisions, Business Incentive Provisions, Savings Provisions, Estate and Gift Tax Provisions, Tax Straddles, Energy Provisions, Administrative Provisions, and Miscellaneous Provisions. Several of these provisions substantially alter the tax liability of individuals and families.

Income tax rates will be reduced by 5 percent in 1981 and 10 percent in 1982 and in 1983. This will result in a cumulative reduction in individual tax rates of 23 percent over the period 1981 through 1984. Beginning in 1985, tax rates, exemptions, and the zero bracket amount will be indexed to reflect annual changes in the Consumer Price Index. This is designed to reduce "bracket creep," whereby tax liability for individuals and families increases when income is increased solely to keep up with inflation. The law also reduces the top marginal tax rate on investment income from 70 percent to 50 percent effective in 1982.

In addition to these broad tax reduction provisions, the Economic Recovery Tax Act also provides tax relief for families with child and dependent care expenses necessitated by gainful employment. Taxpayers with income below $10,000 will be eligible for a child care credit equal to 30 percent of employment-related child care expenses up to $2,400 (one dependent) or $4,800 (two or more dependents). The credit will be reduced by 1 percent for each $2,000 of income above $10,000 down to a credit of 20 percent for taxpayers with income of $30,000 or above.

Other provisions related to individual income taxes allow: (1) Non-itemizing taxpayers to deduct a portion of qualified charitable contributions, beginning in 1982; (2) taxpayers to deduct up to $1,500 of certain expenses associated with the adoption of hard-to-place children, beginning in 1981; (3) taxpayers to defer gain on the sale of a principal residence, if a new residence is purchased within 2 years, on sales and exchanges after July 20, 1981 or for transactions with unexpired rollover periods (18 months under previous law); (4) taxpayers 55 years of age and older to increase the one-time exclusion of gain on principal residences from $100,000 to $125,000, on sales and exchanges after July 20, 1981.

Under the savings provisions of the Economic Recovery Tax Act, individuals will have a lifetime exclusion of $1,000 ($2,000 on joint returns) of interest paid on depository institution tax-exempt saving certificates issued after September 30, 1981. Eligibility for participation in Individual Retirement Accounts (IRA's) will be extended to all workers, regardless of participation in employer-sponsored retirement plans, effective in 1982. In addition, annual contribution limits on IRA's will be increased from $1,500 to $2,000 in 1982.

The gift and estate provisions of the law will exempt an estimated 99.7 percent of all estates from estate tax by 1987. Effective in 1982, the marital deduction will be unlimited. The annual gift tax exclusion will be increased from $3,000 to $10,000 per donee. Most gifts for medical care and tuition will receive unlimited exclusion.

ing single. In 1969 Congress responded to the "singles' penalty" by lowering the tax rates for single individuals.

1969-81. Under the 1969 reforms, the tax rates still remained higher for single individuals than for married couples with equal income; therefore, the tax bonus remained for all one-earner married couples. Nonetheless, the singles' rate schedule would have been advantageous to some two-earner couples. If, by filing separate returns using the singles' tax rate schedule, married earners could take advantage of the low marginal rates at the bottom of two tax schedules, they could reduce their tax liability to less than that of married couples with the same income but with only one earner. To maintain the goal of married couples with equal income paying equal tax, two-earner couples choosing to file separate returns were prohibited from using the singles' tax rate schedule. This created nonneutrality with respect to marriage and generated the "marriage penalty" under which two-earner couples found that the more similar their incomes, the greater their extra tax burden relative to two single persons.

The penalty and bonus structure generated by the separate rate schedules for married and single taxpayers, as it existed in 1980, is illustrated in figure 2. The penalties were greatest for married couples with equally distributed income and increased with level of income. For couples with less than $25,000 in total taxable income and in which one spouse earns less than 20 percent of the income, the tax structure favored or only nominally penalized married taxpayers relative to single taxpayers. However, the marriage penalty increased to almost $3,000 for two married workers each earning $25,000 in taxable income.

An estimated 29 percent of all married couples were potentially subject to the marriage penalty imposed by the separate tax schedules in 1978. This is the percentage of all married couples in which there were two earners each contributing more than 20 percent of earnings (*11*). This represented 18 percent of all households.[2] Some couples were subject to very high marriage penalties. Assuming that married couples are taxed on approximately 75 percent of their total income, approximately 3 percent of all married couples, or just less than 2 percent of all households,

paid penalties in excess of $500.[3] Other factors, including differences in the definition of income as a result of different zero bracket deductions for married and single taxpayers, further exacerbated the marriage penalty for some couples. As part of broader legislation to reduce all Federal income tax rates, Congress in 1981 acted to reduce, and in some cases eliminate, the marriage tax penalty.

1981 Tax Reform

Legislation to reduce the marriage penalty had wide appeal and broad support. Although the proportion of all households penalized by the tax structure in effect from 1969 through 1981 was relatively small, some couples were significantly penalized by the system. What is more, the proportion of couples affected by the marriage penalty was growing at a rapid pace. When the 1969 tax reform was implemented, both spouses were gainfully employed in only about 30 percent of all married couples (*9, 10*). Ten years later, almost 50 percent of all married couples had two earners. Continued growth in the proportion of married couples with two-earners is predicted.

Delegates to the White House Conference on Families in 1980 strongly recommended adoption of "major changes in the tax code to eliminate the marriage tax penalty. . ." as one way to reduce the economic pressures on marriage and family life (*12*). Others advocated reductions in the "working wives' tax" to encourage married women to participate in the paid labor force (*1*). Most of the arguments for reducing or eliminating the marriage tax penalty centered around the issues of economic equity and efficiency.

Equity. Under an equitable tax system, taxpaying units with equal ability to pay are taxed at equal rates. This implies that couples

---

[2] Married couples constituted 62.3 percent of all households. Multiplying the 29 percent of all couples subject to the marriage penalty by 62.3 percent equals 18 percent of all households subject to the marriage penalty.

[3] This includes married couples with two earners each contributing in excess of 20 percent of family income and having total family income greater than $50,000 (taxable income estimated to be in excess of $37,500) and couples with two earners each contributing in excess of 30 percent of family income and having total family income greater than $35,000 (taxable income estimated to be in excess of $26,500).

Marriage Tax Penalties and Bonuses, 1980

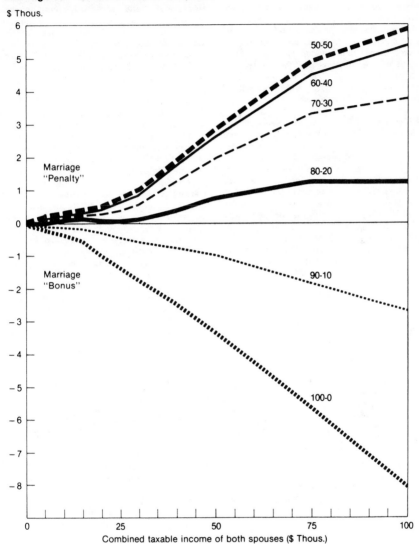

Additional tax liability of married couples compared to tax liability of 2 single taxpayers with the same combined income, by income split and level of income, calculated from 1980 tax schedule.

Figure 2

with the same income pay the same tax. Proponents of the reduction or elimination of the marriage penalty argued that two-earner couples with the same money income as one-earner couples enjoyed less imputed income from home-produced goods and services and incurred higher work-related expenses; therefore, their real income and their taxpaying ability were lower (5). They argued for a deduction to approximate the work-related expenses of secondary workers.

Efficiency. Efficient taxes raise revenue while causing minimal distortion in economic decisions (6). The question of economic efficiency arises in relation to the tax treatment of two-earner couples when labor force decisions of secondary workers are analyzed. Several researchers have reported that the labor force participation rates of wives, who are frequently the lesser earning or secondary workers in families, are highly responsive to changes in tax rates (2, 3, 7). By taxing the first dollar of these workers' income at the same rate as the last dollar of their spouses' income, they are discouraged from entering or fully participating in the paid labor force. Proponents of the 1981 tax reform argued that by deducting part of the secondary worker's earnings from taxable income, labor force decisions of couples would be less distorted by tax considerations.

Implications. Figure 3 illustrates the marriage tax penalties and bonuses projected for 1983 based on the 1981 tax reforms. Overall, the penalties and bonuses will be reduced, narrowing the gap between the tax liability of married couples and equal-income, single taxpayers. The marriage penalties will continue to be greatest for two-earner couples with similar or equal division of earnings between spouses, but unlike the old tax schedules, no two-earner couples with taxable income under $30,000 will be subject to a marriage penalty in excess of $500. At higher income levels, the extra tax liability of two-earner couples over that of two single persons will be significantly reduced from the 1969-81 levels. In 1983, for example, the projected marriage penalty for two married workers each earning $25,000 in taxable income is less than $1,500, compared with almost $3,000 under the previous tax schedule.

Not only do the 1981 tax reforms change the relative tax liability of two-earner married couples and single taxpayers, but also the relative tax liability of two-earner and one-earner married couples. Under the provisions of the 1981 tax reforms, married couples with equal income do not necessarily have equal tax liability. Although the reforms reduce the tax rates for all married couples, two-earner couples benefit from a new deduction not available to one-earner couples. Couples with two earners pay less tax than single-earner couples with the same income because 10 percent of the lesser earning spouse's income, up to a maximum income of $30,000, is tax deductible.

Examples of the differences in tax liability of equal-income, one-earner and two-earner married couples are projected for 1983 in the table on page 10. The differences constitute a "workers' bonus" for two-earner married couples compared with one-earner couples with the same income. The bonus is greater the more similar the division of earnings between spouses. The tax liability of a one-earner married couple earning $50,000 will be more than $400 greater than that of a two-earner married couple in which one spouse earns $10,000 and the other earns $40,000, and more than $1,000 greater than that of a two-earner couple in which each spouse earns $25,000.

Conclusions

The Federal income tax reforms of 1981 reduce the differences between the tax liability of two-earner married couples and two single taxpayers filing as individuals. In this respect, the reforms support the goal of marriage neutrality in the Federal income tax system. Although income tax liability is still influenced by marital status, the marriage penalty for two-earner couples has been significantly reduced.

In deciding in favor of marriage neutrality, Congress implicitly decided in the 1981 reforms to partially relax the goal of equal taxation of married couples with equal income. Recognizing the added expenses of employment in two-earner couples and the home production and leisure that may be foregone, provisions of the 1981 reform allow two-earner couples to adjust their taxable

Marriage Tax Penalties and Bonuses, 1983

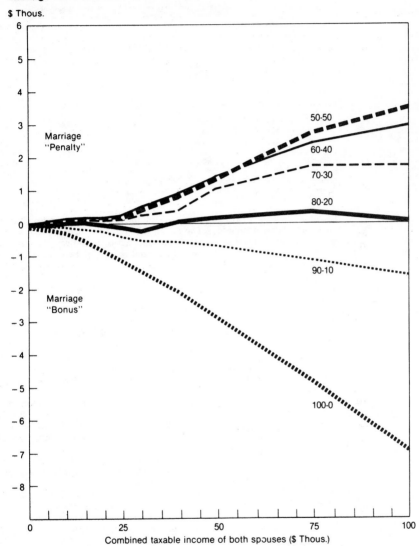

Additional tax liability of married couples compared to tax liability of 2 single taxpayers with same combined income, by income split and level of income, projected for 1983 under 1981 tax reform.

Figure 3

Workers' bonus, 1983[1]

Family income	Share of combined income of lesser earning spouse				
	10%	20%	30%	40%	50%
	Dollars				
$ 0	0	0	0	0	0
$ 5,000	7	8	18	25	30
$ 10,000	15	20	46	61	77
$ 15,000	15	12	39	65	92
$ 20,000	42	82	124	165	206
$ 25,000	68	133	193	253	312
$ 30,000	92	299	256	502	420
$ 40,000	148	295	663	589	736
$ 50,000	181	418	628	838	1,047
$ 75,000	346	692	1,038	1,385	1,385
$100,000	504	1,009	1,513	1,513	1,513

[1] Difference in tax liability of equal-earning married couples with one earner versus two earners, by share of combined income of the lesser earning spouse, projected to 1983, based on 1981 tax reform.

income to lower their tax liability relative to that of equal income, one-earner couples.

The goals of progressivity, equal taxation of married couples with equal income, and marriage neutrality cannot be met simul-taneously in the Federal income tax system. The 1981 tax reforms represent an adjustment in these goals to reflect the growing importance and impact of two-earner couples in the U.S. economic and social systems.

REFERENCES

1. Barrett, Nancy S. 1981. Working couples could use the break. *Washington Post*, March 19, p. A23.

2. Kosters, M. 1969. Effects of an income tax on labor supply. *In* Arnold C. Harberger and Martin J. Bailey, editors. *The Taxation of Income from Capital*. The Brookings Institution.

3. Leuthold, Jane H. 1979. Taxes and the two-earner family: Impact on the work decision. *Public Finance Quarterly* 7(2):147-161.

4. McIntyre, Michael J., and Oliver Oldman. 1977. Treatment of the family. *In* Joseph A. Pechman, editor. *Comprehensive Income Taxation*. The Brookings Institution.

5. O'Neill, June Avis. 1980. The tax treatment of married and single taxpayers. *Journal of Home Economics* 72(4): 32-34.

6. Rosen, Harvey S. 1976. A methodology for evaluating tax reform proposals. *Journal of Public Economics*. Vol. 6, pp. 105-121.

7. _____. 1976. Tax illusion and the labor supply of married women. *Review of Economics and Statistics*. Vol. 58, pp. 167-172.

8. _____. 1977. Is it time to abandon joint filing? *National Tax Journal* 30(4): 423-428.

9. U.S. Department of Commerce, Bureau of the Census. 1975. Projections of the population of the United States: 1975 to 2050. *Current Population Reports*. Series P-25, No. 601.

10. _____. 1979. *Statistical Abstract of the United States*, 100th Edition.

11. U.S. Department of Labor, Bureau of Labor Statistics. 1981. Marital and family characteristics of the labor force March 1979. *Special Labor Force Report 237*.

12. White House Conference on Families. 1980. *Listening to America's Families—action for the 80's*.

Five waves of data from the National Longitudinal Surveys consisting of a sample of 3,690 females age 30 through 44 were analyzed using a cross-lagged panel correlation. In many cases, the results of the analysis were consistent with the view that marital instability increases the need for welfare, AFDC, and food stamps. There was little evidence to support the previously reported effect of public assistance on marital instability.

3

ON THE RELATIONSHIP BETWEEN WELFARE AND MARITAL STABILITY

A Research Note*

*Thomas W. Draper***

The effects of public assistance on the family have been debated for many years. Opinions have varied. Some have viewed welfare programs as humanitarian devices that alleviate need and offer stability and security to families during economic stress. Others have viewed them as insidious "family smashing" devices that encourage husbands to abandon their families and wives to terminate unsatisfactory relationships rather than attempt to improve them (Caplow, 1975).

Bahr (1979) has reviewed investigations of the relationship between welfare and marital stability. He concludes that the methodologies that have been used to explore the relationship were not adequate. Many of these past studies compared the welfare and divorce rates of samples from different populations. Consequently, it has not been possible to tell if causal relationships existed,

even though some apparent effects were noted. Unspecified population differences, which could have affected both marital stability and the need for public assistance, had not been eliminated as alternate explanations.

Bahr (1979) used time-lagged data from the National Longitudinal Survey of Labor Market Experience (NLSLME) to perform a different type of examination of the relationship between welfare and marital stability. Since logic requires that causes precede effects, he hoped that longitudinal data would be useful in drawing inferences about a causal relationship. Using a test of proportionality, Bahr found that women on welfare, as opposed to women without assistance, had significantly higher rates of separation and divorce at time periods of two and seven years after the date of welfare assistance. Receipt of public assistance appeared to be influencing subsequent dissolution. Bahr noted that even though the relationship was occurring over time, it could still be due to some unspecified variable, such as personal instability. Unstable individuals may be more likely to both require public assistance and be involved in divorce than their more stable peers. Although Bahr's analysis did not eliminate all

*I am grateful to J. Allen Watson, John Scanzoni, and Dennis Orthner for comments on an earlier draft of this paper. This work was supported in part by a research excellence award from the University of North Carolina at Greensboro.

**Department of Child Development and Family Relations and Family Research Center, University of North Carolina, Greensboro, North Carolina 27412.

rival explanations, it has yielded the strongest evidence to date of a causal relationship between welfare and marital stability. Bahr (1979) concluded that it was likely that public assistance was contributing to marital dissolution by either directly encouraging divorce or indirectly providing alternate means of support for women who were involved in unsatisfactory marriages.

There are both substantive and technical reasons for questioning Bahr's (1979) findings. His substantive conclusions are markedly more pessimistic than those of other researchers who have studied the relationship between public assistance and welfare. In his classic treatise on welfare, Steiner (1971:85) states that there are "no grounds to conclude that there is any close tie between making a public relief program available to families with a father in the home and the . . . incidence of broken homes." Steiner has pointed out that while the hypothesis that public assistance causes marital dissolution is reasonable on its face, an equally reasonable hypothesis is that such aid is a consequence, rather than a cause, of desertion and divorce. Single-parent families can fall back on public assistance "rather than being forced to fractionalize further by parceling out children among relatives" (Steiner, 1971:82). Bahr's (1979) conclusion appears to reflect the new conservative *zeitgeist* in which negative interpretations of social data are given preeminence.

The technical analysis by which Bahr reached his conclusions does not provide the social policymaker with as much information as it might. First, Bahr (1979) examined data from only two of 10 possible longitudinal comparisons. Data on marital stability, receipt of Aid to Families with Dependent Children (AFDC), food stamps, and welfare were available for comparisons between 1967 and 1969, 1967 and 1971, 1967 and 1972, 1969 and 1971, 1969 and 1972, and 1971 and 1972. Data on marital stability and receipt of welfare were available for comparisons between 1967 and 1974, 1969 and 1974, 1971 and 1974, and 1972 and 1974. Bahr looked at the relationship between data from 1967 and 1969 and 1967 and 1974. It is important to know if the reported causal relationship was present in the majority of longitudinal comparisons or limited to just a few of them. Second, Bahr (1979) did not indicate how

much variation in marital stability can be attributed to welfare status. It would certainly make a difference to the policymaker to know whether the variation in welfare was accounting for 2 percent as opposed to 20 percent of the total variation in marital stability. Such information would be important for any risk-benefits analysis. Third, Bahr (1979) used the time-lagged comparisons to infer a causal relationship between two variables but he discussed only one of two possible relationships within each time-lagged comparison. Not only may welfare status at one time be correlated with marital status at a later time, marital status at the first time may also be correlated with welfare status at the later time. It is impossible to make a strong argument for a cause and effect relationship without considering and comparing both cross-lagged relationships that are present in longitudinal data (Kenny, 1979). As Steiner (1971) has pointed out, one should not consider the effect of welfare on separation and divorce without considering the effects of separation and divorce on welfare. The need for assistance should be considered along with the risks of assisting.

REANALYSIS

A cross-lagged panel correlation (CLPC) technique was selected for a renalysis of the NLSLME data. This cross-over procedure allowed the comparison of the effects of marital stability on welfare with the effects of welfare on marital stability. The use of correlations provided information about the magnitude of the effects.

The data for the present study were derived from the same sample employed in the Bahr (1979) study. The sample consisted of 5,083 mature females, ranging in age from 30 through 44. In collecting these data, an attempt was made to interview each woman in 1967, 1969, 1971, 1972, and 1974. Information on marital status and receipt of AFDC, food stamps, and other welfare had been obtained in each of the first four interviews. Information on marital status and receipt of welfare was obtained in the fifth interview. Marriage was defined as unstable if the respondent was separated or divorced at the time of the interview, and stable if the respondent was married and not separated.

Widows, those who became widows, and those who had never married were excluded from the sample. Each public-assistance variable was defined in the same way: Individuals who received any assistance of the type specified during the previous year were listed by the interviewer as having received assistance. For example, in the statistical analysis, women who received any amount of AFDC during the entire year were placed into one category and women who did not receive AFDC for that year were placed into another.

Comparisons were made between all possible cross-lags over the five waves of data. This resulted in 6 comparisons involving AFDC, 6 involving food stamps, and 10 involving other welfare. For each comparison, only individuals with available data for all of the variables in both time periods were included in the analysis. The correlations between the variables are presented in Table 1 and each set of comparisons may be fitted to the model in Figure 1.

FIGURE 1. TWO-WAVE, TWO-VARIABLE MODEL FOR CROSS-LAGGED PANEL CORRELATIONS

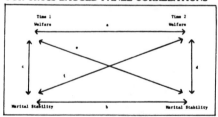

Note. a, b = auto correlations
      c, f = synchronous correlations
      e, f = cross-lagged correlations

The correlations leading from marital stability to welfare were generally larger than the ones leading from welfare to marital stability. This was true for all 6 comparisons involving AFDC, 5 of the 6 comparisons involving food stamps, and 7 out of 10 of the comparisons involving other welfare. In every case where the correlations did not follow this pattern the difference between the cross-lags was less than it was in those cases where the pattern held.

Kenny (1979) has recommended using the Pearson-Filon test for comparing cross-lagged correlations. The testing procedure requires two steps. First, the synchronous correlations are compared to ensure that the relationships being measured are relatively stable. Second, the cross-lagged correlations are compared to determine whether or not they are different. Differences in cross-lagged correlations are easiest to interpret if the synchronous correlations are stable. If the synchronous correlations are themselves quite different, the interpretation of differences in cross-lagged correlations is more difficult.

Kenny (1979) suggests that this statistical test be used with cross-lagged correlations with an absolute value of .3 or higher. Most of the coefficients in Table 1 are lower than that. However, in the formula for the significance test, an unusually large sample size can compensate for somewhat smaller than recommended cross-lagged correlations.

Results of the Pearson-Filon test of statistical significance are reported in the last two columns in Table 1. The synchronous correlations were stable (not significantly different) for 3 of the 6 comparisons involving AFDC, 2 of the 6 comparisons involving food stamps, and 6 of the 10 comparisons involving other welfare. In all comparisons of synchronous correlations, the most recent (Time 2) correlations were the largest. The cross-lagged correlations were significantly different for 3 of the 6 comparisons involving AFDC, 3 of the 6 comparisons involving food stamps, and 5 of the 10 comparisons involving other welfare. In all cases where there was a significant difference between cross-lagged correlations, the correlation leading from marital stability to welfare was larger than the correlation leading from welfare to marital stability.

The logic of CLPC suggests that a dominant crossing is incompatible with most third-factor explanations and, therefore, highly compatible with a causal explanation (Kenny, 1975, 1979; Crano et al., 1972; Baltes et al., 1977; Christensen, 1980). In the present study, the dominant cross-lag was a negative correlation running from marital status at Time 1 to welfare status at Time 2.

There were two causal relationships implied by the dominant cross-lagged correlations. Marital stability may have

TABLE 1. CROSS-LAGGED CORRELATIONS BETWEEN THREE TYPES OF WELFARE AND MARITAL STABILITY COVERING FIVE TIME PERIODS

Times Being Compared	Type of Welfare	Correlations[a]						N	Pearson-Filon Tests	
		Crosslagged		Synchronous		Auto			Synchronous Correlations[c] Z	Cross-lagged Correlations[c] Z
		W_1M_2[b]	M_1W_2	W_1M_1	W_2M_2	W_1W_2	M_1M_2			
Time 1-Time 2										
67-69	AFDC	.278	.318	.313	.325	.555	.830	3657	0.79	2.48*
	Food Stamps	.156	.146	.169	.182	.396	.830	3657	0.71	0.55
	Other	.117	.113	.120	.139	.244	.830	3657	0.90	0.16
67-71	AFDC	.241	.288	.313	.345	.478	.733	3657	1.88	2.59*
	Food Stamps	.133	.196	.169	.231	.286	.733	3657	3.09*	3.11*
	Other	.112	.110	.120	.154	.271	.733	3657	1.64	0.09
67-72	AFDC	.216	.288	.313	.377	.429	.679	3657	3.65*	4.53*
	Food Stamps	.117	.196	.169	.255	.245	.679	3657	4.27*	3.32*
	Other	.118	.118	.120	.156	.183	.679	3657	1.65	0.03
67-74	Other	.126	.266	.120	.349	.225	.629	3657	11.25*	6.72*
69-71	AFDC	.299	.324	.325	.345	.581	.831	3674	1.27	1.58
	Food Stamps	.170	.216	.182	.231	.523	.831	3674	2.87*	2.69*
	Other	.126	.150	.139	.154	.396	.831	3674	0.80	1.26
69-72	AFDC	.277	.322	.365	.377	.527	.756	3674	3.18*	2.65*
	Food Stamps	.186	.218	.182	.255	.497	.756	3674	4.12*	1.79
	Other	.112	.157	.139	.156	.362	.756	3674	0.86	2.26*
69-74	Other	.100	.292	.139	.349	.269	.696	3674	10.62*	9.56*
71-72	AFDC	.332	.351	.345	.377	.682	.889	3685	2.43*	1.37
	Food Stamps	.228	.248	.231	.255	.662	.889	3685	1.70	1.39
	Other	.145	.171	.154	.156	.467	.889	3685	0.10	1.44
71-74	Other	.131	.326	.154	.349	.338	.775	3685	10.35*	10.24*
72-74	Other	.147	.334	.156	.349	.351	.825	3690	10.41*	10.04*

[a]All correlations are significant ($p < .05$).
[b]W_1 = Welfare status at Time 1
W_2 = Welfare status at Time 2
M_1 = Marital status at Time 1
M_2 = Marital status at Time 2
[c]All synchronous and cross-lagged correlations are negative.
*$p < .05$.

decreased welfare or welfare may have increased marital stability. The preferred relationship was determined by noting the sign of the synchronous correlations (Kenny, 1979; Christensen, 1980). The negative synchronous correlations were suggestive of a causal relationship in which marital stability decreased welfare. This relationship could also be restated as marital instability increased welfare. Both statements are consistent with the view that fluctuations in marital status affect welfare status.

This description of the relationship was most appropriate for comparisons where the synchronous correlations were not significantly different, but where the cross-lagged correlations were. These included two comparisons involving AFDC and one involving other welfare. The causal explanation may also have been appropriate for describing comparisons where both the synchronous and the cross-lagged correlations were significantly different. Its appropriateness would depend on the reason for the instability of the synchronous correlations.

If the instability was due to measurement error, the causal relationship would have been less applicable to those comparisons where the synchronous correlations were significantly different. If the instability was the result of a causal effect that increased in size over time, the cause and effect explanation would still apply. The straightforwardness and simplicity of the interviewer's questions about marital and welfare status reduced the likelihood of measurement error. The high auto correlations in Table 1 are also suggestive of a small measurement error. Most of the variation between time periods appear to be due to actual changes in status rather than to unreliable measurement.

Kenny (1979:239) has argued that if a variable becomes more causally effective over time, "this effect would be indicated by not only aysmmetrical crosslags, but also by changing, usually increasing, synchronous correlations. Thus in many non-trivial instances, changing synchronous correlations may be indicative of causal effects." The significantly different cross-lags that were paired with significantly different synchronous correlations did fit this pattern. As can be seen in Table 1, the synchronous correlations

between all three measures of public assistance and marital stability grew larger with each new wave of data.

An increase over time in the causal relationship between marital stability and welfare could have been due to several different things. The women in the sample were growing older as the study proceeded. They were between the ages of 30 and 45 in 1967, but had aged seven years by the last wave of data. It would seem highly plausible that as women become older their alternate means of support when divorced become more limited. This could have increased the demand for welfare, thereby increasing the synchronous correlations. The near doubling of divorces per 1000 married women between 1967 and 1974 also may have played a role (National Center for Health Statistics, 1979). A rapid increase in the number of divorced women may have strained alternative financial-support systems. Economic trends and changes in welfare eligibility criteria, or any interaction of the above variables, could also have resulted in an increase over time in both the causal relationship and the synchronous correlations.

In sum, a causal explanation in which marital status affects welfare status appears to be compatible with half of the time-lagged comparisons of each type of welfare. The remaining comparisons are not exclusively compatible with the explanation. The presence of two statistically significant cross-lagged correlations, neither dominant, suggests one of the two following possible explanations: Unspecified sources of variation, such as personal instability mentioned by Bahr (1979), could have caused both marital status and welfare status to covary. Or, marital status and welfare status may have affected each other over time in a reciprocal cause and effect relationship. Marital instability may have increased the need for public assistance. Public assistance, in turn, may have promoted a smaller increase in marital instability. The likelihood of such reciprocal relationships in complex social phenomena is being recognized at the present time to a greater extent than ever before (cf. Spanier et al., 1978; Klein et al., 1978; Bell, 1979).

CONCLUSIONS

This reanalysis was prompted by several questions that might be of concern to social policymakers:

1. What was the magnitude of the time-lagged relationship leading from welfare status to marital stability that was reported by Bahr (1979)?
2. Was the relationship reported by Bahr (1979) the dominant causal relationship between these two variables?
3. Which conclusion about public assistance and marital stability was most consistent with the NLSLME data, Steiner's (1971) or Bahr's (1979)?

In answer to the first question, it can be seen that the cross-lagged correlations were quite small. Only one of the 22 correlations leading from the different welfare variables to the marital stability variable was greater than .3. More than half of these correlations were less than .2. The amount of covariation explained by such correlations is quite small. In answer to the second question, the overall pattern of results does not support the existence of the causal relationship running from welfare status to marital status that was suggested by Bahr (1979). The effect of welfare status on marital stability was often less than the effect of marital stability on welfare status, and it was never more.

In answer to the third question, the findings are highly consistent with the pattern suggested by Steiner (1971): First, there is little evidence of a strong relationship between public assistance and marital stability. Second, if there is a causal relationship, the only one supported by the present analysis is that divorce and separation cause women to go on welfare, perhaps as a means of keeping the rest of the family together. There is additional evidence that the need for this support may be made greater by aging or by social and economic trends such as a rising divorce rate.

It is possible, of course, to argue that the public aid laws have enticed some people to divorce or separate in order to maximize benefits. The NLSLME data do not allow one to address this issue fully. However, in comparing states where the welfare laws penalize intact families with states where they do not, Steiner (1971) found no evidence that people were dissolving marriages in order to

obtain public assistance. Steiner's conclusions are similar to those of Ryan (1971:106) who states that "To suggest that anyone—or at least more than a tiny handful of erratic or disturbed persons—would choose the bitter existence of AFDC as a way of life except as a last resort, is to demonstrate ignorance either of the basic nature of humanity, or of what life is like on AFDC." Further, if couples were instigating divorce or separation in order to maximize welfare benefits it stands to reason that they would attempt to collect those benefits as quickly as possible. This would result in the shortest possible delay between divorce and the beginning of welfare payments. In order for this "instigation" argument to hold, one would have to argue that the NLSLME interviews just happened to catch a sizeable proportion of individuals who were attempting to maximize their public assistance benefits between the time they had obtained a divorce or separation and prior to the time they began receiving welfare. This argument does not seem very likely unless the processing period for welfare applicants was extremely long.

No doubt, the social consequences of public assistance will continue to be debated. The findings of the present work, involving a nationwide sample of mature women studied over an 8 year span have relevance for that debate. First, there is no evidence of a strong relationship between public assistance and marital stability. Second, there is no compelling evidence of a causal relationship whereby public assistance affects marital stability. Third, there is evidence that public assistance can play a modest positive role in the lives of women who become divorced or separated, particularly as they grow older. The major implication of these findings is that it is inappropriate to attempt to judge the value of AFDC, food stamps, and other welfare in terms of their effects on marital stability. Whatever other positive or negative effects these programs may have, there is little evidence that they influence marital stability in any substantial way.

These findings also have implications for the growth and maintenance of financial independence in adults. It appears that one way for a society to foster independence and reduce the need for public aid is to promote marital stability. This relationship is undoubtedly highly complex and in need of extensive study. These initial findings do suggest, however, that those most concerned with reducing the welfare rolls might do well to support programs designed to stabilize marriages.

REFERENCES

Bahr, S. J.
  1979 "The effects of welfare on marital stability and remarriage." Journal of Marriage and the Family 41 (August):553-560.
Baltes, P. B., H. W. Reese, and J. R. Nesselroade
  1977 Life-Span Developmental Psychology: Introduction to Research Methods. Monterey, California:Brooks/Cole.
Bell, R. Q.
  1979 "Parent, child, and reciprocal influences." American Psychologist 34 (October):821-826.
Caplow, T.
  1975 Toward Social Hope. New York:Basic Books.
Christensen, L. B.
  1980 Experimental Methodology. Boston:Allyn and Bacon.
Crano, W. D., D. A. Kenny, and D. T. Campbell
  1972 "Does intelligence cause achievement?: A cross-lagged panel analysis." Journal of Educational Psychology 63 (June):258-275.

Kenny, D. A.
  1975 "Cross-lagged panel correlation: A test for spuriousness." Psychological Bulletin 82 (November):887-903.
  1979 Correlation and Causality. New York:John Wiley and Sons.
Klein, D. M., S. R. Jorgensen, and B. C. Miller
  1978 "Research methods and developmental reciprocity in families." Pp. 107-135 in R. M. Lerner and G. B. Spanier (Eds.), Child Influences on Marital and Family Interaction: A Life-Span Perspective. New York:Academic Press.
National Center for Health Statistics
  1979 "Divorces by marriage cohort." Vital and Health Statistics. U.S. Department of Health, Education, and Welfare 21(August): Number 34.
Ryan, W.
  1971 Blaming the Victim. New York:Pantheon Books.
Spanier, G. B., R. M. Lerner, and W. Aquilino
  1978 "The study of child-family interactions: A perspective for the future." Pp. 327-344 in R. M. Lerner and G. B. Spanier (Eds.), Child Influences on Marital and Family Interaction: A Life-Span Perspective. New York:Academic Press.
Steiner, G. Y.
  1971 The State of Welfare. Washington, D.C.:The Brookings Institution.

We review the reasons for expecting a negative income tax (NIT) to affect marital dissolution rates and present a stochastic model of marital dissolution. The analysis reveals that the experimental NIT programs increased the marital dissolution rates for blacks and whites but not Chicanos. The differences in the magnitude of the responses by NIT guarantee level suggest that there are nonpecuniary differences between the experimental programs and existing income-support programs. We compare the Seattle and Denver Income Maintenance Experiments findings with the findings from the other income maintenance experiments and discuss implications for welfare reform.

4

THE EFFECTS OF NEGATIVE INCOME TAX PROGRAMS ON MARITAL DISSOLUTION*

Lyle P. Groeneveld, Nancy Brandon Tuma, and Michael T. Hannan

I. INTRODUCTION

Analyses of proposals to replace the current welfare system with a negative income tax (NIT) usually focus on two issues: the effect of the proposed system on incentives to work, and the effect on incentives to marry and stay married. It has been widely agreed that changes in welfare systems alter levels of work effort and that such changes constitute a major component

---

*   The research reported herein was performed pursuant to contracts with the States of Washington and Colorado, prime contractors for the Department of Health, Education, and Welfare under contract numbers HEW-100-78-005 and HEW-100-78-0004, respectively. The opinions expressed in the paper are those of the authors and should not be construed as representing the opinions or policies of the States of Washington and Colorado or any agency of the United States government. We gratefully acknowledge the research assistance of Helen Garrison and Bevery Lauwagie, the helpful comments we received from Douglas Wolf, and the continuing support and encouragement of Robert G. Spiegelman, Director of the Socioeconomic Research Center.

of the net increase in costs under a negative income tax scheme. Until recently there has been no similar consensus that alternative welfare arrangements might substantially alter marital behavior. Hence, policy analysts have tended to understate the importance of effects on marital stability for the long-run cost of an NIT. This situation appears to be changing; the interest in the stabilization of marriage has become the central issue in the welfare reform debate.

This paper has three main purposes. The first is to state the substantive issues—in particular, why an NIT might have an effect on marital stability. The second is to present the results of the Seattle and Denver Income Maintenance Experiments (SIME/DIME) marital dissolution studies in a straightforward manner.[1] Our final purpose is to address the policy relevance of the SIME/DIME findings. We compare our findings with the results from the other income maintenance experiments. Then we discuss some implications of our findings for welfare reform.

II. THE EXPECTED EFFECT OF AN NIT ON MARITAL DISSOLUTION

There are several reasons why one might expect a negative income tax program to affect marital dissolution. First, an NIT would remove the incentives to marital dissolution inherent in the present system. AFDC prohibits benefits to families in which the father is present. The AFDC-UP program eases this restriction somewhat, but only if the father is employed less than some maximum number of days in a period. It is the number of days the father is employed, not the adequacy of the family income, that determines eligibility under the AFDC-UP program. In many states a family unit with the father working full time at the minimum wage has less income (earnings, tax credits, and Food Stamps) than the family would receive from AFDC and Food Stamps if the father were not present. An NIT program with eligibility determined by family income would do away with these restrictions and, thereby, eliminate these incentives for marital dissolution.

No one has yet shown that such financial inducements have important effects on marital dissolution rates. Most research correlates state welfare benefit levels with the number of female-headed households, while controlling for other factors such as the unemployment level or the level of female wages (Honig [93, 94], Ross and Sawhill [187], Minarik and

---

1 We have also analyzed the experimental effects on remarriage, but do not report those results in this paper. In general, we found no significant experimental effect on the rate at which marriages were formed. Our marital formation results are reported in Hannan, Tuma, and Groeneveld [82, 83] and Tuma, Hannan, and Groeneveld [221].

Goldfarb [149]). Data aggregated at the state or SMSA level do not allow one to disentangle the effects of welfare on families from selective migration to areas with high benefit levels. Also, the effect of the benefit levels on the number of female-headed families cannot be distinguished from the effect of the number of female-headed families on the benefit levels. At best, we are ignorant about the effect of the current welfare system on marital stability.

Even if the current welfare system does not promote marital instability, an NIT program may still alter marital dissolution rates by altering levels of family income. Many studies have shown that the probability of marital dissolution is highest for the lowest income families. This relationship can be interpreted in several ways.[2] According to the culture of poverty thesis, the relationship between income and marital instability reflects cultural differences between the poor and the rest of society. Advocates of this position argue that the poor have high rates of marital dissolution because they lack appropriate values and personality traits, not because they lack material resources. If so, altering income levels will not affect marital stability in a low-income population.

Other interpretations of this relationship suggest that an NIT program will stabilize marriage. One holds that changes in income affect the strains to which marriages are exposed and the ability of the families to cope with various problems and dissatisfactions. Another argument contends that personal and social worth are evaluated primarily through consumption activities in our society. Heads of families who cannot provide certain levels of consumption for their families are viewed as failures by themselves and others. One response to such failure is flight from the marriage. Income-supplement progams that substantially improve living standards might reduce the pressures toward dissolution. We refer to such stabilizing effects as *income effects*. We expect that the income effects of an NIT would lower the rate of marital dissolution.

There is another effect of an NIT program that has been overlooked in most discussions of welfare reform. Early in our research we suggested that an NIT would alter the structure of dependence in marriages (Hannan, Beaver, and Tuma [80]). An NIT program that guarantees support to unmarried as well as married people will alter the level of resources available outside the marriage and thereby alter the dependence of the members on marriage. We refer to this as the *independence effect*. If the NIT program increases the level of resources outside of marriage, the independence effect will raise the probability of marital dissolution.

2   Alternative explanations of the relationships between marital dissolution and income are discussed more fully by Hannan, Tuma, and Groeneveld [82, 83].

For an independence effect to be present under an NIT but be of little consequence in the present welfare system, we need to consider the issue of *welfare stigma* and, more generally, the idea of a *welfare discount*. It is often argued that the current welfare system stigmatizes recipients and that an NIT program would reduce the stigma. If participation in the current system is perceived as degrading, both its income and independence effects are muted. Families receiving payments would not experience the full income effect due to the strain induced by stigma. Likewise, dependent spouses would not experience the full independence effect of the welfare system. In particular, women who believe that receiving welfare is degrading may choose to remain in unsatisfying marriages rather than go on welfare. This suggests that the income and independence effects of the current welfare system will be weaker than the effects of an NIT program of the same generosity. Another way of putting this is to say that welfare is "discounted" in its effects on marriage relative to an NIT program.

There are other nonpecuniary differences between welfare and NIT plans that may result in welfare being discounted. Participation in the NIT program involves less effort than going on welfare. Our experimental NIT program has a simpler and presumably less alienating bureaucracy. The rules of the NIT program are carefully explained to the participants. Information about eligibility rules and guarantee levels of welfare are probably not as well known. These three factors (stigma, transaction costs, and lack of information) suggest that the benefits of the current welfare system are discounted.

What, then can be said about the expected impact of an NIT program on marital dissolution rates? For an NIT program that is more generous than the present welfare system, as are most of the treatments in the Seattle-Denver experiments, it is not possible to predict the direction of the net impact a priori. If the income effects dominate, the NIT program will lower the dissolution rate. If the independence effects are stronger, the reverse will hold. Even a less generous program may have both income and independence effects if the changes in the operation of the program affect the rate at which welfare is discounted.

In considering the expected effects of an NIT program on marital dissolution, it is important to consider the ways in which the effects of a short-term experiment such as SIME/DIME might differ from the effects of a permanent national program. During the initial phases of the NIT experiments, many commentators felt that any effects of short-term experiments on marital stability would be too small to be detectable. While a permanent program might affect marital stability, the cost of a marital break-up was thought to be too great to be affected by a short-term experiment. Thus, any estimates of the experimental effects would be underestimates of the effects of a national program.[3]

On the other hand, it is possible that the experiment might be used as an opportunity to get on one's feet after leaving a bad marriage. The short duration of the experiment would give people an incentive to incur such costs during the experimental period when these costs would be subsidized. A permanent program would not have a timing effect in the long run, although the introduction of a permanent program might have such an effect. While many plausible arguments can be offered, there is no clear a priori expectation for the differences between the effects of an experiment and of a permanent program.

III. A MODEL OF MARITAL DISSOLUTION

Because couples dissolve their marriages rather infrequently, we model marital dissolution in a way similar to analyses of other rare events. We chose to model marital dissolution as a discrete-state process in continuous time.[4] We describe the model briefly. A complete discussion of the model can be found in Tuma, Hannan, and Groeneveld [222]. The model is specified in terms of the instantaneous rate at which dissolution occurs at time t given that the couple had not dissolved their marriage at some earlier time t'. Stated formally, the model is:

$$(1) \qquad r(t|t') = \frac{[dF(t|t')]/dt}{1 - F(t|t')}$$

where

$$(2) \qquad F(t|t') = \text{Prob (a couple whose marriage was intact at time } t' \text{ dissolves their marriage before } t)$$

and

$$(3) \qquad F(t|t') = 0 \text{ when } t < t'$$

Equation (1) is a differential equation with the following solution:

$$(4) \qquad F(t|t') = 1 - \exp[-\int_{t'}^{t} r(u|t')du]$$

Equation (4) shows that the rate r specifies the probability that a marriage that existed at t' dissolves before time t. The rate may depend on time and

---

3 The effects of the experiments might also be less than the effects of a national program if people have less confidence in an experimental program than in a national program.

4 In the larger work from which these results are drawn, we also employed a linear probability model of dissolution. The qualitative results of the two models agree closely. In this paper we use only the continuous-time model which we believe to be superior. Results from the linear probability model are reported in Hannan, Tuma, and Groeneveld. [83].

upon exogenous variables. We report here the results from a model in which the rate does not depend on time (i.e., the rate is constant), but does depend on exogenous variables. The particular form we used is:

(5) $$r = \exp(b_0 + b_1 x_1 + b_2 x_2 + \ldots + b_j x_j)$$

where x_j is one of the v exogenous variables and b_j is its coefficient which must be estimated. Equation (5) may be expressed in a log-linear form:

(6) $$\ln r = b_0 + b_1 x_1 + b_2 x_2 + \ldots + b_j x_j$$

The coefficients of the variables are estimated by the method of maximum likelihood from the data on the timing of marital dissolutions.[5]

Because we are interested in the effect of the income maintenance experiments on marital dissolution, we take t' as the date on which we first observe the married couple, that is, the date of their enrollment in the experiment.

In estimating equation (6), we included three kinds of independent variables: assignment variables, characteristics of the couple, and variables describing the experimental treatment. The assignment variables are included to control for the stratified random assignment. Since we are analyzing marital dissolutions and estimate the effects separately for each race-ethnic group, we need only control for normal income level and site. Each equation contains a set of dummy variables for the normal income level categories used in the assignment process. (See Keeley and Robins in this volume for a description of the assignment process.) The experimental site is included as a dummy variable that equals one for Denver couples and zero for Seattle couples. Characteristics of the couple known to affect marital stability are included to increase the precision of our estimates of the experimental effects. These variables are the age and education of the husband and wife, the duration married at enrollment, the number of children in the family, and dummy variables indicating whether the family had a child less than 6 years old and whether the family received AFDC payments in the year before the experiment.

The experimental effects are measured by dummy variables representing the treatments. The manpower program is represented by three dummy variables, one for each manpower treatment condition. We do not focus on this aspect of the experiment in this paper. The financial treatment is represented in two ways in this paper: by a dummy variable that equals one for financial couples and zero for controls, or by a set of three

---

5 The maximum-likelihood estimates of the coefficients and their standard errors are obtained by RATE, a FORTRAN program developed by Nancy Brandon Tuma. Further information can be obtained by writing to Dr. Tuma at the Department of Sociology, Stanford University, Stanford, CA 94305.

dummy variables, one for each guarantee level. In both models the length of the treatment is represented by a dummy variable that equals one for three-year experimental couples and zero for all other couples.

We report the results from two models, differing only in the representation of the financial treatment. The models are estimated in the log-linear form. The first is

$$(7) \qquad \ln r = BX + \alpha F + \gamma Y$$

where X is a vector including the assignment variables, characteristics of the couple, and the manpower variables; B is the vector of associated coefficients; F is the experimental-control dummy variable; α is the coefficient measuring the experimental effect; Y is the dummy variable for the three-year treatment; and γ is the coefficient measuring the difference between the effect of the three-year treatment and the five-year treatment. Thus, the change in the logarithm of the dissolution rate for a couple assigned to a five-year experimental program is α. The change for a couple assigned to a three-year program is $\alpha + \gamma$. The second model is

$$(8) \qquad \ln r = BX + \alpha_1 S_1 + \alpha_2 S_2 + \alpha_3 S_3 + \gamma Y$$

where B and X are as defined in equation (7); S_1, S_2, and S_3 are guarantee-level dummy variables; α_1, α_2. and α_3 are their coefficients; and γ and Y are as defined in equation (7).

While the model is estimated in the log-linear form, the results are easier to interpret if presented in the multiplicative form. The interpretation of e^α is straightforward; it is the ratio of the marital dissolution rates of identical experimental and control couples. If, for example, e^α in equation (7) is 1.50, then the experimental effect is to increase the marital dissolution 1.50 times. The effect may also be expressed as a percent increase by subtracting 1.0 and multiplying by 100. If α equals 1.50, the percentage increase is 50 percent.

One advantage of this model deserves special mention. All panel studies, including SIME/DIME, face the problem of sample attrition. Fortunately, the attrition rate for the two-year period studied here is low: 13 percent for blacks, 8 percent for whites, and 11 percent for Chicanos. The impact of attrition on our results is even less than these figures suggest because the model we use allows us to employ partial observations. If a couple is in the experiment for only part of the time, we analyze their marital behavior up until the time of their attrition. The observation period may be different for each case. For the majority of couples in our analysis, the observation period is two years, but for those couples who attrited, the observation period is shorter. We believe this helps to reduce attrition bias. Other methods more usually employed in panel studies that require cases to be present over some fixed time period are subject to much more attrition bias. We discuss our analysis of attrition after the presentation of our findings.

IV. THE MARRIED-COUPLE SAMPLE

The experimental rules of operation did not require that couples be legally married to be enrolled. Legally married couples could be enrolled whether they had children or not as long as they met the other eligibility criteria. Cohabiting couples, that is, couples who were not legally married, were enrolled as married couples if children were present in the household. Cohabiting childless couples were excluded from the experiment. These rules insured that the "marriages" we study here are not casual or temporary unions, but ones that are intended to be permanent, whether or not they are legal.[6] No attempt was made to record the legal status of marriages at enrollment.

We cannot detect any differences in marital dissolution rates between legal and consensual unions. We do not consider this to be a serious weakness, however. The enrollment criteria insured that the partners in the marital unions we analyzed are committed to the relationships. The majority of the unions are long term; 87 percent had existed two years or longer at the time of enrollment. We do not believe that a national NIT program could ignore consensual unions such as those included in this analysis. The earnings of a cohabitant would not be ignored simply because the couple had never been legally married.

In keeping with the SIME/DIME rules of operation, we defined a marriage as dissolved whenever the couple ceased to cohabit and claimed that the separation was permanent. We learned about these dissolutions in a variety of ways. Couples sometimes contacted our field offices directly or indicated the dissolution on their monthly income reporting form (experimentals) or address reporting form (controls). Dissolutions were also recorded on the periodic interviews that were administered to both controls and experimentals approximately three times a year. No matter what the source of the original report, we included only dissolutions that were confirmed in the interviewing process. This insured that any differences between experimentals and controls would not be due to the greater contact maintained with the experimental families through the payment system.

Although most of the marital dissolutions we observed were permanent, a small percentage resulted in the couple's reconciling. Approximately 10 percent of the dissolutions resulted in reconciliations within six

---

6 These rules are similar to the AFDC eligibility rules which are stated in terms of paternity, not legal marital status.

months. According to our procedures, such separations were treated as dissolutions. Since the period between initial separation and reconciliation was sometimes brief,[7] some have questioned counting such events as dissolutions. We agree that not all dissolutions have equal importance, but we have not found a satisfactory alternative. Moreover, even short separations affect the payments received by family members.

One alternative is to impose some minimum waiting period. For example, we could count as dissolutions only those separations that exceed six months. But, the choice of a waiting period is arbitrary, and we have more confidence in the reports of permanence by the people involved than we have in our ability to choose the appropriate period. Whatever the waiting period, we would lose that much of our observation period because events occurring during that time cannot be verified as permanent. We would lose all observations on couples who dissolve their marriage and then leave the experiment during the waiting period.

The sample used in the analysis reported here includes all 2,771 couples who were married at enrollment. Couples who married after enrollment are excluded.[8] Table 1 reveals some important characteristics of the married sample. The mean duration married at enrollment is 8.73 years. This, when compared with the mean ages of husbands (33.49 years) and wives (30.66 years) is further evidence that our definition of marriage does not result in a sample with a large number of temporary unions. The preexperimental annual family disposable income (i.e., after taxes) is $6,208, substantially above the 1972 poverty level ($4,275 for a family of four). Finally, notice that only 11 percent of the sample attrited during the first two years. This low attrition rate gives us increased confidence in the findings we report.

V. BASIC FINDINGS FROM SIME/DIME

Our analysis of the experimental effect on marital dissolution has used several analytical methods and analyzed data over several time periods. We have consistently found that the experimental NIT plans increased the marital dissolution rates for whites and blacks. We report the results obtained using the instantaneous rate model discussed in Section III. The time period analyzed is the first two years of the experiment. The

---

7 The procedure established to keep track of family composition changes were such that very few dissolutions followed by reconciliation were recorded if the period of separation was less than 30 days.

8 Other reports of our findings [82, 83] included marriages formed during the experiment as well as the marriages observed at enrollment. There is no substantive difference in the results when new marriages are included.

TABLE 1

CHARACTERISTICS OF THE ORIGINALLY MARRIED SAMPLE

Variable	Mean or Proportion
Husband's age (in years)	33.49
Husband's education (in years)	10.90
Wife's age (in years)	30.66
Wife's education (in years)	11.03
Duration married at enrollment (in years)	8.73
Number of children	2.30
Preexperimental annual family disposable income	$6,208
Proportion with at least one child under 10 years old	.75
Proportion who reported receiving AFDC in the year before the experiment	.16
Proportion of wives employed preexperimentally	.48
Proportion white	.47
Proportion black	.34
Proportion Chicano	.19
Manpower treatment	
Control group	.42
Counseling only	.19
Counseling plus 50 percent subsidy	.24
Counseling plus 100 percent subsidy	.14
Financial treatment	
Control group	.45
$3,800 guarantee level	.18
$4,800 guarantee level	.23
$5,500 guarantee level	.14
Proportion of sample enrolled for 5 years on financial treatment	.18
Proportion attriting before 2 years	.11

observation period for each family starts on the day they enrolled and continues for two years unless they drop out before that time.

There are several reasons for reporting the two-year results here rather than using another time interval. First, we are sensitive to the potential attrition bias in our results. Although attrition from SIME/DIME is fairly low and our method makes use of the partial observations for attrited couples, we have less confidence in our findings as the period of observation is increased. Second, in our equations we control for a number of characteristics known to affect marital stability that change over time. The preexperimental values of these variables become less realistic over longer time periods. Third, over longer time periods the restriction of our

TABLE 2
PROPORTION OF ENROLLED MARRIAGES THAT END
BY DISSOLUTION WITHIN TWO YEARS

	Blacks	Whites	Chicanos
Control group	.149	.091	.135
	(435)	(605)	(200)
Financial treatment group	.218	.160	.170
	(504)	(692)	(336)
Experimental group proportion as a percent of the control group proportion	146	176	126

analysis to enrollment couples becomes less realistic. Couples who are most affected by the experiment dissolve their marriages but are not replaced in the sample. Thus, as time goes on, the sample being analyzed becomes less representative of the original sample. Fourth, the experimental effect in the third year may be reduced for those experimental couples whose treatment ends after three years as they anticipate the end of the treatment. This means that the effects averaged over three years will underestimate the effects of the experimental NIT programs. Fifth, we have studied the experimental effects during the first two years most carefully and have greatest confidence in our estimates. These reasons, taken together, provide a strong basis for presenting the two-year findings here. The analysis we have done of longer time periods is qualitatively similar to these findings.

In Table 2, we report the fraction of the experimental and control group that experienced a marital dissolution during the first two years for each race-ethnic group. Dissolutions were 46 percent more likely among the black experimental group than among black controls, 76 percent more likely among white experimentals than controls, and 26 percent more likely among Chicano experimentals than controls.[9] These percentages do not take into account preexperimental differences between the control and experimental treatment groups that might affect the rates of marital dissolution.

To measure the experimental effects controlling for differences between the experimental and control groups, we estimated the models in

---

9 These proportions and the other results reported in this paper differ slightly from earlier published results. These differences are due to the use of a slightly different set of control variables and to corrections made in the marital history data. Earlier reports (Hannan, Tuma, and Groeneveld [82, 83]) analyzed all marriages during the time period, rather than only couples who were married when enrolled.

LYLE P. GROENEVELD et al.

75

TABLE 3
ESTIMATED MULTIPLIERS OF CONTROL MARITAL DISSOLUTION RATE
DUE TO THE EXPERIMENTAL NIT PROGRAMS

	Blacks	Whites	Chicanos
Model I (Equation 7)			
Financial effect	1.56**	1.72**	1.03
Model II (Equation 8)			
Low guarantee effect	1.53	2.14***	1.47
Medium guarantee effect	1.95***	1.67**	.81
High guarantee effect	1.24	1.25	.70
χ^2 test for difference			
between Models I and II	3.24	3.05	5.09**
Number of cases	939	1,297	536

** Significant at the 5 percent level.   *** Significant at the 1 percent level.

equations (7) and (8). Because the change in the logarithm of a rate has little intuitive meaning, we report the experimental effects as multipliers of the control rate. The log-linear coefficients and their standard errors are given in the Appendix. The effects in Table 3 are for couples assigned to the five-year experimental plans. The results for couples assigned to the three-year plans differ from the five-year effects only by a constant (the γ of equations (7) and (8)). The results for three-year couples can be obtained by using both the three-year treatment coefficient and the financial treatment coefficients from the Appendix. The three-year effect is about 80 percent of the five-year effect for blacks and whites and about 114 percent of the five-year effect for Chicanos. The difference between the three- and five-year treatments is not statistically significant for any race-ethnic group. We think that the five-year effect is a better estimate of the effect of a permanent NIT program than the three-year effect.

The top panel of Table 3 compares all experimentals to the controls. Taken together, the experimental NIT programs increased the marital dissolution 56 percent for blacks and 72 percent for whites. Both effects are statistically significant. The effect for Chicanos is negligible. The positive effects are consistent with a model in which the independence effects dominate the income effects for the program tested.

Our most provocative findings concern the effects by guarantee levels. These results are presented in the second panel of Table 3. While the differences in results by guarantee level are not statistically significant, the size and pattern of the guarantee-level effects are of interest. Note a curious result: for each race-ethnic group, the plan that has the highest guarantee, 140 percent of the poverty line, has the smallest impact. The effect of the highest guarantee level is not statistically significant for any race-ethnic group. It appears that at the highest guarantee level, the income and independence effects are approximately equal, but that the independence effects dominate at lower guarantee levels.

The results for the lowest guarantee level hold particular interest because they differ little in financial terms from the existing level of support available from the AFDC and Food Stamps programs. If welfare is not discounted, this program should have no independence effect. The dissolution rate for families on this treatment greatly exceeds that of the control groups. We conclude that the independence effects of welfare are indeed discounted relative to those of an NIT program. This finding emphasizes the need to understand the stigma and information content of NIT schemes in order to compare their effects with the existing system.

The basic results of the experimental analysis in Table 3 are robust. We have found no technical problems that explain the findings.[10] In particular, these results seem to be robust with respect to attrition bias. We lost track of some families, and others refused to participate after a time. A family's decision to remain in the study was probably affected both by the benefits they received from the experiment and by changes in marital status. If control families were more likely than experimental families to leave the experiment at the time of a marital dissolution, our records would undercount dissolutions for controls, inflating experimental-control differences. Fortunately, the attrition rates in this experiment were low— about 11 percent over two years. In studies of rare events such as marital disruptions, even small attrition rates may give misleading results. Our investigations (Hannan, Tuma, and Groeneveld [83]) showed that our results are not very sensitive to attrition. Even if all the controls who left

---

10   It is unlikely that the finding that the NIT treatments increase dissolution rates results from the fraudulent reporting of dissolutions by experimental couples. While it is true that experimental couples with one high-income spouse can gain financially by fraudu- lently reporting that their marriage has ended and covertly maintaining coresidence, we have found no evidence that this practice was widespread enough to affect our findings. First, the couple would have to maintain the fraud throughout the in-home interviews that occurred three times a year. No cases of such fraud were ever proven, and the field operational staff had sufficient evidence to suspect such fraud in only four or five cases. Second, we have studied the behavior of couples who dissolved marriages during the experiment and found no tendency for experimental couples to reunite after their eligibility for the financial program ended. Third, the same reasoning that suggests that experimental couples would fraudulently report dissolutions also suggests that single persons eligible for the NIT plans would fail to report marriages. However, in none of our analyses have we found evidence of any reduction in marriage rates among experi- mentals. In short, the evidence indicates that the observed experimental-control differences cannot be explained as the result of fraudulently reported marital dissolutions.

the experiment had an unrecorded marital dissolution, the experimental-control difference would still be positive for whites and blacks.

The pattern of guarantee-level effects on the marital dissolution rate reported here, although not statistically significant, is one of the most consistent findings in our SIME/DIME analyses. The first report of marital stability results (Hannan, Beaver, and Tuma [80]) noted that the low guarantee level had greater destabilizing effects than the high guarantee level. This pattern has persisted throughout several rounds of analysis and has stimulated much of the discussion surrounding our work.

One explanation that has often been suggested is that the assignment model is responsible for the pattern of effects. Families assigned to the low guarantee level on the average had lower preexperimental incomes than families on the high guarantee level. The assignment model resulted in the low guarantee level families having higher dissolution rates than controls in the absence of an NIT program. To test for this possibility, the hypothesis that the observed guarantee-level effects simply reflect this fact, we must control for the effects of the assignment variables, which we have done in all our analyses. The pattern of guarantee-level effects that we have reported is *always* net of differences in the rates due to pre-experimental income level.

Another explanation that has been suggested is that the response to the experiment depends on the assignment variables—in particular, that lower income families have a greater response than higher income families to the same treatment. This might be due to the partners in low-income families having less commitment to marriage, to wives in low-income marriages having lesser economic alternatives to marriage perhaps because of their lack of labor force participation, or to the greater strains faced by low-income couples. This explanation assumes that there is an experimental-control difference and seeks to explain only the relative magnitudes of the guarantee-level effects. If the magnitude of the experimental effect varies inversely with the level of family income, then having more low-income families on the low guarantee level would result in the observed pattern of effects.

To investigate this hypothesis, we begin by examining the distribution of originally married families by guarantee level and normal income level;[11] see Table 4. Families with unclassified normal earnings and families in the highest normal earnings category ($11,000-$12,999), which

---

11 Normal family income is the expected income of the family in the year prior to the experiment, assuming normal family circumstances. It includes all money and in-kind earnings from paid work or family business but omits transfer payments. In assigning families to the normal income categories, their income was adjusted by a family-size index to the equivalent income for a family of four.

TABLE 4

NUMBER OF CASES: NORMAL INCOME LEVEL BY GUARANTEE LEVEL BY RACE

Normal Income	Controls	Low Guarantee	Medium Guarantee	High Guarantee	Total
Whites					
$0−999	13	9	6	0	28
$1000−2999	41	33	13	2	89
$3000−4999	81	74	46	17	218
$5000−6999	144	95	89	40	368
$7000−8999	190	4	100	70	364
$9000−10,999	120	4	38	51	180
Total	589	219	292	180	1280
Blacks					
$0−999	10	15	3	1	29
$1000−2999	20	16	7	2	45
$3000−4999	55	58	30	6	149
$5000−6999	89	80	58	23	250
$7000−8999	138	1	76	44	259
$9000−10,999	107	0	36	47	190
Totals	419	170	210	123	922

included only control families who were added to the sample after the original assignment process, are excluded. These families were included in the analysis reported in Tables 2 and 3. We restrict our attention to black and white families, for whom we have consistently found statistically significant guarantee-level effects. The marginals of Table 4 show that for both blacks and whites the majority of the originally married couples had normal income between $3,000 and $10,999. Almost no couples above $7,000 were assigned to the low guarantee level and very few couples in the $3,000−4,999 range were assigned to the high guarantee level. The only normal earnings level that has relatively large numbers of couples assigned to all three guarantee levels is $5,000−6,999. The correlation between normal income and guarantee level that is evident in Table 4 will make our investigation of these interactions difficult since we will be limited in our inferences by the small number of cases in some of the cells.

We modify our model to allow full interaction between guarantee levels and normal income categories:

$$(9) \qquad \ln r = AX + BE + CS_e$$

where r is the dissolution rate, X is a vector of background variables, E is a vector of normal income dummies, S_e is a vector of normal income by guarantee level variables, and A, B, and C are vectors of coefficients to be

TABLE 5
GUARANTEE-LEVEL MULTIPLIERS BY NORMAL EARNINGS LEVEL:
24 MONTHS, FIRST DISSOLUTIONS

Normal Income	Low Guarantee	Medium Guarantee	High Guarantee
Whites			
$0–999	3.66	1.84	—
$1000–2999	2.21	2.37	.00
$3000–4999	1.75	2.42*	.53
$5000–6999	3.05***	2.24*	2.06
$7000–8999	1.17	1.30	1.06
$9000–10,999	12.10***	.36	1.38
Blacks			
$0–999	1.09	.87	.00
$1000–2999	.35	1.42	4.95
$3000–4999	2.94**	2.19	.00
$5000–6999	2.39*	4.40***	4.85***
$7000–8999	.00	2.39**	2.13
$9000–10,999	—	1.41	.58

χ^2 tests for guarantee-level normal income level interactions:
Whites   15.03   (14 d.f.) $p > .10$
Blacks   24.87   (14 d.f.) $p < .05$

*Significant at the 10 percent level.   **Significant at the 5 percent level.   ***Significant at the 1 percent level.

estimated. Estimates of the experimental effects over 24 months of data are reported in Table 5. Each entry is the multiplier of the control rate for a particular combination of normal income and guarantee level; that is, the entries are $\exp(cS_e)$. The missing entries, such as the entry for white, high support, $0–999, indicate no cases in that particular cell. Entries of .00 occur in cells with few cases where no dissolutions were observed. We will concentrate on normal income levels $3,000–4,999, $5,000–6,999, and $7,000–8,999 which contain the majority of cases.

For whites, the high guarantee-level multiplier is smaller than the low guarantee-level multiplier in every case, indicating that the pattern of guarantee-level effects remains for whites with these normal income level interactions. For blacks, the results are less clear. For $3,000–4,999, the low-guarantee multiplier is greater than the medium guarantee-level multiplier, and for $7,000–8,999 the medium guarantee-level multiplier is greater than the high guarantee-level multiplier. For $5,000–6,999, the low guarantee-level multiplier is considerably smaller than the medium or high guarantee-level multipliers.

The results in Table 5 indicate that the pattern of guarantee-level effects observed in our earlier reports is not entirely due to the assignment process for whites but may be for blacks. Throughout our analyses, we have found differences between blacks and whites in the experimental effects. These differences may be due to cultural differences between the two racial groups. Blacks and whites may respond differently to the experimental stimulus because of differences in their backgrounds and experiences. On the other hand, the differences may be due to differences in the joint distributions of variables known to affect marital stability in the two groups. For example, the relationship between normal income level and wife's labor supply may differ in the two groups. We plan to examine such differences in future work.

VI. FINDINGS OF THE OTHER INCOME MAINTENANCE EXPERIMENTS

Each of the other income maintenance experiments (New Jersey, Rural, and Gary) has reported analyses of impacts on marital dissolution. Most reported analyses find no significant experimental effects. However, Sawhill et al. [191] report significant effects of the experimental treatments on marital dissolution in their analysis of data from the New Jersey experiment. Their findings are similar to the SIME/DIME findings: the experimental treatment increased the rate of marital dissolution relative to the controls.

There are several reasons why the results of SIME/DIME should carry more weight in any policy discussion than the results of the other experiments. First, large samples are essential for the study of rare events like marital dissolutions. The other three experiments are hampered by relatively small samples. SIME/DIME contains more families than the other three experiments combined.

SIME/DIME also covers a longer time period than the other experiments. The other three experiments lasted three years. In SIME/DIME, approximately three-fourths of the experimental families were enrolled for three years and one-fourth for five years. Approximately 170 Denver families were enrolled for 20 years. A longer term experiment should approximate the impact of a permanent program more closely. The results from SIME/DIME should indicate the effect of a permanent NIT program more closely than the results from the other experiments.

A third reason to give more weight to the SIME/DIME findings is that the rules regarding marital status and program eligibility changed during both the New Jersey and Gary experiments. In New Jersey, the welfare system changed, permitting families with unemployed fathers to receive

AFDC. The AFDC guarantee level also changed substantially during the New Jersey experiment. In the Gary experiment, families on an NIT plan were told that any one-person unit formed as a result of a marital dissolution would not be eligible for the NIT. Though this rule was changed at the end of the first year, it limits the usefulness of any study of marital impacts.

A fourth reason to give greater weight to the SIME/DIME findings is methodological. The methodology used in the SIME/DIME marital stability analysis allows the observation period to be different in each case. Because of this, cases can be included that end prematurely—for example, families who participate for a while and then attrite. As indicated previously, we use the marital history up until the date of attrition. The methodologies used to analyze data from the other experiments necessitated the elimination of cases that were not observed for the entire period under consideration. Those analyses are subject to attrition bias much more than the SIME/DIME analyses and are less representative of the initial experimental population. For these reasons we think that SIME/DIME offers the best opportunity to evaluate the effects of NIT programs on marital stability.

VII. DISCUSSION

Our findings indicate that SIME/DIME increased the rate of marital dissolutions among the experimental families. The size of the increase was least for the most generous programs. Other analyses that we have conducted (Hannan, Tuma, and Groeneveld [81]) indicate that the hypothesized income and independence effects appear to be operating in the experiment. The effects are nonlinear and depend on the level of income as well as on the NIT-induced changes in income. Furthermore, the results indicate that the experimental effect is, in part, due to nonpecuniary differences between the experimental programs and the existing system.

Projecting our findings to a national NIT program is a complicated task. The effects we have reported here are "average" responses that depend on the details of the program and on the characteristics of the individuals assigned to the program. A 30 percent increase in the marital dissolution rate in SIME/DIME cannot be translated into a 30 percent increase due to a permanent national program. Our analyses have revealed that low-income couples respond more than high-income couples. This would mean that the average change in the dissolution rate under a national NIT would be much smaller than the average change observed in SIME/DIME even if the change among low-income couples were similar to that seen in SIME/DIME. We are presently working on a methodology that would allow appropriate projections of the SIME/DIME findings to a national population. Even without such a methodology, the findings from SIME/DIME can be of use to policy-makers.

It is unlikely that any national NIT would be neutral with respect to marital stability. Our findings suggest that a national program that differed little in generosity from the present welfare programs might have large effects on marital stability. This suggests that careful attention be given to the effects on marital stability of nonpecuniary differences among welfare programs. Our findings also suggest that the more generous plans are more stabilizing than the less generous plans. Thus, the level of generosity of any national plan will affect the magnitude of the marital stability effect.

Lastly, we wish to comment on the normative implications of our findings. Our results indicate that the experimental NIT plans increased the rate of marital dissolution. We believe that a permanent national NIT program would have a similar effect, although we doubt that the magnitude of the effect can be estimated. We can say nothing about the desirability (or undesirability) of such effects. The dissolution of a marital union is a major event in the lives of the partners and results from a complex of causes that are not well understood by either social scientists or the participants. The dissolution may make the partners better off or worse off. An NIT plan might improve the situation for wives who are caught in unsatisfactory marriages by economic circumstances. The data from SIME/DIME do not allow us to resolve such questions. They must be left for future research.

APPENDIX

ESTIMATED EFFECTS ON MARITAL DISSOLUTION RATES DURING THE FIRST TWO YEARS USING EQUATION (8): ORIGINALLY MARRIED COUPLES[a]

	Blacks		Whites		Chicanos	
	Parameter	Standard Error	Parameter	Standard Error	Parameter	Standard Error
Normal earnings						
$0–999	.59	.38	.31	.56	−.73	1.12
$100–2999	−.18	.40	.53	.37	−.46	.60
$3000–4999	−.18	.27	.39	.32	.12	.47
$5000–6999	−.37	.24	.30	.31	.13	.45
$7000–8999	−.42*	.23	.20	.31	−.40	.46
$9000–12,999	—		—		—	
Unclassified	−.45	1.03	1.54	1.04	−10.13	377.10
Site (Denver = 1)	.13	.16	−.27	.17	—	
Duration married	−.05**	.02	−.11***	.02	−.05	.03
Wife's age	−.01	.02	.02	.02	−.06	.04
Wife's education	.04	.05	−.07*	.04	−.02	.07
Husband's age	−.04**	.02	−.03	.02	−.02	.03
Husband's education	−.09**	.04	.01	.04	.05	.05
Number of children	.06	.06	.00	.07	.13	.11
1 if child younger than age 6	−.29	.19	−.19	.19	−.51	.32
1 if preexperimental AFDC	.05	.21	.57***	.21	.79***	.27
Manpower treatment						
Counseling only	.08	.22	.35	.21	.54**	.27
50 percent subsidy	.26	.19	.14	.21	.04	.31
100 percent subsidy	.37	.23	.42*	.23	.19	.38

APPENDIX (*Continued*)

	Blacks		Whites		Chicanos	
	Parameter	Standard Error	Parameter	Standard Error	Parameter	Standard Error
3-year experimental	-.26	.21	-.17	.22	.13	.31
Guarantee levels						
Low	.42	.26	.76***	.26	.39	.37
Medium	.67***	.24	.52**	.26	-.21	.38
High	.21	.28	.22	.32	-.35	.45
Constant	-.01	.85	-1.55*	.81	-1.60	1.24

a The estimated coefficients using equation (7) are similar to those reported here for equation (8). The estimated coefficients of the experimental-control dummy and their standard errors in equation (7) are: blacks .45** (.21), whites .54** (.23), and Chicanos -.01 (.28).
* Significant at the 10 percent level. ** Significant at the 5 percent level. *** Significant at the 1 percent level.

PART II

FAMILY STRESS AND COPING

A disturbance and, in some cases, an imbalance in family functioning often emerge in response to stressors from within and outside of the family unit. A family crisis is viewed as an imbalance in one or two critical dimensions of family functioning, namely (a) member-to-family and/or (b) family-to-community relationships. Family effort at adapting to crises is conceptualized in terms of member and system behavioral efforts to achieve a "balance" simultaneously at these two levels of functioning. This theoretical framework, based on observations from a recent longitudinal study of families under stress, involves an expansion of Hill's ABCX Model. This framework attempts to bridge various physical, psychological, and sociological models of stress, coping, and adaptation. Data on family behavior in response to the chronic stresses of raising a handicapped child are presented as an initial test to the efficacy of this framework and line of theory building.

5

FAMILY STRESS AND ADAPTATION TO CRISES

A Double ABCX Model of Family Behavior

Hamilton I. McCubbin and Joan M. Patterson

In the recent Decade Review of Family Stress and Coping (McCubbin et al., 1980), we noted that in general, family stress studies have produced inconclusive and often contradictory results. This wide variance in findings appears to be due to at least three factors: (a) methodological weaknesses in the study designs and in the definitions and measurement of the constructs studied, (b) the use of simplistic conceptualizations in which family outcomes are related in direct and singular fashion to specific social and intrafamilial stressors, and (c) the paucity of concepts and propositions which help to describe the dynamic nature of family behavior in response to crisis and which can be used to explain the variance in family postcrisis outcomes.

The evidence to date (see expanded version of the Decade Review, McCubbin et al., 1981) strongly suggests that family outcomes following the impact of stressor and a crisis are the byproduct of multiple factors in interaction with each other.

In two recent studies (McCubbin et al., forthcoming; McCubbin and Patterson, forthcoming), we suggest that a more productive research approach in the study of family adaptation to crisis would be to employ a multivariate model

AUTHORS' NOTE: Presented at the Theory Construction and Methodology Workshop, National Council on Family Relations annual meeting, October 1981, Milwaukee, Wisconsin.

where psychological, intrafamilial, and social variables identified from prior family stress research would be addressed simultaneously. By so doing, the individual and collective contributions of these variables could be ascertained. The central question for theory building and research in family crisis investigations then becomes how many and what kinds of stressors, mediated by what family coping responses and by what personal, family, and social resources discriminate between adaptive and maladaptive family units.

CONCEPTUAL FRAMEWORK FOR PAST STRESS RESEARCH: ABCX MODEL

Beginning with the early work of Reuben Hill (1949), who studied the stressors of war separation and reunion, family scholars have attempted to identify which families, under what conditions, using what resources and coping behaviors are able to make positive adaptations to stressful situations. The earliest conceptual foundation for research addressing these questions has been the ABCX family crisis model advanced by Hill (1949):

A (the stressor event)—interacting with B (the family's crisis meeting resources)—interacting with C (the definition the family makes of the event)—produce X (the crisis).

STRESSOR, HARDSHIPS, STRESS, AND DISTRESS

In an effort to render clarity to this model and to establish a link to physiological (Selye, 1976) and psychological (Mikhail, 1981; Lazarus, 1966) concepts of stress, we define a *stressor* as a life event or occurrence in or impacting upon the family unit which produces change in the family social system. This change may be in various areas of family life such as its boundaries, goals, patterns of interaction, roles, or values. Such "systemic" change is of a magnitude greater than day-to-day "routine" family change. Family *hardships* are defined as those demands on the family unit specifically associated with the stressor event. An example of hardships would be the family's need to obtain more money or to rearrange family work and recreation plans to accommodate the increased medical expenses and the demand for home care of a handicapped member.

Family *stress* (as distinct from stressor) is defined as a state which arises from an actual or perceived demand-capability imbalance in the family's functioning and which is characterized by a nonspecific demand for adaptive behavior. In other words, stress is not stereotypic, but rather varies depending on the nature of the situation, the characteristics of the family unit, and the psychological and physical well-being of its members. Concomitantly, family *distress* is defined as an unpleasant or dysfunctional state which arises from an actual or perceived demand-capability imbalance in the family's functioning and which is also characterized by a nonspecific demand for adaptive behavior. In other words, stress becomes distress when it is subjectively perceived as unpleasant by the family.

CRISIS-MEETING RESOURCES

The B factor, that family's crisis-meeting resources, has been described as the family's ability to prevent an event of change in the family social system from creating some crisis or disruptiveness in the system (Burr, 1973). Angell (1936), one of the early theorists attempting to describe more specifically what constituted family resources, emphasized the value of family integration—that is, the bonds of coherence and unity running through family life, of which common interests, affection, and a sense of economic interdependence are perhaps the most prominent—and family adaptability, namely the family's capacity to meet obstacles and shift courses as a family. These dimensions have been emphasized repeatedly by other scholars as two central resources to describe family functioning (Olson, Sprenkle, et al., 1979). Cavan and Ranck (1938) and Koos (1946) identified additional resources of family agreement in its role structure, subordination of personal ambitions to family goals, satisfactions within the family obtained because it is successfully meeting the physical and emotional needs of its members, and goals toward which the family is moving collectively. Hill (1958) summarized the B factor as "adequacy-inadequacy of family organization."

FAMILY DEFINITIONS OF THE EVENT

The C factor in the ABCX Model is the definition the family makes of the seriousness of the experienced stressor. There are objective cultural definitions of the seriousness of life events which represent the collective judgment of the social community, but the "C" factor is the family's *subjective* perception of the stressor and its hardships and how they are affected by them. This subjective meaning reflects the family's values and their previous experience in dealing with change and meeting crisis. A family's outlook can vary from seeing life changes as challenges to be met to interpreting a stressor as uncontrollable and a prelude to the family's demise.

CRISIS

These factors taken together: (a) the stressor event, hardships, and stress; (b) the family's resources for dealing with change; and (c) the definition the family makes of this situation all influence the family's vulnerability, that is, their ability to prevent the event of change from creating a crisis (Hansen, 1965). Crisis (the X factor) has been conceptualized as a continuous variable denoting the amount of disruptiveness, disorganization, or incapacitatedness in the family social imbalance. In other words, stress may never reach crisis proportions if the family is able to use existing resources and define the situation so as to restore the imbalance relatively quickly.

LIMITATIONS OF THE ABCX MODEL

The original ABCX Model advanced by Hill (1958, 1949) focuses primarily on precrisis variables which account for differences in family vulnerability to a stressor event and whether and to what degree the outcome is a crisis for the family.

Building on this model, Burr (1973) reviewed the research and attempted to revise and update the list of independent variables (primarily Hill's B factor of resources) that have been related to family vulnerability. In addition, family stress research has focused on variables related to how well families are able to recover from a crisis situation. Drawing from Hansen's (1965) work, Burr (1973) gave prominence to the concept of regenerative power by identifying additional variables that help explain this "variation in the ability of the family to recover from a crisis." Despite the salience of the ABCX Model and variables related to vulnerability and regenerative power for describing family behavior in response to stress at a single point in time, it became apparent from our longitudinal observations of family behavior in response to war-induced separations that a more *dynamic* model was needed to explain the efforts families make over time to adapt to crises.

LONGITUDINAL OBSERVATIONS OF FAMILIES FACED WITH WAR-INDUCED CRISIS: EMERGING CONCEPTS FOR THE DOUBLE ABCX MODEL

The Hill ABCX framework was used to guide the longitudinal study of families who had a husband/father held captive or unaccounted for in the war in Vietnam which was conducted by the family studies branch of the Naval Health Research Center. Observations of the 216 families in crises involved in this study (McCubbin et al., forthcoming; McCubbin and Patterson, forthcoming) suggested that there are at least four additional factors which appeared to influence the course of family adaptation over time: (a) the pile-up of additional stressors, (b) family efforts to activate or acquire new resources, (c) modifications by the family of their perception of the total crisis situation, and (d) the role of family coping strategies in bringing about immediate adjustments and eventual adaptation.

In this article, we propose a Double ABCX Model (see Figure 1) that uses Hill's original ABCX Model as its foundation and adds these postcrisis variables in an effort to describe: (a) the additional life stressors and strains which may make family adaptation more difficult to achieve; (b) the critical psychological, intrafamilial, and social factors families use in managing crisis situations; (c) the

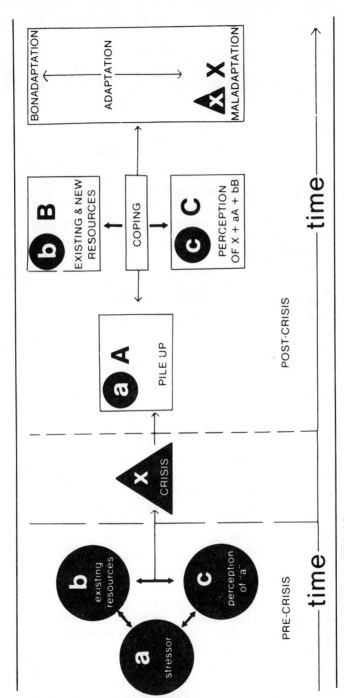

Figure 1: The Double ABCX Model

processes families engage in to achieve satisfactory resolution; and (d) the outcome of these family efforts. The sections which follow set forth the longitudinal observations of these 216 families as they pertain to each factor of the Double ABCX Model, followed by a more generalized explanation of each factor.

PILE-UP: aA FACTOR

Observations from longitudinal study. When a family was called upon to adapt to the absence of a husband/father listed as missing or a prisoner of war, many family changes and hardships evolved naturally from this situation. The extended length of absence for these men (the majority were absent 3-6 years) produced an increasing strain on family relationships as the period of absence increased. Modifications in family roles with accompanying anxieties, frustrations, conflicts, and feelings of insecurity were observed for the wives now taxed with both the traditional and inherited responsibilities of the dual mother-father role (McCubbin et al., 1974). Solo decision making, disciplining of children, handling family finances, and managing children's health problems were cited as hardships. Some child health problems appeared to be a direct consequence of father absence, such as emotional difficulties and conflicts with peers. Many wives experienced serious emotional symptoms as a result of their spouse's prolonged absence and the uncertainty of his return. The hardships which emerged from the stressor of war-induced separation were not readily resolved, and their persistence led to their becoming additional stressors or sources of strain in and of themselves.

In addition, these families had to simultaneously adjust to other life events and changes which are normative occurrences in families over time and which happened independent of the stressor of separation. Childhood accidents and illnesses, deaths and births of extended family members, school transitions, adolescent rebellious behavior, and launching young adults are examples of normative stressors experienced by wives and children which were more difficult to manage without the support of husband/father.

The observations from this longitudinal study revealed that the coping efforts these families used to adjust to the separation produced additional stressors. For example, in order for family life to continue in some routine manner, wives, assuming a dual mother-father role and functioning in the role as head of the household, appeared to become more independent and self-confident. This was especially true when they "closed ranks" (Hill, 1949) and developed a style of life for a family unit without a husband/father. Interestingly enough, social changes which emerged during the same period as the Vietnam War—for example, the women's liberation movement—rendered legitimacy to the wives' efforts to be self-sufficient and independent. This style of coping, which changed a mother's roles and strengthened her authority, was often challenged and questioned by other members of the kin network, particularly in-laws who were concerned about the stability of the family unit and the possibility of divorce. Thus, wives often had to cope with disapproval from other members of the family for the way in which they were handling the separation, and this was a additional stressor.

Not only did specific coping behaviors sometimes become stressors, but two sources of ambiguity for the wives experiencing this separation from their husbands created additional stressors.

Inherent in the event of having a husband/father held captive or missing in action is ambiguity as to whether he will return. Families varied in terms of whether they believed the husband/father would or would not return. On the basis of systems theory and the symbolic interactionist perspective, Boss (1977: 142) has suggested that *boundary ambiguity* within the family system becomes a major stressor in the case of families of the missing: "A system needs to be sure of its components, that is, who is inside system boundaries physically and psychologically, and who is outside, physically and psychologically.... A major consequence of an ambiguous system, that is, a system that is not sure of its components, is that systemic communication, feedback and subsequent adjustment over time are curtailed." This ambiguity also influenced family roles, especially for wives as they struggled with whether and to what degree to take over their husband's role.

Despite the boundary ambiguity inherent in this stressor, our in-depth interviews (McCubbin et al., 1974), and particularly the legal case studies (Nelson, 1974) revealed that families did make a concerted effort to render clarity to the situation, but that in the absence of legitimate paths and procedures for resolution, they faced major roadblocks. *Social ambiguity,* that is, the absence of appropriate norms and procedures for managing this stressful situation, created an additional stressor on family life.

As Hansen and Hill (1964) and Mechanic (1974) have pointed out, the fit between the family and the community may well be the major determinant of successful adaptation to stress. The family's ability to manage stress may depend on the efficacy and/or adequacy of the solutions that the culture, community, or the organization provide. However, these community solutions may lag far behind the times and offer little to families struggling to manage a difficult situation. Social ambiguity emerges when society's blueprints for family behavior under stress are being challenged or are inappropriate and when problem-solving guidelines for family postcrisis behavior are not adequate.

Not only were society's perceptions of this stressor (the war) ambiguous, but the resources (Hill's B factor) available to these families were also ambiguous. For example, powers of attorney, executed by many servicemen to enable their wives to sell jointly held property, expired during the prolonged absence. Families were then left without legal support for their transactions and without guidelines as to how legal power could be achieved.

Wives who wished to move ahead and create a new life by remarrying faced the risk of a bigamy conviction, since declaration of death had not been confirmed. The social stigma of divorce, coupled with the potential loss of military privileges and the possibility of forfeiture of benefits under a husband's estate, also made this option less desirable. While a wife may actively have sought a death determination, parents of the husband strongly resisted this alternative, viewing such a course of action as abandonment of their son and a possible loss of grandchildren (McCubbin et al., 1974; Nelson, 1974). Further, while such an approach would facilitate remarriage and distribution of the husband's estate and insurance settlement, it would have no impact on the military's release of the serviceman's accrued pay and allowances. This fund, which often represented the single most important asset in the estate, could only be released by the Service Secretaries' declaration of death. Thus, many wives were pushed to await an official clarification of this ambiguous situation to realize the full benefits of their husband's estate.

In examining the data from this longitudinal study, these families were faced with a pile-up of stressors resulting from: (a) the hardships of the initial stressor event, which increased and persisted over time; (b) the consequences of family efforts to cope with the separation; (c) additional life changes and events in the family; and (d) ambiguity—both within the family regarding father's return and within society regarding norms and prescriptions for family behavior in this situation.

Generalizations to the Double ABCX Model. Because family crises evolve and are resolved over a period of time, families are seldom dealing with a single stressor. Rather, our studies suggest they experience a pile-up of stressors and strains (or demands or changes), particularly in the aftermath of a major stressor, such as a death, a major role change for one member, or a natural disaster. This pile-up is referred to as the "aA" factor in the Double ABCX Model (see Figure 1). These demands or changes may emerge from (a) individual family members, (b) the family system, and/or (c) the community of which family members and the family unit are a part.

The demands or needs of individuals, families, and society are not static but change over time. For example, the normative growth and development of individuals (involving an increasing need the for independence), life cycle changes of families (beginning parenthood, launching children), and societal changes (such as changing roles of women or declining birth rates) are demands or needs which call for change, and hence are stressor events for the family.

There appear to be at least five broad types of stressors and strains contributing to a pile-up in the family system in a crisis situation. The first is the initial stressor event (the "a" of the aA factor), with its inherent hardships, which played a part in moving the family into a crisis state.

Many of these hardships of the stressor persist because, by their nature, they are unresolvable (for example, ongoing home care of a chronically ill member) or because the family is unable or unwilling to resolve it (such as role overload of dual employed parents or single parents). Thus these persistent hardships become chronic strains—the second aspect of pile-up. It is important to note that these persistent strains are not usually discrete events that can be identified as occurring at a specific point in time. Rather, they usually emerge more insidiously in the family, often as a consequence of some other event. Pile-up as we are defining it includes both stressors and strains.

The third type of stressors and strains contributing to pile-up is normative family life changes and events which occur concomitantly, but appear to be independent of the initial stressor and hardships. Normative developmental changes and transitions such as parenthood or midlife change are examples of this added source of family stress which may also place demands on the family unit already struggling with a specific stressor and its hardships.

The fourth source of pile-up includes stressors and strains that emerge from specific coping behaviors the family may use in an effort to cope with the crisis situation. For example, a second job to cope with inflation or spouse employment to cope with increased medical expenses are likely to introduce added changes to the already "out of balance" family unit.

The fifth source of stressors and strains, also related to coping, is ambiguity. A certain amount of ambiguity is inherent in every stressor since change produces uncertainty about the future. However, as our observations led us to conclude, boundary ambiguity (as in the case of the missing or prisoners of war) is an additional strain on the family system. The concept of boundary ambiguity has also been applied to describe the strains associated with normative life transitions (Boss, 1980), such as the young adult college student who lives at home. Is this person perceived as in or out of the family unit? Additionally, given the expectation that society will offer guidelines or blueprints for families coping with crises, it is probable that families will face the added strain of social ambiguity in those situations where those much needed social prescriptions for crisis resolution are unclear or absent. For example, many families faced with the crisis of a member held hostage (such as Iran 1979-1981) experienced the added strain of contradictory or unclear messages from the community (including government, military, the media, other families, and friends) about what courses to follow which would be helpful to the family and lead to resolution of the crisis.

While a pile-up of stressors and strains may be characteristic of most families at any point in time, it emerges as a significant factor in understanding postcrisis family behavior. Since the system is experiencing an imbalance due to inadequate capabilities to meet the multiple demands, the course of adaptation will be influenced by the number and nature of demands and how these are met or ignored.

RESOURCES: bB FACTOR

Observations from the Longitudinal Study. The literature is replete with observations and concepts around extant psychological (Lazarus, 1966) and community (Caplan and Killilea, 1976) resources used to mitigate the impact of a stressor and facilitate adaptation to crises. Additionally, the family literature (Burr, 1973) has identified numerous family system resources, of which cohesion and adaptability are paramount, that influence a family's regenerative power. From our observations of the families in this war-induced crisis, it was apparent that they drew upon (a) psychological resources like friendships, religious involvement, and mental health professionals; as well as (c) such commonly identified family resources as togetherness, role flexibility, shared values and goals, and expressiveness.

These families were also called upon to expand upon their existing resources in order to manage this crisis situation. Specifically, wives availed themselves of educational opportunities to enhance their earning potential in anticipation of their spouse not returning. These opportunities for personal development also served to enhance their self-esteem and self-sufficiency. Concomitantly, the family unit made internal changes to accommodate the father's absence. They reallocated roles and responsibilities (e.g., oldest child member took a job to increase family income), involved extended kin in meeting family needs, relocated the family in a new community to gain a fresh start, and some remarried. Additionally, the family sought, and in some cases created new community resources tailored to meet their needs. Wives joined the National League of Families, community-based counseling groups, financial investment clubs and groups affiliated with churches. These groups offered various benefits such as encouragement, concrete guidance, empathic understanding, as well as a sense of membership.

Generalizations to the Double ABCX Model. Resources are part of a family's capabilities for meeting demands and needs and include psychological, social, interpersonal, and material characteristics of (a) individual members, (b) the family unit, and (c) the community. Individual resources might include, for example, the ability to manage the home and to function independently, earning potential, or any of a variety of cognitive skills. Family resources could include integration, cohesiveness, flexibility, organization, shared values, expressiveness, and commitment to positive health behaviors. Finally, community-based resources might include social support networks, medical and psychological counseling services, and social policies that enhance family functioning and protect families from harm or breakdown.

When viewed over time and in response to a crisis situation, these resources appear to be of two general types. The first are those existing resources already available to the family which minimize the impact of the initial stressor and reduce the probability of the family entering into crisis, that is, making the family invulnerable (the precrisis "b" factor). The second type are those new resources (individual, family, and community) strengthened or developed in response to the new or additional demands emerging out of the crisis situation or as a result of pile-up. These newly activated resources are the second "B" of the b B factor in the Double ABCX Model.

FAMILY PERCEPTION: cC FACTOR

Observations from the Longitudinal Study. The findings from this study suggest that religion and/or religious beliefs enabled these families to ascribe an acceptable meaning to their situation. This in turn contributed to the maintenance of family unity, the enhancement of member self-esteem, and also served as a source of norms and guidelines for family behavior in this ambiguous situation (McCubbin et al., 1974).

While families struggled, they also appeared to reach a level of adaptive or functional stability, an outcome which could be attributed in part to wives' redefining the situation. For example, Boss's (1977) data revealed that not all of the consequences of boundary and ambiguity were negative. It was positively associated with the interviewer's assessment of child adjustment and the family dimensions of achievement orientation, expressiveness, and organization. Wives appeared to define the ambiguity of father's absence differently for instrumental versus expressive needs: "Although it is financially functional for her (wives) to keep the father present in the instrumental role which offers satisfying financial security, it is at the same time functional for her to psychologically expel him from the emotional support role" (Boss, 1977: 147). Wives appeared to redefine the situation by endowing father's role with some value and meaning (for example, as financial provider) and at the same time legitimate their effort to establish a new life for themselves (for example, developing new ways to meet expressive needs).

Generalizations to the Double ABCX Model. In the Double ABCX Model, the "cC" factor is family perception. Again, there are two forms of perception, depending on whether we are referring to the family's response before or after the crisis. The first "c" factor is the family's perception of the most significant stressor event—the change or demand believed to have caused an imbalance (that is, the crisis) in the family system. The second "C" factor is the family's perception of its total "crisis situation," which includes the added stressors and strains, old and new resources, and estimates of what needs to be done to bring the family back into balance.

Unlike the family's initial perception (c factor) of the situation, which focused on the stressor and related hardships, the family's postcrisis perspective is oriented toward a redefining of the crisis situation. When this effort is constructive, the family attempts to (a) clarify the issues, hardships, and tasks so as to render them more manageable; (b) decrease the intensity of the emotional burdens associated with the crisis situation; and (c) encourage the family unit to carry on with its fundamental tasks of promoting member social and emotional development. This process of redefining the situation involves an effort to integrate individual perceptions which may be discrepant. (For example, the care of a handicapped member may be perceived as a challenge and responsibility by some members of the family and as a burden and major problem by others.) Generally speaking, family efforts to redefine a situation as a "challenge," as an "opportunity for growth," or to endow the crisis with meaning such as "believing it is the Lord's will" appear to play a useful role in facilitating family coping and eventually adaptation. Viewed in this way, the family's perception (the cC factor) becomes a critical component of family coping.

COPING: INTERACTION OF RESOURCES, PERCEPTIONS, AND BEHAVIOR

Observations from the Longitudinal Study. Although family resources and perceptions have been studied independently and offer investigators a gauge of family capabilities used to meet demands, these same observations suggest that we could improve upon our understanding of family adaptation to crises by looking at these two variables simultaneously, along with what families do to cope with the situation. Coping appears to be a multifaceted process wherein resources, perception, and behavioral responses interact as families try to achieve a balance in family functioning.

The wives in this study engaged in *behaviors* to maintain family integration and stability *(resources)* by doing more things with the children, assuming a stronger leadership role in the family, and encouraging the expression of feelings among family members. Perceptually, the wives coped with the ambiguity of their spouses' return by considering him "outside" family boundaries to justify behaviors such as dating to fulfill emotional needs, while at the same time considering him "inside" family boundaries in order to access his military wages to meet the financial needs of the family.

One of the most beneficial coping strategies of these families emerged from wives' efforts to seek a resolution to the many hardships and strains experienced as a result of the separation. The families banded together and formed the National League of Families in an effort to establish a competing form of social organization and, through social action, to change existing military policies and decisions that were seen as inadequate or as threatening to the family unit. Increasingly, it became clear to these families that coping with these major hardships required organized, cooperative efforts that transcended those of any individual family.

These collective group efforts also appeared to provide wives and family members with an important resource called social support. Cobb (1976) defines social support as the exchange of information which provides families with (a) emotional support, leading them to believe they are cared for and appreciated; (b) esteem support, leading them to believe they are valued; and (c) network support, leading them to believe that they have a role to play in the organization and that there is a mutual obligation. Family members pointed out that the National League of Families offered them a social network through which they could obtain understanding, empathy, encouragement, problem-solving information, material assistance, and a sense of belonging.

What also became apparent from our observations of these families is that their coping efforts were directed at multiple stressors and strains (the pile-up) simultaneously. In other words, coping was not stressor-specific. Coping involved efforts to manage various dimensions of family life simultaneously, such as: (a) the maintenance of family bonds of coherence and unity, (b) the maintenance of satisfactory internal conditions for communication, (c) the promotion and enhancement of member independence and self-esteem, (d) the maintenance of family flexibility and autonomy, and (e) the development and maintenance of social supports and other resources in the community (McCubbin et al., 1976; McCubbin, 1979).

As already noted, coping efforts focused on one area of family life may precipitate additional strains. Thus, these families were continually challenged to bring the totality of interactions and transactions into balance simultaneously.

Generalizations to the Double ABCX Model. In the Double ABCX Model, coping becomes a bridging concept linking resources and perception with the family's behavioral responses to the pile-up. Coping has both cognitive and behavioral components that interact with each other in the face of demands. Family coping efforts are directed at eliminating stressors and strains, managing the hardships of the situation, resolving intrafamily conflicts and tensions, as well as acquiring and developing social, psychological, and material resources needed to facilitate family adaptation. This perspective of family coping underscores the importance of family behavior efforts to strengthen and develop itself and draw upon resources from within (including leadership skills, role sharing, income, bonds of family unity, and adaptability) and from the community (such as meaningful friendships, support groups, and professional assistance) which can provide families with much needed information for problem solving and with confirmation that they are understood, accepted, valued, and appreciated.

FAMILY ADAPTATION: xX FACTOR

Hill's X factor (1958), the amount of "crisis" in the family system, generally has been adopted as the major outcome variable describing disruptions in family routines in response to a stressor. Burr (1973) conceived of "crisis" as a continuous variable, denoting variation in the "amount of disruptiveness, incapacitatedness, or disorganization of the family." Given this definition, it might be concluded that the purpose of postcrisis adjustment or the goal of "regenerative power" (Hansen, 1965) is primarily to reduce or eliminate the disruptiveness in the family system and restore homeostasis. It might be argued, however, that family disruptions potentially help to maintain family relationships and may even stimulate desirable changes in family life. Hansen and Johnson (1979: 584) called attention to the restrictive focus of "crisis" and noted that "families are often observed 'accepting' disruptions of habit and tradition not so much as unwelcome problems, but more as opportunities to renegotiate their relationships." Systems theorists (von Bertalanffy, 1968; Hill, 1971) point out that it is characteristic of living systems to evolve toward greater complexity, and that consequently, families may actively initiate changes to facilitate such growth. It is questionable, then, whether "reduction of crisis" alone is an adequate index of a family's postcrisis adjustment.

Observations reviewed in this chapter suggest that family adaptation would be a useful concept for describing the outcome of family postcrisis adjustment. There are three elements to be considered in family adaptation: (a) the individual family member, (b) the family system, and (c) the community of which family members and the family unit are a part. Each of these elements is characterized by both demands and capabilities. *Family adaptation* is achieved through reciprocal relationships where the demands of one of these units are met by the capabilities of another so as to achieve a balance simultaneously at two primary levels of interaction.

At the first level, a balance is sought between *individual family members* and the *family system* (for example, family encouraging and supporting adolescent needs for independence and adolescent family members completing family maintenance tasks or participating in shared family activities). Following the Double ABCX Model, family stress may emerge where there is a *demand-capability imbalance* at this level of family functioning. Specifically, the demands an individual member may place on the family may exceed the family's capability of meeting these demands, thus resulting in an imbalance. For example, the stressor of a member entering adolescence may precipitate an imbalance by virtue of the family's demand for member adherence to rigid rules and by an inability to alter expectations, which would allow for the independence an adolescent needs for personal development. The family is therefore called upon to reconcile this matter and to work to achieve a new "balance" between the individual member and the family unit.

At the second level, a balance is sought between the *family unit* and the *community* of which this family is a part (such as family support of parental involvement in work and community activities and the work community demand for extensive time and personal investment). It has frequently been observed that two social institutions, the family and the work community, compete for the involvement and commitment of family members, which often results in stress— a demand-capability imbalance at this second level of family functioning. For example, the stressor of a wife-mother entering or returning to work may precipitate an imbalance if the family demands that she make a priority commitment to family life and the children. Additionally, the family may be reluctant to modify its rules and behaviors (for instance, toward shared tasks and/or shared responsibilities) in order to permit the transitioning parent to invest in work-for-pay without the added burden of emotional guilt and the felt need to fulfill home and work responsibilities with equal competence. The family is called upon to re-establish and achieve a balance between family and work-community demands and capabilities.

Therefore, family adaptation becomes the central concept in the Double ABCX Model used to describe the outcome of family efforts to achieve a new level of *balance in family functioning* which was upset by a family crisis. In crisis situations, the family unit struggles to achieve a balance at both the individual-family and the family-community levels of family functioning. Since the family is a social system and a change in one level affects the other, family efforts at adaptation always involve an attentiveness and responsiveness to both levels of family functioning simultaneously.

The concept of family adaptation is used to describe a continuum of outcomes that reflect family efforts to achieve a balance in functioning at the member-to-family and family-to-community levels. The positive end of the continuum of family adaptation, called *bonadaptation,* is characterized by a balance at both levels of functioning, which results in (a) the maintenance or strengthening of family integrity; (b) the continued promotion of both member development and family unit development; and (c) the maintenance of family independence and its sense of control over environmental influence. Family *maladaptation,* at the negative end of the continuum, is an outcome characterized by a continued imbalance at either level (member-to-family or family-to-community) of family functioning *or* the achievement of a balance at both levels *but at a price* in terms of (a) deterioration in family integrity; (b) curtailment or deterioration in the personal development of a member or in the family unit's development; or (c) a loss or decline of family independence and autonomy.

Because family adaptation involves the management of often competing dimensions of family life such as member independence and family togetherness, it is likely to involve the element of compromise. Families are called upon to accept or tolerate a less than optimal situation in an effort to preserve family unity and to continue their investment in the development of members and the family unit. The concept of compromise allows social scientists to explain why some families are able to achieve satisifactory adaptation and maintain optimism in the face of prolonged, chronic, and unresolvable stressful situations. Successful forms of family adaptation, therefore, involve compromise that not only preserves the integrity of the family system but also permits the family unit and its members to continue on their developmental course and to maintain a position of self-determination.

At the present time, family adaptation is but a descriptive criterion of family postcrisis outcomes, rather than a clearly defined and operationalized set of measures. One obvious and complicating factor is that any form of adaptation may be viewed as having both long- and short-run consequences. What may be functional in meeting a family's or a member's immediate needs, such as accepting a member who is abusing alcohol, may be maladaptive in light of the long-range, adverse consequences on family stability and the psychological well-being of its members.

INITIAL TESTS OF THE DOUBLE ABCX MODEL

If we were to apply this framework to the study of families faced with raising a handicapped child, we could argue that the pile-up of family life changes interact with parental coping strategies to produce an outcome characterized by a balance or imbalance in family functioning.

One hypothesized paradigm based on the Double ABCX Model is that families characterized by a balance in family functioning (when compared with families who are imbalanced) would show: (a) a higher level of family life changes (pile-up) associated with family efforts to actively manage and accommodate change and keep the family in a balanced state; and (b) a higher level of parental coping responses designed to keep the family unit together, acquire social support, and manage the stressor and related hardships. These factors interact over time as families work to achieve and maintain this balanced family situation.

The study (McCubbin and Larsen, 1981) discussed here is the first in a series of studies designed to test hypotheses from the Double ABCX Model as well as to refine the measurement tools used in stress and family coping research (McCubbin and Patterson, 1981). The principal objective of this study was to determine which independent variable or combination of variables best discriminates between balanced and imbalanced family units faced with the chronic strains of managing a child with cerebral palsy.

Research Method

Subjects were 217 families with a child with cerebral palsy (CP) who were seen at periodic intervals at the Gillette Children's Hospital CP Clinic, St. Paul, Minnesota. The Gillette Clinic is a regional program involving rural and urban families in the treatment of patients from a five-state area: Minnesota, North Dakota, South Dakota, Wisconsin, and Iowa. Families were sent questionnaires designed to obtain independent measures of family life changes and parental coping. Two weeks following receipt of the initial data, families were sent a follow-up questionnaire designed to assess the criterion outcome of family functioning.

Measure of Pile-up. The Family Inventory of Life Events and Changes— FILE (McCubbin et al., 1981) is a 71-item self-report instrument (completed by parents together) designed to measure a family's level of life stressors and strains experienced during a 12-month period. Since families are usually dealing with several life changes and strains simultaneously, FILE provides one index of changes and strains contributing to "pile-up." The 71 items are grouped into ten subscales: (a) intra-family strains, (b) marital strains, (c) pregnancy and childbearing strains, (d) finance and business strains, (e) work-family transitions and strains, (f) illness and family care strains, (g) losses, (h) transitions in and out, (i) family legal violations, and (j) total family life changes. The overall internal reliability (Cronbach Alpha) is .72.

Measure of Coping. The Coping Health Inventory for Parents—CHIP (McCubbin et al., 1979)—is a 45-item questionnaire developed to record information about how parents individually perceive their overall response to the management of a handicapped child. The psychometric details of CHIP are presented elsewhere (McCubbin and Patterson, 1981). Briefly, three coping patterns are measured: (a) Maintaining Family Integration, Cooperation, and Optimistic Definition of the Situation (Alpha, .79); (b) Maintaining Social Support, Self-Esteem, and Psychological Stability (Alpha, .79); and (c) Understanding the Medical Situation Through Communication with Other Parents and Consultation with Medical Staff (Alpha, .71).

Measure of Member-to-Family Adaptation. The Family Adaptability and Cohesion Evaluation Scales—FACES (Olson et al., 1978)—were adopted for this investigation as a criterion measure of balance or imbalance in family functioning. This 111-item self-report questionnaire, completed by parents jointly, is designed to obtain family scores on the two major subscales of cohesion and adaptability. These scores were used to classify each family into one of 16 types according to the family typology established by the Circumplex Model of Marital and Family Systems (Olson, Russell, et al., 1979; Olson, Sprenkle, et al., 1979). For the purposes of this investigation, we focused on those families with cohesion and adaptability scores which placed them in either of two mutually exclusive categories—balanced or imbalanced.

The balanced group (N = 91) of families revealed moderate scores on both the cohesion and adaptability subscales. Families in this group may be characterized as operating at an optimum level (moderate) in promoting individual autonomy and as strengthening the emotional bonds which members have toward one another. Additionally, these families are able to maintain an optimum (moderate) level in their ability to change their power structure, role relationships, and rules in response to stressful situations.

In contrast, the imbalanced group (N = 61) of families included those families that revealed extreme scores on both the cohesion and adaptability subscales. In other words, these families were characterized as being either chaotically disengaged, chaotically enmeshed, rigidly disengaged, or rigidly enmeshed.

Data Analysis

Bivariate group comparisons using tests for significant differences were made across all variables. Finally, a discriminant functional analysis was computed to determine which combination of variables best discriminated between the balanced and the imbalanced family groups. This multivariate statistical procedure is the most appropriate for small sample sizes and for a categorical dependent variable and allows for the relative contribution of each variable to the total discriminant function to be ascertained.

Results

McCubbin and Larsen (1981) found that of the 10 FILE subscales, three discriminated between balanced and imbalanced family groups ($p \leqslant .05$). Family Financial and Business strains (F = 5.33, p = .02), Family Illness strains (F = 4.75, p = .03), and the Total "Pile-up" of Family Life Changes (F = 5.63, p = .01) were, as hypothesized, significantly higher for families in the balanced group. Concomitantly, both mothers and fathers in the balanced group of families scored consistently higher on all three subscales of the parental coping inventory (CHIP). Mothers were significantly higher on Family Integration (F = 39.41, p = .0001), Social Support (F = 25.74, p = .0001) and Medical Consultation (F = 25.24, p = .0001). Fathers were significantly higher on Family Integration (F = 31.67, p = .0001), Social Support (F = 17.08, p = .0001), and on Medical Consultation (F = 20.31, p = .0001).

When these two groups were compared on sociodemographic characteristics (length of marriage, parents' age, education, and family income) there were no statistically significant differences.

TABLE 1   Discriminant Function for Predictions of Balanced
                and Imbalanced Family Groups

Variables	Unstandardized Discriminant Function	Standardized Discriminant Function
Mother's Coping		
Family Integration	−.23	−1.34
Social Support	−.54	−1.04
Medical Consultation	−.59	.09
Father's Coping		
Family Integration	−.81	−.85
Social Support	−.66	−.04
Medical Consultation	−.65	.27
Pile-Up of Family Life Changes		
Financial & Business Strains	−.30	.15
Illness Strains	−.28	−.16
Total Recent Family Life Changes	−.30	−.29

Groups	Centroids Group Means
Balanced Family Group	−.51
Imbalanced Family Group	.76

Classification Accuracy		Predictions		
Actual Group	N	Balanced	Imbalanced	Percentage Correct
Balanced Family Group	91	69	22	76
Imbalanced Family Group	61	24	37	61
		Total Percentage of Cases Correct		70

SOURCE: McCubbin and Larsen, 1981

Given this slice of the total research data, we can render partial support to a multivariate and interactive approach to the study of differences between balanced and imbalanced family groups. However, these results do not indicate the specific contribution or the relative importance of each variable to the group differences obtained. We hypothesized, based on the Double ABCX Model, that (a) not all of the variables would singularly differentiate the groups, (b) the variables would differ in terms of their relative contribution, and (c) the variables (demands—pile-up and capabilities—parental coping) in combination would be the best set of discriminators.

A discriminant analysis procedure was computed to ascertain which pile-up and coping variables would most accurately and reliably discriminate between the groups. The results, as summarized in Table 1, show that the classification accuracy of the discriminant function was 70% and that it was more accurate in classifying cases into the "balanced" group of families (76%) than into the "imbalanced" family group (61%). It appears, then, from these select results, that the most meaningful and useful discriminant function separating the two family groups should include pile-up and parental coping as separate but complementary variables.

SUMMARY AND CONCLUSIONS

The recent developments in family stress and coping research and the opportunity to reexamine data and observations of families in a war-induced crisis situation over time encouraged us to advance concepts and a few hypotheses regarding family adaptation to crisis situations. By building on Hill's (1949) family crisis framework, the Double ABCX Model of family pre- and postcrisis behavior attempts to identify those family variables which appear to explain the wide variability in family postcrisis outcomes. Specifically, this model advances the concepts of pile-up, family resources, perceptions, and coping as critical, if not vital independent variables which interact to shape the course of family adjustment and adaptation. The principal objective of this article was to introduce the basic concepts of the Double ABCX Model and to present observational and empirical data in an effort to render partial support for this line of reasoning and theory building. We propose that the relationship between a stressor and family outcomes, whether it be bonadaptation or maladaptation, should be conceptualized and measured as a complex phenomenon that includes the interaction of family life changes, perception, resources, and coping. From our vantage point, we would argue that a productive direction for future research in this area should not focus on the simplistic design of stressor = family strain = maladaptative relationships. Rather, research efforts should be directed at measuring the relative contributions of defined stressors in interaction with other family system variables, including family life changes, resources, perceptions, and coping patterns. Continued research on populations at risk for maladaptation (such as clinic groups or chronic stress groups) and suffering from a disproportionate exposure to stressors and their deleterious consequences (including racism, war, and poverty) would also seem to offer potential benefits in the elaboration of the Double ABCX Model of family stress. As we move forward with this line of research, we can anticipate a greater number of concepts, propositions, hypotheses, and measures intended to improve upon our understanding of invulnerable and/or resilient families.

REFERENCES

ANGELL, R. D. (1936) The Family Encounters the Depression. New York: Charles Scribner's Sons.
BOSS, P. (1980) "Normative family stress: family boundary changes across the life span." Family Relations 29: 445-450.
——— (1977) "A clarification of the concept of psychological father presence in families experiencing ambiguity of boundary." J. of Marriage and the Family 39: 141-151.
BURR, W. F. (1973) Theory Construction and the Sociology of the Family. New York: John Wiley.
CAPLAN, G. and M. KILLILEA (1976) The Family as a Support System. New York: Grune & Stratton.
CAVAN, R. and K. R. RANCK (1938) The Family and the Depression. Chicago: Univ. of Chicago Press.

COBB, S. (1976) "Social support as a moderator of life stress." Psychosomatic Medicine 38: 300-314.

HANSEN, D. (1965) "Personal and positional influence in formal groups: compositions and theory for research on family vulnerability to stress." Social Forces 44: 202-210.

——— and R. HILL (1964) "Families under stress," in H. Christensen (ed.) Handbook of Marriage and the Family. Chicago: Rand McNally.

HANSEN, D. and V. JOHNSON (1979) "Rethinking family stress theory: definitional aspects," in W. Burr et al. (eds.) Contemporary Theories About the Family, Vol. 1. New York: Free Press.

HILL, R. (1971) "Modern systems theory and the family: a confrontation." Social Science Information 72: 7-26.

——— (1958) "Generic features of families under stress." Social Casework 49: 139-150.

——— (1949) Families Under Stress. New York: Harper & Row.

KOOS, E. L. (1946) Families in Trouble. New York: Kings Crown Press.

LAZARUS, R. (1966) Psychological Stress and the Coping Process. New York: McGraw-Hill.

McCUBBIN, H. (1979) "Integrating coping behavior in family stress theory." J. of Marriage and the Family 41(3): 237-244.

——— and A. LARSEN (1981) "Critical factors in achieving family balance in the care of the chronically ill child." Unpublished.

McCUBBIN, H. and J. PATTERSON (forthcoming) "Family adaptation to crises," in H. McCubbin et al. (eds.) Family Stress, Coping and Social Support. New York: Springer.

——— (1981) Systematic Assessment of Family Stress, Resources and Coping. St. Paul: Univ. of Minnesota Press.

——— and L. WILSON (1981) FILE—Family Inventory of Life Events and Changes. St. Paul: Univ. of Minnesota Press.

McCUBBIN, H., E. HUNTER, and P. METRES (1974) "Adaptation of the family to the prisoner of war and missing in action experience," in H. McCubbin et al. (eds.) Family Separation and Reunion. Washington, DC: Government Printing Office.

McCUBBIN, H., D. OLSON and J. PATTERSON (forthcoming) "Beyond family crisis: family adaptation," in J. Trost (ed.) Families in Disaster. Sweden: International Library.

McCUBBIN, H., M. McCUBBIN, A. CAUBLE, and R. NEVIN (1979) CHIP—Coping Health Inventory for Parents. St. Paul: Univ. of Minnesota Press.

McCUBBIN, H., B. DAHL, G. LESTER, G. BENSON, and M. ROBERTSON (1976) "Coping repertoires of families adapting to prolonged war-induced separations." J. of Marriage and the Family 38: 451-471.

McCUBBIN, H., C. JOY, A. CAUBLE, J. COMEAU, J. PATTERSON, and R. NEEDLE (1980) "Family stress and coping: a decade review." J. of Marriage and the Family 42: 855-871.

McCUBBIN, H., C. JOY, J. PATTERSON, A. CAUBLE, J. COMEAU, and R. NEEDLE (1981) "Family stress, coping, and social support: recent research and theory," in H. McCubbin and J. Patterson, Systematic Assessment of Family Stress, Resources and Coping. St. Paul: Univ. of Minnesota Press.

MECHANIC, D. (1974) "Social structure and personal adaptation: some neglected dimensions," in G. V. Coelho et al. (eds.) Coping and Adaptation. New York: Basic Books.

MIKHAIL, A. (1981) "Stress: a psychophysiological conception." J. of Human Stress 7: 9-15.

NELSON, R. (1974) "The legal plight of the POW/MIA family," in H. McCubbin et al. (eds.) Family Separation and Reunion. Washington, DC: Government Printing Office.

OLSON, D., R. BELL, and J. PORTNER (1978) Family Adaptability and Cohesion Evaluation Scales (FACES). St. Paul: University of Minnesota, Family Social Science.

OLSON, D., C. RUSSELL, and D. SPRENKLE (1979) "Circumplex model of marital and family systems II: clinical research and intervention," in J. Vincent (ed.) Advances in Family Intervention, Assessment and Theory. Greenwich, CT: JAI Press.

OLSON, D., D. SPRENKLE, and C. RUSSELL (1979) "Circumplex model of marital and family systems: cohesion and adaptability dimensions, family types and clinical application." Family Process 18: 3-27.

SELYE, H. (1976) Stress Without Distress. Philadelphia: J. B. Lippincott.

von BERTALANFFY, L. (1968) General Systems Theory (rev. ed.). New York: George Brazilley.

Normative stress in families results whenever components are added to or subtracted from a family system. From birth to death, family boundaries change and remain ambiguous during the process of reorganization after acquisition or loss of a member. The family's perception of who is inside or outside the family system is significantly related to the interaction within that system as well as between that system and the outside world. It is proposed that due to the process of family boundary maintenance, there is little similarity in family structures across time: family structures are constantly changing to facilitate the accomplishment of functions while maintaining family boundaries.

6

NORMATIVE FAMILY STRESS

Family Boundary Changes Across the Life-Span

Pauline G. Boss*

All families, functional and dysfunctional, experience stress—that is, change at various times throughout the family life cycle. However, the question remains as to *why* some families recover from the stress of change and, in fact, become stronger, whereas other families cannot cope and are caught in a downward spiral toward increasing dysfunction.

Issues related to this question were addressed decades ago in the contexts of non-normative crises encountered by families: Angell (1939) and Cavan (1938) on effects of the depression; DuVall (1948), Hill (1949), and Boulding (1950) on the effects of separation and reunion. In the 1970s a number of studies were conducted at the Center for Prisoner of War Studies in San Diego on the effects of military separation (for a review, see McCubbin, Hunter, and Dahl, 1976).

Normative Family Stress and Family Boundaries

Normative life-span stress for the family has been studied much less extensively.

Rhona Rapoport's work (1963) represents a classic in that sparse literature. Though her research centered on the stress of change resulting from "getting married," she focused theoretically on other critical transition points in normal family development: the birth of the first child, children going to school for the first time, death of a spouse, or adolescents leaving home (Rapoport, 1963). These she called "points-of-no-return" which lead either to resolution and growth or to maladaptation and subsequent deterioration of the system. She wrote:

It is postulated that the way these normal "crisis" or status transitions are handled or coped with, will affect outcome—both in terms of the mental health of the individuals, and in terms of the enduring family relationship (Rapoport, 1963, p. 69).

Later Stierlin (1972) referred to family types and the adolescent's struggle to move out of the family system. If the dominant family type is binding and closed, the adolescent's attempt to unbind himself will be crisis-producing for the family, at least for a time. Stierlin sees this struggle for independence as functional for parents as well as adolescents and illustrates this point with the analogy of Martin Luther who forced the sixteenth century church to reform and strengthen itself "while

*Pauline Boss is Associate Professor, Child and Family Studies Program, University of Wisconsin, Madison, WI 53706.

From Pauline G. Boss, "Normative Family Stress: Family Boundary Changes Across the Life-Span," *Family Relations*, 1980, 29, pp. 445-450. Reprinted by permission of the publisher and author.

he, in separating himself from it, bore the onus of rebel . . . " (Stierlin, 1972, p. 174).

More recently, Kantor and Lehr (1975) addressed the issue of the dimensions of family space or boundaries. They defined boundaries as " . . . all the interface rings that constitute the totality of family process interactions . . . " and stated:

Families that adopt the closed-type homeo-static ideal define their boundaries in terms of the fixed constancy feedback patterns. . . . Families that seek the random ideal define their boundaries in terms of variety loops rather than constancy loops. . . . Disequilibrium is the random homeostatic ideal. Families that adopt an open homeo-static ideal opt for a mixture of equilibrium and disequilibrium. . . . Open family boundaries are defined in terms of a combination of constancy and variety loop patterns, employed to maximize the potential for a joint negotiation of distance regulation issues at interface (Kantor & Lehr, 1975, pp. 116-117).

Although Kantor and Lehr's boundary types are not classified as either enabling or disabling, Boss proposes that a high degree of boundary ambiguity in *any* family system may cause dysfunction (Boss, 1975, Note 1; 1977, 1980). If a family member is perceived as psychologically present, but is, in reality, physically absent for a long time, the family boundary is ambiguous and cannot be maintained. The reverse also manifests boundary ambiguity: physical presence with psychological absence, as in some intact families where a parent is consistently preoccupied with outside work (Boss, McCubbin, & Lester, 1979). Operationalization is based on whether or not roles are still being assigned to the absent person and whether or not the absent member is still perceived as present. Thus the premise is based on role theory and symbolic interaction.

This premise of boundary ambiguity plus the works of Kantor and Lehr reflect the influence of earlier works by Piaget and Inhelder (1956), who investigated space as a central aspect of individual perception and cognition. Using this spatial metaphor from early developmentalists, Kantor and Lehr also focused on structuralism for family boundary maintenance as the family responds to everyday life.

At each stage of development in a family's life cycle, new distance-regulation crises appear, stimulating new images and re-emphasizing older ones. The development of family and individual strategies at each stage continues to be dependent on the interaction of family and individual image hierarchies . . . (Kantor & Lehr, 1975, p. 249).

Therefore, in Kantor and Lehr's terms the perception of family boundary (who is inside or outside the family sytem) is a distance-regulation or space-bounding issue. But even before Kantor and Lehr, family therapists proposed the critical nature of both real and perceived family boundaries. Boszormenyi-Nagy and Spark (1973, p. 84) referred to boundaries between the family and the larger world formed by "invisible loyalties" such as family values. From a more microscopic perspective, Minuchin (1974) used boundaries within family sub-systems in clinical assessment of family functioning. He believed that for proper family functioning, the boundaries of subsystems must be clear.

[Boundaries] *must be defined well enough to allow subsystem members to carry out their functions without undue interference, but they must allow contact between the members of the subsystem and others. The composition of subsystems organized around family functions is not nearly as significant as the clarity of system boundaries. A parental subsystem that includes a grandmother or a parental child can function quite well, so long as lines of responsibility and authority are clearly drawn (Minuchin, 1974, p. 54).*

Concomitantly, Minuchin (1974) referred to "diffuse boundaries" (p. 61) as indicators of dysfunctional families. For example diffuse boundaries are found in "enmeshed" families where mother and children are in coalition again the father-husband. In such families, boundaries between the generations, both real and symbolic, remain ambiguous.

Accommodation to Family Stress

Based on the perspective of family therapists and earlier developmentalists and on the initial testing by this author of the boundary ambiguity propositions, it is proposed that individual and family life span perceptions of who is inside or outside the family system are significantly related to the interaction within that system and between that system and the outside world. The specific theoretical proposition is that *the greater the boundary ambiguity at various developmental and normative junctures throughout the family life-cycle, the higher the family and individual dysfunction*. Resolution of the ambiguity is necessary before the family system can reorganize and move on toward new functioning at a lower level of stress. Non-resolution of boundary ambiguity holds the family at a higher stress level by blocking the regenerative power to reorganize and develop new levels of organization. Boundaries of the system cannot be maintained, so the viability of the system is blurred. Dysfunction results.

Change in Family Boundaries

Obviously, some families resolve the stress of membership change much more quickly than do others. For example, roles and tasks may be quickly reassigned when a new baby joins a family. The father takes over the cooking; grandmother or father or a friend takes over the housework temporarily. The theoretical proposition refers operationally to task accomplishment through role performances (function) within the family structure across time. That is, boundaries are maintained after the birth of a baby by a major shifting of roles

and tasks within the family system. Furthermore, interaction of the family with the outside world may be altered: grandmother or a professional support person temporarily becomes active within the system while the new mother temporarily may not be employed outside the home. The latter alone is a major boundary change for many new mothers who are accustomed to daily interaction with colleagues or friends in their outside work world. The task of redefining her family roles after having a new baby is complicated for an employed woman when boundaries remain unclear—in this case, when she isn't sure if she's in or out of the family with respect to her roles and perceptions. She may want to be out in the work world, but she may feel she should be with her new baby, or vice versa. Until she and her family clarify how she is in and how she is out, both perceptually and physically, the family system cannot fully reorganize after the impact of acquiring a new member. Needless to say, the same clarity is necessary to redefine the new father's role.

To emphasize the recurrence and complexity of such situations of change in family systems across time, some examples of Change in Family Boundaries Over the Life-Span are presented in Figure 1. The major assumptions in this model is that *family system boundaries will change over the life-span*. Furthermore, boundary changes resulting from adding and/or losing family members cannot be predicted normatively for diverse American families beyond initial pairing and

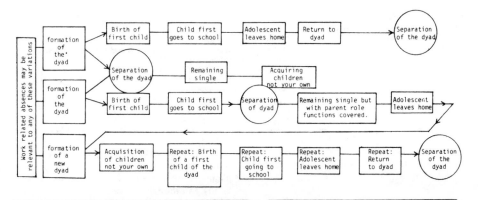

Figure 1. Selective examples of changes in family boundaries over the life-span.

Table 1
Selected References to Illustrate Normative Life-Span Boundary Changes

Type of Life-Span Family Boundary Changes	Boundary Stressors Related to Physical and Psychological Membership in the System
Formation of the dyad Rapoport (1963)	*acquisition of a mate *acquisition of in-laws *realignment with family of orientation *incorporating or rejecting former friendships
Birth of the first child LeMasters, 1957 Russell, 1974 Pridham & Hansen, 1977	*acquisition of a new member *possible separation from extra-familial work world *if so, loss of working colleagues, etc.
Children first going to school Anderson, 1976 Klein & Ross, 1958	*separation of child from the family system to the world of school *acquisition of child's teacher, friends, and peers, i.e., acceptance of them as part of the child's world
Job-related parent/spouse absence or presence Hill, 1949 Boulding, 1950 Boss, 1975, 1980; Note 1 McCubbin et al., 1976 Boss, McCubbin, Lester, 1979 Hooper, J. O., 1979	*fluctuating acquisition *and* separation due to extra-familial role, i.e., military service, routine absence of the corporate executive etc. Stress results from repeated exit and re-entry of the member. Also includes job changes such as return of mother to college or work after she's been a full-time home-maker or retirement of father from work back into the home.
Adolescent children leaving home Stierlin, 1974 Boss & Whitaker, 1979	*separation of adolescent from the family system to his peers, school or job system *acquisition of the adolescent's peers and intimates/same and opposite sex
Taking in child(ren) not your own or blending children from different dyads Duberman, 1975 Visher & Visher, 1978, 1979	*acquisition of another's offspring into the family system, i.e., stepchildren, grandchildren, other nonrelated children.
Loss of a spouse (through death, divorce, etc.) Parkes, 1972 Lopata, 1973, 1979 Bohannan, 1970 Wallerstein & Kelly, Studies from 1974 through 1977 Weiss, 1975 Hetherington, 1971, 1976 Boss & Whitaker, 1979	*separation of mate from the dyad, therefore dissolution of the marital dyad. Note: In case of divorce, the dyad may continue and function on other levels, such as co-parenting, etc.
Loss of parent(s) Sheehy, 1976 Silverstone & Hyman, 1976 Levinson, 1978	*separation of child from parent(s) (child may likely be an adult)
Formation of a new dyad: remarriage Bernard, 1956 Messinger, 1976 Westoff, 1977 Whiteside, 1978 Roosevelt & Lofas, 1976	*acquistion of a new mate *acquisition of a new set of in-laws *realignment with family of orientation and former in-laws, children of former marriage, etc. *incorporating or rejecting former friendships, former spouses etc., former spouse may still be in partnership with a member of the new dyad regarding parenting.
Remaining single Stein, 1976	*realignment with family of orientation *if previously married, realignment with former in-laws *acquisition of friends, intimates, colleagues, etc.

final separation. Hence, various family structural patterns may be exhibited as families progress throughout the life cycle.

Variability in Family Structures for Boundary Maintenance

With an obvious focus on normative function more than on normative structure, it is suggested that there may be no universals in family structural boundaries beyond the original formation of the boundary and its eventual dissolution through family separa-

tion. Between these two stages, it is variance more than universality that allows for coping and functional adaptation across the life-span. Varied structures across *and* among families may support the accomplishment of functions that are necessary for family survival and growth over time. In other words, there may indeed be more than one way for families to reach the same end goal (von Bertalanffy, 1968; pp. 40, 132; Buckley, 1967; Hill, 1971).

The Black American family is an excellent example of adaptive boundary maintenance in the face of severe stress from both inside and outside the family. Such families survived only because of adaptations to the normative family structure, as the television epic *Roots* so clearly illustrated. The Haley family added and exited people as they needed regardless of societal norms or biological destiny. There was no doubt that Chicken George was still the father and husband in his family and that he still performed the necessary functions for his family even though he remained up North for many years. The family boundary stretched, because of necessity, to retain him as a viable member of the system. Indeed, he actively performed the role of provider and purchaser of freedom for the rest of his family system. It was precisely such boundary elasticity that permitted this Black family to perceive his membership within the system despite great physical distance.

To provide examples of the types of boundary changes families appear to encounter in their everyday life over time, selected representative research is noted in Table 1. The boundary changes listed are derived from the classic Rapoport (1963) article, but with these revisions: first, because the "formation of the dyad" is not always synonymous with "marriage," the former term is used. Second, because the "death of a spouse" is not the only recognized way to break up a dyad, "loss of a spouse," which can include death, divorce, or desertion, is used in Table 1. Third, the "acquisition of children not your own" is added because of the frequency of this phenomenon today in remarried or blended families and, traditionally, in the Black American subculture. Fourth, "formation of a new dyad" is added because of the high rate of remarriage today. Finally, "work-related absence" is added to Table 1 because it occurs in so many variations of American families today.

Summary

If it can be assumed that family structural adaptations have been made for the survival of the organism, then these adaptations must be recognized and documented before scientists can proceed toward valid explanation of why some families can cope with the stress of normative membership change whereas others cannot.

Stress continues in any family until membership can be clarified and the system reorganized regarding (a) who performs what roles and tasks, and (b) how family members perceive the absent member. Challenges to the family's capacity for boundary maintenance come not only from outside forces, but also from normal developmental maturation throughout the life cycle. Such challenges are met by families by varying their structure to maintain functions. Recognizing and investigating variability in structure for boundary maintenance offers one promising approach to study the original question of why some families can cope with everyday life stresses whereas others cannot.

REFERENCE NOTE

1. Boss, P. G. *Psychological father absence and presence: A theoretical formulation for an investigation into family systems interaction.* Unpublished doctoral dissertation, University of Wisconsin, Madison, August, 1975.

REFERENCES

Anderson, L. S. When a child begins school. *Children Today,* August 1976, 16-19.

Angell, R. C. *The family encounters the depression.* New York: Scribner's & Sons, 1936.

Bernard, J. *Remarriage.* New York: Holt, Rinehart, and Winston, 1956.

Bohannan, P. *Divorce and after.* Doubleday, 1970.

Boss, P. G. A clarification of the concept of psychological father presence in families experiencing ambiguity of boundary. *Journal of Marriage and the Family,* 1977, **39,** 141-151.

Boss, P. G., The relationship of psychological father presence, wife's personal qualities and wife/family dysfunction in families of missing fathers. *Journal of Marriage and the Family,* 1980, **42,** 541-549.

Boss, P. G., McCubbin, H. I., & Lester, G. The corporate executive wife's coping patterns in response to routine husband-father absence. *Family Process,* March 1979, **18,** 79-86.

Boss, P. G., & Whitaker, C. Dialogue on separation. *The Family Coordinator*, 1979, **28**, 391-398.

Boszormenyi-Nagy, I., & Spark, G. M. *Invisible loyalties.* New York: Harper & Row, 1973.

Boulding, E. Family adjustment to war separation and reunion. *Annals of the American Academy of Political and Social Science*, 1950, **272**, 59-68.

Buckley, W. *Sociology and modern systems theory.* Englewood Cliffs, NJ: Prentice-Hall, 1967.

Cavan, R. S., & Ranck, K. H. *The family and the depression.* Chicago: University of Chicago Press, 1938.

Duberman, L. *The reconstituted family: A study of remarried couples and their children.* Chicago: Nelson-Hall, 1975.

DuVall, E. M. Loneliness and the serviceman's wife. *Marriage and Family Living*, August, 1943, 77-82.

Hetherington, E. M., & Deur, J. The effects of father absence on child development. *Young Children*, 1971, **26**, 233-248.

Hetherington, E. M., Cox, M., & Cox, R. Divorced fathers. *The Family Coordinator*, 1976, **25**, 417-428.

Hill, R. *Families under stress.* Connecticut: Greenwood Press, 1949.

Hill, R. Modern systems theory and the family: A confrontation. *Social Science Information*, 1971, **72**, 7-26.

Hooper, J. O. My wife, the student. *The Family Coordinator*, 1979, **28**, 459-464.

Kantor, O., & Lehr, W. *Inside the family.* San Francisco: Jossey-Bass, 1975.

Klein, D. C., & Ross, A. Kindergarten entry: A study of role transition. In M. Krugman (Eds.), *Orthopsychiatry and the school.* New York: American Orthopsychiatric Association, 1958.

LeMasters, E. E. Parenthood as crisis. *Marriage and Family Living*, 1957, **29**, 352-355.

Levinson, D. J. *The seasons of a man's life.* New York: Ballantine Books, 1978.

Lopata, H. I. *Widowhood in an American City.* Cambridge, MA: Schenkman, 1973.

Lopata, H. I. *Women as widows.* New York: Elsevier, 1979.

McCubbin, H., Dahl, B., & Hunter, E. Research in the military family: A review. In H. McCubbin, B. Dahl, & E. Hunter (Eds.), *Families in the military system.* Beverly Hills: Sage, 1976.

Messinger, L. Remarriage between divorced people with children from previous marriages. *Journal of Marriage and Family Counseling*, 1976, **2**, 193-200.

Minuchin, S. *Families and family therapy.* Cambridge, MA: Harvard University Press.

Parad, H. J. (Ed.) *Crisis intervention: Selected readings.* New York: Family Service Association of America, 1965.

Parkes, C. M. *Bereavement: Studies of grief in adult life.* New York: International Universities Press, Inc., 1972.

Piaget, J., & Inhelder, B. *The child's conception of space.* London: Routledge & Kegan Paul, 1956.

Pridham, K. F., Hansen, M., & Conrad, H. H. Anticipatory care as problem-solving in family medicine and nursing. *Journal of Family Practice*, 1977, **4**, 1077-1081.

Rapoport, R. Normal crises, family structure, and mental health. *Family Process*, 1963, **2**.

Roosevelt, R., & Lofas, J. *Living in step: A remarriage manual for parents and children.* New York: McGraw-Hill, 1976.

Russell, C. Transition to parenthood: Problems and gratifications. *Journal of Marriage and the Family*, 1974, 294-301.

Silverstone, B., & Hyman, H. *You and your aging parents.* New York: Patheon, 1976.

Sheehy, G. *Passages: Predictable crises of adult life.* New York: Dutton, 1976.

Stein, P. *Single.* Englewood Cliffs, NJ: Prentice-Hall, 1976.

Stierlin, H. *Separating parents and adolescents.* New York: Quadrangle, 1974.

Visher, E., & Visher, J. Common problems of step parents and their spouses. *American Journal of Orthopsychiatry*, April, 1978, **48**(2), 252-262.

Visher, E., & Visher, J. *Stepfamilies: A guide to working with step-parents and step-children.* New York: Brunner-Mazel, 1979.

von Bertalanffy, L. *General systems theory* (revised edition). New York: George Brazilley, 1968.

Wallerstein, J. S., & Kelly, J. B. The effects of parental divorce: The adolescent experience. In E. J. Anthony & C. Koupernik (Eds.), *The child and his family: Children at psychiatric risk III.* New York: Wiley, 1974.

Wallerstein, J. S., & Kelly, J. B. The effects of parental divorce: Experiences of the preschool child. *American Academy of Child Psychiatry*, 1975, **14**(4), 600-616.

Wallerstein, J. S., & Kelly, J. B. The effects of parental divorce: Experiences of the child in early latency. *American Journal of Orthopsychiatry*, 1976, **46**, 20-32. (a)

Wallerstein, J. S., & Kelly, J. B. The effects of parental divorce: Experiences of the child in later latency. *American Journal of Orthopsychiatry*, 1976, **46**, 256-269. (b)

Wallerstein, J. S., & Kelly, J. B. Divorce counseling: A community service for families in the midst of divorce. *American Journal of Orthopsychiatry*, 1977, **47**, 4-22 (a)

Wallerstein, J. S., & Kelly, J. B. Brief intervention with children in divorcing families. *American Journal of Orthopsychiatry*, 1977, **47**, 23-37. (b)

Weiss, R. *Marital separation.* New York: Basic Books, 1975.

Westoff, L. A. *The second time around: Remarriage in America.* New York: Viking, 1977.

Whiteside, M., & Auerbach, L. Can the daughter of my father's new wife be my sister? Families of remarriage in family therapy. *Journal of Divorce*, 1978, **1**, 271-283.

Recently, there has been an increased interest in delineating the strategies by which families cope with stressful and challenging events and circumstances. This essay is an effort to explore the range and variety of such coping strategies. More important, it attempts to show how these strategies are related to one another and to more fundamental adaptive capacities of families; these capacities are manifest in the routines that are typical of the quiescent periods of the families' lives. The relationships we posit are shaped by a theory developing out of an extended series of laboratory and field studies in our center. Kuhn's concept of paradigm has been a helpful organizing metaphor for this theoretical work. It has led us to suspect that a family's adaptive capacities—both its everyday routines as well as its attempts to cope with unusual and stressful events—are shaped by its abiding conception of the social world in which it lives.

7

FAMILY PARADIGM AND FAMILY COPING

A Proposal for Linking the Family's Instrinsic Adaptive Capacities to Its Responses to Stress*

*David Reiss** and Mary Ellen Oliveri****

Careful, direct observational studies of families in their natural settings—their homes and communities—are indicating that large segments of family life are humdrum and routine. Although the routines of daily life doubtless serve important functions for families during stable times, occasional events and circumstances challenge the family's well-

*The work described in this paper was supported by DHEW Grant MH 26711.

**David Reiss is Director, Center for Family Research, and Professor, Department of Psychiatry and Behavioral Sciences, The George Washington University School of Medicine, 2300 Eye Street, N.W., Washington, D.C. 20037

***Mary Ellen Oliveri is Investigator, Center for Family Research, and Assistant Research Professor, Department of Psychiatry and Behavioral Sciences, George Washington University School of Medicine, 2300 Eye Street, N.W., Washington, D.C. 20037

formed habits. It is then that the family is called upon to exert some unusual effort: to observe, to experience, to define, to understand and to take some kind of special action so that it can return to the more orderly routines of its daily life. These sequences of experiences and actions, at times of challenge, are occasionally imaginative and inspired, and other times banal and tragic. All of them in their endless variety are coming to be known in our field by the somewhat prosaic term of "coping strategies."

This essay is an attempt to picture some of the variables of these strategies of coping with stress and to show how they derive from underlying intrinsic adaptive capacities of families that, while stable and enduring, may be little noticed during the more ordinary routines of everyday life. More specifically, our aim is to refine a model of family coping so that we may measure a family's intrinsic adaptive capacities at a quiescent period in its

From David Reiss and Mary Ellen Oliveri, "Family Paradigm and Family Coping: A Proposal for Linking the Family's Intrinsic Adaptive Capacities to Its Responses to Stress," *Family Relations*, 1980, 29, pp. 431-444. Reprinted by permission of the publisher and authors.

life, and use those measurements to predict the family's response to stress. Our efforts along these lines have proceeded through three phases. First, we have over many years developed a set of laboratory procedures which highlight variation in how families solve externally-given problems, and we have explored what underlying adaptive capacities are expressed by the various problem-solving styles we observe (Reiss, 1967, 1968, 1969, 1971b, 1971c). This phase of our work has been aided by a developing theory and set of methods which conceive of a broad variety of family problem-solving routines as shaped by an enduring conception each family holds about the fundamental nature of its social world and its place in that world (Reiss, 1971d). Although our theoretical work draws on several sources, Kuhn's (1970) concept of paradigm has been a particularly helpful organizing metaphor. A second phase has been the development of hypotheses about what sorts of coping strategies a family with a particular set of adaptive capacities would develop in the face of stress. Third, we test these predictions by comparing our laboratory findings with assessments of actual coping strategies families use in times of stress. The first of these phases has to some degree been accomplished and is summarized in the first part of this essay. The second phase is outlined in the main portion of this essay. The final phase is under active investigation in our laboratory now.

The Concept of the Family Paradigm

Family Problem Solving and Shared Constructs

For many years we have investigated several aspects of family problem solving. Initially, we used a well-controlled and precise series of laboratory methods, and our interest was in distinguishing different styles or patterns of problem solving. Indeed we found marked differences among families along three principal dimensions (Reiss, 1971d). First, families differed in the extent to which they could detect patterns and organization in the complex stimulus arrays with which we presented them as a group. Second, families differed in their degrees of coordina-

tion, cooperation, and agreement as they progressed through the many phases of our problems. Finally, families differed in their openness to new information: some families reached decisions early whereas others delayed closure as long as possible.

Our first question about these differences in problem solving style concerned their correlates in the actual lives of families, and several studies have suggested that there are some remarkably detailed parallels. For example, in a recent series of clinical studies we have been able to use families' problem-solving styles, measured in the laboratory, to make fine-grained predictions successfully about their patterns of adjustment to the psychiatric hospitalization of an adolescent member (Reiss, Costell, Jones, & Berkman, 1980). Also, in recent studies of nonclinical families, problem-solving styles have correlated with the patterns of relationships between families and their extended kin (Oliveri & Reiss, in press).

Since the problem-solving styles we were observing seemed to reflect more general modes of family adaptation, we wondered what factors or circumstances shaped and controlled them. We examined the most obvious variables to answer this question, but in our samples (we have now tested well over 400 families), social class, family structure, race and the religion of the family, as well as the intelligence, problem-solving skills, and perceptual styles of individual members, have had no relationship with the family group's problem-solving style. However, detailed observation of our families in the laboratory, and interviewing of them after the formal procedures had been administered, gave us our first clue about what did shape their problem-solving styles. It seemed that a specific family's problem-solving style arose less from its understanding of the problems we presented them, and much more from their perception of the research setting and the research team. For all families, the research setting is ambiguous and moderately stressful. Despite the careful oral and written instructions we give them before they come, and once again when they arrive, families really don't know why we are doing the research, what we expect of them, and how they are being assessed. Each family must come to its own conclusions on these matters. These conclusions, we have found, are formed early (often before the family arrives at our doorstep) and seem to determine all that comes afterwards.

For example, some families mistrust us from the outset. They feel we are giving them an insoluble puzzle whose *real* (although concealed) purpose is to humiliate them or strain the ties of one member to another. For them, the true problem is not to solve the logical puzzle we give them but rather to stick together to finish the puzzles and then, as quickly as possible, beat a hasty though decorous retreat. Hence, they show a particular "problem-solving style": very tight consensus, early closure and crude pattern recognition (they haven't really tried to look for patterns). In sharp contrast are families who trust us (whether or not we, in fact, deserve it). They assume right from the start we have given them a soluble puzzle and that we are being honest when we tell them "this is a study to learn more about how families solve problems." They go about their business co-operatively, efficiently, waiting for the maximum amount of data before making a final decision. Thus, they show another kind of "problem solving style": cooperative and effective search for patterns with delayed closure.

From the outset we doubed that these shared family perceptions of the situation resulted from anything we did, purposively or not (Robert Rosenthal, 1969, notwithstanding). First, the reactions of our families were so varied even though our approach to them was relatively uniform. Second, the beliefs about us seemed to be held with great and profound conviction. We began to feel that our laboratory problem-solving procedure had serendipitously uncovered, for each family, a pervasive orientation to the social environment. We reasoned that this orientation might be built into the family and condition the quality of its engagement with any social setting, particularly if the setting were at all ambiguous. This would be a good explanation not only for the variety of problem-solving styles we had observed in the laboratory but, more importantly, for the pin-point predictions regarding families' relationships with

social communities in their everyday worlds (e.g., the social community of the psychiatric hospital or of the extended family).

We have begun to look at this issue directly, and have been developing measures to assess the family's perception of a variety of communities and groups with which it comes into contact. For example, we have recently published a report exploring how a family perceives other families and again have shown surprising, but by now understandable, correlations between problem-solving style and these shared perceptions of other families (Reiss, Costell, Berkman, & Jones, in press). Our recent work has revealed, in each family, a rich and ordered set of beliefs about the social world. These beliefs seem sensibly connected to the ways families actually respond to and interact with their social world.

Our attention has now turned to exploring these shared beliefs, assumptions and orientations families hold. Since our evidence suggests that they are built-in and enduring components of family life, we have asked what function they serve. It was not enough to argue that they played a role in regulating the family's transactions with its social environment. We now want to know why families develop such shared beliefs and assumptions to perform such a function. Equally important, we want to know how such belief systems develop and what circumstances lead to major changes. This line of theorizing has been described in some detail elsewhere (Reiss, in press) along with evidence in support of it. We will only summarize our thinking here in preparation for our discussion of family stress and coping.

The Nature and Function of Shared Constructs

This line of theorizing has been supported and shaped by the ideas on individual psychology of Heider (1958) and Kelly (1955) and on social process by Berger and Luckman (1966). A beginning premise is that each individual must develop his own set of constructs of social phenomena, bound together with his theory of how the social world works. This personal system of ideas, opinions, hunches, assumptions, hypotheses and convictions is a constant guide to individuals in any novel situation. It shapes their hypotheses about that situation, their investigations and conclusions, and is a constant guide for their behavior. In our work on theory, we have added to these familiar notions some ideas about the individual's needs to share with others this task of developing personal theories. Indeed, we have argued with the assistance of thoughts from Berger and Luckman that lengthy, intimate, face-to-face relationships cannot go forward without a reconciliation, integration and shared development of the basic premises of these personal theories. In other words, when two or more individuals develop an intimate relationship, they engage in a process of reconciling the basic premises of their personal construct systems. Thus, a shared system of construing in a family reflects the progressive and crucial integration, over time, of the personal explanatory systems of each member. Conversely, the dissolution or splitting of families develops out of the disavowal of shared premises and personal constructs.

The concept of shared beliefs has been a little difficult to swallow for people who recognize how much disagreement and conflict are invariable components of family life. Our view is that the presence of conflict or disagreement itself does not necessarily mean these underlying shared beliefs are absent. Indeed, what family members often share at times of argument and dissension are beliefs about what is important to argue about and how such arguments may ultimately be resolved. For example, a husband and wife argue bitterly about whose responsibility it is to clean the children's toys from the sidewalk in front of their house. They accuse each other of risking criticism from their neighbors. The wife becomes more strident and the husband sulks away to clean up. We may say this couple, despite its argument, share at least two conceptions. First, both share an extreme sensitivity to the opinion of their neighbors. Second, they share an assumption that the most strident arguer must win out. Underlying, shared beliefs of this kind cannot easily be reported verbally by the family. Often, they must be inferred from observations of the family's behavior. Our own data are tentative

but do seem to support the idea that beliefs or orientations of this kind are truly shared (Reiss, 1971a; Reiss & Salzman, 1973). We also have reported some preliminary evidence that these shared beliefs are more evident in a family's non-verbal behavior than in its discussion (Reiss, 1970).

Our model acknowledges that there are, in all likelihood, several mechanisms by which shared constructs develop and change. Our main interest has been in the role of serious and disabling crisis in family life. We have seen in this circumstance, though rare in the life of an ordinary family, an opportunity to understand some of the fundamental aspects of the development and change of family constructs. Drawing on clinical experience and the recent theoretical work of Kantor and Lehr (1975) we have argued that in severe family crisis, whatever the cause, the family's typical mode of conceptualizing its position in the world becomes more clear, stark, simple. It loses its background position as a gentle coordinator of family affairs and becomes a conspicuous eminence with which no family member feels entirely comfortable. As the crisis becomes more severe, members start to disown this eminence which now seems oppressive. Dissolution of the family or a split of one member from the rest is imminent and often occurs.

At this point in the progressive decay of a family, a reorganization of their mode of construing their position in the world is often possible. In a clinical setting it may be influenced by a therapist; a religious family may draw on a priest or a clerical community. In any case, the recovery and reconstruction from extreme crisis can bring a new organization to family life and more importantly, for our purposes, to their typical mode of construing events. Surface manifestations of these shifts are seen in the way some families respond to the unanticipated death of a child, to a prolonged and disabling illness in an older member, to a move or a job loss. Crisis provides the raw material for a fundamental revision of its shared mode of construing the environment. The new system of constructs can become a point around which the family organizes. Consider, for example, a family that finds it can thrive following the death of a dominant grandmother who controlled the family through dire predictions of danger only she could thwart. A new set of concepts about the family's relationship to the social world can emerge through grief and crisis following grandmother's death. The family can develop an entirely new sense of its own potency. The important point here is that the force, persistence and pervasiveness of the new construct system comes from its initial and continuing role in providing family coherence after a time of crisis. We have argued that this force continues even after the crisis is no longer consciously remembered.

This crisis-oriented group dynamic, as we propose it, bears an interesting relationship to that described by T. S. Kuhn for scientific revolutions (Kuhn, 1970). His familiar formulation pictures, in effect, scientists as a quasi-social group whose behavior is shaped by a set of fundamental assumptions about the natural world. When these assumptions fail to account for new data, dissolution occurs, the community of scientists can no longer function as a smoothly working "group," and crisis arises A clever new solution to existing problems serves as a continuing model or paradigm for the rebuilding of a new system of framing assumptions. Whatever difficulty Kuhn's ideas have encountered in the philosophy of science (Suppe, 1977) they have been a useful set of metaphors for our work. We now refer to the *family paradigm* as that new idea or approach, born in crisis, which serves as a background and orienting idea or perspective to the family's problem solving in daily life. A family paradigm serves as a stable disposition or orientation whenever the family must actively construe a new situation.

We do not have a clear idea, as yet, of the circumstances under which crisis produces a genuine change or "revolution" in family life. After crisis some families return to the old order whereas others undergo major transformations. Some hypotheses in this regard have been formulated elsewhere (Reiss, in press) but this matter is an important area for future investigation.

Dimensions of Family Paradigm

If our argument thus far is on the mark, then it follows that if we know the family's paradigm we should be able to predict a wide range of its responses to ambiguous and stressful events in its social world. We are just beginning to examine these possibilities in a series of related research programs. We are aided by two factors of immense practical importance. First, as we have already indicated. it appears possible to delineate, at least in part, these underlying orientations in family life by our laboratory problem-solving techniques. They serve in part as a group Rorschach: an ambiguous field on which the family can project its own assumptions. However, unlike the Rorschach, our procedures require the family to *act* rather than just talk. These actions are measurable by precise quantitative techniques. A second factor of practical importance is that a great deal of variation in problem-solving behavior, and we believe in the underlying paradigms that produce it, can be accounted for by three conceptually distinct dimensions. Thus, if we know a family's position along each of these three dimensions we should be able to successfully predict a great range of their responses to challenging social situations. It is the burden of this essay to specify these predictions. First, however. we must summarize our cardinal dimensions. The conceptualization and validation of these dimensions is based on work carried out in our own laboratory. Although the findings from this work are internally consistent, it must be emphasized that the findings themselves, and the interpretation we attach to them, need to be corroborated by other investigators in different settings.

Configuration

In our problem-solving tasks we recognize this dimension by the degree to which the family can discover the hidden or underlying patterns in the stimulus arrays we present them. Our data suggest that this problem-solving behavior reflects a fundamental conception, by the family, that the social world in which they live is ordered by a coherent set of principles which they can discover and master through exploration and interpretation (Reiss, 1971b; Reiss, in press, Reiss, et al., 1980). For example, families who recognize patterns in the laboratory problem-solving task also have well-worked out, ordered and subtle conceptions of other families they know (Reiss et al, in press). Also, in our clinical studies, they are sensitive to subtle cues, particularly emotional ones, in developing their impressions of an in-patient treatment program to which their adolescent child has been admitted (Costell et al., in press). The sense of potential mastery over the social environment characterizing families high on configuration has also been revealed in the patterns of social network interactions of nonclinical families; configuration is positively associated with the degree of autonomy of individual family members in relation to the network of extended family (Oliveri & Reiss, in press). Elsewhere, we have proposed that families high or low on configuration can be recognized by observing their everyday household routines. For example, families high on configuration practice rituals which tie them firmly to wider social groups outside the home, such as the home celebration of ethnic rituals or the regular invitation of guests to dinner (Reiss, in press). They also arrange their household activities to clearly reflect an ordered and comprehensive grasp of the family's role in the community. For example, a child will be given space to study and a mother space to conduct meetings if her vocation or avocation requires it. In contrast, the rituals of low-configuration families reflect idiosyncratic ties to their own past and are incomprehensible and separate from the larger community. Their households are either an inchoate jumble or a frozen idealization of the past. An example of the latter is the family of a physician's widow who kept the deceased doctor's desk, medical equipment and books in place for over a decade after his death.

Coordination

We recognize this dimension by the care with which each member dovetails his problem-solving efforts with others in the family. This is more than a measure of simple agreement on the nature of the problem's solution. Our measurement of coordination is based on the degree to which members attend to the details of each other's problem-solving efforts. These problem-solving patterns re-

flect the family's belief that they, in fact, occupy the same experiential world, a world which operates in the same way for all of them. Beyond that, families high on this dimension see themselves as facing their social world as a group; they feel themselves to be a group, but even more important, feel the world treats them as a group. Thus, what happens to one will have implications for the rest. Our data do indeed suggest that families who are high on this dimension carefully compare and integrate their impressions about many aspects of their social world. For example, members in high-coordination families take care to develop similar views of the in-patient treatment program (Costell, Reiss, Berkman, & Jones, in press) and are precisely attuned to one another's efforts to explore and understand other families (Reiss, in press). It is also of interest that these families are embedded in nuclear families who are close and well connected; in these cases the wife's and husband's families often know and relate to one another (Oliveri & Reiss, in press). We have proposed that families high in coordination, as measured in the laboratory, also show a great deal of synchrony and coordination of planning and scheduling in their daily lives. The dimension of coordination is similar, in some respects, to the recently re-conceptualized dimension of cohesion as presented by Olson (1979). Our dimension focuses more specifically on the family's conception or belief about their experiential world. Unlike Olson, we do not regard either the extreme or moderate values on this dimension as adaptive or non-adaptive. As we will briefly review at the end of this essay, in our view family adaptiveness must take into account the family's own goals as well as the social setting in which it lives.

Closure

In our problem-solving situation, this dimension is measured by the degree to which families delay their final decisions until they have all the evidence they can obtain. Families who show delayed closure are rated high on this dimension. They have a strong engagement in the novelty and uniqueness of each new setting which they experience with a relative freshness and little preconception. Low-scoring families reach decisions early and stick with them. They seem dominated by the convictions and forms of their own past. They see the world as constantly reminiscent, as pre-figured and, at most, a modest reshuffling of past experience. In some cases they truly see the world through the eyes of their ancestors. (Olson's dimension of adaptability (1979) is similar in some respects). It is particularly interesting that, in our studies of social network, families with delayed closure are significantly invested in the largest number of extended family members. This is a reflection, we argue, of their thirst for access to maximum breadth and variety of input from the environment that assures continued openness of the family to new experiences (Oliveri & Reiss, in press). We have proposed that, in their own home, early-closure families will show a leisurely pacing of activities, what Kantor and Lehr have referred to as slow "clocking." A more frenetic pacing of events, rapid clocking, will be seen in delayed-closure families. The rituals of early-closure families will invoke the family's past. Consider for example the ritual where every Christmas night a family writes an account of the evening, round-robin style, and then reads the accounts of previous Christmases. In contrast, the rituals of the delayed-closure families will cut them off from the past. For example, a mother and father who have grown up in an orthodox Jewish family fail to celebrate Jewish holidays in their home but annually help their two children to hang Christmas stockings.

In repeated samples of clinic and non-clinic families we have seen that these dimensions are orthogonal. Thus a family may have any combination of high and low scores on all three.

Stress and the Family Paradigm

A Working Definition of Family Stress

In this essay, a preliminary attempt at theoretical synthesis, it seems wise to begin simply. Thus, we will want to consider only those events and circumstances that are relatively brief and circumscribed, lasting weeks or at most months, but not years. Further, we will want to focus on events or circumstances that happen to the family, such as neighborhood changes and physical illness, rather than events that happen within the family, such as marital separations and the birth of children. The latter internal, rather than external, stress events are every bit as important as the former for a general theory of family stress and coping. However, they are particularly difficult conundrums since they are simultaneously stressful events and, in all likelihood, responses to stress. This dual role is easy to see for such an obvious internal event as marital separation. More subtly, La Rossa (1977) has shown quite convincingly how conceiving and bearing children can also be a strategy by which couples cope with preexisting stress. It must be acknowledged, however, that it is no easy matter to distinguish internal and external events. Neighborhood changes, such as a new road or a significant demographic shift, may be relatively beyond the control of the family and hence qualify as truly external. Physical illness, on the other hand, is another matter. Numerous studies have shown that physical illness in one or more member may be part of the family's effort to cope with some other stress, chronic or acute, in their lives. Nonetheless, we will focus on those events and circumstances that seem primarily or substantially to be external.

The next problem concerns some definition of what kinds of external events or circumstances may be regarded as stressful for families. Equally important, for our purposes, is to conceive of a way of judging the magnitude of stress that inheres in the event. Hill (1965) has proposed two factors which interact to establish the stressfulness of an event and the magnitude of that stress. The first is the objective hardships for a particular family which accompany the event. Second is the definition the family makes of the event: how stressful this event seems to them. From our perspective this second factor, the definitional process, is part of the family's *response* to the event; it does not inhere, in any sense, in the stressful qualities of the event itself. Indeed, we will try to show, in the last portion of this essay, that the full range of a family's response to a stressful event can be shown to be related to these definitional processes, not only as their definitional processes are activated at times of stress but as they operate to regulate the routine transactions of a family with its outer world.

Hill's first factor, the actual hardships associated with an event, is not an entirely satisfactory way of judging the magnitude of stress in an event. Hardships do not arrive objectively and unvarnished at the family's boundary for them to define and respond to. Hardships, of whatever magnitude, are transformed by the culture (Hill recognized this process as "cultural definition"). For example, in Navajo society, physical illness is regarded as a failure of fit between the ill person and supernatural forces; it becomes the community's responsibility, under the guidance of the shaman, to provide healing through a reestablishment of harmony between the ill person and the supernatural (Kluckhohn, 1958). All the objective hardships accompanying illness may be identical for a Navajo family and a neighboring Anglo family, but the meaning to the average family within each culture will be different. The Anglo family will see illness as its unique burden to bear, the Navajo as a burden to be shared with its community. It is useful, then, to distinguish conceptually between two aspects of stress. First, the magnitude of a stressful event is determined by the interaction of hardship and cultural definition. Second, the family's definitional processes constitute the core of all the coping responses which follow. Cultural definition shapes the magnitude of the stress; family definition shapes the style of the response.

It is now a practical matter to determine the "cultural definition" of stressful events. Quite unintentionally, the tradition of life events research begun by Holmes and Rahe (1967) has given us some preliminary tools. When these researchers ask a group of judges to rate the "magnitude of stress" inherent in a set of events they are, in effect, asking them to read their own culture. They are asking: "In your culture how much stress or lifechange will this event produce in the average person?" In the most careful study to date, for example, Dohrenwend, Krasnoff, Askenasy, and Dohrenwend (1978) found significant and interpretable differences between Black, Puerto Rican,

and White subcultures in New York City. Our question, however, is somewhat different from investigators in the life events tradition. We want to know, for any particular culture, what events are regarded as stressful for the average *family*. We believe the most sensible approach here requires two steps. The first is to interview a sample of families representative of a particular subculture; in this interview of the whole family as a group the aim is to determine what recent events have significantly altered or disrupted the family's usual routines. The next step is to recruit a second representative sample of families, from the same subculture, and ask each family to work as a group to rate the events, which were provided by the first sample, for the stress or magnitude of change those events will induce in the average family in their community, and for the "externality" of those events. We are already engaged in a study of this kind and have found some intriguing results. For example, families are regularly reporting to us when we interview the family group the importance of neighborhood changes to them. They have included changes such as demographic ones, alterations in the age or race of neighbors, and spatial changes, such as the construction of new highways with consequent changes in traffic patterns and access routes. No events of this kind appear on any of the standard life events lists, constructed for individuals.

Now that we have working concepts and methods to determine the magnitude of stressful events, our interest will focus on events of *moderate* severity. As we have explained elsewhere, severe stress may overwhelm any semblance of family organization. The family's set of beliefs, organized by its central paradigm, may be shattered. Its coping strategies may be determined as much by the nature of the support it receives from the surrounding community (church, neighborhood, therapists, extended family) as from its pre-existing patterns. Thus, it is more difficult to predict from a knowledge of the family's paradigm how it will respond to severe stress. Moderate stress on the other hand will, more often than not, be encompassable by the family paradigm. Here a knowledge of the family's paradigm can help us predict, organize, and understand the family's repertoire of coping strategies.

Stages of a Family's Response to Moderate Stress

It is important to distinguish different phases or stages of a family's responses to moderate stress, since different coping strategies are likely to be employed during different phases. We have drawn on two promising sources. The first has been Joan Aldous' (1971) adaptation of the problem-solving perspectives originally developed by John Dewey (1910) and applied to individuals and families by Brim (1962). This approach views the family's response to any significant problem or stress as a quasi-logical, rational process in which options are developed and explored, and decisions are made based on these options. Aldous lists the following six stages:

1. identification and definition of the problem
2. collection of information about the problem
3. production of alternative solutions
4. deciding among alternatives
5. taking action to solve the problem
6. evaluation of action taken

Although useful, this system of stages implies a stark rationality to family process. It needs to be brought closer to actual sequences in family life. Concepts drawn from work phases in small task groups are useful here. A good source is the work of Chris Argyris who has been a leader in conceptualizing adaptive work in these groups (1965a, 1965b). Borrowing freely from his work, we may revise the specific stages of a family's response to a stressful event as follows:

1. definition of the event; delineating it as a problem or as a routine occurrence; accepting or rejecting group or individual responsibility for response
2. information seeking; encouragement or discouragement of individual explorations
3. self organization, role allocation, selection or confirmation of competent or incompetent leadership in the group
4. trial solutions, risk taking

5. decision-making; consensus or dissension
6. self-evaluation; sense of group confidence; élan
7. commitment or failure of commitment to group decision

There are still problems with this scheme. As Weick (1971) and others have pointed out, any notion of a family's response to a stressful or problematic event must recognize particular features of family life. For example, the stages of a family response may interpenetrate, be skipped entirely, or not follow in an easily-recognizable sequence. Thus, it seems reasonable, at the very least, to combine the stages derived from Aldous and Argyris. Further, it seems best to regard these stages as three conceptual vantage points for examining a family's response to a stressful event rather than considering them as sequential phases which follow one another in regular or predictable order. Somewhat arbitrarily, we have combined the Aldous-Argyris phases as follows:

1. definition of the events and search for additional information
2. initial response and trial solutions
3. final decisions or closing position and family's commitment to this

We regard these as three forms of family process: definition, trial action, and commitment to decision. *They may occur in any order or simultaneously.* As an example of how the order may be reversed, consider the Jones family's response to a new family, the Smiths, who moved in next door. The family who had lived in the house, before the Smiths moved in, was friendly and open. Accordingly, the Jones' first response to the Smiths was on the entirely implicit and unstated assumption that, like the old neighbors, they would be open and friendly as well. However, their first interactions (initial response and trial solution) are unhappy; they are rebuffed by the Smiths. The Jones family begins to develop a shared sense that they have difficult neighbors who must be avoided or closely watched (closing position). Only then do they begin to recognize, after taking trial action and assuming a closing position, that they have defined a difficult problem.

Dimension of Paradigm and Coping Strategies

Let us now consider the relationship between our three cardinal dimensions of paradigm—configuration, coordination and closure—and the three aspects of the family's response to stressful events. Our hypotheses are summarized in Table 1. We have reasoned that each of the three dimensions should relate to each of the three aspects of the family's response to stress.

Configuration, as we have defined it in many contexts, refers to a sense of mastery in the family. Families high on this dimension feel they can gain control in a novel or challenging environment through investigation and understanding. Thus, their definition of a problematic or stressful event is organized around a concept that as a family they can do something in response. In effect, the outcome of solution is, at least in part, their responsibility. Argyris has referred to this as "owning up." Families low on this dimension feel their future is in the hands of fate. Stressful events enhance their sense of being victimized. Rather than owning up, they disown or disavow responsibility. Some of these families will have faith in an abiding and providing destiny; others will feel pessimistic and victimized. In terms of initial responses and trial solutions, families high on configuration should be oriented toward investigation, information gathering and in general exploration and use of people and resources outside the family. Probably there are few instances where families entertain a specific, clearly-articulated hypothesis; nonetheless, high-configuration families during this phase probably have some implicit idea or question which is modified, sharpened, or answered with increasing information and experience. When the high-configuration family reaches a decision, a solution or a closing position, there is some pride, sense of accomplishment, or tangible growth. In contrast, a low-configuration family does not sense any connection between its own response to the problem, the outcome, and its own characteristics as a group. If things have gone well the family feels fortunate; destiny has smiled. If the outcome or closing position is some-

how negative or disappointing, the family's sense of victimization is enhanced.

Coordination refers to solidarity in family organization. Solidarity, then, should be the hallmark of the adaptive or coping style of high-coordination families. These families should often define any problem as one that somehow involves or concerns the whole family. Stressful events in the environment are often experienced as happening to the family as a unitary group rather than to a particular individual. As a result, information and/or feelings about these events are quickly shared. Low-coordination families, in contrast, rarely perceive stress events as happening to the family. Rather they perceive events as befalling individuals only; as a consequence, information about the event is exchanged slowly, if at all. The initial responses and trial solutions of high-coordination families are carefully dove-tailed. People work in recognizable relationships to one another, role allocation is clear and individuals pay attention to what others do and find out. In low-coordination families individuals act on their own; in some families they do so in lonely isolation, and in others in endless struggle and competition. When they finally reach a closing position or decision, high-coordination families forge a genuine agreement. All members remain committed to this position until or unless they forge a new consensus on a new position. In low-coordination families, an apparent consensus will turn out to be forced on the group by a single individual. Quite often the family cannot or does not reach any consensus, or the status of their agreement is unclear.

Closure refers to the role of tradition in the family's attempt to cope with the here-and-now. High-closure (which means delayed-closure) families emphasize the here-and-now; the immediacy of current experience is the major determinant of what they believe and how they act. Families low on closure are oriented toward their past. Over long periods, family traditions and perspectives play an enormous role in their efforts to interpret the present. Over shorter periods, the family cannot tolerate uncertainty; they reach decisions quickly and stand by them rather than remain open to fresh experience and ideas. This

Table 1

Hypothesized Influence of Family Paradigm Dimensions on the Three Aspects of the Family's Response to Stressful Events

Paradigm Dimensions		Definition of the Event and Search for Additional Information	Phases of Family Coping	
			Initial Responses and Trial Solutions	Final Decision or Closing Position and Family's Commitment to This
Configuration: Mastery	High:	1. Owning up Family takes responsibility for event and/or coping	2. Exploration Family's initial responses are designed to seek information and outside resources, or are in response to information and outside support	3. Response to outcome The family is proud of accomplishment, or feels it has learned something of value in failure
	Low:	Family feels victimized and blames outside forces	Initial reactions are unrelated to information or explanation	The family feels fortunate if successful or victimized if not
Coordination: Solidarity	High:	4. Family Identity Readily perceived as family issue; information exchanged quickly	5. Organization or response Organized, integrated response by all family members; roles clear	6. Consensus on decision Decision was reached with clear consensus and family remains committed to it
	Low:	Slowly or not perceived as family issue; information exchanged slowly; events are seen as happening to individual members	Individuals act on own; overt or covert conflict possible	The consensus was forced on the family by a single individual; the status of agreement unclear, or no consensus is reached
Closure: Openness	High: (Delayed)	7. Reference to the past Focuses on current experiences; past family history unimportant	8. Novelty of responses First responses include trying something new; individual experiences, intuitions, and guesses are encouraged	9. Self-evaluation As a result of coping, family alters conception of itself in some way
	Low:	Past determines current perception and action; little interest in raw experience; more interest in convention or tradition	First responses mostly typical or familiar	As a result of coping, family confirms conception of itself

stance toward experience influences families in all three phases of their coping with stressful events. With respect to problem definition, high-closure families value and search for immediate data. The nature of the problem is often left somewhat up in the air; clarification is expected in time, but not necessarily fashioned immediately. The family does not have a rich sense of its own past and a sense of family convention. The initial responses and trial solutions in high-closure families are often novel and intuitive. The family encourages the members to take risks, and to be responsive to idiosyncratic and uncanny experiences. Low-closure families try to routinize experience (Aldous has provided a laboratory study of this form of routinization in family life [Aldous et al., 1974]). The family's initial responses and trial solutions are conservative, drawing on a repertoire of established or traditional behaviors and attitudes in the family. After they come to a closing position, high-closure families will alter the conception of themselves in some way. The decision or closing position will be reached relatively slowly and some aspects or phases of the family's response to the problem should clearly precede the closing position. In low-closure families, the final decision confirms rather than alters the family's conception of itself. Often the decision or closing position is reached early or may even be the family's first recognizable response. In low-closure families the problem definition and trial solutions are shaped by an abiding conception of what the closing position or decision is or should be.

Table 1 identifies nine different tasks of family coping beginning with 1, "owning up," which is the acceptance or rejection of family responsibility for responding to the stressful event; the table ends with 9, the family's evaluation of its own response. The numbering is meant for ease of reference; we do not mean to imply that the coping process is in any sense sequential according to this numbering system. Families may begin almost anywhere, skip some steps, and end almost anywhere else. Within each task are two contrasting coping strategies. Thus, within task 1 a family may either acknowledge responsibility for dealing with the stress or disown that re-

sponsibility. If a family's paradigm is located high on the configuration dimension, we would predict that it would, in most circumstances, own up to its responsibility to meet or deal with the stressful event. Also, a high-configuration family should, during the time when the family makes its initial response (second column), actively explore its environment for useful information, people, and resources. Finally, when at 2 closing position high-configuration families should feel pride in accomplishment, or learn from failure. Likewise, a family's position on the coordination dimension should predict which of the coping strategies it will pick in the task areas: (4) family identity, (5) organization of response, and (6) consensus on decision. A family's position on the closure dimension should predict which of the pair it will pick in: (7) reference to the past, (8) novelty of response, and (9) self-evaluation. We should be able to predict which of these 18 coping strategies any particular family will use based on its typical problem-solving patterns as measured in our laboratory and are currently engaged in a series of investigations to explore just this point.

It is helpful to consider, however briefly, the similarity between the concepts represented in Table 1 and other work on family stress and coping. First consider, in more general perspective, the contents of the three main columns. The coping strategies we list under "definition of the event" are similar to what Hill (1965) has called by the same name. Hill evidently regarded family definitional processes as conceptually and temporally prior to the family's active coping responses to the stressful situation. We see definitional process as more action oriented, as initiating a series of family actions in response to stress, as continuing throughout the family's response to stress, and as ending only when closure is complete (which, in some families, it may never be). Indeed, we see definitional and action processes as intertwined throughout the family's response to and efforts to cope with stress; we do not separate off, as does Hill, the "definition of the event" as a distinct conceptual component. To our knowledge the sequences of action and experience outlined in the last column, "closing position," are ordinarily not viewed as coping strategies by other investigators. In our view, however, the process by which closure is reached, and even more important, the process integrating the family's final resolution in the continuing stream of its life and development, are as critical in coping as the other strategies deployed during other phases of their response. Boss' study of families of servicemen missing in action suggests that some families may never reach a closing position (Boss, 1977). Many of her families could not accept the father's status years after he was reported missing. They continued to act as if he were alive and were thus unable to bring to closure their response to his loss. Her data suggest that, paradoxically, it may be our early-closure families who stand in greatest risk of this form of failed closure. Their inability to make major shifts and the importance to them of maintaining tradition, may make them unable to reach closure in times of grief and give up someone or something that has been treasured

On a more microscopic level some of the strategies we are proposing are similar to coping strategies described by McCubbin (1979) and Boss (1977) for wives of absent husbands. For example, our "exploration" seems a prototype of what they call Establishing Independence and Self-Sufficiency. McCubbin and Boss describe the latter as the wife's acquisition of skills, experience, and training to deal with the objective hardships entailed by her absent husband. They describe another strategy, "Maintaining the Past and Dependence on Religion." This seems similar to, in some respects, each of the lower strategies in cells 7, 8, and 9 of our table. Finally, their strategy of "Maintaining Family Integration and Structure" is similar to the strategy of organizing the family, described in the upper portion of cell 5.

Hill, McCubbin, and Boss, as well as other scholars in this field, have attempted to define strategies that are most adaptive. We, quite emphatically, do not. More specifically, we do not suggest that the strategy labeled "high" within any of the nine cells in Table 1 is more effective or adaptive than the strategy labeled "low." For example, it is likely that the average Navajo family would not "own up"

to its responsibility to bring relief to an ill member but would, in effect, disown such responsibility in the service of joining in communal healing rights. The question of the adaptiveness of coping strategies must take into account the family's own objectives and the nature of the social community in which it lives. In our fledgling science of family stress and coping we may be rushing to judgment, on very slender evidence, concerning which strategies are "best."

Our aim in this paper has been to emphasize the extraordinary variety of coping strategies families employ in response to stress. We have tried to show how these strategies may be related to an enduring structure of beliefs, convictions, and assumptions the family holds about its social world Kuhn's concept of paradigm, used as a metaphor, helps us understand how these shared beliefs shape family action.

REFERENCES

Aldous, J. A framework for the analysis of family problem solving. In J. Aldous, T. Condon, R. Hill. M. Straus. & I Tallman (Eds.). *Family problem solving: A symposium on theoretical, methodological and substantive concerns.* Hinsdale, Ill.: Dryden, 1971.

Argyris, C. Explorations in interpersonal competence—I *Journal of Applied Behavioral Science,* 1965 1, 58-83.

Argyris, C. Explorations in interpersonal competence—II. *Journal of Applied Behavioral Science,* 1965, 1, 147-177

Berger, P. L., & Luckman, T. *The social construction of reality.* New York: Doubleday, 1966.

Boss, P. A clarification of the concept of psychological father presence in families experiencing ambiguity of boundary. *Journal of Marriage and the Family,* 1977, **39,** 141-151.

Costell, R., Reiss, D., Berkman, H., & Jones, C. The family meets the hospital: Predicting the family's perception of the treatment program from its problem-solving style. *Archives of General Psychiatry,* in press.

Dewey, J. *How we think.* New York: D. C. Heath, 1910.

Dohrenwend, B. S., Krasnoff, L., Askenasy, A. R., & Dohrenwend, B. P. Exemplification of a method for scaling life events: The PERI life events scale. *Journal of Health and Social Behavior,* 1978, **19,** 205-229.

Heider, F. *The psychology of interpersonal relations.* New York: Wiley, 1958.

Hill, R. Genetic features of families under stress. In H. J. Parad (Ed.) *Crisis intervention.* New York: Family Service Association of America, 1965.

Holmes, T. H., & Rahe, R. H. The social readjustment rating scale. *Journal of Psychosomatic Research,* 1967, **11,** 213-218.

Kantor, D., & Lehr, W. *Inside the family*. San Francisco: Jossey-Bass, 1975.

Kelly, G. *The psychology of personal constructs*. New York: Norton, 1955.

Kluckhohn, C., & Leighton, D. *The Navajo*. Cambridge: Harvard University Press, 1958.

Kuhn, T. S. *The structure of scientific revolutions*. Chicago: University of Chicago Press, 1970.

LaRossa, R. *Conflict and power in marriage*. Beverly Hills: Sage, 1977.

McCubbin, H. I. Integrating coping behavior in family stress theory. *Journal of Marriage and the Family*. 1979, 41, 237-244.

Oliveri, M. E., & Reiss, D. The structure of families' ties to their kin: The shaping role of social constructions. *Journal of Marriage and the Family*, in press.

Olson, D. D., Sprenkle, D. H., & Russell, C. S. Circumplex model of marital and family systems: I. Cohesion and adaptability dimensions, family types and clinical applications. *Family Process*, 1979, 18, 3-28.

Reiss, D. Individual thinking and family interaction II: A study of pattern recognition and hypothesis testing in families of normals, character disorders and schizophrenics. *Journal of Psychiatric Research*, 1967, 5, 193-211.

Reiss, D. Individual thinking and family interaction III: An experimental study of categorization performance in families of normals, character disorders and schizophrenics. *Journal of Nervous and Mental Disease*, 1968, 146, 384-403.

Reiss, D. Individual thinking and family interaction IV: A study of information exchange in families of normals, those with character disorders and schizophrenics. *Journal of Nervous and Mental Disease*, 1969, 149. 473-490.

Reiss, D. Individual thinking and family interaction V: Proposals for the contrasting character of experiential sensitivity and expressive form in families. *Journal of Nervous and Mental Disease*, 1970, 151, 187-202.

Reiss, D. Intimacy and problem solving: An automated procedure for testing a theory of consensual experience in families. *Archives of General Psychiatry*, 1971, 22, 442-455 (a).

Reiss, D. Varieties of consensual experience I: A theory for relating family interaction to individual thinking. *Family Process*, 1971, 10, 1-28 (b).

Reiss, D. Varieties of consensual experience II: Dimensions of a family's experience of its environment. *Family Process*, 1971, 10, 28-35 (c).

Reiss, D. Varieties of consensual experience III: Contrasts between families of normals, delinquents and schizophrenics. *Journal of Nervous and Mental Disease*, 1971, 152, 73-95 (d).

Reiss, D. *The family's construction of reality*. Cambridge: Harvard University Press, in press.

Reiss, D., Costell, R., Jones, C., & Berkman, H. The family meets the hospital: A laboratory forecast of the encounter. *Archives of General Psychiatry*, 1980, 37, 141-154.

Reiss, D., Costell, R., Berkman, H., & Jones, C. How one family perceives another: The relationship between social constructions and problem solving competence. *Family Process*, in press.

Reiss, D., & Salzman, C. Resilience of family process: Effect of secobartical. *Archives of General Psychiatry*, 1973, 28, 425-433.

Rosenthal, R. Interpersonal expectations: Effects of the experimenter's hypothesis. In R. Rosenthal & R. Rosnow (Eds.), *Artifact in behavioral research*. New York: Academic Press, 1969.

Suppe, F. Exemplars, theories and disciplinary matrices. In F. Suppe (Ed.), *The structure of scientific theories* (Second Edition). Urbana: University Illinois Press, 1977.

Wieck, K. E. Group processes, family processes and problem solving. In J. Aldous, T. Condor, R. Hill, M. Straus, & I. Tallman (Eds.) *Family problem solving: A symposium on theoretical, methodological and substantive concerns*. Hinsdale, IL: Dryden Press, 1971.

The literature concerning dual-career family stress and coping is reviewed. Sources of dual-career strain are delineated, and the coping patterns employed by couples in managing the stress are summarized. Although acknowledging stressful aspects of dual-career living, it was found that most participants defined their lifestyle positively. Achieving a balance between the advantages and disadvantages of the lifestyle appears to be the overriding concern of most dual-career couples. Some implications for family practitioners are discussed.

8

DUAL-CAREER FAMILY STRESS AND COPING

A Literature Review

Denise A. Skinner*

A significant influence on contemporary family living is the increasing rate of female participation in the labor force. Examination of Department of Labor statistics reveals that the married woman is the key source of this growth and helps explain the growing interest in dual-career families reflected in both the professional and popular literature. Although it is difficult to assess the number of married *career* women in the work force, it seems reasonable to assume that the percentage for this group is positively related to the general increase in labor force participation rates of women (Hopkins & White, 1978). As more and more women seek increased education and training. along with an increased demand for skilled labor and a greater awareness of sex-role equality, the dual-career lifestyle is likely to increase in prevalence and acceptability (Rapoport & Rapoport, 1976).

A significant feature of the dual-career lifestyle is that it produces considerable stress and strain. The often competing demands of the occupational structure and those of a rich family life present a number of challenges for dual-career family members. Much of the literature implies that the stress is inherent in a dual-career lifestyle. However, some of the constraints of the lifestyle might be explained by the fact that it is a relatively new and minority pattern. In coping with the pressures of this variant pattern, dual-career couples have been forced to come up with individual solutions as no institutionalized supports exist (Holmstrom, 1973).

The research on dual-career families has been primarily descriptive in nature and has focused on women. Rapoport and Rapoport, who coined the term "dual-career family" in 1969, were pioneers in the study of the impact of career and family on each other. Their research was followed shortly thereafter by other definitive studies on the dual-career lifestyle (Epstein, 1971; Holmstrom, 1973; Garland, 1972; Poloma, 1972). More recent dual-career research has focused heavily on the stresses of the lifestyle and on the management of the strains by the participants (Rapoport & Rapoport, 1978).

The purpose of this literature review is to delineate the sources of dual-career strain and summarize the coping patterns employed

*Denise A. Skinner is Assistant Professor, Department of Human Development, Family Relations, and Community Educational Services, University of Wisconsin-Stout, Menomonie, WI, and a doctoral candidate in the Department of Family Social Science, University of Minnesota, St. Paul, MN.

From Denise A. Skinner, "Dual-Career Family Stress and Coping: A Literature Review," *Family Relations*, 1980, 29, pp. 473-480. Reprinted by permission of the publisher and author.

by dual-career couples in managing stress. Hopefully, this summary will benefit family practitioners as they assist individuals in making adaptive lifestyle choices as well as aid dual-career participants in effective stress-reduction and in developing coping strategies.

The Etiology of Dual-Career Stress

Rapoport and Rapoport (1978) in reviewing the 1960's studies of dual-career families have noted that the stresses of this pattern have been differently conceptualized by various researchers. "The concepts include *dilemmas* (such as) overload, . . . network, identity; *conflicts* between earlier and later norms . . . , *barriers* of domestic isolation, sex-role prejudices . . . , and *problems* such as the wife finding an appropriate job . . . " (p. 5).

Although there is a considerable degree of variation in dual-career stress, there are also common patterns. In the review that follows, an adaptation of the Rapoports' (1971) delineation of strains confronting dual-career families will be used as an organizing framework in highlighting these common patterns reported in the literature. Although interactive and cyclical in nature, strains have been classified as primarily (a) internal: arising within the family; or (b) external: the result of conflict of the dual-career family and other societal structures (Bebbington, 1973).

Internal Strain

Overload issues. The problem of work and role overload is a common source of strain for dual-career families (Epstein, 1971; Garland, 1972, Heckman, Bryson, & Bryson, 1977; Holmstrom, 1973; Poloma, 1972; Rapoport & Rapoport, 1976; St. John-Parsons, 1978). When each individual is engaged in an active work role and active family roles, the total volume of activities is considerably increased over what a conventional family experiences (Portner, Note 1). In dual-career families this can result in overload, with household tasks generally handled as overtime.

The feelings of overload and the degree of strain experienced varied for couples in the Rapoports' study (1976). The Rapoports suggested that overload was affected by four conditions, which were, in part, self-imposed:

(a) the degree to which having children and a family life (as distinct from simply being married) was salient; (b) the degree to which the couple aspired to a high standard of domestic living; (c) the degree to which there was satisfactory reapportionment of tasks; and (d) the degree to which the social-psychological overload compounded the physical overloads (pp. 302-305).

There was a positive relationship between the conditions in items (a), (b), and (d) above, and the degree of strain experienced. Satisfactory reapportionment of tasks was a coping strategy that helped alleviate strain.

Identity issues. The identity dilemma for dual-career participants is the result of discontinuity between early gender-role socialization and current wishes or practices (Rapoport & Rapoport, 1976). The essence of masculinity in our culture is still centered on successful experiences in the work role, and femininity is still centered on the domestic scene (Heckman, Bryson, & Bryson, 1977; Holmstrom, 1973). The internalized "shoulds" regarding these traditional male and female roles conflict with the more androgynous roles attempted by many dual-career couples, resulting in tension and strain.

Bernard, (1974) focusing on professional women, observed that intrapersonal integration of work and domestic roles and the personality characteristics associated with each, does *not* constitute the "psychological work" of the career mother. Rather, the major difficulty, according to Bernard, is that the woman *alone* is the one who must achieve this identity integration.

Role-cycling issues. The dilemma of role-cycling, identified by Rapoport and Rapoport (1976), refers to attempts by the dual-career couple to mesh their different individual career cycles with the cycle of their family. Bebbington (1973) noted that role cycling, unlike other sources of strain, has a developmental pattern. Both employment and family careers have transition points at which there is a restructuring of roles which become sources of "normative" stress.

Dual-career couples attempt to avoid additional strain by staggering the career and family cycles such that transition points are not occurring at the same time. Many couples establish themselves occupationally before having children for this reason (Bebbington, 1973; Holmstrom, 1973; Rapoport & Rapoport, 1976). Stress may also result when the developmental sequence of one spouse's career conflicts with that of the other (Bebbington, 1973). The structural and attitudinal barriers of the occupational world, yet to be discussed, further contribute to the difficulty in role-cycling for many dual-career couples.

Family characteristics. Holmstrom (1973) identified the isolation of the modern nuclear family as a barrier to having two careers in one family. The difficulty of childrearing apart from relatives or other such extended support systems is a source of strain.

The presence or absence of children as well as the stage of the family life cycle seems to affect the complexity of the dual career lifestyle (Holmstrom, 1973, Rapoport & Rapoport, 1976). Heckman, et al. (1977) found that it was the older professional couples and those who had not had children who saw the lifestyle as advantageous. The demands of childrearing, *particularly the problems asssociated with finding satisfactory childcare arrangements*, are a source of strain for younger dual-career couples, especially for the women (Bryson, Bryson, & Johnson, 1978; Gove & Geerken, 1977; Holmstrom, 1973; Orden & Bradburn, 1969; Rapoport & Rapoport, 1971; St. John-Parsons, 1978). In relation to this, a child-free lifestyle has been noted by Movius (1976) as a career-facilitating strategy for women.

External Strains

Normative issues. Despite changing social norms, the dual-career lifestyle still runs counter to traditional family norms of our culture. Rapoport and Rapoport (1976) have explained that although intellectually the dual-career pattern is approved, internalized values from early socialization are still strong and produce tension, anxiety, and guilt. Pivotal points such as career transitions or the birth of a child can activate these normative dilemmas.

One of the more frequently cited problems by dual-career professionals is the expectation on the part of others that the dual-career husband and wife behave in traditional male/female roles (Heckman, et al., 1977). This is consistent with the earlier findings of Epstein

(1971) who indicated that dual-career individuals experienced guilt because they were not conforming to the socially approved work-family structure. Furthermore, the women often had to deal with the implied or overt social controls placed on them by their children according to Epstein's study.

Occupational structure. Holmstrom (1973, p. 517) has commented on the inflexibility of professions noting that "pressures for geographic mobility, the status inconsistencies of professional women because the professions are dominated by men, and the pressure for fulltime and continuous careers" are a source of strain for dual-career couples.

The demand for geographical mobility and its effect on dual-career couples noted earlier by Holmstrom (1973) was also examined by Duncan and Perrucci (1976). They found that the egalitarian orientation toward decision-making promoted in dual-career living was not carried out in job moves with the wives experiencing more of the stress. However, Wallston, Foster, and Berger (1978) using simulated job-seeking situations, found many professional couples attempting egalitarian or nontraditional job-seeking patterns. These authors have suggested that institutional constraints are in part responsible for highly traditional actual job decisions.

Finally, the demands of particular professions for single-minded continuous commitment, for other family members' needs to be subordinated to the job, and for a "support person" (typically the wife) to be available for entertaining, etc., are a source of stress for dual-career couples. The "two-person career" (Papanek, 1973) which depends heavily on an auxiliary support partner is incompatible with the dual-career orientation, according to Hunt and Hunt (1977). Handy (1978) in a study of executive men found that the dual-career relationship was infrequent and difficult when the husband was in such a "greedy occupation."

Social network dilemmas. Maintaining relationships outside the immediate family is a problem for dual-career members for a variety of reasons. The general dilemma exists because of the overload strain discussed earlier, which creates limitations on the availability of time to interact with friends and relatives (Portner, Note 1).

Rapoport and Rapoport (1976) found that the dual-career couples whom they studied reported problems in sustaining the kinds of interaction that their more conventional relatives and friends wanted. Not only was there less time for socializing, but, also, kin were at times asked by the dual-career couples to help out which sometimes produced tension. St. John-Parsons (1978) reported that kin relationships deteriorated when dual-career couples could not meet some of the expected social obligations. The husbands in his study experienced the greater loss as ties to their families of orientation lessened.

The study by St. John-Parsons (1978) revealed that none of the dual-career families maintained extensive social relationships. According to the author, "a salient reason for their social dilemma was their sense of responsibility for and devotion to their children" (p. 40).

Impact of strain

The sources of strain delineated above suggest that dual-career families are vulnerable to a high degree of stress. However, family stress literature has indicated that the family's definition of the situation is an important component influencing the impact of various strains on the family (Burr, 1973). Bebbington (1973) has differentiated between the following two kinds of stress which can co-exist or operate separately in a given lifestyle: "(a) that deriving from an unsatisfactory resolution of conflict as between ideals and behavior; and (b) that deriving from intrinsic properties of the lifestyle, though ideals and behaviors may be consistent" (p. 535). Bebbington has suggested that dual-career participants do not seem to find the principle of "stress minimization" operative with regard to the second type of stress, but rather, accept an orientation of "stress-optimization" in interpreting inherent lifestyle stresses. Dual-career couples have accepted a high degree of the second type of stress as their solution to the dilemma of avoiding the discontinuity stress of the first type, according to Bebbington. They come to view their problems as having both positive as well as negative components and of a more routine than unusual nature.

The cumulative effect of various strains arising from occupational and familial role transitions can be estimated as "transitional density" (Bain, 1978). Bain has hypothesized that the stress experienced and the coping ability of a family in a particular transition is proportional to the stress generated by the transitional density. Applied to dual-career families this idea is specifically related to the particular family characteristics and the multiple role cycling strains previously discussed. The degree of stress experienced from other sources of strain (e.g., overload) may be compounded for a given family by the strain of their family life cycle stage or the newness of the dual-career pattern for them.

Marital Relationship

A considerable portion of the dual career literature focuses on the marital adjustment, happiness, or satisfaction of dual-career couples implying that the stress inherent in the lifestyle has an impact on the marital relationship. In Orden and Bradburn's (1969) study of working wives and marital happiness, they found that a woman's choice of employment (vs. full-time homemaking) strained the marriage-only when there were preschool children in the family. They concluded that the woman's decision to work is associated with a high balance between satisfactions and strains for both partners.

Bailyn (1970) found that an all-consuming attitude toward career was associated with lowered marital satisfaction. Overinvolvement in one's career can result in strain on the marriage, according to Ridley (1973) who found marital adjustment highest when the husband was "medium" and the wife was "low" on job involvement. He concluded that tension in the marital relationship may occur when either partner becomes so highly involved in a job that family obligations are excluded. Occupational practices such as discriminatory sex-role attitudes can also heighten the stress in the dual-career marital relationship (Holmstrom, 1973; Rosen, Jerdee, & Prestwich, 1975). Finally, Richardson (1979) examined the hypothesis that marital stress would be attendant if working wives had higher occupational prestige than their husbands. He found no support for this hypothesis and suggested that its "mythic content" may be sustained, in part, because it is congruent with conventional sex-role orientations.

Rice (1979), focusing on personality patterns, noted the following psychological characteristics as typical of dual-career individuals:

A strong need for achievement, reliance on an extrinsic reward system (promotion, spouse recognition of efforts), hesitancy in making sustained interpersonal commitments, and vulnerability to self-esteem injury through dependency frustrations and fear of failure (p. 47).

The adaptive aspects of, for instance, high achievement may facilitate career advancement for both partners and contribute positively to marital adjustment, or high achievement needs may contribute to competitiveness in the pair.

Sex Differences

An overwhelming proportion of the literature reports that the impact of dual-career stress is felt most by women. Bernard (1974) has noted that a man can combine a professional career and parenting more easily than a woman can because less is expected of the man with regard to familial responsibilities.

Overload strain is a significant issue for dual-career women. Heckman et al. (1977), in assessing problem areas for dual-career couples, found that the women reported more problems in more areas than did men, and that many of the comments about problem areas by husbands were issues that had indirectly affected them because the issue had directly affected their wives. These researchers reported that several women in their study made significant concessions with regard to their careers because of family demands. They concluded that the continued existence of role conflict and overload strain are often at the expense of the woman's personal identity and career aspirations.

Occupationally, it has been the woman more often who takes the risks, sacrifices more, and compromises career ambitions in attempting to make the dual-career pattern operative (Epstein, 1971; Holmstrom, 1973; Poloma, 1972). Interestingly, however, some studies have reported that dual-career wives

are more productive than other females in their respective professions (Bryson, Bryson, Licht, & Licht, 1976; Martin, Berry, & Jacobsen, 1975). One might conclude, as the Rapoports (1978) have done, that the wives were simultaneously exploited and facilitated.

Life for the dual-career male is not without its periods of stress, although the impact of various strains does not appear to be as significant as that reported for women. Garland (1972) reported that dual-career males felt strain in attempting to find free time, but overall, noted the advantages of the lifestyle. The findings of Burke and Weir (1976) do not provide as positive a report for dual-career men, however. While working wives were found to be more satisfied with life, marriage, and job than nonworking wives, husbands of working wives were less satisfied and performed less effectively than husbands of nonworking wives. Burke and Weir indicated that the greater stress experienced by the dual-career husband may be due, in part, to him losing part of his "active support system" when the wife commits herself to a career outside the home, and also to his assuming roles (e.g. housekeeping) which have not been valued as highly in our culture.

Using more sophisticated methodology, Booth (1977) replicated the Burke and Weir study and reported different conclusions. He found very little difference between working and nonworking wives, and reported that the wife's employment had little effect on the stress experienced by the husband. Furthermore, Booth concluded that the dual-career husband may be experiencing less stress than his conventional counterpart as the added income and personal fulfillment of the wife outweigh temporary problems in adjusting to the lifestyle.

Children

Dual-career couples may increase the degree of strain they themselves experience in an attempt to prevent the lifestyle from creating strain for their children. As was noted earlier in the study by St. John-Parsons (1978), some of the social strains the couples experienced was due to their sense of responsibility to their children. There is no evidence to suggest that the dual-career lifestyle, in and of itself, is stressful for children. What may be more significant for the children is the degree of stress experienced by the parents which may indirectly affect the children. In her study of maternal employment Hoffman (1974) concluded that,

. . . the working mother who obtains satisfaction from her work, who has adequate arrangements so that her dual role does not involve undue strain, and who does not feel so guilty that she overcompensates is likely to do quite well and, under certain conditions, better than the nonworking mother (p. 142).

Coping Strategies

Just as the type and degree of strain experienced varies for dual-career families, so do the strategies employed for managing the stress. As was mentioned earlier in this paper, Bebbington (1973) suggested that "stress optimization," the acknowledging of dual-career stress as inevitable and preferable to the stress of alternative lifestyles available, is an orientation of many dual-career couples. Defining their situation as such may serve as a resource in successful adaptation to the stress. Dual-career couples also employ stress-mitigating strategies. These coping behaviors are aimed at maintaining or strengthening the family system and at securing support from sources external to the family.

Coping Behavior Within the Family System

Poloma (1972) outlined four tension-management techniques used by the dual-career women in her study. They reduced dissonance by defining their dual-career patterns as favorable or advantageous to them and their families when compared to other alternatives available. For instance, the career mother noted that she was a happier mother and wife because she worked outside the home than she would be if she were a fulltime homemaker. Secondly, they established priorities among and within their roles. The salient roles are familial ones and if a conflict situation occurs between family and career demands, the family needs come first. A third strategy employed was that of compartmentalizing work and family roles as much as pos-

sible. Leaving actual work and work-related problems at the office would be one way to segregate one's work and family roles. Finally, the women in Poloma's study managed strain by compromising career aspirations to meet other role demands.

Compromise is a common coping strategy noted in much of the dual-career literature as a way of reducing stress and making the lifestyle manageable. Women, in particular, compromise career goals if there are competing role demands (Bernard, 1974; Epstein, 1971; Heckman et al., 1977; Holmstrom, 1973). However, men in dual-careers make career sacrifices also, e.g., compromising advancement opportunities in an attempt to reduce role-conflict.

Prioritizing and compromising are coping strategies employed not only to deal with conflicts between roles but also in resolving competing demands within roles. Domestic overload, for instance, may be managed by deliberately lowering standards. One compromises ideal household standards because of constraints on time and energy in achieving them. Structurally, the domestic overload dilemma can also be managed within the family system by reorganizing who does what, with the husband and children taking on more of what traditionally has been the woman's responsibility. In these instances dual-career families are actively employing coping behaviors within the family aimed at strengthening its functioning and, thus, reducing the family's vulnerability to stress (McCubbin, 1979).

Some dual-career individuals take a more reactive orientation toward stress, and cope by attempting to manage and improve their behavior to better satisfy all of the lifestyle's demands. Holmstrom (1973) reported that the couples in her study adhered to organized schedules and that the women, in particular, were very conscious of how they allocated their time and effort. Flexibility and control over one's schedule are highly valued by career persons in attempting to meet overload and time pressures.

Finally, the presence of what Burke and Weir (1976) have labelled a helping component in the marital relationship can serve a stress-mitigating function within the dual-career family. Qualities such as open communication, empathy, emotional reassurance, support and sensitivity to the other's feelings, characterize this therapeutic role; the presence of these qualities would serve to strengthen the relationship. Related to this, Rapoport and Rapoport (1978) reported that couples established "tension lines," "points beyond which individuals feel they cannot be pushed except at risk to themselves or the relationship" (p. 6). Couples organized their family lives with sensitivity to these tension lines.

Coping Behaviors Involving External Support Systems

Dual-career couples also employ coping strategies aimed at securing support outside the family to help reduce stress. Holmstrom (1973) reported that couples were quite willing to use money to help resolve overload strain. Hiring help, especially for childcare, is a common expense in this lifestyle. Couples also buy time in various other ways such as hiring outside help to do domestic work and purchasing labor- and time-saving devices.

Outside support in terms of friendships were also important to the couples in the Rapoports' study (1976). The dual-career couples formed friendships on a couple basis, associating with other career couples. "Friendships, while gratifying, are also demanding, and in many of the couples there was a relatively explicit emphasis on the mutual service aspects of the relationship as well as the recreational aspect" (Rapoport, p. 316). Thus, establishing friendships with couples like themselves helped to validate the lifestyle for these dual-career couples and provided a reciprocal support structure.

The literature suggests that dual-career couples are increasingly interested in negotiating work arrangements which will reduce or remove some of this lifestyle's stress. Flexible scheduling, job sharing, and split-location employment are used by some dual-career couples as coping mechanisms to reduce the family's vulnerability to overload stress.

Finally, most of the researchers noted that achieving a balance between the disadvantages and advantages of the lifestyle was the overriding concern of dual-career couples.

Although noting the numerous strains associated with the lifestyle, dual-career couples were equally aware of the gains—things like personal fulfillment, increased standard of living, pride in each other's accomplishments, etc. The goal for most dual-career couples, then, is to ". . . plan how to manage the meshing of their two lives so as to achieve an equitable balance of strains and gains" (Rapoport and Rapoport, 1976, p. 298).

Implications for Practitioners

Increasingly, people are choosing dual-career living, a trend that will, no doubt, continue in the future. This has several implications for family life practitioners, particularly given the stress associated with the lifestyle. Certain changes seem necessary in facilitating dual-career living but these changes must occur by concerted efforts at many levels (Rapoport & Rapoport, 1976).

Individuals opting for the dual-career lifestyle, or any other family form for that matter, would benefit from knowledge of the issues central to that lifestyle's functioning. As Rapoport and Rapoport (1976) suggested " . . . the dissemination of a detailed knowledge of a range of lifestyles like the dual-career families will increase the potential for satisfactory choice of options in future" (p. 21). Such an education would enlarge traditional conceptions about men's and women's occupational and familial roles recognizing that different individuals would then have greater opportunities for making adaptive lifestyle choices.

Practitioners in marriage and family therapy may increasingly work with dual-career couples as their numbers increase and as the strains of the lifestyle remain. Rice (1979) has reported that competition, issues of power, and difficulty with the support structure are three common problem areas in dual-career marriages. He has suggested that "the guiding principle in therapy with dual-career couples is to help the partners achieve or restore a sense of equity in the marital relationship" (p. 103). Group-support sessions are suggested by Hopkins and White (1978) as a helpful therapeutic strategy with dual-career couples. Common-problem groups and groups of couples at differing life-cycle stages can provide a supportive structure for mutual sharing of concerns and coping skills. The goal of both preventive and remedial approaches should be to help couples assess their needs, increase interpersonal competencies, and deal constructively with the stress they experience (Rapoport & Rapoport, 1976).

Each family life professional has the opportunity to serve as a spokesperson for societal and institutional changes which would positively affect the functioning of dual-career families. Societal changes which would increase the quantity and quality of all kinds of services (educational, domestic, child-care, etc.) would strengthen the dual career lifestyle. Institutional changes which would increase the flexibility of the occupational structure would also aid significantly in reducing or eliminating some of the stress associated with the lifestyle. Flexible scheduling, increased availability of part-time employment, on-site day care facilities and maternity and paternity leaves are some of the occupational changes advocated to enable individuals to combine work and family roles with less strain. Assuming an advocacy role on behalf of the dual-career lifestyle involves initiating and supporting social policies which promote equity and pluralism (Rapoport & Rapoport, 1976). A society where these values prevail would enhance not only the dual-career lifestyle, but would serve to strengthen family life in general.

REFERENCE NOTE

1. Portner, J. Impact of work on the family. Minneapolis: Minnesota Council on Family Relations, 1219 University Avenue SE, 55414, 1978, 13-15.

REFERENCES

Bailyn, L. Career and family orientations of husbands and wives in relation to marital happiness. Human Relations, 1970, 23(2), 97-113.

Bain, A. The capacity of families to cope with transitions: A theoretical essay. Human Relations, 1978, 31, 675-688.

Bebbington, A. C. The function of stress in the establishment of the dual-career family. Journal of Marriage and the Family, 1973, 35, 530-537.

Bernard, J. The future of motherhood. New York: Penguin, 1974.

Bird, C. The two-paycheck marriage. New York: Rawson, Wade, 1979.

Booth, A wife's employment and husband's stress: A replication and refutation. Journal of Marriage and the Family, 1977, 39, 645-50.

Bryson, R., Bryson, J., Licht, M., & Licht, B. The professional pair: Husband and wife psychologists. American Psychologist. 1976, 31(1), 10-16.

Bryson, R., Bryson, J. B., & Johnson, M. F. Family size, satisfaction, and productivity in dual-career couples. In J. B. Bryson, & R. Bryson (Eds.), Dual-career couples. New York: Human Sciences, 1978.

Burke, R. J., & Weir, T. Relationship of wives' employment status to husband, wife and pair satisfaction and performance. Journal of Marriage and the Family, 1976, 38, 279-287.

Burke, R. J., & Weir, T. Marital helping relationships: The moderators between stress and well-being. Journal of Psychology, 1977, 95, 121-130.

Burr, A. Theory construction and the sociology of the family. New York: Wiley, 1977.

Duncan, R. P., & Perrucci, C. Dual occupation families and migration. American Sociological Review, 1976, 41, 252-261.

Epstein, C. D., Law partners and marital partners: Strains and solutions in the dual-career family enterprise. Human Relations, 1971, 24, 549-563.

Fogarty, M. P., Rapoport, R., & Rapoport, R. N. Sex, career and family. Beverly Hills: Sage, 1971.

Garland, N. T. The better half? The male in the dual profession family. In C. Safilios-Rothschild (Ed.), Toward a sociology of women. Lexington, MA: Xerox, 1972.

Gove, W. R., & Geerken, M. R. The effect of children and employment on the mental health of married men and women. Social Forces, 1977, 56, 66-76.

Handy, C. Going against the grain: Working couples and greed occupations. In R. Rapoport & R. N. Rapoport (Eds.), Working couples. New York: Harper & Row, 1978.

Heckman, N. A., Bryson, R., & Bryson, J. Problems of professional couples: A content analysis. Journal of Marriage and the Family. 1977, 39, 323-330.

Hoffman, L. W. Effects on child. In L. W. Hoffman & F. I. Nye (Eds.), Working mothers. San Francisco: Jossey-Bass, 1974.

Holmstrom, L. L. The two-career family. Cambridge, MA: Schenkman, 1973.

Hopkins, J., & White, P. The dual-career couple: Constraints and supports. The Family Coordinator, 1978, 27, 253-259.

Hunt, J. G., & Hunt, L. L. Dilemmas and contradictions of status: The case of the dual-career family. Social Problems, 1977, 24, 407-416.

Martin, T. W., Berry, K. J., & Jacobsen, R. B. The impact of dual-career marriages on female professional careers: An empirical test of a Parsonian hypothesis. Journal of Marriage and the Family, 1975, 37, 734-742.

McCubbin, H. Integrating coping behavior in family stress theory. Journal of Marriage and the Family, 1979, 41, 237-244.

Movius, M. Voluntary childlessness—The ultimate liberation. The Family Coordinator, 1976, 25, 57-62.

Orden, S. R., & Bradburn, N. M. Working wives and marriage happiness. American Journal of Sociology, 1969, 74, 382-407.

Papanek, H. Men. women and work: Reflections of the two-person career. *American Journal of Sociology*, 1973, **78**, 852-872.

Poloma, M. M. Role conflict and the married professional woman. In C. Safilios-Rothschild (Ed.), *Toward a sociology of women*. Lexington, MA: Xerox, 1972.

Poloma, M. M. & Garland, T. The married professional woman: A study of the tolerance of domestication. *Journal of Marriage and the Family*, 1971, **33**, 531-540.

Rapoport, R.. & Rapoport, R. N. *Dual-career families*. Harmondsworth. England: Penguin, 1971.

Rapoport, R., & Rapoport, R. N. *Dual-career families re-examined*. New York: Harper & Row, 1976.

Rapoport, R.. & Rapoport, R. N. (Eds.), *Working couples*. New York: Harper & Row, 1978.

Rapoport, R. N., & Rapoport, R. Dual-career families: Progress and prospects. *Marriage and Family Review*, 1978, **1**(5), 1-12.

Rice, D. *Dual-career marriage: Conflict and treatment*. New York: Free Press, 1979.

Richardson, J. G. Wife occupational superiority and marital troubles: An examination of the hypothesis. *Journal of Marriage and the Family*, 1979, **41**, 63-72.

Ridley, C. A. Exploring the impact of work satisfaction and involvement on marital interaction when both partners are employed. *Journal of Marriage and the Family*, 1973, **35**, 229-237.

Roland, A.. & Harris, B. *Career and motherhood: Struggles for a new identity*. New York: Human Sciences, 1979.

St. John-Parsons, D. Continuous dual-career families: A case study. In J. B. Bryson & R. Bryson (Eds.), *Dual-career couples*. New York: Human Sciences, 1978.

Wallston, B. S., Foster, M. A., & Berger, M. I will follow him: Myth. reality, or forced choice—Job seeking experiences of dual-career couples. In J. B. Bryson & R. Bryson (Eds.). *Dual-career couples*. New York: Human Sciences. 1978.

This paper discusses the impact of several work role stressors on corporate families: employment insecurity and career mobility, job content and satisfaction, amount and scheduling of work time, geographic mobility, and the corporate wife role. Coping strategies and supports used by corporate families are analyzed briefly.

9

WORK ROLES AS STRESSORS
IN CORPORATE FAMILIES*

Patricia Voydanoff**

There is a growing interest in examining the impacts of executive work roles on corporate families in spite of a general tendency on the part of corporations and executives to ignore or deny the relatedness of work and family roles. This position, referred to by Kanter (1977b) as the denial of connections, has been supported by a strong allegiance to the protestant ethic among corporate executives which includes high priority on work roles, strong dedication to achievement and advancement, and loyalty to the corporation. Executives have been expected to be "good family men" without having family obligations infringe upon work role responsibilities.[1]

Recent work indicates that there are several characteristics of executive employment that serve as family stressors which are related to low levels of marital satisfaction and family

cohesion and to difficulties in performing family roles. Stressors are defined as problems requiring solutions or situations to which the family must adapt in order to maintain the functioning of the family system. Stressors can be of two types: (a) life events or acute changes affecting the family, and (b) relatively enduring situations requiring problem solving behavior or coping strategies (Moen, Note 1; Pearlin, Note 2). Several aspects of executive work roles function as chronic stressors in relation to the family, e.g., routine husband-father absence resulting from long hours and frequent travel, work-related stress associated with time pressure and mobility aspirations, and the tendency for a divergence of interests to develop between husband and wife. In addition to these relatively enduring stressors, more acute life-event stressors occur including geographic mobility and job transfers, nonroutine husband-father absence resulting from long-term travel assignments, and acute stress associated with status changes such as promotions.

Socioeconomic Status and Occupational Success

The literature on the relation between socioeconomic status and family life is extensive and the findings are quite consistent. Socioeconomic status is related to patterns of family behavior including division of labor,

---

*Paper presented at the Annual Meeting of the North Central Sociological Association, May, 1980. Preparation of this manuscript was supported by a grant from the American Council of Life Insurance.

**Patricia Voydanoff is Chairperson, Department of Family and Community Studies, Merrill-Palmer Institute, 71 East Ferry, Detroit, MI 48202.

[1] In this paper analysis is limited to male executives and their families. More research is needed to determine the extent to which the findings and conclusions apply to female executives and their families.

From Patricia Voydanoff, "Work Roles as Stressors in Corporate Families," *Family Relations*, 1980, 29, pp. 489-494. Reprinted by permission of the publisher and author.

marital power and decision-making, and socialization practices and values. In addition, positive relations between socioeconomic status and marital happiness, cohesion and stability are reported from most research. Scanzoni (1970) has developed a model of family cohesion which places major explanatory power on the husband's success in the occupational sphere as measured by socioeconomic status. However, it has been reported recently that the relation between occupational success and marital happiness and cohesion is curvilinear with less satisfactory marital relationships being more prevalent among those who are most and least successful in the occupational world (Aldous, Osmond, & Hicks, 1979). This contrasts with Scanzoni's hypothesis of a direct relation between occupational success and marital happiness and cohesion. Aldous et al. (1979) supported their hypothesis by specifying some of the correlations reported by Scanzoni (1970) and Blood and Wolfe (1960) that indicated a leveling off or decrease in happiness and cohesion among those in higher occupational and income categories. They also cited Dizard (1968) who reported that, in his study of middle-class couples, those who were most successful in their occupations were most likely to have marital relationships deteriorate over time. He explained this finding by suggesting that a gulf develops between the husband and wife because of different life situation requirements.

It has been reported in other literature that a minimum level of income and employment stability are necessary for family stability and cohesion (Furstenberg, 1974). Beyond this minimum the family's subjective perception of adequacy becomes relatively more important in relation to happiness and cohesion (Oppenheimer, 1979; Scanzoni, 1970). Men with middle-level incomes and occupational status may be best able to combine work and family roles whereas those at the lower end have too few economic resources and those at the upper end have difficulty performing family roles (Aldous, 1969; Aldous et al., 1979; Kanter, 1977b). The evidence for this hypothesis is not conclusive; the hypothesis is quite provocative when viewed in the context of the analysis of executive work role stressors.

Executive Work Role Stressors

Job Security and Career Mobility

It has been noted in the recent business literature that executive employment is becoming increasingly insecure due to top-heavy managements, depressed industries, automation and computers, and managerial upheavals. It involves a greater likelihood of unemployment among all levels of management as well as decreasing opportunities for promotion into higher levels of management. Reactions to unemployment among the middle-class are relatively severe in terms of status loss and self-esteem; impacts on the family have not been studied (Braginsky & Braginsky. 1975; Briar, 1978; Elder, 1974; Goodchilds & Smith, 1963; Powell & Driscoll, 1973). Fineman (1979) reported that stress accompanies unemployment among managers in situations where managers are highly involved in their work, where unemployment coincides with family problems, and where repeated job-seeking attempts fail. Stress is lower among managers where job satisfaction and job involvement have been low, where managers interpret job loss as a challenge to meet or a problem to solve, and where they feel confident about their abilities to meet the challenge.

The highest rates of unemployment and economic uncertainty are still found within the lower and working classes. However, strong economic striving and desire for mobility among the middle class may have effects on the family comparable in some ways to the effects of job insecurity and fear of unemployment. In addition, those executives not meeting their achievement aspirations must adjust to the discrepancy between aspirations and accomplishments. Mizruchi (1964) saw the strain associated with this disparity as a major source of anomia in the middle class. Following Durkheim, he referred to this type of anomia as boundlessness. Part of the midlife crisis among executives centers on the need for middle-aged executives to come to terms with the discrepancy between current achievements and aspirations set earlier in their careers. Problems associated with mobility striving and gaps between achievement and aspirations have not been studied in relation to the family except perhaps for Blood and Wolfe (1960) who found that the wives of occupational strivers are less satisfied with their marriages than other wives with husbands in high status occupations.

Job Content and Satisfaction

It has been suggested that the content or requirements of the work roles of successful executives lead to or are accompanied by the development of personality traits or attributes that are inconsistent with successful family life. This incongruence is found on two levels. First, the personal traits needed for a happy family life are not necessarily compatible with those needed to become a successful executive (Bartolomé, 1972; Maccoby, 1976; Zaleznik, Note 3). Managerial careers stress the development of the "head" at the expense of the "heart" (Maccoby, 1976). Second, the husband and wife may grow apart psychologically and develop different interests as the husband grows in his career (Dizard, 1968; Foote, 1963; Levinson, 1964; Seidenberg, 1973). This is especially true if the wife is not employed outside the home.

Research on job satisfaction and the family complements the analysis of occupational success discussed above because job satisfaction may be positively related to family role participation and marital happiness except for those with the highest levels of job satisfaction, i.e., a curvilinear relation may exist (Aldous et al., 1979). Bailyn (1970) found a positive relation between job satisfaction and marital happiness for couples in which the husband was family oriented. However, she found a negative relation between husband's job satisfaction and couple happiness for those couples in which the husband was career oriented and the wife family oriented. Thus, the Aldous et al. (1979) hypothesis that high levels of job satisfaction can hinder marital satisfaction is supported among the couples fitting the general orientation of many corporate families, i.e., a career-oriented husband and a family-oriented wife.

Amount and Scheduling of Time

Executives tend to work long hours and to take work home frequently. Findings on the impact of number of hours spent working on family roles are not conclusive. Time spent working is related to family strain (Mortimer, Note 4); however, the number of hours worked does not significantly influence the performance of family roles except for recreation (Clark, Nye, & Gecas, 1978). Pleck (1977) has suggested that attitudes toward family role performance are more important than work time, i.e., executives can choose to spend their off-work time, limited though it may be, either in family activities or other leisure-oriented pursuits.

It may be that the timing of work role activities has a greater effect on the family than the number of hours worked. Those who travel extensively or work evenings and weekends may find it difficult to fulfill some aspects of family roles including companionship with spouse and children, attendance at family and school functions, and participation in household duties (Culbert & Renshaw, 1972; Kanter, 1977b; Renshaw, 1976; Young & Willmott, 1973).

Geographic Mobility

Frequent transfers have been considered an integral part of moving up the corporate ladder for executives. In recent years, however, some executives and some corporations have been reexamining the costs and benefits associated with corporate transfers. Increasing, though still small, numbers of executives are refusing transfers (Costello, 1976). Personal and family considerations top the reasons for refusal. Corporations are beginning to seek ways to ease the strain of transfers for their employees and their families.

A wide range of family responses to frequent moves has been reported in the literature. In some situations these moves have been found to be stressful for all family members (Tiger, 1974); in others, families have little difficulty adjusting (Jones, 1973; McAllister, Butler & Kaiser, 1973). It is necessary to consider the conditions under which moving is stressful. Factors making a difference in adjustment include the number and timing of moves, degree of family cohesion and integration, ages of children, and the extent to which the wife has difficulty making new friends and transferring her credentials and contacts (Margolis, 1979; Portner, 1978; Renshaw, 1976; Jones, Note 5). After many moves some corporate wives give up trying to become part of yet another community and become isolated and depressed (Seidenberg, 1973).

Role of the Corporate Wife

The executive role has been analyzed as one example of the two-person career, i.e., an occupation in which the wife has well defined duties that are an integral part of the husband's occupational role (Papanek, 1973). These include supporting the husband in his work, taking care of the home so that the husband can spend more time at work and be able to relax when at home, participating in volunteer work to develop business contacts, entertaining work associates, and attending work related social functions (Kanter, 1977a, 1977b). The role also is associated with several problematic characteristics—frequent moves, lack of personal identity development, difficulty in integrating the husband into family activities, lack of parallel growth between husband and wife, and myriad psychological disturbances such as depression and alcoholism (Kanter, 1977a, 1977b; Seidenberg, 1973; Vandervelde, 1979). Information on the prevalence of these problems is limited; most of the data come from corporate wives in clinical settings.

Corporate wives are less likely to be employed than other women partly because their husbands' work roles impose constraints on their employment (Mortimer, Hall, & Hill, 1978). In spite of these constraints, however, wife employment is increasing among women with high educational levels because of changes in sex role orientation and increased occupational opportunities. If the wife also has a career, she is likely to experience role overload because she may continue to fulfill traditional family responsibilities in addition to full-time employment (Holmstrom, 1972).

Coping Strategies and Supports

Within the limits of the current literature, several relations between executive work role stressors, family roles, and cohesion have been documented. Within the context of current employment practices it is important to examine coping strategies and supports used by corporate families to moderate the impact of work stressors.

Boss, McCubbin, and Lester (1979) have outlined three coping strategies used by corporate wives in dealing with husband-father absence: fitting into the corporate life style, developing self and inter-personal relationships, and establishing independence and self-sufficiency. A related study of the wives of Navy servicemen revealed five coping patterns—maintaining family integrity, developing interpersonal relationships and social support, managing psychological tension and strain, believing in the value of spouse's profession and maintaining an optimistic definition of the situation, and developing self reliance and self-esteem (McCubbin, Boss, Wilson, & Lester, Note 6). Mortimer (Note 7) has shown the importance of the wife's support of the husband's work in mediating the relation between job-induced strain and marital satisfaction. Burke and Weir (1975, 1977) also reported that satisfaction with the husband-wife helping relationship effectively mediated between job and life stress and several measures of well-being including job, marital, and life satisfaction and mental and physical well-being. This work suggests the importance of coping strategies and supports within the family itself for limiting the impacts of work role stressors.

Several organizations are attempting to deal with stress in corporate families by holding "executive seminars." In these seminars, the strains and pressure of corporate life are discussed. Executives and their wives are helped to develop personal and family resources to handle their problems. The Harvard Business School offers a course for married students and their spouses on how executives can meet the demands of both work and family responsibilities (Greiff, 1976). The Menninger Clinic seminars on midlife transitions among executives deal with psychological resource development and the integration of work and family roles (Rice, 1979). Others bring together husbands and wives to discuss issues relating to corporate life and marriage (Becerra, 1975). Seminars also have been held to deal with the stresses associated with business travel (Culbert & Renshaw, 1972).

The reduction of work and family stress is also dealt with in the literature for corporate executives and their wives. The American

Management Association recently published
a "how to" book for executives who want to
achieve success in both marriage and corporate careers (Ogden, 1979). Hall and Hall
(1979) have developed many practical suggestions for dealing with stress and role overload
among two-career couples. The literature
written for corporate wives is also changing.
Earlier writings stressed the importance of
the corporate wife in smoothly handling
family life so that her husband could devote
himself to his work. A recent book tells corporate wives how they may become more independent without hurting their husbands'
careers (Vandervelde, 1979).

Much more needs to be done to develop
coping strategies and supports for corporate
families. This work should progress on
several levels—encouraging the development
of internal coping strategies for family units
and individual family members; providing
group supports for families and individual
members, e.g., seminars of various types;
and developing community supports for corporate families, e.g., child care for two-career
families. Based on McCubbin (1979) these
strategies and supports need to be oriented
toward both chronic and acute stressors.

REFERENCE NOTES

1. Moen, P. *Patterns of family stress across the life cycle.*
   Paper presented at the Annual Meeting of the National
   Council on Family Relations, Boston, 1979.
2. Pearlin, L. I. *The life cycle and life strain.* Paper presented at the Annual Meeting of the American Sociological Association, Boston, 1979.
3. Zaleznik. A. D.C.S. *Isolation and control in the family
   and work.* Paper presented at the Symposium on The
   Family: Setting Priorities, Washington, DC, 1978.
4. Jones, S. *Corporate policy on the transferring of employees: Sociological considerations.* Paper presented
   at the Annual Meeting of the North Central Sociological
   Association. Louisville, 1976.
5. McCubbin. H. I., Boss, P. G., Wilson, L. F., & Lester,
   G. R. *Developing family invulnerability to stress: Coping patterns and strategies wives employ in managing
   family separations.* Paper presented at the 9th World
   Congress of the International Sociological Association,
   Uppsala, Sweden, 1978.
6. Mortimer. J. T. *Work-family linkages as perceived by
   men in the early stages of professional and managerial
   careers.* Paper presented at the Annual Meeting of the
   Society for the Study of Social Problems, Boston, 1979.

REFERENCES

Aldous, J. Occupational characteristics and males' role
    performance in the family. *Journal of Marriage and the
    Family*, 1969, **31**, 707-712.
Aldous, J., Osmond, M., & Hicks, M. Men's work and
    men's families. In W. Burr, R. Hill, I. Reiss, & F. I. Nye
    (Eds.), *Contemporary theories about the family.* New
    York: Free Press, 1979.
Bailyn, L. Career and family orientations of husbands and
    wives in relation to marital happiness. *Human Relations*,
    1970, **23**, 97-113.
Bartolomé, F. Executives as human beings. *Harvard Busi-
    ness Review*, 1972, **50**, 62-69.
Becerra, M. Marriage and the corporation. *Nation's
    Business*, 1975, **63**, March, 82-84.
Blood, R. O., & Wolfe, D. M. *Husbands and wives.* New York:
    Free Press, 1960.
Boss, P. G., McCubbin, H. I., & Lester, G. The corporate
    executive wife's coping patterns in response to routine
    husband-father absence. *Family Process*, 1979, **18**, 79-
    86.
Braginsky, D. D., & Braginsky, B. M. Surplus people. *Psy-
    chology Today*, 1975, **9**, 68-72.
Briar, K. H. *The effect of long-term unemployment on
    workers and their families.* Palo Alto: R & E Research
    Associates, 1978.
Burke, R. J., & Weir, T. The husband-wife relationship. *The
    Business Quarterly*, 1975, **40**, 62-67.
Burke, R. J., & Weir, T. Marital helping relationships. *The
    Journal of Psychology*, 1977, **95**, 121-130.
Clark, R. A., Nye, F. I., & Gecas, V. Husbands' work in-
    volvement and marital role performance. *Journal of Mar-
    riage and the Family*, 1978, **40**, 9-21.
Costello, J. Why more managers are refusing transfers.
    Nation's Business, 1976, **64**, October, 4-5.
Culbert, S. A., & Renshaw, J. R. Coping with the stresses
    of travel as an opportunity for improving the quality of
    work and family life. *Family Process*, 1972, 11, 321-337.
Dizard, J. *Social change in the family.* Chicago: University
    of Chicago Press, 1968.
Elder, G. h. *Children of the great depression.* Chicago:
    University of Chicago Press, 1974.
Fineman, S. A psychosocial model of stress and its appli-
    cation to managerial unemployment. *Human Relations*,
    1979, **32**, 323-345.
Foote. N. N. Matching of husband and wife in phases of
    development. In M. B. Sussman (Ed.), *Sourcebook in
    marriage and the family.* Boston: Houghton Mifflin, 1963.
Furstenberg, F. Work experience and family life. In J.
    O'Toole (Ed.), *Work and the quality of life.* Cambridge:
    MIT Press, 1974.
Goodchilds, J. D., & Smith, E. E. The effects of unemploy-
    ment as mediated by social status. *Sociometry*, 1963,
    26, 287-293.
Greiff, B. S. The executive family seminar: A course for
    graduate married business students. *American College
    Health Association*, 1976, **24**, 227-231.
Hall, F. S., & Hall, D. T. *The two-career couple.* Reading,
    MA: Addison-Wesley, 1979.
Holmstrom, L. *The two-career family.* Cambridge: Schenk-
    man, 1972.

Jones, S. B. Geographic mobility as seen by the wife and mother. *Journal of Marriage and the Family,* 1973, **35,** 210-218.

Kanter, R. M. *Men and women of the corporation.* New York: Basic, 1977. (a)

Kanter, R. M. *Work and family in the United States: A critical review and agenda for research and policy.* New York: Sage, 1977. (b)

Levinson, H. *Emotional problems in the world of work.* New York: Harper, 1964.

Maccoby, M. The corporate climber has to find his heart. *Fortune,* December, 1976, pp. 98-108.

Margolis, D. *The managers.* New York: Morrow, 1979.

McAllister, R., Butler, E., & Kaiser, E. The adjustment of women to residential mobility. *Journal of Marriage and the Family,* 1973, **35,** 197-204.

McCubbin, H. I. Integrating coping behavior in family stress theory. *Journal of Marriage and the Family,* 1979, **41,** 237-244.

Mizruchi, E. *Success and opportunity.* New York: Free Press, 1964.

Mortimer, J., Hall, R., & Hill, R. Husbands' occupational attributes as constraints on wives' employment. *Sociology of Work and Occupations,* 1978, **5,** 285-313.

Ogden, R. W. *How to succeed in business and marriage.* New York: AMACOM, 1978.

Oppenheimer, V. K. Structural sources of economic pressure for wives to work: An analytical framework. *Journal of Family History,* 1979, **4,** 177-197.

Papanek, H. Men, women, and work: Reflections on the two-person career. *The American Journal of Sociology,* 1973, **78,** 852-872.

Pleck, J. H. The work-family role system. *Social Problems,* 1977, **24,** 417-428.

Portner, J. *Impacts of work on the family.* Minneapolis: Minnesota Council on Family Relations, 1978.

Powell, D. H., & Driscoll, P. F. Middle-class professionals face unemployment. *Society,* 1973, **10,** 18-26.

Renshaw, J. R. An exploration of the dynamics of the overlapping worlds of work and family. *Family Process,* 1976, **15,** 143-165.

Rice, B. Midlife encounters: The Menninger seminars for businessmen. *Psychology Today,* 1979, **12,** 66-74, 95-99.

Scanzoni, J. H. *Opportunity and the family.* New York: Free Press, 1970.

Seidenberg, R. *Corporate wives-corporate casualties?* New York: AMACOM, 1973.

Tiger, L. Is this trip necessary? The heavy human costs of moving executives around. *Fortune,* September 1974, pp. 139-141.

Vandervelde, M. *The changing life of the corporate wife.* New York: Jecox, 1979.

Young, M., & Willmott, P. *The symmetrical family.* New York: Penguin, 1973.

A majority view in the literature on families of mentally retarded children is that the diagnosis provokes a period of disequilibrium followed eventually by an adjustment to life without undue stress. This conceptual paper contests that position, and argues that there are various stresses which emerge and re-emerge over time. The author suggests that discrepancies between expectations and the performance of the developmentally disabled child continue periodically to bring on a need for information and feelings of grief. Clinicians who understand this can better serve these families and can anticipate periods of difficulty, thus possibly ameliorating some of those stresses.

10

CHRONIC STRESSES OF FAMILIES OF MENTALLY RETARDED CHILDREN

Lynn Wikler*

Families with a child who is mentally retarded are more likely to experience stress, all things being equal, than families who have normal children. This stress may lead to family dysfunction requiring societal intervention. Research on families of mentally retarded children has repeatedly indicated three stressful effects of the mental retardation: (a) social isolation (Cook, 1963; Cummings, Bailey, & Rie, 1966; Davis & MacKay, 1973; Erickson, 1968; Farber, 1968; Holt, 1958; McAllister, Butler, & Lei, 1973); (b) increased indicators of stress in the parents (Barsch, 1968; Cummings, Bailey, & Rie, 1966; Cook, 1963; Erickson, 1968; Levinson, 1975); and (c) a greater incidence of problems at school and mental health clinic visits for normal adolescent sibling(s) (Farber & Jenne, 1963; Fowle, 1968; Gath, 1974). When divorce does occur, the burdens of the single mother of the re-tarded child outweigh those of the single mother of the normal child (Wikler, Note 1). If these problems continue unresolved, the family frequently turns to institutionalization as a way of coping with the stress (Farber, Jenne, & Toigo, 1960; Graliker, Koch, & Henderson, 1965; Saenger (Note 2); Stone, 1965).

Historically, clincial interventions have been *reactive* to these problem situations. However, the delineation of types of stresses and pinpointing of high risk periods for families over the life span of the retarded child could provide information which would enable clinical programs to function from a *proactive* stance. By alerting the clinician to those times when families may need additional attention and support, possibilities for *preventing* problems increase.

This paper contains an overview of stresses in families of mentally retarded children, including the manifestation, etiology and temporal pattern of stress. First, stresses which are chronic for families of mentally retarded children are discussed. Second, the series of potential crises which periodically seem to affect these families is sketched. Finally, a brief account of the implications of this theory of chronic stress is presented. Working hypotheses are presented for further research.

---
*Lynn Wikler is Assistant Professor, School of Social Work and Waisman Center on Mental Retardation and Human Development, University of Wisconsin-Madison, Madison, Wisconsin 53705.

From Lynn Wikler, "Chronic Stresses of Families of Mentally Retarded Children," *Family Relations*, 1981, 30, pp. 281-288. Reprinted by permission of the publisher and author.

Types of Chronic Stresses Unique to Families of Mentally Retarded Children

Parents face stresses that continue over the lifetime of their mentally retarded child. Some are related to the characteristic hardships of mental retardation (stigmatized social interactions and prolonged burden of care) and others are typical parental responses to retardation (realistic parental confusion concerning child care, and periodic parental grieving). All of these are reality stresses resulting from situational demands of raising or caring for a retarded person (Menolascino, 1977).

Stigmatized Social Interactions

Although most mentally retarded people are mildly retarded and eventually function in society with minimal supports, the public (and prior to diagnosis, the parents) stereotype all mentally retarded people as completely lacking in basic competence (Edgerton, 1967). People generally feel uncomfortable with the mentally retarded and strive to avoid interacting with them. Parents must change their own attitudes in order to become advocates for their child. In addition, they must develop competence in managing uncomfortable social transactions (Birenbaum, 1970). They face hostile stares, judgmental comments, murmurs of pity, and intrusive requests for personal information whenever they accompany their child to the grocery store, on the bus, or to the park. Although parents report that they do learn to manage the stigmatized interactions successfully (Voysey, 1972), the growing discrepancy between the child's size and mental functioning tends to increase the number of stressful encounters.

Prolonged Burden of Care

Chronic problems such as managing hyperactivity in a nonverbal child, or lifting a spastic teenager out of a wheelchair are often physically exhausting to the caretakers. As the child grows larger, he becomes more burdensome (Berger & Foster, 1976; Holt, 1958). Even when there are no secondary problems associated with the mental retardation, developmentally delayed children by definition have more prolonged dependency

needs than do normal children. Mothers of older retarded children cannot look forward to engaging in activities comparable to those of parents of normal children now adult age (Birenbaum, 1971; Farber, Note 3). In addition, the prolonged burden of care is continuous. There is no respite from the burden since local babysitters are much less available to families who have mentally retarded children (Moore & Seachore, Note 4).

Recent studies of the effects of respite care on family stress have shown that it leads to a decrease in negative maternal attitudes towards the mentally retarded child (Wikler & Hanusa, Note 5) and increased positive family interaction (Cohen, Note 6).

Lack of Information

In response to offers of therapy, parents of mentally retarded children say that they would *rather* have facts about mental retardation and information about what to do to handle specific child management problems (Matheny & Vernick, 1969; Price-Bonham & Addison, 1978; Puescel & Murphy, 1976; Wolfensberger, 1967). Although parents of normal children can rely on their childhood experiences of being parented, and on advice from friends, relatives, and neighbors, these resources are generally inadequate for parents of children with special needs. Even when these parents go to specialists for advice and information they may find that the general principles presented are inadequate for handling the daily practical tasks of child rearing (Waskowitz, 1959). Moreover, professional texts and behavior management programs tend to focus primarily on the early years of development rather than on management issues that arise *over time* (Berger & Foster, 1976).

The potentially richest source of information is another parent of a mentally retarded child, but here too the parent in need of help may be disappointed because retarded children vary so greatly. The parent of a moderately retarded 12-year-old Down's Syndrome boy would have very different accumulated wisdom from that of the parent of an 8-year-old severely retarded child with uncontrollable seizures or that of a 15-year-old mildly retarded girl with poor social skills. Even when parents are fortunate enough to get the data they need to continue with some confidence, those data do not necessarily generalize to the next complicated situation they confront. The critical, on-going need for information which parents encounter as they pursue long-term care of the mentally retarded person at home, cannot be underestimated as a source of stress (Berger & Foster, 1976).

Grieving

Grieving is extensively described in the clinical literature in relation to the parents' emotional responses to the diagnosis of retardation in their child. The primary cause for the grief at that time is considered to be the loss of the fantasized normal child (Emde & Brown, 1978; Mandelbaum, 1967; Parks, 1977; Solnit & Stark, 1961; Wolfensberger, 1967). Although the parents will regain their sense of equilibrium, the initial apparent adjustment to that disappointment may be temporary. At various points in time, their loss of the fantasized normal child will be restimulated. Depending on the personal fantasies of the individual parent, these moments may occur during holidays, family reunions, birthdays, the wedding of their normal child, watching normal children play, or hearing mothers of normal children chat about their child's successes or failures.

Most important, there are predictable periods when grieving will be reactivated, periods of developmental and transitional crises (described later) in which culturally assumed enactment of parental roles are not fulfilled. When major discrepancies from these expectations occur, most parents will again experience the grieving that they felt at the time of the diagnosis.

Fathers vs. Mothers Stresses

Fathers and mothers perceive and cope with mental retardation in different ways and they may do so at a different pace (Price-Bonham & Addison, 1978). This could be problematic for the marriage. If one parent is grieving and the other is concerned about the burden of care, they are less likely to be responsive to one another. This could also reduce the potential effectiveness of one mate

in ameliorating the impact of the stress for the other. Mother's reports of marital satisfaction are highly correlated with her coping behavior (Friedrich, 1979). On the other hand, many families claim that the stress of the mental retardation has brought the family closer together (Grossman, 1972). Overall, the rate of divorce in families of the mentally retarded (when they have been matched for social class) does not differ significantly from families of normal children (Davis & MacKay, 1973; Schufeit & Wurster, 1976).

Mediating Factors

The extent to which families experience crises is seen as being mediated by (a) the familial interpretation of the stressor event, and (b) the familial resources available for managing that stressor event (Hill, 1958). Certain familial resources for managing the various stresses presented will decrease their impact on the family. For example, a family living in a community which is tolerant of a mentally retarded person—such as a rural community (Dunlop & Hollingsworth, 1977) or a strongly Catholic community (Menolascino, 1977; Saenger, 1960, Note 2)—might experience a significantly decreased number of stigmatized social interactions. A family with strong extended family network, including active involvement in the caretaking, would not find the prolonged special needs as burdensome (Farber, 1959; Waisbren, 1980). Similarly, a mother who has a close friend with a similarly afflicted child and who is consulting regularly with an accepting, specialist pediatrician and social worker team, may have an abundance of relevant information on daily management. Finally, access to a supportive marital partner, close friends and relatives, and non-judgmental professionals may enable a parent to express periodic grieving without being considered pathological.

Periodic Potential Crises Over Time

Although the stresses above occur continuously throughout the life of the mentally retarded person within his/her family, parental awareness of the stresses is periodically increased. An underlying thesis in this paper is that *when a discrepancy emerges between what parents expect of a child's development and of parenting as opposed to what actually takes place when rearing a mentally retarded child*, a crisis may be precipitated.

The anticipation of a crisis can have an ameliorating effect on its impact (Golan, 1980), but parents of the mentally retarded commonly adopt the coping mechanism of living day to day. Although this proves functional in many ways, it becomes problematic if it inhibits their ability to anticipate potential crisis periods over time.

Professionals, as well, have historically been more sensitized to the immediate crisis surrounding diagnosis, and less concerned with ensuing crises. In fact, most of the clinical literature on familial responses to mental retardation suggests that after parents experience three stages of adjustment (e.g. emotional disorganizations, reintegration, and mature adaptation) they learn to live without undue stress (American Medical Association, 1964). The various emotions that parents are said to experience upon learning that their child is mentally retarded, include alarm, ambivalence, denial, guilt, shame, self-pity, sorrow, depression, and a wish for their child's death (Price-Bonham and Addison, 1978; Wolfensberger, 1967). The task of the helping professional is to recognize the "novelty shock" early and to help parents work through that "well circumscribed, definable and time-bound process" (Menolascino, 1977, p. 255).

Although the dominant viewpoint in the psychotherapeutic literature has pointed a series of stages common to parents' reactions to the diagnosis (Berger & Foster, 1976; Jacobsen & Humphrey, 1979) another view of parental response is suggested by a parent of a retarded child.

Professionals could help parents more— and they would be more realistic—if they discarded their ideas about stages and progress. They could then begin to understand something about the deep lasting changes that life with a retarded son or daughter brings to parents and then they could begin to see that negative feelings— the shock, the guilt and the bitterness— never disappear but stay on as part of the parents' emotional life (Searle, 1978, p. 23).

The experience of Mr. Searle suggests that the stresses induced by the addition of a mentally retarded child to the family unit are not one-time phenomenon, and that the stresses cannot be alleviated by a single adjustment. In a pamphlet produced by the National Association of Retarded Citizens on Needs of Parents of Retarded Children, Mrs. Murray writes:

After thirteen years experience as the mother of a retarded child and having talked and corresponded with literally hundreds of other parents, I have come to the conclusion that all of our many, many needs can be covered in one sentence and it is this:

The greatest single need of parents of mentally retarded children is constructive professional counselling at various stages of the child's life which will enable the parents to find answers to their own individual problems to a reasonably satisfactory degree. (Murray, Note 7, p. 11).

An increasing number of clinicians are listening to and supporting the perspective voiced by these parents. Olshansky (1962) coined the term "chronic sorrow" referring to a long term internalization of a depressive mood responding in an understandable, non-neurotic manner to a tragic fact. Farber (Note 3) noted the normality of parental disappointment in response to the tragic crisis, and describes the ongoing disruption of the normal family life cycle resulting from having a mentally retarded child. Menolascino (1977) distinguished three types of crises experienced by parents, including the "reality" crises and the "values" crises that can occur throughout the life span. Peterson & Lippa (Note 8) described seven crises (including diagnostic, informational, socialization, family adjustment, school, social and independence) discussing the parental needs of each one.

What is lacking in these conceptualizations of chronic stresses is an hypothesis for when these crises might occur. The accepted view that a crisis occurs following the diagnosis because of the general disruption of expectancies (Menolascino, 1977) is probably correct; but the conclusion that the gradually regained equilibrium is permanent is probably incorrect. Rearing a mentally retarded child brings with it a whole life of shattered expectations. If tension between what is expected and what occurs produces one crisis (the diagnostic crisis) that dynamic also should hold for later periods of important expectations.

It is hypothesized that ten critical periods are potentially stressful for families of mentally retarded children (Table 1). When these occur, the family would experience a *renewed* emotional upheaval and would need to reactivate their coping mechanisms to reestablish family functioning. Five of the critical periods are defined by the chronological age of the child and are related to an age which for a normal child is characterized by achieving a major developmental milestone. The other five periods are essentially distinctive events not experienced by parents of normal children. There are several instances in which developmental and transitional crises coincide in time.

Crises Arising from Lack of Normal Developmental Progression

One of the most widely shared parental expectations is for normal developmental progression through certain milestones such as baby's first step or first word. These are symbolic markers of important periods of growth towards independence. In the case of the normal child, parents will recall details about each stage of development from their own childhood, will hear about them from their neighbors, will see them demonstrated on television and read about them in magazines and books on rearing children. Children's normal developmental milestones are available as practical information to anyone who wants to measure their child against normality.

The deviance of mentally retarded children lies in the delayed achievement of the developmental milestones. Their rate of development and the discrepancy of that

Table 1
The Hypothesized Effect of Predictable Crises on Types of Stress

Discrepancy in Expectations	Type of Stress			
	Parenting: No Models	Prolonged Burden of Care	Stigmatized Interaction	Grieving
of Child's Development				
Child should have begun walking (12-15 months)	increase	same	increase	increase
Child should have begun talking (24-30 months)	increase	same	increase	increase
Beginning of public school (public label as different in classroom)	decrease	decrease	increase	mixed
Onset of puberty (tension between physical appearance and mental/social ability)	increase	increase	increase	increase
21st birthday (symbolic of independence)	increase	increase	increase	increase
of Parenting Events Experienced Only by Families of the Mentally Retarded				
Diagnosis of mental retardation	increase	increase	increase	increase
Younger sibling with lower CA has MA matching and then higher than MR sibling	increase	same	increase	increase
Serious discussion of placement of MR child outside the home (or placement itself)	increase	decrease	decrease	mixed
Exacerbated behavior, seizure or health problems unique to MR child	increase	increase	increase	increase
Serious discussion about guardianship and care for the MR child	increase	increase	same	increase

development from the norm becomes the area focused upon for diagnosis and treatment and, consequently, the source of heightened stress for the parent. The slow development in mental age in retarded children stands in stark contrast to their chronological age. This disjuncture constitutes the underlying common denominator of the critical period which is here called "developmental crises." Each period involves acknowledgement that the child's performance is discrepant from expectations for what should have occurred had the child been normal. The poignancy lies in the gap between what is expected and what occurs.

Five developmental crises, therefore, can be identified on the bases of the normal child's developmental milestones: (a) the child should have begun to walk (ages 12-15 months); (b) the child should have begun to talk (24-30 months); (c) the child should be starting kindergarten in public school (the child is publicly labeled as "different" and belonging in "special classes"); (d) the onset of puberty (tension between physical appearance vs. mental-social ability); and (e) the 21st birthday (symbolic of independence from the family).

Crises Arising from Transitions in Perception and Services

In the same way that parents have expectations that are culturally derived about normal developmental milestones, they also have expectations about the parenting experience. Certain expectation, will not be fulfilled in the process of rearing a mentally retarded child. The events that occur only in families of the mentally retarded could be critical periods in which the discrepancy between what was expected of parenting and what happened were the greatest. It is at these points that the clinician would expect the greatest potential for stress in families of mentally retarded children.

The most obvious of these crises (the sixth one) is that of the professional diagnosis of the child being mentally retarded rather than normal. The seventh crisis often arises when the parents consider the possibility of having others rear their abnormal child, i.e., placement. The eighth parental crisis occurs

when the normal sibling with a lower chronologicial age performs at a higher developmental level than the retarded child and the retarded child moves functionally into a different ordinal position within the family (Farber, 1959). The ninth crisis arises from child management problems necessitating professional involvement, such as seizure control, stereotypic behavior, and health issues which are unique to the mentally retarded child. The serious discussion about guardianship of the child as the parents grow older and the possibility of having to relinquish guardianship to an outside-the-family member is the tenth crisis.

This second group of crises involves transitions away from the traditional carrying out of parental responsibilities, shifts away from the family and towards professionals in the assignment of decision-making. The process of negotiating with the social service delivery system and the stigma of that process contributes to the stress of the transitional crises. The parents are reminded at each point that had their child been normal this process would not have been necessary. This, in turn, will re-evoke the disappointment about their situation and about the deviant life which they and their offspring are living together.

In a study which was conducted to ascertain parental perspectives on developmental and transitional crises described in this paper, 30 parents retrospectively described their feelings at the times of the 10 critical periods (Wikler, Wasow, & Hatfield, 1981). Data suggest support for the hypothesis that adjustment of parents of mentally retarded children is one of chronic sorrow rather than time-bound adjustment. The data do not, however, indicate that the sorrow is continuous; it seems, rather, to be a periodic phenomenon. Each of the 10 postulated critical periods appeared to precipitate a period of stress for the families. The parents' reported responses to these periods did not decrease in intensity over time. In fact, following the diagnosis, the 21st birthday was the second most stressful of the 10 crises.

The thesis of this paper is that *the various stresses experienced by families of mentally retarded children are exacerbated over time by* unexpected discrepancies between what might have been and what is. The hypothesized interactions of the developmental and transitional crises with the stresses described in the first section are outlined in Table 1.

Implications for Research and Clinical interventions

Although retrospective accounts of parents have provided initial support for the 10 predictable critical periods over the life-span, an in-depth current examination of the manifestations of stress within family interaction is needed. A longitudinal study which measured various indices of stress before, during and after the occurrence of these periods in conjunction with similar cross-sectional data would allow one to compare families in the various stressful and non-stressful periods contemporaneously.

Further investigation of these conjectures are important in light of their clinical implications. First, due to past practices of institutionalization of the mentally retarded, the professional community has not been involved with the *ongoing* stresses that are part of rearing a mentally retarded child within the home. With the current shift towards deinstitutionalization and maintenance in the home, as well as the increased exposure of professionals to mentally retarded children in the school system, more professionals will inevitably become increasingly involved with these families. An awareness of the special difficulties encountered by parents rearing their retarded child at home is necessary before the professionals will be able to make appropriate interventions with those families. Parents as consumers of these services should be considered as rich sources of information for professionals (Wikler, 1979).

Second, since anticipation of crises is itself an ameliorating factor, professional as well as parental awareness of the predictable periods of vulnerability may help to reduce the impact of those stressor events on families. Self-help parent groups could be organized to prepare parents ahead of time for the high risk periods. Third, parents would find themselves being less self-critical about their responses to the difficulties of having a mentally retarded child if they were aware of the normality of these disappointments over time and of the chronic sorrow.

REFERENCE NOTES

1. Wikler, L. *A neglected population: Needs of the single parent of a mentally retarded child.* Paper presented at American Association of Mental Deficiency, Miami, Florida, May, 1979.
2. Saenger, G. *Factors Influencing the Institutionalization of Mentally Retarded Individuals in New York City.* Albany, N.Y.: New York State Interdepartmental Health Resources Board, 1960.
3. Farber, B. Sociological ambivalence and family care: The individual proposes and society disposes. *Family Care of Developmentally Disabled Members Conference Proceedings.* (Available from Department of Psychoeducational Studies, University of Minnesota, August, 1979.)
4. Moore, C., & Seachore, C. *Why do families need respite care? Building a support system.* Unpublished report, 1977. (Available from Montgomery County Respite Care Coalition and Maryland State Planning Council on D.D.)
5. Wikler, L., & Hanusa, D. *The impact of respite care on stress in families of mentally retarded children.* Paper presented at American Association of Mental Deficiency, San Francisco, May, 1980.
6. Cohen, S. *Demonstration model continua of respite care and parent training services for families of persons with developmental disanioties.* Unpublished Annual Report, 1979. (Available from United Cerebral Palsy Associations, Inc., City University of New York.)
7. Murray, M. Needs of parents of mentally retarded children. *National Association for Retarded Citizens.* (Available from 2709 Avenue East, P.O. Box 6109, Arlington, Texas, 76011, 1970.)
8. Peterson, R., & Lippa, S. *Life cycle crises encountered by families of developmentally disabled children: Implications and recommendations for practice.* Paper presented at American Association of Mental Deficiency, Denver, Colorado, May 1978.

REFERENCES

Adams, M. *Mental retardation and its social dimensions.* New York: Columbia University Press, 1971.

American Medical Association. *Mental retardation: A Handbook for the primary physician.* New York: Author, 1964.

Barsch, H. *Parents of the handicapped child.* Springfield, IL: Charles C. Thomas, 1968.

Berger, M., & Foster, M. Family-level interventions for retarded children: A multivariate approach to issues and strategies. *Multivariate Experimental Clinical Research,* 1976, **2**, 1-21.

Birenbaum, A. On managing a courtesy stigma. *Journal of Health and Social Behavior,* 1970, **11**, 106-206.

Birenbaum, A. The mentally retarded child in the home and the family cycle. *Journal of Health and Social Behavior,* 1971, **12**, 55-65.

Cook, J.J. Dimensional analysis of child-rearing attitudes of parents of handicapped children. *American Journal of Mental Deficiency*, 1963, **8**, 354-361.

Cummings, S. T., Bayley, H. C., & Rie, H. E. Effects of the child's deficiency on the mother: A study of mothers of mentally retarded, chronically ill, and neurotic children. *American Journal of Orthopsychiatry*, 1966, **36**, 595-608.

Davis, M., & MacKay, D. Mentally subnormal children and their families. *The Lancet*, October 27, 1973.

Edgerton, R. *The cloak of competence: Stigma in the lives of the mentally retarded.* Berkeley: University of California Press, 1967.

Emde, R. & Brown, C. Adaptation to the birth of a Down's Syndrome infant: Grieving and maternal attachment. *American Academy of Child Psychiatry*, 1978, **17**, 299-323.

Erickson, M. T. MMPI comparisons between parents of young emotionally disturbed children and mentally retarded children. *Journal of Consulting Clinical Psychology*, 1968, **32**, 701-706.

Farber, B. Family adaptations to severely mentally retarded on family integration. *Monographs of the Society for Research in Child Development*, No. 71, 1959.

Farber, B. *Mental retardation: Its social context and social consequences.* Boston: Houghton Mifflin Co., 1968.

Farber, B. Family adaptations to severely mentally retarded children. In M. J. Begals and S. A. Richardson (Eds.), *The mentally retarded and society: A social science perspective.* Baltimore: University Park Press, 1975.

Farber, B., & Jenne, W. C. Family organization and parent-child communication: Parents and siblings of a retarded child. *Monographs of the Society for Research in Child Development*, 1963, **7,28**.

Farber, B., Jenne, W., & Toigo, R. Family crisis and the decision to institutionalize the retarded child. Washington, D.C.: Council for Exceptional Children, NEA Research Monograph Series, 1960, No. A-1.

Fowle. C. M. The effect of the severely mentally retarded child on his family. *American Journal of Mental Deficiency*, 1968, **73**, 468-476.

Friedrich, W. Predictors of the coping behavior of mothers of handicapped children. *Journal of Consulting and Clinical Psychology*, 1979, **47**, 1140-1141.

Gath, A. Sibling reactions to mental handicap: A comparison of the brothers and sisters of mongol children. *Journal of Child Psychology and Psychiatry*, 1974, **15**, 187-198.

Graliker, B., Koch, R., & Henderson, R. A study of factors influencing placement of retarded children in a state residential institution. *American Journal of Mental Deficiency*, 1965, **69**, 553-559.

Golan, N. Interventions at times of transition: Sources and forms of help. *Social Casework*, 1980, **61**, 259-266.

Grossman, F. K. *Brothers and sisters of retarded children: An exploratory study.* Syracuse, N.Y.: Syracuse University Press, 1972.

Hill, R. Generic features of families under stress. *Social Casework*, 1958, **39**, 139-150.

Holt, K. Home care of severely retarded children. *Pediatrics*, 1958, **22**, 744-754.

Illingworth, R. S. Counseling the parents of the mentally handicapped child. *Clinical Pediatrics*, 1967, **6**, 340-348.

Jacobsen, R. B., & Humphry, R. Families in crisis: Research and theory in child mental retardation. *Social Casework*, 1979, **60**, 597-601.

Levinson, R. Family crisis and adaptation: Coping with a mentally retarded child. Unpublished Dissertation, University of Wisconsin, 1975.

Mandelbaum, A. The group process in helping parents of retarded children. *Children*, 1967, **14**, 227-232.

Matheny, A., & Vernick, J. Parents of the mentally retarded child: Emotionally overwhelmed or informationally deprived? *Journal of Pediatrics*, 1969, **74**, 953-959.

McAllister, R., Butler, E., & Lei, T. J. Patterns of social interaction among families of behaviorally retarded children. *Journal of Marriage and the Family*, 1973, **35**, 93-100.

Menolascino, F. J. *Challenges in mental retardation: Progressive ideology and services.* New York: Human Sciences Press, 1977.

Olshansky, S. Chronic sorrow: A response to having a mentally defective child. *Social Casework*, 1962, **43**, 190-193.

Parks, R. M. Parental reactions to the birth of a handicapped child. *Health and Social Work*, 1977, **2**, 52-66.

Price-Bonham, S., & Addison, S. Families and mentally retarded children: Emphasis on the father. *The Family Coordinator*. 1978, **27**, 221-230.

Pueschel, S., & Murphy, A. Assessment of counseling practices at the birth of a child with Down's Syndrome. *American Journal of Mental Deficiency*, 1976, **81**, 325-330.

Schufeit, L. J. & Wurster, S. R. Frequency of divorce among parents of handicapped children. *Resources in Education*, 1976, **11**, 71-78.

Searle, S. J. Stages of parent reaction: Mainstreaming. *The Exceptional Parent*, 1978, April, 23-27.

Solnit, A., & Stark, M. Mourning and the birth of a defective child. *Psychoanalytic Studies of the Child*, 1961, **16**, 523-536.

Stone, N. M. Family factors in willingness to place the mongoloid child. *American Journal of Mental Deficiency*, 1965, **72**, 16-20.

Voysey, M. Impression management by parents with disabled children. *Journal of Health and Social Behavior*, 1972, **13**, 80-89.

Waisbren, S. Parents' reactions after the birth of a developmentally disabled child. *American Journal of Mental Deficiency*. 1980, **34**, 345-351.

Waskowitz, C. The parents of retarded children speak for themselves. *The Journal of Pediatrics*, 1953, **54**, 319-329.

Wikler, L. Consumer involvement in training of social work students. *Social Casework*, 1979, March, 145-149.

Wikler, L., Wasow, M., & Hatfield, E. Chronic sorrow revisited: Attitudes of parents and professionals about adjustment to mental retardation. *American Journal of Orthopsychiatry*, 1981, **51**, 63-70.

Wolfensberger, W. Counseling parents of the retarded. In A. Baumeister (Ed.), *Appraisal, education, rehabilitation.* Chicago: Aldine, 1967.

PART III

DIVORCE AND CHILD CUSTODY

This paper reviews research on the antecedents and the consequences of divorce for adults. Divorce is discussed as part of a continuum of marital instability. Research on historical and sociological causes of divorce and theoretical models for the study of divorce are reviewed. The changes in health status and the role redefinitions experienced by the divorced are discussed. The contribution of unmodifiable and modifiable factors in easing adjustment to divorce is examined. The paper concludes with a discussion of issues relating to sampling and measurement that need to be addressed in future research in order to improve and expand upon previous studies.

11

DIVORCE RESEARCH

What We Know; What We Need to Know

Gay C. Kitson and Helen J. Raschke

Compared with other family phenomena, divorce, its antecedents, and especially its consequences for adults, have been little studied. This article will review sociological and social psychological causes and consequences of divorce, highlight some of the little studied topics, and suggest ways to address these issues.

America has the highest marriage and divorce rates in the world (Carter & Glick, 1976; Norton & Glick, 1979). Although the marriage rate declined from the mid-1950s until 1976, from 1976 through 1979 it increased. The divorce rate began a precipitous increase in the early 1960s which continued into the mid-1970s. Since then, the rate of increase has not been as rapid (Glick & Norton, 1979; Monthly Vital Statistics Report, Note 1). The crude divorce rate for 1979 was 5.3 per 1,000 population, compared

Dr. Kitson is Assistant Professor in the Department of Family Medicine, School of Medicine, and Adjunct Assistant Professor of Sociology at Case Western Reserve University, Cleveland, OH 44106. Dr. Raschke is Associate Professor, Department of Psychology and Sociology, Austin College, Sherman, TX 75090.
The writing of this paper was supported in part by National Institute of Mental Health Grant MH-22575. We are grateful to Randal D. Day for his comments on an earlier version of this paper.

with 5.2 for 1978. From the 1979 crude rate, Paul Glick (Note 2) of the U.S. Bureau of the Census estimates the refined divorce rate for 1979 to be 23 per 1,000 married women. The frequency of divorce is indicated by the fact that 17% of all women ages 16 to 75 have been divorced at least once as of June 1976; this ranges from a low of 4.3% for 16 to 20 year olds to a high of approximately 20% for women ages 40 to 55 (U.S. Bureau of the Census, 1976).

The Census Bureau predicts that about 38% of women, ages 25 to 29 in 1975, may eventually end their first marriages in divorce, if their future divorce experience mirrors that of older adults. Of the three-fourths who will later remarry, about 44% may redivorce (Norton & Glick, 1979).

Shifting to a different perspective, in March 1976, there were 2.8 million men and 4.4 million women who were reported as currently divorced. There were 75 divorced persons per every 1,000 persons in intact marriages—twice as high as the corresponding ratio (35) for 1960 (U.S. Bureau of the Census, 1977).

These data on the increase in divorce raise the question of whether divorce or unhappy marriage is the problem. The answer depends, in part, on the theoretical perspective one uses. From an institutional perspective, the continuity of the family system is more important than the needs and interests of individual members. From the viewpoint of the society, the primary purpose of the family is producing and socializing new members. Breaks in the family through death, divorce, or desertion are thought to affect this purpose adversely. Similarly, divorce has been viewed by some psychiatrists as an indicator of individual disfunction. To them, divorce is a product of neurotic marital interaction patterns. From this perspective, *Divorce Won't Help* (Bergler, 1948) because each partner's interpersonal difficulties will continue in new relationships unless or until therapeutic intervention occurs.

Despite varying degrees of disapproval of and consequent ease in obtaining one, the option of divorce is almost universally recognized as a regrettable necessity (Murdock, 1950; Goode, 1963). "It represents merely a practical concession to the frailty of mankind, caught in a web of social relationships and cultural expectations that often impose intolerable pressure on the individual personality" (Murdock, 1950:201). From such an individual perspective, the health and well-being of the marital partners, rather than the institutional needs of the family unit, are of primary importance (Winch, 1971).

Despite continuing discussion (Lasch, 1977) about the demise of the family, we know relatively little about how much marital instability there actually is (for a recent discussion, see Lewis & Spanier, 1979). Divorce is, after all, only one solution to the problem of an unsatisfactory marriage. Still others are continuing to live in "empty shell" marriages (Goode, 1966), permanent separation, separation and reconciliation, and interventions that modify the marriage for the better. Before we can adequately address the question of whether and to what extent divorce is a problem, we need to know more about the varieties of marital instability.

Marital Instability

Recent data suggest that there may be more instability and, at the same time, more effort to save marriages than was previously thought. Instability may be higher in that substantial numbers of couples are sufficiently unhappy or uncertain about their relationships that they separate at some point in their marriages. We do not know much about the average length of such separations or their outcome, but Weiss (1975) estimates that approximately half of all American married couples separate at least once. If we take the recent estimate of a lifetime divorce rate of 38% (Glick & Norton, 1979) then 12% of these separated couples are likely to remain together either with some degree of continuing dissatisfaction or by having developed methods of handling their difficulties. Figures from Bloom, Hodges, Caldwell, Systra, and Cedrone (1977) and Kitson, Holmes, and Sussman (Note 3) support this estimate.

Another step in this process is thinking about divorce. Booth and White (1980) report that 10% of a random sample of married Nebraskans report having thought about divorce. Although thinking about divorce is correlated in their sample with low marital satisfaction, there are some differences. Regardless of marital satisfaction, factors such as marriage at a young age, low religiosity, shorter length of marriage, low satisfaction with family income, and reported spouse abuse are independently associated with divorce. Employment for wives also seems to enable women to think about the possibility of divorce. Further, thoughts about divorce are more likely when there are preschoolers at home. The meaning of these findings is uncertain. They may reflect the strains of full-time child tending or increased financial pressures when the husband and/or wife are in the early stages of their careers, a stage which generally coincides with the beginning of the family life cycle (Aldous, 1978). The average divorce occurs within the first 8 years of marriage, again coinciding with the early stages of the family life cycle. The strains of the first years of marriage and the changing composition of the family unit may make this a particularly vulnerable period. One way to examine the influence of these variables would be to look at couples married before and after the age of 20 in the first 10 years of marriage, with and without preschool children, perhaps controlling for perceived economic problems and other variables that could be causal. There may be other vulnerable periods in the family life cycle that produce a greater likelihood of divorce but they have not yet been examined in detail.

Another category of unstable marriages includes those who separate instead of divorce. While such separations may be legal (separate maintenance), others are informal and may be a step in the divorce process since couples generally separate before deciding to file for divorce. Separation may also be a euphemism for divorce for couples who never married but who have children. We know little about those who choose to separate instead of divorce. One characteristic we do know about is race. In the 1970 census, 8% of black males and 15% of black females (ages 35-44) were reported to be separated versus less than 2% of white males and females. It is also likely that those who feel they cannot afford the cost of divorce and those from religious groups opposed to divorce are more likely to separate. Separation may create greater distress than divorce for those experiencing it because of the ambivalence of the status as they are neither married nor legally free to establish a new relationship. Permanent separations seem to be decreasing as the stigma and, with Legal Aid, the cost of divorce decrease.

It is difficult to estimate what proportions of intact marriages are unhappy (for discussions of the concepts of marital satisfaction and happiness, see Burr, 1973; Lewis & Spanier, 1979). The number of such unions is likely to be substantial, however, if for no other reason than that many couples contemplate divorce for some time before actually filing. As an example of this, Kitson et al. (Note 3) report that 42% of the divorced suburban residents in their longitudinal study drawn from court records had separated and reconciled before initiating their current divorce action.

We also know relatively little about the efficacy of self-help or counseling efforts designed to improve the quality of deteriorated relationships. A review of marital counseling outcome studies with control groups reports that the majority of the couples in therapy did make improvements (Beck, 1975). It is not known how many of these couples were still living together or were separated when they entered therapy or whether such indicators of the stage of difficulty in the relationship make a difference in outcome. Little is known about the stability and satisfaction of these marriages post counseling (see Gurman, 1973, for a review of the few follow-up studies available).

Another small but growing segment of the population likely to be exhibiting relationship instability includes couples who are living together without being married. As of March 1977, nearly two million adults were living with an unrelated person of the opposite sex. This is an 80% increase since 1970 but accounts for only 2% of the nation's 48 million couple households (Norton & Glick, 1979). The dissolution rate among such persons is likely to be high, and for some the period of adjustment is not unlike that of the legally divorced (see, for example, Hill, Rubin, & Peplau, 1976). No method has yet been devised to account for the dissolution of unions of cohabiting couples since they are not required to go through a legal process.

While these data on the extent of marital instability do not answer the question of whether divorce is a problem for society, they do more accurately shift the focus of the discussion to the foundations for the instability of relationships whether or not instability in turn leads to dissolution.

Antecedents

DATA SOURCES

A common query is what has caused the increase in divorce. In this section we shall examine historical, sociological, and social psychological findings on the antecedents or causes of divorce. (For other recent reviews see Levinger, 1965, 1976; Nye, White, & Frideres, 1973; Brandwein, Brown, & Fox, 1974.)

Although there are currently a number of studies underway, there has until recently been relatively little primary research on divorce. With the exception of Robert Weiss's (1975) outstanding qualitative analysis of the divorce process and his more recent discussion of single parent families (1979), the most recent sociological monograph on the topic was written by William Goode in 1956 based on survey data collected in 1948. While an excellent book, its findings need replicating and updating. Furthermore, Goode only looked at divorced mothers age 38 or less. He did not look at the divorce process for males, older women, or women without children.

Because divorce has to a great extent been ignored as a primary subject of study since Goode's work, much of what we know about divorce has been a by-product of research on other topics such as mental health and life satisfaction (Gurin, Veroff, & Feld, 1960; Srole, Langner, Michael, Opler, & Rennie, 1962; Langner & Michael, 1963; Campbell, Converse, & Rodgers, 1976), race relations (Moynihan, 1967; Crain & Weissman, 1972), economic and occupational surveys (Ross & Sawhill, 1975; Hampton, 1979; Cherlin, 1979, Mott & Moore, 1979), and population control (Bumpass & Sweet, 1972). Still another important source of data has been the U.S. Census with all the assets and liabilities of such demographic research (Udry, 1966, 1967; Bernard, 1966; Carter & Glick, 1976). Findings based on these data sources mean that we know more about who divorces than why they divorce or what happens to them after divorce and, as we shall see, the whos of divorce are changing.

In the majority of cases, these studies have been cross-sectional which can produce various kinds of biases. Such studies provide a "snapshot" of marital status at one point and self-reports of previous marital statuses; subjects have not been followed over time. The lack of longtitudinal data produces additional problems since three out of four divorced persons eventually remarry (Glick & Norton, 1979). Because of the high remarriage rate, the proportion of currently divorced persons is much smaller than the proportion of persons who have ever experienced a divorce. In addition, divorced men are consistently undernumerated because they are more difficult to locate and remarry faster than women (Norton & Glick, 1979).

Many conclusions drawn about causes of divorce and post-divorce adjustment have been based on samples of the currently divorced. These findings, while useful, are suspect for drawing conclusions about the divorced without more data on the representativeness of this subpopulation of the divorced. With this reminder of the potential for bias, we shall use findings from many such studies to explore the antecedents, or causes of divorce.

While there is clearly overlap in these categories, for organizational purposes our discussion is divided into historical and sociological and social psychological factors.

HISTORICAL

A frequent explanation for the increase in divorce involves changes in the organization of the family over the past several hundred years. As the dominant family form shifted from a multigenerational, extended system that fulfilled a variety of functions for the members to a nuclear, or conjugal, form based on wage labor in an increasingly urban, industrial, and bureaucratic environment, the utility and influence of the family for its members decreased (Goode, 1963; Winch, 1977). Cross-cultural ethnographic and demographic studies support the view that greater gender equality and economic independence play roles in the increase in divorce. In tribal societies, when women's status is equal or close to the status of men, as measured by such variables as women's ability to inherit property and be involved in religious or political activities, divorce rates are high (Pearson & Hendrix, 1979). Using the variables of percent of females in universities and whether societies have a socialist form of government that fosters such civil rights as divorce, Anderson and Troost (Note 4) report similar findings for modern nations over five million in population. Such data, however, are on the national or societal level and cannot address the important issue of subcultural variation in divorce rates within societies. Within the United States, groups such as the Jews, Amish, Chinese-Americans, and rural populations continue to emphasize the importance of the extended family. Such subcultural variations provide a contemporary way of examining the impact of familism on marital relationships.

Goode (1963) notes that industrialization seems to produce a similar rate of marital dissolution around the world. In some cases, such as Japan, it led to a decrease in divorce rates; in others, such as some western countries, an increase. An additional question is why, given similar levels of industrialization, is the rate of divorce higher in the United States than in other industrial societies and why is it higher in certain parts of the United States than in others? Weiss (1975) postulates that the United States has a particularly individualistic emphasis that focuses on self-realization and therefore may foster divorce as people seek to maximize their personal fulfillment. There is some support for this explanation within the United States from data collected by Pang and Hanson (1968) and by Fenelon (1971) showing higher divorce rates in western states. Rates were higher in states with higher numbers of in-migrants, low numbers of foreign born, fewer Roman Catholics, and a stronger emphasis on individualism.

Additional factors to which the recent increase in divorce has been attributed include the prolonged Vietnam War in the 1960s and 1970s, the subsequent readjustment to a peace time economy with a recession which did not reduce the divorce rate as it has in other periods, the renewal of the women's movement giving women more options for education and jobs, more liberal attitudes toward personal behavior among most religious denominations, and the liberalization of divorce laws in most states (Glick & Norton, 1979). While plausible, such explanations, particularly those relating to the impact of the Vietnam War and changing religious standards, await testing. The economic slowdown of the early 1980s also provides an opportunity to re-examine the relationship between economic conditions and divorce.

It is commonly held that the liberalization of the divorce laws has increased divorce. Although additional analysis on this important issue is needed, to date the data suggest that laws which legislate family patterns and moral standards generally change slowly and lag behind everyday standards of behavior (Brody, 1970). Wright and Stetson (1978) and Sell (1979) found little difference in divorce rates of states which liberalized their laws and states which had not. While Schoen, Greenblatt, and Mielke (1975) report similar findings in California, Stetson and Wright (1975), using 1960 census data gathered prior to the major liberalization of the divorce laws, found that the more permissive the divorce laws the higher the divorce rate, even when economic factors and social costs such as ethnicity, religion, and population stability were controlled. It would be useful to replicate this study with 1980 census data.

SOCIOLOGICAL AND SOCIAL PSYCHOLOGICAL

Socioeconomic status. A first set of relationships to report upon is that the likelihood of divorce varies inversely with occupational status, education, and income, that is, there are more divorces among people in low status occupations, among people with less education, and among those with less income. Until Goode's 1948 survey, it was commonly assumed that higher status occupational groups had the higher divorce rates; in fact, Goode (1956) discounted pretest data for his survey because it did not comply with the common notion of divorce patterns.

While these relationships are still true, comparisons between the 1960 and 1970 census suggest a shift in the distribution so that the status differences in divorce rates are less striking. While those of lower status still account for more of the divorces, the percentage increase in divorce is greater among higher status groups. Norton and Glick (1979, p. 14) note: "The important conclusion that can be drawn from these trends is that the recent increase in divorce has been pervasive with regard to social and economic level but that socioeconomic differences in divorce are now smaller than they used to be."

High status occupational groups have lower divorce rates than do low, but within occupational groups there are also differences. As an example, the likelihood of divorce varies within the professions. Using data from California divorce records for 1968, Rosow and Rose (1972) report variations in divorce rates among professional occupations. Of 12 professional occupations examined, the rates were highest for authors followed by social scientists, architects, college faculty, lawyers and judges, engineers, chemists, editors and reporters, accountants and auditors, dentists, physicians and natural scientists who had the lowest rates. Even within occupational groups Rosow and Rose found that physicians in specialties with more patient contact at more irregular hours were more likely to divorce. Generalizing from Rosow and Rose's research, we might expect that the likelihood of divorce will vary directly with occupational stress. More data are needed on the impact of different kinds of occupations on marital instability. Levinger (1965) hypothesizes that irregular work hours which disrupt home life or occupations that bring individuals into greater contact with members of the opposite sex are more likely to lead to divorce.

Although the stigma of being divorced seems to have diminished somewhat, there are relatively few studies of the impact of divorce on occupational careers. In one such study, Hutchison and Hutchison (1979) report that divorced Presbyterian clergymen are more geographically but less upwardly mobile than nondivorced clergy. Additional research on divorce and occupational contingencies would be particularly useful.

Another related factor is employment status. The likelihood of divorce is greater in households in which the husband is unemployed periodically (Coombs & Zumeta, 1970). It would appear that it is not simply unemployment per se which leads to divorce since the divorce rate generally has gone down in periods of recession or depression (Ferriss, 1970), but rather that unemployment highlights other problems in the family. One might rephrase the question to ask why some families with unemployed males break up while the majority remain intact. Scanzoni (1968) suggests, as does Goode (1956), that a key factor is the different meanings which husbands and wives place on being employed and the type or level of employment. Scanzoni found that compared with still married women, divorcing women were more dissatisfied with their husbands' occupational achievement, whatever it was. He also found that the meaning of work is more likely to differ when the husband and wife come from different family backgrounds. A variety of researchers have found that marital dissatisfaction and divorce are more likely when husbands and wives come from different social backgrounds (e.g., Burgess & Cottrell, 1939; Goode, 1956; Levinger, 1965; Bumpass & Sweet, 1972).

Recent studies report contradictory findings on the role of income in marital dissolution. Cutright (1971) found, using census data, that income was the most powerful predictor of instability, with those with lower incomes being substantially more likely to divorce. Using survey data, Ross and Sawhill (1975) report that level of family income does not predict instability but that unemployment and lower than usual income do. Cherlin (1979) also reports that instability of income, not its amount, predicts divorce. Reporting on data from the National Longitudinal Survey of Labor Market Behavior of Young Women Ages 14 to 28 in 1968, Mott and Moore (1979) found that for whites debt accumulation and for blacks the same or lower income than previously reported were more strongly associated with disruption than were husband's earnings. On the other hand, in the recent income maintenance experiments, families with higher level subsidies were more likely to separate or divorce than those with low or no subsidies (Hannan, Tuma, & Groeneveld, 1977; Steiner, Note 5). This suggests, again, that there actually may be more unhappiness and latent marital instability than is illustrated by the rate of separation and divorce. The role that income and the perception of the economic status of the family play in the divorce process needs further specification. Women employed outside the home are more likely to be divorced than those who are not (Glick & Norton, 1979). The direction of causality is unclear. Scanzoni (1968) found that employed women in intact families reported approval and support of their husbands for their employment while those who were divorced did not. Couples who divorce may have different views of marital roles than do those who remain married, or the wife's employment outside the home may be a symptom of other family conflicts. It may also be that women who are employed can afford to think about divorce or be divorced (Booth & White, 1980); that is, they can support themselves without a spouse (Cherlin, 1979; Kitson et al., Note 3). Alternatively, divorced women may have to work to make ends meet. These issues need further clarification.

Race.   Another factor, which is tied to many of the previous ones, is race. Many studies report blacks to be more likely to divorce than whites and much more likely to separate (Udry, 1966; Bernard, 1966; Crain & Weisman, 1972; Norton & Glick, 1979). Blacks are also more likely to remain divorced thereby magnifying the differences. Drawing upon data from the Current Population Series, Moynihan (1967) traced the higher rates of marital dissolution for blacks back to 1940. Controversy continues concerning the Moynihan report. Briefly, Moynihan's argument concerning marital instability in the black community is that rates of family breakup are high because discrimination led to an inability to obtain skilled employment that would provide adequate income for family life. This in turn produced a situation in which the sons of these marriages were unskilled, unhappy, and unable to provide the economic resources needed for stable homes of their own. The pattern, therefore, was perpetuated. The root of the problem according to Moynihan is the matrifocal structure of the black family; this structure emasculates the male and puts an immense burden on the female. It is therefore a subculture which supports divorce. Moynihan's solution for changing this situation was to strengthen the black family.

More recent data throw this notion of subcultural approval of divorce as a cause of the high divorce rates among blacks into question. Glick and Norton (1971) using data from the Economic Opportunity Survey, a probability sample of 28,000 families, indicate that while blacks divorce more often than whites, they wait longer before doing so. In their survey, half of the divorces among whites took place within less than eight years of marriage while for blacks it was a little over eight years. This suggests the possibility that many blacks may have tried for a longer period of time to make their marriages work. In other words, there may be greater pressure for the marriage to succeed rather than a subculture of divorce. Other evidence supports this view. Hampton (1975), using data from the University of Michigan panel study of economic progress in 5,000 families, shows that when income, home ownership, and differences in family size—all factors highly correlated with race—are taken into account, black families experience separation or divorce 6% *less* often than whites. Farley and Hermalin (1971) report similar findings concerning the proportion of black male headed households. Crain and Weisman (1972) also indicate that blacks who come from homes broken by divorce are *not* more likely to divorce; they are more likely to remain in an unhappy marriage while those with homes broken by the death of a parent are more likely to divorce. They suggest that those with divorce in their family backgrounds have seen that divorce does not always solve marital problems; the effect is, in fact, stronger for males than for females. Crain and Weisman therefore endorse the view that social psychological and economic pressures encourage divorce among blacks rather than that there is a subcultural predisposition to this solution.

Despite the frequency of divorce among blacks, there is practically no research, other than economic, on the causes or effects of divorce in this population group. Studies of blacks and whites matched on economic factors would be a way of addressing the issue of race. The process of marital dissolution is thought to be similar for blacks and whites, as Hampton (1979) notes, but the competing explanatory models have not been adequately studied.

Age. Age at first marriage is inversely related to divorce. Couples who marry in their teens are twice as likely to divorce as those who marry in their 20s (Norton & Glick, 1979). Census data report that marriages are also somewhat less stable for women who marry in their 30s (Bauman, 1967; Glick & Norton, 1979). Although a number of explanations have been advanced to account for these findings, the reasons for this relationship are still unclear. It has been suggested that those who marry at a younger age do not have the emotional, educational, or economic resources to make a success of marriage. Invoking an individual psychopathology model in analysis of data from the National Fertility Study, Bumpass and Sweet (1972) found, adjusting for length of marriage, level of education, and premarital pregnancy, that separation and divorce rates are higher for marriages contracted before the age of 20. They suggest that life cycle issues need to be examined, such as adolescents' unrealistic expectations for adult roles and difficulties in pulling away from their families of orientation. Those who marry at a later age more readily dissolve their marriages because they have the economic and educational resources and previous experience living independently to be able to live separately if the relationship goes badly. It is also suggested that those who marry later may have emotional problems that help to account for their late marriages and higher marital instability. With the increase in the age at marriage this explanation may be called into question. These issues need to be further explored using multivariate techniques that allow for simultaneous testing of the influence of the various dimensions hypothesized to account for the relationship.

Premarital pregnancy. Premarital pregnancy has also been shown to be correlated with divorce (Christensen & Meissner, 1953; Christensen & Rubenstein, 1956; Coombs & Zumeta, 1970; Bumpass & Sweet, 1972; Furstenberg, 1976; Hampton, 1979). While, as we have seen, divorce is inversely associated with age at marriage, when controls have been introduced for age, premarital pregnancy continues to have a small effect (Bumpass & Sweet, 1972). Furstenberg's (1976) analysis suggests that lack of preparation for marriage, truncated courtship patterns, and economic problems are the most compelling factors influencing marital stability.

Intergenerational transmission of divorce. A number of studies have reported a small but consistent relationship for the intergenerational transmission of marital instability (Gurin et al., 1960; Langner & Michael, 1963; Bumpass & Sweet, 1972; Heiss, 1972; Pope & Mueller, 1976; Mueller & Pope, 1977; Kulka & Weingarten, 1979; Mott & Moore, 1979).

Various explanations have been advanced for this finding (for a review, see Pope & Mueller, 1976) including one which states that the personality problems and characteristics of the divorced parents produce similar problems in their children leading to further marital instability; an economic explanation that the reduced family income and downward social mobility often associated with divorce reduces the kinds of marital choices available; a role model rationale positing that the predivorce conflict and the postdivorce broken home produce inappropriate sex role learning that reduces the likelihood of a successful marriage. Mueller and Pope (1977) provide support for a social control hypothesis that parental marital instability leads to high risk mate selection. They found that children of divorce are more likely to marry at younger ages, be pregnant at marriage, and marry husbands with lower status occupations. This occurs, they suggest, because of lack of adequate parental supervision. In support of this hypothesis, they find that high risk mate selection is more likely for women when other siblings are present than for those who are only children. Although a relatively weak relationship has generally been reported, given the currently high divorce rate, if divorce begets more divorce, the issue raised by intergenerational transmission of divorce is an important one bearing more study.

CAUSE OF DIVORCE

We have so far examined a number of causes, or correlates, of divorce. Another meaning of the term *cause* as applied to divorce is why the couple decided to split up (for descriptions of reasons for marital breakdown see Goode, 1956; Albrecht, 1979; Kitson & Sussman, 1982). Determining the cause(s) of marriage breakdown is difficult in part because there is what "really" broke the marriage from the viewpoint of an outside observer, such as marrying at too young an age without the occupational resources to provide adequately for the couple's needs, and what the couple itself sees as the cause. Further, if both partners are studied, their perceptions of the reasons for the break may be radically at variance, as if they were talking about different marriages. Weiss (1975) calls these perceptions *accounts*—histories of the breakdown with a beginning, a middle, and an end. Accounts focus on a few dramatic events or a few factors which run through the marriage. Each partner's account of the breakdown is likely to differ. As an example, using data on the reasons given for marital breakup obtained from court-required interviews for child custody in Cleveland, Levinger (1966) reports that wives were significantly more likely to complain of physical and verbal abuse, financial problems, mental cruelty, drinking, neglect of home or children, and lack of love, while husbands were more likely to complain of in-law troubles or sexual incompatibility.

Rasmussen and Ferraro (1979) argue that causes for divorce, such as excessive drinking, financial problems, and extramarital affairs, may have existed for years in ongoing marriages but become escalated to real causes of crisis proportions when one or both partners decide they want out of the marriage. More data are needed linking self-described causes of divorce to the demographic antecedents of divorce.

THEORETICAL PERSPECTIVES

As the research cited above indicates, divorce in the United States has been studied theoretically and empirically from a variety of perspectives. These include divorce as an index of social disorganization (Faris, 1955; Pinard, 1966; Scanzoni, 1965, 1966), as an index of family disorganization or disintegration (Mowrer, 1927; Burgess & Locke, 1953; Elliot & Merrill, 1961; Kirkpatrick, 1963; Winch, 1971), as an indicator of marital maladjustment (Sprey, 1966), as an index of personal disorganization and/or pathology (Waller, 1967; Loeb & Price, 1966; Loeb, 1966; Blumenthal, 1967; Ackerman, 1969; Chester, 1971), as an index of social change (Ogburn, 1953; Goode, 1956), as a form of redefined deviance (Reiss, 1976), as a case of low cohesiveness (Levinger, 1965, 1976), as a necessary adjunct to our contemporary family system to relieve the pressure of unworkable marriages (Goode, 1956, 1966; Hunt, 1966; O'Neill, 1967; Reiss, 1976), as a strategy of conflict resolution (Scanzoni, 1965; Sprey, 1969), as dysfunctional for the individual and the family (Burgess & Locke, 1953), and also as functional for the individual and the family (Farber, 1964). The variety of often contradictory explanations highlights the important role of the social era in which research is done in focusing researchers' perspectives to a problem.

Currently the most common microexplanation of divorce is exchange theory (Levinger, 1965; 1976; Scanzoni, 1972; 1979; Scanzoni & Scanzoni, 1976; Nye et al., 1973; Nye, 1979; Lewis & Spanier, 1979). Exchange theory provides a useful model for categorizing and testing data that were previously loosely organized conceptually. From this perspective, divorce is likely when the rewards for maintaining a relationship are lower and the costs higher than those available in another relationship or by living alone. While exchange theory is commonly used as a theoretical explanation, there have been fewer empirical tests of the utility of the model. When used, such efforts have focused more on structural variables such as income, age, presence or absence of children, and employment of the wife (Levinger, 1979; Kitson et al., Note 3), rather than evaluation of intrapsychic measures (Johnson, Note 6). This may, however, illustrate the primacy of such structural variables in enabling evaluation of more personal influences to come into play. Several of these efforts (Levinger, 1979; Kitson et al., Note 3) have examined divorce versus the decision to withdraw the divorce petition. This is in part due to methodological problems of lack of comparable data on the married or on the married studied in sufficient numbers and at sufficient length to produce a large enough pool of divorces. There is a paucity of theoretical frameworks and, furthermore, few empirical attempts to test those that are available. More effort needs to be addressed to developing and testing models of "divorce proneness."

Consequences of Divorce

In this section we shall explore what happens during and after a divorce. Considerably more emphasis has been given in divorce research to the causes, or correlates, of the decision to divorce than to what happens during the separation and after the divorce. This lack of attention is probably due in part to the relative ease with which data on correlates of divorce can be obtained versus the time and expense involved in obtaining process data. Further, as we shall see, much of the research has focused on the deleterious consequences of divorce for health status with little effort expended distinguishing between adequate and inadequate adjustment to divorce.

ADJUSTMENT

While some might maintain that good adjustment to divorce is remarriage, it is our view that adjustment to divorce means an ability to develop an identity for oneself that is not tied to the status of being married or to the ex-spouse and an ability to function adequately in the role responsibilities of daily life—home, family, work, and leisure time.

HEALTH STATUS AND ADJUSTMENT

A key element in research on adjustment has been an examination
of the impact divorce has on physical and mental well-being (for
recent reviews, see Bachrach, 1975; Bloom, Asher, & White,
1978). Study after study reports that the divorced are less well
adjusted than the married or the widowed. They are more likely
to have symptoms of physical and psychological disturbance (Gurin et al., 1960; Srole et al., 1962; Langner & Michael, 1963;
Blumenthal, 1967; Bellin & Hardt, 1958; Berkman, 1969; Gove,
1972a, 1972b, 1973; Briscoe, Smith, Robins, Marten, & Gaskin,
1973; Briscoe & Smith, 1973, 1974; Rushing, 1979; Somers, 1979;
Verbrugge, 1979). But what do these findings mean? Were the
parties disturbed *before* the divorce, so psychologically disturbed
that they could not function adequately in marriage? Or, did the
process or events leading up to the divorce, the new coping skills
required, and the generally negative views society has concerning
divorce produce the frequently reported health and role inadequacies? Although these questions have been repeatedly
raised, lack of longitudinal data on the divorce process has made
the cause and effect relationship difficult to determine. The issue
is further clouded because, for some, the individual and social
causation models are likely to be correlated; that is, previously
existing psychological problems may be exacerbated by the crisis
of divorce.

A common thread in much of the divorce literature has been
not only that divorce is a negative event, but also that people who
divorce are psychologically less fit than those who do not;
"healthy" people stay married and the less healthy divorce. Some
data suggest that it may in fact be the healthier who are able to
make the break from their spouses in unsatisfactory marriages. In
a probability sample of Alameda County, California residents,
Renne (1971) found, controlling for race, sex, and age, that unhappily married persons were less healthy than divorced or happily married ones. Further, those divorced persons who remarried and considered themselves happy in their marriages reported fewer symptoms of physical or mental illness than did
unhappily married individuals who had never divorced, supporting the view that at least for some divorced persons, disturbance
was apparently exogenous, or event related.

There are clearly some people who divorce who have diagnosed
psychiatric disease which probably did contribute to their divorces

as Briscoe and Smith (1973), Briscoe et al. (1973), and Rushing (1979) demonstrate. There are others for whom divorce is likely to be a negative event with a whole series of negative consequences. For still others, while divorce is a disruptive event which produces a period of turmoil, it may in the long run lead to no change in or improved psychological functioning (Weiss, 1975; Wiseman, 1975). The proportions in each of these categories are unknown. Since most divorced people remarry, cross-sectional surveys of the relationship between marital status and health cannot address the issue accurately. A cohort of the divorced including those who remarry needs to be studied prospectively.

ROLE REDEFINITIONS

It has often been suggested (Waller, 1951, 1967; Goode, 1956, 1964; Parkes, 1972; Blau, 1973; Marris, 1974; Weiss, 1976, 1979) yet infrequently examined empirically that many of the characteristics of the process of adjusting to the loss of a spouse in divorce are similar to those in widowhood. Response to the two events differs, however, in that the role and cultural expectations established for the widow are missing for the divorcee (see Weiss, 1979, for other differences). While such role ambiguity and the greater likelihood of ambivalent feelings about the ex-spouse might be expected to lead to greater difficulties in adjustment for divorcees, life events ratings (Holmes & Rahe, 1967; Dohrenwend, Krasnoff, Askenasy, & Dohrenwend, 1978) rank being widowed as requiring more adjustment than being divorced. These rankings of events based on votes of judges may reflect the long standing stigma attached to the divorced status which leads to the belief that losing someone loved should be more distressing than losing or leaving someone about whom one's feelings are mixed. Yet, it is often such ambivalence that produces psychological and physical distress. The feeling of stigma and lack of support experienced by the divorced is illustrated in a recent report by Kitson, Lopata, Holmes, and Meyering (1980). After adjusting for the age differences of the samples used, divorcees were found to have more restricted relationships with others than do widows. The divorcees felt more like a fifth wheel, more taken advantage of, and less supported by others. Additional study on age-matched samples of the widowed and divorced would not only help to clarify the characteristics of the formerly married as a group but also highlight the differences and similarities between the widowed and divorced.

In the transition from the married to the divorced status, old roles are lost or must be transformed, and many new roles must be created and added. The accompanying norms for these new roles are often ambiguous. Bohannan (1970) suggests that in developing role redefinitions for themselves, the divorced experience six overlapping processes that vary in intensity and in order of occurrence. All must be dealt with at least on a minimal level, but eventually each must be dealt with fully. These include the emotional, legal, economic, coparental, community, and psychic divorce. In addition, individuals have often lost the habit of seeing themselves as individuals instead of as part of a couple. This is exacerbated for those who married in order to avoid becoming autonomous individuals in the first place. For these individuals, role redefinition is probably especially difficult.

On the psychological level, individuals are often blocked in developing role redefinitions, autonomy, and adjustment to the divorced status by continuing attachment to the former spouse (Weiss, 1975). This lingering attachment, or the feelings of comfort and support provided by the other, often remains after all other components of love have dissipated. In using the attachment measure described by Kitson (1981), Marroni (1977) and Hynes (1979) replicated their findings that the higher the lingering attachment for the former spouse, the higher the distress associated with the divorce. In a sample of separate persons who had contacted a marriage counseling service, Brown, Felton, Whiteman, and Manela (1980) report similar findings. Hence, lingering attachment could act as a deterrent to role redefinition and autonomy. The frequency and duration of feelings of attachment need to be further researched. While Weiss (1975) suggests that virtually all divorced persons experience continuing feelings of attachment to their ex-spouses, Spanier and Casto (1979) report that slightly over a quarter of their respondents did not evidence any signs of continuing attachment.

In summary, there has been little research involving the role redefinitions required for the shift from the married to the divorced status. In general, we do know that the lack of societal norms for the divorced status makes the transition and the accepting or forging of new norms and role redefinitions difficult, but there is little empirical research describing this process of adjustment in detail.

The studies which have been done can be grouped into two broad categories of factors affecting adjustment: (1) unchangeable factors generally outside the individual's control and (2) factors which are potentially modifiable or changeable. Until recently, most research examined factors that could not be changed, perhaps reflecting the emphasis on the individual pathology model of divorce. In both categories, the findings are inconclusive probably due to differences in the samples, measurement instruments, and methods of data collection and analysis. Below we shall examine some of the unchangeable and modifiable factors that influence divorce adjustment.

UNMODIFIABLE FACTORS INFLUENCING ADJUSTMENT

Gender. Thus far, the findings on whether males or females have more difficulty adjusting to divorce are contradictory. This is evidenced by the differences found in studies of Parents Without Partners, an organization for divorced or widowed parents (Raschke and Barringer, 1977), in which an urban sample revealed that females perceived greater distress than males, while the small town-small city sample reported the opposite. Weiss (1975), in his work on Seminars for the Separated, found no differences between males and females in experiencing distress after a separation or divorce. Chiriboga and Cutler (1977), in their random sample court record survey, report greater distress for women in the predivorce decision period. Deckert and Langelier (1978), in their convenience sample of late divorces (marriages of 20 years or longer) in Canada, discovered no difference in the reported distress between males and females in the separation period, but found females higher than males after the divorce in what they refer to as long-term divorce stress.

In a convenience sample of divorced men in which they looked for factors in marriage that affected postdivorce adjustment, White and Asher (Note 8) found postdivorce adjustment was easier for those who had not been totally emotionally dependent on their wives and for those who had established a social life which was independent of the marriage. Gove (1973), in reviewing studies of marital status and mental illness, found that divorced men have more symptoms of disturbance than women. He suggests that social supports ease adjustment and that men generally have fewer social supports than women.

Brown and Fox (1978, p. 119), in their review of sex differences in divorce adjustment, conclude that, in general, "Women experience both more situational stress and more conscious feelings of subjective distress than men during a divorce." They qualify this difference as being influenced by economic resources, custody of children, and early socialization patterns, all of which tend to be gender linked. We need more research controlling for the influence of these variables in order to determine if gender differences in adjustment to divorce really exist. In doing such research, particular attention needs to be paid to gender differences in methods of displaying distress (for a discussion of this issue in mental health research see Dohrenwend & Dohrenwend, 1976).

Children.   The findings are also inconsistent on whether having children or having custody of the children adversely affects adjustment to divorce. Goode's (1956) study of divorced mothers showed having more children associated with greater trauma, as did Pais' (1978). Two studies of members of Parents Without Partners report conflicting results. Neither females' nor males' adjustment was affected by number of children in Barringer's (1973) Iowa study, while only females' distress was unaffected in Raschke's (1974) Minnesota–Virginia study. (For a comparison of these data with those of Goode, 1956, see Raschke & Barringer, 1977.) Marroni (1977) in his Catholic sample found having more children was associated with less distress. Meyers (1976) found absence of children was related to the easiest postdivorce adjustment. These findings suggest there is some association between number of children involved in divorce and subsequent adjustment of parents. However, this relationship may be spurious as we do not know what role is played by variations in economic resources, parenting ability, social support networks, role of ex-spouse, and social and psychological attitudes toward children such as those that could be encouraged by religion and other institutions. (For recent research on children of divorce see Levitin, 1979.)

While the financial and emotional strains associated with the presence of children in divorce have been a research focus, less attention has been paid to the kinds of help, assistance, or support that children may provide for the custodial parent, thereby reducing distress. Weiss (1975) suggests that responsibility for the children may also help the parent keep going. Pais (1978) found that satisfaction with mother-child interaction was positively related to mothers' adjustment. Since women still generally obtain custody of minor children, they may constitute an adjustment asset which partially accounts for the gender differences in adjustment upon which Gove (1973) reports. The findings of Brown et al. (in press) also support this interpretation.

In general, most of the postdivorce adjustment studies find that individuals who take an active role in the divorce decision, either as the initiator or in a mutual decision, have an easier time adjusting (Goode, 1956; Blair, 1970; Raschke, 1974; Meyers, 1976; Marroni, 1977; Pais; 1978; Brown et al., 1980; Kitson, 1982; Davis, Note 9). Weiss (1975), however, did not find much difference between "the leaver" and "the left" in adjustment, but did report differences in the kinds of distress experienced by each partner, with the initiator experiencing more guilt and the party left feeling hurt and abandoned.

Divorce complaints. Weiss (1976) and Kitson and Sussman (1982) found that the type of divorce complaint affected the subsequent adjustment, with those complaints which reflect on the character of the divorced individual, such as the partner's alcoholism or marital infidelity, being more difficult to adjust to. On the other hand, Raschke (1974) found little relationship.

Length of Separation.   The time immediately preceding and following the physical separation has generally been shown to be the most difficult period with a variety of psychophysiological symptoms reported. These include headaches, dizziness, skin rashes, asthma, loss of appetite, pains in the chest and stomach, weight change, sleep difficulties, difficulty concentrating, heavier smoking and drinking, tiredness, and self-neglect. In addition, the amount of time lapsed since the physical separation is related to adjustment; the longer the time, the lower the distress and adjustment problems (Goode, 1956; Blair, 1970; Chester, 1971; Barringer, 1973; Raschke, 1974; Chiriboga & Cutler, 1977; Pais, 1978). The exceptions to this finding are Deckert and Langelier's (1978) study which found females' distress increased after the divorce, and Hetherington, Cox, and Cox's (1976) report of increased distress for both males and females two years after the divorce followed by a reduction of distress. Both of these studies, however, used nonrepresentative samples. It may be that there are differences in the characteristics of those who agreed to participate in the research. Another possible explanation is the distinction that Weiss (1975, 1976, 1979) has made between short-term and long-term adjustment difficulties: when does divorce adjustment end and the deleterious consequences of the social isolation of being single begin?

The Legal System.   It is thought (Rheinstein, 1972) that no-fault divorce decreases the amount of animosity, tension, and polarization in the divorce process thereby easing adjustment. However, the negative impact attributed to the fault-based legal system is itself brought into question by Spanier and Anderson's (1979) report that while over half of their respondents were dissatisfied with aspects of Pennsylvania's fault-based legal system, such dissatisfaction did not produce poorer divorce adjustment. Even with easier legal arrangements, we feel that for many, the divorce process itself, with its wrenches in accustomed ways of thinking and acting, its assaults on self-image, and the emotional turmoil produced by breaking up a once meaningful relationship, is likely to remain an important cause of distress. In support of this view, the research of Hill et al. (1976) on the end of cohabiting relationships illustrates the emotional impact of dissolution without any legal intervention. The key test of the impact of the legal system on adjustment is to compare and contrast responses to divorce in states with pure no-fault, mixed fault and no-fault, and fault-based legal systems.

Age and Length of Marriage.   It is difficult to disentangle the effects of age and length of marriage on adjustment since the two are generally correlated, but more work is needed on these two variables. Goode's (1956) and Blair's (1970) studies of divorced women, both based on in-depth interviews, and Pais' (1978) study, based on information from questionnaires, showed that the ending of a longer marriage produced more traumatic effects and more difficult adjustment. Chiriboga, Roberts, and Stein, (1978) found that divorced women over age 40 who had been married for longer periods of time were less happy than those under 40. On the other hand, Granvold, Pedler, and Schellie (1979), in a convenience sample, found that older women and those who had been married longer were better adjusted. Duration of marriage had no effect on adjustment or distress in the Barringer (1973) or Raschke (1974) studies.

Most studies dealing with age and adjustment find that older individuals, older women in particular, have more distress and a more difficult time adjusting than younger individuals (e.g., Goode, 1956; Blair, 1970; Barringer, 1973; Meyers, 1976; Marroni, 1977; Chiriboga et al., 1978; Pais, 1978), although the Granvold et al. (1979) study produced contradictory results. More data are needed on whether it is a lowered sense of "marketability" for remarriage or lowered self-esteem and insecurity concerning re-entering the singles scene after a long absence that accounts for these findings.

MODIFIABLE FACTORS INFLUENCING ADJUSTMENT

The second group of factors that affect adjustment are those that are potentially modifiable by the individuals themselves or by some kind of social intervention. The major research question remains: what differentiates those able to adjust adequately to divorce in a reasonable length of time from those who have more difficulty in making this major role transition? Robert Weiss (1975, 1979) follows the lead of Parents Without Partners in stating that it takes from 2 to 4 years to recover completely from a divorce. Given Glick and Norton's (1971) findings from the Economic Opportunity Survey that a quarter of the divorced remarry within a year and one-half within 3 years, continuing adjustment to divorce may be made more difficult by the changes required in a new marriage. Few cohorts of the divorced have been followed prospectively to address these issues. Research in this area is still relatively new and sparse, although there is work in progress that should give new and better insights.

Socioeconomic Status.   Most studies have found that level of education has little effect on trauma, distress, or adjustment (Goode, 1956; Barringer, 1973; Raschke, 1974; Marroni, 1977; Smith, Marder, & Kramer, Note 10). However, Everly (1978) found higher current education to be related to less conflict reaction (strain) and to an easier role transition from married to divorced. Spence and Lonner (Note 11) report that some of the women in their small study experienced difficulties with adjustment during separation. They then withdrew their divorce petitions and went back to school or obtained jobs before filing again. These data suggest that educational and occupational preparations for divorce need to be examined.

Some research has been done on the economic effects of divorce specifically on low-income mothers, perhaps because these are the women who are most likely to end up on public assistance (Kriesberg, 1970; Stack, 1974; Ross & Sawhill, 1975; Hynes, 1979; Guttentag, Salasin, Leege, & Bray, Note 15). Ross and Sawhill (1975) illustrate that AFDC payments may ease adjustment and avoid hasty remarriage by giving families some resources to get back on their feet. Income—actual amount, source, anticipated amount, and stability of income—is related to adjustment. The higher the actual amount of income, the better the adjustment and/or the lower the trauma or distress (Goode, 1956; Blair, 1970; Raschke, 1974; Marroni, 1977; Bould, 1977; Pais, 1978). The more economically independent individuals are, particularly women, the better their adjustment or the higher their sense of fate control (Raschke, 1974; Bould, 1977; Everly, 1978). Finally, Kitson and Sussman (Note 7) found that the higher the anticipated income, the lower the subjective distress. Similarly, Spanier and Lachman (1980) found greater economic stability related to better adjustment.

The perspective that divorce is something from which a person recovers rather than a permanent blotch on one's character and life treats the process as a crisis (Weiss, 1975; Wiseman, 1975). Part of the crisis model is the increasingly documented belief that structural, social, and personal characteristics can be modified or manipulated to ease life transitions (Hill, 1958; Weiss, 1975; Caplan & Killilea, 1976).

Social Support. By *social support* we mean formal and informal contacts with individuals and groups that provide emotional or material resources that may aid a person in adjusting to a crisis such as separation and divorce. Studies have found that higher social participation is correlated with lower distress, better adjustment or better coping, and personal growth (Goode, 1956; Edwards & Klemmack, 1973; Raschke, 1974; Weiss, 1975; Brown, 1976; Marroni, 1977; Hynes, 1979; Smith et al., Note 11). Goode (1956) dichotomizes social activities into those most likely to help in finding new friends and eligible partners (associated with least trauma) and those least likely to lead in these directions, e.g., women's club at church (associated with higher trauma). Weiss (1973) also discusses Parents Without Partners in terms of this dichotomy for those who find people to date through the organization and those who do not.

In most studies, higher dating activity was related to lower trauma or distress and higher adjustment (Goode, 1956; Barringer, 1973; Raschke, 1974; Hetherington et al., 1976; Spanier & Lachman, 1980; Lachman, Note 13), although for Raschke (1974) the relationship held for males only. Higher sexual permissiveness was found to be related to lower postdivorce stress by Raschke (1974) in her predominantly Protestant sample, while Marroni (1977) found no relationship in his Catholic sample. Over 90% of Hunt and Hunt's (1977) respondents in their nationwide convenience sample of divorce report postseparation or postdivorce sexual activity. Hunt and Hunt conclude that sexual activity, for the most part, has a positive influence on adjustment. Hunt's (1966) typology of sexual styles—abstainers, users (using others sexually without regard to feelings), and addicts (promiscuous sexuality)—provides a model for looking at this phenomenon further. Few research studies have examined the relationship between sexual activity and postdivorce adjustment.

The role of social supports for separated and divorced individuals is now being researched heavily although few results have actually been published. In a study of low-income single parent mothers, Hynes (1979) found higher levels of social support, provided through friends and family, organizational participation, and public agencies, to be related to lower distress. In a study of low- and moderate-income divorced mothers with a control group of married mothers, Colletta (1979) illustrates that social support and satisfaction with the degree of support provided affects child-rearing practices. Mothers with social support, generally provided by friends and family, were less punitive and less restrictive with their children than those with fewer supports. Kitson, Moir, and Mason (1982) report that provision of help by family members is related to their reported approval of the decision to divorce. Regardless of approval of the divorce decision, if other life events occur simultaneously to the divorced person, family members provide help. This reinforces the point made by Blau (1973) and Weiss (1975, 1979) concerning the continuing presence of stigma attached to the status of being divorced. Stigma may modify the amount of support and understanding provided to those experiencing marital dissolution.

Although it is assumed that counseling can aid people in adjusting to distress, we are aware of few studies that explore the relationship between counseling and adjustment to divorce. In Chiriboga, Coho, Stein, and Roberts' (1979) research, those who report high distress are more likely to seek help from a counselor, friends, or family, but this research does not demonstrate that counseling or other forms of social support lessens distress. (For data on client satisfaction with marital and divorce counseling see Brown & Manela, 1977:) Briscoe and Smith (1973) also report that a number of the divorced respondents in their study had sought counseling, but they do not report that individuals differ in adjustment as a result of having or not having received assistance. Additional research is needed to examine the impact of formal and informal types of social support on adjustment.

Psychological Resources.   Even though the interrelationships are not clear, there appears to be some dimension of internal resources, whether in the form of traditional religion or other psychological factors, that affects postseparation/divorce adjustment. For example, Brown (1976) found that having a religious affiliation enhanced personal growth, Barringer (1973) and Marroni (1977) found that higher religiosity related to better adjustment and lower distress, while Raschke (1974) found no relationship.

Other psychological characteristics that affect adjustment include gender role attitudes and dogmatism. Nontraditional and/or equalitarian gender role attitudes in divorced women have been related to more personal growth, less distress, and better adjustment (Meyers, 1976; Brown, Perry, & Harburg, 1977; Granvold et al., 1979). Higher tolerance for change and lower dogmatism (open-mindedness versus closed-mindedness) were associated with lower distress in Raschke's (1974), Marroni's (1977), and Hynes' (1979) studies. Both high anxiety and low self-esteem were related to poorer postdivorce adjustment in Blair's (1970) and Pais' (1978) research. Colletta (1979) also suggests that characteristics such as independence and self-esteem may ease adjustment. Finally, internal locus of control (as opposed to external) was associated with better adjustment in Bould's (1977) and Pais' (1978) studies. In addition, variables related to coping styles need to be examined more fully.

Conclusion

Our review has highlighted some issues that need addressing in the continuing effort to describe and predict who divorces, why, and with what consequences. We have divided our concluding comments into methodological and theoretical and substantive issues. While these two categories obviously overlap, some of the gaps in the research can begin to be addressed with greater attention to various methodological issues.

First, concepts such as adjustment and distress need to be more carefully defined and operationalized so that research can be replicated more easily. Attention also needs to be paid to potential gender biases in the kinds of mental health indicators used. For example, a focus on depression and anxiety may elicit more disturbance for divorced females, while inclusion of measures on which males score more highly, such as acting out behavior, may produce a different distribution of distress (see, for example, Dohrenwend and Dohrenwend's, 1976, review of mental health measures).

Another important sampling issue relates to the gender of divorced subjects. Despite evidence suggesting significant health disturbance among divorced males, we are aware of few in-depth studies that have examined divorced males with and, more importantly, without children. A body of literature is developing on fathering and parenting issues in divorce (cf. the special issue of *The Family Coordinator,* "Fatherhood", 1976) but not on these broader issues of relevance.

A variety of other sampling issues also need attention. Compared to many other special kinds of populations, the divorced are easy to identify. Divorce filings are public information available through county court records. While there are missing cases, losses, and duplicate filings, the samples drawn through such methods are vastly superior to those drawn through convenience methods (for early discussions of the use of court record samples, see Mowrer, 1927; Locke, 1951; Goode, 1956). Despite the relative ease of drawing representative samples of the divorced, potentially biased convenience samples continue to be widely used. This occurs in spite of the fact that even specialized representative samples can be drawn using court records. For example, it is possible to maximize the frequency of certain structural characteristics of potential interest such as age, social class, length of marriage, presence or absence of children and then to randomly draw the records of respondents from the targeted populations. County or community differences in divorce rates can also be used as a basis for selecting a sample from divorce records. Attention also needs to be paid to the cyclical variation in the number of divorces filed by month. Unless an effort is made to account for such variations, biased samples may result.

There are problems in using divorce records in that individuals are identified after they have filed for divorce. This, however, is a problem which can only be dealt with by following a sample of the married, some of whom may move into separation and divorce. Another method of doing this, which is less time consuming, is to draw a matched sample of married persons at the same time as the divorced and compare and contrast the characteristics of the two groups. Efforts must be made to improve sample quality in divorce research so that findings may be more readily and confidently generalized.

Another important methodological issue is the need to follow a cohort of the divorced over time, including their movement into new marriages. To draw conclusions about the consequences of divorce from those who remain or those who are divorced at the time of an interview is misleading at best. Furthermore, issues concerning the individual pathology, social causation, and crisis models of divorce cannot be adequately addressed without samples that include a longitudinal dimension. Prospective studies are expensive and have their own difficulties in terms of attrition and test-retest effects. One method of dealing with these issues might be to take a leaf from the models for lifespan development research. This would involve an in-depth look at certain stages in the divorce process combined with following a group of respondents for a length of time.

Although it appears that divorce is much less stigmatized than it was previously, more data on public attitudes toward marital dissolution and acceptance of divorce are needed. There is a continuing undercurrent in the literature that the divorced are still being treated as a deviant group. To the extent that this is true, such attitudes may affect the availability of resources for them to turn to and therefore, possibly, their ability to adjust.

More data on societal variations in divorce patterns comparing and contrasting adjustment patterns and the impact of differing cultural contexts would also be useful. Further use of data sources such as the Ethnographic Atlas (Murdock, 1967) and the standard cross-cultural sample (Murdock & White, 1969) would also broaden our perspective.

More attention needs to be placed on multivariate statistical techniques that look at the simultaneous and relative impact of a number of variables. These methods are useful in developing and testing models of divorce. At the same time, in an increasingly quantitatively oriented world of research, we can lose sight of the utility and necessity of carefully done qualitative research studies of the divorce process. Such research needs to be encouraged for the richness of the data and its utility in generating hypotheses.

With a growing recognition of the presence of potentially modifiable aspects of the divorce process, more efforts are needed to assess the impact of social supports, a seemingly important manipulable component. In particular, evaluations are needed of the impact of professional and self-help groups in easing adjustment. Further research is needed on the timing and efficacy of early interventions designed to ease marital strains that might otherwise lead to divorce. For example, is it possible to develop clinically useful predictors of the potential for marital instability?

Efforts need to be made to develop integrated models of the divorce process. It seems unlikely to us that the causes and consequences of divorce are unrelated to one another, yet relatively little effort is made to tie these factors together. One avenue of approach is the use of exchange theory, but other models, such as systems theory, need to be explored as well.

Finally, despite the fact that it takes two to marry and two to divorce, there is almost no research on couple adjustment to divorce. There are enormous methodological difficulties in terms of obtaining cooperation of both partners and in analyzing such correlated data, but the research payoff would appear to be tremendous, particularly for an area such as divorce which involves issues of attachment, loss, and change. If, as a system, a family is more than the sum of the parts, what happens to the participants when a split occurs? With the exception of the research of Hetherington et al. (1976, 1978) and that of Wallerstein and Kelly (1977, 1980), there are few studies that look at the interaction of all the family members, including the children. Such constellations need examination.

Another issue which the examination of marital dissolution raises is its obverse, namely, marital continuity. With all the factors and pressures that can pull a marriage apart, in some ways the more interesting issue is why and how do so many couples remain together and what distinguishes them from the divorced? Data on the frequency of marital separations and reconciliations suggest the possibility of an even greater amount of marital ambivalence and discontent than was previously thought. Despite this, what are the factors that press toward continued commitment and continuity in relationships? Well-designed divorce research can help us look at these issues as well.

REFERENCE NOTES

1. Monthly Vital Statistics Report. Provisional statistics from the National Center for Health Statistics, Births, Marriages, Divorces and Deaths for 1979, DHEW Publication No. (PHS)80-1120, *28*, 1980.
2. Glick, P. C. Personal communication, June 9, 1980.
3. Kitson, G. C., Holmes, W. M., & Sussman, M. B. *Withdrawing divorce petitions: A predictive test of the exchange model of divorce.* Unpublished manuscript, Case Western Reserve University, 1979.
4. Anderson, T. R., & Troost, K. M. *International comparisons of national divorce rates.* Paper presented at the meeting of the American Sociological Association, New York, 1976.
5. Steiner, G. Y. Family stability and income guarantees. In *The Washington COFO Memo,* 1979, *2*, 2–6.
6. Johnson, F. C. *A test of a social exchange model of marital stability.* Paper presented at the meetings of the Western Association of Sociology and Anthropology, Calgary, Alberta, Canada, 1977.
7. Kitson, G. C., & Sussman, M. B. *The processes of marital separation and divorce: Male and female similarities and differences.* Paper presented at the meetings of the American Sociological Association, New York, 1976.
8. White, S. W., & Asher, S. J. *Separation and divorce: A study of the male perspective.* Unpublished manuscript, University of Colorado, 1976.
9. Davis, J. A. *Perceptions of control over separation: A potential resource.* Research report, University of California, San Francisco, 1977.
10. Smith, J. E., Marder, C., & Kramer, P. *Marital dissolution and life satisfaction: A comparison between formerly married and never married adults.* Paper presented at the annual meetings of the Southern Sociological Society, Atlanta, 1979.
11. Spence, D. L., & Lonner, T. D. *Divorce and the life course of middle-aged women.* Paper presented at the annual meeting of the American Sociological Association, Denver, 1971.
12. Guttentag, M., Salasin, S., Legge, W. W., & Bray, H. *Sex differences in the utilization of publicly supported mental health facilities: The puzzle of depression.* Unpublished manuscript, Harvard University, 1976.
13. Lachman, M. *Dating: A coping strategy during marital separation.* Research report. University of California, San Francisco, 1977.

REFERENCES

Ackerman, N. W. Divorce and alienation in modern society. *Mental Hygiene,* 1969, *53,* 118-126.

Albrecht, S. L. Correlates of marital happiness among the remarried. *Journal of Marriage and the Family,* 1979, *41,* 857-868.

Aldous, J. *Family careers: Developmental change in families.* New York: John Wiley and Sons, 1978.

Bachrach, L. L. *Marital status and mental disorder: An analytical review.* (DHEW Publication # (ADM) 75-217). Washington, D.C.: U.S. Government Printing Office, 1975.

Barringer, K. D. *Self perception of the quality of adjustment of single parents in divorce participating in Parents-Without-Partners organizations.* Unpublished doctoral dissertation, University of Iowa, 1973.

Bauman, K. E. The relationship between age at first marriage, school dropout, and marital instability. *Journal of Marriage and the Family,* 1967, *29,* 672-680.

Bellin, S. S. and Hardt, R. H. Marital status and mental disorders among the aged. *American Sociological Review,* 1958, *23,* 155-162.

Beck, D. F. Research findings on the outcomes of marital counseling. *Social Casework,* 1975, *56,* 153-181.

Bergler, E. *Divorce won't help.* New York: Harper Bros., 1948.

Berkman, P. Spouseless motherhood, psychological stress and physical morbidity. *Journal of Health and Social Behavior,* 1969, *10,* 323-334.

Bernard, J. Marital stability and patterns of status variables. *Journal of Marriage and the Family,* 1966, *28,* 421-429.

Blair, M. Divorcee's adjustment and attitudinal changes about life. *Dissertation Abstracts International,* 1970, *30,* 5541B-5542B. (University Microfilms No. 70-11,099)

Blau, Z. *Old age in a changing society.* New York: Franklin-Watts, 1973.

Bloom, B. L., Hodges, W. F., Caldwell, R. A., Systra, L., & Cedrone, A. R. Marital separation: A community survey. *Journal of Divorce,* 1977, *1,* 7-19.

Bloom, B. L., Asher, S. J., & White, S. E. Marital disruption as a stressor: A review and analysis. *Psychological Bulletin,* 1978, *85,* 867-894.

Blumenthal, M. D. Mental health among the divorced. *Archives of General Psychiatry,* 1967, *16,* 603-608.

Bohannan, P. The six stations of divorce. In P. Bohannon (Ed.), *Divorce and after.* Garden City, New York: Doubleday, 1970.

Booth, A., & White L. Thinking about divorce. *Journal of Marriage and the Family,* 1980, *42,* 605-616.

Bould, S. Female-headed families: Personal fate control and the provider role. *Journal of Marriage and the Family,* 1977, *39,* 339-349.

Brandwein, R. A., Brown, C. A., & Fox, E. M. Women and children last: The social situation of divorced mothers and their families. *Journal of Marriage and the Family,* 1974, *36,* 498-514.

Briscoe, C. W., Smith, J. B., Robins, E., Marten, S., & Gaskin, F. Divorce and psychiatric disease. *Archives of General Psychiatry,* 1973, *29,* 119-125.

Briscoe, C. W., & Smith, J. B. Depression and marital turmoil. *Archives of General Psychiatry,* 1973, *29,* 811-817.

Briscoe, C. W., & Smith, J. B. Psychiatric illness—marital units and divorce. *Journal of Nervous and Mental Disease,* 1974, *158,* 440-445.

Brody, S. A. California's divorce reform: Its sociological implications. *Pacific Law Journal,* 1970, *1,* 223-232.

Brown, P. *Psychological distress and personal growth among women coping with marital dissolution.* Unpublished doctoral dissertation, University of Michigan, 1976.

Brown, P., & Manela, R. Client satisfaction with marital and divorce counseling. *The Family Coordinator,* 1977, *26,* 294-303.

Brown, P., Perry, L., & Harburg, E. Sex role attitudes and psychological outcomes for black and white women experiencing marital dissolution. *Journal of Marriage and the Family,* 1977, *39,* 549-561.

Brown, P., & Fox, H. Sex differences in divorce. In E. Gomberg and V. Frank (Eds.), *Gender and psychopathology: Sex differences in disordered behavior.* New York: Bruner-Mazel, 1978.

Brown, P., Felton, B. J., Whiteman, V., & Manela, R. Attachment and distress following marital
separation. *Journal of Divorce*, 1980, *3*, 303-317.
Bumpass, L. L., & Sweet, J. A. Differentials in marital instability: 1970. *American Sociologi-
cal Review*, 1972, *37*, 754-766.
Burgess, E. W., & Cottrell, L. S., Jr. *Predicting success or failure in marriage*. New York:
Prentice-Hall, 1939.
Burgess, E. W., & Locke, H. J. *The family: From institution to companionship* (2nd ed.). New
York: American Book, 1953.
Burr, W. R. *Theory construction and the sociology of the family*. New York: John Wiley and
Sons, 1973.
Campbell, A., Converse, P. E. & Rodgers, W. L. *The quality of American life: Perceptions,
evaluations and satisfactions*. New York: Russell Sage Foundation, 1976.
Caplan, G., & Killilea, M. (Eds.). *Support systems and mutual help: Multidisciplinary explorations*.
New York: Grune and Stratton, 1976.
Carter, H., & Glick, P. C. *Marriage and divorce: A social and economic study* (Rev. ed.).
Cambridge, Mass.: Harvard University Press, 1976.
Cherlin, A. Work life and marital dissolution. In G. Levinger & O. C. Moles (Eds.), *Divorce
and separation: Context, causes, and consequences*. New York: Basic books, 1979.
Chester, R. Health and marriage breakdown: Experience of a sample of divorced women.
British Journal of Preventive and Social Medicine, 1971, *25*, 231-235.
Chiriboga, D. A., & Cutler, L. Stress responses among divorcing men and women. *Journal
of Divorce*, 1977, *1*, 95-105.
Chiriboga, D. A., Roberts, J., & Stein, J. A. Psychological well-being during marital separa-
tion. *Journal of Divorce*, 1978, *2*, 21-36.
Chiriboga, D. A., Coho, A., Stein, J. A., & Roberts, J. Divorce, stress, and social supports: A
study in helpseeking behavior. *Journal of Divorce*, 1979, *3*, 121-136.
Christensen, H. T., & Meissner, H. H. Studies in child spacing: III—Premarital pregnancy
as a factor in divorce. *American Sociological Review*, 1953, *18*, 641-644.
Christensen, H. T., & Rubinstein, B. B. Premarital pregnancy and divorce: A follow-up
study by the interview method. *Marriage and Family Living*, 1956, *18*, 114-123.
Colletta, N. D. Support systems after divorce: Incidence and impact. *Journal of Marriage
and the Family*, 1979, *41*, 837-846.
Coombs, L. C., & Zumeta, Z. Correlates of marital dissolution in a prospective fertility
study: A research note. *Social Problems*, 1970, *18*, 92-102.
Crain, R. L., & Weisman, C. S. *Discrimination, personality and achievement: A survey of northern
blacks*. New York: Seminar Press, 1972.
Cutright, P. Income and family events: Marital instability. *Journal of Marriage and the Family*,
1971, *33*, 291-306.
Deckert, P., & Langelier, R. The late-divorce phenomenon: The causes and impact of
ending 20-year-old or longer marriages. *Journal of Divorce*, 1978, *1*, 381-390.
Dohrenwend, B. P., & Dohrenwend, B. S. Sex differences and psychiatric disorders. *Ameri-
can Journal of Sociology*, 1976, *81*, 1447-1454.
Dohrenwend, B. S., Krasnoff, L., Askenasy, A. R., & Dohrenwend, B. P. Exemplification
of a method for scaling life events: The PERI life events scale. *Journal of Health and Social
Behavior*, 1978, *19*, 205-229.
Edwards, J. N., & Klemmack, D. L. Correlates of life satisfaction: A re-examination.
Journal of Gerontology, 1973, *28*, 497-502.
Elliot, M. A., & Merrill, F. E. *Social disorganization* (4th ed.). New York: Harper, 1961.
Everly, K. *Leisure networks and role strain: A study of divorced women with custody*. Unpublished
doctoral dissertation, Syracuse University, 1978.
Farber, B. *Family: Organization and interaction*. San Francisco: Chandler Publishing Com-
pany, 1964.
Faris, R. E. L. *Social disorganization* (2nd ed.). New York: Ronald Press, 1955.
Farley, R., & Hermalin, A. I. Family stability: A comparison of trends among blacks and
whites. *American Sociological Review*, 1971, *36*, 1-17.
Fatherhood. *The Family Coordinator*, 1976, *25*, 335-512.
Fenelon, B. State variations in United States divorce rates. *Journal of Marriage and the
Family*, 1971, *33*, 321-327.

Ferriss, A. An indicator of marriage dissolution by marriage cohort. *Social Forces,* 1970, *48,* 356-365.

Furstenberg, F. F., Jr. Premarital pregnancy and marital instability. *Journal of Social Issues,* 1976, *32,* 67-86.

Glick, P. C., & Norton, A. J. Frequency, duration, and probability of marriage and divorce. *Journal of Marriage and the Family,* 1971, *33,* 307-317.

Glick, P. C., & Norton, A. J. Marrying, divorcing, and living together in the United States today. *Population Bulletin,* 1979, *32,* Washington, D.C.: Population Reference Bureau, Inc. (Updated reprint)

Goode, W. J. *After divorce.* New York: Free Press, 1956.

Goode, W. J. *World revolution and family patterns.* New York: Free Press, 1963.

Goode, W. J. *The Family.* Englewood Cliffs, N.J.: Prentice-Hall, Inc., 1964.

Goode, W. J. Family disorganization. In R. K. Merton & R. A. Nisbet (Eds.), *Contemporary Social Problems.* New York: Harcourt Brace and World, 1966.

Gove, W. R. Sex, marital status, and suicide. *Journal of Health and Social Behavior,* 1972, *13,* 204-213. (a)

Gove, W. R. The relationship between sex roles, marital status, and mental illness. *Social Forces,* 1972, *51,* 34-44. (b)

Gove, W. R. Sex, marital status, and mortality. *American Journal of Sociology,* 1973, *79,* 45-67.

Granvold, D. K., Pedler, L. M., & Schellie, S. G. A study of sex role expectancy and female postdivorce adjustment. *Journal of Divorce,* 1979, *2,* 383-393.

Gurin, G., Veroff, J., & Feld, S. *Americans view their mental health.* New York: Basic Books, 1960.

Gurman, A. S. The effects and effectiveness of marital therapy: A review of outcome research. *Family Process,* 1973, *12,* 145-170.

Hampton, R. L. Marital disruption: Some social and economic consequences. In J. N. Morgan (Ed.), *Five thousand American families.* (Vol. 3). Ann Arbor: Institute for Social Research, 1975.

Hampton, R. L. Husband's characteristics and marital disruption in black families. *The Sociological Quarterly,* 1979, *20,* 255-266.

Hannan, M. T., Tuma, N. B., & Groeneveld, L. P. Income and marital events: Evidence from an income-maintenance experiment. *American Journal of Sociology,* 1977, *82,* 1186-1211.

Heiss, J. On the transmission of marital instability in black families. *American Sociological Review,* 1972, *37,* 82-92.

Hetherington, E. M., Cox, M., & Cox, R. Divorced fathers. *The Family Coordinator,* 1976, *25,* 417-428.

Hetherington, E. M., Cox, M., & Cox, R. The aftermath of divorce. In J. H. Stevens, Jr. & M. Matthews (Eds.), *Mother-child, father-child relations.* Washington, D.C.: NAEYC, 1978.

Hill, C. T., Rubin, Z., & Peplau, L. A. Breakups before marriage: The end of 103 affairs. *Journals of Social Issues,* 1976, *32,* 147-168.

Hill, R. Social stresses on the family. In M. B. Sussman (Ed.), *Source-book in marriage and the family.* Boston: Houghton Mifflin, 1968 (Reprinted from *Social Casework,* 1958, *39,* 139-150).

Holmes, T. H., & Rahe, R. H. The social readjustment rating scale. *Journal of Psychosomatic Research,* 1967, *11,* 213-218.

Hunt, M. *The world of the formerly married.* New York: Fawcett World Library, 1966.

Hunt, M., & Hunt, B. *The divorce experience.* New York: McGraw-Hill, 1977.

Hutchison, I. W., & Hutchison, K. R. The impact of divorce upon clergy career mobility. *Journal of Marriage and the Family,* 1979, *41,* 847-856.

Hynes, W. J. *Single parent mothers and distress: Relationships between selected social and psychological factors and distress in low-income single parent mothers.* Unpublished doctoral dissertation, The Catholic University of America, Washington, D.C., 1979.

Kirkpatrick, C. *The family: As process and institution.* New York: Ronald Press, 1963.

Kitson, G. Attachment to the spouse in divorce: A scale and its application. *Journal of Marriage and the Family,* 1982, *44,* 379-393.

Kitson, G., Moir, R., & Mason, P. Family social support in crises: The special case of divorce. *American Journal of Orthopsychiatry,* 1982, *52,* 161-165.

Kitson, G., & Sussman, M. Marital complaints, demographic characteristics, and symptoms of mental distress in divorce. *Journal of Marriage and the Family,* 1982, *44,* 87-100.

Kriesberg, L. *Mothers in poverty: A study of fatherless families.* Chicago: Aldine Publishing Co., 1970.

Kulka, R. A., & Weingarten, H. The long-term effects of parental divorce in childhood on adult adjustment. *Journal of Social Issues,* 1979, *35,* 50-78.

Langner, T. S., & Michael, S. T. *Life stress and mental health.* New York: Free Press of Glencoe, 1963.

Lasch, C. *Haven in a heartless world: The family beseiged.* New York: Basic Books, 1977.

Levinger, G. Marital cohesiveness and dissolution: An integrative review. *Journal of Marriage and the Family,* 1965, *27,* 19-28.

Levinger, G. Sources of marital dissatisfaction among applicants for divorce. *American Journal of Orthopsychiatry,* 1966, *36,* 803-807.

Levinger, G. A social psychological perspective on divorce. *Journal of Social Issues,* 1976, *32,* 21-47.

Levinger, G. Marital cohesiveness at the brink: The fate of applications for divorce. In G. Levinger & O. C. Moles (Eds.), *Divorce and separation: Context, causes, and consequences.* New York: Basic Books, 1979.

Levitin, T. E. (Ed.), Children of Divorce. *Journal of Social Issues,* 1979, *35,* 1-186.

Lewis, R. A., & Spanier, G. B. Theorizing about the quality and stability of marriage. In W. R. Burr, R. Hill, F. I. Nye, & I. L. Reiss (Eds.), *Contemporary theories about the family* (Vol. 1). New York: The Free Press, 1979.

Locke, H. L. *Predicting adjustment in marriage: A comparison of a divorced and a happily married group.* New York: Henry Holt, 1951.

Loeb, J. The personality factor in divorce. *Journal of Consulting Psychology,* 1966, *30,* 562.

Loeb, J. and Price, J. R. Mother and child personality characteristics related to parental marital status in child guidance cases. *Journal of Consulting Psychology,* 1966, *30,* 112-117.

Marris, P. *Loss and change.* New York: Pantheon Books, 1974.

Marroni, E. L. *Factors influencing the adjustment of separated or divorced Catholics.* Unpublished master's thesis, Norfolk State College, 1977.

Meyers, J. C. *The adjustment of women to marital separation: The effects of sex-role identification and of stage in family life, as determined by age and presence or absence of dependent children.* Unpublished doctoral dissertation, University of Colorado, 1976.

Mott, F. L., & Moore, S. F. The causes of marital disruption among young American women: An interdisciplinary perspective. *Journal of Marriage and the Family,* 1979, *41,* 355-365.

Mowrer, E. R. *Family disorganization.* Chicago: University of Chicago Press, 1927.

Moynihan, D. P. The Negro family: The case for national action. In L. Rainwater & W. L. Yancey (Eds.), *The Moynihan report and the politics of controversy.* Cambridge, Mass.: The M.I.T. Press, 1967.

Mueller, C. W., & Pope, H. Marital instability: A study of its transmission between generations. *Journal of Marriage and the Family,* 1977, *39,* 83-93.

Murdock, G. P. Family stability in non-European cultures. *Annals of the American Academy of Political and Social Science,* 1950, *272,* 195-201.

Murdock, G. P. Ethnographic atlas: A summary. *Ethnology,* 1967, *6,* 109-236.

Murdock, G. P., & White, D. R. Standard cross-cultural sample. *Ethnology,* 1969, *8,* 329-369.

Norton, A. J., & Glick, P. C. Marital instability in America: Past, present, and future. In G. Levinger & O. C. Moles (Eds.), *Divorce and separation: Context, causes, and consequences.* New York: Basic Books, 1979.

Nye, F. I., White, L., & Frideres, J. A preliminary theory of marital stability: Two models. *International Journal of Sociology of the Family,* 1973, *3,* 102-122.

Nye, F. I. Choice, exchange, and the family. In W. R. Burr, R. Hill, F. I. Nye, & I. L. Reiss (Eds.), *Contemporary theories about the family* (Vol. 2). New York: The Free Press, 1979.

Ogburn, W. F. The changing functions of the family. In R. F. Winch & R. McGinnis (Eds.), *Selected studies in marriage and the family.* New York: Henry Holt, 1953.

O'Neill, W. L. *Divorce in the progressive era.* New Haven: Yale University Press, 1967.

Pais, J. S. *Social-psychological predictions of adjustment for divorced mothers.* Unpublished doctoral dissertation, University of Tennessee, Knoxville, 1978.

Pang, H., & Hanson, S. M. Highest divorce rates in western United States. *Sociology and Social Research,* 1968, *52,* 228-236.

Parkes, C. M. *Bereavement: Studies of grief in adult life.* New York: International Universities Press, Inc., 1972.

Pearson, W., Jr., & Hendrix, L. Divorce and the status of women. *Journal of Marriage and the Family,* 1979, *41,* 375–385.

Pinard, M. Marriage and divorce decisions and the larger social system: A case study of social change. *Social Forces,* 1966, *44,* 341–355.

Pope, H., & Mueller, C. W. The intergenerational transmission of marital instability: Comparisons by race and sex. *Journal of Social Issues,* 1976, *32,* 49–66.

Raschke, H. J. *Social and psychological factors in voluntary postmarital dissolution adjustment.* Unpublished doctoral dissertation, University of Minnesota, Minneapolis, 1974.

Raschke, H. J. The role of social participation in postseparation and postdivorce adjustment. *Journal of Divorce,* 1977, *1,* 129–139.

Raschke, H. J., & Barringer, K. D. Two studies in postdivorce adjustment among persons participating in Parents-Without-Partners organizations. *Family Perspective,* 1977, *11,* 23–34.

Rasmussen, P. K., & Ferraro, K. J. The divorce process. *Alternative Lifestyles,* 1979, *2,* 443–460.

Reiss, I. L. *Family systems in America* (2nd ed.). Hinsdale, IL.: The Dryden Press, 1976.

Renne, K. Health and marital experience in an urban population. *Journal of Marriage and the Family,* 1971, *33,* 338–350.

Rheinstein, M. *Marriage stability, divorce, and the law.* Chicago: The University of Chicago Press, 1972.

Rosow, I., & Rose, K. D. Divorce among doctors. *Journal of Marriage and the Family,* 1972, *34,* 587–598.

Ross, H. L., & Sawhill, I. V. *Time of transition: The growth of families headed by women.* Washington, D.C.: The Urban Institute, 1975.

Rushing, W. A. Marital status and mental disorder: Evidence in favor of a behavioral model. *Social Forces,* 1979, *58,* 540–556.

Scanzoni, J. A reinquiry into marital disorganization. *Journal of Marriage and the Family,* 1965, *27,* 483–491.

Scanzoni, J. Family organization and the probability of disorganization. *Journal of Marriage and the Family,* 1966, *28,* 407–411.

Scanzoni, J. A social system analysis of dissolved and existing marriages. *Journal of Marriage and the Family,* 1968, *30,* 452–461.

Scanzoni, J. *Sexual bargaining: Power politics in the American marriage.* Englewood Cliffs: Prentice-Hall Spectrum, 1972.

Scanzoni, J. A historical perspective on husband-wife bargaining power and marital dissolution. In G. Levinger & O. C. Moles (Eds.), *Divorce and separation: Context, causes, and consequences.* New York: Basic Books, 1979.

Scanzoni, L., & Scanzoni, J. *Men, women and change.* New York: McGraw-Hill, 1976.

Schoen, R., Greenblatt, H. N., & Mielke, R. B. California's experience with non-adversary divorce. *Demography,* 1975, *12,* 223–243.

Sell, K. Divorce law reform and increasing divorce rates in the United States. In J. G. Wells (Ed.), *Current issues in marriage and the family,* 2nd ed. New York: Macmillan, 1979.

Somers, A. R. Marital status, health, and use of health services. *Journal of the American Medical Association,* 1979, *241,* 1818–1822.

Spanier, G. B., & Anderson, E. A. The impact of the legal system on adjustment to marital separation. *Journal of Marriage and the Family,* 1979, *41,* 605–613.

Spanier, G. B., & Casto, R. F. Adjustment to separation and divorce: A qualitative analysis. In G. Levinger & O. C. Moles (Eds.), *Divorce and separation: Context, causes, and consequences.* New York: Basic Books, 1979.

Spanier, G., & Lachman, M. Factors associated with adjustment to marital separation. *Sociological Focus,* 1980, *13,* 369–381.

Sprey, J. Family disorganization: Toward conceptual clarification. *Journal of Marriage and the Family,* 1966, *28,* 398–406.

Sprey, J. The family as a system in conflict. *Journal of Marriage and the Family,* 1969, *31,* 699–706.

Srole, L., Langner, T. A., Michael, S. T., Opler, M. K., & Rennie, T. A. C. *Mental health in the metropolis: The midtown study* (Vol. 1). New York: McGraw-Hill Book Co., 1962.

Stack, C. B. *All our kin: Strategies for survival in a black community.* New York: Harper and Row, 1974.

Stetson, D. M., & Wright, G. C., Jr. The effects of laws on divorce in American states. *Journal of Marriage and the Family*, 1975, *37*, 537–547.

Udry, J. R. Marital instability by race, sex, education, and occupation using 1960 census data. *American Journal of Sociology*, 1966, *72*, 203–209.

Udry, J. R. Marital instability by race and income based on 1960 census data. *American Journal of Sociology*, 1967, *72*, 673–674.

U.S. Bureau of the Census. Number, timing, and duration of marriages and divorces in the United States: June 1975. *Current Population Reports*, Series P-20, No. 297, Washington, D.C.: U.S. Government Printing Office, 1976.

U.S. Bureau of the Census. Marital status and living arrangements: March, 1976. *Current Population Reports*, Series P-20, No. 306. Washington, D.C.: U.S. Government Printing Office, 1977.

Verbrugge, L. M. Marital status and health. *Journal of Marriage and the Family*, 1979, *41*, 267–285.

Waller, W. *The family: A dynamic interpretation* (Revised by R. Hill). New York: Holt, Rinehart, and Winston, 1951.

Waller, W. *The old love and the new: Divorce and readjustment.* New York: Liveright, 1930. (Reprint, Carbondale: So. Illinois University Press, 1967.)

Wallerstein, J. S., & Kelly, J. B. Divorce counseling: A community service for families in the midst of divorce. *American Journal of Orthopsychiatry*, 1977, *47*, 4–22.

Wallerstein, J. S., & Kelly, J. B. *Surviving the breakup: How children and parents cope with divorce.* New York: Basic Books, 1980.

Weiss, R. S. The contributions of an organization of single parents to the well-being of its members. *The Family Coordinator*, 1973, *22*, 321–326.

Weiss, R. S. *Marital separation.* New York: Basic Books, 1975.

Weiss, R. S. The emotional impact of marital separation. *Journal of Social Issues*, 1976, *32*, 135–145.

Weiss, R. S. *Going it alone: The family life and social situation of the single parent.* New York: Basic Books, 1979.

Winch, R. F. *The modern family* (3rd ed.). New York: Holt, Rinehart and Winston, 1971.

Winch, R. F., with Blumberg, R. L., Garcia, M. P., Gordon, M. T., & Kitson. G. C. *Familial organization: A quest for determinants.* New York: The Free Press, 1977.

Wiseman, R. S. Crisis theory and the process of divorce. *Social Casework*, 1975, *56*, 205–212.

Wright, G. C., Jr., & Stetson, D. M. The impact of no-fault divorce law reform on divorce in American states. *Journal of Marriage and the Family*, 1978, *40*, 575–580.

There is little current or systematic information concerning the nature of relationships between former spouses who continue to share child rearing. In this study, based on a General Systems Theory paradigm, 129 former spouses in mother-custody postdivorce families participated in an in-depth, semistructured interview. Descriptive findings on multiple dimensions of former spousal relationships, from the perspectives of both male and female members of the divorced couple, are presented. The former spousal relationship emerges as a vital component of the reorganized, postdivorce family system.

12

RELATIONSHIPS BETWEEN FORMER SPOUSES

Descriptive Findings

Jean Goldsmith

The relationship between former spouses who continue to share child rearing responsibilities has recently emerged as a critical variable in understanding postdivorce family functioning (Hetherington et al., 1976; Wallerstein & Kelly, 1975). This new focus may be accounted for by changes in the conceptualization of postdivorce families. Initially, such families were essentially defined as single-parent; both research and treatment consequently focused on the mother-child dyad (Biller, 1974). With increased recognition of shared parenting postdivorce, the paradigm was altered to accommodate the noncustodial parent (usually father) and the father-child dyad (Keshet & Rosenthal, 1978). Only recently have researchers and clinicians recognized that the mother-father dyad may also

Jean Goldsmith, PhD is a faculty member, Center for Family Studies and Assistant Professor, Department of Psychiatry and Behavioral Sciences, Northwestern University Medical School, Ten East Huron, Chicago, IL 60611.
This is a revised version of a paper presented at the National Council on Family Relations meetings, Boston, 1979. Data reported here were collected in 1978. Data analysis was supported in part by Grant RR-05370 from the U.S. Public Health Service, National Institutes of Health. The author gratefully acknowledges Constance Ahrons for her contribution to the design of the study; Gary Bond for data analysis consultation; Alan Tepp and Nydia Welles for research assistance; and Gary Bond, Larry Feldman, William Pinsof, Alan Tepp, and Mary Zaglifa for their helpful feedback on this paper.

be a vital component of the reorganized postdivorce family when parenting is shared.

There is, however, little current or systematic information concerning the nature of former spousal relationships. In the absence of this information [what Mead (1977) has termed an "information vacuum"], former spouses face the formidable task of terminating their marital relationship while reorganizing their relationship to one another as parents, without knowing how this is accomplished by others in similar circumstances. In a pilot study with former spouses (Ahrons & Goldsmith, 1978), the most frequently registered concern was the lack of knowledge about how other divorced parents were working out this relationship. Moreover, an increasing number of professionals who are attempting to help parents develop satisfactory postdivorce relationships do so with little information on what, in fact, constitutes normative behavior for this population.

This paper addresses the need for knowledge concerning the nature of former spousal relationships in which both persons continue to participate in child rearing. It is the first report of a study of such relationships based on a General Systems Theory paradigm (Buckley, 1968). This paradigm has been successful in guiding research and intervention (Weiting, 1976) with "married" families. Within it, divorce is seen as a crisis in the life cycle of a family which results in reorganization of the original family system, but not necessarily in its dissolution. When the two adults divorce as spouses, but continue to share child rearing functions, members of the original family, *including both former spouses*, still function as a self-regulating system, although the characteristics (e.g., rules, roles, functions, etc.) of the system will (probably) have been altered. Among other things, this means that the members of the original family continue to be interdependent (mother's behavior affects father, and vice versa), and that the relationships developed within any two-member subsystem, including the former spousal dyad, can be expected to have repercussions throughout the family. The present study focused on the former spousal subsystem within the overall postdivorce family system.

This paper presents descriptive findings for multiple dimensions of former spousal relationships including frequency, content, and quality of the interaction and of the feelings and attitudes which former spouses have toward one another. The dimensions selected for examination were those reported by previous investigators as relevant to an understanding of postdivorce family functioning. For this study, the coparental divorce (Bohannan, 1971), described as one of the most difficult tasks facing divorcing/ divorced adults, was defined as involving two kinds of relationships: the relationship that each parent develops with the children (parent-child) and that which former spouses develop with one another about the children (the coparental relationship). This distinction was necessary because, for example, father and mother may spend equal amounts of time with their children while having little to do with one another, or the divorced parents may actively plan for or talk about the children even though the noncustodial parent may spend little time directly with them. With regard to the parent-child relationship, continued access to both parents has been found to have a positive influence on children's adjustment to divorce (Wallerstein & Kelly, 1975). There is little agreement, however, on what the ideal kind of interaction is with regard to the frequency and content of the coparental relationship (Suarez et al., 1978; Goldstein et al., 1973). On the other hand, there is consensus that a successful coparental relationship involves mutual support and cooperation between former spouses and has optimal impact on postdivorce adjustment of family members, particularly children (Kressel & Deutsch, 1977).

Not only do former spouses maintain coparental relationships, but they may also continue to relate to one another in ways that have nothing to do with the parenting function. Such relating may range from friendly or "kin" type interaction to more romantic involvements. There have been contradictory interpretations of such relationships; some view this relating as a healthy outcome of the divorce process, and others view it as a pathological inability to separate (Kressel & Deutsch, 1977). Certainly, both coparental and nonparental role relationships must be examined to provide a complete description of the divorced couple relationship.

In addition to overt interaction, former spouses are expected to experience continued feelings toward one another as part of an emotional process following separation and divorce (Weiss, 1975). There is considerable agreement that termination of a marriage may be accompanied by a corresponding set of feelings toward the separated spouse which may include hostility, caring, guilt, and preoccupation or pining. Maintaining these feelings is expected not only to affect individual adjustment (Kitson & Sussman, 1976), but also to influence overt interaction with the former spouse (Weiss, 1975).

The present study investigates former spousal relationships from the perspectives of both members of divorced couples who are involved in the most common postdivorce custody situation, in which the mother has custody of the children. Thus, it yields information relevant to the as yet unresolved question of whether the divorce experience is a "human" phenomenon experienced in a similar way irrespective of sex (Weiss, 1975) or whether men and women experience their divorce in different ways, e.g., the woman perceived as the victim (Goode, 1956). Additionally, it sheds light on the issue of whether, as recent research would indicate (Keshet & Rosenthal, 1978), the role of the noncustodial father carries with it greater difficulties and dissatisfactions than that of the custodial mother. Lastly, it permits examination of whether there is consensus among former spouses in perceptions of their relationships or whether one must describe "his" and "her" divorces in the same way that others have described "his" and "her" marriages (Bernard, 1972).

The following research questions regarding the nature of relationships between former spouses who continue to participate in child rearing provided the basis for the present paper:

1. To what extent are parenting tasks shared, that is, how extensive is the noncustodial father's involvement with his children?
2. To what extent does divorce result in termination of the relationship between former spouses; specifically, what is the frequency, content, and quality of their involvement in terms of both coparental and nonparental relationships?
3. To what extent do former spouses maintain various kinds of feelings toward one another?
4. To what extent are there differences in perceptions and experiences between female members of divorced couples who have custody and male members who do not?

Method

SAMPLING PROCEDURE

Divorced couples were selected to participate in the study on the basis of the following criteria: (a) they were divorced approximately one year prior to sampling period; (b) mother was granted custody of the children, and the minor children lived with her; (c) former spouses lived within 2-1/2 hours (by ground transportation) of each other; (d) father saw the child at least once during the 2 months preceding the sampling period; (e) former spouses had not remarried one another and did not live in the same dwelling; (f) they were both Caucasian. These criteria were selected to permit assessment of the former spousal relationship after the initial family disequilibrium was over and to generate a sample likely to represent the most common divorced family form (Hetherington et al., 1976).

The names of 225 divorced couples were randomly selected from the Divorce Division records of the Circuit Court of Cook County, Illinois, a demographically heterogeneous major urban area including the city of Chicago. Names were selected from pro-

gressive months of the year to keep the 1-year postdivorce time period constant as interviewing progressed, and to minimize the likelihood that the data would be specific to
people divorced in one particular month or time of year. This sampling method has
proved feasible in prior studies (Kitson & Sussman, 1976; Cohen, 1977) and has the
advantage of avoiding biases inherent in samples restricted to specific groups, e.g.,
"Parents Without Partners," or to people volunteering for clinical and educational
programs.

A letter requesting participation in the study with an accompanying letter of support
by the presiding judge of the Circuit Court was followed up one week later with a telephone call from an interviewer. Both members of each divorced couple were contacted
whenever possible; however, individual members were interviewed whether their
former spouses did or did not participate. Thus, the sample included couples where
the perspective of each member could be obtained, as well as couples with only one
member responding. Although this sampling strategy added to the complexity of the results, it made possible identification of potential sources of bias resulting from restricting a sample to only those divorced couples where both members were willing to
participate.

INTERVIEW PROCEDURE

Each former spouse participated in an individual interview procedure developed in extensive pilot work and conducted in the interviewee's home.[1] The interviews ranged in
time from between 1-1/4 hour to over 2 hours in length. The format of the interview involved both open-ended and closed-ended questions, a modified Q-Sort procedure, and
a paper and pencil test. Where response choices to questions exceeded three, a card list
of response choices was presented to the respondent to reduce possibility of error due to
memory loss and to facilitate speed of the interview. Card lists utilized both likert-type
responses and multiple-choice selections. The order of choices was varied to reduce response bias. Questions were based on modification and extension of the work of prior
investigators (Cohen, 1977; Hetherington et al., 1976; Goode, 1956) and included an
attachment index (Kitson & Sussman, 1976).

The interviewers were male and female Caucasians having at least a bachelor's degree in a mental health field and at least minimal clinical experience. Interviewers were
randomly assigned, subject to the condition that both members of a divorced couple
would not be seen by the same interviewer. A detailed interview guide developed in
pilot work was used to train interviewers.

Interview items were designed to elicit the characteristics of former spousal relationships which have been described by previous investigators as relevant to an understanding of postdivorce family functioning. Items were grouped a priori into the following
categories: (a) amount and content of coparental communication; (b) quality of the coparental relationship (mutual support and cooperation); (c) amount and content of
nonparental relating; (d) amount and content of father's involvement in child rearing;
(e) feelings of attachment, hostility, caring, guilt toward the former spouse and attitude
toward the former spouse as a parent.

---

[1]The interview was developed in collaboration with Constance R. Ahrons, PhD.

SAMPLE OBTAINED

Of the 225 divorced couples selected from the court records, 56 couples (25%) did not meet one or more of the selection criteria, as determined during the initial telephone call, and they were, therefore, excluded from the study. Nineteen of these couples were excluded because the father did not maintain contact with the children. Of the remaining 169 eligible couples: 85 (50.3%) had one or both members participating; both members of six couples (3.5%) refused; in 29 couples (17.2%), one member refused while the other could not be contacted; and neither member of 49 couples (29%) could be contacted. The main reasons for being unable to contact former spouses were incorrect or unavailable addresses and telephone numbers. A greater number of females (77) than males (52) participated in the study. The larger percentage of males that could not be contacted (50.3%), as compared to females (36.7%), accounted for this difference: The refusal rates among contacted males and females were approximately equal.

To assess sample bias, comparisons of demographic variables were drawn between the interviewed group of divorced couples and the group of couples where neither member was interviewed. Data derived from court records was used for this purpose. As can be seen in Table 1, the interviewed sample was older, had been married longer, and was better educated than the noninterviewed sample. However, when the interviewed sample was broken down into couples where both members were interviewed (both-member interviewed) and those where only one member was interviewed (one-member interviewed), there were no significant differences between the one-member interviewed group and no-member interviewed group. Thus, while the both-member interviewed group provided the most complete and heterogeneous sample, the one-member interviewed group was more representative of the divorced couple population as a whole. For the sake of brevity and clarity, this report will present results based on the couples where both members were interviewed. It will then evaluate generalizability by comparing results obtained from the one-member interviewed couples to determine whether there were significant differences.

MEASURE DEVELOPMENT

As can be seen in Table 2, reliability and validity were evaluated for each of nine scales (eight of which were newly constructed for this study) measuring the dimensions of the relationships between former spouses as defined a priori. Internal consistency reliability was evaluated for each scale, and a Cronbach's alpha coefficient of .80 or above was

TABLE 1. COMPARISON OF INTERVIEWED TO NON-INTERVIEWED COUPLES ON DEMOGRAPHIC VARIABLES
          OBTAINED FROM COURT RECORDS

Demographic characteristics	Mean for Divorced Couples			Tests of significance between interviewed (N=85) & non-interviewed (N = 84) groups
	Both-member interviewed N = 44	One-member interviewed N = 41	No-member interviewed N = 84	
Length of marriage (years)	14	11	10	t = 7.4*
Age of adult male (years)	40	37	35	t = 2.6*
Age of adult female (years)	37	34	32	r = 2.8*
Males having some college educ. (%)	55	36	32	x^2 = 4.8*
Females having some college educ. (%)	55	40	28	x^2 = 6.8*
Number of children under 18	2	2	2	t = .004

*$p < .01$

TABLE 2. MEASURES OF THE RELATIONSHIP BETWEEN FORMER SPOUSES (F.S.): RELIABILITY AND VALIDITY

Scale name	Example of scale item[a]	Number of items	Reliability coefficient N = 129	Correlations between f.s. reports N = 44 couples	Correlations between self-report of feeling and f.s. perception of feeling	
					Male self-report N = 44 couples	Female self-report N = 44 couples
Amount of coparental communication	Has discussing your child's school or medical problems been shared between you and your f.s.?	10	.93	.71***	--	--
Quality of coparental relationship Support subscale	Would you say that your f.s. is a resource to you in raising the children?	10	.87	.54***	--	--
		5	.82	.51***	--	--
Conflict subscale	When you & your f.s. discuss parenting, how often does an argument result?	4	.85	.35*	--	--
Amount of non-parental relating	In the past several months how often have you & your f.s. talked about old friends in common?	13	.86	.73***	--	--
Amount of father involvement in child rearing	How involved is father in running errands with/for the children?	10	.90	.73***	--	--
Attachment (Kitson & Sussman, 1976)	I find myself wondering what my f.s. is doing.	4	.81	--	.63***	.30*
Hostile feelings	I want revenge for wrongs done to me.	8	.86	--	.57***	.43**
Caring feelings	I have warm feelings for my f.s.	4	.83	--	.50***	.35*
Guilt feelings	I wish I could make up for the hurt I've caused him/her.	4	.82	--	.24	.15
Attitude that f.s. is a good parent	My f.s. is an irresponsible parent.	4	.91	--	.45**	.62***

[a]Each item was rated on a 5 point scale (1 = always, to 5 = never) except Amount of non-parental relating items which were rated on a 6 point scale (1 = daily, to 6 = never). * = $p < .05$, ** = $p < .01$, *** = $p < .001$

TABLE 3. DESCRIPTION OF BOTH-MEMBER INTERVIEWED COUPLES ON BACKGROUND VARIABLES

Background Variable	Percentage		
	Divorced Couples[a]	Female Former Spouses	Male Former Spouses
Divorce History			
Number of Separations			
One	74	--	--
More than one	26	--	--
Grounds for Divorce			
Mental Cruelty	82	--	--
Physical Cruelty	2	--	--
Adultery	0	--	--
Desertion	16	--	--
Court Visits Subsequent to Divorce			
Yes	14	--	--
No	86	--	--
Decision Regarding the Divorce			
Wife Decided	61	--	--
Mutual Decision	12	--	--
Husband Decided	27	--	--
Family Composition			
Sex of Child			
Male Child	73	--	--
Female Child	77	--	--
Age of Child			
Pre-school Age (1-5)	25	--	--
Latency Age (6-12)	61	--	--
Adolescent Age (13-18)	57	--	--
Young Adult Age (19-23)	23	--	--
Total Yearly Income[b]			
0,000 to 9,999	--	51	7
10,000 to 19,999	--	40	34
20,000 to 29,999	--	7	37
Over 30,000	--	2	22
Occupation[c]			
Professional, Technical, etc.	--	25	25
Managers & Administrators	--	5	29
Sales	--	5	14
Clerical	--	39	2
Craftsman	--	0	18
Service Workers	--	14	5
Transport Equipment Operatives	--	0	5
Housewife	--	6	0
Unemployed	--	6	2
Current Marital Status			
Remarried	--	14	16
Therapy Experience			
Obtained therapy or counseling			
(individual, group, or couple)	--	67	53

[a]As there were no significant sex differences at the .05 level, couple percentages are based on female respondents' reports.

[b]Men reported significantly higher income levels than women ($\underline{t}$ (43) = 6.9, p $<$ .001).

[c]Based on 1970 Census of Population, Alphabetical Index of Industries & Occupations, Washington, D. C., U. S. Govt. Printing Office, 1977.

used as a criterion indicating that internal consistency reliability had been achieved. The nine scales mentioned above achieved the criterion level for internal consistency, with reliability coefficients between .82 and .93.

Preliminary evaluation of validity was also undertaken and was supported for each scale except Guilt feelings. For the scales measuring amount and quality of coparental communication, amount of nonparental communication, and father involvement in child rearing, evaluation of validity was made by comparing former spouses' perceptions. As shown in Table 2, correlations between former spouses' reports were all highly significant and provided support for the validity of the scales. For the scales measuring feelings and attitudes toward the former spouse, evaluation was made of the congruence between self-report of feelings and former spouses' perception of those feelings. There were significant correlations between feelings and attitudes and former spouses' perception of same for every scale except Guilt feelings.

Findings based on these scales are presented in the Results section. In addition, for descriptive purposes, findings for specific items are also reported. To simplify data presentation, when analyses yielded no significant differences on the basis of sex, an average item score for former spouses (male and female) is presented. Moreover, the responses to items are grouped according to endorsement (a rating of always, usually, or sometimes) and nonendorsement (a rating of rarely or never) to maximize clarity of presentation.

Results

BACKGROUND VARIABLES

Table 3 presents a description of the both-member interviewed couple sample through a number of relevant background variables. Of particular note are the results indicating that it was primarily the women who decided to divorce rather than the men, and that few decisions were mutual. The congruence between former spouses' perceptions of the decision-making process ($r = .84$, $p < .001$) supports the validity of this information.

AMOUNT OF FATHER PARTICIPATION IN CHILD REARING

How much and in what way is the noncustodial father involved with his children after divorce? Results indicate that the answer depends on whom you ask: Fathers report that they are significantly more involved with their children than mothers report them to be ($t(43) = 4.3$, $p < .001$). This perception is consistent across all 12 areas assessed (see Table 4). In terms of actual frequency of father-child contact, 42% of fathers report that they see their children at least twice weekly, but only 17% of mothers report this same frequency. Perceptions of length of visits, however, are not significantly different (60% of visits are all day or less and 40% are overnight or more).

As can be seen in Table 4, the amount of father-child involvement reported by both sexes varies with the specific child rearing area; celebrating holidays and special events is the most frequent area of involvement. While the vast majority (91%) of divorced parents feel that it is important for the father to stay involved with the child, one half still feel that his fre-

TABLE 4. FATHER'S PARTICIPATION IN CHILD REARING: MOTHER vs. FATHER REPORTS

Area of father-child involvement[a]	% of mothers reporting father very much, much, or somewhat involved N = 44	Rank order from most to least involved	% of fathers reporting father very much, much, or somewhat involved N = 44	Rank order from most to least involved
Celebrating significant events	82	1.0	86	2.0
Celebrating holidays	76	2.0	89	1.0
Recreational activities	59	3.0	74	4.0
Discussing problems	56	4.0	81	3.0
Vacations	45	5.0	56	6.0
School or church functions	44	6.0	55	7.0
Religious or moral training	36	7.5	52	8.0
Running errands	36	7.5	48	9.0
Discipline	35	9.0	57	5.0
Dress and grooming	16	10.0	47	10.0
Mean percentage	48.5		64.6	

[a]Each item was rated on a 5 point scale (1 = very much, 2 = much, 3 = somewhat, 4 = little, 5 = not at all).

quency and manner of involvement make the father "like a visitor in the children's lives." Half of the divorced parents feel satisfied with this situation; half have mixed feelings or are dissatisfied. There were no significant differences between mothers and fathers in their satisfaction.

AMOUNT AND CONTENT OF COPARENTAL COMMUNICATION

Unlike the findings for father-child involvement, there are no significant differences in mothers' and fathers' perceptions of the amount of involvement they maintain with one another as parents ($t (43) = .9, p > .05$). Former spouses generally do maintain a continuing relationship to one another as parents: 84% of them report telephone and/or in-person contact about child rearing issues. Just over half communicate with one another three times a month or more, and the contact is generally of fairly short duration (70% spend 15 minutes or less on the average). Although former spouses in general do maintain a coparental relationship, there is wide variation among divorced couples in their amount of involvement. For example, while 19% of couples communicate with one another quite frequently, i.e., twice a week or more, 16% do not communicate at all.

As can be seen in Table 5, the majority of former spouses continue, to some extent, to share, discuss, and plan most child rearing events, joys, and responsibilities with one another. The amount of coparental communication, however, varies with the child rearing area involved. Although the majority of divorced parents do communicate with one another about most child rearing matters, at least some of the time, school and/or medical problems initiate the highest frequency of communication between the divorced parents. Other child rearing areas, such as everyday decisions involving the children, are much less likely to be shared.

In addition to communicating about child rearing issues, the majority (55%) of divorced couples also report that, on occasion, they do spend time with one another *and* with the children together as a "family." These tend to be special occasions (birthdays, Christmas), periodic outings (museum, dinner), school or church functions, and visits to grandparents, e.g., "Tonight we are all having dinner together with both grandmothers to celebrate one grandmother's birthday."

While the majority of former spouses of both sexes are satisfied with the amount of coparental communication between them, there are significant differences in amount of satisfaction between male and female former spouses (t (43) = 2.1, $p < .05$). The noncustodial father is more dissatisfied than the custodial mother: 41% of fathers are dissatisfied as compared to 20% of mothers. The consistent reason given for dissatisfaction on the part of both sexes is that more interest and involvement is desired from the other parent. The noncustodial fathers, in particular, express feelings of dissatisfaction that stem from a sense of being excluded from knowledge about their children by their former wife, e.g., "I feel shut out. I don't know what is happening in my children's lives."

QUALITY OF THE COPARENTAL RELATIONSHIP

Regarding the extent to which former spouses maintain a mutually supportive and cooperative coparental relationship with one another, there are no significant differences between males and females in mean ratings

TABLE 5. AMOUNT AND CONTENT OF COPARENTAL COMMUNICATION BETWEEN FORMER SPOUSES (F.S.)

Child rearing areas that F.S.s discuss, plan or share[a]	% rating always, usually or sometimes N = 88	Rank order from most to least communication
School and/or medical problems	77	1
Child's progress and accomplishments	70	2
Child's personal problems	63	3
Major decisions	58	5
Special events	58	5
Finances	58	5
Problems raising the children	54	7
Problems with coparenting	44	8
Child's adjustment ot divorce	40	9
Day to day decisions	23	10
Mean % for all child rearing areas	54.5	

[a]Each item was rated on a 5 point scale (1 = always, 2 = usually, 3 = sometimes, 4 = rarely, 5 = never).

TABLE 6. PERCEIVED QUALITY (COOPERATION AND MUTUAL SUPPORT) OF DIVORCED COPARENTAL
          RELATIONSHIPS

Characteristics of the coparental relationship between former spouses (f.s.)[a]	% rating always, usually, or sometimes N = 88	Rank order from most to least characteristic
You are willing to accommodate to f.s.'s needs	95	1
You side with the children against f.s.	87	2
You are a resource to f.s. in child rearing	79	3
F.s. is willing to accommodate to your needs	78	4
There are arguments	76	5
There is an atmosphere of hostility	73	6
You and f.s. have basic differences of opinion	71	7
Conversation is stressful	67	8
F. s. is supportive to your needs	64	9
F. s. is a resource in child rearing	49	10
You seek help from f.s. in child rearing	48	11

[a]Each item was rated on a 5 point scale (1 = always, 2 = usually, 3 = sometimes, 4 = rarely, 5 = never).

of quality of their coparental relationships (t (43) = .08, p > .05). As seen in Table 6, three quarters of divorced parents describe their relationships as conflictual, stressful, or involving basic differences of opinion in child rearing. Divorced parents also perceive their relationships as mutually supportive, at least some of the time, but both sexes describe themselves as more accommodating, resourceful to, and supportive of their former spouses than they describe their former spouses as being toward them.

Divorced fathers are significantly less satisfied with the quality of their coparental relationships than are divorced mothers (t (43) = 2.7, p < .01); 51% of the men, in contrast to 19% of the women, report that they are dissatisfied. Common problems reported by both sexes are disagreements and arguments about raising children, problems with how the other parent "uses" the child (e.g., as a go-between or to get back at the other parent), problems with how the other parent relates to the child, problems with former spouse's personality (e.g., "too immature"), living arrangements (e.g., lives with friend of opposite sex), and competition with the other parent. Problems raised exclusively by mothers include the father spoiling the children and lack of support and caring from the father. Problems reported exclusively by men include lack of input into, and control over, the child rearing process because of the former spouse.

While problems are common among divorced parents, it would appear that a small subgroup of former spouses perceive themselves as having developed high quality divorced coparenting relationships. Several spontaneously report that they have what they would call an ideal relationship with their former spouse. Moreover, based on items on the "Quality" scale, 13% report that their parenting relationships are supportive and cooperative almost all of the time.

NONPARENTAL RELATIONSHIP

There are no significant differences in mean amount of nonparental relating reported by males and females (t (43) = 1.4, p > .05). As seen in Table 7, continued interaction between former spouses in areas that do not involve child rearing is common, but is restricted to certain ways of maintaining contact and not others. Friendly or "kin" type contacts (e.g., talking about family other than children) are maintained by the majority of divorced couples. It is unusual for a couple not to maintain this type of contact. Romantic sexual involvement, however, is quite unusual; for example, no former spouses report that they continue to have sexual intercourse with one another.

There are no significant differences in mean satisfaction with the nonparental relationship between males and females (t (43) = .10, p > .05). The majority of former spouses of both sexes report that they are *not* satisfied with this aspect of their relationship. The reasons for dissatisfaction, however, differ; some former spouses report dissatisfaction because they want more contact and more intense involvement, but others because they desire less contact and involvement.

FEELINGS AND ATTITUDES TOWARD THE FORMER SPOUSE

There are no significant (p > .05) differences in feelings of attachment, hostility, caring, and guilt between male and female former spouses (t (43) = 1.6, .12, .76, and 1.6, respectively). Out of 20 statements describing possible feelings toward one's former spouse, five statements are reported by a majority of both sexes as, in fact, reflecting their own feelings. Com-

TABLE 7. AMOUNT AND CONTENT OF NON-PARENTAL INVOLVEMENT

Area of involvement[a]	% involved in these areas in the past several months	Rank order from most to least involvement
Talking about your families (not children)	89	1.0
Talking about friends	64	2.5
Talking about new experiences	64	2.5
Discussing finances not related to the children	57	4.0
Talking about your past marriage	48	5.0
Talking about personal problems	44	6.0
Talking about why you got divorced	36	7.0
Helping each other with household tasks	35	8.0
Physical contact without sexual intercourse	25	9.0
Talking about reconciling	10	10.5
Dating each other	10	10.5
Going out to dinner	9	12.0
Having sexual intercourse	0	13.0

[a]Each item was rated on a 6 point scale (1 = daily, 2 = once a week, 3 = twice weekly, 4 = once a month, 5 = every few months, 6 = never). All those who rated 1-5 were designated as being involved.

mon feelings include both positive types (caring about his/her welfare, 82%; compassion, 77%; warm feelings, 57%) and negative (blame, 62%; angry feelings, 57%). Extreme feelings of either a positive (love, 30%) or a negative nature (feel former spouse should be punished, 10%), however, are not common. Neither attachment to the former spouse nor guilt feelings are reported by a majority. Less than one third are preoccupied and pining for the former spouse (items ranged from 24% to 31% endorsement), and approximately 40% experience guilt feelings (items ranged from 38% to 43% endorsement).

The majority of former spouses (59%) report that their feelings toward one another have changed since the divorce was first filed. Changes are in both directions on all feelings (e.g., some say they are now more attached, others less). Former spouses attribute these changes in feelings not only to the passage of time, but also to counseling, adjustment to a new life, remarriage of self or former spouse, personal growth and maturity, and subsequent interaction with the former spouse.

THE EFFECT OF WHO MADE THE DECISION TO DIVORCE

As reported earlier, significant differences were obtained between male and female members of divorced couples on a number of former spousal relationship variables. It can be argued that these findings result from differences between males and females with respect to who made the decision to divorce, with women more likely to have decided. In order to evaluate this possibility, a series of t tests were performed comparing those who decided to divorce to those whose former spouses made the decision. The tests were applied to those variables where there had been significant sex differences. Results indicate that men whose former spouses decided to divorce report significantly less satisfactioin with the coparental relationship than men who decided themselves, both in terms of amount shared (t (42) = 2.9, $p < .01$) and quality (t (42) = 2.0, $p < .05$). There were no other significant differences for either sex.

FINDINGS FOR THE ONE-MEMBER INTERVIEWED SAMPLE

In order to evaluate generalizability of the findings from the divorced couple sample where both members were interviewed, tests of significance between both-member interviewed and one-member interviewed groups (t tests and chi squares) were computed for all variables. There are no significant differences between males from couples where only the male member was interviewed (N = 8) and males from couples where both members were interviewed (N = 44) on any variable. While the perceptions of females from couples where only the female member was interviewed (N = 33) and females from couples where both members were interviewed (N = 44) are similar on most variables, there were several significant differences. Females whose former spouses refused to participate or could not be contacted report that they spend less time together with their former husband and the children as a "family" (x^2 = 7.4, p < .01), that their coparental relationships are of poorer quality (t (75) = 2.3, p < .05), and that their former spouses are less competent parents (t (75) = 2.1, p < .05). Thus, while the results from the both-member interviewed couple sample appear to be representative of the overall divorced population in most areas, there are several key ways in which results from couples where the father participated yield a different picture of divorced couples from that provided by women whose former husbands were either not available or not willing to participate.

Discussion and Conclusions

The findings support the basic General Systems Theory paradigm as applied to postdivorce families. Divorce does not necessarily result in the dissolution of the original family system; rather, all of its members generally continue to be interdependent, even though reorganization of the system takes place. When the noncustodial father remains involved with the children, it is normative for both spouses to remain involved with each other and to continue to share responsibilities, concerns, and joys of child rearing.[2]

This continuity of coparental relationships between former spouses calls into question the term "single-parent" family as a description of the postdivorce situation. The mother-father, as well as the noncustodial parent-child relationships, are vital components of many postdivorce families. While the custodial mother continues to maintain primary reponsibility for child rearing, it is the more unusual postdivorce family that is truly "single-parent." These findings also have implications for the vocabulary commonly used to describe postdivorce relationships. The term "copar-

---

[2]There is a subsample of couples who not only maintain coparental relationships but also spend time together with one another and their children as a family unit. This is more likely to be the case in families where the father was available and willing to participate in the study. For postdivorce families that maintain such ties, it is particularly difficult to support the position that divorce means family dissolution.

ents" might well be used to supplement the term "ex-spouses" in describing many divorced couple relationships. The latter describes what they were but no longer are to one another, while the former may more accurately describe their current relationship.

The coparental relationship is an important element in most postdivorce families, although it is not generally characterized by day-to-day involvement. Instead, the contact, while regular, is episodic and is more likely to occur around special events or problems. Most former spouses of both sexes are satisfied with this type of contact. However, the noncustodial fathers, particularly those who were not supportive of the decision to divorce, feel more dissatisfied with their coparental relationship; they often feel "shut out" of their parenting role as a result of this kind of contact.

The majority of former spouses, particularly those women whose former husbands did not participate, report stress and conflict in their coparental relationships. This is true even though many report that they in particular, but also their former spouses, try to be supportive and accommodating to one another. There is a subgroup of couples, however, who believe that they have developed relatively problem-free and successful coparental relationships. Investigation of the factors that account for this positive outcome is underway.

While the coparental interaction is probably the most important aspect of former spousal relationships, it is certainly not the only one; rather, maintenance of friendly or "kin" type interaction, separate from parenting, is normative among former spouses. Friendly interaction must be differentiated from an intense romantic involvement; most former spouses talk to one another about their respective families and friends, but few are involved with one another sexually.

With regard to the process of emotional separation, the findings indicate that by 1 year postdivorce, the majority of former spouses are not feeling emotionally preoccupied with one another and do not experience extreme feelings, either positive or negative, about each other. Unlike the majority of divorced women in Goode's (1956) study who had feelings of wanting revenge, divorced adults of both sexes in the present study experience only mildly hostile feelings. Consistent with Weiss' (1975) findings, former spouses generally experience positive, caring feelings toward one another concurrent with negative ones. In fact, caring and compassion for the former spouse is the most frequently acknowledged feeling. It may be argued that these findings reflect social desirability bias to report positive rather than negative feelings. This may be the case to some extent, although it is unlikely that there is strong social sanction for reporting positive feelings toward one's former spouse. In fact, positive feelings toward the former spouse are, at times, confusing to divorced adults who experience them (Weiss, 1975).

The findings on "kin" type interaction and positive feelings point to the need for a more careful clinical understanding and definition of what is considered pathological in the relationships of former spouses with each other. Caring feelings and friendly interaction appear to be normative and should not be "automatically" considered indicative of an unhealthy entanglement or an inability to separate. Differentiation should be made between "attachment" defined as preoccupation and pining and which has been found to be associated with psychiatric problems (Kitson & Sussman, 1976) and "attachment" defined as continued caring and friendship with the former spouse, which is not necessarily a negative outcome of the divorce process.

Former spouses are generally not satisfied with the way they have worked out their relationships with one another in areas other than parenting. Some believe that there is too much involvement, and others feel that there is too little. An absence of norms, as well as confusion over the "meaning" behind this kind of relating, may contribute to their struggle. Perhaps a key element is not whether former spouses interact in friendly ways, but whether the boundaries (i.e., rules for relating about some areas or in some ways, and not others) are clear and agreed upon (Minuchin, 1974).

The present study compared the perceptions and experiences of male and female members of divorced couples. Restricted to mother-custody families, sex was directly linked to custodial status. This linking is typical of the general divorced population but is not a one-to-one relationship; recently more fathers are obtaining custody, and there are more joint-custody couples. It is apparent in the present study that the female who has custody of the children cannot be characterized as a victim of the divorce process (Goode, 1956): Women are more likely to decide to divorce and men more likely to be "left." This finding supports the experience of on-line clinicians working with the divorced population (Levit, 1979). In addition, consistent with recent work of other investigators (Kitson & Sussman, 1976), the emotional separation process appears to be a "human" phenomenon with similar feelings experienced by both sexes.

The inclusion of both members of divorced couples in the present study allowed for evaluation of congruence between individual former spouses' perceptions of their relationships. Surprisingly, in light of the problem of achieving consensus in research with "married" couples (Booth, 1978),

there was generally high congruence between former spouses' perceptions. It may be that the divorced relationship with less involvement and
more formalized interaction yields greater consensus in reports. There
were significant differences, however, between noncustodial fathers and
custodial mothers in their perceptions of amount of father-child involvement; fathers saw themselves as more involved than mothers saw them.
Noncustodial fathers may overrate their involvement, perhaps because
they want to see themselves as more significant family members, and/or
custodial mothers may underrate fathers' involvement out of a need to see
fathers as comparatively less centrally involved. Such differences in perceptions between fathers and mothers support the importance of including
both former spouses when examining the postdivorce family.

Whether the noncustodial father was available or willing to participate
in the study emerged as an important factor in evaluating former spousal
relationships. Couples in which the father did not participate differed from
both-member interviewed couples on several substantive variables; their
coparental relationships were more troubled, and they were less likely to
spend time together as a family unit. Inclusion of both "types" of couples
provided for the most complete picture of the overall divorced population.

With regard to generalization of the results from this study, several cautions must be noted. Limited to mother-custody, Caucasian couples where
the father continued to see the children, these results cannot be generalized to other kinds of postdivorce families. Also, an effort was made to
maximize generalizability by including both-member interviewed couples,
as well as the one-member interviewed couples who were more demographically representative of the noninterviewed population. The study,
however, does not permit evaluation of the perceptions of noncustodial
fathers who were unavailable or unwilling to participate.

Results of the present study underscore the need for future research on
former spousal relationships. Such relationships were examined at 1 year
postdivorce. Examination at later points in the reorganization process
would be fruitful, and, therefore, follow-up of the present sample at 3
years postdivorce is planned. The present study did not evaluate the role
of children as they relate to the former spousal subsystem. This restriction
was necessitated by the relative absence of prior work on the former
spousal dyad itself. Certainly, to provide a complete description of the
postdivorce family system, future research must include the children as
part of that system.

The present study provides a first step toward a description of former
spousal relationships as a vital component of the postdivorce family sys-

tem. The findings have implications for the direction of intervention programs aimed at the divorced population. First, an understanding of the
former spousal subsystem must be included as an integral part of any
assessment of postdivorce family functioning. Moreover, although mutually supportive and cooperative coparental relationships are optimal for
children's postdivorce adjustment (Hetherington et al., 1976), the present
study shows that many former spouses have difficulty actually working out
this kind of mutually supportive and cooperative relationship. There is a
need for intervention programs aimed at helping them to do so. Finally, a
great deal of emphasis has appropriately been placed on helping the
"single-parent" mother cope with increased parenting responsibilities.
However, if the child is to maintain continued access to both parents postdivorce, it is also necessary to find ways to help the noncustodial father
who feels shut out of child rearing functions to develop a more satisfying
role vis-a-vis both his former spouse, now coparent, and his children.

REFERENCES

Ahrons, C., & Goldsmith, J. *The coparental divorce: Preliminary research findings with implications for family policy.* Paper presented at the National Council for Family Relations meetings, Philadel-phia, October 1978.

Bernard, J. *The future of marriage.* New York: Bantam Books, 1972.

Biller, H. B. *Paternal deprivation.* Lexington, MA: Lexington Books, 1974.

Bohannan, P. (Ed.). *Divorce and after.* New York: Doubleday, 1971.

Booth, A., & Welch, S. Spousal consensus and its correlates: A reassessment. *Journal of Marriage and the Family,* 1978, *40,* 23-32.

Buckley, W. *Modern systems research for the behavioral scientist.* Chicago: Aldine, 1968.

Cohen, S. *Impact of divorce on children and their parents: Interview schedule.* Unpublished manuscript, 1977.

Goldstein, J., Freud, A., & Solnit, A. J. *Beyond the best interests of the child.* New York: The Free Press. 1956

Goode, W. J. *After divorce.* New York: Free Press, 1956.

Hetherington, E. M., Cox, M., & Cox, R. Divorced fathers. *The Family Coordinator,* 1976, *25,* 417-428.

Keshet, H. F., & Rosenthal, K. M. Fathering after marital separation. *Social Work,* 1978, *23,* 11-18.

Kitson, G.C., & Sussman, M. B. *The processes of marital separation and divorce: Male and female similarities and differences.* Paper presented at American Sociological Association meetings, New York, August 1976.

Kressel, K., & Deutsch, M. Divorce therapy: An in-depth survey of therapists' views. *Family Process,* 1977, *16,* 413-443.

Levit, L. Personal communication, April 1979.

Mead, M. Anomalies in American postdivorce relationships. In P. Bohannan (Ed.), *Divorce and after.* New York: Doubleday, 1971.

Minuchin, S. *Families and family therapy.* Cambridge: Harvard University Press, 1974.

Suarez, J., Weston, N., & Hartstein, N. Mental health interventions in divorce proceedings. *American Journal of Orthopsychiatry,* 1978, *48,* 273-283.

Wallerstein, J. S., & Kelly, J. B. The effects of parental divorce: Experiences of the pre-school child. *Journal of the American Academy of Child Psychiatry,* 1975, *14,* 600-616.

Wallerstein, J. S., & Kelly, J. B. Divorce counseling: A community service for families in the midst of divorce. *American Journal of Orthopsychiatry,* 1977, *47,* 4-22.

Weiss, R. S. *Martial separation*. New York: Basic Books, 1975.

Weiting, S. G. Structuralism, systems theory and ethnomethodology in the sociology of the family. *Journal of Comparative Family Studies*, 1976, *7*, 375-395.

Recent research in the area of marital dissolution has attended primarily to the presence or absence of problems related to divorce without assessing the extent to which the problems influence the process of adjustment. Through multivariate techniques, the present study first examines the effect of divorce-related problems on perceived distress. Second, the role of various coping strategies in mediating distress is examined. The results indicate that only interpersonal and familial problems have a major effect on overall mood state. In addition, involvement in social activities, expressing feelings, and developing autonomy are highly related to greater postdivorce adjustment.

13

ADAPTATION TO DIVORCE

Problems and Coping Strategies*

William H. Berman and Dennis C. Turk**

The phenomenon of divorce is receiving increasing attention as a stress-inducing life crisis that affects over two million adults and one million children annually (Dohrenwend and Dohrenwend, 1974; Norton and Glick, 1976). The divorce rate in the United States has been steadily increasing during the past 15 years and shows no sign of levelling off (National Center for Health Statistics, 1977).

Divorced people are consistently overrepresented in all psychiatric populations (Crago, 1972; Redick and Johnson, 1974; Bloom, 1975), with as many as 40 percent of all divorced people receiving some form of psychiatric care (Bloom et al., 1978). This does not include those who seek pastoral counseling or other less formal interventions (Kressel et al., 1978). Divorced people are also more likely to develop physical illnesses (Holmes and Masuda, 1974) and have higher morbidity rates (Bloom et al., 1978) than comparable married people.

*This research was conducted from June to December, 1978. The authors would like to thank Robert Schorman, Toni Suarez, and especially Lurline deVos and Robert Sternberg for their contributions to earlier drafts of this paper.

**Department of Psychology, Yale University, Box 11A Yale Station, New Haven, Connecticut 06520.

Awareness of the extent of the impact of divorce on the individual and on society has resulted in increasing interest in ways of controlling and minimizing the disruptive experiences of the divorcing adult. Recently, Bloom et al. (1978:888) suggested, "Marital disruption is an irresistible candidate for preventive intervention programs that are well thought out, economically feasible, and subject to careful evaluation." As Lazarus (1978) points out, any intervention designed to facilitate adaptation and social competence assumes a knowledge of the specific difficulties confronted by the population, their contribution to distress, and the range and relative efficacy of coping strategies that may be employed. Current research on the process of divorce has focused only on the specific difficulties, and few data are available regarding their impact or the more commonly used coping strategies.

The problems and stresses encountered by the divorced fall roughly into three major categories: pragmatic concerns, interpersonal and social problems, and family-related stresses. These problems have been discussed elsewhere (Hetherington et al., 1976, 1977; Bloom et al., 1978; Berman, 1979) and will

From William H. Berman and Dennis C. Turk, "Adaptation to Divorce: Problems and Coping Strategies," *Journal of Marriage and the Family*, 1981, 43, pp. 179-189. Reprinted by permission of the publisher and authors.

be summarized only briefly here. A large number of problems occur in the area of pragmatic issues. Both men (Hetherington *et al.*, 1976; Mendes, 1976) and women (Goode, 1956; Glasser and Navarre, 1965; Bohannon, 1970; Brandwein *et al.*, 1974; Yates, 1976; Hetherington *et al.*, 1977) encounter difficulties in such areas as home repair and maintenance, work efficiency and performance, household organization, and finances. Moreover, divorced people express a general feeling of being overwhelmed, of not having enough time to do everything, and of not knowing what to do or how to do it.

The interpersonal-social sphere is the second major area of disruption for divorced people. Goode (1956) notes that although old friends are initially supportive and helpful, they rapidly place themselves at a distance, often as a result of conflicting loyalties to the two former spouses. Goode also reports a reduction in the number of people—especially men—who are willing to be involved with divorced women with children. Both Brandwein *et al.* (1974) and Miller (1970) describe a number of attitudes that develop among friends of the divorced person, including ambivalence regarding the divorce, sexual attraction to the divorced person, stereotypes of a divorced woman, and an unconscious fear in couples that the same process will happen to them. Divorced individuals themselves change both attitudes and feelings regarding interpersonal involvements. Both the fear of involvement in another long-term relationship and a sense of vulnerability influence the level of social activity for many divorced individuals (Bohannon, 1970; Weiss, 1975; Brown, 1976).

Family interactions comprise the third major problem domain contributing to post-divorce distress. The prolonged, negatively toned contact between the spouses preceding, during, and following the divorce often interferes with effective adaptation. Hetherington *et al.* (1976) and Weiss (1975, 1976) describe the continued attachment and conflictual involvement of the former spouses. It has also been reported that regular child-rearing practices and communication become disrupted during a divorce (Hetherington *et al.*, 1976; Kressel and Deutsch, 1977). Problems in this latter aspect of the family area are exacerbated when

children, especially male children, become more resistant and less compliant with the custodial parent (Hetherington *et al.*, 1976; Mendes, 1976).

A central component of the post-divorce adjustment process is the individual's emotional reactions to the divorce and to life after the break. The affective responses begin long before the divorce is final (Levinger, 1976), and intensifies after the legal aspects are completed. Following the divorce, both men and women experience similar patterns of personal and emotional problems; they are initially more severe for men (Hetherington *et al.*, 1976; Bloom *et al.*, 1978) but more sustained for women (Hetherington *et al.*, 1977). During the first year following a divorce, both men and women report low self-esteem, confusion concerning social and sexual roles, and feelings of anger, anxiety, ambivalence, and depression. Men report a lack of both structure and coherent personal identity, and feelings of rootlessness, guilt, and loss (Hetherington *et al.*, 1976; Mendes, 1976). Women report feeling unattractive, helpless, and personally and socially incompetent (Hetherington *et al.*, 1977).

These emotional reactions should not be viewed as isolated experiences independent of the other problems of post-divorce life. Rather, the affective responses influence and are influenced by problems in other areas and affect subsequent difficulties in interpersonal, family, and practical spheres. Although the existence of problems in these spheres has been identified, their contribution to distress is unclear, and it requires empirical examination.

Many of the problems arising during and after a divorce recede with time, and the individual eventually reaches an equilibrium and a reintegration into society (Bohannon, 1970; Hetherington *et al.*, 1976, 1977; Kressel and Deutsch, 1977). Although some people require counseling, many seem to adjust without formal intervention. Very little is known of the adaptive mechanisms and strategies that facilitate the process of adjusting to divorce. Hetherington *et al.* (1977:17) suggest that "the most important factor in changing the self-concept two years after the divorce was the establishment of a satisfying intimate heterosexual relationship." They also suggest that the flurry of social activities, noted for men, at one year after divorce may be important in reestablishing a sense of identity and improving self-concept. An independent pre-divorce social life reportedly facilitates post-divorce adjustment for men (Bloom *et al.*, 1978). Further, Weiss (1975) has noted the adaptive value of the continued former spouse attachment.

Research on coping with other forms of life stress has identified numerous active coping strategies that facilitate adjustment and reduce perceived distress. Pearlin and Schooler (1978) identified several types of coping strategies used to deal with different life stresses, including self-reliance, emotional discharge, positive comparisons, and selective ignoring. And McCubbin *et al.* (1976) have observed several specific strategies used by prisoner-of-war wives to deal with spouse absence, including social involvement, home activities, and emotional expression. The role of such adaptive mechanisms has yet to be examined with respect to divorce.

In short, the current literature on divorce leaves many questions unanswered. Hetherington *et al.*'s work (1976, 1977) suggests that real-world problems affect the individual's self-esteem and emotional state, but their differential contribution to distress has not been explored. Previous research on divorce has treated post-divorce adjustment as a passive phenomenon, in contrast to the active process of coping with stress as seen in other life-stress research (Roskies and Lazarus, 1979; Turk, 1979).

The present study is designed to confirm and clarify the specific problem areas confronting the divorced adult, and further,

to examine the specific contribution of family, interpersonal, and practical problems to overall adjustment. In addition, this study is designed to identify those coping strategies that help to alleviate post-divorce distress, and to examine the relationship between the reported effectiveness of coping strategies and their impact on adaptation.

METHODS

Subjects

Since the presence of children in families of divorce has been shown to be a central component of post-divorce distress (*e.g.*, Hetherington *et al.*, 1976), all of the subjects in this study have children. The subjects were 65 female and 25 male volunteers from chapters of Parents Without Partners. In addition, questionnaire data from another 16 female subjects who participated in a separate study being conducted concurrently were included in certain aspects of the data analysis. Subjects in this latter group were selected randomly from the Superior Court records of all women who received a divorce within the past two years and who had at least one minor child at home. Ages of the 106 subjects ranged from 23 to 60 years; the mean age was 40.8. Time elapsed since separation ranged from three months to 15 years; the mean length of separation was 3.23 years. The sample was predominantly middle class: 63.5 percent were from Hollingshead's (1957) social classes III and IV (middle class); the median was 3.42, with the remaining 36.5 percent distributed among the other three classes. The demographic data are summarized in Table 1. The subjects in the Parents Without Partners and Superior Court

TABLE 1. DEMOGRAPHIC CHARACTERISTICS OF DIVORCED SAMPLE

Variable	Mean	Mode	Standard Deviation
Age	40.80		8.59
SES	3.17		1.00
Current income[a]		$14,000	
Pre-divorce income [a]		$20,000	
Number of children	2.54		1.20
Minor children	1.76		0.97
Minor male children	0.88		0.81
Length of marriage (years)	14.74		8.04
Length of separation (years)	1.29		1.23
Length of divorce (years)	3.23		3.60

[a]Income was rated on a 6-point ordinal scale, from 1 = $33,000 or more, to 7 = < $6,000.

subgroups did not differ significantly on any
of the demographic variables and thus were
combined for subsequent analyses.

Measures

Checklist of problems and concerns.[1] A
Checklist of Problems and Concerns (CPC)
was developed to assess the nature of
problems encountered during the process of
adapting to divorce. The 45 items on this
scale were obtained from a review of the
relevant literature and pilot interviews with
divorced people. The items described problems contained in the four major areas
previously identified, including practical
(*e.g.,* "Taking care of my car"), interpersonal (*e.g.,* "Maintaining old friendships"),
family (*e.g.,* "Having enough time for my
children"), and emotional difficulties (*e.g.,*
"Losing my temper at my family," "Being
lonely"). Subjects were instructed to rate
each item on a 4-point scale according to the
frequency with which each item was perceived
to be a problem or worry during the past
month.

Coping strategies and resources inventory.
The Coping Strategies and Resources Inventory (CSRI) was adapted from a scale
developed by McCubbin *et al.* (1976) for use
with a population of prisoner-of-war wives.
The coping strategies included various social
and personal activities, family interactions
and supports, avoidance and withdrawal
techniques, and other adaptational behaviors. For example, strategies included
"talking to others who are divorced or
widowed," "punishing myself" and "taking
medications." Subjects rated the perceived
efficacy of 53 coping strategies on a
4-point scale from "not at all helpful" to "very
helpful."

Current mood state. The current mood
state of these subjects was assessed on a
9-item short form of a scale used by Pearlin
and Schooler (1978). Each subject rated, on a
5-point scale, the frequency with which they
had felt specific emotions during the past
three months. These emotions included conditions of being: unhappy, bothered, worried,
bored, lonely, frustrated, tense, neglected,

contented. A sum of the first eight item scores
minus the score of the ninth item (contented)
was used to assess current mood state.

Finally, subjects were asked to rate, on
5-point scales: (1) the level of satisfaction
with their marriage, their pre-divorce life,
and their current life; (2) desire for divorce;
and (3) attitudes toward eight specific aspects
of their current life concerns. Desire for
divorce and current life satisfaction were used
as dependent variables in the analyses.

Procedure

The first author administered the questionnaires to several groups of between 20 and 50
subjects at monthly meetings of different
chapters of Parents Without Partners, or
individually to the group identified from
court records. One hundred thirty-nine
questionnaires were distributed, of which 115
were returned. Of these, nine were excluded
because of numerous omissions of data. (Six
had omitted one or both questionnaires, and
three omitted at least half of the demographic
data.)

Data Analyses

Factor analysis. In order to examine the
underlying relationships among the problem
items and among the coping strategies, both
the CSRI and the CPC were subjected to
principal-factors factor analyses with varimax
rotation (PA2 and varimax routines, Nie *et
al.,* 1975). Factor scores for each subject were
computed by summing subjects' standardized
scored for those items that loaded above .35
on the different factors (Nie *et al.,* 1975).
This method of using equal weights for each
item rather than weighted values was used to
enhance the reliability of the results. Equal
weights for variables above the cutoff are not
subject to capitalization on chance and can
not be influenced by outliers, a potential
problem with the estimated weights (Wainer,
1976).

Canonical correlation analysis. This analysis was performed to determine the presence
of a relationship between sets of problem
factors and particular sets of coping factors.
Is there a relationship between the occurrence
of some problems and the usefulness of
certain coping strategies, or do these two sets
of behaviors occur independently?

Multiple regression analysis. The relationships between the derived factors from the

[1] Copies of the CPC and the CSRI are available from
the authors upon request.

CPC and CSRI and the dependent variables of mood disturbance and life satisfaction were investigated by stepwise multiple regression analyses (Nie et al., 1975).[2]

These analyses serve two purposes. First, they provide data regarding the extent to which certain types of problems, or, similarly, types of coping strategies, contribute to an individual's subjective experience of his or her life. Second, they provide a test of the construct validity of the scales. Since the factors are orthogonal, multiple correlations provide a more accurate assessment of the similarities between dependent and criterion variables than do separate bivariate correlations. In addition, demographic and attitudinal variables were used to identify individuals who were more susceptible to distress.

RESULTS

Current Mood State

In order to assess the reliability of the Current Mood State scale. Cronbach's *alpha* was computed for all nine items. For this sample, $a = .926$, indicating a high degree of internal consistency for the items in the scale.

Problems and Stressors

The frequency distribution of the 45 items in the CPC was examined to identify items that were not indicated as problems and thus unlikely to be of value in this scale. Ten items were eliminated from further analyses because they were rated as never a problem by at least 50 percent of the sample. The factor analysis performed on the remaining 35 items yielded six orthogonal factors that had *eigenvalues* greater than 1.0 and were easily interpretable. These six factors accounted for 79.5 percent of the variance in the scale. Internal consistency was consistently high for the items in the factors, with Cronbach's *alpha* ranging from .66 to .84.

As expected, the six factors that emerged identify several independent areas of social,

emotional, and environmental disturbances. The first factor we have labelled *Former Spouse Contacts*, $\lambda = 5.88$. The items comprising this factor are concerned with talking with the former spouse about money or children, meeting the former spouse through visitation and social situations, and the feelings these contacts elicit. Factor 2 is labelled *Parent-Child Interactions*, $\lambda = 2.80$, and measures the degree of difficulty people experience in communicating with their children, both regarding the divorce and in more general areas. *Interpersonal Relations* is the third factor identified, $\lambda = 2.39$. The items making up this factor include both intimate and casual relationships with the same and opposite sex. Factor 4 is comprised of several items that are related to *Loneliness*, $\lambda = 1.95$.

The last two interpretable factors are concerned with less interpersonal themes; rather, they involve common concerns and problems of a pragmatic nature. Factor 5, $\lambda = 1.68$, deals with *Practical Problems* in day-to-day living, such as cooking, cleaning, and shopping. The other items in this factor deal with the lack of time divorced people feel they have, both for practical and family activities. Factor 6, $\lambda = 1.27$, addresses the *Financial Concerns* of divorced people; specifically, having enough money to make ends meet. The items in each factor, the factor loadings, factor labels, and the percent of variance accounted for are presented in Table 2. Cross-validation of this factor structure was provided by identical factor analyses on random halves of the sample. The factor structures produced by these analyses were similar to the factor structure for the whole sample, suggesting that the results were not due to chance.

The impact of these factors on post-divorce adjustment was examined by regression analysis. Five of the six problem factors were regressed onto mood state and life satisfaction for the 86 subjects in the survey sample for whom there were no missing data. Factor 4, *Loneliness*, was eliminated from this analysis, since this factor is, in effect, measuring the individual's reported mood disturbance, $r = .63$. Of the five remaining factors, three were significantly related to mood disturbance. Difficulties in *Interpersonal Relations* is most highly related to a poorer mood state, followed by *Former*

---

[2] The stepwise multiple regression begins by entering into the regression equation the independent variable with the highest zero-order correlation with the dependent variable. It then computes partial correlations between the dependent variable and the remaining independent variables, controlling for the variable in the equation. This process is then repeated, entering the variables with the largest partial correlations, until all independent variables are used.

TABLE 2. FACTORS DERIVED FROM THE
CHECKLIST OF PROBLEMS AND CONCERNS

Factor Items	Factor Loadings
Factor 1: Former Spouse Contacts	
Talking with my former spouse about money matters	.857
Talking with my former spouse about the children	.767
Visitation	.643
Resenting my former spouse	.535
Meeting my former spouse in social situations	.494
Percent variance accounted for	29.3
Factor 2: Parent-Child Interactions	
Talking with a child about my life	.815
Talking with a child about his/her life	.766
Expressing my feelings to my children	.626
Talking with my children about the divorce	.553
Being too independent	.384
Percent variance accounted for	13.9
Factor 3: Interpersonal Relations	
Dating new people	.830
Developing an intimate relationship	.715
Making new friends	.547
Getting involved in social activities	.412
Percent variance accounted for	11.9
Factor 4: Loneliness	
Being depressed	.784
Being lonely	.720
Getting involved in social activities	.420
Keeping a close family without my former spouse	.373
Feeling adequate as a person	.355
Percent variance accounted for	9.7
Factor 5: Practical Problems	
Cooking meals for the family	.623
Not having enough time to get things done	.620
Cleaning the house	.595
Going to the market	.440
Having enough time for my children	.361
Percent variance accounted for	8.4
Factor 6: Financial Concerns	
Having enough money	.892
Making ends meet	.732
Percent variance accounted for	6.3
Total percentage variance accounted for	79.5

Spouse Contacts and *Parent-Child Interactions*. Neither *Practical Problems* nor *Financial Concerns* yielded significant *beta* weights. This regression was repeated using only those three variables with significant *betas* in the first analysis: *Interpersonal Relations, Former Spouse Contacts,* and *Parent-Child Interactions*. This provides a final model for the relationship of these variables to post-divorce adjustment that is not contaminated by the insignificant variables (Sternberg, 1979). The second analysis produced a highly significant multiple $R = .417$, accounting for 17.3 percent of the variance in mood state, $F(3, 81) = 5.68$, $p < .005$.

Overall life satisfaction has a different pattern of relationships to the various problem factors. In this equation, *Interpersonal Relationships* was significantly related to improved life satisfaction. However, neither *Former Spouse Contacts* nor *Parent-Child Interactions* was related to the criterion variable. Both *Practical Problems* and *Financial Concerns* did have significant or near-significant *beta* weights. A second regression equation using the three significant variables was highly significant, $R = .448$, $F(3, 81) = 6.79$, $p < .001$. It is interesting to note that a high level of practical problems is correlated with a high level of life satisfaction, while the other two factors have the inverse relationship. These data are presented in Table 3.

Coping Strategies

As with the CPC, the individual items in the CSRI were examined in order to eliminate any that were too infrequently used to be considered common coping strategies. Eight items were rated as never being employed by at least 50 percent of the sample and had a restricted range of responses. These eight were deleted from further analyses. The principal factors analysis produced six orthogonal factors with *eigenvalues* greater than 1.0 that were easily interpretable. As with the problem factors, reliability was high, ranging from $a = .675$ to $a^c = .793$.

The six factors produced by this analysis account for 71.5 percent of the total variance. Factor 1, $\lambda = 7.58$, contains five items that identify a variety of intimate and casual *Social Activities,* including involvement in Parents Without Partners. The second factor we have called *Learning,* $\lambda = 2.66$, and involves seeking education and professional support. We labelled the third factor *Personal Understanding,* $\lambda = 2.56$. It involves both reflection and understanding of the divorce, and efforts toward developing a positive self-image by one's self, that is, without external help. Factor 4, $\lambda = 1.87$, is

TABLE 3. MULTIPLE REGRESSION OF PROBLEM FACTORS WITH MOOD STATE AND LIFE SATISFACTION

Dependent Variable	Independent Variables	First Regression	Final Regression		
		Beta	Beta	R	F
Mood state	Interpersonal Relations	.326*	.327	.385	14.50***
	Former Spouse Contacts	.159*	.134	.407	8.16***
	Parent-Child Interactions	.130*	.090	.417	5.68***
	Practical Problems[a]	−.118	—	—	—
	Financial Concerns[a]	.096	—	—	—
Life satisfaction	Interpersonal Relations	.384**	.415	.376	13.65***
	Former Spouse Contacts[a]	.017	—	—	—
	Parent-Child Interactions[a]	.095	—	—	—
	Practical Problems	−.215*	−.232	.427	9.14***
	Financial Concerns	.120*	.140	.448	6.79***

[a]These factors were eliminated in the final regression equation due to lack of significance in the initial equation.
*$p < .05$.
**$p < .01$.
***$p < .001$.

comprised of items related to *Expressing Feelings*, especially anger. Factor 5 identifies an important component of the divorcing process, the development of *Autonomy*, $\lambda = 1.54$. This includes working, personal strength, and independence. The sixth factor is concerned with the role of *Home and Family Activities*, $\lambda = 1.37$, in the coping process. The items, their factor loadings, and the percent of common variance are included in Table 4. Cross-validation factor analyses on random halves of the sample produced similar factor structures, confirming the reliability of the full-sample analysis.

All six coping factors were regressed onto overall mood disturbance. Three of these factors had significant *beta* weights and accounted for a significant portion of the variance in mood. Using these three factors, the final regression equation accounted for 20.9 percent of the variance, $R = .458$, $F(3, 81) = 7.34$, $p < .001$. Involvement in *Social Activities* and *Autonomy* activities was positively correlated with a favorable mood state; in contrast, a greater mood disturbance correlated with higher ratings of *Expressing Feelings*. *Home and Family Activities, Learning,* and *Personal Understanding* appeared to be unrelated to mood disturbance.

The regression of coping strategies onto life satisfaction revealed that four of the six factors are related to positive feelings about post-divorce life. *Social Activities, Home and Family Activities* and *Autonomy* were positively related to high life satisfaction, and the belief that *Expressing Feelings* is helpful was correlated with a low level of life satisfaction. The second regression equation for these four variables produced a multiple

TABLE 4. FACTORS DERIVED FROM THE COPING STRATEGIES AND RESOURCES INVENTORY

Factor Items	Factor Loadings
Factor 1: Social Activities	
Dating	.852
Developing intimate sexual relationships	.703
Developing new friendships	.570
Getting involved in social activities with others	.491
Involvement with Parents Without Partners	.450
Percent of variance accounted for	30.8
Factor 2: Learning	
Going to school	.888
Taking evening courses	.748
Talking to a therapist or counselor	.424
Learning new skills	.406
Percent of variance accounted for	10.8
Factor 3: Personal Understanding	
Learning new things about myself	.654
Talking with others who are divorced	.573
Telling myself I'm a good person	.515
Trying to understand what went wrong	.419
Taking a more positive attitude toward life	.392
Establishing a new life for myself	.373
Percent of variance accounted for	10.4
Factor 4: Expressing Feelings	
Blowing up	.748
Allowing myself to get angry	.620
Crying	.605
Percent of variance accounted for	7.6
Factor 5: Autonomy	
Establishing a new life for myself	.626
Becoming more independent	.582
Working: outside employment	.434
Showing I am strong	.378
Taking a more positive attitude toward life	.363
Percent of variance accounted for	6.3
Factor 6: Home and Family Activities	
Taking care of my home	.655
Doing more things with the children	.573
Doing things with the whole family	.504
Keeping an organized, stable household	.360
Percent of variance accounted for	5.6
Total percentage variance accounted for	71.5

TABLE 5. REGRESSIONS OF COPING FACTORS WITH MOOD STATE AND LIFE SATISFACTION

Dependent Variable	Independent Variables	First Regression	Final Regression		
		Beta	Beta	R	F
Mood state	Social Activities	−.318**	−.349	.353	12.09***
	Expressing Feelings	.323**	.310	.442	10.21***
	Autonomy	−.132*	−.144	.458	7.34***
	Home and Family Activities[a]	−.101	—	—	—
	Learning[a]	−.029	—	—	—
	Personal Understanding[a]	.018	—	—	—
Life satisfaction	Social Activities	−.345**	−.347	.451	21.76***
	Home and Family Activities	−.223*	−.224	.482	12.76***
	Expressing Feelings	.224*	.226	.517	10.07***
	Autonomy	−.105*	−.134	.528	7.93***
	Learning[a]	−.032	—	—	—
	Personal Understanding[a]	−.024	—	—	—

[a]These factors were eliminated in the final regression equation due to lack of significance in the initial equation.
*p < .05.
**p < .01.
***p < .001.

$R = .528$, $F(4, 80) = 7.93$, $p < .001$. As in the regression of coping with moods, neither *Personal Understanding* nor *Learning* was related to life satisfaction. The results are presented in Table 5.

The work of Pearlin and Schooler (1978) suggests that coping strategies are problem specific, and are not equally effective with all types of life stresses. The relationship between the six problem areas and the six coping factors identified in this study was examined through canonical correlation. This analysis indicated that involvement in *Social Activities* and activities that promote *Autonomy* are significantly related to a reduced level of problems with *Loneliness* and *Interpersonal Relations*. This single pair of canonical variates had a multiple $R = .59$, $x^2 = 59.59$, $p < .007$. None of the other problem factors was significantly related to the other coping factors. This supports Pearlin and Schooler's (1978) argument that some coping strategies are problem-specific, rather than global attempts at adaptation.

Demographic Characteristics

Multiple regression analysis was also used to identify what constellation of independent variables predicts subjects' overall mood disturbance. The predictor variables used in the following analysis include: sex, age, length of marriage (in years), number of children, number of minor male children, current yearly income, change in income due to the divorce, socioeconomic status (SES), and desire for divorce.

The regression of these variables onto current mood disturbance approached significance after five variables were included in the equation, $R = .404$, $F(5, 60) = 2.34$, $p = .055$. People experiencing greater mood disturbance tended to have fewer children, but more minor males, had less desire for divorce, had a lower current income, and had a longer marriage. Neither sex nor age contributed significantly in this equation.

DISCUSSION

The results of the present study clearly indicate that, for a wide range of divorced individuals, both the problems encountered after the divorce and the coping strategies used contribute greatly to post-divorce adjustment. The emergence of several distinct problem areas and coping patterns emphasizes the utility of a multivariate approach to the study of life stress in general, and marital disruption specifically. These data demonstrate that neither problems alone nor coping alone are sufficient to understand the phenomenon of divorce; on the contrary, both aspects should be examined concurrently to understand accurately the process of adjustment to divorce.

The present study demonstrated that there are six major areas of concerns and problems that affect divorced individuals. Hetherington *et al.*'s (1976-1977) that problems arise in practical, interpersonal, emotional, and family-related areas is basically corroborated but has been clarified by the present research. Family related problems should be considered as two distinct sets of problems: (1) interactions with the children, and (2) interactions with the former spouse. These two problem areas account for separate amounts of variance in the scale, as well as in overall mood disturbance and life satisfaction. In addition, practical problems in daily living—such as marketing, cleaning, and finding the time to accomplish everything—are statistically orthogonal to concerns about financial difficulties.

These problem areas do not contribute equally to distress, however. Difficulties with peer and social relations are most highly related to both greater mood disturbance and lower life satisfaction. Increased mood disturbance is also affected by problematic family interactions. In contrast, family problems involving either former spouse or children have relatively little relation to life satisfaction. Rather, financial and practical concerns are related to this measure. This may indicate that dysphoric mood and other affective disturbances are influenced by interpersonal factors, while one's cognitive appraisal of his or her life situation is affected by more pragmatic issues of day-to-day concern.

It is interesting to note that problems in daily living correlate significantly with a higher level of reported life satisfaction. A possible explanation for this is that practical problems often have simple solutions and provide the divorced adult with feelings of competence and control, enhancing self-esteem and self-worth. Alternatively, practical problems may facilitate avoidance of the potentially more distressful interpersonal problems.

The absence of the problem item "keeping control of a male child" in any of the interpretable problem factors was surprising in light of Hetherinton et al.'s data (1976). However, the significant contribution of the *number of male children* to distress suggests that caring for male children is in general a problem for these people and that the physical presence of male children is more predictive of distress than the relative difficulty they present for discipline.

The various alternatives available for coping with the stresses of divorce also combine into meaningful factors. Expressing feelings, social and interpersonal activities, involvement in the home and family, personal understanding, autonomy, and learning activities account for a significant proportion of the variance in the scale. These factors are similar to those obtained by McCubbin et al. (1976), and are based on a larger, more diverse sample.

However, these coping factors have differential effects on post-divorce adjustment. Social and interpersonal involvements are directly related to lower mood disturbance and heightened life satisfaction, as are the development of autonomy and independence. In addition, these coping strategies are related to problems only in the interpersonal and emotional spheres, and have little effect on former spouse or family problems. Expressing feelings, or catharsis, is related to high mood disturbance and low life satisfaction and is not related to any specific problem area. Neither learning activities nor personal understanding appears to be related to post-divorce adjustment. These differential effects emphasize the importance of identifying empirically the impact of coping strategies, as well as their presence or absence in someone's repertoire.

The positive correlation between the usefulness of cathartic activities and heightened emotional distress can be explained in at least two ways. First, those people who report high levels of distress are more willing to view expression of affect as helpful and are more willing to acknowledge negative feelings in general, while low distress individuals deny any expression of their negative feelings. An alternative is that emotional expression is most helpful for those people who are highly distressed, while social and personal activities are only effective once the emotional distress is reduced to a manageable level. While we favor the latter explanation, additional research using longitudinal designs and multiple measures of adjustment should clarify the role of the different coping strategies in reducing distress over time.

Taken as a whole, these data clearly demonstrate important interrelationships among a variety of coping patterns, problems, and life assessments in the divorced adult. Several separate and distinct problem areas contribute to post-divorce distress, although in different ways. And several classes of coping strategies are used by the adult in divorce, although only a few of these classes contribute to the adaptational process. It must be noted that the results of this study may be biased due to the use of a sample primarily from Parents Without Partners. Generalizations must be made cautiously until cross-validation studies using alternate populations are performed. Whether these subjects are idiosyncratic in the problems they encounter, coping strategies, mood states, or life satisfaction remains to be determined. However, since over 100,000 divorced people are currently involved in Parents Without Partners, it seems that these results should be considered in their own right. Additional research on life stress in general and divorce in particular should evaluate carefully both the problems and the coping strategies encountered throughout the process of adjustment.

REFERENCES

Berman, W. H.
1979   "Coping strategies and the problems of divorce: A multivariate study." Unpublished master's thesis, Yale University.
Bloom, B. L.
1975   Changing Patterns of Psychiatric Care. New York:Human Services Press.
Bloom, B. L., S. J. Asher, and S. W. White
1978   "Marital disruption as a stressor: A review and analysis." Psychological Bulletin 85 (June): 867-894.
Bohannon, P.
1970   "The six stations of divorce." Pp. 29-55 in P. Bohannon (Ed.), Divorce and After. Garden City, New York:Doubleday and Company.
Brandwein, R. A., C. A. Brown, and E. M. Fox
1974   "Women and children last: The social situation of divorced mothers and their families." Journal of Marriage and the Family 36 (August):498-514.
Brown, E.
1976   "Divorce counseling." Pp. 202-232 in D. H. Olson (Ed.), Treating Relationships. Lake Mills, Iowa:Graphic Publishing Company.
Crago, M. A.
1972   "Psychopathology in married couples." Psychological Bulletin 77 (1):114-128.
Dohrenwend, B. S., and B. P. Dohrenwend (Eds.)
1974   Stressful Life Events: Their Nature and Effects. New York:John Wiley and Sons.

Gettleman, S., and J. Markowitz
1974   The Courage to Divorce. New York:Simon and Schuster.
Glasser, P., and E. Navarre
1965   "Structural problems of the one-parent family." Journal of Social Issues 21 (January): 98-109.
Goode, W. J.
1956   After Divorce. Glencoe, Illinois:The Free Press.
Hetherington, E. M., M. Cox, and R. Cox
1976   "Divorced fathers." Family Coordinator 25 (October):417-428.
1977   "Beyond father absence: Conceptualization of effects of divorce." Pp. 149-177 in E. M. Hetherington and R. D. Parke (Eds.), Contemporary Readings in Child Psychology. New York:McGraw-Hill.
Hollingshead, A. B.
1957   "Two-factor index of social position." Unpublished manuscript, Yale University.
Holmes, T. H., and M. Masuda
1974   "Life change and illness susceptibility." Pp. 45-72 in B. S. Dohrenwend and B. P. Dohrenwend (Eds.), Stressful Life Events: Their Nature and Effects. New York:John Wiley and Sons.
Kressel, K., and M. Deutsch
1977   Divorce therapy: An in-depth survey of therapists' views." Family Process 16 (December):413-444.
Kressel, K., M. Lopez-Morillas, J. Weinglass, and M. Deutsch
1978   "Professional intervention in divorce: A summary of the views of lawyers, psychotherapists, and clergy." Journal of Divorce 2 (Winter):119-155.
Lazarus, R.
1978   "Strategy for research in hypertension." Journal of Human Stress 4 (September):35-39.
Levinger, G.
1976   "A social-psychological perspective on marital dissolution." Journal of Social Issues 32:21-47.
McCubbin, H. I., B. Dahl, G. R. Lester, D. Benson, and M. L. Robertson
1976   "Coping repertoires of families adapting to prolonged war-induced separations." Journal of Marriage and the Family 38 (August): 461-472.
Mendes, H. A.
1976   "Single fathers." Family Coordinator 25 (October):439-444.
Miller, A. A.
1970   "Reactions of friends to divorce." Pp. 46-77 in P. Bohannon (Ed.), Divorce and After. New York:Doubleday and Company.
National Center for Health Statistics
1977   "Final divorce statistics, 1975." Monthly Vital Statistics Report 26 (2, Supplement 2), May 19. Washington, D.C.:U.S. Government Printing Office.

Nie, N. H., C. H. Hull, J. G. Jenkins, K. Steinbrenner, and D. H. Bent
  1975   Statistical Package For The Social Sciences (2nd ed.). New York:McGraw-Hill.
Norton, A. J., and P. C. Glick
  1976   "Marital instability: Past, present and future." Journal of Social Issues 32 (Winter):5-20.
Pearlin, L. I., and C. Schooler
  1978   "The structure of coping." Journal of Health and Social Behavior 19 (March):2-21.
Redick, R. W., and C. Johnson
  1974   "Marital status, living arrangements, and family characteristics of admissions to state and county mental hospitals and outpatient psychiatric clinics, United States, 1970." Statistical Note 100. National Institute of Mental Health. Washington, D.C.:U.S. Government Printing Office.
Roskies, E., and R. S. Lazarus
  1979   "Coping theory and the teaching of coping skills." Pp. 127-141 in P. Davidson (Ed.),

Behavioral Medicine: Changing Health Life Styles. New York:Brunner/Mazel.
Sternberg, R. J.
  1979   Personal communication. July 27.
Turk, D. C.
  1979   "Factors influencing the adaptive process with chronic illness: Implications for intervention. Pp. 291-311 in I. Sarason and C. Spielberger (Eds.), Stress and Anxiety, (Vol. 6). Washington, D.C.:Hemisphere Publishing Corporation.
Wainer, H.
  1976   "Estimating coefficients in linear models: It don't make no never mind." Psychological Bulletin 83 (March):213-217.
Weiss, R. S.
  1975   Marital Separation. New York:Basic Books.
  1976   "The emotional impact of marital separation." Journal of Social Issues 32 (Winter):135-145.
Yates, M.
  1976   Coping: A Survival Manual For Women Alone. Englewood Cliffs, New Jersey:Prentice-Hall.

This paper presents a conceptualization of a normative process of divorce as a crisis of family transition. With the integration of family stress and systems theories, a series of five transitions are identified as normative. Within each of these transitions, stresses associated with major role transitions and common family coping strategies are identified. Rather than dissolving the family, divorce culminates in its redefinition from a nuclear to a binuclear system. The continuation of meaningful attachment bonds between parents and children can reduce major stresses associated with this complex process of family change.

14

DIVORCE
A Crisis of Family Transition and Change*

*Constance R. Ahrons***

Traditional views of divorce as an indicator of deviance are outdated since the divorced family is a variant life style selected by many American families (Glick & Norton, 1978). A recent increase in divorce research has yielded a greater focus on outcomes, yet the adjustment of individual family members, primarily women and children, still receives the greatest attention (Luepnitz, 1978; Magrab, 1978). Although some stages of the divorce process have been identified for adults (Brown, 1976; Wiseman, 1975) and for children (Gardner, 1976; Tessman, 1978; Wallerstein & Kelly, 1980), no literature exists which integrates the interaction between parents and children throughout the divorce process (Levitin, 1979). The practice literature has fol-lowed a similar pattern and developed therapeutic approaches oriented toward individuals, primarily women and children. Published articles that include the divorced family in their treatment programs are rare (Goldman & Coane, 1977; Weisfeld & Laser, 1979).

The scarcity of research on the family processes of the divorced family results in part from the fact that the postdivorce family has no historical precedent in western society (Bohannan, 1971; Mead, 1971). Two recent studies, however, have included both parents and children in their designs and have contributed new knowledge about the effects of divorce of family members (Hetherington, Cox & Cox, 1976; 1978; Wallerstein & Kelly, 1980). These studies strongly suggest a process-orientation: the findings indicate a positive correlation between the divorced parents' relationship and their children's psychological adjustment.

Based on these and other results (Ahrons, 1979, 1980; Note 1) this paper focuses on relationships between former spouses in postdivorce families and is an initial step in conceptualizing divorce as a process of family change. The central assumption is that divorce is a crisis of family transition which causes structural changes in the family system. These transitions and the accompanying stresses

*Work on this paper was supported by a Biomedical Research Support Grant (Project #110824), University of Wisconsin Graduate School, and HEW-AoA Grant #90-A-1230 for Multidisciplinary Research on Aging Women, awarded to the Faye McBeath Institute on Aging and Adult Life, University of Wisconsin, Madison. The author wishes to thank Morton S. Perlmutter for his critical review and valuable comments.

**Constance R. Ahrons is Assistant Professor, School of Social Work, University of Wisconsin, Madison 53706.

From Constance R. Ahrons, "Divorce: A Crisis of Family Transition and Change," *Family Relations*, 1980, 29, pp. 533-540. Reprinted by permission of the publisher and author.

can be understood through a synthesis of general systems and family stress theories. The process of divorce results in changes in the family system's characteristics (i.e., the rules by which family members relate), but it does not necessarily obliterate the parent-child unit. Systems theory helps describe this process of family change. Family stress theory (Burr, 1973) provides constructs for identifying and explaining the relationships between major stressors in the divorce process and their impact on the family and allows the further construction of a model for clarifying normative family transitions that result from the divorce process.

Transition and Family Stress

The divorce process can be viewed as a series of transitions that mark the family's change from married to divorced status, from nuclearity to binuclearity (Ahrons, 1979). Erickson's (1968, p. 96) concept of transition as "a turning point, a crucial period of increased vulnerability and heightened potential within the life cycle" has been expanded to include periods which may encompass entire series of events. Characterized by affective and cognitive distress, they often result in disequilibrium reaching crisis proportions (Golan, 1978). Watzlawick, Weakland and Fisch's (1974) concept of second-order change (i.e., radical or ruleless) sought to explain this process. Although we usually define transitions within developmental frameworks (e.g., birth of first child, retirement), some life transitions are unrelated to developmental or social time clocks (Neugarten, 1979). Divorce is an unscheduled life transition, and one-third to one-half of the married population will experience these stresses of transition in the life cycle of their family.

Unlike family crises of sudden onset, the divorce process begins long before the actual decision to obtain a legal divorce. It need not be a crisis of dismemberment (Hansen & Hill, 1964), nor does it necessarily follow the stages of other family crises (e.g., dying or alcoholism). Unlike a crisis precipitated by war or death, in which external causes separate marriage partners, divorce is an internal crisis of relationship. It is a deliberate disso-

lution of the primary subsystem of the family and because of the sociotheologic sanctity of marriage, the family's identity appears shattered.

The degree of crisis, however, that the family experiences depends on a complex interaction of individual and family variables which act to mediate the individual and cumulative impact of the transitions. The dramatic role changes which accompany divorce are identified as major sources of divorce-related stress: the ambiguity that surrounds roles in the postdivorce family further complicates these role changes.

Based on Burr's (1973) propositions, it can be argued that the lack of clear role models for the divorcing relates inversely to the amount of crisis experienced: the less role clarity, the greater the crisis. In addition, McCubbin (1979) has postulated that the family's vulnerability to stress is influenced by the clarity of community expectations and norms. Given the role ambiguity for the divorced in our culture, the divorcing family is in a highly vulnerable state.

Our culture presently provides largely negative role models for the divorcing family. The focus of divorce literature on clinical samples of maladaptive responses to divorce has given rise to a distorted perception. Language for divorced families lacks the capacity to describe a present relational system except in terms of a past relationship, e.g., broken home, ex or former spouse. In his recent appraisal of divorce's effect on the institution of marriage, Weiss (1979) suggests we recognize the marriage of uncertain duration as a new marital form. If we follow Weiss's suggestion, we would then be normalizing divorce, enabling and allowing the eventual definition of a wide range of roles for postdivorce family relationships. The basis emerges for a model of the divorce process as normative, allowing for development of appropriate role models for divorcing families, thereby alleviating some of the major stresses currently necessitated by family change. While the divorce process includes the dissolution of many aspects of the nuclear family system, it also requires redefinition of the postdivorce family such that basic family needs, specifically the needs of the children, continue to be met.

Transitions and Family Change

In this framework five transitions are identified in the divorce process: (a) individual cognition, (b) family metacognition, (c) systemic separation, (d) systemic reorganization, and (e) family redefinition. Although they are presented sequentially in their ideal developmental order, *they usually overlap*. Each transition includes social role transitions encompassing a complex interaction of overlapping experiences. Bohannan (1971) has identified these experiences as: (a) the emotional divorce, (b) the legal divorce, (c) the economic divorce, (d) the coparental divorce, (e) the community divorce, and (f) the psychic divorce. These "stations of divorce" form some of the basic tasks to be accomplished in the transitions leading to family change.

Individual Cognition

Most spouses are slow to cognize the marital relationships as causing distress in the family. Spouses may acknowledge personal distress, but they then search frantically for less threatening causes, e.g., the need for more extrafamilial interests, a new house, or even another baby. Family conflicts may intensify during this period.

Characteristic of the coping mechanisms in this transition is the denial of marital problems (Wiseman, 1975; Weiss, 1976). Childhood depression or acting-out and clinical depression in one of the spouses are common responses to marital distress.

Spouses also resort to blaming to obtain respite from a situation perceived as intolerable. The marital conflict escalates and the search for the fault in the other spouse often results in his or her being labeled the culprit. This time can be a highly stressful one, especially for the children who often become pawns in the marital strife. Conflict-habituated marriages are less threatening to some families than the uncertainty and change that accompanies separation and divorce. When compared with divorced families, these highly conflictual "intact" marriages appear more damaging to children than the disorganization associated with divorce (Lamb, 1977; Magrab, 1978).

After one of the spouses (or sometimes both) has identified the source of stress as

the marital relationship itself, they seek a solution. The type of resolution chosen during this transition may vary with the couple's history of coping patterns (Hansen & Hill, 1964). They frequently decide the best resolution is to delay divorce until a less disruptive time. For example, they will have made a pseudodecision to stay in the marriage until, for example, the kids are grown. Other coping strategies include the decision to alter lifestyles and invest energy in extrafamilial interests while attempting to maintain the facade of an intact family. This process of emotional divorce, the withdrawing of emotional investment in the marital relationship, is self-protective and may have some positive individual benefits. Although withdrawal by one member will reverberate throughout the system, it is usually only one member who benefits. Emotional withdrawal may occur early in the cognition transition or only after many other coping behaviors have failed.

The duration of this transition depends on the coping behaviors employed and other factors related to the family's vulnerability to stress. Equilibrium in the family is usually maintained, albeit precariously, during this transition. Role patterns may remain undisrupted. Families frequently manifest internal stress by assigning one member the role of family scapegoat (Vogel & Bell, 1968).

Family Metacognition

The metacognitive process is family stocktaking. Information is exchanged, more or less openly in the family, of the realization that the problem is essential to the system (Flavell, 1979). This exchange of information sums up each family member's anticipatory anxieties. The metacognition is that the marriage is the source of the problems and may itself perish because of them. If the family can cope well enough to survive this transition, the physical separation will occur after assimilation of the problem, its potential solutions and anticipated family changes. This time can be used to prepare for the changes caused by physical separation without decisions based on anger. If the family has not employed this method of problem solving in past crises, however, it is not apt to do so at this time. Due to the persistent emotional bonds between spouses, regardless of quality, this period is marked by ambivalent feelings of love and hate, euphoria and sadness (Weiss, 1976).

The amount of crisis experienced may depend on whether the crisis is voluntary or inflicted (Hansen & Hill, 1964). Although Weiss (1976) noted no long-range differences between those who did and those who did not choose divorce, this factor appears critical in determining coping behaviors and the degree of crisis experienced in the early stages of the marital disruption. Based on the mutuality of the decision to separate or divorce, the leavers are more likely to feel guilt about disrupting the family; those left, more likely to experience anger and/or depression (Brown, 1976).

For some families this is the time of greatest disequilibrium: old roles have disappeared and new ones have not yet developed. The future appears ambiguous, and the family searches for role models. In striving for homeostasis the family may try to preserve old rules and rituals, but old patterns fail to provide comfort or unity. Children often begin to research divorce by seeking friends whose parents are divorced.

Systemic Separation

The actual physical separation may be met with great variations in family coping patterns. The degree of crisis depends on whether the family has completed the work of the other transitions prior to the physical separation. When spouses separate reactively, prior to metacognizing separation or divorce as a solution to the problem, crisis in the family system is more likely to arise. This frequently results in premature contact with the legal system: the adversarial nature of the system is readily available to punish the spouse. When the first two transitions have not been completed, the crisis at the physical separation transition is more likely to be disruptive to the family.

Couples commonly engage in a long transition of separation and reconciliation. In many families, parents separate and reconcile briefly, perhaps several times, because of feelings of ambivalence or guilt over the

children's distress. The stress in families during these intermittent periods of separation and reconciliation may resemble the stress experienced by the MIA wives (Boss, 1977) and corporate wives (Boss, McCubbin, & Lester, 1979). In the most common divorced family form, mother and children remain as one unit while father moves out and functions as a separate unit. The mother-headed household faces a dilemma: should it reorganize and fill roles enacted by the physically absent father, or should it maintain his psychological presence in the system by not reorganizing. If the mother/children unit tries to reassign roles, the father's return will be met with resistance. If, on the other hand, they deal with father as psychologically present, they perpetuate family disequilibrium and stress. This cycle is typical of the stress endured during this period. The children face a difficult and very stressful transition with the family in a constant state of disequilibrium characterized by the boundary ambiguity (Boss, 1977) created by the father's intermittent exit and return. This "on-again-off-again" marital relationship often continues for years as the spouses resolve their ambivalences and make the transition to reorganization. This length of time is particularly required if a crisis of the first transition precipitated the physical separation without allowing for a reorganization.

Even families that have successfully completed the earlier transitions suffer stress during this period, although they may not face severe disruption. At this time they share their marital separation with extended family, friends, and the community as they begin the tasks of the economic and legal divorce. These mediating factors can help and/or hinder the transitional process. The family usually encounters the legal system at this time and faces additional stress as they confront hard economic and child-focused realities. This may also escalate the crisis, since spouses now need to divide what they had shared.

Although no-fault divorce legislation reflects changing social attitudes, the legal system still operates on an adversarial model. Based on a win-lose game, the legal divorce frequently escalates the spousal power struggle, adding additional stress to the already disorganized system.

Systemic Reorganization

The concept of family boundaries, rules which determine the parameters of the family system (Minuchin, 1974), helps to understand a major stress of this transition. In the earlier transition, the absence of clear boundaries creates much of the confusion and stress; in this transition, the clarification of boundaries generates the distress.

Rules defining when and how each of the parents continues to relate to the children are critical to the child's understanding of the divorce and to the consequent stabilization of the parent-child relationship. Each parent must establish an independent relationship with the child to pass this transition successfully, but the continuation of each parent-child relationship unit requires the continued interdependence of the former spouses. This paradoxical and complex process requires the clarification of roles and boundaries between parental and spousal subsystems (Ahrons, Note 2). The lack of role models and the absence of societal norms for a continuing relationship between divorced parents complicate this transition.

The final stage of adjustment has been traditionally the exclusion of the "problem member" from the family system. This process of "freezing out" (Farber, 1964), "closing ranks" (Hill, 1949), or "closing out" (Boss, 1977) is functional only when the father remains absent in the system. While the literature has not directly identified this final stage as part of the divorce process, ample evidence suggests that this coping strategy has been common both to divorced families and to our thinking about them. Clinical literature often cites a healthy adjustment to divorce as associated with termination of relationships between former spouses (Kressel & Deutsch, 1977). The label "single parent family" as a descriptor of divorced families indicates the assumption that divorce results in one parent leaving the system.

Recent research, however, revealed that this pattern of coping with postdivorce family reorganization results in increased individual stress and family dysfunction: the more the noncustodial father is "closed out" of the system, the more dysfunctional stress the system experiences. Noncustodial fathers with infrequent postdivorce contact with their children were reported to be more depressed (Greif, 1979), more dissatisfied with their relationships with their children (Ahrons, 1979), and more stressed regarding role loss (Keshet & Rosenthal, 1978; Mendes, 1976). Sole custody mothers were more depressed and overburdened by the responsibilities resulting from role overload (Brandwein, Brown & Fox, 1974; Hetherington et al., 1976; Weiss, 1980). Children with very limited or no father contact suffered the most severe developmental and emotional distress (Hetherington, 1979; Wallerstein & Kelly, 1980).

The nuclear family's reorganization through divorce creates new households with single parents *only* when one parent has no further contact with the family and no longer performs parental functions. The frequent creation of interrelated maternal and paternal households creates two nuclei which form one family system—*a binuclear family system* (Ahrons, 1979, 1980, Note 1).

Family Redefinition

This transition is a metacognition and conclusion to the reorganizational transition. How the divorced family defines itself, both to itself and to community and friends, is critical to the family's struggles with identity, boundaries, and individuation. Society's labeling of postdivorce families as deviant only increases the stress of this final transition. Postdivorce households "have one thing in common; they show an individual adaptation to an overall social situation that is poorly defined and morally unresolved" (Bohannan, 1971, p. 290).

The redefinition of relationships in the divorced family depends on the relationship between the parents. Although a continued, cooperative, and mutually supportive relationship between divorced parents reduces the crisis potential associated with divorce, its dynamics remain largely unexplored. The growing debate about custody rights reveals our lack of knowledge about the time-honored concept, "best interests of the child," and brings the custom of sole custody into serious question. A trend toward shared custody and coparenting seems to be emerging ("One child . . . ," 1979) which should have profound implications for the postdivorce family. Given current societal changes such as increased role sharing and equality in marriage, increase of women in the labor force, and increased parental involvement of fathers, the issue is clearly no longer *whether*, but *how* divorced parents can continue to share parenting effectively.

Although current research on joint custody is necessarily limited to small samples, an increasing pool of data suggests a range of coparental relationship patterns which permits both parents an active role in their children's lives (Sell, Note 3). One major component of the redefinitional process appears to be the parents' ability to maintain a child-centered relationship. For some this includes a personal continuing friendship, but for most it is less intimate and more instrumental (Ahrons, 1979, 1980, Note 1). Parents who share custody, however, experience great distress as they interact with social institutions, family, and friends. Institutions based on the nuclear family strongly resist the changes introduced by the binuclear family. For example, the desire of *both* parents to receive copies of their children's report cards and school announcements commonly meets with resistance. Extended family and friends view such relationships as embarrassing, deviant, or in some way pathological. However, observations reveal normative changes which may assist in postdivorce family redefinition. Greeting cards are not available to announce a divorce and to send to the newly divorced. Language norms also reflect change: phrases like "my son's mother" and "my coparent" are no longer so rare.

A family redefinitional process frequently includes remarriage and the introduction of stepparents into the postdivorce family. Remarriage creates a series of transitions beyond the scope of this paper, but which are part of the ongoing transition of family redefinition. For some families, a potential remarriage partner or spouse-equivalent may become part of the family system prior to the legal divorce and at the early phases of the reorganization transition. Some unnamed and thus unsanctioned relationships within the binuclear family structure take on an importance in the redefinitional transition (see Fig. 1). They are kin or quasi-kin relationships in the context of the postdivorce family.

Relationships between stepparents and parents in the binuclear family system provide an important emotional continuity for both parents and children. It facilitates this transition by redefining the divorced family so that the amount of relationship loss experienced by children and parents is minimized.

Conclusions and Speculations

The dramatic role transitions and systemic reorganization necessitated by divorce puts stress on the whole family. This can bring on critical family dysfunctioning in all the major transitions. Rather than dissolving the family, divorce creates the need to develop a new equilibrium over time, with specific structural and behavioral rules for a binuclear family system.

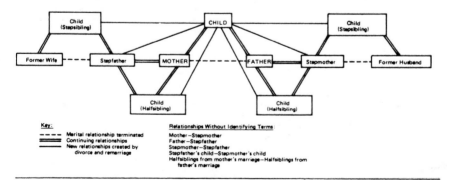

Figure 1. THE CHILD'S BINUCLEAR FAMILY SYSTEM

While this paper does not aim to present an intervention model, some clinical guidelines emerge. The maintenance of a good parenting relationship requires the redefinition of the divorced family to include both parents. The divorced spouses must be helped to disengage from spousal roles, at both the individual and interactive levels, while developing new rules and metarules for their continued relationship. Any attempt to redefine the boundaries of the coparental relationship must clarify boundaries within and between all the subsystems so that spousal roles do not contaminate parental roles. Therapists must especially work to clarify their personal perceptions and values about divorce, and to recognize the divorced family as a continuing family system. The transition from married to divorced can be less threatening if divorced parents know they can continue a coparental relationship. The binuclear family provides a family style which does not force the child to sever the bond with either parent, but which allows both parents to continue their parental roles postdivorce.

REFERENCE NOTES

1. Ahrons, C. R. *The continuing coparental relationship between divorced spouses.* Paper presented at the American Orthopsychiatric Association, Annual Meeting, April. 1980. Toronto. Canada.

2. Ahrons, C. *Redefining the divorced family: A conceptual framework for postdivorce family system reorganization. Social Work.* in press.

3. Sell, K. *Joint custody and coparenting.* Unpublished paper, Catawba College, North Carolina, 1979.

REFERENCES

Ahrons, C. The binuclear family: Two households, one family. *Alternative Lifestyles,* November, 1979, **2,** 499-515. 515.

Ahrons, C. Joint custody arrangements in the postdivorce family. *Journal of Divorce,* Spring, 1980, **3,** 189-205.

Bohannan, P. (Ed.) *Divorce and after.* New York: Anchor Books, 1971.

Boss, P. A clarification of the concept of psychological father presence in families experiencing ambiguity of boundary. *Journal of Marriage and the Family,* 1977, **39,** 141-151.

Boss, P., McCubbin, H. I., & Lester, G. The corporate executive's wife's coping patterns in response to routine husband-father absence. *Family Process,* 1979, **18,** 79-86.

Brandwein, R. A., Brown, C. A., & Fox, E. M. Women and children last: The social situation of divorced mothers and their families. *Journal of Marriage and the Family,* 1974, **36,** 498-514.

Brown, E. M. A model of the divorce process. *Conciliation Courts Review,* 1976, **14,** 1-11.

Burr, W. *Theory construction and the sociology of the family.* New York: Wiley, 1973.

Erikson, E. *Identity, youth and crisis.* New York: Norton, 1968.

Farber, B. *Family organization and interaction.* San Francisco: Chandler, 1964.

Flavell, J. Metacognition and cognitive monitoring: A new area of cognitive-developmental inquiry. *American Psychologist,* 1979 **34,** 906-911.

Gardner, R. A. *Psychotherapy with children of divorce.* New York: Jason Aronson, 1976.

Glick, P. G., & Norton, A. J. Marrying, divorcing and living together in the U.S. today. *Population Bulletin,* 1978, **32,** 3-38.

Golan, N. *Treatment in crisis situations.* New York: Free Press, 1978.

Goldman, J. & Coane, J. Family therapy after the divorce: Developing a strategy. *Family Process,* 1977, **16,** 357-362.

Greif, J. B. Fathers, children and joint custody. *American Journal of Orthopsychiatry,* 1979, **49,** 311-319.

Hansen, D. & Hill, R. Families under stress. In H. T. Christensen (Ed.), *Handbook of marriage and the family.* Chicago: Rand McNally, 1964, 782-819.

Hetherington, E. M. Divorce: A child's perspective. *American Psychologist.* October, 1979, **34,** 851-858.

Hetherington, E. M., Cox, M., & Cox, R. Divorced fathers. *The Family Coordinator,* 1976, **25,** 417-428.

Hetherington, E. M., Cox, M., & Cox, R. Stress and coping in divorce: A focus on women. In J. E. Gullahorn (Ed.), *Psychology and women in transition.* New York: John Wiley, 1979.

Hill, R. *Families under stress.* New York: Harper, 1949.

Keshet, H. F., & Rosenthal, K. M. Fathering after marital separation. *Social Work,* 1978, **23,** 11-18.

Kressel, K., & Deutsch, M. Divorce therapy: An in-depth survey of therapists' views. *Family Process,* 1977, **16,** 413-443.

Lamb, M. E. The effects of divorce on children's personality development. *Journal of Divorce,* 1977, **1,** 163-174.

Luepnitz, D. A. Children of divorce: A review of the psychological literature. *Law and Human Behavior,* 1978, **2,** 167-179.

Magrab, P. R. For the sake of the children: A review of the psychological effects of divorce. *Journal of Divorce,* 1978. 1, 233-245.

McCubbin, H. I. Integrating coping behavior in family stress theory. *Journal of Marriage and the Family,* 1979, **41,** 237-244.

Mead, M. Anomalies in American postdivorce relationships. In P. Bohannan (Ed.), *Divorce and after.* New York: Anchor Books, 1971, 97-112.

Mendes, H. Single fatherhood. *Social Work,* 1976, **21,** 308-312.

Mendes, H. A. Single fathers. *The Family Coordinator*, 1976, **25**, 439-449.

Minuchin, S. *Families and family therapy*. Cambridge, MS: Harvard University Press, 1974.

Neugarten, B. L. Time, age, and the life cycle. *The American Journal of Psychiatry*, 1979, **136**, 887-894.

One child, two homes. *Time*, Jan. 29, 1979, p. 61.

Tessman, L. H. *Children of parting parents*. New York: Aronson, 1978.

Vogel, F. & Bell, N. W. The emotionally disturbed child as the family scapegoat. In N. Bell and E. Vogel (Eds.), *A modern introduction to the family*. New York: Free Press, 1968, 412-427.

Wallerstein, J. S., & Kelly, J. B. *Surviving the breakup: How children and parents cope with divorce*. New York: Basic Books, 1980.

Watzlawick, P., Weakland, J., & Fisch, R. *Change: Principles of problem formation and problem resolution*. New York: Norton, 1974.

Weisfeld, D., & Laser, M. Divorced parents in family therapy in a residential treatment setting. *Family Process*, 1977, **16**, 229-236.

Weiss, R. S. The emotional impact of marital separation. *Journal of Social Issues*, 1976, **32**, 135-146.

Weiss, R. A new marital form: The marriage of uncertain duration. In H. Gans, N. Glazer, J. R. Gusfield, & C. Jencks (Eds.), *On the making of Americans: Essays in honor of David Reisman*. Philadelphia: University of Pennsylvania Press, 1979.

Wiseman, R. S. Crisis theory and the process of divorce. *Social Casework*, 1975, **56**, 205-212.

This paper focuses on four major areas of child custody in transition: parental preference, child preference, rights and responsibilities of custodial and noncustodial parents, and joint custody. These issues are addressed with regard to parent vs. parent custody decisions. Current legal and psychological trends in custody contests are reviewed.

15

CHILD CUSTODY IN TRANSITION*

Robin L. Franklin and "B" Hibbs**

The historical shifts in presumption to custody reflect societal and legal assumptions regarding what constitutes the "best interests of the child." The child is singled out by law for special consideration; he is viewed as an incomplete person, unable to safeguard his rights. Law is then society's response to the need for assuring that a child's environment is suitable for his continued growth and development. The evolution of judicial decision making in custody placement mirrors societal practice and understanding of the best interests of the child. Historically, this is demonstrated in the shifting emphasis from the father's to the mother's to the child's rights. Paternal preference, rooted in the presumption of the child as property, gradually was displaced in this century in favor of maternal preference. This was based on the traditional role of the mother as the primary physical and psychological caretaker of the child.

Recently, the courts have held that the best interests of the child are not always represented by the unilateral judgments of the divorcing parents. What appears to be emerging is a consideration for the rights and responsibilities of all parties. Several state legislatures are beginning to show support for alternatives other than the traditional ones. Court affiliated reconciliation services, mandatory divorce counseling, and joint custodial arrangements are current reflections of changes in this area. This paper will address major transitions in custody arrangements by reviewing parental and child preferences, the rights and responsibilities of the custodial and non-custodial parent, and joint custody.

Paternal Preference

The distinction between the physical and psychological well-being of the child is a relic of Roman law (circa 500 B.C.). In that era the child was regarded as property, whose physical care should be provided by the father. This was supported legally by the doctrine of patria potestas, charging the father with the power of life or death over his progeny (Derdeyn, 1976a). This fundamental view of the child as property and later a provider of services and income, did not assume a philosophical shift until the 16th century. Still the

*The authors gratefully acknowledge the contributions of Florence Kaslow, PhD, and Margaret Controneo, MSN, MA.

**Robin L. Franklin, MEd, MFT and "B" Hibbs, MS, MFT co-authored this paper at Hahnemann Medical College, Philadelphia, Pennsylvania.

Reprinted from Volume 6, Number 3 of *Journal of Marital and Family Therapy*, pp. 285-291. Copyright © 1980 American Association for Marriage and Family Therapy. Reprinted by permission.

law was slow to reflect changing cultural views. When a marriage dissolved, the child, whose custody was based on the presumption of property rights, went to the father. If for some reason the father was deprived of his child, he was also absolved of any responsibility to support the child financially (Duncan, 1978). The state did not intrude in the father's common law right to custody except in cases of paternal default (Solow & Adams, 1976). The Anglo-Saxon court broke the tradition of non-interference in 1839 with the Talfourds Act. The doctrine of parens patriae was established and the court assumed the power to decide custody for children under seven (Derdeyn, 1976a.) This act set the stage for one of the main governing principles of custody decisions, the Tender Years Presumption.

Maternal Preference

In a tradition-breaking precedent, a judge presiding over the Hart v. Hart (1880) custody dispute ruled in favor of the mother with this argument: "the claim of a mother during the early years of an infant's life to the care of her child is to be preferred to that of the father" (Duncan, 1978, p. 464). This ruling reflected an initial, though tentative, move towards a consideration of the psychological well-being of the child. Though precedent setting, maternal custody was regarded as a temporary exception to the rule. The court often returned the child to the father after its early years. (Cases cited include return of the child at age four, Derdeyn, 1976a.)

This narrowly defined maternal claim to custody gradually broadened, and by the late 19th century, the question was raised as to which parent should retain custody of the child. The concept of a father's duty to support a child not in his custody developed in statutes and case law in the early 1900s. Contemporaneous with this development was the mother's right to custody. This grew out of a moral and cultural climate in which the assumption was that the mother was best suited for the physical and psychological care of the child (Derdeyn, 1976a).

Both paternal and maternal presumptions to custody reflected unilateral parental rights rather than the interests of the child. Judge Cordoza in the 1925 Finlay v. Finlay decision was credited with the development of the "best interests of the child" standard. He ruled that [the judge] "Does not proceed upon the theory that the petitioner, whether father or mother, has a cause for action against the other or indeed against anyone. He acts as parens patriae to do what is best for the interests of the child" (Duncan, 1978, p. 464). The traditional 20th century guidelines for establishing the best interests of the child dictates that (Derdeyn, 1976b, p. 165):

(1) The young child should be placed with the mother.
(2) A girl should be in the mother's custody, a boy in the father's (providing he no longer requires mother's constant care).
(3) If the child is old enough, he can voice his preference.
(4) There will be rights of visitation by the non-custodial parent (except in case of harm to the child).

These presumptions, based on English common law, were designed to insure the interests of the child. These standards have, however, generally supported maternal presumption. As Woody (1977, p. 879) documents: "For the better part of this century the law, though based on the assumption of equity, has delivered four-fifths of custody cases to the mother, one-tenth [to] the father and the rest to both parents or the relatives are made guardians of the children."

Maternal custody has recently been accused of being based on acts, not facts. What maternal preference acknowledged was that the traditional role of the mother was for the primary care of the child in its early years. What the courts are now asked to recognize, by critics of maternal preference, is that with changing roles, it may be the father who assumes the nurturant, "mothering" role. The essential shift would be from maternal to primary caretaker preference.

The current challenge by some fathers for their right to custody has suggested a move toward legally enforceable equity of custody decisions. The Tender Years Presumption is subject to question under Amendment Fourteen, because its bias for women defies the protection of equality guaranteed in the Constitution.

In a period when fathers have made renewed claims for custody, the courts have expressed a growing concern that the rights of the child may not be best represented by parent-oriented advocacy. The next transition in custody considerations occurred with an emphasis away from the rights of the parents to the rights of the child.

Best Interests of the Child Standard

The protection of the child is most often expressed, informally, by adherence to "the best interests of the child" standard. Currently maternal preference is being displaced by an insistence of a neutral application of the best interests guideline. Thirty-one states have statutes providing for a best-interests of the child standard, while others rely on their courts to develop best interest guidelines. Basic considerations, which are included in this standard, are (Mnookin, 1978, p. 636):

(1) The relationship of the children to each parent prior to the commencement of the action or any subsequent hearing;
(2) The desires and wishes of the children if of an age of comprehension regardless of their chronological age, when such desires and wishes are based on sound reasoning; and
(3) The general health, welfare, and social behavior of the children.
(4) In determining with which of the parents the children, or any of them shall remain, the court shall not give preference to either parent based on the sex of the parent and no presumption shall exist that either parent is more fit to have custody of the children than the other.

These broad guidelines do not represent substantive standards, nor do they offer a predictability for what would insure the child's best interests. Mnookin (1978, p. 488) notes: "An inquiry about what is best for a child often yields indeterminate results because of the problems of having adequate information, making the necessary predictions, and finding an integrated set of values by which to choose." What is in the child's best interest may then be decided by default. In place of imposing stringent rules for best interest considerations, there has been an increasing trend toward court appointment of a guardian ad litem or a lawyer to represent the child's interests and preference.

Child Preference

The Uniform Marriage and Divorce Act (model legislation approved by the American Bar Association in 1974) attempts to establish legal guidelines for divorce in the child's best interests. Its three major standards are (Duncan, 1978, p. 464):

(1) The access to litigation to modify custody is prohibited for two years after the issuance of the custody decree (in the absence of serious harm to the child).
(2) The court may appoint an attorney for the child (in contested cases or in cases of concern for the best interests of the child).
(3) The court may order a custody investigation.

Other issues are questions of the child's right to participate and express a preference. As Mnookin (1978, p. 480) notes, "Normally parties most affected by a dispute have the right to participate in the adjudicatory process." While a parent can appeal a custody decision, a child cannot. Even with independent representation afforded by a guardian ad litem or by an attorney, the representative must define for himself the child's best interests (except in the case of older children).

Twenty states now have statutes that require a consideration of the child's preference of custodial parent. The remaining thirty have case law dealing with this consideration. The guidelines for establishing competency to testify vary from state to state. Twelve states have "10-year statutes," under which a child less than 10 is judged not a competent witness. The common law competence to testify includes five criteria (Wynne & Cohen, 1979):

(1) His understanding of the obligation to speak the truth on the witness stand.
(2) His mental capacity at the time of the event about which he is to testify.
(3) Whether his memory is sufficient to retain an independent recollection of the occurrence.
(4) His capacity to express in words his memory of the occurrence.
(5) His capacity to understand simple questions about it.

Schowalter (1979) raises further considerations regarding how much weight to give a child's preference. From a developmental perspective, the child has a poor ability to project the idea of self into the future prior to the acquisition of formal operational thought (which occurs around age eleven, Guber & Voneche, 1977). This has obvious implications for weighting of the child's preference. Other considerations include ascertaining if the preference has been coached and how strong it is. A strong depressive reaction is often observed in children who express a preference, no matter which parent is granted custody (Schowalter, 1979). Whether or not the child's preference is heavily weighted in the decision, the child lives with the fantasy that he is responsible for his parents' separation (and divorce). This choice further divides the child's loyalties to his parents. Out of a concern for insuring the child's right to choose between parents, it seems that the legal and cultural system often parentifies the child it seeks to protect.

This historical overview provides a perspective on the shifting emphasis from the rights of the father, to the rights of the mother, to the rights of the child. In the most recent trend, the court no longer assumes that the divorcing parents are able to make the unilateral judgment which will reflect the child's best interests.

Rights and Responsibilities

The exclusive rights and responsibilities of custodial and non-custodial parents are defined with little specificity in the statutes. "The distinctions that are made, in fact, are based either on certain generally held notions on what custody permits or on such other grounds as custom, common sense and/or expediency" (Kiefer, 1979, p. 373). In practice, the non-custodial parent has substantially fewer parental rights than the custodial parent. The non-custodial parent may or may not have visitation rights. When he/she does, the frequency and duration of visitation tends to come under the control of the custodial parent. Therefore, in a traditional custody arrangement, one parent has close to total control of a child's life.

In an analysis of federal and state statutes, Kiefer (1979) found only two statutes which distinguished between the parent who was awarded custody and the parent with factual possession of the child. One statute grants the custodial parent the right to invoke criminal penalties if there is a violation of the custodial interference statute. While the custodial parent can take the child and leave the state permanently without having violated the law, the non-custodial parent does not have the same right.

It appears that a second statutory advantage is given to the custodial parent for income tax deductions. However, a dependency exemption given by the Internal Revenue Code, actually makes distinctions according to support and possession—and not necessarily on the legal award of custody. Kiefer (1979, p. 375) quotes the following from the Internal Revenue Code: "The parent who has custody of the child for the greater part of the year is treated as the parent who furnishes more than half the child's support . . ."

Sole custody has been the subject of extensive analysis in both the legal and mental health literature. Controversy tends to surround the area of one parent carrying all of the parenting responsibilities versus joint or shared responsibilities by both parents. The presumption of sole custody in the legal arena is set forth in the book, *Beyond the Best*

Interests of the Child (Goldstein, Freud, and Solnit, 1973). This book proposes that continuity of relationship with the custodial parent is necessary for the child's development; and that this development may be disrupted and hindered by a continued relationship with the non-custodial parent.

One criticism of Goldstein, *et al.* is that they " . . . ignore the child's right to maintain an ongoing relationship with each parent, emphasizing only the hazards but none of the benefits of such a course" (Duncan, 1979, p. 465). This can be seen when visitation disputes between parents are found to be damaging to the child. Duncan (1979, p. 465) further states that "Visitation controversy provides an avenue for sustained marital warfare and conflicts of loyalty in the children." The custodial parent may deny or discourage the non-custodial parent's visitation with the child. Contrary to this view, Goldstein, *et al.* (1973, p. 38) state that " . . . the noncustodial parent should have no legally enforceable right to visit the child, and the custodial parent should have the right to decide whether it is desirable for the child to have such visits." The visitation provisions that are put forth in the Uniform Marriage and Divorce Act (1979) state:

Visitation
    (a) A parent not granted custody of the child is entitled to reasonable visitation rights unless the court finds, after a hearing, that visitation would endanger the child's physical health or significantly impair his emotional development.
    (b) The court may modify an order granting or denying visitation rights whenever modification would serve the best interests of the child; but the court shall not restrict a parent's visitation rights unless it finds that the visitation would endanger the child's physical health or significantly impair his emotional development.

Inherent in all custody arrangements is the fact that one parent will have less than all of the parental rights that would be included in an intact family. However, when child custody is considered on the basis of one parent versus the other, perhaps the result is in no one's best interest. In the last few years a contextual integration (Cotroneo, Krasner and Nagy, 1980), which considers the best interests of all parties, has appeared in the legal structure. This multilateral approach surfaces the rights of a child to be parented by both his parents. Legally, the rubric of this concept is joint custody.

Joint Custody

Joint custody is a legal disposition for shared parental responsibility for a child. It does not necessarily imply "co-parenting," which is a relational arrangement where the parents work together jointly to raise their child. Joint custody is not a new procedure, though traditionally the courts in most states have viewed it as undesirable. Lawyers have been trained to work out settlements for sole custody with visitation for the non-custodial parent primarily because sole custody is perceived as bringing an end to litigation. However, it has been strongly suggested by several authors that the concept of joint custody is not adverse to the present legal system. Parley (1979, p. 315) states that, "Once joint custody has been translated into a decree, there is an interest on the part of the parents to conform their behavior to "the law," but prior to the decree, "lawlessness" and self interest have greater leeway."

In fact, there is evidence to the contrary—that the classical custody situation increases the likelihood of further litigation. "In many private disputes, the court must often choose between parties who each offer advantages and disadvantages, knowing that to deprive the child completely of either relationship will be disruptive" (Mnookin, 1978, p. 489).

In a study by Judith Grief (1979), the argument is presented that children of divorce, as well as children of intact families, need loving relationships with both parents. The study addresses the three most common myths associated with joint parenting arrangements.

One myth is that it would be disruptive for a child to have two homes rather than one. The results of her research showed that a child who lived in a two-home situation had adjusted well to the routine and that separations were made with much less pain than in families with sole custody arrangements. "The joint custody fathers reported that they and their children could more easily separate, knowing they would soon have a long period of time together again" (Grief, 1979, p. 318).

Another myth is what has been called the "yo-yo" problem. This refers to a belief that a child in this situation will wind up being bounced from parent to parent, that he will become a pawn in his parents' marital battle, and that his loyalties will be divided. Grief found that this situation was more likely to occur in sole custody arrangements. "In joint custody arrangements, . . . parental power and decision-making are equally divided, so there is less need to use children to barter for more" (Grief, 1979, p. 318).

The third myth is that joint custody can only work when the parents can get along—and if they get along so well, then why did they get divorced? The research on joint custody families has shown that despite hostilities within the marriage, these couples are able to work well together because of their shared commitment to the child. The joint custody couples in Grief's study were largely able to separate out their parental responsibilties from their marital problems (1979, p. 318).

Joint custody is only one alternative to the traditional custody arrangements. There are those who feel that there should be a legal presumption for joint custody. In this case, it would be up to the divorcing parents to prove that sole custody would be in the child's best interests. This is a fairly radical approach; however, there have been cases where joint custody has been ordered despite the objections of one parent (Mnookin, 1978, p. 643). In the majority of cases, joint custody is considered only when sole custody has not worked. Legal counsel is very important in this regard.

Mandatory counseling is one form of coercion the court can use to encourage people to work out custodial decisions. This process is built into the no-fault divorce laws in some states. However, implementation of these procedures is a problem. Suggestions have been made for the entire custodial process to be moved out of the adversarial arena into a more conciliatory and mediating one. The contextual approach to child custody decisions, developed by Cotroneo, Krasner & Nagy (1980), represents one attempt to bridge this traditional adversarial position.

The contextual approach is an adjunctive one, which advocates for flexibility in custody decisions, rather than for an inflexible position of either sole or joint custody. The presumption is that:

> . . . judicial decision making should aim at providing the child with an on-going relationship to both biological parents and with as many members of the child's family of origin as possible. It follows then that the best custodial parent is the one who is most able to tolerate and collaborate in maintaining an ongoing relationship to all or as much of the child's family of origin as possible. (Cotroneo, Krasner & Nagy, 1980)

Co-parenting, regardless of custodial arrangement, is the relational goal which is seen to serve the best interests of both the parents and the child.

The transitional nature of child custody decisions is reflected in these current legal alternatives, as well as in the shifting emphasis from parental to child's rights. Historically, the legal and cultural paternal presumption to custody gave way in the first quarter of this century to maternal preference. The factual and psychological assumptions regarding maternal preference are now being questioned. More dramatically, a concern for the rights of the child is represented in the therapeutic literature on custody and in the legal commitment to the best interests of the child. Recently, an integration of these unilateral arrangements has resulted in the legal structure of joint custody. The underlying premise of this concept, as well as of the contextual approach to child custody decisions, appears to be the child's right and need for conjoint parental accessibility. With this in mind, child custody contests begin to have new meaning for the courts, as well as for parents and their children.

REFERENCES

Cotroneo, M., Krasner, B., & Boszormenyi-Nagy, I., Contextual approach to child custody decisions, in P. Sholevar (Ed.), *Marriage is a family affair.* New York: Spectrum, in press, 1980.

Derdeyn, A. Child custody contests in historical perspective. *American Journal of Psychiatry,* 1976, *133*, 1369–1376. (a)

Derdeyn, A. A consideration of legal issues in child custody cases. *Archives of General Psychiatry,* 1976, *33*, 165–171. (b)

Duncan, J. W. Medical, psychologic, and legal aspects of child custody disputes. *Mayo Clinic Process,* 1978, *53*, 463–468.

Goldstein, J., Freud, A., & Solnit, A.J. *Beyond the best interests of the child.* New York: The Free Press, 1973.

Grief, J. B. Fathers, children, and joint custody. *American Journal of Orthopsychiatry,* 1979, *49*, 311–319.

Guber, E. H. & Voneche, J. J. (Eds.) *Jean Piaget: The essential Piaget.* New York: Basic Books, 1977.

Kiefer, L. Custody meanings and considerations. *Connecticut Bar Journal,* 1979, *53*, 371–386.

Mnookin, D. S. *Child, family and state.* Boston: Little Brown & Co., 1978.

Parley, L. Joint custody: "Traces" in the legal system. *Connecticut Bar Journal,* 1979, *53*, 310–319.

Schowalter, J. E. Views on the role of the child's preference in custody litigation. *Connecticut Bar Journal,* 1979, *53*, 298–300.

Solow, R. A. & Adams, P. L. Custody by agreement: Child psychiatrist as child advocate. *Bulletin of the American Academy of Psychiatry and Law,* 1976, *4*, 77–94.

Woody, R. H. Sexism in child custody decisions. *Personnel and Guidance Journal,* 1977, 168–170.

NOTES

[1]Wynne, M. E. & Cohen, G. I. *The role of the child's preference in custody proceedings: Legal aspects.* Paper presented at the Yale University Child Custody Symposium, New Haven, April, 1979.

PART IV

MARITAL AND FAMILY VIOLENCE

This paper reviews research on family violence in the seventies. The issue of family violence became increasingly visible as a social and family issue in the decade of the seventies. Whereas research in the sixties tended to view domestic violence as rare and confined to mentally disturbed and/or poor people, research in the seventies revealed family violence as an extensive phenomenon which could not be explained solely as a consequence of psychological factors or income. Students of domestic violence grappled with the problems of defining abuse and violence, sampling problems, and measurement issues as they focused their efforts on measuring the incidence of family violence, the factors related to violence in the family, and the development of causal models to explain family violence. The review concludes by discussing research needs and future issues in the study of violence in the family.

16

VIOLENCE IN THE FAMILY

A Review of Research in the Seventies

Richard J. Gelles*

The *Journal of Marriage and the Family* Decade Review of family research and action in the sixties did not contain a review of research on family violence. This is not surprising in light of O'Brien's (1971) report that the Index of the *Journal*, from its inception in 1939 through 1969, did not include even one article with the word "violence" in the title.[1]

RESEARCH IN THE SIXTIES

That there was not any article on family violence in the first 30 years of publication of the JMF does not necessarily mean that there was no research on family violence carried out prior to 1969. There was burgeoning interest in the topic of child abuse, commencing with

the publication of Kempe *et al.*'s seminal article, "The Battered Child Syndrome," which appeared in the *Journal of the American Medical Association* in 1962. The majority of published work on child abuse in the decade of the sixties was written by and for medical or mental health professionals.

Scholarly and even popular literature on wife abuse was virtually nonexistent in the sixties. Snell *et al.* (1964) wrote a profile of battered wives, while Schultz (1960) examined wife assaulters. Violence toward husbands, parents, and the elderly was neither recognized nor reported in scholarly or lay literature prior to the seventies.

The knowledge base on family violence (in reality this applies mostly, if not only, to child abuse) in the sixties was characterized by singular and narrow theoretical and methodological approaches to the problem. No reliable statistics on the incidence of family violence existed in the sixties. Estimates of child abuse varied widely, from thousands to tens of thousands (Kempe, 1971; Steele and Pollock, 1968). In 1965, David Gil and the National Opinion Research Council collaborated on a household survey of attitudes,

*Department of Sociology and Anthropology, University of Rhode Island, Kingston, Rhode Island 02881.

[1] It is noteworthy that O'Brien's article, containing this quote, was published in a special issue of the *Journal of Marriage and the Family* published under the guest editorship of Felix M. Berardo in 1971 on the topic of family violence. This was perhaps the first such special issue published on family violence by a scholarly journal.

From Richard J. Gelles, "Violence in the Family: A Review of Research in the Seventies," *Journal of Marriage and the Family*, 1980, 42, pp. 873-885. Reprinted by permission of the publisher and author.

knowledge, and opinions about child abuse. Of a nationally representative sample of 1,520 individuals, 45, or 3 percent of the sample, reported knowledge of 48 different incidents of child abuse. Extrapolating this to the national population, Gil estimated that between 2.53 and 4.07 million adults knew of families involved in child abuse (Gil, 1970). A 1968 survey yielded a figure of 6,000 *officially reported and confirmed* cases of child abuse (Gil, 1970). The problem with the latter estimate was that all 50 states did not, at the time of the survey, have mandatory child-abuse reporting statutes, and only a fraction of known cases of abuse were being reported to official agencies. The institution of uniform reporting laws by 1968 made it seem as though there were an exponential leap in child abuse in the seventies as more and more cases of abuse were actually reported.

Gil's estimate of millions of cases of child abuse was the exception and, by and large, the prevailing attitude in the sixties was that child abuse and other forms of family violence were rare occurrences in family life.

Early research and writing on family violence were dominated by the psychopathological model (Gelles, 1973; Spinetta and Rigler, 1972). Child abuse researchers discounted social factors as playing any causal role in violence towards children (see for example, Steele and Pollock, 1968, 1974). Rather, the explanation was thought to lie in personality or character disorders of individual battering parents (Steele and Pollock, 1968; Galdston, 1965; Zalba, 1971). The exception to this point of view was Gil's (1970) multidimensional model of child abuse which placed heavy emphasis on factors such as inequality and poverty. The rare reports on wife abuse portrayed both the battering husband and his victim as suffering from personality disorders (Schultz, 1960; Snell *et al.*, 1964).

The similarity of theoretical focus in the field of family violence was probably a product of the similar methods of procedure employed by investigators. Nearly all published work on child abuse and family violence was based on clinical samples (*e.g.*, hospitalized children, patients of psychiatrists or social workers) or officially reported cases of child abuse. Early studies of family violence typically failed to employ control or comparison groups, based conclusions on *post-hoc* explanations, and were based on small, nonrepresentative samples (Spinetta and Rigler, 1972).

RESEARCH ISSUES IN THE SEVENTIES

It would be fair to say that the issue of family violence, especially forms of violence other than child abuse, suffered from "selective inattention" (Dexter, 1958) prior to 1970. It would be equally fair to conclude that the decade of the seventies witnessed a wholesale increase in attention to and published reports on various aspects of violence in the home.

Straus attempted to explain the shift from "selective inattention" to "high priority social issue" by positing that the emergence of family violence as an important research topic was the result of three cultural and social forces (1974a). First, social scientists and the public alike became increasingly sensitive to violence due to a war in Southeast Asia, assassinations, civil disturbances, and increasing homicide rates in the sixties. Second, the emergence of the women's movement played a part—especially by uncovering and highlighting the problems of battered women. One of the the first major books on the topic of wife battering was written by Del Martin (1976), who organized and chaired the National Organization for Women task force on wife battering. The third factor postulated by Straus was the decline of the consensus model of society employed by social scientists and the ensuing challenge by those advancing a conflict or social action model.

Perhaps a fourth factor should be added. Someone had to demonstrate that research on family violence could be conducted. Researchers commencing projects in the early seventies were constantly told that reliable and valid research on domestic violence could not be carried out. Investigators were reminded that they would literally have to ask, "Have you stopped beating your wife?" Early studies, such as those by O'Brien (1971), Levinger (1966), Straus (1971), and Steinmetz (1971) demonstrated that research could be done (using nonclinical samples) and outlined appropriate methods and sampling strategies for conducting research on domestic violence.

Difficulties Confronting Early Research

There were a number of obstacles which faced researchers interested in the study of domestic violence. Among these obstacles was the need for an adequate nominal and operational definition of domestic violence.

Defining abuse and violence. One of the main problems which caused, and still causes, confusion for those involved in the study of child abuse, wife abuse, and family violence is that the terms "abuse" and "violence" are not conceptually equivalent. In some instances, abuse refers to a subset of violent behaviors—those which result in injury to the victim. An example is Kempe *et al.'s* (1962) definition of child abuse in which abuse was seen as a clinical condition (*i.e.,* with diagnosable medical and physical symptoms) having to do with those who have been deliberately injured by physical assault. In addition, Straus *et al.*'s (1980) definition of child and wife abuse referred to only those acts of violence which had a high probability of causing injury to the victim.

Other definitions of child and wife abuse refer to mistreatment including, but extending beyond, acts of injurious violence. Malnourishment, failure to thrive, and sexual abuse are among the nonviolent phenomena included in many definitions of child abuse (Giovannoni and Becerra, 1979). Some definitions of wife abuse include sexual abuse and marital rape. Some groups see the portrayal of women in degrading images (such as in pornography and some advertising) as constituting the abuse of women (London, 1978).

In short, while definitions of violence can refer to all forms of physical aggression, definitions of abuse often refer to only physical aggression that can or does cause injury and also to nonphysical acts of maltreatment which are considered to cause harm.

"Violence" has proved to be a concept which also is not easy to define. Some early researchers attempted to distinguish between legitimate acts of force between family members and illegitimate acts of violence (Goode, 1971). This was a consequence of the fact that much of the hitting in families is culturally approved and normatively accepted. Most individuals believe that spanking a child is normal, necessary, and good (Straus *et al.*, 1980). One in four men and one in six women report that they think it is

acceptable for a man to hit his wife under some circumstances (Stark and McEvoy, 1970).

However, research on family violence has found that offenders, bystanders, agents of social control, and even victims of family violence often accept and tolerate many acts which would be considered illegitimate violence if they occurred between strangers (Gelles, 1974; Steinmetz, 1977; Straus *et al.*, 1980). Thus, it has proven to be impossible to distinguish neatly and precisely between legitimate force and illegitimate violence in the family.

One frequently used nominal definition of violence was proposed by Gelles and Straus (1979). They defined violence as "an act carried out with the intention, or perceived intention of physically hurting another person." This definition includes spankings and shoving as well as other forms of behavior which do not actually typically lead to injury. Thus, the definition covers considerably more behavior than that viewed as physical abuse. [2]

Operational definitions of abuse and violence. While there was considerable variation in nominal definitions of abuse and violence, there was surprising similarity in the way researchers operationally defined abuse and violence in the seventies. In short, abuse was typically defined in an operational sense as those instances in which the victim became publicly known and labeled by an official or professional. Most studies of child abuse drew cases or subjects from two sources. The first were patients labeled victims of abuse by physicians. The second were children who had been reported to state or local child protection agencies and who were found, upon investigation, to be abused.

A major problem with these methods of operationally defining child abuse is that they overlook the fact that there is bias in the labeling process (Gelles, 1975a). Newberger *et al.* (1977) report that lower-class and minority children seen with injuries in a private hospital are more likely than middle- and upper-class children to be labeled as "abused." Turbett and O'Toole (1980), using an experimental design, found that physi-

---

[2] These same researchers (*e.g.*, Gelles, 1978) frequently found themselves defining their interest as violence towards children and then using "violence towards children" and "child abuse" interchangeably in their reports.

cians are more likely to label as abused minority children or lower-class children (a mock case was presented to the physicians with the injury remaining constant and the race or class of the child varied). Giovannoni and Becerra (1979) found that attitudes toward and definitions of child abuse varied by professional group. In all, operationally defining "child abuse" as pertaining only to those children publicly labeled "abused" produced a major problem; that is, the factors causally associated with abuse became confounded with factors related to susceptibility or vulnerability to having an injury diagnosed as abuse.

Those studying wife abuse frequently develop similar operational definitions. A number of studies of battered women operationally defined wife abuse as pertaining to those women who publicly admitted they were battered. This could range from responding to an advertisement placed in a popular periodical asking for battered women to complete a questionnaire, as was done by Prescott and Letko (1977), to interviewing women in a shelter for battered women, as was done by Walker (1979) and Dobash and Dobash (1979). Another technique was to identify families through police records or social service agency files (Gelles, 1974). Again, since women who answer advertisements, flee to a shelter, or become known to public and private agencies are but a nonrepresentative portion of the total number of abused wives, such techniques of operationally defining abuse produced systematic bias in the study results—ranging from lack of generalizability to confounding of variables.

One possible reason for the reliance on officially reported cases of abuse as the method of operationalizing the concepts of violence and abuse is the belief that reliable and valid research on family violence cannot be based on self-reports (Pelton, 1979). But, the early and continuing research of Straus and Steinmetz demonstrated that research could be conducted using nonclinical, nonofficially-reported cases. Both Straus and Steinmetz utilized the Conflict Resolution Technique [later renamed the Conflict Tactics Scales (Straus, 1979b)] in their early research using college students as subjects (Straus, 1971, 1974b; Steinmetz, 1971). Steinmetz (1977) was perhaps the first family

violence researcher to attempt to study a representative sample of families. Finally, Straus, Gelles, and Steinmetz administered the Conflict Tactics Scales to a nationally representative sample of families. The rates of family violence reported by subjects responding to the Conflict Tactics Scales demonstrated that one could develop a rigorous operational definition of family violence and expect to obtain reliable data based on self-reports (Straus, 1979b).

RESEARCH FINDINGS

As we stated earlier, the prevailing attitude in the sixties was that family violence was rare, and when it did occur, was the product of mental illness or a psychological disorder. Research in the seventies was largely aimed at refuting these conventional wisdoms and replacing them with informed data. Researchers struggled to overcome the definitional problems involved in the study of family violence, and they also aimed at correcting the major methodological problems (such as lack of comparison groups) which plagued research in the sixties.

In reviewing research on domestic violence conducted in the seventies, it appears that the major research issues were to: (1) establish a reliable estimate of the incidence of family violence; (2) identify the factors associated with the various types of violence in the home; and (3) to develop theoretical models of the causes of family violence.

The Extent of Family Violence

Among those who were concerned with the problem of family violence, one central research goal was to establish reliable and valid estimates of the incidence of various types of family violence—if only to answer the first and most obvious question asked by others—how much child, wife, husband, parent, or elderly abuse is there?

There were no shortages of estimates and extrapolations generated. Estimates of child abuse ranged from a low of 6,000 (Gil, 1970) to a high of one million (*New York Sunday Times*, November 30, 1975).[3] There were many problems with the various estimates of child abuse. Most estimates were based only on officially reported cases of child abuse

---

[3]The latter figure became the semiofficial estimate since it was frequently quoted by officials of the National Center on Child Abuse and Neglect.

(The American Humane Association, 1979). This is problematic because: (1) not all instances of child abuse come to public or official attention and (2) the definition of child abuse varies at least from state to state, if not from tabulator to tabulator (Giovannoni and Becerra, 1979).

Estimates of the extent of wife abuse were even more variable. Since there are no laws mandating the reporting of wife abuse, as there are in the case of child abuse, investigators had to make use of indirect measures of wife abuse, such as the percentage of homicides which involve domestic killings, number of wife-abuse claims handled by family courts, number of domestic disturbance calls responded to by police departments, and the number of cases of battered women treated by hospital emergency rooms (Martin, 1976; Walker, 1979). Estimates ranged from thousands to the nearly unbelievable estimate of 28 million battered wives (Langley and Levy, 1977).

Estimates of the incidence of abusive violence are at best limited by definitional problems and nonrepresentative samples and at worst are based on no empirical data whatsoever. Moreover, the crude estimates provide little or no information on age-specific or gender-specific rates.

One study which was based on a nationally representative sample of families and which used a standard operational definition of violence was conducted by Straus *et al.* (1980) in the mid-seventies. These investigators based their estimates of violence and abuse on self-reports of a nationally representative sample of 2,143 individual family members who responded to Straus's Conflict Tactics Scales measure of violence (1979b).

The national survey yielded an incidence rate of 3.8 percent of American children aged 3 years to 17 years abused each year (see Table 1). Projected to the 46 million children aged 3 to 17 who lived with both parents during the year of the survey, this meant that between 1.5 and 2 million children were abused by their parents (Gelles, 1978; Straus *et al.*, 1980).

Focusing on violence between marital partners, the investigators report that 16 percent of those surveyed reported some kind of physical violence between spouses during the year of the survey, while 28 percent of those interviewed reported marital violence at some point in the marriage (Straus, 1978; Straus *et al.*, 1980).

In terms of acts of violence which could be considered "wife beating," the national study revealed that 3.8 percent of American women were victims of abusive violence during the 12 months prior to the interview (see Table 2).

The same survey found that 4.6 percent of the wives admitted or were reported by their husbands as having engaged in violence which was included in the researchers' "Husband Abuse Index." This piece of data, as reported by Steinmetz (1978a) in her article on "battered husbands" set off a major controversy in the study of family violence in the seventies. Steinmetz was accused by her critics (see Pleck *et al.*, 1978) of having misstated and misrepresented the data. While there were significant political overtones to the debate and discussion, it became apparent that the presentation of only the incidence data did not fully represent the different experiences and consequences of violence experienced by men as opposed to women. As the decade closed, the investi-

TABLE 1. TYPES OF PARENT-TO-CHILD VIOLENCE (N=1,146)[a]

	% Occurrence in Past Year				
Incident	Once	Twice	More Than Twice	Total	Occurrence Ever
Threw something	1.3	1.8	2.3	5.4	9.6
Pushed/Grabbed/Shoved	4.3	9.0	18.5	31.8	46.4
Slapped or Spanked	5.2	9.4	43.6	58.2	71.0
Kicked/Bit/Hit with Fist	0.7	0.8	1.7	3.2	7.7
Hit with Something	1.0	2.6	9.8	13.4	20.0
Beat Up	0.4	0.3	0.6	1.3	4.2
Threatened with Knife/Gun	0.1	0.0	0.0	0.1	2.8
Used Knife or Gun	0.1	0.0	0.0	0.1	2.9

[a]On some items, there were a few responses omitted, but figures for all incidents represent at least 1,140 families (from Gelles, 1978).

TABLE 2. COMPARISON OF HUSBAND AND WIFE VIOLENCE RATES

| | Incidence Rate (%) | | Frequency | | | |
| | | | Mean | | Median | |
	H	W	H	W	H	W
Wife-Beating and Husband-Beating (N to R)	3.8	4.6	8.0	8.9	2.4	3.0
Overall Violence Index (K to R)	12.1	11.6	8.8	10.1	2.5	3.0
K. Threw something at spouse	2.8	5.2	5.5	4.5	2.2	2.0
L. Pushed, grabbed, shoved spouse	10.7	8.3	4.2	4.6	2.0	2.1
M. Slapped spouse	5.1	4.6	4.2	3.5	1.6	1.9
N. Kicked, bit, or hit with fist	2.4	3.1	4.8	4.6	1.9	2.3
O. Hit or tried to hit with something	2.2	3.0	4.5	7.4	2.0	3.8
P. Beat up spouse	1.1	0.6	5.5	3.9	1.7	1.4
Q. Threatened with knife or gun	0.4	0.6	4.6	3.1	1.8	2.0
R. Used a knife or gun	0.3	0.2	5.3	1.8	1.5	1.5

*For those who engaged in each act, i.e., omits those with scores of zero. (from Straus, 1978).

gators were still attempting to clarify and interpret the data on violence towards men (Gelles, 1979; Straus, 1980).

While the national survey met the objective of basing an estimate of the incidence of family violence on a representative sample, there were methodological difficulties with the survey. Most obvious, the data were based on self-reports and it is probable that the data underrepresented the true level of family violence. Second, no data on violence towards children under 3 years of age was provided, and there were no data on parental violence in single-person families (see Straus et al., 1980 for a complete explanation of the methodology). But, even with the methodological problems, the study fulfilled the objective of exploding the myth that family violence is infrequent and rare in society. The data clearly present the American family as one of society's most violent institutions and social groups.

Factors Associated With Family Violence

The extensive search for personality and psychological factors related to child abuse, wife abuse, and other forms of family violence did not end in the sixties. Well into the seventies, investigators continued to concentrate on the intra-individual factors which were thought to be related to various forms of family violence. However, as the conceptual model used to examine family violence expanded in the seventies, research on intra-individual correlates with family violence was augmented by investigations which studied the social factors thought to be related to violence. This section draws both on key empirical studies and reviews of literature to identify social factors which were found related to abuse and violence.[4]

1. *The cycle of violence.* One of the consistent conclusions of domestic violence research is that individuals who have experienced violent and abusive childhoods are more likely to grow up and become child and spouse abusers than individuals who have experienced little or no violence in their childhood years (Spinetta and Rigler, 1972; Parke and Collmer, 1975; Kempe et al., 1962; Straus, 1979a; Steinmetz, 1977; Gayford, 1975; Owens and Straus, 1975; Byrd, 1979; Gelles, 1974; Flynn, 1975). Steinmetz (1977) reports that even less severe forms of violence are passed on from generation to generation. Straus et al. (1980) not only find support for the hypothesis that "violence begets violence," but they also provide data which demonstrate that the greater the frequency of violence, the greater the chance that the victim will grow up to be a violent partner or parent.

2. *Socioeconomic status.* Research on child and wife abuse in the sixties claimed that social factors were not related to acts of domestic abuse. Yet, the same articles which made these claims offered empirical evidence that abuse was more prevalent among those with low socioeconomic status (Gelles, 1973). Research on family violence in the seventies supported the hypothesis that domestic violence is more prevalent in low socio-

---

[4] Space precludes providing a complete and exhaustive reference list of articles and papers documenting each relationship. We have chosen to cite key studies and major review articles to document each relationship. The review articles (Maden and Wrench, 1977; Parke and Collmer, 1975; Byrd, 1979; and Steinmetz, 1978b) should be consulted for the exhaustive documentation.

economic status families (Byrd, 1979; Gelles, 1974; Levinger, 1966; Gayford, 1975; Maden and Wrench, 1977; Elmer, 1967; Gil, 1970; Parke and Collmer, 1975; Straus et al., 1980). This conclusion, however, does not mean that domestic violence is confined to lower-class households. Investigators reporting the differential distribution of violence are frequently careful to point out that child and spouse abuse can be found in families across the spectrum of socioeconomic status (Steinmetz, 1978b).

3. Stress. A third consistent finding of most domestic violence research is that family violence rates are directly related to social stress in families (Gil, 1970; Maden and Wrench, 1977; Parke and Collmer, 1975; Straus et al., 1980). In addition to reporting that violence is related to general measures of stress, investigators report associations between various forms of family violence and specific stressful situations and conditions, such as unemployment or part-time employment of males (Gil, 1970; Parke and Collmer, 1975; Prescott and Letko, 1977; Straus et al., 1980), financial problems (Prescott and Letko, 1977), pregnancy—in the case of wife abuse (Gelles, 1975b; Eisenberg and Micklow, 1977), and being a single-parent family—in the case of child abuse (Maden and Wrench, 1977).

4. Social isolation. A fourth major finding in the study of both child and spouse abuse is that social isolation raises the risk that there will be severe violence directed at children or between spouses (Gil, 1970; Maden and Wrench, 1977; Parke and Collmer, 1975; Gelles, 1974; Ball, 1977; Borland, 1976).

In addition to these four general social factors found related to both violence towards children and between spouses, there have been studies directed at identifying specific factors related to child or spouse abuse.

In the case of violence towards children, some of the factors are: larger than average family size (Light, 1974; Gil, 1970; Maden and Wrench, 1977; Parke and Collmer, 1975; Elmer, 1967; Straus et al., 1980); low birth-weight child (Parke and Collmer, 1975); prematurity of the child (Elmer, 1967; Maden and Wrench, 1977; Parke and Collmer, 1975; Steele and Pollock, 1974); lack of attachment between mother and child—sometimes as a result of low birth weight or prematurity (Klaus and Kennell,

1976). In addition, females are found to be slightly more likely to abuse their children (Maden and Wrench, 1977) and males are slightly more likely to be the victims of child abuse (Gil, 1970; Maden and Wrench, 1977). Researchers have also proposed that handicapped, retarded, developmentally-delayed children, or those perceived by their parents as being "different" are at greater risk of being abused (Friedrich and Boriskin, 1976; Gil, 1970; Steinmetz, 1978b).

Students of wife abuse have reported abuse more common when husband and wife report low job satisfaction of the husband (Prescott and Letko, 1977), when the husband has no religious affiliation (Prescott and Letko, 1977), and when there are alcohol problems (Byrd, 1979; Gelles, 1974; Gayford, 1975; Eisenberg and Micklow, 1977). Furthermore, investigators have pointed out that there is an interrelationship between spouse abuse and child abuse (Rounsaville and Weissman, 1977-1978; Straus et al., 1980).

Important Caveats in Understanding the Relationship Between Social Factors and Family Violence

While there appears to be consistent support for the existence and persistence of the associations between family violence and the four major factors and many of the minor factors, it is important to point out some caveats in accepting these findings uncritically.

For example, in the case of the proposed cross-generational pattern of violence, Potts and Herzberger (1979) explain that the hypothesis relating abuse as a child with adult abusive behavior is overstated. Potts and Herzberger argue that, while some authors state that there is near unanimity among researchers that abusing parents were themselves abused or neglected physically or emotionally (Spinetta and Rigler, 1972), the evidence on which this claim is based must be examined more critically. First, Potts and Herzberger note that some publications which are widely cited as supporting the cycle of violence hypothesis actually present no empirical data (see for example, Curtis, 1963, and Spinetta and Rigler, 1972). Second, where data exist, they typically are based on small case studies. Other papers present data, but the study designs include no comparison group(s) so that no actual evidence of a statistical association exists. Finally, Potts and Herzberger note that, where reasonably reliable data are presented (*e.g.*, Straus, 1979a), the actual magnitude of the association is modest compared to the claims made by many researchers concerning the importance of violent childhood socialization in explaining later adult abusive acts.

Potts and Herzberger (1979) identify problems which are applicable to other areas of study in family violence research. One general problem is what Houghton (1979) calls the "Woozle Effect" (based on a Winnie the Pooh story). The "Woozle Effect" begins when one investigator reports a finding, such as Gelles's (1974) report that 55 percent of his sample of families reported one instance of conjugal violence in their marriage. The investigator may provide qualifications to the findings. In Gelles's case, it was that the sample was small, nongeneralizable, and the sampling technique was designed to draw cases from police and social service agency files which would insure that a large portion of the sample would have engaged in spousal violence. In the "Woozle Effect," a second investigator will then cite the first study's data, but without the qualifications (such as done by Straus, 1974a). Others will then cite both reports and the qualified data gain the status of generalizable "truth." In the case of the Gelles statistic, by the time Langley and Levy cited the figure in 1977, it had become so widely cited that Langley and Levy used it to extrapolate an incidence estimate for all married women and concluded that 28 million women were abused each year!

A second problem, indirectly noted by Potts and Herzberger (1979), is that evidence will accumulate for an association without any measures of the magnitude of that association. Within a short time, the fact that many researchers find an association between a certain factor and family violence will come to be interpreted as meaning that this factor is *strongly* associated with family violence. While most investigators find socioeconomic status, stress, isolation, and history of violence statistically related to family violence, the associations have, in large part, been relatively modest both for each individual factor and for the factors combined.

A third problem is that the methodological shortcomings which existed in the sixties still

persisted in the seventies. Researchers continued to operationalize child abuse and wife abuse as involving solely those cases which are known by social agencies, police, or hospitals. Such operational definitions continue the problem of being unable to partial out the factors that lead a family to be identified as abusive from those factors actually related to abuse. The introduction of survey research methods and operational definitions of abuse and violence which are not tied to those families known to agents of social control does not completely solve the problem. Straus *et al.*, (1980) based their research on a nationally representative sample and used a self-report measure of violence. There are problems with their data. Most obviously, the use of a self-report measure of violence leaves open the plausible rival hypothesis that many of the relationships discussed were the result of respondents' selective reporting, rather than true associations. When the Conflict Tactics Scales (Straus, 1979b) were administered to a representative sample of 1,900 women in Kentucky (see Schulman, 1979) by telephone interview (Straus *et al.*, relied on face-to-face interviews), the difference between the rates of interspousal violence in lower-class homes and middle- and upper-class homes was much less than the difference reported by Straus *et al..*[5]

The final problem is that, while there have been factors found related to domestic violence (even considering methodological problems), these factors have remained largely *unexplained*. To date, few studies have employed multivariate methods of analysis which would allow for explaining, interpreting, or specifying relationships. This problem brings us to the final issue in the study of family violence in the seventies, the development of theoretical models to explain family violence.

Theoretical Approaches to Family Violence

Family violence has been approached from three general theoretical levels of analysis: (1) the intra-individual level of analysis or the psychiatric model; (2) the social-psycho-

[5] Obviously, this could be the result of the different populations sampled. However, the results of the CTS administered in Kentucky and the one administered to the national sample showed no major differences between the two samples (Schulman, 1979).

logical level of analysis; and (3) the socio-logical or sociocultural level of analysis (Burgess and Conger, 1978; Justice and Justice, 1976; Gelles and Straus, 1979; Steinmetz, 1978b; Parke and Collmer, 1975).

The psychiatric model. The psychiatric model focuses on the offender's personality characteristics as the chief determinants of violence and abuse. The psychiatric model includes theoretical approaches which link mental illness, alcohol and drug abuse, and other intra-individual phenomena to acts of family violence.

The social-psychological model. The second approach assumes that violence and abuse can be best understood by a careful examination of the external environmental factors which impact on the family. In addition, this model considers which every-day family interactions are precursors to violence. Theoretical approaches which ex-amine stress, the transmission of violence from one generation to another, and family interaction patterns fit into the social-psycho-logical model. Such general theories as learning theory, frustration-aggression theory, exchange theory, and attribution theory, all approach violence from the social psychological level of analysis (Gelles and Straus, 1979).

The sociocultural model. The socio-cultural, or sociological model provides a macro-level analysis of family violence. Violence is considered in light of socially-structured inequality and cultural attitudes and norms about violence and family rela-tions. Structural-functional theory and sub-culture of violence theory are two of the better known theoretical approaches which come under the sociocultural level of analysis.

The seventies produced a number of extensive reviews of theories of violence in the family. Gelles and Straus (1979) listed, reviewed, discussed, and attempted to inte-grate propositions from 15 theories of violent behavior. In addition, they examined two theories which were developed to explain the specific case of family violence. Steinmetz (1978b) also provided a succinct review of theories which have been used to explain family violence. While a number of investi-gators attempted to apply existing theories of interpersonal violence to the family (Gelles, 1974; Erlanger, 1974), others developed new or integrated theoretical approaches to family

violence. Still others attempted to apply existing theories of family relations to the phenomenon of violent behavior. The following section briefly reviews some of the approaches which developed new theories of violence in the home.

Five Theories of Family Violence

Resource theory. Goode's (1971) Resource Theory of Intrafamily Violence was the first theoretical approach applied explicitly to family violence. Goode states that all social systems "rest to some degree on force or its threat." Goode explains that within a social system, the greater the resources a person can command, the more force he can muster. However, the more resources a person can command, the less he will *actually deploy* violence. Thus, violence is used as a last resort when all other resources are insuf-ficient or lacking. Applying this set of as-sumptions to the family, Goode explains that a husband who wants to be the dominant family member but has little education, job prestige, or income, and lacks interpersonal skills may be likely to resort to violence in order to be the dominant person. Empirical data from O'Brien (1971) and Gelles (1974) support this theory.

General systems theory. The second theory developed in the seventies to explain intra-family violence was Straus's General Systems Theory (1973). Straus attempts to account for violence in the home by viewing the family as a purposive, goal-seeking, adaptive social system. Violence is viewed as a system product, or output, rather than an individual pathology. Straus specified "positive feed-back" in the system which can create an upward spiral of violence, and "negative feedback" which can maintain, dampen, or reduce the level of violence.

An ecological perspective. Later in the seventies, Garbarino (1977) proposed an "ecological model" to explain the complex nature of child maltreatment. First, the eco-logical, or human development approach, fo-cuses on the progressive, mutual adaptation of organism and environment. Second, it focuses on the interactive and overlapping set of sys-tems in which human development occurs. Third, the model considers "social habitabil-ity"—the question of environmental quality. Lastly, the model assesses the political, eco-nomic, and demographic factors which shape the quality of life for children and families. Garbarino identified cultural support for the use of physical force against children and the inadequacy and inadequate use of family support systems as two necessary conditions for child maltreatment. In short, maltreatment is believed to arise out of a mismatch of parent to child and family to neighborhood and community.

An evolutionary perspective. At the end of the seventies, Burgess (1979) proposed an evolutionary perspective for understanding child abuse. In it, Burgess attempts to go beyond intra-individual or social psychological levels of analysis to provide a model that can explain both the current phenomenon of abuse as well as the socially-patterned occurrence of abuse over time and across cultural groups. Using the concept of "parental investment," Burgess explains that, in situations such as lack of bonding and parental uncertainness, the risk of child abuse would be increased [as has been found by investigators who report higher levels of abuse in families in which the victims were stepchildren (Burgess *et al.*, in press)]. Burgess also proposes that an inadequate parenting resource base would decrease the probability of parental investment and, thus, raise the risk of abuse. Lack of parental resources would then explain the inverse relationship proposed between abuse and social class and the proposed positive relationship between family size and abuse. Burgess (1979) also points to problems with children that decrease parental investment and increase the risk of abuse—such as developmental problems, retardation, Down's syndrome, etc.

Patriarchy and wife abuse. Dobash and Dobash (1979) see the abuse of women as a unique phenomenon which has been obscured and overshadowed by what they refer to as the "narrow" focus on domestic violence. The Dobashes attempt to make the case that, throughout history, violence has been systematically directed at women. Their central thesis is that economic and social processes operate directly and indirectly to support a patriarchal social order and family structure. Their central theoretical argument is that patriarchy leads to the subordination of women and contributes to a historical pattern of systematic violence directed against wives.

The Dobashes' theory, while perhaps the most macro-level approach to wife abuse developed in the seventies, has the major drawback of being a theory which is essentially a single-factor (patriarchy) explanation of violence towards women.

LOOKING AHEAD

Midway through the seventies, Zigler (1976), in an important and pessimistic paper titled "Controlling Child Abuse in America: An Effort Doomed to Failure," stated that the cumulative knowledge in 1976 about the nature of child abuse was comparable to what was known about mental illness in 1948! While Zigler may have been overly gloomy, the knowledge base on the nature and causes of family violence is indeed modest compared to the knowledge generated in the other areas of family study reviewed in the volume. In the first decade of intensive research on all aspects of violence in the family, investigators wrestled with definitional issues, tried to estimate the incidence and nature of the problem, inventoried social-psychological factors associated with or presumed to be associated with violence, and tentatively proposed theories and theoretical frameworks to explain violence in the home.

No doubt, researchers in the eighties will continue to find these issues compelling and significant. Nevertheless, having assessed what is known about family violence, we see some specific areas where knowledge is needed.

Theory Testing and Building

While research in the seventies was hardly atheoretical, the compelling issues of definition, incidence, and relationships meant that research was guided primarily by pragmatic goals (*e.g.*, answering the question: How much child abuse exists?) rather than theoretical goals. The seventies produced no shortage of theoretical frameworks and theories which were applied to family violence. However, what the decade did not produce was a systematic program of research to empirically test theories and also to use available data to build new theories of family violence. The work of Garbarino (1977) and Burgess (1979) speak to the kind of theory building which is needed. But, even more than that, investigators must design their research so as to *test theories*. By far the greatest limitation of our current theoretical knowledge of family violence is that it is built on *post hoc* explanations of data.

Longitudinal Designs

While investigators have demonstrated that certain social factors are related to family violence and abuse, many of the associations found could be symmetrical. In other words, stress could lead to abuse or abuse could create family stress. A major gap in research in family violence is that there have been few longitudinal studies which could be used to reduce plausible rival hypotheses concerning time order and causal direction.

More Nonclinical Samples

Researchers in the seventies demonstrated that one could actually interview door-to-door and obtain reliable, if not valid, information about family violence. Social scientists no longer need to assume that subjects for studies of child and wife abuse can only be located in large numbers in police files, emergency rooms, and public welfare offices. By using more nonclinical samples, researchers can begin to overcome the confusion which arises out of confounding factors which lead to public identification of family violence with those factors causally related to violent behavior in the home.

Methodological Triangulation

There is a need for increased diversity of measurement instruments and data collection techniques to be used in the study of family violence. By and large, most research in the seventies employed survey research designs and gathered data through questionnaires and interviews. Steinmetz's (1977) use of daily diaries to record conflict and violence is a notable exception to this trend. Straus's Conflict Tactics Scales (1979b), since it is one of the only standardized measures of violence available, has been used and adapted in numerous investigations. It would be tragic if the field of family violence research changed from one "easy" research design (clinical case study of known abuse victims) to another easily available methodology (surveys using the CTS). Just as the study of family power has benefited from a concern for developing more adequate means of measuring power, so

too will the study of family violence benefit from diversity and refinement of measures and designs.

SUMMARY

The harshest critics of research on family violence have been those who viewed the study of violence in the home as only another "hot topic" or fashionable field of study. This criticism, while perhaps grossly unjust, could become true unless those interested in the study of family violence become increasingly sophisticated both theoretically and methodologically. There has been a major growth of knowledge in the seventies in this field. Where, formerly, conventional wisdom and myths prevailed, now there are empirical data and tested propositions. Data exist on many more aspects of family violence than existed 10 years ago. However, theoretical development and methodological refinement will be necessary to keep this field of study vital and viable.

REFERENCES

The American Humane Association
   1979   National Analysis of Official Child Neglect and Abuse Reporting. Englewood, Colorado: Author.
Ball, Margaret
   1977   "Issues of violence in family casework." Social Casework 58(January):3-12.
Borland, Marie (Ed.)
   1976   Violence in the Family. Atlantic Highlands, New Jersey:Humanities Press.
Burgess, Robert L.
   1979   "Family violence: Some implications from evolutionary biology." Paper presented at the annual meetings of the American Society of Criminology, Philadelphia (November).
Burgess, Robert L., and Rand D. Conger
   1978   "Family interaction in abusive, neglectful, and normal families." Child Development 49 (December):1163-1173.
Burgess, Robert L., Elaine A. Anderson, and Cynthia J. Schellenbach
In press   "A social interactional approach to the study of abusive families." In J. P. Vincent (Ed.), Advances in Family Intervention, Assessment, and Theory: An Annual Compilation of Research (Vol. 2). Greenwich, Connecticut:JAI Press.
Byrd, Doris E.
   1979   "Intersexual assault: A review of empirical findings." Paper presented at the annual meetings of the Eastern Sociological Society, New York (March).

Curtis, George C.
  1963 "Violence breeds violence—perhaps." Ameri-
         can Journal of Psychiatry 120(4):386-387.
Dexter, Louis
  1958 "A note on selective inattention in social
         science." Social Problems 6(Fall):176-182.
Dobash, Rebecca E., and Russell Dobash
  1979 Violence Against Wives. New York:The Free
         Press.
Eisenberg, Sue E., and Patricia L. Micklow
  1977 "The assaulted wife: 'Catch 22' revisited."
         Women's Rights Law Reporter 3-4(Spring-
         Summer):138-161.
Elmer, Elizabeth
  1967 Children in Jeopardy: A Study of Abused
         Minors and Their Families. Pittsburgh:Uni-
         versity of Pittsburgh Press.
Erlanger, Howard
  1974 "Social class and corporal punishment in child-
         rearing: A reassessment." American Socio-
         logical Review 39(February):68-85.
Flynn, John P.
  1975 "Spouse assault: Its dimensions and charac-
         teristics in Kalamazoo County, Michigan."
         Unpublished manuscript, Western Michigan
         University.
Friedrich, William N., and Jerry A. Boriskin
  1976 "The role of the child in abuse: A review of
         literature." American Journal of Orthopsy-
         chiatry 46(October):580-590.
Galdston, Richard
  1965 "Observations of children who have been physi-
         cally abused by their parents." American Jour-
         nal of Psychiatry 122(4):440-443.
Garbarino, James
  1977 "The human ecology of child maltreatment."
         Journal of Marriage and the Family 39(Novem-
         ber):721-735.
Gayford, J. J.
  1975 "Wife battering: A preliminary survey of 100
         cases." British Medical Journal 1(January):
         194-197.
Gelles, Richard J.
  1973 "Child abuse as psychopathology: A socio-
         logical critique and reformulation." Ameri-
         can Journal of Orthopsychiatry 43(July):611-
         621.
  1974 The Violent Home. Beverly Hills:Sage Publica-
         tions.
  1975a "The social construction of child abuse."
         American Journal of Orthopsychiatry 43(Octo-
         ber):611-621.
  1975b "Violence and pregnancy: A note on the ex-
         tent of the problem and needed services." The
         Family Coordinator 24(January):81-86.
  1978 "Violence towards children in the United
         States." American Journal of Orthopsychiatry
         48(October):580-592.
  1979 "The myth of battered husbands—and other
         facts about family violence." Ms 8(October):
         65-73.
Gelles, Richard J., and Murray A. Straus
  1979 "Determinants of violence in the family: To-

ward a theoretical integration." Pp. 549-581 in
         Wesley R. Burr, Reuben Hill, F. Ivan Nye, and
         Ira L. Reiss (Eds.), Contemporary Theories
         About the Family (Vol. 1). New York:The Free
         Press.
Gil, David
  1970 Violence Against Children: Physical Child
         Abuse in the United States. Cambridge:Har-
         vard University Press.
Giovannoni, Jeanne M., and Rosina M. Becerra
  1979 Defining Child Abuse. New York: The Free
         Press.
Goode, William J.
  1971 "Force and violence in the family." Journal of
         Marriage and the Family 33(November):
         624-636.
Houghton, Beverly
  1979 "Review of research on women abuse." Paper
         presented at the annual meetings of the Ameri-
         can Society of Criminology, Philadelphia
         (November).
Justice, Blair, and Rita Justice
  1976 The Abusing Family. New York:Human
         Sciences Press.
Kempe, C. Henry
  1971 "Pediatric implications of the battered baby
         syndrome." Archives of Disease in Children
         46:28-37.
Kempe, C. Henry, Frederic N. Silverman, Brandt F.
Steele, William Droegemueller, and Henry K. Silver
  1962 "The battered child syndrome." Journal of the
         American Medical Association 181(July):
         107-112.
Klaus, Marshall H., and John H. Kennel
  1976 Maternal-Infant Bonding. St. Louis: C. V. Mos-
         by Company.
Langley, Roger, and Richard C. Levy
  1977 Wife Beating: The Silent Crisis. New York:
         Dutton.
Levinger, George
  1966 "Sources of marital dissatisfaction among ap-
         plicants for divorce." American Journal of
         Orthopsychiatry 26(October):803-897.
Light, Richard J.
  1974 "Abused and neglected children in America: A
         study of alternative policies." Harvard Educa-
         tional Review 43(November):556-598.
London, Julia
  1978 "Images of violence against women." Vic-
         timology 2(3/4):510-524.
Maden, Marc F., and David F. Wrench
  1977 "Significant findings in child abuse research."
         Victimology 2 (2):196-224.
Martin, Del
  1976 Battered Wives. San Francisco:Glide Publica-
         tions.
Newberger, Eli H., R. B. Reed, J. H. Daniel, J. N. Hyde,
Jr., and M. Kotelchuck
  1977 "Pediatric social illness: Toward an etiologic
         classification." Pediatrics 60(August):178-185.
O'Brien, John E.
  1971 "Violence in divorce prone families." Journal
         of Marriage and the Family 33(November):
         692-698.

Owens, David, and Murray A. Straus
  1975 "Childhood violence and adult approval of violence." Aggressive Behavior 1(2):193-211.
Parke, Ross D., and Candace W. Collmer
  1975 "Child abuse: An interdisciplinary analysis." Pp. 1-102 in Mavis Hetherington (Ed.), Review of Child Development Research (Vol. 5.). Chicago: University of Chicago Press.
Pelton, Leroy G.
  1979 "Interpreting family violence data." American Journal of Orthopsychiatry 49(April): 194.
Pleck, Elizabeth, Joseph Pleck, Marilyn Grossman, and Pauline Bart
  1978 "The battered data syndrome: A comment on Steinmetz's article." Victimology 2(3/4):680-683.
Potts, Deborah, and Sharon Herzberger
  1979 "Child abuse: A cross generational pattern of child rearing?" Paper presented at the annual meetings of the Midwest Psychological Association, Chicago (May).
Prescott, Suzanne, and Carolyn Letko
  1977 "Battered women: A social psychological perspective." Pp. 72-96 in Maria Roy (Ed.), Battered Women: A Psychosociological Study of Domestic Violence. New York:Van Nostrand Reinhold.
Rounsaville, Bruce J., and Myrna A. Weissman
  1977- "Battered women: A medical problem requir-
  1978   ing detection." International Journal of Psychiatry in Medicine 8(2):191-202.
Schulman, Mark A.
  1979 A Survey of Spousal Abuse Against Women in Kentucky. New York:Louis Harris and Associates.
Schultz, Leroy G.
  1960 "The wife assaulter." Journal of Social Therapy 6(2):103-111.
Snell, John E., Richard J. Rosenwald, and Ames Robey
  1964 "The wifebeater's wife: A study of family interaction." Archives of General Psychiatry 11(August):107-113.
Spinetta, John J., and David Rigler
  1972 "The child abusing parent: A psychological review." Psychological Bulletin 77(April): 296-304.
Stark, Rodney, and James McEvoy
  1970 "Middle class violence." Psychology Today 4(November):52-65.
Steele, Brandt F., and Carl Pollock
  1968 "A psychiatric study of parents who abuse infants and small children." Pp. 103-147 in Ray E. Helfer and C. Henry Kempe (Eds.), The Battered Child. Chicago:University of Chicago Press.
  1974 "A psychiatric study of parents who abuse infants and small children." Pp. 89-134 in Ray E. Helfer and C. Henry Kempe (Eds.), The Battered Child (2nd ed.). Chicago:University of Chicago Press.

Steinmetz, Suzanne K.
  1971 "Occupation and physical punishment: A response to Straus." Journal of Marriage and the Family 33(November):664-666.
  1977 The Cycle of Violence: Assertive, Aggressive, and Abusive Family Interaction. New York: Praeger Publishing Company.
  1978a "The battered husband syndrome." Victimology 2(3/4):499-509.
  1978b "Violence between family members." Marriage and Family Review 1(3):1-16.
Straus, Murray A.
  1971 "Some social antecedents of physical punishment: A linkage theory interpretation." Journal of Marriage and the Family 33(November): 658-663.
  1973 "A general systems theory approach to a theory of violence between family members." Social Science Information 12(June):105-125.
  1974a "Forward." Pp. 13-17 in Richard J. Gelles, (Ed.) The Violent Home: A Study of Physical Aggression Between Husbands and Wives. Beverly Hills:Sage Publications.
  1974b "Leveling, civility, and violence in the family." Journal of Marriage and the Family 36(February):13-30.
  1978 "Wife beating: How common and why?" Victimology 2(3/4):443-458.
  1979a "Family patterns and child abuse in a nationally representative American sample." Child Abuse and Neglect: The International Journal 3(1):213-225.
  1979b "Measuring intrafamily conflict and violence: The conflict tactics (CT) scales." Journal of Marriage and the Family 41(February):75-88.
  1980 "Husbands and wives as victims and aggressors in marital violence." Paper presented at the annual meetings of the American Association for the Advancement of Science, San Francisco (January).
Straus, Murray A., Richard J. Gelles, and Suzanne K. Steinmetz
  1980 Behind Closed Doors: Violence in the American Family. Garden City, New York:Doubleday.
Turbett, J. Patrick, and Richard O'Toole
  1980 "Physician's recognition of child abuse." Paper presented at the annual meetings of the American Sociological Association, New York (August).
Walker, Lenore E.
  1979 The Battered Woman. New York:Harper and Row, Publishers.
Zalba, Serapio
  1971 "Battered children." Transaction 8(July-August):58-61.
Zigler, Edward
  1976 "Controlling child abuse in America: An effort doomed to failure." Paper presented at the First National Conference on Child Abuse and Neglect, Atlanta (January).

The physical abuse of children by their parents is a family matter and should be viewed within the context of the family unit. Unfortunately, few child abuse studies have directly examined the family unit. Rather, most studies focus on characteristics of individual members of abusing families or on dyadic relationships within abusing families. Therefore, the present paper examines the family-related variables that might contribute to child abuse. This review is divided into two parts. Part I discusses methodological considerations and parent-related aspects of abusing families, including: characteristics of abusing parents, childhood experiences of abusing parents, marital relationships of abusing parents and the perceptions and expectations that abusing parents have of their abused children. Part II of this review, which will appear in a later issue, will cover child-related aspects of abusing families, parent-child interactions in these families, environmental conditions associated with child abuse and typologies of abusing families.

17

THE CHILD ABUSING FAMILY

I. Methodological Issues and Parent-Related Characteristics of Abusing Families

Audrey M. Berger

The physical abuse of children occurs most often at the hands of the child's parents and, consequently, it can be viewed as a family problem. It is, therefore, surprising to find that little direct attention has been given to the family unit in the child abuse literature. Rather, the focus of much work has been either on the abused child or on the abusing parent. Family relationships and dynamics have been mentioned in many articles on child abuse, but only a few investigators have studied the family unit. Consequently, in order to obtain a picture of what these families are like, it is necessary to pool bits and pieces of information from articles which do not focus on the family as a unit. There is a need for a more systematic examination of the characteristics of abusing families.

This paper will review, in two parts, the available literature on aspects of family life in child abusing families. It will cover only the literature on physical abuse of children. Part I will review various methodological issues, characteristics of abusing parents, multigenerational patterns of abuse, the marriages of abusing parents and the perceptions and expectations that abusing parents have of their abused children. Part II, which will appear in a later issue, will cover: characteristics of abused children, patterns of child-rearing in abusing families, siblings of abused children, the abusing family's relationship to the environment and typologies of abusing families.

The author would like to thank Neil Jacobson, Ph.D. and John Knutson, Ph.D. for their helpful comments and suggestions. Reprint requests should be sent to Audrey Berger, The University of Rochester Medical Center, Dept. of Psychiatry, Div. of Psychology, 300 Crittenden Blvd., Rochester, NY 14642.

From Audrey M. Berger, "The Child Abusing Family: I. Methodological Issues and Parent-Related Characteristics of Abusing Families," *American Journal of Family Therapy*, 1980, Volume 8, Number 3, pp. 53-66. Reprinted by permission of the author and publisher.

THE PROBLEM: INCIDENCE AND IMPACT

It is difficult to estimate the incidence of child abuse because it often goes unrecognized. Nevertheless, the statistics based on reported cases are impressive. Light (1973) estimated that 1% of the children under 18 years of age in the United States are subjected to physical or sexual abuse, or severe neglect. Denver and New York City report between 250 to 300 cases of child abuse per million population annually (Kempe and Helfer, 1972). In the state of Iowa, 3,328 cases, out of a population of around three million, were reported in 1977 (Iowa Department of Social Services, 1977). Baldwin and Oliver (1975) reported a rate of one per 1000 children under four years of age in northeast Wiltshire, England, demonstrating that the problem of child abuse is not restricted to the United States.

The number of reported incidents of child abuse has risen steadily over the years. The report of the New York State Assembly Select Committee (Besharov and Duryea, 1974) showed a jump from 211 cases reported between August 1964 and January 1965 to 3,224 cases reported in 1971; this is a 536% difference in reported cases of child abuse. It seems likely that this increase in reported cases is due to more accurate reporting rather than to an increase in the actual numbers of abused children.

The magnitude of the problem may still be much greater than is currently recognized. A number of factors contribute to the difficulty of correctly estimating the incidence of child abuse (Parke and Collmer, 1975): 1) Parents may not seek medical attention for the child; 2) in cases of repeated abuse, parents may change hospitals in order to obscure the cause of the injury; 3) sometimes the injuries inflicted may not be easily discernible; 4) some doctors may not report cases of child abuse;* 5) definitions of child abuse vary.

Definitions of child abuse not only differ between states, but they also differ within states over time. In compliance with the Mondale act,** some states now include physical and sexual abuse as well as neglect, while other states include only physical abuse. The rate of reported abuse will obviously vary significantly with the type of definition employed. In the present review, the term child abuse will refer exclusively to the physical abuse of children.

DEFINITIONS OF CHILD ABUSE

In the child abuse literature, different authors use different definitions of child abuse, which makes comparison among studies difficult. The problem of defining physical child abuse can be divided into three general issues: 1) broad versus narrow definitions; 2) definitions based on the intent of the aggressor versus the outcome of the aggressor's behavior; and 3) definitions which consider the cultural context of the abuse versus those which do not.

Broad definitions of child abuse (e.g., Kempe and Helfer, 1972) usually place no requirement on the nature of the injury and, hence, can encompass a rather wide range of injuries. Some (e.g., Gil, 1970) require only that the parent use excessive force with the child, regardless of whether or not the child is actually injured. Narrow definitions of child abuse (e.g., Baldwin and Oliver, 1975) generally consider as abused only those children with severe injuries (e.g., multiple fractures,

---

* Gil (1970) found that private physicians were contacted first in 5.1% of the cases, but they only filed 2.8% of the reports. However, all states currently require by law that physicians report any cases of suspected abuse.
** PL 93-247, 1974.

brain damage, skull or facial bone fractures, etc.). Others may require that there be evidence of repeated abuse (e.g., Green et al., 1974).

In practice, broad degnitions of child abuse are likely to include numerous false positives, whereas narrow definitions are likely to miss many cases of abuse. It is not clear which type of definition is most useful for research purposes, although use of a narrow definition is more likely to yield a homogeneous group. In terms of intervention, however, the use of a narrow definition may have very serious consequences: A child who has been abused is at risk for being abused again, possibly with severe consequences, if someone does not intervene.

Both broad and narrow definitions of child abuse can include cases based on either the intent of the aggressor or the impact of the aggressor's action (i.e., the existence of injury). Both approaches present difficulties. Definitions based on intent require an ability to assess intent, which is extremely problematic, if not impossible.

Adopting a definition of abuse based on the existence of injury regardless of intent runs the risk of including a large number of false positives. Children are prone to accidents and sometimes sustain rather severe injuries from them, even in the presence of cautious parental care. Reports suggest that some proportion of abused children are very active (Baldwin and Oliver, 1975; Johnson and Morse, 1968; Knutson, 1978), and one might reasonably assume that active children are more likely to have accidents, independent of parental behavior. Furthermore, Galdston (1971) notes that the abused children in his study utilized their bodies in an aimless, purposeless manner. The point is that what may look like abuse may sometimes be truly accidental—even when there are recurrent injuries.

Cases of child neglect would be included in a group defined by the existence of injuries. There is some evidence to suggest that abuse and neglect are associated with very different variables, and that they differ markedly in terms of their impact upon the child. Abusing and neglecting families do, however, appear to have certain characteristics in common (Disbrow et al., 1977; Gaines et al., 1978; Kent, 1976; Martin, 1972; Ruppenthal et al., 1976; Suomi, 1978; Young, 1964). Nevertheless, at this stage it seems best to study abuse and neglect separately, which requires the use of definitions which distinguish between them.

A number of authors have argued that definitions of child abuse should consider the cultural context in which the abuse occurs (Garbarino, 1976; 1977; Gelles, 1973; Gil, 1970; Korbin, 1977). They point out that accepted child-rearing practices vary widely between different cultural groups. Thus, it has been proposed that child abuse should be defined as a deviation from the child-rearing norms of the relevant cultural group. This approach has the advantage of distinguishing between situations where physical punishment is a deviant child-rearing technique, suggesting deviance in the parent or in the family interactions, versus those situations where the use of physical punishment is a normal child-rearing technique, suggesting that the parent is behaving in accord with cultural expectations.

However, there are problems involved in basing a definition of child abuse on cultural norms. In the first place, child-rearing practices often vary widely within cultural groups. Thus, defining child abuse within a cultural group would not simply be a matter of identifying a group of parents who are aberrant with respect to child-rearing practices of their cultural group. More likely, it would be necessary to determine a cut-off point on a continuum of child-rearing practices. Determining that cut-off point would be a difficult, and using it would mean that there might be little difference between those families whose child-rearing practices place them just below, and those who fall just above, the cut-off point.

Secondly, it seems impractical to use such a definition in the United States. Although it is possible to identify subcultures within the United States, determining the presence or absence of child abuse on the basis of subculture child-rearing norms would be an onerous task. In practice, such an approach would mean that two children might be experiencing the exact same parental treatment and might have the same injuries, yet one might be considered abused while the other might not be considered abused.

Since little is known about the importance of the cultural context in child abuse, it seems more useful at this point to define child abuse without reference to cultural context, and to examine the cultural context as an independent variable.

SUBJECT POPULATION AND SAMPLING BIAS

Differences between subject populations complicate attempts to compare findings of studies on child abuse. One variable which differs across studies is the age of the children in the subject population. Many authors assert that child abuse primarily involves children under three years of age (Cohen et al., 1966; Ebbin et al., 1969; Gelles, 1973; Kempe et al., 1962). Consequently, some studies include only abused children under three years of age (e.g., Galdston, 1965). Gregg and Elmer (1969) studied children who were abused when they were less than 13 months of age. Other investigators have entended the age of children studied to five years (e.g., Baldwin and Oliver, 1975; Friedman and Morse, 1974). Still other studies place no restriction on age.

There may be little justification for restricting the subject population to infants and young children. In his nationwide survey, Gil (1970) found that almost one half of the abused children were over six years of age. He concluded that younger children are more severely injured, probably because they are less able to withstand the impact of abuse, and so they are more likely to come to the attention of hospitals. In addition, the Iowa Department of Social Services (1977) report on child abuse showed that during that year, 46% of the children were older than six years of age, and 70% were older than three years of age. However, there may be justification for distinguishing between children who are first abused at a very young age and continue to be abused as they grow older, versus children who are first abused at an older age. Some researchers have inferred that physical abuse which begins when the child is older bears more relationship to sexual issues (Steele, 1970; Steele and Pollack, 1974).

Socioeconomic class of the abusing families is another factor which differs across studies. Most studies have found a large proportion of the families to be from the lower socioeconomic classes; however, there is some variability within and between studies. It seems reasonable to consider the possibility that there may be some important differences between abusing families from different socioeconomic classes.

The overrepresentation of lower-class families may be partly a function of sampling bias. Parents in the middle and upper social classes may be more capable of concealing child abuse. They are more likely to seek medical attention from private physicians who have, in the past, been reluctant to report parents. Also, middle- and upper-class parents may have more mobility and resources which would enable them to obtain medical assistance in various locations to obscure any repeated episodes of abuse. Nevertheless, it seems probable that the overrepresentation of lower-class families in the child abuse statistics is not solely a function of sampling bias (Pelton, 1978).

HETEROGENEITY OF ABUSING FAMILIES

It seems clear that, although abusing families share certain characteristics, they constitute a heterogeneous group. A few authors have suggested subtypes of abusing families in an attempt to decrease this heterogeneity (Dubanoski et al., 1978; Gil, 1970; Knutson, 1978; Walters, 1975; Young, 1964; Zalba, 1967), but generally speaking, abusing families are studied as a group. A priori it seems reasonable to consider the possibility that there may be important differences in the characteristics associated with abuse in intact versus broken homes, in lower social class versus upper and middle social class families, by the father versus the mother, by psychotic versus nonpsychotic parents, of one child in the home versus all children in the home, in repeated versus isolate incidents, and so on.

An additional distinction which is not addressed in the literature is the possible difference between impulsive, explosive abuse where the implement of destruction is the hands of the parent or some readily accessible device, versus abusive episodes where the implement of destruction requires some amount of preparation and, hence, might be indicative of premeditated action (e.g., placing a child in a pot of scalding water, tying a child to be beaten, wrapping newspapers around the child's arm and setting it on fire, etc.). Knutson (1978) has recently suggested that child abuse researchers should distinguish between two types of behavior that are addressed in the aggression literature: irritable aggression and instrumental aggression.

METHODOLOGICAL PROBLEMS

Additional methodological problems abound in the literature on child abuse: 1) much of the work is ex post facto; 2) much of the work is purely correlational, with little hypothesis testing; 3) control groups are conspicuously rare, and matched control groups are practically nonexistent; 4) much of the information collected in these studies is based on parental self-report; 5) the subject population tends to be rather small.

CHARACTERISTICS OF ABUSING PARENTS

Two separate but overlapping questions can be asked about abusing parents: 1) Are abusing parents mentally ill? 2) What particular traits or characteristics, if any, differentiate abusing from nonabusing parents?

There is considerable consensus in the literature that very few abusing parents are psychotic (Blumberg, 1974; Cohen et al., 1966; Flynn, 1970; Fontana and Bernard, 1971; Galdston, 1971; Parke and Collmer, 1975; Steele, 1970; Steele and Pollack, 1974; Wasserman, 1968). However, there is also fair agreement that abusing parents manifest high rates of behavioral and social deviance. In his nationwide study, Gil (1970) found that in the year prior to the reported abusive incident, nearly half of the abusing mothers and fathers were judged to be deviant. In their epidemiological study of child abuse in northeast Wiltshire, England, Baldwin and Oliver (1975) found that abusing parents showed high rates of psychiatric disturbance and criminality.

Smith, Hanson and Noble (1973) compared a group of abusing parents with the parents of nonabused children who were admitted to a hospital emergency room. These authors used pyschiatric interviews, standard personality inventories and the Wechsler Adult Intelligence Scale to evaluate the parents in both groups. They found that abusing parents had significantly more personality disorders, were more neurotic, were more frequently of borderline intelligence and more often had criminal records than the parents in the control group.* Steele and Pollack (1974) used clinical interviews and psychological tests to examine 60 abusing parents. They reported that most of the abusing parents had enduring emotional problems.

Thus, clinical observations and assessment data seem to indicate that abusing parents are frequently emotionally, behaviorally and socially abnormal, but that they are rarely psychotic. However, the data suggest that the type of psychopathology varies considerably within the abusing population (Blumberg, 1974; Boszormenyi-Nagy and Spark, 1973; Gelles, 1973; Green et al., 1974; Morse et al., 1970; Spinetta and Rigler, 1972; Steele and Pollack, 1974).

A number of specific personality traits have been reported for many abusing parents. Theoretically, abusing parents could constitute a diagnostically heterogeneous population and yet still be homogeneous with respect to certain traits that might cut across diagnostic classes. Furthermore, abusing parents could be homogeneous with respect to traits that would not necessarily be considered pathological. However, Gelles (1973) reviewed the literature and concluded that there is a striking lack of agreement on the personality traits of abusing parents.

The most frequent observation is that many of these parents are narcissistic, immature and have poor impulse control (Blumberg, 1974; Bennie and Sclare, 1969; Johnson and Morse, 1968; Kempe et al., 1962; Nurse, 1964; Terr, 1970; Wasserman, 1968; Zalba, 1967). Abusing parents have also been described as rigid and compulsive (Fontana and Bernard, 1971), as having low self-esteem (Blumberg, 1974; Green et al., 1974; Spinetta and Rigler, 1972; Steele and Pollack, 1974) and as anxious, hostile and depressed (Johnson and Morse, 1968).

One of the problems with the literature on characteristics of abusing parents is that conclusions are frequently reached on the basis of clinical observation alone. However, a few studies have addressed this issue carefully, with appropriate concern for methodological considerations, and some consistencies do appear to emerge.

Disbrow, Doerr and Caulfield (1977) compared 37 abusive or neglecting parents with 32 control parents in an attempt to develop a battery of tests with which to identify parents who have the potential for abusing or neglecting their children. They interviewed the parents, had the parents complete questionnaires that assessed parental attitudes and empathy, and they measured physiological responses (i.e., heart rate, GSR, skin temperature and respiration rate) to videotapes of neutral, pleasant and unpleasant family scenes. More abusers than neglectors and controls were found to lack empathy and to have low self-esteem. Both abusers and neglectors were found to have lower heart rate variability than the controls; that is, physiological measures showed that the control parents differentiated between pleasant, unpleasant and neutral videotaped family scenes, while abusers and neglectors did not. Also, the abusers and neglectors showed greater physiological arousal throughout the entire videotape presentation.

Melnick and Hurley (1969) compared 10 abusing mothers with 10 matched control mothers on a number of personality measures. Like Disbrow et al. (1977), these authors found that abusing mothers had lower self-esteem and greater difficulty empathizing with others than the control mothers. They also concluded that abusing mothers had more frustrated dependency needs and showed less need to be nurturant.

---

* The authors only administered four subtests of the Wechsler Adult Intelligence Scale (vocabulary, block design, comprehension and picture arrangement). It is not clear that this procedure is an appropriate way to derive an I.Q. Score. For further discussion of this issue, see: C. A. Hyman. I.Q. of parents of battered babies. *British Medical Journal*, 1973, 4, 739.

The physiological responses of abusing and control parents to the smiling and crying of an infant were compared in a study by Frodi and Lamb (1978). These authors found that the infant's crying was perceived as aversive, while the infant's smiling produced more positive responses, in all the parents. However, the abusing mothers reported more marked aversion to the crying and less marked positive reaction to the infant's smiling. The heart rate data suggested that the abusing mothers were less responsive to changes in the infant's signals. These results appear to be consistent with Disbrow et al.'s (1977) findings, which raised the possibility that abusing mothers are less responsive to positive stimuli and somewhat more responsive to certain aversive stimuli than are normal parents. However, since Disbrow et al. (1977) found this pattern of physiological responding to be characteristic of both abusers and neglectors, this variable might not be specific to abusing parents. In fact, these results suggest that abusers and neglectors may share certain characteristics.

The few studies that compared abusing parents with controls on the variables of empathy and self-esteem support the clinical observations that abusing parents are low on both of these variables. The suggestion that abusing parents have difficulty empathizing with others is intriguing in light of Feshbach and Feshbach's (1969) findings that the inhibitory effect of pain cues on aggression may depend upon the development of empathy. However, measures used to assess self-esteem and empathy may be of questionnable validity and reliability.

It is difficult to interpret the findings on the personality traits of abusing parents because of the methodological flaws in most of the studies. Few studies used control groups, standardized testing or blind interviewing. Many conclusions have been reached on the basis of inference rather than through rigorous scientific investigation.

It may well be that many or most abusing parents are emotionally, behaviorally and socially deviant, but so are many parents who do not abuse their children; thus, psychopathology cannot be considered a sufficient condition for abuse. Furthermore, since not all abusing parents are found to be deviant, psychopathology is not a necessary condition for abuse. Certain personality characteristics may be found frequently in abusing populations, but they can also be found in nonabusing parents; so, once again, these characteristics cannot be considered sufficient or necessary conditions for abuse.

Child abuse is a complex phenomenon that involves more than one individual; a unidimensional model of child abuse based on parental characteristics would seem to be far too simplistic to be useful. Gaines et al. (1978) found that while certain characteristics of abusing mothers (e.g., a sense of coping failure) did differentiate them from neglecting and normal mothers, these characteristics accounted for very little of the variance. Thus, other contributing factors must be explored. Since child abuse occurs primarily in the context of the family, it seems crucial to examine other characteristics of abusing families.

MULTIGENERATIONAL ABUSE

Most investigators have found that abusing parents report a history of abuse, neglect or rejection in their own childhood (Baldwin and Oliver, 1975; Blumberg, 1974; Cohen et al., 1966; Fontana and Bernard, 1971; Gelles, 1973; Gil, 1970; Green et al., 1974; Johnson and Morse, 1968; Justice and Justice, 1976; Kempe and Helfer, 1972; Nurse, 1964; Oliver and Taylor, 1971; Paulson and Chaleff, 1973; Silver et al., 1969; Smith, 1975; Spinetta and Rigler, 1972; Steele, 1970; Steele, 1976; Steele and Pollack, 1974; Van Stolk, 1972; Walters, 1975; Young,

1964; Zalba, 1967). This observation appears so frequently in the literature that it is almost given axiomatic status.

The data, however, do not appear to warrant such strong conviction. First, most of the data on this issue are self-reports. One might more accurately state, therefore, that most abusing parents *perceive* (or report) their own childhood as excessively difficult. Second, the significance of this perception of childhood is not altogether clear, since we have no data on the frequency of similar perceptions of childhood among matched nonabusing parents.

Nevertheless, for a number of reasons it seems logical to hypothesize that these parents do have a history of abuse and/or neglect in their childhood. Parents serve as role models for their childhood and abusing parents might have learned their child-rearing techniques from their own parents. There is a good deal of evidence that learning plays an important role in the etiology of aggressive behavior (Bandura, 1973; Bandura et al., 1961; Lefkowitz et al., 1963; Owens and Straus, 1975; Sears et al., 1974). Some data will be presented in Part II of this review which show that abused children are frequently considered to be aggressive, suggesting that they may be learning aggressive behavior from their parents. It is possible that some personality traits which could be passed from one generation to the next are involved in the abuse of children, although this remains to be shown.

Animal data seem to suggest that infants reared in very unfavorable circumstances become very poor mothers. Ruppenthal, Arling, Harlow, Sackett and Suomi (1976) found that monkeys separated from their mothers shortly after birth and reared in a bare cage, with a cloth surrogate mother, or with peers, showed a high frequency of abnormal mothering behaviors when they produced offspring. In particular, those reared in a bare cage or with cloth surrogate mothers were likely to be either indifferent or abusive to their offspring. Those raised with peers were more likely to show adequate maternal behavior than the other "motherless monkeys," but were much less likely to provide adequate maternal care than monkeys who received normal mothering. "Motherless mothers" who were reared in bare wire cages were the most likley to be abusive with their offspring.

These findings appear to have some relevance to neglecting and abusing parental behavior in humans. They suggest that harsh experiences in infancy and early childhood may relate to abnormal parenting behaviors. Alternatively, these data raise the possibility that the lack of opportunity to learn appropriate child rearing behaviors may lead to deviant parenting behavior. But these data must be interpreted with caution since there are many problems involved in using animal data as a model for human behavior, and since this model does not really parallel the supposed childhood experiences of abusing parents.

The maternal behavior of the neglected and abused offspring of the "motherless monkey mothers" might serve as a more appropriate analogue to child abuse and neglect. To date, most of the abused and neglected monkeys have not produced offspring, but Suomi (1978) presented data on the maternal behavior of three such monkeys. The two monkeys who were reared by "indifferent" mothers have provided their offspring with adequate maternal care. But the one monkey reared by an abusive mother has been abusive to her offspring. These findings are provocative; they suggest that neglecting and abusive mothering behaviors in monkeys are different though related phenomena, and that abusive behavior can be learned. More work is needed to determine the adequacy of this model as an analogue to child abuse and neglect.

The actual statistics on early abuse and neglect in the childhood of abusing parents are difficult to interpret since some authors report only childhood abuse (e.g., Gil, 1970), while others combine abuse with neglect and rejection (e.g., Blumberg, 1974). Furthermore, it is rarely clear how these terms are defined. The proportion of abusing parents that report a history of childhood abuse, neglect and/or rejection varies widely between studies. For example, Gil (1970) found that 11% of the abusing parents in his study reported being abused in childhood, while other studies report rates close to 100% (e.g., Blumberg, 1974). As would be expected, the studies which include childhood neglect and rejection report much higher rates than those that report only a history of abuse.

A few studies have carefully traced the histories of abusing parents and have found high rates of maltreatment in their family histories. Oliver and Taylor (1971) studied five generations of one family in which child abuse was identified. They examined 49 members of this family and found that: six babies were dead (excluding stillbirths); three babies were abused; 10 children were abandoned one or more times; 11 children were unsupervised or left to fend for themselves. Adequate information could not be obtained on six individuals, but of the 49 individuals studied, only seven appeared to have escaped maltreatment in childhood. Silver, Dublin and Lourie (1969) studied the history of abusing parents by searching police records and records from other agencies. These authors found that many of the abusing parents were on record as having been abused in childhood.

It is possible that, despite high rates of abuse in the histories of abusing parents, a history of childhood abuse might not be predictive of abusive parental behavior. Knutson (1978) points out that, to determine more accurately the impact of childhood abuse or neglect on future child-rearing behaviors, we need longitudinal data. To date, no such data are available, so it is presently not possible to determine the proportion of abused children that are likely to become abusing parents. However, on the assumption that a history of abuse in childhood constitutes a risk factor for becoming an abusing parent, it might be worth comparing individuals who are known to have been abused as children but who are providing their own children with adequate care, with those who were abused in childhood and are known to abuse their own children. If it were possible to identify variables that seem to protect an abused child from growing up to become an abusing parent, it might be possible to use such information in working with abusing families to break the "cycle of abuse."

Although many abusing parents report having been abused in chilhood, there are a large number of abusing parents who do not report a history of maltreatment in childhood. Thus, a history of abuse in childhood may increase the probability that parents will abuse their children, but it constitutes neither a necessary nor a sufficient condition.

MARITAL RELATIONSHIPS IN ABUSING FAMILIES

A number of authors have observed that, more often than not, the marital relationship in abusing families is either highly conflicted or nonexistent.

Ebbin et al. (1969) found that only 30% of abusing parents in their study had intact marriages, as compared with 53% in the pediatric outpatient control group. Elmer (1977) compared a group of 17 abused children with a matched control group of 17 children who had sustained serious accidental injuries. She found that 53% of the abusing parents were single, separated, divorced or widowed, as compared with 35% of the control parents. In addition, 35% of the abusing parents were living without an adult companion, while only 12% of the control parents were living alone with their children. In his nationwide survey, Gil (1970) found that 30% of the abusing mothers were single, separated, divorced, deserted or widowed and 30% of the mothers lived without a male partner. Among the 20 cases of abusing parents in her sample, Nurse (1964) found that 75% of the marriages had a history of unsettled relationships, with many divorces and separations. Smith, Hanson and Noble (1974) compared abusing families with families who had a child admitted to the emergency room of a hospital for reasons other than an accident. They reported that 29% of the abusing mothers in their sample were unmarried, as compared with 6% of the mothers in their control group. Young (1964) reported that many parents in her sample were separated, divorced or single.

Numerous authors have observed that abusing parents with intact marriages appear to experience a good deal of marital conflict (Blumberg, 1974; Flynn, 1970; Galdston, 1971; Gelles, 1973; Green et al., 1974; Johnson and Morse, 1968; Smith, 1975; Steele and Pollack, 1974; Young, 1964). Marital distress in these families is usually found to take the form of frequent fighting, spouse abuse and lack of emotional support from the spouse. Smith (1975) reported that more abusing than matched control parents were dissatisfied with their marriage. The abusing parents in this sample reported more recent quarrels with their spouse, and the mothers frequently reported a lack of spouse cooperation in child-rearing. Young (1964) examined the case records of 300 abusing or neglecting families and found high rates of marital distress in both types of families. She reported that fighting and lack of support between the spouses were common in both abusing and neglecting populations. She also found that sometimes the child abusing parent abused the spouse as well. Nurse (1964) and Green et al. (1974) reported a high rate of physical violence between the spouses in their samples. Bennie and Sclare (1969) found that, during the weeks preceding the reported child abuse incident, marital conflict tended to be especially severe, and the parents often become violent with one another. In Baldwin and Oliver's (1975) sample, most of the child abuse incidents occurred soon after marriage or the start of cohabitation.

In none of the above studies was marital conflict or spouse interaction ever formally assessed. Rather, judgments on the marital relationship were made on the basis of informal observation or parental report.

In addition to the reports of marital conflict, a number of other observations have frequently been made about the marital relationships of abusing parents. It has been suggested that the marriages of some abusing parents are characterized by dominant-submissive patterns (Boszormenyi-Nagy and Spark, 1973; Kempe and Helfer, 1972; Terr, 1970; Young, 1964). It has also been hypothesized by some authors that the nonabusing parent may play a role in the child abuse. Steele and Pollack (1974) state that the nonabusing parent contributes to the abuse by: 1) open acceptance or more subtle encouragement; 2) urging the other parent to discipline the child; 3) accusing the spouse of not being a good parent; 4) rejecting the spouse, thereby causing the rejected partner to turn to the child with increased demands. Boszormenyi-Nagy and Spark (1973) and Zalba (1967) have suggested that, in abusing families, marital conflict is displaced onto the child, who serves as a scapegoat. According to this perspective, the nonabusing parent benefits from the child abuse and, therefore, passively allows it to continue or, perhaps, even encourages it.

A major problem with the literature on the marriages of abusing parents, as with so many other characteristics discussed in this review, is that correlational data are used to suggest causal explanations. While it is certainly possible that broken or turbulent marriages may instigate child abuse in some cases, a definitive conclusion is unwarranted at this point. An additional problem with much of the research on the marriages of abusing parents is that control groups are rarely included. In order to effectively analyze the data, it is essential that the marriages of matched non-abusing parents be studied.

DISTORTED PERCEPTIONS, ROLE REVERSAL AND INAPPROPRIATE EXPECTATIONS

There is fair agreement among investigators that, although very few abusing parents are psychotic, they frequently have very distorted perceptions of the abused child. Based on interviews with abusing mothers and the reports of caseworkers, Green et al. (1974) concluded that abusing mothers "projected" negative attitudes onto the child and, consequently, used the child as a scapegoat. Steele and Pollack (1974) mention a phenomenon that they call "reverse identification"; that is, abusing parents sometimes state that the abused child has "all my bad qualities." Gregg and Elmer (1969) found that abusing mothers often thought the baby was troublesome, while the research team felt that the babies were somewhat easier to care for than usual; in addition, this misperception of the child's behavior was not found among the mothers in the matched control group. Smith (1975) reported similar discrepancies between the perceptions of the research team and those of the abusing mothers toward the abused children. In a group therapy project for abusing parents, Galdston (1971) found that the abusing mothers described their abused children in an inconsistent and exaggerated manner.

Despite the fact that abusing parents are frequently found to have distorted perceptions of their abused children, it cannot be concluded that these perceptions play an etiological role in child abuse. Brock and Pallak (1969) have presented evidence which shows that after behaving aggressively individuals will frequently change their perceptions of their victims, ostensibly in an attempt to justify the aggressive behavior. For example, the aggressor will often devalue the victim following the aggressive encounter. Thus, it is conceivable that the distorted perceptions that some abusing parents have of their abused child may actually be a consequence, rather than an antecedent, of the abuse.

It is also conceivable that, in many cases, the perceptions that abusing parents have of their children are based on reality more than is generally acknowledged. Gelles (1973) points out that unwanted newborn children may cause a great deal of financial and emotional stress within a family and that the child may not, in such cases, be a projected source of the parent's problems, but rather, a real source of family stress. It is also possible that the abused children are the cause of some of the marital conflict which is thought to characterize many intact abusing families; if so, the child would be a likely target for parental aggression. In addition, there is some evidence that abused children are sometimes more difficult to raise than their siblings and peers.

If abusing parents do in fact have distorted perceptions of the abused child, the question then becomes: do abusing parents have similarly distorted perceptions of all children? Frodi and Lamb (1978) found that abusing parents reported the crying of an infant to be more aversive, and the infant's smiling to be less positive, than was true for control parents, suggesting that abusing parents may in fact perceive child behavior differently than nonabusing parents.

Another phenomenon which is frequently mentioned in the literature is role reversal (Morris and Gould, 1963); that is, many authors have argued that abusing parents demand of the abused child, gratification and fulfillment of their unmet dependency needs (Boszormenyi-Nagy and Spark, 1973; Johnson and Morse,

1968; Oliver and Taylor, 1971; Steele, 1970; Steele and Pollack, 1974; Van Stolk, 1972). Smith and Hanson (1975) tested the role-reversal hypothesis by a semantic differential technique developed to allow parents to communicate their reactions to difficult child behavior. After comparing the ratings of the abusing parents with those of a control group, Smith and Hanson concluded that they found no support for the role reversal hypothesis.

Except for the Smith and Hanson (1975) study, the literature on role reversal is largely inferrential in nature. It may well be that this hypothetical phenomenon is important in understanding child abuse, but it is essential that the concept be operationally defined and tested empirically.

It is also frequently reported that abusing parents expect their children to behave in a manner that is far in advance of their capabilities, given their developmental level. Based on his clinical work with abusing parents, Galdston (1965) noted that abusing parents speak of their children as if they were adults; they expect them to have an adult's ability for intentional, purposeful and organized behavior. Smith and Hanson (1975), Steele (1970) and Wasserman (1968) also point out that abusing parents often make unrealistic demands of their children. The Iowa Department of Social Services (1977) report shows that 19% of the parents who abused their children had inappropriate expectations of these children.

Thus, there appears to be fair agreement in the literature that abusing parents frequently believe that children exist to satisfy the needs and desires of their parents, and that they expect their children to be capable of adult behaviors. This is only an hypothesis at present; nevertheless, it is alluring because it lends itself nicely to empirical testing. If parental expectations differentiate between abusing and nonabusing parents, measurement of parental expectations might enable workers to predict more accurately which parents are at risk for abusing their children; ultimately, parental expectations might easily be assessed by self-report questionnaires or interviews even before the child is born. Nurses working on maternity wards might be able to collect such information. Inappropriate expectations of their children could, in some cases, be based on ignorance about child development. Elmer (1977) found that abusing mothers were drastically deficient in knowledge about child development. Such knowledge might easily be conveyed to high-risk mothers while they are still in the hospital. Before parental expectations can be used as a predictor variable, however, data are needed that compare the expectations of abusing and nonabusing parents; the groups should be matched on variables such as age, social class and number of children. Of course, the crucial test of the predictive utility of this variable will come only from longitudinal research with high-risk populations.

REFERENCES

BALDWIN, J. A. and OLIVER, J. E. Epidemiology and family characteristics of severely abused children. *British Journal of Preventive Social Medicine,* 1975, 29, 205-221.

BANDURA, A. Social learning theory of aggression. In J. Knutson (Ed.), *Control of Aggression: Implications from Basic Research.* Chicago: Aldine-Atherton, 1973.

BANDURA, A., ROSS, D., and ROSS, S. A. Transmission of aggression through imitation of aggressive models. *Journal of Abnormal and Social Psychology,* 1961, 63(3), 575-582.

BENNIE, E. H. and SCLARE, A. B. The battered child syndrome. *American Journal of Psychiatry,* 1969, 125(7), 975-979.

BESHAROV, D. J. and DURYEA, P. B. Report on the New York State Assembly Select Committete on child abuse, April, 1972. In R. E. Helfer & C. H. Kempe (Eds.), *The Battered Child.* 2nd edition. Chicago: The University of Chicago Press, 1974.

BLUMBERG, M. L. Psychopathology of the abusing parent. *American Journal of Psychotherapy,* 1974, 28, 21-29.

BOSZORMENYI-NAGY, I. and SPARK, G. M. *Invisible Loyalties*. Hagerstown, Md.: Harper & Row, 1973.

BROCK, T. C. and PALLAK, M. S. The consequences of choosing to be aggressive: An analysis of the dissonance model and review of relevant research. In P. G. Zimbardo (Ed.), *The Cognitive Control of Motivation*. Glenview, Ill.: Scott, Foresman & Company, 1969.

COHEN, M. I., RAPHLING, D. L., and GREEN, P. E. Psychological aspects of the maltreatment syndrome in childhood. *Journal of Pediatrics*, 1966, 69, 279-284.

DISBROW, M. A., DOERR, H., and CAULFIELD, C. Measuring the components of parents' potential for child abuse and neglect. *Child Abuse and Neglect*, 1977, 1, 279-296.

DUBANOSKI, R. A., EVANS, I. M., and HIGUCHI, A. A. Analysis and treatment of child abuse: A set of behavioral propositions. *Child Abuse and Neglect*, 1978, 2, 153-172.

EBBIN, A. J., GOLLUB, M. H., STEIN, A. M., and WILSON, M. G. Battered child syndrome at the Los Angeles County General Hospital. *American Journal of Diseases of Children*, 1969.

ELMER, E. *Fragile Families, Troubled Children*. Pittsburgh: The University of Pittsburgh Press, 1977.

FESHBACH, N. and FESHBACH, S. The relationship between empathy and aggression in two age groups. *Developmental Psychology*, 1969, 1, 102-107.

FLYNN, W. R. Frontier justice: A contribution to the theory of child battery. *American Journal of Psychiatry*, 1970, 127(3), 375-379.

FONTANA, V. J. and BERNARD, M. L. *The Maltreated Child*. Springfield, Ill.: Charles C Thomas, 1971.

FRIEDMAN, S. B. and MORSE, C. W. Child abuse: A 5-year follow-up of early case finding in the emergency department. *Pediatrics*, 1974, 54(4), 404-410.

FRODI, A. M. and LAMB, M. E. Psychophysiological responses to infant signals in abusive mothers and mothers of premature infants. Paper presented to The Society for Psychophysiological Research. Madison, Wisconsin, 1978.

GAINES, R., SANDGRUND, A., GREEN, A. H., and POWER, E. Etiological factors in child maltreatment: A multivariate study of abusing, neglecting and normal mothers. *Journal of Abnormal Psychology*, 1978, 87(5), 531-540.

GALDSTON, R. Observations on children who have been physically abused and their parents. *American Journal of Psychiatry*, 1965, 122, 440-443.

GALDSTON, R. Violence begins at home. *Journal of the American Academy of Child Psychiatry*, 1971, 10, 336-350.

GARBARINO, J. A preliminary study of some ecological correlates of child abuse: The impact of socioeconomic stress on mothers. *Child Development*, 1976, 47, 178-185.

GARBARINO, J. The human ecology of child maltreatment: A conceptual model for research. *Journal of Marriage and the Family*, 1977, 39(4), 721-735.

GELLES, R. J. Child abuse as psychopathology: A sociological critique and reformulation. *American Journal of Orthopsychiatry*, 1973, 43(4), 611-621.

GIL, D. G. *Violence Against Children*. Cambridge, Mass.: Harvard University Press, 1970.

GREEN, A. H., GAINES, R. W., and SANDGRUND, A. Child abuse: Pathological syndrome of family interaction. *American Journal of Psychiatry*, 1974, (131(8), 882-886.

GREGG, G. S. and ELMER, E. Infant injuries: Accident or abuse? *Pediatrics*, 1969, 44(3), 434-439.

Iowa Department of Social Services, Report Series A-4, Statistical data on child abuse cases, 1977.

JOHNSON, B. and MORSE, H. A. Injured children and their parents. *Children*, 1968, 15(4), 147-152.

JUSTICE, B. and JUSTICE, R. *The Abusing Family*. New York: Human Sciences Press, 1976.

KEMPE, C. H. and HELFER, R. E. *Helping the Battered Child and His Family*. Philadelphia: J. B. Lippincott, 1972.

KEMPE, C. H., SILVERMAN, F. N., STEELE, B. F., DROEGEMUELLER, W., and SILVER, H. K. The battered child syndrome. *Journal of the American Medical Association*, 1962, 181(1), 17-24.

KENT, J. T. A follow-up study of abused children. *Journal of Pediatric Psychology*, 1976, 1(2), 25-31.

KNUTSON, J. F. Child abuse research as an area of aggression research. *Pediatric Psychology*, 1978, 3(1), 20-27.

KORBIN, J. Anthropological contributions to the study of child abuse. *Child Abuse and Neglect*, 1977, 1, 7-24.

LEFKOWITZ, M. M., WALDER, L. O., and ERON, L. D. Punishment, identification and aggression. *Merrill-Palmer Quarterly of Development and Behavior*, 1963, 9, 159-174.

LIGHT, R. J. Abused and neglected children in America: A study of alternative policies. *Harvard Educational Review*, 1973, 43, 556-598.

MARTIN, M. The child and his development. In C. H. Kempe and R. E. Helfer (Eds.), *Helping the Battered Child and His Family*. Philadelphia: J. B. Lippincott, 1972.

MELNICK, B. and HURLEY, J. R. Distinctive personality attributes of child-abusing mothers. *Journal of Consulting and Clinical Psychology*, 1969, 33(6), 746-749.

MORRIS, M. G. and GOULD, R. W. Role-reversal: A necessary concept in dealing with the "battered child syndrome." *American Journal of Orthopsychiatry*, 1963, 33, 298-299.

MORSE, C. W., SAHLER, O. J. Z., and FRIEDMAN, S. B. A three-year follow-up study of abused and neglected children. *American Journal of Diseases of Children*, 1970, 120, 439-446.

NURSE, S. M. Familial patterns of parents who abuse their children. *Smith College Studies in Social Work*, 1964, 32, 11-25.

OLIVER, J. E. and TAYLOR, A. Five generations of ill-treated children in one family pedigree. *British Journal of Psychiatry*, 1971, 119, 473-480.

OWENS, D. J. and STRAUS, M. A. The social structure of violence in childhood and approval of violence as an adult. *Aggressive Behavior*, 1975, 1, 193-211.

PARKE, R. D. and COLLMER, C. W. *Child Abuse: An Interdisciplinary Analysis*. Chicago: The University of Chicago Press, 1975.

PAULSON, M. J. and CHALEFF, A. Parent surrogate roles: A dynamic concept in understanding and treating abusive parents. *Journal of Clinical Child Psychology*, 1973, 2, 38-40.

PELTON, L. H. Child abuse and neglect: The myth of classlessness. *American Journal of Orthopsychiatry*, 1978, 43(4), 608-617.

RUPPENTHAL, G. C., ARLING, G. L., HARLOW, H. F., SACKETT, G. P., and SUOMI, S. J. A ten-year perspective of motherless-mother monkey behavior. *Journal of Abnormal Psychology*, 1976, 85(4), 341-349.

SEARS, R. R., MACCOBY, E. E., and LEVIN, H. The sources of aggression in the home. In S. K. Steinmetz & M. A. Straus (Eds.), *Violence in the Family*. New York: Dodd, Mead & Company, 1974.

SILVER, L. B., DUBLIN, C. C., and LOURIE, R. S. Does violence breed violence? Contributions from a study of the child abuse syndrome. *American Journal of Psychiatry*, 1969, 126(3), 404-407.

SMITH,, S. M. *The Battered Child Syndrome*. London: Butterworths, 1975.

SMITH, S. M. and HANSON, R. Interpersonal relationships and child-rearing practices in 214 parents of battered children. *British Journal of Psychiatry*, 1975, 125, 513-525.

SMITH, S. M., HANSON, R., and NOBLE, S. Parents of battered babies: A controlled study. *British Medical Journal*, 1973, 4, 388-391.

SMITH, S. M., HANSON, R., and NOBLE, S. Social aspects of the battered baby syndrome. *British Journal of Psychiatry*, 1974, 125, 568-582.

SPINETTA, J. J. and RIGLER, D. The child-abusing parent. *Psychological Bulletin*, 1972, 77, 296-304.

STEELE, B. F. Parental abuse of infants and small children. In E. J. Anthony and T. Benedick (Eds.), *Parenthood: Its Psychology and Psychopathology*. Boston: Little, Brown & Company, 1970.

STEELE, B. F. Violence within the family. In R. E. Helfer and C. H. Kempe (Eds.), *Child Abuse and Neglect: The Family and the Community*. Cambridge, Mass.: Ballinger, 1976.

STEELE, B. F. and POLLACK, C. B. A psychiatric study of parents who abuse infants and small children. In R. E. Helfer and C. H. Kempe (Eds.), *The Battered Child*. 2nd edition. Chicago: The University of Chicago Press, 1974.

SUOMI, S. J. Maternal behavior by socially incompetent monkeys: Neglect and abuse of offspring. *Journal of Pediatric Psychology*, 1978, 3(1), 28-34.

TERR, L. C. A family study of child abuse. *American Journal of Psychiatry*, 1970, 127(5), 665-671.

VAN STOLK, M. *The Battered Child in Canada*. Toronto: McClelland & Stewart, 1972.

WALTERS, D. R. *Physical and Sexual Abuse of Children: Causes and Treatment*. Bloomington, Indiana: University of Indiana Press, 1975.

WASSERMAN, S. The abused parent of the abused child. *Children*, 1968, 14(5), 175-179.

YOUNG, L. *Wednesday's Children: A Study of Child Neglect and Abuse*. New York: McGraw-Hill, 1964.

ZALBA, S. R. The abused child: II. A typology for classification and treatment. *Social Work*, 1967, 12, 70-79.

A number of family variables associated with child abuse are reviewed. Few studies have examined the abusing family as a unit, so it is necessary to pool bits and pieces of information on individuals or dyads in these families to get a sense of what they are like. Part I of this review (Berger, 1980) covered methodological issues in the child abuse literature and parent-related characteristics of abusing families. Part II, the present paper, reviews child-related characteristics of abusing families, child-rearing patterns in these families, the abusing family's relationship to the extra-familial environment, and typologies of abusing families. Finally, the material covered in Parts I and II is summarized and discussed. Suggestions are made for improving the quality of future studies in this area.

18

THE CHILD ABUSING FAMILY

II. Child and Child-Rearing Variables, Environmental Factors and Typologies of Abusing Families

Audrey M. Berger

Family variables in child abuse have not been systematically investigated. Variables which affect family life have received a large amount of attention, but the interested reader must combine information from different sources to get a picture of what abusing families are like. The purpose of this review is to organize this information to highlight family variables that relate to child abuse and to emphasize the importance of studying the family as a unit. This review deals with only the physical abuse of children.

In Part I (Berger, 1980), methodological issues were discussed. It was pointed out that the definition of child abuse is problematic, that different studies have used different definitions, and that abusing families constitute a heterogeneous population. As a result, it is often difficult, and possibly even misleading, to compare the findings of different studies. Nevertheless, this review attempts to synthesize the child abuse data to find the consistencies that have emerged across studies.

CONTRIBUTIONS OF THE CHILD

The literature suggests that abused children are different from their nonabused siblings and from other nonabused children. Many authors have proposed that

Reprint requests should be sent to Audrey Berger, The University of Rochester Medical Center, Dept. of Psychiatry, Div. of Psychology, 300 Crittenden Blvd., Rochester, NY 14642.

The author would like to thank Dr. Neil Jacobson and Dr. John Knutson for their helpful comments and suggestions.

From Audrey M. Berger, "The Child Abusing Family: II. Child and Child-Rearing Variables, Environmental Factors and Typologies of Abusing Families," *American Journal of Family Therapy*, 1980, Volume 8, Number 4, pp. 52-68. Reprinted by permission of the author and publisher.

certain characteristics of abused children may play an eliciting role in abuse (Friedrich and Boriskin, 1976; Gelles, 1973; Green, 1978; Johnson and Morse, 1968; Kempe and Helfer, 1972; Knutson, 1978; Lynch, 1976; Lynch and Roberts, 1977; Martin, 1976; Milow and Lourie, 1964; Reid and Taplin, 1976; Walters, 1975). The most common characteristics found among populations of abused children can be divided into two categories. The first category includes those characteristics which are known to have existed prior to the abuse and may have some as yet unspecified effect on the child's behavior, as well as on the parent-child interaction. The second category includes mental, physical and behavioral attributes of these children which could have either existed prior to the abuse or resulted from it, and which most certainly affect the parent-child relationship.

Characteristics in the first category include *prematurity* and *low birth weight, premarital conception, illegitimacy* and *congenital defects.* Of these, prematurity and low birth weight are the most commonly reported. Friedrich and Boriskin (1976) reviewed the literature and concluded that there is a much higher rate of prematurity and low birth weight among abused children than in the population at large. Klein and Stern (1971) found that 23.5% of their sample of 51 abused children were low birth weight infants, a rate much higher than is found in the general population. Baldwin and Oliver (1975) reported that 21% of the abused children in their sample were premature, in contrast to the general population rate of 6.7%. Smith (1975) found four times the rate of low birth weight among the abused children in his sample than in the general population. Lynch (1976) compared the prenatal, perinatal and early life histories of abused children with those of their nonabused siblings and found striking differences between the groups. There was a much higher rate of pregnancy and birth complications and of medical difficulties and unusual circumstances during the first year of life for the abused group than for their nonabused siblings. On the basis of hospital records, Lynch and Roberts (1977) compared a group of abused children with a group of nonabused children born at the same hospital. Admission of the infant to a special care baby unit was among the many variables which were found to characterize the abused children. Although it was not explicitly stated, low birth weight and prematurity were likely to have been the reason for the infant's need for special care.

What factors might account for the apparent relationship between prematurity and low birth weight and later child abuse? Although there are presently no definitive answers to this question, the literature does point to some intriguing possibilities. Friedrich and Boriskin (1976) note that the premature child is often restless, distractible and difficult to care for. Martin (1976) proposes that the child at high risk for abuse is one who is difficult to care for, but not obviously different, and thus does not elicit social support for the mother; premature and low birth weight infants may fit this description.

Frodi and Lamb (1978a, 1978b) have conducted a series of ingenious studies to assess the impact of the premature infant on normal adults. In these studies, adults have viewed videotapes of either premature or full-term infants. They have used a 2 × 2 design so that in two conditions the subjects heard the cry of the infant they were viewing; in two other conditions the crying was dubbed in so that one group saw a full-term infant but heard the cry of a premature infant, and another group viewed a premature infant but heard the cry of a full-term infant. These authors found that crying by both full-term and premature infants elicited marked autonomic arousal and was perceived as irritating and annoying by normal adults. However, the cry of the premature infant elicited a greater autonomic response and was perceived as more aversive than the cry of the full-term infant. This difference was even more pronounced when the cry and face of the premature infant were presented together.

There is some evidence that the premature infant may be at greater risk for abuse due to early difficulties in the attachment process between the mother and her infant. After birth, premature infants are generally separated from their mothers for a longer period of time than are full-term infants. Klaus and Kennell (1976) suggest that early contact between a mother and her infant importantly influences their future relationship. In a study on visiting patterns of mothers in a nursery for premature infants, Farnoff, Kennell and Klaus (1972) found that 25% of the mothers who were infrequent visitors later exhibited "disorders of mothering," one of which was child battering. These data support the hypothesis that maternal-infant bonding may importantly influence later mother-child relationships. But it is also possible that mothers who do not visit their hospitalized infant are simply the type of mothers who would in general be more likely to abuse children. Infrequent visits could also indicate that the child is unwanted.

Lynch's (1976) data, described earlier, support the notion that early separation between a mother and her infant may place that infant at risk for abuse. Lynch found a much higher rate of mother-child separations during the first six months of life for the abused children than for their nonabused siblings. Hyman (1977) compared the interactions of abusing mothers and their infants, aged six to 20 months, with the interactions of a matched control group of mother-infant dyads. Hyman found that the mothers and infants in the abuse sample were much less responsive to one another than those in the control sample; furthermore, the abused infant was more likely to cry on reunion with the mother. The author suggested that these data may indicate a disturbance in the mother-infant attachment in the abuse dyads.

It should be noted that prematurity and low birth weight are not always found with high frequency in samples of abused children. For example, of the abused children surveyed in the Iowa Department of Social Services Report (1977), only a few were born prematurely.* Also, Gaines, Sandgrund, Green and Power (1978) found that neonatal complications requiring hospitalization did not successfully discriminate between the abusing, neglecting and control groups. Thus, they found no support for the hypothesized relationship between interruptions in the early mother-child attachment process and child abuse. Perinatal complications could, in fact, be found with high frequency among samples of abused children yet still not be predictive of abuse; that is, the available data have not documented that the variables of low birth weight and prematurity predict abuse better than base rate.

It is frequently reported that many abused children were conceived premaritally, were born out of wedlock, or were unwanted (Cohen et al., 1966; Johnson and Morse, 1968; Kempe et al., 1962; Nurse, 1964; Steele, 1970). Nurse (1964) found that, of her sample of 20 abused children, five were premaritally conceived and six were born out of wedlock. In their sample of 101 abused children, Johnson and Morse (1968) found that one-half were unwanted and one-fourth were born out of wedlock. Cohen et al. (1966) reported that three of the four abused children that they studied were conceived premaritally. Smith, Hanson and Noble

---

* The children included in the statistics of the Iowa Department of Social Services Report (1977) were simply reported as abused. Upon investigation, some of these reports were found to be unsubstantiated, so the children included in those statistics may be significantly different than the children included in other studies on child abuse.

(1974) found that 71% of the abused children in their sample versus 33% of the control children were premaritally conceived, and that 36% of the abused children were illegitimate, whereas this was true for only 6% of the control group. However, Lynch (1976) found that the abused children in her sample were less likely to be illegitimate and more likely to have been planned than their nonabused siblings, showing that the relationship between abuse and illegitimacy is not a consistent one.

Abused children have also been reported to have a higher frequency of congenital defects. Baldwin and Oliver (1975) found that 10% of the abused children in their study had congenital defects as compared with the 3% reported in surveys of the general population.

The second category of child characteristics associated with abuse includes *mental retardation, physical handicaps* and *behavioral deviations*. These characteristics differ from prematurity, illegitimacy and congenital defects in that it is frequently difficult to ascertain their onset; this is particularly true for behavioral deviations. Even if these deviations are known to have existed prior to the identified episode of abuse, there is no assurance that previous unidentified episodes of abuse are not responsible for the deviations. Therefore, it is unclear whether these characteristics played an eliciting role in the abuse or resulted from the abuse. However, since abuse is only one aspect of a more general pattern of parent-child interaction, behavioral deviations may be seen as a product of the general pattern rather than exclusively as a product or precipitant of the abuse. As will be discussed shortly, Patterson and Reid's (1970) coercion construct proposes that it is the general pattern of parent-child interactions which leads to abuse. However, even if the mental retardation, physical handicaps or behavioral deviations are specific products of the abuse, it is certainly possible that the existence of these characteristics will then serve to increase the probability of the recurrence of abuse.

Friedrich and Boriskin (1976) concluded from their review of the literature that there is a high incidence of mental retardation and physical handicaps among abused children, but they point out that the etiology of these deviations is unclear. In contrast, the Iowa Department of Social Services (1977) reported that only 4% of the abused children identified were mentally retarded or physically handicapped; 85% of the abused children were found to be physically and behaviorally normal.

The Iowa Department of Social Services (1977) report also found a relatively low incidence of behavioral deviations in the abused children. However, most studies report much higher rates of behavioral deviations. Gil (1969, 1970) found that the frequency of behavioral deviance in his sample of abused children was much higher than is found in the general population. Gil also reported that 30% of the abused children had shown noticeable behavioral deviations during the year prior to the identified abusive episode. In their study of abused children under five years of age, Baldwin and Oliver (1975) found a high frequency of: 1) fear of parents or other adults; 2) withdrawal, listlessness or drowsiness, hyperactivity or repetitive motor activity; 3) persistent irritability. Galdston (1971) reported that the abused boys in his sample were often thought to display unpredictable, unpremeditated and apparently purposeless violent behavior, while the girls tended to be isolated or clinging. Children of both sexes were felt to be preoccupied with attaining adult attention. Johnson and Morse (1968) reported that within the abusing family, the child most likely to be the target was usually hyperactive or difficult to control. Social worker reports indicated that 70% of this sample of 268 abused children showed physical or behavioral abnormalities before the identified abusive incident. These children had few friends, and approximately 10% were thought to be treated badly by their siblings, while about 20% were thought to mistreat their siblings.

Green (1978) reported on the behavioral deviancy of 60 abused children seen in an outpatient clinic. On the basis of psychiatric evaluation, psychological testing and observation during therapy, Green described these children as: often hyperactive and impulsive, with minimal frustration tolerance; aggressive and destructive, self-destructive and accident prone; and provocative. Kent (1976) compared a large sample of abused children with neglected children and with nonabused children from low SES families that manifested some evidence of dysfunction. Based on social worker reports, Kent concluded that the abused children were more aggressive, more disobedient and had poorer peer relationships, than children in the other groups, while the neglected children showed more developmental delays than the abused children. Martin (1972) proposes that there are two types of abused children: One type is apathetic and relatively unresponsive to the environment; the other type is aggressive. He argues that the apathetic type is more frequent than the aggressive type.

PARENT-CHILD INTERACTIONS

Recent literature suggests that the behavior of both the abusing parent and the abused child should be viewed in light of the interaction patterns characterizing the entire family. Blumberg (1974) noted that abused children often act out. He hypothesized that the abusing family is caught in a vicious cycle: Abuse leads to retaliation by the child which leads to further abuse.

Burgess and Conger (1977) compared the interaction patterns of 10 abusing families with those of 10 neglecting families and 10 matched normal control families. "Blind" observers coded the behaviors of the family members using the Behavioral Observation Scoring System. These authors found high rates of coercive and noncompliant behaviors and low rates of reciprocity among all members of abusing families. However, neglecting families showed interaction patterns that were similar to those of abusing families. These findings raise the possibility that family interaction patterns may not discriminate between distressed families. Alternatively, it could be that the observational code used in this study was insensitive to differences between abusing and neglecting families.

Reid and Taplin (1976) compared child and parent behaviors in abusing families, distressed nonabusing families and nondistressed nonabusing families. All families were observed for six to 10 sessions. The results showed that abusing families engaged in a significantly greater frequency of aversive interactions than the distressed nonabusing families. Both parents and children in the abusing families manifested consistently higher rates of physically aggressive behaviors than did the parents and children in the distressed nonabusing families. The authors concluded that abused children participate in their own abuse.

Reid and Taplin's (1976) work is outstanding in the child abuse literature. Their systematic use of a rather complex observational system and the relative lack of inference in their behavioral measures could have made these results the least ambiguous in the literature. However, there are a few reasons why this impressive study should be interpreted cautiously. First, the abusing families were selected in a very unusual manner. A group of 88 families was originally selected, for a study of distressed families, from the families who had been referred to the clinic because of child conduct problems. After reviewing their clinic records it was discovered that 27 of the 88 distressed families also had a history of child abuse; these 27 families constituted the sample of abusing families, while the distressed but nonabusing families constituted the control. Second, the abusing and distressed nonabusing families were not matched. The abusing families were more frequently low SES than the comparison families. Nevertheless, Reid and Taplin's findings are provocative, and similar work should be done with matched groups.

Patterson and Reid (1970) have proposed a pattern of interaction they call the "coercion process," which may be helpful in attempting to understand the role of children in their own abuse, the sequence of events which could lead to an abusive episode, and how abuse could become a high probability outcome of future noxious encounters. In the coercion process, the participants emit aversive behaviors, leading to further escalation of aversive behaviors. The process ends when one participant emits some behavior which causes a cessation of further aversive behaviors. By capitulating, one participant reinforces the other for emitting some highly aversive behavior. Since Gil (1970) found that 63% of the abusive incidents occurred in a disciplinary context, the coercion process may indeed prove to be a useful model for conceptualizing abusive interactions.

Knutson (1978) has also noted that aversive events may immediately precede abusive incidents and that intrusive behaviors may constitute noxious stimuli. He hypothesizes that some abused children may have circadian rhythms which are asynchronous with the rest of the family and therefore may be more likely to intrude on the activities of other family members. Knutson reports that some data collected by John Reid are consistent with this hypothesis.

Some evidence from the aggression literature supports the hypothesis that certain characteristics of the child may play a role in abuse. Berkowitz (1973) showed that the target's stimulus characteristics, because of the meaning they have for the aggressor, can serve to increase the intensity of the aggressor's attack. Berkowitz and Frodi (1978) showed that female undergraduates were likely to punish an unattractive child more severely than an attractive child for an incorrect response in a learning task.

It is important to bear in mind that these characteristics of the abused child gain their significance from the impact that they have on the parent. They are not high-risk variables in and of themselves, but only when they exist in combination with other parental or situational characteristics. For example, the crying of premature infants may in fact be perceived as more aversive by all parents, but most parents will not abuse their premature infant. However, if the mother and child have failed to develop a strong bond, or if the mother is hyperreactive to crying, and so on, then the premature child may be at risk for abuse.

The finding that some abused children may, in fact, be especially difficult to discipline supports the hypothesis that children actively contribute to their own abuse. However, since it is not possible to determine whether aversive behaviors emitted by these children existed prior to the abusive behavior of the parents, only longitudinal data on high-risk families can determine the sequence of events. In any event, since abused children are often considered hard to handle, it seems reasonable to hypothesize that repeated episodes of abuse may, in part, be a function of the child's behavior, regardless of the cause for the initial abusive incident.

PATTERNS OF CHILD REARING

It has been found that a significant proportion of abusive incidents occur within the context of disciplinary action by the parents (Dubanoski et al., 1978; Gil,

1970), and that abusing parents may lack an adequate disciplinary repertoire (Reid and Taplin, 1976). Reid and Taplin (1976) propose that abusing parents discipline their children inconsistently and ineffectively, and consequently are unable to control their children's behavior. During home observations, abusing parents displayed more verbal and physical aggressive behaviors and used threats more frequently than distressed nonabusing and nondistressed parents. In addition, children in abusing families had an almost equal probability of obtaining positive reinforcement for aversive behaviors as for pro-social behaviors. The authors concluded that abusing parents lack child-management skills.

Friedman and Morse (1974) found that abusing mothers had a great deal of difficulty setting and maintaining limits for their children. However, this was also found to be true for the mothers of neglected children and for the mothers whose children were classified as accident victims.

Some mothers in the Morse, Sahler and Friedman (1970) study reported difficulty controlling or disciplining their children. These mothers were also confused by their children's behavior. It should be noted, however, that this study was conducted three years after the abusive episode was reported, and it is possible that the disciplinary difficulties began after the abusive incident.

Smith and Hanson (1975) reported that in battering families physical punishment is used to excess and that the discipline is inconsistent. The mothers were overly concerned and punitive about some things and careless about others. Young (1964) reported that inconsistent discipline was the rule in all the severe abuse families and in 91% of the moderate abuse families in her study. However, this was also true of 97% of the severe neglect and 88% of the moderate neglect families. She also found that 88% of the severe abuse, 81% of the moderate abuse, 94% of the severe neglect and 82% of the moderate neglect parents had no consistent expectations of their children. Only 22% of the severely abused and 27% of the moderately abused children had defined responsibilities. Only 5% of the severe abuse parents and 8% of the moderate abuse parents shared and discussed their problems with their spouse. Thus, both abusing and neglecting families in Young's study lack a consistent disciplinary structure, the children probably have difficulty knowing what's expected of them, and the parents probably do not work together to achieve control over their children's behavior.

Young (1964) also found that abusive language, nagging and scolding were significantly more characteristic of abusing than neglecting families. The abusing parents also consistently prevented their children from participating in a variety of "normal" childhood activities.

Although the literature is laden with methodological problems (i.e., lack of matched control groups, mostly self-report data, etc.), it seems highly probable that disciplinary skills are severely lacking in the repertoire of at least some abusing parents. Lack of an appropriate disciplinary repertoire may conceivably be a necessary condition, but it is not a sufficient condition for the occurrence of abuse. In the first place, the data suggest that neglecting parents may be equally ineffective at disciplining their children. Since many (if not most) neglected children are not abused, some additional component or components must be necessary for an episode of abuse to occur. Second, inconsistent discipline may account for the child's behavior, but it does not account for the parent's use of physical violence. However, if we consider the fact that inconsistent discipline may lead to an increase in deviant child behaviors (Patterson and Reid, 1970) and that such behavior on the part of the child is likely to lead the parents to feel helpless and frustrated, then the import of disciplinary techniques for the parents' behavior begins to make sense.

It may well be true that many abusive episodes are a response to an escalation in aversive behaviors on the part of the child, but it is often the case that the events reported to have triggered the abusive episodes would probably be considered by most people to be normal, though aversive, behaviors of children (Gil, 1970). Weston (1974) presents 36 cases of severe abuse that led to the child's death and the precipitants that triggered the incident. Twelve of the caretakers said that the child cried too much, 11 reported that the baby soiled him or herself, three spoke of feeding problems, one reported that the child "splashed water," and another complained that the child "needed love and attention."

It may be that abusing parents tend to apply disciplinary action to different behaviors than nonabusing parents. (Data bearing on this issue were discussed in Part I in the section on parental perceptions of their children.) In support of this view, Knutson (1978) has hypothesized that these parents may be hyperreactive to certain noxious stimuli. If the noxious stimuli that are so very aversive to these parents also happen to be behaviors that are part and parcel of normal child development, it becomes more understandable that some of these parents perceive their seemingly normal or helpless child as bad, hard to handle, etc. This is not to suggest that some abused children are not hard to handle; rather, it might explain why infants of nonpsychotic parents and children who do not seem particularly aggressive or unmanageable are subjected to abuse.

If, as this review suggests, abusing parents lack child-management skills and are hyperreactive to certain types of stimuli, it would seem important to ask whether other children in the family are also abused; and if they are not abused, why not?

THE SIBLINGS OF ABUSED CHILDREN

The statistics indicate that some moderate proportion of the siblings of abused children are also abused (Baldwin and Oliver, 1975; Friedman and Morse, 1974; Gil, 1970; Johnson and Morse, 1968; Kempe et al., 1962; Nurse, 1964). If the locus of the problem is presumed to lie within the parents, it makes sense that more than one child in the family is sometimes abused. However, if the parents typically make excessive demands on the children, use inconsistent discipline, are hyperreactive to noxious stimuli, etc., why would some of the children in abusing families escape abuse? Some of the data bearing on this question were discussed earlier and in Part I, but it seems worthwhile to review briefly some of the possible implications of the data on children's contributions to their own abuse:

1) The abused child might have some characteristic which is particularly aversive to the parent. For example, the child might be very irritable, mentally retarded or a new financial burden. If the parent is differentially hyperreactive to certain stimuli, the child with those characteristics might be at high risk for abuse. For example, the child who cries a lot might be more at risk for abuse than an aggressive child, or vice versa.

2) If marital problems exist, the child who is favored by the other parent, the child who is most like the other parent or the child who has precipitated marital stress might be the target.

3) In cases where the abuse occurs only once, the target child may simply be at the wrong place at the wrong time, when the abusing parent is under a great deal of stress.

ABUSING FAMILY-ENVIRONMENT RELATIONSHIPS

Isolation

It is frequently reported that abusing families are socially isolated and lack contextual support (Elmer, 1977b; Morris and Gould, 1963; Nurse, 1964; Parke and Collmer, 1975; Smith and Hanson, 1975; Smith et al., 1974; Spinetta and Rigler, 1972; Steele and Pollack, 1974; Young, 1964). Young (1964) found that 95% of the severe abuse and 83% of the moderate abuse families in her study had no continuing relationship with people outside the nuclear family. Young also found that, when abusing parents did develop friendships, they rarely lasted more than a few weeks and usually ended in a violent quarrel. Only 15% of the abusing families in Young's study belonged to an organized group.

Abusing families are thought to be alienated not only from the community, but also from their own extended families. Numerous investigators have noted that these families receive little or no support from relatives (Bennie and Sclare, 1969; Green et al., 1974; Johnson and Morse, 1968; Nurse, 1964; Parke and Collmer, 1975; Smith et al., 1974; Spinetta and Rigler, 1972).

Another frequently reported characteristic of abusing families is a high mobility rate (Gil, 1969, 1970; Spinetta and Rigler, 1972) which could contribute to the isolation which may be experienced by many abusing families.

In some cases, abusing parents also appear to work actively to ensure that their children also remain isolated from the community. Young (1964) found that more than half of the abusing families consistently denied their children normally accepted activities, and 59% of the severe abuse families refused to allow their children to become attached to anyone outside the family.

If, in fact, these families lack contextual supports, this could function to increase stress within the family and to decrease the likelihood that stress will be handled effectively. Under such circumstances, the parent who has primary responsibility for child care may well be pushed too far by seemingly harmless behaviors of the children. Parents who receive support from their family and community might be less likely to feel so desperately trapped and frustrated by their children's behavior.

Environmental Stressors

Many authors have argued that environmental stressors impinging on the family play an important role in child abuse (e.g., Erlanger, 1974; Garbarino, 1976, 1977; Gelles, 1973; Gil, 1970; Justice and Justice, 1976; Kempe and Helfer, 1972; Parke, 1978; Parke and Collmer, 1975). Abusing families often live under highly stressful conditions. Some of the stressors commonly found are related to socio-economic status (Elmer, 1977a; Gelles, 1973; Gil, 1969, 1970; Gregg and Elmer, 1969; Johnson and Morse, 1968; Nurse, 1964). Gil (1970) found that the occupational and educational status of the abusing families in his study was low, and that the fathers often had an unstable work history. Not surprisingly, these families had low incomes, while also having more mouths to feed than the average American family.

Stress may be an important antecedent to abuse. However, since lower class families experience a disproportionate number of stressors, and since most identified abusing families are from the lower social classes, stress and socioeconomic class are confounded. Since most lower class families do not abuse their children, it cannot be concluded on the basis of most available data that the stressors associated with poverty cause child abuse.

A number of approaches could, however, be taken to investigate the role of environmental stressors in child abuse. One would be to show that abusing families experience more and/or different types of stressors than matched nonabusing lower class families. Another would be to identify particular types of stressors that are found with greater frequency in abusing families of all social classes. A third would be to show that certain types of crises (i.e., sudden exacerbation of stress or new severe stressors) consistently precede abusive episodes.

If it were repeatedly found that abusing families do not experience more or different stressors than matched nonabusing families, it would not necessarily mean that stress does not play an important role in child abuse. It could mean that stress must interact with some other variables that are found with greater frequency in abusing families in order to snowball into an episode of abuse. Variables that could exacerbate the impact of a stressor have been discussed in Parts I and II of this paper. The tendency for abusing parents to be social isolates may be particularly relevant here. Rabkin and Struening (1976) have suggested that the unavailability of social supports may be a crucial factor in determining the detrimental effects of stress.

Garbarino (1976) presented some data which support the importance of social supports. He examined the ecological correlates of child abuse and maltreatment in 58 New York state counties. He generated regression equations using various indices of socioeconomic and demographic characteristics of the counties. The results showed that child abuse and maltreatment rates were highest in counties where there was a high rate of poor, single mothers who had few child-care facilities and resources available to them. Although these data are suggestive, they are correlational, and therefore no conclusions can be drawn regarding causation. In addition, the variables included in Garbarino's analysis accounted for 36% of the variance, leaving 64% of the variance unexplained. It is conceivable that the unexplained variance can be accounted for by including additional ecological variables in the equation, but it seems more likely that variables specific to the abusing families are more crucial, since not all mothers in such situations abuse their children. Furthermore, Gaines et al. (1978) concluded, on the basis of a stepwise discriminant analysis on 12 variables associated with child maltreatment, that stress played only a minor role in the abuse. Of the six variables found to discriminate abusing, neglecting and normal mothers, environmental stress accounted for a very small portion of the discriminant space. Furthermore, neglecting mothers reported higher levels of stress than did abusing mothers, suggesting that environmental stress is related to parenting difficulties in general, rather than to child abuse per se. The authors concluded that stress is relevant to the maltreatment syndrome (abuse and neglect), but that it leaves much of the phenomenon unexplained.

A few studies have found environmental stressors to be importantly related to abuse, independent of social class. Burgess and Conger (1977) administered the Schedule of Recent Events and found that abuse families tended to show more life changes than neglecting and control families. Justice and Justice (1976) used the Holmes and Rahe Social Readjustment Rating Scale (SRRS) to evaluate the level of life changes experienced by abusing and nonabusing parents from varying economic groups. They found that the abuse group reported significantly more, and more serious, life crises than the nonabusing group. The authors argued that life crises predispose parents to abusive behavior, and that these life crises are not a function of socioeconomic status. Although the group differences obtained in this study are intriguing, their meaning is not immediately clear. The SRRS includes numerous items which refer to events that could easily be self-induced, for example, getting fired from a job. So, these results could indicate that the stress produced by life changes may contribute to abuse, or alternatively, these results could simply reflect a general tendency for abusing parents to cause themselves a lot of problems; most likely, it's combination of the two.

There are many methodological problems involved in the assessment of stressors and they have been virtually ignored in the abuse literature. It is imperative that researchers consider these issues in any investigation of the role of stress in child abuse. The reader is referred to Rabkin and Struening (1976) and Brown, Harris and Birley (1973) for in-depth discussions of the methodological problems involved in assessing stressors.

TYPOLOGIES OF ABUSING FAMILIES

The numerous factors associated with the family life of abusing families may constitute necessary conditions for child abuse, but none of them appear to be a sufficient condition for abuse. Furthermore, it is probable that none of these factors alone are necessary for child abuse to occur, since no one factor has been reported as present in every abusive family studied. It seems more likely that different combinations of certain factors might constitute necessary and sufficient conditions for child abuse. Thus, it appears important to shift the focus to the family unit.

By looking for clusters of factors associated with the family unit, rather than just looking at the presence or absence of each of these factors in isolation, it may be possible to find meaningful patterns that have some descriptive and predictive validity. It appears improbable that any one cluster of factors characterizes all abusing families, since these families appear to be so heterogeneous. Therefore, it may prove fruitful to search for the different clusters of factors which characterize different types of abusing families. A typology of abusing families might help clarify the relationships between the variables associated with abuse.

A typology can be developed a priori on the basis of some hypotheses, and then tested empirically to determine whether subgroups of abusing families do fit into the predicted categories; or it can be developed empirically by first identifying attributes associated with abusing families and then cluster analyzing those attributes to identify clusters of factors which characterize different types of abusing families (Frederiksen, 1972).

A number of typologies of child abuse have been proposed (e.g., Gil, 1970; Walters, 1975; Zalba, 1967), but only Zalba's is concerned exclusively with types of abusing families. Zalba developed his categories of abusing families a priori, and they remain to be validated empirically. His typology describes six types of abusing families and each category is defined by a number of factors including the type of parent, the type of child, the nature of the abuse, and treatment implications.

Zalba divided his classification scheme into "controllable" and "uncontrollable" abuse. Uncontrollable abuse was defined as situations in which only the removal of the child from the abusing family (temporary or permanent) could insure the child's safety. Three types of abusing families were included in this category: 1) families with a psychotic parent; 2) families with a pervasively angry and abusive parent; and 3) families with a depressive, passive-aggressive parent. Note that in all three cases, the locus of the problem is presumed to lie within the abuser's personality system.

In cases where Zalba classifies the abuse as controllable, he predicts that treatment can generally progress without removing the child from the home. The prognosis for these families, according to Zalba, is significantly better than for the families who fall into the uncontrollable abuse categories. Three types of families are included under controllable abuse: 1) families with a cold, compulsive, disciplinarian parent—here again, the locus of the problem is presumed to lie within the abuser's personality system; 2) families with an impulsive but generally adequate parent, and where there's marital conflict—in this case, the locus of the problem is thought to lie within the family system; 3) families where a parent has an identity/role crisis—the locus of the problem is hypothesized to lie within the family-environment system.

Zalba's typology still remains to be validated, but it provides much opportunity for hypothesis testing. It does not account for numerous factors, however. It does not directly address the possible role of disciplinary techniques, isolation, the abuser's own upbringing, ecological variables, etc. There may also be other factors which might distinguish between types of abusing families. It should be noted that a typology developed either in an a priori or empirical manner could have excellent descriptive validity but little predictive validity. Both types of validity must be addressed in determining the utility of any typology.

Except for Zalba's typology, the characteristics associated with abusing families have not yet been formulated into meaningful or consistent patterns. Since abusing families appear to be a heterogeneous group, since different types of abusing families may require different treatment strategies, and since the identification of families at high-risk for abuse is a major concern, it seems imperative that more energy be devoted to the identification of meaningful classifications of abusing families.

CONCLUSIONS

A review of the available literature on child abuse has shown that there are a wide array of factors which have been hypothesized to contribute to this syndrome. In Part I of this review it was concluded that abusing parents as a group manifest high rates of psychopathology, but they appear to be diagnostically heterogeneous. Very few abusing parents are found to be psychotic, and some abusing parents appear to be normal. Abusing parents also seem to be heterogeneous with respect to a wide variety of personality traits. A few of the more methodologically sound studies suggest that many or all abusing parents may have low self-esteem and low empathy. Some abusing parents may be less physiologically responsive to changes in the environment and generally more physiologically aroused when viewing videotapes of children or families than comparison subjects. Many abusing parents report that they were abused by their own parents, but other abusing parents report no such history of maltreatment. With only a few exceptions, however, investigations of the characteristics of abusing parents are methodologically inadequate. They rely largely on the verbal reports of these parents and the inferences of the investigators, and rarely include adequate control groups or blind interviews.

Abusing parents are frequently found to be single parents or, if their marriage is intact, to experience a good deal of marital conflict. Although the data on marital status are clear-cut and rather intriguing, the data on marital conflict leave much to be desired; once again, investigators have relied almost exclusively on the verbal reports of the parents for their assessment of marital conflict, and control groups are conspicuously absent. It has also been frequently suggested that abusing parents have distorted perceptions and inappropriate expectations of their abused child, but the methodological flaws of these studies require that their "findings" be considered hypotheses until methodologically sound studies confirm or discredit these reports.

In Part II of this review, characteristics of abused children were discussed. Certain characteristics of these children may play a role in eliciting their abuse. Prematurity and low birth weight, illegitimacy, premarital conception, congenital defects, mental retardation, physical handicaps and behavioral deviations have been found with high frequency in populations of abused children. Obviously, the characteristics associated with conception, pregnancy and birth exist prior to the abusive episodes, and so may contribute to the abuse in some unknown manner. It is, however, more difficult to isolate the onset of intellectual, physical and behavioral deviations; it is frequently unclear whether they are products of the abuse or whether they played a role in provoking the abuse.

The aggressive/coercive behaviors manifested by some of these children may be partly a consequence of the general child-rearing techniques utilized by their parents. Recent observational data support earlier clinical observations that these parents use inconsistent discipline, that the family interactions are characterized by abnormally high levels of verbal aggression, and that the family members behave coercively toward one another. However, since it is often found that only one child in the family is abused, it seems likely that general patterns of family interaction are not sufficient to explain why a particular child is targeted.

Finally, abusing families have been found to be isolated from their extended family and from their community and seem to experience a great deal of environmental stress. Since the abusing families studied are usually from the lower social classes, and since lower social class families generally experience a disproportionate number of stressors, social class and stress are confounded in most studies of abusing families, making it difficult to draw any conclusions about the contribution of stress to child abuse. A few studies, however, do seem to suggest that abusing families experience a disproportionate number of stresses, independent of social class, although those studies do not overcome the methodological difficulties involved in the assessment of environmental stressors.

In sum, a variety of factors have been observed more frequently among samples of abusing families than among nonabusing families. However, methodological flaws in many of the studies render their findings very tentative. It appears from the literature that abusing families are quite heterogeneous, making it unlikely that any variable or cluster of variables will consistently be found to discriminate abusing from nonabusing families. But, the literature does suggest that a number of the variables reviewed in this paper may, in fact, be implicated in child abuse. The important question is: How do these variables interact to lead to an episode of child abuse? No one variable is likely to be sufficient cause for abuse to occur. Rather, it might be more fruitful to look for patterns of variables, paying particular attention to possible subtypes of abusing families. The family unit should be the focus of investigation rather than just the characteristics of individuals in the family. However, in searching for patterns of variables, characteristics of each of the individual family members should be considered, in addition to the patterns of family interaction. It may be possible to find subtypes of abusing families where each subtype is defined by clusters of certain variables, and where each differs on some or all of those variables from nonabusing families and from other subtypes of abusing families. What is now an inconsistent and confusing array of variables associated with abuse might then be found to form meaningful patterns with descriptive and predictive utility. The confusion and inconsistency that now characterizes the literature on child abuse may be partly a function of the fact that a heterogeneous population is studied as though it were a homogeneous group.

Of course, it is also possible that the literature on characteristics of abusing families is inconsistent and confusing because the significant variables related to abuse lie in the extra-familial environment; for example, Gil (1970) has hypothesized that the cultural context is the most significant causal variable in child abuse. Although cultural influences and environmental stressors may, in fact, be causally related to abuse, these variables would appear to operate through their impact on the functioning of the family system. It is here proposed that the extra-familial environmental variables should most certainly be examined in studies on child abuse, but that they should be viewed as a set of variables impinging on the family unit that must interact with other characteristics of the family unit and its members to lead to an episode of child abuse.

It is likely that the major reason for the confusion in the child abuse literature is the dearth of appropriate methodology and systematic investigation. The lack of consistency in criteria used to select abused subjects is problematic. It would be preferable for a standard definition of child abuse to be adopted by all researchers, but in the absence of a standard definition, researchers should be careful to clearly delineate their criteria for subject inclusion. Also, control groups are urgently needed, but finding an appropriate control group is difficult. Investigators have used neglecting families (Disbrow et al., 1977; Gaines et al., 1978; Young, 1964), children who have sustained some traumatic injury but not as a result of abuse (Elmer, 1977a, 1977b), children who were admitted to the emergency room of a hospital for reasons other than an accident (Smith, 1975; Smith and Hanson, 1975; Smith et al., 1974), and behaviorally deviant children and their families (Reid and Taplin, 1976) as controls. Each type of control has drawbacks and advantages. Some investigators have used two comparison groups: a normal control group and a comparison group with some type of pathology. This latter approach provides the most information, but is more difficult to conduct.

Where possible, comparison groups should be matched on relevant factors. The most appropriate factors for matching depend partly on the goal of the investigation. Since social class is a major factor that could spuriously affect the results and lead to inaccurate conclusions, it must be taken into account. Unfortunately, it is sometimes difficult to match subjects on social class in child abuse studies. Smith and Hanson (1975) were unable to match on social class, so they dealt with the problem by weighting the results of their sample of abusing families, equating them for the social class of the controls. At the very least, the investigator should specify any social class differences not controlled.

Demographic characteristics of the subjects should be clearly specified, since abusing families appear to be a rather heterogeneous group. In reporting a study, the methodology should be clearly described; far too often in the child abuse literature, it is difficult to tell precisely how the authors conducted their investigation. If an interview format is used, it might be helpful to use a structured interview schedule that could easily be obtained and used again by other investigators interested in studying the same or similar problems. Also, it would be helpful if investigators would use standardized assessment techniques. For example, in attempting to measure marital conflict in these families, the Locke-Wallace Marital Adjustment Scale (Locke and Wallace, 1959) might be appropriate. Similarly, the use of standardized observational techniques, such as that utilized by Reid and Taplin (1976) would greatly augment our knowledge and understanding of the interactional patterns in these families.

It is important that investigators use more caution when interpreting the results of their studies. The child abuse literature is filled with examples of causal inferences made on the basis of correlational data, and with examples of inferences presented as scientific data. Also, investigators sometimes state that retrospective data on abusing parents or abused children can be used to predict the occurrence of child abuse. Follow-back studies sometimes yield very different kinds of data than follow-up studies, so investigators should be careful to recognize the limitations of the methodology used.

The type of research that has been proposed in this paper is time-consuming and costly. Relative to the magnitude of other social and health problems in our society, the incidence of child abuse may seem so small as to make it a low priority problem. However, a number of considerations argue for making child abuse a high priority social and health problem: 1) the true incidence of child abuse is unknown, and most workers believe that current statistics grossly underestimate the magnitude of the problem; 2) the impact of abuse on the victimized children may well be physically and psychologically devastating, or even life-threatening; 3) abused children may be at risk for becoming abusing parents, thus perpetuating the cycle; and 4) as noted by Oliver and Taylor (1971), abusing families sometimes make disproportionate demands on community resources.

To develop effective prevention programs, it will be necessary to know a good deal more about abusing families than is known at present. It therefore seems appropriate to devote some of our research efforts to investigating the problem of child abuse. In particular, the abusing family should be studied as a unit, since the factors relevant to child abuse may begin to form a more meaningful pattern in the context of this primary unit. But most important, we should make every effort to insure that our research endeavors will enable us to go beyond the stage of hypothesis, and will take us into the realm of concrete, replicable findings.

REFERENCES

BALDWIN, J. A. and OLIVER, J. E. Epidemiology and family characteristics of severely abused children. *British Journal of Preventive Social Medicine,* 1975, 29, 205-221.

BENNIE, E. H. and SCLARE, A. B. The battered child syndrome. *American Journal of Psychiatry,* 1969, 125(7), 975-979.

BERGER, A. The child abusing family: Part I. Methodological issues and parent-related characteristics of abusing families. *American Journal of Family Therapy,* 1980, 8(3), 53-66.

BERKOWITZ, L. Words and symbols as stimuli to aggressive responses. In J. F. Knutson (Ed.), *Control of Aggression: Implications from Basic Research.* Chicago: Aldine-Atherton, 1973.

BERKOWITZ, L. and FRODI, A. Reactions to a child's mistakes as affected by her/his looks and speech. Unpublished paper, 1978.

BLUMBERG, M. L. Psychopathology of the abusing parent. *American Journal of Psychotherapy,* 1974, 28, 21-29.

BROWN, G. W., HARRIS, T. and BIRLEY, J. L. T. Life-events and psychiatric disorders. Part I: Some methodological issues, *Psychological Medicine,* 1973, 3, 74-87.

BURGESS, R. L. and CONGER, R. D. Family interaction patterns related to child abuse and neglect: Some preliminary findings. *Child Abuse and Neglect,* 1977, 1, 269-277.

COHEN, M. I., RAPHLING, D. L. and GREEN, P. E. Psychological aspects of the maltreatment syndrome in childhood. *Journal of Pediatrics,* 1966, 69, 279-284.

DISBROW, M. A., DOERR, H. and CAULFIELD, C. Measuring the components of parents' potential for child abuse and neglect. *Child Abuse and Neglect*, 1977, 1, 279-296.

DUBANOSKI, R. A., EVANS, I. M. and ITIGUCHI, A. A. Analysis and treatment of child abuse: A set of behavioral propositions. *Child Abuse & Neglect*, 1978, 2, 153-172.

ELMER, E. A follow-up study of traumatized children. *Pediatrics*, 1977, 59(2), 273-279. (a)

ELMER, E. *Fragile Families, Troubled Children*. Pittsburgh: The University of Pittsburgh Press, 1977. (b)

ERLANGER, H. S. Social class differences in parents' use of physical punishment. In S. K. Steinmetz and M. A. Straus (Eds.), *Violence in the Family*. New York: Dodd, Mead & Co., 1974.

FARANOFF, A., KENNELL, J. and KLAUS, M. Follow-up of low birth weight infants— the predictive value of maternal visiting patterns. *Pediatrics*, 1972, 49, 287-290.

FREDERICKSEN, N. Toward a taxonomy of situations. *American Psychologist*, 1972, 27, 114-123.

FRIEDMAN, S. B. and MORSE, C. W. Child abuse: A 5-year follow-up of early case finding in the emergency department. *Pediatrics*, 1974, 54(4), 404-410.

FRIEDRICH, W. N. and BORISKIN, J. A. The role of the child in abuse: A review of the literature. *American Journal of Orthopsychiatry*, 1976, 46(4), 580-590.

FRODI, A. M. and LAMB, M. E. Fathers' and mothers' responses to the signals and characteristics of young infants. Paper presented at the International Conference on Infant Studies. Providence, Rhode Island, 1978. (a)

FRODI, A. M. and LAMB, M. E. Fathers' and mothers' responses to the faces and cries of normal and premature infants. *Developmental Psychology*, 1978, 14, 190-198. (b)

GAINES, R., SANDGRUND, A., GREEN, A. H. and POWER, E. Etiological factors in child maltreatment: A multivariate study of abusing, neglecting and normal mothers. *Journal of Abnormal Psychology*, 1978, 87(5), 531-540.

GALDSTON, R. Violence begins at home. *Journal of the American Academy of Child Psychiatry*, 1971, 10, 336-350.

GARBARINO, J. A preliminary study of some ecological correlates of child abuse: The impact of socioeconomic stress on mothers. *Child Development*, 1976, 47, 178-185.

GARBARINO, J. The human ecology of child maltreatment: A conceptual model for research. *Journal of Marriage and the Family*, 1977, 39(4), 721-735.

GELLES, R. J. Child abuse as psychopathology: A sociological critique and reformulation. *American Journal of Orthopsychiatry*, 1973, 43(4), 611-621.

GIL, D. G. Physical abuse of children. *Pediatrics*, 1969, 44, 857-864.

GIL, D. G. *Violence against Children*. Cambridge: Harvard University Press, 1970.

GREEN, A. H. Psychopathology of abused children. *Journal of Child Psychiatry*, 1978, 17(1), 92-103.

GREEN, A. H., GAINES, R. W. and SANGRUND, A. Child abuse: Pathological syndrome of family interaction. *American Journal of Psychiatry*, 1974, 131(8), 882-886.

GREGG, G. S. and ELMER, E. Infant injuries: Accident or abuse? *Pediatrics*, 1969, 44(3), 434-439.

HYMAN, C. A. Preliminary study of mother/infant interaction. *Child Abuse and Neglect* 1977, 1, 315-320.

Iowa Department of Social Services, Report Series A-4. Statistical data on child abuse cases, 1977.

JOHNSON, B. and MORSE, H. A. Injured children and their parents. *Children*, 1968, 15(4), 147-152.

JUSTICE, B. and JUSTICE, R. *The Abusing Family*. New York: Human Sciences Press, 1976.

KEMPE, C. H. and HELFER, R. E. *Helping the Battered Child and His Family*. Philadelphia: J. B. Lippincott, 1972.

KEMPE, C. H., SILVERMAN, F. N., STEELE, B. F., DROEGEMUELLER, W. and SILVER, H. K. The battered child syndrome. *Journal of the American Medical Association*, 1962, 181(1), 17-24.

KENT, J. T. A follow-up study of abused children. *Journal of Pediatric Psychology*, 1976, 1(2), 25-31.

KLAUS, M. H. and KENNELL, J. H. *Maternal-infant bonding*. St. Louis: The C. V. Mosby Company, 1976.

KLEIN, M. and STERN, L. Low birth weight and the battered child syndrome. *American Journal of Diseases of Children*, 1971, 122, 15-18.

KNUTSON, J. F. Child abuse research as an area of aggression research. *Pediatric Psychology*, 1978, 3(1), 20-27.

LOCKE, H. J. and WALLACE, K. M. Short marital adjustment and prediction tests: Their reliability and validity. *Marriage and Family Living*, 1959, 21, 251-255.

LYNCH, M. A. Risk factors in the child: A study of abused children and their siblings. In H. P. Martin (Ed.), *The Abused Child: A Multidisciplinary Approach to Developmental Issues and Treatment*. Cambridge: Ballinger, 1976.

LYNCH, M. A. and ROBERTS, J. Predicting child abuse: Signs of bonding failure in the maternity hospital. *Child Abuse and Neglect*, 1977, 1, 491-492.

MARTIN, M. The child and his development. In C. H. Kempe and R. E. Helfer (Eds.), *Helping the Battered Child and His Family*. Philadelphia: J. B. Lippincott, 1972.

MARTIN, H. P. Which children get abused: High risk factors in the child. In H. P. Martin (Ed.), *The Abused Child: A Multidisciplinary Approach to the Developmental Issues and Treatment*. Cambridge: Ballinger, 1976.

MILOW, I. and LOURIE, R. The child's role in the battered child syndrome. *Society for Pediatric Research*, 1964, 65, 1079-1081.

MORRIS, M. G. and GOULD, R. W. Role-reversal: A necessary concept in dealing with the "battered child syndrome." *American Journal of Orthopsychiatry*, 1963, 33, 298-299.

MORSE, C. W., SAHLER, O. J. Z. and FRIEDMAN, S. B. A three-year follow-up study of abused and neglected children. *American Journal of Diseases of Children*, 1970, 120, 439-446.

NURSE, S. M. Familial patterns of parents who abuse their children. *Smith College Studies in Social Work*, 1964, 32, 11-25.

OLIVER, J. E. and TAYLOR, A. Five generations of ill-treated children in one family pedigree. *British Journal of Psychiatry*, 1971, 119, 473-480.

PARKE, R. D. Child abuse: An overview of alternative models. *Journal of Pediatric Psychology*, 1978, 3(1), 9-13.

PARKE, R. D. and COLLMER, C. W. *Child Abuse: An Interdisciplinary Analysis*. Chicago: The University of Chicago Press, 1975.

PATTERSON, G. R. and REID, J. B. Reciprocity and coercion: Two facets of social system. In C. Neuringer and J. L. Michael (Eds.), *Behavior Modification in Clinical Psychology*. New York: Appleton-Century Crofts, 1970.

RABKIN, J. G. and STRUENING, E. L. Life events, stress and illness. *Science*, 1976, 194, 1013-1020.

REID, J. B. and TAPLIN, P. S. A social interactional approach to the treatment of abusive families. Paper presented to The American Psychological Association, Washington, D.C., 1976.

SMITH, S. M. *The Battered Child Syndrome*. London: Butterworths, 1975.

SMITH, S. M. and HANSON, R. Interpersonal relationships and child-rearing practices in 214 parents of battered children. *British Journal of Psychiatry*, 1975, 125, 513-525.

SMITH, S. M., HANSON, R. and NOBLE, S. Social aspects of the battered baby syndrome. *British Journal of Psychiatry*, 1974, 125, 568-582.

SPINETTA, J. J. and RIGLER, D. The child-abusing parent. *Psychological Bulletin*, 1972, 77, 296-304.

STEELE, B. F. Parental abuse of infants and small children. In E. J. Anthony and T. Benedick (Eds.), *Parenthood: Its Psychology and Psychopathology*. Boston: Little, Brown and Company, 1970.

STEELE, B. F. and POLLACK, C. B. A psychiatric study of parents who abuse infants and small children. In R. E. Helfer and C. H. Kempe (Eds.), *The Battered Child*. (2nd edition) Chicago: The University of Chicago Press, 1974.

WALTERS, D. R. *Physical and Sexual Abuse of Children: Causes and Treatment*. Bloomington: University of Indiana Press, 1975.

WESTON, J. T. A summary of neglect and traumatic cases (pathology). In R. E. Helfer & C. H. Kempe (Eds.), *The Battered Child*. (2nd edition) Chicago: The University of Chicago Press, 1974.

YOUNG, L. *Wednesday's Children: A Study of Child Neglect and Abuse*. New York: McGraw-Hill, 1964.

ZALBA, S. R. The abused child: II. A typology for classification and treatment. *Social Work*, 1967, 12, 70-79.

An intervention for child abusers was evaluated using multiple outcome criteria and extended follow-up. Families were assigned to treatment (n = 8) and control (n = 8) groups on a first-come basis. All families were supervised by protective services, and none had requested help voluntarily. A treatment program involving group parent training in the clinic and competency-based training and rehearsal in the home was provided. The findings indicated that training abusive parents in child-management and self-control techniques resulted in improvements in parenting skills as measured by home observations, parental reports of child-behavior problems, and caseworker reports of family problems. A 1-year follow-up indicated that no incidences of child abuse among treatment families had been reported to or suspected by caseworkers. Implications for integrating an educational training approach into major services for abusive and high-risk families are discussed.

19

A COMPETENCY-BASED PARENT TRAINING PROGRAM FOR CHILD ABUSERS

David A. Wolfe, Jack Sandler, and Keith Kaufman

Researchers currently estimate that between 1.4 and 1.9 million children experience physical injury each year as a result of the types of violent behaviors parents use to resolve conflicts with their children (Straus, Gelles, & Steinmetz, 1979). Child abuse, according to research consensus, appears to be not an isolated act but rather the culmination of excessive use of aversive control tactics, corporal punishment, and ineffective coping on the part of the parent and is due to many interrelated causes and circum-

stances (see Friedman, 1975, and Parke & Collmer, 1975, for reviews). Developers of an effective intervention strategy for child abusers will have to tolerate the many intervening variables that often affect the degree of success in changing patterns of interaction that have been in operation for a long period of time.

A functional analysis of child-abusive behavior (Friedman, Sandler, Hernandez, & Wolfe, 1981) underscores the interrelationship of many factors in the abuse process and has provided clarity and direction for intervention/prevention plannning. The child's aversive behavior (e.g., crying, screaming, wetting) and marital conflicts are two commonly reported antecedent stimuli of aggression and abuse (Friedman et al., 1981). The parents' behavioral capabilities (i.e., predisposed to using aggressive conflict-resolution tactics, poor knowledge of child development and unrealistic expectations and demands of the child, isolation from appropriate parenting models and re-

This research was conducted as part of a doctoral dissertation and was presented at the meeting of the Association for Advancement of Behavior Therapy, New York, November 1980. The authors gratefully acknowledge the cooperation and support of the Department of Health and Rehabilitative Services, Tampa, Florida, and the important contributions of Vicky Wolfe, Robert Friedman, Bill Kinder, William Hutchinson, Cindy Stoeffel, Robert Brubaker, Joseph Denicola, and Nick Kuiper.

Requests for reprints should be sent to David A. Wolfe, Department of Psychology, University of Western Ontario, London, Ontario, Canada N6A 5C2.

sources) are often not adequate to deal effectively and nonviolently with these aversive stimuli, leading to aggression toward a child (or spouse). The aggressive response, furthermore, may be reinforced by its short-term consequences (e.g., tension reduction, termination of aversive stimulus) and may escalate as a function of its long-term consequences (e.g., child's habituation to punishment, creating an increase in intensity). This formulation of child abuse is consistent with the social learning, interactional approach to family dysfunction (Parke & Collmer, 1975; Patterson, 1976). Such an approach emphasizes the parent's lack of skill in using effective, nonabusive techniques to teach his/her child prosocial skills and to handle discipline situations, which may lead to high rates of aversive behavior by both parents and children (Friedman et al., 1981). One of the major gains of this model is its empirically derived conceptualization of child abuse as being similar to related problems of family dysfunctioning. Through the utilization of the extensive data base that has evolved from research with problem families, this conceptual model of high-risk parent/child interactions in abusive homes is well-suited for the formulation of assessment and intervention procedures with this population.

Although behavioral parent-training methods have received wide recognition for their efficacy in modifying maladaptive family interactions with voluntary, nonabusive parents (e.g., Forehand & Atkeson, 1977; Johnson & Christenson, 1975), few treatment studies have involved parents who abuse their children. Unfortunately, treatment of child abuse has been addressed only recently by social scientists, and thus few data are presently available to evaluate appropriate intervention methods with this population (Burgess, 1979; Starr, 1979). This is most likely due to the difficulty of providing treatment services to this population (e.g., poor attendance, denial of a problem, adherence to harsh physical punishment, etc.) as well as to the difficulty of studying and recording low-frequency behaviors (i.e., abuse) either directly or indirectly.

In the past 3 years, several small-N studies have reported treatment findings that provide preliminary support for the social learning model's prediction that improvement in parents' child-management skills may result in less coercive child-rearing methods and fewer child-behavior problems in the home. For example, Sandler and his colleagues (Denicola & Sandler, 1980; Sandler, Van Dercar, & Milhoan, 1978; Wolfe & Sandler, 1981) and Crozier and Katz (1979) investigated the effects of training child abusers in more effective child-management and anger-control skills. These researchers provided intensive training to abusive parents by combining several important behavioral methods into a comprehensive treatment program focusing on parenting skills, including didactic instruction, problem solving, rehearsal, self-control training, and home implementation. Each study has reported that these training methods produced important changes in several parenting dimensions and parent/child interactional patterns, as determined by observation in the home, and these changes were partially maintained over time. Typically, the parents' aversive behavior toward their children was substantially reduced, and positive behavior showed corresponding improvements. Concomitant prosocial changes were observed in the target children.

These initial studies have provided the groundwork for more extensive investigation of the generalizability and long-term efficacy of behavioral parent training as a treatment and prevention method with child abusers and high-risk families. To provide cost-effective, practical intervention for the many families in need, however, these methods must undergo more rigorous investigation of their benefit and utility with a larger sample of child abusers. The present study was conducted to determine the relative importance of child-management training with abusive parents in comparison with a control group of abusers who received the standard services provided by the state child-welfare agency. This study extended the procedures of previous treatment studies using a group research design and employed multiple outcome measures to corroborate expected improvements in child-management skills following treatment. Goals for this study were based on the following considerations: (a) the clear demonstration of appropriate child-management skills in the home; (b) requirements for the provision of services to abusive parents, based on court and child-welfare agency guidelines; and (c) the parent's own identified problems in child-rearing.

Method

Subjects

Sixteen family units, composed of at least one adult and one child per unit, were included in this study. Families were referred to the Child Management Program for High-Risk Families (CMP) by the local child-welfare agency following an investigation of a complaint of physical child abuse that had been substantiated by physical and/or circumstantial evidence (i.e., high-risk characteristics).

The majority of the referrals were Caucasian females with low incomes (less than $6,000 per year). All families participating in the study were either directly court-ordered to attend family therapy sessions ($N = 6$) or had been nonjudicially ordered to attend by the child-welfare agency to avoid possible court action ($N = 10$). No self-referrals were included in this study. The children ranged in age from 2 through 10 years, with a mean of 4½ years. No significant chi-square differences were found between the treatment and control groups on any demographic variables.[1]

Outcome Measures

Improvement in the parents' child-management skills was the primary focus of intervention, and this was assessed by independent observation in the home. Corroborative measures of improvement in family functioning were obtained from family caseworkers and from parental reports of child-behavior problems.

Parent–Child Interaction Form (PCIF). The PCIF (adapted from Sweitzer & Boyd, Note 1) is a criterion-based observational system for scoring parents' appropriate uses of antecedents and consequences while interacting with their children. Three categories of parent performance are analyzed by this system: positive reinforcement, commands/prompts, and appropriate punishment. Each category comprises several behavioral units specifying parents' usages of these skills (e.g., reinforced immediately, stated contingency if necessary, used appropriate intensity of punishment, etc.), which results in a score based on the percentage of appropriate child-rearing skills demonstrated by the parents during 30 minutes of home observation (described below). The PCIF offers several advantages over other family observation systems (i.e., reliability, situation-specific assessment), and provides a measurement basis to competency-based training procedures (Friedman et al., 1981).

Eyberg Child Behavior Inventory (ECBI). The ECBI (Eyberg & Ross, 1978) was administered to the target parent to obtain the parent's description of child-behavior problems. This inventory contains 36 behaviorally specific items (e.g., fights with sibling) and enables an assessment of child behavior on two dimensions: (a) problem score—the number of specific problem behaviors that parents endorse as a problem for them (range = 0–36) and (b) intensity score—the sum of the frequencies with which all problem behaviors are reported to occur (range = 36–252). The ECBI was chosen as an outcome measure because of its simple wording and instructions, and the instrument has been shown to provide a reliable and valid assessment of parental perceptions of child-behavior problems (Eyberg & Ross, 1978).

Agency Referral Questionnaire. A questionnaire was developed to serve two purposes: (a) as a screening/referral device to identify treatment priorities for the families and (b) as an assessment device to quantify the caseworker's perceptions of the severity of the family's treatment needs. The questionnaire required each family's caseworker to rate the importance of treatment on a 7-point scale (1 = no importance—needs no treatment in this area; 7 = highly important) in 10 common problem areas (e.g., child management, anger control). Ratings in the three areas of child management, anger control, and child development were combined to assess the impact of treatment from the caseworker's perspective, since these areas were treatment targets.[2]

Procedures

An initial interview was conducted by the program coordinator with the parent(s) to gather descriptive information and to discuss their home situation vis-à-vis child-rearing problems, their perceptions toward changing the problems, and any attempts they had made to resolve these difficulties. Details and requirements of the Child Management Program were explained in full to them, and their consent to treatment was obtained. There was no fee for their participation.

Families were assigned to treatment and control conditions on a first-come basis, as dictated by methodological and practical considerations. The treatment sample comprised the first eight abusive families who were referred to the program.[3] The control sample consisted of abusive families who were referred for treatment after the first group was formed, and these families were placed on a waiting list for 8 weeks. During this time, the control families continued under the normal supervision of their child-welfare worker, receiving the services provided by the state. Assignment to groups in this manner assured the support and cooperation of the agency caseworkers, who were informed of the necessity to establish a waiting list once treatment had begun. Moreover, the child was never placed in further jeopardy, since caseworkers maintained supervision of both the treatment and control families at all times. All control families who desired treatment following the waiting period were offered treatment.

Pretest assessment. The Agency Referral Questionnaire was completed by the family's assigned caseworker preceding the initial family interview with the CMP staff. The Eyberg Child Behavior Inventory was administered to the target parent in all families during the initial interview. Within 1 week following this interview, raters visited the home to complete the Parent–Child Interaction Form. Raters had been trained to use the PCIF by observing videotaped and "live" normal families who volunteered to serve as "subjects" until 80% reliability was obtained, and raters were not aware of the treatment status of the family or the nature of the study. During home observations, the target parent was told to interact with the target child in three separate situations: (a) free interaction—no structure imposed

---

[1] More details of the characteristics of these families are available from the first author.
[2] Copies of all assessment devices and a complete treatment manual are available from the first author.
[3] The Child Management Program had been operating for 3 years at the time this study began.

by the raters; (b) teaching—teaching the child an un-familiar task slightly above his/her age level (e.g., puzzle assembly); and (c) command/compliance—requiring the child to comply to several distinct commands (e.g., pick up toys). Each task/situation continued for a period of 10 minutes, for a total of 30 minutes of observation time. Interrater reliability on the PCIF was calculated using Cohen's (1960) kappa to correct for chance agreements, which indicated that the observations were reliable (positive reinforcement = .87; commands/prompts = .81; appropriate punishment = .88; total PCIF score = .85).

Group treatment components. The parent training group was held one night per week for 2 hours, with an average of 82% group attendance for the target parents. The group training sessions consisted of three related components:

1. Instruction in human development and child management. Each family received a copy of *Parents Are Teachers* (Becker, 1971), which provided a systematic means for training and evaluating the group's development of child-management skills. Filmstrips on human development were shown at the beginning of each session, and behavioral principles as applied to parenting were reviewed and discussed each week (e.g., positive reinforcement, time out, shaping, appropriate punishment).

2. Problem solving and modeling of appropriate child management. Videotaped vignettes of common child-management problems were presented at each session, and parents were required to problem solve the situation based on prior reading. Parents were shown the problem scene once again, with an appropriate resolution modeled on the tape.

3. Self-control. Initially, as a group, all parents were taught deep muscle relaxation (Wolpe, 1969). They were then instructed via audiotape in impulse-control procedures that could be applied to their individual problem situations (i.e., preparing for the stressor, handling the stressor, coping with anger, and reinforcing self-statements; Meichenbaum, 1975).

Individualized home-based training procedures. A treatment coordinator (clinical psychology graduate student) visited the families in their homes once a week for the purpose of implementing the new techniques in relevant child-rearing situations. Initially, the parent was instructed to identify and to record any child-related problem that occurred during the following week. Each week the parent(s) selected a target situation and decided on a positive approach to its resolution, which was rehearsed with the treatment coordinator and/or the child. Since training in the home was criterion-based, the treatment coordinator did not progress to more difficult behavioral skills on the Parent–Child Interaction Form until proficiency was demonstrated at more basic levels. The majority of the families attained skill proficiency after eight home sessions (an average of 8.9 professional hours in the home per family).

Standard services to abusive families (control condition). Families assigned to the waiting control sample received the standard services provided to abusive families by child-welfare workers. These agency services consisted of regular (biweekly) monitoring of the child's safety in the home and/or the provision of community resources (e.g., welfare support, homemaker services) to the family members as needed during the crisis period.

Posttest and follow-up assessment. The three assessment procedures (Agency Referral Questionnaire, ECBI, and PCIF) were repeated following the 8-week treatment or control period for the 16 families to obtain posttest measurements. In addition, 5 treatment families were assessed with the ECBI and PCIF measures at a 10-week follow-up (3 treatment families were unavailable at 10 weeks due to relocation). Since control families began treatment after posttest of the first treatment phase, no untreated follow-up data were collected for these families.

A 1-year follow-up probe was conducted to determine the long-term status of the families involved in this study. Permission was obtained from the juvenile court to review the child-welfare agency's records of reported abusive incidences and case dispositions for each of the eight treatment and eight control families.

Results

Table 1 presents the pre- and posttest group means for the four dependent variables: percentage of appropriate child-management skills demonstrated by parents in the home, parental report of the number of specific child-behavior problems and the summed frequency of their occurrence, and caseworker ratings of family treatment needs. Adjusted means are also presented for the posttest measure. Significant pretest group differences were found on the parental report data (both problem and intensity scores). To determine the significance of the treatment program across all measures in relation to control subjects, the effect of groups was analyzed with a one-way multivariate analysis of covariance (MANCOVA). The four pretest scores served as covariates for each posttest score. Only the results of Wilks's lambda are reported, since the significance levels for Wilks's, Hotelling's, and Pillais's tests of significance were identical. Following this analysis, the Roy-Bargman step-down F test (Bock & Haggard, 1968) was performed for the purpose of interpreting the multivariate effect, as recommended by Kaplan and Litrownik (1977).

The results of the MANCOVA analyzing the effects of the parent training program are shown in Table 2. A significant overall treatment effect was demonstrated by this multivariate analysis, multivariate $F(4, 7) = 16.13$, $p < .001$. Subsequently, the four variables were entered into the step-down analysis in the order of theoretical importance

Table 1

Treatment and Control Group Means for PCIF Child-Management Skills, ECBI Child-Behavior Problems and Frequencies, and Caseworker Ratings

Variable	Treatment	Control
Child-management skills (PCIF)[a]		
Pre	17.6	19.8
Post	91.1	14.8
Adjusted post[b]	84.8	21.1
Number of child-behavior problems (ECBI problem score)		
Pre	11.6	24.1
Post	1.8	22.4
Adjusted post[b]	7.2	17.0
Summed frequency of problem occurrences (ECBI intensity score)		
Pre	130.0	184.0
Post	83.0	155.0
Adjusted post[b]	114.6	123.0
Caseworker ratings of family treatment needs[c]		
Pre	17.9	16.8
Post	7.0	17.0
Adjusted post[b]	7.5	16.4

Note. PCIF = Parent–Child Interaction Form; ECBI = Eyberg Child Behavior Inventory. $n = 8$ for both groups. [a] Percent correct. [b] Regression of posttest on the pretest scores. [c] Range = 3–21; lower score indicates low treatment needs.

in accounting for the treatment effect; that is, the measure of child-management skills was the variable of primary interest and was entered first, followed by parent and caseworker report data. As shown by the step-

Table 2

Multivariate Analysis of Covariance for the Effects of Competency-Based Parent Training With Abusive Parents

	Treatment effect[a]		
Variable	F[b]	df	p
Child-management skills	68.93	1, 10	.001
Problem score	1.98	1, 9	.19
Intensity score	.007	1, 8	.94
Caseworker ratings	.42	1, 7	.54

[a] Multivariate F (Wilks's lambda) = 16.13; $df = 4, 7$; $p < .001$.
[b] Roy-Bargman step-down F tests.

down test, the treatment effect was due primarily to the acquisition and performance of appropriate child-management skills by the parents in the treatment group, and this effect was corroborated by related outcome measures.[4]

Table 3 shows mean pretest, posttest, and follow-up data for five treatment families who were available for home observation 10 weeks following conclusion of treatment. Maintenance effects were analyzed by comparing mean scores of pretest and follow-up using t test planned comparisons. The results indicated that these five treatment families maintained improvement in their child-management methods during this period. Significant pretest–follow-up mean comparisons were found for child-management skills, $t(4) = 12.88$, $p < .01$; number of child-related problems, $t(4) = 5.68$, $p < .01$; and intensity of child problems, $t(4) = 4.82$, $p < .01$. Although follow-up means showed some decrement over time, posttest–follow-up comparisons of these changes were not statistically or clinically significant.

The critical 1-year follow-up probe of agency records revealed that none of the eight treatment families had been reported or suspected of child abuse or maltreatment since the group completed treatment. Two of the three families who had relocated to other counties were followed by local child-welfare caseworkers and had not been suspected of abuse; the status of the other family could not be determined by the agency, due to out-of-state relocation. The agency and the court closed the local supervision of all eight treatment families over the course of the year and viewed the families as functioning effectively. An abuse charge was re-

---

[4] Univariate F tests on all four measures revealed significant findings for both child-mangement skills and caseworker reports, $F(1, 10) = 68.9, p < .001$, and $F(1, 10) = 12.0, p < .01$, respectively. However, the significant correlation between these two measures, $r(16) = -.95, p < .001$, reduced the unique variance accounted for by caseworker data to nonsignificant levels, as shown in the step-down analysis in Table 2. Pearson product-moment correlations between the PCIF and ECBI data compiled from both groups were also significant, $r(16) = -.91, p < .001$ (problem score), $r(16) = -.70$, $p < .001$ (intensity score), which corroborates the high congruence between the measure of child-management skills and the ancillary measures.

Table 3
Mean Pretest, Posttest, and Follow-Up Scores for Five Treatment Families

Variable	Pretest		Posttest		Follow-up	
	M	SD	M	SD	M	SD
Child-management skills	18.2	7.7	89.6	8.2	84.6	11.9
Problem score	12.6	3.2	.6	.9	2.6	2.7
Intensity score	126.4	19.4	76.4	12.4	80.2	12.5

corded for one of the control families 6 months after declining treatment. Six families in the control group completed treatment, and their cases were closed by the agency and court; the remaining control family who declined treatment was still under active agency and court supervision.

Discussion

The present study provides overall support for training abusive parents in appropriate child-management and self-control techniques. Competency-based training resulted in improvements in parent effectiveness as measured by observations of parenting skills in the home, parental reports of child-behavior problems, and caseworker reports of family problems. Furthermore, a 1-year review of agency records revealed no further suspected or reported child abuse only for those families (treatment and control) who completed the treatment program.

The finding that abusive parents interact in a more positive, constructive manner with their children following training in child-management skills supports the results of earlier studies (Denicola & Sandler, 1980; Sandler et al., 1978; Wolfe & Sandler, 1981). Moreover, current findings indicated that improvements in parents' appropriate child-management skills were related to favorable changes in family functioning, as assessed by corroborative measures. The use of effective child-rearing techniques by parents in the treatment group was significantly related to the low number of child-rearing problems indicated by parents and caseworkers. Conversely, the lack of child-management skills among control families was related to the greater number of child-rearing problems reported by these parents and caseworkers.

An important comparison in this study involved the use of a control group of abusive families who were under continual state supervision and receiving the normal services provided to abusive parents by the child-welfare agency. Since the present treatment program accomplished these favored goals with an average of 8.9 individual hours in the home and 16 hours in the group, the cost-effectiveness and importance of child-management training compared with routine supervision with abusive parents was supported.

The present data point to more effective and efficient methods by which to train abusive parents (i.e., competency-based progression) and support a comprehensive evaluation system to assess changes in parenting methods. The use of multiple outcome criteria to evaluate the effectiveness of treatment from three perspectives resulted in several interesting findings. First, the home observation data determined that abusive parents do acquire child-management skills in a reasonable length of time and that these new skills are applicable to common child-rearing situations. The temporal and situational generalizability of these skills, however, remains to be more thoroughly demonstrated. Second, data from the caseworker ratings of family problems provided supportive evidence for the effectiveness of treatment. These data suggest that caseworkers were satisfied with the outside services provided to their clients, and they viewed the families as functioning more effectively following child-management training than state supervision alone. If replicated, these findings have implications for the development of large-scale intervention/ prevention programs for abusive families, which would involve the cooperation, support, and training of existing child-welfare departments.

Although these findings provide strong support for the efficacy of a broad-based behavioral approach to treating child abusers, caution must be taken in generalizing these findings to all abusive families. The type of intervention strategy employed must be integrated with other procedures or programs to deal with a wide range of problems that may surface, such as social isolation, economic deprivation, and other situational factors often associated with child abuse. Ideally, the child-welfare agency may be able to offer these latter services in conjunction with referral to a parenting program. A major benefit of an educational training approach with abusive families may lie in its ability to provide critical structure and direction for case planning, which may disburden social agencies and allow for increased flexibility in meeting the needs of these families.

The present findings lend support to the social learning hypothesis that abusive parents have not learned (or do not perform) even minimal levels of appropriate child-management skills and experience a great deal of difficulty controlling their children. Obviously, many other variables contribute to the manifestation of parent aggression toward offspring (e.g., social isolation, Garbarino, 1977; financial and job stress, Light, 1973; marital conflict, Friedman et al., 1981; history of family violence, Steele & Pollock, 1974). Since the present findings indicated that effective child-management skills were taught to abusive parents with a relatively small investment of time and labor and parents were able to avoid serious conflict with their children over several months, the inclusion of parent training procedures in child-abuse intervention/prevention planning seems warranted. Future efforts may be focused on the development of parenting competency programs for at-risk parents at an earlier stage in order to establish effective, appropriate child-rearing methods and

to prevent parents' reliance on harsh, punitive controls.

Reference Note

1. Sweitzer, M., & Boyd, A. *Parent Performance Checklist: A behavioral assessment of parenting skills.* Unpublished manuscript, Florida Mental Health Institute, 1979.

References

Becker, W. C. *Parents are teachers.* Champaign, Ill.: Research Press, 1971.

Bock, R. D., & Haggard, E. A. The use of multivariate analysis of variance in behavioral research. In D. K. Whitla (Ed.), *Handbook of measurement and assessment in behavioral sciences.* Reading, Mass.: Addison-Wesley, 1968.

Burgess, R. L. Child abuse: A behavioral analysis. In B. Lahey & A. Kazdin (Eds.), *Advances in clinical child psychology.* New York: Plenum Press, 1979.

Cohen, J. A coefficient of agreement for nominal scales. *Educational and Psychological Measurement,* 1960, 20, 326-330.

Crozier, J., & Katz, R. C. Social learning treatment of child abuse. *Journal of Behavior Therapy and Experimental Psychiatry,* 1979, 10, 213-220.

Denicola, J., & Sandler, J. Training abusive parents in cognitive-behavioral techniques. *Behavior Therapy,* 1980, 11, 263-270.

Eyberg, S., & Ross, A. Assessment of child behavior problems: The validation of a new inventory. *Journal of Clinical Child Psychology,* 1978, 7, 113-116.

Forehand, R., & Atkeson, B. M. Generality of treatment effects with parents as therapists: A review of assessment and implementation procedures. *Behavior Therapy,* 1977, 8, 575-593.

Friedman, R. Child abuse: A review of the psychosocial research. In *Four perspectives on the status of child abuse and neglect research.* Springfield, Va.: National Technical Information Service, 1975.

Friedman, R., Sandler, J., Hernandez, M., & Wolfe, D. Behavioral assessment of child abuse. In E. Mash & L. Terdal (Eds.), *Behavioral assessment of childhood disorders.* New York: Guilford Press, 1981.

Garbarino, J. The human ecology of child maltreatment: A conceptual model for research. *Journal of Marriage and the Family,* 1977, 39, 721-735.

Johnson, S., & Christenson, A. Multiple criteria follow-up of behavior modification with families. *Journal of Abnormal Child Psychology,* 1975, 3, 135-154.

Kaplan, R. M., & Litrownik, A. J. Some statistical methods for the assessment of multiple outcome criteria in behavioral research. *Behavior Therapy,* 1977, 8, 383-392.

Light, R. J. Abused and neglected children in America: A study of alternative policies. *Harvard Educational Review,* 1973, 43, 556-598.

Meichenbaum, D. Self-instructional methods. In F. Kanfer & A. Goldstein (Eds.), *Helping people change.* New York: Pergamon Press, 1975.

Parke, R., & Collmer, C. Child abuse: An interdisciplinary analysis. In M. Hetherington (Ed.), *Review of child development research* (Vol. 5). Chicago: University of Chicago Press, 1975.

Patterson, G. R. The aggressive child: Victim and architect of a coercive system. In L. Hamerlynck, L. Handy, & E. Mash (Eds.), *Behavior modification and families, Vol. 1: Theory and research.* New York: Brunner/Mazel, 1976.

Sandler, J., Van Dercar, C., & Milhoan, M. Training child abusers in the use of positive reinforcement practices. *Behavior Research and Therapy,* 1978, *16*, 169–175.

Starr, R. A. Child abuse. *American Psychologist,* 1979, *34*, 872–878.

Steele, B. F., & Pollock, C. B. A psychiatric study of parents who abuse infants and small children. In R. E. Helfer & C. H. Kempe (Eds.), *The battered child* (2nd ed.). Chicago: University of Chicago Press, 1974.

Straus, M. A., Gelles, R. J., & Steinmetz, S. K. *Behind closed doors: Violence in the American family.* Garden City, N.Y.: Doubleday, 1979.

Wolfe, D., & Sandler, J. Training abusive parents in effective child management. *Behavior Modification,* 1981, *5*, 320–335.

Wolpe, J. *The practice of behavior therapy.* New York: Pergamon Press, 1969.

This paper presents a theoretical perspective that integrates elements of social structural and social psychological explanations of spouse abuse. In particular, the relationships between the educational and occupational attainments of individuals and marital partners are examined as risk factors in abusive behavior. Status inconsistency of either partner and status incompatibility between partners are hypothesized to be associated with an increased risk of abusive behavior within the couple. A modification of the Conflict Tactics Scale is used to measure the incidence and 1-year period prevalence of three levels of spouse abuse: psychological abuse, physical aggression, and life-threatening violence. The data are drawn from a random survey of Kentucky women who were 18 years of age or older and were married or had been living with a male partner during the study period. The results show that, in general, both status inconsistency and status incompatibility are associated with an increased risk of psychological abuse, an even greater increased risk of physical aggression, and a still greater increased risk of life-threatening violence. Certain types of status inconsistency (i.e., under-achievement in occupation by the husband) and certain types of status incompatibility (i.e., when the woman is high in occupation relative to her husband) involve very high risks of spouse abuse, particularly life-threatening violence. Other types of inconsistency (i.e., over-achievement in occupation by the husband) seem to protect couples from abusive behavior. These findings are discussed in detail and promising areas of future analyses are noted.

20

STATUS RELATIONSHIPS IN MARRIAGE

Risk Factors in Spouse Abuse*

*Carlton A. Hornung,** B. Claire McCullough,***
and Taichi Sugimoto***

*This article is a revision of a paper presented at the annual meetings of the American Sociological Association, August, 1980, New York. Please address all correspondence to the first author. We would like to thank Mark Schulman of Louis Harris and Associates for providing the data for this analysis and Richard J. Gelles for encouraging us in this line of inquiry. We would also like to thank our colleagues Greg Alexander and Robert Lewis for helpful comments on the analysis of these data and the preparation of this report. Special thanks are also due to Cheryl Harwell and Pat Mielke for their expert secretarial assistance.

**Department of Preventive Medicine and Community Health, School of Medicine, University of South Carolina, Columbia, South Carolina 29208.

***Computer Services Division, University of South Carolina, Columbia, South Carolina 29208.

Family violence has recently become a topic of national concern and has come to be defined as an important social problem affecting every stratum of American society. This has been prompted, at least in part, by the many publications of Straus, Gelles, and Steinmetz (cf. Straus et al., 1980). In spite of the large increase in research in the area in recent years, a coherent theoretical understanding is absent and much remains to be learned about the problem.

The theoretical perspective offered here integrates elements of social structural and social psychological explanations. In particular, the analysis focuses upon structural

From Carlton A. Hornung, B. Claire McCullough, and Taichi Sugimoto, "Status Relationships in Marriage: Risk Factors in Spouse Abuse," *Journal of Marriage and the Family*, 1981, 43, pp. 675-692. Reprinted by permission of the publisher and authors.

relationships between the educational and occupational dimensions of the stratification system, status expectation processes, and norms of equity within marriage.

The lack of comprehensive understanding of the causes as well as the incidence and prevalence of family violence stems not only from limited theoretical formulations but also from methodological inadequacies in empirical studies. One critical problem that has plagued the majority of studies is that of nonrepresentative and frequently very small samples. These samples are often drawn from police records (Gelles, 1974), outpatient hospital records (Stark et al., 1979), or from clinical settings (Rosenbaum et al., 1980). Each of these sources of data is likely to introduce a Berksonian or sampling bias in several ways. The types of agencies from which data are typically collected serve a segment of the population that is limited with respect to socioeconomic, sociocultural, and demographic characteristics. In addition, violent families are more likely to come into contact with such agencies than are families in which violence is absent or extremely rare. Since the majority of studies on the subject have been based on such nonrepresentative samples, a comprehensive empirical examination of family violence with generalizable conclusions is difficult to find. Straus, Gelles, and Steinmetz's (1980) analysis of data from a large, representative national sample and Louis Harris and Associates' (1979) analysis of a survey of women in Kentucky provide notable exceptions.

A further type of bias that often occurs stems from the assumption that women are the only victims of spouse abuse. This assumption frequently results in the collection of data that are concerned solely with violence against women. Even though some researchers (Gelles, 1974; Straus, 1974; Steinmetz, 1977; Straus et al., 1980) recognize that men are also potential victims of violence, family violence is still often equated with wife abuse.

A further methodological weakness of much of the research on family violence is that it tends to be largely descriptive rather than analytical. This results in part from the newness of the area and partly from the large public interest in the topic. However, this descriptive approach does not promote a thorough understanding of the problem, and in fact, may generate even more unfounded speculation about its extent and causes.

The research reported on here avoids some of these methodological weaknesses. The present analysis utilizes data from a survey of Kentucky women collected by Louis Harris and Associates for the Kentucky Commission on Women. Data were collected by telephone interviews in households selected by random-digit dialing of numbers that had been stratified by geographic location. According to Louis Harris and Associates (1979), 89 percent of the households in Kentucky had telephone service. Interviewers enumerated women in each household who were currently married or who had lived with a male partner (approximately 1 percent of the sample) within the preceding year and randomly selected a respondent from this list. Only 9 percent of these respondents either refused to be interviewed or to complete the interview once it was started. Such a low rate of nonresponse was accomplished by making appointments to call back if the respondent indicated in any way that she was not free to talk at the time of initial contact. Harris reported that 18 percent of the interviews were completed in a subsequent contact, which resulted in a sample size of 1,793 women. This is one of the most comprehensive, statistically defensible, and generalizable samples on which data about family violence have been collected. Because of missing data on the education or occupation of either the woman or her male partner, 1,553 couples are analyzed here.

Although only women were interviewed, they were also asked about violence they had inflicted upon their husbands or male partners. The present analysis makes use of this additional data by considering violence *within a couple* instead of just violence against one partner or the other. Although the analysis focuses upon couple violence, it should be kept in mind that the data reflect wives' reports of couple violence. This analysis also goes beyond a simple description of the incidence of spouse abuse or what violent families are like in general. Instead, it focuses upon a set of structural conditions and thoroughly analyzes how they affect the incidence and prevalence of spouse abuse. The establishment of an all-encompassing explanation of spouse abuse is of less interest here than is the examination of spouse abuse as one of many possible outcomes of various status relationships between husbands and wives.

STATUS RELATIONSHIPS IN
MARRIAGE

The focus of this paper is the extent to which patterns of educational and occupational attainments of women and their male partners are associated with an increase risk of spouse abuse. In previous research (Hornung and McCullough, 1977, 1981), we have presented a theory of status relationships in marriage that relates status inconsistency and status incompatibility to psychological well-being, measured in terms of marital and generalized life dissatisfaction. Stated briefly, this theory begins with the proposition that each of the many status characteristics of the individual gives rise to expectations about other characteristics possessed by the individual, as well as the status attributes of his or her spouse. These status expectations are anticipatory (Berger *et al.*, 1972), for example, an individual is anticipated to have completed a certain level of education and earn a level of income that depends upon his or her occupational status. Status expectations are normative in that the expected levels of education and income come to be defined as what the individual *should* have attained, given his or her occupation. Finally, status expectations are asymmetric in that a certain level of education may be expected among individuals in a given occupation, but all individuals with the same level of education are not necessarily expected to be in the same occupation. For example, skilled trades workers may be expected to have completed high school but all individuals who have completed high school are not anticipated to be skilled trades workers.

The theory further proposes that the expectations of what status attributes will and should be possessed concurrently are predicted upon frequency of occurrence in the population. If most individuals with characteristic X also possess characteristic Y, then Y comes to be expected of individuals with X. For example, most but not all individuals in professional occupations have completed some post-college education. Education beyond the bachelor's level is therefore expected and in many instances legally required of persons in professional jobs. And educational attainment below the post-college level violates this expectation and is, therefore, inconsistent with a professional occupation. There is evidence to support this proposition in

work reported by Alves and Rossi (1978) and by Webster and Driskell (1978).

Defining combinations of statuses as consistent or inconsistent based upon the frequency of their concurrent occupancy is a significant departure from most previous work which has defined status consistency in terms of equally ranked positions in multiple status hierarchies. The revised definition, in effect, incorporates the concept of status integration (Berry, 1963; Gibbs and Martin, 1964) into the formulation of status consistency. This synthesis of status consistency and status integration has important conceptual implications. Whereas the original formulation of status consistency initiated by Lenski (1954, 1956) postulated psychological stress to be a consequence of simultaneously occupying positions of unequal rank across multiple status hierarchies, the revised formulation postulates psychological stress to be a consequence of occupying an *atypical* combination of status characteristics. At an even more primitive level, the revised formulation postulates that frequently occurring combinations of status characteristics, *which may or may not be equally ranked in their respective hierarchies,* engender expectations of behavior that involve a minimum role conflict for their incumbents and for others with whom they are associated.

A further consequence of the synthesis of the status consistency and status integration concepts is that combinations of statuses, that are unequally ranked and would be defined as inconsistent according to the traditional approach to consistency, would be defined as consistent in the revised formulation if they occurred frequently within the population. For example, clerical workers are higher in occupational prestige than are workers in skilled trades, but skilled workers generally earn higher wages than clerical workers. According to the traditional approach to measuring status inconsistency, skilled workers are considered to be status inconsistent by virtue of their relatively high income and lower occupational prestige. However, the formulation of consistency followed here would define individuals in both occupations to be status consistent if their level of income was equal to others in the same job.

The anticipatory, normative, and asymmetric quality of relationships between statuses occupied by an individual can be generalized to status positions occupied by different persons within a group such as the marital dyad. The status characteristics possessed by one person give rise to expectations about the status attributes of others with whom he or she is associated. In the case of marital partners, the educational attainment of the husband is a basis for anticipating the years of education that his wife will have completed, just as the educational attainment of the wife is a basis for anticipating her husband's years of education.

The combination of husband's and wife's statuses that are expected to go together are based upon their empirical distribution in the population. Combinations that are atypical come to be defined as incompatible; a term which is used in this instance to denote a status relationship involving more than a single individual. Moreover, these status relationships are asymmetric, partly because of the differential attainment of men and women in the various status hierarchies. For example, more men than women drop out of school before earning a high school diploma while, at the same time, more men than women go on to post-college training, particularly in the professional schools. This is one important reason why men with few years of education tend to marry women with a greater number of years of formal education while post-college educated men tend to marry women with fewer years of education. However, women who have completed schooling beyond the college level may marry similarly educated men partly because men at this level of educational attainment are in relatively abundant supply.

It is important to note that the combinations of husband's and wife's statuses that are expected to go together are not necessarily equally ranked and that the characteristics of the husband that are expected on the basis of those of the wife are not symmetric to the characteristics of the wife that are expected on the basis of the husband's attainments. These ideas contrast sharply with most of the previous research that has examined the impact of simple status differences between husbands and wives on a number of behavioral and attitudinal outcomes, including marital stability. As formulated here, *it is not simple rank differences between the positions of the husband and his wife that are the source of stress and discord within the relationship, but rather it is atypical combinations of status characteristics that presage personal and marital difficulties, including spouse abuse.*

The final proposition of the theory being tested here is that combinations of statuses that come to be defined as consistent or compatible serve as "distribution laws" (Cook, 1975) that define the equity of status investments and status rewards. Combinations of statuses that occur infrequently, and hence are inconsistent or incompatible, violate these distribution laws and subject their incumbents to feelings of deprivation or inequity-disadvantage, *i.e.*, when rewards are low relative to the amount of investments (*e.g.*, occupation low for a given level of education), or feelings of guilt or inequity-advantage, *i.e.*, when investments are low relative rewards (*e.g.*, education low for a given occupation). This social comparison process implies that others in the same occupation and others with the same amount of education constitute referential structures or equity groups (Kemper, 1968). It is in terms of these groups that the equity of rewards in the occupational structure is evaluated relative to the level of investments in education, and vice versa. In the case of the marital dyad, this further implies that the status investments and rewards of one's marital partner are evaluated in equity terms relative to one's own investments and rewards and that one's own positions are similarly and asymmetrically evaluated in terms of the positions attained by one's partner.

It is through these evaluative social psychological comparison processes that the structural conditions of status inconsistency and status incompatibility lead to psychological stress for the individuals involved and subsequently to a range of documented outcomes, including dissatisfaction with life in general and dissatisfaction with marriage (Hornung and McCullough, 1981). It is the working hypothesis of this analysis that these structural conditions, and the stress they engender, predispose couples to violent behavior. Thus, one would expect to find more violence in couples in which one or the other partner is status inconsistent and in couples that are incompatible in educational or occupational attainments.

MEASUREMENT OF STATUS INCONSISTENCY AND INCOMPATIBILITY

The measures of status inconsistency of the

woman and her husband or male partner were constructed by cross-classifying the individual's years of education and the Census categories of their current occupation. Separate computations were made for men and women because of gender differences in the relationship between years of education and occupational attainment (Treiman and Terrell, 1975). The levels of education that were attained by the middle 70 percent of the workers in each occupation were defined as being consistent with that job. The levels of educational attainment exhibited by the lowest 15 percent of the sample in each occupational category were defined as "inconsistent-low" for that occupation while the educational levels for the 15 percent that were the most highly educated were defined as "inconsistent-high." If it is assumed that years of education is normally distributed within categories of occupations, then the middle categories that contain 70 percent of the cases correspond closely to the area plus or minus one standard deviation from the mean (and median and mode).[1]

The procedure was reversed to determine whether the individual's occupation was consistent or inconsistent with his or her education. Specifically, for each level of education, the Census categories of occupations that contained the middle 70 percent of the cases were defined as status consistent for that particular level of schooling. Those occupations employing the lowest 15 percent of individuals with the same education were defined as "inconsistent-low" for that education while those categories of occupations employing the highest 15 percent were defined as "inconsistent-high."

There are some noteworthy exceptions to these procedures. First, in defining education as consistent or inconsistent with occupation, no levels of educational attainment were determined to be inconsistent-low for service workers and no levels of education were determined to be inconsistent-high for individuals in professional occupations. In other words, there was no basis for saying that individuals in the lowest category of oc-

cupations were under-educated for their job or that individuals in the highest category of occupations were over-educated for their profession. Second, in defining occupation as "inconsistent-low" for individuals with the least amount of education and no occupations were defined as "inconsistent-high" for individuals with post-college training. In other words, there was no basis for saying that individuals with less than 7 years of education were occupational "under-achievers" nor was there a basis for saying that individuals with post-college degrees were "over-achievers." Finally, all levels of education were defined as consistent with the status of housewife and farm occupations and, conversely, farm occupations and housewife were defined as occupations consistent with all levels of education. The decisions concerning the occupation of farmer were based on an inability to distinguish between types of farm occupations. Whether or not a given level of education is high or low for a farm occupation depends upon the size and type of farm; however, this information was not collected. Similarly, the expectations of what is an appropriate level of education for housewives is highly ambiguous, partly because of the ambiguity about where housewife stands in the hierarchy of occupations. Moreover, the education that is expected of a housewife is likely to be a function of her husband's status characteristics more than of the status of housewife *per se.*

The measures of the eight types of status incompatibilty that involve comparisons of the status attainments of women and their male partners were constructed in the same fashion. Two types of incompatibility involve the educational attainments of women and their partners, two types involve occupational comparisons, and the remaining four types involve compatibility of the education of one partner and the occupation of the other. An individual's status was defined as compatible with his or her partner's if it was within the middle 70 percent of the distribution given the partner's position. Values below and above this range were defined as "incompatible-low" and "incompatible-high," respectively.

Again, an exception to this strategy was made in the case of the status of housewife. There was no basis for defining any level of education or any occupational attainment of the husband to be incompatible with a

---

[1]A measure of *degree* of status inconsistency could be constructed by expressing an individual's deviation from the mean in standard deviation units (see Hornung and McCullough, 1977, 1981) or in percentile deviations from the median (see Hornung, 1972, 1980). Further, the measure of type of inconsistency presented here is easily applied to three or more status variables (see Hornung, 1972, 1977).

woman's position as housewife. Conversely, there was no basis for defining a woman's status as housewife to be incompatible with any level of education or occupation of husbands. In other words, it was not *atypical* for men at each level of education and occupation to be married to or to be living with a woman who reported herself to be a housewife. Further, there were no atypical levels of education or occupation among the husbands or male partners of housewives. This measurement strategy gives rise to four comparisons involving status inconsistency and eight comparisons involving status incompatibility, each of which can be either high or low. There are, therefore, eight possible types of inconsistency and 16 possible types of incompatibility.

MEASUREMENT OF SPOUSE ABUSE

The analysis reported here utilizes a modification of the Conflict Tactics Scales described by Straus (1974). The items in the original scale are reported in Table 1. Factor analysis of the items measuring the woman's behavior and an analysis of the items measuring the behavior of the husband or male partner, as well as an analysis of the woman's and man's behavior together, confirmed the presence of three distinct dimensions or components (*eigenvalues* greater than one) of spousal violence. The first component pertains to psychological abuse (loading above

.5) as indicated by: (1) one partner insulting or swearing at the other; (2) one or the other sulking or refusing to talk about an issue; (3) stomping out of the house or room; (4) doing or saying something to spite the other; and (5) one partner threatening to hit or throw something at the other. The analysis revealed a second dimension which was labeled physical aggression. This dimension involves five aggressive acts: (1) whether one partner ever threw something at the other; (2) whether there was pushing, grabbing or shoving; (3) whether one partner slapped the other; (4) whether there was kicking, biting, or hitting with a fist; and (5) whether one partner hit or tried to hit the other with something. The third component revealed in the analysis was life-threatening violence. The acts involved in this dimension include: (1) one partner beating up the other; (2) threatening violence with a knife or gun; and (3) actually using a knife or gun against one's partner.

One intriguing aspect of the factor analyses that confirmed the presence of three analytically distinct dimensions of violence was the fact that threatening to hit or throw something at one's partner had equally high loadings of approximately .54 on both the psychological abuse and physical aggression dimensions. On the one hand, this means that a *threat* to throw something at or hit one's spouse is both an act of psychological abuse and an act of physical aggression. On the

TABLE 1. THE CONFLICT TACTICS SCALE

Each female respondent was asked how often each of the following behaviors were committed by her husband or male partner against her, and how often she committed each behavior against him during the past year. Responses were coded: never, once, twice, 3-5 times, 6-10 times, 11-20 times, and more than 20.

Psychological Abuse	1. Discussed an issue calmly.
	2. Got information to back up his side of things.
	3. Brought in or tried to bring in someone to help settle things.
	4. Insulted you or swore at you.
	5. Sulked or refused to talk about an issue.
	6. Stomped out of the room or house or yard.
	7. Cried¹.
	8. Did or said something to spite you.
	9. Threatened to hit you or throw something at you.
	10. Threw or smashed or hit or kicked something¹.
Physical Aggression	1. Threw something at you.
	2. Pushed, grabbed, or shoved you.
	3. Slapped you.
	4. Kicked, bit, or hit you with a fist.
	5. Hit or tried to hit you with something.
Life-Threatening Violence	1. Beat you up.
	2. Threatened you with a knife or gun.
	3. Used a knife or fired a gun.

¹This item was omitted in the present study.

other hand, the pattern of factor loadings suggest that the threat to hit or throw something at one's spouse is a transition point in the escalation of conflict from acts and language that are psychologically abusive to acts that involve physical aggression.

Two measures of each component of spouse abuse were constructed. The first is a measure of the incidence rate of each component of spouse abuse in the couple per couple year at-risk. This measure reflects whether or not one or more acts of the various types of spouse abuse occurred during the 12 months preceding the time of the interview (adjustments, *i.e.*, weighting, were made for couples that had been living together less than the one-year study period). The second measure of each component of spouse abuse is the period prevalence. This measure reflects the number of acts of psychological abuse, physical aggression, and life-threatening violence, per couple year at-risk.

It is important to note that the incidence and prevalence rates reported here pertain to spouse abuse within the couple, without regard to whether the abuse was directed against the man or the woman. Thus, in the analysis of incidence rates, a couple was defined as violent if the man was abusive, aggressive, or employed lethal force against his wife or female partner during the year; if the woman was abusive, aggressive, or used lethal force against her husband or male partner during this time; or if both were abusive, aggressive, or used deadly force against each other at any time during the year. The measures of incidence of psychological abuse, physical aggression, and life-threatening violence differentiate couples in which there was at least one abusive, aggressive, or life-threatening act from couples that were free of these acts for the entire 12 months prior to the time of the interview. The incidence rate is therefore a dichotomy that is expressed as a percentage of couples in which there was one or more acts of violence during the one-year study period. In contrast, the measures of period prevalence indicate the total number of psychologically abusive acts, the total number of physically aggressive acts, and the total number of acts that were life threatening per couple year at-risk. The measures of period prevalence should not be confused with the number of *episodes* of violence. The latter would be lower to the extent that an episode of violent conflict between part-

ners involves multiple abusive, aggressive, and perhaps life-threatening acts committed by the man and/or by the woman.

RESULTS

In Table 2, an analysis of variance of the incidence rates according to the years of education completed is presented. Psychological abuse was a very common event. More than two thirds of the couples reported at least one incident in the 12 months preceding the time of the interview. Physical aggression was substantially less common among couples, but nearly 16 percent of the couples studied reported at least one act of physical aggression. The most severe type of violence was even rarer. Nevertheless, life-threatening violence occurred during the year in nearly 3 percent of the couples studied. In other words, 1 out of every 35 couples studied reported that either the woman or the man or both had been beaten up, threatened with a knife or gun, or actually had a weapon used against them by their partner. In the final column in Table 2, a measure of total strife within the couple is reported. This measure was calculated on the bases of whether or not any of the components of spouse abuse had occurred at least once during the year. The fact that the incidence rate for total strife is nearly equal to the rate for psychological abuse indicates that couples who experienced physical aggression and/or life-threatening violence also experienced one or more acts of psychological abuse.

A more detailed analysis of these incidence rates reveals that while the educational attainment of both men and women is significantly ($p < .001$) related to psychological abuse, the relationship is not inverse as might be expected. Instead, the relationship is nonlinear with higher rates of incidence at the higher levels of education. However, the incidence rate for both aggression and violence are particularly high in couples where the man or the woman has either some high school training or a 2-year technical degree.

While an examination of the incidence of the three components of spouse abuse is interesting in its own right, it is especially instructive to compare the incidence rates for men and women at each level of education. Such a comparison suggests that *it is not educational attainment per se that is associated with increased risk of violence, but rather that it is an incompatibility in the educational levels of couples that is the*

TABLE 2. INCIDENCE OF PSYCHOLOGICAL ABUSE, PHYSICAL AGGRESSION, LIFE-THREATENING VIOLENCE, AND TOTAL STRIFE WITHIN COUPLES BY WOMAN'S AND MALE PARTNER'S EDUCATIONAL ATTAINMENT

Education	Sample Size		Psychological Abuse		Aggression		Violence		Total Strife	
	Women	Men	%Women	%Men	% Women	% Men	% Women	% Men	% Women	% Men
None	8	10	50.0	30.0	0.0	10.0	0.00	0.00	50.0	30.0
1-7 Years	71	96	36.9	47.1	11.4	10.5	7.09	3.14	36.9	47.1
8 Years	158	203	46.7	53.6	11.4	12.8	1.90	3.46	46.7	53.6
9-11 Years	303	264	70.9	73.1	21.7	19.3	4.13	4.17	70.9	73.1
12 Years	628	515	70.7	68.7	15.5	15.5	2.31	2.82	71.0	69.1
1-3 Years College	153	178	71.1	71.6	14.8	16.9	2.62	1.69	71.1	71.6
2 Years Technical	78	64	80.7	75.0	17.4	18.0	5.81	0.00	80.7	75.0
College Graduate	92	125	70.0	76.4	13.7	17.2	0.00	2.40	71.0	77.2
Post College	65	99	81.5	76.1	10.0	13.2	1.54	3.05	81.5	76.1
Grand Mean			67.6	67.6	15.7	15.7	2.87	2.87	67.8	67.8
Probability			<.001	<.001	<.10	n.s.	n.s.	n.s.	<.001	<.001

important risk factor. For example, note that psychological abuse occurred in more than 4 out of 5 couples (81.5 percent) in which the woman had a post-college education. Not only is this high relative to the overall incidence rate of 67.6 percent, but it is also higher than the 3 out of 4 couples (76.1 percent) who reported psychological abuse when the husband had post-college training. The difference in these percentages, although small, is a clue that it is not so much that the partners of post-college trained men experience psychological abuse, either as a victim or as a perpetrator, but rather it is that couples are at high risk of psychologically abusive behavior when the woman has achieved a post-graduate education that exceeds the educational attainments of her husband or male partner.

Additional evidence of an education incompatibility effect is provided by the incidence rates of physical aggression and life-threatening violence when one or the other partner has gone beyond a college education. Here, however, the apparent incompatibility effect is opposite in direction to what is observed for psychological abuse. While 10 percent of the post-college-trained women are in relationships in which there has been some physical aggression and 1.5 percent are in relationships where life-threatening force has been used, the percentages for similarly educated men are 13.2 and 3.1, respectively. This suggests that it is not couples in which there is a woman with education beyond college that are at higher risk of these more severe forms of spouse abuse, but rather it is couples comprised of a post-college-trained man and a woman with less education that are at higher risk.

Table 3 presents the relationships between the three components of violence and the occupational attainments of men and women. It is especially informative to note that in couples in which the woman reports her occupational status as housewife, the incidence rate of psychological abuse, physical aggression, and life-threatening violence are all lower than the over-all incidence rates among working women. In other words, it is couples in which the woman is working that are most likely to experience all three forms of spouse abuse and *not* couples in which the woman is a housewife. Couples in which the woman is in a sales or clerical position or the man is in a skilled trade or is a manager-official exhibit particularly high rates of psy-

TABLE 3. INCIDENCE OF PSYCHOLOGICAL ABUSE, PHYSICAL AGGRESSION, LIFE-THREATENING VIOLENCE, AND TOTAL STRIFE WITHIN COUPLES BY WOMAN'S AND MALE PARTNER'S OCCUPATIONAL ATTAINMENT

Occupational Attainment	Sample Size		Psychological Abuse		Aggression		Violence		Total Strife	
	Women	Men	% Women	% Men	% Women	% Men	% Women	% Men	% Women	% Men
Housewife	887		66.2		14.4		2.59		66.4	
Farm	11	141	45.5	48.8	9.1	8.9	0.00	1.42	45.5	48.8
Service	111	80	69.7	65.6	22.6	14.4	4.52	2.50	69.7	65.6
Unskilled	122	430	66.4	66.6	18.9	18.5	4.10	3.84	66.4	66.8
Skilled	16	364	61.3	73.4	22.6	19.2	3.23	4.40	61.3	73.6
Sales	44	68	77.3	66.7	25.0	16.3	0.00	1.48	77.3	66.7
Clerical	160	35	75.0	65.7	15.9	12.9	1.88	2.86	75.0	65.7
Small Business Proprietor	26	73	46.2	64.4	11.5	9.6	3.85	0.00	46.2	64.4
Manager-Official	36	147	66.7	73.0	18.1	12.3	5.56	2.05	66.7	73.7
Professional	141	217	71.3	70.9	12.4	13.4	3.55	1.39	72.0	70.9
Grand Mean			67.6	67.6	15.7	15.7	2.87	2.87	67.8	67.8
Probability			<.10	<.001	n.s.	<.10	n.s.	n.s.	<.10	<.001

chological abuse (between 70 and 75 percent). Conversely, couples in which the woman is a small business proprietor or the man or woman works in farming exhibit relatively low rates of psychological abuse (less than 50 percent).

The incidence of physical aggression is particularly high, 20 percent or more, among couples in which the woman is employed in a sales, service, or skilled position; while the lowest incidence rate (9.1 percent) occurs among farm women. However, there is very little difference in the incidence rates by the occupational attainment of men, with no occupational group having a rate above 20 percent and farm men having the lowest incidence rate of 9 percent.

Couples in which the woman is in a sales position or a farm occupation, as well as couples in which the man is a small business proprietor, did not report the occurrence of any episodes of the most severe form of violence during the study year. However, the highest rates of this form of violence are exhibited by couples in which the woman is a manager-official (5.6 percent) or the husband is employed in a skilled trade (4.4 percent).

Table 3 suggests that occupational incompatibilities are more important than occupation per se-for increasing the risk of all three components of violence. The increased risk is more apparent in the case of life-threatening violence. While women in the top two occupational strata of manager-official and professional are highly likely, relative to other women, to be in couples characterized by the incidence of life-threatening violence, men in these occupational strata are unlikely, relative to other men, to be in couples in which this most severe form of violence occurs. It follows, therefore, that many of the violent couples where the woman is in the two highest occupational strata involve men with lower status occupations. In other words, a couple consisting of a woman with a high-occupational status and a man with a lower-occupational position is at increased risk of violence involving the use of a weapon.

In Table 4, the period prevalence rates for the three components of spouse abuse and total strife within couples are reported. In the case of prevalence, the rate consists of the sum of the prevalence rates for abuse, aggression, and violence. The average number of psychologically abusive acts is 14.4 per year

TABLE 4. PREVALENCE OF PSYCHOLOGICAL ABUSE, PHYSICAL AGGRESSION, LIFE-THREATENING VIOLENCE, AND TOTAL STRIFE WITHIN COUPLES BY WOMAN'S AND MALE PARTNER'S EDUCATIONAL ATTAINMENT

Education	Psychological Abuse		Aggression		Violence		Total Strife	
	Women	Men	Women	Men	Women	Men	Women	Men
None	15.75	5.20	0.00	0.10	0.00	0.00	15.75	5.30
1-7 Years	10.26	8.16	2.06	2.09	0.57	0.33	12.88	10.59
8 Years	8.28	11.88	1.64	1.68	0.10	0.40	10.02	13.96
9-11 Years	16.78	17.86	3.09	2.63	0.37	0.27	20.25	20.76
12 Years	15.10	13.97	1.67	1.66	0.22	0.12	17.00	15.76
1-3 Years College	13.74	15.51	0.65	1.93	0.07	0.39	14.46	17.83
2 Years Technical	20.41	20.90	2.01	0.69	0.20	0.00	22.62	21.59
College Graduate	11.52	15.19	0.57	1.27	0.00	0.10	12.10	16.56
Post College	14.64	12.63	0.45	0.90	0.03	0.07	15.12	13.60
Grand Mean	14.42	14.42	1.75	1.75	0.22	0.22	16.39	16.39
Probability	<.01	<.01	n.s.	n.s.	n.s.	n.s.	<.05	<.10

per couple. Psychological abuse is most prevalent among couples in which one or the other partner has earned a two-year technical degree in which the man has no formal education.

It should be kept in mind that the prevalence rate of 14.4 abusive acts is the mean number of acts based upon all couples in the study, even though only 66.7 percent of the couples reported any psychological abuse. Accordingly, among couples in which psychological abuse occurred, it happened on the average of more than 22 times or about once every other week during the year.

An examination of the prevalence of physical aggression shows it to be unrelated to the education of men and women. Physically aggressive acts occur most often among couples in which the woman has no formal education. The overall prevalence rate of 1.75 translates into more than 11 aggressive acts during the year in couples evidencing this form of violence.

A comparison of the prevalence rates for men and women at the same level of education also suggests the presence of status incompatibility effects. This is seen by comparing the prevalence of life-threatening force among individuals with the most education. Couples that include post-college-educated men evidence more than twice as many acts of the most severe form of violence than couples in which the woman has some education beyond the college level. An even more striking comparison is the high frequency of life-threatening violence in couples in which the man has a college degree compared to the absence of extremely violent acts in couples where the woman has a college degree. This means that college-educated women are not the victims of extremely violent acts nor do they inflict this type of violence upon their husbands or male partners. But, in contrast, women with less than a college education are either the victims of extreme violence at the hands of more highly educated men, or college- and post-college-educated men are the victims of life-threatening violence at the hands of their less-highly-educated wives or female partners.

Additional insight into the problem of violence can be gained by comparing incidence and prevalence rates. A low rate of incidence combined with a high prevalence rate suggests that violence is confined to a few couples who experience repeated violent acts. Such situations provide a clue to the types of relationships in which the abused person has few avenues of escape or other options and is, to one degree or another trapped by his/her situation. This would be anticipated to be the case when the individual has few educational resources to translate into viable alternatives to the current situation. Support for this conjecture is seen in a comparison of the incidence and prevalence of life-threatening violence among women with only an eighth grade education. These women are in marriages that are not only the most likely to involve at least one episode of violence with a weapon, but marriages in which, if severe violence occurs at all, it happens about once every 6 months.

In contrast to this pattern, a low prevalence rate, especially when combined with a high rate of incidence, indicates marriages in which acts of violence do not become a recurrent pattern of behavior. The failure of these patterns to become recurrent may perhaps be due to the fact that the initial episode initiates help-seeking behavior to correct the underlying problem or because the behavior or its recurrence results in the termination of the relationship. This would be anticipated to be the case when individuals have resources at their disposal that allow them to change their situation. For example, men with a graduate education are in marriages with a relatively high incidence rate of lethal violence combined with a low rate of prevalence; the same is true for professional women whose jobs may provide economic resources enabling them to change their situations.

Table 5 gives prevalence rates according to occupational status. Each of the three components of violence tends to be highly prevalent among couples in which either the man or woman is in a blue collar occupation, while prevalence is lowest in couples in which the man is a small business proprietor. However, women who are small business proprietors, as well as women managers and officials, experience a high prevalence of physical aggression and life-threatening violence. Women managers and officials are in marriages in which there are 45 times as many acts of life-threatening violence than couples in which the man is a manager-official.

Several clues to the presence of status incompatibility effects in these incidence and prevalence rates have already been indicated.

TABLE 5. PREVALENCE OF PSYCHOLOGICAL ABUSE, PHYSICAL AGGRESSION, LIFE-THREATENING VIOLENCE, AND TOTAL STRIFE WITHIN COUPLES BY WOMAN'S AND MALE PARTNER'S OCCUPATIONAL ATTAINMENT

Occupation	Psychological Abuse		Aggression		Violence		Total Strife	
	Women	Men	Women	Men	Women	Men	Women	Men
Housewife	13.32		1.50		0.16		14.97	
Farm	13.27	7.29	1.45	0.83	0.00	0.03	14.73	8.14
Service	17.96	15.77	3.15	3.91	0.34	0.78	21.45	20.46
Unskilled	14.46	16.52	2.10	2.50	0.40	0.40	16.96	19.41
Skilled	17.29	16.72	6.45	1.98	0.19	0.21	23.94	18.91
Sales	19.07	13.41	2.68	1.24	0.00	0.12	21.75	14.77
Clerical	17.09	13.31	1.01	0.64	0.07	0.03	18.17	13.99
Small Business Proprietor	7.77	8.83	1.42	0.18	0.38	0.00	9.58	9.00
Manager-Official	12.96	14.39	5.85	1.05	1.78	0.04	20.58	15.48
Professional	15.46	12.94	1.08	1.06	0.13	0.03	16.67	14.03
Grand Mean	14.42	14.42	1.75	1.75	0.22	0.22	16.39	16.39
Probability	n.s.	<.01	n.s.	n.s.	<.05	n.s.	n.s.	<.01

There are also several findings that portend the presence of status inconsistency effects. Consider, as an example, the high incidence of severe violence for men with post-college education and the low incidence rate of this type of spouse abuse for men in professional occupations. This suggests that it is not couples which include professional men with post-college educations (status consistent for their job) that experience life-threatening violence, but that it is couples which include men with graduate training who fail to attain professional occupational status. In other words, it is men whose jobs are status inconsistent low for their level of education. Consider also the reverse pattern of incidence of lethal violence for post-college-educated women and women in professional jobs. Couples in which women have graduate training are at a low risk of life-threatening violence yet couples in which the woman is in a professional job are at much higher risk. This indicates that it is probably couples which include professional women with less than graduate training (in other words women who are education low for their job) that are at increased risk.

In the next two tables, the relative risk associated with types of status inconsistency and status incompatibility are addressed. The figures for relative risk given in the right-hand panel of each table reflect the increased or decreased incidence and frequency of violence among couples exposed to a type of inconsistency or incompatibility relative to the incidence rate and frequency among couples in which the particular type of inconsistency or incompatibility is absent. For example, the 80 percent incidence rate of psychological abuse among couples in which the woman has an occupation that is high, given her level of education, translates into a relative risk of 1.19 when compared to the incidence rate of 67 percent among couples in which the woman is employed in an occupation that is consistent with her educational attainment. This relative risk means that couples in which the woman is "occupation-high" inconsistent are 1.19 times more likely to experience at least one act of psychologically abusive behavior than are couples in which the woman is occupation-education consistent.

Epidemiologists generally regard a relative risk of 2.0 to signify an important risk factor as evidenced, for example, by the very large amount of money spent on anti-smoking efforts based, in part, upon a relative risk of coronary heart disease of 2.0 among smokers compared to nonsmokers. However, the generally accepted critical value of a twofold risk cannot be uniformly applied here. The exception to this rule of thumb is a consequence of the high incidence rate of psychological abuse in the population of couples studied and the low proportion of couples defined as status inconsistent or status incompatible. Since the incidence rate of 67.6 percent for psychological abuse in the population is greater than the approximately 10 percent of couples exposed to each type of inconsistency and incompatibility, there is a finite upper limit to the value for relative risk. This occurs because, even if the incidence rate among couples exposed to a particular risk factor was 100 percent, the incidence rate among the nonexposed couples would still be approximately 63 percent. Accordingly, in the analysis of the incidence of psychological abuse the upper limit is approximately 1.6 and the relative risk associated with a particular type of inconsistency or incompatibility should be interpreted with this maximum value in mind. However, the figures for the relative risk of physical aggression and life-threatening violence are not constrained in this way nor are the figures for relative frequency of each type of violence. In the analysis of these, several relative risk values greater than 2.0 and some types of inconsistency and incompatibility that involve a sixfold risk of violence can be noted.

The incidence rates given in Table 6 reveal a general pattern in which the relative risk associated with many types of status inconsistency and incompatibility increases from psychological abuse to the most severe form of violence. In other words, for most types of inconsistency and incompatibility, the risk of life-threatening violence is greater than the risk of physical aggression and the risk of physical aggression is greater than the risk of psychologically abusive behavior. However, for some types of inconsistency and incompatibility the reverse is true, suggesting that some status relationships somehow protect couples from violence.

The pattern of increasing risk associated with status inconsistency is clearest in the case of women who have less educational

TABLE 6. INCIDENCE AND RELATIVE RISK OF PSYCHOLOGICAL ABUSE, PHYSICAL AGGRESSION, LIFE-THREATENING VIOLENCE, AND TOTAL STRIFE WITHIN COUPLES BY STATUS CONSISTENCY AND COMPATIBILITY

		N	Incidence Rate (%)				Relative Risk			
			Abuse	Aggression	Violence	Strife	Abuse	Aggression	Violence	Strife
Status Consistency										
Woman's Education	Low	(85)	64.1	23.5	7.1	64.1	.96	1.57	2.74	.95
Given	Cons.	(1378)	67.0	14.9	2.6	67.2	1.00	1.00	1.00	1.00
Her Occupation	High	(90)	80.0	19.4	3.3	80.0	1.19	1.30	1.28	1.19
Woman's Occupation	Low	(113)	78.8	23.0	3.5	78.8	1.18	1.52	1.32	1.17
Given	Cons.	(1360)	66.9	15.2	2.7	67.2	1.00	1.00	1.00	1.00
Her Education	High	(80)	62.9	13.8	5.0	62.9	.94	.91	1.88	.94
Man's Education	Low	(306)	58.8	13.7	3.3	58.8	.85	.88	1.18	.85
Given	Cons.	(1064)	68.9	15.6	2.8	69.2	1.00	1.00	1.00	1.00
His Occupation	High	(183)	74.6	19.4	2.7	74.6	1.08	1.24	.99	1.08
Man's Occupation	Low	(135)	69.9	20.5	4.5	69.9	1.03	1.29	1.46	1.03
Given	Cons.	(1227)	67.7	15.9	3.1	67.9	1.00	1.00	1.00	1.00
His Education	High	(191)	65.5	11.0	.5	65.5	.97	.69	.17	.96
Status Compatibility										
Woman's Education	Low	(245)	62.0	18.4	3.9	62.0	.90	1.15	1.47	.90
Given	Cons.	(1082)	68.5	16.0	2.6	68.8	1.00	1.00	1.00	1.00
Man's Education	High	(227)	69.3	11.3	2.9	69.3	1.01	.73	1.09	1.01
Man's Education	Low	(161)	64.5	12.5	2.5	64.5	.95	.79	.85	.95
Given	Cons.	(1218)	67.9	15.9	2.9	68.1	1.00	1.00	1.00	1.00
Woman's Education	High	(175)	68.5	17.5	2.9	68.5	1.01	1.10	.98	1.01
Woman's Occupation	Low	(116)	71.6	22.4	4.3	71.6	1.06	1.48	1.66	1.06
Given	Cons.	(1364)	67.3	15.1	2.6	67.5	1.00	1.00	1.00	1.00
Man's Occupation	High	(73)	67.1	15.8	5.5	67.1	1.00	1.04	2.11	.99
Man's Occupation	Low	(61)	69.7	18.9	4.1	69.7	1.04	1.24	1.42	1.04
Given	Cons.	(1419)	67.1	15.3	2.9	67.3	1.00	1.00	1.00	1.00
Woman's Occupation	High	(73)	76.0	21.2	1.4	76.0	1.13	1.39	.47	1.13
Woman's Education	Low	(215)	53.7	14.2	3.3	53.7	.78	.91	1.25	.78
Given	Cons.	(1150)	68.6	15.6	2.6	68.8	1.00	1.00	1.00	1.00
Man's Occupation	High	(188)	77.1	17.9	4.0	77.6	1.12	1.14	1.53	1.13
Man's Education	Low	(94)	58.5	18.6	4.3	58.5	.86	1.22	1.49	.86
Given	Cons.	(1383)	67.8	15.3	2.9	68.0	1.00	1.00	1.00	1.00
Woman's Occupation	High	(76)	75.5	19.9	1.3	75.5	1.11	1.30	.46	1.11
Woman's Occupation	Low	(118)	70.6	20.4	4.3	70.6	1.05	1.31	1.57	1.04
Given	Cons.	(1347)	67.6	15.6	2.7	67.8	1.00	1.00	1.00	1.00
Man's Education	High	(89)	64.4	11.3	3.4	64.4	.95	.73	1.25	.95
Man's Occupation	Low	(158)	69.8	14.6	1.9	69.8	1.04	.92	.61	1.04
Given	Cons.	(1133)	67.0	15.9	3.1	67.3	1.00	1.00	1.00	1.00
Woman's Education	High	(262)	68.9	15.3	2.3	68.9	1.03	.96	.73	1.03

training than most other women in the same occupation. These "education-low" women, when compared to women with educational attainments that are consistent for their occupations, are .96 times as likely to be in marriages involving physical aggression and nearly three times more likely to be in marriages in which there has been at least one act of life-threatening violence during the year. This pattern also occurs when the man is "education-low" but is more pronounced in couples in which the man has achieved an occupational status that is lower than most other men with the same amount of education. Couples in which the man is "occupation-low" (in other words, couples where the man is an underachiever) are at 1.03 times the risk of psychologically abusive behavior, 1.29 times the risk of physically aggressive behavior, and 1.46 times the risk of life-threatening violence.

The opposite pattern, which suggests a "protective" effect of status inconsistency, is clearest when the man has achieved a position in the occupational hierarchy that is above what most other men with his level of education have attained. Couples in which the man is "occupation-high" (in other words when the man is an "overachiever") are at .97 the risk of psychological abuse, .69 times the risk of physical aggression, and only .17 times the risk of life-threatening violence. It is interesting to note that the apparent protective effect of overachievement does not occur when the couple includes a woman with this type of status inconsistency. Although couples in which the woman is an over-achiever in occupational attainment are at reduced risk of psychological abuse and physical aggression, these couples are at a nearly twofold risk of life-threatening violence.

Several types of status incompatibility conform to the pattern of increasing risk for the more severe forms of spouse abuse, while only incompatibilities between the man's occupation relative to the woman's education are associated with decreasing risks of physical aggression and life-threatening violence. In general, incompatibilities between the occupational attainments of the man and woman involve higher risks than incompatibilities between their educations or incompatibilities between the occupation of one and the education of the other. Particularly high risks are found when the woman's occupation is in-

compatible with her partner's job. Couples in which the woman has a job that is higher than anticipated in view of her partner's occupation are not at increased risk of psychological abuse or physical aggression, but they are more than twice as likely to experience life-threatening violence than are partners who are occupationally compatible. Increased risk of all forms of spouse abuse occurs when either the woman's job is low relative to her partner's, in which case the relative risks are 1.06, 1.48, and 1.66, or when the man's job is low relative to his partner's, in which case the relative risks of psychological abuse, physical aggression, and lethal violence are 1.04, 1.24, and 1.42, respectively. However, when the man's job is high relative to his partner's occupation, there is an appreciably increased risk of psychological abuse and physical aggression but a significant reduction in the risk of life-threatening violence. These couples are less than one half as likely as occupationally compatible couples to experience lethal violence in their relationship.

A significant reduction in the risk of life-threatening violence also occurs when the woman's occupational status is high in view of her partner's level of education. This is a particularly intriguing finding in view of the fact that couples in which the woman is high in occupation relative to her partner's job are at a twofold risk of life-threatening violence. Together these findings suggest that couples in which the woman holds a job that is higher than normal given her partner's occupational position are at reduced risk of severe violence *if the man is an occupational overachiever.* In other words, while marriages involving a woman with an occupation that is high relative to her partner's are at high risk of lethal violence, this increased risk is apparently tempered by the presence of a man who has achieved more occupationally than other men with a comparable amount of education.

Table 7 presents the prevalence and relative frequency of violence, by types of inconsistency and incompatibility. These figures dramatically show the increased risk of spouse abuse, particularly in its most severe form, when either the man or woman is status inconsistent and when there is an incompatibility in their occupational attainments.

When the woman's occupation is inconsistent-high for her educational level, there is more than five times the number of life-

TABLE 7. PREVALENCE AND RELATIVE FREQUENCY OF PSYCHOLOGICAL ABUSE, PHYSICAL AGGRESSION, LIFE-THREATENING VIOLENCE, AND TOTAL STRIFE WITHIN COUPLES BY STATUS CONSISTENCY AND COMPATIBILITY

		Prevalence (Mean No.)				Relative Frequency			
		Abuse	Aggression	Violence	Strife	Abuse	Aggression	Violence	Strife
Status Consistency									
Woman's Education Given Her Occupation	Low	15.9	2.9	.62	19.5	1.12	1.69	3.13	1.21
	Cons.	14.1	1.7	.20	16.2	1.00	1.00	1.00	1.00
	High	16.7	.9	.11	17.7	1.18	.54	.56	1.10
Woman's Occupation Given Her Education	Low	18.1	2.1	.22	20.4	1.28	1.31	1.27	1.28
	Cons.	14.1	1.6	.17	15.9	1.00	1.00	1.00	1.00
	High	14.1	3.7	.96	18.7	1.00	2.29	5.50	1.18
Man's Education Given His Occupation	Low	12.3	2.0	.39	14.7	.85	1.22	2.96	1.90
	Cons.	14.5	1.6	.13	16.2	1.00	1.00	1.00	1.00
	High	17.7	2.0	.44	20.2	1.22	1.24	3.40	1.24
Man's Occupation Given His Education	Low	18.2	4.5	1.05	23.7	1.27	2.88	6.61	1.48
	Cons.	14.3	1.6	.16	16.0	1.00	1.00	1.00	1.00
	High	12.7	1.0	.01	13.7	.89	.66	.07	.86
Status Incompatibility									
Woman's Education Given Man's Education	Low	13.2	1.9	.21	15.3	.87	1.02	.99	.89
	Cons.	15.1	1.9	.21	17.2	1.00	1.00	1.00	1.00
	High	12.6	.9	.24	13.8	.83	.50	1.10	.80
Man's Education Given Woman's Education	Low	9.5	1.4	.27	11.1	.63	.76	1.21	.65
	Cons.	15.1	1.8	.23	17.1	1.00	1.00	1.00	1.00
	High	14.3	1.6	.10	16.1	.95	.90	.46	.94
Woman's Occupation Given Man's Occupation	Low	18.3	2.9	.33	21.6	1.31	1.88	1.98	1.37
	Cons.	14.0	1.6	.17	15.7	1.00	1.00	1.00	1.00
	High	15.6	3.7	1.01	20.3	1.11	2.38	6.13	1.23
Man's Occupation Given Woman's Occupation	Low	22.6	5.9	1.10	29.6	1.60	3.69	5.78	1.86
	Cons.	14.1	1.6	.19	15.9	1.00	1.00	1.00	1.00
	High	14.5	1.2	.01	15.7	1.03	.73	.00	.99
Woman's Education Given Man's Occupation	Low	11.1	1.9	.25	13.2	.75	1.01	1.11	.79
	Cons.	14.7	1.8	.23	16.7	1.00	1.00	1.00	1.00
	High	16.7	1.2	.13	18.0	1.14	.63	.55	1.07
Woman's Occupation Given Man's Occupation	Low	12.5	2.1	.35	15.0	.85	1.21	1.60	.90
	Cons.	14.6	1.8	.22	16.6	1.00	1.00	1.00	1.00
	High	13.6	1.0	.01	14.7	.93	.59	.06	.89
Man's Education Given Woman's Occupation	Low	17.6	2.9	.32	20.8	1.23	1.68	1.53	1.28
	Cons.	14.4	1.7	.21	16.3	1.00	1.00	1.00	1.00
	High	11.1	1.0	.16	12.3	.77	.60	.75	.75
Man's Occupation Given Woman's Education	Low	15.2	2.4	.44	18.0	1.05	1.35	1.97	1.09
	Cons.	14.6	1.7	.23	16.5	1.00	1.00	1.00	1.00
	High	13.3	1.4	.05	14.8	.92	.82	.20	.90

threatening events than when she is status consistent. Greatly increased risk of severe violence occurs when the man has a job beneath his level of education, whereas having a job well above his level of training is associated with a greatly reduced risk of lethal violence in the relationship. It is interesting to note that, as is the case with the incidence of violence, a man's overachievement is occupation somehow protects the couple with respect to the prevalence of violence, but overachievement by the woman does not function in this way. Rather, couples in which the woman is an overachiever in occupation experience 5.50 times the number of life-threatening acts as when the woman is status consistent.

The relative frequency of life-threatening events is also very high when the man and woman are in jobs that are incompatible. When the woman's job is high relative to her partner's, life-threatening acts occur more than six times more often than when their jobs are compatible. Similarly, when the man's job is lower than expected in view of the woman's occupation, life-threatening violence also occurs about six times more frequently than when the partners are compatible in occupational attainment. But when the man's job is high relative to either his partner's education or her occupation, the risks of life-threatening violence are significantly below the risks for couples which are compatible in these status hierarchies.

SUMMARY AND CONCLUSIONS

Spousal violence, particularly psychologically abusive behavior, is a more common problem than is generally recognized. These data reveal that 68 percent of the couples studied experienced at least one act of spousal violence during the year. Moreover, among couples that did experience spousal violence, an act of psychological abuse, physical aggression, or life-threatening violence occurred, on the average, about once every two weeks. Although life-threatening violence and physical aggression between marital partners have received considerable attention, largely because of their more serious immediate consequences for the well-being of the individual, the potential long-term serious consequences of psychological abuse for mental as well as physical health and the incidence of stress-induced

illnesses cannot be ignored. It is possible that (long-term) exposure to a psychologically abusive marital relationship contributes significantly to an increased risk of such stress-related conditions as chronic depression, cardiovascular disease, etc. If this is true, then the high incidence and prevalence of psychological abuse within couples may prove to have higher social costs in terms of morbidity and mortality than either physical aggression and/or life-threatening violence.

Although spousal violence is very common, the present analyses have shown that not all couples are equally likely to experience violence. Contrary to what is generally believed, housewives are *less* likely than working women to be in a marital relationship that involves violence. This finding may be due to a true lower incidence of spousal violence in couples in which the woman is not employed, or it may be a function of under-reporting of violence by housewives. This latter explanation has a certain appeal in that one would hypothesize that housewives, who are typically, to a large degree, dependent upon their husbands, would under-report the occurrence of spousal violence out of a belief or fear that reporting such behavior would jeopardize whatever economic security they had in the relationship. Although this hypothesis is reasonable it is not probable that under-reporting accounts for all of the differences between housewives and working women in both the incidence and prevalence rates. To account for these differences, the incidence rate for housewives would have to have been under-reported by nearly 5 percent and then, with under-reporting of incidence adjusted for, the average number of violent acts would still have to have been under-reported by 10 percent.

Finally, these analyses support the hypothesis that the incidence and prevalence of spousal violence are related to the inconsistency and incompatibility of educational and occupational attainments of men and women. It is important to note that those types of inconsistency and incompatibility that were found to be associated with increased or decreased risk of spousal violence in the present study are the same types of inconsistency and incompatibility that were found to be associated with high levels of satisfaction or dissatisfaction with marriage and life in general in an earlier study utilizing a different sample of cases (Hornung and McCullough, 1981). For example, in the present study it was found that overachievement in occupation by the man is associated with a lower incidence and prevalence of spousal violence, while in the earlier study this type of status inconsistency was associated with a high level of marital satisfaction among men. In contrast, overachievement by the woman is associated with a high incidence and prevalence of spousal violence while the earlier study showed this type of inconsistency to be related to high levels of marital dissatisfaction among women. With respect to the effects of status incompatibility, the earlier study showed that educational incompatibilities were related to husbands being dissatisfied with their marriages. In the present study, it has been found that couples in which the woman is educationally incompatible with her partner, particularly if her attainments are low relative to his, experience a high incidence of spousal violence, especially in the form of life-threatening violence.

The results presented here, like those in the earlier study, are probably conservative and underestimate the effects of status inconsistency and status incompatibility, if only because the analyses are based upon currently intact marriages or cohabitational arrangements. It is suspected that a stronger relationship would be found between inconsistency and incompatibility and spousal violence in a retrospective study of marital relationships that ended in divorce (or suicide or homicide). Further, it is suspected that an analysis that distinguished between violence directed against the woman and that directed against the man would sharpen greatly the relationship between types of status inconsistency, incompatibility, and the incidence and prevalence of spousal violence. Analyses are also needed to explore factors that exacerbate or mollify the stresses engendered by status inconsistency and incompatibility (e.g., achievement motivation, Hornung, 1980; Hornung and McCullough, 1981). An especially significant line of needed inquiry is an investigation of factors that constrain men and women to remain in violent marital or cohabitational relationships. These constraints may include strongly held religious beliefs against divorce, the presence of children, the lack of economic resources, or the unavailability of social support systems that are essential to change one's life situation.

In spite of the need for further analysis, if marital dissatisfaction and abusive and violent behavior against one's spouse is considered to be related in a reciprocal cause and effect way, or even as spuriously correlated outcomes of a common cause, then these analyses, combined with the earlier work, provide strong evidence that status inconsistency and status incompatibility, conceptualized and measured as atypical combinations of status, can have serious disruptive consequences for an individual and a marital relationship.

REFERENCES

Alves, M. A., and P. H. Rossi
1978   "Who should get what? Fairness judgements of the distribution of earnings." American Journal of Sociology 84 (November):541-564.
Berger, J., M. Zelditch, Jr., B. Anderson, and B. P. Cohen
1972   "Structural aspects of distributive justice: A status value formulation." Pp. 119-146 in J. Berger, M. Zelditch, Jr., and B. Anderson (Eds.), Sociological Theories in Progress (Vol. 2). Boston:Houghton Mifflin Company.
Berry, K. J.
1968   "Status integration and morbidity." Unpublished doctoral dissertation, University of Oregon.
Cook, K. S.
1975   "Expectations, evaluations and equity." American Sociological Review 40 (June):372-388.
Gelles, R. J.
1974   The Violent Home: A Study of Physical Aggression Between Husbands and Wives. Beverly Hills:Sage Publications.
Gibbs, J., and W. T. Martin
1964   Status Integration and Suicide. Eugene, Oregon:University of Oregon Press.
Harris, L., and Associates
1979   A Survey of Spousal Violence Against Women in Kentucky. Report prepared for the Kentucky Commission on Women.
Hornung, C. A.
1972   "Status consistency: A method of measurement and empirical examination." Unpublished doctoral dissertation, Syracuse University.
1977   "Social status, status inconsistency and psychological stress." American Sociological Review 42 (August):623-638.
1980   "Status inconsistency, achievement, motivation and psychological stress." Social Science Research 9 (December):363-380.

Hornung, C. A., and B. C. McCullough
1977 "Status relationships in marriage: Consequences for life and marital dissatisfaction." Paper presented at the annual meetings of the American Sociological Association, Chicago (August).
1981 "Status relationships in dual-employment marriages: Consequences for psychological well-being." Journal of Marriage and Family 43 (February):125-141.
Kemper, T.
1968 "Reference groups, socialization and achievement." American Sociological Review 33 (February):31-46.
Lenski, G.
1954 "Status crystallization: A non-vertical dimension of social stratification." American Sociological Review 19 (August):405-413.
1956 "Social participation and status crystallization." American Sociological Review 21 (August):458-464.
Rosenbaum, A., D. Goldstein, and K. D. O'Leary
1980 "An evaluation of the self-esteem of spouse abusive men." Paper presented at the American Psychological Association annual meetings, Montreal (September).
Stark, E., A. Flitcraft, and W. Frazier
1979 "Medicine and patriarchal violence: The social construction of a private event." International Journal of Health Services 9 (November):461-488.
Straus, M. A.
1974 "Leveling, civility, and violence in the family." Journal of Marriage and the Family 36 (February):13-29.
Straus, M. A., R. J. Gelles, and S. K. Steinmetz
1980 Behind Closed Doors: Violence in the American Family. New York: Anchor Books.
Steinmetz, S. K.
1977 "Wife beating, husband beating: A comparison of the use of physical violence between spouses to resolve marital fights." Pp. 63-96 in M. Roy (Ed.), Battered Women. New York: Van Nostrand Reinhold.
Treiman, D., and K. Terrell
1975 "Sex and the process of status attainment: A comparison of working men and women." American Sociological Review 40 (April):174-200.
Webster, M., Jr., and J. E. Driskell, Jr.
1978 "Status generalization: A review and some new data." American Sociological Review 43 (April):220-236.

Previous research on cohabitation and Levinger's (1965) model of marital cohesiveness and dissolution lead to the hypothesis that there is a higher level of violence in ongoing marriages than in ongoing cohabiting relationships. Data from a national sample of 2,143 adults did not support this hypothesis. Instead the reverse was found: cohabitors are more violent than marrieds. However, cohabitors who are over 30, divorced women, those with high incomes, and those who had been together for over ten years, had very low rates of violence. The fact that some cohabitors are much more violent than marrieds, whereas others are appreciably less violent, provides evidence that cohabitation should not be seen as a unitary phenomenon. Of the different types of cohabiting relationships, only a portion can be regarded as a liberal alternative to traditional marriage. The social, legal and educational implications of these findings are discussed.

21

INTERPERSONAL VIOLENCE AMONG MARRIED AND COHABITING COUPLES*

Kersti Yllo and Murray A. Straus**

Recent studies of family violence indicate that physical aggression between spouses is often viewed as legitimate (even if not mandated) in family relations. The tolerance, and sometimes approval, of spousal violence is not just a part of the folk culture. It is also embedded in the legal system (Straus, 1976). Suits and new legislation have been necessary to force the police and courts to treat husband-wife assaults as they would other assaults. Public tolerance of marital violence is also quite high. About 25% of a national sample of Americans stated that they would approve a husband or wife hitting one another under certain circumstances (Stark & McEvoy, 1970). This tolerance is further illustrated by the results of an unpublished experiment by Churchill and Straus. Subjects were presented with identical descriptions of an assault by a man on a woman. Those who were told that the attacker and victim were husband and wife recommended much less severe punishment for the man than those who were told that the two were dating. Such evidence has led some family violence researchers to adopt the notion that the marriage license is, in effect, a hitting license (Straus, 1976).

Living Together Without the Marriage License

Researchers concerned with alternative family forms, particularly cohabitation, have also attempted to assess the effect of the license and legal contract on intimate relationships (Whitehurst, 1974). Marriage brings with it not just a change in the legal status of the couple, but also a change in the whole set of social expectations and assumptions regarding the couple. The marriage ceremony

*Based on a paper presented at the 1978 annual meeting of the National Council on Family Relations, Philadelphia, PA.

This paper is part of the University of New Hampshire Family Violence Research Program, supported by NIMH grants MH27557 and T32 MH15161, and the University of New Hampshire. A program bibliography and list of available publications may be obtained on request to Straus.

We wish to thank Ursula G. Dibble, Joni Benn, and Cathy S. Greenblat for the valuable comments and suggestions on an earlier draft.

**Kersti Yllo is a Post-Doctoral Research Associate with the Family Violence Research Program at the University of New Hampshire, Durham, NH 03824. Murray A. Straus is Director, Family Violence Research Program, and Professor, Department of Sociology and Anthropology, University of New Hampshire, Durham, NH 03824.

From Kersti Yllo and Murray A. Straus, "Interpersonal Violence Among Married and Cohabiting Couples," *Family Relations*, 1981, 30, pp. 339-347. Reprinted by permission of the publisher and authors.

transforms a private relationship into a public one in which social norms more closely govern the behavior of the couple.

Nevertheless, the behavioral importance and impact of the marriage license remains unclear. Much of the research has been limited by various methodological problems, in particular inadequate samples and lack of empirical comparison with married couples (Cole, 1977). Still, some interesting findings have emerged from two studies which overcome these problems. There are *few* differences between marital and living-together relationships in such areas as division of labor, decision-making power, and communication and satisfaction with the relationship (Stafford, Backman, & Dibona, 1977; Yllo, 1978).

Theoretically, cohabiting couples might be expected to have lower rates of violence than married couples. Since they are not legally bound to their relationship, they may be more likely to leave an unsatisfactory situation. If the marriage license is, in effect, a covert hitting license (that cohabitors do not have), cohabitors might be expected to view violence as less legitimate and also feel less bound to tolerate it. However, violence in marriage may be a reflection of the intense conflict which occurs in all intimate relationships (Foss, 1980; Gelles & Straus, 1979). It is difficult to speculate about how cohabitors react to violence (Hennon, 1976).

The prediction of lower violence among cohabitors is appropriate if the ideological basis of their relationship includes rejecting the traditional rules and rights of marriage, such as male leadership, the right to hit and so on. Unfortunately, we have no basis upon which to argue that all or even most cohabiting relationships are based on this type of counter-culture ideology. Empirical knowledge about the nature of cohabitation is limited (Cole, 1977). Almost all studies of cohabitation are based on college student samples. These studies provide no information on the nature of cohabitation in the population as a whole. Consequently, the expectation that cohabitors are less violent than marrieds because of counter-culture life styles is quite tentative.

Levinger's Cohesiveness-Dissolution Model

George Levinger's (1965) conceptual model of marital cohesiveness and dissolution iden-

tifies factors which may serve to keep intact a relationship in which violence has occurred and those which facilitate its breakup. The rates of violence in marriages and cohabiting relationships can be assessed within this framework.

Levinger conceives of marriage as a special case of all two-person relationships and marital cohesiveness as a special case of group cohesiveness. He defines group cohesiveness as "the total field of forces which act on members to remain in the group" (1965, p. 19). Inducements to remain in the group include the attractiveness of the group and the strength of restraints against leaving it. Inducements to leave the group include the attractiveness of alternative relationships. Levinger proposes that the strength of the marital relationship is a direct function of (a) the attractions within and (b) the barriers around the marriage, and (c) an inverse function of such influences from alternative relationships (1965, p. 19). Thus, the strength of the intimate relationship is regarded as a function of bars as well as bonds. The relative stability of marriage as opposed to cohabitation may be considered in terms of the three dimensions Levinger outlines.

Attractiveness of the Relationship

The cohabitation research discussed above indicates that the attractions within marriage and cohabitation should be fairly similar. Both are intimate relationships with similar internal structures. Cohabitors and marrieds do not differ significantly in their feelings of satisfaction with the relationship (Yllo, 1978).

A key difference between marriage and cohabitation in relation to attractiveness may be differences in the degree to which the two types of relationships are embedded in kin support networks. The new husband and wife officially become members of one another's families and receive support (both financial and emotional) from kin (Sussman, 1959). The cohabiting couple, on the other hand, seems more likely to be isolated from such a support network. The data on cohabitors indicate that their parents often do not even know of the relationship (Henze & Hudson, 1974; Macklin, 1972; Peterman, Ridley, & Anderson, 1974).

However, the involvement of family in the marriage may be regarded as interference rather than support. From this perspective, the relative isolation of cohabitors from their kin may be regarded as an advantage.

It is difficult to assess the relative attractiveness of marriage as opposed to cohabitation. The societal stigma or acceptance is an important consideration. It also depends to a great extent on the individual couple and their values. In content and intimacy these relationships differ little. These factors lead us to assume that there would also be little difference in conflict and violence between marrieds and cohabitors.

Barriers to Dissolution

Levinger points out that it is also important to consider the barriers around the relationship. It is with regard to barriers that there are important differences between marrieds and cohabitors.

Levinger maintains that barrier forces exist both inside and outside the individual. Feelings of obligation to the marital bond are an important barrier to the dissolution of a marriage. Little information is available on feelings of obligation which living together couples feel for their relationships. However, it seems reasonable to assume that, while cohabitors may feel as satisfied and as strongly about the importance of the relationship to them as marrieds, their commitment is more dependent on the attractions within the relationship.

The social and legal status of marriage is a source of barrier strength outside of the individuals. The most obvious barrier to the dissolution of marriage, which does not exist for cohabitors, is the necessity of a legal divorce. Resources such as time, effort, and money are required to obtain a divorce and work to make the break-up of a marriage a costly option.

The legal system serves opposite ends for cohabitors. In many states it is still a criminal offense to live together unmarried. This prohibition makes it difficult for cohabiting couples to establish the same kind of financial interdependence as marrieds. In addition, it is sometimes difficult for cohabitors to find a place to live and there are even more problems when it comes to major purchases which require credit (Gagnon & Greenblat, 1978, p. 191).

In addition to the legal boundary around marriage, there are numerous informal social forces which maintain the relationship. For example, religious proscriptions against divorce may influence a couple to stay together, even at the cost of tolerating some violence. Another informal barrier which Levinger discusses is kinship affiliation. As pointed out earlier, the networks of family relations are different for marrieds and cohabitors. Whereas family members may support the efforts of the married couple to work out their differences and avoid the turmoil and social stigma of divorce, they may actively encourage the break-up of a cohabiting relationship which they regard as illicit.

Alternatives

The third dimension which Levinger discusses is attractiveness of alternative relationships. While there is no empirical evidence on this issue, the case can be made that alternative attractions would be stronger for cohabitors. If one's parents oppose living together unmarried, the desire to reestablish relations with one's family may serve to weaken the relationship.

Also, alternative sexual and emotional involvements seem more available to cohabitors. The advances of others are less likely to be deterred. The fact that one is living with someone is not usually as widely known as the fact than one is married. In addition, marriage carries with it stronger expectations of sexual and emotional exclusivity. Adultery is a legally defined act. Involvement with another person when one is cohabiting receives fewer negative sanctions.

The increased possibility for outside involvement among cohabitors seems to carry the potential for increased conflict among them. However, the greater chance for and acceptability of outside involvement may also be considered positively. An outside affair may have a much more serious impact on a marriage than on a cohabiting relationship. Within marriage such an act constitutes the breaking of a legal contract and the public marriage vows.

Hypothesis

Previous theoretical and empirical research (Gelles & Straus, 1979; Straus, 1976) indicates a high level of violence in family relationships. The discussion in this paper of the nature of marital and cohabiting relationships and sources of attractiveness and conflict within them, suggest that this is likely to also apply to cohabiting couples. However, consideration of the barriers against dissolution of the relationships has emphasized that marriage is a much more binding commitment and would be more likely to stay intact despite problems, including violence. These factors lead to the following hypothesis:

There is a significantly higher level of interpersonal violence in ongoing marriages than in ongoing cohabiting relationships.

The Sample

The data for this study were obtained from a survey conducted in January and February of 1976. Interviews were conducted with a national area-probability sample of 2,143 adults. To be eligible for inclusion in the sample each respondent had to be between 18 and 70 years of age and living with a member of the opposite sex as a couple. However, the couple did not have to be formally married. A random half of the respondents were female and half were male. Each interview lasted approximately one hour and was completely anonymous. Furthermore, interviewers were of the language or racial group which was predominant in the sampling area for which they were responsible. Further details on the sample are given in Straus, Gelles, and Steinmetz, 1980.

Interviews were completed with 40 persons who were not legally married to their partners. The 40 cohabitors make up 1.9% of the sample. This figure corresponds quite closely with the most recent census estimate of 2% (Glick & Norton, 1977). It is important to note that both our figures and the census estimate are probably underestimates of the actual rate of cohabitation. It is quite likely that a number of cohabitors, particularly those with long-established relationships, reported themselves as married.

Concepts and Measures

There has been considerable confusion regarding definition of concepts in both cohabitation and family violence research. It is, therefore important to specify both the nominal and operational definitions of the central concepts used in this paper.

Cohabitation

The concept of cohabitation has been somewhat unclear because researchers of the phenomenon have used a variety of terms interchangeably. "Living together unmarried," "quasi-marriage," "trial-marriage," "shacking up," and "nonmarital cohabitation" have been used synonymously by some and defined differently by others. For the purposes of this research, the terms "living together" and "cohabitation" will be used interchangeably to refer to a more or less permanent relationship in which two unmarried persons of the opposite sex share a living facility without legal contract (Cole, 1977, p. 67).

In this study, the marital status of respondents was determined on the basis of questions on family composition. All respondents who listed the marital status of both partners as "married" were coded as legally married couples and are referred to as marrieds. Those respondents who reported the marital status of partners as "single," "divorced," "widowed," or "separated" were coded as cohabitors. All of the relationships were intact and ongoing at the time of the interviews.

Violence

In this study, the terms violence and physical aggression will be used synonymously and are defined as "an act carried out with the intention of, or perceived as having the intention of, physically hurting another person" (Gelles & Straus, 1978, p. 16). Although violence connotes a more negative and political evaluation of an act than does physical aggression, the terms are used here to refer to the same actual behavior.

The data on violence were obtained using the Conflict Tactics Scales (Straus, 1979). The overall violence scale contains eight items, starting with "mild" acts such as pushing, shoving, slapping, throwing things. For purpose of this paper, the Severe Violence Index will be used; this includes acts of violence that carry with them a high risk of physical injury, specifically: punching, biting, kicking, hitting with an object, beating up, and any attack in which a knife or gun was actually used. The violence rates reported are the percentage of couples in which someone did one or more of these things in the year prior to the interview. Violence rates will be reported for male-to-female violence and for couple violence. The former is a measure of violence in which the woman is the victim and the latter is a measure of all violent acts, whether directed at the male or the female.

It is important to note that our data provide information only on the extent to which violent acts were carried out and not on the consequences of those acts, i.e., severity of injury.

Violence Rates

The findings of this research indicate that our assumptions about marial cohesiveness, the nature of cohabitation, and factors influencing the level of violence in both types of relationships need to be reconsidered. Not only was the hypothesis not supported, but the actual rates are significantly different in the reverse direction. Cohabitors appear to be more violent than their married counterparts.

As Table 1 indicates, cohabiting women are almost four times more likely to suffer severe violence as married women. The data on total couple violence indicate that cohabiting women are not just the victims of high rates of violence but that they are quite violent to their partners as well. The cohabitors are almost five times more likely to have a severe violent incident than are the marrieds. The rates of violence among cohabitors given in Table 1 are not highly reliable due to the small number of cohabitors in the sample. There-

fore, these findings must be considered with caution.

As the overall violence rates parallel the severe violence rates in this analysis (and all others), only the latter will be reported in the remainder of the paper, so as to avoid the complexity of two sets of data presentations.

In order to insure that the above differences in levels of violence are not spurious, the relationship between marital status and violence was controlled for a number of key variables. Previous comparisons of these samples of marrieds and cohabitors showed that cohabitors are significantly younger and more likely to be divorced or separated. Also, the duration of the cohabiting relationships was found to be significantly shorter than that of marriages (Yllo, 1978). These variables were introduced as control factors. In addition, the relationship was controlled for level of family income.

The analyses indicate no evidence that other variables account for the higher rates of violence among cohabitors. The difference in male-female rates of severe violence between marrieds and cohabitors remained significant at the .01 level under all control conditions. The difference in *couple* violence between marrieds and cohabitors was reduced by the introduction of control variables, with the result that four of the F ratios do not quite reach the .05 level.

The more interesting findings from the two-way analyses of variance are in respect to the interaction effects discussed below, even though most of these are not statistically significant.

Income

It is clear from Table 2 that income has a direct effect on level of interpersonal violence. There is an inverse relationship between income and rate of physical aggression

Table 1
Interpersonal Violence Rates for Married and Cohabiting Couples

	Married ($n = 2,049$)	Cohabiting ($n = 37$)	Chi-square	p ($df = 1$)
Male-to-Female, Severe	3.6	13.5	7.251	.05
Total Couple, Severe	5.6	27.0	25.847	.05
Male-to-Female, Overall	11.6	32.4	9.048	.05
Total Couple, Overall	15.1	37.8	12.690	.05

Table 2
Severe Interpersonal Violence Rates for Married and
Cohabiting Couples, Controlling for Key Variables

	% Violent			
	Male to Female Violence		Couple Violence	
Control Variables	Married ($n = 2,049$)	Cohabiting ($n = 37$)	Married ($n = 2,049$)	Cohabiting ($n = 37$)
Income				
High (over $20,000)	1.6	0.0	2.9	0.0
Middle ($10,000-$19,000)	2.4	10.0	4.4	20.0
Low (under $10,000)	8.4	20.0	11.5	40.0
Marital Status	$F = 7.61**$		$F = 3.71*$	
Income	$F = 1.24$		$F = 1.51$	
Interaction	$F = 5.67**$		$F = 3.83*$	
Age of Respondent				
Thirty and under	8.4	21.7	13.3	43.5
Over thirty	1.8	0.0	2.7	0.0
Marital Status	$F = 6.72**$		$F = 3.40$	
Age of Respondent	$F = 2.90$		$F = 2.19$	
Interaction	$F = 2.48$		$F = 1.73$	
Female Previously Divorced or Separated				
No	3.1	16.1	5.0	36.0
Yes	7.4	0.0	9.8	0.0
Marital Status	$F = 7.06**$		$F = 3.64$	
Female Previously Divorced/ Separated	$F = 0.259$		$F = 1.38$	
Interaction	$F = 0.652$		$F = 0.53$	
Male Previously Divorced or Separated				
No	3.5	16.0	3.6	36.0
Yes	4.6	9.1	7.6	9.1
Marital Status	$F = 6.59**$		$F = 3.11$	
Male Previously Divorced/ Separated	$F = 2.23$		$F = 1.62$	
Interaction	$F = 4.00$		$F = 2.64$	
Duration of Relationship				
Under 2 years	10.0	12.5	18.2	31.2
3 to 10 years	5.8	30.0	8.7	50.0
Over 10 years	1.7	0.0	2.3	0.0
Marital Status	$F = 7.24**$		$F = 3.28$	
Duration of Relationship	$F = 2.94*$		$F = 1.96$	
Interaction	$F = 0.178$		$F = 0.197$	

$*p < .05.$
$**p < .01.$

for both married and cohabitors. However, this effect seems much more dramatic for those living together. Cohabitors earning over $20,000 annually reported no violent incidents. In contrast, a full 40% in the low income group (family income under $10,000) indicated that they had had at least one incident of severe violence in the last year. In contrast, the rate of couple violence for marrieds ranged from 2.9% in the high income group to 11.5% in the low income group. It appears that the stresses of living on low income are somehow compounded for couples living together unmarried.

Age

Age also has a strong effect on interpersonal violence for both marrieds and cohabitors. The rates of wife-beating and total couple violence are considerably greater for those under 30. Again, this factor has greater impact for cohabitors. Those over 30 who were living together reported no violence at all within the previous year. But, as Table 2 shows, 43.5% of cohabitors under the age of 30 had been involved in one or more violent episodes within that year.

Previous Divorce or Separation

As reported in an earlier paper (Yllo, 1978) many more cohabiting than married couples reported that a previous marriage had ended in divorce. Divorce is introduced as a control on the assumption that the different marital histories of the two groups might differentially affect levels of violence. As Table 2 illustrates, previous divorce appears to have opposite effects for marrieds and cohabitors as far as physical aggression is concerned.

For marrieds, the rate of severe violence is somewhat higher for those who had previously been divorced. Perhaps these couples are willing to tolerate a higher level of violence in order to avoid the stigma of a second divorce.

The rate of violence for cohabitors who had been divorced or separated, in contrast, was lower than for those who had not been previously married. Among those cohabiting couples in which it was the woman who had been married, the violence rate is zero. For those living together couples who had not been previously married the rate of wife-beating is 16% and total couple violence is 36%. Perhaps those people who choose to cohabit rather than remarry are quite cautious about their new involvement and are less inclined to tolerate any abuse.

Duration of the Relationship

The duration of cohabiting relationships is significantly shorter than that of marriages. Further, this relationship remains significant when controlled for age of respondent.

Controlling the marital status-violence relationship for the duration variable also produced differences between marrieds and cohabitors. The meaning of those differences is far from clear, however. While the rate of total couple violence decreases from 18.2% for those married under two years to 2.3% for those married over ten years, this trend is not clearly paralleled among cohabitors. For the under two year cohabiting group, the rate is about double that of the newly marrieds (31.2%). Instead of declining as length of relationship increases, the violence rate goes up to a full 50% for those who have been living together for three to ten years. The rate then drops to zero for those couples who have been living together for over ten years.

The barriers to dissolving a marriage may explain why longer established marriages are more violent than cohabiting arrangements of similar duration. However, it does not explain why the rate of violence is appreciably higher for cohabiting couples who have lived together from one to ten years.

Summary and Conclusions

The hypothesis that the rate of violence among marrieds is higher than among cohabitors was not supported. The data show the reverse relationship to be significant. Overall, cohabitors are more violent than marrieds. However, certain cohabitors, in particular those who are over 30, divorced women, those with high incomes, and those who had been together for over ten years, had very low rates of violence. In fact, cohabitors with these characteristics were less violent than their married counterparts.

These differences in rates of violence in cohabiting as opposed to marital relationships are striking, fascinating, and difficult to interpret adequately. Because of the small number of cohabitors in the sample, these results must be treated cautiously. Overall, the findings suggest that the idea that relationships of cohabitors are less violent because of a commitment to non-violent counter-culture ideology or because such relationships can be dissolved more easily due to the lack of legal and social barriers around them, may be ill-founded. It appears that both marriage and cohabitation, as intimate relationships, involve conflict and, often, violence.

One possible reason that rates of violence are so high among cohabitors is that violence may be interpreted as a symbol of love by some. The joke about the woman who is concerned that her husband doesn't love her anymore because he hasn't smacked her in a week illustrates this point. Love, intimacy, conflict, and violence are closely entwined in our culture (Foss, 1979). It may be that for *some* cohabitors physical violence toward one's partner serves as a symbol of closeness and ownership in the absence of a legal license and label.

The fact that some cohabitors are more violent than marrieds, whereas cohabitors with the characteristics listed above appear less violent, provides empirical evidence for the view that cohabitation should not be seen as a unitary phenomenon. In attempting to understand various aspects of cohabitation it is important to avoid thinking in terms of the stereotype of living together couples which has been perpetuated by the presently available research. That research, having focused almost entirely on college students, tends to portray such relationships as liberal and avant-garde. Cole's (1977, p. 76) review of the cohabitation literature, suggests that more attention needs to be given to distinguishing between the types of cohabitation because couples differ in their motives for entering such relationships. Data from the present study support the idea that there may be a number of *different* types of cohabiting relationships, and that only a portion of such unions can be regarded as a liberal alternative to traditional marriage.

The findings of this research also help to clarify the nature of violence among intimates. Of the several factors affecting violence which were considered, marrieds and cohabitors differed, in terms of direction of the relationship, only where divorced women were involved. Overall, the findings indicate that the same variables which explain spousal violence in marriage, explain violence among cohabitors, only more so. Cohabitors and marrieds who are over thirty, have a high income, or have been together for over ten years have very low violence rates. In general, rates of violence are higher among the young and the poor, whether they are married or living together. However, the married couples within this group seem to be ahead in coping with their problems, as they are less violent than cohabitors with the same characteristics. The greater social support and integration in the kin network of the married couple may explain this difference.

A number of implications emerge from the findings of this research. First, the high rate of violence among cohabitors has legal implications which should be investigated further. We know little about the response of police and the legal system to an unmarried woman with a violent partner. While the married woman may receive little help from the police, the cohabiting woman may receive none at all. Since her relationship is still illegal in many states, the cohabiting woman may be regarded as less moral and less deserving of protection than her married counterpart. She may be trapped in a relationship because of a tangle of emotional and financial reasons, yet her legal recourses are limited.

These findings also have implications for social services. The image that cohabitation is a liberal lifestyle, freely chosen as an alternative to traditional marriage, may obscure the need which many cohabitors have for the support of social agencies. The isolation or estrangement of living-together couples from the support of kin networks may enhance their need for help from other sources.

Finally the finding that cohabitors are more violent than marrieds has implications for family life educators. This research underscores the inherent conflict in all intimate relationships. It is important for students to understand that the avoidance of legal marriage, alone, will not eliminate the problems which wives and husbands must face within their relationship. In fact some of the problems may be exacerbated. The ability to discuss, negotiate, and manage conflict nonviolently are important skills for all, regardless of the type of intimate lifestyle they choose.

REFERENCE NOTE

1 . Hennon, C. *Interpersonal violence and its management by cohabiting couples.* Paper presented at the Western Social Science Meeting, Tempe, Arizona, April 29-May 1, 1976.

REFERENCES

Cole, C. Cohabitation in social context. In R. Libby & R. Whitehurst (Eds.), *Marriage and alternatives: Exploring intimate relationships.* Glenview, III.: Scott Foresman, 1977.

Foss, J. E. The paradoxical nature of family relationships and family conflict. In M. A. Straus & G. T. Hotaling, *The social causes of husband-wife violence.* University of Minnesota Press, (In press).

Gagnon, J., & Greenblatt, C. S. *Life designs.* Glenview, Illinois: Scott, Foresman, 1978.

Gelles, R. J., & Straus, M. A. Determinants of violence in the family: Toward a theoretical integration. In W. R. Burr, R. Hill, F. I. Nye, & I. L. Reiss (Eds.), *Contemporary theories about the family.* New York: Free Press, 1979.

Glick, P. C., & Norton, A. J. *Marrying, divorcing, and living together in the U.S. today.* Washington, D.C.: Population Reference Bureau, 1977.

Henze, L., & Hudson, J. Personal and family characteristics of cohabiting and non-cohabiting students. *Journal of Marriage and the Family*, 1974, **36**, 722-727.

Levinger, G. Marital cohesiveness and dissolution: An integrative review. *Journal of Marriage and the Family*, 1965, **27**, 19-28.

Macklin, E. D. Heterosexual cohabitation among unmarried college students. *The Family Coordinator*, 1972, **21**, 463-472.

Peterman, D., Ridley, C., & Anderson, S. Comparison of cohabiting and non-cohabiting students. *Journal of Marriage and the Family*, 1974, **36**, 344-354.

Stark, R., & McEvoy, J. Middle class violence. *Psychology Today*, 1970, **4**, 52-65.

Stafford, R., Backman, B., & Dibona, P. Division of labor among cohabiting and married couples. *Journal of Marriage and the Family*, 1977, **39**, 43-57.

Straus, M. A. Sexual inequality, cultural norms, and wife-beating. *Victimology*, 1976, **1**, 54-76. Also reprinted in E. C. Viano (Ed.), *Victims and society*. Washington, D.C.: Visage Press, 1976, and in J. R. Chapman & M. Gates (Eds.), *Women into wives: The legal and economic impact on marriage*. Sage Yearbooks in Women Policy Studies, Vol. 2, Beverly Hills, Calif.: Sage, 1977.

Straus, M. A. Measuring intrafamily conflict and violence: The Conflict Tactics (CT) scales. *Journal of Marriage and the Family*, 1979, **41**, 75-88.

Straus, M. A., Gelles, R. J., & Steinmetz, S. K. *Behind closed doors: Violence in the American family*. New York: Anchor/Doubleday, 1980.

Sussman, M. B. The isolated nuclear family: Fact or fiction?" *Social Problems*, 1959, **6**, 333-339.

Whitehurst, R. N. Violence in husband-wife interaction. In S. K. Steinmetz & M. A. Straus (Eds.), *Violence in the Family*. New York: Harper & Row, 1974.

Yllo, K. Non-marital cohabitation: Beyond the college campus. *Alternative Lifestyles*, 1978, **1**, 37-54.

PART V

ALCOHOLISM, DRUG ABUSE, AND THE FAMILY

This article examines these myths and presents the realities as perceived by the author at this time.

22

MYTH AND REALITY IN THE FAMILY PATTERNS AND TREATMENT OF SUBSTANCE ABUSERS*

Edward Kaufman

MYTHS IN FAMILY PATTERNS

1. Families where the identified patient (IP) has a drug problem are different from families wherein the IP has an alcohol problem.

2. Family relationships are relatively unimportant in the genesis and perpetuation of substance abuse.

3. Family relationships are the key factors in causing and maintaining most if not all substance abuse.

4. The intense transgenerational coalition between mother and son is unique to substance abuse and is the most important pathologic factor in these families.

5. Fathers in this group are disengaged, brutal, and/or alcoholic.

6. Familial factors are so inconsistent that they are generalizable to all social classes and ethnic groups.

7. Familial factors in male substance abusers are generalizable to females.

*Based on the 15th Donovan Memorial Lecture delivered for Eagleville Hospital on May 15, 1980 in Valley Forge, Pennsylvania.

From Edward Kaufman, "Myth and Reality in the Family Patterns and Treatment of Substance Abusers," *American Journal of Drug and Alcohol Abuse,* 1980, 7, pp. 257-279. Reprinted by permission of the publisher and author.

8. The addict-parental pair triangle is so crucial that the role of siblings can be overlooked.

9. Family structures observed at one point in time are generalizable to other time periods in the family's life cycle.

10. We are presently knowledgeable about the family structures of substance abusers.

MYTHS IN FAMILY THERAPY

The major myths in family therapy deal with whether therapy does or does not work and what the techniques and parameters are which enable it to work best. These myths include:

A. Family therapy can be done while a family member is dysfunctional on chemicals.

B. Family therapy can be successful if limited to dyads, either addict-spouse or addict-single parent.

C. Family therapy alone is sufficient to reverse the problem.

D. Family therapy techniques which work with one socioethnic group will work with all or most groups.

E. All information revealed in individual sessions should be shared with the entire family.

F. Family therapy of substance abusers is best done in individual family therapy, exclusive of multifamily groups.

G. Psychoanalytic and psychodynamic family therapies have no role in substance abuse.

H. It is unnecessary for a family therapist to have his/her own family therapy or family work.

I. Family therapy can be successful when the family therapist has no significant responsibility for overall treatment.

J. Paradoxical therapeutic techniques are an essential part of an effective family therapist's armamentarium.

K. The efficacy of family therapy with substance abusers has been adequately demonstrated.

FAMILY PATTERN MYTHS AND REALITIES

Myth 1: *Families where the identified patient (IP) has a drug problem are different from families wherein the IP has an alcohol problem.* Most of the research on this myth has been done by researchers at Eagleville Hospital, and their detailed work in this field will be summarized.

A major issue about these differences which is frequently overlooked has to do with the age and generation of the index patient. The literature on the family patterns of alcoholics deals with individuals who are mainly in their 40s. Thus the focus has been on their family of procreation which is also called the nuclear family. Studies of drug abusers generally deal with patients in their 20s and thus focus on their family of origin. Many arguments about differences are ludicrous as we are frequently addressing different generations of the same family. In over half of families with an IP who has a serious drug problem, there is also a parent with alcoholism [1, 2].

In the Eagleville study [1], where the age range between alcoholics and drug abusers tends to be less than in most noncombined facilities, the ages were 33 and 26 respectively. Sixty-two percent of alcoholics participated with their families of origin, as did 68% of drug dependents. Sixty-three percent of drug abusers and 68% of alcoholics had substance abusing relatives. Over half the substance abusing relatives in both groups were fathers who abused alcohol. One difference in the two groups was that single parent families constituted 28% of alcoholics and 14% of drug dependents. Despite this, both groups of families were highly reactive to the substance abuse problem and included a substance abuser who was, in turn, highly dependent on parental figures.

Sixty-four percent of families of origin had an absent or peripheral father figure, with this occurring 5 to 1 in Black vs White families. Thus this conceptualization of the father is skewed by the 69% Black population in this study. The differences in Black families will be discussed under Myth 6. The occasional parental child role of the IP was also noted.

Olson [3] has pointed out that families should not be stereotyped based on presenting complaint (drugs or alcohol), but rather should be classified as to the way a specific system makes use of the system.

Myth 2: *The unimportance of family relationships.* Alexander and Dibb [4] have stated that "a minority of opiate addicts maintain close emotional and financial relationships with their parents." However, this statement was based on methadone patients in British Columbia. Methadone maintenance patients, in my experience, tend to insulate their families from therapy more than addicts in any other form of treatment. In the 18 families studied, it was noted that, when the father was present, he was dominant in 11 of 18 cases. However, their treatment sample was limited to Caucasians. Noone and Reddig [5] found that a majority of drug abusers and addicts, despite many mock separations, maintain close ties with their families or origin.

In a study of 85 addicts, Stanton *et al.* [6] noted that of male addicts with living parents, 82% saw their mothers and 58% saw their fathers at least weekly; 66% either lived with their parents or saw their mothers daily. In 1966, Vaillant [7] reported that 72% of addicts still lived with their mothers at age 22, and 47% continued to live with a female blood relative after age 30. Interestingly, Vaillant also noted that of the 30 abstinent addicts in his follow-up study, virtually all were living independently from their parents.

In a typology of alcoholic families which I developed with Pattison [8], the alcoholic is continuously and intimately involved with his or her family in three of four subtypes. It is only in the skid-row type of alcoholic that the family is absent. The Eagleville study mentioned previously also emphasizes the ongoing involvement of the family of origin and the family of procreation with the alcoholic [1].

Myth 3: *Family relationships are the key factors in causing and maintaining most if not all substance abuse.* Though this myth may be supported by the reality of Myth 2, it is included as a myth here to warn against overgeneralizing the crucial aspects of the family. My own family studies in two treatment programs in New York and Los Angeles included only one-quarter of the patients in each program [9]. My findings are therefore biased because I have only studied the types of families who come for treatment and excluded those who do not. My hypothesis is that enmeshed families come to treatment more often than disengaged ones. Thus these findings should not be generalized to the 75% of families who did not come in for treatment and study.

Binion [10] has studied a group of women heroin users from Detroit in comparison with a matched demographic sample. She found that differences between the two groups' perceptions of their family were minimal. She also stated that the control group was *three times* as likely to live at home. Although her study was based on interviews of only one person in the family and included no contact with the rest of the family, it emphasizes the importance of matched control groups before we make specific statements about addicts.

In one family I worked with, where the father and five of the six children were heroin addicts, there was considerable overt disengagement between family members. This family highlights the importance of the social milieu in producing and perpetuating substance abuse, particularly in urban ghettos.

As we emphasize the importance of the family, we should also not overlook genetic factors as well as the contributions of peer pressure and drug availability. However, the family's influence "accentuates or attenuates the impact of such external forces" [6]. Individual psychopathology and psychodynamics are critical etiologic factors but are also interwoven with family dynamics.

Myth 4: *The intense transgenerational coalition between mother and son is unique to substance abuse and is the most important pathologic factor in these families.* Many authors have noted the primary importance of the mother-son dyad in substance abuse. However, their contributions were made in the early years of family observation when dyads were emphasized over total family systems. Fort [11] noted that such mothers were "overprotective, controlling, and indulgent" and "they were willing to do anything for their sons, except let them alone." In a comparison of mothers of drug addicts, schizophrenics, and normal adolescents, the mother's symbiotic need for the child was highest in the mothers of drug abusers [12]. In my own studies of the mothers of heroin addicts, I found that 88% were enmeshed with the IP. Only 2.6% were classified as disengaged [9]. A critical issue about this myth is the uniqueness of the mother-son transgenerational coalition to substance abuse. Indeed, the enmeshment between mother and IP has been cited as the primary family pattern in schizophrenia, male homosexuality, childhood asthma, school phobias, and anaclytic depressions. I have begun a study in which families of alcoholics are compared with families of hospitalized, depressed patients to determine if the family structures of these two groups differ significantly from each other.

Another problem with overemphasizing the primacy of the mother-son dyad is the lack of daughter-mother and daughter-father data in the field. Alexander and Dibb [4] have speculated that the same sex parent may be as overinvolved, indulgent, and overprotective of the addict as the opposite sex parent in middle class families.

Alcoholism programs, on the other hand, have not focused on the relationships between the male alcoholic and his mother but on the alcoholic-spouse dyad. They have all too frequently overlooked the importance of the alcoholic-parent dyad, as it produces and perpetuates alcoholism, as well as shapes the relationship of the alcoholic to his/her spouse.

Myth 5: *Fathers are disengaged, brutal, and/or alcoholic.* This myth may be reality for a simple majority of substance abusers; however, it is not the case in many instances. In my own work, 43% of fathers were disengaged, but 41% were enmeshed [9]. This is related to the specific ethnic biases in my sample, which will be discussed shortly, but emphasizes the importance of the father in many middle class ethnic groups as well as when the IP is female. Also, some paternal disengagement may be reactive to early enmeshment patterns such as incest or disappointment with a child's not living up to expectations. Paternal disengagement is facilitated by a society which sanctions the father's involvement with job-related, social, and recreational activities. Some paternal disengagement, even physical separation, may be superficial as deep emotional ties are maintained.

Brutality and disengagement are not synonymous. In fact, a great deal of brutality takes place in enmeshed families. In my study, physical brutality was common between Italian fathers and their sons [9]. However, this was a multigenerational problem which was a part of enmeshed intimacy. Italian fathers felt that their own fathers who had beaten them loved them deeply, and so passed this legacy on to their sons. It is much easier for enmeshed fathers to hit a child once or twice than enforce a discipline over hours and days. Also, in my study [9], many sons worked directly for their fathers, particularly in construction fields. They were frequently protected in this way from having to meet the usual demands of employment and were locked into their fathers 24 hr a day. These sons are nevertheless preoccupied with how unfair their fathers are to them. In the Binion survey [10], female addicts saw their fathers as "helpful, loving people" although they "slightly favored their mothers."

Myth 6: *Familial factors are so consistent that they are generalizable to all social classes and ethnic groups.* There have been very few attempts to delineate family patterns in different social classes and ethnic groups. My own studies are just a beginning and are limited by small samples in each ethnic group, as well as by variation in participation. When the resident was Italian or Jewish, his/her entire family of origin almost always attended family therapy. Hispanic spouses came but not their families of origin. A few Black mothers came, and Protestant families stayed away. There are many regional differences within ethnic groups. In particular, Puerto Rican and Mexican-American families have many similarities as well as differences. So do northern and southern Italian families, urban and rural Blacks, and so forth.

In the majority of Italian and Jewish families that I studied, the entire family, including the father, was quite enmeshed. Puerto Rican and Protestant fathers were quite disengaged and/or absent from therapy. Most of the Black families had strong, involved mothers and absent or passive fathers. One Greek family had three totally enmeshed generations, which is quite typical of Greek families without an addict.

Binion's [10] studies also emphasize the importance of comparing matched samples of nonaddicted comparable ethnic groups before we confirm that family patterns are related to disease rather than ethnicity. Ablon [13], in a study of middle-class Catholic families who were primarily Irish, German and Italian, has pointed out that cultural prescriptions regarding behavior and attitude directly and indirectly relate to drinking patterns and contribute to the mode of the "alcoholic family" system.

These ethnic differences within addict families are related to normal relationship trends within these families when there is no addict present. Teasing out family sustaining ethnic patterns from those which cause and perpetuate substance abuse is a difficult but exciting prospect.

Myth 7: *Familial factors in male substance abusers are generalizable to females.* Colten [14] compared male and female addicts from Detroit, Los Angeles, and Miami. She found that women addicts, compared with addicted men, are lower in self-esteem, higher in anxiety and depression, less assertive, and have less control over their lives. Women addicts are more feminine and less adrogynous than a matched control group. They are more frequently separated, divorced, or never married than addicted men. The fathers and mothers of women addicts are more poorly educated than a control group. One evidence of paternal disengagement in this study is that "addicted women are a little more than twice as likely not to know the level of their father's education."

Also, despite their idealization of their parents, women were more likely to be punished by restriction, extra work and "being screamed and yelled at." They also listed hassles from parents as the third most important reason they used heroin [14].

As expected, drinking was a problem in 60% of addicts' families and, perhaps surprisingly, in 43% of controls' families.

In my own work, I found that the relationship between mothers and daughters tended to be extremely hostile, competitive and, at times, chaotic. Half the mother-daughter relationships were severely enmeshed. When her mother suicided, a severely enmeshed daughter also made a serious suicide attempt. I have also seen fathers deeply enmeshed with their addict daughters in much the same way that mothers are with addict sons. The incidence of incest in the histories of female addicts has been found to be quite high, and in later years this generally leads to reactive disengagement, particularly after father-daughter incest.

My observations of female addicts who are spouses of male addicts are that these women are generally quite passive [9]. They have frequently been introduced to drugs by their male partners who feel a strong need to control their heroin use. They buy for them, inject them, and beat them if they buy heroin from someone else, discouraging and prohibiting any autonomy including that associated with drug use. There is also a significant minority of assertive female addicts, particularly those who have come to addiction on their own rather than having been led to it by a mate. Parenthetically, some of these assertive women addicts have the capacity to become excellent therapists and program directors.

There is also a rapidly emerging literature on the differences between female and male alcoholics. Female alcoholics tend to marry male alcoholics, but male alcoholics rarely marry female alcoholics [8]. Individuals tend to choose spouses with equal levels of ego strength and self-awareness but with opposite ways of dealing with stress. We see frequently that opposites attract in male-female relationships, particularly obsessives and hysterics. In such relationships each person sees him-herself as giving in to the other. The one who gives in the most becomes "deselfed" and is vulnerable to a drinking problem [15]. If it is the wife, she begins drinking during the day to help her through her chores, hiding it from the husband to be ready for ideal togetherness when he returns—until she passes out several times and the problem is recognized.

Women's drinking tends to be more hidden and more triggered by specific life events than their male counterparts [16]. Women alcoholics are more likely to have affective disorders and men to be sociopathic. Thus males are less accepting of their wives' drinking and tend to leave alcoholic wives more easily [8]. Women tend to start heavy drinking later than men, when their personal inadequacy and lack of self-realization lead to an awareness that the promises of youth cannot be fulfilled. The empty nest etiology of alcoholism focuses mainly on women.

Thus we see, and not surprisingly so, that familial factors in female substance abusers are quite different from those in males. Yet the literature is replete with assumptions about family dynamics based on studies of male patients.

Myth 8: *The addict parental pair triangle is so crucial that the role of siblings can be overlooked.* This is obviously a myth, yet it is often treated as fact, particularly in treatment. In my studies [9], siblings tended to fall equally into two basic categories: one group was composed of fellow addicts whose drug dependence was inextricably fused with that of the resident; the other group was composed of "good" siblings. These were parental children who assumed an authoritarian role when the father was disengaged and/or were themselves highly successful. Some of these successful siblings had individuated from the family, but many were still enmeshed. A small group of "good" siblings were quite passive and not involved with substance abuse. Some of these developed psychosomatic symptoms like headaches. Enmeshed addicted siblings buy drugs for and from each other, inject one another, set each other up to be arrested, or even pimp for one another. At times, a large family may show sibling relationships of all of the above types. Many successful older siblings were quite prominent in their fields, and in these cases the addict sibling withdrew from any vocational achievement rather than compete.

At times, the addict's sibling role in the family is as a parental child where he/she has no way of asking for relief from responsibilities except through the use of drugs and ultimate collapse through drugs.

Myth 9: *Family structures observed at one point in time are genralizable to other time periods in the family's life cycle.* We frequently assume that what we find in the families of substance abusers predates and helps cause substance abuse. My impression is that this is basically true, but that most problems and pathological sets are greatly intensified after substance abuse develops. Thus it is difficult to say how much substance abuse has intensified a "normal" ethnically determined pattern. There are no longitudinal studies which have demonstrated these patterns prior to substance abuse. Valliant's [17] prospective study of 184 50-year-old alcoholics, who were first studied during their college years, showed no correlation between poor childhood, early personality instability, and alcoholism. Kammeier *et al.* [18] demonstrated that pathologic MMPI profiles in alcoholics were not observed in the same individuals 15 years before they became alcoholic.

Another challenge of this myth is that families change structures and move through phases of enmeshment and disengagement after substance abuse develops [6]. For example, co-alcoholics become progressively more deeply enmeshed as the alcoholic worsens. Much disengagement is reactive to enmeshment. This is particularly true when there are incestuous enmeshed relationships as these invariably lead to disengagement. This may also happen when parents expect a child to fulfill all their wished-for achievements. When the child does not, this type of parent will cut off all ties as a reactive disengagement.

Olson has described one family as "The Chaotic Flippers." This alcoholic family vacillated rapidly from disengaged to enmeshed [19]. Aponte [20] has also noted that poverty stricken families (which constitute the majority of all addict families) are frequently underorganized. He points out that boundaries shift rapidly in such families as a result of each individual's inability to find constancy, differentiation, and flexibility in society.

Myth 10: *We are presently knowledgeable about the family structures of substance abusers.* The obvious summation based on my first nine myths is that we are not. One reason our knowledge is so limited is that our research base is so poor. Studies in this field have been limited to two basic types:

observation of family behavior and interview/questionnaires of the substance abuser. The two major problems with family observation studies to date are that they are almost exclusively limited to families who volunteer for treatment, and that they have not been quantified. We cannot assume that families who volunteer for treatment are similar to those who do not. It is a reasonable hypothesis that families who readily become involved in treatment are more enmeshed than those who do not. As we involve more resistant and probably more disengaged families, we will obtain a more balanced view. Stanton and Todd have demonstrated that, with great effort, resistant families can become engaged in treatment [21]; their success in recruiting 89% of families, once they have the IP's permission to contact them, may indicate that their research encompasses families who do not have the biases of limitation to those who volunteer for treatment. Hopefully the field in general will progress to a broader base of families upon which to base our observations.

With the exception of Stanton *et al.*'s work [2] there has been very little published work on quantifiable studies of family structures of substance abusers. Fortunately, there are at present studies under way by Olson, Wellisch, and Steinglass using such quantifiable instruments as Olson's FACES [22] and Moos's FES [23] to study family structures.

Studies which are solely limited to the index patient's opinions of his/her family can of course be done in an entire treatment population. These studies have serious limitations because of the IP's bias. In addition, they tell us nothing about the families of substance abusers when neither the IP nor the family enters treatment. Surveys of all drug abusers, whether in treatment or not, have also been done in high schools or catchment areas, but these also tend to be biased by presenting only the observations of the interviewee, invariably emphasizing the importance of peers over family.

In my early years in this field, I attempted to survey family dynamics of Columbia University heroin users who were not in treatment, through the use of a technique known as the "psychoanalytic interview" [24]. This involves a 1:1 unstructured interview which emphasizes dreams and fantasies. In this study, fathers were described as cold, distant, sadistic, competitive with their sons, and seductive with their daughters. Mothers were perceived as distant or overtly seductive. Although these findings were quite different from family observational studies, this study noted the symbiotic tie between addict siblings and helped alert me to this factor in my later work.

I hope that ongoing research in this field will clarify these issues. One study which should be done is a comparison of families with a substance abusing IP who volunteer for an intensive family treatment program with similar families who do not. In the summer of 1980 I began a study of two matched groups of families; one group with a depressed IP and the other with an alcoholic IP to determine what, if any, differences there are between "alcoholic" families and "depressed" families. In addition, the insider/outsider approach to family evaluation as developed by Olson [25] will be utilized. Thus each family member will rate the family through the 111-question FACES and, in addition, the family will be observed and rated through the Clinical Rating Scale [26]. This permits a cross validation between the families' views of themselves and a trained observer's view.

FAMILY THERAPY MYTHS AND REALITIES

All myths in family therapy deal with the effectiveness of this technique— whether it works or not, for whom it is necessary or contraindicated, when it works best, and how to make it work. My general view is that family therapy is a very helpful if not essential aspect of the treatment of substance abuse. The better and more flexible the treatment program, the more effective will be the family therapy, particularly if the parameters of reality delineated in these myths are followed.

A. *Family therapy can be done while a family member is dysfunctional on chemicals.* Family therapy is difficult when a non-IP is substance dysfunctional and, in my experience, almost impossible when the IP is substance dysfunctional. On the other hand, many families in which one or more members continue to use substances desperately need family intervention and will not accept a therapy which expects them to cease substance abuse as a precondition for beginning therapy. My basic premise is that if the substance abuser's intake is so severe that he or she is unable to attend sessions without being under the influence and/or if functioning is severely impaired, then the first priority is interrupting the pattern of abuse, at least temporarily. Thus my first goal is to persuade the family to pull together to initiate detoxification or at least some measure to achieve temporary abstinence. Generally, this is best done in a hospital and, if the abuse pattern is severe, I will require this in the first session or very early in the therapy. If the drinking is only moderately severe or intermittent, such as binge alcoholism or stimulant abuse, then I would offer the family alternatives as to how to initiate this temporary substance-free state. These include social detoxification centers, regular attendance at Alcoholics Anonymous, and Antabuse for alcoholics or detoxification and methadone maintenance for heroin addicts. Antabuse should generally not be given to a family member for daily distribution, as this tends to reinforce the family's being locked into the alcoholic's drinking or not drinking. Benzodiazepines are discouraged because they tend to become a part of the problem rather than a solution. In general, treatment begins in a much more effective way if the patient is totally immersed in a 28-day residential treatment program which includes detoxification, individual and group therapy, AA and/or Narcotics Anonymous, and family therapy. This type of short-term residential program can be a most effective introduction to therapy. It seems to be more effective with alcoholics than with drug abusers, perhaps because of the power of AA as aftercare. For many drug abusers and particularly addicts, insistence on long-term residential treatment is the only alternative. Most families will not accept this until other methods have failed. In order to accomplish this, a therapist must maintain long-term ties with the family, even through multiple treatment failure.

Bowen [15] and Berenson [27] have developed treatment approaches for working with families while a member continues to drink problematically. I know of no successful programs for working with the families of presently addicted drug abusers, through some structuralists may theoretically feel this could be done by first changing family structures. Berenson [27] offers a series of steps and chores for the nonalcoholic spouse which I have found clinically useful, particularly when the drinking member refuses to enter or return to treatment:

Step 1. Calm down system and provide clarity.
Step 2. Create a support system for family members so that the emotional intensity isn't all within the session or relationship with the alcoholic. This can be done by jobs, housing, recreation, friendships, social agencies, vocational training, or Al-Anon. In Al-Anon the group and/or the sponsor may provide emotional support and calm down the situation.

Steps 1 and 2 may also be facilitated by a group for spouses and significant others which they attend in addition to Al-Anon. This group provides support to the spouse, and frequently, after several months, the alcoholic will join the spouse in a couples group. In this group and in individual therapy the spouse can be given three choices [27]: (a) keep doing exactly what you are doing, (b) detach or emotionally distance from the alcoholic, or (c) separate or physically distance. When the client chooses to not change, it is overt; in this case, it is the first choice (a). When clients do not choose (b) or (c), the therapist can point out that they are in effect choosing (a). Spouses are helped to not criticize drinking, to accept it, to live with the alcoholic, and to be responsible for their own reactivity regarding drinking.

The spouse is presented with three choices, all of which seem impossible to carry out. The problem is resolved by choosing one of three courses of action and following through, or by experiencing the helplessness and powerlessness of these situations being repeated and clarified. The spouse then shares despair and "hits bottom" sufficiently to become responsible for himself or herself rather than continuing to try to change the alcoholic. When the spouse distances, the alcoholic will get worse in order to get the spouse back into the entanglement. The therapist must predict and prepare the spouse for this situation. If the spouse can say "I prefer you not to kill yourself (or me), but I am powerless to do so," it is unlikely that the alcoholic will kill himself or someone else [27]. As part of the initial contract that I make with a couple where one member is abusing substances, I request that the spouse commit him/herself to continue in the spouse group if the IP drops out, generally because of resuming heavy substance abuse.

Whenever we maintain therapy with a "wet" alcoholic or drug abusing system, we have the responsibility of not maintaining the illusion that families are resolving problems, while in fact they are really reinforcing them.

The problem of the family that comes to therapy for an identified substance abuser, but that has one or more other abusers in the family, is a difficult but common one. In general, the rules of thumb just discussed are applicable here; that is, family therapy is difficult or impossible to initiate while there is dysfunctional substance abuse. However, there is a difference here. One rule of structural family therapy is to alleviate the symptom of the IP *before* focusing on symptoms in other family members. When these other symptoms are dealt with, they should then be reframed in the context of helping the IP. The most common situation of this type is a family that enters treatment for help with a drug-abusing teenager. We generally learn in the first session that father drinks, and shortly thereafter that he is an alcoholic, which he in turn usually denies. This family must ultimately be treated as if the father were the IP. However, in the type of family I've described, it cannot be done too early, or the father, feeling scapegoated, will retaliate by attacking everyone else and force the family out of treatment. Thus the best sequence is joining the entire family, alleviating the IP's symptoms, and dealing with parental alcoholism later. At times, the parental alcoholism must be dealt with first when this is necessary to begin to alter the IP's symptoms. If the total family is joined with first, this can be done. However, the more severely an alcoholic drinks the more difficult it is to join with him/her.

As we work with wet systems over long periods of time, we risk becoming like the parent or spouse who supports substance abuse to maintain contact, in the hope that this contact will lead to abstinence. We must avoid promoting this type of regressive step. The balance required in maintaining contact without infantilizing and in timing an interdiction about substance abuse is a vital part of the art of psychotherapy.

B. *Family therapy can be successful if limited to dyads, either addict-spouse or addict-single parent.* In my experience, family therapy limited to any dyad is most difficult. The mother-addicted son dyad is an almost impossible one to treat if no other family member is involved. Someone else *must* be brought in if treatment is to succeed. This may be a drug-free sibling, grandparent, aunt, uncle, cousin, or the mother's lover or ex-spouse. If there is absolutely no one else available, multiple family therapy provides surrogates to facilitate restructuring and other family approaches.

Therapy limited to alcoholics and their spouses has been a traditional family approach to alcoholism. All too often, this has excluded the crucial parents or progeny of the alcoholic. Children are not just victims of alcoholic families. By their reciprocating involvement in these sytems, they contribute to the problem and are a necessary part of the solution regardless of age. A young child may encourage a parent to drink in order to dampen violence or to loosen controls to a point where affection is shown. Alcoholic parents may drink because they are unable to curb their adolescent children's drug and/or alcohol abuse. Adolescents may provoke a cycle of drinking and fighting in parents so that they then are unable to set limits and enforce punishments. A 14-year-old, whenever limits were placed on him to tidy his room, would point out to his mother that his father (dry for 3 years) did not tidy his, thereby undermining their beginning efforts to jointly set limits for him, as mother accepted the "old tape" and restarted her old arguments with her spouse. The parents of alcoholics stay involved as long as drinking continues. Thus the most effective family approach to alcoholism is one which involves the entire family network and works with individual subsystems as tailored to the needs of each family.

Treatment which focuses on drug addicts and their spouses has been less effective than with alcoholic couples. This had led Stanton and Todd [21] to suggest that family treatment of narcotic addicts begin with their parents, and that the addict-spouse couple should not be worked with until his parents are brought to a point of cooperation and can "release" him to his spouse. Phoenix House has found so much difficulty with addicted couples that they insist on separate residences for such couples. At The Awakening

Family, in California, we have met with some success with treating addicted couples in the same program. Success is enhanced by insisting on couple therapy throughout the duration of their stay in the program. Another essential aspect of treating such couples when they have children is focusing on their function as a parenting team. The addict has always neglected his/her function as a parent, and therapy which involves progeny has the distinct advantage of developing parenting skills *in vivo*.

Thus I strongly advise the importance of a four-generational approach, involving grandparents, parents, spouse, and children. When most other family problems are resolved, a couples group can be very helpful, but it should never be the sole modality of family therapy.

C. *Family therapy alone is sufficient to reverse the problem.* I feel that this myth has been propagated and perpetuated by family therapists who have approached substance abusers without prior experience in working with this type of patient. With drug addicts and abusers my family approach would be useless without methadone, propoxyphene or clonidine detoxification, methadone and LAAM maintenance, Naltrexone, residential therapeutic communities, hospital detoxification, Narcotics Anonymous, specialized vocational rehabilitation, individual and group psychotherapy, particularly the techniques of ex-addicts [29], and so on. Similarly with alcoholics, I would feel powerless without AA, Al-Anon, Al-Ateen, Antabuse, specialized alcohol residential treatment, relaxation techniques, or medication to treat underlying affective and psychotic disorders.

D. *Family therapy techniques which work with one socioethnic group will work with all or most groups.* We must know the social and cultural patterns of each group that we work with if we are to join with and change that group. Without that knowledge, joining and change are almost impossible. My own success with Jewish families is not a coincidence but a reflection of my knowledge of their cultural norms, how these affect family function, and their amenability to intervention. This knowledge helps me work well with similar families ·such as Italians and Greeks, although this may be explained more by the emotional kinship between these families and myself than by knowledge. Cultural knowledge of Hispanic families teaches us to expand the social phase of family contact, to respect machismo; of Blacks to respect the strong matriarchy and the parental child and to search for the everpresent but hidden male. Asking a three-generational Italian family to not eat together daily is assigning a difficult task, but one which we accomplished with the support of a multiple family group. On the other hand, first generation Hispanics do not share well in such groups, particularly when they are in the minority. The list of cultural taboos and strengths is endless, and the more one understands these, the better one will be able to work with each group.

  E. *All information revealed in individual sessions or sessions with particular dyads and subsets should be shared with the entire family.* This principle is based on the finest motives: honesty, integrity, openness, and avoiding coalitions between the therapist and family members which exclude others. Yet family therapy requires more flexibility than this. To encourage a married couple, or an entire family, to share everything with one another is to forfeit their boundaries and encourage enmeshment [30]. At times, one can only learn critical information, such as the existence of an affair, if one pledges total confidentiality. In general, it is best to be flexible about sharing information, while remaining aware that withholding information forms coalitions with the therapist which (a) may or may not be compatible with goals for restructuring and (b) may render the therapist impotent to bring about change.

  F. *Family therapy of substance abusers is best done in individual family therapy exclusive of multifamily groups.* My broad use of multiple family therapy (MFT) has already been discussed. I feel that MFT is a very helpful and at times necessary adjunct to family therapy. It is particularly helpful, as cited earlier, with single parent families. MFT offers relief from the loneliness and pain of having a substance abuser in the family. It forms a new supportive network, a family of families which offers an alternative to a network of drug abuse facilitators and substance abusers. It is easy for parents to offer conflict-free parenting to the children of others and then apply these principles to their own family. Substance abusers also gain insights from the family work of others which they apply to themselves. They may also act as therapist and enforcers of tasks when they accompany their peers on family visits [31].

  In MFT, members make changes through group pressure and support that would be otherwise impossible. One of the most striking examples of this is "closing the back door" (i.e., helping parents to not take their children back home in a conspiracy to undermine and terminate treatment), which is a prime goal of any MFT in a residential setting. Without MFT, many substance abusers will persuade their families to take them back to protect them from "unfairness" and "harsh discipline" in much the same way as they have manipulated their families to protect them from jail, overdoses, and creditors. To work this problem through in individual family therapy requires interruption of the patterns of guilt and severe enmeshment, and considerable restructuring. In MFT it is done much more easily by group support and insight [31]. A mother will say, "Yes, I thought I was protecting my child from jail and suicide by giving him money for durgs. Now I know that was what was killing him. To take him back before he has graduated would also be killing him, and I must not kill my child by taking him back now." This group pressure is so strong that one psychotic mother, whose episodes were triggered by her son to continue her overprotection, was able to say to her son in MFT—right after she emerged from psychosis, "I will not hold you to me anymore" [31].

G. *Psychoanalytic and psychodynamic family therapy has no role in substance abuse.* A basic premise which answers this myth is: The more you know about a family, the better a therapist you will be for that family. I do not feel that extensive information about a family limits the spontaneity of the therapist. At the very least, a detailed genogram should be done on every family at the first session. This can be done without miring the family in the past, their using the past as a cop-out, or encouraging the replay of "old tapes."

Understanding the family's past permits the most detailed treatment plan, providing the therapist with a framework which he/she can use as a basis for spontaneous interaction with the family. In this way, detailed knowledge of the family facilitates free interaction rather than dampens it.

The second major issue in answer to this myth deals with the use of psychodynamic interpretations. Such interventions first require confrontation of the family's misuse of the past. These interpretations use Menninger's [32] triangle of insight—the past, the present, and the relationship with the therapist—to create change in the present. Insight is only intellectual until the psychoanalytic work of working through and working over is done, and then it is real or emotional insight. The psychoanalytic technique of working through is not substantially different from the structural technique of giving tasks in the session and at home and reassigning similar tasks until change takes place.

Thus interpretations utilizing the past are helpful if they are done without blaming, guilt induction, and dwelling on the hopelessness of long-standing patterns. A psychoanalytic interpretation can be used directively to accomplish immediate shifts in the family system. For example, a family presented with a 17-year-old son who had lost his license as the result of an accident while intoxicated. Immediately after disciplining the son for driving in a car where beer was consumed, the mother embraced and kissed him because she could not bear to have him suffer the pain of punishment. When she was given the task of disciplining him without embracing him, she was asked to remember that all discipline did not include being held by the feet and dipped head first into a bucket of water, as she had been "disciplined" as a child. Another mother who could not ask for support from her husband was reminded that she was not a Cossack army officer, as her rigid father had been and had demanded that she be, and was able to ask for the support she needed in session.

H. *It is unnecessary for a family therapist to have his/her own family therapy or family work.* Proponents of this myth (Haley, Minuchin, Stanton) believe that therapists, like families, can change their behavior without understanding their dynamics. The arguments for my rebuttal of this myth are similar to those in Myth G. The more a therapist understands his/her own family, the more the therapist will be able to use him/herself as a facilitator of restructuring. To join a family and not be drawn into antitherapeutic coalitions requires insight about one's position in one's own family. A living family sculpture of one's own family, utilizing classmates as family members, can bring about a great deal of affective laden understanding. My own 6-year personal psychoanalysis has given me a great deal of understanding of my own family, though a course of family therapy might have given me greater knowledge in a much shorter period of time. Having been a student and teacher in several T.O.E. courses has also helped me understand my own family patterns.

I. *Family therapy can be successful when the family therapist has no significant responsibility for overall treatment* [28]. That this is a myth is obvious, yet it is reenacted repeatedly in most treatment programs. Without responsibility for treatment, the family therapist will be triangulated with the primary therapist by the patient and will be relegated to the role of the weaker parent. One can work very hard with a family to facilitate methadone detoxification but, without control over the dosage, be defeated by a coalition between the IP and the methadone staff. In an MFT in a residential treatment center, the younger addicted brother's repeated undermining and devastation of the IP became clear. However, the information that the former revealed was sufficient to cause the IP to become discharged from the treatment center and led to such chaos that a junior staff member also resigned. The family therapist's control of treatment could have avoided this repetition, but it would have been at the cost of overlooking a basic policy of the program. The more responsibility we as family therapists have for treatment, the more effective we are, and hopefully the more effective the overall treatment program is.

J. *Paradoxical therapeutic techniques are an essential part of an effective family therapist's armamentarium.* Paradox is one of the most exciting techniques to be applied recently to the family therapy of substance abusers. It seems to work particularly well with these family systems because their rigidity and circularity resist intrusive therapeutic techniques. The paradox uses unexpected, puzzling, and creative techniques which are quite seductive to therapists [33]. Writers on this subject [30, 33] use their very persuasive style to convince us as therapists/readers to use these techniques, perhaps too frequently and with inappropriate patients. Although the reader is warned against abuses of the paradox by these writers, this may have a paradoxical effect on the beginning family therapist who may try to prove he can use the paradox when he/she should not (e.g., telling a suicidal patient to take his life). In addition, the proper use of paradox requires a certain personality style that one sees in hypnotherapists or in individuals who can readily assume a variety of roles. Many of us will never be able to adapt these techniques to our personalities and, when we try, we succeed only in alienating families. Minuchin [34] pointed out that "the road is how you walk it," which means that we must know ourselves in order to know those techniques which we can best use.

As we study paradoxical theory and technique, we must not lose sight of the extent to which families will change directly. This is done by skillful joining, and facilitated by the talent, reputation, charisma and, to borrow from Castenada, the "personal power" of the therapist. The support of their own extended family or of an MFT will also help many family members to change.

An example of a family who did well with nonparadoxical directives follows. This family saw me intermittently for over a year, initially because two teenage sons were arrested for marijuana possession. This family has made many gains, all based on direct restructuring tasks. They have learned to let their 5-year-old pick up his own toys in session and at home, to permit their 18-year-old daughter to move out, and to diminish the three older siblings parenting of the 5-year-old. The parents agreed on the punishments for future pot use and the mutual enforcements of them. They hired a part-time babysitter, facilitating the parents' spending regular quality time together at home and with friends. With several months' work, they were able to move their 5-year-old out of the family bedroom. Recently the husband has been able to ask for money due to his business in order to minimize their arguing about financial problems. He has been able to disengage from his family of origin so that they no longer impair his mutuality with his wife.

K. *The efficacy of family therapy with substance abusers has been adequately demonstrated.* Those of us who use family therapy know that it works. However, this knowledge is not sufficient proof of effectiveness. One problem is that all family therapy is not the same; thus it is difficult to generalize success or failure from one program or individual to another or to the field in general. Perhaps I should have included a myth that all family therapy is the same but that seems too obvious. Another problem is that the entire field of family therapy is just entering a phase of scientific evaluation, a phase which, fortunately or unfortunately, will be more rigorous an evaluation than individual therapy has ever had. Certainly the efficacy of any system of psychotherapy presently in use could be similarly questioned.

Papers have been published on the success or failure of family therapy dealing with a single case [35]. These can be dismissed with the same ease as our own opinions of efficacy. That single case studies continue to be published emphasizes the virginity of family therapy evaluation. I will not attempt to thoroughly review the literature on the family therapy of substance abusers. Stanton [36] and Janzen [37] have already provided us with excellent reviews of drug abuse and alcoholism, respectively. However, I will discuss several examples of family therapy evaluation in this field.

In drug abuse, Silver *et al.* [38] describe a methadone program for pregnant addicts and their addicted spouses which included 40% of the women becoming drug-free in treatment and the male employment rate increasing from 10 to 55%. Both rates are much higher than those achieved by traditional methadone programs without family treatment. The problem with this study, as with most evaluations of family approaches to drug abuse, is the lack of follow-up data or control groups.

Ziegler-Driscoll [1] has reported an Eagleville study which found, on 4-6 month follow-up, no difference between treatment groups with family therapy and those without. However, the therapists were new to family therapy and the supervisors new to substance abuse. As therapists became more experienced, their results improved. Stanton *et al.*'s [2] evaluation of family therapy with heroin addicts on methadone is perhaps the most outstanding one with hard-core drug addicts. They compared paid family therapy, unpaid family therapy, paid family movie "treatment," and nonfamily treatment with random assignment. The results of a 6-month posttreatment follow-up were that the two family therapy treatments produced much better outcomes than nonfamily treatments in the use of drugs. The nonfamily treatment and movie groups did not differ from each other.

Hendricks [39] followed-up 5½ months of MFT 1 year after treatment and found double the continued attendance in therapy of narcotics addicts who attended the MFT. Kaufmann's work has shown that adolescent addicts with MFT have half the recidivism rate of clients without it [31]. Stanton [36] noted that of 68 studies of efficacy in the family therapy of drug abuse, only 14 quantify their outcome. Only six of these provide comparative data with other forms of treatment or control groups.

Although there has been more detailed evaluation of the family therapy of alcoholism than of drug abuse, Janzen [37], in a 1977 review, stated that "it is not possible to show that family treatment is as good or better than other forms of treatment for alcoholism." However, he also stated that such treatment has advantages to the family and the alcoholic which other treatments do not offer. Despite their methodological shortcomings, all the studies he cited reported positive results. Meeks and Kelly [40] demonstrated the success of family therapy with five couples, but without comparison with another group who had the same program but with no family therapy. They emphasized abstinence in two alcoholics and "improved drinking patterns" in the other three, but with no objective measures of family function. Cadogan [41] compared marital group therapy in 20 couples with 20 other couples in a waiting list. After 6 months of therapy, nine couples in the treatment group but only two couples in the control group were abstinent. However, again there was no follow-up or use of objective measures.

Steinglass [42], utilizing a comprehensive battery of evaluative instruments with alcoholic families before treatment and at 6-month follow-up, found that five of nine alcoholics were drinking less at follow-up. Overall positive changes in psychiatric symptomatology were minimal. However, when the results of the two therapists were analyzed, the directive, forceful therapist was much more successful than the passive one. Steinglass also proposes that brief, intense family therapy programs may shift rigid systems but may not provide sufficient time for beneficial shifts to be permanently incorporated.

It is only with the recent development of such instruments as Moos's FES [23], Olson's FACES [22], and CRS [26] that quantitative and objective evaluation of the families of substance abusers has become possible. I have recently begun to utilize the FACES and CRS and plan to compare a group of alcoholic families who participate in an intensive 1-week family program with a group of families who do not volunteer. The treatment group will, in turn, be divided into those who participate in continued outpatient family therapy and those who do not. Families will be assessed by the FACES' which is an 111-item questionnaire filled out by each family member (the insider's viewpoint), and the CRS, in which the family therapist (outsider's viewpoint) rates the family on similar parameters. To be effective, the study will have to be conducted for the duration of outpatient treatment and for several years thereafter, at 6-month intervals, and involve the treatment groups as well as the controls.

I hope that the reader has been stimulated to think about these ideas, and that they will be food for thought in work with families. If our field can find definitive realities to replace these myths, we and our clients will be more than satisfied. At the very least, these points should function as probes to stimulate ideas in discussions, research, and work with families.

REFERENCES

[1] Ziegler-Driscoll, G., Family research study at Eagleville Hospital and Rehabilitation Center, *Fam. Process* **16**:175-189 (1977).

[2] Stanton, M. D., *et al., Family Characteristics and Family Therapy of Heroin Addicts: Final Report, 1974-1978,* NIDA Grant #RD1 DA 01119, October 1979.

[3] Olson, D. H., Russell, C. S., and Sprenkle, D. H., Marital and family therapy: A decade review, *J. Marriage Fam.* **42** (1980), In Press.

[4] Alexander, B. K., and Dibb, G. S., Opiate addicts and their parents, *Fam. Process* **14**:499-514 (1975).

[5] Noone, R. J., and Reddig, R. L., Case studies on the family treatment of drug abuse, *Fam. Process* **15**(3) (September 1976).

[6] Stanton, M. D., *et al.,* Heroin addiction as a family phenomenon: A new conceptual model, *Am. J. Drug Alcohol Abuse* **5**:125-150 (1978).

[7] Vaillant, G., A 12-year follow-up of New York narcotic addicts, *Arch. Gen. Psychiatry* **15**:599-609 (1966).

[8] Pattison, E. M., and Kaufman, E., Family therapy in the treatment of alcoholism, in *Major Psychopathology and the Family* (M. Lansky, ed.), Grune and Stratton, New York, In Press.

[9] Kaufman, E., and Kaufmann, P., From a psychodynamic orientation to a structural family therapy approach in the treatment of drug dependency, in *Family Therapy of Drug and Alcohol Abuse* (E. Kaufman and P. Kaufmann, eds.), Gardner, New York, 1979, pp. 43-54.

[10] Binion, V. J., A descriptive comparison of the families of origin of women heroin users and non-users, in *Addicted Women: Family Dynamics, Self-Perceptions and Support Systems,* NIDA, HEW, 1979, pp. 77-113.

[11] Fort, J. P., Heroin addiction among young men, *Psychiatry* **17**:251-259 (1954).

[12] Attardo, N., Psychodynamic factors in the mother-child relationship in adolescent drug addiction: A comparison of mothers of schizophrenics and mothers of normal adolescent sons, *Psychotherapeutic Psychosomatic* **13**:249-255 (1965).

[13] Ablon, J., The significance of cultural patterning for the "alcoholic family," *Fam. Process* **19**(2):127-144 (1980).

[14] Colten, M. E., A descriptive and comparative analysis of self-perceptions and attitudes of heroin-addicted women, in *Addicted Women: Family Dynamics, Self-Perceptions and Support Systems,* NIDA, HEW, 1979, pp. 7-36.

[15] Bowen, M., Alcoholism as viewed through family systems theory and family psychotherapy, *Ann. N. Y. Acad. Sci.* **233**:115-122 (1974).

[16] Winokur, G., *et al.,* Alcoholism. III. Diagnosis and familial psychiatric illness in 259 alcoholic probands, *Arch. Gen. Psychiatry* **23**:104-111 (1970).

[17] Vaillant, G. E., Natural history of male psychological health. VIII. Antecedents of alcoholism and "orality," *Am. J. Psychiatry* **137**:181-186 (1980).

[18] Kammeier, M. L., Hoffman, H., and Coper, R. G., Personality characteristics of alcoholics as college freshment and at time of treatment, *J. Stud. Alcohol* **34**:390-399 (1973).

[19] Olson, D. H., Russell, C. S., and Sprenkle, D. H., Circumplex model of marital and family systems. II. Empirical studies and clinical intervention, *Adv. Fam. Intervention, Assessment Theory* **1**:129-176 (1980).

[20] Aponte, H., Underorganization in the poor family, in *Family Therapy: Theory and Practice* (P. Guerin, ed.), Gardner, New York, 1976, pp. 432-448.

[21] Stanton, M. D., and Todd, T. C., Engaging "resistant" families in treatment. II. Principles and techniques in recruitment, *Fam. Process* (1980), In Press.

[22] Olson, D. H., Bell, R., and Portner, J., *FACES: Family Adaptability and Cohesion Evaluation Scales,* Family Social Science, University of Minnesota, St. Paul, Minnesota, 1978.

[23] Moos, R. H., Insel, P. M., and Humphrey, B., *Combined Preliminary Manual for Family, Work and Group Environment Scales,* Consulting Psychologists Press, Palo Alto, California, 1974.

[24] Kaufman, E., The psychodynamics of opiate dependence: A new look, *Am. J. Drug Alcohol Abuse* 1:349-370 (1974).

[25] Olson, D. H., Insiders' and outsiders' views of relationships: Research studies, in *Close Relationships* (G. Levinger and H. Rausch, eds.), University of Massachusetts Press, Amherst, Massachusetts, 1977.

[26] Olson, D. H., *Clinical Rating Scales for the Circumplex Model of Marital and Family Systems,* Family Social Science, University of Minnesota, St. Paul, Minnesota, 1980.

[27] Berenson, D., The therapist's relationship with couples with an alcoholic member, in *Family Therapy of Drug and Alcohol Abuse* (E. Kaufman and P. Kaufman, eds.), Gardner, New York, 1979, pp. 233-242.

[28] Stanton, M. D., and Todd, T. C., Structural family therapy with drug addicts, in *Family Therapy of Drug and Alcohol Abuse* (E. Kaufman and P. Kaufmann, eds.), Gardner, New York, 1979, pp. 55-70.

[29] Kaufman, E., Group therapy techniques used by the ex-addict therapist, *Group Process* 5:3-14 (1973).

[30] Haley, J., *Problem Solving Therapy,* Jossey-Bass, San Francisco, 1977.

[31] Kaufman, E., and Kaufmann, P., Multiple family therapy: A new direction in the treatment of drug abusers, *Am. J. Drug Alcohol Abuse* 4:467-478 (1977).

[32] Menninger, K. A., and Holzman, P. S., *Theory of Psychoanalytic Technique,* 2nd ed., Basic Books, New York, 1973.

[33] Watzlawick, P., Weakland, J. H., and Fisch, R., *Change: Principles of Problem Formulation and Problem Resolution,* Norton, New York, 1974.

[34] Minuchin, S., *Families and Family Therapy,* Harvard University Press, Cambridge, Massachusetts, 1974.

[35] Dinaburg, D., Glick, I. D., and Feigenbaum, E., Marital therapy of women alcoholics, *J. Stud. Alcohol* 36:1245-1257 (1975).

[36] Stanton, M. D., Family treatment approaches to drug abuse problems: A review, *Fam. Process* 18:251-280 (1979).

[37] Janzen, C., Families in the treatment of alcoholism, *J. Stud. Alcohol* 38:114-130 (1972).

[38] Silver, F. C., Panepinto, W. C., Arnon, D., and Swaine, W. T., A family approach in treating the pregnant addict, in *Developments in the Field of Drug Abuse* (E. Senay *et al.,* eds.), Shenkman, Cambridge, Massachusetts, 1975.

[39] Hendricks, W. J., Use of multifamily counseling groups in treatment of male narcotic addicts, *Int. J. Group Psychother.* 21:34-90 (1971).

[40] Meeks, D. E., and Kelly, C., Family therapy with families of recovering alcoholics, *Q. J. Stud. Alcohol* 31:399-413 (1970).

[41] Cadogan, D. A., Marital group therapy in the treatment of alcoholism, *Q. J. Stud. Alcohol* 34:1184-1194 (1973).

[42] Steinglass, P., An experimental treatment program for alcoholic couples, *J. Stud. Alcohol* 40:159-182 (1979).

In questioning many of the myths in this field, Kaufman has made an important contribution to the literature. Much of the material he presents deserves wider dissemination. However, at least four of his 21 "realities" are overstated, and another four are not well founded or are amenable to alternative explanations. The present paper is generally supportive of Kaufman's presentation while also attempting to place certain of the issues in perspective so as to avoid the creation of new myths.

23

A CRITIQUE OF KAUFMAN'S "MYTH AND REALITY IN THE FAMILY PATTERNS AND TREATMENT OF SUBSTANCE ABUSERS"

M. Duncan Stanton

In his paper [1], Kaufman has done us a valuable service. Applying his broad knowledge and experience in the family and substance abuse area, he has challenged a number of notions that have prevailed in the field—fortifying his arguments with good clinical and empirical data where available. Kaufman wants to keep us aware that, while a particular conclusion or finding may apply, for example, in 80% of the cases, we must not overgeneralize to the 20% which it does not encompass.

Many of Kaufman's antidotes to these myths need to be emphasized repeatedly. He has stated them and it is encumbent on us to promulgate them.

From M. Duncan Stanton, "A Critique of Kaufman's 'Myth and Reality in the Family Patterns and Treatment of Substance Abusers," *American Journal of Drug and Alcohol Abuse*, 1980, 7, pp. 281-289. Reprinted by permission of the author and publisher.

As André Gide once asserted, "It has all been said before. But you have to say it again, because nobody listens."

Other of his arguments are overstated. As implied above, Kaufman is not really attacking myths in some instances, but is questioning general findings that do not apply in every case. In addition, at times he presents one side of an issue but neglects an opposing position which is just as well-founded and valid. It will be the purpose, in part, of the present paper to restore some balance to these particular issues and to fill in a few gaps in order to offset the risk that Kaufman's paper does not itself generate any new myths.

Each of the myths will be listed, in abbreviated form, below. Those most completely and cogently dealt with by Kaufman will not be discussed, aside from an occasional plaudit. Others will receive more attention.

MYTHS IN FAMILY PATTERNS

1. *Differences in drug and alcohol families.* Kaufman's point about ostensible differences between these groups being due to generational and family life-cycle differences is an excellent one. Are NIDA and NIAAA listening?

2. *Unimportance of family relationships.* Hear! Hear!

3. *Family relationships as the key factors.* Kaufman overstates his case here and uses selected data. It is unlikely that anyone knowledgeable in the field would say that family factors are the *only* ones operating. On the other hand, all the available data are not derived from as select a sample as Kaufman's. Our own research [2, 3] was based on a much less "volunteer" population, as are a number of other studies, reviewed by the author [4, 5], which document the importance of family factors. Further, the Binion [6] study is offset by the research of Perzel and Lamon [7] in which male and female drug abusers were six times as likely to live with their parents than normal controls (42-45 vs 7%) and also more likely to be in daily telephone contact with one or both parents (51-64 vs 9%).

4. *Mother-son coalitions.* It is doubtful that anyone who is up-to-date in the family field would subscribe to this myth as stated here. To begin with, it is dyadic, and thinking has shifted almost entirely from dyads to triads and larger units since this necessity was identified 25-30 years ago. Recent work with substance abusing families (e.g., Refs. 5 and 8) has also emphasized triads. Nonetheless, if some people continue to hold onto the dyadic myth, Kaufman is correct in challenging it.

5. *Disengaged, brutal alcoholic father.* The points are well taken.

6. *Generalizing to all classes and ethnic groups.* Bravo! The conclusions Kaufman has drawn from his own work, in particular, are insightful and helpful.

One minor point on the enmeshment-disengagement continuum. I have found this to be a less and less useful dimension as it pertains to substance abusing families. As Haley [9] observes, often the "disengaged" or "distant" member of a severely dysfunctional family becomes extremely involved and upset when change starts to occur in the family system. Such members may ostensibly appear to be disengaged, but in reality are quite tied in or enmeshed.

7. *Families of female substance abusers.* We are in debt to Kaufman for pointing out the misperceptions and inadequate information that exist on this topic.

On a minor point, caution should be exercised regarding the results of the Colten [10] study: the fact that the parents of female addicts and controls differed on education level might indicate that the two groups were not equated on socioeconomic status (SES). One of the two factors in Hollingshead and Redlich's [11] Two Factor Index of Social Position is father's education level. Perhaps differences in education and SES were the major contributory variables in Colten's findings, rather than family patterns, *per se.*

8. *The addict-parental triangle and siblings.* A good point, but a bit over-stated. In some cases it is necessary to involve siblings and in others it is not.

9. *Family structures and the life cycle.* Kaufman is certainly right on this. No facet of family factors in substance abuse has been more neglected than that of the family life cycle and its attendant notion of families getting "stuck" at certain stages. This paradigm is of considerable theoretical importance [8, 12].

10. *Knowledge of family structures.* Another overstatement. We certainly know a great deal more in this area than we did 10 years ago. Unless Kaufman defines "knowledgeable" as knowing all there is to know, he has misused the term and in the process has (perhaps inadvertently) slighted the dozens of researchers who have been working in the field [5]. Instead, he should have challenged the myth that "We do not have much to learn."

FAMILY THERAPY MYTHS AND REALITIES

A. *Doing therapy with a member who is dysfunctional on chemicals.* Most people in the field, including myself [13], agree with Kaufman on this. The clinical material he provides here is clear and cogent. However, he should be challenged on the notion of using long-term hospitalization for drug addicts. The field of family therapy developed in part because such methods did not work; symptoms recurred soon after discharge. This is an expensive and time-consuming modality, even when it is effective, and emerging data indicate that it is an unnecessary and increasingly outmoded one [14]. Indeed, Haley [9] has noted that hospitalizing the "sick" family member can crystalize a symptom and make it chronic. Hopefully we are ready to move on to more cost-efficient methods.

B. *Dyads in treatment.* Amen!

C. *Family therapy alone.* Perhaps Kaufman has not seen a successful substance abuse case in which family therapy was the only modality. I have encountered many of them. The point here is not that ancillary and parallel treatments are not necessary: They often are. The point is that Kaufman is too categorical in demanding them in all cases.

D. *Generalizing to all socioeconomic groups.* Excellent point, well stated.

E. *Sharing information from individual sessions.* This is a tricky area. There are times when confidences must be protected. The danger, as Kaufman notes, is that such information is sometimes used by a family member as a ploy to reduce the therapist's effectiveness and thus undercut his/her efforts to induce change.

F. *Individual family versus multiple family therapy.* I am sympathetic to Kaufman's view here and there are some data to support it [14]. Once again, though, he goes too far by implying treatment is *most* effective in an MFT setting, and the data do not necessarily support such a parochial position.

G. *Psychoanalytic and psychodynamic family therapy.* Here Kaufman introduces an issue that has been debated in the family therapy field for 25-30 years. There is not space to adequately deal with it in the present paper, but certain alternative points need to be made in order to regain perspective.

First, Kaufman's admonition about "knowing more" about a family, if not tempered by the constraints of time and efficiency, could turn into a ludicrous exercise. Carried to its logical extreme, a therapist could spend his or her whole professional life with a single family so as to "know" all there is to know about it. The more important questions are: (a) how much knowledge is necessary before starting to intervene effectively?; (b) what kind of knowledge—historical or interactional—is needed?; and (c) how is this knowledge used to bring about change? Therapists differ in their emphases and choices on these matters, and a therapist of a different persuasion than Kaufman might criticize him for paying too much homage to his psychoanalytic mentors while postponing the work of inducing real change. For my own part, I feel that obtaining some history is necessary, especially as it might (a) indicate areas for "ascribing noble intentions" to the family [13] and (b) dictate which family subsystems need to be altered.

In raising the "insight" issue, Kaufman confuses two different levels of integration: that of the individual and that of the interpersonal system. Certainly individuals in a family may develop "insight" from events occurring in family therapy. They are also having their biochemical compositions changed and their central nervous systems altered. One can look at therapy session events from any number of perspectives. A problem with the insight paradigm is that it is inadequate for explaining changes in the interpersonal/family system and, since it focuses on "in the head" phenomena, it less readily dictates the *direction for treatment* of such a system.

One final point on "insight." If it were such a valuable technique or goal, why have insight-oriented individual therapies shown such miserable results with the addictions? What is important is showing *actual change* in behavior, and this has not been the forte of the insight therapies, at least in terms of cost efficiency. In fact, it is my experience that in family treatment "insight," if it occurs at all, lags about 3 months behind actual change, indicating that the insight was not particularly necessary. It is one thing to try to make a family more "insightful" and quite another to try to change its patterns and structures within the session. In the latter, the members may not actually be aware of "why" things have changed, but they are nonetheless able to do something in a new way. This is not insight in the usual sense, but a change in the pattern or sequence of behaviors within an interpersonal system. From all this, I would substitute the following (alternative) myth in Kaufman's list: *Insight is necessary for changing a substance abuse pattern.*

H. *Personal therapy for therapists.* This is the weakest point in Kaufman's paper. It is also a controversial one in the family therapy field, with no firm evidence one way or the other. Certainly there are times when certain family therapists need therapy. Also, personal family work is rarely harmful and may be helpful to many therapists. However, to taut it as a necessity or requisite as Kaufman does here is to take an unjustifiably extreme position, and one that I feel too frequently leads to misdirected, wasteful effort and, perhaps, a new myth. (At its logical extreme it would also mean that a therapist could never do therapy unless he has gone through some sort of detailed family work over years.) I have known, observed, or worked with too many excellent family therapists who have never undertaken such an endeavor to give this notion much credence. To paraphrase Haley [15], requiring personal therapy as part of a therapist's training is (a) demeaning to the therapist; (b) distracts him/her from the work at hand; (c) in its requirement for personal insight is antithetical to a therapeutic approach which deemphasizes insight; and (d) gives less recognition to the fact that the therapist grows with success in his/her work, and that the first task is to train him/her to solve problems met in therapy—for example, by coaching a therapist with "authority conflicts" in specific ways for dealing with, say, grandfathers, rather than steering him/her toward on "understanding" of his/her personal authority-figure problems [16].

I. *Therapists' responsibility for treatment.* An excellent point and example. The challenge to this myth probably originated as much from our own work as from any other source [13]. We found early on that lack of case control by family therapists was killing our treatment efforts and we had to alter the ways in which the treatment system handled clinical responsibility.

J. *Paradoxical techniques.* I was a bit surprised to see Kaufman include this as a myth, since paradoxical techniques have been minimally applied in the substance abuse field. Further, it is unlikely that many family therapists would hold that they be used in all cases. Like Kaufman, Papp [17] and I [16, 18] have advocated applying them only after more direct methods have failed, while Haley [9] recommends against their use with families of schizophrenics and addicts, especially if the therapist is inexperienced. In addition, Haley [15], Papp [17], Rohrbaugh *et al.* [19], and especially Weeks and L'Abate [20] have been very explicit about the inappropriate use of such techniques, giving multiple examples of when they should not be applied (such as in suicidal cases) and of the safeguards necessary while training therapists in their use. There are always dangers that any kind of therapeutic procedure will be misused, and paradoxical instructions are no exception. A reading of any of the aforementioned publications [15, 17, 19, 20] could only lead to the conclusion that the authors take these dangers seriously, and have set forth their caveats in a sincere and concerned way. It is hard to imagine even a naive therapist misconstruing them on this. Thus Kaufman's (undocumented) allusion that they are trying to trick parvenu therapists into indiscriminate use of paradox (such as prescribing a suicidal attempt) is a cheap shot, and not on par with the quality and general scholarship shown in the remainder of his article.

K. *Efficacy of family therapy.* One always runs into problems when discussing the efficacy of a therapy approach. To a great extent, efficacy lies in the eye of the beholder. It depends on the standards one sets. For example, is a modality efficacious if it shows better results than other existent modes? Must it "cure" all cases, 90% of the cases, or only the majority? How many studies are needed to demonstrate its effectiveness? What about cost efficiency? Who defines the yardstick, what are his/her preferred modalities, and will these modalities be supplanted if the new method is embraced? Generally, new psychotherapy approaches have been adopted more because of the values underlying them, and the political/social Zeitgeist, than for their demonstrated efficacy; if it were otherwise, certain modalities would have been abandoned long ago. Kaufman is sensitive to these issues, and notes that, fairly or not, family therapy will probably undergo much greater scrutiny than did its predecessors. This is partly because family and interpersonal systems therapies require a paradigm shift. They demand that one apply new ways of thinking about symptoms and human problems which are discontinuous with conventional thought. Thus there will be those who will never understand them, making the efficacy dilemma even more formidable.

Kaufman has treated this subject in fine and sophisticated fashion. Consequently, I would like only to supplement his presentation with two additional points. First, it is important to note that one of Janzen's major conclusions from his review of the relevent alcoholism literature was that "there is strong indication that family treatment for alcoholism can be successful" and that its success "does not appear to be contingent on additional (ancillary) treatment. Treatment which begins with the family is apparently successful in producing change both in the alcoholic and the family" [21, p. 128].

The second notion concerns Kaufman's point that there are different kinds of family therapy and that outcomes for them may be different in general and may also differ for various patient populations. This point needs special emphasis, as the myth that the various family approaches are pretty much the same is rather pervasive within the drug abuse field. Moreover, there are some data which speak to it. While outcome data on some family approaches are practically nonexistent, a review of the literature [14] reveals that particular family modalities and approaches with drug abusers are superior to others, or to certain nonfamily treatments. On the other hand, one or two other family approaches have been shown, from the available information, to be *less* effective than nonfamily modes; for example, the Bowen approach does not seem to work well with drug abusers' families, perhaps because it is not oriented toward dealing with the kind of crises which these families so frequently generate. In a recent review, Olson *et al.* [22] compare 10 types of family therapy across nine types of presenting problems (symptoms) and conclude that three (structural, strategic, and MFT) have shown some degree of documented effectiveness with drug abusers, and two (behavioral exchange contracting, conjoint couples groups) with alcoholism. These various reviews would indicate that while the jury may still be out on the efficacy of family therapy with substance abusers, it seems safe to conclude from the existent research that certain family approaches show considerable promise for dealing with problems of this type.

CONCLUSION

In taking to task a number of myths on the family and substance abuse, Kaufman has made a constructive and valuable contribution to the literature. Many of these myths have gone unchallenged in the past. Most of Kaufman's antidotes to them need to be echoed repeatedly. While he has overstated his case on some points, and needs to be challenged on others in order to prevent the formation of *new* myths, there is no doubt the paper will stimulate the kind of vigorous discussion and activity which he has intended.

REFERENCES

[1] Kaufman, E., Myth and reality in the family patterns and treatment of substance abusers, *Am. J. Drug Alcohol Abuse* 7:257-280 (1980).

[2] Stanton, M. D., Todd, T. C., Steier, F., *et al.*, *Family Characteristics and Family Therapy of Heroin Addicts: Final Report, 1974-1978*, NIDA Grant #R01 01119, October 1979.

[3] Stanton, M. D., and Todd, T. C., Engaging "resistant" families in treatment. II. Principles and techniques in recruitment, *Fam. Process* **20** (1981).

[4] Stanton, M. D., *Drug Misuse and the Family*, Report Prepared for the White House Office of Drug Abuse Policy, Washington, D.C., October 1977.

[5] Stanton, M. D., Drugs and the family: A review of the recent literature, *Marriage Fam. Rev.* **2**(1):1-10 (1979).

[6] Binion, V. J., A descriptive comparison of the families of origin of women heroin users and non-users, in *Addicted Women: Family Dynamics, Self-perceptions and Support Systems*, NIDA, DHEW Pub. (ADM) 80-762, 1979.

[7] Perzel, J. F., and Lamon, S., *Enmeshment within Families of Polydrug Abusers*, Paper Presented at the National Drug Abuse Conference, New Orleans, August 1979.

[8] Stanton, M. D., Todd, T. C., Heard, D. B., *et al.*, Heroin addiction as a family phenomenon: A new conceptual model, *Am. J. Drug Alcohol Abuse* **5**:125-150 (1978).

[9] Haley, J., *Leaving Home: The Therapy of Disturbed Young People*, McGraw-Hill, New York, 1980.

[10] Colten, M. E., A descriptive and comparative analysis of self-perceptions and attitudes of heroin-addicted women, in *Addicted Women: Family Dynamics, Self-Perceptions and Support Systems*, NIDA, DHEW Pub. (ADM) 80-762, 1979.

[11] Hollingshead, A. B., and Redlich, F. C., *Social Class and Mental Illness*, Wiley, New York, 1958.

[12] Stanton, M. D., A family theory of drug abuse, in *Theories on Drug Abuse* (D. Lettieri, M. Sayers, and H. Pearson, eds.), NIDA Research Monograph 30, DHEW Pub. (ADM) 80-967, 1980.

[13] Stanton, M. D., and Todd, T. C., Structural family therapy with drug addicts, in *Family Therapy of Drug and Alcohol Abuse* (E. Kaufman and P. Kaufmann, eds.), Gardner, New York, 1979.

[14] Stanton, M. D., Family treatment approaches to drug abuse problems: A review, *Fam. Process* 18:251-280 (1979).

[15] Haley, J., *Problem Solving Therapy*, Jossey-Bass, San Francisco, 1976.

[16] Stanton, M. D., Strategic approaches to family therapy, in *Handbook of Family Therapy* (A. Gurman and D. Kniskern, eds.), Brunner-Mazel, New York, 1981.

[17] Papp, P., The Greek chorus and other techniques of paradoxical therapy, *Fam. Process* 19:45-57 (1980).

[18] Stanton, M. D., Marital therapy from a structural/strategic viewpoint, in *Marriage Is a Family Affair: Textbook of Marital and Family Therapy* (G. P. Sholevar, ed.), S. P. Medical and Scientific Books, Jamaica, New York, 1981.

[19] Rohrbaugh, M., Tennen, H., Press, S., *et al., Paradoxical Strategies in Psychotherapy*, Symposium Presented at the American Psychological Association, San Francisco, 1977.

[20] Weeks, G. R., and L'Abate, L., A compilation of paradoxical methods, *Am. J. Fam. Ther.* 7:61-76 (1979).

[21] Janzen, C., Families in the treatment of alcoholism, *J. Stud. Alcohol* 38:114-130 (1977).

[22] Olson, D. H., Russell, C. S., and Sprenkle, D. H., Marital and family therapy: A decade review, *J. Marriage Fam.* 42:973-993 (1980).

Seventy-six wives of alcoholics were interviewed in depth concerning how they acted once they were certain their husbands had a drinking problem. Findings indicate that long before the husband seeks professional help, his wife is attempting to treat his alcoholism at home through a sequence of strategies which reflect her changing beliefs about the nature of alcoholism, her assessment of her current relationship with her husband, and her reaction to the failure of her most recent attempt to cope with this problem. Some of these wives' unsuccessful attempts at home treatment may be the behavior which professionals often view as pathological. Additionally, the home treatment represents strategies of amelioration under stress which probably contribute to such stress as well.

24

THE "HOME TREATMENT"

The First Steps in Trying to Cope With an Alcoholic Husband*

*Jacqueline P. Wiseman***

It is now recognized that alcohol addiction generates problems that extend beyond the heavy drinker to the family and particularly the spouse. Yet for several decades, when the spouse (and especially the wife) was the focus of research, primary emphasis was on her as an unwitting causal agent in her husband's problem drinking, due to the presumed presence of "pathological" personality traits such as dominance, dependency, or sadomasochism.[1] More recently, Steinglass and others (i.e., Steinglass [1976]; Steinglass, Weiner, and Mendelson [1971], Steinglass and Meyer [1977] and Paredes [1973])have taken a functionalist, systems approach and attempted to show that the wife is a part of a family "system" that may help maintain the husband's problem drinking. Where the focus has been on the coping behavior of wives of alcoholics, investigators have been concerned with her management of the problem over a considerable time span of his drinking career and do not detail early attempts to get him to stop or cut down (Jackson, 1954, 1956, 1959, 1962; Oxford & Guthrie, 1968). This effort to fit

*This research was supported by NIAAA Grant No. 2 ROIAA 01456-03. I am indebted to members of the Social Research Group, University of California-Berkeley, who offered suggestions and criticisms when I presented an earlier version of this paper.

**Jacqueline P. Wiseman is Professor of Sociology, University of California—San Diego.

[1]See, for instance, de Saugy (1962), Futterman (1953), Kalashian (1959), Lewis (1937), Price (1945), and Whalen (1953). This research has been refuted to a great extent by

studies which compared the personality traits of wives of alcoholics with control groups (Corder, Hendricks, & Corder, 1964; Kogan, Fordyce, & Jackson, 1963; Kogan & Jackson, 1963; Mitchell, 1959; Rae & Forbes, 1966). Edwards, Harvey, and Whitehad (1973) examined this literature and concluded that wives of alcoholics exhibit stress that women with any marital problem might have. Paolino and McCrady (1977) report that evidence is lacking on both the existence of pathological traits of wives of alcoholics, as well as their apparent unconscious desire to keep their husbands drinking.

From Jacqueline P. Wiseman, "The 'Home Treatment': The First Steps in Trying to Cope With an Alcoholic Husband," *Family Relations*, 1980, 29, pp. 541-549. Reprinted by permission of the publisher and author.

the wife into the etiology of alcoholism, or condense her attempts to cope with a husband's long drinking career into major stages, has resulted in ignoring what might be the first line of defense in the battle with a man's compulsive drinking behavior—the wife's early intervention efforts.

This paper contains a delineation of the many aspects of what will be referred to as the "home treatment" attempted by wives of alcoholic men as they try to handle their husbands' problem drinking in the privacy of their homes when they first become aware that he may be an alcoholic. Like the proverbial iceberg below the surface, there exists a career of amateur therapy by the wife of an alcoholic which is enacted long before her drinking husband comes to the attention of professionals in the field.

Shibutani (1961) has pointed out that all acts, even coping ones, depend on how the individual actor defines the situation and how he or she defines and symbolizes the meaning of any attempt at amelioration and the counterreactions these inspire. In the course of such definitions, the social actor takes into account how others feel about the action, and then moves tentatively toward it, "building it up" piece-by-piece, checking and re-checking the usefulness of the decision. Reports on the hidden drama of the home treatment indicate that maneuvers by the wife reflect her understanding of the nature of alcoholism, her adjustments to the reactions of her husband to reform attempts, and her changing perception of their relationship and her subordinate status vis-à-vis her spouse. Furthermore, there appears to be an *approximate* time order to the methods that are tried.

Wives of alcoholics who attempt to cope alone with the heavy drinking of their spouses find themselves in dual and somewhat contradictory roles: both therapist and close kin. Like the professional therapist, the wife searches for ways to help her husband with what she perceives to be a serious problem affecting both him and the entire family. Like many cases that therapists handle, the husband-client seldom admits he drinks too much. Again, like the professional, the wife gropes for ways of helping her "patient" in the face of his denial and even hostility to her efforts.

However, unlike the professional, the wife usually has an established and close relationship with the patient that existed *prior* to her attempts to help him stop his drinking. This has both advantages and disadvantages. Although this relationship may give the wife an edge over the professional in empathetic understanding, she is often, unlike the professional, the person with the *least power* in the dyad. This is quite the opposite from the professional relationship, where the therapist is seen to be of higher (or dominant) status in the role relationship with his client due to his acknowledged expertise.

Without this advantage, the wife of the alcoholic is forced to use approaches to her husband's problem drinking that do not depend on role power based on authority of knowledge and training. Thus, the stage is set for strategic interaction, since it is lack of power that is usually the genesis of inferior role position strategies. Yet, as will be seen, the approaches wives develop through trial and error bear a striking resemblance to some professional therapeutic stances.

Methodology

Seventy-six wives of alcoholics were interviewed in depth and also answered a five-page structured questionnaire concerned with pertinent background data. Wives were asked to discuss how they decided their husbands were alcoholics, what they did after they decided this, what persuaded them to try to get their husbands into professional treatment, how they handled this matter, their experiences (and their husbands') with professional treatment, and what effects the alcoholism of the husband had on their marital relationship and their lives in general.

Wives were recruited through an advertisement placed in newspapers in the city selected for the study. This approach is preferred over recruiting through Al-Anon because the latter offers a distinct philosophy of life to wives of problem drinkers, a fact which could confound the findings. Thus, Al-Anon members were interviewed only as they surfaced through advertisements.

Although the actual universe of wives of alcoholics is unknown, and thus cannot be compared with the sample, important demographic characteristics of the sample indicate

that a desirably broad range of women participated in the study. The distribution by age,
yearly income, education, and length of time
drinking of wives (and the husbands they are
reporting on) can be seen in Tables 1 through
4.

The wife's word that her husband is an alcoholic was accepted, because there was no
way to check back with the husband inasmuch
as many women came in secret to be inter-

Table 1
Age Distribution of Sample of Wives
of Alcoholics and Their Husbands

Age	Wives (n = 76) %	Husbands[a] (n = 76) %
20 or under	1	1
21-30	20	8
31-40	22	26
41-50	30	32
51-60	22	27
Over 60	5	6

[a]Age of husband was supplied by wife.

Table 2
Distribution of Yearly Family Income
of Sample of Wives of Alcoholics[a]

Total Yearly Income before Taxes	Wives (n = 72)[b] %
Under $5,000	7
$5,000-$7,499	8
$7,500-$9,999	5
$10,000-$14,999	35
$15,000-$19,999	15
$20,000 and over	15
Don't know	15

[a]Data were gathered in 1976 and 1977. Relatively low yearly income levels may reflect the
marginal employment status of some men or a
family dependent on a wife's income only.
[b]Refusals were excluded from the base.

Table 3
Educational Attainment of Sample of
Alcoholic Men and Their Wives[a]

Year in School Completed	Husbands (n = 72)[b] %	Wives (n = 72)[b] %
Elementary school only	7	—
Some high school	16	22
Vocational school	3	12
High school graduate	36	32
Some college	24	22
College graduate	6	8
Post graduate	8	4

[a]Educational attainment was thought to be a
more stable social class indicator for the purposes
of this study than occupation, since many men had
lost their jobs or been demoted because of their
drinking.
[b]No answers were excluded from the base.

Table 4
Length of Time Husband Has Had Drinking
Problem as Perceived by Wives of Alcoholics

Husband Has Had Drinking Problem	Wives (n = 76) %
Less than a year	1
1 to 5 years	9
6 to 10 years	21
11 to 15 years	13
16 to 20 years	26
21 to 30 years	11
31 years or more	15
Not certain, drank before marriage, etc.	4

viewed. However, there were reassuring indicators that the husbands who were discussed
by their wives were indeed alcoholics: first, all
had undergone some sort of treatment for their
alcohol problem at least twice; additionally,
the consistencies in the behavior of the husbands, as described by the wives, lend
credence to the belief that a uniform population (in terms of the existence of problem
drinking) was being tapped.

The Home Treatment

Wives of alcoholics were asked, "When you
first decided that your husband was an alcoholic, what did you do? What did you do next?
What did you do after that? Then, what did you
do?" The aggregate behaviors reported had a
time order—that is, almost all wives tried the
same first approach to the problem of their
husbands' alcoholism, and almost all adjusted
their approaches to a series of failures in the
same ways. However, many of these wives
were offering retrospective data that spans 10
to 25 years of marriage. Some have said that
they tried one thing and then another and then
they would go back and try the entire repertoire
again. Thus, the exact order of home treatment
attempts cannot be known, although it would
appear that the time order presented here is at
least indicative of the general progression of
events.[2]

The Direct Approach

At the outset, the wife saw her task as providing logical reasons to her husband for quitting his heavy drinking—arguments so persuasive that they outweigh any motives her

[2]It would be erroneous to perceive the ordered aspects of
the wives' strategies as "stages" in the way that Jackson
(1954,1956) describes wives of alcoholics as they cope with
their husbands' drinking over the years. They are, rather a
logical (to the wives) trial-and-error progression.

husband may have for continuing. Although the wife probably had been told that alcoholism is a "disease," at this point she still believed her husband's drinking was voluntary. Thus, she initially proceeded on the theory that the use of alcohol can be halted or reduced if the drinker is persuaded of the necessity to do so.

Logical persuasion and its fate. When wives tried to "talk things over" with their husbands, most started out rather low key, affecting a casual attitude while still making their concern clear.

> *Usually, when we are alone, I tell him, "You gonna start to drink again, you better be careful." But I would not nag him. I'd say, "You're drinking again; you better be careful or you'll end up in trouble." Usually he says, "No, I won't, Babe."*

> *(I'd say) "John, do you have to drink that much? Now is it really necessary?"*

As can be seen, the early approach centers on suggestions for more moderate drinking, rather than stopping altogether. The responses by the men were, however, primarily defensive.

> *I'm taking care of myself. I'm not drinking so much now. Don't worry.*

> *I'm not drinking too much. It's your imagination.*

When convinced that a gentle nudge toward cutting down on alcohol intake is not going to work, wives escalated to "presenting a case." Their arguments usually had three major foci:

1. The husband had better start realizing that he has a real drinking problem, and his drinking has gotten out-of-hand.
2. His drinking is adversely affecting other areas of his life and relationships with others.
3. His drinking, if continued, will ruin his health.

Sample comments from wife-respondents were:

> *I told him that if he kept drinking, he'd be out of a job.*

> *I tried to show him what was bothering me. The fact that we didn't have any money; the car; he has ulcers also . . . the fact that he was always complaining about a headache, his stomach and everything.*

Wives reported that the reaction of some husbands to these stronger arguments remain mild, and even become conciliatory as they offer agreement and promises to cut down their drinking. However, these promises rarely were kept for long.

> *He was very intelligent, and he would always agree. Then he would really get drunk and get a big hangover and say, "That is it. You are right, honey, no more." I live in hope until the next time (he starts drinking again).*

Nagging—Wives Escalate Their Campaign. If social bonds, especially those in the marriage relationship, are based on shared meanings, reciprocity, and trust, then it is not surprising that a great deal of strain was felt by the wife as she experienced the disappointment of a succession of such broken promises and that she moved from logical discussion to nagging.

> *I felt let down, you know. Somebody didn't keep their end of the bargain. Now I just don't believe him, and tell him so.*

> *I'd be a screaming, nagging bitch, that's what I've become.*

Husbands did not react to a wife's nagging and quarreling with the same equanimity they showed when she attempted logical persuasion. A frequent reaction was to suggest to the wife that she was driving him to drink by her continual complaining.[3]

> *Well, he said I was nasty when he drank, so this is why he drank. Who wants to come home to a nasty woman? I admit I did start to get nasty.*

It is at this juncture that men used counter criticism to end the nagging *and* to explain their drinking.

> *Once he said, "You're too fat. Stop eating and I'll stop drinking."*

The above strategy placed the wife in a no-win position. Logical discussion and sweet reasonableness do not result in any long-term reform. When she became more forceful, he began to blame her for his excessive drinking.

---

[3]Some social workers believe that complaining wives do drive their husbands to drink, and take as one therapeutic mandate teaching the wife not to be hostile to her husband. See, for instance, Cheek, Franks, Laucius, & Burtle (1971).

In despair and desperation, these women turned to a persuasive strategy used by many women in other situations—emotional pleading and threatening (Safilios-Rothschild, 1969).

Emotional pleading and threats to leave. Wives' descriptions of how they acted when they became too emotional to continue to discuss their husbands' drinking dispassionately indicated they still believed that their spouses could stop drinking if they wished. Wives also hoped their husbands' love would cause these men to cease their excessive alcohol intake in order to end her unhappiness.

I begged him. I pleaded, I cried. I was very emotional and I cried and said that if loved me, he wouldn't do this to me and the children.

Husbands who were constrained when their wives raised the subject of their heavy drinking calmly and who limited themselves to countercharges when wives made accusations produced some defensive escalation (Schelling, 1963) and exhibited anger when approached by an emotion-wrought wife.

He said, "Well, you go your way and I'll go mine. I am not an alcoholic."

With talk on all levels failing, but still holding to the belief that their husbands could voluntarily stop their drinking, wives of alcoholics often turned next to threats of separation or divorce. The purpose, however, was to hasten reform and ultimately to salvage the marriage. These women hoped *not* to have to carry through on their threat.

At that time, I threatened: "You either stop or I will leave." I guess that when I said I would leave him, I hoped that it would sort of, you know, make him realize.

Husbands responded to these threats primarily with cavalier disinterest, although remorseful promises (such as they made in response to tearful pleas) were sometimes forthcoming. These drinking husbands appeared to be guessing that there was a lack of real seriousness in the threat. They may have known that it is economically very difficult for the average wife to manage such a move on her own—especially if small children are involved. They also may have counted on their wives lacking the courage for such a drastic

action. Women, themselves, admitted these problems. They said:

The threats I used to use on him would roll off his back and he would say, "Well, maybe you're right, maybe we should give up and quit and get a divorce."

James and Goldman (1971) and Estes (1974) have noted that wives of alcoholics often develop an entire repertoire of coping styles for living with an alcoholic. As one fails to produce the desired results, another is tried. The findings of this study—more narrowly focused on the early period of trying to get alcoholic husbands to stop drinking excessively—substantiate these two reports. Starting with the direct approach, wives passed through logical discussion, emotional pleading, nagging, and threats, and then often go back to some one of these methods in the hope that they would yet be effective. It is at this juncture of failing several times at various direct approaches that wives began to develop indirect moves—strategies they hoped would help the husband cut down on his drinking *without his being aware of the fact the wife was trying to change his behavior.*

The Indirect Approach

The development of hidden anti-drinking strategies signals a turning point in the wife's view of alcoholism and her power to do anything about it. She no longer sees excessive drinking as so completely voluntary and is beginning to consider the possibility that his drinking is a compulsion.

Her assessment of their relationship changes as well. She has learned that he will not stop drinking just for her sake, nor does he show concern at the ritual threat of separation. Because of this, she often feels a loss of closeness with her husband. At the same time, she may also experience feelings of being more aware than her husband of the danger he is in. Using a type of reasoning that is startlingly like that of professional therapists, wives try out a range of behind-the-scenes manipulative approaches to managing the husband's environment in such a way that he either has less desire or less opportunity to drink.

Acting "normal" or "natural". One indirect approach is not unlike the so-called therapeutic milieu that enjoyed popularity in treating mental illness in the 1960's (Rapoport, 1959). The essence of the method is that professional therapists construct the environment of the alcoholic in such a way that he will experience less stress and have a reduced desire to drink. The wife, lacking the resources of an institution, must therefore create the non-stressful environment within her limited sphere of power and competence.

The wifely version of the therapeutic milieu is what wives referred to as acting "normal" or "natural."[4] The wife stopped trying to persuade her husband to stop his heavy drinking. Instead, she pretended the drinking or the drunken behavior was not occurring. Often the wife will try this method after deciding that the daily hassle of the direct confrontation was useless, as well as being hard on her emotions. It should be stressed, however, that "acting normal or natural" was more than just resignation. It was a mode of "reasonable" behavior that wives assumed in reaction to their husband's drinking; it was intended to elicit the same type of "reasonable" behavior in return.

I acted a lot of ways when he was drunk. Inside, I acted like, "Let's pretend it is not happening." Now, I try to act like a normal person (like he thought I was abnormal) because I thought if I acted normal in some way, that he would act normal . . .[emphasis added]

A major setting for these attempts to act natural was the home at the end of the day when the husband returned quite obviously drunk. The wife then tried to act like she thought she would act if her spouse were sober.

(When he came home) I just talked to him like I'm talking to you. I just pretend like nothing is wrong. Sometimes it would work and other times he would keep at me 'til I got mad.

In an effort to reduce such strain, wives of alcoholics used props and activities to aid in acting natural. Often they went on a self-conscious and feverish round of cleaning and cooking activities when their husbands came home drunk, for it is easier to play-act at "naturalness" if one has some concrete routine involving behavior that will take up excess nervous energy.

(I act normal by) being in the garage washing, in the den, or finding something to do—nervous energy. I am so busy with things that I don't even pass the kitchen to see what he is doing.

Goffman (1968) discussed the strains that develop in the family of a deviant (in this case, a mentally ill member) when loved ones try to help him, and keep him from harming himself, while at the same time working hard at appearing "normal" so that such surveillance is not noticed. The problematic person also notices the forced normalcy but pretends to be unaware of being watched. Thus, the interaction becomes stilted and the home becomes "an insane place."

Taking over. A touching extension to acting natural is added by the wives who actively attempted to make all facets of the home and marriage better for their husbands by taking over anything that might put demands on their mates or upset them. In addition to trying to be better wives and housekeepers, such women took care of more details of running the house and other areas of life. Their hope was that an extremely pleasant, burden-free atmosphere would reduce their husband's need for liquor.[5] It is quite possible that this coping approach is the foundation for the traits of "dominance" and "desiring a dependent marriage partner" that were earlier ascribed to the wife of an alcoholic by psychiatrists and social workers.[6]

---

[5] Obviously, as the drinking continues, the wife must take over for practical as well as altruistic reasons.

[6] Like all research topics, interest in the coping patterns of wives of alcoholics, the psychological sources of her reactions to her husband's drinking, as well as the effect of her behavior on his imbibing have been in and out of fashion. In the 1940s, 1950s and early 1960s, emphasis was on her "pathological" personality traits. It was also suggested that she somehow manipulated her husband into being an alcoholic and/or remaining one. Thus, the wife was seen as an important link in the etiology of alcoholism. In the late 1960s, studies failed to find personality differences between these wives and women in marriages

---

[4] The strategy of "acting natural" appears to transcend cultural boundaries. Finnish wives of alcoholics also described this ploy (Wiseman, 1976).

I do all the shopping. I take him to work and bring him home, pick him up from work, and I pay the bills and, you know, things like that. Well, I thought it would help him, that I could, you know, help with some of the responsibilities. I thought maybe he could have been tired—they need a drink to relax. I thought that might be the problem.

Another indirect strategy involved selecting "safe," non-drinking companions or visitors for social occasions.

I tried getting us involved with people that didn't drink as much as we did, but he found them very dull.

If he would say, "I am going to go out for a little while," I'd say, "Take Mike with you." He is five years old. I figure if he (the husband) has the child with him, he would not go to the pub.

Wives also tried to manipulate the money available to their husbands for alcohol. Those wives who had direct access to the family money and got the paycheck first, hid the checkbook or hid extra money. Wives who found it difficult to physically withhold or hide money, however, took a more indirect course and often attempted to spend so much that there was little or no money left for alcohol.

Neither approach was successful in preventing most husbands from getting money to buy alcohol. Desperation finally drove the wife of an alcoholic at one time or another to try and curtail the supply of liquor available in the home. They poured out liquor, smashed bottles wherever they found them, or hid the liquor supply from their husbands. This direct

---

where alcoholism was not a problem, and it was thought that any emotional problems a wife might have were the result of the stress caused by living with him. At this time, there was more focus on how this stress, however understandable, might result in her acting in ways to undermine his treatment —however sincerely she might want to help her husband stop drinking. Thus, emphasis was on how to counsel her to help him. In the 1970s, these two concerns were, to some extent combined in the systems approach to alcoholism. Here, the wife was seen as part of a family system which when adjusted to his drinking unknowingly perpetuated it. Practical focus here is on family therapy to make wives of alcoholics aware of the system which has been created and to enable them to handle their behavior in such a way as not to perpetuate it.

and time-worn strategy is more histrionic than really helpful to finding a solution for the problem.

Industrial therapy. Quite often part of the therapeutic milieu in the mental hospital or institutional setting is what has been termed "industrial therapy" (Belknap, 1956; Wiseman, 1970). This "I.T." refers to routine work around the ward, which is assigned to patients in an attempt to keep them out of trouble, taking up free time with a "useful pursuit." A variation of this approach has been invented by wives of alcoholics, who exhibit great versatility in the creation of tasks and a subtlety of task management. Because their rather special form of industrial therapy grew out of their subordinate position in the marriage dyad, however, wives attempted to increase the number of activities where their husbands usually and voluntarily drink less. By this strategy, women reduced their spouses' intake without creating an awareness of manipulation.

I try to keep him busy. I bought paintings for him . . . You know, those paint-by-the-numbers things.

I tried to interest him in reading, but that didn't work. (I tried) gardening . . . We did a lot of gardening together. We planned out our landscaping and, of course, the house which I thought was the final, ultimate . . . Eventually, I had to subcontract practically everything, because he just could not grasp hold of it . . . it didn't work.

Drinking along with him. With some vague intent of forcing him to "share the supply," or "showing him," or "letting him see what it is like to be living with an alcoholic," or forcing him to "cut down in order to be a better example to her," some wives turned to a dangerous and dramatic strategy—they tried to drink as much as the men did. Most wives found this an impossible task; they usually were unable to match their alcoholic spouses drink for drink. Either they became ill and passed out, or they retreated from the approach upon becoming frightened that they themselves might be developing a serious drinking problem.

Other wives reasoned that if a husband's drinking could be restricted to the home, he would drink less. To get him to drink at home, they start drinking with him, trying to create a party atmosphere that would be competitive with the inviting social milieu of the bars he frequented. But, as with "use the supply" and "fighting fire with fire" approaches, most wives found the "home party" strategy failed because they couldn't match their husband's intake stamina.

It was great (drinking with him at home), but then after two or three drinks, I had enough and I was ready to go to bed. By then he was so happy . . . he'd want me to sit with him 'till three o'clock, and if I refused, and say, "I have to go to work, I don't want to drink more," then, well, he'd go out. So you see, there was no way of stopping him.

Miscellaneous indirect strategies. In their desperation to turn back the tide of their husbands' increasingly heavy drinking, wives also tried a variety of other strategies—all covert in nature and some reflecting what stress can do to a person's powers of reasoning.

I tried behavior modification. The biggest behavior mod I've done is definitely withhold sex.

I remembered he loved his boots, and I thought somehow, if I do something to these boots so he can't wear them to go out drinking, then he won't go; (so) I hid them.

The "Hands-off" Approach

After extensive efforts at various aspects of home treatment, wives began to feel (sometimes through counseling or at Al-Anon) that they personally could do little about their husband's drinking. McNamara (1960) has pointed out that for many wives, this is a relief.

I figure after trying everything out, I figure let me leave him alone. It will either kill him or cure him, or something, but let him do it on his own. I cannot fight him. I fight, I get less results, so I figure let me let it be.

After allowing the problem to lie fallow for a time, however, the wife finally turned to professional help for her husband. She realized at last her inability to do anything to help him. This awareness signals a greater acceptance of the illness theory of problem drinking, as well as a definite end to any hope of handling the problem within the family. The home treatment was terminated. Coping began to focus on how to adjust to an alcoholic in the family. Parenthetically, contact with alcoholism treatment professionals, initially on behalf of her husband, may eventually result in the wife arranging for counseling for herself.

Summary and Conclusions

Well before a man's drinking problem emerges to engage the attention of professionals in the field, his wife is usually attempting to cope through what might be termed "the home treatment." Wives start out certain their special marital relationship, plus the objective facts of their husband's increased alcohol intake and its obvious results, will mean that the spouse will yield to a logical argument. They soon discover that they are trying to dissuade a man from a behavior that at present defies logic.

Wives turn next to emotional pleading and threats followed by a series of indirect strategies that signal a change from perceiving the husband's heavy drinking as a voluntary act to viewing it as a compulsion or illness. Among the indirect strategies are some intended to create a stress-free environment for the husband and thus eliminate his need to drink. These strategies are what wives refer to as "acting natural" (pretending he is not drunk and making no fuss about it), and "taking over" (handling all tasks and chores connected with the household). Wives also will drop drinking friends of their husbands and take up non-drinking companions; they will attempt to keep their husbands from having money to spend on alcohol; and sometimes they will destroy the home supply of liquor. They also may attempt to drink with him as a means of getting him to reduce his own intake. None of these efforts work.

These home treatment approaches remind us that the first type of coping behavior people select when a stressful problem strikes seldom includes adjustment to the many facets of their changed circumstances created by the problem. More often it is a valiant attempt to return to some less painful *status quo.* Furthermore, as with the case of alcoholism, many coping efforts take place in a knowledge vacuum, without counseling or professional help. These coping strategies by wives of alcoholics are the individualistic (and somewhat naïve) attempts to handle things alone with methods that have the potential of doing more harm than good.

Additionally, a most important aspect in understanding each spouse's effect on the other is that the wife must live, in a very literal sense, with her therapeutic failures. She gets no surcease on nights or weekends. That is the hardest part of all for her and an important factor for the study of interaction with an alcoholic over time. One wife[7] who had been both in the role of a professional (a social worker) and the wife of an alcoholic was quite aware of this:

I tried to think of him as sick, but it was hard to do. I knew he was sick, but I had to stand him. I had worked with alcoholics as a social worker, but it's different living with one.

If these wives could be reached by educators and counselors in this early stage of their husbands' problem drinking, they might be saved the disappointment of futile attempts to "cure" their husband's alcoholism single-handedly. Furthermore, the emotional stress and ultimate alienation these efforts cause in both spouses (which may actually exacerbate the drinking) could be avoided. Most important, wives might be given instructions on more fruitful approaches to handling an alcoholic husband in the beginning stages of his drinking career.

---

[7]This quote comes from a Finnish wife, indicating, again, how the effects of an alcoholic in the family are strikingly similar, despite cultural differences (Wiseman, 1976).

REFERENCES

Belknap, L. *Human problems in a state mental hospital*. New York: McGraw-Hill, 1956.

Cheek, F. E., Franks, C. M., Laucius, J., & Burtle, V. Behavior-modification training for wives of alcoholics. *Quarterly Journal of Studies on Alcoholism*, 1971, **32**, 456-461.

Corder, B. F., Hendricks, A., & Corder, R. F. An MMPI study of a group of wives of alcoholics. *Quarterly Journal of Studies on Alcohol*, 1964, **25**, 551-554.

deSaugy, D. L'alcoolique et sa femme: Etude psychosociale et statistique sur les conditions de leur developpement individuel et de leur vie en commun. *Hygiene Mental*, 1962, **51**, 81-128, 145-201.

Edwards, P., Harvey, C., & Whitehead, P. C. Wives of alcoholics: A critical review and analysis. *Quarterly Journal of Studies on Alcohol*, 1974, **34**, 112-132.

Estes, N. J. Counseling the wife of an alcoholic spouse. *American Journal of Nursing*, 1974, **74**, 1251-1255.

Futterman, S. Personality trends in wives of alcoholics. *Journal of Psychiatric Social Work*, 1953, **23**, 37-41.

Goffman, E. Insanity of place. *Psychiatry*, 1968, **32**, 357-388.

Jackson, J. K. The adjustment of the family to the crisis of alcoholism. *Quarterly Journal of Studies on Alcohol*, 1954, **4**, 562-586.

Jackson, J. K. The adjustment of the family to alcoholism. *Journal of Marriage and the Family*, 1956, **18**, 361-369.

Jackson, J. K. Family structure and alcoholism. *Mental Hygiene*, 1959, **43**, 403-406.

Jackson, J. K. Alcoholism and the family. In D. J. Pittman & C. R. Snyder (Eds.), *Society, culture, and drinking patterns*. New York: Wiley, 1962.

James, J. E., & Goldman, M. Behavior trends of wives of alcoholics. *Quarterly Journal of Studies on Alcohol*, 1971, **32**, 373-381.

Kalashian, M. M. Working with the wives of alcoholics in an out-patient clinic setting. *Journal of Marriage and the Family*, 1959, **21**, 130-133.

Kogan, K. L., Fordyce, W. E., & Jackson, J. K. Personality disturbances in wives of alcoholics. *Quarterly Journal of Studies on Alcohol*, 1963, **24**, 227-238.

Kogan, K. L., & Jackson, J. K. Role perceptions in wives of alcoholics and of non-alcoholics. *Quarterly Journal of Studies on Alcohol*, 1963, **24**, 627-639.

McNamara, J. H. The disease conception of alcoholism: Its therapeutic value for the alcoholic and his wife. *Social Casework*, 1960, **41**, 460-465.

Mitchell, H. E. The interrelatedness of alcoholism and marital conflict. *American Journal of Orthopsychiatry*, 1959, **29**, 547-559.

Orford, J. F., & Guthrie, S. Coping behavior used by wives of alcoholics: A preliminary investigation. *International Congress of Alcohol and Alcoholism, Proceedings*, 1968, **1**, 97.

Paolino, T. J., & McCrady, B. S. *The alcoholic marriage: Alternative perspectives*. New York: Grune & Stratton, 1977.

Paredes, A. Marital-sexual factors in alcoholism. *Medical Aspects of Human Sexuality*, 1973, **7**, 98-115.

Price, G. M. A study of the wives of twenty alcoholics. *Quarterly Journal of Studies on Alcohol*, 1945, **5**, 620-627.

Rae, J. B., & Forbes, A. R. Clinical and psychometric characteristics of the wives of alcoholics. *British Journal of Psychiatry*, 1966, **112**, 197-200.

Rapoport, R. N. *Community as doctor: New perspectives on a therapeutic community*. London: Tavistock, 1959.

Safilios-Rothschild, C. Patterns of familial power and influence. *Sociological Focus*, 1969, **2**, 7-19.

Schelling, Thomas C. *The strategy of conflict*. New York: Oxford University Press, 1963.

Shibutani, T. *Society and personality*. Englewood Cliffs: Prentice-Hall, 1961.

Steinglass, P. Experimenting with family treatment approaches to alcoholism, 1950-1975: A review. *Family Process*, 1976, **15**, 97-123.

Steinglass, P., & Moyer, J. K. Assessing alcohol use in family life: A necessary but neglected area for clinical research. *The Family Coordinator*, 1977, **26**, 53-60.

Steinglass, P., Weiner, S., & Mendelson, J. H. A systems approach to alcoholism: A model and its clinical application. *Archives of General Psychiatry*, 1971, **24**, 401-408.

Wiseman, J. P. *Stations of the lost: The treatment of skid row alcoholics*. Englewood Cliffs, NJ: Prentice-Hall, 1970.

Wiseman, J. P. Early diagnosis and therapeutic strategies on the home front. (Part I of *The other half: Wife of an alcoholic in Finland*.) *Alkoholipolitikka*, 1976, **41**, 62-72.

This paper presents findings from a recent study of a population of middle-class Catholic families, primarily Irish, German, and Italian, among whom alcohol-related problems are frequent and severe. To understand alcohol usage in this population, a knowledge of the historical and cultural roles of drinking in the relevant ethnic or national groups and a holistic view of contemporary family life are essential. It is suggested that massive social controls in major areas of family life are closely related to problematic drinking behavior. The delineation of cultural prescriptions regarding behaviors and attitudes directly and indirectly related to drinking patterns may contribute a significant cultural dimension to proposed models of the "alcoholic family" system.

25

THE SIGNIFICANCE OF CULTURAL PATTERNING FOR THE "ALCOHOLIC FAMILY"*

Joan Ablon†

FOLLOWING THE REALIZATION that most alcoholics were not homeless derelicts, a florescence of clinical literature dealing with family-related aspects of alcoholism began to appear in the 1950s and 1960s. The evolution of research orientations may be traced through several distinct phases that have focused on psychological features of individual family members and interactional aspects of the family as a closed system (1). Little or no attention is given in most of these works to the cultural, social, or economic aspects of family life or to what extent role behavior of family members is the living-out of cultural expectations or prescriptions. This paper will present findings from a recent study of nonlabeled, "normal," middle-class Catholic families, largely Irish, German, and Italian, in which alcohol-related problems are frequent and severe. The findings suggest that to understand the role of alcohol usage in this population, an understanding of the historical and cultural role of drinking in the relevant ethnic or national groups and a holistic view of contemporary family life are essential.

Early "family" studies documented the pathology of the nondrinking spouse. The most persistently explored subject has been the personality and role of "the wife of the alcoholic" in relation to the inception and maintenance of her husband's excessive drinking problem. She has usually been considered either the culprit or, less commonly, the martyr in this portrayal. Clinically oriented studies portrayed the wife as a disturbed pathological personality with dependency conflicts and complex needs

* The research on which this paper is based was supported by Grants Number 2 R01 AA00180, NIAAA and MH-08375, NIMH. I wish to thank Dr. Betty Kalis for her criticisms of a previous draft of this paper.

† Associate Professor of Medical Anthropology, Departments of Psychiatry and Epidemiology and International Health, University of California School of Medicine, San Francisco.

From Joan Ablon, "The Significance of Cultural Patterning for the 'Alcoholic Family,' " *Family Process*, 1980, 19, pp. 127-144. Reprinted by permission of the publisher and author.

that directed her to choose as a husband an alcoholic or someone with a personality type susceptible to alcoholism (if it were not full-blown at the time of marriage) and further to maintain the excessive drinking patterns of her spouse. She dominated the marriage by taking over the roles he, by default, could not fulfill because of his drinking and then castigated him for his insufficiencies. For examples of such studies, see Price (26), Futterman (14), and Macdonald (22).

A contrasting point of view emphasizing family stress was first presented in the works of Jackson (17, 18, 19), who focused on how the family as a unit adjusted to the alcoholism of one of its members. From her systematic observation of women in Al-Anon Family Groups in Seattle over nearly a decade, Jackson presented in various papers a natural history of the phases of the alcoholic process. Jackson was skeptical about the validity of hypothesizing that current pathological characteristics of the wife constituted a set personality type that existed in the predrinking or premarriage period. In rebuttal to the typologies of wives of alcoholics presented by clinicians, she presented the alternative suggestion that the particular so-called "pathological" behavior constellations described might represent these women as they coped in particular ways appropriate to stresses of the various stages of family adaptation to alcoholism. Kogan, Fordyce, and Jackson (21), and Corder, Hendricks, and Corder (10) presented evidence from a variety of studies that a conceptualization of the unitary personality for wives of alcoholics is not tenable. For comprehensive literature reviews, see Ablon (1), Edwards, Harvey, and Whitehead (12), and Paolino and McCrady (25).

A series of papers that implicitly or explicitly regarded the total family unit as the necessary functional context for an understanding of the individual alcoholic's drinking patterns began to appear in the late 1960s. These studies utilized systems and interactional theories, positing that the major perpetuator of drinking patterns is the overriding need for the maintenance of the status quo or family homeostasis that has developed within the family system. Ewing and Fox (13) presented the best early statement of this approach. Steinglass, Weiner, and Mendelson (30, 31), Steinglass (29), Davis et al. (11), Wolin et al. (36), Bowen (6), Berenson (5), and Ward and Faillace (34) explicated a variety of theoretical and practical aspects inherent in the viewing of alcohol-related problems within a systems approach. The realistic unit for research and treatment is recognized to be the "alcoholic system" rather than the alcoholic family member.

Steinglass et al. (31) presented a model detailing the manner in which family members are involved in an ongoing alcoholic bargain that functions for the maintenance of the system. The authors suggest that family members as component parts of a system "manipulate" other members and adjust their behavior as is necessary to maintain a "complementary relationship of psychopathology, needs, strengths, cultural values, etc. within the family" (31, p. 405). This maneuvering is necessary for the ongoing existence of the family group as a functioning system. Drinking behavior may operate in either of two forms: (a) The drinking behavior of one member may serve as a symptom or expression of stress created by conflicts within the system. In this way the drinking may serve, as it were, as an escape valve for such stress. Or, (b) drinking may constitute an integral part of one of the working programs within the system. In this form it might serve unconscious needs of family members in its effect on such areas as role differentiation or the distribution of power or "might express culturally learned attitudes toward alcohol" (31, p. 406).

This model offers a bridge between the psychological and sociological theories presented previously by pointing up differing functions of excessive drinking for individual family members and for the maintenance of the ongoing family system.

Sociocultural Factors

The significance of cultural patterning for family roles and behavior has been given scant attention in any of the foregoing literature. Although the importance of sociocultural factors as one significant determinant in stimulating or maintaining the specific drinking behavior of the alcoholic individual has been considered by Bales (2, 3), Snyder (28), and Ullman (33), the role of these factors in relation to the behavior of the spouse or other family members has been ignored. For example, the majority of the studies dealing with alcoholism and the family present little or no comment on the sociocultural contexts within which their subjects exist. The drinking patterns and attitudes of the nuclear family, the extended family, the friendship circle or church mates of the alcoholic or even of the community caregivers in the larger society are not considered or even mentioned. Although Steinglass, Weiner and Mendelson's highly sophisticated model (31) allows for cultural considerations, no exploration of the implications of sociocultural affiliation were made in the published case studies of Steinglass or his colleagues, nor were sociocultural features held constant to allow an analysis of their significance.

The data presented in this study illustrate the case of families in which the excessive use of alcohol indeed fulfills *all* of the functions for individual members and for the maintenance of the system as outlined in the model above, yet the homeostatic theme or *cultural* paradigm that perpetuates heavy drinking has been handed down through the generations and is a strong and encompassing one, perhaps as significant as the individual "pathological needs" of any one family member.

Traditional Drinking Patterns and Family Life

This study deals with Irish, German, and Italian Catholic families in a metropolitan

area of Southern California. Survey research data rank Catholics nationally and locally the highest among religious groups for prevalence of alcohol-related problems. Among American ethnic groups, the Irish rank the highest or near highest in terms of heavy intake, loss of control, untoward social consequences, and the provision of social support for heavy drinking among associates. Germans and Italians traditionally have low rates of problem drinking within their European contexts or as defined ethnic groups in the United States. Although systematic moderate to heavy drinking is widespread in both groups, chronic alcoholism or related problems are not attributed to either (7, 8).

The Irish in their homeland have ranked internationally among the highest groups for prevalence of alcohol-related problems. The literature on the Irish in Ireland is replete with statements about the prevalence of hard drinking among males and the purported relation of this pattern to characteristics of the family, social, and economic systems. Bales (2) cited a variety of historical, economic and cultural factors that contributed to drinking patterns: poverty, the substitution of drink for food, harsh childrearing practices and family conflict. Bales suggested that the fact that drinking in Ireland was carried out within convivial and utilitarian contexts rather than in a sacred context also contributed to widespread excessive drinking. He further posited the function of male peer group drinking for suppression of forbidden aggression and sexuality.

Hard drinking has been related by a number of researchers to Irish family life. Marriage, Messenger noted, is primarily an economic relationship. The relation between spouses is one of accommodation, and affection, when present, lacks depth. "She keeps the fire going, has the tea ready, and listens to a man's troubles" (24, p. 77).

The Irish mother has been portrayed vividly as a controlling matriarch by many writers. Men tend to relate to their wives as they have related to their mothers. The wife is the strong person on whom the husband is emotionally dependent, even when their relationship is one of mutual withdrawal and uncooperativeness.

Attitudes of the Irish toward marriage and sex were and are, even today, problematic. Irish marriages are fewer and occur later than in any Western country. Messenger (24), who studied life in a contemporary Irish village Inis Beag, stated:

> Marriage is looked on with trepidation, or at least as something less than desirable. The marriageable man in his late twenties and thirties is usually sexually repressed to an unbelieveable degree, has been dominated by parents who have allowed him to take on few responsibilities, has a mother who acts as a wife surrogate in all but the sexual sphere (at least consciously), has established a routinized existence, and has male companions for whom he feels affection and with whom he shares numerous work and recreational activities. [24, pp. 68–69]

Messenger (24) stated that the most prominent characteristic of Inis Beag (and Irish) personality probably was sexual puritanism. Messenger (24), Connery (9), and Scheper-Hughes (27) have well documented the obsessive fears and avoidance of sex among contemporary Irish populations. Sexual activities are avoided when possible by late marriage and by choosing religious vocations, the latter demanding a lifetime status of celibacy. One female informant told Messenger, "Men can wait a long time for 'it,' but we can wait a lot longer" (24, p. 109).

Stivers (32) presented an incisive analysis relating economic and social factors to drinking patterns of Irish and Irish-Americans. He suggested that hard drinking, which only occasionally became drunkenness and alcoholism, was used by Irish men to reaffirm their identity in times of collective and individual crisis. The collective crisis was caused by the traditional family "stem" system of inheritance in which only one son, usually the eldest, inherited the

farm. Often he had to wait into his middle years until his father was willing to give up the farm and the status it carried. Although the eldest son could not marry until he was a landholder, younger siblings were even more disadvantaged. They remained landless or had to emigrate. Hard drinking among men became a basis for status in the bachelor group, membership in which constituted the redeeming masculine identity for landless, single males.

Stivers traced the history of Irish immigration to this country and pointed up the severe early discrimination against the Irish. He built a case for the view that hard drinking in the United States was disembodied from its cultural context in Ireland and became important among Irish immigrants as a national identifying trait, both to Irishmen and to their fellow Americans. "In Ireland drink was largely a sign of male identity; in America it was a symbol of Irish identity" (32, p. 129). Stivers further traced the uneasy passage from hard drinking to drunkenness:

> Thus, in the Irish-American family, the mother held up to her children two ideal sexual roles: the chaste Irish woman and the saintly Irish man (the priest). In contradistinction to this, adult males proffered to the adolescent male the hero of the political boss, reputed to be the epitome of a man of the world, a force to be reckoned with, and among other things, a hard drinker. Irish-American literature indicates also that some mothers caviled about their husband's or brother's drunkenness to their sons. So, hard drinking or drunkenness also became a negative identity, something to be avoided at all costs.

> The upshot of this discussion is that some adolescent males could handle the positive identity of hard drinker provided by adult male companions and synthesize it together with their mother's valuation of priestliness; but others were doomed to choose the negative identity of drunkard, which on the surface met the requisites of the male group. It was their mothers' inability to tolerate their sons' drinking in any form that contributed to their choice of the negative identity. Added to this

was the stereotype of the Irish-American as drunkard, which confirmed on the cultural level what was in some instances being foisted on the Irish male on the psychological level. [32, pp. 134–135]

No formal ethnographic descriptions of contemporary Irish-American family life exist. Greeley (15), with characteristic Irish wit and the temerity only an Irishman may exhibit in writing about the Irish, has presented a sharp commentary on the affective characteristics of the Irish family. He stated that the Irish have "practically no capacity to give themselves in intimate relationships. Emotions are kept under control by internal guilt feelings and external ridicule" (15, pp. 104–105). Tenderness is not tolerated. Greeley presented a dim view of sexual relations among Irish-Americans.

One has the impression—obviously from the secure but biased perspective of the celibate—that many, if not most, Irish-Americans get rather little enjoyment out of sex and are not very skillful in the art of lovemaking. This may stem from the fact that the Irish are generally not very good at demonstrating tenderness or affection for those whom they love. The Irish male, particularly in his cups, may spin out romantic poetry extolling the beauty of his true love, but he becomes awkward and tongue-tied in their presence and clumsy, if not rough, in his attempts at intimacy. She, on the other hand, finds it hard to resist the temptation to become stiff, if not frigid, in the face of his advances, however much warmth she may feel. For her especially, sexual relationships are a matter of duty, and if she fails in her "duty" to her husband she will have to report it the next time she goes to confession. Some Irish women, with obvious pride, will boast that they have never once refused the "duty" to their husbands, even though in twenty years of marriage they have not got one single bit of pleasure out of it. A sex encounter between a twosome like that is not likely to be pleasurable. [15, p. 114]

Greeley stated that the Irish often tend to drink for reassurance and escape from their "intolerable" psychological burdens and their need to repress sexuality and ag-

gressiveness. He described the domination of the Irish-American mother who rules her family by her strong will or by subtly manipulating the sympathies and guilts of her husband and children. Greeley noted that "many, if not most of the alcoholic Irishmen I know come from families where the mother rules the roost and have married women who are very much like their mothers." [15, p. 135]

In sum, a number of social scientists clearly have pointed up a variety of common economic, social, and personal characteristics shared by hard-drinking Irish and Irish-Americans.

The Population

The families described here resided in a middle-class, Catholic parish of a West Coast metropolitan area. A year-long, ethnographic survey of the parish produced a social and economic profile of a relatively homogeneous population constituting some 80 per cent of the 2000 parish families and representing demographically a significant proportion of the total population of their metropolitan area according to census statistics. The majority of families were second and third American-born generations of European stocks, chiefly Irish, German, and Italian. They exhibited remarkably similar marital and family histories and were employed within several discrete occupational clusters—civil service, large utility companies, and small business operations. Features of family life style and social, political, and economic values were predictably similar. Thirty families were chosen for more intensive family study as highly representative of the ethnicity, lifestyle, and values of the parish population. The sample then is a carefully *selected* one, rather than a statistically representative one. All families who were contacted agreed to participate in the project.

A focused study of family dynamics and interaction was carried out by the author with these 30 families through interviews and observations over a four-year period.

The wife in every case was the principal informant. In one-third of the families, husbands were also interviewed. The wife was chosen as the key informant primarily in keeping with her central affective and functional position in the family vis-à-vis husband and children. Furthermore the wife was much more readily accessible around the clock to the female investigator than the husband because of male work schedules. However, the logistic accessibility of wives was secondary to the consideration of their appropriateness for the gathering of material on total family interaction. Although the potential for perceptual bias was recognized, interviews with other family members, statements about family dynamics by other parish informants outside of the family, and ongoing systematic observation for cross-checking the validity of wives' statements by the researcher were felt to control effectively for the wife-informant as a potential problem. Knupfer (20), from a comparison of wives' and husbands' responses to questions about husbands' drinking problems found a high degree of reliability in wives' responses. In fact she noted that the spouse was the more reliable source in cases of contradictory information. Guze (16) found that criminals queried about their drinking problems gave more frequent positive responses concerning their drinking histories than did their relatives. McCrady, Paolino, and Longabaugh (23) reported positive correlations between reports of drinkers and their spouses about the drinkers' behavior and impairment. It should be noted that in all of the above cases any disparity was in the spouses' *underreporting* of drinking behavior. The danger that spouses would exaggerate the alcoholics' drinking does not seem great on the basis of these reports.

Participant observation of family activities in a wide variety of contexts provided a wealth of material complementary to that elicited in the interviews. For instance, the observer was present at varying times of the day—mornings, afternoons, and eve-nings—in many households. Family behavior was observed at meal times and during varied social and recreational activities in the home, at church, at parties and weddings, and out of the city at vacation resort areas.

In 21 cases, the marital unions represented a mixture of ethnic strains, predominately Irish and German, or Irish and Italian. Often the parents of each spouse also represented differing ethnic groups. Very few "pure" Irish, Italians, or Germans were encountered unless the parents of informants were the migrant generation. In most instances informants were third generation (second American-born generation). Census materials and interviews with local population specialists reflected clearly that the mixture found in these families was highly typical of the larger population of old European Catholic settlers in this metropolitan area.

Although the researcher initially classified families' ethnicity for sampling by the ethnicity of husband and classified individuals by father's ethnicity, it later became evident that informants, when asked, tended to vary in how they defined their own ethnic identity. Some classified themselves by their father's chief ethnic identification (which also was mixed) and some by the mother's. Furthermore they might change this classification depending upon the context and their humor at that time. Any Irish identity on one or both sides often predominated in identification. (Table I shows the ethnic mix of the thirty families in the sample. Table II shows the ethnic identification of husbands and wives.)

Although this study reveals the significance of the mother's ethnicity as well as the father's for prediction of drinking problems, survey research data customarily do not distinguish with specificity the ethnicity of parents or grandparents. For example, Cahalan and Room (8, p. 203), one of the most useful compilations available, classified subjects by their responses to the ques-

TABLE I

Ethnic Mix of Families as Classified by Fathers

Husband's Father	Wife's Father	N
Irish	Irish	6
German	Irish	6
Italian	Italian	2
Irish	German	1
Irish	Italian	1
Irish	Other	1
German	Other	3
Italian	Irish	1
Italian	German	1
Italian	Other	1
Other	Irish	2
Other	Italian	1
Other	Other	4
		30

TABLE II

Ethnic Identification of Husbands' and Wives' Parents

	Ethnicity of Fathers		Ethnicity of Mothers	
	Husbands	Wives	Husbands	Wives
Irish	9	15	14	14
German	9	2	6	6
Italian	5	5	3	2
Mixed, Other*	7	8	7	8

* Other nationalities represented in the sample are English, Scotch-English, French, Dutch, Mexican, and Middle-Eastern.

tions, "What country or countries did most of your ancestors come from?," and "Which one do you feel closest to?," if there was more than one country of ancestry. Thus, ethnicity was an approximate conception rather than a specific empirical one.

Ethnicity has differing meanings for each family. Relatively few informants exhibited outward social indicators such as belonging to national clubs. The most significant elements remaining, although not in the consciousness of informants, appeared to be particular elements of traditional childrearing and role behavior differentially present when the mother or father was of Irish heritage. The Irish and German mothers described were the strong, dominating forces in their families of orientation, and their daughters, the subjects of this study, likewise were strong wives and mothers.

Irish and, in fewer cases, German fathers typically were described as nice, quiet men who had frequently displayed excessive drinking patterns, as did many of their adult sons.

Ages of subjects ranged from 34 to 64 with a mean of 50 for the men and 47 for the women. The normative level of educational attainment for both men and women was high school graduation. The economic pursuits of two-thirds of husbands were in city or federal civil service. The remaining one-third were employed in about equal numbers in large utility companies, and the management of their own small businesses. This occupational breakdown was representative of the parish population at large.

Most of these couples were reared in an older part of their city and attended parochial schools there, being educated in a "parochial school culture" that homogenized most aspects of life. Couples met in school or in their home neighborhoods, in Catholic young peoples' groups, or at work. Early marriage was the expectation, and most couples married before age 21. It appears that couples often were propelled into marriage because of premarital sexual restrictions and family pressures before they had the opportunity for social maturation. Nonetheless, whatever the age at marriage and the place of meeting, informants married persons who brought similar backgrounds, values, and expectations to the union. The population was remarkably homogeneous in lifestyle and values. The marital contract in these Catholic families was, in almost every case, an all-encompassing lifeway of shared goals and role expectations. The marriage relationship was seen as an organic, going concern that had to and would work out.

Families tended to be child-centered, with planning of daily, weekly, and yearly activities built around children's school and recreational needs. Large families were highly valued. Most families in the sample, as well as in the parish at large, had from three to five children. Some families in keeping with the Church's strictures against birth control, produced more children than the parents were emotionally able to cope with or economically equipped to maintain in the manner considered appropriate. About one-third of the women spontaneously brought up the issue of difficulties in their family life that they felt had been caused by the Church's attitudes toward birth control. Many of these women stated that if they were newly married now they would not hesitate to use some form of birth control.

The parish population unequivocally was a drinking population, and liberal alcohol usage was an expected part of the good life. Alcohol abuse and alcohol-related family problems were common, although hidden to the larger society. Massive denial existed in regard to help-seeking by problem drinkers, and to a lesser degree, by their families. Families were divided into categories according to husbands' drinking patterns. Drinking patterns labeled here as "problematic" were defined as such by the wife and in some cases also the husband in interviews. In most instances the problematic (i.e., disruptive) nature of patterns was clearly witnessed by the researcher during participant observation of family life. Fourteen families exhibited nonproblematic drinking patterns, also normative in drinking frequency to the parish population (one to two drinks or less daily). Sixteen currently had or had had in the past severe drinking problems. Five men were totally abstinent or drank rarely as a consequence of a severe drinking problem in the past. Five fairly distinct categories of drinking patterns were delineated:

1. "Normative" drinking of one to two drinks daily with no problem indicated (N = 11).
2. Rare drinking in the home with guests or at parties or on trips out of the home with no problem indicated (N = 3).
3. Abstinence or rare drinking as a consequence of a severe drinking problem in the past (N = 5).
4. Continuous drinking in the home at

nights or on weekends, defined as a problem (N = 7).
5. Periodic but frequent binge drinking (five hours to overnight) outside of the home, defined as a problem (N = 4).

Although a few wives were observed to be heavy systematic drinkers, only one self-acknowledged alcoholic woman existed within this sample. No more than two or three others within the parish were reported or known to the researcher over the four-year period.

Excessive drinking patterns appeared to be a core element of family conflict. For example, families were divided into four categories in accordance with reported and observed conflict. Twelve families were normatively or reasonably functioning with a minimum of conflict, two had had severe conflict in the past but were reasonably functioning at present, nine had stabilized in a condition of ongoing conflict, and seven were acutely conflicted. Of the 18 making up the last three categories, strikingly, 16 have or had-alcohol abuse as a clearly expressed core element of family conflict.

Initial surveys of the population pointed up two aspects of family life that appeared to be related: a prevalence of alcohol-related problems and the existence of strong, culturally patterned controls encompassing almost all features of individual and family life.

The pattern of tradition in these families functioned in a variety of ways; it constituted the superstructure that made for strong, stable families. There was essentially no divorce or separation. Young people followed a relatively traditional pathway through high school graduation into college or employment, and they ultimately married—normative life career rituals that have disappeared for many young people in contemporary society. Family members worked at the jobs that are basic to the maintenance of American life as we know it. They provided the essential routine of the work-a-day world; they were proud to be civil servants and to serve the taxpayers.

The traditional pattern of social controls

was maintained in large part by the almost unchanging nature of primary relationships in these families. The relationships were constituted by extended kin and friends from high school, and in many cases, even early childhood. Continuing weekly social activities with persons in these categories were typical. The pattern of primary relations tended to be extended throughout the lifetime, but narrow in breadth and parochial, allowing for few new persons and ideas to be introduced. This social pattern in most cases served to steer both men and women into highly stylized sex and work roles and to preclude new behaviors.

These massive social controls stood in anomalistic relief to the permissive and alternative lifestyles of the metropolitan area in which this population lived. Histories revealed that throughout their lives the pattern of social controls often served to lock both men and women into painful family roles and to stifle personal and family interaction, creativity, and freedom of choice in major areas of the life career.

The chief areas of control are best conceptualized as interrelated constellations of features central to family life. The most significant dealt with marital roles and relationships. For instance, adherence to religious strictures against premarital sex, birth control, and abortion often resulted in inhibiting spontaneous sexual expression and producing more children than the family could financially support in the manner perceived as necessary. Adults frequently were still subject to the expectations and ongoing coercive presence of family of orientation, and as a result were not able to grow in new and potentially productive ways in their family of procreation.

Problematic drinking patterns occurred with greatest severity in the families of cultural groups exhibiting the highest levels of expressed and accepted family and subgroup societal controls concerning the above important areas of family life. Thus Irish Catholics, who have traditionally exhibited the greatest amount of control in all features of life, also exhibited more problem drinking than other Catholics.

The significance of oppressive social controls as they related to problem drinking are suggested here to lie in the *interrelationship* of certain *peculiar* characteristics of specific religious and ethnic groups and not in the nature of *individual* elements as they might appear in many populations. For example, perhaps the most important single area, that of religious strictures dealing with sexual behavior, was pervasive, affecting almost all other areas of family life. It also was specific to the Catholic subculture and within this, occurred even more rigidly among Irish Catholics. Other areas of control are commonly found among many groups—for instance, Jews, who have a particularly low rate of alcoholism.

Ethnicity and Problematic Drinking Patterns

Problematic drinking in the sample was linked most closely to the Irish (see Tables III & IV). In *all* cases (N = 8) in which men had an Irish father *and* an Irish mother there was or had been a serious alcohol problem. In cases in which husbands had an Irish mother but father of another ethnicity, if that father was characterized at least as a *heavy* drinker even if not "alcoholic," the subject also had a drinking problem (N = 3). In one instance in which the mother was Irish and the father (French) was said to have been an alcoholic before the subject's birth, the subject drank normatively. Where there was an Irish mother and the son did not have a drinking problem, the *absence* of another variable was striking—the role model of an alcoholic father (N = 3).

Many of the same family characteristics that have been posited by researchers to contribute to excessive drinking patterns in Ireland appeared to persist remarkably intact in this group of families with the traditions of the old country. Child-rearing and marital roles appeared strikingly similar to those common to historical and contemporary Ireland, despite the seeming acculturation and homogenization of the Irish

TABLE III

Ethnic Background of Husbands in Relation to Drinking Problems

	N	Irish Mother	Other Mother	Irish Father	Other Father
Problems	16	11	5	8	8
No Problems	14	2	12	1	13

TABLE IV

Husband's Drinking Patterns × Parents' Ethnicity

	N	Father-Mother IR-IR	Father-Mother IR-Non Ir	Father-Mother Non Ir-IR	All Others
Drinking Problem	16	8	0	3	5
No Problem	14	0	1	3	10

in American society. Elements that appear unique to American society in fact parallel old constrictive patterns. Constrictive cultural features that locked the Irish male and female into frequently painful and problematic family roles and behavior patterns were evidenced in significant themes that pervaded family life.

Normative Life Career Themes that Involve Critical Elements of Control

Because the Irish cultural tradition has prevailed in American Catholic life, the themes presented here, although a part of the life experiences of most Catholics in the study, appeared most clearly in families that had the most significant Irish heritage. The themes emerged from family case materials as features of life and marriage that often appeared to be injurious, according to the subjects, or less frequently as defined by the researcher, to the marital relationship by precluding or diminishing communication and growth of positive, expressive relationships between spouses or between spouses and children. The themes are vividly illustrated through cases materials.

1. *Domineering Mothers.* Wives frequently spoke of the domineering nature of their husbands' mothers (and often their own) in contrast to the passivity of their husbands' fathers (and often their own). The controlling nature of these mothers was much more obvious when the mothers were Irish.

For example, one informant, herself a strong Irish woman, continually talked about her mother-in-law, a remarkable prototype of the Irish matriarch who ruled the social life of her (middle-aged) adult children and their families until her death only a few years ago. Another, herself Irish on both sides, commented on how much her husband was like his father and his uncles, all of whom were alcoholics:

> J's father was German, but he was very inert. He would come to our house and just sit and not do much of anything. J's mother (Irish) was a very pushy kind of woman. When she died, J's father kept saying, "My mamma sure took good care of me." Here was a big six-foot man saying, "My mamma sure took good care of me." I just wasn't going to take that kind of care of J. I didn't want him to get into that.

Another informant, married to a man whose father was Italian and Irish, was tracing the roots of their marital problems. In talking of her husband's mother she noted:

> E's father was Italian, and his mother was Irish. His mother was a very strong woman and did everything for his father. She had definite views on what men did and what women did. When E and I married, his mother told me, "Now E doesn't go to funerals, and E doesn't do this, and E doesn't do that, and E doesn't do the other thing." And I just went along with it because I was young and didn't know anything.

2. *Religious Sanctions Related to Sex.* Strong religious sanctions and the negative

mystique surrounding premarital sexual experimentation and expression caused couples to marry more quickly than wisely. Some informants thought they also caused young men to drink heavily.

One informant articulated this when asked about pressures she may have felt toward early marriage:

Well, being devout Catholics we really couldn't have any sexual relations outside of marriage. If you wanted to pet or do anything like that, you had to do it within marriage. Most of us, most of the people I knew, got married so they could have sexual relations. I knew my husband was a virgin and B (an alcoholic friend) too. That is why I think there was a lot of drinking among these young men—they couldn't have sexual relations because that was so disapproved.

(Drinking wasn't disapproved?)

No, that is just it. The disapproval from the families and the church went to the sex, and it didn't go to the drinking.

(Did you think the Irish drank more than the others?)

Well I think the people in public school drank less than those in parochial school, and those were mostly Irish.

I guess we had abstinence for so long—I remember lying in bed feeling frustrated all those years. Maybe I've tended to sublimate it. So I feel strongly for young people today that they can show their love and not abstain. I feel we have been sexually damaged. That's why young men drank before and during marriage. I think this was a real contributing factor. B's father was a drinker. Maybe he had the same problem.

Or another:

(Did most young people date very much?)

They dated, but I think there was this urgency.

(Did the boys feel the same way in terms of sex as the girls?)

Oh yes, they were devout. I think the fellows were the same way. I think there was a lot of drinking then by young people, young men, because they couldn't go out and have sex. I think there was a lot of drinking in lieu of having sex.

3. *Little Premarital Factual Knowledge About Sex.* Both men and women had little knowledge about sex or intimate relationships. Newlyweds encountered the physical and psychological aspects of marriage with few guidelines. Although sex was considered central to marriage in relation to its procreative function, young people were assiduously protected from information about sexual matters. Newlyweds rarely received any sexual counseling, and the extreme shame and reticence hovering about sex also worked against seeking such counseling at a later time in life. Only when a couple was forced into marital counseling or psychotherapy, usually late in married life, were sexual issues broached, and then it was far too late to be of much help. It is significant that wives often perceived the biggest family problem to be alcohol abuse, but husbands often stated the biggest problem was sex—sexual incompatibility or the unwillingness of their wives to have sexual relations. In these cases, almost invariably women commented on their ignorance of sexual matters when they married—and in fact, to the present day. For example, one informant, who had among the most severe contemporary sexual problems, stated that when she married some twenty years ago, she did not know what to expect from sex. She asked a girlfriend who had married a few months earlier for advice, and the friend told her little more than the informant knew herself at that time. She spoke of her husband as a "sex fiend" when referring to his weekly petitions for relations. After listening to a radio talk show extolling the pleasures of orgasm, she asked the researcher what an orgasm is. "Here," she said, "I've been married over twenty years and have six children, and I don't know if I've had an orgasm."

Another woman, one of the youngest in the sample, at 34 after 16 years of marriage and the mother of five children, asked the researcher to recommend a sexual counseling center she could go to for help.

> I'm just so confused. Several people have told me I should go to one of those sex clinics. I'm afraid they are quacks. Do you know anything about them? He says sex is a big part of the problem and that it's all me. Well, I wonder how I got this way since I've only been with him. It's been a problem for a long time, and he blames everything on that and it seems to be getting worse and worse. I don't think that it's all sex. *Sex* couldn't be *that* important to *anybody*.

Sex for middle-aged Catholic women often is couched in difficulties. Early taboos and ignorance almost certainly set a pattern for an uncomfortable ambivalence at best about sexual relations. Added to this, relationships between spouses often lack romantic feeling or intimacy as defined by the sharing of personal thoughts or desires. Many find little physical pleasure in sexual activities. This is compounded by memories of husbands' perceived insensitivities or obnoxious drinking habits.

> Whenever he'd come near me, I'd remember all those terrible things he did when drunk and my cleaning up the bathroom and all that. I just didn't want him near me.

Some wives commented that excessive drinking contributed to their husbands' loud snoring or unpleasant breath and body odor, which also served to inhibit their positive desires for sex.

Even though wives knew that the "giving" of sex often helped the relationship, on a short-term basis at least, patterned reservations and willful begrudging usually won out. In the possession of the decision to give or not to give, the woman controlled this key to her husband's physical needs.

4. *Strictures Against Birth Control.* Strictures against birth control and the cultural prescriptions exhorting procreation in Catholic family life led to the production of children before couples could work out their own dyadic relationship. Children came quickly in the first years of marriage and

young parents sometimes found themselves totally enveloped in childrearing with little understanding of what their responsibilities as parents meant.

> I guess it was terrible, but within a month or two after we got married I was pregnant. I was embarrassed, but he had a lot of mixed feelings. I had a lot of mixed feelings, too, because we weren't ready for it. You know, we couldn't tell each other. He couldn't tell me how he felt, and I couldn't tell him. He just took it out on me. Then he was happy to have a baby, but he just didn't want it.

> (Do you think he was ready to get married and have children?)

> Oh, I don't know if he'd ever have been ready to get married or have children. He was really terrible to the oldest child. He used to hit her, and he was really rough with her. Even today she's 30 years old and still goes to a psychiatrist. Her father treated her so roughly that she just doesn't feel he ever cared for her. This was before the drinking.

One informant frequently expressed her past and current fears and confusion about childrearing to the researcher. As newlyweds, when she and her husband learned they were going to have a baby, they were both terrified. When the new baby would cry, she said she was so frightened she thought of committing suicide. It was at this time that her husband began drinking heavily.

Fear of pregnancy often constituted a divisive element in relationships, thwarting spontaneity of sexual expression and resulting in prolonged periods of sexual abstinence. The use of birth control devices or obtaining a vasectomy often caused great guilt and alienation from the Church and Holy Sacrament if priests refused to give absolution for these actions. One informant vehemently talked about the negative effect the Church's teaching against birth control had on her marriage and also her sister's.

> R. and I dated five years before we married. We played it straight and were both virgins.

After we married, we stuck strictly to the rhythm method—that meant that for more than half of the month we couldn't sleep together. When you finally can legally have an intimacy, you should be able to go through with it. ... Then when I nursed my four children, I did not have periods for seven months each time, so we abstained from sex. It seemed all right then; maybe we didn't have such a sex drive. But looking back, maybe it bothered him more than he said. ... You can't imagine how regimented this whole thing made our lives. I'm an orderly person about a lot of things, but I'm not that organized about my emotions. When you have a feeling for intimacy or closeness you should be able to go through with it. Here half of the month we couldn't do that, or if he came to me, I'd say well OK, but you know this is the time we shouldn't. Well, he wouldn't. ... Besides, I didn't want a family of ragamuffin children. When you have so many children, it's not just the economics of it; you can't relate to each one. I didn't want to have seven or eight children. I wouldn't know where they were, out on the street or whatever. I want to be able to know each one.

One informant expressed the views of many when she said, "Many people just abstain, particularly the Irish." As Messenger's (21) informant was noted above to have told him, "Men can wait a long time for 'it,' but we can wait a lot longer."

5. *Husbands' Irregular Work Hours.* Many men were in occupations requiring them to work afternoons or night shifts. Others were able to meet the economic demands of large families only by carrying extra jobs. Some attended night school for specialized training. Thus, economic patterns resulted in an absentee father. Although the family was not socially stigmatized in the manner that female-headed welfare-based families are, the father essentially still relinquished household responsibilities and childrearing, including the discipline of children, to his wife. Commenting on the early years of her marriage, a police officer's wife said:

You know I felt like divorcing H. many times.

For years he was just never there. I had to raise my children alone. I had to be mother *and* father. I had to do everything, and then when the husbands come home for a day or a week, they just start ordering you around. It's terrible.

A senior policeman stated:

I worked twelve years before I saw the light of day (day shift) because of the seniority thing.

Wife (*nodding disgustedly*): Yeah, five kids.

Said a fireman, in the context of speaking about his oldest son's personality problems:

When boys grow up today, 90 per cent of all contacts they have are with women. Some of them grow up and hate women. It was the same with my son. He would come home and I wasn't there, so he would have his mother tell him what to do. He didn't want to listen to that.

One particularly reflective informant (who has had occasion to analyze her own marriage in the process of therapy) stated:

I see all around me in my friends that women do all the controlling. The men do practically nothing, and it gets to a point that all they are doing is bringing the paycheck. The women make all decisions and do all the things with the kids. They start saying, "Don't take it to your father, he is too tired." Within a few years the fathers aren't involved in the child-raising at all.

The husband's early dependency on a strong mother appears to feed into an easy capitulation to dependency on the wife, often forced by the issue of occupational time schedules. Thus, whatever the conscious or unconscious intents, men frequently move from the domination of strong mothers to that of equally strong wives who also "take care" of them and their family.

6. *Failure to Separate from Family of Orientation.* Adults often fail to separate from the expectations and ongoing coercive presence of their family of orientation. This does not allow spouses to grow in new and potentially productive ways in their family

of procreation. Continuing responsibilities owed to parents and siblings that take a great deal of time and energy, preclude the development of nuclear family activities not dominated by family and old friends. A vigorous pattern of socializing with extended kin often continues throughout life. This is particularly critical in the early years of marriage when spousal communication is developing. Continuous group activity is a way of life that contributes to the production of a publicly social "hail-fellow" who cannot talk privately to his wife and children. One informant when talking about her long-standing problems in communicating with her husband was asked if she had good communication when they dated and when they first were married, some twenty years ago.

> Well, we were always socially in a crowd. We were never alone. We never worked out a relationship by ourselves. We were either with his family or my family or out with friends. We always had a big circle of my friends from school and his friends. ... The only time in our life we've ever been alone was on our honeymoon and even then there was a couple in the cabin next to us who'd been married a year and were on a second honeymoon. So we spent a lot of time with them.

Thus, despite the great amount of family activity and necessity for conversation about logistical matters, a significant characteristic of family life was a lack of communication between spouses. For instance, 18 of the 30 wives talked about their difficulties in communicating feelings about important issues to their spouses. The husbands in these families illustrate what has been called by Balswick and Peek (4) the "uncommunicative" or "inexpressive American male." The lack of communication in males may be related also to common masculine role behavior in the ethnic groups represented, particularly Irish and German. These men, while bringing home an income insuring a comfortable lifestyle, helping to a limited degree with home

chores and with children, and fostering their wives' own activities in a number of areas, often felt no need to communicate their feelings about their families or about continuing personal events. Many related little of what happened at work. Some wished to talk but not listen to what their wives cared to share. In the husbands' perception, their *doing* has fulfilled their part of the domestic bargain. An informant who continually complained about her husband's chronic silence and sullen moods was asked:

> (Did you have trouble talking when you first got married?)
>
> We didn't have to talk. We didn't have anything to talk about.
>
> (How can you live together and not have anything to talk about?)
>
> We just didn't. It's impossible to have a conversation with A. He's either bathing, sleeping, eating, watching television, or resting (sarcastically). Or he's painting or doing something else. You can't get him to take a walk around the block (to talk away from the children). You just can't communicate. Or he yells. When we go out, I talk. He never says anything.

7. *The Nature of Employment.* Most men in this population worked either in civil service occupations or large utility companies—large impersonal bureaucracies; they had little control over their own careers. For example, advancement in the police department was very slow; it was not unusual for a man to remain a patrolman for fifteen years, still working nights and having only rare weekends off. Tests for advancement were given only three to five years on an average. Competition was keen and preparation uniformly was said to require six months of continuous study (outside of work hours). New quotas for advancement of minorities and women exacerbated the situation for white males. It should be noted, however, that work in large bureaucracies like the civil service or utility companies was consciously and de-

liberately chosen for what perhaps was considered the overriding positive feature of such employment—security.

8. *The Importance of Men's Peer Groups.* Many of the values and functions of the Irish bachelor group were taken over by the chief peer groups of the husband. His referents for masculine values and behavior tended to be male relatives, workmates, parishmates and early parochial school friends. Because of the stable and homogeneous nature of this population and lack of geographic mobility, these persons all tended to come from the same sociocultural roots and, in fact, might be the same persons. One aspect of expected masculine role behavior was heavy drinking.

Five families of the 30 exhibited six or more of the eight themes presented. In three of these five families, husbands had both Irish fathers and mothers. In the remaining two, husbands had Irish mothers and German alcoholic fathers. Husbands in two other families exhibited at least four themes; both husbands had Irish fathers and mothers. It is of particular interest that *all seven* of these husbands had current and severe alcohol problems. The prevalence of the themes varied within the other 23 families, with most exhibiting from one to three. For every theme the number of problem drinkers exceeded the number of nonproblem drinkers. (See Tables V and VI.)

The Role of the Wife

The life career of women was as equally circumscribed as that of men. They grew up with the model of an energetic, highly capable mother who somehow kept her family going in the throes of poverty. The father was remembered as a good quiet man who was rarely at home or, if so, was alone in his room silently drinking. Stivers (32) and Greeley (15) discussed the frequent cases of absentee fathers among Irish immigrants in the nineteenth century. The demands of economic reality, then as now, compounded further the propensity of the mother to be a strong and dominating figure.

Many of the subjects of the present study, as their mothers before them, managed and disciplined large families essentially alone, ran the household, and took care of aging relatives. Thus, in the tradition of cultural continuity, most of the wives inherited the pattern that often emerges when the husband, because of occupation-related work schedules *or* alcohol-related problems, defaults on family responsibilities that must then be picked up by the wife. As noted above, clinicians have pointed up this pattern and read into it a neurotic wife whose conflicting dependency needs have caused her to force such a situation by choosing and maintaining an alcoholic spouse. Yet it appears that in the population described here, the realities of husbands' occupations, as exemplified by the police profession, might contribute heavily to such a domestic situation, re-

TABLE V

Number of Theme Characteristics Exhibited by Problem Drinkers

	N	6 or more	4 or more	3 or fewer
Problem	16	5	2	9
No Problem	14	0	0	14

TABLE VI

Themes Characteristic of Families

	N	1* N	%	2 N	%	3 N	%	4 N	%	5 N	%	6 N	%	7 N	%	8 N	%
Problem	16	9	56	6	37.5	8	50	5	31	11	69	7	44	14	88	8	50
Nonproblem	14	5	36	1	7	0	0	2	14	6	43	1	7	8	57	1	7

*1 Insufficient information on four cases.

gardless of the wife's wishes, unless one might say that this is so because she *chose* a policeman for a husband (although most married before their husbands joined the police force), anticipating that he *might* work nights and also *might* become an alcoholic. It should be noted, however, that a great proportion of Irish Catholics enter the police force and significant proportions of both Catholics and policemen (not necessarily overlapping) are alcoholics, thus confusing the issue of independent and dependent variables.

Discussion

A study of 30 families selected as typical of the life style and cultural and economic values of a much larger population from which the families were drawn has been presented to illustrate a family system that controls the behavior of its members in both dramatic and significantly subtle ways. Although generalization from a small number of cases must be considered as tentative, the data are nonetheless provocative in their implications for studies of larger populations. At a time when American society seemingly offers the individual more options for freedom of action each day, most of the persons in this sample appear to live out their lives locked within a pattern of cradle-to-the-grave moral, social, and economic expectations. The data presented here relate excessive drinking with massive social controls in *all* cases in which men had an Irish father and an Irish mother (N = 8) and in *all* cases in which men had an Irish mother and father of other ethnicity who was reported to have had an alcohol problem and to have been alive in the husband's youth (N = 3). Key variables in this scenario might appear to be, then, an Irish mother who is the primary maintainer of the Irish tradition and the highest level of controls, and second, a father who provides an alcoholic role model. Excessive drinking may be prescribed in a situation in which a man had an Irish mother and an Irish *or*

non-Irish alcoholic father. One inference from these data could be that many men drink to dull their sexual needs and to blot out the frustrations linked to massive personal and social controls in almost every aspect of their lives. *Excessive drinking (with all of its adhering, untoward consequences) is an effective and culturally sanctioned way of rattling the cage, while not breaking out of it.* Wives and mothers in culturally appropriate roles have helped fashion this cage and, more so than the men, may indeed hold the keys to it. Basic intervention techniques that focus on establishing spousal communication and breaking the continuity of culturally inherited role patterns may offer an indirect but effective avenue through which to approach problematic drinking behavior.

Summary

The literature on alcoholism and the family has characteristically focused on individual pathology of family members or on interaction between members within a closed context of the family as a functional unit. Little or no mention is made of cultural, social, or economic factors that contribute to individual and group interactive behavior. This study of a specific group of families at high risk for frequent and severe alcohol problems illustrates the importance of looking at the behavior of family members as they relate to each other in a complex of social and cultural expectations rather than focusing only on individuals as interacting bundles of pathological needs. In contrast to labeling the wife (or any other family member) as culprit or martyr, in this population of families, a perpetuating, encompassing, culturally defined family system may be perceived as both culprit and martyr. A holistic perspective allowing the delineation of cultural prescriptions and expectations regarding behavior and attitudes directly and indirectly related to drinking patterns may contribute another dimension to the systems model proposed by clinicians. Furthermore, detailed knowledge of family lifestyle and behavior may provide a rich and educated basis for the effective planning of preventive community programs as well as therapeutic interventions for specific families.

REFERENCES

1. ABLON, J., "Family Structure and Behavior in Alcoholism: A Review of the Literature," in B. Kissin and H. Begleiter (Eds.), *The Biology of Alcoholism 4*, New York, Plenum, 1976.

2. BALES, R. F., "Attitudes Toward Drinking in the Irish Culture," in D. J. Pittman and C. R. Snyder (Eds.), *Society, Culture, and Drinking Patterns*, New York, Wiley, 1962.

3. ——, "Cultural Differences in Rates of Alcoholism," *Quart. J. Stud. Alc.* 6: 480–499, 1946.

4. BALSWICK, J. and PEEK, C., "The Inexpressive Male: A Tragedy of American Society," *Fam. Coord.* 20: 363–368, 1971.

5. BERENSON, D., "A Family Approach to Alcoholism," *Psychiat. Opin.* 13: 33–38, 1976.

6. BOWEN, M., "Alcoholism as Viewed Through Family Systems Theory and Family Psychotherapy," *Ann. N.Y. Acad. Sci.* 233: 115–122, 1974.

7. CAHALAN, D., *Problem Drinkers: A National Survey*, San Francisco, Jossey-Bass, 1970.

8. CAHALAN, D. and ROOM, R., "Problem Drinking Among American Men," *Monographs of the Rutgers Center of Alcohol Studies 7*, New Brunswick, N.J., Publications Center of Alcohol Studies, 1974.

9. CONNERY, D. S., *The Irish*, rev. ed., New York, Simon and Schuster, 1970.

10. CORDER, B. F.; HENDRICKS, A.; and CORDER, R. F., "An MMPI Study of a Group of Wives of Alcoholics," *Quart. J. Stud. Alc.* 25: 551–554, 1964.

11. DAVIS, D. I.; BERENSON, D.; STEINGLASS, P.; and DAVIS, S., "The Adaptive Consequences of Drinking," *Psychiat.* 37: 209–215, 1974.

12. EDWARDS, P.; HARVEY, C.; and WHITEHEAD, P. C., "Wives of Alcoholics: A Critical Review and Analysis," *Quart. J. Stud. Alc.*, 34: 112–132, 1973.

13. EWING, J. A. and FOX, R. A., "Family Therapy of Alcoholism," *Curr. Psychiat. Ther.* 8: 86–91, 1968.

14. FUTTERMAN, S., "Personality Trends in Wives of Alcoholics," *J. Psychiat. Soc. Work* 23: 37–41, 1953.

15. GREELEY, A., *That Most Distressful Nation*, Chicago, Quadrangle Books, 1972.

16. GUZE, S. B., et al., "The Drinking History: A Comparison of Reports by Subjects and Their Relatives," *Quart. J. Stud. Alc.* 24: 249–260, 1963.

17. JACKSON, J. K., "The Adjustment of the Family to the Crisis of Alcoholism," *Quart. J. Stud. Alc.* 15: 562–587, 1954.

18. ——, "Alcoholism and the Family," *Ann. Am. Acad. Polit. Soc. Sci.* 315: 90–110, 1958.

19. ——, "Alcoholism and the Family," in D. J. Pittman, and C. R. Snyder (Eds.), *Society, Culture and Drinking Patterns*, New York, Wiley, 1962.

20. KNUPFER, G. "The Validity of Survey Data on Drinking Problems: A Comparison Between Respondents' Self Reports and Outside Sources of Information," n.d. Mimeo.

21. KOGAN, K. L.; FORDYCE, W. E.; and JACKSON, J. K., "Personality Disturbances in Wives of Alcholics," *Quart. J. Stud. Alc.* 24: 227–238, 1963.

22. MACDONALD, D. E., "Mental Disorders in Wives of Alcoholics," *Quart. J. Stud. Alc.* 17: 282–287, 1956.

23. McCRADY, B. S.; PAOLINO, T. J.; and LONGABAUGH, R., "Correspondence Between Reports of Problem Drinkers and Spouses on Drinking Behavior and Impairment," *J. Studies Alc.* 39: 1252–1257, 1978.

24. MESSENGER, J. C., "Inis Beag," volume in series: in G. Spindler and L. Spindler (Eds.), *Case Studies in Cultural Anthropology*, New York, Holt, Rinehart, and Winston, 1969.

25. PAOLINO, T. J. and McCRADY, B. S., *Alcoholic Marriage: Alternative Perspectives*, Grune, Stratton and Company, 1977.

26. PRICE, G. M., "A Study of the Wives of 20 Alcoholics," *Quart. J. Stud. Alc.* 5: 620–627, 1945.

27. SCHEPER-HUGHES, N., "Saints, Scholars

and Schizophrenics: Mental Illness and Irish Culture," Ph.D. dissertation, University of California, Berkeley, 1976.

28. SNYDER, C. R., "Culture and Jewish Sobriety: The In-Group—Out-Group Factor," in D. J. Pittman and C. R. Snyder (Eds.), *Society, Culture, and Drinking Patterns*, New York, Wiley, 1962.

29. STEINGLASS, P., "Family Therapy in Alcoholism," in B. Kissin and H. Begleiter (Eds.), *The Biology of Alcoholism*, New York, Plenum, 1977, pp. 259–299.

30. STEINGLASS, P., WEINER, S. and MENDELSON, J. H., "Interactional Issues as Determinants of Alcoholism," *Am. J. Psychiat.* 128: 275–280, 1971.

31. ———, "A Systems Approach to Alcoholism: A Model and its Clinical Application," *Arch. Gen. Psychiat.*, 24: 401–408, 1971.

32. STIVERS, R., *The Hair of the Dog*, University Park, Penn State University Press, 1976.

33. ULLMAN, A., "Sociocultural Backgrounds of Alcoholism," *Ann. Am. Acad. Polit. Soc. Sci.* 315: 48–62, 1958.

34. WARD, R. F. and FAILLACE, G. A., "The Alcoholic and His Helpers," *Quart. J. Stud. Alc.* 14: 632–641, 1953.

35. WHALEN, T., "Wives of Alcoholics: Four Types Observed in a Family Service Agency," *Quart. J. Stud. Alc.* 14: 632–641, 1953.

36. WOLIN, S.; STEINGLASS, P.; SENDROFF, P.; DAVIS, D. I.; and BERENSON, S., "Marital Interaction During Experimental Intoxication and the Relationship to Family History," in M. Gross (Ed.), *Alcohol Intoxication and Withdrawal, Experimental Studies*, New York, Plenum, 1975.

Reprint requests should be addressed to Joan Ablon, Ph.D., Medical Anthropology Program, Departments of Psychiatry and Epidemiology and International Health, University of California, 1320 Third Avenue, San Francisco, California 94143.

Research and clinical interest in the alcoholic family has tended to outpace the development of family-oriented conceptual models of alcoholism. A family development perspective has been almost totally absent, despite the chronic, longitudinal nature of alcoholism. A life history model is proposed that uses the concepts of the "alcoholic system," family homeostasis, and the "family alcohol phase" as its building blocks. Chronic alcoholism tends to produce distortions in the normative family life cycle. These distortions and their clinical implications are discussed, using four case histories as illustrations of the concepts proposed. The model is also examined in the light of current research findings about the alcoholic family.

26

A LIFE HISTORY MODEL OF
THE ALCOHOLIC FAMILY*

Peter Steinglass†

A FTER MANY YEARS of clinical and research neglect, the alcoholic family appears to have come of age. Clinical interest, most clearly represented in the increased application of family therapy techniques to alcoholism problems (24) and the phenomenal growth of Al-Anon (1), Alateen, and Alafam (the first two organizations offer help to family members but tend to exclude the alcoholic from group meetings; Alafam includes the entire family), has been particularly strong. Family-oriented research efforts, although hardly keeping pace with the changes in clinical practice outlined above, have also been attracting increasing interest (2).

Unfortunately, this growing research and clinical interest in the alcoholic family has tended to outpace the development of conceptual models useful in viewing alcoholism from a family perspective. Although several

* This work is part of a larger research project entitled "Factors Maintaining Drinking in Alcoholic Families," supported by Grant No. RO AA 01441 awarded by the National Institute on Alcohol Abuse and Alcoholism. The project is being carried out by Peter Steinglass, M.D., and the research staff of the Center for Family Research, Department of Psychiatry and Behavioral Sciences, George Washington University School of Medicine.

† Center for Family Research, Department of Psychiatry and Behavioral Sciences, George Washington University School of Medicine, Washington, D.C.

From Peter Steinglass, "A Life History Model of the Alcoholic Family," *Family Process*, 1980, 19, pp. 211-226. Reprinted by permission of the publisher and author.

interesting stabs have been made at explaining aspects of family interaction related to alcoholism from transactional (23), systems (8), psychoanalytic (19), and behavioral perspectives (15), there still appears to be ample room for additional theory-building in this area.

One notable oversight in previously suggested conceptual models has been a failure to incorporate a developmental perspective. Although the chronic nature of alcoholism as a clinical condition has obviously been acknowledged, the long-range developmental implications for the family of having to live side by side with such a condition has rarely, if ever, been addressed. Some attention has been paid to the notation that families go through an identifiable sequence of stages in their adjustments to alcoholism (14, 17), and keen interest has been expressed in the role the family plays in the *maintenance* of chronic drinking patterns (27, 28), but these models have tended to focus almost exclusively on family life during periods of active drinking.

By way of contrast, the model presented in this paper has a strong developmental orientation. It has been derived by applying the developmental construct of the family life cycle to the unique life history of the alcoholic family. The model grew out of a longitudinal study in which families were intensively observed over a six-month period in three different locations: in their homes on nine separate occasions; in multifamily discussion groups for 24 weekly, 90-minute meetings; and once in the family interaction laboratory. The longitudinal perspective gained from this study tended to underscore the potential usefulness of a model that traces the ebbs and flows of alcoholism over an extended time period, as a supplement to models that focus more microscopically on behavior associated with periods of active drinking.

In presenting this new conceptual model, we will proceed as follows: first, review the basic concepts of the family developmental approach; second, apply these concepts to the alcoholic family and outline a proposed family-level life history model of alcoholism; third, provide some illustrative clinical examples from our current study; and, finally, discuss some clinical implications of approaching alcoholism from a family-developmental perspective.

The Developmental Approach to the Family

Developmental approaches to the family, first introduced by sociologists as research models (13), have subsequently gained wide popularity both as conceptual frameworks for family life education (3, 6) and as models for clinical intervention (5, 10, 22). The core of the family developmental framework is a series of "concepts dealing with orderly sequences, the sequential regularities observable in the family over its life history, such as role sequences, careers of family positions, intercontingencies of careers, and stages of development (12, p.11)." The family is presumed to have a life cycle or life history that can be divided into a series of recognizable stages, each stage in turn associated with a series of developmental tasks. Drawing heavily on Erikson's (7) model of the individual life cycle, it is postulated that the family must also pass sequentially through this series of stages and that inability to manage successfully the tasks associated with an earlier stage will compromise family resources in dealing with subsequent stages. Although individual variation is acknowledged, the usefulness of identifying "normative" tasks associated with each life cycle stage is also stressed. A number of life cycle schema have been proposed by sociologists; all of these schema, however, tend to emphasize family composition (births, deaths, children leaving home, etc.) as defining points for the different stages.

Clinicians, on the other hand, have been more interested in what has been called "transitional" behavior (11). Whereas the sociologist might use the developmental model as a framework for gathering information about such aspects as family role behavior, the clinician focuses on aspects of family life that seem to interfere with normal growth and development. Although not exclusively so, clinical problems seem to emerge most frequently during periods of transition between life stages (21). New demands are placed on the family, and existing resources or patterns of behavior are inadequate to meet these demands. These transitional periods also frequently highlight competing developmental needs either of separate individuals within the family or competing needs of an individual and the family itself.

At the very least, therefore, the developmental perspective helps alert the clinician to potential stress points along the life cycle (including the impact of physical or emotional illness), and to set priorities for issues that are being presented by a family in a clinical setting. When the issue at hand is the consequence for the family of having to manage a *chronic* illness, the developmental perspective offers the clinician an additional advantage. Here one begins to focus on potential *distortions* in the customary life cycle introduced by the particular chronic pathological condition of interest. What, for example, are the changes in the family life cycle associated with chronic alcoholism and what are the clinical implications of these distortions? We will focus on these questions in the suggested life history model of alcoholism presented in this paper.

The Family Life History Model

In attempting to apply these developmental concepts to families with alcoholic members, we have constructed a model built around three central concepts: the alcoholic system; family homeostasis; and the family alcohol phase.

1. *The Alcoholic System.* The concept of the alcoholic system is drawn from my earlier thinking about the relation between interactional behavior and chronic alcoholism (27, 28). It was postulated that in certain interactional systems (families being one of them), alcohol use might come to play such a critical role in day-to-day behavior as to become a central organizing principle around which patterns of interactional behavior might be shaped. In this sense, major aspects of behavior would be so flavored by the style and consequences of alcohol use as to warrant the term, "an alcoholic system." This term, we felt, was particularly applicable in those circumstances in which families remained economically and structurally intact despite (or to use this different way of thinking, assisted by) the presence of chronic alcoholism in their midst. In such families, during periods of active drinking, we proposed that the family actually cycled between two predictable interactional states, one associated with sobriety and one associated with intoxication. These were not merely differential patterns that the family used in dealing with its identified alcoholic member. These were truly different interactional states at the family level. The repetitive and stereotyped aspect of behavior within the family during periods of actual intoxication, we proposed, might actually be associated with certain aspects of problem-solving by the family, and it might also serve to reduce uncertainty. In this sense, intoxicated interactional behavior might become as habitual as the alcohol consumption itself.

2. *Family Homeostasis.* Don Jackson first proposed that Cannon's physiological concepts of homeostasis used to describe feedback mechanisms responsible for controlling certain internal physiological processes within the body might be an appropriate metaphor to describe similar processes of interactional systems such as families. The notion is that families tend to establish a sense of balance or stability, and have built-in mechanisms to resist any change from that predetermined level of stability.

Chronic illnesses, if only by dint of their

persistence over time, tend to be associated with repetitive, stereotyped patterns of behavior. These patterns of behavior in turn can become integrated into the family's homeostatic mechanisms and thereby paradoxically become associated with long-term family stability. Crises tend to disrupt or overwhelm family homeostatic mechanisms, creating periods of instability associated with profound subjective dysphoria and family-level stress. Our model, therefore, attempts to track and separate periods of stability from periods of instability in family life and suggests different roles for alcoholism in each of these periods.

3. *The Family Alcohol Phase.* The cyclical use of alcohol has both a microscopic (day-to-day) and macroscopic (longitudinal) dimension. Our primary interest in the life history model is the macroscopic dimension—those long periods of months or years that can be characterized as "dry" or "wet" by the family. Although such distinctions are obviously tied to the drinking behavior of one (or perhaps two) family members, it is our perception that the entire family not only can clearly demarcate these time periods one from another, but tends to associate these different periods with profoundly different life experiences and patterns of behavior. In this sense these different time periods can be thought of as *family-level alcohol life phases.* In the life history model we have specifically identified three such phases: a dry phase; a wet phase; and a transitional phase (transitions both from wet to dry and dry to wet time frames).

These three elements—alcoholic system, importance of alcohol use for family homeostatic mechanism, and family alcohol life phase—have been combined in a life history model that is diagrammatically outlined in Figure 1. As can be seen, major phases are identified by two criteria: (a) stable or unstable; and (b) wet, dry, or transitional. In addition, the alcoholic family is differentiated from a non-alcoholic family counterpart.

The family's life history has been somewhat arbitrarily divided into five major periods. Although each of these periods may include a number of separate stages and transitions (as we have defined these concepts above), they form convenient bench marks for following the family developmentally through its life history. It should also be obvious that there will be as many deviations from this typical pattern as there are inventive solutions to cohabitation. However, it is still conceptually useful to discuss these issues from the point of view of a typical life history. Let us therefore follow a typical family through this suggested life history model, and discuss the various options available to the family.

In the *premarriage* period one of three possible combinations can occur: an alcoholic can marry a non-alcoholic; two alcoholic individuals can decide to join forces; or two non-alcoholics may choose each other. This phase of mate selection is subject to a wide range of psychological and cultural variables. Although the possible combinations of these variables are virtually limitless, the suggestion has been frequently made that alcoholism has already been predetermined by the time individuals come to select their marital partners and that the process of mate selection is often in the service of setting the stage for a life centered around alcoholism. It has also been suggested that cultural variables play a major role at this point in life and that cultural values regarding the use of alcohol and attitudes toward alcoholic behavior predetermine the kinds of marital selections people within that culture ultimately make. The life history model acknowledges the potential importance of each of these issues. For example, although it is certainly likely that many non-alcoholic individuals choose to marry alcoholic partners with full knowledge of their existing difficulties, it is also probable that most people do not anticipate a life organized around alcohol at the time they take their marriage vows.

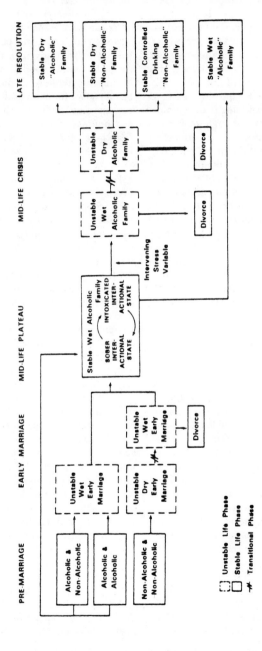

PRE-MARRIAGE EARLY MARRIAGE MID-LIFE PLATEAU MID-LIFE CRISIS LATE RESOLUTION

Fig. 1: A diagramatic representation of the developmental life history of alcoholic families.

Alcoholic & Non-Alcoholic

Alcoholic & Alcoholic

Non-Alcoholic & Non-Alcoholic

Unstable Wet Early Marriage

Unstable Dry Early Marriage

Unstable Wet Early Marriage

Divorce

Stable Wet Alcoholic Family
SOBER INTER-ACTIONAL STATE
INTOXICATED INTER-ACTIONAL STATE

Intervening Stress Variable

Unstable Wet Alcoholic Family

Unstable Dry Alcoholic Family

Divorce

Divorce

Stable Dry "Alcoholic" Family

Stable Dry "Non-Alcoholic" Family

Stable Controlled Drinking "Non-Alcoholic" Family

Stable Wet "Alcoholic" Family

Unstable Life Phase
Stable Life Phase
Transitional Phase

The *early marriage* period is almost always one of relative instability. Organized patterns of behavior have yet to be established, distribution of role function and rules regarding management of the internal and external environment of the family are gradually worked out during the early marriage phase. This phase is usually a critical formative phase in the life of the family, and although frequently quite stressful, allows the family to experiment with a number of different approaches in organizing its life, and in fine-tuning the relationships within the marriage and family.

It would be during this period of early marriage that the future role of alcohol use in family life would most likely be determined. Such aspects of alcoholism as unstable work patterns, heightened affect during periods of intoxication, the high incidence of intrafamily violence associated with alcoholism, and conflicts between spouses and extended family members all presumably increase the difficulties for the couple in completing the normative developmental tasks of the early marriage period. It is also during this period that alcohol use becomes incorporated into important family behavior patterns and family rituals. The stressful aspects of alcoholism are probably contributing factors to the incidence of divorce during this period, especially if alcoholism emerges after rather than before marriage. On the other hand, the desire for long-term stability on the part of the family increases efforts to incorporate alcoholism into family life in some fashion that the family can "live with." The end product of this latter process is a conversion from a "family with an alcoholic member" to an "alcoholic family." At this point alcohol use has become incorporated into the homeostatic mechanisms of the family. Overall stability has been achieved despite the more superficial evidence that alcohol use has acted as a disruptive force in daily family life.

As the family moves into the *mid-life plateau* period, alcohol use and consequent behavior have become central organizing principles for interactional life within the family. The family has entered a *stable-wet* alcohol phase. We have already described an earlier theoretical model developed in response to the need to understand the relative stability of this phase in the life of the alcoholic family (28). Figure 1 incorporates this earlier model in suggesting that during the stable wet phase families cycle between two fundamentally different interactional states, one associated with sobriety and one associated with intoxication, and that this cycling is an important mechanism used by the family in maintaining long-term stability.

For some families this mid-life plateau proceeds year after year with remarkably little change in patterns of alcohol consumption, family attitudes, or family behavior. For most families, however, the plateau is not so level. A wide variety of intervening stress variables impinge on the family from within and without, tending to disrupt the steady-state behavior associated with the stable-wet phase. Intrafamily stress variables might include normal developmental changes (such as births and deaths or the growth of children), changing role functions, or physical illness. Extrafamily stresses might include economic crises, job changes, and physical relocations. Although one possible consequence of the family's having to deal with an intervening stress variable is an increase in alcoholic behavior, a second alternative is an actual cessation of drinking—going "on the wagon." At the very least, however, these stressor events invariably create an instability in what was previously a homeostatic system. The customary coping mechanisms of the family (including those associated with alcoholism) are overwhelmed, and the family experiences a new instability in its life.

If the response to this challenge to family stability is merely increased alcohol consumption, that is, if the solution is simply "more of the same," then this now *wet unstable* alcoholic family may dissolve under the continuing pressures brought to bear by its inability to deal successfully with this superimposed stress. The second alternative, the conversion to a dry state, has its own difficulties and uncertainties. This initial conversion of the wet alcoholic family to a dry alcoholic family, especially when the alcoholic history predates marriage, has long been associated in the clinical literature with an increased rate of divorce. The conventional wisdom suggests that the alcoholic behavior was satisfying intrapsychic needs of both spouses. The absence of alcoholic behavior creates a psychological void that is subsequently reflected in efforts by the non-alcoholic spouse to encourage the alcoholic to return to drinking. If these efforts are unsuccessful, divorce often results. If the transition from the wet to dry state is successfully managed, then the family enters a *dry stable* alcohol phase.

For some alcoholic families the transition from the wet to dry state is a dramatic one that occurs only once in its lifetime. For many families, however, the mid-life period is characterized by a cycling between periods of wetness and dryness, each of which might encompass periods of months or years. This cyclical process seems to represent, at a macroscopic level, a pattern analogous to the more microscopic cycling between sober and intoxicated states we have proposed occurs as a component of the stable-wet alcohol phase. The mid-life period in such instances might be diagrammed as a linear chain of stable wet phase → transitional phase → stable dry phase → transitional phase → stable wet phase → transitional phase → stable dry phase, etc. In the discussion section we will mention some compelling evidence suggesting that these transitional phases are associated with characteristic patterns of family behavior irrespective of whether the transition is from wet to dry or from dry to wet.

Finally, the alcoholic family enters a period of *late resolution*. Just as we have been suggesting alternative pathways for the al-

coholic family during earlier life periods, all alcoholic families do not seek the same resolution of this problem. In our current study, we have identified four distinct late resolution patterns that appear to represent different family level solutions.

The first solution, the *stable-wet alcoholic family* appears to be merely a continuation of the steady-state solution established by the family during its mid-life period. Perhaps because this family's life has been relatively aproblematic (especially when external stressor events have not occurred) or perhaps by dint of the magnitude to which family life has become organized around alcohol, these families have continued year after year with remarkably little change either with regard to alcohol use or the consequences of alcoholism for family life. They remain alcoholic systems; they remain remarkably stable; but they also have an unchanging quality, a sense of being "locked in concrete."

A second possible resolution is the *stable-dry alcoholic family*. This family has successfully converted to the dry state and maintained this state for an extended time period. However, despite the fact that its alcoholic member is no longer drinking, the family's life, to a remarkable degree, continues to be organized around alcohol. Family members are active participants in AA, Al-Anon, and Alateen groups. Reading material and family discussions frequently return to topics related to alcoholism as reminders of past difficulties. Individuals within the family have made career changes that incorporate alcoholism as a work focus (e.g., alcoholism counselors, alcoholism lobbyists). Family life is organized to maximize the prevention of slippage back to a wet state. Social life, family rituals such as holidays and dinner time behavior, vacation planning, are all restuctured with this alcoholism component in mind. Although the quality of solutions worked out by these stable-dry alcoholic families in their late resolution periods might vary widely—from highly adaptive and flexible to quite rigid and restrictive—all these families appear to share in common their continued propensity to organize major aspects of family life around alcoholism as the central focus.

A third solution, the *stable-dry non-alcoholic family*, differs from the second group in the single parameter that this family should no longer be thought of as an alcoholic system. Alcohol has been eliminated not only in a physical sense, but in a subjective and emotional sense as well. These families might continue to be curious about their earlier experiences with alcoholism, but there is little concern that alcoholism will emerge again as a significant problem in their lives. In all likelihood, there is some relation between the magnitude of alcoholism in such families and the ability to move on to a stable-dry non-alcoholic family resolution. However, properties inherent in the family itself probably also contribute to the question of which families remain alcoholic systems and which families do not.

The fourth type of late resolution is the *stable controlled-drinking, non alcoholic family*. The ability of chronic alcoholic individuals to return successfully to a controlled drinking or social drinking pattern is a highly controversial topic in the alcoholism field (4, 9). However, a growing series of reports tend to support such a possibility (20). Our current study included one family that we felt had achieved such a status. Therefore, although apparently occurring infrequently, this late resolution possibility should be included in our model.

Four Case Histories

The four families described below have all participated as subjects in our research study. They have been selected to illustrate both the protean nature of alcoholism and family life and the four types of resolution phases suggested by our model.

1. *A Stable-Wet Alcoholic Family*

Dr. S., a 62-year-old science administrator, and Mrs. S., a 59-year-old part-time secretary, have been married 28 years. Of their three children, only the youngest son is still living at home. For the past eight years Mrs. S. has been engaged in an alcoholic drinking pattern that has become increasingly fixed and has proven resistant to external changes in the family's life or to medical advice (she has both cardiac and hepatic difficulties). A recent hospitalization secondary to mild congestive heart failure has not deterred her from returning to drinking; she claims she enjoys it and plans to continue, although she feels her drinking is elective, that is, she can stop whenever she chooses to.

An infrequent social drinker during the early years of her marriage, Mrs. S. dramatically increased her drinking when her oldest son was imprisoned after being convicted on a drug-manufacturing charge. Although this son had a chronic history of delinquent behavior and although marital conflict secondary to the strain of managing their son's difficulties had brought the couple to seek counseling, these earlier troubles had not stimulated a change in Mrs. S.'s drinking habits prior to her son's enforced separation from the family. At the time of his arrest, she felt as though a huge burden had been lifted from her, that she could at last begin to relax, and that drinking was one way of doing so. She now admits that drinking was her way of attempting to forget about her son's leaving.

For the past five years, Mrs. S.'s drinking pattern has "stabilized." During the six months of the study, she consumed an invariant amount of alcohol during the same late afternoon and evening time period, ostensibly unnoticed by her husband and son. The regularity of this drinking pattern is illustrated in Figure 2, a drinking histogram compiled from a six-month behavioral log of alcohol consumption.

Family life during this stable-wet phase has been characterized by a high level of isolation of individual family members, consistent with the family rule that Mrs. S.'s drinking is to go unnoticed. Mr. S. is seldom

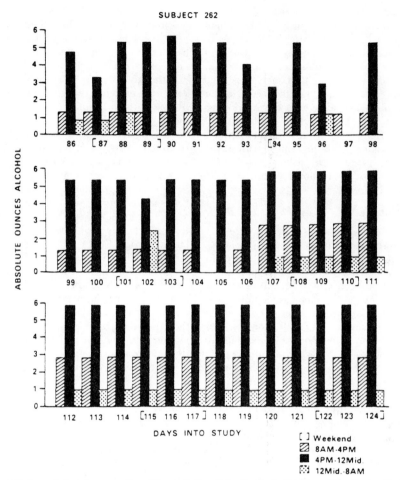

SUBJECT 262

ABSOLUTE OUNCES ALCOHOL

DAYS INTO STUDY

[ ] Weekend
▨ 8AM-4PM
■ 4PM-12Mid.
▦ 12Mid.-8AM

Fig. 2: Pattern of alcohol consumption of the alcoholic wife/mother in the "stable wet" family vignette. This histogram was compiled from a daily log of drinking behavior kept by the subject. Note that consumption is recorded as absolute ounces of alcohol. Each ounce of a 100-proof distilled beverage contains one-half ounce of absolute alcohol. Therefore, if this subject reported drinking six ounces of absolute alcohol during a 4:00 pm to 12.00 midnight time period, it meant she was consuming 12 ounces of 100-proof vodka or 14 ounces of 86-proof scotch.

at home, involved in either work activities or extra-marital relationships. When at home, he is usually working in his study. The youngest son spends almost all his free time working at a local tennis club. Home is primarily a place to eat and sleep. Mrs. S., on the other hand, spends most of her time at home, except when working in the mornings or attending a weekly art class. Although separation or divorce have been considered from time to time, the couple sees it as unnecessary unless one of them intends to remarry.

And so the family's life goes on from day to day with remarkably little variation. Despite their apparent lack of emotional and physical involvement with each other, they have managed to establish a stable, albeit vacuous, family life. Mrs. S. continues to drink regularly and heavily but within limits that make it possible for her to carry out her work responsibilities and household chores. Her son does not feel her behavior is in any way affected by her drinking, except that perhaps she is forgetful at times. Her husband adds only that perhaps her drinking makes her a little withdrawn. Mrs. S. responds by asking rhetorically, "Withdrawn from whom? Who is there to withdraw from?"

2. A Stable-Dry Non-Alcoholic Family

Mr. and Mrs. N. have been married 18 years and have three children, ages 14, 12, and 8. The family is vigorous, energetic, and economically successful. Their one major current concern is Mrs. N.'s chronic back ailment that has necessitated her spending extended time periods on total or partial bed rest. The family, however, has been able to accommodate its daily life to meet the needs of this chronic illness.

Mr. N., the identified alcoholic, had a drinking history beginning in college. Periodic episodes of drunkenness and occasional blackouts gradually increased in frequency over the first ten years of his marriage. During these years he would begin drinking at home after work, continue through dinner, and finally sequester himself in a basement TV room where he would eventually pass out and be awakened in the early morning by his wife. His wife and children rarely went down to the basement while he was drinking. His meaningful interaction with other family members was therefore minimal. Although the couple's social life and Mr. N.'s work were clearly affected by the magnitude of his drinking, the family made little or no effort to alter his behavior.

The critical event initiating the conversion from stable-wet to stable-dry phases was a weekend drinking binge that culminated in Mr. N.'s passing out while in an upstairs bathroom. For the first time he was found by one of his children rather than his wife. He admitted himself to a hospital shortly thereafter, was detoxified, and has been abstinent ever since.

Although obviously a dry family, there is very little evidence that alcohol remains a live issue for his family. It is viewed primarily as an episode from the past, quite distressing in retrospect, but clearly behind them and therefore of no immediate relevance. There is no involvement with AA or Al-Anon. No family members are currently in psychiatric treatment, nor have there been any efforts to seek treatment since Mr. N. became abstinent. Mrs. N. continues to drink socially, and alcohol is served at family parties.

Interestingly, however, the family's management of mother's curent ailment has striking parallels to their behavior during their stable-wet phase. Just as father previously retreated to the basement level of their home to drink in solitude, leaving mother and children to interact freely in the living room–dining room–kitchen complex of the house, during mother's extended illness she has encamped herself in a bedroom on the second floor of their house and managed much of the family's daily routines from this location. Her children meet with her after school in her bedroom, she hands out housekeeping assignments, and after dinner family entertainment occurs on the second floor. Father, on the other hand, tends to remain on the ground floor where he moves from room to room carrying out household chores. In this sense, the family's structural patterns of interaction are still clearly visible and unaltered in the conversion from a stable-wet to a stable-dry alcohol phase (merely moved up one floor in the house).

3. A Stable-Dry Alcoholic Family

Mr. D., a 43-year-old architect and Mrs. D., a 40-year-old housewife have been married eight years, the first six of which were plagued by the couple's profoundly disturbing behavior related to alcoholism. This is Mrs. D.'s third marriage and the fourth time in her life she has been involved in a family situation centered around alcoholism. It is Mr. D.'s second marriage but his first run-in with alcoholism. The household also includes four children, two from Mrs. D.'s second marriage and two from the current marriage. This complicated history of alcoholism and family life can perhaps be most easily traced using Mrs. D. as the protagonist.

The product of an alcoholic father and non-alcoholic mother, Mrs. D. was unaware of her father's drinking habits while she was living at home. Drinking rarely occurred in front of her, she claims, and it was only recently that she discovered her father had "quite a problem with alcohol when he was younger."

She began experimenting with alcohol as an adolescent, got drunk on numerous occasions, and had several episodes of blackouts. In her early twenties she married a man who "drank too much." He became physically abusive when drunk but drank heavily primarily outside the home. She would drink only at special family occasions. The marriage ended in divorce after several years.

Mrs. D. remarried in her late twenties, and her second husband also proved to be a heavy drinker, probably at an alcoholic level. This time, however, drinking was a mutual affair. Evenings always included constant drinking, and social life also seemed to revolve around drinking parties. Although Mrs. D.'s behavior when drinking in company tended to be restrained, drinking episodes at home were invariably associated with bitter quarrels and verbal abuse. This second marriage also ended in divorce. During the divorce proceedings, however, and for a period of several years postdivorce, Mrs. D.'s drinking diminished dramatically. She married her third husband, Mr. D., when she was 32 years old. He came from an Italian-American family that was accustomed to drinking wine

freely but had no history of alcohol abuse or alcoholism. The couple drank moderately during courtship without difficulty, but shortly after getting married drinking again increased to abusive levels. Although Mrs. D. appeared to lead the way, Mr. D. initially followed willingly. Several times a week they would meet for lunch, begin drinking, and would have an extended drinking session that would continue into the late evening at bars and dancing clubs. Once again, she begain experiencing bitter feelings about her husband, and frequent verbal fights errupted at home.

After several years of this style of interacting, Mr. D. apparently unilaterally decided to back out, reducing both his own drinking and the intensity of their social contact outside the home. Mrs. D. shortly thereafter retreated into the home, isolating herself and drinking almost constantly. Drinking became more secretive, but her quantity of alcohol consumption reached its highest point during this phase. At around this time she admitted to her husband that she was an alcoholic, a conclusion he, however, refused to accept.

Mrs. D. attended her first AA meeting at this point and initially remained sober for two months. She began drinking again during a reception following her son's marriage but contacted her AA sponsor and was brought to an alcoholism treatment unit and detoxified. She has remained sober since that time. Throughout this time her husband openly disparaged AA and the alcoholism treatment program, viewing these people as intruders in the family. Following a transitional period, however, Mr. D. began attending Al-Anon meetings and now openly acknowledges the family's past difficulties with alcoholism.

What is the family's current stance regarding alcohol? Mrs. D. remains abstinent; Mr. D. occasionally drinks wine in moderate amounts. Both Mr. and Mrs. D. attend twice-weekly Al-Anon and AA meetings, respectively, at the alcoholism treatment unit attached to their community hospital.

Mrs. D. regularly serves as a sponsor for new AA members and talks warmly about her satisfaction with this role. During our study the D.'s would regularly drive ten or fifteen miles out of their way to pick up one or two couples and bring them to the multiple family group meetings when these other couples had transportation problems. In particular, Mrs. D. "attached herself" to another family with an active drinking husband and made herself available to both this husband and his non-alcoholic wife for support and guidance. The family's past difficulties with alcohol were a live issue in family discussions, with frequent reminders about the contrast in family life between past and present. Mrs. D.'s involvement with AA and her "social work" role in dealing with other families in our study group was, as an organized series of activities, the closest analogy to a job or outside employment she has experienced in her adult life.

4. A Stable, Controlled-Drinking, Non-Alcoholic Family

Mr. C. a 38-year-old salesman and Mrs. C. a 29-year-old program analyst have been married for five years (his second marriage, her first) and live with his two daughters by a previous marriage (ages 15 and 11). Both spouses have active careers and are hard-working. For the past several years they have routinely enjoyed one or two predinner cocktails to help them "relax and unwind from the day's pressures." Although drinking is currently confined to this postwork ritual, such "controlled" drinking has not always been the case for Mr. C.

An occasional social drinker during his early 20's, Mr. C.'s alcohol consumption changed following his marriage and the birth of his children, eventually increasing to a daily consumption of six to eight beers plus four to five ounces of bourbon. He attributes the onset of alcoholism to an attempt on his part to escape from the pressures of problems in his parent's family and his marriage. Drinking began at 11:00

in the morning and would continue until bedtime. Over a 13-year period, this persistent pattern resulted in gradual loss of friends, work deterioration and minor arrests, but the family remained intact (we would label this period a stable-wet phase during a mid-life plateau).

Eventually he and his first wife separated and were then divorced. Two months after his divorce and despite his continued drinking, he and Mrs. C. were married. However, when Mr. C.'s alcoholism began to threaten this second marriage, he undertook to control his problem and admitted himself to a local hospital for treatment. He was abstinent for the next nine months, then gradually assumed the controlled drinking posture that has remained in a stable pattern for the past four years.

Mr. C.'s control over his drinking continues despite some tension and problems in the household. Mrs. C. and her stepdaughters are not so close. Never having raised children of her own, Mrs. C. has difficulty managing and communicating with the girls, and the resulting tension within the family further isolates them from her. Anne, the younger, and Mrs. C. have frequent arguments, and Anne spends a great deal of time in her room. Mr. C., of course, is often caught between his wife and daughters in attempts to mediate, soothe feelings, and struggle to remain neutral.

The children are part of their parents' dinner routine but little more. Typically, Mr. and Mrs. C. spend the evening together, either sharing an activity or doing separate things in the same room while the girls spend this time each in their own rooms—considered their private places. It is in their rooms that they most often entertain their friends. Mr. and Mrs. C.'s bedroom is likewise off-limits to the children. On weekends, the family spends a large part of its time out of the house, parents on family errands, the girls with their friends.

Despite the obvious difficulties experienced by this "blended" family in developing a sense of itself as an integrated unit

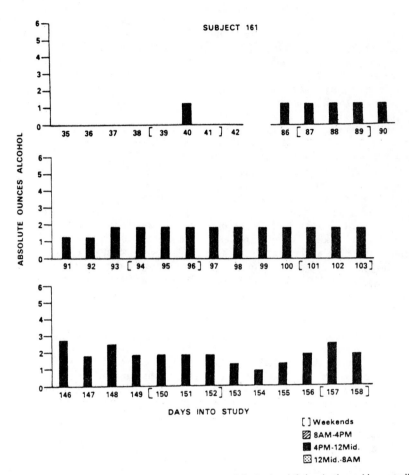

Fig. 3: A histogram of the pattern of alcohol consumption of the husband/father in the stable, controlled drinking, non-alcoholic family vignette.

and the attendant pressures brought to bear on Mr. C., he feels he has control of his drinking and says that he intends to continue to enjoy a few drinks a day as long as it does not lead to heavier drinking.

Research and Clinical Implications of the Model

What evidence can be marshalled from research findings in support of our proposed life history model of the alcoholic family? We would point to two major lines of evidence.

The first line of evidence comes from our own study of interactional behavior of alcoholic families in home, MFG, and laboratory settings (the study already cited as our impetus for looking at alcoholic families from a developmental perspective). Completed analyses of data from home and laboratory settings indicate that the family's current alcohol life phase is a powerful discriminator of statistically discernable patterns of interactional behavior. In the home, three distinct family-level interactional patterns could be clearly identified depending upon whether families were in stable-wet, stable-dry, or transitional phases (26). Furthermore, the family-level behavioral patterns associated with the transitional phase were similar in character for both wet-to-dry and dry-to-wet transition families. In the laboratory, dramatic differences emerged in interactional styles of families on a problem-solving task when stable-wet families were contrasted with stable-dry families (25). It is important to underscore that these findings relate to family-level patterns of behavior, not merely the differential treatment by the family of its alcoholic member.

The second line of evidence is the persistent inability to identify specific patterns of interactional behavior that distinguish alcoholic families as a group from non-alcoholic families (2, 28). These findings suggest that research designs examining within-group variation rather than, or in addition to, across-group variation is the more prudent way to investigate the relationship between alcoholism and family life. Therefore, models that suggest potential typologies of alcoholic families (such as the life-history model) are preferable to models that attempt to identify uniform characteristics invariably associated with alcoholism.

What are the potential clinical implications of the life history model? Major implications stem most directly from the three constructs that were the major building blocks for the model: the alcoholic system; the importance of alcohol use for family homeostasis; and the concept of the family alcohol life phase.

The distinction made in the model between the alcoholic and non-alcoholic family, an extension of the concept of the alcoholic system, suggests the importance of making a clinical distinction between those families that have introduced alcohol use as a central organizing principle for interactional behavior and those families that seem to treat the drinking of their alcoholic member as an isolated or circumscribed

symptom. Although in both instances the presence of alcoholism presents a problem for the family, in the first instance the family appears to embrace the alcoholic condition, whereas in the second the family tries to wall off and isolate the pathology.

In discussing this same phenomenon from the perspective of family rituals, Wolin and his colleagues (30) have introduced the terms "distinctive" versus "subsumptive," to indicate instances in which families have maintained the integrity of such areas of ritualized behavior as holidays and dinner time by refusing to allow alcoholic behavior to alter the structural content of these rituals (distinct from alcoholism), versus instances in which family rituals have succumbed to alcoholism. Wolin et al. suggest that the ability of the family to prevent alcoholism from invading family rituals is associated with an ability of the family to prevent the emergence of alcoholism in subsequent generations. Studies of coping styles used by spouses of chronic alcoholics have also suggested that styles that appear to challenge or confront alcoholic behavior ultimately are more successful in long-term recovery from alcoholism than styles associated with a tacit acceptance of the behavior (18).

The suggested role of alcohol as part of family homeostatic mechanisms emphasizes the relation between alcohol use and long-term stability in alcoholic families. To the extent that alcoholism and stability have become synonymous for these families, an obvious resistance would occur if the clinician attempted willy-nilly to remove the alcoholic symptom without first understanding the role it played in the family homeostasis and supporting efforts on the family's part to develop alternative mechanisms for stabilizing family life. It also suggests, however, that these families may place such a high value on stability as to be willing to trade long-term growth for short-term stability. These families, for example, have been repeatedly described in the clinical literature as rigid, unchanging, highly resistant to change, locked in concrete, stunted, etc.

The most important feature of the life history model, however, is the family-alcohol-phase concept. It is this concept that gives the model its developmental focus. How does the presence of this chronic disease alter the family life cycle?

The most striking difference suggested by the family-life-phase concept is that the developmental history of the alcoholic family, rather than consisting of a series of progressive stages, is instead organized in a cyclical fashion. The family returns repeatedly to stages already experienced rather than moving ahead in stepwise fashion to deal with a progressive series of tasks and stages as outlined by Duvall (6) in the classical family-life-cycle model. At the microscopic level, the cycling between sober and intoxicated interactional states produces the inflexible stability associated with the stable-wet phase. At the macroscopic level the cycling between stable-wet and stable-dry family life phases during the mid-life period produces a plateauing effect that profoundly alters the customary slope of family development. In this regard, there are in all likelihood marked similarities between the pattern of family development associated with alcoholism and the effect of other chronic illnesses, such as end stage renal disease or physical disability, on family development. The unique flavor associated with alcoholism comes from the physiological effect of the drug on the individual and on interactional behavior.

This is not to propose the total absence of customary patterns of family development in alcoholic families. Surely one is still able to perceive the effects of such developmental benchmarks as birth and death on such families. But the life history model proposes that the impact of such events on the developmental course of the alcoholic family would be blunted and very much colored by the family's current alcoholic life phase and the behavioral patterns it tends to develop around this alcohol-related issue.

REFERENCES

1. ABLON, J., "Al-Anon Family Groups: Impetus for Learning and Change Through the Presentation of Alternatives," *Amer. J. Psychother.* 28: 30–45, 1974.

2. ———, "Family Structure and Behavior in Alcoholism: A Review of the Literature," in B. Kissen and H. Begleiter (eds.) *The Biology of Alcoholism*, Plenum Press, 1976.

3. ALDOUS, J., *Family Careers: Developmental Change in the Family*, New York, Wiley, 1978.

4. ARMOUR, D.; POLICH, J.; and STAMBUL, H., *Alcoholism and Treatment*, Santa Monica, Rand Corporation, 1976.

5. BARNHILL, L. R. and LONGO, D., "Fixation and Regression in the Family Life Cycle," *Fam. Proc.* 17: 469, 1978.

6. DUVALL, E., *Family Development*, New York, Lippincott, 1971.

7. ERIKSON, E. H., *Childhood and Society*, New York, Norton, 1963.

8. EWING, J. A. and FOX, R. E., "Family Therapy of Alcoholism" in J. H. Masserman (ed.) *Current Psychiatric Therapies*, vol. 8, New York, Grune & Stratton, 1968.

9. EWING, J. A. and ROUSE, B. A., "Failure of an Experimental Treatment Program to Inculcate Controlled Drinking in Alcoholics," *Brit. J. Addiction* 71: 123–134, 1976.

10. GARTNER, R. B.; FULMER, R. H.; WEINSHEL, M.; and GOLDKLANK, S., "The Family Life Cycle: Developmental Crises and Their Structural Impact on Families in a Community Mental Health Center," *Fam. Proc.* 17: 47–58, 1978.

11. HAMBURG, D. A. and ADAMS, J. E., "A Perspective on Coping Behavior: Seeking and Utilizing Information in Major Transitions," *Arch. Gen. Psychiat.* 17: 277–284, 1967.

12. HILL, R., "Modern Systems Theory and The Family: A Confrontation," *Soc. Sci. Inform.* 10: 7–26, 1971.

13. HILL, R. and RODGERS, R., "The Developmental Approach," in H. Christensen (ed.), *Handbook of Marriage and Family*, Rand McNally, 1964.

14. JACKSON, J. K., "The Adjustment of the Family to the Crisis of Alcoholism," *Quart. J. Studies on Alcohol* 15: 562–586, 1954.

15. JAMES, E. and GOLDMAN, M. "Behavior Trends of Wives of Alcoholics," *Quart. J. Studies on Alcohol* 32: 373–381, 1971.

16. KENNEDY, D. L., "Behavior of Alcoholics and Spouses in a Simulation Game Situation," *J. Nerv. Ment. Dis.* 162: 23–34, 1976.

17. LEMERT, E. M., "The Occurrence and Sequence of Events in Adjustment of Families Through Alcoholism," *Quart. J. Studies on Alcohol* 21: 679–697, 1969.

18. ORFORD, J.; GUTHRIE, S.; NICHOLLS, P.; OPPENHEIMER, E. EGEIT, S.; and HENSMAN, C., "Self-Reported Coping Behavior of Lives of Alcoholics and Its Association with Drinking Outcome," *J. Studies on Alcohol* 36: 1254–1267, 1975.

19. PAOLINO, T. J. and MCCRADY, B. S., *The Alcoholic Marriage: Alternative Perspectives*, New York, Grune & Stratton, 1977.

20. PATTISON, E. M., "On Abstinence Drinking Goals in the Treatment of Alcoholism," *Arch. Gen. Psychiat.* 33: 923–930, 1976.

21. RAPOPORT, R., "Normal Crises, Family Structure, and Mental Health," *Fam. Proc.* 12: 68–80, 1963.

22. SOLOMON, M., "A Developmental, Conceptual Premise for Family Therapy," *Fam. Proc.* 12: 178–188, 1973.

23. STEINER, C. M., *Games Alcoholics Play*, New York, Grove Press, 1971.

24. STEINGLASS, P., "Experimenting with Family Treatment Approaches to Alcoholism, 1950–1975: A Review," *Fam. Proc.* 16: 97–123, 1976.

25. ———, "The Alcoholic Family in the Interaction Laboratory," *J. Nerv. Ment. Dis.* 167: 428–436, 1979.

26. STEINGLASS, P., "The Alcoholic Family at Home: Patterns of Interaction in Dry, Wet, and Transitional Stages of Alcoholism," *Arch. Gen. Psychiat.*, in press.

27. STEINGLASS, P.; WEINER, S.; and MENDELSON, J. J., "A Systems Approach to Alcoholism: A Model and Its Clinical Application," *Arch. Gen. Psychiat.* 24: 401–408, 1971.

28. STEINGLASS, P.; DAVIS, D. I.; and BERENSON, D., "Observations of Conjointly Hospitalized 'Alcoholic Couples' During Sobriety and Intoxication: Implications for Theory and Therapy," *Fam. Proc.* 16: 1–16, 1977.

29. WARD, R. F., and FAILLACE, L. A., "The Alcoholic and His Helpers," *Quart. J. Studies on Alcohol* 31: 684–691, 1970.

30. WOLIN, S. J.; BENNETT, L. A.; and NOONAN, D. L., "Family Rituals and the Recurrence of Alcoholism over Generations," *Amer. J. Psychiat.* 136: 589–593, 1979.

Reprint requests should be addressed to Peter Steinglass, M. D., Center for Family Research, George Washington University School of Medicine, 2300 Eye Street, N.W. Washington, D.C. 20037.

PART VI

WORK AND THE FAMILY

Work provides economic resources that are essential to the well-being of families. Connections between work and family life are very complex, especially when more than one family member is employed. In this article, linkages between work and two-earner families are examined in the areas of financial security, status, conflicting obligations, and role strains. Issues are raised about how the structure of occupations and family roles might change as more families have two earners and as workplaces and government policies increasingly recognize employees as family members.

27

THE TWO-PROVIDER FAMILY
Problems and Potentials

Phyllis Moen

INTRODUCTION

One of the most striking social trends of the century is the progressive influx of married women into the labor force. In 1979, half of all married women in the United States were either employed or looking for a job. This compares to only 4.5% of married women in the labor force in 1890 (Smith, 1979). Indeed, the two-provider family is rapidly becoming the norm. From 1960 to 1975 the proportion of two-earner husband/wife families grew from 23% to 30% of all households (Masnick & Bane, 1980; p. 8). The greatest change in recent years has been the increase in two-provider families with children. In 1979, over 52% of married woman with children under the age of 18 were in the labor force. Included in this group were 59% of the married mothers of school-aged children to 43% of those with children younger than 6. (US Department of Labor, 1980). Moreover, it is expected that by 1990 fully half of all mothers with preschool children will be in the labor force (Smith, 1979).

Foremost among the reasons for this remarkable growth of two-provider families are increased family financial need (especially in inflationary times), opportunities for women in service-type industries, the declining birthrate, and changes in social attitudes and prescriptions concerning the roles of women and men (Hoffman & Nye, 1974; Moore and Hofferth, 1979; Sweet, 1973). Scholars have documented the social, family, and individual factors that affect the decisions of married women to work (Moore and Hofferth, 1979; Sobol, 1974; Sweet, 1973), but there has been little systematic study of the *consequences* for families of having two earners. This chapter examines what is know as well as what is unknown about two-provider families.

Underlying Assumptions

Two assumptions guide the discussion that follows: (1) recognition of the pro-
cessual aspects of the work–family connection; and (2) a picture of the active,
systematic nature of families. Individuals pursue a number of "careers"; for
two-provider families what is significant is the interface of the occupational and
family careers. It is important to remember that the term *career* connotes change.
Both work and family activities alter in intensity and significance over time;
moreover, changes in one role may have inevitable consequences for the other
role. For example, couples may work longer or shorter hours as a result of
changes in family economic needs. Similarly, there may be changes in labor-
force activity to accompany changes in a parent's time requirements—for instance, with the birth of a new baby. Investigating families with two incomes
while ignoring the dynamic nature of both jobs and families would only produce
a distortion of the issues.

A second assumption is a perception of the two-provider family as *active*
rather than *passive*. Families can be viewed as merely responding to their existing situations or as decision-making units that make choices within the contexts of
constraints, needs, and opportunities at hand. This chapter is oriented more
toward the second perspective. The decision to have both husband and wife
employed involves a number of considerations, including the problems and benefits that will accrue to the family as a whole.

Both opportunity factors in the labor market and family economic needs have
fostered the employment of married women. But the large-scale forces producing
and perpetuating the two-provider family must be considered in the light of
individual families making *individual decisions* concerning the amount and form
of each member's labor-force participation. Working couples are not merely
passive victims of inflation or workplace demands. These families may resist,
negotiate, or collaborate with the demands of work to varying degrees—taking
another job rather than moving, for example, or refusing to work overtime.
Because working husbands and wives are seen as actors rather than reactors, it is
important to understand their perceptions of the problems and potentials of work,
for themselves and for their families.

Major Issues

The two-provider family underscores a key issue for those concerned with
families and with family well-being: *What is the nature of the relationship
between families and the world of work?* When both spouses are employed, the
intrusion of work into family life (and vice versa) becomes readily apparent.

A second vital concern is with *the impacts of having two earners on the family
and on particular family subsystems* (such as the marital dyad or the parent–child
linkage). What are the costs, in terms of family resources, of having both spouses

work? Do working couples experience greater or less marital satisfaction? What are the implications of having both parents employed for the care and the socialization of their children?

Equally salient are *the impacts on society as a whole*. Individual families, across the nation, are making choices concerning who in the family will be employed outside the home. These individual decisions collectively result in widespread social change—in the make up of the labor force, in the structure of families, in the need for services, programs, and policies that take into account the phenomenon of the two-provider family.

Organization of the Chapter

The plan of the chapter is as follows: First, the more general issue of work–family linkages is discussed. Then both problems and payoffs in the form of family resources are described. Outcomes in terms of family roles and responsibilities—the division of household labor, child rearing, the marital relationship—are highlighted. The chapter concludes by placing two-provider families within the contexts of the life-course perspective as well as within a larger, societal framework.

WORK–FAMILY LINKAGES

An important outgrowth of research on two-provider families is the explication of the links between family life and the world of work. For years, scholars, employers, unions, and even workers themselves have harboured a myth of separate worlds (Kanter, 1977). Job and home life have been neatly compartmentalized; any overlap and attendant strain between them has been ignored.

But the separation of the worlds of work and family life is more illusionary than real. Notwithstanding the physical and temporal segregation of workplace and home, family and job roles clearly converge. Recent qualitative studies of individual families convincingly document the many ways in which work intrudes into the home, as well as how family life affects experiences on the job (Piotrkowski, 1979; Rapoport & Rapoport, 1976). The magnitude of this work–family conjunction is clearly suggested by findings of a recent national survey of employed workers, the 1977 Quality of Employment Survey, in which 34% of the respondents reported various forms of interference between work and family (Quinn & Staines, 1978).

In the two-provider family the links between home and work cannot be ignored, as problems from one domain are most apt to intrude upon the other. For example, couples may have difficulties in finding two jobs that mesh with their family needs. As Berger and his colleagues (1978; p.23) point out, couples seek employment opportunities: (1) in the same geographical area; (2) with hours that are compatible with household and child-care responsibilities; (3) that will allow time for them to pursue joint as well as individual interests; (4) that meet their current job expectations; and (5) that will contribute to long-term career goals. The task of locating jobs that are personally rewarding is difficult enough. Finding and maintaining two links to the labor force while at the same time meeting family obligations becomes a way of life for two-provider families that may be fraught with problems and is rarely easy.

Work–Family Strains

Strains between job and family obligations may well be inevitable in families where both spouses work. Difficulties faced by working couples have been described as *overload,* where the totality of job and family demands is simply too great, or as work–family *interference* or *conflict,* where the demands of one's job and one's family are actually contradictory (Voydanoff, 1980).

The Rapoports (1976) outline five types of dilemmas faced by working couples. The first is *overload,* which can involve social–psychological strain as well as time pressures. In the second category are *normative* dilemmas, brought about by discrepancies between one's own life-style and that valued by society. For example, a mother who is employed may feel she is not properly caring for her child according to social expectations regarding the maternal role. *Identity* dilemmas represent discontinuities between early internalized norms about the roles of men and women and the actual behavior of two-provider couples. A husband, for example, may feel that a wife's place is at home, even though his wife is employed. *Social–network* dilemmas reflect the inability of working couples to meet the expectations of and obligations to family and friends. There is little time on weekends and in the evenings for socializing when both spouses have jobs. Finally, there are *role-cycling* dilemmas, involving decisions that must be made about starting a family and the timing of major career decisions. Family and job events must be scheduled in ways that integrate childbearing and child rearing with career patterns. Moreover, couples may try to schedule job stresses so that heavy job pressures are not simultaneously experienced by both spouses.

In her study of 53 dual-career couples, Poloma (1972) found that this sample of professional women used four coping strategies in dealing with work–family overload and conflicts: (1) defining the situation of having a two-career family as positive; (2) creating a hierarchy of values (family responsibilities supersede job demands); (3) compartmentalizing home and work into separate spheres; and (4) compromising (one's career goals). A companion study of the husbands of these women (Garland, 1972) reports that the men regarded the dual-career arrangement as generally beneficial to their lives and did not feel personally threatened by their wives' careers.

The strains that Poloma and the Rapoports describe are those faced by *dual-career* families, "the type of family in which both heads of household pursue careers and at the same time maintain a family life together [Rapoport & Rapoport, 1971, p. 18].'' In comparison, working-class couples, holding down two *jobs,* not commonly regarded as careers, may well experience a different set of strains (see, for example Lein et al., 1974). In fact, a distinction is often made between dual-*worker* and dual-*career* families (Mortimer, 1978; Mortimer, Hall, and Hill, 1978). Unfortunately, most studies of two-provider families have investigated professional (career) families (Bailyn, 1970; Garland, 1972; Holmstrom, 1973; Poloma, 1972; Rapoport & Rapoport, 1971). Consequently, little is known about the experiences, orientations, and coping strategies of working-class couples (an exception: Lein et al., 1974; Working Family Project 1978), where two incomes may be defined a necessity and the requirements of jobs may be relatively inflexible and permit little freedom to deal with family concerns. For example, time off for dental appointments or for care of a sick child is much more difficult to secure in lower-level occupations (i.e., "jobs") than in professional "careers."

Differences in Work–Family Linkages

Families where both spouses are employed differ considerably, not only from single-provider families, but among themselves. For example, it is clear that dual-worker and dual-career families reflect variations in the objective requirements of the job. But working spouses may also differ in their general level of commitment to employment and the meaning they ascribe to work. Some may value work principally for the economic return it provides. Others may stress the status and social identity that are attached to particular occupations. And still others may see employment as an opportunity to socialize, to learn new skills, or to occupy otherwise unused time. These different values sought in and through employment may vary not only across working couples but within them. For example, a husband may enjoy his job principally because of its intrinsic rewards whereas his wife may be working because she appreciates the feeling of economic independence her job encourages.

Families can differ as well in terms of their ability to withstand the *costs* of the employment of both husband and wife. Dual-*career* families can usually afford to hire adequate household and child-care help to ease the domestic burden, and they may easily purchase services and laborsaving devices to reduce demands (dining out, hiring a housekeeper, household appliances, etc.) on their time and energies (Holmstrom, 1972). In working-class families, on the other hand, caring for the children and the home cannot be so easily dealt with; these couples often must juggle schedules, compromise needs, or just let things slide.

The costs of two jobs also vary by family structure and stage of the life cycle. Families with a large number of children or with preschoolers are more likely to experience difficulties meshing work and family responsibilities than are smaller families or families with school-age children. Similarly, parents who start their families relatively late in life, after job security has been achieved, are likely to experience less stress than are young parents who are simultaneously launching both their work and their family careers. To avoid or reduce the strains of coping with work and family obligations, couples may decide to delay the period of childbearing and/or choose to have smaller families (although the direction of causality is not entirely clear—see Smith-Lovin & Tickameyer, 1978; Waite & Stolzenberg, 1976). Another variation involves the patterning of labor-force patterns over the life cycle. Husbands and wives may work continuously over the life course, or one (almost always the wife) may interrupt his or her employment during the early years of childbearing and child rearing (Rapoport & Rapoport, 1976).

Finally, two-provider families can differ in terms of the employment conditions that serve to hamper or to facilite the meshing of work life with family life. Some jobs have great flexibility in terms of working hours and individual discretion, whereas others impose strict requirements concerning where and when work is accomplished. For example, college professors, among other professionals, may choose to do some of their work at home. The preponderance of jobs, however, must be performed exclusively at the workplace. Still other differential demands concern such requirements as geographical mobility, business travel, and overtime. Employers typically view their employees only as individuals and not as members of families (Renshaw, 1976), and thus are not inclined to tailor employment conditions to meet family needs. The degree to which organizations provide maternity (or parental) leaves, flexible hours, time off for the care of a sick child, and the availablity of convenient, reliable, inexpensive child-care arrangements can markedly affect the individual worker's roles both as employee and as family member.

Summary

In discussing the links between work and family life it is important to recognize the differences across two-provider families. The majority of couples do not regard their situation as voluntary; for many, two jobs are an economic necessity rather than an option. Neither do all working couples experience the same strains or the same benefits from the two-provider life-style. Some couples may take pride in meeting the challenges that jobs and family pose (Rapoport & Rapoport, 1976); others may find the same kinds of problems overwhelming. The costs and benefits of having two earners are not equally distributed among all families. It is important to remember, however, that there *are* positive as well as negative aspects of having both spouses employed. The following section discusses both the problems and potentials of this family form in terms of family resources.

FAMILY RESOURCES

Life-styles in two-provider families differ from those in traditional single-provider families, in part because of the different roles that family members play, but also because of the different resources that each family type generates. Time and money are the most obvious resources that help to determine the quality of family life. But energy and commitment are also important, as is the availability of social supports. In a somewhat different vein, personal feelings of self-worth also can be considered a "resource" that enhances the lives of working couples and can have indirect repercussions as well on the lives of their children.

The work–family connection can be conceptualized as a system of exchange (Fig. 2.1). Husbands and wives give of their skills, energies, and time in order to gain economic security, status, and a sense of purpose and identity. The nature of the exchange depends on both the structure of the family (for example, family size) and the stage of the family life cycle. For most families the benefits of having two earners far outweigh the costs. But all pay a price, particularly in respect to one scarce resource, time to get things done.

Time

The principal family resource involved in labor-force activity is time. As a fixed commodity, time allocated to employment is necessarily unavailable for other activities, including family activities. Time spent at work, therefore, offers an important and concrete measure of one dimension of employment affecting individuals and their families. The amount of time spent working, as well as which family members are employed, varies widely, both across families and within the same family over the life course.

Studies of dual-provider families too often treat employment as a simple dichotomous variable; one is either employed (or looking for employment) or out of the labor force. But treating work in this simplistic fashion may well *obscure* as much as it reveals. Employment may be full-time, part-time, or overtime, and it may involve one family member working at two jobs or two family members working at one or two jobs.

The number of work hours and their scheduling are significant because of the

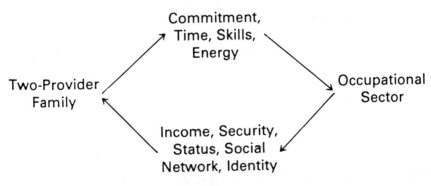

FIG. 2.1.   Labor Force Participation as Exchange

strains they may induce between employment and family life (Quinn & Staines. 1978). Time constraints imposed by having two earners in the family have inevitable ramifications for the frequency and quality of family interaction and for the division of labor within the family. The employment of both parents typically creates problems of child care and conflicts between occupational and family responsibilities. Because of the cultural definitions of men's and women's roles, these burdens brought about by time constraints are apt to be disproportionately borne by the wife.

The *scheduling* of hours spent at work is no less important than their number when considering the character and quality of time available for family activities. There obviously must be a synchronization of job and family schedules (Aldous. 1969), yet such a synchronization can be problematic. Many dual-worker couples are able to use shift work as a way of reconciling the demands of two jobs with child-care responsibilities (Lein et al., 1974; Mott et al., 1965). But shift work can also impose serious strains on family life. For example, studies of fathers on afternoon shifts document the fact that these men often feel they see too little of their children because of the timing of their work (Mott et al., 1965). Mortimer's (1979) study of midwestern male college graduates revealed that 59% of those men found that the long hours and the need to work at night or on weekends was disruptive of their family life. Similarly, men and women interviewed for the Quality of Employment Survey most often mentioned time and scheduling problems as the primary form of work–family interference (Quinn & Staines, 1978).

Not enough is known about the effects of both spouses working on the amount of time for family activities. Couples may adapt to the high time demands of jobs by forgoing leisure rather than family activities. A study of couples in Seattle (Clark, Nye, & Gecas, 1979), revealed that husbands' work time was not related to marital role performance but was linked to reduced participation in recreational activity. However, for couples with preschool children a negative relationship was found between the husband's hours on the job and his participation in the child-care role (Clark & Gecas, 1977). These kinds of studies are suggestive, but far from definitive. The complex relationships among work time, family time, and leisure time are substantially underresearched. What is required are investigations that take into account the detailed work patterns of each spouse in order to trace out the specific family impacts of the time and timing of work.

Energy and Commitment

Closely related to time is another resource that is "spent" in the market place: energy. Research has convincingly documented that work can be a physical and emotional drain, and a major impediment to achieving a satisfactory and satisfying non-work life (Kornhauser, 1965; Work in America, 1973; Young & Willmott, 1973). Moreover, these are costs born not only by working parents but by their children as well. It is only reasonable to expect that parents fatigued by physically and psychologically demanding jobs will have insuffient energy to devote to family matters.

Still another resource that is related to time involves the significance of the work role, the degree of commitment to the job. Commitment is apt to be thought of as a undimensional, fixed quantity variable, with high work involvement on one end of the continuum and high family involvement at the other. Although this is a realistic portrayal of the quantity of involvement—of the relative amount of time devoted to work and family—it is not necessarily an accurate reflection of psychological investments. For example, it would be possible for parents to rate themselves as highly committed to *both* parenting and employment. It is in this instance that the strains produced by the two roles are likely to be most pronounced.

The "absorptiveness" of jobs, the degree to which one's occupation demands high emotional involvement, is a prime example of the "spillover" of work into home (Kanter, 1977). When either partner (or both) is on a career ladder, high commitment is demanded; this is often at the time of life when family responsibilities are the greatest (Mortimer, Hall, & Hill, 1978). Parents highly committed to their work have been shown to experience frequent conflict in relation to their family responsibilities (Young & Willmott, 1973). In Mortimer's study of midwestern college graduates, over half of her sample felt their families suffered strain as a result of their own fatigue or irritability due to tensions or problems at work, and 41% reported their preoccupation with work-related problems or demands was disruptive to their families.

In this area of work–family concern as in others, research to date has been provocative but incomplete. What is not known is how commitment to work and family changes over time, and research is needed to document variations in the absorptiveness of jobs over the family life cycle. Additional study of the consequences of high work commitment—for child care and family life in general—is also required.

Economic Security

The multiworker family is one remedy for the financial press of inflation, low wages, and the progressively increasing costs of raising a family. In 1978, the median family income of families in which both husband and wife were employed was $22,109 compared to $16,156 in families where the husband alone worked outside the home (US Department of Labor, 1980). This represents a significant difference in the ability of families to provide for their needs and live comfortably.

The presence of secondary earners is thus an important family resource in achieving economic security and well-being. In 1977, wives' earnings represented about one-fourth of family income. Wives working full time and year round contributed nearly 40% of their family's income (Hayghe, 1978). However, whether the earnings potential of wives can in fact be realized in order to provide for their families is determined by a host of cultural and institutional factors, including employment opportunities, prevailing wage rates, and the "costs" of employment. For women with preschool children, for example, the expenses incurred in order to work full time may be quite high (e.g., substitue child care), and they may at best be able to manage temporary or part-time employment.

Work obviously is critical to the economic well-being of families; but, by the same token, unstable or low-paying jobs can undermine that well-being. One survey reported that most American wage earners rank job security higher in importance than increased income (Yankelovich, Skelly, & White, 1975). Seventy percent of those with young children agreed with the statement that it is better to have a secure job than one that pays a lot, compared with only 44% of those families having no children.

Which two-provider families are the most economically insecure? Understandably, insecurity is most common among couples who have little education and few marketable skills. Parents in families with young children also tend to be insecure, because they more frequently lack the seniority and experience that insures stable employment and higher wage rates. A recent study found that breadwinners with children under 6 were the most likely to be unemployed, to have a longer period of unemployment in the event of job loss, and to have inadequate income in the face of unemployment (Moen, 1979, in press).

Here again, more research is needed—to clarify further the contributions to family life made by secondary wage earners, as well as the problems created in the course of making these contributions. The role of the second income in easing pressure points, especially during the early stages of child rearing, is most in need of investigation, with particular attention paid to the costs of substitute child care.

Status and Social Placement

In considering the financial benefits of having both spouses employed it is important to recognize an additional social reward in the form of *status* or, more broadly, what Scanzoni (1970) terms "integration into the opportunity structure." The location of individuals and their families within the social structure is contingent on the power, prestige, and resources that are earned through the family's linkage to the economic system. The social standing of families within the community is a critical determinant of life circumstances and experiences, the quality of the life of parents and their children. Although it is difficult, if not impossible, to separate the effects of social status from the effects of income per se, it is important to acknowledge the differential payoff that accrues to parents employed as professionals compared to that received by persons situated on the lower rungs of the occupational ladder. Success in the occupational sphere is reflected in the "respectability" of the family; moreover, parents who are ascribed low prestige may limit the occupational aspirations as well as the opportunities of their children. Status becomes a life-style contingency, opening or closing options not only to the individual worker, but to his or her family as well. (For a discussion of status mobility, see Blau & Duncan, 1967; Duncan, Featherman, & Duncan, 1968). Wives and children in an early study of blue-collar families were found to be aware of the low status of the father's occupation and expressed dissatisfaction with the low prestige of his job (Dyer, 1956). Social scientists are just beginning to examine status in two-earner families by evaluating the jobs of both spouses. Of particular interest in such research are the implications, for families, of status differentials between husbands and wives, situations where the spouses occupy widely separated positions in the occupational hierarchy.

Social Network

Another "resource" that emerges from the work–family connection is the development of a network of social contacts and relationships. In fact, one of the major complaints of mothers who are not in the labor force is their sense of social isolation (Ferree, 1976). The workplace constitutes a social setting where friendships may be fostered and information is transmitted. These, in turn, can become important family resources, social supports that are invaluable to working couples not only in times of crisis, but also in managing day-to-day problems of living. When both spouses are employed, their potential network is doubled. On the other hand, their nonworking hours are often occupied in the care and maintainance of the home and the children. This leaves little time for leisure and for social activities (Mortimer, Hall, & Hill, 1978). Even relationships with relatives may be quite circumscribed (St. Johns-Parsons, 1978). One of the limitations faced by two-earner families is the physical and social isolation of the nuclear family (Holmstrom, 1973). Working parents rarely have relatives living in the home or nearby to share the burden of child care. This isolation is compounded because of the scarcity of time for socializing with friends or those relatives who are accessible (Rapoport & Rapoport, 1976). One solution to the lack of leisure time may be socializing with others in similar circumstances and with similar time constraints. The Rapoports' study (1976) of dual-career couples reported the importance of social linkages with other dual-career families for exchanging services as well as support for their shared life-style.

Friends, neighbors, and relatives constitute an informal source of support for the two-provider family, but there are also formal ties to the community. Public and private agencies can be sources of information, child care, counseling, recreational activities, and emergency aid. Research is required to investigate the use by working couples of community services as well as informal social networks and the factors that contribute to the isolation of some families and the integration of others. The distinctions between dual-worker and dual-career families may be important in describing the utilization of social services as well as the tapping of one's personal network of kin, friends, and neighbors to ease the strains in coordinating work and family roles.

Identity and Self-Esteem

Work serves as a major basis for evaluating oneself and being evaluated by others in our society. This is especially true for men, whose identities are closely bound to their occupational positions. Although our society has long recognized the importance of work as a "validating activity" for men (Kahn, 1972; Mortimer, 1979; Rainwater, 1974a, 1974b), evidence suggests that it is now becoming increasingly salient for women as well (Hoffman, 1974; Sobol, 1974). Studies of employed mothers have shown that they express higher levels of self-esteem, competence, and general satisfaction with life than mothers not engaged in paid employment (Feld, 1963; Hacker, 1971; Hoffman, 1974). A recent study of working-class mothers of grade school children underscores the fact that women who are employed are more satisfied with themselves and their lives than are full-time homemakers (Ferree, 1976).

For women, however, the importance of work as a source of identity is less than it is for men. Historically, the wife's identity has been synonomous with the family. According to Oakley, 1976: Our language contains the phrase "a family man," but no such phrase for women—since family, for all practical purposes means women. Women's evaluation of their work experience depends heavily on their motivation and commitment (Bailyn, 1970; Dubin, 1976: Haller & Rosenmayer, 1971; Parnes, et al., 1970; Safilios-Rothschild, 1970), but it is becoming clear that the work role and its identity-bestowing qualities are significant for many wives.

What are the psychological implications of being a partner in a two-earner family? Most research has examined the consequences for employed *mothers,* rather than fathers, assuming that the strain of work–family conflicts is borne principally by the woman of the house. Some studies (Birnbaum, 1971) have found a positive link between a woman's employment and feelings of anxiety or guilt. Hoffman (1974), on the other hand, emphasizes psychic satisfactions of work and the feelings of achievement, competence, and contribution it fosters. More recent research reveals that employed women have a more positive self-image than do full-time homemakers. A study of 83 dual-career and traditional families found that the husbands and wives with dual careers were more inner-directed than traditional couples, although it fails to document differences in self-regard between working and nonworking wives (Huser & Grant, 1978). Research on married women has shown that the nature of their work experience can exert a powerful effect on their self-conceptions, social orientations, and even intellectual functioning (Kohn et al, 1979). Moreover, this research has shown that dimensions of occupation, such as time pressure, substantive complexity, and closeness of supervision have psychological consequences for both men and women. The role of the other spouse's orientations toward the two-earner family as well as attitudes concerning his or her own job may be an important factor in the mental health of the individual.

Scholars looking at two-earner families must also be sensitive to the drudgery of some jobs and to the fact that employment is not always perceived as desirable, especially for working couples with jobs, rather than careers. Although work can be a source of satisfaction and self-esteem (Form, 1973; Seeman, 1971; O'Toole, 1974), it also can foster dissatisfaction, depression, and despair (Blauner, 1964; Kornhauser, 1965; Seligman, 1965). Much of the meaning of work depends on the role orientations of the individual worker as well as the particular characteristics of the job. Whether one's job is seen as a career or an occupation—contributing both to society and to individual fulfillment—or whether it is seen as a task requiring certain skills or merely a way of earning money affects both the salience and the satisfactions of employment (Fried, 1966). For example, professionals report higher levels of job satisfaction than do workers in lower occupational categories (Kahn, 1974). Studies have found not only consistent differences in health and self-esteem by occupational level, but progressive changes in health and self-esteem as one moves up or down the occupational ladder (French, 1963; Kahn & French, 1970). A study in Baltimore and Detroit of employed, married men with small children found a positive relationship between social status (higher income and educational levels) and feelings of effectiveness and control (Gurin & Gurin, 1976). One's job status serves as an indicator of public esteem (French, 1963). Those holding low-status jobs and those whose work linkage is marginal at best are most likely to be evaluated and to evaluate themselves as inadequate and incompetent.

What is the relative importance of job and family in accounting for feelings of self-worth and general life satisfaction? Although, as suggested in the foregoing, work is a key element in individual well-being, studies of the mental health of both men and women have underscored the centrality of the family in people's lives. Douvan and colleagues (1979), for example found that the family role, pitted against work, is valued at a ratio of three to one by both men and women. And research has shown that family roles are an important source of life satisfaction. People who are happy in their marriage and family life tend to consider themselves happy in general (Gurin, Veroff, & Feld, 1957). But there is unquestionably variability in the salience of work and family across two-provider families and in the consequent effects of each on feelings of well-being.

Summary: Resource Distribution

The sharing of the breadwinning role by husbands and wives has obvious implications for the quality of family life. Financial well-being is clearly improved; the cushion of a second income also provides an added measure of economic security. But other resources—time and energy—are often constrained when both spouses are employed, curtailing opportunities for family activities and relationship among family members.

Existing knowledge and understanding about the resources of two-provider families are far from complete. Research needs to be undertaken not only on the *availability* of particular resources such as time and money but on the configuration or *distribution* of resources across families and within the same family over its life cycle. Duel-*career* couples may be able to "purchase" time, for example, by engaging domestic help or eating at restaurants. But dual-*worker* families may well have neither time nor money and may, therefore, be less equipped to manage reoccurring work–family strains. It is also likely that families with limited resources are less able to cope with unanticipated stresses, such as a sick child, than can those families with more bountiful resources. What is not clear is the relative utility or the substitutability of different types of resources. Are social supports more valuable for procuring emergency child care than is income? Similarly, how important is flexibility of working hours, relative to the income that a job generates, in dealing with points of stress in the work–family junction? Questions need to be asked, as well, about the impacts of *changes* in family resources on the relationships between husbands and wives, parents and children.

Resources constitute the materials and the tools by which families shape their day-to-day experiences, their relationships, their dreams for the future. The amount and type of resources available to two-provider families have direct repercussions for the functioning of the family. The following section examines three facets of life for two-provider families: the division of labor, the marital relationship, and parenting.

FAMILY FUNCTIONING

Household Division of Labor

In considering the division of labor within the home a distinction should be made between *participation* in domestic activities and *responsibility* for these activities. When both spouses work, husbands may share in the household tasks, but domestic roles usually remain the principal responsibility of the wife (Holter, 1970; Pleck, 1977; Slocum & Nye, 1976). Holmstrom (1973), in as study of 27 professional couples, found that most of the husbands did in fact "help out" with the domestic chores. Poloma and Garland (1971) report similar conclusions in a study of 53 employed professionals but found that only one couple shared the housework equally. Research on male managers in Britian documented that these men put in long hours on the job and did little housework (Young & Willmott, 1973). Time-budget studies in the last half of the 1960s (Robinson, 1977; Walker & Woods, 1976) reported that the amount of time wives spent working outside the home did not markedly affect the amount of time that husbands devoted to household activity, including time for child care. A more recent national time-budget study by the University of Michigan's Survey Research Center compares time use in 1975 with that in 1965 and continues to reflect the minimal involvement of husbands in domestic activities (Hill & Stafford, 1980; Stafford, 19-80).However, Hoffman (1977) notes that husbands of employed wives are more likely to help with the care of children than are husbands of nonemployed wives. And in a recent national survey of employed workers (the 1977 Quality of Employment Survey), husbands in two-provider families reported spending 1.8 hours per week more in housework and 2.7 hours per week more in child care than did husbands of nonemployed wives (Pleck, 1979).

It is reasonable to expect that the division of labor between husband and wife varies according to the nature of each spouse's employment. When both spouses pursue uninterrupted careers one would anticipate that household chores are equitably divided between them. But this need not be the case, as is reported in a study (St. Johns-Parsons, 1978) of 10 dual-career families in which the wife had been continuously employed. There was no sharing of household tasks, and the husband's was seen as the more important career.

The distribution of domestic chores may differ somewhat between families in which wives work full time and in those in which wives work less than full time. Weingarten (1978), in interviews with 32 Boston couples, found that professional families with wives working part time were less likely to share the household chores than were full-time employed couples. But if one considers both work on the job and domestic ''work'' at home, the division of labor may be more equitable in families where the wives are employed less than full time. Vickery (1979) notes that the part-time employed wife and her husband are more likely to have evenly distributed work loads than are full-time working couples, with the wife assuming major responsibility for the domestic chores, and the husband devoting most of his time to his job.

One factor that may affect the amount of time husbands devote to domestic activities is the scheduling of each spouse's job. A recent study of 750 households using time diaries found that men were more likely to do housework and care for children if their wives worked in the late afternoon or evening (Berk & Berk, 1979). This well may be the pattern of many working-class couples, who use shift work as a means of sharing the child-care role (Lein et al., 1974). However, because most research on the division of labor has focused on professional couples, little is known about the patterns of domestic activity in working-class families. In one intensive study of 14 dual-worker families, it was found that although both parents participated in child care, the responsibility for the children remained with the wife (Lein et al., 1974). And Bahr (1974) also found that even though husbands may participate more in domestic activities the *responsibilities* for home and child care remain with the wife.

The Rapoports (1976) have underscored the importance of looking at the division of responsibility as well as the actual participation of husbands and wives in domestic chores. From the literature review it would appear that what Myrdal and Klein (1956) describe as a married woman's second "primary" role, her employment, more often than not takes a back seat to her first primary role within the home. Although men may be "helping out" at home, particularly with child care, the responsibility for the household maintenance and child rearing remains with their wives. This may represent a deliberate limitation of both partners' involvement in various spheres (Bailyn, 1978); men may still be responsible for breadwinning, whereas women are accountable for the maintenance and smooth functioning of the family. But it may also reflect the difficulty of truly sharing responsibilities for work and family equally (Pleck, 1977). What Young and Willmott (1973) describe as *symmetrical* patterning, where neither spouse has a monopoly in either work or homelife, may be exceedingly difficult to achieve when both societal norms and job expectations are geared to a sexual division of labor. In traditional single-earner families the presence of two adults in the household has facilitated the occupational attachment of one by providing a "homemaker" to accomplish the nonmarket work (Hunt & Hunt, 1977). This division of labor places a serious limitation on the occupational opportunities of married women. Until normative prescriptions concerning the roles of men and women change and the structural constraints of occupations have been altered, time will be especially scarce for working wives. In addition, fathers will continue to put most of their time into providing for the family, which means a minimal involvement for them in child care and other domestic responsibilities. The full ramifications of this situation in terms of the emotional relationships between husband and wife, parent and child remain to be developed through further research. What is required is a thorough investigation of the consequences for couples and their children of various patterns of work, especially as they pertain to caring for children and maintaining a home. Potential consequences for both men and women of a decrease in the standard work week and/or greater opportunities for part-time employment are particularly deserving of attention.

The Marital Relationship

Strains resulting from simultaneously managing a job and family responsibilities may well influence the emotional relationship between husband and wife. The hidden contract in most marriages contains certain implicit expectations regarding the roles played by husbands and wives (Gowler & Legge, 1978). When working couples develop relationships that radically depart from those in conventional single-provider families, both spouses may be dissatisfied with the marriage. An extensive review of the literature on the relationship between marital problems and the wife's employment suggests that in lower-class families there is more marital satisfaction when the wife is not in the labor force (Hoffman & Nye, 1974). However, studies of middle-class families reveal no such differences; indeed, when the wife enjoys her work, working couples appear to experience greater marital satisfaction than do traditional single-earner couples (Hoffman & Nye, 1974, p. 206).

Research suggests that characteristics of the jobs as well as husbands' and wives' attitudes toward their own work and the employment of the spouse may be important conditioners of the quality of the marital relationship. For example, a study of male shift workers (Mott, et al., 1965) found that those on rotating shifts had a great deal of difficulty in coordinating family activities with their wives and reported problems in a number of areas in their roles as husbands (p. 101–130). Staines and his colleagues (1978) found that role overload of women (defined as wishing for domestic help from husbands and feeling rushed) was an important correlate of marital problems in two-earner families. Bailyn (1970) found that marital happiness in two-career families was related to the family orientations of the husbands. She suggests that: "identifying the conditions under which men find it possible to give primary emphasis to their families while at the same time functioning satisfactorily in their own careers may become more relevant to the problems of careers for married women than the continued emphasis on the difficulties women face in integrating family and work [p. 112]."

In spite of the work–family strains, couples may benefit from sharing the provider role. In a study of 54 professional couples Weingarten (1978) found that these couples were intensely involved with each other as well as with their careers using "interdependence" as a strategy for coping with the complexities of their lives. The younger couples in her sample were particularly close emotionally, sharing the setbacks as well as the successes of their respective careers. A study (Huser & Grant, 1978) of 83 university faculty couples found no difference between single breadwinner and dual-career couples in the number and types of interests shared and, in fact, found that the two-career spouses were more flexible than the more conventional couples in the sample. In considering the quality of marriage, it is important not to equate recognition of problems with marital dissatisfaction. A recent survey found, for example, an increase in awareness of difficulties concurrently with an increase in reported happiness in marriage from 1957 to 1976 (Douvan et al., 1979, p. 63).

Some writers have expressed concern that working couples might compete with one another in terms of their careers (Parsons, 1959, Parsons & Bales, 1955). The potential for marital conflict as a result of direct competition in the world of work, however, is not apt to be great because, as Oppenheimer (1977, p. 404) points out, husbands and wives rarely work in the same occupation or even in the same organization. Still while there may be no direct on-the-job conflicts, the fact that a wife earns money changes the family distribution of resources and, hence, her relative power in the marriage and in family decision making (Scanzoni, 1978).

Whether or not working couples experience marital strain or conflict it is clear that social attitudes toward the roles of husbands and wives are changing. A study by Thornton and Freedman (Institute for Social Research, 1980), using data collected from a panel of women at various intervals from 1962 through 1977, found a major shift in attitudes concerning sex roles. For example, there was an increase of 21 percentage points in the number of women who disagreed with the statement: "Some work is meant for men and other work is meant for women." Similarly, whereas two-thirds of the respondents in 1962 agreed that panel study concerning the following item: "Most of the important decisions in the life of the family should be made by the man of the house," only one-third endorsed this statement in 1972. Thornton and Freedman report that the greatest changes in sex-role attitudes has occurred among younger women, those with more education, those with better educated husbands, and those who were working in 1962.

Additional research is required to investigate the effects of such changes in sex-role attitudes. Differences in marital satisfaction between working-class couples and professional couples is another area requiring study. Much of the difference may be due to socioeconomic status and resources rather than the work roles of either spouse. Further study is also needed to examine the attitudes and behavior of spouses in "successful" two-provider families, those who appear to manage work–family overloads and conflicts with relative ease, to determine how they achieve an effective blending of roles.

Childrearing

It is commonly believed that the development of children can be enhanced by their participation in activities with valued adults (Bronfenbrenner, 1979). In our society, with the isolation of the nuclear family, the burden of the caretaking of children falls principally on the parents (Holmstrom, 1973). There are few social supports—formal or informal—to share this task. The conditions of child rearing and development are necessarily transformed when both parents work, but it is still unclear just how and to what extent parents' jobs limit their full participation in the child-care role.

One should not look at the implications for children of having both mothers and fathers employed without first placing the two-provider family in its social and historical context. In March 1977 nearly half (47.7%) of all children under 18 had mothers who were employed (Grossman, 1978). Moreover, the labor force reentry rate of employed women who bear their first child is greater than 50% (Mott & Shapiro, 1977). Thus being a child in a two-earner family is becoming the norm. Much of the literature on the effects of having both parents work is therefore dated, looking at maternal employment at a time when it was far less commonplace.

Characteristics of parent's occupations "spill over" into the lives of their children in both direct and indirect ways. For example, a parent's job responsibilities necessarily take away from the hours available to spend in family activities. In fact, it may well be that time demands are the most formidable problem of child rearing faced by two-provider families (Vickery, 1979). Because of the separation of work and home that has been a fact of life since the Industrial Revolution, hours spent on the job are almost always hours that a parent is away from the child (Oakley, 1976; Young & Willmott, 1973).

Scarcity of time is especially problematic for parents of young children who simultaneously face both high time demands for child care and high financial needs. As Rallings and Nye (1979, p. 222) point out, the years with preschool children are the most costly—both economically and psychologically—for two-provider families. The early years of child rearing are likely to be the peak years of job demands of working parents (Wilensky, 1963). They also are likely to be the period when job and financial security are the lowest (Moen, 1981).

One means of accommodating to the conflicting demands of working and parenting is to reduce working time. Women with small children who remain in the labor force are more likely to work less than are women with older children. Not quite 20 % of the employed mothers of preschoolers were working full time for 50 weeks per year in 1977, compared to over 50% of the wives without children (US Dept. of Labor, 1979). Many of those working full time would prefer to work fewer hours. A recent study (Moen & Dempster-McClain, 1981) of the working parents of preschoolers found that nearly half the mothers employed full time expressed a preference for working fewer hours in order to spend more time with their children. Noteworthy too, nearly a third of the fathers of preschoolers also would have preferred a reduced work week. A study of the work-leisure preferences of workers in California found that parents of young children were more willing to trade in income for time off than were workers at other stages of the life cycle (Best, 1978).

Time is a precious commodity for working parents of young children. One reflection of this is reduced family size. The high labor-force participation rate of married women during their childbearing years has meant a postponement in starting families as well as having fewer children (Hoffman & Nye, 1974; Waite & Stolzenberg, 1976). Another indicator of the scarcity of time is the curtailment of domestic activities. Employed mothers spend considerably less time on housekeeping chores than do mothers not working outside the home (Robinson, 1977; Walker & Woods, 1976), though differences between employed women and homemakers in time spent on housework appears to be diminishing (Pleck, 1979). Nevertheless, working mothers, in particular, are vulnerable to role overload in trying to meet the competing demands of a job and home life (Rapoport & Rapoport, 1972). This overload often results in the requirement that children assist with the housework—and in the process develop independence and resourcefulness through helping with the household task assignments—(Elder, 1974; Propper, 1972). Fathers as well as mothers are handicapped in the child-care role as a result of the hours they work. A study of 78 Seattle couples with preschoolers found that there was a negative relationship between a husband's work time and his sharing of the child-care role (Clark & Gecas, 1977).

Working parents must not only find adequate child-care arrangements, but also mesh the scheduling of these arrangements for different children of different ages with their own work schedules. When emergencies such as a child's illness or a school holiday create disruptions in the arrangements, couples must resort to their own makeshift solutions. Such problems of child care are particularly stressful for working parents of preschoolers (Bryson, Bryson, & Johnson, 1978; Rapoport & Rapoport, 1971; St. Johns-Parsons, 1978).

When the occupation of either parent requires frequent travel or relocation the whole family is affected. Jobs requiring geographical mobility mean that children must face new neighborhoods, schools, and friends. Still, geographical mobility may not be as disruptive as one might think. In one study of families who had moved, most parents said their children had little difficulty in adjusting and making new friends (Barrett & Noble, 1973).

There are also more subtle ways in which the world of work touches the lives of children. Children traditionally have seen work as something appropriate for fathers and not for mothers (Goldstein & Oldham, 1979). Changes in women's and men's roles, as well as attitudes towards them are not faithfully mirrored in the socialization process. A study of children's attitudes towards employment found that 41% of the sample of children in grades one, three, five, and seven saw women as nonworkers (Goldstein & Oldham, 1979, p. 43). The younger children were especially likely to see mothers as exempt from employment outside the home. But conventional views of the sexual division of labor are giving way to more egalitarian orientations. Children of working mothers are more likely to approve of maternal employment than are children of nonemployed mothers (Hoffman, 1977).

Working parents also serve as role models for their children. For example, daughters of all ages, from grade school through college level, are more likely to want and intend to work if their mothers worked than are daughters of nonworking mothers (Almquist & Angrist, 1971; Hartley, 1960; Smith, 1969). Several studies have shown that daughters of working mothers are also more likely to have higher career aspirations than daughters whose mothers are not employed (Almquist & Angrist, 1971; Tangri, 1972). Furthermore, the fact that fathers are taking a more active role in child rearing when the mother is employed may well lead to reduction in the sex differences between boys and girls and may facilitate the development of independence and achievement in girls. But as Hoffman (1977) notes: "the shift in women toward work is more clearly documented than is the shift in the role of men toward parenting [p. 655]."

Child rearing has traditionally been the province of the mother. Consequently, it has been logical, from a research point of view, to look at the effects of the *mother's* employment on the parenting role. But clearly the father's job also has socialization effects. Kohn (1972) has documented the effects of the father's occupational experience on parental values such as encouraging self-direction. He found that middle-class fathers (who are more likely to be rewarded on the job for self-reliance and ambition) were more likely to stress achievement values for their children, whereas blue-collar fathers underscored the importance of obedience (see review by Gecas, 1979). Although children no longer learn job skills sitting at the working parent's knee, they are taught behaviors and attitudes about work by their parents—both intentionally and unintentionally. As two-provider families become commonplace and increasingly an accepted family form, fathers may participate more fully in the care and socialization of their children. Additional research is required to examine the separate and joint effects of both parents' jobs on socialization processes and outcomes as well as the role of supplementary caregivers in the socialization process (see chapters by Belsky, Steinberg, & Walker on day care and by Lamb on maternal employment).

A LIFE-COURSE PERSPECTIVE

Families are dynamic institutions with continously changing membership, functions, and needs over time. Work careers are similarly dynamic, changing over the years in both form and function. The two-provider family must be viewed within this context of change in order to understand fully the variations in the costs and benefits of this type of work–family linkage over the life course.

Parents with young children are the most likely to experience conflicts between work and family obligations. As children grow older, the time demands of both work and family may be considerably reduced, and the role overload of working parents should be similarly lessened. But other problems may be exacerbated at the same time. For example, the high income requirements of families with adolescents may pressure either or both parents to put in more hours on the job and, at times, take second jobs. And the degree of involvement of husbands and wives in careers over the years may make geographical mobility difficult. The Rapoports (1976) label the meshing of individual job careers with the family life cycle "role cycling." In order to understand the problems and potentials of the two-provider family the stage of the family in terms of life-cycle events needs to be considered as well as the stage of both spouses in their respective employment.

Because the existing body of knowledge is so inadequate, future research needs to explore the expanding and contracting demands of both home and work life. It has been suggested that when family and occupational responsibilities peak at the same time the husband's satisfaction with both work and family declines (Aldous, Osmond, & Hicks, 1979). But it could be that high involvement in one role encourages high involvement in another. The degree of absorption—in family and in work—over the life course is another area worthy of investigation, as are critical transition points in work and in family life.

Pleck (1980) has suggested that work–family interference may be more correctly regarded as work-*parent* interference because parents as revealed in the 1977 Quality of Employment Survey—both fathers and mothers—are more likely than nonparents to experience conflict concerning work and family roles. A far more central research question is to what extent family adjustments to having both parents employed outside the home are a function of: (1) characteristics of each spouse's job; and (2) the availability and use of community services (such as day care). In addition, the effects on families of continuities and discontinuities of each spouse's work role need to be documented, as do the impacts of transitions (as, for example from single-earner family to having both spouses work). "Career" implies an occupation with a sequential patterning that includes progressively greater responsibility, and greater rewards (Wilensky, 1961); but "career" need not necessarily imply a hierarchial sequence (as, for example, in Wilensky's discussion of "disorderly careers" 1961). Researchers need to pay greater attention to how both mothers and fathers schedule their work careers over the life cycle—in terms of moonlighting, overtime, and part-time work as well as withdrawing from the labor force—and to link this patterning with outcomes such as time spent with family, quality and quantity of parenting, and marital, parental, and work satisfactions.

Change can be viewed from the perspective of individual families as they pass through stages of the life cycle; it can also be examined from a larger historical perspective. Two-provider families are becoming the rule rather than the exception. Projections into the future indicate that there will be a substantial decrease in the number of one-provider husband/wife households, from the current 25% to about 14% of all households by 1990, whereas two-provider husband/wife households will remain at about 31% (Masnick & Bane, 1980, p. 9). (Projections also suggest an increase in both single-parent and single-*person* households.) As an increasing number of families confront the task of integrating work and family roles, new coping strategies for doing so—both formal and informal—can be expected to emerge. The sheer magnitude of this development is likely to become a potent force for change in the amount and types of support provided to working couples.

TWO-PROVIDER FAMILIES IN A SOCIETAL CONTEXT

Families do not exist in isolation; their borders are crossed, even trespassed daily. The family is vulnerable—sometimes painfully so—to the forces exerted by the structures and cultures in which it is embedded. These forces differ over time, both in strength and centrality. For example, in the Middle Ages the church was a significant shaper of European family life. In the United States, in the 1980s, there are two institutions that penetrate the lives of families in both overt and subtle ways: the economic system and the political system. This chapter concentrates on one strand of influence in which each of these institutions shares a hand: the world of work as it relates to two-provider families.

The family is an appropriate vantage point from which to examine work, because the family provides the forum through which labor-force involvement decisions are structured. It is also the filter through which labor-force activity affects dependent persons, be they children, youth, nonworking adults, or the aged. The problems of working parents are an inevitable consequence of the juxtaposition of conflicting roles. The personal crises faced by two-provider families in the management of both work and family roles are specific examples of the general, cultural ambivalence towards the responsibilities of society toward families. In the United States we view the difficulties faced by working couples (especially working parents) as essentially personal problems rather than public issues. Parents must, for the most part, manage their own problems of child care, shiftwork, geographical mobility, job security, and the rising costs of living. Working couples today deal with the strains between work and family essentially on their own. Their "coping" strategies include establishing priorities for work and family responsibilities, reducing involvement in one role (e.g., working part time, having fewer children, postponing childbearing, temporarily dropping out of the labor force) or seeking outside support (such as child-care assistance). But the real task ahead is to recast the complex social and economic environments that structure both family and work roles.

The proliferation of families in which both spouses work has implications beyond the borders of the individual family units. The economic system and society at large are shaped to a great extent by the decisions made in individual families concerning the nature and extent of their attachments to the labor force. Consequently, public policies must attend more closely and deliberately to the two-earner phenomenon or fail to respond appropriately and effectively to this emerging family form. Similarly, the private policy decisions of individual firms and labor unions must also begin to take closer account of the family contexts of worker's jobs.

Solutions to the major problems of two-provider families turn on achieving an optimal balance of work and family obligations. Provision for child care is one obvious need in families where both parents work. Equally important are options in work hours and the scheduling of work. Much of the role conflict and strain experienced by working parents emanate from the absence of such flexibility. Jobs are designed for individuals, not family members; yet, for optimal family functioning, the family roles of working parents must be coordinated with the work roles of both spouses, even as the two jobs must be coordinated one with the other.

Two possible options for two-provider families are the sharing of the same position ("job sharing") or sharing of the provider role by each working part time ("work sharing"). Job sharing has been seen by some academic couples as beneficial in reducing work–family strains (Arkin & Dobrofsky, 1978), but it may well be an opportunity limited to a few occupations. When each spouse holds a part-time job the overloads of family and work demands are considerably reduced. Gronseth (1978), in a study of 18 Norwegian couples, found that this "work-sharing" pattern was highly satisfactory to both husbands and wives. But both job sharing and part-time employment may be unrealistic for couples with high financial needs and/or low wages.

Policies concerning childbearing and infant care should be developed so as to facilitate the maintenance of stable links of both parents to the labor force where such are preferred. In addition, provision should be made to enable either fathers or mothers to interrupt their work careers in order to begin their families without sacrifice of position, benefits, or status. Temporary reductions in responsibilities and in hours on the job when children are small should be an option in all occupations, for both men and women.

A variety of points have been suggested where policy intervention might facilitate satisfactory work–family integration. Focusing on two-provider families calls attention to the constraints making labor-force attachment problematic at different stages in the life cycle, especially for women. It also underlines the strains faced by working parents. As Kanter notes, people come to work in organizations as members of families; the families are themselves affected by the policies and practices of the organization (1977, p. 3). Needs of families may well have to be taken into consideration in future organizational and public policies. Problems of part-time work, flexible hours, geographical mobility, child care, and maternal (and paternal) benefits are already intruding into the policy debate (Kreps, 1976; O'Toole, 1974; Work in America, 1974).

The larger issue of social change in the patterns of labor-force participation really turns on the changing roles of men and women—within the occupational sphere and within the family itself. Studies have documented that even when women are employed, the burden of the household and child-care tasks remain theirs. It has been suggested that this is indicative of normative constraints concerning the roles of husband and wife as well as the occupational constraints of the husband's job (Pleck, 1977). The issue of scheduling of work becomes central when facing the problems of moving from role separation to joint role performance of husband and wife in the occupational and family spheres (Bott, 1957). Changes from one earner per family to two requires corresponding changes in the workplace and in the provision of social services to meet new family "needs." Government, organizations, and families will have to re-negotiate the forms and functions of work, especially the amount and flexibility of time for work.

The connections between work and family cannot be viewed apart from their environmental context—from the structural, cultural, and occupational milieu in which families are located. An important mediator of the environment is government. The United States does not have a formal "family policy." But, if we define such a "policy" as the things government does to and for the family (Kamerman & Kahn, 1978), then government is very much involved in constraining, facilitating, and mediating the family/labor-force transaction—both deliberately and unintentionally.

CONCLUSIONS

This chapter has underscored the linkages between work and family in two-provider families as they are manifested in the form of financial security, status, conflicting obligations, and role strains. Work is essential to the economic well-being of the family; it offers parents the means to maintain or even improve the quality of their lives and the lives of their children. By the same token, the absence of a satisfactory job linkage at a living wage can be a serious impediment to husbands and wives struggling to make ends meet.

Time constraints necessarily limit the number of joint activities working couples can engage in—with their children and with each other. While this can be problematic for all families, it is especially straining in those families in which both parents work. The conflicts between work and family roles are seldom resolved, rather, they are "juggled" in a time-budgeting process that is often unsatisfactory. Because of the traditional division of labor within the family it is the woman who is seen as principally responsible for the domestic chores, including child care. The strain of role overload is most often felt, therefore, by the mother who works.

These two aspects of work—money and time—are not separate from one another; husbands and wives trade their time and skills for income, status, and security. What is particularly significant in these days of inflation is that a single income is often insufficient for a family to meet the rising costs of living. Families are being forced to give increasing amounts of time—in the form of moonlighting, overtime, as well as having two earners—in order to meet the economic squeeze. Although there are many reasons for the increase in the participation of married women in the labor force, an accurate and important point to note is that in an increasing number of cases, two earners are required to support a family.

Much of the stress of work for two-provider families is socially determined—a consequence of the structure of occupational roles and the fundamental cultural contraditions built into the economic and family systems as they exist in the United States today. Governmental as well as organizational policies have underscored these strains by viewing the worker as an individual, apart from any family context. The difficulty lies not in the family or the workplace, but in the articulation of the two.

Both public and private policies can do much to alleviate the strains faced by parents who work by altering the structure and scheduling of employment. A number of options are possible: flexible working hours, substitute child care, part-time employment (with fringe benefits and opportunities for promotion), maternal and paternal leaves of absence, a reduced work week for parents who choose to work less while their children are young, moving into regular working hours as their children grow older.

The issues raised in this chapter are important, not only from the perspective of today's two-provider families, but from the vantage point of families of the future. For a number of reasons—both ideological and economic—two-provider families are here to stay. A study of the orientations of men and women found that young women are closer to young men in the choice of work-related "self-actualization" as an important value than they are to the values of older women (Douvan et al., 1979). Moreover, evidence from the younger cohorts of men and women suggests that the attachments of mothers to the labor force are likely to become more similar to those of fathers; married women will in even greater numbers work continuously at full-time jobs (Masnick & Bane, 1980). The question remains as to whether to design of work will be transformed to enable family life to thrive within the context of two jobs.

ACKNOWLEDGMENTS

The author appreciates the comments and suggestions made by Jeylan Mortimer, Richard P. Shore, Paula Avioli, and Donna Dempster McClain on an earlier draft of this chapter.

REFERENCES

Aldous, J. Occupational characteristics and males' role performance in the family. *Journal of Marriage and the Family*, 1969, *31*, 707–712.

Aldous, J., Osmond, M., & Hicks, M. Men's work and men's families. In W. Burr, R. Hill and I. Nye (Eds.), *Contemporary theories about the family*. New York: Free Press, 1979.

Almquist, E. M. & Angrist, S. S. Role model influences on college women's career aspirations. *Merrill-Palmer Quarterly*, 1971, *17*, 265–269.

Andrisani, P. J. & Nestel, G. Internal-external control as contribution to and outcome of work experience. *Journal of Applied Psychology*, 1976, *61*, 156–165.

Arkin, W. & Dobrofsky, L. R. Job Sharing. in R. Rapoport & R. N. Rapoport (eds.), *Working couples*. New York: Harper Colophon Books, 1978.

Bahr, S. J. Effects on power & division of labor in the family. In L. W. Hoffman & F. I. Nye (Eds.), *Working mothers*. San Francisco: Jossey-Bass, 1974.

Bailyn, L. Career and family orientations of husbands and wives in relation to marital happiness. *Human Relations*, 1970, *23*, 97–113.

Bailyn, L. Accomodation of work to family. In R. Rapoport & R. N. Rapoport, eds., *Working couples*. New York: Harper Colophon, 1978.

Barrett, C. & Noble, H. Mothers' anxieties versus the effects of long distance move on children. *Journal of Marriage and the Family*, 1973, *35*, 181-188.

Bell, C. S. Should every job support a family? *Public Interest*, 1975, *40*, 109-118.

Berger, M., Foster, M. & Wallston, B. S. Finding Two Jobs. in R. Rapoport & R. N. Rapoport (eds.), *Working couples*. New York: Harper Colophon books, 1978.

Berk, R. A. & Berk, S. F. *Labor and leisure at home*. Beverly Hills, Sage, 1979.

Best, F. Preferences on worklife scheduling and work-leisure trade offs. *Monthly Labor Review*, 1978, *101*, 31-37.

Birnbaum, J. A. Life patterns and self-esteem in gifted family-oriented and career-committed women in M. M. T. Shuch (Ed.), *Women and achievement: social and motivational analyses*. New York: Wiley, 1971.

Blau, P. M. & Duncan, O. D. *The American occupational structure*. New York: Wiley, 1967.

Blauner, R. *Alienation and freedom*. Chicago: University of Chicago Press, 1964.

Bott, E. *Family and social networks*. London: Tavistock Publications, 1957.

Bronfenbrenner, U. *The ecology of human development*. Cambridge, MA: Harvard University Press, 1979.

Bryson, R., J. Bryson, & Johnson, M. Family size, satisfaction and productivity in dual-career couples. In. R. Bryson and J. Bryson (eds), *Dual career couples*. New York: Human Science, 1978.

Clark, R. A. & Gecas, V. The employed father in America: A role competition analysis. Paper presented at the annual meeting of the Pacific Sociological Association, 1977.

Clark, R. A., Nye, F. I., & Gecas, V. Husbands' work involvement and marital role performance. *Journal of Marriage and the Family*, 1978, 9-21.

Douvan, E., Veroff, J. & Kulka, R. Family roles in a twenty year perspective. *Economic Outlook USA*, 1979, *6*, 60-63.

Dubin, R. Work in Modern Society. In R. Dubin (ed.), *Handbook of Work, Organization and Society*. Chicago: Rand McNally, 1976.

Duncan, O. D., Featherman, D. L. & Duncan, B. *Socioeconomic background and occupational achievement*. U.S. Department of HEW, Office of Education, 1968.

Dyer, W. G. The interlocking of work and family social systems among lower occupational families. *Social forces*, 1956, *34*, 230-233.

Elder, G. H., Jr. *Children of the great depression*. Chicago: University of Chicago Press, 1974.

Feld, S. Feelings of Adjustment. In F. I. Nye and L. W. Hoffman (Eds.), *The employed mother in America*. Chicago: Rand McNally, 1963.

Ferree, M. M. Working-class jobs: Housework and paid work as sources of satisfaction. *Social Problems*, 1976, *23*, 431-441.

Form, W. H. Auto workers and their machines: A study of work, factory and job satisfaction in four countries. *Social Forces*, 1973, *52*, 1-15.

French, J. R. P., Jr. The social environment and mental health. *Journal of Social Issues*, 1963, *19*, 39-56.

Fried, M. A. The role of work in a mobile society. In S. B. Warner (ed.), *Planning a network of cities*. Cambridge, Mass.: MIT Press, 1966.

Garland, T. The better half? The male in the dual profession family. In C. Safilios Rothschild (Ed.), *Toward a sociology of women*. Massachusetts: Xerox Publishing, 1972.

Gecas, V. The influence of social class on socialization. in W. R. Burr, R. Hill, F. I. Nye, I. L. Reiss (eds.), *Contemporary theories about the family*, Vol. I. New York: The Free Press, 1979.

Goldstein, B. & Oldham, J. *Children and work: A study of socialization*. New Brunswick, NJ: Transaction, Inc., 1979.

Gowler, D. & Legge, K. Hidden and open contracts in marriage. in R. Rapoport & R. N. Rapoport (eds.), *Working Couples*. New York: Harper Colophon Books, 1978.

Gronseth, E. Work sharing: A Norwegian example. In R. Rapoport & R. N. Rapoport (eds.), *Working Couples.* New York: Harper Colophon Books, 1978.

Grossman, A. S. Children of working mothers. *Monthly Labor Review,* 1978, *101,* 30-33.

Gurin, G. & Gurin, P. Personal efficacy and the ideology of individual responsibility. In B. Strumpel (ed.), *Economic means for human needs.* Ann Arbor, Michigan: Institute for Social Research, 1976.

Gurin, G., Veroff, J. & Feld, S. Americans view their mental health, 1957.

Hacker, H. M. The feminine protest of the working wife. *Indian Journal of Social Work,* 1971, *31.*

Haller, M. & Rosenmayer, L. The pluridimensiondity of work commitment. *Human Relations,* 1971, *24,* 501-518.

Hartley, R. What aspects of child behavior should be studied in relation to maternal employment on children. A. Siegel (Ed.). PA: Social Science Research Center, 1960.

Hayghe, H. Marital and family characteristics of workers, March 1977. *Monthly Labor Review,* 1978, *3,* 51-54.

Hill, C. R. & Stafford, F. P. Parental care of children time diary estimates of quantity, predictability and variety. *Journal of Human Resources,* 1980, 219-39.

Hoffman, L. W. Changes in family roles, socialization, and sex differences. *American Psychologist,* 1977, *32,* 644-657.

Hoffman, L. W. Psychological factors. In L. W. Hoffman and F. I. Nye (eds.), *Working mothers,* San Francisco: Jossey-Bass, 1974.

Hoffman, L. W. & Nye, F. I. *Working mothers.* San Francisco: Jossey-Bass, 1974.

Holmstrom, L. L. *The two-career family.* Cambridge, Mass: Schenkman, 1973.

Holter, H. *Sex roles and social structure.* Oslo: Universitetsforlkaget, 1970.

Hunt, J. G. & Hunt, L. L. Dilemmas and contradictions of status: The case of the dual-career family. *Social problems,* 1977, *19,* 412-416.

Huser, W. R. & Grant, C. W. A study of husbands and wives from dual-career and traditional-career families. *Psychology of Women Quarterly,* 1978, *3,* 78-79.

Institute for Social Research Fifteen year study documents tremendous change in women's sex-role attitudes. *ISR Newsletter,* 1980, p. 3.

Kahn, R. L. The meaning of work. In *The human meaning of social change* ed. by Angus Campbell & Philip E. Converse. NY: Russell Sage, 1972.

Kahn, R. L. The work module: A proposition for the humanism of work. In J. O'Toole (Ed.), *Work and the quality of life.* Cambridge, MIT Press, 1974.

Kahn, R. L. & French, J. R. P., Jr. Status and conflict: Two themes in the study of stress. In J. E. McGarth (ed.), *Social and Psychological Factors in Stress.* New York: Holt, Reinhart and Winston, 1970.

Kamerman, S. & Kahn, A. J. (eds.) *Family Policy: Government and families in fourteen countries.* New York: Columbia University Press, 1978.

Kanter, R. *Work and family in the United States: A critical review and agenda for research and policy.* New York: Russell Sage, 1977.

Kanter, R. M. Families, family processes, and economic life: Toward systematic analysis of social historical research. *American Journal of Sociology,* 1978, *84,* supplement, 316-340.

Kohn, M. L., Miller, J, Miller, K. A. & Schooler, C. Women and work: The psychological effects of occupational conditions. *American Journal of Sociology,* 1979, *88* 66-95.

Kornhauser, A. *Mental health of the industrial worker.* New York: Wiley, 1965.

Kreps, J. (ed.) *Women and the American Economy* Englewood Cliffs, New Jersey: Prentice-Hall, 1976.

Lein, L., Durham, M., Pratt, M., Schudson, M., Thomas, R. & Weiss, H. Final report: Work and family life. National Institute of Education Project, No. 3-3094. Cambridge, MA: Center for the Study of Public Policy, 1974.

Masnick, G. & Bane, M. J. *The nation's families: 1960-1990.* Cambridge, Mass.: Joint Center for Urban Studies, 1980.

Moen, P. Family impacts of the 1975 recession: Duration of unemployment. *Journal of Marriage and the Family,* 1979, *4,* 561-572.

Moen, P. Preventing financial hardship: Coping strategies of families of the unemployed. In H. McCubbin (ed.), *Family stress, coping and social support* (in press).

Moen, P. & Dempster-McClain, D. Work time preferences of parents of preschoolers. Unpublished draft, 1981.

Moore, K. A. & Hofferth, S. L. Women and their children. In R. E. Smith (ed.), *The Subtle Revolution.* Washington, D.C.: The Urban Institute, 1979.

Molm, L. D. Sex role attitudes and the employment of married woman: The direction of causality. *The Sociological Quarterly,* 1978, *19,* 522-533.

Mortimer, J., R. Hall & Hill, R. Husbands' occupational attributes as constraints on wives' employment. *Sociology of Work and Occupations,* 1978, *5,* 285-313.

Mortimer, J. T. Dual career families: A sociological prespective. In S. S. Peterson, J. M. Richardson, G. V. Kreuter (eds.), *The two-career family—Issues and alternatives.* Washington, D.C.: University Press of America, 1978.

Mortimer, J. T. Work-family linkages as perceived by men in the early stages of professional and managerial careers. In H. Z. Lopata (ed.), *Research in the interweave of social roles: Women and men.* Greenwich: JAI Press, 1979.

Mott, F. L. & Shapiro, D. Work and motherhood: The dynamics of labor force participation surrounding the first birth. In H. S. Parnes (ed.), *Years for decision: A longitudinal study of the educational and labor market experience of young women,* Vol. 4. Columbus, Ohio: Ohio State University Center for Human Resource Research, 1977.

Mott, P. E., Mann. F. C., McLaughlin, Q., & Warwick, D. P. *Shift work: The social, psychological, and physical consequences.* Ann Arbor: University of Michigan Press, 1965.

Myrdal, A., & Klein, V. *Women's two roles: home and work.* London: Routledge & Kegan Paul, 1956.

Nye, F. I. Sociocultural context. In Lois W. Hoffman & F. I. Nye (Eds), *Working mothers.* San Francisco: Jossey-Bass, 1974.

Oakley, A. *The housewife: Past and present.* New York: Vintage Books, 1976.

Oppenheimer, V. K. The life cycle squeeze: The interaction of men's occupational and family life cycles. *Demography, 11,* 227-246.

Oppenheimer, V. K. The sociology of women's economic role in the family. *American Sociological Review,* 1977, *42,* 387-405.

O'Toole, J. *Work and the quality of life: Resource papers for work in America.* Cambridge, Mass.: MIT Press, 1974.

Papanek, H. Men, women, and work: Reflections on the two-person career. *American Journal of Sociology,* 1973, *78,* 852-872.

Parnes, H. S., Shea. J. R., Spitz, R. S. & Zeller, F. A. *Dual careers: A longitudinal analysis of the labor market experience of women,* Vol. I. (Manpower Research Monograph). Washington, D.C. U.S. Government Printing Office, 1970.

Parsons, T. The social structure of the family. In R. Anshen (ed.), *The family: Its function and destiny.* New York: Harper, 1959.

Parsons, T. & Bales, R. F. *Family socialization and interaction process.* Glencoe, Illinois: The Free Press, 1955.

Piotrkowski, C. S. *Work and the family system: A naturalistic study of working class and lower-middle class families.* New York: The Free Press, 1979.

Pleck, J. H., Staines, G. L., & Lang, L. Conflicts between work and family life. *Monthly Labor Review,* 1980, March, 29-31.

Pleck, J. H. The work-family role system. *Social Problems,* 1977, *24*(4), 417–427.

Pleck, J. Men's family work: Three perspectives and some new data. *The Family Coordinator,* 1979, *28,* 481–487.

Poloma, M. Role conflict and the married professional women. In C. Safilios-Rothschild (ed.), *Toward a sociology of women.* Lexington, Mass.: Xerox College Publishing Co., 1972.

Poloma, M. M. & Garland, T. N. The myth of the egalitarian family: Familial roles and the professionally employed wife. In Athena Theodore (Ed.), *The Professional Woman.* Cambridge, MA: Schenknon Books, 1971.

Propper, A. The relationship of maternal employment to adolescent roles, activities, and parental relationships. *Journal of Marriage and the Family,* 1972, *34,* 417–421.

Quinn, R. P. & Staines, G. L. *The 1977 Quality of Employment Survey.* Ann Arbor, Michigan: Institute for Social Research, University of Michigan, 1978.

Rainwater, L. *What money buys: Inequality and the social meaning of income.* New York: Basic Books, 1974a.

Rainwater, L. Work, well-being and family life. In J. O'Toole (Ed.), *Work and the quality of life.* Cambridge, Mass.: MIT Press, 1974b.

Rallings, E. M. & Nye, R. I. Wife-mother employment: Family & society. In W. R. Burr, R. Hill, F. I. Nye, I. L. Reiss (Eds.), *Contemporary theories about the family,* Vol. I. New York: Free Press, 1979.

Rapoport, R., & Rapoport, R. *Dual-career families.* Baltimore, MD: Penguin, 1971.

Rapoport, R., & Rapoport, R. The Dual-career family: A variant pattern and social change. In Safilios-Rothschild, C. (Ed.), *Toward a sociology of women.* Lexington, MA: Xerox, 1972.

Rapoport, R., & Rapoport, R. *Dual-career families re-examined: new integrations of work and family.* New York: Hoper Colophon, 1976.

Renshaw, J. An exploration of the dynamics of the overlapping worlds of work and family. *Family Process,* 1976, *15,* 143–65.

Robinson, J. *How Americans use time: A social-psychological analysis.* New York: Praeger, 1977.

Safilios-Rothschild, C. The influence of wives' degree of work commitment upon some aspects of family organization and dynamics. *Journal of Marriage and the Family,* 1970, *24,* 681–691.

Scanzoni, J. *Opportunity and the family: A study of the conjugal family in relation to the economic opportunity structure.* New York: Free Press, 1970.

Scanzoni, J. *Sex roles, women's work and marital conflict.* Lexington, Mass.: Lexington Books, 1978.

Seeman, M. The urban alienations: Some dubious theses from Marx to Marcuse. *Journal of personality and social psychology,* 1971, *19,* 135–143.

Seligman, B. B. On work, alienation and leisure. *American Journal of Economics and Sociology,* 1965, *24,* 337–339.

Slocum, W. L. & Nye, F. I. Provider and housekeeper roles. In F. Ivan Nye et al. (Eds.), *Role structure and analysis of the family.* Beverly Hills: Sage Foundation, 1976.

Smith, H. C. *An investigation of the attitudes of adolescent girls toward combining marriage, motherhood, and a career.* Unpublished doctoral dissertation, University microfilms 69–8089, Columbia University, 1969.

Smith, R. E. *The subtle revolution.* Washington, D.C.: The Urban Institute, 1979.

Smith-Lovin, S. & Tickameyer, A. S. Non-recursive models of labor force participation, fertility behavior and sex role attitudes. *American Sociological Review,* 1978, *43,* 541–547.

Sobol, M. G. Commitment to work. In L. W. Hoffman and F. I. Nye (Eds.), *Working mothers.* San Francisco: Jossey-Bass, 1974.

St. Johns-Parsons, D. Continuious dual-career families: A case study. *Psychology of Women Quarterly,* 1978, *3,* 30–42.

Stafford, F. P. Women's use of time converging with men's. *Monthly Labor Review,* 1980, 57–59.

Staines, G. L., Pleck, J. H., Shepard, L. J., & O'Connor, P. Wives' employment status and marital adjustment: Yet another look. In Bryson & Bryson (eds.), *Dual-career couples*. New York: Human Services Press.

Sweet, J. A. *Women in the labor force*. New York: Seminar, 1973.

Tangri, S. S. Determinants of occupational role innovation among college women. *Journal of Social Issues*, 1972, *28*, 177-199.

U.S. Department of Labor *Marital and family characteristics of workers, 1970 to 1978*. Special Labor Force Report 219. Washington: Bureau of Labor Statistics, 1979.

U.S. Department of Labor *Perspectives on working women: A databook*. Bulletin 2080. Washington, D.C.: U.S. Bureau of Labor Statistics, 1980.

Vickery, C. Women's economic contribution to the family. In R. E. Smith (Ed.), *The subtle revolution*. Washington, D.C.: Urban Institute, 1979.

Voydanoff, P. Work-family life cycles. Paper presented at Workship on Theory Construction, National Council on Family Relations, October, 1980.

Waite, L. J. & Stolzenberg, R. M. Intended childbearing and labor force participation of young women: Insights from nonrecursive models. *American Sociological Review*, 1976,*41*, 235-51.

Waldman, E. et al. Working mothers in the 1970's a look at the statistics. *Monthly Labor Review*, 1979, 39-48.

Walker, K. E. & Woods, M. E. *Time use: A measure of household production of family goods and services*. Washington, D.C.: American Home Economics Association, 1976.

Weingarten, K. The employment pattern of professional couples and their distribution of involvement in the family. *Psychology of Women Quarterly*, 1978, *3*, 43-52.

Wilensky, H. L. The moonlighter: A product of relative deprivation. *Industrial Relations*, 1963, *3*, 105-124.

Wilensky, H. L. The uneven distribution of leisure. *Social Problems*, 1961, *9*, 32-56.

Work in America. Report of a Special Task Force to the Secretary of Health, Education and Welfare. Cambridge, Mass.: MIT Press, 1973.

Working Family Project. Parenting. In R. Rapoport and R. Rapoport (eds.), *Working couples*. New York: Harper Colophon Books, 1978.

World of Work Report. *Part-time workers constitute fast-growing work force segment*, 1977.

Young, M. & Willmott, P. *The symmetrical family*. New York: Pantheon Books, 1973.

Yankelovich, Skelly, & White. *The general mills American family report 1974-75*. Minneapolis, Minn., 1975.

We propose a role homophily theory which posits that marriages are enhanced when spouses' roles are similar. We use cross-sectional survey data to determine how respondents' marital solidarity is affected by whether wives are employed, and by the occupationally derived socioeconomic status of both husbands and wives. We find that wives' employment has a positive effect on marital solidarity as perceived by both husbands and wives. This finding is consistent with role homophily theory, but inconsistent with the predictions of both sex-role differentiation and bargaining theories. When we examine effects of husbands' and wives' socioeconomic status on marital solidarity we find little support for any of the three theories. We conclude that role homophily theory is the best supported of the three theories.

28

CONJUGAL WORK ROLES AND
MARITAL SOLIDARITY*

Ida Harper Simpson and Paula England

The continuing increase in women's employment outside the home lessens the sex differentiation of conjugal roles. This research explores the effects of this dedifferentiation on marital solidarity. We use cross-sectional survey data to determine how respondents' marital solidarity is affected by whether wives are employed, and the occupationally derived socioeconomic status of both husbands and wives. Our findings dispute both a sex-role differentiation and a bargaining perspective on marital solidarity. We find that marital

Authorship is joint and equally shared. We acknowledge helpful comments from Richard L. Simpson, as well as NIMH grant 5T 32 MH 14670 03, which supported Paula England during a 1979-1980 postdoctoral fellowship at Duke University Medical Center, and Biomedical Research Support Grant 303-3188 to Ida Harper Simpson. Data from the Quality of American Life Survey were made available by the ISR Social Science Archive, University of Michigan. Data from the 1970 Occupation-Industry classification were made available by Kenneth Spenner. We bear full responsibility for our analysis and interpretation of these data.

interaction is enhanced when both spouses are employed, and that marriages do not benefit from the socioeconomic superiority of the male. We propose what we call the role homophily theory of marital solidarity.

THREE THEORIES AND SOME EVIDENCE

Aldous et al. (1979: 242-248) identify two main theoretical perspectives on the linkage between the occupational system and the family: the role differentiation theory and bargaining theory. We derive a third from literature on companionship marriage and homogamous mating; we call it *role homophily* (see Lazarsfeld and Merton, 1954). The three perspectives lead to different predictions about the effects of wives' employment and occupational status on marital solidarity. This disagreement of the three theories is mirrored by inconsistent findings of earlier research regarding the effects of wives' employment on marriages. (For a review of literature on the effects of wives' employment, see Rallings and Nye, 1979.) Little research has looked at effects of wives' employment on their husbands' marital satisfaction (Rallings and Nye, 1979), nor has it considered, as an independent variable, wives' occupational status singly or in relation to their husbands'. Our research deals with these neglected areas. Table 1 charts the predictions generated from the three theories.

PARSONS'S SEX-ROLE DIFFERENTIATION THEORY

Parsons (1942, 1949, 1955) saw the family as a reproductive organization based on sex differentiation of roles within and outside the family. The husband's role is in the economic system outside the family domain and is concerned with procurement of resources for family livelihood. The wife's role is centered within the family and is oriented to procreative and sustaining functions. The husband's occupation links the family to the socioeconomic system. The wife adapts her roles to her husband's occupational role; the husband does not

TABLE 1

Predictions about the Effects of Wives' Employment and Spouses' Socioeconomic Status from Three Theories of Marital Solidarity

Effect of:	Wife's Employment		Wife's SES		Husband's SES		Male SES Superiority[a]		SES Congruity[b]	
Theories \ Effect on:	Husbands	Wives	Husbands	Wives	Husbands	Wives	Husbands	Wives	Husbands	Wives
Sex role differentiation	-	-	-	-	+	+	+	+	No prediction	
Bargaining	$-^c$	+	$-^c$	+	+	$-^c$	$+^c$	$-^c$	No prediction	
Role Homophily	+	+	No prediction		No prediction		-	-	+	+

a. Husband's SES minus his wife's (HSES–WSES).

b. Negative of absolute value of husband's SES minus wife's SES (–|HSES–WSES|).

c. These predictions hold only when total resources brought into the family are controlled. Without this control the positive effect of the additional resources for the unit might outweigh the negative effect of having less resource-based personal bargaining power.

adapt to his wife. The sexual division of labor between the husband and wife corresponds to Durkheim's organic solidarity. Role complementarity builds marital solidarity. Parsons saw conjugal relations as a structure that articulates the family system with the economic system of industrial society. His concern was the needs of the family system rather than spouses' satisfactions from marital interactions. (For an exposition and criticism of the Parsonian perspective on female employment, see Oppenheimer, 1977.)

An extension of the Parsonian perspective to a consideration of wives' labor force participation posits deleterious effects on marital solidarity. When a wife and her husband both seek success in work, they are competitors. Aldous et al. (1979: 242-243) assess research literature to test the proposition that "marital role differentiation with the husbands performing the occupational role and wives the family caretaker role is positively related to marital stability." At the time when Parsons wrote, data on divorce supported the proposition. But times have changed; it is now normative for wives to work (Rallings and Nye, 1979: 214-215). Some worked when Parsons wrote. About them he said, "The large proportion do not have jobs which are in basic competition for status with those of their husbands" (Parsons, 1942: 608-609). According to the role differentiation perspective, the adverse effects of wives' working should be reduced by their being in occupations that are not in status competition with their husbands' occupations.

Even since the 1950s, when wives began to work in large numbers, some research findings are consistent with Parsons's predictions. Employed women are more apt to divorce if they have relatively high earnings (Ross and Sawhill, 1975: 57) or potential earnings (Cherlin, 1979) and are highly educated (Glick and Norton, 1977). Several studies have also shown that wives' employment adversely affects marital satisfaction and/or adjustment (Nye, 1961; Gover, 1963; Michel, 1970; Scanzoni, 1970; Bean et al., 1977). Few studies have considered the impact of wives' occupational status on wives' and husbands' perceptions of their marriages (Rallings and Nye, 1979).

BARGAINING THEORY

The bargaining perspective of exchange theory (Homans, 1961) emphasizes the separate interests of the two individual spouses. Each spouse bargains to have decisions made in his or her individual interest. Bargaining power rests on resources one can offer or withhold. Resources may be generated within the marriage through nurturance and sustenance activities, or outside the marriage through socioeconomic rewards. Resources generated from extrafamilial socioeconomic systems give more bargaining power than within-family role contributions such as affection, housework, and child care. The perspective assumes that individuals try to maximize their resources and their bargaining power.

We must deal with an ambiguity in the bargaining theory before making our predictions. Resources are valuable to both spouses and they try to maximize them. Socioeconomic rewards that are a bargaining tool for one spouse are also a resource consumed jointly. The effects of access to shared resources and of one's own relative bargaining power may have counteracting effects on marital satisfaction. While one spouse's high socioeconomic position weakens the other's relative bargaining power, it also increases the resources the other has access to. For this reason, we need to hold constant combined family resources to make predictions about the effects on marital satisfaction of either spouse's contributions.

When we hold constant the level of socioeconomic resources coming into the family, the bargaining theory predicts that marital satisfaction depends on the relation of the spouse's externally generated resources to those of his or her mate. A gain in resources and resulting bargaining power for one entails a loss for the other. Wives' employment should have a positive effect on wives' marital satisfaction, but a negative effect on that of husbands. Two studies have found such a negative effect of wives' employment on husbands' satisfaction, together with a positive effect on wives' satisfaction (Scanzoni, 1970, 1972; Burke and Weir, 1976). (See also Ferree, 1976, who found that wives' employment increased their marital satisfaction; no data on husbands were gathered.) The effects of one spouse's socioeconomic status on the other have not been studied as far as we know. But the general notion that a couple is happier when the family's total financial, educational, and status resources are greater is supported by many studies (Terman, 1938; Blood and Wolfe, 1960; Gurin et al., 1960; Renne, 1970; Scanzoni, 1970; Miller, 1976). This notion is compatible with all three theories.

ROLE HOMOPHILY THEORY

We propose a perspective which we term role homophily. Its basic tenet is the opposite of that of the role differentiation theory. It is based on the argument that similarity of roles builds marital solidarity. When the home and the socioeconomic system are each the locus of a role for each spouse, spouses bring similar objective interests into their marriages. The problems of one spouse can be more readily appreciated by the other. Similar locations promote commonality in social outlooks. An effect of this commonality is to enhance marital communication and companionship. Marital solidarity is also increased when wives and husbands share responsibility for the family livelihood. Both spouses must contribute inputs if solidarity is to be maximized; neither of them, alone, can bring inputs sufficient to compensate for a lack of inputs by the other. Conjugal interests that grow from congruity of their socioeconomic positions are not reducible to the constituent parts. Our view of role homophily corresponds to Durkheim's notion of mechanical solidarity.

Our perspective is consistent with findings from several bodies of research. The notion that shared world views enhance solidarity is compatible with the theory of homogamous mate selection, as well as with research showing that communication is the social-psychological variable that best predicts marital satisfaction (Navran, 1967; Snyder, 1979). Sex-role differentiation has divisive effects; it separates the worlds of husbands and wives and this separation impedes mutual understanding and companionship. At a time when instrumental functions of the family have given way to companionate functions (Hicks and Platt, 1970; Nye, 1974), mechanical solidarity arising from role congruity becomes increasingly important for marital solidarity. The kind of marital structure that we predict will be experienced most positively by husbands and wives corresponds to the "symmetrical family" that Young and Willmott (1972) see as having emerged recently in industrial societies.

Our contention that role congruity enhances marriage takes support from the U-shaped curve of marital satisfaction over the life cycle; the greatest satisfaction occurs before child rearing and after children are launched from the home (Bernard, 1934; Terman, 1938; Gurin et al., 1960; Burr, 1970; Rollins and Feldman, 1970; Rollins and Cannon, 1974; Aldous, 1978: 202; and Schram, 1979). The dip in satisfaction may simply indicate the rigors of child rearing, but we find it suggestive that the greatest satisfaction coincides with those periods with the least sex-role differentiation. The enhancing effect of role congruity is shown more directly in studies that show that marital satisfaction benefits from equality of power (Bean et al., 1977) and flexible sex-role differentiation (Michel, 1970).

Our theory deals with marital solidarity, not the survival and disolution of marriages. It is ironic that while role congruity occasioned by the wife's employment enriches marital interaction, the wife's work may also give spouses the independence to dissolve the marriage if a bad situation arises. When wives lack financial independence, they cannot afford to dissolve marriages, even when they are dissatisfied with them; many such marriages remain intact (Cuber and Haroff, 1965; Levinger, 1965).

Some studies support none of the three theories of marital solidarity we have described; they find no effects on marriages of the socioeconomic status of either spouse (Glenn and Weaver, 1978; Jorgensen, 1979) or of wives' employment (Blood and Wolfe, 1960; Campbell et al., 1976; Booth, 1977; Glenn and Weaver, 1978; Wright, 1978).

RESEARCH PROCEDURES

DATA

To test our predictions from the three theories we have used data from the Quality of American Life Survey conducted by Campbell, Converse, and Rodgers in 1971 (described in Campbell et al., 1976). From their national probability sample of 2164 adults we selected all white, married respondents with children (including those whose children had left home). We restrict our study to whites because black women have a work tradition different from that of whites. The restriction to married persons with children is made because Parsons's theory attributes the sex differentiation of roles to the procreative function of the family.

Our subsample averaged 43 years of age. The husband respondents had a mean age of 44.2 years and the wife respondents 42.5 years. Slightly over 60% of the families represented by husband and wife respondents had children under 18 living at home (61% of the husbands and 63% of wives), and nearly 40% were in the postparental stage. The average education of husbands and wives was a little less than 12 years. Wives were employed in 40% of the families. Around one-half of the families in the sample had combined family incomes over $10,000. The average employed wife (respondent and spouse of husband respondent) earned considerably less than her husband—$3000 versus $8000 in 1971. But spouses differed little in occupational prestige and education requirements of their jobs. Wives exceeded their husbands' status about as often as husbands exceeded that of their wives. This reflects the concentration of wives in white-collar clerical and sales work; these jobs had higher prestige and educational requirements than many predominantly blue-collar ones held by husbands, but had lower earnings.

DEPENDENT VARIABLES

The dependent variables in our analysis are indicators of what we call marital solidarity; we divide these into four categories of variables: mutuality, marital commitment, marital satisfaction, and family satisfaction. The questionnaire items in each category are listed below.

Mutuality:

How often do you disagree with your husband/wife about how much money to spend on various things?—very often, . . . never (5 categories);

How well do you think your husband/wife understands you—your feelings, your likes and dislikes, and any problems you may have: Do you think he/she understands you not well at all, . . . very well? (4 categories);

How well do you understand your husband/wife?—not well at all, . . . very well (4 categories);

How much companionship do you and your husband/wife have—how often do you do things together?—hardly ever, . . . all the time (5 categories).

Marital commitment:

Have you ever wished you had married someone else?—never, . . . often (5 categories);

Has the thought of getting a divorce ever crossed your mind?—never, . . . often (5 categories).

Marital satisfaction:

How much satisfaction do you get from your marriage?—none, . . . a very great deal (7 categories). (This item is asked amid questions on satisfaction from a variety of life domains, such as work, hobbies, and so on.)

Family satisfaction:

How much satisfaction do you get from your family life?—none, . . . a very great deal (7 categories). (This question is asked amid questions on satisfaction from a variety of life domains, such as work, hobbies, and so on.)

INDEPENDENT VARIABLES

Our independent variables include wives' employment status, and several measures of the occupationally derived socio-economic status of each spouse. Wives' employment status was dichotomized as employed or not employed.[1] We did not take into account the number of hours wives worked because this information was not obtained from male respondents about their wives. For this reason we cannot examine the effects of the number of hours wives worked on husbands' perceptions of their marriages. Since we want our analyses of husbands and wives to match, we will not do the analysis for wives. The fact that these data are missing is unfortunate. Some past research has found that the effect of wives' employment depends on whether it is part-time or full-time (for a summary, see Rallings and Nye, 1979). The data we use show no differences in women's perceptions of marital solidarity between those employed full- and those employed part-time (Campbell et al., 1976: 440).

Our second set of independent variables consists of occupationally derived socioeconomic characteristics of husbands and wives. The Quality of American Life data provide few measures of occupational characteristics. To get these, we merged two socioeconomic attributes of respondents' occupations into the file. Codes of two occupational characteristics were provided by Spenner (1977): the occupation's requirement for formal schooling, measured by the *Dictionary of Occupational Titles* (DOT) scale of general educational development; and occupational prestige, measured by Temme's (1975) scale. Our third socioeconomic indicator is income. The income information is in the Quality of American Life data set. Respondents were asked about their family incomes and personal incomes. For a measure of spouse's income, we subtracted respondent's income from family income.

ANALYSIS PROCEDURE

We use the partial Pearson correlation coefficient to test our predictions. Since financial resources affect marital solidarity, we have controlled family income in all analyses so that we can isolate the effects that are predicted differently by the theories. In examining the effect of each spouse's socioeconomic status, we control the status of the other spouse. When we assess the impact of differences between husbands' and wives' socioeconomic status, we control for the husband's status level.

Since marital understanding and satisfaction are curvilinear over the life cycle of a family (see Aldous, 1978: 202 for a summary of research), we do all of our analysis within life-cycle stages or control for age and presence of children at home as proxies of family life cycle. We consider only the parental and postparental life-cycle stages: parental with children in the dwelling unit and the youngest under 6 years of age; parental with children in the dwelling unit and the youngest aged 6 to 17; and postparental with children, but none 18 or younger in the dwelling unit. (The Quality of American Life data set does not distinguish children 18 and over who live at home from those who do not.)

In interpreting our findings, we take into account problems inherent in the measures of quality of life in the data set. Campbell et al. (1976) report two limitations of these items, including the marital solidarity ones. The variance in each item is small and the responses are skewed toward the positive end. They surmise from this that respondents adjust the scale to their circumstances rather than rate their subjective feelings on an objective scale. They found low correlations of demographic variables with the quality of life items. Indeed, few correlations reached .20. These limitations were not unique to marriage but were true for all subjective measures of quality of life. For these reasons, we decided to consider the directions of correlation coefficients when they had probability levels of .25 or less. Our tables report numerical coefficients significant at the .05 level and signs (but not numerical values) of coefficients with probabilities from .05 through .25. Since we have multiple indicators of marital solidarity, we use the sign test to infer statistical significance from a consistent pattern of same-signed coefficients, even if the single correlations are not significant at the .05 level. We use one-tailed tests of significance throughout, since all our predictions involve signs.

FINDINGS

WIFE'S EMPLOYMENT

The role differentiation theory predicts that employment of the wife impairs marital solidarity. The bargaining theory predicts that it benefits the wife's marital situation but adversely affects the husband's. Our findings on the effects of the wife's employment on wives' and husbands' perceptions of marital solidarity within life cycle stages are given in Table 2. They show that employment of the wife has salutary effects on marital solidarity as perceived by both husbands and wives.

All significant relationships between wives' employment and marital solidarity are positive; most of the signs of nonsignificant coefficients are positive as well. Out of 24 coefficients estimating the effects of wives' employment on wives' perception of marital solidarity, 10 are positive with a significance level at or below .25. Of the 24 effects of wives' employment on husbands, 15 are positive and significant at or below .25. If we look at each of these coefficients as an independent test of the relationship between wives' employment and marital solidarity, we would expect only one-fourth to be positive and significant at the .25 level in a population with no relationship. A (binomial) sign test indicates that the number of pluses with significance levels of .25 or below for wives (10 out of 24) has a probability of .055 of occurring by chance. For husbands, the 15 out of 24 can be expected to occur by chance less than 5% of the time. The total for husbands and wives combined (25 of 48) also would occur by chance less than 5% of the time. Although interpretation of the sign of any one nonsignificant coefficient entails a greater than 5% risk of Type I error, the consistent pattern of positive signs of the nonsignificant coefficients, in combination with the several significant positive correlations, gives us confidence in concluding that wives' employment helps marital solidarity.

Wives' employment serves both husbands and wives, but it is more beneficial for husbands, particularly during the parental stages. The effects on the spouses differ most when they have

TABLE 2
Partial Correlations[a] Between Wives' Employment and Marital Solidarity, Controlling for Family Income

Marital Solidarity Indicators[b]	Wives			Husbands		
	With child under 6 years	With >1 child, but none under 6 years	Post-parental (no child under 18 at home)	With child under 6 years	With >1 child, but none under 6 years	Post-parental (no child under 18 at home)
Mutuality						
Disagree about spending	+			+		+
Spouse understands respondent		+		+	+	+
Respondent understands spouse		+	-	.23	+	
Companionship		+	-	.18	.16	-
Marital Commitment						
Wished married someone else	-			.15	-	
Thought of divorce		+	.13	+		-
Satisfaction						
Satisfaction from marriage		+	.14	+	+	+
Satisfaction from family life		+	.17	+	+	.13
N[c]	127-130	129-131	208-213	115-116	106-107	206-208

a. A sign without a correlation coefficient in this table and the one to follow indicates that the relationship is not significant at the .05 level, but $p \leqslant .25$.

b. All correlations in this table and the one to follow reflect scaling of variables such that greater marital solidarity receives a higher score. Positive coefficient means that employment of the wife increases marital solidarity.

c. Ns within a column within this table and the one to follow vary because missing values differ between marital solidarity items.

children under 6 years old in the home. During this period, wives' employment exerts a positive effect on husbands' marital experience, but its effects on wives are almost nil. This sex difference in the timing of the effects of wives' employment may reflect sex differentiation of domestic responsibilities. When children are under 6, child care responsibilities are very time consuming and cannot be scheduled to suit the convenience of the parent. Since wives do the preponderance of domestic work even when employed (Walker, 1970; Meissner et al., 1975; Robinson, 1977; Berk and Berk, 1979; Pleck, 1979), our findings suggest that a domestic work overload may cancel out positive effects of employment for wives. It is significant, however, that during this time of heavy child care responsibilities, employment does not adversely affect wives' perceptions of their marital solidarity.

As children age, the employment of wives comes to affect them in more nearly the same way as it affects husbands. When the youngest child is between 6 and 17, and in the postparental stage, the patterns of influence on wives and husbands are very similar. But the effects differ for both spouses between the two life-cycle stages. In the postparental stage, the point in the family life cycle when marital satisfaction reverses an earlier downward slope and begins to rise (Aldous, 1978: 202) and parenthood is no longer a basis of sex differentiation between spouses, wives' employment no longer promotes mutuality for husbands and wives. Spouses' worlds within the family are now more similar; perhaps this dedifferentiation of family roles serves mutuality earlier served by wives' employment. Wives' employment continues to aid marital and family satisfaction in the postparental stage. (Of our coefficients, three are positive and significant at the .05 level.)

All in all, our findings show that the wife's employment benefits marital relations the most during the parental stage of the family, when marital and parental relations compete, and that husbands are the main beneficiaries. Why might this be? A wife's employment links her to collective life. This link is particularly important for marital solidarity from the view of

husbands during the stage of preschool children. The extrafamilial work role seems to keep wives' interests from narrowing to an exclusive concern with children. Without this
institutionalized link that employment provides, demands of
child rearing could more easily lead to an overabsorption in the
mother role. The employed wife may well have more "wifely"
vitality than the full-time mother. She shares an extrafamilial
role with her husband to make her world more like his.
Husbands benefit much from their wives' work roles.

Our findings on wives' employment support the role homophily theory, and disconfirm the bargaining and sex-role
differentiation theories of marital solidarity. Wives' employment has a stronger positive effect on husbands than on wives,
just the opposite of what bargaining theory would predict. The
salutary effect of women's employment on both husbands and
wives is consistent with the role homophily theory that we
advance. Communication and commonality are facilitated
when wives' worlds are similar to husbands' because both work
outside the home.

SOCIOECONOMIC CHARACTERISTICS OF SPOUSES

The effects of socioeconomic status on the perception of
marital solidarity differ for husbands and wives. For wives,
marital solidarity is increased by having a high-status occupation as well as by having a husband with high status. Table 3
shows that all 14 significant coefficients for wives are positive
and most of the signs of the coefficients we consider are also
positive. A sign test of such an occurrence of positive coefficients shows a probability below .05. In contrast, husbands'
marital perceptions are little affected by their own status or
that of their wives. Husbands and wives differ more in the
effects of income than in the effects of other status attributes.
An increase in the wife's or her husband's income improves her
perception of her marriage, but a wife's income has less effect
on her husband than his own income, and any effect is
negative. The differences between husbands and wives are also

striking with respect to occupational prestige. The wife's prestige benefits both spouses more than the husband's (see Simpson and Mutran, forthcoming).

Again, our findings are inconsistent with both the bargaining theory and role differentiation theory. In Parsons's theory, a high-status wife is competing with her husband in his role as provider. Parsons's perspective suggests positive effects on both spouses' perceptions of marital solidarity when the husband has high status, but negative effects on both spouses' perceptions of the marriage when the wife has high occupational status. This latter prediction is contradicted by our findings. Bargaining theory predicts a positive effect on either spouse of his or her own socioeconomic status, controlling for the total level of family resources. It is the prediction of a negative effect of one's spouse's socioeconomic status that our analysis challenges; we find a positive effect on wives of their husbands' socioeconomic status and essentially no effect on husbands of their wives' status. Role homophily theory makes no prediction about the direction of effects of either spouse's socioeconomic status on marital solidarity. The finding that women are more affected by their own and their spouses' status than men are is not predicted by any of the three theories. Future research should seek to explain this sex difference.

A more direct test of the predictions of the role differentiation and bargaining theories compares the socioeconomic status of the spouses. We construct a difference score by subtracting the wife's status from her husband's; a high score indicates the husband's socioeconomic superiority and a low score indicates the wife's superiority. The role differentiation theory predicts that the husband's socioeconomic superiority enhances marriage for both spouses; the bargaining theory predicts that husbands' ascendancy improves husbands' perceptions of their marriages but detracts from that of wives. The findings do not support either theory. (These data are not reported.) Using the sign test we find that husbands' higher status does reduce wives' perception of marital solidarity, as bargaining theory predicts, but it does not improve the

TABLE 3
Partial Correlations Between Socioeconomic Status and Marital Solidarity, Controlling for Respondent's or Spouse's SES,[a] Age, Children in Household,[b] and Family Income

	Wives						Husbands					
	Income[c,d]		Educ. Requirement of Occupation		Occupational Prestige		Income[c,d]		Educ. Requirement of Occupation		Occupational Prestige	
Marital Solidarity Indicators	Respondent	Spouse's	Respondent	Spouse's	Respondent	Spouse's	Respondent	Spouse's	Respondent	Spouse's	Respondent	Spouse's
Mutuality												
Disagree about spending	.08	.08		+	+	+	+					+
Spouse understands respondent	+	.08	+	.13	+	+	+		.13	+	+	++
Respondent understands spouse	+	.09	+	.13	+	−			+	+	+	++
Companionship	+		+		+							
Marital Commitment												
Wished married someone else	+		.19	+	.14		−	−				
Thought of divorce			.15	.13	.16		−					+
Satisfaction												
Satisfaction from marriage	+	+	.15		.13	−						+
Satisfaction from family life	.07	+	+							+		+
N	575–580	575–580	202	190	202	202	531–535	531–535	199	185	199	199

a. Spouse's score on a given SES indicator is controlled in correlation with own score on that indicator and vice versa. For example, own income is controlled in the correlation between spouse's income and marital solidarity; spouse's income is controlled in the correlation between own income and marital solidarity.

b. Dichotomized so respondents with children in the dwelling unit are scored 1; others are scored 0. Since we have removed nonparents, only post-parental respondents (those with no child under 18 at home) are scored 0.

c. Family income in this table cannot be controlled for in correlations with own and spouse's income since it is a linear function of these variables.

d. Persons with no income in the year prior to the survey are scored as having 0 income; they are not missing cases. Persons not employed last year are treated as missing cases in correlations with occupations' educational requirements and prestige.

marriage for husbands. The failure of husbands' higher socioeconomic status to enhance marriages as viewed by husbands and wives contradicts the prediction of role differentiation theory.

We have not yet given a direct test of the predictions of role homophily theory with respect to socioeconomic status. Such a test requires a measure of spouses' status similarity to each other. We measure the similarity of status by taking the negative of the absolute value of their difference score used above. If socioeconomic similarity improves marital solidarity, as the homophily theory posits, similarity should correlate positively with marital solidarity. Since the similarity score does not distinguish which spouse is higher, neither bargaining nor role differentiation theory makes a prediction about its effects on marital solidarity. We computed partial correlations of this similarity measure with the indicators of marital solidarity, controlling for age, presence of children, and family income. The findings show only 4 of 48 coefficients significant. Of the 24 signs of effects on males, 19 are negative; a sign test shows the chance probability of this patterning to be less than .05. There is no consistent pattern of the signs of the effects on women of socioeconomic congruity. (These data are not reported here.) These findings do not support the role homophily prediction that socioeconomic congruity aids marriage.

We speculate that as women's employment becomes increasingly continuous and norms that prescribe similar work careers for both sexes become more widespread, socioeconomic congruity will increasingly benefit marriage. But at this point in history the relevant role similarity for a theory of homophily is that both spouses have jobs. Wives' employment makes the worlds of husbands and wives more symmetrical; they both have extrafamilial and familial roles.

DISCUSSION

We have considered three theories on the effects of dedifferentiation of spouses' work roles on marital solidarity. Our findings are not consistent with either of the two prominent theoretical perspectives on marital and occupational linkages. We find partial support for a third hypothesis, role homophily. We suggest a need to reassess the view that role differentiation promotes marital solidarity and the notion that one's marital satisfaction depends on one's bargaining position relative to one's spouse.

We show that wives' employment supports marital solidarity as perceived by both husbands and wives. This finding supports the role homophily theory but contradicts predictions derived from the bargaining and role differentiation theories. We suggest that the similarity of wives' and husbands' worlds when both have extrafamilial roles promotes marital solidarity.

But when we look for possible effects of husbands' and/or wives' positions in the socioeconomic system on the perceived solidarity of their marriages, we find little support for any of the three theories. Bargaining theory predicts high satisfaction when one's own status is higher than one's spouse's. Role differentiation theory predicts that marriage is enhanced when the husband's status is high, absolutely and relative to his wife's. Role homophily theory predicts that marriage is enhanced when spouses have similar socioeconomic status. In fact, our findings show that wives' perceptions of their marriages benefit from high socioeconomic status regardless of whether it is derived from their own or their husbands' occupations. But husbands' perceptions of marital solidarity are little affected by either their own or their wives' socioeconomic status. None of the theories offers predictions about the effects of socioeconomic status on marital solidarity that are consistently upheld.

In summary, we derived hypotheses from role differentiation, bargaining, and role homophily theories to explain the effects of spouses' linkage to the occupational system on marital solidarity. Our findings consistently support only one of the predictions. The wife's employment enhances marriage as perceived by both the husband and wife. This prediction comes from role homophily theory. We conclude that the role homophily theory is the best supported of the three.

It is appropriate to reflect on why the bargaining and role differentiation theories have led to erroneous predictions about the effects of wives' employment on marriage. Parsons's theory of sex-role differentiation suffers from an overemphasis on the functional and consensual aspects of arrangements that were current at the time he wrote. The theory posits a *particular* normative structure that relates the family to the socioeconomic system. It is a static conception, and fails to take account of the fact that the normative structure it posits rests on a historically specific complex of societal conditions. Those conditions have changed (Young and Willmott, 1972). Wives leave their homes along with their husbands to go to work and, like their husbands, bring the influence of their work into their marriages. This change in wives' roles has paralleled a shift from instrumental to companionate family functions. The isolation and subordination of wives inherent in Parsons's views on sex-role differentiation impair the companionship that couples now seek. Parsons is correct that the sex-differentiated nuclear family is one way to articulate child rearing with the economic system, but it is only one way and one that is rapidly fading.

The atomistic individualism assumed by bargaining theory gives a very incomplete view of marriage. To be sure, spouses sometimes have conflicts of interest which lead to bargaining for individual gain. But when the quality of the process of interacting is as important to spouses as any limited benefits that can be extracted and taken away from an interaction, there is no such thing as zero-sum game; what one gains at the expense of the other will detract from the "public good" of marital solidarity. Work changes people in ways that affect their empathy, vitality, and the commonality of their marital interaction. It is the contribution of these qualities to marital solidarity that bargaining theory is unable to predict.

Our theoretical reassessment and empirical analysis have led us to propose a theory of role homophily. The theory posits that women's employment increases the role congruity of husbands and wives and thus has positive effects on both husbands' and wives' perceptions of marital solidarity. Our findings support this view. Socioeconomic congruity appears unrelated to marital solidarity; perhaps this is because occupational sex segregation is so pervasive (England, forthcoming) that congruity of socioeconomic status still means substantially different kinds of work for husbands and wives.

Our analysis of the effects of wives' employment on marriages joins a large literature riddled with conflicting findings. In response to the question of why the reader should believe our conclusions when they conflict with those of other empirical analyses, we point out four assets of our study that recommend its findings. We have used a survey which is more nationally representative and has a larger number of respondents than those used in some past studies. Because we have used multiple indicators of both marital solidarity and socioeconomic status, we can identify consistent patterns in the effects even when the effects are too small to be significant when taken one by one. The most important way in which our analysis differs from many we have reviewed is in statistical partialling to remove spurious effects of variables the literature suggests as important controls. Many of the studies we cite did not control for either life-cycle stage or family income. Finally, our analysis has considered the effects on marriage of wives' employment *and* the status of their jobs; few past studies have dealt with the effects of women's occupationally derived socioeconomic status on subjective indicators of marital solidarity.

We began this article with reference to our interest in the macrosocial effects of sex-role dedifferentiation. Our findings have implications for that question. Since current sex role change is increasing the number of dual-worker families, our findings suggest a positive aggregate impact of such changes on marital solidarity.

NOTE

1. The question on spouses' employment simply asked men if their wives were doing any work for money now. Housewives, students, or those who were unemployed were all coded together as not employed. Respondent's own employment status was coded in more detail, distinguishing housewives from students and the unemployed. But for comparability we used the dichotomous coding both for female respondents'

reports of their own employment status and for male respondents' reports of their wives' employment status. To see the effects of this coding decision we recomputed the effects on wives in Table 2, counting only housewives as not employed, and counting students and the unemployed as missing values. This change in coding had negligible effects on the results.

REFERENCES

Aldous, J.
1978   Family Careers: Developmental Change in Families. New York: John Wiley.
Aldous, J., M. W. Osmond, and M. W. Hicks
1979   "Men's work and men's families," pp. 227-256 in W. R. Burr et al. (eds.) Contemporary Theories about the Family: Research Based Theories. Volume I. New York: Macmillan.
Bean, F. D., R. L. Curtis, Jr., and J. P. Marcum
1977   "Familism and marital satisfaction among Mexican Americans: the effects of family size, wife's labor force participation, and conjugal power." J. of Marriage and the Family 39 (November): 759-767.
Berk, R. and S. F. Berk
1979   Labor and Leisure at Home. Beverly Hills, CA: Sage.
Bernard, J.
1934   "Factors in the distribution of marital success." Amer. J. of Sociology 49 (July): 49-60.
Blood, R. O. and D. M. Wolfe
1960   Husbands and Wives: The Dynamics of Married Living. New York: Macmillan.
Booth, A.
1977   "Wife's employment and husband's stress: a replication and refutation." J. of Marriage and the Family 39 (November): 645-650.
Burke, R. and T. Weir
1976   "Relationship of wives' employment status to husband, wife and pair satisfaction and performance." J. of Marriage and the Family 38 (May): 279-287.
Burr, W.
1970   "Satisfaction with various aspects of marriage over the life cycle: a random middle class sample." J. of Marriage and the Family 32 (February): 29-37.
Campbell, A., P. Converse, and W. Rodgers
1976   The Quality of American Life. New York: Russell Sage.
Cherlin, A.
1979   "Work life and marital dissolution," pp. 151-166 in C. Levinger and O. C. Moles (eds.) Divorce and Separation: Context, Causes and Consequences. New York: Basic Books.
Cuber, P. and J. Haroff
1965   Sex and the Significant Americans. New York: Viking.

England, P.
  1981 "Assessing trends in occupational sex-segregation, 1900-1976," pp. 273-295 in I. Berg (ed.) Sociological Perspectives on Labor Markets. New York: Academic.
Ferree, M.
  1976 "Working class jobs: housework and paid work as sources of satisfaction." Social Problems 23 (April): 431-441.
Glenn, N. D. and C. N. Weaver
  1978 "A multivariate, multisurvey study of marital happiness." J. of Marriage and the Family 40 (May): 269-282.
Glick, P. C. and A. J. Norton
  1977 "Marrying, divorcing, and living together in the U.S. today." Population Reference Bureau 32 (October): 3-38.
Gover, D. A.
  1963 "Socio-economic differentials in the relationship between marital adjustment and wife's employment status." Marriage and Family Living 25 (November): 452-456.
Gurin, G., J. Veroff, and S. Feld
  1960 How Americans View Their Mental Health. New York: Basic Books.
Hicks, M. W. and M. Platt
  1970 "Marital happiness and stability: a review of the research in the sixties." J. of Marriage and the Family 32 (November): 553-574.
Homans, G. C.
  1961 Social Behavior: Its Elementary Forms. London: Routledge & Kegan Paul.
Jorgensen, S. R.
  1979 "Socioeconomic rewards and perceived marital quality: a re-examination." J. of Marriage and the Family 41 (November): 825-835.
Lazarsfeld, P. F. and R. K. Merton
  1954 "Friendship as a social process," pp. 18-67 in M. Berger et al. (eds.) Freedom and Control in Modern Society. New York: Litton.
Levinger, C.
  1965 "Marital cohesiveness and dissolution: an integrative review." J. of Marriage and the Family 27 (February): 19-28.
Meissner, M., E. Humphreys, S. Meis, and W. Scheu
  1975 "No exit for wives: sexual division of labor and the accumulation of household demands." Canadian Rev. of Sociology and Anthropology 12: 424-439.
Michel, A.
  1970 "Wife's satisfaction with husband's understanding in Parisian urban families." J. of Marriage and the Family 32 (August): 351-360.
Miller, B. C.
  1976 "A multivariate developmental model of marital satisfaction." J. of Marriage and the Family 38 (November): 643-657.
Navran, L.
  1967 "Communication and adjustment in marriage." Family Process 6 (September): 173-184.

Nye, F. I.
  1974 "Emerging and declining family roles." J. of Marriage and the Family 36 (May): 238-245.
  1961 "Maternal employment and marital interaction: some contingent conditions." Social Forces 40 (December): 113-119.
Oppenheimer, V.
  1977 "The sociology of women's economic role in the family." Amer. Soc. Rev. 42 (June): 387-406.
Orden, S. R. and N. M. Bradburn
  1968 "Working wives and marriage happiness." Amer. J. of Sociology 74 (January): 715-731.
Parsons, T.
  1955 "The American family: its relations to personality and to the social structure," pp. 3-33 in T. Parsons and R. F. Bales (eds.) Family, Socialization and Interaction Process. New York: Macmillan.
  1949 "The social structure of the family," pp. 173-201 in R. Anshen (ed.) The Family: Its Function and Destiny. New York: Harper & Row.
  1942 "Age and sex in the social structure of the United States." Amer. Soc. Rev. 7 (October): 604-616.
Pleck, J.
  1979 "Men's family work: three perspectives and some new data." Family Coordinator 28 (October): 481-488.
Rallings, E. M. and F. I. Nye
  1979 "Wife-mother employment, family and society," pp. 203-226 in W. R. Burr et al. (eds.) Contemporary Theories about the Family: Research Based Theories. Volume 1. New York: Macmillan.
Renne, K. S.
  1970 "Correlates of dissatisfaction in marriage." J. of Marriage and the Family 32 (February): 54-67.
Robinson, J.
  1977 How Americans Use Their Time. New York: Praeger.
Rollins, B. C. and K. L. Cannon
  1974 "Marital satisfaction over the family life cycle: a re-evaluation." J. of Marriage and the Family 36 (May): 271-282.
Rollins, B. C. and H. Feldman
  1970 "Marital satisfaction over the family life cycle." J. of Marriage and the Family 32 (February): 20-28.
Ross, H. and I. V. Sawhill
  1975 Time of Transition. Washington, DC: Urban Institute.
Scanzoni, J.
  1972 Sexual Bargaining. Englewood Cliffs, NJ: Prentice-Hall.
  1970 Opportunity and the Family. New York: Macmillan.
Schram, R. W.
  1979 "Marital satisfaction over the family life cycle: a critique and proposal." J. of Marriage and the Family 41 (February): 7-12.

Simpson, I. H. and E. Mutran
    1981   "Women's social consciousness; sex or worker identity," pp. 335-350 in
           R. L. Simpson and I. H. Simpson (eds.) Research on the Sociology of Work.
           Volume 1. Greenwich, CT: JAI.

Snyder, D. K.
    1979   "Multidimensional assessment of marital satisfaction." J. of Marriage and
           the Family 41 (November): 813-823.

Spenner, K. I.
    1977   "From generation to generation: the transmission of occupation." Ph.D.
           dissertation, University of Wisconsin, Madison.

Temme, L. V.
    1975   Occupations: Meanings and Measures. Washington, DC: Bureau of Social
           Science Research.

Terman, L. M.
    1938   Psychological Factors in Marital Happiness. New York: McGraw-Hill.

Walker, K.
    1970   "Time spent by husbands in household work." Family Economic Rev. 2
           (June): 8-11.

Wright, J. D.
    1978   "Are working women really more satisfied? Evidence from several national
           surveys." J. of Marriage and the Family 40 (May): 301-313.

Young, M. and P. Willmott
    1972   The Symmetrical Family. London: Routledge & Kegan Paul.

Ida Harper Simpson is Associate Professor of Sociology at Duke University. Her research focues on occupations, work, and their interrelations with family and other institutions.

Paula England is Associate Professor of Sociology and Political Economy at the University of Texas at Dallas. She is presently engaged in research projects dealing with occupational sex segregation, portrayals of males and females in advertisements, and links among work, leisure, and psychological well-being.

This study assessed the effects of a flexible work schedule ("flextime") on time allocated to children and spouse by federal workers. Direct behavioral observations of family, home, and work functions were precluded because of the cost involved in observing many people for long periods of time. In order to obtain detailed individual data, participants completed hour-by-hour activity logs a mean of twice per week for 35 weeks. Participants received prior training on log completion, initial feedback on the detail of their log entries, and were prompted to complete the forms. Four different procedures assessing reliability indicated a corroboration rate of 80% with other sources. Log data were reliably reduced to nine categories such as "PM time with children" and 37 subcategories such as "time at dinner." The log data were presented in time-series form and the use of a quasi-experimental design showed that participants who altered their work schedule were able to spend more PM time with their families. The log data demonstrated that the capacity exists to assess closely the effects of large-scale changes at a micro-behavioral level, but other methods are needed to make complex self-reporting systems less expensive and more capable of immediate monitoring of the intervention's effects.

29

FLEXIBLE WORK SCHEDULES AND FAMILY TIME ALLOCATION

Assessment of a System Change on Individual Behavior Using Self-Report Logs

Richard A. Winett and Michael S. Neale

One important trend in the evolution of behavior analysis involves efforts at large-scale system modifications (Glenwick & Jason, 1980). The principles and methodologies of behavior analysis have recently been extended, for example, to such areas as organizational behavior management (Prue, Frederiksen, & Bacon, 1978), community health education (Meyer, Nash, McAlister, Maccoby, & Farquhar, 1980), and transportation management (Everett, Hayward, & Meyers, 1974). Often the dependent measures in such investigations are system or setting focused, or aggregate counts of individual behavior, rather than analyses of the same individual's behavior under varying conditions. For example, in community litter programs, the primary dependent measure has generally been litter counts made in designated areas (Geller, Brasted, & Mann, 1980). Transportation interventions have used bus ridership counts to assess effectiveness (Everett et al., 1974), and health-care programs have focused on aggregate appointment data (Reiss, Piotrow-

Data were collected while the authors were at the Institute for Behavioral Research. This research was supported by Grant No. MH-30585 from the Center for Metropolitan Problems of the National Institute of Mental Health. Reprint requests should be sent to Richard Winett, Psychology Department, Virginia Polytechnic Institute and State University, Blacksburg, Virginia 24061.

ski, & Bailey, 1976). Obviously, in many instances, having the level of the independent and dependent variables closely match is an appropriate strategy, e.g., system-level intervention with system or aggregate individual data.

However, there are also some situations in which detailed analyses of the interactions of system-level change with individual behavior change may also be highly appropriate (Meyer et al., 1980; Willems, 1974). For example, Bronfenbrenner (1979) has recently proposed a framework for developing and evaluating what he described as "macro-level" changes (system, organization) on "micro-level" events (individual behavior). Bronfenbrenner's formulations are specifically directed to family policy. In particular, he has proposed that ("macro") changes in work patterns, including instituting flexible work schedules and career-oriented part-time work, should be developed and longitudinally analyzed for their ("micro-level") benefits to families with young children.

Such investigations will require methods to assess in detail various aspects of family life, for many families, studied over relatively long periods of time. However, observational procedures typically used for most behavioral research would appear to be too expensive (and possibly obtrusive) for the proposed family life and work-patterns studies, or for other large-scale studies of the effects of system-level change on individual behavior. Other, less expensive methods that still yield reliable, fine-grain individual data seem needed.

This paper will report on one type of benefit that may accrue to young families when a worker from the family is allowed to temporally alter his or her work schedule—increased time for family-related activities. However, the major purpose of the paper is to describe the methodology involved in collecting detailed time-allocation data for such activities as commuting, work, spouse, child, and family interactions, and a range of highly specific events such as time spent in dinner, exercise, or TV watching. These data were collected from hour-by-hour *time-activity logs* kept by participants in two studies on flexible work hours. The methodology for collecting these data, examples of outcomes, and costs and benefits of such fine-grained data for analyzing system changes will be discussed.

METHOD

Background

Two studies were conducted with employees of two large federal agencies (see Winett & Neale, 1980*a* and Winett, Neale, & Williams, Note 1, for a complete summary of this work). All participants (N = 97) were volunteers, and in both agencies, workers could adopt a minimal flexitime system that allowed them to alter their work schedule by about one hour. Political and logistical considerations did not allow random or staggered (e.g., multiple baseline) assignment of workers to flexitime and regular hour conditions, necessitating that a quasi-experimental (nonequivalent control group) design be used for evaluation (Campbell, 1969).

The studies involved a baseline period when all workers were on regular work hours and a flexitime period when some workers then chose to change their work schedule. For study two, which will be the focus of this report, the baseline (regular hours) lasted for seven weeks and data were collected for 28 weeks during the flexitime period. The limited flexitime system allowed workers to arrive or depart 45 min earlier or later than the original 8:15 AM to 4:45 PM schedule, with an eight-hour work day (plus 1½ hour for lunch) still required. Employees (N = 24) were considered to have changed their schedules if they always came to work at least 30 minutes earlier (e.g., all opted for an earlier schedule) than regular hours during the flexitime system. *No change* employees (N = 26) retained their original schedule, and 15 employees varied their schedule. Results for this latter group will not be presented here.

A major objective of the studies was to ascertain how even minimal alteration of the work schedule affected time allocated to family activities. For example, there may be some benefits in arriving home somewhat earlier, e.g., more time with children, less traffic. Such changes in schedule could also have qualitative benefits as certain difficult situations (e.g., having time to prepare dinner) now could become easier. However, given the number of participants in the study (N = 65 for study two) who lived in diverse locations, the length of the data collection period (35 weeks), and the fact that the activities to be investigated primarily took place in the home, ethical, fiscal, and logistical constraints precluded direct observation of participants in their homes.

Instead of direct observations, time allocation data were obtained through the use of standardized and detailed logs recorded by participants two to three times per week. Reviews (Ciminero, Nelson, & Lipinski, 1977; Kazdin, 1974; Nelson, 1977) of self-reporting/self-monitoring of overt and covert events through the use of different written instruments have cautioned about the accuracy of such data and the persistence of data recording. Despite these possible limitations, our studies used the log instrument for a number of reasons: (a) as noted above, direct observation was precluded; (b) cross-sectional time-allocation research investigating similar issues had reported acceptable reliability with a log instrument (Robinson, 1977); (c) it was possible to train participants in log recording, and (d) to prompt log completion; and (e) reliability of the logs could be assessed through multiple methods.

Participants

Participants were 65 federal employees performing administrative work at the agency's headquarters who volunteered (see Winett, Neale, & Williams, 1979, for recruitment procedures) for the project. Participants spanned a complete range of federal job levels and had a mean 1978 gross income of approximately $20,000. As noted above, data will be presented only on workers who either changed (N = 24) or did not change (N = 26) their work schedule. The change group consisted of four males from dual-earner families; two males from families where the wife worked part-time; seven males from single-earner (male) families; five females from dual-earner families, and six females from single-parent families. The *no-change* group included two males from dual-earner families; two males from families where the wife worked part-time; 10 males from single-earner (male) families; five females from dual-earner families,

and seven females from single-parent families.

The mean age of *change* participants was 33.4 years and spouse mean age was 31.1 years. Change families had a mean of 1.8 children with a mean age of 5.7 years. The means for the *no change* group were age, 34.4 years; spouse age, 32.6 years; number of children, 1.8; child age, 5.9.

Mean job level (specific to the setting) was about the same, but the no-change group had been on the job for more years ($\bar{x} = 7.4$) than the change group ($\bar{x} = 5.3$ years). Thus, on most age, familial, and employment variables, the two groups were quite comparable.

Instrument and Completion Schedule

The time-activity log was an 8½″ × 14″ form that required participants to record the main activity engaged in; the time each activity began and ended; the setting for the activity; person interacted with for each activity; other secondary activities occurring while engaged in the primary activity noted (e.g., eating dinner is the main activity but also watching TV), and a rating of "enjoyment" of each main activity on a 5-point scale. Thus, the log potentially could yield a wealth of self-reported data on activities, interactions, time-allocations, and perceptions.

For the first 16 weeks (starting in April) of the project, seven of which were for the baseline period, logs were completed for Tuesday, Wednesday, and Thursday. For the next 10 weeks, logs were completed for Tuesday and Wednesday, and for the final 9 weeks (ending in December), logs were completed for only Wednesday. Logs were not completed on weekday holidays and there was a total of 75 possible log days. The rationale for the log schedule was to focus on typical weekdays, across a spring baseline period and across flexitime periods in the late spring, summer, and fall, while gradually decreasing the number of logs completed each week. The data to be presented below, do not indicate differential outcomes by day or schedule, suggesting the feasibility of the recording schedule. In addition, participants were allowed by agreement with management to complete logs during work hours.

Training

Training for log completion consisted of providing each participant with a model sample form and giving written feedback for the first six weeks of the project on the quality of detail provided on his or her log. Feedback was given using one of three $8\frac{1}{2}'' \times 11''$ forms placed in each participant's weekly folder (see below). A gold form with a large smile on it was given if a project staff person judged the detail of a participant's logs for the week to be of a quality equal to or greater than the sample. A yellow form with a small smile, which listed all possible recording deficiencies, was given when it was judged that the participant's logs displayed less than four problems, with the problems specified by a check on the form. For more than four problems, a green form identical to the yellow form, but with a lesser smile, was given with the appropriate deficiencies checked.

Delivery and Retrieval of Log Forms

Log forms and other data instruments were placed in a folder and hand-delivered to each participant's desk, and hand-retrieved at the desk following a schedule of delivery on Tuesday morning and retrieval on Friday morning throughout the entire study. During the 35 weeks of the study, about 90% of distributed forms were completed and returned by the participants.

Reliability

The reliability of the logs was assessed using four different procedures as shown in Table 1 and as discussed in more detail in Winett et al. (1979). Despite the use of different modalities of information (e.g., telephone and time records versus logs); time between a spouse's log completion and the corresponding day for the participant's log (see Table 1); no training of the spouse in log completion, and a conservative estimate of spouse and participant agreement on

the logs (see Table 1), the correspondence of log data with the four different corroborating sources at an 80% agreement level appears to meet acceptable standards (Kazdin, 1975).

Reliability and the Process of Reduction of Log Data

The log data were reduced to nine standard categories (work time, and AM or PM time with spouse, children, spouse and children, or alone) and 37 subcategories (such as time in exercise, commuting, dinner, or TV) by six trained coders following reliability procedures involving independent matching of activity category and time entries to a "master" coder (author two), and independent agreement between individual coders. Reliability checks were done in such a way that coders were unaware they were being checked, and were done throughout a 3-mo data reduction period. Agreement with the master coder and between coders was approximately 90%. The exact criteria and procedures are specified in detail in Winett et al., 1979.

Thus, the log data as recorded by participants appear to be of acceptable reliability and log data were reliably reduced to standard categories.

RESULTS

Overall Outcomes

For each participant, a maximum of 75 logs were available. However, this total was reduced in several ways. Logs were not completed during sick days or vacation days, and across participants, 10% of the logs were simply not completed. Logs were not included in analyses when less than 23 hours of time were found during data reduction procedures to be accounted for on a log; when a participant worked more than 570 min or less than 450 min (e.g., 510 min was the regular day); or when children were not at home (e.g., summer vacations) for three or more consecutive days, retroactively effective to the first day of the series.

Overall analyses of the log data based on

Table 1

Methods, Criteria, and Correspondence Rate for Assessing Log Reliability

Method	Criteria	Correspondence
Telephone calls to participants by "blind" assistant. Participants called a mean of 2.2 times during the middle of the project. Participant recounts activities during last 30 min, notes settings, and people involved.	Checked by other staff person. Activity, settings, persons noted the same, and time within 15 min, between telephone report and log.	155 calls made; 222 reports of activities, 204 reports corresponded (92%).
The *recording of a known event* checked by staff. Home interviews were conducted as part of the study on certain weeknights that logs were to be (independently) completed. Participants were not told of checks. Interviews conducted during first third of the study.	Checked later by staff person. The interview had to be indicated on the log at the same time it was scheduled.	30 of 34 (88%) interviews correctly listed.
Informant reports were obtained during the baseline, and middle of the study, by having the spouse complete a time-activity log during a home interview for a day corresponding to the last recording day for the participant. A mean of 2.7 days existed between the spouse and participant recording days, and no training was given to the spouse.	Checked later by staff person. Activity, settings, persons noted the same and time within 30 min.	296 of 325 (91%) of activities reported by both spouse and participant agree. However, 106 activities were not noted by each other. When these were included as "disagreements," the correspondence rate was 296 of 431 (69%).
Archival records were kept at the work site by a designated department timekeeper on arrival, departure, and lunch time. Records were obtained at the 7-mo point in the study for 10 specified days that had occurred at the 6-mo point.	Timekeeper records and participant reports on logs within 15 min of each other.	432 of 664 lunch time agreed (65%); 779 of 842 (93%) of arrival and departure times agreed; overall, 1,211 of 1,506 (80%) times agreed.
TOTAL		Including 106 activities not reported by spouse and participant (see above), 1,741 agreements were scored on 2,193 checks (80%).

mean participant scores for the baseline, spring, summer, and fall periods and reported elsewhere (Winett & Neale, 1980a; Winett et al., Note 1) indicated that the group of workers changing to an earlier schedule significantly increased their PM time with their children, and decreased their commute time. The no change group showed stability across these measures. However, rather than simply shifting time-allocation patterns, change group participants reported on other data instruments that the increase in PM time alleviated some of the difficulties involved in coordinating a number of work and home life situations (see Winett

& Neale, 1980a; Winett et al., Note 1). The time and qualitative data outcomes of the second study were congruent with the results of a prior small-scale study (reported in Winett and Neale, 1980b), suggesting the generality of the time effects of the alteration in work schedule and family life. And, in both studies, the flexitime program was rated highly by management and employees (see Winett & Neale, 1980a and Winett et al., Note 1).

Fine-Grained Data

Figure 1 shows the "composite PM time spent with the family" for the change and no change group for 75 log reporting days. Composite family PM time is comprised of data from PM "time with spouse," "time with children," and "time with spouse and children." Each reporting day's data represent a mean for those participants in each group completing a log for that day and within the criteria for work-time and children at home noted above.

The data show considerable day-to-day variability that did not, however, appear to be a function of the inclusion of individuals in a reporting day's mean, or as a function of day of the week. Particularly for the no change group, a pattern existed for days of high time with the family to be followed by low time days during all the phases of the study. The pattern was less apparent during the fall when recording was reduced to one day per week. We have no explanation for this pattern. Despite the variability, consistent group trends for change of level are apparent. During the baseline period, the group spent a mean of 237 min per recording day in composite family time compared to a mean of 226 min by the no change group.

Mean time was increased by 36 min ($x = 273$) for the change group during the spring, but only by 6 min by the no change group ($x = 232$). During the summer, however, the change group again showed an increase of 36 min from baseline ($x = 273$), but the no change group showed an increase of 22 min ($x = 248$). During the fall, the change group showed an increase from baseline of 31 min ($x = 268$), while the no change group only increased 4 min ($x = 230$).

The daily patterns of the two groups shows considerable overlap in data points during the baseline period, some overlap during the summer, and virtually no overlap during the spring and fall. Both groups, however, show a trend for decreased family time as the fall phase progressed. These results suggest some seasonal interactions with family time and the effects of an alteration in work schedule.

Data similar to those shown in Figure 1 were available for each participant and for all main category time-allocation data, plus all subcategory data (e.g., "time in dinner"). Thus, it was possible to analyze outcomes for any participant

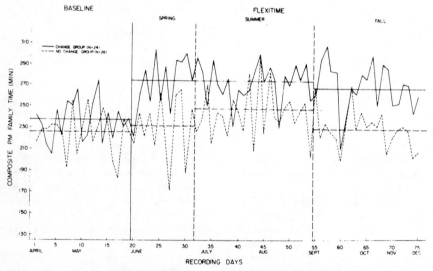

Fig. 1. Mean composite PM family time in minutes for the change and no change groups for each recording day across the baseline and flexitime phases of the study. Mean group times for the baseline period, and the spring, summer, and fall flexitime periods are indicated by horizontal lines.

and for any activity category included in the standard data-reduction procedures.

DISCUSSION

The time-activity log data that were presented demonstrated that relatively complex, written reports of events can be reliably recorded for long periods of time when people are provided with appropriate forms, training, feedback, and minimal prompting (e.g., form delivery and retrieval). This method may be particularly valuable when detailed behavioral observations of individuals are precluded for a variety of poential reasons.

In the present example, individually based, but group-presented, time-allocation data indicated that the introduction of a fleximite system that allowed employees to come to work earlier resulted in these workers being able to spend more time with their families during PM hours. A comparison group who retained their original schedule showed only minimal changes. A seasonal interaction effect was also identified.

Besides focusing on major categories of behavior (e.g., time with children), the time-activity log procedure also allowed assessments of more micro-level events (e.g., time for dinner, exercise, TV) that were also reliably recorded and reduced (Winett et al., 1979). For example, it was ascertained that the mean time in exercise on recording days for all study participants was 10.5 min. Time in exercise was not influenced by the fleximite system, but, not surprisingly, showed a seasonal effect with more exercise related activity reported in the summer. Similar data were analyzed for time in dinner, watching TV, and commuting, with commuting time showing significant reductions for the "change" group (see Winett & Neale, Note 2). Thus, the potential seems to exist to perform rather fine-grained, micro-analyses of diverse behaviors that may be affected by interventions at macro-levels. Such analyses may be helpful in planning public policies by pinpointing the costs and benefits to different types of individuals

as a result of existing or proposed policies (Bronfenbrenner, 1979).

We are, however, by no means offering the time-activity log as the best means of securing such data. When used in its present form with many people, the time-activity log, though much less expensive than on-site observations (see Winett et al., Note 1), is still very expensive in terms of data reduction. For example, after training, the persons reducing the log data at a rate of $4.25 per hour, could only complete about six logs per hour, or about $.71 per log.

Further, the cost and subsequent time involved in data-reduction eliminated the possibility of continuous monitoring of the effects of the fleximite system. Without a continuous monitoring system, the potential to perform true behavioral analyses of a variety of fleximite/ alternative work pattern programs, or other large-scale changes, is sharply reduced. Therefore, we are turning our attention to the development of methods using forms allowing direct computer entry. For the research on alternative work patterns, direct computer entry may allow continual assessment of how changes at work are affecting reported family behaviors for employees from different kinds of families, and help to develop more optimal *matches* between work arrangement and family life. Our goal is to use such instruments to evaluate, and "fine-tune" diverse alternative work pattern systems that are much more innovative than the fleximite system evaluated in the present study.

Thus, as behavior analysis evolves to frequent investigation of system-level change, we may still be able to ascertain reliably how such changes affect complex human behaviors even in circumstances where direct behavioral observations are not possible.

REFERENCE NOTES

1. Winett, R. A., Neale, M. S., & Williams, K. R. *The effects of flexible work schedule on urban families with young children: Quasi-experimental, ecological studies.* Unpublished manuscript. Psychology Department, Virginia Polytechnic Insti-

tute and State University, Blacksburg, Virginia 24061.
2. Winett, R. A., & Neale, M. S. *Work and the quality of urban family life: Innovations and temporal constraints.* Unpublished manuscript. Psychology Department, Virginia Polytechnic Institute and State University, Blacksburg, Virginia 24061.

REFERENCES

Bronfenbrenner, U. *The ecology of human development. Experiments by nature and design.* Cambridge, Massachusetts: Harvard University Press, 1979.

Campbell, D. T. Reforms as experiments. *American Psychologist,* 1969, **24,** 409-424.

Ciminero, A. R., Nelson, R. O., & Lipinski, D. P. Self-monitoring procedures. In A. R. Ciminero, K. S. Calhoun, & H. E. Adams (Eds.), *Handbook of behavioral assessment.* New York: Wiley, 1977.

Everett, P. B., Hayward, S. C., & Meyers, A. W. The effects of a token reinforcement procedure on bus ridership. *Journal of Applied Behavior Analysis,* 1974, **1,** 1-9.

Geller, E. S., Brasted, W. S., & Mann, M. F. Waste receptacle designs as interventions for litter control. *Journal of Environmental Systems,* 1980, **9,** 145-160.

Glenwick, D., & Jason, L. (Eds.). *Behavioral community psychology: Progress and prospects.* New York: Praeger Press, 1980.

Kazdin, A. E. Self-monitoring and behavior change. In M. J. Mahoney & C. E. Thoresen (Eds.), *Self-control: Power to the person.* Monterey, Calif.: Brooks-Cole, 1974.

Kazdin, A. E. *Behavior modification in applied settings.* Homewood, Ill.: Dorsey Press, 1975.

Meyer, A. J., Nash, J. D., McAlister, A. L., Maccoby, N., & Farquhar, J. W. Skills training in a cardiovascular health education campaign. *Journal of Consulting and Clinical Psychology,* 1980, **48,** 129-142.

Nelson, R. O. Methodological issues in self-monitoring. In J. D. Cone & R. P. Hawkins (Eds.), *Behavioral assessment.* New York: Bruner/Mazel, 1977.

Prue, D. M., Frederiksen, L. W., & Bacon, A. Organizational behavior management. An annotated bibliography. *Journal of Organizational Behavior Management,* 1978, **1,** 216-257.

Reiss, M. L., Piotrowski, W. D., & Bailey, J. S. Behavioral community psychology: encouraging low-income parents to seek dental care for their children. *Journal of Applied Behavior Analysis,* 1976, **9,** 387-398.

Robinson, J. P. *How Americans use time: A social-psychological analysis of everyday behavior.* New York: Praeger Press, 1977.

Willems, E. P. Behavioral technology and behavioral ecology. *Journal of Applied Behavior Analysis,* 1974, **7,** 151-166.

Winett, R. A., & Neale, M. S. Flexitime and family life: Experimental methods and outcomes with federal workers. *Monthly Labor Review,* November, 1980, 29-32. (a)

Winett, R. A., & Neale, M. S. Modifying settings as a strategy for permanent, preventive behavior change: Flexible work schedules and family life as a case in point. In P. Karoly & J. J. Steffen (Eds.), *Improving the long-term effects of psychotherapy.* New York: Gardner Press, 1980, 407-436. (b)

Winett, R. A., Neale, M. S., & Williams, K. R. Effective field research procedures: Recruitment of participants and acquisition of reliable, useful data. *Behavioral Assessment,* **1,** 1979, 139-155.

Received November 29, 1979
Final acceptance August 28, 1980

Official statistics do not reveal the nature of the contribution which farmers' wives make to the farm labour force. On the basis of a pilot study, three roles for women on farms were identified. Main distinguishing features were division of labour between husband and wife, frequency of manual work, responsibility for farm enterprises, participation in formal organisations and approach to housework. Home-centred farm housewives only work on the farm occasionally, working farmwives assist their husbands regularly while women farmers threaten male status by doing "man's" work. Reasons for women playing one role rather than another are discussed. Trends in agriculture suggest that the farmer's wife contribution to the farm business will become still more significant in future.

30

ROLES OF WOMEN ON FARMS
A Pilot Study

Ruth Gasson*

"The concept of 'the farmer and his wife' so often used by agricultural economics is far from having universal validity" (Ashby, 1953: 97).

1. Official Statistics

Agricultural economists studying farm businesses tend to set up stereotypes such as "the farmer and his family" or "farmer's plus wife's labour." Rarely, it seems, do they stop to consider the meaning of these concepts. This paper attempts to penetrate the façade by considering some of the roles which women play on farms nowadays.

How important is the contribution of farmers' wives to the farm labour force nationally? On this question the Agricultural Census has been extremely reticent. Until 1976 the occupier of an agricultural holding completing the labour section of his June Return form was instructed to "exclude the wives of farmers, partners and directors, even though the wives themselves may be partners or directors". Attempts have been made elsewhere to estimate the work done by farmers' wives. While between 80 and 90 per cent of male farmers in this country are married, not all wives are willing, able or expected to work on the farm. The 1975 EEC Farm Structure Survey estimated that the spouse of the occupier helped on 59 per

---

* The writer wishes to thank the Women's Farm and Garden Association for supporting the research project on which this paper is based, the Economic Development Committee for Agriculture for permission to use data from the national survey of the farm labour force, the Social Science Research Council Survey Archive for providing tapes of the Agriculture EDC data and an anonymous Editorial Consultant for comments on an earlier draft of this paper.

From Ruth Gasson, "Roles of Women on Farms: A Pilot Study," *Journal of Agricultural Economics*, 1981, 32, pp. 11-20. Reprinted by permission of the publisher and author.

cent of full time holdings in England and Wales (Ministry of Agriculture, Fisheries and Food, 1976). The Economic Development Committee for Agriculture concluded that 52 per cent of farmers on full time holdings were assisted by their wives who contributed 17 hours a week on average throughout the year (Agriculture EDC, 1972). (Comparable figures for the United States in 1964 were 43 per cent of farmers and 20 hours a week (Huffman, 1976).) Farmers' wives supplied 5 or 6 per cent of the total hours worked on farms in England and Wales in 1970/1 (Sparrow, 1972; Britton and Hill, 1975). These results together with local surveys carried out by Ashby (1953), Hine and Gregory (1972) and Newby and colleagues (1978) suggest that between half and two-thirds of all farmers' wives in this country do some manual work on the farm while up to three-quarters are involved in the farm business in a manual, managerial or administrative capacity.

Women can be farmers as well as farmers' wives. While the Agricultural Census does not record the sex of farmers, the last Population Census reported nearly 25,000 female farmers, farm managers and market gardeners in England and Wales in 1971 (Office of Population Censuses and Surveys, 1976). This is broadly in line with Harrison's estimate that 20,000 farm business principals in England in 1969 were women (Harrison, 1975). He puts the proportion of female farmers at 9 per cent, the Population Census at 11 per cent while in the EEC as a whole, women represent 10 per cent of farmers.

How many female farmers are sole operators, how many farm actively in partnership with others and how many, accorded the legal status of partner or director for tax purposes, are farmers in name only? Official statistics shed little light on the question. Acording to Harrison (1975: p.22), only about 1 per cent of all farmers were principals "in their own right as it were, and their husbands were not farmers". Other sources put the proportion of female sole or principal farmers nearer 3 per cent (Agriculture EDC, 1972; MAFF, 1976). None of these sources reveals how many women farming in partnership with their husbands are active and how many only nominal farmers.

2. The Concept of "Role"

Part of the problem with official labour statistics is that labels like "farmer, partner or director" or "spouse assisting with farm work", which are in any case very broad categories, shed little light on the activities of those so described. In this journal Errington (1980) has argued the case for classifying farm occupations according to tasks undertaken rather than relying on job titles which are often misleading. Logically one might go further and adopt role as the unit of analysis for, as the author of a recent COPA paper on European women farmers pointed out, "As the role of women working and living in the agricultural sector is not well defined, the statistics logically do not draw up a clear picture of the situation" (Tazza, 1979).

"Role" means more than a job title or even the sum of activities undertaken by a person pursuing an occupation. A person who performs a role is like an actor who steps into a part with all its associated actions, responsibilities and relationships. One who takes up the role of farmer, for example, engages in characteristic activities and assumes responsibilities such as "good stewardship of the land". As a farmer he enters into previously defined relationships with other groups like farm workers or the National Farmers' Union.

An actor is not left to play his dramatic role in a vacuum. While there may be room for individual interpretation, he has to observe cues, lines and stage directions. So in real life, a person playing a role models his behaviour on the performance of others, seeks instruction, accepts advice, judges from the reactions of others whether his performance is acceptable. Guidelines for role performance are "role expectations" or "norms". Those who do not conform to the prevailing norms are subjected to social sanctions which are intended to bring them into line. Sanctions vary in severity from the merest hint of reproach to outright criticism, ridicule or even ostracism.

Role expectations may vary from one economic, social or cultural setting to another. Nevertheless, in any given context, social pressures to conform impose a certain regularity on role behaviour. Therefore by observing the behaviour of individuals in an occupation it should be possible to identify whole constellations of tasks, responsibilities and relationships which amount to *ideal role types.* This paper describes three such role types for women on farms and goes on to consider some of the implications for the industry.

3. Farm Survey—Sampling and Approach

Information on farm women's roles was gathered during a pilot survey in 1979. Aims of the survey included documenting activities of farm women and collecting background information which might account for variations in roles. Since subjects were to be interviewed in depth, no attempt was made to draw a random sample, contacts being made on the basis of personal acquaintance or recommendation. The sample was not representative, being biased towards large farms, women active in farming and women with agricultural qualifications. The strength of the approach lay in the quality of the response, the wealth of information and depth of insight it provided on farm women's roles.

The sample included forty-four women from the south of England. All but three were or had been married to farmers or farm managers, the exceptions being two farmers whose husbands were not farming and one retired farmer who had never married. Although respondents shared a common bond of farming, in most other respects such as age, background, education, training and previous work experience, the sample was extremely varied. Farm size ranged from under 5 to over 200 hectares. Enterprises included dairying, extensive and intensive livestock units, cereals, fruit, hops and vegetable crops.

4. Three Ideal Role Types

The forty-four respondents approximated to one of three ideal role types which will be called "farm housewife", "working farmwife" and "woman farmer". Main distinguishing features were frequency of manual work on the farm, responsibility for a farm enterprise, division of labour between spouses, participation in formal organisations and attitude to housework.

The first ideal type, *farm housewife,* accounted for twenty women in the sample. In this group, division of labour and interest between husband and wife is marked; It is *his* farm, *her* farmhouse. The woman does not work regularly on the farm and is not responsible for any farm enterprise, although she is expected to be available in emergencies and to lend a hand at busy times like haymaking and harvest. Rounding up straying livestock, bottle feeding lambs and watching the grain drier were typical duties for farm housewives in the survey.

Only eight of the farm housewives interviewed were business principals. Being somewhat remote from day-to-day events on the farm, they had little control over short term management decisions, although they felt they would be consulted on matters with longer term implications. Most believed they would have a say, but not the last word, on major policy issues such as land transactions or succession. Farm housewives are often responsible for the farm accounts and invariably expected to answer the telephone, see callers and run errands.

The farm housewife is a home centred person. Nearly all respondents said that domestic and family tasks absorbed the greater part of their time and all agreed that this was their most important responsibility. Far from viewing housework as an imposition, however, they tend to make an art of it. More than half the farm housewives baked their own bread, for instance. Any surplus time and energy is channelled into off-farm activities, sometimes gainful but more often voluntary. Farm housewives in the sample belonged to 3.4 formal organisations on average, one being active in nine organisations. Notably these women support the Women's Institute and community services organisations such as the parish council, Parent Teachers' Assocation and Women's Voluntary Service.

Ten respondents fitted the description of *working farmwife*. The farmwife spends part of every day working manually on the farm, possibly more time than she spends in the house. She probably prefers farm work to housework, too. She and her husband make a good team, working together for much of the time but with a clear division of labour. Typically she feeds calves and he drives the tractor; he repairs fences but she fetches hammer and nails. The working farmwife's place is to assist her husband and she is rarely put in charge of a farm enterprise. Control rests with the man who makes day-to-day decisions affecting them both, although major policy decisions are likely to be shared. The wife may be a legal partner in the business, as were half of those interviewed. Like the farm housewife, she may be responsible for farm accounts and will certainly answer the telephone and see callers.

Although working farmwives in the sample tried to keep household chores to a minimum, at least half would have preferred less to do. Half were involved in farm based enterprises such as farm gate sales or farmhouse accommodation, which may be the modern counterpart to the traditional farmwife's poultry flock or farmhouse cheese enterprise. Domestic help was rarely employed, however. Women in this group are less likely than farm housewives to join voluntary organisations, six of the ten interviewed belonging to none.

Fourteen *women farmers* were identified, eight farming actively in partnership with husbands and six farming alone because they were single or widowed or their husbands were not farmers. Like working farmwives they work regularly on the farm, possibly spending more hours outside than in. Most women farmers interviewed regarded farming as their most time consuming, most important and most enjoyable occupation. Unlike the working farmwife, however, the woman farmer does not merely assist her husband but has some clearly defined responsibility of her own. Several respondents managed beef units, for example, and some also ran farm based enterprises such as pick-and-pay. Further, tasks undertaken by women farmers need not be those regarded as "suitable" for women; one respondent was in charge of baling, another for farm building repairs. All but one was a business principal and most had at least equal responsibility with their partners for long term policy decisions. Compared with the others, women farmers had greater influence over short and medium term management decisions.

Turning to the farmhouse, half the women farmers interviewed objected to housework but they were more likely than the others to employ domestic help. The woman farmer is nearly as ready as the farm housewife to support formal associations. Typically, though, she belongs to the National Farmers' Union or a farming discussion group rather than the Women's Institute. Table 1 illustrates some salient features of the three role types as revealed in the pilot survey.

Table 1 Women's involvement in the farm business by role type

Responsibility for major policy decisions:	Farm housewife	Working farmwife	Woman farmer
entirely or mainly woman's	—	—	5
shared equally with others	6	6	5
mainly others' but woman consulted	10	3	4
entirely others'	4	1	—
Woman a business principal	8	5	13
Woman not a business principal	12	5	1
Woman personally responsible for:			
whole farm	—	—	8
major enterprise (eg beef unit)	—	2	6
minor enterprise (eg farmhouse poultry)	5	2	—
no enterprise	15	6	—
Woman works on farm:			
regularly	3	8	11
occasionally	15	2	2
never	2	—	1
Number in sample	20	10	14

This threefold classification of roles, derived from a small sample, provided a useful framework for analysing data gathered in the pilot survey. This is not to deny that better schemes may be developed when more data become available or that different versions might prove more appropriate in other settings. For instance Pearson (1979) produced the following classification of farm women's roles in southern Colorado:

— independent producers who manage farms or ranches largely by themselves

— agricultural partners who share all aspects of work, responsibility and decision making with husbands

— agricultural helpers who only participate in farm work at busy times when extra help is needed and

— farm homemakers who contribute to farm production only indirectly by preparing meals and running errands for those who work in the fields.

Craig (1979) recognised these roles types in Australia and added a fifth category, the matriarch who manages a farm but does not contribute any labour.

5. Towards an Explanation of Variations in Roles

What causes women on farms to adopt one role pattern rather than another? Results of the pilot study suggest that farm housewives and working farmwives both conform to traditional role expectations, socio-economic status discriminating between them. Women farmers, on the other hand, play a non-traditional role.

Size of farm business goes a long way to account for role differences between working farmwives and farm housewives. Farms in the sample where the woman was a working farmwife averaged only 36 hectares. None of these farms employed regular non-family labour and half the farmers had only their wives to help them. Working regularly on the farm, these women felt competent to advise on major decisions. With manual work and possibly farm based enterprises to cope with as well as the family, working farmwives had little time left for voluntary organisations.

Farms where the woman played the farm housewife role averaged 92 hectares. At least one man was employed on all but three, so wives were only needed occasionally. Being somewhat out of touch with daily farm events, they were unable to contribute as much to management decisions. Instead they concentrated their energies on children, homes and gardens. Any surplus creative ability was directed away from the farm to the local community, welfare work and women's organisations.

The tendency for the wife's involvement in the farm to decline as size of farm increases has been documented frequently. In the Agriculture EDC survey, for instance, the proportion of wives doing farm work fell from 71 per cent on farms without regular workers to 43 per cent on farms with five men or more. Britton and Hill (1975) calculated from Farm Management Survey data that the wife's contribution peaked in the 400 to 500 standard man day group and declined to negligible proportions on farms of over 2,000 standard man days. Similar patterns have been described for Denmark (Mørkeberg, 1978), British Columbia (Sawer, 1973) and Wisconsin (Wilkening and Bharadwaj, 1968).

Two other socio-economic variables appear to reinforce the differences in roles expected of farm housewives and working farmwives. One is the woman's social background. Working farmwives tend to come from working class families where, it is suggested, the idea of a woman doing routine farm work would not be unacceptable. Most working farmwives in the sample had had manual jobs before marriage. By contrast farm housewives are likely to come from rural middle class families where, perhaps, ideas about "suitable" work for women might be more rigid. It could be argued, too, that participation in formal associations, so characteristic of the farm housewife, is essentially a middle class trait.

The husband's position at marriage, another reflection of socio-economic status, could also affect the woman's role in the business. If a woman marries a man who is already an established farmer, her scope for sharing in the running of the farm will probably be less than if husband and wife start farming together after marriage.

Most husbands of working farmwives and farm housewives in the sample came from farming backgrounds and a majority had succeeded to family farms. With a small farm, usually only one son can inherit and not before the father retires or dies. Working farmwives in the sample had mostly married younger sons or sons who would not inherit a farm for some years. Only three had married established farmers, as Table 2 shows. Consequently, most of these couples embarked on farming after marriage and the wife was as much involved in the venture as the husband. The larger the parental farm, the greater the probability that sons wanting to farm can be established in farming before the father dies or retires. Twelve of the twenty farm housewives in the sample had married men who were already farm business principals (Table 2) and therefore accustomed to making decisions without a wife's help. Where the husband was in partnership with parents or brothers, the new wife had to tread very warily. Young wives in this situations had the least influence over farm business decisions.

Table 2 Respondents' means of entry to farming

Women acquired status in farming by:	Farm housewife	Working farmwife	Woman farmer
marrying an established farmer	10	3	—
marrying successor to a family farm	2	2	1
couple buying or renting farm after after marriage	5	4	6
husband obtaining manager's post after marriage	3	1	1
inheritance or other means, independent of marriage	—	—	6
Husband from farming family	15	9	6
Husband not from farming family	5	1	8

Eleven of the fourteen women playing the non-traditional role of woman farmer had decided on a farming career before meeting their future husbands. Eight had been to agricultural college and all eleven had worked on farms before they married. Agricultural training and farming experience were not usual among more traditional farmers' wives. Six women farmers were farmers' daughters and none of them had brothers. It is possible that as children they had been brought up to help father on the farm rather than mother in the house. Six women, including most of these "substitute sons", had inherited or acquired farms of their own independent of marriage (Table 2). If a wife brings the farm or most of the capital to a marriage, she might well be expected to exercise more control over it than her husband.

A farm background was not sufficient to explain why some women played the farmer role, for eight of them were not from farming families. They were mostly city-born daughters of business or professional men. Their parents encouraged them to choose careers and they attended the kind of school which, before the 1944 Education Act, fostered career aspirations in girls. In this they probably differed from most of their contemporaries who were brought up to see marriage as the ultimate goal of a woman.

This section has suggested that a woman's role is influenced by such variables as size of farm business and social origins of spouses. This is not to imply that a woman is necessarily tied to the same role all her life. Widowhood might push a woman into the role of farmer. Other milestones in the family cycle, such as sons coming home to work, might edge a working farmwife into the farm housewife role. Although the pilot study produced little evidence of women changing roles, further research with a more representative sample could throw new light on the dynamics of role determination.

6. Population Frequencies

Over the country as a whole, working farmwives, associated with family farms employing no outside labour, are likely to be the largest group. Over three-quarters of the agricultural holdings in Britain today are without full time hired workers, nearly half the farmers and spouses being on holdings where they provide at least 80 per cent of the labour (Britton, 1979).   Data from the Agriculture EDC survey reveal that working wives are typical of small, full time dairy farms, farms in the western half of England and in Wales, farms where husbands spend most of their time in manual work.   Britton and Hill (1975) confirm that wives make the greatest labour contribution on small dairy farms.

According to the Agriculture EDC study, wives are least likely to do manual work on very large arable farms, those employing five or more workers and farms in the eastern counties.   If the husband is a farm manager or if he spends much of his time in managerial rather than manual work, his wife is unlikely to work regularly on the farm.   These conditions add up to the woman playing the role of farm housewife.

Women farmers are probably the smallest group, if only because few women choose a farming career independent of marriage.   The Agriculture EDC data suggest that farms run by women are smaller than men's farms and employ fewer workers.   Women farmers are relatively numerous in south east England, Wales and the south west and quite rare in the eastern counties.   Women farmers tend to specialise in horticulture, dairying or breeding pedigree livestock and to eschew large scale arable farming.

This pilot study, based on a small and unrepresentative sample, has uncovered an aspect of farming business which, though far reaching in its implications, has been neglected by agricultural economists.   It points to the need for a more comprehensive study of the contribution which farmers' wives make to agriculture.   A wider survey might bring to light significant variations in the woman's role related to such variables as source of capital, tenure and stage of family cycle, to mention but three.   It would be useful to test for regional differences as well, to determine whether there are cultural variations in female role expectations exerting an influence independent of the effects of farm size and type.

7. Trends and Implications

Post-war trends in British agriculture have tended to increase women's participation in farm work.   Mechanisation has reduced the need for physical strength in many operations while "the drift from the land" has left many farmers mainly dependent on their wives for help with farm tasks.   Growing size and complexity of farm businesses has increased the need for accurate farm records and accounts, activities in which wives are often involved.   (Nearly half the women interviewed had sole reponsibility for farm accounts.)

Looking to the future, the pace of farm mechanisation and the rate of outflow of hired labour may slacken in the 1980s but the demand for farm records, physical and financial planning and controls will increase steadily (Nix, 1980).   Thus the woman's role as farm secretary is likely to gain significance.   The pilot survey showed, too, that most farmers consult their wives over major issues such as obtaining finance or development plans.   Soaring land prices and high interest rates must underline the need for informed decision making.   All this suggests that farm women could benefit from training in farm business management.   A number of respondents in the survey had experience of office work and others were hoping to learn book-keeping or typing, but only a few recognised a need for courses in financial management and control.

Some individuals who provide services to agriculture also need educating about the woman's role. It is common for a woman trying to transact farm business, being fobbed off because the agent insists on dealing with the male partner. The pilot survey found instances, too, of women farmers not being taken seriously by their political organisation, the National Farmers' Union. Wives are welcomed at social functions but not expected to voice opinions at business meetings.

Turning to manual work, most farmers expect their wives to help on the farm at least occasionally. Demands are likely to increase as the hired labour force shrinks. Socialisation of women, even those reared on farms, tends to neglect skills which would be valuable to a farmer's wife, such as carpentry and mechanical engineering. More encouragement might therefore be given to farmers' wives to attend training courses in order to acquire farm skills. Several respondents felt they would benefit from machinery courses, a sensible suggestion since it is often the farmer's wife who is sent to collect a spare machine part in an emergency.

A hardening of the cost-price squeeze, which has been predicted for British agriculture in the 1980s (Nix, 1980) could result in a growth of multiple job holding among farm families. Women farmers and working farmwives might well respond by developing lucrative farm-based enterprises or by releasing husbands for off-farm employment. Farm housewives, unaccustomed to regular farm work, might contribute more by taking off-farm jobs themselves. (The pilot survey found that 17 out of 20 farm housewives had trained for careers, mainly as teachers, nurses or secretaries.) Relevant considerations here include the marketable skills of spouses, jobs available and transport.

Changing values of society also have implications for the farm woman's role. Women's liberation has come to mean freedom for women to be employed outside the home. Now that half the married women in Britain go out to work, those who stay at home are beginning to appear deviant. Some farm housewives in the survey wanted off-farm jobs but were prevented by the fact that husbands expected them to be available on the farm when needed. Voluntary activities served a valuable function for these women, offering a means of self-expression and a source of status independent of marriage, without demanding rigid hours. For how long, though, will intelligent women be content with *substitute* careers?

Women's liberation is likely to mean fewer women content with traditional, subordinate roles in farming, more determined to become farmers. These women risk opposition on all sides. Society expects women to have jobs nowadays, it is true, but not in occupations which threaten the status of men. On a farm a woman may undertake "suitable" work but not "masculine" tasks like marketing livestock, ploughing or driving a combine. For a woman to do these things well undermines the traditional authority of men. Nearly all the women farmers interviewed had bitter experiences of discrimination directed against them for presuming to compete in a man's world.

Like most working wives in Britain today, the woman farmer is faced with dual role expectations. As a farmer she will be judged by the yardstick of full time male farmers, regardless of her additional responsibilities in the home. Equally as a woman she is judged against the full time farm housewife, irrespective of her farm commitments. In the pilot survey there was a subtle inference that a woman was allowed to "indulge" in farming so long as the family did not suffer in any way. Farming has to be treated as an additional role rather than an alternative to the more traditional wife-mother role.   Moreover, housework and childcare are areas in which British women are investing more, not less, time and emotional energy.   Despite the increase in domestic technology, housework hours have increased this century because standards have risen.   Although having children occupies less of a woman's life today, rearing children has become more complex and demanding (Oakley, 1979).   Without a re-evaluation of the woman's role in the home, therefore, little real progress can be made towards liberation for women.

References

Agriculture EDC, (1972). *Agricultural Manpower in England and Wales.* HMSO.
Ashby, A. W., (1953). "The farmer in business", *J. Proc. agric. Econ. Soc.,* **10**, 91 - 126.
Britton, D. K. and Hill, B., (1975). *Size and Efficiency in Farming.* Farnborough, Saxon House: 102 - 105.
Britton, D. K., (1979). *Age Structure of Farmers in UK, 1975.* Unpublished paper.
Craig, R. A., (1979). "Down on the farm: role conflicts of Australian farm women". Paper presented at national conference on *The Woman in Country Australia Looks Ahead.* McMillan Rural Studies Centre, Victoria.
Errington, A., (1980). "Occupational classification in British agriculture", *J. agric. Econ.,* **31**, 73 - 81.
Harrison, A., (1975). *Farmers and Farm Businesses in England.* University of Reading, Department of Agricultural Economics and Management, Miscellaneous Study 62.
Hine, R. C. and Gregory, G. N. F., (1972). *A Study of the Labour Force on Small Farms.* University of Nottingham, Department of Agricultural Economics.
Huffman, W. E., (1976). "The value of the productive time of farm wives: Iowa, North Carolina, and Oklahoma". *Am. J. agric. Econ.,* **58**, 836 - 841.
Ministry of Agriculture, Fisheries and Food, (1976). *EEC Survey on the Structure of Agricultural Holdings, (1975): England and Wales.* Government Statistical Service.
Mørkeberg, H, (1978). "Working conditions of women married to self-employed farmers", *Sociol Rur.,* **18**, 95 - 106.
Newby, H. Bell, C. Rose, D. and Saunders, P. (1978). *Property, Paternalism and Power* Hutchinson University Library, 67 - 72.
Nix, J., 1(979). "British agriculture into the 1980s", *J. R. agric. Soc.,* **140**, 43 - 50.
Oakley, A., (1979).   "The failure of the movement for women's equality", *New Society* 23 August, 392 - 394.
Office of Population Censuses and Surveys, (1976). *Economic Activity Tables Census 1971 Great Britain, Part II.* HMSO.
Pearson, J., (1979). "Note on female farmers". *Rural Sociology,* **44**, 189 - 200.
Sawer, B. J., (1973).   "Predictions of the farm wife's involvement in general management and adoption decisions". *Rural Sociology,* **30**, 412 - 426.
Sparrow, T. D., (1972). "The use of agricultural manpower". *J. agric. Lab. Sci.,* **1**, 3 - 10.
Tazza, A., (1979). *The Working and Living Conditions of the European Women Farmers.* COPA, Brussels.
Wilkening, E. A. and Bharadwaj, L. K., (1968). "Aspirations and task involvement as related to decision making among farm husbands and wives". *Rural Sociology,* **33**, 30 - 45.

Using data from a random sample of 790 Nebraska parents, this paper reports on extent of children's involvement in the household division of labor and the meaning of this work for the family. These data indicate that children's chores are an ubiquitous feature of family life. Based on parental report, four rationales for these chores are discussed: developmental, reciprocal obligation, extrinsic, and task learning. The relationships between these meanings of work and structural and family characteristics are explored. It is suggested that these meanings form a family theme, providing insight into values surrounding the parent-child bond and the duties that parents and children owe one another.

31

CHILDREN'S WORK IN THE FAMILY
Its Significance and Meaning

Lynn K. White and David B. Brinkerhoff***

A prominent belief about the classic family of Western nostalgia is that "children used to work long and hard in the home, in the factory, on the farm" (Ingoldsby and Adams, 1977). In contrast, most contemporary observers believe that today's children do not work, that outside of schoolwork, their primary obligation is to enjoy childhood. Boocock (1975:421) writes that "almost none do errands or chores or contribute in any other way to the running of the household." Similarly, Campbell (1969:824) argues that adolescents "possess only the shadow of significance and usefulness."

While some observers decry this state of affairs and compare it unfavorably with our nostalgic (but undocumented) picture of the past, there are others who clearly feel that work is a burden which children are well rid of and which, when present, represents neglect or exploitation of the child. There is, for example, a significant literature showing that children do more work around the house when

their mother works outside of the home (Hedges and Barnett, 1972; Propper, 1972). The interpretation of this finding has often been that this is a burden which inhibits the child from achievement in school or social life (Roy, 1961). McClelland (1961), in his studies of child-rearing practices related to achievement training, argues that making children do regular chores or pick up after themselves is a sign of rejection.

There thus is considerable ambivalence in the literature both in regard to the extent of children's work and its meaning. Almost universally, however, children's work has been a sidelight rather than a focus of research and there is little accurate descriptive data on children's work in the family. Nor has there been any systematic consideration of the meaning of children's work for family organization and interaction.

This paper attempts to fill some of these gaps by reporting on a study of children's domestic work. It is concerned with the extent to which children work and the tasks they are given. Most importantly, it is concerned with the meanings families attach to children's work, *i.e.*, their rationales and interpretations. Finally, it is interested in integrating these findings with theoretical approaches

*Bureau of Sociological Research and Department of Sociology, University of Nebraska-Lincoln, Lincoln, Nebraska 68508.

**Department of Sociology, University of Nebraska-Lincoln, Lincoln, Nebraska 68508.

From Lynn K. White and David B. Brinkerhoff, "Children's Work in the Family: Its Significance and Meaning," *Journal of Marriage and the Family*, 1981, 43, pp. 789-798. Reprinted by permission of the publisher and authors.

within the social-psychological and sociological literature.

CHILDREN'S WORK: LITERATURE AND CONCEPTUALIZATION

With a few recent exceptions, children's work—or the lack of it—has been a concern of psychologists rather than sociologists.[1] Household chores as a means to individual development, particularly in regard to responsibility and morality, has been the major focus of the literature. Sociological concerns, such as the effect of children's work on the family, have been almost totally ignored. The existing research in children's work is briefly reviewed below, followed by a development of ideas drawn from the broader literature.

The Psychological Literature

A major research tradition in psychology has been the development of moral character in the child, *i.e.*, the development of responsibility, self-control, and service (Piaget, 1948; Kohlberg, 1964). As part of this concern, Harris *et al.* (1954) investigated the common-sense notion that children who are assigned home duties will be quicker to develop these notions of service and responsibility to others. They measured the extent of home duties by a simple checklist of chores that the children had ever done and responsibility by: (1) a teacher rating and (2) a student questionnaire on citizenship values. Data collected from 3,000 Minnesota school children showed no relationship between home duties and the development of responsibility. Although their measures can be faulted, in particular for using number of chores *ever* done as a measure of home responsibility, their research remains widely cited. For example, largely on the basis of their findings, Kohlberg (1964:425) concluded that "strong training demands which serve the parents' convenience (cleanliness,

---

[1] A third area of research regarding children and work is not concerned with children's work at all, but with children's socialization into adult work roles. The best and most recent work in this tradition is Goldstein and Oldham's (1979) comprehensive study of the development of children's ideas about work and exchange, and, in particular, about specific occupations, occupational prestige, and occupations as intrinsic to a system of social inequality. Unique among such studies, the authors recognize that children do work themselves and that their own experiences, as well as other influences around them, may affect their work socialization.

chores, neatness, [control of] aggression in the home) are, if anything, negatively related to moral response."

Elsewhere in the psychological literature, children's household chores have been investigated in terms of their relationship to the achievement syndrome. McClelland (1961) felt that requiring chores of children would reduce their opportunities to strive for excellence, and Smith (1969) noted that the skills and attitudes involved in doing routine chores may be actively contradictory to those demanded by a competitive drive for achievement. Nevertheless, Smith did find a significant correlation between having required chores and achievement motivation and concludes that chores may represent legitimate demands for independence and responsibility.

Apart from the above, the developmental literature has not included any theoretical or empirical work on the meaning of children's household chores. While the general tone of this literature is somewhat negative, the outstanding characteristic of the psychological literature on the developmental outcomes of children's contributions is the lack of research attention.

The Sociological Literature

Sociological research on children's work is meager. An exception is the early work by Straus (1962), comparing work behavior of urban and farm boys. Straus included a thoughtful analysis of the implications of children's chores for development, noting that further research was badly needed in order to learn the values parents were trying to teach their children through work, the parental motivations behind asking children to work, and the importance of children's work in preparing them for adult roles.

These issues have not been addressed within sociology. Rather, sociological concern with children's work has been an empirical interest in the functional contributions of children's work to the family division of labor. Unfortunately, this interest in children's work has existed only to the extent that it has clarified the role of working mothers and their participation in the family division of labor. Generally, the research has shown that, when wives work, children rather than husbands increase their involvement in housework to make up for wives' decreased availability (Hedges and

Barnett, 1972; Thrall, 1978). In spite of some early concerns that this additional demand on children might negatively (and, it was implied, unfairly) affect children's social life, more recent studies suggest that housework has no adverse consequences for children's social or school life (Nye and Hoffman, 1974).

The Sociological Perspective

The literature that deals explicitly with children's work recognizes only a relatively narrow set of implications: Psychological interest has focused on the developmental impact of work on the child and sociologists have concentrated on the functional impact of work on the family division of labor. A broader sociological perspective on the meaning of children's work, however, yields provocative insights.

First, picking up on Strauss' early ideas, one should consider the implications of children's work for adult roles. The work children do is not simply a practice exercise which may prepare them for real, *i.e.*, paid work, but rather consists of domestic chores that are likely to form part of their lifelong tasks. General socialization theory suggests that childhood experiences in this regard will have consequences for later roles in their own families. This expectation is supported by Thrall's (1978) finding that both men and women rely heavily on their childhood experiences when devising their own marital division of labor.

An additional perspective on children's work is drawn from the broader literature on the meaning of work. With reference to adult work, Menninger (1964:xiv) characterized the sociological approach as a recognition that "work is a method of relating meaningfully to the family and the community—a group process by which the individual becomes an entity, but, at the same time, is identified with the group." Application of this idea to children's work suggests that the coparticipation of children and adults in household tasks may contribute to increased family solidarity.

If the literature on the meaning of adult work is any guide,[2] there are undoubtedly additional and more subtle meanings of chil-

dren's work. The literature reviewed above, however, is sufficient to suggest that children's work may have important functional, integrative, and developmental implications, both for the child and for the family. Children's household work may have further outcomes for their performance in school, in the community, and on the job, but initially and intrinsically, it is a family matter.

Consequently, this paper concerns itself with the child's experiences with work in the family and the meanings of this work for the family. Because of the absence of any other holistic approaches to the role of children's work in the family, this research is necessarily exploratory. The preceding ideas, however, form a backdrop to the present exploration and additional sociological research is drawn upon throughout the discussion in order to put the findings into context.

STUDY DESIGN

Data for this study come from telephone interviews with parents collected as part of the Nebraska Annual Social Indicators Survey. Over 1,800 randomly selected adults from Nebraska were interviewed for this study in February-March, 1979. This research reports on the 790 homes in which there was a child under age 18. In each household, a child was randomly selected to be the subject of the interview and the parent was asked whether the child was regularly required to do chores around the house or yard. Parents were also asked to provide some details about these activities and to give their reasons for requesting their children to work around the house. The rest of the questions in the interview consisted of general indicators of quality of life, including detailed background descriptions of family composition and history as well as information on the family's current situation.

FINDINGS

This paper represents an exploratory study of the role of children's work in the family. As a preliminary step in this inquiry, the extent of children's involvement with household work is documented. The bulk of this paper, however, is concerned with exploring the meaning which children's work has for their families.

Extent of Children's Work

Table 1 presents data on the extent to which children engage in regular chores, categorized

[2] There is a considerable amount of literature on the meaning of work for adults. Of particular interest is Berger's (1964), *The Human Shape of Work*, and Tilgher's (1930), *Work: What It Has Meant to Man Through the Ages*.

TABLE 1. PERCENT OF CHILDREN REGULARLY REQUIRED TO DO CHORES AND WEEKLY MEDIAN HOURS SPENT ON CHORES BY AGE AND SEX

Age Group	Percent with Chores		Of Those with Chores Median Hours		Number
	Boys	Girls	Boys	Girls	
Total	82	78	3.4	4.6	790
0 - 4	40	36	2.1	1.7	189
5 - 9	91	87	2.3	4.0	207
10 - 14	98	92	4.1	4.7	220
15 - 17	94	93	4.2	6.1	174

by sex and age. These findings indicate clearly that being assigned chores around the house and yard is a developmental process. In some households it apparently begins very early and, by the time children are 9 or 10, well over 90 percent are involved in regular chores. Participation tends to fall off slightly in the late teens as adolescents reduce their participation in all family activities, but chores remain a near universal. Although there is a consistent tendency for parents to report that their sons are more likely than their daughters to have chores, these differences are not statistically significant.

While these data indicate that children are increasingly involved with regular household chores as they get older, few of these children are required to put in gruelling hours. The median number of hours spent by children on chores is 4.0 per week. Even for the hardest working group, older girls, the median is only 6 hours per week. Still, on top of schoolwork, homework, and extra-curricular activities, chores can add a significant additional demand on children.

Children begin their involvement in household chores by assuming responsibility for themselves: picking up their own toys, making their own beds, and cleaning up their own rooms. By the time they are 10 years old, however, most children have moved beyond purely self-centered chores and are doing work for their family. As children grow older they move from helping their parents, say by setting the table or folding the clothes to replacing their parents by assuming full responsibility for some tasks.[3]

The Meaning of Children's Work

The data reviewed above indicate that most

[3] A detailed analysis of age and sex differences in the content of children's work appears in White and Brinkerhoff (forthcoming).

parents assign regular chores to children and that this is a significant activity in terms of hours per week. The question remains, however, as to what this activity means for the child and the family. As Murray Straus (1962) noted 20 years ago, it is frequently less trouble to do a task oneself than to nag a child into doing it and then supervise and help. Until adolescence, children's chores probably represent more, rather than less, work for the parent. The following section empirically addresses some of the meanings parents attribute to assigning their children chores.

Parental responses to the question: "Why do you ask your children to work?" are illuminating. The key word for most parents is "responsibility." In fact, over 25 percent of the parents surveyed spontaneously used the word responsibility in their reply. For example, parents made such remarks as:

[Work] gives them a sense of responsibility. Makes them appreciate what they have. I think it helps them grow into responsible adults. (Parent of 8-year-old girl.)

I think it develops the character. Unless they do it, it won't get done. It builds their responsibility —his own responsibility toward others. (Parent of 14-year-old boy.)

Regardless of the specific words used, the majority of parents gave character building as the primary reason for assigning their children chores. In fact, many parents reported that it was their duty to give children chores:

I feel children have to learn to work while young and it stays with them. We do them an injustice as a parent if we let them do nothing. (Parent of 13-year-old boy.)

Because he's a member of the family, because there's too much work for me to do it all. The main reason, he has to be responsible and I would be very derelict as a parent not to. (Parent of 12-year-old boy.)

Some parents also expressed a specific belief that household chores were a means to integrate the family and to provide greater cohesiveness among family members. A few of these parents sounded as if they had just finished reading Durkheim's classic treatise on the moral functions of the division of labor; they are clearly convinced that joint responsibility is positive and vital.

> We think it makes them a part of the family; they're living at home. It makes them know they have their duties and share in making it a home. (Parent of 6-year-old girl.)

> Their responsibility to help their family. A family becomes a family when we all take part and they have to learn that. (Parent of 14-year-old boy.)

> They need to know how to do some things. They need to help the family in their everyday living. They become a part of the family that way. (Parent of 15-year-old girl.)

There are a few parents (22 out of 669) who gave purely extrinsic reasons for asking their children to work, such as, "I need the help." A much larger number included remarks about wanting the help within a longer reply stressing character building. A few of these parents specifically noted that the work accomplished was a secondary consideration and that it was really for the child's benefit that they assigned them chores.

These verbatim responses from parents give an illuminating picture of the variety of meanings associated with children's work and an overall impression of concern with developmental outcomes. For a more careful analysis of the meaning of children's work, parental responses were coded into five categories of meaning corresponding roughly to the four *a priori* meanings developed above plus one residual category. These categories and some typical responses are:

Developmental: Doing chores builds character, develops responsibility, helps children learn.
Reciprocal obligations: It is their duty to help the family; working together is part of being a family; occasionally, more bluntly, "they live here, don't they?"
Extrinsic: Parents need help.
Task learning: Children need to learn how to do these tasks.
Residual: All other reasons, most often that child has to earn an allowance or needs something to do in order to keep busy.

Each response was coded twice by independent coders. Because many parents gave complex reasons, each answer was given as many as three codes. For example, the response for the 15-year-old girl cited above was coded for both the second and fourth category. Table 2 presents the distribution of the reasons given by parents for having their children work.

Clearly, most parents' responses fall into the developmental category. However, the age pattern for this meaning is in sharp contrast to the others: While the proportion assigning a developmental reason declines with the age of the child, the likelihood of giving all of the other reasons increases with age. While parents of older children still most commonly give a developmental reason, an increasing number report that they rely on the help of older children, see them as having some obligation to their family, or as needing to learn some basic domestic skills. There is a subtle change from "helping will build his responsibility" to "it is his responsibility to help" by late teens.[4] Note that compared with age the

'The first reason in this example would be coded as developmental and second as reciprocal obligation.

TABLE 2. REASONS GIVEN FOR ASSIGNING CHILDREN CHORES, BY AGE AND SEX OF CHILD[a]

Reason	Total (Percent)	Age				Sex	
		0-4	5-9	10-14	15-17	Male	Female
Developmental	72.4	80.5	78.2	74.7	59.2	72.5	72.2
Reciprocity	24.8	12.2	19.9	24.7	36.8	27.2	22.0
Extrinsic	22.7	18.3	14.1	23.6	32.9	21.4	24.3
Learn Tasks	12.1	8.5	9.6	13.5	15.1	10.4	14.3
Other	9.2	6.1	6.4	12.4	9.9	10.4	7.7
N	568	82	156	178	152	309	259

aPercents do not add to 100 because some parents gave more than one reason for assigning children chores.

differences by sex are small and statistically insignificant.

The developmental response is so frequent across age and sex categories that it bears the characteristics of a normative or socially desirable response. It is suspected that most parents, without having given the matter a lot of thought, adhere to the conventional wisdom that chores are good for children. Or perhaps, parents give this socially desirable response in order to rationalize more extrinsic or selfish reasons.

The approximately 45 percent of the sample who gave a nondevelopmental response express a view of the family as a working unit, not merely as a child-rearing agency. While this position is not always clearly articulated, the responses of many parents indicate a firm belief that "the family that works together, stays together," and a belief that children can be expected to contribute to the family regardless of developmental outcomes.

The strong moral tone that pervades many of these diverse replies suggests that the meanings of children's work may be part of a family ethos, what Hess and Handel (1959) have called family themes. Conceiving of a family theme as a pattern comprising "some fundamental view of reality and some way or ways for dealing with it," Hess and Handel (1959: 11) argue that families develop "themes" which then affect the way they, as a group, structure their environment, process new information, and perceive reality. These responses to children's work may be part of such a theme, providing significant insight into those family values surrounding the parent-child bond and the obligations that parents and children have to one another. A much broader study of family values and outcomes would be necessary to determine whether interpretations of children's work are part of such a theme. With data only on children, this larger interpretation must remain a speculation. It is possible, however, to explore the possibility that the different interpretations of children's work are products of different family environments. In the following section, the family characteristics that may affect assigned meanings are examined. In particular, the analysis attempts to determine whether the values assigned to children's work are simply another instance of social-class differentials or whether they are primarily reflective of structural differences among families.

The Determinants of Meaning

In order to answer these questions, multiple-classification analysis is used to investigate differentials related to the three major categories of meaning.[5] This form of analysis is well suited to this type of exploratory research: It is designed to evaluate the impact of categorical independent and control variables and offers a unique opportunity to examine the form of the relationships rather than just a measure of association (Andrews and Messenger, 1973). This analysis is presented in two parts in Table 3. The first panel shows the independent effect of measures of family structure controlling for age and sex of child. The second panel shows the independent effect of each family background characteristic.

The results of the first panel indicate that there is no relationship between parents assigning developmental meaning to children's work and family structure: All types of families appear to attribute this category of meaning to children's work. On the other hand, family structure shows some relationship to the other two categories of meaning. Urban families are significantly more likely than rural families to believe that children have an obligation to do chores; more predictably, families with working mothers or single parents are more likely to say that they ask their children to work because the work needs to be done and they need the help. While the B^2 does not reach significance, there is also a linear increase in the percent saying they need help as household number rises. To a smaller extent, this same pattern appears between household size and a belief in reciprocal obligation.

In the next panel of Table 3 findings are presented on the effect of family background

---

[5] Task learning was dropped from further analysis, in part because of the smaller number of cases, but also from a conviction that this was the weakest coding category. Responses in this category were the most vague and the least likely to carry the moral overtone that characterizes the other three categories, an overtone which may represent a configuration of family values. When the analysis in Table 3 was performed for task learning, no significant relations were found.

TABLE 3. DETERMINANTS OF MEANING ASSIGNED TO CHILDREN'S WORK

	Adjusted Percent Giving Each Meaning			
	Developmental	Reciprocal Obligation	Extrinsic	Number
Grand Mean	72	25	23	548
Structural Characteristics[a]				
Mother's Employment				
Full-time	67	27	28	162
Part-time	76	23	28	133
Other	73	25	18	273
B^2	.0064	.0009	.0144*	
Number in Household				
Two	74	16	8	13
Three	72	24	19	124
Four	70	25	22	209
Five	74	23	25	132
Six or more	74	31	30	90
B^2	.0009	.0049	.01	
Household Type				
Husband-wife family	72	25	21	508
Single-parent family	70	21	52	43
Other	79	20	19	17
B^2	.0009	.0009	.04*	
Residence				
Rural farm	75	19	20	91
Rural nonfarm	70	19	26	116
Urban	72	29	23	361
B^2	.0016	.0121*	.0016	
Family Background Characteristics[b]				
Parental Respondent's Education				
0-11 years	70	18	17	
12 years	74	21	21	
13-15 years	71	31	24	
16 or more years	75	31	29	
B^2	.0025	.0169*	.0064	
Subjective Family Income				
Below average	73	21	20	106
Average	72	26	22	319
Above average	76	25	22	123
B^2	.0016	.0016	.0004	
Religion				
Catholic	73	24	25	157
Other	73	25	21	391
B^2	.0000	.0000	.0025	
Satisfaction with Marital Division of Labor				
Completely satisfied	72	27	13	231
Fairly well satisfied	73	23	26	218
Somewhat dissatisfied	73	23	34	61
B^2	.0004	.0016	.0324*	

[a]Adjusted for age and sex of child plus the other three structural characteristics.
[b]Adjusted for age of child and structural characteristics shown to have a significant effect and other family background characteristics.
*Significant at the .05 level.

on the meaning of children's work controlling for the structural variables previously found to have an impact: age of child, mother's work status, household type, and rural-urban residence. This analysis evaluates the independent effects of the four measures of family background: parent's education, family income, religion, and parental respondent's satisfaction with the family division of labor. The first two variables are routine measures of family's socioeconomic background. The measure of religion is included because earlier studies have found this to be related to work attitudes (Smith, 1969). The measure of satisfaction with the marital division of labor is included in order to see the contextual effect of family attitudes toward household work on the meaning assigned to children's work.

The results again indicate that the developmental response is so standard that it is almost invariant across families. This strongly suggests the presence of a cultural norm. To the extent that this response is given as a socially desirable rather than an honest answer, the normative interpretation is strengthened. A nearly constant three quarters of our sample believes or feels it ought to believe that chores are assigned to children for the benefit of the child.

The other two reasons, however, show some patterns. The belief that children have a duty to their family is significantly related to parents' education and positively, though not significantly, related to family income. The evidence is rather convincing that, for this sample, the "work as duty" ethic is positively associated with social class. Purely extrinsic meaning is significantly associated with only one variable: parental satisfaction with the marital division of labor. Parents who are dissatisfied with their own domestic share (presumably because they are over- rather than under-worked) are more apt to demand work from their children for purely extrinsic reasons. There is also a linear relationship between extrinsic reasons and parental education, though this is not statistically significant.

In summary, there do appear to be some differences in the kinds of families that give one meaning for work as opposed to another. While approximately three quarters of all kinds of families assign developmental reasons to children's work, higher-status and well-educated parents are more apt to attribute reciprocal obligations among family members as a reason and families with higher work loads—working mothers, single parents, or those with large households—are most apt to assign extrinsic meaning to children's work. It is important to bear in mind, however, that the meanings are not mutually exclusive: Two thirds of the parents who gave an extrinsic meaning to children's work also cited a developmental meaning.

Consequences of Meaning

The previous analysis has demonstrated that there are some significant differences among families in assigning different mean-

ings to children's work. Before attaching undue importance to this finding, however, it is important to evaluate whether these meanings have any significant consequences. Following Hess and Handel's (1959) lead, this study is concerned with whether these differences in meanings reflect underlying family values that have consequences for family organization. Specifically, do these differences in meaning affect what family members do?

This question can only be answered in terms of the consequences for children's labor, i.e., how many hours children are asked to work each week and whether their parents pay them for work around the household. In the present study, children were regarded as being paid for their labor if their parents gave them an allowance and said that they thought of this primarily as payment for work around the household or if, aside from a regular allowance, parents paid their child for work done around the household.

In order to show the independent effect of family themes on children's behavior, multiple classification analysis was again used. This time, the analysis looked at the effect of family theme on children's work hours and children's pay controlling for the background factors found to be important in Table 3: parental education, mother's employment, residence, family income, child's age, and satisfaction with family division of labor.[6]

The results in Table 4 show that family meaning has a small, but systematic, effect on the amount of work children do and their payment for this work. The data show that children whose work is given an extrinsic interpretation are likely to work the longest hours and the most likely to get paid for their work. Similarly, those whose work is seen as part of a reciprocal obligation are, not sur-

---

[6] It was necessary to make the categories of work meaning mutually exclusive for this analysis. In order to retain as many families as possible in the two smaller categories, parents who gave a reciprocal obligation or extrinsic reason as well as a developmental reason are coded only in the former categories. Families who gave both reciprocal obligation and extrinsic reasons ($N = 23$) were excluded from the analysis. This coding scheme produces three mutually exclusive categories: (1) families who see duty as a meaning ($N = 118$), (2) families who see extrinsic reasons for children's work ($N = 106$), and (3) families who see only developmental reasons ($N = 344$).

TABLE 4. ADJUSTED PERCENT OF CHILDREN WHO GET PAID FOR THEIR WORK AROUND THE HOUSE AND MEAN HOURS OF WORK PER WEEK BY FAMILY WORK ETHIC

Family Work Ethic	Percent Paid[a]	Mean Hours/Week[a]	Number
Total	38	4.55	493
Developmental	38	4.40	295
Reciprocal Obligation	35	4.71	110
Extrinsic	42	4.86	88

[a]Controlling for age of child, parent's education, mother's employment, family income, residence, and parental satisfaction with marital division of labor.

prisingly, least likely to get paid for their work. The number of hours this latter group works is a little above average, but not as high as the children who work for extrinsic reasons. Finally, the children whose work is assigned only a developmental meaning work the fewest hours.

While not significant, the pattern of results in Table 5 supports the idea that, controlling for family background and structure as well as child's characteristics, the way a family thinks about work has consequences for family organization.

SUMMARY

Parental reports from a random sample of 790 Nebraska youngsters have been used to investigate the extent and the meaning of children's participation in the family division of labor. The data indicate that children begin having regular chores very early and, as they get older, are assigned more extensive and responsible work. The chores themselves change from self-centered to family-centered activities. Analysis of responses from parents indicates that most parents report assigning chores to children as a means of building character. A minority of parents additionally see their children's chores as either the child's duty to his or her family or as a fair demand from overburdened parents.

Analysis of differentials in the interpretation of children's work suggests that there are systematic differences in the meanings assigned to children's chores. While a developmental or child-centered explanation appears to be normative in all categories of families, there are some significant patterns. Subjectively and objectively overworked parents are most apt to give extrinsic meaning to children's work, i.e., to see the work accomplished as an important part of the exercise. On the other hand, a belief that coparticipation in the household division of labor is an individual duty to the family is a value associated with higher-status parents. Further analysis shows that the meaning parents assign to children's work has consequences for the number of hours children work and whether they are paid for their work.

CONCLUSIONS

The findings suggest that children's work around the house is an ubiquitous and value-laden feature of family life. And, while there is only a limited literature to support it,['] it is speculated that the parent-child division of labor (chores) may create almost as much family tension as does the husband-wife division of labor. Given the centrality of chores for the experiences of children and families, further research is necessary in order to document the vital role of work and work ethos in family life and the consequences (developmental and otherwise) of children's involvement in the family division of labor.

More generally, there should be an increased inclusion of children in studies of family structure and process. Whether the topic is the division of labor, power relationships, or family conflict, the role of children in the family has been neglected. Rather, family sociologists have largely been content to leave the subject of children to developmental scholars. Hopefully, this research on the integrative and functional, as well as developmental, significance of children's work will be a step in this direction.

REFERENCES

Andrews, F. M., and R. C. Messenger
1973 Multivariate Nominal Scale Analysis. Ann Arbor:Institute for Social Research.

['] Griffiths (1954) found that in response to a question about what they could do that would please their parents most, the large majority of elementary school children responded that they could do their chores better.

Berger, P. L.
1964 The Human Shape of Work. New York:Macmillan.

Boocock, S. S.
1975 "The social context of childhood." Proceedings of the American Philosophical Society, 119 (December):419-429.

Campbell, E. O.
1969 "Adolescent socialization." Pp. 821-859 in Goslin (Ed.), Handbook of Socialization Theory and Research. New York:Russell Sage Foundation.

Goldstein, B., and J. Oldham
1979 Children and Work: A Study of Socialization. New Brunswick, New Jersey:Transaction Books.

Griffiths, W.
1954 "Behavior difficulties of children as perceived and judged by parents, teachers, and the children themselves." Unpublished manuscript, cited in Harris *et al.*, 1954.

Harris, D. B., K. E. Clark, A. M. Rose, and F. Valasek
1954 "The relationship of children's home duties to an attitude of responsibility." Child Development 25 (March):29-33.

Hedges, J. N., and J. K. Barnett
1972 "Working women and the division of household tasks." Monthly Labor Review 95 (January):9-14.

Hess, R., and G. Handel
1959 Family Worlds: A Psychosocial Approach to Family Life. Chicago:University of Chicago Press.

Ingoldsby, B. B., and G. R. Adams
1977 "Adolescence and work experiences: A brief note." Adolescence 12 (Fall):339-343.

Kohlberg, L.
1964 "Development of moral character and moral ideology." Pp. 383-431 in L. W. Hoffman and M. L. Hoffman (Eds.), Review of Child Development Research (Vol. 1). New York:Russell Sage Foundation.

McClelland, D. C.
1961 The Achieving Society. New York:The Free Press.

Menninger, W. C.
1964 "The meaning of work in western society." Pp. xiii-xvii in Borow (Ed.), Man in a World at Work. Boston:Houghton Mifflin Company.

Nye, F. I., and L. Hoffman
1974 Working Mothers. San Francisco:Jossey-Bass.

Piaget, J.
1948 The Moral Judgment of the Child. Glencoe, Illinois:The Free Press. (Originally published, 1932.)

Propper, A. M.
1972 "The relationship of maternal employment to adolescent roles, activities, and parental relationships." Journal of Marriage and the Family 34 (August):417-421.

Roy, P.
1961 "Maternal employment and adolescent roles: Rural-urban differences." Marriage and Family Living 23 (November):340-349.

Smith, C. P.
1969 "The origin and expression of achievement-related motives in children." Pp. 102-150 in C. P. Smith (Ed.), Achievement-Related Motives in Children. New York:Russell Sage Foundation.

Straus, M. A.
1962 "Work roles and financial responsibility in the socialization of farm, fringe, and town boys." Rural Sociology 27 (September):257-274.

Thrall, C. A.
1978 "Who does what? Role stereotyping, children's work, and continuity between generations in the household division of labor." Human Relations 31 (March):249-265.

Tilgher, A.
1930 Work: What It Has Meant to Man Through the Ages. New York:Harcourt, Brace. (Translation by Dorothy Fisher, printed 1977.)

PART VII

FAMILY ECONOMICS

A survey of almost 2000 families in 1976 found that 59 percent had fallen behind rising prices and almost as many, 52 percent, were hurting because of inflation. The families most affected by inflation and recession were the less privileged ones, those of low income, the retired, the semiskilled and unskilled, and members of minority groups, the Blacks and Spanish speaking. A variety of coping mechanisms were identified, ranging from income-raising strategies such as taking second jobs, having additional family members go to work, and working more overtime, to lowering consumption, greater self-reliance, bargain hunting, and sharing with others. Lowering consumption was almost the universal response to inflation as families in all walks of life reported cutting back on food, clothing, and entertainment expenditures. About one third of the respondents reported that financial pressures from inflation and recession were causing problems for their marriages, and more than one fourth said that financial pressures had damaged their mental health. The pressures of inflation and recession generated considerable hostility toward government and politicians, who were blamed for the economic ills. Confidence in government was virtually nonexistent among those hard hit by inflation and recession.

32

MAKING ENDS MEET

How Families Cope With Inflation and Recession

David Caplovitz

David Caplovitz received his Ph.D. in sociology at Columbia University in 1961. He has taught sociology at the University of Chicago (1962–64), Columbia University (1964–70), Hunter College (1971–73), and the Graduate School of the City University of New York from 1973 to the present, where he is a full professor of sociology. Through the years he has directed numerous research projects that have led to a number of books including The Poor Pay More, Reports on Happiness, The Merchants of Harlem: Small Business in a Black Community, Consumers in Trouble: A Study of Debtors in Default, *and* Making Ends Meet: How Families Cope with Inflation and Recession.

NOTE: This article is an extract from David Caplovitz, *Making Ends Meet: How Families Cope with Inflation and Recession* (Beverly Hills, CA: Sage Publications, 1979).

From David Caplovitz, "Making Ends Meet: How Families Cope With Inflation and Recession," *The Annals of the American Academy of Political and Social Science*, 1981, 456, pp. 88-98.

I HAVE been asked to write this article because a few years ago a book of mine was published, *Making Ends Meet: How Families Cope with Inflation and Recession*. That book in turn was based on a study I did of almost 2000 families back in 1976. The idea for that study developed in 1974 when, for the first time in modern history, our economy was being wracked by the twin evils of inflation and recession. Until then economic theory held that inflation and recession were opposite phenomena that could occur sequentially, but never simultaneously. This bizarre state of affairs has now been with us for seven years and has given rise to a new word, stagflation, to connote rampant inflation at a time of high unemployment.

My interest in the problem of inflation was aroused by an article I read in the *Wall Street Journal* about the unemployed. I had naively assumed that the unemployed were people who had lost their jobs, but from the *Wall Street Journal* article I learned that a substantial number of the unemployed were people looking for their first job. It suddenly dawned upon me that rampant inflation could be causing unemployment by forcing new breadwinners into the labor force in efforts to make ends meet. From this insight grew the idea of studying the impact of inflation and recession on American families, and a grant from the National Institute on Mental Health made the research possible.

A review of the sociological literature revealed that sociologists have virtually ignored the phenomenon of inflation. I was able to find only one dissertation in 1962 that dealt with this topic and that was a study of the role of inflation in the demands of members of the steel work-

ers union.[1] In contrast, the Great Depression of the thirties spawned a large literature dealing with the consequences of unemployment.[2]

The primary source of data in my study was a survey of almost 2000 families in four cities: New York, Detroit, Atlanta, and San Francisco. The cities were selected to represent different regions of the country, and within each city four groups were sampled: the poor and the retired, the two groups commonly believed to be the hardest hit by inflation, and working-class and middle-class families. In addition to the survey, we conducted in-depth interviews with some 90 heads of households in the New York metropolitan region. The book that emerged from this research is a

1. Sam Sieber, *Union Members, the Public and Inflation* (unpublished diss., Columbia University, 1962).
2. Among the classics on unemployment are the following: Maria Jahoda, Paul F Lazarsfeld, and Hans Zeisel, *The Unemployed of Marienthal* (Allensback und Bonn: Verlag Fur Demoskopie, 1960, reprinted by Aldine Press, Chicago, 1974); Mirra Komarovsky, *The Unemployed Man and his Family* (New York: Dryden Press, 1940); W. Wight Bakke, *The Unemployed Worker: A Study of the Task of Making a Living without a Job*, (New Haven, CT: Yale University Press, 1940); and Robert Cooley Angell, *The Family Encounters the Depression*, (New York, Charles Scribner's Sons, 1936). The most ambitious project to assess the impact of the depression on American society was carried out in 1936 and 1937 by the Social Science Research Council (SSRC). The SSRC sponsored a series of 13 studies assessing the impact of the depression on various facets of American society and institutions. The title for the overall series was *Studies in the Social Aspects of the Depression* and each volume was entitled *A Research Memorandum on——and the Depression*. The topics that filled the blank included crime, recreation, the family, consumption, minority groups, education, religion, health, and rural life.

blend of the statistical material from the survey and the qualitative data from the depth interviews.

THE TYPES OF FAMILIES AFFECTED BY INFLATION

The research had two major objectives: first, to describe the types of families that were hard hit by inflation and recession; and second, to study the responses of families to these economic ills, how they were coping and not coping with these problems.

To measure the impact of inflation, we drew a distinction between what we called objective and subjective inflation crunch. By objective inflation crunch we meant the degree to which family income had fallen behind rising prices. By subjective inflation crunch, we meant the degree to which families were hurting because of rising prices.[3] Objective inflation crunch was measured by a question that asked families to compare their current financial situation with what it had been a few years earlier. The families could respond by saying they were actually better off financially than a few years earlier, that their financial situation had remained pretty much the same as it had been, that they were a little worse off financially, or that they were now much worse off financially than in the past.

3. The word "objective" is used loosely here, for it is based on information provided by the respondents about their financial situation, namely, whether their income kept up with inflation. A truly objective measure would be one based on some external source like income tax returns. We use the term to describe what the respondents' tell us is a fact, how their income compares with what it was two years previously. In contrast, what we call subjective crunch refers to feelings, complaints and accounts of suffering, that is, to an internal state of affairs.

Were families asked such a question in noninflationary times, undoubtedly a substantial majority would have said they were better off financially, for the trend since World War II has been a steady rise in family income. But during the period of rampant inflation in which we conducted our survey, only 16 percent said they were better off now, and 25 percent said they had stayed even with rising prices, for a total of 41 percent who were untouched by inflation. In contrast, 37 percent said they were a little worse off than previously, and 22 percent said they were a lot worse off, for a total of 59 percent whose income had fallen behind rising prices.

Having found out how many families were affected by inflation, our next task was to learn what types of families were falling behind rising prices, that is, were worse off now financially than previously. This analysis showed that inflation was primarily a problem of the less privileged groups in society, the poor, the retired, the semiskilled and unskilled workers, and those of low education and members of minority groups, the blacks and Spanish speaking. For example, of families with incomes under $7000, 81 percent were worse off financially, compared with 69 percent in the $7000 to $13,000 range, 57 percent of those earning between $13,000 and $20,000, and only 38 percent of those earning over $20,000.

Those living on fixed income, the retired, were almost as hard hit as the poor. Whereas 81 percent of the poor were worse off financially, this was true of 66 percent of the retired, compared with 59 percent of blue-collar workers and 49 percent of white-collar workers.

In terms of race–ethnicity, we found that whereas 53 percent of the whites had fallen behind rising prices, this was true of 75 percent of the blacks and 83 percent of the Spanish speaking. Further analysis disclosed that income largely explained the differential impact of inflation on the various occupational and educational groups. Once income was taken into account, the occupational and educational differences largely disappeared. But this was not true for race–ethnicity. On every income level, the blacks and Spanish speaking had more difficulty than whites in keeping up with rising prices.

These findings were corroborated by the findings on the impact of the recession. Recession impact was measured in a variety of ways. In addition to unemployment, we counted, as part of recession impact, having to work harder because other people had been laid off, worry over losing one's job, and being unable to work as much overtime as previously. The impact of the recession was even more sharply limited to the have-nots, the underprivileged, than was that of inflation. For example, unemployment turns out to be almost exclusively a problem of the poor and those in the lower reaches of the occupational structure. Thus hardly any white-collar workers lost their jobs during the recession, whereas a substantial minority of the poor did lose their jobs.

Using a more general measure of recession impact than unemployment alone, we find the impact to increase enormously as income falls. Among those earning over $20,000, only 8 percent were hard hit by the recession, a figure that climbs to 54 percent of those earning under $7000. The same pattern holds for ethnicity. Only 17 percent of the whites scored high on the recession impact measure, compared with 38 percent of the

blacks and 52 percent of the Spanish speaking.

What these findings indicate is that inflation and recession exacerbate the class cleavages found in society. When the economy runs amok, the class divisions suddenly become more visible and the myth of America as one big happy homogeneous family is shattered. Quite apart from all the other benefits of wealth, these findings show that it largely immunizes the people who have it from the hazards of inflation and recession.

In addition to measuring the extent to which family income fell behind rising prices, what we called objective inflation crunch, we also measured the degree to which families were hurting because of inflation, what we called subjective inflation crunch. The respondents were asked an array of questions that tapped this dimension: for example, whether inflation was making them depressed, whether they felt their money was becoming worthless, whether they had had to dip into their savings, whether they felt everything was turning into a hardship, whether they had had to stop buying things they needed, and so forth. In all, nine such questions were used to measure subjective inflation crunch.

The findings for subjective inflation were much like those for objective crunch and recession impact. The poor, those of low education, those with semiskilled and unskilled jobs, and the blacks and Spanish speaking were much more likely to be hurting from inflation than the well-to-do, the well educated, the professionals and business executives, and the whites.

There was, however, one significant exception to the similarities in the findings for objective and subjective inflation crunch. As I have noted, the retired were almost as likely as the poor to have their incomes fall behind rising prices. But the retired were not nearly as likely as the poor to be suffering from inflation. Thus 84 percent of the poor were suffering from inflation, 60 percent of the blue-collar sample, but only 45 percent of the retired. In this respect, the retired were like the white-collar sample, which had 37 percent suffering from inflation.

Although it is not immediately clear why the retired should be experiencing more inflation but suffering less from it—66 percent of them had their income fall behind rising prices, but only 45 percent of them were hurting from inflation— I suggest in my book that one reason for this is that the retired are much less active as consumers than those still in the labor force. They have many fewer consumer needs, such as automobiles and new appliances, than families in the earlier stages of the life cycle.

When the results for objective inflation crunch are compared with those for subjective crunch, an interesting pattern emerges. The more privileged groups, those of higher income and higher occupational status and whites, are more likely to report that their income has failed to keep up with rising prices than they are likely to report that they are suffering from inflation. In short, the two dimensions of objective and subjective inflation crunch are highly related to each other, but there are a number of exceptions, people who are high on one dimension and low on the other. Those whose incomes fell behind rising prices but were not suffering from it, I call the stoics, and conversely those who reported suffering from inflation, even though their incomes kept up with prices, I call the complainers. As I have

noted, the more privileged groups in terms of occupation, income, education, and ethnicity were likely to be stoics, that is to have their incomes fall behind without their suffering from it. This strongly suggests that the more privileged groups have resources that enable them to ride out the storm of inflation.

The chief economist in the Ford administration, Alan Greenspan, has identified what one of these resources is: homeownership. It turns out that a substantial majority of American families, particularly the more privileged ones, own their own home and, as we all know, homes have appreciated enormously in value under inflationary pressures. Greenspan had argued that many families have capitalized on the rising value of their homes by obtaining new mortgages and using the proceeds to tide them over the hard times. To test this theory, we devoted an entire chapter of our book to the role of homeownership in mitigating the pain of inflation. We found that the more privileged groups were more likely to own their home and that homeowners in every group were more likely than nonowners to avoid the stresses and strains of inflation. Homeownership, which is so widespread in America, may well be the chief reason why people are more equanimical in the face of the economic calamities of today than during the Great Depression of the thirties. Thus in spite of high unemployment and rampant inflation, we have had no marches on Washington and no rush to radical political parties.

The quantitative data generated by the survey painted a picture of the underprivileged being hard hit by inflation and recession while the more privileged groups were able to escape these twin evils. The qualitative data generated by approximately 90 depth interviews provide more subtlety to this picture of how the haves differ from the have-nots with regard to inflation. A number of welfare mothers were interviewed in depth, and their stories dramatize the hardships inflation imposes on the poor. These mothers pointed out that even in relatively good times they had to tighten their belts and scrimp on food and clothing in order to get by. Inflation has forced them to tighten their belts even further. Some women told us that they have cut down on the number of meals in their families from three to two or one and half. And they limit their shopping for clothes to thrift shops. Inflation forces upon the family in poverty a host of undesirable choices, such as which child to buy clothes for, since there is not enough money to buy clothes for more than one child, and which teenaged child should go to work and which one should be allowed to stay in school. These hard choices involving denial to family members are the burden of the poor; the middle class never has to face such choices. For the poor, inflation means a struggle for survival in the present. The poor cannot afford the luxury of thinking ahead or planning for the future; they must struggle to survive in the present.

The depth interviews with middle-class people showed a sharply different picture. In keeping with the quantitative data, most of the middle-class people interviewed had little difficulty keeping up with rising prices. Except for some economizing in their food budgets—they did not eat as much steak and lobster, they told us—they had no difficulty maintaining their standard of living. Where the middle class was affected by inflation was not in their present day-to-day lives, but rather

in their plans for the future. Middle-class people told us they could not save as much money as they used to. This in turn meant that their plans for the future were being undermined. If they did not already own their own home, they found that they had to postpone purchasing a house until their income improved substantially. Instead of buying a Cadillac, the middle-income family found it had to buy a less expensive car. In short, inflation has had a major impact on the aspirations of middle-class families. Their dreams of upward social mobility symbolized by a new car, a house, and a swimming pool have been shot down by inflation. As a result, many in the middle class are also angry about inflation, even though they are not suffering in the ways that the poor are suffering.

COPING STRATEGIES

Having described some of the answers to the first question we raised in our research, namely, who is being hurt by inflation, I shall now turn to the second question that guided our work, How have families tried to cope with inflation and recession, and what has been the impact of these calamitous events on their lives?

In examining the role of homeownership in mitigating the pains of inflation, I have suggested one coping mechanism, what might be called cashing in on assets. Another chapter of the report deals with other coping mechanisms. Underlying these mechanisms is an input–output model much like that of energy utilization. Inflation, and for that matter recession, represent a sudden disparity in the family's income–expenditure pattern. Families that were accustomed to a given standard of living suddenly find that they are unable to maintain that standard of living on their current income.

One solution to this problem would be to raise income, equivalent to turning up the power in some energy system. In our research we asked about several income-raising strategies that the family might have employed. For example, a second member of the family, such as the wife, might have entered the labor force. Or the chief wage earner might have taken a second job or worked more overtime. As important as raising income is for families, only a minority were able to find a way of earning more money. In 16 percent of the families, a second member did go to work, and only 60 of the more than 1600 chief wage earners in the sample held a second job, a mere 4 percent of the sample. Working more overtime is a more popular strategy, as 26 percent of the workers told us that they did. In all, 38 percent of the families employed at least one of these income-raising strategies.

Still another strategy for closing the gap between income and standard of living would be to curtail expenditures, that is, to lower the standard of living. Curtailing expenditures was by far the most popular coping strategy. Some 50 percent of the respondents told us that they had economized on their food expenditures, and almost as many cut back on entertainment, eating out, and buying of clothes. One third of the families told us that they had cut back on vacations, and most of the poor told us they never had vacations to cut back. Some families, 15 percent of the total sample, told us they were even cutting back on medical and dental care. In such a fashion, even physical health can suffer from the ravages of inflation.

Finally, the gap between income and expenditures might be narrowed by increasing efficiency, that is, by getting more return for a given level of income. We managed to identify and study three ways of increasing efficiency. The first, what we called "bargain hunting," refers to shopping around, making use of coupons, and taking advantage of sales. The second, "greater self reliance," refers to doing for oneself what formerly was done by others—for example, repairing one's own car, making one's own clothes, painting one's house, and so forth. The third way of increasing efficiency is to share with others, whether this be in the form of food co-ops, car pools, exchanging clothing, or lending each other money.

Needless to say, the more hard hit the family was by inflation and recession, the more likely was it to employ these various coping strategies. And on any given level of inflation crunch or recession impact, the underprivileged were more likely to engage in these various coping strategies than the more privileged groups. The one exception to this rule occurred on the strategy of raising income.

It turns out that, unlike curtailing consumption, or shopping around, or sharing, or becoming more self-reliant, income raising is not merely a matter of choice, of making the effort. The poor have much less opportunity to raise their income than do the more privileged groups. They have trouble enough finding one job, much less two, and they may be unable to work overtime even though they want to. And the housewife in the poor family may be unable to find work. Thus when it comes to raising income, the poor did much less well those of higher income. But in every other respect, the poor were more likely than the well-to-do to employ the coping strategy.

The development of self-reliance under inflationary pressures is symbolic of the silver lining in the cloud of inflation. Many people surprised themselves by discovering they had hidden talents for fixing things and making repairs. The poor were especially likely to become more self-reliant. Another favorite coping strategy for the poor is bargain hunting, as they were much more likely to shop around.

Although we asked about second jobs in the survey, we did not do a good job of tapping underground sources of income, that is, working off the books. We had no questions that dealt directly with this. And yet the approximately 90 depth interviews that we conducted suggested that participation in the underground economy might well be one of the major strategies for coping with inflation. A working-class man told us he spent his weekends helping his father-in-law in his moving business. Another man washed automobiles on his weekends, and a third installed carpets for a friend who had such a business. One woman helped her friend in a jewelry business, and another told us that she did sewing for another friend. One woman told us that she did bookkeeping for her boyfriend, who had his own illegal bookmaking—betting—business. One man we interviewed, a bachelor in his late twenties who had an administrative job with a hospital, told us that he had become a fence in order to make extra money. He told us that he bought stolen merchandise and then sold it through a network of friends and acquaintances. A welfare mother told us that she was able to buy, on a regular basis, stolen meat on the street. I suspect that the under-

ground economy is playing an important role in these inflationary times, and although it would be hard to do, research on the underground economy should prove rewarding.

SOME CONSEQUENCES OF INFLATION

A final concern of the research was to see how inflation and recession had affected the lives of people. By impact on lives I mean the extent to which these economic calamities affected people's mental health, marriages, and basic value orientations and attitudes.

As our client was the National Institute on Mental Health, we were quite eager to explore whatever connection might exist between economic stress and mental health. The psychologist Harvey Brenner has done extensive research documenting a strong connection between the state of the economy and various measures of mental health. He has shown that suicide rates, admissions to mental hospitals, and serious illnesses increase sharply in times of high unemployment.[4] We developed two measures of mental health. One was a general measure of psychological well-being based on the balance of positive and negative feelings, a measure first developed by a University of Chicago psychologist, Norman Bradburn. The second measure inquired more directly about the impact of financial pressures on mental health. The respondents were asked, for example, whether they were worrying a lot about making ends meet, whether financial pressures had caused them

4. See Harvey M. Brenner, *Mental Illness and the Economy* (Cambridge, MA: Harvard University Press, 1973); and idem, "Unemployment, Economic Growth and Mortality," *Lancet*, 24 March 1979.

to become depressed, and whether financial pressures had made them angry. Not surprisingly, the greater the impact of inflation and recession on people, the more likely was their mental health to suffer both in terms of the general measure of psychological well-being and the more specific measure of stress induced by financial pressures. For example, of those who claimed that their financial situation had actually improved, only 4 percent experienced stress from financial pressures, compared with 25 percent who said their financial situation was a little worse and fully 46 percent of those who said their situation was much worse. For the balance of feeling index, the percentages of negative feelings ranged from 10 to 53 percent as inflationary pressures increased.

The types of people who suffered most from inflation were also the types most likely to have their mental health impaired. Thus the poor, the semiskilled and unskilled workers, the poorly educated, and the blacks and Spanish speaking experienced more mental stress than their more privileged counterparts. In sum, our study has documented what many have suspected, that economic stress readily translates into mental stress.

In addition to exploring mental health, we wanted to examine the impact of economic stress on the respondents' marriages. Two questions tapped a positive impact and two questions a negative impact. On the positive side, the respondents were asked whether financial pressures had drawn them closer to their spouse and whether pressures had led the spouses to understand each other better. On the negative side, the respondents were asked whether financial pressures had con-

tributed to tensions in their marriage and whether there were more quarrels over money. On the basis of these measures, we found that 40 percent of the sample reported no change in their marriages as a result of economic pressures; some 28 percent reported that financial pressures had made their marriages better; 19 percent gave a mixed response, that is, they reported both positive and negative consequences of financial pressures for their marriage; and 14 percent reported only negative consequences. All told, 33 percent, that is, one third of the sample, reported at least some negative consequences for their marriage stemming from economic pressure. Needless to say, the greater the impact of inflation and recession on the family, the more likely was there to be marital strain, and the families that suffered most from inflation— the poor, those toward the bottom of the occupational hierarchy, and the blacks and Spanish speaking—were most likely to have marital strain. In sum, economic stress not only causes mental stress, but is also contributes to marital instability.

Finally, we explored the impact of inflation and recession on some basic value orientations, notably, commitment to free enterprise and the capitalistic system, level of aspirations in light of inflation and recession, and confidence in the federal government. In spite of the economic calamities that were wracking the country in the mid-seventies, commitment to free enterprise and capitalism was quite strong. A substantial majority said our free enterprise system is the best economic system, and a similar majority rejected the idea that socialism is a better system; finally, 57 percent of the respondents rejected the socialistic idea that government should guarantee a job for everyone who wants to work. When these items are combined into an index, we find that 62 percent of the sample endorsed two or three of these free enterprise ideas, 22 percent endorsed at least one of these ideas, and only 16 percent rejected all three. Needless to say, the victims of inflation and recession were most likely to question the value of free enterprise, and the underprivileged were much more critical of free enterprise than the privileged, whatever the impact of inflation.

To measure level of aspirations, the respondents were asked whether they had decided to lower their standard of living in order to make ends meet, whether they had lost interest in owning expensive things, and whether they had lost confidence in the American dream of success. In every instance, only a minority, about one third, gave the response suggesting a lowering of aspirations. Although they had been buffeted by the economy, a substantial majority, 65 percent, still had confidence in the American dream. But perhaps it is somewhat disturbing that 35 percent had indeed lost confidence in the American dream. When combined into an index of lowering aspirations, we find that those who were hard hit by inflation and recession were most likely to lower their aspirations and those who were untouched by inflation retained their high level of aspirations. Clearly, lowering aspirations is one mode of adjustment to inflation and recession.

The last attitude area explored had to do with confidence in the institutions of the federal government, Congress, the presidency and the Supreme Court. In the post-Watergate era in which these interviews were conducted with the sharp downturn in the economy, most people told us that they had lost confidence in the federal government. This response was particularly typical of those who suffered the most from inflation and recession. The people interviewed in the survey and in the depth interviews were given the opportunity to explain who they blamed most for the economic difficulties. By far the most popular villain was government and politicians. The research we conducted uncovered a wide reservoir of hostility toward government and politicians. The average citizen blames his government and the politicians who man it for his economic ills. The poor and well-to-do alike did not hesitate to express their bitterness over politicians and particular governmental policies such as foreign aid and defense spending and welfare programs. Reading through the data we collected, I could not escape the feeling that people are ready to explode unless the economic ills are somehow corrected. The poor and the downtrodden are close to exhaustion in their efforts to get through each day. And the more comfortable middle classes are bubbling with anger as they discover that they cannot save for a better day and that their aspirations for making it big are coming to naught.

The time is getting ripe for fundamental changes in our society, and the new administration seems determined to make those changes. The Great Society is being dismantled, and even the New Deal is being threatened. And yet at the same time that important social programs such as food stamps, The Comprehensive Training and Employment Act (CETA), and legal services for the poor are being sharply curtailed and even abolished, the defense budget is growing by leaps and bounds. It is now approaching $200 billion a year, and by the mid-eighties it will reach $300 billion a year. The Reagan administration is so nickle and diming it that it wants to abolish the Consumer Product Safety Commission (CPSC) that has a paltry budget of $39 million a year. The CPSC is responsible for saving thousands of lives a year by its regulations banning dangerous products. At the same time the administration wants to build the B-1 bomber, which is estimated to cost $180 million. Not only inflation, but a myriad of other problems, such as unemployment, poverty, reindustrialization, and national health insurance, could be solved if only we had the resolve to reduce the defense budget instead of expanding it.

This paper reports on the development of measures of family material well-being, based on observations of ownership and consumption behavior in a sample of 1,169 New Zealand families. Factor analysis of 49 indicator measures revealed that the material well-being of the families could be measured along two distinct yet correlated dimensions: the level of family ownership and the amount of economizing behavior the family was required to undertake. Both dimensions were of moderate to good reliability and showed systematic correlations with a series of concurrent and predictive validity measures. The advantages of direct measures of family material well-being over the traditional alternatives of income, expenditure, or family budget information are discussed.

33

THE MEASUREMENT OF FAMILY MATERIAL WELL-BEING*

*D. M. Fergusson,** L. J. Horwood,** and A. L. Beautrais***

Research into family living standards has been hampered by the fact that there is no generally agreed upon method of measuring this concept. Broadly speaking, three approaches have been used to measure variations in levels of family material well-being (Harding, 1978):

1. Income-based methods: These methods assume that a family's level of material well-being can be measured by the level of income it receives. Attempts to produce income-related indices of material well-being have ranged from relatively simple measures, based on family income adjusted for the effects of family size and other variables, to more complicated estimation procedures, derived from the life-cycle hypothesis of saving developed by Duesenberry (1949), Friedman (1957), and Ando and Modigliani (1963). (See also Moon, 1977; Morgan et al., 1974; Garfinkel and Haveman, 1977.)

2. Expenditure-based methods: These methods assume that a family's level of material well-being may be measured by its level of expenditure. The approach was first developed by the 19th-century German statistician Ernst Engels, who observed that as family income rose, expenditure on food increased, but the proportion of income spent on food declined. On the basis of this observation, sometimes called Engel's Law (Wynn, 1970), Engels concluded that proportionate expenditure on food and other necessities was a good measure of family living standards. This approach has been employed by many studies (e.g., Wynn, 1970) as a means of estimating poverty lines for various countries.

3. Budget-based methods: These methods were first developed by Rowntree (1899) in his study of the poor in the city of York at the turn of the century. The method measures family living standards by comparing family income with the costs of some idealized mix of goods and services (the basket of goods) which are deemed to be necessary for the family's continued welfare.

All three measurement approaches, and their many variants, share a common problem in that it is assumed that measures of family *economic* well-being, based on actual or imputed family income or expenditure, are good measures of family *material* well-being.

*This research was funded by grants from the Medical Research Council of New Zealand and the National Children's Health Research Foundation.

**Christchurch Child Development Study, Department of Paediatrics, Christchurch Clinical School of Medicine, Christchurch Hospital, Christchurch, New Zealand.

From D. M. Fergusson, L. J. Horwood, and A. L. Beautrais, "The Measurement of Family Material Well-Being," *Journal of Marriage and the Family*, 1981, 43, pp. 715-725. Reprinted by permission of the publisher and authors.

It is clear, however, that, theoretically, the two concepts are quite distinct: Family economic well-being describes the level of financial input received by the family and the transactions are that (or may be) performed on this input; family material well-being refers (or should refer) to the mix of goods, commodities, and services to which family members *actually* have access. Since it is unlikely that there will be a one-to-one relationship between family economic well-being and family material well-being, it follows that measures of family economic well-being will be imperfect indicators of family material well-being. What seems to be needed to measure family material well-being is some index or measure based directly on family ownership and consumption patterns, rather than on the economic inputs and processes which contribute to these patterns.

Jensen (1978) has suggested that family material well-being may be thought of as a latent dimension which is reflected in a series of observable indicator variables relating to family ownership and consumption behavior. He illustrated this idea by developing scenarios of three families: the Frugals, the Modests, and the Affluents. The Frugals, as their name implies, have little and consume little; the Modests fare somewhat better, but they are completely overshadowed by their neghbors, the Affluents, who appear to live in the lap of luxury. Jensen suggested that these three families may be thought of as lying on three different points on some underlying dimension (or dimensions) of family material well-being, with the Frugals having a poor standard of material well-being, the Modests having an average standard, and the Affluents having a high standard of material well-being.

Given this intuitive background, it would seem that the appropriate measurement model for assessing family material well-being is one in which a series of observable indicators of family ownership and consumption behavior are combined to recover estimates of the underlying but nonobservable dimension(s) of family material well-being.

This paper describes the results of a research project into the living standards of a sample of New Zealand families with 1-year-old children. The aim of the research was to examine the extent to which it was possible to devise valid and interpretable measures of family material well-being based on direct measures of family ownership and consumption behavior.

METHOD

The data were collected during the third stage of the Christchurch Child Development Study. In this study, a birth cohort of all children born in maternity units in the Christchurch urban region has been studied at birth, four months, and one year. The initial sample comprised 1,262 infants born to 1,248 mothers; at one year, 1,180 children and 1,169 families remained in the research. These numbers represented 97 percent of the sample who were alive and resident in New Zealand and 94 percent of the original cohort.

At each point of study, mothers were given an hour-long structured interview which dealt with various aspects of the child's health, well-being, and family situation (Fergusson, Horwood, Wright, and Stewart, 1978; Fergusson, Horwood, Shannon, and Taylor, 1978; O'Donnell et al., 1978). At one year, considerable attention was paid to the family's general level of economic and material well-being. The following measures were obtained:

1. Indicators of family material well-being: A total of 49 indicator measures of variations in family material well-being were collected. These measures fell into two classes:
   a. Family ownership: Home, car, television, refrigerator, telephone, radio, and so on.
   b. Family economizing behavior: Respondents were asked whether they had been forced to cut down or reduce their expenditures in the last year in a number of areas of consumption. These economies ranged from the mild (reducing expenditure on holidays) to the stringent (postponing visits to the doctor, buying secondhand shoes).

Responses to these items were probed thoroughly to ensure that reports were related to economies made because of actual or perceived financial reasons.

The 49 items and the conventions used to score these items are shown in the appendix.

Selection of the 49 items was determined by two major considerations. First, a factor analytic study conducted by the New Zealand Department of Social Welfare (1975), using data from a sample of subjects aged 65 years and over, suggested that family living standards varied along two correlated dimensions: the level of family ownership and the level of family economizing behavior. Many of the discriminating items from this previous study were incorporated, sometimes in modified form, in the list of items shown in the appendix. A second consideration was that, since the data were collected as part of a large longitudinal study of child health and welfare, the amount of interviewing time that could be devoted to collecting information on family material well-being was limited to approximately 15 minutes. Pilot testing, at four months, revealed that, providing the items were administered in a precoded checklist form, the required information could be collected within 15 minutes.

2. Estimated family gross income: Respondents were asked to provide estimates of both their own and their husbands' gross weekly income. Income was measured by a series of 31 income brackets ranging from $0 to $300 and over, per week. Estimated family income was the sum of the median incomes for both husband and wife. In cases where the wife was unwilling or unable to provide family income estimates, the husband was contacted and asked to provide an estimate. For families receiving nontaxable social welfare benefits, an estimate of the corresponding gross income value was obtained by weighting the welfare payment by a coefficient of 1.2. The value of 1.2 was somewhat arbitrary, but sensitivity analysis revealed that the properties of the data were virtually unaffected by weighting benefit levels over a plausible range of values in the region of 1. to 1.5.

   It was not possible to provide direct validation of income estimates, but measures of the reliability of the estimates were obtained by correlating the estimate given at four months with the estimate provided at one year. Overall, the correlation between the two estimates was .77.

3. Family assets: Respondents were asked to estimate the total value of their savings and investments in such places as savings banks, life insurance, stocks and shares, property and real estate, and so on. The asset estimate excluded the value of the respondent's present housing accommodation. Asset estimates were coded into 34 brackets ranging from $0 to $20,000. The test/retest reliability for asset estimates between four months and one year was .73.

4. Family weekly expenditure: Respondents were asked to provide estimates of the family's weekly expenditure on food and household products, electricity, rental, mortgage or taxes, medical care, and running a car. These estimates were likely to be inexact, since they were based on respondent's recall, supplemented by existing receipts, rather than on an exact diary record. To measure variability in expenditure levels, an approximate index of the proportion of family income spent on necessities was obtained by dividing total estimated expenditure by estimated gross weekly income.

5. Socioeconomic status of principal earner: This measure was based on the Elley and Irving (1976) scale of occupational status for New Zealand. This scale classifies occupations into six groups, based on median income and education values. The scale is based on male occupation only. However, 89 of the families were single-parent families in which the mother received social welfare benefits. These families were classified as falling on the lowest step of the Elley and Irving scale in view of their low income levels.

6. Ethnic status of principal earner: This measure was classified as Pakeha (European) versus Maori, Pacific Island, or Other. A two-category division of ethnic status was necessary, as relatively few of the sample fell into the categories of Maori, Pacific Islander, or Other.

7. Educational level of principal earner: This measure was classified as secondary school only (no formal educational qualifications); secondary school qualifications (i.e., New Zealand School Certificate, University Entrance); or tertiary qualifications (including university degree, technical qualifications). (Broadly speaking, the New Zealand education system has three levels: primary education, 5-12 years; secondary education, 13-15 years (minimum); and tertiary education, provided by universities and technical institutes, 16 years and over.)

8. Number of parents: One-parent family versus two-parent family.

9. Interviewer and respondent ratings of family living standards: To provide concurrent validation of the derived scale measures, a series of living standard ratings was obtained from the respondent and interviewer. These measures included: the respondent's assessment of the adequacy of family income to meet everyday living costs, made on a 4-point scale from "income very inadequate" to "income more than adequate"; an interviewer rating of the degree of apparent financial hardship the family was facing, made on a 4-point scale ranging from "family obviously in difficulty" to "family obviously has no difficulty"; and an interviewer rating of the overall living standards of the family made on a 5-point scale ranging from "very poor" to "very good."

Method of Analysis

Identification of scale dimensions. The measurement model assumed that the total variance of the standard of living indicators could be partitioned into two additive components: one component reflecting the effects of the common standard of living dimensions and another component, unique to each item, which reflected the effects of such variables as individual preferences, measurement error, and so on. To derive estimates of the common factors, the matrix of correlations of the 49 items was subjected to Principal Factors Analysis (Harman, 1976) with both oblique (Oblimin) and orthogonal (Varimax) rotations.

The criteria for factor extraction were based on Cattell's (1966) scree test, with the upper limit boundary of the number of factors set by Guttman-Kaiser criterion of *eigenvalues* greater than unity.

Derivation of scale scores. Scale scores for the extracted factors were obtained by standard regression methods by weighting each item (in standard score form) by the least squares estimate of the factor score coefficient. Estimates of the fit of the factor scores to the true but nonobserved factors were obtained by standard factor analytic solutions (Harman, 1976). Approximations to the factor scores were also constructed by summing the raw scores of items loading on each factor.

Reliability. The reliability of the scale scores was estimated using coefficient *alpha* (Cronbach, 1951).

Scale validity. Validity was assessed using three methods:

1. Face validity: Impressions of face validity were obtained by deriving the item/score distributions for each factor and all relevant items to show the way in which scale scores varied with the mix of family ownership and consumption behaviors.
2. Concurrent validity was assessed by generating the matrix of product moment correlations between the derived factor scores and interviewer and respondent ratings of family living standards.
3. Predictive validity was assessed by correlating the factor scores with a series of measures generally assumed to be indicative of family living standards: family income, assets, expenditure, socioeconomic status, ethnic status, education, and number of parent figures. To test for curvilinearity, all bivariate correlations were compared with nonmetric correlation ratio: *eta*. This comparison showed a significant nonlinear relationship between family assets and scale scores. To take account of this, asset values were transformed to logarithmic units.

Social and Demographic Characteristics of the Sample

To provide some indication of the general characteristics of the sample, Table 1 shows descriptive statistics on the age and ethnic status of the family's principal earner; family size and composition; family socioeconomic status and income levels. The results show that the sample was comparatively young (the median age of principal earner was 29 years); predominantly Caucasian; family sizes were relatively small and children mainly in the preschool age group.

While detailed population figures are not available for comparison, the general impression conveyed by the results was that the families were likely to be fairly typical of New Zealand families at an early stage of family life cycle who have one or more preschool children.

RESULTS

Table 2 shows the factor loading and factor pattern matrices for the Varimax and Oblimin rotations. The following results are evident from the table:

TABLE 1. SOCIAL AND DEMOGRAPHIC CHARACTERISTICS OF THE SAMPLE

Measure	N	Percentage of Sample	Measure	N	Percentage of Sample
Age of Principal Earner			Family Type		
25 or under	299	25.6	Single-parent family	89	7.6
26-30	440	37.6	Two-parent family	1,080	92.4
31-35	271	23.2			
36 or over	159	13.6			
Ethnic Status of Principal Earner			Number of Children in Family		
Pakeha (European)	1,052	90.0	1	471	40.3
Maori, Pacific Islander, Other	117	10.0	2	426	36.4
			3 or more	272	23.3
			(mean age of children = 3.0 years)		
Socioeconomic Status of Family[a]			Gross Family Income (per annum)		
Levels 1, 2 (professional, executive)	242	20.7	$0 - 6,500	231	19.8
			$6,501 - 8,000	230	19.7
Levels 3,4 (clerical, technical, skilled)	574	49.1	$8,001 - 9,500	186	15.9
			$9,501 - 11,500	183	15.7
Levels 5,6 (semiskilled, unskilled)	353	30.2	$11,501 and over	218	18.6
			Data not available	121	10.4

[a]Based on Elley and Irving (1976) scale of socioeconomic status for New Zealand.

1. The common factor variance of the items is explained by two factors which account for 18.4 percent and 9.3 percent of the total item variance, respectively. The appropriateness of a two-factor solution may be judged from the plot of *eigenvalues* given in Figure 1.
2. The first rotated factor for both solutions shows a consistent pattern of loadings on all items relating to economizing behavior within the family and as a consequence may be described as "economizing."
3. The second rotated factor has consistent loading on all items relating to family ownership and as a consequence may be labelled as "ownership."
4. The Oblimin solution shows that both factors are moderately correlated ($r = -.25$).

Factor scores were estimated by weighting the items in standard score form by the least squares estimates of the factor score coeffi-

cients. The correlation between the estimated factor score and the true but nonobserved factor was in excess of .99 for both factors, suggesting that despite the relatively small amount of total item variance explained by the factors, the items provided good estimates of the common factors.

To examine the extent to which the factor score estimates could be approximated by an unweighted sum of the items, economizing and ownership scores were also estimated by summing the raw scores of items having loadings of greater than .3 on each factor. The resulting composites were very good approximations to the factor scores: The correlation between the factor score and the unweighted sum for the ownership dimension was .99; the

TABLE 2. FACTOR LOADING AND FACTOR PATTERN MATRICES[a]

Item	Orthogonal Rotation		Oblique Rotation	
	Factor 1	Factor 2	Factor 1	Factor 2*
Consumer Durables and Accommodation				
Color television		.347		.347
Automatic washing machine		.531		.538
Tumbler clothes drier		.495		.501
Separate deep freeze		.495		.498
Automatic stove		.547		.558
Wall-to-wall carpet		.400		.401
Central heating		.408		.421
Vacuum cleaner		.401		.409
Stereo		.367		.373
Telephone		.619		.623
Power mower		.375		.378
Family car		.522		.522
Second car		.488		.452
Home ownership		.655		.660
Rated standard of interior		.614		.610
Standard of surrounding housing		.381		.388
Economizing				
Reduced holidays	.532		.553	
Reduced car usage	.506		.523	
Reduced entertaining of friends	.593		.615	
Reduced eating at restaurants	.612		.644	
Reduced visiting hotel	.621		.628	
Reduced home heating	.537		.547	
Reduced hobby materials	.576		.588	
Reduced theatres, concerts, other entertainment	.633		.652	
Degree of difficulty saving	.509	−.351	.475	
Savings drawn on to meet expenses	.365		.358	
Postponed visits to doctor	.368		.343	
Postponed visits to dentist	.494		.483	
Postponed purchase of clothes	.578		.557	
Old clothes worn because could not afford replacements	.604	−.300	.578	
Secondhand clothes bought for family or self	.391	−.415	.345	−.376
Secondhand shoes bought for family or self	.314	−.352		−.322
Something sold to raise money	.359		.351	
Money borrowed to meet everyday living costs	.393	−.315	.360	
Reduced weekly shopping to save money	.580		.581	
Percentage of Variance	18.4	9.3	18.4	9.3

[a]For simplicity of presentation, factor loadings less than .3 have been omitted from the table. Variables which had loadings of less than .3 on both factors are omitted.
*Factor 1-Factor 2 correlation = −.25.

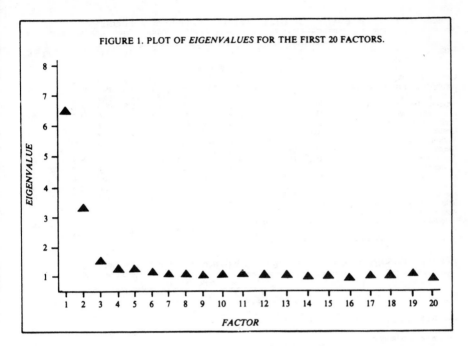

FIGURE 1. PLOT OF *EIGENVALUES* FOR THE FIRST 20 FACTORS.

correlation between the factor score and the unweighted sum for the economizing dimension was .95.

Tables 3 and 4 show the distributions of the items over each factor. In these tables, factor scores are grouped into 10 percent groups (deciles) and scored using the convention that a high score (or decile) implies a high standard of living. The degree of discrimination achieved by each item is measured by the point biserial correlation ($r_{pbis.}$) between the item and the factor score. Inspection of the tables suggests the following conclusions:

1. For the ownership dimension, the item endorsement frequencies show a clear monotonic tendency to increase with the factor scores. The impression of face validity conveyed by the table is reinforced by the fact that item/score distributions vary in systematic ways. Items relating to basic necessities (*e.g.*, vacuum cleaner) show a convex distribution which rises rapidly over the first few deciles and reaches an asymptote at around the fourth or fifth decile. Items relating to semiluxury durables (*e.g.*, color television, stereo, automatic washing machine) show a more or less linear trend over the deciles, and items relating to luxury items (*e.g.*, central heating, high-quality residential area) show a concave distribution in which

ownership is very low over the first five or six deciles and then rises rapidly.

2. The profile of the economizing dimension is more skewed, with most items showing a rapid decline over the first five or six deciles. One of the implications of this property is that the economizing measure is likely to be insensitive in its upper range.

Reliability and Validity

Coefficient *alpha* was .85 for the economizing dimension and .83 for the ownership dimension, suggesting that both scales had moderate to good reliability.

Table 5 shows the matrix of correlations between the 10 concurrent and predictive validity measures and two standard of living scales. Again, both scales are scored so that a high score indicates a high standard of living. The results suggest that the scales satisfy some of the conditions for validity. First, both scales have significant correlations with all validity measures. Further, the degree of correlation between the scale scores and the validity measures varies directly with the extent to which each validation measure may be thought of as a direct measure of the scale con-

TABLE 3. ITEM ENDORSEMENTS FOR THE OWNERSHIP SCALE BY SCALE DECILES

Item	Decile										$r$pbis.
	1	2	3	4	5	6	7	8	9	10	
	Percentages										
Color television	12.3	17.1	27.6	20.9	36.9	33.0	44.0	51.9	58.4	65.2	.36
Automatic washing machine	9.6	18.8	31.9	46.1	54.1	58.9	71.8	79.8	89.4	93.0	.54
Tumbler clothes drier	12.3	21.4	37.9	53.0	54.1	61.6	68.0	82.7	84.1	92.2	.50
Separate deep freeze	11.4	26.5	44.0	54.8	61.3	63.4	78.4	78.8	87.6	90.4	.51
Automatic stove	15.8	24.1	33.6	49.6	63.1	72.3	81.6	88.5	95.6	96.5	.55
Wall-to-wall carpet	50.0	61.5	75.9	80.9	87.4	90.3	92.8	96.2	99.1	99.1	.40
Central heating	0.0	3.4	0.9	6.1	2.7	8.9	14.4	19.2	35.4	60.9	.40
Vacuum cleaner	71.9	92.3	96.6	100	100	100	100	100	100	100	.40
Stereo	42.1	60.7	76.7	80.0	81.1	81.3	90.4	85.6	92.9	96.5	.37
Telephone	21.1	44.4	71.6	90.4	91.9	99.1	99.2	100	98.2	99.1	.63
Power mower	21.9	39.3	50.9	56.5	58.6	70.5	68.0	74.0	84.1	83.5	.38
Family car	43.0	71.8	87.1	91.3	96.4	99.1	100	100	100	100	.53
Second car	3.5	6.0	9.5	13.9	18.0	20.5	31.2	50.0	64.6	71.3	.46
Home ownership	4.4	23.9	34.5	64.3	76.6	86.6	92.8	92.3	98.2	99.1	.67
Below average interior	48.3	15.4	12.1	8.7	4.5	0.9	0.8	0.0	0.0	0.0	−.64
Above average surrounding housing	0.9	0.9	0.0	0.9	4.5	7.1	3.2	10.6	17.7	59.1	.38
N	114	117	116	115	111	112	125	104	113	115	

TABLE 4. ITEM ENDORSEMENTS FOR THE ECONOMIZING SCALE BY SCALE DECILES

Item	Decile										$r$pbis.
	1	2	3	4	5	6	7	8	9	10	
	Percentages										
Reduced holidays	55.6	52.6	27.8	28.0	9.5	7.9	3.1	0.0	0.0	0.0	−.52
Reduced car usage	54.7	38.8	34.8	22.0	19.0	6.7	7.3	0.0	0.0	0.0	−.49
Reduced entertaining of friends	58.1	37.1	21.7	7.6	6.9	0.0	0.0	0.0	0.0	0.0	−.57
Reduced eating at restaurants	74.4	47.4	42.6	24.7	17.2	19.1	1.0	0.0	0.0	0.0	−.58
Reduced visiting hotel	72.6	32.8	23.5	12.7	1.7	1.1	1.0	0.0	0.0	0.0	−.62
Reduced home heating	70.1	39.7	23.5	20.3	14.7	13.5	13.1	0.0	0.0	0.0	−.53
Reduced hobby materials	60.7	37.9	24.3	11.0	6.9	1.1	1.0	0.0	0.0	0.0	−.57
Reduced theatre, concerts, other entertainment	70.1	45.7	27.0	15.3	7.8	1.1	0.0	0.0	0.0	0.0	−.62
Impossible to save	63.2	31.9	31.3	25.4	17.2	14.6	25.0	0.0	0.0	0.0	−.56
Savings drawn on to meet expenses	52.1	46.6	34.8	43.2	27.6	19.1	16.7	19.1	0.0	0.0	−.38
Postponed visits to doctor	25.6	13.8	5.2	0.0	0.9	1.1	0.0	0.0	0.0	0.0	−.40
Postponed visits to dentist	55.6	33.6	21.7	12.7	7.8	2.2	5.2	0.0	0.0	0.0	−.52
Postponed purchase of clothes	82.9	60.3	46.1	42.4	31.9	14.6	3.1	3.1	0.0	0.0	−.61
Old clothes worn because could not afford replacements	85.5	57.8	51.3	34.8	31.0	9.0	0.0	0.0	0.0	0.0	−.64
Secondhand clothes bought	50.4	31.9	27.8	11.1	13.8	9.0	5.2	1.0	0.0	0.0	−.45
Secondhand shoes bought	24.1	14.7	11.3	7.6	2.6	3.4	2.1	0.0	0.0	0.0	−.37
Something sold to raise money	35.0	18.1	10.4	8.5	5.2	3.4	4.2	0.0	0.0	0.0	−.38
Money borrowed to meet living costs	34.2	16.4	13.9	6.8	1.7	0.0	0.0	0.0	0.0	0.0	−.43
Reduced weekly shopping	81.2	58.6	55.7	42.4	29.3	22.5	13.5	4.1	0.0	0.0	−.58
N	117	116	115	118	116	89	96	98	152	149	

struct. Thus the economizing dimension has its highest correlations with interviewer assessments of financial difficulty ($r = .54$) and respondent assessments of adequacy of income ($r = .48$); the absolute size of the correlation diminishes for the income, assets, and expenditure variables ($r = .27$ to $.35$); and it reduces even further for the social background measures ($r = .10$ to $.19$).

A similar pattern is evident for the ownership dimension: Interviewer ratings of level of financial hardship and family living standards correlate .60 with ownership; family income, assets and expenditure correlate from .57 to -.24 with ownership; and family social background correlates between .46 to .30 with ownership.

Multiple correlations between each scale score and all validation measures were computed to measure the amount of information in common between the two sets of measures. The multiple correlation between the ownership dimension and the validation measures was .76 ($p < .0001$); the correlation between the economizing dimension and the validation measures was .62 ($p < .0001$). The lower multiple correlation for the economizing measure reflects the fact that the correlations of this scale with the validation variables are consistently lower than those for the ownership scale.

DISCUSSION

The findings of this research suggest that it has been possible to devise scale scores which appear to measure variations in levels of family material well-being. Evidence for the validity of this interpretation can be drawn from several sources. First, the item/score distributions convey a strong impression of face validity in that, from the response profiles of various groups, it is possible to form an intuitive picture of the living standards of families who fall into various decile groups. Second, both scale scores show systematic correlations with a series of concurrent and predictive validity measures. Finally, the results of this analysis produced factors which were similar in content to the factors obtained in the study of persons aged 65 years or over, conducted by the New Zealand Department of Statistics and Social Welfare (1975). While both studies used similar items and methods of analysis, the samples on which these analyses were based differed markedly. The fact that the same factor structure can be found in two very different New Zealand subpopulations suggests that the ownership and economizing dimensions identified in these analyses are of considerable generality.

However, there are several *caveats* that must be placed on the results. First, since the scale items are based on respondent reports, the validity of the results depends heavily on the accuracy of these reports. For the ownership scale, there can be little question about the accuracy of the items, since these items

are related to matters of fact which could be cross-checked during the course of the interview. For the economizing scale, matters are a little less clear. In particular, the subject's likelihood of responding positively to an item was apt to be conditioned by a variety of factors, including family aspirations and the threshold at which the family began to economize. It is a matter of common observation that families vary in their response to financial stress; in some families minor economic perturbations precipitate major economizing, whereas other families contemplate complete ruin with equanimity. These variations in family responsiveness to financial stress are likely to introduce sources of variation into the economizing items which are unrelated to actual variations in family living standards. It seems possible that these sources of variation may account for the generally lower validation coefficients obtained for the economizing dimension.

A second point concerns the effects of family preference on the scale items. It could be argued that the factor score distributions reflect variations in family consumption preferences and choices rather than variations in living standards. This criticism can be answered by examination of the results. The factor analytic approach used in this analysis explicitly assumed that each item is influenced by two general sources of variation: the common variation of family living standards and unique variation relating to variation in family preferences and other factors. The results show that relatively little (27 percent) of the total item variance is explained by the common factors, suggesting that family preferences and other variables dictate patterns of ownership and consumption to a considerable extent. However, while the factors explain relatively little of the item variance, the converse is not true: The true factor scores are well estimated by the items. Assuming the appropriateness of a factor model, the results suggests that this model is capable of extracting good estimates of the common living standard factors from the background noise created by variations in family choice and preference.

A third point relates to the range of items on which the scales are based. It is quite clear that this study did not collect a fully comprehensive range of family living standard indicators. Obvious omissions are items relating

TABLE 5. MATRIX OF CORRELATIONS FOR TWO SCALE SCORES AND TEN VALIDATION MEASURES[a]

Variable	Factor 1	Factor 2	SOL	Financial Difficulty	Adequacy of Income	Assets (Logarithmic Units)	Gross Income	Proportion Spent on Necessities	SES	Education	Ethnic Status	Number of Parents
Economizing (Factor 1)	1	.40	.32	.54	.48	.35	.27	−.29	.19	.13	.11	.10
Ownership (Factor 2)		1	.60	.60	.35	.57	.48	−.24	.46	.31	.33	.30
Interviewer rating of standard of living (SOL)			1	.61	.40	.39	.43	−.25	.31	.27	.18	.15
Interviewer rating of financial difficulty				1	.49	.52	.46	−.34	.39	.29	.23	.20
Respondent rating of adequacy of income					1	.36	.39	−.30	.25	.23	.15	.08
Family assets (logarithmic units)						1	.42	−.25	.42	.30	.22	.42
Gross family income							1	−.53	.44	.32	.14	.42
Proportion of gross income spent on necessities								1	−.21	−.16	−.11	−.10
Family socioeconomic status (SES)									1	.61	.22	.43
Education of principal earner										1	.17	.18
Ethnic status of principal earner											1	.07
Number of parents												1

[a]To interpret this matrix it is important to note that: (1) both factors are scored so that a high score implies a high standard of living (*i.e.*, high levels of ownership and low levels of economizing); (2) standard of living, financial difficulty, adequacy of income, and socioeconomic status are scored using a similar convention—a high score implies a high standard of living.

to the quality of consumer durables, the intensity of economizing, and such areas as adequacy of diet. The effects of such omissions are open to question. If the omitted items relate to the same common factors identified in this analysis, the effects of their omission will be benign and merely result in a lowering of the scale reliability (which could stand some improvement). If the omitted factors relate to different scale dimensions, then the effects of omissions could be more far-reaching.

Further, it is not clear to what extent the results are specific to New Zealand conditions and to what extent the scales may be applied in other societies. However, it is important to note that New Zealand is, socially and economically, a relatively homogeneous society in which extremes of wealth and poverty are rare. Because of this, many of the items which prove discriminating in the New Zealand context may be rather "middle class" when applied to other societies. The effect of this would be to reduce the discriminating power of the scales at the extremes, and it seems likely that if the approach described here were to be applied to more economically heterogeneous societies, further items would need to be added to tap extremes of wealth and poverty. For example, at one extreme items relating to rodent infestation may improve discriminating power, while at the other, information on the number of color televisions owned by the family may discriminate between the affluent and the very affluent.

While it is clear that the measurement approach described in this paper is open to considerable refinement and modification, two major advantages over the traditional methods of measuring family living standards can be claimed. First, the use of direct measures of family ownership and consumption provides a more theoretically sound basis for measuring family living standards and, in particular, avoids the possibly incorrect assumption that levels of family material well-being are synonymous with levels of family economic well-being.

A second advantage of the method is that it provides a means of interpreting standard of living measures directly in terms of patterns of family ownership and economizing behavior. A problem common to most economic indicators of family material well-being is that

it is often difficult to visualize the living conditions of families having different standard of living scores. However, the scales described in this paper may be directly interpreted in terms of patterns of family ownership and consumption behavior by deriving response profiles characteristic of given scale levels. This property would appear to have multiple applications in the area of setting poverty lines and assessing the effects of social and economic policies on levels of family material well-being.

REFERENCES

Ando, A., and F. Modigliani
1963 "The 'life cycle' hypothesis of saving: Aggregate implications and tests." American Economic Review 53 (1):55-84.

Cattell, R. B.
1966 "The scree test for the number of factors." Multivariate Behavioral Research 1 (2):245-276.

Cronbach, L. J.
1951 "Coefficient alpha and the internal structure of tests." Psychometrika 16 (3): 297-334.

Department of Social Welfare, New Zealand.
1975 Survey of Persons Aged 65 Years and Over: Report of Results Relating to Social Security Benefit Rates. Wellington:New Zealand Government Printer.

Duesenberry, J. S.
1949 Income, Saving, and the Theory of Consumer Behavior. Cambridge:Harvard University Press.

Elley, W., and J. Irving
1976 "Revised socio-economic index for New Zealand." New Zealand Journal of Educational Studies 11 (1):25-36.

Fergusson, D. M., L. J. Horwood, R. Wright, and C. R. Stewart
1978 "Factors associated with planned and unplanned nuptial births." New Zealand Medical Journal 88 (617):89-92.

Fergusson, D. M., L. J. Horwood, F. T. Shannon, and B. Taylor
1978 "Infant health and breast-feeding during the first 16 weeks of life." Australian Paediatric Journal 14 (December):254-258.

Friedman, M.
1957 A Theory of the Consumption Function. Princeton:Princeton University Press.

Garfinkel, I., and R. H. Haveman
1977 Earnings Capacity, Poverty and Inequality. New York:Academic Press.

Harding, S.
1978 Survey of the Aged. Literature review, unpublished report, Department of Social Welfare, New Zealand.

Harman, H. H.
1976 Modern Factor Analysis. Chicago:University of Chicago Press.

Jensen, J.
  1978   Minimum Income Levels and Income Equiva-
         lence Scales. Unpublished report, Department
         of Social Welfare, New Zealand.
Moon, M.
  1977   The Measurement of Economic Welfare. New
         York:Academic Press.
Morgan, J. N., K. Dickinson, J. Dickinson, J. Benus,
and G. Duncan
  1974   Five Thousand American Families—Patterns
         of Economic Progress, Volume 1. An Analysis

of the First Five Years of the Panel Study of
Income Dynamics. Ann Arbor:Institute for
Social Research, University of Michigan.
O'Donnell, J. L., D. M. Fergusson, L. J. Horwood, and
  F. T. Shannon
  1978   "Health care in early infancy." New Zealand
         Medical Journal 88 (622):315-317.
Rowntree, B. S.
  1899   Poverty:A Study of Town Life. London:Nelson
Wynn, M.
  1970   Family Policy. London:Michael Joseph.

APPENDIX

Definitions of 49 Items Relating to Living Standards

Ownership and Accommodation[a]

1. Television*
2. Fully automatic washing machine
3. Tumbler clothes drier
4. Refrigerator
5. Separate deep freeze
6. Automatic stove
7. Wall-to-wall carpet in living area
8. Central heating
9. Air conditioning
10. Vacuum cleaner
11. Radio
12. Stereo
13. Telephone
14. Garbage disposal
15. Power mower
16. Family car
17. Second family car
18. Boat or yacht
19. Home ownership (home freehold or mortgaged)
20. Interviewer rating of interior of accommodation**
21. Interviewer rating of exterior of accommo-
    dation**
22. Interviewer rating of quality of surrounding
    housing**
23. Separate laundry
24. Separate dining room
25. Crowding index***

Economizing[b]

26. Reduced holidays
27. Reduced car usage
28. Reduced entertaining of friends
29. Reduced eating at restaurants
30. Reduced visiting hotel
31. Reduced home renovations or repairs
32. Reduced home heating
33. Reduced hobby materials
34. Reduced membership of clubs or associations
35. Reduced attendance at theatres, concerts, other
    entertainment
36. Postponed visits to doctor
37. Postponed visits to dentist
38. Meals omitted (to save money)
39. Postponed purchase of (needed) clothes
40. Old and worn-out clothes worn because could not
    afford replacements
41. Secondhand clothes bought for family or self
42. Secondhand shoes bought for family or self
43. Something sold (because money was needed)
44. Money borrowed to meet everyday living costs
45. Moved to cheaper accommodations
46. Goods bought on installment plan returned
47. Reduced weekly shopping to save money
48. Degree of difficulty saving****
49. Savings drawn on to meet everyday expenses
    (food, rent, etc.)

[a]Items without asterisks were scored: has = 1, otherwise = 0.
[b]Items without asterisks were scored: reduced, postponed, or other action taken to save money or to meet ex-
penses = 1, otherwise = 0.
*No T.V. = 1; black and white T.V. only = 2; color T.V. = 3.
**Far below average = 1; below average = 2; average = 3; good = 4; very good = 5.
***Persons in house/number of bedrooms.
****Easy to save = 1; can save with some difficulty = 2; difficult to save = 3; impossible to save = 4.

Little is known about how families use the additional income earned by working wives and mothers. A wife's earnings are important because they increase the amount of family income available for either raising the standard of living or for savings and investments. This article explores the relationship between wife employment and family net worth accumulation. Findings indicate that the absolute amount of family income, rather than who earns it, is most important in determining the amount of family net worth accumulation. However, family net worth accumulation is lower in families where the wife earns part of the income than in families at the same income level with only the husband employed. This might be due to increased job-related expenditures, substitution of market goods and services for home production, or preference for increased standard of living over net worth accumulation in working-wife families.

34

WIVES' EARNINGS AS A FACTOR IN FAMILY NET WORTH ACCUMULATION

Ann C. Foster

Wives' earnings as a factor in family net worth accumulation

ANN C. FOSTER

Over the last decade, the dramatic increase in the proportion of married women who are in the labor force has had a profound impact on both the family and the economy. By March 1979, the labor force participation rate of married women was 49.4 percent — up nearly 9 percentage points since 1970.[1] The earnings of wives often allow their families to enjoy a higher level of living than that provided by husbands' earnings alone. In 1978, for example, median income among families in which both husband and wife were employed was $22,109, compared with the $15,796 reported for families of wives who did not work outside the home.[2] In many cases, the additional earnings have lessened the inroads that inflation has made on family purchasing power.[3]

Previous research[4] has shown that wives' labor force participation tends to be higher when husbands' income is relatively low, indicating that economic need is a major influence on wives' employment. Although labor force participation is still greater among wives of men at the lowest earnings levels, the largest increase in recent years has been among those whose husbands are in the upper earnings ranges.[5] There is evidence that income distribution between working-wife and nonworking-wife families has become more unequal over the years,[6] and increased labor force participation among wives of high earners could further widen the differential.

Of particular interest to many concerned with the effects of married women's employment is whether the pattern of consumption and saving in a family in which the wife works differs from that in a family in which the same amount of money is earned by the husband alone. This question is significant because the family's allocation of its human and material resources affects its economic well-being and ultimately its quality of life.

The purpose of this study is to explore the relationship between a wife's earnings and family net worth accumulation. Do working-wife and nonworking-wife families have comparable net worth, given similar composition and income, and to what extent do earnings affect net worth? Because the labor force participation rate of married women is predicted to increase, the relationship between a wife's earnings and net worth accumulation should be clarified.

Ann C. Foster is an assistant professor of consumer affairs at Auburn University, Auburn, Alabama.

From Ann C. Foster, "Wives' Earnings as a Factor in Family Net Worth Accumulation," *Monthly Labor Review*, 1981, 104, pp. 53-57. Reprinted with the author's permission.

Theoretical background

A wife's employment is not without cost. Part of her earnings may have to be used to purchase goods and services she formerly provided at home, such as cooking and child care. An additional portion may also be claimed by transportation and other job-related expenditures. These factors may account for previous findings that, other things being equal, working-wife families have higher consumption-to-income ratios than non-working-wife families.[7]

Family goals also greatly influence the use of financial resources. Among these goals is improvement in the level of living—the quantity and quality of goods and services consumed. Another goal is financial security, or the assurance that resources will be available to meet future needs. During a particular period, a family may use its total current income to meet consumption needs and enhance its level of living, or it may choose to save some of this income to increase net worth and financial security. Similarly, assets may be liquidated and the proceeds used to increase or maintain current consumption, or they may be held in reserve to provide for financial security.

Methodology

Data underlying this study of the impact of wives' earnings are from the 1967 and 1972 National Longitudinal Surveys of Labor Market Experience, conducted by the Ohio State University Center for Human Resources Research under contract to the U.S. Department of Labor, and relate to the cohort of mature women (age 30 to 44) in mid-1967.[8] The initial multistage probability sample of 5,083 women was drawn by the Census Bureau in 235 areas of the United States to represent the Nation's noninstitutionalized mature female population at the time of data reference.[9] For purposes of this study, that sample was further refined to include only those respondents who were married for the first time prior to 1967 and who resided with their husbands during the 1967–72 period. In addition, each respondent must have provided information on all characteristics of interest in this research. Despite these eligibility criteria, the net sample size of 807 is quite large compared with those used in other studies of the allocation of family financial resources.

It should be noted here that economic and social changes took place after this sample was drawn which might significantly alter the results of the following analysis. For example, the sharp increase in married women's labor force participation over the last decade probably reflects a different mix of reasons why women work. At the same time, inflationary pressures may have considerably changed the distribution of family income between current consumption and net worth accumulation. And finally, the appreciation of housing since 1967 would make homeownership a much more important factor in explaining the stock of and change in family net worth.

Dependent variables

In the cross-sectional analyses of the relationship between wife's earnings and family net worth, the dependent variable of interest was family net worth in 1967 and 1972. Data for 2 years were analyzed because of the recent changes in the social and economic roles of American women. As previously indicated, intervening events during the period covered by the study could mean that variation in 1972 net worth was the result of factors different from those affecting 1967 net worth.

Net worth was determined by subtracting a family's total liabilities from its total assets. Assets used in the computation of net worth were:

Savings and checking accounts
U.S. savings bonds
Stocks, bonds, and mutual funds
Home
Farm
Business
Other real estate

The value of savings and checking accounts was the dollar amount on deposit at the time of the interview, while face value was used in determining the worth of U.S. savings bonds. For remaining assets, current market value was used to assess worth. Liabilities used in the computation included obligations, such as mortgages and back taxes, connected with the ownership of home, farm, business, or other real estate, as well as debt for other goods and services.

In the longitudinal analysis of the effect of wife's earnings on net worth change, the dependent variable of interest—dollar change in family net worth during the 1967–72 period—was computed by subtracting 1967 net worth from 1972 net worth.

Independent variables

The following independent variables were included in the cross-sectional analyses:

Respondent's earnings
Family income
Respondent's occupation, current or last job
Respondent's age
Respondent's race
Respondent's education
Number of family members
Number of years married
Homeownership status
Number of durables purchased in previous year

In addition, the "employment-to-marriage" ratio was included in the 1967 analysis. This ratio consisted of the number of years in which a respondent worked 6 months or more between marriage and 1967, divided by the number of years married.[10]

Respondent's earnings, the major independent variable of interest, was the total of her pretax earnings in the calendar year prior to the survey from wages, salaries, commissions, tips, or operation of her own business. Family income was the total pretax income received from all sources over the same period. In addition to earnings of all family members, these sources included interest, dividends, rent, and social insurance and public assistance payments. Except for homeownership status and race, all independent variables were treated as continuous variables. Homeownership status was a dichotomous variable; nonhomeowners were coded 0, and homeowners, 1. Race was treated as a set of dummy variables based on the categories white, black, and "other"; the latter category was the reference category embodied in the regression constant.

Independent variables employed in the longitudinal analysis of change in net worth were:

Respondent's earnings (1966)
Change in respondent's earnings (1966–1971)
Number of weeks respondent worked between 1967 and 1972 surveys
Family income (1966)
Change in family income (1966–1971)
Net worth (1967)
Respondent's age (1967)
Respondent's education (1967)
Respondent's race
Number of family members (1967)
Change in number of family members (1967–1972)
Change in homeownership status (1967–1972)

Change in homeownership status was a set of dummy variables based on the following categories: (1) nonhomeowner 1967 and 1972, (2) nonhomeowner 1967—homeowner 1972, (3) homeowner 1967 and 1972, and (4) homeowner 1967—nonhomeowner 1972. The latter category was the reference category. Except for race, which employed the same measurement used in the cross-sectional analyses, the remaining independent variables were treated as continuous variables.

Multiple regression model

In each analysis, independent variables were entered into an initial stepwise multiple regression model which was then refined to include only those variables which would collectively have the greatest impact on net worth or change in net worth. An independent variable was left in the final model if it explained at least 1 percent of total variance in the dependent variable or if it had a zero-order correlation coefficient of $\pm.25$, indicating a moderate degree of association with the dependent variable. A variable was also included in the final model if mandated by conceptual considerations, as in the case

of respondent's earnings. To facilitate comparisons between the two cross-sectional analyses, variables which met any criterion in one analysis were automatically included in the other.

Results of cross-sectional analyses

The final multiple regression model explained 29.7 percent of total variance in 1967 net worth and 25.5 percent in 1972. As tables 1 and 2 show, the relative importance of factors influencing net worth varied somewhat between the 2 years. In both analyses, family income made by far the greatest contribution to explained difference in net worth, although the variable's contribution was substantially less in 1972 than in 1967. B values indicate that for each additional dollar of family income, net worth was \$1.98 higher in 1967 and \$1.51 higher in 1972. It should be noted that a family's net worth at any time is, in large measure, a result of past saving behavior. Current income may be influential because it reflects a relatively high past income which allowed saving to occur and thus, net worth to increase.

Although much smaller than that of family income, the second greatest contribution to total variance in both analyses was made by homeownership status. The amount contributed to explained variance by this variable was greater in the 1972 study. Families who were homeowners in 1967 had net worth positions \$5,914 higher than nonhomeowners, but in 1972, homeownership was associated with an \$11,227 differential.

Respondent's earnings were not significant in explaining variance in 1967 net worth. The moderately high zero-order correlation coefficient of .23, however,

Table 1. Multiple regression of selected variables on 1967 net worth

[Sample size = 807]

Independent variables	Coefficient of determination[1] (R^2)	Variable contribution to final coefficient of determination (ΔR^2)	Coefficient of correlation (r)	[2] b
Family income	274	.....	52	[3] 1.98 (0.15)
Respondent's earnings	276	002	23	−0.26 (0.23)
Respondent's education	276	.....	22	−112.91 (219.75)
Homeownership status	296	020	27	[3] 5,913.76 (1,253.51)
Race — white			19	−3,563.36 (3,411.93)
Race — black	297	001	−22	−3,292.08 (3,571.99)

[1] Each entry represents the contribution to the ratio of explained variation to total variation in net worth made by the associated variable and those variables which precede it.
[2] Partial regression coefficient, in dollars. Each b value indicates how much a one-unit change in the independent variable affects net worth when the effects of other independent variables in the multiple regression model are controlled. Standard error of the estimate is shown in parentheses.
[3] Significant at the .01 level.

Table 2. Multiple regression of selected variables on 1972 net worth

[Sample size = 807]

Independent variables	Coefficient of determination [1] (R²)	Variable contribution to coefficient of determination (ΔR²)	Coefficient of correlation (r)	[2] b
Family income	196		44	[3] 1.51 (0.15)
Respondent's earnings	209	013	11	[3] 1.09 (0.29)
Respondent's education	218	009	26	[4] 709.66 (337.06)
Homeownership status	247	029	28	[3] 11,226.90 (2,101.83)
Race — white			25	-8,186.60 (5,101.72)
Race — black	255	008	-28	[4] -12,923.94 (5,323.97)

[1] Each entry represents the contribution to the ratio of explained variation to total variation in net worth made by the associated variable and those variables which precede it.
[2] Partial regression coefficient, in dollars. Each b value indicates how much a one-unit change in the independent variable affects net worth when the effects of other independent variables in the multiple regression model are controlled. Standard error of the estimate is shown in parentheses.
[3] Significant at the .01 level
[4] Significant at the .05 level

indicates that net worth, in the absence of other factors, was greater among working-wife families. A fairly high degree of association found between respondent's earnings and family income (r = .51) suggests that the effect of the former variable may have been indirect. It was determined that without a respondent's earnings, total income among working-wife families would have been substantially below that of nonworking-wife families in both 1966 and 1971. The fact that a working wife's contribution increased family income substantially appears to have had an important influence on net worth position in 1967. It seems that the amount, not the source, of family income was relevant in determining the level of net worth.

In 1972, however, respondent's earnings did make a statistically significant contribution to total variance in net worth. Although there was a slight positive zero-order correlation between respondent's income and net worth, when other factors were held constant, there was a weak negative association. For each additional dollar earned by a respondent in 1971, net worth in 1972 was lower by $1.09. As in the previous analysis, it appears that the influence of a wife's earnings was indirect, increasing the financial resources available for strengthening net worth position.

The negative relationship is not inconsistent. Given two families of equal income and composition, a lower saving-to-income ratio, and thus lower net worth, would be expected in the family in which a wife earns a portion of this income. One explanation for the lower saving-to-income ratio is increased job-related expenditures and more frequent substitution of market goods and services for household production. These factors

would reduce discretionary income available for saving, relative to that of a nonworking-wife family. Another explanation is that the economic hazards of unemployment, death, and disability would be less in a family with more than one earner. Therefore, a working-wife family may feel less need to increase its financial security.

Factors influencing net worth change

The greatest influence on net worth change was exerted by the family income variables. As table 3 illustrates, both dollar change in family income and 1966 family income were positively associated with the dependent variable. It would appear that, among these families, the goal of financial security was sufficiently strong for at least a portion of any income increase to be allocated to net worth accumulation. Because 1966 family income had a fairly high zero-order correlation (r = .52) with 1967 net worth, its influence on net worth change may have been due to its being a proxy for initial net worth. Other factors being equal, families with high levels of income in 1966 probably experienced increased net worth accumulation relative to those at

Table 3. Multiple regression of selected variables on dollar change in net worth, 1967-72

[Sample size = 807]

Independent variables	Coefficient of determination (R²) [1]	Variable contribution to final coefficient of determination (ΔR²)	Coefficient of correlation (r)	b [2]
Change in family income, 1966-77	039		20	0.74 [3] (0.13)
Family income in 1966	069	030	17	0.63 [3] (0.16)
Change in homeownership status				
Nonhomeowner in 1967 and 1972			-18	1,961.11 (3,824.66)
Nonhomeowner in 1967, homeowner in 1972	089	019	-01	6,930.07 [4] (3,917.87)
Homeowner in 1967 and 1972			17	8,219.29 [3] (3,592.01)
Change in respondent's earnings, 1967-72	091	002	02	-0.71 [3] (0.31)
Total weeks worked	092	001	05	14.21 (8.49)
Respondent's earnings in 1966	095	003	07	-0.62 (0.37)

[1] Each entry represents the contribution to the ratio of explained variation to total variation in net worth made by the associated variable and those variables which precede it.
[2] Partial regression coefficient, in dollars. Each b value indicates how much a one-unit change in the independent variable affects net worth when the effects of other independent variables in the multiple regression model are controlled. Standard error of the estimate is shown in parentheses.
[3] Significant at the .01 level
[4] Significant at the .05 level

lower levels because of subsequent appreciation of assets which comprised 1967 net worth.

Homeownership also had a positive influence on the dependent variable. Families who were homeowners in both 1967 and 1972 or who became homeowners by 1972 experienced increased net worth compared to families who were homeowners in 1967 only.

Of the remaining variables, only change in respondent's earnings was significant in explaining net worth change. Controlling for the effects of other factors uncovered a negative association; for each additional dollar increase in respondent's earnings change in net worth was $.71 less. These findings indicate that in two families experiencing similar income increases, net worth accumulation was lower in the family in which the wife's earnings accounted for part of this change than in the family in which the wife made no monetary contribution. Again, factors such as increased job-related expenditures, substitution of market goods and services for household production, or preference for improvement in standard of living over financial security in working-wife families could account for these findings. It should be noted that change in respondent's earnings and change in family income had a moderately strong positive zero-order association (r = .38). This finding would indicate that by increasing the level of family income available for saving, change in respondent's earnings may have had an indirect positive influence on change in net worth.

Implications

Findings clearly indicate that the absolute amount of family income, rather than its sources, was the most important factor in determining the extent of net worth accumulation among sample families. Without a wife's earnings, however, income among working-wife families would have been appreciably lower than that of nonworking-wife families. Thus, a wife's earnings were important because they increased the family income available for transformation into both an improved level of living and increased financial security.

As noted earlier, the trend toward increased labor force participation among women whose husbands are at the highest earnings levels could increase the income inequality between working-wife and nonworking-wife families. Although they would have more time available

for household production and leisure than working-wife families, this increased income inequality would most likely be reflected in a lower level of living among nonworking-wife families. Research findings of a positive association between level of family income and net worth accumulation suggest that, in the future, working-wife families should also have more favorable net worth positions and increased financial security compared to nonworking-wife families.

FOOTNOTES

Beverly L. Johnson, "Marital and family characteristics of the labor force, March 1979," *Monthly Labor Review*, April 1980, p. 48.

Money Income of Families and Persons in the United States: 1978, Current Population Reports, Consumer Income, Series P-60, No. 123 (Bureau of the Census 1980), p. 6.

See, for example, Howard Hayghe, "Families and the rise of working wives — an overview," *Monthly Labor Review*, May 1976, p. 18.

' This relationship has been uncovered in a number of studies. For example, see William C. Bowen and T. Aldrich Finegan, *The Economics of Labor Force Participation* (Princeton University Press, 1969); Glen C. Cain, *Married Women in the Labor Force: An Economic Analysis* (University of Chicago Press, 1966); and Jacob Mincer, "Labor force participation of married women: A study of labor supply," in National Bureau of Economic Research, ed., *Aspects of Labor Economics* (Princeton University Press, 1962).

Paul Ryscavage, "More wives in the labor force have husbands with 'above-average' incomes," *Monthly Labor Review*, June 1979, pp. 40–42.

' Dong W. Cho, "Working women and family income distribution," *The Collegiate Forum*, Winter 1979, p. 5.

Myra H. Strober, "Wives' labor force behavior and family consumption patterns," *American Economic Review*, February 1977, pp. 410–17.

' Previous research in this area includes "Survey of financial characteristics of consumers," *Federal Reserve Bulletin*, March 1964, pp. 285–92; Ruth E. Deacon and Janet A. Krofta, *Economic Progress of Rural Nonfarm and Part-time Farm Families*, Research Bulletin 1976 (Wooster, Ohio, Agricultural Research and Development Center, December 1965); Flora L. Williams and Sarah L. Manning, "Net worth change of selected families," *Home Economics Research Journal*, December 1972, pp. 104–13; Rosemary Walker, *Wife's Hours of Market Work Related to Family Saving Behavior*, Ph.D. dissertation (Purdue University, 1978); and Colien Hefferan, "Saving behavior in multiple earner families," in *Proceedings 25th Annual Conference of the American Council on Consumer Interests* (Columbia, Mo., American Council on Consumer Interests, 1979), pp. 177–78.

' For a more detailed description see, *The National Longitudinal Surveys Handbook* (Columbus, Ohio State University, Center for Human Resources, 1976).

This variable was not used in the 1972 analysis because data on the number of years in which a respondent worked 6 months or more between 1967 and 1972 were unavailable.

Committee proposes four budget levels applicable to six different types of families, and based on median expenditures, rather than detailed commodity lists.

35

SPECIAL PANEL SUGGESTS CHANGES IN BLS FAMILY BUDGET PROGRAM

Harold W. Watts

The Bureau of Labor Statistics' Family Budget Program produces one of the most popular and widely publicized series in the repertoire of labor statistics. It provides annual estimates of the cost of purchasing hypothetical "market baskets" of goods that represent "lower," "intermediate," and "higher" standards of living. The budgets are styled for the traditional four-person family, and for a retired couple. For the worker's family, they estimate a corresponding total income, which provides for taxes and expenses consistent with the three consumption expenditure levels. These budgets are replicated for major cities and for regional averages. They provide the only available basis for inter-area comparisons of living costs or "real" income levels.[1]

In 1978, the Bureau of Labor Statistics contracted with the Wisconsin Institute for Research on Poverty to recommend revisions in the Family Budget Program. The Institute appointed the Expert Committee on Family Budget Revisions, which embodied a wide range of experience related both to methods of developing budget standards and to uses of the standards. The Bureau used similar outside expertise when it reviewed the budgets in 1948 and 1967. The committee and staff, which included members of the Poverty Institute, reviewed the existing program in detail, analyzed new evidence on

Harold W. Watts is a professor of economics at Columbia University and chairperson of the Expert Committee on Family Budget Revisions.

spending patterns based on the 1972–73 Consumer Expenditure Surveys, and assessed the enlarged possibilities provided by the projected continuous Consumer Expenditure Survey. The panel heard testimony from government experts familiar with the development of the current budgets and commissioned several papers by other experts.

The committee recommended that four American Family Budget Standards be developed in place of the current three budgets. The revised standards have been designed to take advantage of the new information on family behavior collected in the new Consumer Expenditure Surveys. These recommendations have been submitted in the committee's report to the Commissioner of Labor Statistics and are now being considered.

This article explains the basic recommendations and the reasoning behind them. Although the proposed new standards are based on methods that diverge from past practices, they will yield budget totals that are very much in line with the existing series. But a more important continuity—the aim to express normative and quantitative standards that can be used to evaluate relative levels of living among groups, between times and across regions—has been maintained. Because such comparisons yield valuable insights and are widely used in the design and implementation of policy, it is important that they be based on clear and understandable principles. The committee, with only one dissenting vote, believes this report proposes a sound and improved basis

From Harold W. Watts, "Special Panel Suggests Changes in BLS Family Budget Program," *Monthly Labor Review*, 1980, 103, pp. 3-10. Reprinted with the author's permission.

for such comparisons and unanimously recommends a program to study the direct estimation of standards from household attitude surveys. Refinement and validation of the direct methods hold the promise of still further improvements in the Family Budget Program.

Principal recommendations

Budget levels. The committee recommends four levels to replace the existing three budgets:

- Prevailing Family Standard
- Social Minimum Standard
- Lower Living Standard
- Social Abundance Standard

The Prevailing Family Standard, designed to reflect the level of living achieved by the typical family, is set at the median expenditure of two-parent families with two children. In the judgment of the committee, this standard affords a family full opportunity to participate in contemporary society, and to enjoy the basic options it offers. This level is the conceptual descendant of the intermediate budget, but it is also closely related to the traditional "modest but adequate" level of living or the "prevailing standards" of ordinary moderate living.

The other three levels are determined in fixed proportion to this basic standard; standards for other family sizes or types are also expressed relative to the archetypical four-person family. The Lower Living Standard,

		The committee members	
Harold W. Watts (Chairperson)	Columbia University Department of Economics
Anne Draper	American Federation of Labor and Congress of Industrial Organizations, Department of Economic Research; and member, Labor Research Advisory Council, Bureau of Labor Statistics
Lawrence Gibson	General Mills, Marketing Research; and member, Business Research Advisory Council, Bureau of Labor Statistics
James E. Jones, Jr.	University of Wisconsin Law School
Bette Silver Mahoney	System Development Corporation Human Systems Division
Lee Rainwater	Harvard University Department of Sociology
Eugene Smolensky	University of Wisconsin Department of Economics
Barbara Starfield	The Johns Hopkins University School of Hygiene and Public Health

Table 1. Recommended equivalence scale and updated values of American family expenditure standards for 1979

Number of persons	Equivalence scale	Social Minimum Standard	Lower Living Standard	Prevailing Family Standard	Social Abundance Standard
1 aged	50	$ 4,032	$ 5,376	$ 8,064	$12,096
1 nonaged	54	4,355	5,806	8,710	13,064
2 aged	61	4,919	6,559	9,839	14,758
2 nonaged	67	5,403	7,204	10,806	16,210
3	80	6,452	8,602	12,903	19,355
4	1 00	8,064	10,753	16,129	24,193
5	1 20	9,677	12,903	19,355	29,032
6	1 39	11,210	14,946	22,419	33,629
7	1 57	12,661	16,882	25,323	37,984
8	1 74	14,032	18,710	28,064	42,097
9	1 90	15,322	20,430	30,645	45,968
10	2 05	16,532	22,043	33,064	49,597
11	2 19	17,661	23,548	35,323	52,984
12	2 32	18,710	24,946	37,419	56,129
13 +	2 32 + 12 for each over 12	18,710 + 967 for each over 12	24,946 + 1,290 for each over 12	37,419 + 1,935 for each over 12	56,129 + 2,903 for each over 12

NOTE Assumes no real growth in median income from 1978 value for four-person household

set at two-thirds of the Prevailing Family Standard, is a successor to the current lower budget. It represents a level that the committee regards as requiring frugal and careful management, leaving little room for choice in achieving what Americans regard as an acceptable standard of living. The Social Minimum Standard is set at half of the Prevailing Family Standard and lies, in the committee's judgment, in a boundary zone below which issues of deficiency and deprivation are appropriate matters of social concern. The Social Abundance Standard, set 50 percent higher than the Prevailing Family Standard (or three times the Social Minimum Standard), rounds out the set by providing a balancing view of a higher living standard. The committee regards this standard as marking the beginning of the expenditure range that increasingly affords choices in the luxury categories of consumption.

The interfamily equivalence scales. To allow for different family sizes, the expenditure standards for the four-person household are varied using an equivalence scale. The scale recommended has been adapted from the updated "poverty cut-offs" developed by Mollie Orshansky and Carol Fendler, which rely in turn on the relative cost of the "Thrifty Food Plans" provided by the U.S. Department of Agriculture.[2] The proposed scale sets the current expenditure levels for an aged single-person household at 50 percent of the four-person reference standard. A non-aged couple's standard is set at 67 percent of a four-person standard, and that of a family of eight at 174 percent. Table 1 shows the equivalence scale and the full set of levels evaluated for 1979.

The following estimates, based on the 1972-73 Consumer Expenditure Survey, give some idea of the distribution of the population relative to the proposed standards. More than two-thirds of the population lives between the Social Minimum Standard and the Social Abundance Standard; 13 percent are below the Social Minimum Standard, and 18 percent are above the Social Abundance Standard; more than one in four persons live below the Lower Living Standard. The all-too-familiar finding of lower incomes for black persons shows here as a rate of 36.1 percent below the Social Minimum Standard, in contrast to only 10.4 percent for nonblack persons. Children and older persons also show distinctly higher likelihood of living below the minimum and lower chances of living in abundance.

Methods of annual updating. A major objective in developing the recommendations was to provide continuous updating of the standards, based on current information and relatively free of discretionary choices. The recent BLS decision to conduct Consumer Expenditure Surveys on a continuous basis provides a way to keep the budgets up to date that has not existed in the past. The committee recommends that the median expenditures for the reference family type be estimated directly from the annual waves of survey data (using adjacent size groups if needed to enhance precision). For the interim until the survey estimates are available, an estimated expenditure can be obtained by adjusting annual income medians from the Current Population Survey.

Linking the structure of expenditure standards to the median level of the four-person reference family assures that the standards will not be made obsolete by changing economic conditions. Short-run variations in median expenditure levels should not, however, be reflected in norms or standards that gain much of their usefulness from their stability. Consequently, the committee recommends that the expenditure standards be maintained at their previous peak in real terms until a higher real median level is observed. This feature is called a "ratchet." The Consumer Price Index would be used for making the required estimates of real expenditure, thus preventing any decline in the real level of the various standards. During periods of constant or declining real median expenditures the nominal standards would continue to rise in tandem with the general price level, thus staying constant in "real" terms.

Detailed budgets and total income estimates. The new standards have been defined and expressed in terms of expenditure totals. But for many kinds of comparisons and to communicate the meaning of the standards more clearly, further detail is needed. An allocation of expenditures among major categories can be derived from the Consumer Expenditure Surveys. Average allocation patterns can be estimated for each of several types of families at each of the expenditure standards. It must be noted that for any level of total expenditure apparently

identical families spend their money differently. These differences are surely due in part to different, but unobserved, circumstances, but there are also differences in tastes and preferences that lead a household to favor one line of consumption over another. Such differences have no apparent ill effect on the interests of the general public and are evidently preferred by the individuals concerned; consequently, the committee feels that to invest the average, or any other allocation, with normative or prescriptive significance is unjustified. The average patterns recommended show plausible allocations because they are based on observed behavior. However, equally plausible allocations can be obtained by trading some expenditures for others, and within a wide range there is no basis for authorative judgment that one is better than another.

The committee proposes that detailed allocations be developed and displayed for six different types of families:

- Two parents and two children (the reference family)
- An aged couple 65 and over
- A non-aged single person
- A one-parent, two-child family
- A two-parent, five-child family
- An aged single person

The budgets would be shown in detail for all four standards, except that the Social Abundance Standard should be omitted for the last three types. There are too few families of those kinds at that level to permit reliable estimation of allocation patterns.

For the non-aged family types, it is also necessary to estimate the level of gross income that will enable a worker's family to spend the amount specified for a given standard. Several adjustments apply here, but income and payroll tax adjustments are the most important and vary from State to State. The committee proposes that calculations based on current Federal and State laws be carried out to determine the tax adjustments needed to arrive at the appropriate equivalent gross income for each State.

Interarea differentials. The committee recommends the introduction of an interarea price index program based on fixed-weight or market-basket procedures. This program should provide price comparisons among all city and regional aggregates for which sufficient price data are regularly collected. While basic price comparisons are useful for many purposes, they do not show the cost of achieving equivalent living levels in different places. This second problem, the "true cost of living" question, cannot be directly resolved by reference to price data *or* to observed expenditure patterns. The committee urges continuing research on this problem, but for the imme-

One committee member dissents

The present BLS Family Budgets are based on detailed cost estimates of items necessary for a worker's family to maintain or achieve specified living standards. Under the proposal of the majority of the Expert Committee on Family Budget Revisions, these would be replaced by a set of declaratory judgments by the committee as to levels of total expenditure, tied to median consumption, that are designated as representing particular living standards.

Even the committee appears rather uncomfortable with this. It produces an ultimate proposal for surveys, that would ascertain public opinion on what is needed to maintain various living standards. Such a project has many useful possibilities as an adjunct to family budget research, and I support it. However, I do not believe it can substitute for systematic budget cost calculations from customary statistical data. In any case the results of such explorations lie far in the future. The immediate question is whether to adopt the committee's specific proposals, based on its judgments.

Why should we accept the committee's judgments? Its answer, in effect, is that the present budgets are equally based on judgments, although less obviously. Thus is discarded a history of Bureau budget-making and evolutionary development that spans more than 70 years. Has the Congress, in commissioning, accepting, and using such budgets, been fooled all this time?

The committee majority objects to the present budgets for their commodity lists, their use of scientific standards and expert opinion, and their elements of relativism. This fails to recognize the purpose of budget-making: estimating costs and making their nature explicit in terms of specific items of purchase, quantity, and price. Necessary costs for a given standard of living are not a mirror image of expenditures taken from a Consumer Expenditure Survey.

The Bureau's work in budget-making, in accordance with Congressional directives, has been skilled and honest.

I would have interpreted the mandate of the committee as that of recommending improvements in the methodologies for selecting goods and services to be priced for the worker budgets, not that of overturning the bases of the present budgets in their entirety.

It would be difficult to describe the committee's declaratory judgments on expenditure totals as "methodology." The judgments were not, however, picked out of thin air. Essentially, they were arrived at by consulting the results of other people's judgments, including those of the rejected BLS budget-makers, and converting them to percentage relationships with median consumption figures. It was felt to be important not to have the dollar results diverge markedly from existing numbers that have already been accepted. With acceptable "number" results, the methodology, or lack of it, would not matter.

Thus, the choice of median consumption to represent the Prevailing Family Standard rests essentially upon the present Intermediate Family Budget, which the committee observes to have fallen historically "within the middle range of family incomes." The establishment of the Lower Living Standard at two-thirds of median consumption is pegged at the consumption level of the existing Lower Budget, and is further buttressed by Gallup poll opinion data on "how much it takes to get along." The Social Minimum Standard, set at 50 percent of the consumption median, is similar to other estimates for poverty threshold. When nonconsumption items and taxes are included, it will also be about 70 percent of the Lower Living Standard as referenced in the Comprehensive Employment and Training Act. The Social Abundance Standard, at 150 percent of the median, is simply the obverse of the Social Minimum and rests upon no particular observations or other reference data.

The committee's living standard lines essentially are derivative judgments based on existing estimates, rather than

diate future, it recommends that adjustments in fuel and clothing that can be explicitly related to climate differences be recognized as the only basis for interarea adjustments. It is likely that additional adjustments are warranted, but in the absence of consistent evidence of their direction or size, differentials that are based on conjecture may cause more mischief than no adjustments at all.

Measuring popular conceptions of norms. The principles and basic notions that have inspired the new standards suggest the possibility of eliciting normative standards through general public surveys. Recent work in Europe and the United States suggests that people can be asked how much it takes to live comfortably, for example, or to just get along. Their answers can be related to their own income or expenditure levels. From these relationships a consensus can be derived that directly reflects popular views about standard living levels.

Potentially, a measure of this kind could replace the median expenditure standard that forms the basis of the committee's recommendations. All four standards might be estimated separately, for example, and the proportional relationship among them validated or improved. The system of interfamily equivalence scales could also be examined in light of directly expressed requirements of differently composed households. Direct survey questions could also produce independent evidence of interarea differentials.

But at present these approaches need further study and experimental implementation. The committee urges an extensive effort to evaluate these promising new methods. An experimental survey program is practical because the questions required could be added to both the new Consumer Expenditure Survey and other large-scale surveys. The survey program should be carefully designed to identify the best form for the questions. A coordinated analytic program, inside or outside the Bu-

resting upon independent findings or methodologies developed by the committee.

The percentages arrived at are further mandated to remain indefinitely in the same fixed relationships. The Social Minimum is always to be 50 percent of the current year's median, the Lower Living two-thirds, and so forth.

The postulate that adequacy at prevailing levels of living is always at median consumption, and that other standards remain in fixed percentage relationships to the median, is inherently insupportable. In a very poor society, for example, or even our own at different periods in history, median consumption may be the minimum of needed consumption. At other times, median consumption may be well above such a minimum.

The committee's formula is particularly troublesome to contemplate in what may become an era of falling real living levels. There is no genuine safety net to protect whatever is represented in terms of necessary consumption, particularly at the Lower and Social Minimum levels. For the short term, the committee has devised a "ratchet" mechanism. This would obviate the problem by mandating that the median will always be at the real levels of 1972–73, or any subsequent higher real level, as determined through the Consumer Price Index. Under this specification, the "formula" median can readily exceed the actual median, producing a need for complicated explanations. If real living levels are reduced over a long period, the Bureau of Labor Statistics must drop the ratchet and presumably revise the percentages. No guidance is offered concerning when to drop the ratchet or what to do about the percentages. Quantity-cost budgets would no longer be available for guidance.

Regarding geographical or place-to-place variations for national median consumption, the logic of using expenditure totals instead of calculated costs is questionable. Obviously the committee would not want area median expenditures to be the basis for area variations from the national total. This is a problem the committee has not truly resolved, and on which it urges "continuing research." It has endorsed development of an interarea fixed-weight price index, which would ignore local area usage differences for such items as fuel, transportation, clothing, and food preferences. On a separate track, it suggests "climate adjustments" for home fuel use (and possibly clothing) based on degree days in each State; this to represent "living cost" differences on a State basis. The recommendations are incomplete and ad hoc.

The production of equivalent consumption totals for families of different sizes through use of the Orshansky scales is not necessarily objectionable. But, as the committee itself recognizes, this entails no real advance over existing methodologies, all of which are tied to food consumption. The main defect is the failure to detail what any of the budgets actually contain, in terms of tangible goods and services. In the committee formulations, "detail" consists only of percentages allocated to different categories, such as food, clothing, and housing.

In conclusion, I believe that abandonment of the Bureau's traditional quantity-cost budgets would be a grave loss. The budgets have made an independent and substantial contribution to studies of income adequacy. The explicit lists they provide of the commodities and services that go into the budgets are a crucial part of their value. People can judge for themselves whether the lists are reasonably representative of living standards at specified levels.

—ANNE DRAPER
Department of Economic Research, AFL–CIO,
and Labor Research Advisory Council,
Bureau of Labor Statistics

---

reau of Labor Statistics, should also be developed in order to explore all possible uses of directly elicited living standard estimates.

New socioeconomic report. The final recommendation calls for the design of a new report that can take advantage of the evidence in the continuous Consumer Expenditure Survey, as well as other major Federal surveys, to illuminate the condition of American families and households as consumers. The new budget standards provide a framework in which the population of households and persons can be distributed and the latest information on spending patterns can also be displayed. Such a report would also explicate the annually updated living standards and combine them with revised tax and related adjustments in order to determine the income standards appropriate for each State. In addition to reporting on standard annual series, the report could offer interpretative analytical articles based on expenditure data and methodological articles on possible improvements to the Family Budget Standards Program.

Rationale for the changes

To the small and select group of individuals closely familiar with the Family Budgets Program, it will be evident that these recommendations depart sharply from existing practices. For readers who have used and followed the budget series, but are less familiar with the details of the series construction, this section will point out the main contrasts. The reasoning behind the changes is presented for both groups of readers.

Dollar totals vs. shopping lists. A major and far-reaching departure is proposed in the basic formulation of the budget. The existing budget total can be regarded as the cost of a specific list of goods and services drawn from a variety of sources to characterize a "modest but adequate" standard of living. The proposed Prevailing Family Standard aims at the same general level, but arrives at it by: (1) examining the living standards of a specified and familiar category of household spending a median number of dollars on current consumption relative to others of that type; and (2) taking that level as typifying the ordinary concept of prevailing living standards. Subtotals of expenditure for categories of consumption such as food, shelter, or clothing can be based upon average patterns observed for households at the median level. Illustrative lists of quantities of goods affordable within those totals can also be compiled on the basis of average price data. The critical difference is that the new procedure abandons the notion of a rigidly fixed list of things that are interpretable as minimum *needs* in achieving a given level of living.

Because of evidence that different families commanding the same set of choices select rather different commodities without apparent deterioration in health, vitality, or human dignity, the committee found mistaken the belief that there is a best or unique "recipe" for attaining a living standard. More important, careful examination showed that the existing lists of commodities were in fact not based on objective assessment of needs.

The idea that there are experts who can prescribe what is necessary for a working family to live decently is both widespread and attractive. It promises a basis for claims to "just wages" or "fair treatment" that are apparently supported by the absolute authority of science. Such claims are generally regarded as harder to refute than those based on relativistic standards such as the ones proposed by the committee. The committee might have embraced a set of well-authenticated needs that could be translated directly into costs. But no experts could be found who were willing to formulate such requirements. Nutritional experts can combine agreed-upon nutritional requirements (that can, in themselves, be satisfied at very low cost) with palatability limits and evidence related to food preferences to produce any number of need-filling food quantity lists. These lists have differing costs, and most people would prefer a higher cost "food plan" over a lower one. But the nutritional criteria provide no basis for choosing one plan over another, and the actual choice of a plan for the existing budget depends on relativistic measures that are no less arbitrary than the committee's proposal to assign median total expenditure as a standard of comparison.

Physical standards for housing have also been used in forming the budgets but, again, the standards do not determine a unique cost. The selection from among the wide range of values and prices of units that meet the standard is made by applying arbitrary and relativistic standards. Yet food and housing are usually considered the best cases for application of expert or scientifically

sanctioned standards. The same recourse to arbitrary and essentially relative criteria was apparent at all stages of development of the quantity lists currently used for the family budgets.

The majority of the committee concluded that the main claimed advantage of lists of qualities of goods and services — that such lists assure the meeting of authoritatively established needs — was in fact illusory. Any cost total derived from lists of commodities has perforce been based on a myriad of individual judgments. Consequently, the committee majority, recognizing that a judgment based on individual values and *not* on scientific requirements must be made at some stage whatever the method used, decided to exercise that judgment in the choice of an expenditure *total* rather than in several hundred item choices.

It must be emphasized that the decision did not involve rejection of scientific or expert-based cost of living criteria. What was rejected was a complex and often obscure set of judgmental choices that has often and mistakenly been confused with scientific or expert-based standards. The theoretical and practical possibility of deriving genuine scientific quantity standards was also explored, but no promising new approach to determining detailed quantity lists was discovered. Finding no alternative to relying on its collective experience and judgment in assigning numerical totals to the more abstract notion of living standards, the committee chose an alternative that makes the exercise of judgment both explicit and "out front." The committee believes that family budgets based on its recommendations will be at least as useful as the current budgets but very much hopes that unsupportable claims will *not* be made by those who use them.

However, the family budgets do need an explicit conceptual base, and if the authoritative list of needs is abandoned, what is the alternative that informs the recommendations? The alternative is the notion of a popular or democratic consensus about norms or standards of comparison. The committee asserts that there is a general consensus about how much it takes for an ordinary family to "get along" — perhaps not an exact figure, but rather a range or "band" of total expenditure levels that contains what most people would agree is the "get along" amount. Similar consensus may be defined for thresholds for deprivation or abundance, and survey research, both in Europe and the United States, has been able to measure these levels.[3]

Assuming the existence of such norms as social facts, the committee addresses the task of finding acceptable ways of eliciting and expressing them in quantitative detail. The majority of the committee believes the reason the existing practice has been acceptable is that the numbers arrived at are consistent with the popular norms, not that they were derived from expert judgment. If "experts" had decided that everyone must have new shoes every week, for example, resulting budgets would have been widely rejected as outside the consensus for such norms. But it also follows that any method of establishing norms that succeeds in approximating the consensus will be reasonably well-received and found useful.

But this view of norms also suggests that a more direct way to elicit them would be to inquire about them in surveys. For this reason the committee recommends a major effort to evaluate and perfect the survey method so that it eventually may be considered in designing possible alternatives for the methods already recommended in this report.

In short, this report recommends a basic shift toward a more populist or democratic framework — the notion that ordinary people, not experts, know what they need in order to get along or to prosper. Thus, recommendations for new measurement are directed toward the task of finding stable and reproducible estimates of those levels.

Related differences. There are several implications of the basic change. First of all, in order to determine the cost of the shopping list, the existing budgets require current price data on the listed items; the process of updating the cost, between list revisions, similarly depends on a continuous flow of appropriate price data. The proposed approach does not require price data to establish a "bottom line" total cost number, but it does require continuous survey data on household expenditure behavior both for the total cost and for the current allocation among different lines of expenditure. Since price data would no longer be needed for the Family Budget Program (except for the "ratchet" computation which prevents reductions in real budget levels), the committee recommends that fixed-weight price index numbers be developed for inter-city and inter-regional comparisons. The existing budgets provide cost differentials that are often used as price differentials. The committee urges that the price data be kept separate from the budgetary norms but recognizes that each has its legitimate use and urges that both be surveyed and published.

Unlike the existing budgets which are shown only for specific cities and for regional aggregates that do not have homogeneous tax laws or climate, the new budget standards would be designed to cover all areas, State by State. In the event that dependable and consistent estimates of differential living costs according to urbanization can be formed, they could be added to the array of variations. But this should be done on a size or type-of-place basis rather than for specific cities. Because price data are collected only for specific cities, the committee recommends that the price comparisons be limited to those same cities.

The change in concept also implies a shift from an "absolute" to a "relative" standard, at least to the extent that the underlying, popularly conceived norms will be based on what the individuals are experiencing directly and on what they see going on around them. If the underlying norms can be faithfully reflected in the family budgets, they will automatically keep pace with the constantly changing levels and patterns of expenditure that correspond to the different standards. The absolute standards embodied in detailed lists of commodities must be overhauled periodically; only for a very short time do they approximate the patterns and items of actual current spending. (Pedal pushers, for example, are among the anachronistic items in the current budgets.)

Equivalence scales and family types. The proposed approach to the family budgets allows for extension of the budget levels and allocations to as many family types as desired. The committee recommends only six, but it would be possible to prepare other budgets of the same type on short notice if needed for special purposes. The equivalence scale provides an adjustment factor for calculating the appropriate budget total for any kind or size of family, and the most recently estimated expenditure allocation system will yield average patterns of spending for each. Finally, the tax and "other expense" categories can be calculated and added to yield a total "gross income" requirement for maintaining the standard for each kind of family. With the existing system a whole new list of goods and services must be specified for each separately budgeted family type. Clearly the size of this task has been an obstacle to providing coverage for a wider variety of family types. While the existing program has its own set of equivalence scales that can be used to adjust the four-person spending totals, they have never been widely used or given prominent attention.

ALTHOUGH THE COMMITTEE recommends substantial changes in the way family budgets are conceived, estimated, and presented, the new standards are very much in line with the traditional ones. The levels that have been chosen provide essential continuity with those that have been developed and found useful in the existing program. Consequently, the typical user will not notice any sharp change in the overall appearance of the budgets despite the sharp change in methodology. If the recommendations are accepted the committee believes that the broader coverage of the budgets, both as to family types and areas, will make the budgets useful for a wider range of users and that the proposed new Report on Household Consumption will add an important dimension to our array of social indicators. □

——— *FOOTNOTES* ———

¹ A large part of the estimates were based on analysis of the 1960–61 Survey of Consumer Expenditures. Given the availability of data from the 1972–73 Consumer Expenditure Survey and the mandate of the Comprehensive Employment and Training Act (CETA) of 1973 that "the Secretary (of Labor) shall develop methods to establish and maintain more comprehensive household and budget data at different levels of living, including a level of adequacy, to reflect the differences of household living costs in regions and localities, both urban and rural," the Bureau of Labor Statistics began to plan for a comprehensive revision of the Family Budget Program.

² See Carol Fendler and Mollie Orshansky, "Improving the Poverty Definition" in *Statistical Uses of Administrative Records with Emphasis on Mortality and Disability Research: Selected Papers given at the 1979 Annual Meeting of the American Statistical Association*, Washington, D.C., August 1979. Social Security Administration, Office of Research and Statistics, pp. 161–68.

³ See Denton Vaughn and S. Lancaster, "Income Levels and Their Impact on Two Subjective Measures of Wellbeing: Some Early Speculation from Work in Progress," *1979 Proceedings of the Section on Survey Research Methods, American Statistical Association*, Forthcoming; and Frank M. Andrews and Stephen B. Withy, *Social Indicators of Wellbeing: Americans' Perceptions to Life Quality* (New York, Plenum Press, 1976.)

Serious consideration of housework is usually neglected or analyzed in market economy terms. Home production is, however, a major determinant of our well-being, and it is different than the production of goods and services in the marketplace. The market economy is characterized by mass production and distribution of goods and services, whereas the home economy specializes in nurturing family members by the personalized provision of food, clothing, and shelter. In this article, home and market economies are contrasted on the dimensions of supervision, pay, mobility, measures of values, and personalization. As increasing numbers of women are employed in the marketplace, questions arise about the decline of the home economy.

36

HOME PRODUCTION FOR USE
IN A MARKET ECONOMY

Clair (Vickery) Brown

> *"How would I describe myself? It'll sound terrible—just a housewife.* (LAUGHS.) *It's true. What is a housewife? You don't have to have any special talents. I don't have any.*
>
> *"Oh—I even painted the house last year. How much does a painter get paid for painting a house?* (LAUGHS.) *What? I'm a skilled craftsman myself? I never thought about that. Artist? No.* (LAUGHS.) *I suppose if you do bake a good cake, you can be called an artist. But I never heard anybody say that. I bake bread too. Oh gosh, I've been a housewife for a long time.* (LAUGHS.)
>
> *"I never thought about what we'd be worth. I've read these things in the paper: If you were a tailor or a cook, you'd get so much an hour. I think that's a lot of baloney.*
>
> *"What am I doing? Cooking and cleaning.* (LAUGHS.) *It's necessary, but it's not really great."*
>
> *Theresa Carter,*
> *from Stud Terkel's* WORKING

Housework is taken for granted in our postindustrial economy, although the work done within the privacy of the home com-

Barrie Thorne, David Matza, Lois Greenwood, Lenore Weitzman, Todd Easton, Myra Strober, Harold Wilensky, and Joanne Kliejunas provided helpful comments and discussions on a previous draft.

prises the number-one full-time occupation and virtually all adults engage in it to some degree. Why have we largely ignored an essential work activity that is a major determinant of our well-being? Precisely because it is so essential and because, until recently, it has changed little.

Housework, or the work performed within the home economy, consists of child rearing and the provision of food, clothing, and shelter. This work satisfies basic human needs, and the functioning of the home economy must be taken for granted in order to ensure reproduction and to free part of the adult population for work activities outside the home. Even the threat of a disruption of basic housework services affects the smooth functioning of the society and the market economy. No wonder, then, that the recent rapid changes we have been witnessing in our family structure have precipitated the declaration of social crisis along with political resistance to change. The future of the family, which serves as a catchword for the future of women's role within the society, has gained high priority on the agenda of national social problems.

This essay analyzes the structural characteristics of home production and then uses the analysis to discuss how the home economy is related to the growing market economy. A source of conflict between these two economies stems from the fact that the production processes in the home economy are time-intensive and fulfill basic human needs, yet the work done in the home has declined in relative (although not absolute) importance as a determinant of the family's material standard of living because the goods and services purchased in the marketplace have become more important in defining the family's consumption position.

This analysis delineates the interactions between the home and market economies by two stages. During the first stage, many of the production processes of the home economy were taken over by the market economy. During the second stage, which has been underway for at least half a century, the market economy provided new goods and services never produced by the home economy. If the family wanted to consume these goods and services, they had to enter the marketplace both as workers (to earn money) and as consumers (to purchase the goods).

After discussing these historical trends, this essay documents how the shift toward fewer people per household has increased the resources needed per person to meet the basic needs of shelter, transportation, and housework. In addition, more fluid marital patterns have undermined the role of the family in providing income security for wives and have increased wives' need for an independent, dependable source of income other than their husband's income.

The essay then discusses the problems inherent in switching one's work effort between the home and market economies because of the different work and value structures of the two economies. These differences post barriers to rapidly and smoothly changing the current division of labor by sex between the two economies.

Housework: The Provision of Essential Services

As feminist social historians have noted, the stability of the family has long been a social concern, and keeping women's primary work role within the home has been the major focus of this concern.[1] The threatened disruption of the family, and along with it a breakdown in the functioning of the home economy, is distinguished in the current crisis by the rise in the importance of paid work for wives and mothers outside the home. In order to discuss the economic importance of ongoing change in the family, we need to understand the basic characteristics of housework and how the home economy has been affected by economic growth.

The home economy produces a "good home life," primarily through providing the four basic housework services (child rearing and the provision of food, clothing, and shelter) along with satisfying personal relationships. Even the adult without children must take care of her (his) food, clothing, and shelter needs. Because some housework is a necessity, it must be readily obtainable under normal circumstances; otherwise, it could not have become a necessity.

"Necessity" is a nebulous concept because it is defined precisely only through death, and the point of death comes at different levels of deprivation for different individuals. This approach to absolute necessity became economically obsolete before it was ever adequately defined. Since an economically mature country can afford the broader test of relative deprivation, the concept of necessity expanded beyond those items necessary for the support of life to include items that are necessary to be integrated into the society. This broader concept of necessity is even more muddled, however, as the determination of "socially necessary" becomes a political football.

Housework has components that fit into both concepts of necessity—some housework is needed to support and reproduce life at a subsistence level, and other housework is needed to reproduce child and adult behavior that is socially acceptable. Housework activities above these two levels can be viewed as producing value above necessity (e.g., leisure for the housewife or nonnecessity work that enhances the family's life). An outsider's division of these categories of housework most likely would differ from the housewife's categorization of her own work, but the categorization provides a division of housework into the two groups of necessity and above-necessity activities.

When the wife has primary responsibility for the home, she can engage in paid labor only after making sure the necessity housework activities are done. Then she can compare the value to the family of the above-necessity housework with the value of the goods and services she can buy with her paycheck. Part of the analysis by economists of women's work decisions has been misdirected because the necessity component of housework has either been ignored (or judged to be significantly small) or has been assumed to be available for purchase in the marketplace.

The family's valuation of the fruits of the wife's work does not occur in a vacuum. For example, the family's comparison of the mother's supervision of children after school with a large entertainment budget depends to a large extent on what other families in the neighborhood are doing. And although the primary determinant of the amount of necessity housework is the family composition, especially the number and ages of the children, this too is affected by social custom.

The housewife performs a broad range of daily services at times that are dictated by human needs—for example, satisfying the need for food must be done at specified times and responding to a baby's needs must occur as the need arises. Other activities may be performed at times chosen by the homemaker—for example, housecleaning and shopping. Most importantly, a full-time homemaker is on call twenty-four hours a day, and she provides her family with flexibility in using her services, especially in providing personalized care and attention.

These timing problems characterize both necessity and above-necessity chores and constrain the homemaker's ability to decide how to allocate her time among different work activities. In addition, market work must be done in blocks of time at specified hours. But these scheduling rigidities are only part of the limitations faced by the wife in her "choice" of work activities. Most importantly, she faces the situation that most services provided within the home cannot be substituted with goods and services bought in the marketplace. This point has not been obvious to economists and needs elaboration.

What's Wrong with Economic Analyses of the Home Economy

In most economic models, the household is viewed as producing consumption by combining time with market goods and services (e.g., meals are produced with the time spent shopping for and preparing store-bought items). The family is viewed as facing a large array of possibilities of how to use its time and money to produce a given set of consumption bundles. More specifically, the wife is viewed as having a great deal of flexibility in deciding how to combine her time with market goods in producing her "output," such as meal preparation, a clean house, and neat clothing. However, very little substitution between the homemaker's time and market goods has actually been observed in the homemaking process. There is evidence that both employed and full-time homemakers use the same techniques in running their homes, with the employed wife using few market goods and services to substitute for her own input of time.[2] The main substitution tends to be between the wife's market work and her leisure time. Lack of substitution of time and market goods in housework means that the way a family lives—its material standard of living versus its personalized care—is dramatically affected by whether the wife works full-time at home or whether she also works for pay outside the home.

The lack of substitution between housework and purchased goods and services reflects the more basic lack of comparability between services provided by the homemaker and the goods and services purchased in the marketplace. The home economy specializes in producing mothering and the nurturing of family members along with personalized care in providing food, clothing, and shelter. The marketplace produces sophisticated medical care, advanced education, the means for transportation and communication, urban housing, and the ability to pool risk through insurance, as well as mass-produced food, clothing, cars, and other consumer durables. The family's evaluation of these dissimilar home-produced and market-produced goods and services will be a major determinant of whether the wife works exclusively at home or also has a job. The family's evaluation will vary with its circumstances and experiences over time.

The wife's work decision about having a paid job should be viewed as a decision by her and her husband (although not necessarily without conflict) about the family's needs or desire for her mothering and nurturing services weighed against its needs or desire for the market goods and services that can be purchased with her paycheck. Although the cost to the family of the wife's housework is her foregone earnings in the labor market, her market wage will not accurately reflect the marginal cost of her time because of the constraints she faces in scheduling her activities at home and at a job. In addition, the full-time homemaker's provision of round-the-clock care of family members' needs makes it impossible to equate the value of her time with her replacement cost (i.e., the wage rate such services would command in the marketplace). The personalized and on-call nature of her work prevents us from evaluating the services of the housewife as a combination of so many hours of chauffeur, cook, babysitter, and laundress per day. In the real world, the household could not contract to buy these services in the small amounts of time and at the random hours that the housewife actually performs these duties. Even in those instances where the contracting of some services occurs, the service is more impersonalized and must be directed by someone (usually the housewife). The purchased services usually do not reflect the kind of service the housewife provides because she intimately knows the family members she is serving and takes responsiblilty for organizing and providing the care as it is needed.

The "new home economics," the name adopted by the neoclassical school for their work on the family,[3] has done little to increase our understanding of the home economy because its positivist methodological approach only provides a logical, rationalistic framework for a *post hoc* measurement of family behavioral response to economic variables. Because a family is assumed to make the best of its given economic situation, its observed behavior is optimal by assumption, and the differences between households that appear to be economically identical are theoretically "explained" by unidentified preference structures. Problems of conflict among family members are admitted but ignored.

Even more seriously, the question of what options are available to the family is not addressed, since one of the tenets of neoclassical theory is that the marketplace responds to people's needs and desires rather than that people's needs and desires are formed by the marketplace. Choice, in an economic sense, is assumed to exist on the basis that if people are willing to pay the market value (i.e., the opportunity costs or exchange value of the resources used) for a good or service, then the market will provide the good or service. However, when there are large fixed costs and information problems, such as in housing, few people may be willing to take the risk associated with individually experimenting with different kinds of housing that would allow for more flexibility in family arrangements, even though collectively the demand for experimental housing might justify the cost. Since the functioning of the home economy is intimately tied to the family arrangement and the housing situation, people's choice of how to provide the necessities produced by the home economy depends on the options available to them in how they set up their households. If the housing stock does not include certain arrangements, such as communal kitchens and dining rooms, we cannot automatically assert that people have voluntarily rejected this housing arrangement in favor of private kitchens.

The importance of this point will become clearer after we look at how the relative importance of the home economy for family consumption standards has declined with economic growth and how the absolute importance of the home economy in the national economy has increased with changes in family arrangements.

The Impact of Rising Standards of Living on the Contribution of Housework

The relationship between the home and market economies has gone through two distinct stages. Early industrialization began the process of transferring some production processes (e.g., clothmaking, sewing, canning foods) from the home to the marketplace. Although the home economy could still produce these goods, the processes were arduous and the market economy was usually more efficient. Soon, the more important second stage was evident—the marketplace began producing goods and services that had never been produced by the home economy, and the home economy was unable to produce them (e.g., electricity and electrical appliances, the automobile, the telephone, television, advanced education, sophisticated medical care). In the second stage, the question of whether the home economy was less efficient in producing these new goods and

services was irrelevant; if the family were to enjoy these fruits of industrialization, they would have to be procured in the marketplace. The
traditional ways of taking care of these needs in the home, such as in
nursing the sick, became socially unacceptable (and, in most serious cases,
probably were less successful). Just as the advent of the automobile made
the use of the horse-drawn carriage illegal and then impractical, and the
advent of television changed the radio from a source of entertainment to a
source of background music, so most of the fruits of economic growth did
not increase the options available to the home economy to either produce
the good or service or purchase it in the market. Growth brought with it
increased *diversity* in consumption goods, but *not* increased flexibility for
the home economy in procuring these goods and services. Instead,
economic growth brought with it increased consumer reliance on the marketplace. In order to consume these new goods and services, the family
had to enter the marketplace as wage earners and consumers. The neoclassical model that views the family as deciding whether to produce goods
and services directly or to purchase them in the marketplace is basically a
model of the first stage. It cannot accurately be applied to the second (and
current) stage.

The process of urbanization was an important part of the economic
growth that changed consumption patterns to include market goods and
services that made living in dense areas more feasible and desirable. The
movement of the population from the farm or from abroad to the city or
the suburb displayed distinct but complex patterns. In 1910, one-third of
all households still lived on a farm; by 1970, fewer than 1 in 20 households
lived on a farm. Urban population rose from 46 percent in 1910 to 73
percent in 1970. After World War II, the suburban population doubled
from 14 percent in 1950 to 27 percent in 1977.[4] Urban distribution networks facilitated the mass marketing of the modern consumer goods made
possible by technological innovation and capital formation.

Advances in medical technology and the growing social acceptance of
birth control and abortion increased women's control over the number
and, more importantly, the timing of their children. As a result, the
number of years devoted to child rearing declined. Currently the median
age of the mother at the birth of her last child is under thirty years.[5] In a
majority of families, the mother has completed her childbearing and has
her youngest child in public school by the time she has turned thirty-five.
Faced with a life expectancy of over seventy years, women can no longer
view the time-intensive role of mothering as a lifetime career.

The dramatic improvement in the material standard of living since
World War II can be demonstrated with a few observations from the
Consumer Expenditure Surveys of 1950 and 1972 (for the average
middle-income family of four):

1. The percent of after-tax income spent on recorded expenditures declined from 111 percent to 92 percent.
2. The percent of after-tax income spent on food declined from 33 percent to 19 percent.
3. The percent of after-tax income spent on clothing declined from 12 percent to 6 percent.
4. The proportion of after-tax income spent on transportation increased from 13 percent to 18 percent, primarily reflecting the increased ownership of cars.
5. Insurance and retirement increased from 5 percent to 7 percent.
6. Shelter expenditures increased from 11 percent to 13 percent (as home ownership increased from 57 percent to 72 percent for this group), and house furnishing expenditures declined from 7 percent to 4 percent.[6]

The primary housework activities of meal preparation and clothing care have been using a declining share of the family's budget; hence a housewife's efforts to decrease expenditures in these areas by direct work activities (e.g., baking from scratch) or more careful shopping made less difference in their relative impact on the family's budget in 1972 than they did in 1950. This decrease in the relative economic importance of housework probably also affects the significance a wife attaches to her work in the home. Purchases of food and clothing, 45 percent of the average middle-income family's disposable income in 1950, accounted for only 25 percent of their income in 1972. Twenty percent of the family's budget that had previously been spent on food and clothing now became freed for other kinds of expenditures, primarily transportation, insurance and retirement, and homeownership.

As a growing proportion of the family's budget is being spent on market goods and services that are not directly related to housework activities, the family's ability to consume these items depends primarily on its purchasing power (i.e., its money income) and not on its time available for housework activities. The output of the home economy has declined in relative importance as a determinant of the family's total consumption standard; however, housework still remains important as a necessity.

Budget studies show that families have used economic growth both to increase the command over material goods and to lessen financial strain by reducing expenditures as a proportion of disposable income. However, most families have not used increasing affluence to increase their time available for leisure or other nonpaid activities. To the contrary, the hours devoted to market work per family have increased, as have the number of activities that go through the marketplace. Some social scientists have viewed this unfolding of events as a paradox; the Greek philosophers had predicted that an affluent society would use time above that needed to produce necessities to enjoy the good life, defined in terms of noneconomic satisfactions.[7] This has not occurred, as the following figures show.

Real per capita income in 1972 was 60 percent higher than in 1950, and this increase reflected both higher real wages and more workers per family. If we look at the families in the top 60 percent of the income distribution, we see that only 20 to 30 percent of the wives in husband-wife families were in the labor force in 1950; by 1972, 60 percent of the families in these middle- and upper-middle-income groups had more than one earner in the labor market, and 10 to 30 percent had more than two earners. In addition, nonearned income, primarily transfer payments and income from assets, became increasingly important over the period. In 1972, the typical middle-income family had at least two earners and income in addition to their earnings.[8] At the same time, changes were occurring in living arrangements, and these changes have important implications for how we use our economic resources, especially the time required for housework.

The Resources Needed by Different Families

The living arrangement of families simultaneously determines their needs, which reflect the age and number of family members, and their resources, which reflect the economic power of the adults (i.e., their control over wages and hours of work). Setting up a household entails large fixed costs that include procuring shelter, household furnishings, and a means of transportation. These fixed costs result in economies of scale with increased family size, since it involves the sharing of capital among household members. As a result, a decline in the nation's average household size means an increase in the resources needed to provide the basic housing and equipment needed by the population.

The period from 1940 to 1975 witnessed a decline in average household size from 3.7 to 2.9 persons.[9] This decline reflects primarily an increase in the number of unrelated individuals living alone, reinforced by a decrease in families living together as well as a decrease in the number of children per family since the mid-1960s. Over this period, the population of the country grew 62 percent, the number of nuclear families increased 76 percent, and primary individuals (i.e., individuals who do not live with relatives) increased an astonishing 352 percent.

The phenomenal growth in primary individuals resulted from an increased tendency for both younger and older adults to maintain their own households. In 1950, only 43 percent of unrelated individuals lived alone; by 1975, 73 percent did. The one-adult household jumped from 7 percent of all households in 1940 to 21 percent in 1976.

Although families sharing housing were never a large group during this period, group-family housing became almost nonexistent. Less than 5 percent of all families shared homes in 1976 (down from around 16 percent in 1940). Family groups that in the past tended to double up and young and retired adults who tended to live with their families are now buying more privacy. Whatever the reasons for the rapid growth of one-person households, the economic outcome is clear: Our society is using an increasing amount of resources per capita to provide housing, household furnishings, and transportation. To what extent this reflects our state of affluence or to what extent this reflects the inflexibility of our existing institutions remains an open question.

The fixed money costs of setting up a household are only part of the relatively large fixed costs associated with smaller households; in addition there are time economies of scale. Table 1 gives the economies of scale observed at the poverty threshold. For example, a one-adult household required $43 of income per week in 1973 and 31 hours of household work time to stay above poverty. By contrast, the one adult with one child household required $58 per week, an increase of $15 (35%); it also required 57 hours of housework time, an increase of 26 hours (84%). With the

Table 1. Economies of Scale at the Poverty Threshold

Household	One-Adult Income Index	One-Adult Time Index
	Weekly Figures	
One adult with:		
0 children	1.00	1.00
1 child	1.35	1.84
2–3 children	1.81	1.97
4–5 children	2.47	2.03
6 or more children	3.16	2.23
Two adults with:		
0 children	1.35	1.39
1 child	1.63	2.00
2–3 children	2.19	2.13
4–5 children	2.98	2.19
6 or more children	3.26	2.39

Source: The "one-adult indices" were calculated by dividing the time or money requirements for each household type by the corresponding requirement for the one-adult household. The calculations for the income figures are based on the Social Security Administration's poverty thresholds, and the calculations for the time figures are based on the time requirements derived in Clair Vickery, "The Time Poor: A New Look at Poverty," *Journal of Human Resources* 12, no. 1 (Winter 1977).

addition of one to two more children, the money needed increased $20 (81%), while the time needed increased 4 hours (97%). Major economies of scale in terms of income are experienced with the addition of the first (and additional) children, and major economies of scale in terms of time are experienced with the addition of the second (and additional) children. In the two-adult household, money economies of scale also begin with the second person; time economies of scale also begin with the second child. In both kinds of households, the first child substantially raises the required housework time, and additional children only slightly increase the (already substantial) time required.[10]

As family groupings have become more fragmented, the home economy has become less efficient because the smaller household does not capture the benefits of the scale economies. The impact has been most obvious in the growing housing shortage where the rapid proliferation of new households has pushed vacancy rates downward and housing prices upward. In addition, the unforeseen increases in the price of energy over the past six years have caused energy costs to become a large part of shelter costs. This price development makes the smaller household even less efficient because energy usage is part of the scale economies of shelter.

The growth in real income has allowed the individualization of consumption activities as the economic need to band together as family members has declined and the ability to buy privacy has increased. The result has been an increase in our work activities and resources that go toward fulfilling necessities, as well as an increased reliance on the marketplace. Economic analyses of the family have ignored this source of inefficient behavior and instead have focused on the economic returns from specialization in housework. These trends toward fragmentation of family groupings and equalization of work roles by sex are inefficient in terms of producing the resources used to satisfy basic needs, although they may not be inefficient in terms of the more general efficiency criteria of satisfying needs or desires above the level of necessity. Unfortunately, economists have not addressed the more general question of whether there is a more efficient way of satisfying the observed quest for greater flexibility in household arrangements and for women's economic independence. Both goals have a major impact on the functioning of the home economy.

The Changing Role of the Home Economy

The demand by the women's movement for economic independence and the equalization of sex roles has brought into clear relief the contrasts and contradictions between the home economy and the market economy, for these differences between the two economies have helped perpetuate the inequality between the sexes. Because women have been prepared to run the home economies when they assume their roles as wives and mothers, their sense of identity and personal power are grounded in this economy. The market economy and home economy have their own value structures, their own work structure, and reward different behaviors. For this reason, movement between the two economies is difficult and usually involves personal conflict.[11] The two economies can be contrasted by five major characteristics:

1. *Supervision.* The housewife is her own supervisor during the day as she performs her chores within the home. Although she responds to the demands and needs of other family members, she is in charge of deciding how to provide the personalized care. At a paid job, most workers have a formal supervisor who decides what work needs to be done in what manner and ensures that the work is actually performed.

2. *Pay.* The housewife gives her services within the home economy; in return, the family shares the husband's earnings (or in the absence of the children's father, she qualifies for a government welfare check or a government-enforced maintenence check from the father). Although the work performed within the home economy varies little by the income of the husband, the earnings that the wife and children share vary tremendously. There is no systematic relationship between the output of her work efforts and the family income. No provision is made for sickness, and the housewife is on call twenty-four hours a day. In a paid job the worker has a formal or informal contract that stipulates a rate of pay for a job performed. Rules govern behavior on the job, sick leave, vacation days, and hours of work.

3. *Mobility.* The housewife's job in the home economy depends on the agreement with her husband to share his income and her labor as a family unit. If she becomes dissatisfied with her job, her choices are to improve the job (or otherwise to change her attitude toward her job) or to quit. Quitting is not a clear-cut option, however, since some home economy must still exist in order to provide food, clothing, and shelter for the children and the separated parents. Because of the essential nature of the housewife's job, "changing jobs" for her boils down to continuing working (i.e., caring for the children) without a guarantee of pay; "changing jobs" means a complete change in life style with a greatly reduced income. The market economy provides for less dramatic changes if a worker is dissatisfied with a job and is unable to effect changes at the current workplace. Although options are restricted by the market jobs available, and changing jobs is a stressful process, the worker still faces more than the two options of continuing on the current job or working for little or no pay.

4. *Measure of Value.* The housewife works in a personalized economy that caters to children's and husband's needs, and the measure of value is

not quantified. In fact, economists have tried unsuccessfully to quantify the value of the home economy through its reflection in the market economy, primarily because the outputs of the home and market economies are not the same. The home economy focuses on individual and family well-being, and its personalized care and nurturing cannot be given a price tag by comparing the services of the home economy with what a family is willing to pay for occasional substitutes (e.g., child care, meals out, maid service), since the occasional substitute is not comparable to a permanent replacement. Asked about the comparison, many housewives would agree with Theresa Carter quoted at the start of this essay: "I think that's a lot of baloney." So far the marketplace has not provided a permanent replacement for the services provided in the home economy. In contrast, the employed woman knows precisely the value of her work since the marketplace uses the exchange value (i.e., the rate of pay) as its measure of value for the work performed.

5. *Personal behavior.* The home economy is based on the concept of mutual aid and service to others, and this cooperative behavior is necessary for the home economy to function. It can be viewed primarily as a noncompetitive economy, while the market economy is a competitive economy that rewards the individual. A woman who has worked primarily in the home economy is at a disadvantage in the market economy, which has a different reward structure and different value system. If the woman carries with her cooperative and service values of the home economy, she is likely to end up working for a low monetary reward when she seeks the approval of others and a sense of worth from service to others, both reflections of the reward system of the home economy. Since money and individual advancement are not part of the reward structure of the home economy, a woman who takes the value structure of the home economy with her into the market economy will be at a disadvantage in demanding equitable compensation for her work according to the values of the market economy.

These conflicts between the value and reward structures of the home and market economies have caused deep divisions among feminist social scientists in discussing the future of the home economy. Women, who have had responsibility for running the home economy, realize the importance of the home economy for rearing children. At the same time, they realize the role the home economy has played in keeping women in a subordinate role through economic dependence on the husband. Since the home economy takes care of necessities, we cannot hold its functioning in abeyance until we agree on how to restructure it. At one extreme we hear cries for saving the values of the home economy at the expense of equality for women; at the other extreme, we hear cries for destroying the home economy and turning its functions over to the marketplace or state in order to achieve equality for women. Faced with these two dismal prospects, many women (and men) have had to search for some alternative. As is usually the case, compromise positions seem to promise too much to everyone and please no one, since they tend to gloss over the underlying conflict between the home and market economies.

As the household has shrunk in size and as market activities have become more important, the dichotomy between the large, impersonal, efficient market economy and the small, personalized, inefficient home economy grows. Do viable alternatives to these extremes exist? If they exist, are there any signs of the mechanisms that will produce the necessary insitutional changes? Although more and more people are experimenting with nontraditional family arrangements, these experiments do not yet point to the widespread acceptance of new family forms. Possible ways for families or individuals to pool capital equipment, share housing, and engage in a quasi-barter system of exchanging skills within a neighborhood setting remain unexplored. Examples of such potentially pooled activities include car repair, plumbing and household repairs, small carpentry and remodeling jobs, gardening, electrical work, as well as the traditional jobs of child care and meal preparation. Although the social institutions through which these exchanges might occur do not yet exist, the economic forces promoting such changes are increasing. One example of a possible pooling arrangement is to allow neighborhoods to use the public school system to set up systems of car repair and small carpentry jobs. Another possibility is for the government to experiment with setting up new-style apartments for older people that would allow each person to have a separate living space and at the same time share kitchens or bathrooms. This set-up would allow the sharing of food preparation, which is their major housework activity.

The Future of Home Economy

As the social customs enforcing lifetime marriages have weakened, marriage with its explicit sharing of money income and housework no longer provides income security for the wife. These shifts in family institutions have increased the need for most adults to have some direct control over their money income, and this control is usually achieved through paid labor.

Wives' work responsibilities in the home have been influenced by these social changes and by economic growth in two important ways. First, their homework-based bargaining power diminished as homemaking activities declined in value relative to the family's total consumption activities. As the jobs available to women expanded and as their control over conception grew, the wife was drawn to paid labor in order to in-

crease her economic contribution to the family, her input in family decision making, and her own self-esteem, as well as to increase her financial
security in the event of divorce. Second, since the majority of families
came to have a wife employed at least part of the time, each family became
increasingly dependent on the wife's earnings to maintain its relative income position and participate in consuming the fruits of economic growth.

At the same time that each adult's need for economic independence
has grown, the family and the individual have both become more dependent on the marketplace, this dependence on wage labor mitigated somewhat by government programs of unemployment compensation, welfare
benefits, and social security. This long-run trend toward the marketplace
producing more and better goods and services that have become part of the
commonly accepted living standard for most families raises the question of
how much economic growth has reduced financial strain. The entrance of
the wife into paid labor also does not necessarily reduce the family's
financial stress, especially when one spouse is unemployed. Although the
risk of the family having no money income declines when both spouses are
in the labor market, the family's incidence of unemployment increases as
each worker faces the risk of unemployment. Unless the wife's working
increases the family's savings and decreases its financial commitments, her
employment will not decrease the financial strain that accompanies unemployment. Once the wife becomes regularly employed, she can no
longer act as a buffer stock of labor, entering the labor market as a temporary waitress or office clerk when her husband is unemployed or involved
in a work stoppage. The family's financial pressures will continue to be
determined not only by their income level but also by their material
aspirations, which may be fueled by economic growth and the wife's
entrance into paid labor.

As the number of paid work hours per family has grown, the time
available for nonmarket work, for interpersonal relationships, and for family life in general has declined. How can we get off this treadmill? The
decisions of each family and society as a whole are interrelated, so that no
family feels it can cut back its market work until other families also cut
back their market work. Otherwise, the family's economic position relative to its peer group will fall. The labor movement and the government
could both promote social discussion of policies that would allow families
greater flexibility in organizing the husband's and wife's work and simultaneously encourage a better balance of paid and nonpaid activities. Programs such as legislation to do away with mandatory overtime or to decrease the standard workweek through amendment of the Fair Labor
Standards Act would be steps in the right direction of reducing the paid
work hours for both men and women.

In looking at the role that families play in our economy, I conclude that as the home economy's functions decline in relative terms, the family's ability to procure higher earnings by increasing the paid work time of its members will reach a dead end. As we experience the personal costs of our economic gains, then perhaps we will be willing to rethink the relative importance of economic gains versus our noneconomic needs for love, self-development, and satisfying relationships that come with good home and community life. Central to these issues are the evolving work roles of men and women in the home and market economies. If our society goes toward more equal work roles between men and women, we will necessarily go toward increasing the work done by men within the home and the time spent by men in family life. One role of the economist in this analysis is to reevaluate the gains from specialization of work roles at a time when the activities performed in the home have become less important in determining the living standards of the family. At the same time, we need to search for alternative ways of providing the services normally produced by the home economy, such as meal preparation and child care, that are no longer provided efficiently by small households and yet need to be produced within a cooperative setting that reflects the values of the home economy.

As Theresa Cook said, "Cooking and cleaning. It's necessary, but it's not really great."

Notes

1. See Barbara Ehrenreich and Deirdre English, *For Her Own Good* (New York: Doubleday Anchor 1978); and Sheila M. Rothman, *Woman's Proper Place* (New York: Basic, 1978).

2. Clair Vickery, "Women's Economic Contribution to the Family," in *The Subtle Revolution: Women at Work*, ed. Ralph Smith (Washington, D.C.: Urban Institute, 1979); Myra H. Strober and Charles B. Weinberg, "Stragegies Used by Working and Nonworking Wives to Reduce Time Pressures," *Journal of Consumer Research*, March 1980, pp. 338–48.

3. See, for example, Gary S. Becker, "A Theory of the Allocation of Time," *Economic Journal*, September 1965, pp. 493–517; idem, "The Economics of Marriage," *Journal of Political Economy*, July/August 1973, pp. 813–46; Supplement on New Economic Approaches to Fertility, *Journal of Political Economy*, March/April 1973, pt. 2; and Jacob Mincer, "Labor Force Participation of Married Women," in

Aspects of Labor Economics, ed. H. Gregg Lewis (Princeton: Princeton University Press, 1962), pp. 63–105.

4. U.S. Bureau of the Census, *Historical Statistics of the United States, Colonial Times to 1970*, 1976, Series A-73, A-82, A-350, A-352. The definition of "urban area" varies by year.

5. Hugh Carter and Paul C. Glick, *Marriage and Divorce: A Social and Economic Study* (Cambridge, Mass.: Harvard University Press, 1976), p. 145; updated by Glick in a paper presented at the annual meeting of the Population Association of America in Montreal, 30 April 1976.

6. This analysis of expenditure patterns draws from my earlier work, "Women's Economic Contribution." These same patterns of *changes* in expenditures are observed across all income groups in addition to the middle-income family reported here.

7. Staffan B. Linder, *The Harried Leisure Class* (New York: Columbia University Press, 1970); see also Harold Wilensky, "The Uneven Distribution of Leisure: The Impact of Economic Growth on 'Free Time,'" *Social Problems* 9 (Summer 1961).

8. U.S. Bureau of the Census, *Statistical Abstract of the United States: 1976*, Table Nos. 636, 630, 2; U.S. Bureau of the Census, *Current Population Reports*, Series P-60, Nos. 80 and 90.

9. This discussion of changes in living arrangements draws from Clair Vickery, "The Changing Household: Implications for Devising an Income Support Program," *Public Policy*, Winter 1978, pp. 121–51.

10. Similar economies of scale are observed at other income levels. Equivalency tables for the hypothetical Department of Labor budgets (lower, moderate, and higher cost budget) for urban families can be found in U.S. Bureau of Labor Statistics, *Revised Equivalence Scale for Estimating Equivalent Incomes or Budget Costs by Family Type*, Bulletin No. 1570-2, November 1968. Time-budget studies across income groups are reported in Kathryn E. Walker and Margaret E. Woods, *Time Use: A Measure of Household Production of Family Goods and Services* (Washington, D.C.: American Home Economics Association, 1976).

11. A study of these issues as they relate to the displaced homemaker has been done by Lois Greenwood, *Toward a Theory of Women and Powerlessness: A Study of the Displaced Homemaker*, forthcoming Ph.D. dissertation, University of California, Berkeley.

PART VIII

MARITAL ENRICHMENT
AND PREMARITAL PREPARATION

Marriage enrichment is viewed as a philosophy, a process, and a variety of programs. The philosophy of marriage enrichment is based on a positive, growth-oriented, dynamic view of marriage which suggests that people and relationships have strengths and resources which can be tapped and developed. The process of marriage enrichment has three major theoretical bases: the Rogerian emphasis on providing an empathic environment, the behavioral emphasis on learning and practicing specific skills, and the use of group process for providing a safe learning environment. The process is dynamic, experiential, educational, and preventive in nature. The variety of marriage enrichment programs is described and a historical overview of the research literature on marriage enrichment is provided. A detailed review of the research literature on marriage enrichment leads to the conclusion that the appropriate attitude about the effectiveness of marriage enrichment programs is one of cautious optimism. The results of outcome studies have generally been positive, but much of the existing research has been conducted with limited samples of couples or has been poorly designed.

37

MARRIAGE ENRICHMENT

Larry Hof and William R. Miller

Introduction

Marriage Enrichment is a philosophy, a process, and a variety of programs. Although the programmatic expressions are many and the structure, content, and setting are greatly varied, all of the programs share at least several things in common. They are

> concerned with enhancing the couple's communication, emotional life, or sexual relationships; with fostering marriage strengths, personal growth, and the development of marriage and individual potential while maintaining a consistent and primary focus on the relationship of the couple (Otto, 1976, p. 14).

Mr. Hof is Director of Group and Enrichment Programming, Marriage Council of Philadelphia, and Associate in Psychiatry, University of Pennsylvania School of Medicine. Dr. Miller is Director of Research, Marriage Council of Philadelphia, and Assistant Professor of Psychology in Psychiatry, University of Pennsylvania School of Medicine, 4025 Chestnut Street (2nd Floor), Philadelphia, Pennsylvania 19104. Preparation of this article was supported in part by National Institute of Health Grant RR-09069 to Dr. Miller.

This article appeared in a revised form in *Marriage Enrichment: Philosophy, Process and Program* by Larry Hof, MDiv, and William R. Miller, PhD.

The most popular programs (in terms of numbers of actual participants) have been designed "for couples who have what they perceive to be fairly well-functioning marriages and who wish to make their marriages even more mutually satisfying" (Otto, 1976, p. 13; see also Clinebell, 1975; Hopkins & Hopkins, 1975; Hopkins, Hopkins, Mace, & Mace, 1978; Koch & Koch, 1976; Mace & Mace, 1976a; Miller, 1975). However, an increasing number of practitioners are employing marriage enrichment procedures and programs with couples identified as "troubled," "dysfunctional," or "clinical," viewing such procedures and programs as important and beneficial adjuncts to marital and relationship therapy (Bolte, 1975; Clinebell, 1975; Gottman, Notarius, Gonso, & Markman, 1976; Guerney, 1977; L'Abate, 1977; L'Abate & Weeks, 1976; Schauble & Hill, 1976; Smith & Alexander, 1974; ·Wright & L'Abate, 1977; Mace, Note 1).

Marriage Enrichment is one of a newly emerging group of programs and services which is attempting to bring about a synthesis between the personal and the social (cf. Glasser & Glasser, 1977). Sensing the serious problems facing marriage and the family in our society (e.g., rising divorce rates, violence between marital partners and within families, etc.), and at the same time affirming the need for personal growth and fulfillment, the proponents of marriage enrichment have made a commitment to stabilize the marriage relationship in our society, and to enable it to become a mutually satisfying relationship. It is hoped that this can be accomplished by making it possible for individuals to develop (not "find") fulfillment within the marital relationship. The emphasis on development is a clear statement of marriage enrichment's belief that relationships need to be worked at continually, mutually, and reciprocally, in a disciplined, committed, and responsible way (Benson, Berger, & Mease, 1975; Buckland, 1977; Lederer & Jackson, 1968; Mace, 1975b; Mace & Mace, 1975; Miller, Nunnally, & Wackman, 1976b; Otto, 1969; Vincent, 1973). If this occurs, then it is thought that the synthesis of the social and the personal can occur within the marital relationship, and the goal of interpersonal intimacy can be achieved.

The origin of the term "marriage enrichment" is unclear, but synonyms such as "marital enrichment," "marital growth," "marital health," and "preventive marital health" are frequently used. Apart from Otto's quote in the previous paragraph, there are few clearly stated definitions of marriage enrichment. Mace and Mace (1974) have defined marriage enrichment as "drawing out potentialities in the marriage that are already there, unrealized and underdeveloped" (p. 96), and making a conscious commitment to marital and individual growth, to in-depth involvement and sharing with each other, to open communication, to effective conflict utilization, and to the experience of deep intimacy. L'Abate (Note 2) defines enrichment as "the use of structured, manual-dictated programs chosen from a large library to fit the needs of a particular couple or family" (p. 2), and he links the use of the term enrichment with semi-professional personnel working under the supervision of a trained therapist (L'Abate, 1977). This latter definition is much too restrictive and does not accurately express the thinking of many of the other people involved in the marriage enrichment movement, though it may well serve L'Abate's purposes. The statements of Otto and the Maces come closest to being a sufficiently broad definition of the term.

The lack of a generally accepted definition of marriage enrichment, and the fact that different clinicians and researchers have defined the term in a variety of ways, poses at least one serious problem for reviewing the literature. It is difficult to determine whether a particular study should be included or excluded from a review of research on enrichment. For example, Beck (1975) classified only five of the outcome studies of marital counseling she reviewed as studies of marriage enrichment. Yet, many of the 29 studies Gurman and Kniskern (1977) included in their review of marriage enrichment programs can be found in Beck's article, but listed by Beck as studies of marital counseling or communication training.

The great diversity in marriage enrichment programming, the lack of a clearly developed and enunciated theoretical base for many of the programs (which contributes to the diversity of programs), and the lack of sufficient empirical research on most of the programs, when combined with the definitional problem noted above, makes an in-depth review rather difficult. However, problems such as these appear with any movement in its infancy, and marriage enrichment is still in the early stages of development. The Maces (Mace & Mace, 1974), Otto (1969), the Smiths (Mace & Mace, 1978; Smith & Smith, 1976), and the leaders of Marriage Encounter (Bosco, 1973) were conducting programs in the early and middle 1960s. But, Otto (1975, 1976), in a survey of 30 professionals involved in marriage enrichment programming, found that 90 percent of respondents conducted their first program in 1973 or later.

The focus of this article will be upon a brief discussion of the philosophy, process, and programmatic expressions of marriage enrichment; an overview of the history of marriage enrichment; and an in-depth review of the research assessing the outcome of marriage enrichment programs.* A more detailed discussion of these issues is contained in Hof and Miller (Note 3).

Philosophy, Process, and Programs

PHILOSOPHY OF MARRIAGE ENRICHMENT

Marriage enrichment is based on a philosophy of growth and the human-potential hypothesis that all persons and relationships have a great number of strengths and resources and a tremendous amount of unused potential which can be tapped and developed (Mace & Mace, 1975; Otto, 1976). All relationships and individuals thus have a need and potential for growth, and all persons, given the appropriate environment and conditions, can choose and learn how to change and maintain significant interpersonal relationships, and can experience increased satisfaction in life and in relationships with other people (Clinebell, 1975, 1976; Luthman & Kirschenbaum, 1974; Mace & Mace, 1976a; Miller et al., 1976b; Otto, 1976).

Proponents of marriage enrichment have a positive, growth-oriented, and dynamic view of marriage. It is affirmed that the marriage relationship can still provide opportunities for individual and couple growth and fulfillment, and for acceptance and love, as each partner is known and loved by the other in an interdependent way (Mace & Mace, 1974; Otto, 1969). Marriage is seen as a growing, dynamic, constantly changing relationship (Mace & Mace, 1974; Otto, 1969), a complex system based on "the dynamic interplay of the unique and changing needs, expectations, and skills of the two partners themselves" (Sherwood & Scherer, 1975, p. 14; cf. Lederer & Jackson, 1968).

This positive, growth-oriented and potential-oriented, dynam-

---

*This article focuses exclusively on marriage enrichment. A consideration of family enrichment programs is beyond the scope of this review.

ic philosophy and view of the individual and the marriage relationship is at the core of marriage enrichment. To actualize it in relationships, proponents of marriage enrichment employ a variety of voluntary processes and programs focusing on the individual and the marital dyad. The general goal is to enable partners to create a climate between them which will enable them to increase self- and other-awareness and awareness of the growth potential of the marriage; to explore and express their thoughts and feelings with honesty and empathy; and to develop and use the skills needed to relate together effectively, solve their problems, and resolve their conflicts (Guerney, 1977; Mace & Mace, 1974, 1977; Miller et al., 1976b). In such a climate, it is believed that the individual and the couple are best able to maximize their potential for relationship satisfaction and personal and couple growth.

Mace and Mace (1974, 1975) have noted a shift that has occurred in our society with regards to how we view marriage. They suggest the shift has been from the concept of marriage as a rigid and hierarchical institution to the concept of companionship marriage, which is a relationship based on intimacy, equality, and flexibility in interpersonal relationships (Burgess & Locke, 1945). We believe that the ultimate goal, and underlying value, of most marriage enrichment programs is the attainment and maintenance of such as relationship. We chose to label it the "intentional companionship marriage."

Intentional companionship marriage is a relationship in which there is a strong commitment to an enduring marital dyad in which each person experiences increasing fulfillment and satisfaction. There is a heavy emphasis on developing effective interpersonal relationships and on establishing and maintaining an open communication system. There is the ability to give and accept affection in an unconditional way, to accept the full range of feelings towards each other, to appreciate common interests and differences and accept and affirm each other's uniqueness, and to see each other as having equal status in the relationship.

There is a commitment to expanding and deepening the emotional aspects of the relationship, including the sexual dimension, and developing and reinforcing marital strengths. It is characterized by a mutual affection, honesty, true intimacy, love, empathy, and understanding. There is an awareness of changing needs, desires, and aspirations, and appropriate responses to them. There is also a sense of self-worth in each partner and a balance between autonomy and interdependence, with each partner accepting equal responsibility for the success of the relationship.

The intentional compansionship marriage is imbued with a conscious realization that marriage is not a static system with inflexible roles, but is a dynamic, changing relationship, calling for continued commitment to appropriate openness, creative use of differences and conflict, negotiation and renegotiation of roles and norms, and continued individual and couple awareness and growth. There is an *intentional* commitment by both partners to work on the process of the relationship, and to develop the skills needed to insure the continued growth and vitality of the relationship. (The preceding discussion of intentional companionship marriage is drawn from Buckland, 1977; Luthman & Kirschenbaum, 1974; Mace & Mace, 1974, 1975, 1977; Rogers, 1972; Satir, 1975; Stapleton & Bright, 1976; Travis & Travis, 1975, 1976a; Vincent, 1973, 1977; as well as our own experience and values.)

Perhaps we can appropriately say that the intentional companionship marriage is an unachievable goal. Yet, we believe it is the goal and process to which the marriage enrichment movement has committed itself. It is a continually developing and expanding goal, and in a real sense, the process of working towards the goal is the fulfillment of it.

PROCESS OF MARRIAGE ENRICHMENT

Ideally, the process and programs of marriage enrichment should be built upon a sound theoretical foundation, a theoretical base which should also be clearly linked to the philosophy of marriage enrichment. Unfortunately, only a few proponents of marriage enrichment have developed and presented a clear statement of the theoretical framework of their particular program. The lack of clearly enunciated theoretical bases has contributed to the diversity of programs and has contributed to the lack of much needed empirical research on most of the programs.

Otto (1976) notes that many marriage enrichment programs are eclectic, in that they draw from a variety of contributors and theoretical frameworks, such as those expressed by Satir, Perls,

Frankl, Rogers, and Berne. However, "eclectic" seems to be used by some practitioners as synonomous with "hodge-podge" or "smorgasbord," and to cover for, or rationalize away, the lack of a well-developed theoretical framework. We can only hope that proponents of marriage enrichment will acknowledge the need to develop and clearly enunciate their theoretical base (cf. Guerney, 1977; Miller et al., 1976b), and will then follow that acknowledgement with appropriate action.

Marriage enrichment has clear roots in the human-potential movement, humanistic psychology, and affective education (Clinebell, 1975; Miller, 1975; Otto, 1976). More specifically, we have identified three major, theoretical bases. First, we have the Rogerian emphasis on providing an empathic environment in which participants can freely express their feelings and experience increased self-acceptance and self-knowledge, and increased acceptance of others and from others, especially their marital partner. The assumption is that this will contribute to changes in cognition and the attitudes which underlie behavior (Guerney, 1977), and will lead the participants to change their behavior. Secondly, there is an equal behavioral emphasis on enabling participants to learn and practice specific skills they can use to change their own behavior and create effective interpersonal relationships, on the assumption that repeated practice and reinforcement will lead to enduring positive change (cf. Jacobson, 1977; Miller et al., 1976b). Lastly, there is an emphasis on the use of group process to provide a temporary and safe learning environment in which various growth and curative factors can be experienced (e.g., social learning, support, feedback, sense of universality, etc.) (Egan, 1970; Guerney, 1977; Mace, 1975b; Mace & Mace, 1976b; Miller et al., 1976b; Yalom, 1970).

The process of marriage enrichment has certain common features in spite of the diversity of programs. The process is dynamic, experiential, educational, and preventive in nature (e.g., Buckland, 1977; Clinebell, 1976; Harrell & Guerney, 1976; Guerney, 1977, 1978; L'Abate, 1977; Mace & Mace, 1975, 1978; Otto, 1976; Sherwood & Scherer, 1975). The process typically promotes a balance between relational and individual growth (e.g., Mace & Mace, 1977; Miller, Nunnally, & Wackman, 1975; Otto, 1969, 1976; Travis & Travis, 1975, 1976a). The process of marriage enrichment is ongoing, not restricted to participation in one weekend experience or a time-limited group. Many practitioners and participants emphasize that such participation is a beginning, not an end, of the process of marital and relationship growth and enhancement (Mace & Mace, 1976a). There is an increasing emphasis upon the need for an ongoing support system, an ongoing or time-limited group, and continued growth experiences after the initial experience (Clinebell, 1975; Hopkins et al., 1978; Mace, 1975b; Otto, 1975; Rappaport, 1976).

Marriage enrichment has a pronounced focus upon identifying, sharing, and developing positive aspects of the marital relationship (e.g., Clarke, 1970; Clinebell, 1975; Mace & Mace, 1976b, 1977; Otto, 1972, 1976). Most programs actively avoid confrontation as part of the process (Mace & Mace, 1974; Otto, 1976), although there are exceptions (e.g., Zinker & Leon, 1976).

Most marriage enrichment programs emphasize increasing the ability to communicate effectively (Collins, 1977; Epstein & Jackson, 1978; L'Abate, 1977; Mace & Mace, 1974, 1975, 1977; Miller, Corrales, & Wackman, 1975; Miller et al., 1976b; Otto, 1975, 1976; Regula, 1975), and increasing appropriate self-disclosure (Miller, Corrales, & Wackman, 1975; Otto, 1976; Regula, 1975). Some multiweek marriage enrichment programs employ a variety of homework assignments, involving reading and skill practice, for couples to complete between group meetings (e.g., Guerney, 1977; L'Abate, 1977; Liberman, Wheeler, & Sanders, 1976; Miller et al., 1976b; Paul & Paul, 1975; Schauble & Hill, 1976; Shelton & Ackerman, 1974). Finally, marriage enrichment programs are led by a variety of people (married couples, nonmarried couples, individuals) with varying professional and nonprofessional backgrounds, degrees of training, and styles of leadership (participant, nonparticipant). However, regardless of the background, training, or leadership style, most writers agree on the importance of the leaders modeling the skills they propose to teach and the growth-oriented relationship they value and espouse (Guerney, 1977; Mace & Mace, 1976b; Regula, 1975).

MARRIAGE ENRICHMENT PROGRAMS

Marriage enrichment can take place in a variety of formal or informal ways (Hopkins et al., 1978), but the three most common are the following: (1) the intensive retreat, conference, or marathon which can last from a weekend to a five-day experience, with the weekend being most common (e.g., Bosco, 1973; Demarest, Sexton, & Sexton, 1977; Genovese, 1975; Mace & Mace, 1976b, 1977); (2) a marital growth group, which meets for a series of weekly meetings in the participants' home community (Hopkins et al., 1978); and (3) couple communication programs (e.g., Guerney, 1977; Miller, Nunnally, & Wackman, 1975, 1976b; Nunnally, Miller, & Wackman, 1975; Stein, 1975).

These different types of marriage enrichment programs vary greatly in terms of design, format, and techniques and resources used. Programs vary in their use of total group interaction, dyadic interaction, small groups of several couples, individual reflection time, and free or fun time. Areas covered include the following: expressing wants, needs, expectations, feelings, and intentions; goals and values (cf. Piercy & Schultz, 1978); communication skills; conflict-utilization skills; intimacy and affection; individual and marital strengths; negotiating marital roles; sexual fulfillment; parenting; decision making and contracting; the list could go on endlessly.

Programs vary in their degree of structure, with a continuum ranging from highly structured and couple centered, some almost to the point of being programmed instruction (e.g., Marriage Encounter, Marriage Enrichment, Inc.) (cf. Wright & L'Abate, 1977), to relatively nonstructured and centered on the couple-group. Another continuum could be established between the poles of the interactionally oriented programs (e.g., "Quaker Model"; Mace & Mace, 1976b) and the strict behaviorally oriented programs (e.g., Behavioral Exchange Model: Rappaport & Harrell, 1975), with a program like the Marriage Communication Lab (Smith & Smith, 1976) lying somewhere between the two poles. As Wildman (1977) has observed, it is often difficult to determine where enrichment ends and training in communication or behavioral skills begins.

Programs also vary with regard to the extent that leaders are permitted and encouraged to change and modify the program format for each client group and even during a particular experience (e.g., Marriage Enrichment, Inc. — no flexibility; Marriage Communication Lab — great flexibility and encouragement for the leader and participants to develop their own program and be able to modify it according to the emerging needs of a particular group of couples). We need to note here that our value system requires that a clear theoretical rationale be present for all experiences in which clients are required to participate.

The association of many marriage enrichment programs with organized religious bodies is an inducement to attend such programs for some couples who might otherwise fear a "psychologically oriented" program. For other couples, the religious association is contrary to their value system, and they self-select themselves out of participation in those programs.

History of Marriage Enrichment

The marriage enrichment movement has emerged from a variety of sources. The Roman Catholic Marriage Encounter program began in Spain in 1958, under the initiative of Father Gabriel Calvo. It grew out of a desire to enable families to relate more effectively together and Father Calvo's belief that it was necessary to start with the relationship of the marital dyad (Bosco, 1973; Demarest et al., 1977; Genovese, 1975; Mace & Mace, 1978). The program reached the United States in 1967, and over 200,000 couples in the United States have participated in the Marriage Encounter program since 1967 (Genovese, 1975). Because of the strong links with the Roman Catholic Church, some perceived sense of exclusivism, and differing needs, several Protestant and Jewish "expressions" of Marriage Encounter have been developed.

David and Vera Mace began their work in marriage enrichment with retreats for the Quakers in 1962 (Mace & Mace, 1974, 1978). Herbert Otto was conducting a variety of experimental programs in the area of marital and family enrichment as early as 1961 (Mace & Mace, 1978; Otto, 1969). Leon and Antoinette Smith were conducting programs in the mid 1960s, and they initiated the first leadership training program for couples in the United Methodist Church in 1966 (Mace & Mace, 1978; Smith & Smith, 1976). Sherod Miller and his associates were conducting their studies in marital communication in the late 1960s, and they eventually developed the Minnesota Couples Communication Program (now known as the Couples Communication Program) (Mace & Mace, 1978). Undoubtedly, many other people were doing concurrent exploratory work in the area of marriage enrichment and marital communication (cf. Guerney, 1977; L'Abate, 1977).

In 1973, thirty delegates of various denominations, who were conducting programs or were interested in marriage or family enrichment, met in Indianapolis, under the auspices of the National Council of Churches. The purpose of the meeting was to share information and discuss the future of marriage and family enrichment (Otto, 1976). In that same year, the Association of Couples for Marriage Enrichment (ACME) was founded by David and Vera Mace (Hopkins et al., 1978). In 1975, the Council of Affiliated Marriage Enrichment Organizations (CAMEO) was formed, and has concerned itself primarily with developing leadership and training standards.

Marriage enrichment programs are not limited to the United States, but this country does appear to be the leader in the field at present (Otto, 1975). The human potential movement and the encounter and small-group movement have clearly been the forerunners of the marriage enrichment movement in America, contributing greatly to the philosophy, process, and program design of most programs (Otto, 1976). The movement in America, since its inception, has also had strong roots in many religious or faith systems (Hopkins & Hopkins, 1975), because of their keen interest in the family and their concern for the future of marriage and the family. Of the 20 national marriage enrichment organizations listed in the ACME handbook (Hopkins et al., 1978), 14 are directly connected to an established religious organization or church. However, there are other programs listed which do not have religious affiliations, such as the Couples Communication Program, Family Service Association of America, Marriage Effectiveness Training, and the Relationship Enhancement Programs listed under Ideals, Inc.

Many of the marriage enrichment programs which have been developed to date are local in scope, in that they have been developed and are used, for the most part, by a particular individual or couple and associates within a small geographical area. The Pairing Enrichment Program (Travis & Travis, 1975) and the MARDILAB (Stein, 1975) are examples of such programs. Other programs are national in scope, in terms of organization, leadership training, and/or programs conducted throughout the country. Some of the programs which are included in this latter category are the following: Marriage Encounter (Bosco, 1973; Demarest et al., 1977; Genovese, 1975), Marriage Communication Labs (Smith & Smith, 1976), Relationship Enhancement Programs (Guerney, 1977),

Couples Communication Program (Miller et al., 1976a), the programs of the Association of Couples for Marriage Enrichment (ACME) (Hopkins et al., 1978), and the enrichment programs developed by L'Abate and collaborators (1975; cf. L'Abate, 1977).

There are at least 50 different programs known to the authors, some of which have been attended by as few as 10 couples, and others that have been attended by thousands of couples (Otto, 1976). In that group of 50 are included several "educational therapy" programs developed and conducted by marital therapists and counselors (e.g., Bolte, 1975; Smith & Alexander, 1974). Otto (1976) has edited a volume which describes the goals, structure, and process of four family-centered enrichment programs and 14 marriage or couple-oriented enrichment programs. L'Abate (1977) and Miller (1975) have edited similar volumes. In 1977, Mace (Note 4) placed notices in the newsletters of the American Association of Marriage and Family Counselors and the National Council on Family Relations requesting information on innovative programs in the fields of marriage and the family. He received 40 replies, representing 37 different programs. The programs were divided into the following four categories: Premarital or Neomarital programs (5), Marriage Enrichment programs (12), Parenthood Enrichment programs (11), and Family Enrichment programs (9).

Otto (1976) has surveyed various marriage and family enrichment programs in the United States and Canada, and has concluded that at least 420,000 couples have attended programs reported by his respondents (e.g., over 3,500 for the Couples Communication Program, over 7,000 for the United Methodist Marriage Communication Labs, over 400,000 for the various expressions of Marriage Encounter). He estimates that at least twice that number have participated in enrichment programs, and bases his estimate on the increasing number of facilitators and programs which have come to his attention since his initial survey was conducted in 1973 and 1974. Such numbers, if anywhere near accurate, indicate that the marriage enrichment movement is at least peripherally touching the lives of enormous numbers of people. Such numbers clearly indicate the need for an in-depth examination of the movement, and the programs represented by it, by all concerned with improving the quality of marital and family relationships.

Outcome Research

Research on marital and premarital enrichment programs is still in its infancy. When viewed within the context of the large number of couples who have been participants in enrichment programs, the number of research studies done on marital enrichment seems very small. Evaluation of the effectiveness of marital enrichment programs is difficult. Furthermore, the programs are interactionally oriented, and any control over the process, including provisions for research on outcome, is often not valued or sought (L'Abate, 1977; Otto, 1976).

For the present review of research results, we have included studies of nonclinical couples who have participated in programs designed to increase the couples' relationship skills or to enhance the quality of their relationship. The enrichment programs studied differ markedly in their definition of marital enrichment, format, goals, and scope. These programmatic differences, as well as differences in research methodology, and in the type of dependent measures used, make it difficult to draw general conclusions from the studies reviewed.

With few exceptions, research on the outcome of martial enrichment experiences has involved a pre-post assessment format with two groups, the treatment group and a waiting-list or no-treatment control group. Due to this similarity in research design across studies and due to the fact that Gurman and Kniskern (1977) have recently reviewed most of the studies reported on here, we have decided not to present a detailed examination of each study. Rather, our intention is to summarize what is and is not currently known about the effectiveness of marital enrichment. The reader who is interested in the specific details of any of the studies reviewed is referred to the original reports and to Table 1.

Table 1 presents some basic information about 34 different studies of marital enrichment. (There are 36 listings in the table, but two studies are referenced under each of two different program formats.) As mentioned above, marital enrichment programs vary considerably in format and structure. In order to facilitate comparisons between studies, we have identified three general types of marital enrichment programs: (1) those which focus primarily on communica-

TABLE 1

Author	Control Groups[a]			Outcome Measures[b]				Results[c]
	WL/NT	Pl.	A.T.	Class	Self Report	Independent Ratings	Follow-up	
A. Mixed Experiences/Exercises								
Bruder (1972)	Y	N	N	MA,P,RS	Y	N	N	P = +; MA,RS, = −
Burns (1972)	Y	N	N	P	Y	N	Y	±
Huber (Note 5) (Marriage Encounter)	Y	N	N	P	Y	N	Y	Mostly +
Kilmann, Moreault, & Robinson (1978)	Y	N	Y	MA, P	Y	N	Y	+
L'Abate (1977)	Y	N	N	P	Y	N	Y	+
Swicegood (1974) (ACME)	Y	N	N	P,RS	Y	Y	Y	Mostly +
Travis & Travis (1976a) (Pairing Enrichment Program)	Y	N	N	P	Y	N	N	Mostly −
Travis & Travis (1976b)	N	N	N	P	Y	N	N	+
Weinstein (1975)	Y	N	N	P	Y	N	N	+
B. Communication Training								
1. Minnesota Couples Communication Program								
Campbell (1974)	Y	N	N	RS	N	Y	N	+
Larsen (1974)	N	N	N	P,RS	Y	N	N	±
Miller (1971)	Y	N	N	P,RS	Y	Y	N	P = ±, RS = +
Nunnally (1971)	Y	N	N	RS	Y	Y	N	Mostly +
Schwager & Conrad (1974)	N	N	N	P	Y	N	N	+
2. Conjugal Relationship Enhancement Program								
Collins (1971)	Y	N	N	MA,RS	Y	N	N	±
D'Augelli, Deyss, Guerney, Hershenberg, & Sborofsky (1974)	Y	N	N	RS	N	Y	N	+
Ely, Guerney, & Stover (1973)	Y	N	N	RS	N	Y	N	±
Rappaport (1976)	Y	N	N	MA,P,RS	Y	N	N	+
Schlien (1971)	Y	N	N	P,RS	Y	Y	N	Mostly +
Wieman (1973)[d]	Y	N	Y	MA,RS	Y	Y	Y	+

TABLE 1 (cont.)

Author	Control Groups[a]			Outcome Measures[b]				Results[c]
	WL/NT	Pl.	A.T.	Class	Self Report	Independent Ratings	Follow-up	
3. Other Communication Training								
Epstein & Jackson (1978)	Y	N	Y	RS	Y	Y	N	Mostly +
Hines (1976)	Y	N	Y	RS	N	Y	N	+
Nadeau (1971)	Y	N	N	P, RS	Y	Y	Y	±
Neville (1971)	N	N	N	P,RS	Y	N	N	+
Orling (1976)	Y	N	N	MA,P	Y	N	N	+
Pilder (1972)	Y	N	N	P,RS	Y	Y	N	±
Van Zoost (1973)	N	N	N	P,RS	Y	N	N	±
Venema (1976)[d]	N	N	Y	MA,P,RS	Y	N	N	Mostly −
Williams (1975)	Y	N	Y	MA,RS	Y	N	N	−
C. Behavior Exchange								
Dixon & Sciara (1977)	N	N	N	P,RS	Y	N	N	Mostly +
Fisher (1973)	Y	N	Y	P	Y	N	N	Mostly +
Harrell & Guerney (1976)	Y	N	N	MA,P,RS	Y	Y	N	RS= ±; MA,P = −
McIntosh (1975)	Y	N	Y	MA,P,RS	Y	N	N	−
Roberts (1975)	Y	Y	N	MA,P	Y	N	N	+
Venema (1976)[d]	N	N	N	MA,P,RS	Y	N	N	Mostly −
Wieman (1973)[d]	Y	N	Y	MA,RS	Y	Y	Y	+

Note. −Y = Yes, N = No

[a] WL/NT = Waiting-List or No-Treatment Group; Pl. = Placebo-Control Group; A.T. = Alternate Therapy, i.e., the experimental group is compared with another therapy or enrichment group.

[b] Outcome measures are divided into three classes or groups: MA = measures of marital adjustment, P = perceptual and personality measures, RS = relationship-skill measures. Measures may also be based on self-report or ratings by independent observers or judges.

[c] + = statistically significant pre-post change and, when used, greater change than control group; ± = mixed results; − = negative results.

[d] Two studies, Venema (1976) and Wieman (1973), are listed twice, since each study can be grouped under two different categories of enrichment.

tion training, (2) those based mainly on behavioral exchange principles, and (3) those programs which offer a varied mix of experiences and exercises. The various outcome measures used have been separated into the three categories suggested by Gurman and Kniskern (1977): overall adjustment; perceptual and individual personality variables, such as perception of spouse, self-esteem and self-actualization; and relationship skill variables, such as communication and problem-solving skills, self-disclosure, and empathy.

The most basic question to be addressed by outcome research is whether the intervention procedure is followed by specific affective, attitudinal, cognitive, and/or behavioral changes. As Table 1 shows, most of the outcome studies reviewed do report positive changes on at least some measures following a marital enrichment experience. Furthermore, significant changes are not restricted to any particular type or class of variables.

Are the changes that follow participation in marital enrichment programs a result of the enrichment experience, the passage of time, or nonspecific, i.e., placebo, effects? Table 1 shows that 27 of the 34 studies (79%) used either a waiting-list or no-treatment control group. Since the general finding for these studies has been that significantly greater change occurs for the marital enrichment group than for the control group, we can view the changes as being due to factors other than the simple passage of time.

Table 1 also indicates that only one study used an attention-placebo control group. Roberts (1975) formed a placebo condition by placing five couples in an unstructured group setting in which issues could be discussed, but where the various enrichment experiences and exercises were not present. This placebo condition controlled for changes that might occur as a result of group participation and discussion in the absence of the specific enrichment experiences. Roberts (1975) reported that greater changes did occur in the placebo group than in a waiting-list control group. The marital enrichment group was, however, superior to both control groups. Thus, although nonspecific treatment factors did produce positive changes, the enrichment experience itself resulted in greater changes.

Dixon and Sciara (1977) attempted to demonstrate a causal relationship between treatment intervention and changes in self-ratings of the relationship through use of a multiple baseline procedure, rather than a placebo control group. Their results suggested that changes in ratings were contingent upon the introduction of specific, reciprocity-exchange procedures.

It is unfortunate that only two of the studies reviewed included some type of control for placebo effects. Such a group is particularly necessary, because, as Roberts (1975) demonstrated, nonspecific treatment factors can lead to significant changes in self-reported marital adjustment and in relationships. This finding raises the obvious question of whether some of the significant changes reported in the other studies reviewed here are due to so-called placebo effects, and not to the marital enrichment experience itself.

Are the measurements made with reliable and valid instruments and are independent ratings, as well as self-report measures, used? Only 13 of the 34 studies (38%) have included independent raters or judges, whereas 31 of the studies (91%) have used self-report measures. Although self-report is more economical and convenient to obtain than ratings of objective observers, there are serious dangers in relying exclusively on measures that are so easily influenced by response biases, social desirability, and demand characteristics. Another drawback to the studies which have used only self-report as a measure of outcome is that often the instruments used are of unknown reliability and validity.

Do the reported outcomes represent stable or temporary changes in the participants? Six of the 34 studies (18%) included some type of follow-up assessment. Burns (1972) and Huber (Note 5) reported maintenance of changes in self-perception and perception of spouse, respectively, from posttest to followup, and Wieman (1973) found that changes in marital adjustment, expressive and responsive skill, and specific target behaviors were stable over a 10-week follow-up period. Nadeau (1971) and Swicegood (1974) also reported some stability in changes following a marital enrichment experience. However, in Nadeau's (1971) study, self-report changes were better maintained than behavioral changes, while in Swicegood (1974), some of the changes in perception of the relationship, marital integration, and communication were not maintained at follow-up. Kilmann, Moreault, and Robinson (1978) also found that some changes were maintained at followup, while others were not. In addition, significant improvement did not emerge for some variables until follow-up testing. Although these results are encouraging, more studies need to be done with follow-up measures before we can conclude that marital enrichment does lead to stable changes in relationships.

Are different types of marital enrichment experiences more or less effective than others? Eight of the 34 studies (24%) have directly compared two types of marital enrichment programs (see Table 1).

Wieman (1973) contrasted the Conjugal Relationship Enhancement (CRE) program, a behavioral exchange program, and a waiting list control group. Both enrichment programs resulted in significant increases in marital adjustment, in communication skill, and in target behaviors, and there were no differences between the two programs. Kilmann et al. (1978) contrasted two formats of the same program and a no-treatment control group. The sequence of treatment experiences did not affect outcome, and both treatment formats were superior to no treatment. Two additional studies which used alternative treatments found, as did Wieman (1973), no differences between the various treatments (McIntosh, 1975; Williams, 1975). These studies, however, reported no significant changes for any of the enrichment experiences.

In contrast to the results of Kilmann et al. (1978), McIntosh (1975), Wieman (1973), and Williams (1975), four studies reported superiority of one treatment format over another. Epstein and Jackson (1978) included communication training, interaction-insight, and no-treatment groups in their study. Both treatment groups reduced verbal disagreements. Only the communication training group, however, led to increases in assertive requests, decreases in verbal attacks, and increases in spouse-rated empathy. Hines (1976) also reported superiority of a communication training experience over both an insight and a control group, using a rater's estimate of the couples' mutual helpfulness as the outcome measure. Fischer (1973) found that a behaviorally oriented group made significant gains in prediction of attitudes and preferences of spouses relative to a control group and to a facilitative group based on Adlerian and functional methods. Finally, although Venema (1976) found very little change for any of these treatments, a combination of communication training and behavioral exchange led to greater change on a number of measures than did either communication training or behavioral exchange alone.

In summary, there is some evidence from comparative studies for differential effectiveness of different marital enrichment formats. The research suggests that communication training (Epstein & Jackson, 1978; Hines, 1976) and behavioral exchange (Fisher, 1973) are superior to insight-oriented group experiences. Behavioral and communication-training programs appear to be similar in their effects. We must, however, be cautious in making conclusions at this point, since the number of relevant studies is very small.

Do programs with different formats and content produce different types of changes? The comparative studies described above provided no evidence for this possibility. Comparing the results of the various studies in Table 1 does, however, suggest a possible difference in the types of changes produced by different marital enrichment experiences. Positive changes on all three general types of outcome measures — marital adjustment, perceptual and personality measures, and relationship skill measures — have been obtained in many of the studies of communication training and behavior exchange programs. For programs consisting of mixed experiences and exercises, there is consistent evidence for positive change only on perceptual and personality measures. Of course, only two of the studies of the "mixed" type of enrichment experience have included marital adjustment or relationship-skill measures. Thus, we cannot draw any conclusions about different types of changes occurring with different programs until more comparative studies, which include all three types of outcome measures, have been completed.

For particular interventions that result in positive change, what are the effective components of the program that produce the change? For what types of participants are the enrichment programs effective? The study by Roberts (1975) is the only one we have located which sought to identify an effective component of a marital enrichment experience. Roberts (1975) examined differences in outcome as a function of therapists' experience level, using novice paraprofessional, experienced paraprofessional, and graduate student therapists. He found that outcome was positively related to the experience level of the therapists, i.e., the groups led by more experienced therapists had better outcome. Clearly, many other variables, e.g., the inclusion or exclusion of specific exercises, the time format, number of leaders per group, and social class of participants (most programs have been limited to middle-class couples) need to be related to outcome.

Two studies have examined the response of different types of participants to marital enrichment experiences. Neville (1972) used the Myers Briggs Type Indicator to identify personality types among participants in a marital enrichment experience. He found that a significantly greater proportion of volunteer participants were "intuitive-feeling" types as opposed to "sensing-thinking" personality types. Neville concluded that these two personality types differed in their comfort and compatibility with the enrichment process, but that both groups, nevertheless, responded well to the experience. Huber (Note 5) assessed the outcome of a Marriage Encounter experience using the Caring Relationship Inventory (CRI) (Shostrom, 1967). He reported that only the male participants showed significant positive change on CRI scales; females' scores did not change.

Thus, one of these studies (Neville, 1972) suggests that, although individuals with certain personality types may be more likely than others to volunteer for marital enrichment experiences, the outcome of the experience may not be affected by the participant's personality type. The second study (Huber, Note 5), on the other hand, suggests that males may be more likely than females to change following participation in at least some marital enrichment programs. More research is needed before we can determine whether enrichment programs are more or less effective for different types of participants.

We can conclude from this examination of the research that some optimism about the effectiveness of marital enrichment programs is appropriate. We must however, be very cautious in our optimism. Although generally positive results have been reported, we must await the presentation of more well-designed research before we can comfortably conclude that marital enrichment produces stable, positive change in couples.

Conclusion

If marriage enrichment or preventive marital health is to become a significant area of emphasis which impacts upon a truly broad spectrum of the population, some real changes will have to be made within and outside the movement. People within the movement will need to actively seek, and open their programs to, the careful scrutiny of appropriate empirical research, so that we can identify the effective component parts of each program and, as a result, create more effective and efficient programs. For this to happen, proponents of marriage enrichment will have to realize and accept the fact that the enthusiastic testimonies of participants and leaders is not sufficient (though the quantity of them requires careful notice). Explicit, carefully developed, and defined theoretical frameworks for the various programs and techniques used need to be developed (cf. Guerney, 1977; Mace, 1975a). Some of the almost fanatical, cult-like, "ours is the best program," enthusiasm will have to be replaced with a more open and flexible approach to marriage enrichment programming which is based upon matching programs to the specific needs and abilities of specific individuals and couples. The need for appropriate and ongoing training of nonprofessional and professional leaders must continue to be addressed, with an emphasis on the cognitive and theoretical areas as well as the experiential and interpersonal relations areas.

The professional community of marital and family counselors, therapists, researchers, and educators will need truly to accept and acknowledge that significant learning, change, and growth can occur within and through a learning experience led by (and even created by) nonprofessionals (cf. Collins, 1977; Goldstein, 1969; Guerney, 1969, 1977; Truax & Carkhuff, 1967). With that acceptance can come open support of such programs and a specific and planned effort to utilize professional skills in the development and training of appropriate nonprofessional leaders (L'Abate, 1977).

With Vincent (1973, 1977), we wonder why the helping professions have been so slow to accept the viability of a marital health or marriage enrichment approach to dyadic interactions and relationships. Part of the answer may lie in the failure of many proponents of marriage enrichment to have been seriously concerned with appropriate research and theoretical considerations. However, that is possibly only part of the reason. Could there also be fears of diminished stature on the part of professionals (i.e., "if they can really help themselves so much, or can be helped by someone with much less training than I have, then what will happen to me")? Could there be fears that if people can be helped by "marital enrichers" all that will be left for the trained professional therapist will be the very difficult cases (Vincent, 1973)?

We believe there will always be a need for the highly skilled, trained, and qualified professional in the field of marital and relationship therapy. Many couples and individuals simply cannot benefit from marriage enrichment experiences, or benefit from them as much as from conjoint or individual therapy. But, can the trained professional content himself/herself with the offering of these traditional services? We think not, especially, if research demonstrates that a marriage enrichment or preventive marital health approach is as helpful and efficient as traditional methods, or more so, or provides a helpful adjunct to therapy. If this is the case, then there is a need for the trained professional therapist to learn and develop specific skills in preventive marital health and marriage enrichment in order to help couples to develop their potential for effective relationships (cf. Wright & L'Abate, 1977).

With the acceptance of a philosophy of prevention and marriage enrichment by the professional community, it is hoped that marital health could be developed as a multidisciplinary and interdisciplinary and interprofessional specialty field (Vincent, 1973, 1977), and that appropriate degree programs in the area of enrichment could be developed (L'Abate, 1977). Even without the establishment of a separate specialty field or degree programs, however, there is a current need for the various training programs in marriage counseling to focus on marital enrichment and preventive marital health. Trainees need to be exposed to growth-oriented and preventive approaches and models as well as to models which focus upon the treatment of dysfunctional relationships or systems. That exposure needs to include appropriate theory and practical experiences, with couples in therapy as well as those from the broader community (cf. the training program of the Interfaith Pastoral Counseling Center/Family Therapy Training Program of Kitchener, Ontario, in Guldner, 1978).

Agencies which serve the family need to be encouraged to include positive and preventive programming in their services to clinical and nonclinical populations. Marriage enrichment programming needs to be extended to those preparing for marriage and to senior citizens (cf. Ginsberg & Vogelsong, 1977; Mace, 1972; Mace & Mace, 1977). The lack of a specific focus on sexuality in many marriage enrichment programs needs to be corrected (Otto, 1975).

The list could go on indefinitely but, in brief, what is needed is for the various proponents and practitioners of marriage enrichment (professional and nonprofessional) and marital counselors, therapists, researchers, and educators to join in a truly collaborative and concerted effort to make the benefits of marriage enrichment available to all couples who could benefit from such a service and program. A united effort, welcomed and sought by all groups, could conceivably exert significant political pressure, could encourage the federal government to develop a focused emphasis and policy on marriage (Mace & Mace, 1975), and could tap the financial and personnel resources of various government agencies to provide positive, growth-oriented services.

As some of these hopes and dreams (many of which are currently being pursued) become integrated realities, preventive marital health and the philosophy, process, and programs of marriage enrichment will achieve a new and deeper level of significance in our society. The development, implementation, and assimilation of a growth-oriented marital philosophy throughout our society could have a significant impact upon marital and family life in the future. But, in the final analysis, it will take commitment on the part of the individual couples to the continuing process of marriage enrichment. For many couples (if not most), that will mean an ongoing, disciplined involvement in a personally meaningful program of marriage enrichment designed to enable the participants to fulfill their potential as individuals and as married couples.

REFERENCE NOTES

1. Mace, D. R. Personal communication, March 22, 1978.
2. L'Abate, L. *Enrichment as prevention: Some possibilities.* Paper presented at the Family Therapy Conference on the Roots of Mental Health, Urban Life Center, Georgia State University, Atlanta, January 1978.
3. Hof, L., & Miller, W. R. *Marriage Enrichment: Philosophy, process, and program.* Book in preparation, 1978.
4. Mace, D. R. *Preventive training for creative family relationships: Some experiential programs in North America.* Unpublished manuscript, 1978. (Available from Dr. David R. Mace; P.O. Box 5182; Winston-Salem, North Carolina 27103.)
5. Huber, J. W. *Measuring the effects of Marriage Encounter experience with the Caring Relationship Inventory.* Manuscript submitted for publication, 1977.

REFERENCES

Beck, D. F. Research findings on the outcomes of marital counseling. *Social Casework,* 1975, *56,* 153-181.
Benson, L., Berger, M., & Mease, W. Family communication systems. In S. Miller (Ed.), *Marriages and families: Enrichment through communication.* Beverly Hills: Sage, 1975.

Bolte, Gordon L. A communications approach to marital counseling. In A. S. Gurman & D. G. Rice (Eds.), *Couples in conflict.* New York: Jason Aronson, 1975.

Bosco, A. *Marriage Encounter, a rediscovery of love.* St. Meinard, Ind.: Abbey, 1973.

Bruder, A. H. *Effects of a marriage enrichment program upon marital communication and adjustment.* Unpublished doctoral dissertation, Purdue University, 1972.

Buckland, C. M. An educational model of family consultation. *Journal of Marriage and Family Counseling,* 1977, *3*(3), 49-56.

Burgess, E. W., & Locke, H. J. *The family: From institution to companionship.* New York: American Book, 1945.

Burns, C. W. *Effectiveness of the basic encounter group in marriage counseling.* Unpublished doctoral dissertation, University of Oklahoma, 1972.

Campbell, E. E. *The effects of couple communication training on married couples in the child-rearing years.* Unpublished doctoral dissertation, Arizona State University, 1974.

Clarke, C. Group procedures for increasing positive feedback between married partners. *The Family Coordinator,* 1970, *19,* 324-328.

Clinebell, H. J. *Growth counseling for marriage enrichment.* Fortress, 1975.

Clinebell, H. J. Cassette programs for training and enrichment. In H. A. Otto (Ed.), *Marriage and family enrichment: New perspectives and programs.* Nashville: Abingdon, 1976.

Collins, J. D. *The effects of the Conjugal Relationship modification method on marital communication and adjustment.* Unpublished doctoral dissertation, Pennsylvania State University, 1971.

Collins, J. D. Experimental evaluation of a six-month conjugal therapy and relationship enhancement program. In B. G. Guerney, Jr., *Relationship Enhancement.* San Francisco: Jossey-Bass, 1977.

D'Augelli, A. R., Deyss, D. S., Guerney, B. G., Jr., Hershenberg, B., & Sborofsky, S. L. Interpersonal skill training for dating couples: An evaluation of an educational mental health service. *Journal of Counseling Psychology,* 1974, *21,* 385-389.

Demarest, D., Sexton, J., & Sexton, M. *Marriage Encounter.* St. Paul: Carillon, 1977.

Dixon, D. N., & Sciara, A. D. Effectiveness of group reciprocity counseling with married couples. *Journal of Marriage and Family Counseling,* 1977, *3*(3), 77-83.

Egan, G. *Encounter: Group process for interpersonal growth.* Belmont, Calif.: Brooks/ Cole, 1970.

Ely, A. L., Guerney, B. G., Jr., & Stover, L. Efficacy of the training phase of conjugal therapy. *Psychotherapy: Theory, Research and Practice,* 1973, *10,* 201-207.

Epstein, N., & Jackson, E. An outcome study of short-term communication training with married couples. *Journal of Counseling Psychology,* 1978, *46,* 207-212.

Fisher, R. E. *The effect of two group counseling methods on perceptual congruence in married pairs.* Unpublished doctoral dissertation, University of Hawaii, 1973.

Genovese, R. J. Marriage Encounter. *Small Group Behavior,* 1975, *6,* 45-46.

Ginsberg, B., & Vogelsong, E. Premarital relationship improvement by maximizing empathy and self-disclosure. In B. G. Guerney, *Relationship enhancement.* San Francisco: Jossey-Bass, 1977.

Glasser, L. N., & Glasser, P. H. Hedonism and the family: Conflict in values? *Journal of Marriage and Family Counseling,* 1977, *3*(4), 11-18.

Goldstein, A. P. Domains and dilemmas. *International Journal of Psychiatry,* 1969, *7,* 128-134.

Gottman, J., Notarius, C., Gonso, J., & Markman, H. *A couple's guide to communication.* Champaign, Ill.: Research Press, 1976.

Guerney, B. G., Jr. *Psychotherapeutic agents: New roles for nonprofessionals, parents and teachers.* New York: Holt, Rinehart & Winston, 1969.

Guerney, B. G., Jr. *Relationship enhancement.* San Francisco: Jossey-Bass, 1977.

Guerney, B. G., Jr. Evaluation of consultation-supervision in training conjugal therapists. *Professional Psychology,* 1978, *9,* 203-209.

Guldner, C. A. Family therapy for the trainee in family therapy. *Journal of Marriage and Family Counseling,* 1978, *4*(1), 127-132.

Gurman, A. S., & Kniskern, S. P. Enriching research on marital enrichment programs. *Journal of Marriage and Family Counseling,* 1977, *3*(2), 3-11.

Harrell, J., & Guerney, B. G., Jr. Training married couples in conflict negotiation skills. In D. H. L. Olson (Ed.), *Treating relationships.* Lake Mills, Iowa: Graphic, 1976.

Hines, G. A. Efficacy of communication skills training with married partners where no marital counseling has been sought (Doctoral dissertation, University of South Dakota, 1975). *Dissertation Abstracts International,* 1976, *36,* 5045-5046A.

Hopkins, L., & Hopkins, P. Marriage enrichment and the churches. *Spectrum,* 1975, *Fall.*

Hopkins, L., Hopkins, P., Mace, D., & Mace, V. *Toward better marriages.* Winston-Salem: ACME, 1978.

Jacobson, N. S. Training couples to solve their marital problems: A behavioral approach to relationship discord. *International Journal of Family Counseling,* 1977, *5*(1), 22-31.

Kilmann, P. R., Moreault, D., & Robinson, E. A. Effects of a marriage enrichment program: An outcome study. *Journal of Sex and Marital Therapy,* 1978, *4,* 54-57.

Koch, T., & Koch, L. Marriage enrichment courses: The urgent drive to make good marriages better. *Psychology Today,* September 1976, *10,* 33-35; 83; 85; 95.

L'Abate, L. *Enrichment: Structured interventions with couples, families, and groups.* Washington, D.C.: University Press of America, 1977.

L'Abate, L. *Manual: Enrichment programs for the family life cycle.* Atlanta: Social Research Laboratories, 1975.

L'Abate, L., & Weeks, G. Testing the limits of enrichment: When enrichment is not enough. *Journal of Family Counseling,* 1976, *4*(1), 70-74.

Larsen, G. R. An evaluation of the Minnesota Couples Communication Program's influence on marital communication and self and mate perceptions (Doctoral dissertation, Arizona State University, 1974). *Dissertation Abstracts International,* 1974, *35,* 2625-2628A.

Lederer, W. J., & Jackson, D. D. *The mirages of marriage.* New York: Norton, 1968.

Liberman, R. P., Wheeler, E., & Sanders, N. Behavioral therapy for marital disharmony. *Journal of Marriage and Family Counseling, 1976, 2,* 383-395.

Luthman, S. G., & Kirschenbaum, M. *The dynamic family.* Palo Alto: Science and Behavior, 1974.

Mace, D. R. *Getting ready for marriage.* Nashville: Abingdon, 1972.

Mace. D. R. Marriage enrichment concepts for research. *The Family Coordinator,* 1975, *24,* 171-173. (a)

Mace. D. R. We call it ACME. *Small Group Behavior,* 1975, *6,* 31-44. (b)

Mace, D., & Mace, V. *We can have better marriages if we really want them.* Nashville: Abingdon, 1974.

Mace, D., & Mace, V. Marriage enrichment—wave of the future? *The Family Coordinator,* 1975, *24,* 131-135.

Mace, D., & Mace, V. Marriage enrichment—a preventive group approach for couples. In D. H. L. Olson (Ed.), *Treating relationships.* Lake Mills, Iowa: Graphic, 1976. (a)

Mace, D., & Mace, V. The selection, training and certification of facilitators for marriage enrichment programs. *The Family Coordinator,* 1976, *25,* 117-125. (b)

Mace, D., & Mace, V. *How to have a happy marriage.* Nashville: Abingdon, 1977.

Mace, D., & Mace, V. The marriage enrichment movement: Its history, its rationale, and its future prospects. In L. & P. Hopkins & D. & V. Mace, *Toward better marriages.* Winston-Salem: ACME, 1978.

McIntosh, D. M. A comparison of the effects of highly structured, partially structured, and nonstructured human relations training for married couples on the dependent variables of communication, marital adjustment, and personal adjustment (Doctoral dissertation, North Texas State University, 1975). *Dissertation Abstracts International,* 1975, *36,* 2636-2637A.

Miller, S. *The effects of communication training in small groups upon self-disclosure and openness in engaged couples' systems of interaction: A field experiment.* Unpublished doctoral dissertation, University of Pennsylvania, 1971.

Miller, S. (Ed.). *Marriages and families: Enrichment through communication.* Beverly Hills: Sage, 1975.

Miller, S., Corrales, R., & Wackman, D. B. Recent progress in understanding and facilitating marital communication. *The Family Coordinator,* 1975, *24,* 143-152.

Miller, S., Nunnally, E., & Wackman, D. B. *Alive and aware.* Minneapolis: Interpersonal Communications Programs, 1975.

Miller, S., Nunnally, E. W., & Wackman, D. B. A communication training program for couples. *Social Casework,* 1976, *57,* 9-18. (a)

Miller, S., Nunnally, E. W., & Wackman, D. B. Minnesota Couples Communication Program (MCCP): Premarital and marital groups. In D. H. L. Olson (Ed.), *Treating Relationships.* Lake Mills, Iowa: Graphic, 1976. (b)

Nadeau, K. G. *An examination of some effects of the marital enrichment group.* Unpublished doctoral dissertation, University of Florida, 1971.

Neville, W. G. An analysis of personality types and their differential response to marital enrichment groups (Doctoral dissertation, University of Florida, 1971). *Dissertation Abstracts International,* 1972, *32*(12-A), 6766.

Nunnally, E. W. *Effects of communication training upon interaction awareness and empathic accuracy of engaged couples: A field experiment.* Unpublished doctoral dissertation, University of Minnesota, 1971.

Nunnally, E. W., Miller, S., & Wackman, D. B. The Minnesota Couples Communication Program. *Small Group Behavior,* 1975, *6,* 57-71.

Orling, R. A. The efficacy of proactive marital communication training (Doctoral dissertation, New Mexico State University, 1974). *Dissertation Abstracts International,* 1976, *36,* 3618-3619B.

Otto, H. A. *More joy in your marriage.* New York: Hawthorne, 1969.

Otto, H. A. *The utilization of family strengths in marriage and family counseling.* Beverly Hills: Holistic, 1972.

Otto, H. A. Marriage and family enrichment programs in North America—Report and analysis. *The Family Coordinator,* 1975, *24,* 137-142.

Otto, H. A. (Ed.). *Marriage and family enrichment: New perspectives and programs.* Nashville: Abingdon, 1976.

Paul, N., & Paul, B. *A marital puzzle.* New York: Norton, 1975.

Piercy, F., & Schultz, K. Values clarification strategies for couples' enrichment. *The Family Coordinator,* 1978, *27,* 175-178.

Pilder, S. J. *Some effects of laboratory training on married couples.* Unpublished doctoral dissertation, United States International University, 1972.

Rappaport, A. F. Conjugal Relationship Enhancement Program. In D. H. L. Olson (Ed.), *Treating relationships.* Lake Mills, Iowa: Graphic, 1976.

Rappaport, A. F., & Harrell, J. E. A behavioral exchange model for marital counseling. In A. S. Gurman and D. G. Rice (Eds.), *Couples in conflict.* New York: Jason Aronson, 1975.

Regula, R. B. Marriage Encounter: What makes it work? *The Family Coordinator,* 1975, *24,* 153-159.

Roberts, P. V. The effects on marital satisfaction of brief training in behavioral exchange negotiation mediated by differentially experienced trainers (Doctoral dissertation, Fuller Theological Seminary, 1974). *Dissertation Abstracts International,* 1975, *36,* 457B.

Rogers, C. R. *Becoming partners: Marriage and its alternatives.* New York: Delacorte, 1972.

Satir, V. M. Family life education—a perspective on the educator. In S. Miller (Ed.), *Marriages and families: Enrichment through communication.* Beverly Hills: Sage, 1975.

Schauble, P. G., & Hill, C. G. A laboratory approach to treatment in marriage counseling: Training in communication skills. *The Family Coordinator,* 1976, *25,* 277-284.

Schlien, S. R. *Training dating couples in empathic and open communication: An experimental evaluation of a potential preventative mental health program.* Unpublished doctoral dissertation, Pennsylvania State University, 1971.

Schwager, H. A., & Conrad, R. W. *Impact of group counseling on self and other acceptance and persistence with rural disadvantaged student families* (Counseling Services Report No. 15). Washington, D.C.: National Institute of Education, 1974.

Shelton, J. L., & Ackerman, J. M. *Homework in counseling and psychotherapy.* Springfield, Ill.: Thomas, 1974.

Sherwood, J. J., & Scherer, J. J. A model for couples: How two can grow together. In S. Miller (Ed.), *Marriages and families: Enrichment through communication.* Beverly Hills, Sage, 1975.

Shostrom, E. L. *Caring Relationship Inventory.* San Diego: EDITS/Educational and Industrial Testing Service, 1967.

Smith, L., & Smith, A. Developing a national marriage communication lab training program. In H. A. Otto (Ed.), *Marriage and family enrichment: New Perspectives and programs.* Nashville: Abingdon, 1976.

Smith, R. L., & Alexander, A. M. *Counseling couples in groups.* Springfield: Thomas, 1974.

Stapleton, J., & Bright, R. *Equal marriage.* Nashville: Abingdon, 1976.

Stein, E. V. MARDILAB: An experiment in marriage enrichment. *The Family Coordinator,* 1975, *24,* 167-170.

Swicegood, M. L. *An evaluative study of one approach to marriage enrichment.* Unpublished doctoral dissertation, University of North Carolina at Greensboro, 1974.

Travis, R. P., & Travis, P. Y. The Pairing Enrichment Program: Actualizing the marriage. *The Family Coordinator,* 1975, *24,* 161-165.

Travis, R. P., & Travis, P. Y. Self-actualization in marital enrichment. *Journal of Marriage and Family Counseling,* 1976, *2,* 73-80. (a)

Travis, R. P., & Travis, P. Y. A note on changes in the caring relationship following a marriage enrichment program and some preliminary findings. *Journal of Marriage and Family Counseling,* 1976, *2,* 81-83. (b)

Truax, C. B., & Carkhuff, R. R. *Toward effective counseling and psychotherapy.* Chicago: Aldine, 1967.

Van Zoost, B. Premarital communication skills education with university couples. *The Family Coordinator,* 1973, *22,* 187-191.

Venema, H. B. Marriage enrichment: A comparison of the behavior exchange negotiation and communication models (Doctoral dissertation, Fuller Theological Seminary, 1975). *Dissertation Abstracts International,* 1976, *36,* 4184-4185B.

Vincent, C. E. *Sexual and marital health.* New York: McGraw-Hill, 1973.

Vincent, C. E. Barriers to the development of marital health as a health field. *Journal of Marriage and Family Counseling,* 1977, *3*(3), 3-11.

Weinstein, C. G. Differential change in self-actualizing and self-concept, and its effect on marital interaction, as an outcome of a selected growth group experience (Doctoral dissertation, University of Southern California, 1975). *Dissertation Abstracts International,* 1975, *36,* 4067-4068A.

Wieman, R. J. *Conjugal relationship modification and reciprocal reinforcement: A comparison of treatment for marital discord.* Unpublished doctoral dissertation, Pennsylvania State University, 1973.

Wildman, R. W., II. Structured versus unstructured marital intervention. In L. L'Abate, *Enrichment: Structured interventions with couples, families, and groups.* Washington: University Press of America, 1977.

Williams, A. M. *Comparison of the effects of two marital enrichment programs on marital communication and adjustment.* Unpublished master's thesis, University of Florida, 1975.

Wright, L., & L'Abate, L. Four approaches to family facilitation. *The Family Coordinator,* 1977, *26,* 176-181.

Yalom, I. D. *The theory and practice of group psychotherapy.* New York: Basic Books, 1970.

Zinker, J. C., & Leon, J. P. The Gestalt perspective: A marriage enrichment program. In H. A. Otto (Ed.), *Marriage and family enrichment: New perspectives and programs.* Nashville: Abingdon, 1976.

Various models have been proposed for classifying marriage and family skill training programs. The ERA model described in this article goes beyond the content and target population criteria commonly used and places major emphasis on the three dimensions of Emotions, Reasons, and Actions. Each of these modalities are considered essential in therapeutic change. The classification of present marriage and family skill training programs is offered as a heuristic tool to help therapists and researchers visualize program approaches to these modalities.

38

THE E-R-A MODEL

A Heuristic Framework for Classification of Skill Training Programs for Couples and Families

Donna Ulrici, Luciano L'Abate, and Victor Wagner*

The purpose of this paper is to provide a model for categorizing marital and family skill training programs according to their theoretical orientation. Our concerns are both empirical and clinical. The former is to provide researchers with a framework for more explicit investigation of program outcomes. The latter is to alert counselors and clinicians to the significant psychological dimensions operating within various skill training programs and to the effect that these variables may have on program clientele.

Structured skill training programs designed to enhance marriage and family life cover a wide range of interests and concerns, including (a) communication skills, (b)

*Donna Ulrici is a Ph.D. candidate in the Family Psychology Program at Georgia State University and Psychologist, Developmental Services of Cobb/Douglas Counties, GA. Luciano L'Abate is Director, Family Study Center, Psychology Department, Georgia State University, University Plaza, Atlanta, GA 30303. Victor Wagner is a Post-Doctoral Fellow in the Division of Family Studies, Department of Psychiatry, University of Rochester, School of Medicine, Rochester, NY.

couples encounters, (c) couples enrichment, (d) fair fighting, (e) problem solving training, (f) parenting skills, and (g) family enrichment. These diverse programs vary on dimensions of content area, target populations, methods of instruction, length of training, therapeutic objectives, and psychological rationales. However, classification of these programs has primarily focused on two areas, *what* the program teaches, i.e., content, and *who* the program addresses, i.e., target population (Miller, 1975; Otto, 1976; L'Abate, 1977, 1980).

Structural skill training programs have recently gained prominence as a viable means for preventive and quasi-therapeutic intervention within family systems (Gurman & Kniskern, 1977; L'Abate, 1980). Therefore, classification in terms of *how* each program deals with interventions, i.e., theoretical orientation and methodological emphasis, has become more relevant vis-a-vis the issue of attempting a greater specificity of matching problems with programs.

Major research on family and marital programs has examined the efficacy of a particular program content to improve the skill of a

From Donna Ulrici, Luciano L'Abate, and Victor Wagner, "The E-R-A Model: A Heuristic Framework for Classification of Skill Training Programs for Couples and Families," *Family Relations*, 1981, 30, pp. 307-315. Reprinted by permission of the publisher and authors.

Table 1

Classification of Intervention Methods According to the E-R-A Model

Emotions	Reasons	Actions	
		Behavioral	Systemic
Methods focus on experiential exercises which differentiate feeling states of solitude and solidarity.	Methods focus on the development of conscious understanding which supports rational control of emotions and behavior.	Methods focus on the application of scientific principles to shape and control behavior.	Methods focus on adjusting dimensions of cohesion and adaptability which maintain family functioning.
1. Developing intrapersonal awareness through individual exercises of meditation, fantasy trips, imaginary dialogues, here and now awareness.	1. Teaching new facts, concepts and theories through lectures, readings and discussions.	1. Solving behavioral problems through experimental analysis—quantifying behavior, determining controls, implementing interventions and evaluating.	1. Restructuring operations in response to situational stress or developmental changes through: (a) Reorganization of family interactions within the session (e.g., enactment, increasing intensity, reframing) (b) Liner task assignments to directly change operations (e.g., rescheduling family duties, assigning age appropriate task) (c) Paradoxical task assignments that emphasize operational problems and points out complementary relationships (e.g. role reversals, behavioral extremes).
2. Developing awareness of interpersonal relationships through interactional task of role play, sculpting, etc.	2. Relating past influence to present functioning through cognitive recreation of past events, (e.g., psychoanalytic dialogues, genograms, rational reevaluations.)	2. Teaching and increasing desired behavior and extinguishing unappropriate techniques of operant conditioning. (e.g., negative and positive reinforcement, extinction, punishment, differential reinforcement.)	Establishing appropriate boundaries for cohesion and autonomy through a) Directives given within the session e.g., spacial rearrangement, demanding interactions, blocking interactions, unbalancing the social network). b) Liner and paradoxical assignments for daily context. (e.g., rituals, activities to support coalitions or limit enmeshment.)
3. Developing bodily awareness through physical exercises of creative movement and interpersonal body contacts.	3. Developing insight to differentiate feelings from actions through analysis of one's present and past relationships, (e.g., working through transference, understanding defense operations and ego controls)	3. Regulation of overt behavior through symbolic mediational processes (e.g., observational learning), and cognitive mediational processes (e.g., modification of set interpretations.)	
4. Teaching skills of interpersonal sensitivity and communication through lectures, readings,	4. Teaching skills of rational thinking and ego control through lectures, discussions, and practice at rational	4. Extinguishing unappropriate or undesirable behavior through deconditioning (e.g., flooding;	

Table 1 (Cont'd)
Classification of Intervention Methods According to the E-R-A Model

Emotions	Reasons	Actions	
		Behavioral	Systemic
demonstrations and practice exercises.	problem solving and decision making.	desensitization techniques) and adverse conditioning procedures. 5. Practice application of learned behavior through behavioral rehearsal (e.g., role play, simulation exercises) 6. Implementing desired behavior or its approximation through behavioral task performed in daily context. 7. Teaching behavioral principles through lectures, models and practice exercises.	

target sample. Findings report the degree of change between pretest and posttest evaluations of a designated program (Gurman & Kniskern, 1977). Few studies have compared the relative effectiveness of one approach to training a skill to that of another approach (L'Abate, 1980; L'Abate & Rupp, Note 1). Categorization and investigation of skill training programs which do not examine how programs operate to effect change appear contrary to the prevailing needs of family facilitators who strive to implement the most beneficial approach to intervention.

L'Abate and Frey (in press, 1981) have suggested a classification framework for therapeutic approaches to intervention based on their orientation to change. They proposed *Emotions, Reasons,* and *Actions* are the three major modalities or aspects involved in therapeutic change. The model explains that there is a separate yet interdependent relationship among these modalities of Experiencing, Reasoning, and Acting: "Our emotions (E), reasoning (R), and actions (A) systems are all the major resources we have for dealing with our internal and external environments" (L'Abate & Frey, in press, 1981). None of these three aspects is more important or takes primacy over the other two, but rather, we need access to all three aspects to reach our potential as human beings. This classification system can be used diagnostically to differentiate qualities of persons as well as taxonomically to categorize therapeutic approaches to intervention and their methodological techniques. Although this model may have important implications for most methods of marital and family interventions, the focus of this paper is on the application of this model to skill training programs for couples and families. We want to demonstrate the applicability of this model for a classification of these programs.

The following section provides a description of Emotional, Reasoning, and Action approaches to intervention. Table 1 presents a specific classification used by the three approaches. Based on the criteria of content, method of instruction, and psychological rationale, family and marital skill training programs are delineated and categorized according to the E-R-A model.

Table 2
Emotionally Oriented Skill Training Program

Program	Content Focus	Methods of Training	Theoretical Rationale
1. Catholic Encounter (Bosco, 1976)	Couples, spiritual feelings, interpersonal commitment.	Interactional task to develop interpersonal awareness.	Need periodically to experience rebirth of communications, feelings and commitment.
2. Marriage Enrichment Program-Reformed Church (Vander Haar & Vander Haar, 1976; VanEck & VanEck, 1976)	Couples-Search for meaning in life and marriage	*Phase I*-Task and exercises developing interpersonal awareness. *Phase II*-Exercise of interpersonal awareness and bodily contact. Teaching skills of sensitivity and communication.	Couples can express intimacy and meaning in life through marriage.
3. Christian Marriage Enrichment Retreat (Green, 1976)	Couples-Defining priorities, values and the meaning of love. Improving intimacy and communication.	Interactional exercises, bodily awareness techniques and written exercise of intrapersonal awareness. Group Task developing individual awareness and couples task of interpersonal communication.	A retreat can provide opportunity to integrate religious values and married life and to foster growth.
4. Marriage Rebirth Retreat (Schmitt & Schmitt, 1976)	Couples-the experience of separation and reunion		Rankian concepts of experience and meaning in life through a marriage relationship.
5. Gestalt Marriage Enrichment (Zinker & Leon, 1976)	Couples-Creative use of conflict in a relationship	Exercises of interpersonal and bodily awareness. Task to develop awareness of interpersonal transactions. Teaching communication process skills.	Gestalt concepts of experiencing reconstruction of relationships and using conflict for growth.
6. Conjugal Relationship Enhancement (CRE) (Rappaport, 1972, 1976)	Couples, increasing intimacy and improving communications	Teaching skills of interpersonal sensitivity and effective communication	Although behavioral principles are used in teaching, the primary focus is on Rogerian concepts of positive regard and empathic listening. (Same as CRE)
7. Filial Therapy and PARD (Guerney, 1969)	Parent/child improving communications	(Same as CRE)	
8. Second Chance Family (Malamud, 1975)	Family-Accepting one's human fallability and conflict with others	Exercise of intrapersonal awareness and interactional task for interpersonal awareness	Experiential encounters can build understanding of self and others.

Table 3

Reason Oriented Skill Training Programs

Programs	Content Focus	Method of Training	Theoretical Rationale
1. Preventive maintenance model (Sherwood & Sherer, 1975)	Couples-How relationships are established, maintained and changed.	Teaching a theoretical model to understand marriage interactions. Giving rational labels to feeling states and teaching how rational language can be used for decision making.	Rational-emotive theory—Developing new concepts to understand relationships and the use of reasoning to guide behavior.
2. Family Evening Home-Mormon Church (Cowly & Adams, 1976)	Family and extended family—Psychological and theological concepts.	Preplanned programs teaching psychological and theological concepts through family discussions.	Marriage and parenthood are a sacred obligation. Religious concepts can be used to solve family problems.
3. Jewish Marriage Encounter (Kligfield, 1976)	Couples-meaning marriage and Jewish family life in terms of "cosmic" significance and the techniques of an "I-Thou" dialogue.	Teaching a communication and unification theory as a foundation for a marriage relationship. Differentiating love as a feeling from love as an act of will. Formulating a decision to love. Engaging in couples' dialogue.	Buber's concept of marriage as a state of communication, i.e., I-Thou dialogue and a unification where eternal "Thou" is always present. Unification through communication is a sacred goal.
4. Institute for Transactional Analysis (Capers & Capers, 1976)	Couples-Understanding various ego states and their controls. Achieving intimacy through ego control.	Teaching a transactional theory of behavior. Using verbal and non-verbal exercises to differentiate different ego states.	Transactional theory of parent, child, and adult ego states within each person. Awareness of different states can help one control their ego and renegotiate marriage on adult terms.
5. Jealousy Program (Constantine, 1976)	Couples-Defining types of jealous behavior and the process of jealous behavior.	Teaching new concepts of jealousy, and teaching ways to apply these concepts to jealousy problems.	An understanding of jealousy processes can control jealous behavior.

Classification of Marital and
Family Skill Training Programs

According to the E-R-A model, family interventions with an emotional orientation focus on content that is concerned with the immediate here and now, with consideration being given to how feelings are expressed and translated within couples, families, or group transactions. Humanistic schools of existential, experiential, and phenomenological psychology have provided rationales that are congruent with an emotional, empathic orientation. Intervention methods within the emotional orientation usually take place within the structured program context. They often are directed toward increasing sensitivity to emotional messages and developing skills involved in making positive contact with others. Table 2 presents skill training programs which focus on an emotional orientation. These programs strive to support marriage relationships or family life by improving how individuals experience and express intimate feelings. Programs 6 and 7 focus directly on teaching effective skills of interpersonal sensitivity and communication. Programs 1, 3, and 8 use exercises that develop a sense of self and others and provide experiences of separation and sharing as a means for facilitating intimate relationships. Programs 2, 4, and 5 have incorporated touch and awareness exercises and direct training of communication skills to reach their goals.

Reasoning schools tend to focus on content and deal with knowledge of and reasons about the family's or couple's intrapsychic and interpersonal processes. Their methodology focuses on cognitive representations of reality—the past as well as the immediate is considered. There are hypothetical and rational discussions of specific problems and emotional issues. Calm, logical approaches to behavior and feelings are emphasized. The reasoning approach to intervention is based on theories presented by psychoanalytic and cognitive schools of psychology. Table 3 presents the reason oriented skill training programs. Although the content focus of their programs is diverse, all are based on the idea that a better theoretical understanding of interpersonal interaction and family transaction will help to solve daily problems and improve relationships. Programs 1, 2, and 5

are primarily educational, while programs 3 and 4 have included exercises to provide an experiential understanding of new concepts presented.

Action oriented programs focus on defining and solving specific family and/or marriage problems. They aim at preventing future problems. These methods include behavioral techniques and principles, practice tasks to be performed during the structured program, and task assignments to be implemented in daily life. Action approaches have emerged from distinctly different psychological positions of behaviorism, family systems, and Adlerian theories. Although these theories disagree on many of the processes that operate to control interaction, all three agree that change is best effected through active behavioral tasks directed at changing one's everyday observable interactions. Programs 1 through 5 use behavioral principles to teach couples new and more effective courses of action. Programs 6, 7, and 8 develop new structures of family transactions through behavioral tasks that engage families in a new system of communication and involvement with each other or with members of their social network.

From an examination of Tables 2, 3, and 4, it is apparent that the training programs presented here are more or less representative of one of the three modalities, and programs with a more eclectic approach are not included. One should note that the classification of a program in one of the three modalities does not demand purity in focus but rather is based on evaluation of the major assumed or alleged emphasis of the program. Therefore, this classification of skill training programs involves interpretation of the major theoretical emphasis as well as an evaluation of specific areas of emphasis. As long as interpretation and evaluation by their nature are subjective processes, we are aware that our designation and weighting of criteria for classification may not be absolute. These limitations withstanding, this classification system is offered as a viable structure to determine dimensions of skill training programs that may significantly affect program outcome.

Table 4

Action Skill Training Program

Program	Content Focus	Method of Training	Theoretical Rationale
1. Behavioral Exchange Negotiations A. Liberman Program (Liberman, 1970, 1976) B. Stuart Program (Stuart, 1976)	Couples-Communication. Skills tracking of positive and negative interpersonal behavior, conflict negotiations and contingency contracting.	Teaching behavioral principles for interpersonal communications. Reinforcement of positive interactions. Instruction, practice exercises and task assignments for negotiation skills.	Couples can use behavioral principles to improve communications and solve problems.
2. Communication Skill Training CST (Miller, Nunnally, 1974, Miller, 1975)	Couples-(Training can be used separately or as a part of other programs) Sending and receiving clear direct communications.	Teaching communication skills through lectures, models, practice exercises and evaluative feedback.	Communication problems can occur due to skill deficit couples can benefit from learning new behavioral skill.
3. Assertiveness Training (Fensterheim and Baer, 1975, Baer, 1976)	Couples-Self enhancing behavior that does not deny rights of others.	Teaching assertive behavior through instructions, modeling, role play, task assignments, and evaluative feedback.	Aggressive and nonassertive behavior is learned and more appropriate assertive behavior can be learned and used to benefit couples interaction.
4. Problem solving A. Blechman & Olsen (1976); B. Kieren et al. (1975)	Couples-Effective means of problem solving through specific steps of deductive reasoning and outcome evaluations.	Teaching problem solving steps. Simulated practice exercises with positive reinforcement for following steps.	Behavioral concept that empirical principles can be used to solve daily problems.
5. Behavioral programs for Parents (Patterson & Gullion, 1971)	Parents-Behavioral management principles of conditioning and social learning.	Teaching of behavioral principles or programmed self instruction to learn principles.	Behavioral principles of learning can be used to manage child behavior.
6. Adlerian Parent-Child Programs (Dreikurs & Sultz, 1967)	Family-Birth orders, family constellations, rules, consequences of positive and negative transaction.	Discussions, family conferences for problem solving and task assignments.	Adlerian concepts that family life education can prevent future problems.
7. Family Growth Group (Anderson, 1976)	Families—Making families more adaptable systems. Developing awareness of family growth, potential. Developing cohesion between families that share a larger community.	Directing exchange of information within and between families. Task assignments that build support systems within and between families.	Systematic concept of families as a system—family potential can grow from transactions with other family systems.
8. Family Communication Systems Program (Benson et al., 1975)	Parents-Presenting families as an enmeshed system, clarifying needs and problems of families in terms of systems relationships.	Using objective directives to develop family goals and teach listening skills. Behavioral task of active involvement to teach parents ways to effectively intervene in their family relationships.	Systematic concepts that families should clarify problems and needs in terms of their family relationship systems.

Discussion and Conclusions

Logically, one may surmise that to provide the most effective outcome for program participants, program selection should be based on a match that goes beyond content concerns and population specifications. It should also consider what psychological orientation to programming best fits the needs and characteristics of the family, couple, or groups of clients. For example, recognition of the strengths and the weaknesses on Emotional, Reasoning, and Action modalities could enable one to choose a preexisting skill training program which emphasized aspects more relevant to existing characteristics and needs of a couple or a family. Presently, investigators are only beginning to consider the significance of matching specific characteristics of the clientele with complementary treatment modalities (L'Abate & Frey, in press; Frey, L'Abate, & Wagner, Note 2). The question of whether program selection should be based on a matching of strengths, that is, choosing a program orientation which emphasizes the clientele's strong resources, or on a matching of weaknesses, that is, choosing a program orientation which concentrates on the clientele's least effective domain, remains open for theoretical debate. However, classification of skill training programs according to Emotions, Reasons, and Actions provides a framework within which researchers and clinicians can examine the interplay between the clientele's characteristics and intervention approaches.

Research on the relative effectiveness of different program approaches for specific clientele could not only benefit selection of skill training programs but also provide insight into how different psychological approaches operate to effect change. It follows that empirical and clinical application of this model could extend to most methods of marital and family interventions. However, we must conclude that the formulation of this classification framework is just the beginning. The value of this model remains heuristic, and the therapeutic significance is still dependent upon the effective outcome of its application. Therefore, we welcome clinical and empirical evidence in support or consideration of this classification system.

REFERENCE NOTES

1. L'Abate, L., & Rupp, G. Enrichment: *Skill training for family life*. (Manuscript submitted for publication).
2. Frey J., L'Abate, L., & Wagner V. Further implications and elaborations of the E-R-A model for family therapy (Manuscript submitted for publication).

REFERENCES

Anderson, D. A. The family growth group: Guidelines for an emerging means of strengthening families. In H. A. Otto (Ed.) *Marriage and family enrichment: New perspectives and programs*, Nashville: Abington, 1976.

Baer, J. *How to be an assertive not an aggressive woman in life, love and on the job*. New York: Signet, 1976.

Benson, L., Berger, M., & Mease, W. Family communication systems. In S. Miller (Ed.), *Marriage and family enrichment through communications*. Beverly Hills: Sage Publications, 1975.

Blechman, E. A., & Olson, D. H. L. The family game: Description and effectiveness. In D. H. L. Olson (Ed.), *Treating relationships*. Lake Mills, IA: Graphic Publications, 1976.

Bosco, A. Marriage encounter: An eciemenical enrichment program. In H. A. Otto (Ed.), *Marriage and family enrichment: New perspectives and programs*. Nashville: Abington, 1976.

Capers, H., & Capers, B. Transactional analysis tools for use in marriage enrichment programs. In H. A. Otto (Ed.), *Marriage and family enrichment: New perspectives and programs*. Nashville: Abington, 1976.

Constantine, L. L. Jealousy: From theory to intervention. In D. H. L. Olson (Ed.), *Treating relationships*. Lake Mills, IA: Graphic Publishing Co., 1976.

Cowly, A. J., & Adams, R. S. The family home evening: A national ongoing enrichment program. In H. A. Otto (Ed.), *Marriage and family enrichment: New perspective and programs*, Nashville: Abington, 1976.

Dreikers, R., & Sultz, V. *Children: The challenge*. Chicago: Adlerian Institute, 1976.

Fensterheim, H. & Baer, J. *Don't say yes when you want to say no*. New York: Dell Publishers, 1975.

Green, H., A Christian marriage enrichment retreat. In H. A. Otto (Ed.), *Marriage and family enrichment: New perspectives and programs*. Nashville: Abington, 1976.

Guerney, B. G. (Ed.) *Psychotherapeutic Agents: New roles for nonprofessional parents and teachers*. New York: Holt, Rinehart & Winston, 1969.

Gunman, A. S., & Kniskern, D. P. Enriching research on marital enrichment programs. *Journal of Marriage and Family Counseling*, 1977, **3**, 3-9.

Kieren, D., Henton, J. & Marotz, R. *Her and his: The problem solving approach to marriage*. Hinsdale, IL: Dryden Press, 1975.

Kligfeld, B. The Jewish marriage encounter. In H. A. Otto (ed.), *Marriage and family enrichment: New perspectives and programs*. Nashville: Abington, 1976.

L'Abate, L. ENRICHMENT: *Structured interventions with couples, families and groups*. Washington, D.C.: University Press of America, 1977.

L'Abate, L. Skill training programs for couples and families: Clinical and non clinical applications. In A. S. Garmant & D. Kriskern (Eds.), *Handbook of Family Therapy*, New York: Brunner/Mazel, 1980.

L'Abate, L. Toward a theory and technology of social skills training: Suggestions for curriculum development. *Academic Psychology Bulletin*, 1980, **2**, 207-228.

L'Abate, L., & Frey, J. The E-R-A Model: The role of feeling in family therapy reconsidered: Implications for theories of family therapy, *Journal of Marriage and Family Therapy*, in press, 1981.

Liberman, R. P. Behavioral approaches to family and couple therapy. *American Journal of Orthopsychiatry*, 1970, **40**, 106-118.

Liberman, R. P., Wheeler, E., & Sanders, N. Behavior therapy for marital disharmony: An educational approach, *Journal of Marriage and Family Counseling*, 1976, **2**, 383-396.

Malamud, D. I. Communication training in the second chance family. In S. Miller (Ed.), *Marriage and families: Enrichment through communication*. Beverly Hills: Sage Publications, 1975.

Miller, S. (Ed.) *Marriage and families: Enrichment through communication*. Beverly Hills: Sage Publications, 1975.

Miller, S., Nunnally, E., Wackman, D., & Brazman, R. *Alive and aware, improving communication in relationships*. Minneapolis: International Communications Programs, Inc., 1974.

Otto, H. A. (Ed.). *Marriage and family enrichment: New perspectives and programs*. Nashville: Abington, 1976.

Patterson, G. R. & Gullion, E. M. *Living with children: New methods for parents and teachers*. Champaign, IL: Research Press, 1971.

Rappaport, A. F. The effects of an intensive conjugal relationship modification, *Dissertation Abstracts International*, 1972, **32**, 6571-6572A.

Rappaport, A. I. Conjugal relationship enhancement program. In Olson (Ed.), *Treating relationships*, Lake Mills, IA: Graphic Publishing Co., 1976.

Schmitt, A., & Schmitt, D. Marriage renewal retreats. In H. A. Otto (Ed.), *Marriage and family enrichment: New perspectives and programs*. Nashville: Abington, 1976.

Sherwood, J. J., & Scherer, J. J. A model for couples: How two can grow together. In S. Miller (Ed.), *Marriage and families enrichment through communication*, Beverly Hills: Sage Publications, 1975.

Stuart, R. B. An operant interpersonal program for couples. In D. H. Olson (Ed.), *Treating relationships*. Lake Mills, IA: Graphic Publishing Co., 1976.

Vander Haar, D. and Vander Haar, T. The marriage enrichment program, phase I. In H. A. Otto (Ed.), *Marriage and family enrichment: New perspectives and programs*. Nashville: Abington, 1976.

VanEck, B. & VanEck, B. The Phase II marriage enrichment lab. In H. A. Otto (Ed.), *Marriage and family enrichment: New perspectives and programs*. Nashville: Abington, 1976.

Zinker, J. C., & Leon, J. P. The besalt persective: A marriage enrichment program. In H. A. Otto (Ed.)., *Marriage and family enrichment: New perspectives and programs*. Nashville: Abington, 1976.

There has been much controversy over the effectiveness of marital enrichment programs. Sources of controversy include the questionable quality of existing outcome studies, failure to differentiate varieties of enrichment programs that have different goals, and lack of consensus in defining what is a valid, clinically relevant effect. In this paper, an important distinction is made between valid and illusory effects of marital enrichment experiences. A three-stage model of marital enrichment designed to maximize valid effects and integrate participants' attitudinal and behavioral changes is presented. Goals of the three stages are differentiated, their advantages and limitations are discussed, and suggestions for well-designed research on the sequential model are presented.

39

INTEGRATING ATTITUDINAL AND BEHAVIORAL CHANGE IN MARITAL ENRICHMENT*

*Larry Hof, Norman Epstein, and William R. Miller***

The proliferation of marital enrichment programs designed to enhance basically well-functioning relationships (Mace & Mace, 1976; Otto, 1975) has been associated with highly enthusiastic testimonials by participants and program leaders. Similar reports are emerging as enrichment programs are conducted for couples described as "troubled," "dysfunctional," or "clinical." However, reviewers of research evaluating the outcome of a variety of these growth-oriented enrichment programs (Gurman & Kniskern, 1977; Hof & Miller, in press) conclude that although outcome data generally are encouraging,

over-reliance on participant self-reports and use of inadequate control groups in most existing studies limit one's confidence in drawing firm conclusions regarding the effectiveness of such programs. For example, couples' positive changes cannot be attributed with certainty to specific enrichment experiences rather than to participation in treatment per se. In addition, existing studies have not adequately addressed the question of whether or not observed changes are more than superficial impressions of couples that their relationships are "better."

Critics of some enrichment programs (e.g., Doherty, McCabe, & Ryder, 1978) go so far as to suggest that benefits may be illusory (invalid) and may produce painful disillusionment when the emotional "high" is replaced by the stark realities of continued marital conflict and unfulfilled needs. Unfortunately, adequate research to answer these questions has yet to be produced, and both proponents and critics of marital enrichment are limited to speculating about its effectiveness. The purposes of this paper are to describe a strategy for differentiating valid from invalid effects of enrichment experiences and to propose a sequential model for maximizing and

*Work on this paper was supported in part by NIMH Grant No. RR-09069. The first and second authors contributed equally to the paper and the order of listing was determined by a coin flip.

**Larry Hof is Associate in Family Study in Psychiatry, Marriage Council of Philadelphia, Department of Psychiatry, University of Pennsylvania; Norman Epstein is Assistant Professor of Psychology in Psychiatry, Marriage Council of Philadelphia, Department of Psychiatry, University of Pennsylvania; William R. Miller is Assistant Professor of Psychology in Psychiatry, Marriage Council of Philadelphia, Department of Psychiatry, University of Pennsylvania, Philadelphia, PA 19104.

From Larry Hof, Norman Epstein, and William R. Miller, "Integrating Attitudinal and Behavioral Change in Marital Enrichment," *Family Relations*, 1980, 29, pp. 241-248. Reprinted by permission of the publisher and authors.

integrating valid attitudinal and behavioral changes in marital enrichment programs.

Before questions of treatment effectiveness can be addressed, proponents and critics alike must avoid evaluating marital enrichment programs as an undifferentiated mass. The global term "marital enrichment" has been used to describe a wide variety of interventions, including communication training, behavior exchange programs, and mixtures of affective and skill-training experiences (Gurman & Kniskern, 1977; Hof & Miller, in press). Consequently, it is crucial that systematic evaluations carefully differentiate programs according to their theoretical bases, specific goals, and procedures. The utility of each program should be judged according to two criteria: (a) whether it lives up to its proponents' claims (i.e., produces valid, intended change) and (b) if effective as intended, whether it is appropriate for the specific needs of a particular couple. General reviews such as that by Gurman and Kniskern (1977) are informative, but they do not differentiate subcategories of enrichment experiences that have different goals and should be evaluated accordingly. Since research comparing effects of different marital enrichment programs is at present scanty (Hof & Miller, in press), more comparative studies will be needed in order for clinicians to be able to select programs as primary or adjunctive interventions for couples with particular characteristics.

Differentiating Valid and Illusory Effects of Marital Enrichment

As noted above, a major concern of reviewers has been the possibility that changes attributed to enrichment programs may be illusory. Doherty et al. (1978) suggest that widely attended Marriage Encounter programs (cf., Bosco, 1973; Genovese, 1975) establish unrealistically positive expectations of marriage that are bound to be shattered. Gurman and Kniskern (1977) argue that because enrichment experiences "are conducted in very accepting, even loving, atmospheres, there is a very real possibility that changes reported, coming as they do primarily from participants at the end of the program, represent global 'halo' or placebo effects" (p. 8). Although there is a strong possibility that changes, particularly on self-report measures, may be superficial and invalid (e.g., when participants report positive change *that does not exist*, in order to please program leaders or to reduce their own cognitive dissonance over effort expended), such false reports must be distinguished from effects that are real but not due to the theoretically based, specific treatment components. Care is required in using the term "placebo effect," which was borrowed from medicine and is intended to describe actual behavior change not attributed to the *known* active (theoretically relevant) ingredients of a treatment. In medicine, a placebo effect has occurred when an inert treatment (e.g., a sugar pill) produces changes in target symptoms.

Researchers such as Jacobson and Baucom (1977) refer to the determinants of such placebo effects as *nonspecific factors;* i.e., variables associated with the treatment (e.g., therapist activity level or attention) but not *hypothesized* to be change-inducing. Both specific and nonspecific treatment factors can produce valid effects in treated clients. In treatment outcome research, it typically is the experimenter's task to demonstrate that specific components of a theoretically active intervention are effective over and above the effects due to nonspecific factors associated with treatment procedures. Researchers evaluate experimental treatments by comparing their effects on targets (overt behavior, feelings, etc.) with changes produced by placebo treatments matched as closely as possible to experimental treatments in terms of possible nonspecific factors.

Nonspecific or placebo factors have been considered "nuisance" variables, as somehow not real or significant, when in fact such factors have been shown to produce valid change. The difference between valid specific effects and valid nonspecific effects is that the theoretical reasons for the latter's impact have not yet been understood (Bernstein & Nietzel, 1977; O'Leary & Borkovec, 1978). Bernstein and Nietzel argue that such factors can be used as legitimate influence tactics and propose research to identify the determinants of valid nonspecific effects so that they may be administered to clients in a systematic manner. The crucial issue, in regard to evaluation of marital enrichment programs, is the need to distinguish among valid specific effects (those that are theoretically active), valid nonspecific effects (that can become theoretically specific effects), and truly illusory (invalid) effects.

A related area of confusion in evaluations of marital enrichment involves a failure to distinguish between illusory (invalid) treatment effects and those that may not generalize beyond the treatment setting to couples' everyday lives. For example, Gurman and Kniskern (1977) refer to limitations in the duration and generalizability (from an accepting treatment atmosphere to the home environment) as placebo effects. However, effects that are real but short-lived and effects that are real but do not generalize well to other environments are neither placebo nor illusory. The former may necessitate *more* training in relationship skills or "booster" sessions in order to increase the longevity of treatment effects, and the latter may necessitate more *in vivo* practice and role-playing in order to increase transfer of learning from the training environment to the home. The crucial issue is that a weak or short-lived effect still is an effect, and if it is a desirable effect it is our task to maximize and utilize it rather than dismissing it as somehow illusory. Thus, Gurman and Kniskern's statement that short-lived "peak" experiences reported by marital enrichment participants do not, by themselves, indicate that a program was effective requires qualification. Such a statement would be valid if the theoretically based goals of marital enrichment involve only long-term effects. However, many existing programs include a primary orientation toward rapidly shifting couples' motivation and attitudes about their marriages, as well as facilitating long-term relationship changes through skill training. Both short-term and long-term attitudinal and motivational changes are expected. If the "emotional highs" produced by a marital enrichment program in fact represent valid motivational and attitudinal changes, then at least one of the program's short-term goals has been achieved, and the program was *partly* effective. Of course, valid short-term effects will be of little value if they are not extended or used to produce long-term effects.

If an enrichment program does not also in-crease relationship skills to the point of effective integration, couples may experience disillusionment over time as their initial good intentions toward change are frustrated by their inability to solve problems and resolve conflicts. We propose that attitudinal and motivational changes produced in the short run will facilitate the learning of skills, but also that skill training needs to be of sufficient duration and depth to enable participants to integrate and use their new skills effectively in daily living.

In light of the above discussion, evaluation of any marital enrichment program necessitates a clear specification of its theoretical goals, the treatment components expected to produce specific desired changes, treatment characteristics that may produce valid nonspecific effects, and factors that may produce illusory effects (invalid outcome data). Only the illusory effects will be of no positive utility, and any limitations (e.g., duration, generalizability) of valid specific and nonspecific treatment effects can be addressed by either modifying the enrichment experiences or supplementing them with other treatments.

Integrating Attitudinal and Behavioral Change in Marital Enrichment

In the following discussion, the generally accepted goals of marital enrichment are outlined and possible limitations of existing types of programs for achieving this set of goals are noted. It is proposed that the strengths of the various programs be combined into a sequential model for marital enrichment. This multiple component approach is believed to lead to more stable and enduring changes other than approaches. Subsequently, a research strategy for evaluating the proposed sequential enrichment model is described.

General Goals and Limitations of Marital Enrichment Programs

Although marital enrichment programs for nonclinical couples (couples who do not identify themselves as distressed) vary widely in format, the most common goals are: (a) to increase spouses' self-awareness and mutual empathy; (b) to increase their awareness of their positive characteristics, strengths, and potential as individuals and as a couple; (c) to increase mutual self-disclosure of thoughts and feelings; (d) to increase intimacy; and (e) to develop relationship skills in communication, problem solving and conflict resolution (Hof & Miller, in press). The means for achieving these goals vary considerably across programs, and some programs may pay minimal attention to one or more of them. For example, Marriage Encounter programs have been criticized for overemphasizing marital unity and failing to prepare couples to deal with interpersonal differences and conflict (Doherty et al., 1978; Hof & Miller, in press). Marriage Encounter attempts to build communication skills by means of a narrowly focused and highly structured "dialogue" technique that may increase couples' self-disclosure but by itself may be insufficient for dealing with day-to-day marital conflicts. The failure to teach other skills such as conflict management may limit the effectiveness of this program.

Other weekend programs such as the Creative Marriage Enrichment Program (Hof & Miller, in press) introduce couples to a wider range of relationship skills (listening, self-disclosure, noncontingent behavioral contracting, role renegotiation, and conflict resolution). Although these programs provide couples with a fairly broad repertoire of skills, their effectiveness may be limited by insufficient practice of each skill.

In spite of these possible shortcomings in the area of skill development, numerous testimonials that cannot simply be dismissed suggest that an initial marital enrichment weekend experience such as Marriage Encounter (Demarest, Sexton, & Sexton, 1977), Marriage Communication Lab (Smith & Smith, 1976), the model developed by Mace and Mace (1976, 1977), or the Creative Marriage Enrichment Program (Hof & Miller, in press) creates an interpersonal atmosphere of acceptance and trust which is conducive to increased mutual self-disclosure and awareness of marital strengths. Many couples report an increase in positive feelings toward their partner and their relationship as a result of participating in such a program. If these experiences increase couples' positive motivation to work on their relationships and if they reduce couples' resistance to change, such experiences can be highly valuable adjuncts to, or

preludes to, more skill-oriented programs (e.g., Relationship Enhancement Program: Guerney, 1977; Couples Communication Program: Miller, Nunnally, & Wackman, 1976).

Integrating Complementary Program Components

While the relative strengths and weaknesses of different enrichment programs still must be determined through controlled comparative studies, it is likely that each of the various approaches may be quite limited in some respects yet have positive potential in others. Positive and complementary components of various programs that can be validated in research might be utilized in the formation of new enrichment programs. For example, enrichment programs that focus primarily on attitudinal/motivational change may not develop couples' relationship skills sufficiently, and positive attitudes developed in the absence of skills are likely to sour. On the other hand, skill training programs that lack sufficient grounding in attitudinal change may encounter significant resistance to change from participants. Couples who are not motivated to expend considerable effort are unlikely to change long-standing relationship patterns. Motivation can be low if they either are not aware that more satisfying alternative ways of interacting exist, or do not believe that old patterns can be changed. Couples commonly resist change in their relationships due to anxiety regarding possible negative consequences of change, comfort with the familiar, and positive payoffs ("secondary gain") of even problematic interactions. Professionals who work with couples are all too familiar with limited positive motivation and resistance to change even in the best intentioned clinical *and* nonclinical clients.

Even when skill training is successful in modifying participants' overt behaviors, couples may fail to perceive their relationships as significantly different or improved. Spouses may attribute each other's behavioral changes to negative motivation (e.g., being coerced to change) rather than to positive motivation (e.g., changing because one cares about one's partner and is committed to improving the relationship). Epstein and Jackson's (1978) finding that attitudinal change (couples' perceptions of change in their relationships) lagged behind overt behavioral change in a communication training program is not unusual. Although attitudes may be modified gradually as newly skilled couples experience changes in their daily interactions, this process might be facilitated by adding another treatment component to the training program. This component would focus directly on the areas of mutual acceptance, caring, intimacy, individual and marital strengths, and commitment to the development of the relationship. Goals would include (a) increasing each couple's awareness and expression of these factors, and (b) increasing the levels of the factors in their relationship. This attitudinal-affective component already exists in many intensive weekend enrichment programs. Rather than dismissing the reported attitudinal and motivational changes in these programs as illusory, those committed to the development of effective, broad-based programs should evaluate the potential of such effects and use those components found to increase motivation and pair-bonding.

A Sequential Enrichment Model

The prior discussion leads us to propose a model of sequential enrichment experiences, designed to integrate and maximize attitudinal/motivational and skill development. Our model is based on the belief that a comprehensive marital enrichment program must (a) increase couples' positive motivation for expending considerable effort to change; (b) reduce resistance to change stemming from anxiety and "secondary gains" accrued from existing interactional patterns; (c) build specific relationship skills for communication, problem solving, and conflict resolution; (d) develop generalization of gains from the treatment setting to the home environment; and (e) maximize longevity of positive gains. In the absence of sufficient comparative research, this model is based on assumptions regarding the strengths of each treatment component. It is hoped that presentation of the model will stimulate evaluative research. In this vein, the authors currently are conducting a series of outcome studies assessing valid specific, valid nonspecific, and (invalid) illusory effects of various marital enrichment experiences, individually and in sequence.

We hypothesize that a marital enrichment program will be most likely to produce broad, enduring positive behavioral and attitudinal change when it includes three major stages, in the following order. First, an intensive experience (e.g., a weekend retreat) would be used to increase positive feelings between partners, positive attitudes toward the relationship, and motivation for change. The first stage also would *introduce* participants to relationship skills. The second stage would be a highly structured multiweek training program in which each of several specific skills (e.g., communication, conflict-resolution) would be taught in depth. The third stage would involve an ongoing (perhaps peer-led) marital growth or support group in which couples' positive changes can be maintained and increased. In this latter group, couples could give and receive reinforcement for changes, discuss obstacles to change and strategies for coping with them, and practice skills further.

Intensive Retreat. This format, in which couples meet for a few days (most commonly a weekend) in a setting removed from daily routines, distractions and stresses, has been used widely in enrichment programming, including Marriage Encounter (Demarest et al., 1977), Marriage Communication Lab (Smith & Smith, 1976), the model developed by Mace and Mace (1976), and the Creative Marriage Enrichment Program utilized by the authors at the Marriage Council of Philadelphia (Hof & Miller, in press). Couples have an opportunity, in an atmosphere of seclusion and leisure, to take an uninterrupted look at their marriages (Mace & Mace, 1974). While some enrichment programs (notably Marriage Encounter) minimize total group or small group interaction and focus on the marital dyad, others, such as the Marriage Communication Lab (Smith & Smith, 1976), utilize group process through interaction in the total group and smaller sub-groups of several couples.

The major theoretical advantages of intensive retreats are (a) a facilitative function, in which leadership modeling, group process (e.g., support and feedback from other couples), and physical environment produce an atmosphere conducive to exploration of self, partner, and relationship; and (b) a diagnostic/motivational function in which couples' awareness of their relationships' strengths and weaknesses, as well as alternative ways of relating, is increased. The intensive nature of the experience, the focus on positive aspects of the marriage as well as its growth potential, and the introduction provided to useful relationship skills can produce a highly satisfying emotional experience for participants. Many couples report a renewed or deepened sense of intimacy and commitment to their relationships, and increased estimates of the potential and strength of the relationships (Hof & Miller, in press).

There are several potential limitations of retreat experiences. L'Abate (1977) cautions that couples may engage in "self-presentational" (socially desirable) behavior rather than true self-disclosure in enrichment groups. The intensity of this potential problem, which exists in *any* group setting and is likely to be a function of the degree of trust actually achieved in such a brief experience, is an important topic for future research. Secondly, there may be insufficient practice of relationship skills, such that participants do not integrate the new knowledge well enough to modify long-standing patterns of marital interaction. Thirdly, there may be insufficient support in each couple's daily environment for the maintenance of changes initiated in the atypical retreat setting. Support involves a social system that "encourages" constructive interaction. In behavioral terms, this environment includes stimulus conditions likely to elicit desired marital·interactions (in a sense, reminders to practice good relationship skills), minimal stimuli likely to elicit competing problematic responses such as fights, and positive consequences (reinforcement) for constructive responses. Retreat experiences on their own generally do not address these issues, with the exception of recommendations given to couples that they regularly set aside some time to be together, away from distractions. (A few programs offer ongoing support groups after the initial weekend experience, but the percentage of couples who participate in such groups is extremely small.) Repeated practice in using constructive relationship skills such as conflict resolution strategies under unfavorable conditions (those unlike peaceful retreat environment) rarely occurs.

The limitations of the initial retreat compo-

nent of the proposed enrichment sequence may be offset by following the motivational experience with more extensive skill practice (including *in vivo* practice, to maximize generalization) and ongoing support groups to maintain a high level of motivation.

Spaced Relationship Skill Training. A variety of well developed, structured programs for teaching specific relationship skills exist, with some research evidence attesting to their efficacy in changing couples' behaviors (Hof & Miller, in press; Jacobson & Martin, 1976; Williams & Miller, 1979). Couples can be taught communication skills (Epstein & Jackson, 1978; Guerney, 1977; Thomas, 1977), decision-making skills (Thomas, 1977), and behavioral contracting skills (Jacobson & Martin, 1976; O'Leary & Turkewitz, 1978; Weiss, Hops, & Patterson, 1973), among others. Most of these programs are administered in a series of weekly sessions (typically six to eight), each session lasting an average of two hours.

Theoretical advantages of structured skill training programs include (a) teaching of specific skills with sufficient practice (in the group setting and also between sessions at home) and time for couples to integrate the material that has been presented; and (b) a preventive function, such that couples can use their new skills not only to solve current problems but also to prevent the development of future problems.

Potential disadvantages include (a) a lack of intensity and broken continuity over a series of weeks; (b) resistance to change, which may be alleviated or reduced by means of participation in a prior retreat experience; (c) limited generalization to the home environment, which may be addressed by attempting to create practice conditions similar to the home, by encouraging repeated practice of new skills under home conditions, and by instructing couples in modification of the home environment (e.g., putting a lock on their bedroom door to ensure more privacy; implementing more effective discipline techniques with children); and (d) limited longevity of treatment effects, which can be extended by modifying the home environment and/or providing ongoing support groups for participants.

Ongoing Support Group. An ongoing marital support or growth group would follow the initial, intensive weekend experience and the multiweek training program. These groups of four to five couples frequently meet on a monthly basis for two to four hours, and are generally peer-led (see Hopkins, Hopkins, Mace, & Mace, 1978). Members develop their own agendas and focus on areas of special interest. They utilize the leadership skills of group members, resources garnered from a variety of books or audiotaped programs, and they occasionally contract for an intensive program with professional leadership (e.g., sexual enrichment program).

In such a group setting, couples have the opportunity to give and receive feedback, support, and reinforcement for changes. They can discuss obstacles to changes in their relationship (e.g., inability to establish and maintain sufficient private time together) and strategies for coping with them. There are ongoing opportunities to experience a variety of "curative" and "growth" factors such as "universality" (i.e., a sense of "I am not alone with this problem or concern") and "altruism" (a sense of helping other group members through support, suggestions, etc.) (Egan, 1970; Yalom, 1970). Participants can also practice skills further and learn new skills in a supportive atmosphere.

There are at least two possible limitations of such support groups. First, the lack of appropriately trained professional leadership may make the development of effective programs and the "working through" of blocks to group and couple growth more difficult. Secondly, couples may feel the need (as noted above) to engage in "self-presentational" (L'Abate, 1977) or socially desirable behavior rather than true self-disclosure. Training programs designed to enable selected couples to become effective facilitators of such support groups may be an effective means of reducing the negative effects of these two potential problems (cf. Hopkins et al., 1978).

Suggestions for Research

Systematic evaluation of an integrative, comprehensive marital enrichment program such as the sequential model proposed in this paper would involve two major steps. First, the theoretical effects of the three major program stages (retreat, extended skill train-

ing, and support groups) should be validated independently. Second, effects of combining the three types of enrichment experiences should be assessed.

To date, research on relationship skill programs (e.g., Guerney, 1977; Jacobson & Martin, 1976; O'Leary & Turkewitz, 1978) is the most advanced, but more data regarding generalizability and stability of learned skills are needed. Research on retreat experiences has been more limited. Studies should test whether retreats increase spouses' awareness of marital strengths and problems, motivation for working toward change, awareness of feelings, self-disclosure, mutual acceptance and trust, and awareness of relationship skills that can be practiced. Enrichment retreats should be compared not only with no-treatment control conditions but also with treatments controlling for particular nonspecific variables such as leader activity level. The importance of the physical setting (e.g., need it be like a resort?), isolation from daily stresses, leader modeling of desired behaviors, and other factors as determinants of participants' valid attitudinal and behavioral changes could be assessed.

Since participants' self-reports of change may be biased, outcome studies should include behavioral measures as well. For example, behavioral indices of motivation might include measures of the amount of time spouses spend together performing relationship-enhancing tasks (e.g., practicing communication skills). Possible social desirability bias in participants' self-reports can be evaluated and statistically controlled by including marital social desirability scales (e.g., Edmonds, 1967). Follow-up assessments and measures of marital interaction in the home (e.g., Christensen, in press) would address issues of retreat treatment longevity and generalizability.

Effects of marital support groups have received little attention as yet. First, measures of group process are needed to insure that couples are interacting in the intended manner. Trained judges could make behavioral ratings of participants' mutual support, feedback and reinforcement. In addition, the extent to which participants identify obstacles to growth and engage in both group and couple problem-solving can be coded. Second, as recommended for retreat and skill training treatment components, both short-term and long-term *outcome* should be measured in terms of attitudinal and behavioral changes.

Research on the effects of combining retreats, extended skill training and support groups as an integrated enrichment program should address three major issues: (a) whether or not the proposed ordering of the three stages is most effective in producing desired changes; (b) what the optimal timing (spacing and duration) of the stages should be; and (c) whether all three stages are necessary for maximal treatment effectiveness. The possibility that different combinations of enrichment experiences are needed for different kinds of clients (e.g., by age or personality) also should be evaluated. Clearly, a series of well controlled experimental studies is needed to answer these questions and determine how attitudinal and behavioral changes can best be integrated in marital enrichment.

REFERENCES

Bernstein, D. A., & Nietzel, M. T. Demand characteristics in behavior modification: The natural history of a "nuisance." In M. Hersen, R. M. Eisler, & P. M. Miller (Eds.), *Progress in behavior modification* (Vol. 4). New York: Academic, 1977.

Bosco, A. *Marriage Encounter, a rediscovery of love.* St. Meinrad, IN: Abbey, 1973.

Christensen, A. Naturalistic observation of families: A system for random audio recordings in the home. *Behavior Therapy,* in press.

Demarest, D., Sexton, J., & Sexton, M. *Marriage Encounter.* St. Paul, MN: Carillon, 1977.

Doherty, W. J., McCabe, P., & Ryder, R. G. *Marriage Encounter: A critical appraisal. Journal of Marriage and Family Counseling,* 1978, **4**, 99-107.

Edmonds, V. H. Marital conventionalization: Definition and measurement. *Journal of Marriage and the Family,* 1967, **29**, 681-688.

Egan, G. *Encounter: Group process for interpersonal growth.* Belmont, CA: Brooks/Cole, 1970.

Epstein, N., & Jackson, E. An outcome study of short-term communication training with married couples. *Journal of Consulting and Clinical Psychology,* 1978, **46**, 207-212.

Genovese, R. J. Marriage Encounter. *Small Group Behavior,* 1975, **6**, 45-56.

Guerney, B. G., Jr. *Relationship Enhancement.* San Francisco: Jossey-Bass, 1977.

Gurman, A. S., & Kniskern, D. P. Enriching research on marital enrichment programs. *Journal of Marriage and Family Counseling,* 1977, **3**, 3-11.

Hof, L., & Miller, W. R. *Marriage enrichment: Philosophy, process, and program.* Bowie, MD: Charles Press, in press.

Hopkins, L., Hopkins, P., Mace, D., & Mace, V. *Toward better marriages.* Winston-Salem: ACME, 1978.

Jacobson, N. S., & Baucom, D. H. Design and assessment of nonspecific control groups in behavior modification research. *Behavior Therapy,* 1977, **8**, 709-719.

Jacobson, N. S., & Martin, B. Behavioral marriage therapy: Current status. *Psychological Bulletin,* 1976, **83**, 540-556.

L'Abate, L. *Enrichment: Structured interventions with couples, families, and groups.* Washington, DC: University Press of America, 1977.

Mace, D., & Mace, V. *We can have better marriages if we really want them.* Nashville: Abingdon, 1974.

Mace, D., & Mace, V. Marriage enrichment—A preventive group approach for couples. In D. H. L. Olson (Ed.), *Treating relationships.* Lake Mills, IA: Graphic, 1976.

Mace, D., & Mace, V. *How to have a happy marriage.* Nashville: Abingdon, 1977.

Miller, S., Nunnally, E. W., & Wackman, D. B. Minnesota Couples Communication Program (MCCP): Premarital and marital groups. In D. H. L. Olson (Ed.), *Treating Relationships.* Lake Mills, IA: Graphic, 1976.

O'Leary, K. D., & Borkovec, T. D. Conceptual, methodological, and ethical problems of placebo groups in psychotherapy research. *American Psychologist,* 1978, **33**, 821-830.

O'Leary, K. D., & Turkewitz, H. Marital therapy from a behavioral perspective. In T. J. Paolino, Jr. & B. S. McCrady (Eds.), *Marriage and marital therapy: Psychoanalytic behavioral and systems theory perspectives.* New York: Brunner/Mazel, 1978.

Otto, H. A. Marriage and family enrichment programs in North America—Report and analysis. *The Family Coordinator,* 1975, **24**, 137-142.

Smith, L., & Smith, A. Developing a national marriage communication lab training program. In H. A. Otto (Ed.), *Marriage and family enrichment: New perspectives and programs.* Nashville: Abingdon, 1976.

Thomas, E. J. *Marital communication and decision making.* New York: Free Press, 1977.

Weiss, R. L., Hops, H., & Patterson, G. R. A framework for conceptualizing marital conflict, a technology for altering it, some data for evaluating it. In L. A. Hamerlynck, L. C. Handy, & E. J. Mash (Eds.), *Behavior change: Methodology, concepts, and practice.* Champaign, IL: Research Press, 1973.

Williams, A. M., & Miller, W. R. Outcome and evaluation in marital therapy. In G. P. Sholevar (Ed.), *Marriage is a family affair: A textbook of marriage and marital therapy.* New York: Wiley/Spectrum, 1979.

Yalom, I. D. *The theory and practice of group psychotherapy.* New York: Basic, 1970.

Premarital counseling programs have been proliferating in the United States since their appearance in the 1930s. In order to evaluate the success such programs have had in preparing couples to build successful marriages, reduce the incidence of divorce and prevent unsuccessful marriages from occurring, the authors reviewed those programs which outlined standardized intervention procedures and utilized dependent measures to assess the program's effectiveness. Thirteen programs met these criteria. In general, premarital counseling programs were found to be atheoretical in their approach to intervention, loosely designed and nonspecific as to their goals.

40

PREMARITAL COUNSELING

Appraisal and Status

Dennis A. Bagarozzi and Paul Rauen

In the United States, marriages are being terminated in unprecedented numbers. This country now has one of the highest marriage/divorce ratios of all industrialized nations. In 1976 there were 2,133,000 marriages and 1,077,000 divorces (Glick & Norton, 1977). Prior to marriage, many engaged couples hold a variety of romantic notions about married life as well as a number of unrealistic expectations and untested assumptions about their future mates (Goode, 1959; Kephart, 1966; Schulman, 1974; Walster & Walster, 1978). Such unfounded optimism often prevents engaged couples from critically examining and evaluating their relationship before they are formally wedded.

In order to help prospective mates evaluate their relationship and acquaint them with the ways by which they might build a more happy and successful marriage, premarital counseling programs have been proliferating throughout the country for over four decades since the first premarital educational program was developed at the Merrill-Palmer Institute in 1932. One of the earliest premarital counseling programs was established at the Philadelphia Marriage Council (Mudd et al., 1941). The primary goals of this standardized program were: (a) to provide

---

For reprints please contact Dennis A. Bagarozzi, Ph.D., University of Georgia School of Social Work, Tucker Hall, Athens, GA 30602.

From Dennis A. Bagarozzi and Paul Rauen, "Premarital Counseling: Appraisal and Status," *American Journal of Family Therapy*, 1981, 9(3), pp. 13-30. Reprinted by permission of the publisher and authors.

education and information about married life to couples contemplating marriage and (b) to help prospective spouses work out whatever interpersonal difficulties they were experiencing at the time.

Premarital counseling programs have been devised to meet the needs of a variety of populations, for example: dating couples (Schlein, 1971), couples living with their parents (Rolfe, 1977a), the handicapped and disabled (Stallings, 1968; Walker, 1977), couples where one of the partners is a minor (Shonick, 1972), teenage couples (Reiner & Edwards, 1974; Rolfe, 1976; Rue, 1972), West Point cadets (Glendening & Wilson, 1972), members of particular religious denominations (Apple, 1970; Boike, 1977; Gangsei, 1971; Microys & Bader, 1977; Oates & Rowatt, 1975; Rolfe, 1975; Wright, 1977), college students (D'Augelli et al., 1974; Hinkle & Moore, 1971; Jackson, 1972; Meadows & Taplin, 1970; Miller et al., 1976a; Van Zoost, 1973), and the general public (Bernstein, 1977; Bienvenu, 1974; Freeman, 1965; Holoubek & Holoubek, 1973; Holoubek et al., 1974; Levine & Brodsky, 1949; Mace, 1972; McRae, 1975; Ridley et al., 1979; Rolfe, 1973; Ross, 1977).

While the long-term effects of premarital counseling have yet to be determined, some states have passed laws requiring all couples with a member under the age of 18 applying for marriage licenses to receive some type of premarital counseling (Ehrentraut, 1975; Elkin, 1977; Leigh, 1976; Shonick, 1975).

In an attempt to evaluate the effects of premarital counseling programs as currently practiced, the authors chose to review only those premarital counseling programs that met the two criteria listed below. The authors believe that these criteria represent the minimum standards without which meaningful analyses cannot be conducted.

1) Standardized procedures and intervention techniques were employed and followed systematically during the premarital counseling process.
2) Some type of outcome measure was employed by the investigator to assess the treatment's effectiveness.

The analysis of premarital counseling programs in this article, will be limited to the 13 studies which fulfilled these minimum requirements.

Two analyses are presented below. Table 1 offers a descriptive account of each program. Table 2 provides an analysis of the research methods and procedures used by each investigator to evaluate the program's effectiveness.

Program Analysis

The authors believe that for clinical intervention to be most effective it should be guided by sound theoretical reasoning and that intervention into family systems should be based upon a coherent theory of family process and family development. Such a theory should describe the normal course of family development and optimal family functioning as well as explain the etiology of deviant family processes and the development of aberrant interaction patterns. Premarital counseling is intervention which takes place at the initial stage of the family developmental life cycle. As such, its goals are more likely to be preventive and educational rather than remedial and therapeutic. One would expect a well-designed premarital counseling program, therefore, to have a developmental orientation or at least to take into consideration some of the developmental tasks that all couples must resolve successfully if they are to go on to enjoy a mutually rewarding life together

Table One

Summary of Formal Programs for Premarital Counseling

Investigator and Program Orientation	Articulation with a Theory of Family Development or Family Process	Goals of the Program	Procedures Employed to Attain These Goals	Number of Issues or Topics Dealt With	Specific Skills Taught to Couples	Program's Duration
1. Boike (1977) Pre Cana, religious.	Family development, family systems and family crisis.	Personal awareness for couple of implications of their decision to marry. Discuss aspects of themselves and partner that may affect their marriage.	Didactic groups.	Communication, expectations, sexuality, finances, & religion (5).	None.	10 hours, 4 sessions
2. D'Augelli et al. (1974) PRIMES,[1] nonreligious.	Not specified.	To acquire functional communication skills.	Didactic & experiential groups.	Interpersonal communication. Couples choose issues.	Communication, empathy and openness.	16-20 hours, 8-10 sessions.
3. Freeman (1965) Group Process, nonreligious.	Not specified.	Help couple become aware of what type of marriage is appropriate for them. To understand the stresses and satisfactions of marriage.	Experiential groups.	Open to group members.	None.	Hours not reported, 6-10 sessions.
4. Glendening & Wilson (1972) Premarital Counseling, nonreligious.	Not specified.	To help couples gain insight into themselves and relationship. To offer couples a positive experience. To become aware of and express feelings. To establish a belief that a deep emotional relationship brings joy and to teach techniques for maintaining an enriching relationship.	Didactic & experiential groups.	Communication, conflict resolution, sex, religion, parents, in-laws, parenting and living arrangements (7).	None.	22 hours, 3-day weekend.

Program		Objectives	Format	Content	Skills taught	Length
5. Hinkle & Moore (1971) Couples Program, nonreligious.	Not specified.	Not stated.	Didactic & experiential groups.	Verbal and nonverbal communication, constructive fighting (3).	Communication.	14½ hours, 7 sessions.
6. McRae (1975) Behavioral, nonreligious.	Not specified.	Partners learn to state specifically their expectations for self and other and their marriage. To learn how to request change in a positive manner. To negotiate contracts, to compromise and to make joint decisions.	Didactic & experiential groups.	Caring behaviors, nonverbal behaviors and sex (3).	Negotiation, compromise and how to establish contingency contracts.	12 hours, 6 sessions.
7. Meadows & Taplin (1970) Premarital education model, nonreligious.	Not specified.	Insight into self and partner, understanding self and partner's perceptions concerning marital roles and communication. The competence of developing problem-solving skills as a couple.	Experiential dyads.	Expression of affection, finances, in-laws and use of authority by spouses (4).	None.	Hours not reported, 2-7 sessions.
8. Microys & Bader (1977) Small group course, religious and nonreligious.	Not specified.	Not reported.	Didactic & experiential groups.	Communication, family influences, finances, sex, the law and the ceremony, conflict in marriage, roles and building a better relationship (8).	None.	Hours not reported, 8 sessions.

(continued)

Investigator and Program Orientation	Articulation with a Theory of Family Development or Family Process	Goals of the Program	Procedures Employed to Attain These Goals	Number of Issues or Topics Dealt With	Specific Skills Taught to Couples	Program's Duration
9. Miller (1971) Minnesota Couples Communication Program, nonreligious.	Family development, family systems theory and communication theory.	Awareness of couples' interactions and processes, exploration of one's contribution to the dyadic interaction and rules of the relationship, especially in conflict situations. How each partner maintains own esteem and that of mate. Improve communication.	Didactic & experiential groups.	Left up to couple	Communication skills and interaction awareness skills.	12 hours, 4 sessions.
10. Ridley et al. (1979). Conflict management, behavioral, nonreligious.	Social exchange theory of family process and reciprocity.	Training couples in problem-solving process using positive control procedures.	Didactic & experiential groups.	Communication skills and positive control techniques (2).	Communication and 10-step problem-solving process utilizing behavioral technology.	24 hours, 8 sessions.
11. Ross (1977) Premarital counseling workshop, nonreligious.	Not specified.	To help couples pass beyond romantic conceptions of marriage and to approach marriage in a more realistic way.	Didactic & experiential groups and dyads.	Communication, constructive fighting, love, children, sex, vocation, finances, religion, in-laws and leisure (10).	Communication skills.	12 hours, 6 sessions.
12. Schlein (1971) PRIMES,[1] nonreligious.	Not specified.	Help participants become aware of and express feelings to partner in more effective manner. Emphasis is upon empathic understanding and self-awareness.	Didactic & experiential groups.	Interpersonal communication, couples choose issues.	Communication skills.	20 hours, 10 sessions.
13. Van Zoost (1973) Communication skills education, nonreligious.	Not specified.	To acquaint participants with basic principles of communication and to have them observe others and participate themselves in effective communication practices.	Didactic & experiential groups and dyads.	Nonverbal communication, communication and marital conflict (3).	Communication and conflict resolution.	10 hours, 5 sessions.

1 PRIMES (Program for Relationship Improvement)

(Duvall, 1971; Hill et al., 1970; Rogers, 1973). In addition, premarital counseling programs should help prospective spouses focus on and begin to discuss some of these critical tasks and issues that they eventually will face and to help them acquire behavioral skills and problem-solving strategies that will enable them to overcome these developmental crises when they arise.

Duvall (1971) has outlined a number of developmental tasks which newly married couples must resolve in order to build a solid foundation for the future development of their relationship. Some of these are: (a) preparing for the physical maintenance of the couple, (b) securing, allocating and planning the use of financial resources, (c) devising patterns of authority and control, (d) arranging for the assignment of familial roles and tasks, (e) developing a mutually satisfying sexual relationship, (f) establishing a system of intellectual and emotional communication, (g) establishing a workable relationship with relatives and friends, (h) planning for a family, if desired, and (i) evolving patterns of decision making, problem solving and conflict negotiation.

Finally, premarital programs should afford couples the opportunity to evaluate and reconsider whether they are suited for each other and whether they believe they can build a satisfying relationship together.

In Table 1, one can see that only three of the programs reviewed explicitly identified a theory or theories of family behavior which served as a guide for their intervention attempts (Boike, 1977; Miller, 1971; Ridley et al., 1979). Of these three programs, only two stress a developmental viewpoint (Boike, 1977; Miller, 1971). When one looks at all the programs where goals have been articulated, however, one finds that each of them addresses at least one or more of the developmental tasks considered to be important by family developmentalists (Duvall, 1971; Hill et al., 1970; Rogers, 1973). Eight of these programs recognize the role that functional communication plays in the development and maintenance of intimate relationships and, therefore, include communication training as an essential skill that is taught to the participants (D'Augelli et al., 1974; Hinkle & Moore, 1971; McRae, 1975; Miller, 1971. Ridley et al., 1979; Ross, 1977; Schlein, 1971; Van Zoost, 1973). The importance of functional communication for resolving interpersonal conflicts has been advocated by family systems theorists (e.g., Satir, 1964; Watzlawick et al., 1967), and family developmentalists also have stressed the role played by functional communication for successfully accomplishing developmental tasks. Only three of these programs (McRae, 1975; Ridley et al., 1979; Van Zoost, 1973), however, include problem solving and conflict negotiation as skills that ought to be taught to couples contemplating marriage. Finally, only two programs (Boike, 1977; Freeman, 1965) attempt to have couples reevaluate their decision to marry.

A variety of techniques are utilized by the different programs: (a) didactic lectures and discussions, (b) structured and unstructured group and dyadic experiences, and (c) a combination of both didactic and experiential methods. The behavioral skill most frequently taught to couples who participate in premarital counseling programs is communication. None of the programs reviewed, however, used the same model of communication training to teach couples effective communication skills, and none used the same dependent measures to evaluate effectiveness. As a result, comparisons between and among various programs to determine their relative effectiveness in teaching communication skills to premarried couples cannot be made.

Of the eight programs whose goal was to teach communication skills, only three used control groups to evaluate the effectiveness of communication training

(D'Augelli et al., 1974; Miller, 1971; Schlein, 1971). In these three studies, all experimental groups improved significantly over their control counterparts, but no follow-up evaluations were undertaken so the long-term effects of communication training cannot be determined.

METHODOLOGICAL ANALYSIS

As can be seen in Table 2, only six of the 13 programs reviewed employed control groups against which the effects of intervention could be evaluated (Boike, 1977; D'Augelli et al., 1974; Microys & Bader, 1977; Miller, 1971; Schlein, 1971; Ridley et al., 1979), and one program (McRae, 1975) compared two counseling approaches developed by the investigator. All but one of these seven studies (Microys & Bader, 1977) used random assignment to insure the equivalence of experimental and control groups. Of these seven programs, four used behavioral coding systems which can be considered to reflect actual changes in the participants' communication patterns and problem-solving styles rather than changes in responses to questions about these behaviors (Boike, 1977; Microys & Bader, 1977; Miller, 1971; Ridley et al., 1979). Only one of these studies (Miller, 1971), however, used a standardized observational procedure which was developed specifically for measuring dyadic interactional processes (Hill, 1965). Of the remaining three studies where either a control group or a comparison group was used, only one investigator (Schlein, 1971) employed standardized paper and pencil scales and inventories to assess changes.

Of the six studies where control groups were used, all but one (Boike, 1977) failed to demonstrate significant changes in the desired direction on one or more of the dependent measures for participants assigned to the experimental group. No differences were found, however, between groups in the only study which compared the outcomes of two premarital counseling approaches. McRae (1975) found that combining counseling with didactic lectures had the same effect on treatment outcome as did a treatment approach which used a combination of individual and conjoint counseling sessions. Both groups improved as a result of their experiences. The effect of the order in which treatments were delivered could not be determined, however, since a counterbalanced design was not used.

In the only two studies where follow-up evaluations were undertaken (Microys & Bader, 1977; Ridley et al., 1979), only subsamples of the original experimental and control groups were used.

Microys and Bader (1977) used trained raters to evaluate audiotaped discussions of a subsample of 17 couples of the original 119 couples seen in the premarital counseling groups. Only seven of the 34 couples who were assigned to the control group were seen in follow-up interviews. No follow-up data were collected, however, from any of the 25 couples who attended a second treatment condition. This treatment consisted of didactic courses which offered couples the opportunity to discuss a variety of topic areas considered to be important for later marital adjustment. These investigators found at six-month- and one-year-after posttests that the majority of couples who participated in the counseling sessions continued to believe that confronting conflict openly in marriage had a positive effect upon their relationship. The majority of control couples, on the other hand, continued to see confronting marital problems openly as having either a neutral or negative impact on their marriage.

These findings are suspect for a number of reasons: (a) random assignment to various groups was not used and assignment procedures were not specified; (b) the

TABLE TWO
Methodological Analysis

Study	Therapists' or Leaders' Training	Years of Experience	Participants	Assignment Procedures Employed and Number of Participants	Use of Control Group	Dependent Measures Used	Results	Follow-Up
1. Boike (1977)	Nonprofessionals. Trained married couples.	Not reported.	Engaged persons 18-29 years old.	Random assignment. Experimental group, N = 139 couples. Control group, N = 99 couples.	No treatment control group used.	MCI, MRI, T-JTA.[1]	No evidence of change in the communication patterns of experimental couples, communication facilitativeness, perception of one's own personality traits, or perception of partner's personality traits. These findings did not differ significantly from control group.	None.
2. D'Augelli et al. (1974)	Not reported.	Not reported.	Dating couples.	Random assignment. Experimental group, N = 34 couples. Control group, N = 34 couples.	No treatment control group used.	EUIP, CRIP, IRIP, HSIP.[2]	Experimental group had increased awareness in empathy and self-exploration relative to control group.	None.
3. Freeman (1965)	Not reported.	Not reported.	Engaged couples.	Author's selection of participants from group of volunteers.	None.	Group members' statements about how they feel as a couple as a result of the group experience.	Couples are reported as having found the experience helpful.	None.

(continued)

TABLE TWO (continued)

Study	Therapists' or Leaders' Training	Years of Experience	Participants	Assignment Procedures Employed and Number of Participants	Use of Control Group	Dependent Measures Used	Results	Follow-Up
4. Glendening & Wilson (1972)	Authors: social worker and student in pastoral counseling.	Not reported.	Engaged West Point cadets.	Volunteers, N = 15 couples.	None.	Self-report.	Couples thought the experience had been a good investment in terms of time and money.	None.
5. Hinkle & Moore (1971)	Authors and graduate students: experienced counselors and students in training.	Not reported.	Engaged and married couples.	Volunteers, N not reported.	None.	Self-report.	Participants reported the experience to be positive.	None.
6. McRae (1975)	Author: graduate student.	Not reported.	Engaged couples or couples thinking of marriage.	Random assignment to two groups: counseling and lecture 1-4, individual sessions and 1-3 conjoint sessions. N not specified.	None; comparison of two methods.	Premarital inventory, marriage prediction schedule and course evaluation form. Nonstandardized measures developed by author.	No differences found between groups on dependent measures.	None.
7. Meadows & Taplin (1970)	Authors: professional counselors.	Not reported.	Engaged college students.	Volunteers, N = 6 couples.	None.	Questionnaire.	No posttest results, only follow-up evaluation.	One month after treatment 3 couples had broken off their engagement. Two of these couples reported the experience to have been very helpful. The remainder reported the program to be somewhat helpful.

8. Microys & Bader (1977)	Medical doctors, counselors, psychologists, social workers, clergy, and students.	Varied.	Engaged couples.	Assignment to small group discussion N = 60, didactic course N = 25, or no treatment control N = 34. Assignment procedures not specified.	No treatment control group.	Questionnaire and nonstandardized behavioral ratings of audiotapes of a subsample of 17 small group discussion couples and of couples from the no treatment control group.	No posttest results, only 6-month and 1-year follow-up evaluations.	Premarital counseling was found to have a significant effect upon a subsample of group participants, N = 17, and no treatment control, N = 7, couples at both 6 months and 1 year on their perception as to whether confronting conflict in marriage had a positive effect on their relationship. Group participants saw confronting problems as having a positive effect on the relationship.	None.
9. Miller (1971)	Author: graduate student.	Not reported.	Engaged couples.	Random assignment, Experimental group, N = 17 couples. Control group, N = 15 couples.	No treatment control group.	SDQ, HIM, IMC, PRQ, and EAS.[3]		Experimental group had increased awareness of dyadic interaction and greater use of communication styles appropriate to work on relationship issues.	

(continued)

TABLE TWO (*continued*)

Study	Therapists' or Leaders' Training	Years of Experience	Participants	Assignment Procedures Employed and Number of Participants	Use of Control Group	Dependent Measures Used	Results	Follow-Up
10. Ridley et al. (1979)	Authors: professional counselors and graduate students.	Not reported.	Dating couples.	Random assignment. Experimental group, N = 26 couples. Control group, N = 28 couples.	No treatment control group.	Behavioral rating of problem-solving skills by trained raters.	Experimental group showed a significant increase in problem-solving ability as determined by trained raters immediately following treatment.	6-month follow-up of 53% of original experimental sample & 78% of control sample. Experimental group had maintained its superior performance as evaluated by raters.
11. Ross (1977)	Author: graduate student.	Not reported.	Dating and engaged couples.	12 volunteer couples.	None.	Premarital inventory and intimacy rating scale developed by author.	Both self-report and objective raters revealed a positive evaluation of workshop and partner.	None.
12. Schlein (1971)	Author: graduate student and other trained graduate students.	Not reported.	Undergraduate dating couples.	Random assignment. Experimental group, N = 15 couples. Control group, N = 27 couples.	No treatment control group used.	LAS, SFAS, PCI, PCI-P, HPCS, IRS, RS-S, RCS, SCS.[4]	Experimental group improved in interpersonal communication relative to control group. Experimental group showed greater gains in overall relationship.	None.
13. Van Zoost (1973)	Author: experienced counselor.	Not reported.	6 dating couples.	Volunteers.	None.	ASS-C, SDQ, ICI, CKT.[5]	Couples increased their knowledge about communication significantly and increased the amount of self-disclosure to partner.	None.

[1] MCI (Marital Communication Inventory), MRI (Marital Relationship Inventory), T-JTA (Taylor-Johnson Temperament Analysis).
[2] EUIP (Empathic Understanding in Interpersonal Processes), CRIP (Communication of Respect in Interpersonal Processes), IRIP (Immediacy of Relationship in Interpersonal Processes), HSIP (Helpee Self-Exploration in Interpersonal Processes).
[3] SDQ (Self-Disclosure Questionnaire), HIM (Hill Interaction Matrix), IMC (Inventory of Marital Conflicts), PRQ (Prediction and Recall Questionnaire), EAS (Engagement Adjustment Scale).
[4] LAS (Listener Acceptance Scale), SFAS (Speaker Feelings Awareness Scale), PCI (Premarital Communication Inventory), PCI-P (Primary Communication Inventory, Partner), HPCS

effects of different treatments could not be ascertained because follow-ups were conducted only with one treatment group; (c) subsamples were too small and unequal in number so statistical analyses could not be performed; and (d) since the investigators do not describe how subsamples were selected, one does not know whether they are representative of the two groups from which they were drawn.

Ridley et al. (1979) used behavioral raters to evaluate the maintenance of problem-solving skills of a randomly selected subsample of 53% of the couples who were assigned to the experimental condition and 78% of control group participants. Unlike Microys and Bader (1977), however, these researchers did collect posttest data on all couples in both conditions. Ridley et al. found that the experimental subsample did retain its superior performance over the control subsample in dyadic problem-solving ability when six-month follow-ups were conducted. While the Ridley et al. study is methodologically more sound than that of Microys and Bader, both studies fail to describe the procedures used to train raters, and both studies did not use standardized coding systems specifically developed to evaluate dyadic interaction.

The use of control groups and long-term follow-ups are essential if the effects of premarital counseling programs are to be determined. While control groups are important, they can tell us only whether premarital counseling programs have been more successful in producing immediate attitudinal and/or behavioral changes in couples than no treatment at all. They cannot provide us with any information, however, concerning whether increased sensitivity to critical issues which all couples must face in marriage and the acquisition of certain communication skills and problem-solving strategies do increase later marital success or satisfaction for couples who participate in such programs when compared with couples who do not. Similarly, follow-up evaluations of one year or less are of limited value in helping one determine the success that premarital counseling might have in preventing later marital distress or dissolution, because the majority of divorces in this country take place after the first year of marriage with divorces occurring most frequently during the third year after the ceremony (Norton & Glick, 1979).

NONEXPERIMENTAL STUDIES

Of the six nonexperimental programs, five utilized nonstandardized self-report questionnaires devised by the authors to evaluate their program's effectiveness (Freeman, 1965; Glendening & Wilson, 1972; Hinkle & Moore, 1971; Meadows & Taplin, 1970; Ross, 1977). In the only program where standardized measures were used in addition to nonstandardized instruments (Van Zoost, 1973), questions concerning the validity of measurement arise. Van Zoost (1973) used the Affective Sensitivity Scale (Danish & Kagan, 1971) as one of his dependent measures. This instrument, however, was developed to evaluate the trained therapist's ability to identify and recognize client's feelings and to be sensitive to the meaning of a client's communications. Since the validation sample consisted of trained therapists, the validity of using this measure to assess the progress made by dating couples who have not received any formal training in counseling is questionable. It is no wonder that no pretest-posttest changes were observed on this instrument for couples participating in the program. Similarly, Van Zoost used the Interpersonal Communication Inventory (Bienvenu, 1970) to assess marital communications. The validity of this instrument as a measure of communication between individuals, however, has been questioned (Schumm et al., 1979). No significant pretest-posttest differences were recorded on this measure.

This study underscores a number of common methodological inadequacies which typify the nonexperimental evaluations of premarital counseling programs: (a) the use of nonstandardized dependent measures, (b) the acceptance of participants' self-reports, paper-and-pencil tests and questionnaires as valid indicators of behavior changes, and (c) the inappropriate use of standardized measures.

PREMARITAL COUNSELING: A CLOSER LOOK

In addition to the methodological questions raised above, a number of important issues surface when one attempts to evaluate the field as a whole. For example, in their discussion of "trends" in premarital counseling, Schumm and Denton (1979) cite four programs as examples of well-controlled experimental studies (Ginsberg & Vogelsong, 1977; Miller et al., 1976a, 1976b; Schlein, 1971). What these authors fail to note, however, is that there are in fact only two studies. The Miller, Nunnally and Wackman (1976a, 1976b) studies actually are later reports and discussions of the original doctoral work done by Miller (1971). This same program with some modifications has been discussed again by Miller, Corrales and Wackman (1975). Similarly, the PRIMES program described by Ginsberg and Vogelsong (1977) actually is a discussion of the original research done by Schlein (1971).

Numerous descriptions of the premarital counseling process have been presented by Rolfe (1973, 1977a) whose work appears more frequently in the literature than any other author. Unfortunately, when he reports his findings (Rolfe 1976, 1977b), he fails to outline the research methods employed, the procedures followed, and no statistical analyses are presented.

THE RELEVANCE OF PROGRAM GOALS

In order to ascertain whether a premarital intervention program has been effective, one must not only ask if the program has achieved its desired goals and whether these goals are maintained over time, but one must also evaluate whether the stated goals are relevant and meaningful. For example, many of the premarital programs reviewed in this paper have specified improved or functional communication as a treatment goal, and each program which taught skills to participants, except McRae (1975), included communication training as an essential skill to be mastered. The importance of clear and open communication as a major correlate of marital satisfaction has been well documented (Lewis & Spanier, 1979), but many of the programs that offer communication training to participants and nothing more (D'Augelli et al., 1977; Hinkle & Moore, 1971; Miller, 1971; Ross, 1977; Schlein, 1971) fail to recognize that teaching communication skills to couples without providing them with the means to negotiate conflict, to solve problems, and to make structural changes in dysfunctional interaction patterns will probably not produce lasting changes nor create satisfying marital relationships (Bagarozzi, in press; Haley, 1978; Rogers & Bagarozzi, in press).

In our opinion, premarital intervention programs should attempt to achieve at least the following goals in order for them to offer the participant more than an "experience":

1) To provide prospective spouses with the opportunity to become aware of and discuss the developmental tasks that they will face in the early stages of their marriage.

2) To teach couples a variety of behavioral skills that will enable them to successfully resolve these developmental tasks and make structural changes in their

relationship. These skills should include, but should not be limited to, (a) conflict negotiation, (b) problem solving, (c) communication training, and (d) positive behavior change strategies.

3) To provide the couple the opportunity to reevaluate their decision to marry.

EVALUATION OF PROGRAM EFFECTIVENESS

Evaluation of program effectiveness requires assessment at both the individual and dyadic levels (Gurman & Kniskern, 1980; Kniskern & Gurman, in press) and should take into account the two vantage points suggested by Olson (1974), i.e., the "insider's" (participant's) perception and the "outsider's" (researcher's) perspective. For assessment to be comprehensive, it should include all six levels of inference described by Gurman and Kniskern (1980) and Kniskern and Gurman (in press).*

Although immediate posttest assessments can be used to determine whether a program has been successful in achieving its stated goal, they cannot help the investigator evaluate the relevance of the program or its long-term effects. Since premarital intervention programs are designed to increase marital satisfaction and avert divorce, only longitudinal follow-ups of both treatment and matched control groups can provide us with some indication of their effectiveness. Similarly, if one assumes that one goal of premarital intervention is to prevent potentially unsuccessful marriages from occurring (Mace, 1972), long-term follow-ups of individuals who decide not to marry their partners as a result of their participation in premarital counseling programs can help determine whether program participants: (a) were able to build more successful and satisfying marriages with different partners than control couples who married without the benefit of premarital counseling; and (b) had more successful marriages than program participants who married their original partners.

One should not assume that marital stability is a valid criterion for evaluating a program's effectiveness. Many marriages are stable (i.e., remain intact for decades), but the spouses are dissatisfied and distressed because they perceive themselves as trapped in a nonvoluntary relationship (Bagarozzi & Wodarski, 1977). In order to assess a program's effectiveness, one should try to determine whether spouses stay together because they evaluate their interpersonal exchanges as equitable and rewarding (Bagarozzi & Wodarski, 1977, 1978) or whether they remain married because perceived barriers to separation and divorce prevent them from terminating an unhappy relationship (Bagarozzi, in press).

A number of assessment instruments are available which can assist the researcher in his/her attempt to evaluate the intervention process. For example, in order to obtain an "insider's" view of the relationship from a family systems perspective, one might use the Family Adaptability and Cohesion Evaluation Scale (Olson et al., 1979) which focuses on the two dimensions of dyadic and family process—adaptability and cohesion (Olson et al., 1979; Russell & Olson, in press). For an "in-

---

* Gurman and Kniskern (1980) and Kniskern and Gurman (in press) have suggested that in assessing changes in marital and family systems there are six possible levels of inference that can be identified, each level having its own best source of assessment. These include: Level Ia = simple behavior counts—machine or trained objective raters; Ib = performance on clinically relevant, objective criteria—institutional records; II = perceived interaction patterns —trained observers; III = behavioral self-reports—family members; IV = nonbehavioral self-reports—intrapersonally focused—family members; V = nonbehavioral reports of self in relationship to others—family members; VIa = individual psychodynamics or personality structure —expert judges; VIb = family psychodynamics—therapist or expert judges; VIc = inferred family systems properties—professional judges.

sider's" view of the social exchange process and the degree to which a spouse perceives his/her relationship as dissatisfying and nonvoluntary, the researcher can use the Spousal Inventory of Desired Changes and Relationship Barriers (Bagarozzi, in press). For an "insider's" evaluation of marital satisfaction, a variety of measures are available (e.g., Locke & Wallace, 1959; Orden & Bradburn, 1968). "Insider's" perceptions of the communication control patterns can be obtained by using the Relationship Style Inventory (Christensen & Scoresby, 1975).

For an "outsider's" behavioral evaluation of dyadic processes from a systems perspective, one can use the Relational Communication Coding System (Ericson & Rogers, 1973). This highly sophisticated coding system was developed and refined to assess changes in communication control patterns of dyadic interaction (Rogers & Bagarozzi, in press). This is an excellent tool for evaluating whether communication training actually does alter dysfunctional relationship patterns by introducing structural changes that are essential for improved systems functioning (Watzlawick et al., 1974). The objective evaluation of dyadic problem solving and conflict negotiation from a social-learning perspective can be gained by using the Marital Interaction Coding System-Revised (Weiss, 1975). Finally, for a unique blend of "insider's"-"outsider's" views of the same communication-interaction process, one can use the Hill Interaction Matrix (Hill, 1965). This procedure requires the interactants to rate and evaluate their own videotaped interactions and to indicate how satisfied they were with their interaction process. These videotapes also are rated by trained coders.

The instruments and rating systems cited above will provide the researcher with both "insider" and "outsider" perspectives and offer the opportunity to assess process and outcome from a variety of inference levels.

CONCLUSION

Although premarital counseling programs are on the rise in the United States, no empirical data exist to support the notion that these programs reduce the incidence of divorce or separation for those couples who participate, because the follow-up evaluations which have been conducted thus far have not allowed sufficient time to elapse after treatment to obtain a valid measure of their effectiveness. Similarly, no data exist which indicate that couples who participate in premarital counseling programs are more satisfied or successful in their marriages than those who do not. Finally, we do not know whether premarital counseling practices serve any prophylactic functions; for example, do they prevent bad marriages from taking place?

A concerted effort should be undertaken by those individuals who conduct premarital counseling programs to evaluate their effectiveness.

REFERENCES

APPLE, J. Premarital counseling techniques. *Your Church,* 1970, March/April 30-31, 51-54.
BAGAROZZI, D. A. Methodological developments in measuring social exchange perceptions in marital dyads (SIDCARB): A new tool for clinical intervention. In D. A. Bagarozzi, A. P. Jurich and R. W. Jackson (Eds.), *New Perspectives in Marital and Family Therapy: Issues in Theory, Research and Practice.* New York: Human Sciences Press, in press.
BAGAROZZI, D. A. and WODARSKI, J. S. A social exchange typology of conjugal relationships and conflict development. *Journal of Marriage and Family Counseling,* 1977, 3, 53-60.
BAGAROZZI, D. A. and WODARSKI, J. S. Behavioral treatment of marital discord. *Clinical Social Work Journal,* 1978, 6, 135-154.
BERSTEIN, B. Lawyer and counselor as an interdisciplinary team: Premarital counseling. *The Family Coordinator,* 1977, 26, 415-420.

BIENVENU, M. J., Sr. Measurement of marital communication. *The Family Coordinator,* 1970, 19, 26-31.

BIENVENU, M. J., Sr. Talking it over before marriage: Exercises in premarital communication. *Public Affairs Pamphlet No. 512.* New York: Public Affairs Committee, 1974.

BOIKE, D. The impact of a premarital program on communication process, communication facilitativeness, and personality trait variables of engaged couples. Unpublished doctoral dissertation. Florida State University, 1977.

CHRISTENSEN, B. and SCORESBY, A. L. The measurement of complementarity, symmetrical and parallel interaction in family dyads. Unpublished manuscript. Brigham Young University, 1975.

DANISH, S. J. and KAGAN, N. Measurement of affective sensitivity. *Journal of Counseling Psychology,* 1971, 18, 51-54.

D'AUGELLI, A., DEYSS, C., GUERNEY, B., HERSHENBERG, B. and SBORDFSKY, S. Interpersonal skills training for dating couples: An evaluation of an educational mental health service. *Journal of Counseling Psychology,* 1974, 21, 385-389.

DUVALL, E. M. *Family Development.* Philadelphia: J. B. Lippincott, 1971.

EHRENTRAUT, G. The effects of premarital counseling of juvenile marriages on marital communication and relationship patterns. Unpublished doctoral dissertation, United States International University, 1975.

ELKIN, W. Premarital counseling for minors: The Los Angeles experience. *The Family Coordinator,* 1977, 26, 429-443.

ERICSON, P. M. and ROGERS, L. E. New procedures for analyzing relational communication. *Family Process,* 1973, 12, 244-267.

FREEMAN, D. Counseling engaged couples in small groups. *Social Work,* 1965, 10, 36-42.

GANGSEI, L. *Manual for Group Premarital Counseling.* New York: Association Press, 1971.

GINSBERG, B. and VOGELSONG, E. Premarital relationship improvement by maximizing empathy and self-disclosure: The PRIMES program. In B. G. Guerney, Jr. (Ed.), *Relationship Enhancement: Skill Training Programs for Therapy, Problem Presentation and Enrichment.* San Francisco: Jossey-Bass, 1977.

GLENDENING, S. E. and WILSON, A. Experiments in group premarital counseling. *Social Casework,* 1972, 53, 551-562.

GLICK, P. and NORTON, A. Marrying, divorcing and living together in the United States today. *Population Bulletin,* 1977, 32.

GOODE, W. The theoretical importance of love. *American Sociological Review,* 1959, 24, 38-47.

GURMAN, A. S. and KNISKERN, D. P. Family therapy outcome research: Knowns and unknowns. In A. S. Gurman and D. P. Kniskern (Eds.), *Handbook of Family Therapy.* New York: Brunner/Mazel, 1980.

HALEY, J. *Problem Solving Therapy.* San Francisco: Jossey-Bass, 1978.

HILL, R., FOOTE, N., ALDOUS, J., CARLSON, R. and MacDONALD, R. *Family Development in Three Generations.* Cambridge: Schenkman Publishing, 1970.

HILL, W. F. Hill interaction matrix. Monograph. Los Angeles, University of Southern California, Youth Studies Center, 1965.

HINKLE, J. E. and MOORE, M. A student couples program. *The Family Coordinator,* 1971, 20, 153-158.

HOLOUBEK, A. and HOLOUBEK, J. Pre-marriage counseling. *Journal of the Arkansas Medical Society,* 1973, 70, 176-178.

HOLOUBEK, A., HOLOUBEK, J., BERGERON, J., BACARISSE, A., INAINA, J., SANDERS, A. and BAKER, D. Marriage preparation: An interdisciplinary approach. *Journal of the Louisiana State Medical Society,* 1974, 126, 313-316.

JACKSON, R. W. Simulation as an adjacent in premarital counseling: A theoretical examination. Unpublished master's thesis. Purdue University, 1972.

KEPHART, W. *The Family, Society and the Individual.* Boston: Houghton Mifflin, 1966.

KNISKERN, D. P. and GURMAN, A. S. Future directions for family therapy research. In D. A. Bagarozzi, A. P. Jurich and R. W. Jackson (Eds.), *New Perspectives in Marital and Family Therapy: Issues in Theory, Research and Practice.* New York: Human Sciences Press, in press.

LEIGH, D. An exploration of Ohio's premarital counseling requirement in Ohio Appalachia: A descriptive and comparative analysis of responses. Unpublished doctoral dissertation. Ohio University, 1976.

LEVINE, L. and BRODSKY, J. Group premarital counseling. *Mental Hygiene,* 1949, 33, 577-587.

LEWIS, R. A. and SPANIER, G. B. Theorizing about the quality and stability of marriage. In W. R. Burr, R. Hill, F. I. Nye and I. L. Reiss (Eds.), *Contemporary Theories about the Family,* (Vol. 1). New York: Free Press, 1979.

LOCKE, H. J. and WALLACE, K. M. Short marital adjustment and prediction tests: Their reliability and validity. *Marriage and Family Living,* 1959, 21, 251-255.

MACE, D. *Getting Ready for Marriage.* Nashville: Abingdon Press, 1972.

McRAE, B. A comparison of a behavioral and a lecture discussion approach to premarital counseling. Unpublished doctoral dissertation. The University of British Columbia, 1975.

MEADOWS, M. E. and TAPLIN, J. Premarital counseling with college students: A promising triad. *Journal of Counseling Psychology,* 1970, 17, 516-518.

MICROYS, G. and BADER, E. Do premarital programs really help? Unpublished paper. Department of Family and Community Medicine, University of Toronto, 1977.

MILLER, S. The effects of communication training in small groups upon self disclosure and openness in engaged couples' system of interaction: A field experience. Unpublished doctoral dissertation. University of Minnesota, 1971.

MILLER, S., CORRALES, R. and WACKMAN, D. B. Recent progress in understanding and facilitating marital communication. *The Family Coordinator,* 1975, 24, 143-152.

MILLER, S., NUNNALLY, E. W. and WACKMAN, D. B. A communication training program for couples. *Social Casework,* 1976, 57, 9-18. (a)

MILLER, S., NUNNALLY, E. W. and WACKMAN, D. B. Minnesota Couples Communication Program (MCCP): Premarital and marital group. In D. H. Olson (Ed.), *Treating Relationships.* Lake Mills, IA: Graphic Publishing Co. 1976. (b)

MUDD, E., FREEMAN, C. and ROSE, E. Premarital counseling in the Philadelphia Marriage Council. *Mental Hygiene,* 1941, 25, 98-119.

NORTON, H. J. and GLICK, P. C. Marital Instability in America: Past, present, and future. In G. Levinger and O. C. Moles (Eds.), *Divorce and Separation.* New York: Basic Books, 1979.

OATES, W. and ROWATT, W. *Before You Marry Them: A Premarital Guidebook for Pastors.* Nashville: Broadman Press, 1975.

OLSON, D. H. Insiders and outsiders view of relationships. Research strategies. Paper presented at the Symposium on Close Relationships, University of Massachusetts, 1974.

OLSON, D. H., BELL, R. and PORTNER, J. Family adaptability and cohesion evaluation scale (FACES). Unpublished manual. University of Minnesota, 1979.

OLSON, D. H., SPRENKLE, D. H. and RUSSELL, C. S. Circumplex model of marital and family systems: I. Cohesion and adaptability dimensions, family types, and clinical applications. *Family Process,* 1979, 18, 3-28.

ORDEN, S. R. and BRADBURN, N. M. Dimensions of marriage happiness. *American Journal of Sociology,* 1968, 73, 715-731.

REINER, B. and EDWARDS, R. Adolescent marriage—social or therapeutic problem? *The Family Coordinator,* 1974, 23, 383-390.

RIDLEY, C., AVERY, A., HARRELL. J. E., LESLIE, L. A. and O'CONNOR, J. Conflict management: A premarital training program in mutual problem solving. Unpublished study. Texas Tech University, 1979.

ROGERS, L. E. and BAGAROZZI, D. A. An overview of relational communication and implications for therapy. In D. A. Bagarozzi, A. P. Jurich, and R. W. Jackson (Eds.), *New Perspectives in Marital and Family Therapy: Issues in Theory, Research and Practice.* New York: Human Sciences Press, in press.

ROGERS, R. *Family Interaction and Transaction: The Developmental Approach.* Englewood Cliffs, NJ: Prentice-Hall, 1973.

ROLFE, D. Preparing groups of engaged couples for marriage. Paper presented at the National Council on Family Relations, Toronto, Canada, October, 1973.

ROLFE, D. *Marriage Preparation Manual.* New York: Paulist Press, 1975.

ROLFE, D. Premarital assessment of teenage couples. *Journal of Family Counseling,* 1976, 4, 32-39.

ROLFE, D. Premarital contracts: An aid to couples living with parents. *The Family Coordinator,* 1977, 26, 281-285. (a)

ROLFE, D. Techniques with pre-marriage groups. *British Journal of Guidance and Counseling,* 1977, 5, 89-97. (b)

ROSS, J. The development and the evaluation of a group premarital counseling workshop. Unpublished doctoral dissertation. University of Northern Colorado, 1977.

RUE, J. Premarital counseling for teenagers. *Marriage,* 1972, 54, 60-66.

RUSSELL, C. S. and OLSON, D. H. Circumplex model of marital and family systems: Review of empirical support and elaboration of therapeutic process. In D. A. Bagarozzi, A. P. Jurich and R. W. Jackson (Eds.), *New Perspectives in Marital and Family Therapy: Issues in Theory, Research and Practice.* New York: Human Sciences Press, in press.

SATIR, V. *Conjoint Family Therapy.* Palo Alto: Science and Behavior Books, 1964.

SCHLEIN, S. Training dating couples in empathic and open communication: An experimental evaluation of a potential preventive mental health program. Unpublished doctoral dissertation. Pennsylvania State University, 1971.

SCHULMAN, M. Idealization in engaged couples. *Journal of Marriage and the Family,* 1974, 36, 139-147.

SCHUMM, W. R. and DENTON, W. Trends in premarital counseling. *The Journal of Marital and Family Therapy,* 1979, 5, 23-32.

SCHUMM, W. R., FIGLEY, C. R. and JURICH, A. P. Dimensionality of the marital communication inventory: A preliminary factor analytic study. *Psychological Reports,* 1979, 45, 123-128.

SHONICK, H. Premarital counseling in California. *Health Service Report,* 1975, 87, 304-310.

STALLINGS, J. Premarital counseling with the deaf. *American Annals of the Deaf,* 1968, 113, 918-919.

VAN ZOOST, B. Premarital communication skills education with university students. *The Family Coordinator,* 1973, 22, 187-191.

WALKER, P. Premarital counseling for the developmentally disabled. *Social Casework,* 1977, 58, 475-479.

WALSTER, E. and WALSTER, G. *A New Look at Love.* Reading, MA: Addison-Wesley, 1978.

WATZLAWICK, P., BEAVIN, J. and JACKSON, D. D. *Pragmatics of Human Communication.* New York: W. W. Norton, 1967.

WATZLAWICK, P., WEAKLAND, J. H. and FISCH, R. *Change: Principles of Problem Formation and Problem Resolution.* New York: W. W. Norton, 1974.

WEISS, R. L. Marital interaction coding system—revised. Unpublished manuscript. University of Oregon, 1975.

WRIGHT, H. *Premarital Counseling.* Chicago: Moody Press, 1977.

This paper reports on the development, implementation, and evaluation of an innovative marriage preparation program. The program used a small discussion-group format, had pre- and post-wedding sessions, and emphasized the importance of communication patterns and conflict resolution. It was hypothesized (1) that spouses who took part in such a program would be less likely to engage in destructive conflict with each other than those who had not taken part; and (2) that spouses who took part in the program would seek assistance in solving either individual or marital problems more readily than those who did not take part. The data supported both hypotheses.

41

DO MARRIAGE PREPARATION PROGRAMS REALLY WORK?

A Canadian Experiment*

Edward Bader, Gisele Microys, Carole Sinclair,
*Elizabeth Willett, and Brenda Conway***

The development and implementation of marriage preparation programs has been advocated by numerous authors over the past 25 years. In 1953, Burgess and Locke proposed that the causes of marital failure can be dealt with best before marriage and in the early years of marriage. Baber (1958) believed that marriage would be immeasurably strengthened and the frequency of divorce correspondingly reduced if couples would work out their philosophy of marriage before they marry. Mace (1972) laid much stress on the importance of the first few months of marriage, believing that couples can drift into unsatisfactory and destructive ways of interacting, sowing the seeds for later trouble and conflict. All of these authors suggested that marriage preparation programs could act as a preventive measure for later marital breakdown.

Criticisms of Existing Programs

In Canada, most marriage preparation programs have been sponsored by church groups. Several unpublished studies of these programs have been done in recent years.

*This research was supported by grants from the Physicians Services Incorporated Foundation, Toronto, Canada; the Family Service Association of Metropolitan Toronto; the Vanier Institute of the Family, Ottawa, Canada; and the Anglican, Roman Catholic and United Church of Canada National Offices. A version of this paper was presented at the AAMFC meeting, San Francisco, October, 1977. The authors are indebted to Sonja Poizner, PhD, for her contribution to the marital conflict stories; to Stephanie Wilson, BEd, for rating the taped disagreement discussions, and to Carol McLaughlin for both coding and coordinating the interviews.

**Both Edward Bader, MA, and Gisele Microys, MD, are Assistant Professors, Department of Family and Community Medicine, University of Toronto. Carole Sinclair, PhD, is a Psychologist at the Dellcrest Children's Centre, Downsview, Canada; Elizabeth Willett, PhD, is a Psychologist in Toronto, Canada; and Brenda Conway, MA, is Coordinator of the Separation Counseling Project for the Family Service Association in Toronto.

Although generally favorable to the goals of such programs, the studies are quite critical of some of their dimensions. Oussoren (1972) believed that the programs were not geared to the needs of the couples involved and were generally inadequate in preparing couples for the realities of marriage. Kondrath (1974) commented on the lack of coordination and creativity in the area of marriage preparation. Both authors pointed out that criticisms and recommendations made in 1964 by the Social Planning Council of Metropolitan Toronto had not been put into effect in any pre-marriage programs in that city. The Council had criticized the information-giving focus, the minimal use of audio-visual materials, and the discontinuity in leadership of some programs in that there was a different leader for each session.

In addition to the above criticisms, another frequently expressed (Clinebell, 1975; Schumm and Denton, 1979) is that there is a lack of well designed research into the effectiveness of marriage preparation programs. Although Clinebell believes that "much so-called pre-wedding counseling" is of questionable effectiveness, there has been little use of objective measures and control groups to test his belief.

The Present Project

The project described in this paper represents an attempt both to develop an innovative marriage preparation program which takes into account previous criticisms and suggestions, and to test objectively the effectiveness of the program on later marital adjustment.

In order to make the content of the sessions as relevant and useful as possible to couples from a broad range of socio-economic backgrounds, two themes were emphasized: communication and conflict resolution. The importance of communication patterns in marriage has received much emphasis (Bach and Wyden, 1969; Miller, Corrales, and Wackman, 1976). Modes of conflict resolution have also been viewed as crucial to the course of marriage (Rausch, Goodrich, and Campbell, 1963; Barry, 1970). In particular, Deutsch (1969) distinguishes between destructive modes of conflict resolution and constructive modes. Through a search of the literature, several common areas of conflict were identified: roles (Spiegel, 1957); kin (Leichter and Mitchell, 1967; Irving, 1972); sexuality (Burgess and Wallin, 1953); and finances (Peterson, 1964).

Combining the themes of communication patterns and conflict resolution and attending to specific common sources of conflict in marriage, an eight-session marriage preparation program was designed. The following titles evolved for each session: (a) Communication in Marriage, (b) Family Influences, (c) Finances, (d) Sexuality, (e) The Law and the Ceremony, (f) Conflict in Marriage, (g) Changing Roles in Marriage, and (h) Building a Better Relationship.

In addition to a new approach to establishing the content, the present project also made use of several previous recommendations concerning the format of marriage preparation programs. In contract to the lecture-oriented format of many other programs, a small group discussion format was used. No more than six couples were included in each group. This approach has been thought to be more educational for everyone involved and more likely to result in effective communication training (Miller, Nunnally, and Wackman, 1976). Film segments were used in each session to stimulate discussion and to dispel fears that the sessions were a type of "group therapy". Each group of couples was led by two leaders throughout the eight sessions, allowing for continuity from session to session. (Two of the authors of this paper were the primary leaders, each leading 50% of the groups, with a resident in family practice or a nurse practitioner as co-leader. Each group had one male and one female leader/co-leader.)

A further innovation adopted was the division of the program into pre- and post-wedding sessions. Guldner (1971) had experimented with post-wedding sessions at one month, three months, and six months after the wedding. He found that couples who had been married only one month were still in "a state of marital bliss" and were not open to looking in depth at their marriage. In contrast, most of the couples married either three months or six months when the sessions began were open and appreciative of the opportunity. The most open and positive response came from couples who had been married six months. In the present project, the more traditional approach of pre-wedding sessions was combined with the innovative approach of post-wedding sessions. The first five sessions were held about three months before the wedding, and the final three sessions (Conflict in Marriage, Changing Roles in Marriage, and Building a Better Relationship) were held about six months after the wedding.

Evaluation of the Present Project

Two major methodological problems occur in attempts to evaluate the effectiveness of marriage preparation programs; that is, the self-selection of participants in such programs, and the general use of subjective measures of "happiness" and "success" in marriage. The present study has attempted to deal with both of these problems.

As participants in marriage preparation programs usually make a personal decision that they want to participate, it is difficult to draw conclusions about the effect of the program on their marriages. If compared with couples who do not participate and if found to have "more successful" or "happier" marriages, it can always be argued that those who choose to participate probably do not need such programs and would have "better" marriages anyway. To avoid this problem, the present project involved a population of couples for whom a marriage preparation program was not readily available. The couples were randomly assigned to experimental (program) and control (no program) conditions.

The second methodological problem was resolved by borrowing and developing objective measures of "success" rather than relying mainly on subjective self-report. Objective measures were developed to test the effect of the couples' main area of disagreement on their relationship and to test the couples' pattern of resolving hypothetical marital conflict situations. A third set of measures looked at couples' constructive use of their support systems (Irving, 1972) when they needed help.

Two major hypotheses were formulated: (a) Spouses who have taken part in a marriage preparation program will be less likely to engage in destructive conflict with each other than those who have not taken part in such a program. (b) Spouses who have taken part in a marriage preparation program will seek assistance in solving either individual or marital problems more quickly than those who have not taken part in such a program.

Method[1]

The Sample—Nineteen Toronto churches of different denominations and with congregations which varied widely in both social and educational backgrounds participated in the project. With the permission of the clergy involved, couples who had already arranged to be married in the churches were approached. The couples were contacted on a random basis until the desired numbers of experimental and control couples were reached. From a list of six couples, one, three, four and five were invited to take the marriage preparation program. Couples two and six were asked to grant an interview with no reference being made to the program. The acceptance rate was 41% for the experimental group and 37% for the control group.

Those taking the marriage preparation program were interviewed for the first time about one month prior to the pre-wedding sessions (which were held two to three months before the wedding); for the second time about one month prior to the post-wedding sessions (which were held six to seven months after the wedding); and for the third time within a week or two of the first anniversary of their wedding. The Control group was interviewed according to the same timetable.

Interviews—Each interview consisted of a questionnaire and two couple tasks. The questionnaire was completed by each partner separately and was designed to elicit both sociological and psychological information such as, demographic material, family relationships, attitudes, disagreements, and help-seeking behavior. Most of the questions in the interview had been used in previous research (Blood and Wolfe, 1960; Turk, 1970; Irving, 1972). One couple task involved the selection of their main area of disagreement and a guided discussion of its effect on their relationship. The second task involved the couple attempting to resolve hypothetical marital conflict situations. Six situations were constructed using the marital conflict stories developed by Rausch, Barry, Hartel and Swain (1974) as models. The six stories were randomly distributed across all three phases of the study, but in such a way that each couple had been exposed to all six stories by the end of the third phase. Two stories were used in the interview at each phase.

Both couple tasks were taped. However, the first task was done with the interviewers present, and the second task was done with the interviewers absent.

The majority of the interviewers were married couples who conducted the interviews either in their own homes or in the homes of those being interviewed. They were trained by the project staff. A "Master Instrument" contained explicit instructions for conducting the interviews so that comparability was retained. All scoring of data obtained from the interviews was done blind, with no knowledge of whether the interview was of Control or Experimental group or at which phase (first, second or third interview) of the program. Inter-rater reliability checks varied from 80% to 100%, depending on data being scored.

Over the course of the project, 229 interviews were carried out, 94 (60 Experimental and 34 Control) prior to marriage, 72 (48 Experimental and 24 Control) six months after marriage, and 63 (41 Experimental and 22 Control) one year after marriage. Most couples who dropped out between phases had moved and could not be located or could not be interviewed because of distance. Only 10 couples (9.4%) refused to be interviewed a second time. The refusal rate for the third interview at one year was even lower (8.3%).

Results

Comparability of Experimental and Control Groups.—For the entire sample, a multivariate analysis was carried out for the two groups on the following nine variables: couples' mean education in years, the difference in couples' mean family closeness between growing up and pre-marriage, discrepancy in couples' ages, couples' mean church attendance, couples' mean family closeness growing up, discrepancy in couples' incomes, length of engagement, history of family disruption, and difference in couples' religion. The multivariate ($n = 60$) was not significant (Hostelling-Lawley Trace $F = 1.57, p = .15$). From this analysis, it can be concluded that the Experimental and Control groups were comparable.

Conflict Resolution

The couples' ability to deal positively with conflict situations was examined through their discussion of their main area of disagreement and its effect on their relationship and through the marital conflict stories.

Disagreement Discussions.—Temporal as well as budgetary considerations precluded the hours of coding required for the complete analysis of the disagreement discussions. Therefore, a sub-sample of 20 Experimental and 10 Control couples was drawn randomly. The Experimental couples were found to differ from the Control couples in two ways: the main area of disagreement; and, the effect of this disagreement on their relationship.

1. Fifteen general problem areas mentioned by the couples in the written question-naires were collapsed into five larger areas. The first (I) of these included roles, affection, sexual relationship, personality and behavior, and the couple's relationship. The second area (II) included problems related to job and money, and the third (III) focused upon relationships with family and friends, and children. The fourth problem area (IV) included religion, values and residence, while the fifth area (V) involved issues revolving around social activities and time and attention. As shown in Table 1, the Experimental couples slowly decreased in reporting conflict about those interpersonal topics of Area I, whereas Control couples seemed to avoid these topics totally at the six-month interview, concentrating on the "safer" topics of Areas II and III. At the one-year interview, however, the Control couples dramatically increased in their reporting of conflict in the interpersonal area (I).

Table 1. Percentages of Couples in Each Group Whose Disagreement Area Fell Within Five Major Problem Categories (N = 30)

Area	Experimental (n = 20)			Control (n = 10)		
	Pre	Six-Month	One-Year	Pre	Six-Month	One-Year
I	35	35 .	25	30	0	50
II	15	30	30	30	70	20
III	25	25	30	10	30	10
IV	15	5	10	10	0	10
V	10	5	5	20	0	10·

2. The effect of the couple's main area of disagreement on their relationship was coded as positive, neutral, or negative. The results indicate that whereas the Experimental and Control groups reported a similar degree of positive effect of their main area of disagreement on their relationship at the first interview (61% vs. 56%), this positive effect decreased sharply for the Control group over the next two interviews (to 29%), but not for the Experimental group (to 53%).

The data from the disagreement discussions lend support to the first hypothesis. Spouses who have taken part in a marriage preparation program experience a more constructive effect of their main area of disagreement than those who have not taken part in such a program, and seem ready to deal with the more sensitive conflict areas earlier in their marriage.

Solutions to Marital Conflict Stories.—As a further test of the first hypothesis, the couples' taped discussions of the hypothetical conflict stories were scored. The same sub-sample of 20 Experimental and 10 Control couples mentioned above were used. Transcripts of the taped discussions were rated on a three-point rating scale of positive conflict resolution. The results of this segment of the study can be seen in Figure 1.

The Control couples as a group showed no change in their mean degree of positive conflict resolution over the three interviews of the study. On the other hand, the Experimental couples showed an increase in their degree of positive conflict resolution at both the second and third interviews of the study.

A sign test (Siegel, 1956) was applied to the data to test the significance of the changes. As expected, no significant differences between interviews were found for the Control group. In the Experimental group, no significant difference was found between the first and second interview. However, a significant difference was found between the second and third interview ($p = .033$).[2]

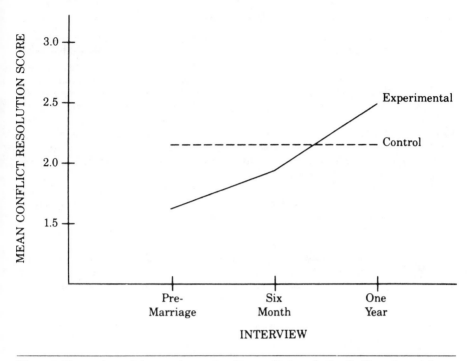

Figure 1. Comparison of changes in constructive conflict resolution for Experimental and Control groups over the three phases of the study.

Once again, the first hypothesis is supported. The Experimental group showed a significant change in resolving conflict more positively while the Control group showed no change.

Help-Seeking Patterns

The second major hypothesis was that couples taking part in the program would seek assistance in solving either individual or marital problems more readily than those who did not take part. When the questionnaires were examined, differences between the two groups were apparent in two help-seeking patterns: seeking help from any possible helper; and, seeking help from professionals.

The Experimental couples named more types of helpers than the Control couples at both the six-month ($M = 3.69$ vs. 2.91) and one-year ($M = 3.13$ vs. 2.65) interviews, even though they had named fewer than the Controls at the pre-marriage interview ($M = 4.00$ vs. 4.76). A repeated measures analysis of variance indicated a significant interaction between group and interview ($F = 3.40, p = .04$).

The second difference in help-seeking was found in the analysis of the incidence of professional help-seeking which again showed a significant interaction between group and interview ($F = 3.71, p = .03$). The Control couples showed a marked decrease in their mean use of professional help (.69 pre-marriage to .23 at one year) while the Experimental couples showed a small, but steady, increase (.35 pre-marriage to .45 at one year).

These results support the second hypothesis. Couples who participated in the marriage preparation program reported use of a broader support system than did couples who did not participate.

Discussion

One of the most interesting findings of this study was that couples who participated in the marriage preparation program showed a decrease in reporting conflict about interpersonal topics over the three interviews, whereas couples who did not participate seemed to avoid these topics totally at the six-month interview, but dramatically increased in their reporting of conflict in this area at the one-year interview. As Rausch, et al. (1974), so aptly stated, "A way out of interpersonal conflict is to deny the problem, . . . that is, pretend that no conflict exists" (p. 64). It appears that Control couples could successfully avoid the more sensitive interpersonal issues at the six-month point, concentrating on the "safer" areas of job, money, and relationships with people outside of the marital couple, but ended up having to spend an inordinate amount of energy on the interpersonal issues at the one-year point.

If Rausch, et al. (1974), were accurate when they stated that "facing up to the issues of conflict obviously offers greater hope for constructive outcomes" (pp. 84–85), it may be said that couples who participated in the program engaged in this constructive process earlier in their marriage than couples who did not attend a marriage preparation program.

Overlapping with the above is the finding that, once married, couples who participated in the program reported a continuing high positive effect of their main area of disagreement on their relationship, whereas the other couples report a sudden drop in positive effect. In other words, in the day-to-day living situation which is marriage, conflict is more likely to result in a negative effect on the relationship of couples who did not participate in marriage preparation, possibly giving them good reason to avoid dealing with conflict.

The results of the Marital Conflict Stories offer a possible explanation for the confronting vs. avoiding style of the two groups. Whereas the Control couples neither increased nor decreased in their overall ability to resolve hypothetical conflict situations, the Experimental couples showed a steady and significant increase. The skills of the latter group to resolve conflict appear to have increased, possibly contributing to more confidence about their ability to face conflict and to a more positive effect of conflict on their relationship.

Further support for this explanation comes from the finding that even when the Control couples increased their confrontation of interpersonal conflict at the one-year point, their reporting of a positive effect of their main area of disagreement on their relationship did not increase. This suggests that although they avoided conflict less at this point, their lack of improvement in ability to resolve conflict constructively diminished the positive effect that confronting conflict can have on a relationship.

Although help-seeking is sometimes viewed as an indication of trouble in a marriage, in the present study it was viewed as an indicator of a couple's use of resources in their support network. Conflict in marriage is normal. The seeking of help around resolving both intrapersonal and interpersonal conflict can be both appropriate and constructive. Although the helper horizon narrowed for both Experimental and Control couples after marriage, it narrowed much more for the Control couples. Viewed within the context of their apparent conflict avoidance, it is not surprising that Control couples decreased use of their support network substantially. The much smaller decrease on the part of the Experimental couples probably reflects the growth of an identity as a couple, but not to the point of cutting themselves off from resources outside themselves.

One further finding of interest is that the Experimental couples' ability to resolve hypothetical conflict constructively increased significantly from the six-month to the one-year interview, but not from the pre-marriage to the six-month interview. This suggests that the sessions after marriage were more effective than those before marriage.

However, the authors believe that a change from providing all sessions before marriage to providing all sessions after marriage in marriage preparation programs would be premature. The provision of pre-wedding sessions may be crucial to the motivation of couples to attend such programs. Further research is needed to determine if post-wedding sessions alone would be sufficient to effect the changes found in this study. In any case, the present results indicate the importance of including post-wedding sessions in marriage preparation programs.

Conclusions

This study has demonstrated the positive effect that marriage preparation can have on a couple's ability to confront marital conflict, to resolve their conflicts constructively, and to seek appropriate help when needed. However, the study is not without limitations. For instance, the analyses only scratched the surface in evaluating the taped tasks. As video-tape was not available, it was not possible to take into account the whole range of non-verbal communication. Audio-tapes of only 30 of the 63 couples were examined. In addition, the interviews themselves may have been a significant intervention in the lives of the couples who were interviewed and therefore the Control couples may not be representative of couples who have had no intervention at all (Rubin and Mitchell, 1976). A further limitation is that the study explored the effectiveness of marriage preparation over a time frame of only one year. As pointed out by Schumm and Denton (1979), this time frame is the maximum explored by any previous research, but longer time frames are needed to evaluate the overall impact of marriage preparation programs. (The project reported in this paper has recently been granted extended funding and the same couples will be interviewed after four years of marriage.)

In spite of these limitations, the authors believe that the present project has meaningfully supported the potential value of well-designed marriage preparation programs and wish to emphasize the importance of further innovation, effort, and research in the area.

REFERENCES

Baber, R. *Marriage and the family.* New York: McGraw-Hill, 1958.
Bach, G. & Weyden, P. *The intimate enemy.* New York: W. Morrow, 1969.
Barry, W. Marriage research and conflict. *Psychological Bulletin,* 1970, *73,* 41–53.
Blood, R. & Wolfe, D. *Husbands and wives.* New York: Free Press, 1960.
Burgess, E. & Locke, H. *The family.* New York: American Book Co., 1953.
Burgess, E. & Wallin, P. *Engagement and marriage.* Philadelphia: Lippincott, 1953.
Clinebell, H.J. *Growth counseling for marriage enrichment.* Philadelphia: Fortress Press, 1975.
Deutsch, M. Conflicts: Productive and destructive. *Journal of Social Issues,* 1969, *25,* 7–41.
Guldner, C. The post-marital: An alternative to pre-marital counseling. *The Family Coordinator,* 1971, *20,* 115–119.
Irving, H. *The family myth.* Toronto: Copp-Clark, 1972.
Kondrath, W. *Marriage preparation.* Unpublished manuscript, University of Toronto, 1974.
Leichter, H. & Mitchell, W. *Kinship and casework.* New York: Russell Sage Foundation, 1967.
Mace, D. *Getting ready for marriage.* Nashville, Tenn.: Abingdon, 1972.
Miller, S., Nunnally, E. & Wackman, D. A communication training program for couples. *Social Casework,* 1976, *57,* 9–18.
Miller, S. Corrales, R. & Wackman, D. Recent progress in understanding and facilitating marital communication. *The Family Coordinator,* 1975, *24,* 143–152.
Oussoren, A. H. *Education for marriage.* Unpublished manuscript, Ontario Institute for Studies in Education, 1972.
Peterson, J. *Education for marriage.* New York: Scribners, 1964.

Rausch, H., Barry, W., Hertel, R. & Swain, M. A. *Communication, conflict and marriage.* San Francisco: Jossey-Bass, 1974.

Rausch, H., Goodrich, D. & Campbell, J. Adaptation to the first years of marriage. *Psychiatry,* 1963, *26,* 368–380.

Rubin, Z. & Mitchell, C. Couples research as couples counseling. *American Psychologist,* 1976, *31,* 17–25.

Rutledge, A. *Pre-marital counseling.* Cambridge, Mass.: Schenkman, 1966.

Schumm, W. & Denton, W. Trends in pre-marital counseling. *Journal of Marital and Family Therapy,* 1979, *5* (4), 23–32.

Siegel, S. *Nonparametric statistics for the behavioral sciences.* New York: McGraw-Hill, 1956.

Social Planning Council of Metropolitan Toronto. *Marriage education.* Toronto: 1964.

Turk, J. *The measurement of intra-familial power.* Unpublished doctoral dissertation, University of Toronto, 1970.

NOTES

[1] Further details of individual sessions and measures used can be obtained from the primary author, E. L. Bader.

[2] It should be noted that chi-square analyses indicate no significant differences between the two groups at any of the three interviews of the study. It is when changes within each group, over interviews, are analyzed that significant differences occur.

PART IX

MARITAL THERAPY

Excerpts from a couple therapy case are cited to illustrate the practical significance of a multi-level framework in understanding couple interactions. The clinical implications of the metacommunicational framework, as a metaphor for examining and understanding relational processes, are discussed. Also, the pragmatics of following "process" at a variety of levels when working with punctuational differences, developing therapy strategies and goals, and measuring the progress of couple therapy are discussed.

42

MULTI-LEVEL COUPLE THERAPY

Applying a Metacommunicational Framework of Couple Interactions*

Guillermo Bernal† and Jeffrey Baker‡

IN A PREVIOUS REPORT (5), we presented a multi-level framework to understand couple interactions. This article describes the applications of the framework for understanding process in couple therapy. The conceptual framework of metaphor, still in the formative stages, is the natural outgrowth of our research (4, 5) and clinical work (6). Initial applications of the framework with couples in therapy suggest that trainees and beginning therapists, as well as more experienced therapists, find it use-ful as a cognitive map by which they can follow transactional processes as well as define the stages in couple therapy.

The framework was derived from the early work of various communication theorists and family therapists on the levels of communication (1, 2, 3, 9, 14, 16). These contributors referred to two levels of communication. One level was defined as the "content," another as the "command" or "relationship" component of a message. Because the content of a message is logically contained within the relationship component, the relational message constitutes a higher order of logic. The relational message defines the relationship (3, 7, 9, 10, 11, 16) and may be nonverbal or verbal. If verbalized explicitly, these relational components become content. When this happens, we may call it interpretation or metacommenting, from which "insight" may or may not follow. Note, however, that even when couples make relationship the content of their discussion, the concept of metalevels continues to apply.

* A version of this paper was presented at the annual meeting of the American Psychological Association, Toronto, Canada, August, 1978.

The senior author wishes to express his gratitude to Ivan Boszormenyi-Nagy, M.D., for the clinical supervision on the case presented. Additionally, we are indebted to Frank A. Johnson, M.D., for his helpful comments and careful review of the manuscript.

† Assistant Professor, Department of Psychiatry, University of California, San Francisco General Hospital, 1001 Potrero Avenue, San Francisco, California 94110.

‡ Clinical Psychologist, Charles River Hospital, Wellesley, Massachusetts.

A Metacommunicational Framework[1]

The levels framework to be illustrated in its clinical application has been described in an earlier paper (5). The framework developed originally from a research study of punctuational differences (15) with couples (4). The classic illustration of punctuational differences is that of the husband and wife who are locked into a pattern in which he withdraws and she nags or complains. Each sees the other as the stimulus for his or her responses, viewing the other as the cause of the difficulties. Each spouse "punctuates" or groups the same set of interactions quite differently.

To establish a punctuational framework for clinical and research purposes, five interactional levels, progressively increasing in abstraction, were defined by content. Capsule descriptions are offered here for ready reference. In addition, Figure 1 illustrates the five levels using Venn diagrams. The interactional *content* (shaded at each level) is the primary criterion defining that level.

Level 1—Object: Transactions at this level are focused on an issue. For example, a couple's interaction may be about finances, in-laws, a stomach or back pain, recreation, division of labor (i.e., who cleans the house), etc. If a member of a pair discussing housework were asked to draw his

or her transaction, the resulting picture would be one of the housework finished or undone (5). The interactions take the form: "The back pain/housework is a source of frustration"; "The problem is finances," etc.

Level 2—Individual: At this level, the content is focused on one of the individuals in the interaction. Often interactions at this level include mutual accusation and blaming that may be represented as punctuational differences (15), when each person views the other as the reason for his or her behavior. "Members of the couple view their own actions as reactions. The individuals now are the content of the transactions, illustrated in Figure 1 as a figure superimposed on a ground of object content. Interactions may take the following form: 'I am/you are a nag,' or 'It's your fault the house is a mess,' or 'You are a spendthrift with our money,' etc. (5). If a member of the couple were asked to draw the interaction, the emerging image would be of the other person.

Level 3—Transactional: The Transactional level represents a change in content from a focus on individuals (i.e., "I am the problem," "You are the problem," "It's your fault," etc.) to a focus on discussing explicitly the patterns of interaction ("It's you *and* I"). The Transactional level is distinguished from the Individual level by the couple's acknowledgment of a connection between their behaviors more complex than cause-and-effect, e.g., recognizing "vicious circles" such as, "You nag me about cleaning the house and I keep forgetting to do it," or "You stay out late and I get headaches." At the Transactional level couples may be acknowledging implicitly such dynamics in their relationship as passive-aggressive acting-out, but not yet explicitly at the more abstract level of generalized relationship dynamics (see Level 4). As Figure 1 illustrates, "transactions are now the content focus with both individuals as figure for a ground of people discussing issues" (5, p. 295).

Level 4—Relational: At this level, the

[1] A word of caution about conceptual schemes in general seems appropriate. All attempts at describing ongoing process fall short in the depiction of reality. The problem is two-fold. On the one hand, we run the risk of mistaking our abstractions for genuine human experience. On the other, we confront the paradox of unitizing information that may not be suitable for a grouping or classification. For instance, when process is stopped, whether for descriptive or analytical purposes, the act of stopping the process is itself an arbitrary grouping of events; that grouping of groupings, of course, represents still a different process. It is probable that frameworks attempting to describe human experience are inherently inadequate and cannot do justice to the complexity of the material at hand. As we proceed, it may be worthwhile to avoid the tendency to reify by reminding ourselves of the dialectic between experience and the description of experience.

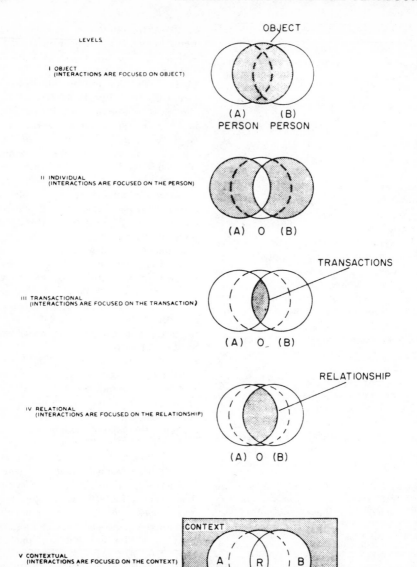

Fig. 1. Levels for understanding couple interactions: Object, individual, transactional, relational and contextual.

focus changes from an acknowledgment of patterns (Level 3) to a focus on the relationship itself. "Assumptions, definitions, questions, and rules about the relationship are discussed and explicitly negotiated, e.g., 'Neither housework nor who's right or wrong is really the issue. Let's talk about what this says about our relationship,' or

'I'm unhappy with this rule by which I'm the teacher and you're the student,' etc. In Figure 1 the relationship, as content focus, is figure against the ground of specific transactions, the individuals involved, and concrete object or issue." (5, p. 294)

Level 5—Contextual: The next shift in content is toward discussion of growth in the context of life goals. Interactions may focus on any material that sets the context for the current relationship. This contextual material may be psychohistorical, political, economic, ethnic, developmental (life cycle crisis), intergenerational, etc. Whatever the nature of the material at hand, this level entails an exploration of contextual issues that may relate to marital history or take the form of individual psychotherapeutic work in the presence of a spouse. As Figure 1 shows, "Content at this level subsumes relationship, transactions, individuals, and the object perhaps at issue." (5, p. 295) Members of a couple may reflect and examine past incidents, relational debts, loyalty conflicts, etc., in terms of the relationship or perhaps specific incidents or experiences that set the context for the current relationship, e.g., "My father used to get headaches whenever he felt my mother was ignoring him."

Applying the Frame to Couples in Therapy

Material from a couple therapy case will illustrate the practical significance of the framework. At the outset, however, it is important to note that although an immediate goal in the examples to follow has been to help the couple encounter each other at the same level (so that they may talk directly, for example, and in doing so find confirmation and test the realities of their assumptions) this in itself comprises only one possible therapeutic move and need not be an end in itself. What is more appropriate in one instance may not be so in another. Similarly, just as helping couples meet at the same level need not imply a therapeutic endpoint, the examples

that follow, in which couples are aided to move to increasingly abstract levels, are not intended to imply that movement up the hierarchy of communicational content levels is movement ascending toward health. For example, couples will at times need to find more concrete levels of discourse to overcome avoidance of feeling through overabstraction. Indeed, developing the ability to move flexibly among levels, often meeting and sometimes diverging, may be the best specific indicator of movement toward health. The model proposed is intended primarily as an aid in enabling therapists to define process, and although some suggestions for its use as technique are offered, its best application remains as a conceptual schema to promote creative experimentation and flexibility of technique.

We begin with some brief details about the couple.[2] The clients were a working-class couple from North Philadelphia in their early thirties. The wife was four years older than her husband. They had no children, had been married for six years, and were high school graduates. Initially, the wife had sought help at a community mental health center for depression. Notes from the intake interview described an obese, diabetic woman who complained about marital problems and was frightened by recurring thoughts of her own death. She was diagnosed as a depressive neurotic. Beginning five months after the first interview, she was seen individually in "supportive" therapy for four months. During this time there were many cancellations, little progress, and a progressive deterioration that led to hospitalization for an angina attack. Notes from the final individual session reported "poor sleep," rambling conversations, the "marriage in a crisis," and medical complications connected to the patient's fluctuating blood sugar levels.

Prior to hospitalization, upon the sugges-

---

[2] Names and some facts have been changed to ensure anonymity.

tion of the wife's therapist, the husband had requested the services of the clinic. This occurred two months after the wife had entered individual therapy. The husband was described as "casually dressed, unshaven, eager to speak, and appearing older than his age." He attributed his problems to a dishonorable discharge because of a mismanagement of funds while he was in the Army. He had difficulty keeping a job and at the time was unemployed. Further, he openly discussed his aggressive and assaultive behavior toward his wife and reported periods of brooding when "everything builds up." He had been taking antidepressants prescribed by a private physician and was diagnosed as having a passive-aggressive personality disorder. After two sessions, he had not returned for other individual therapy appointments.

Because of increasing signs of deterioration in the wife, her individual therapist[3] asked for a marital therapy consultation, and the senior author joined the therapy sessions. The husband was invited to a conjoint interview, and the couple agreed to participate in a set of five couple therapy evaluation sessions (16). After the "evaluative" sessions, further treatment was recommended. The couple agreed to continue weekly therapy sessions.

At the beginning of treatment the couple complained of frequent fights, some of which escalated to physical violence with the destruction of household property. They also reported periods of depression, poor sexual relations, and financial problems. The initial stage of treatment, the engagement (16) or joining (13) phase, was characterized by interactions occurring at the Object and Individual levels. The couple repeatedly engaged in heated, mutually blaming arguments about finances, relatives or friends, and their "accidents." The therapists worked at establishing

dyadic situations (i.e., where the couple was instructed to talk to each other rather than to the therapists) and slowing down the process with specific questions. The therapists were in "side-taking" and "go-between" roles (16), working with basic communicational techniques (14).

The following is an illustration of a typical discussion about what the wife called "someone getting hurt," taken from the sixth session (inclusive of the evaluation). The wife tended to accuse and blame her husband, and he blamed her. The dialogue was as follows:

H: It was an accident, and you don't know the difference between an accident and when something is done on purpose.

W: You don't know the difference between affection and brutality.

H: Yes I do.

W: No.

H: As far as this morning is concerned, that there was taken out of proportion out of something that was a pure accident.

W: Why is it that every time I reach out to you, you hurt me?

H: Maybe your timing is wrong.

W: My timing is wrong?

H: And when I make wrong moves at the wrong times as you make it, sometimes you wind up getting hurt.

W: Do I have to make an appointment?

H: No. And don't make a joke out of it neither.

There are two salient elements to these interactions. One is that the wife is in an attacking stance, and the husband defends by focusing the discussion on the accidents. While she blames him for being rough (Individual level), he may attack in return, but ends up by talking about "accidents" (Object level) that are beyond his control. One goal during this session was to synchronize the interactions so that both would be talking to each other on the same level. The immediate therapy goal was to facilitate finishing transactional sequences. To these ends, the husband was encouraged to talk

---

[3] The cotherapist was Ms. Daisy Negroni. The senior author is indebted to her for her helpfulness throughout the year.

with his wife about the specifics of the situation while she listened to him. For instance, the therapists would make comments of the following type: "Instead of talking about who was at fault, let's talk only about what happened." The following illustrates the Object level, where the content of discussion was primarily their "accidents."

> H: For instance, OK, I don't know the exact wording used, but we were playing. And I poke my finger and you said, "Well, I'm going to bite your finger if you stick it in my face again." So I stuck it in your face and you grabbed hold of it and so, before you could bend my finger, I bent your finger. Then you grabbed it and I bent your hand with my finger before you could bend it. And then you went to hug me. I thought you were coming after me, so I lowered my head. When I lowered my head, you were coming toward me. My head ran into your chest, knocking the wind out of you and everything blew up.
>
> W: No. You hit the bedpost.
>
> H: It was taken as if it was done deliberately. I just lowered by head and hadn't expected to make contact with you. You said, "Well, there's too many accidents." And everything blew up.

The four or five sessions following the evaluation phase dealt with the specifics of their arguments (Object and Individual levels). Both spouses were encouraged to describe concretely each of their views of what happened and, together, to explore each of their views of how events came about. This resulted in certain plans of action resembling quid pro quo negotiations on the basis of which tasks were assigned to the couple. During this period, their fighting diminished, the wife appeared less depressed, and the husband found a job.

The next phase of the therapy, beginning with the tenth session, was less behaviorally focused and dealt with identifying patterns of transaction. The therapists commented on how the spouses acted and reacted toward each other. The goal was to move toward Transactional and Relational levels.

For instance, the therapists repeatedly commented on the process of the couple's immediate and reported interactions, focusing on situations in which the wife "bugged" her husband and he "pulled away" or withdrew. When the couple began to identify the presence of a pattern, the therapists encouraged them to talk about it. The therapists interpreted the pattern explicitly for the couple to examine more closely when the couple appeared ready to do so. This pattern occurred for them verbally, socially, and sexually. The wife's attempts at affection often ended in heated arguments over her husband's withdrawal or rebuffs, and they would return to the Individual level of interactions with mutual accusations. Consider the following dialogue from the tenth session:

> W: A brief encounter . . . we get started out trying to be affectionate and wind up, somebody gets hurt, usually me. We both woke up with a cold . . . all of a sudden it turns into a disaster. I was totally insulted and I got bombastically mad. The result was that we were being affectionate and everything was going all right until I was told, "You're bugging me."
>
> H: It was taken completely wrong. You go ahead and explain it your way and I'll explain it my way.
>
> W: Well, the way it came out was, you know.
>
> H: You explain it your way and I'll explain it mine.
>
> W: The way it came out was that I went to hug you and all of a sudden you say, "Leave me alone."
>
> H: I told you I had an upset stomach. You don't bug me.
>
> W: You didn't say that.
>
> H: I told you I had an upset stomach.
>
> W: You didn't say that. You said, "You make me sick."

As the interactions continued, it became increasingly obvious to the couple themselves that, when the wife tried to get close, "accidents" seemed to occur. The following vignette illustrates the couple, moving from the Object to the Transactional level: Transactional rather than Relational in that the discussions stop at the specifics of a pattern of behavior.

> H: Majority of times you are more passionate than I am.
> W: But that is as far as it goes.
> H: Let me finish. You are more passionate toward me than I am toward you.
> W: No.
> H: No, wait a minute. We've been talking about this for weeks, and you know you have. And I haven't really said much. So don't go changing your mind and take the blame for something you aren't to blame for.
> W: All right, I'll shut up.
> H: Right. First time we agreed on something.
> W: It's usually a slight accident, a collision, when it should be a little bit of tenderness, love . . .
> H: (Interrupts) You know what she's telling me? She's telling me that consciously I'm causing these accidents. That's what she's saying. I'm saying they are not intentional. I don't believe they are happening all the time, and that makes me feel subconsciously I'm producing these accidents to avoid her. Do you believe that?
> T: Do they happen all the time?
> W: The majority of the times.
> H: Let's see here, how many times have you tried to hug me this week?
> W: Seven.

After they discussed the number of weekly accidents during the previous three weeks, a clear pattern emerged. The tenth session marked a transition, because the couple was entering the Transactional level by discussing their interactions with honesty and openness. Their dialogue continued in the following way:

> H: I feel that shows a lessening. It shows that the pattern of accidents is going down.
> W: We were fighting all week over this.
> H: Right, all week over this.
> W: Over this one issue, no. This one issue. You haven't been able to recognize it.

> H: We have been fighting all week over it?
> W: Yes.
> H: There is a pattern here.
> T: Can you talk about it?
> H: There is a pattern, true. But isn't the pattern going down?
> T: It sounds like it is, somewhat. The cycle of you going after him and his blocking you used to happen a lot, and it happens less now.
> W: Instead of it being something pleasurable, it winds up in an argument.
> T: At the same time, it also happens the other way around. This is the same as before, where you bug him and he pulls away.

The couple's interactions moved from the Transactional to Relational levels during a discussion of her feelings about her husband not sharing more with her. At first the husband would say, "If you weren't so demanding, then I wouldn't withhold so much." She would say, "If you would tell me things, I wouldn't be so demanding." (Although their statements are mutually blaming, the conditional "if" is taken to signify the acknowledgment of a pattern; optimistically and pragmatically, "if" statements that include the behavior of both parties are assigned the Transactional designation.) After they talked about their Transactional pattern, the couple were encouraged to discuss the more general issue of trust. The therapist directly inquired about trust in one of the following ways: "I wonder what has happened in your marriage that there seems to be so little trust?" or, "Can you two talk about the lack of trust in your relationship?" The interactions were now focused on the nature of the relationship—that is, they were at the Relational level. Both acknowledged their difficulty in trusting each other, and the events leading to the erosion of trust were discussed subsequently. Additionally, the couple were able to work on a plan of action to build relational trustworthiness (8). Their plan was related to issues concerning extended family members and involved interactions at the Contextual level.[4]

Transition to contextual material was facilitated by the therapists' inquiring about the families of origin. For instance, the therapists asked if certain issues (e.g., trust) reminded either of them of events when they lived with their families. Such comments moved the subject of discussion to the context and contributed to the rebuilding of trust in relatedness, because such dialogues are usually characterized by important disclosures, support, and mutual helpfulness.

The following segment is an illustration of interactions at the Contextual level that were extensions of relational issues of trust, indebtedness, and entitlement that surfaced during the twelfth session. Through the therapists' intervention, the husband was encouraged to talk to his spouse about his difficulty with his mother, who had abandoned him several times when he was a child.

H: There were arguments and fights with my mother since 1953 when she forced me from my foster home where I had lived for ten years. We fought and argued. She put me in a boys' home. Then I came out of there. My mother is the type of person with whom you can have an argument and you come back years later and she'll act as if nothing happened. Forgive and forget, she says. But I forgave and forgot too many times.

W: Not really.

H: No. No. No.

W: It will always be there.

H: Oh, yeah, It'll be there, but I've given too many times.

---

[4] Given the nature of the clinical supervision on this case, the interactional material that emerged in the Relational and Contextual levels reflected a particular family therapy orientation (Boszormenyi-Nagy and Spark, 1977) which in a sense biased this data a la Nagy (e.g. prominance of the concepts of trustworthiness, justice, loyalty conflicts, etc.). Therapists working from other theoretical orientations (e.g., psychoanalytic, behavioral, etc.) may elicit different material at these levels.

W: Before we got married, everything was terrific.

H: I put out and put out from 1953 till now. I had to draw the line.

W: I agree with you. But before we got married, everything was terrific between you and your mom.

H: For the past year or so. That's all.

W: When we got married, there was nothing.

H: That only lasted a year and a half. You see, my sister threw me out of my mother's house when I came back from Vietnam because I visited my foster parents for a couple of weeks. They were my family, too. My sister threw me out of my mother's house, and that led to a silence between my mother and me that lasted years.

The interactions continued in the above contextual manner, and the couple related a number of issues from their families of origin to issues in their relationship. This became an openly acknowledged "reflection" on their lives and history, occurring in an atmosphere of openness and mutual helpfulness.

The contextual interactions added meaning to the couple's difficulties. Both were entitled to have received more from their parents, particularly the husband. Both were parentified children (8) and were remaining "invisibly loyal" to their families by maintaining a balance of distance by means of the back-and-forth trading of distancer and pursuer transactional roles. The long-range therapeutic goal with this couple was to enhance trustworthiness in the marriage by helping them to work through their loyalty conflicts. They worked on developing an action plan whereby both could remain loyal to each other and develop or maintain meaningful connections to their families of origin.

Discussion and Conclusions

Applying the multi-level interactional frame to the transactions of couples in clinical as well as research settings (5, 4) reveals that distressed couples are often locked into a particular level, demonstrating limited movement among the levels. Specifically, initial work with couples may reveal patterns of mutual accusation and blame characteristic of *Level 2* interactions. When the intensity of conflict is reduced, movement across the communicational levels is more likely and therapeutic work leading toward clear relationships, self-understanding, tolerance of differences, rebuilding of trust, and shared responsibility becomes feasible.

Clinical experience with the multi-level framework suggests that beginning therapists and trainees find it useful as a schema with which to follow transactional processes and develop intervention strategies. A therapist may attempt to synchronize couples at one level (for example, by allowing one member to speak while the other listens) or may choose to work at moving couples, or one or another member of a couple, from one level to another by both implicit and, in time, explicit encouragement, as earlier illustrated. Transition from level to level presupposes an appreciation for the engagement process in couple and family therapy (16). In some situations, this movement may require weeks of therapeutic work.

In the case presented, shifts from *Level 2* to *Level 3* occurred after the contracted five-session "evaluation" period, which primarily focused on *Level 1* and *Level 2* interactions. The couple had to be helped to engage at *Level 1* before they could move beyond blaming to *Level 3*. The evaluation phase facilitated the couple's engagement in a therapy process within which a wide range of issues could be explicitly brought up for examination and reality-tested in a relatively safe setting. Movement from *Level 2* to *Level 3* was further facilitated by comments on the couple's process and other interventions that moved the clients toward a position of taking more responsibility. For example, once the couple had engaged at Level 1, the therapist said, "You two argue a lot about the accidents. And the more you try to get close to your husband, the more he tries to get away and the more accidents

happen." Other alternatives might be for a therapist to prescribe more concretely a paradoxical task to make covert patterns more overt. For example, a couple may be asked to go home and do more of the same (e.g., husband withdraw and wife nag, etc.). Another possibility would involve a role-reversal sequence to exaggerate the couple's particular pattern or the couple could be provided with video-taped feedback of their process, thus removing them from the immediacy and intensity of the situation and facilitating their engaging in *Level 3* discussions.

In general, "interactional movement may be facilitated by a therapist's offering comments, challenges, tasks, paradoxes, exercises" (5, p. 300) or directives. For example, vituperations at *Level 2* may be effectively dealt with by slowing down the blaming process with highly specific questions about the issue or with questions about each member's own feelings. With the former, the couple may be moved to interact at the Object level. The behaviorally oriented therapist might stay with this alternative, working with the couple on quid pro quo negotiations. Asking each member of the couple to talk about his or her feelings may move the interaction to the Transactional, Relational, or—through associations—to the Contextual level.

Therapists can facilitate interactional shifts from lower levels to *Level 4* or *Level 5* by direct demonstration, suggestion, or inquiry. With our exemplary couple, movement to *Level 4* was achieved when the therapist directly inquired about issues such as trust and commitment. At one point, the therapist said: "Your wife wants to talk about your commitment to the relationship, and you tend to shift the topic to the accidents." At another point, the therapist asked: "Can the two of you talk about your commitment to the relationship?" At the relational level, the focus is on relationship properties; this may reveal disagreements "over existing definitions and/or rules for relatedness" (5, p.300), or differing perceptions of the same, for example, "You have to understand that my feeling a little gloomy or quiet doesn't mean I don't love you."

The family of origin always plays a role that may become the level of exploration and rebalancing work (8) for one or both members of the couple. In the above case, shifts to *Level 5* occurred when the therapists linked current problematic issues and patterns to similar difficulties in the family of origin. For example, during a discussion of difficulties with trust, the therapist asked: "Does this talk about trust and trustworthiness remind you of anything?" On other occasions, the therapist made connections between imbalances in the marital relationship and imbalances in the family-of-origin relationships as a way to focus on contextual transgenerational processes. Clearly, shifts to Relational and Contextual levels may signify greater degrees of involvement in a therapeutic process, as demonstrated by the case study above.

The clinician new or experienced in working with couples encounters not only a bewildering array of interactional patterns and choices of perspectives, but also, as in the case illustrated, rapidly shifting resistances and a high degree of emotional reactivity. All can contribute to a sense of therapist helplessness as "the monkey in the middle" or an experience of being "stuck" along with the couple in a recalcitrant therapy. It is hoped that the framework presented here may serve both a differentiating and creative function for therapists working with couples. Therapists may use the framework in helping couples to make pragmatic changes and to become more sympathetically self-reflective while consistently encouraging in couples an awareness of the multiple levels of interactional meaning.

REFERENCES

1. BAKER, J., "Family Systems: A Review and Synthesis of Eight Major Concepts," *Fam. Ther.* 1: 1-27, 1976.
2. BANDLER, R. and GRINDER, J., *The Structure of Magic:* Vol. 1. Palo Alto, California, 1976.
3. BATESON, G., *Steps to an Ecology of Mind*, New York, Ballantine, 1972.
4. BERNAL, G. and GOLANN, S. E., "Couple Interactions: A study of the Punctuation Process," *Int. J. Fam. Ther.* 2: 47-56,1980.
5. BERNAL, G. and BAKER, J., "Toward a Metacommunicational Framework of Couple Interactions," *Fam. Proc.* 18: 293-302, 1979.
6. BERNAL, G. and VANDE KEMP, H., "Marital Therapy: Experiential Perspectives of Two Developing Clinicians," *Fam. Ther.* 2: 109-122, 1976.
7. BOSZORMENYI-NAGY, I., "A Theory of Relationships: Experience and Transaction," in I. Boszormenyi-Nagy and J. L. Framo (Eds.), *Intensive Family Therapy: Theoretical and Practical Aspects*, New York, Harper and Row, 1965.
8. BOSZORMENYI-NAGY, I. and SPARK, G. M., *Invisible Loyalties*, New York, Harper & Row, 1973.
9. HALEY, J., *Problem Solving Therapy*, San Francisco, Jossey-Bass, 1976.
10. HARPER, J. M.; SCORESBY, A. L.; and BOYCE, W. D., "The Logical Levels of Complementary, Symmetrical, and Parallel Interaction Classes in Family Dyads," *Fam. Proc.* 16: 199-210, 1977.
11. KARPEL, M., "Individuation: From Fusion to Dialogue," *Fam. Proc.* 15: 65-82, 1976.
12. LANGS, R., *The Bipersonal Field*, New York, Jason Aronson, 1976.
13. MINUCHIN, S., *"Families and Family Therapy."* Cambridge, Mass., Harvard University Press, 1974.
14. SLUZKI, C. E., "Marital Therapy From a Systems Theory Perspective," in T. J. Paolino, Jr., and B. S. McCrady (Eds.), *Marriage and Marital Therapy: Psychoanalytic, Behavioral, and Systems Theory Perspectives*. New York, Brunner/Mazel, 1978.
15. WATZLAWICK, P.; BEAVIN, J. H.; and JACKSON, D. D. *Pragmatics of Human Communication*, New York, Norton, 1967.
16. ZUK, G. H., *Family Therapy: A Triadic Based Approach*, New York, Behavioral Publications, 1972.

Distressed couples were assigned to Behavioral Marital Therapy, Communication Therapy, or a Wait-List. Treated couples demonstrated more change than controls in marital problems and general communication patterns, but not in feelings toward spouse or communication during conflict resolution discussions. Wives in treatment reported more positive change in personal, nonmarital problems than control wives. There were no overall differences between treatment groups; treated couples reported increases in marital satisfaction and communication from pretreatment to the 4-month follow-up. There was an interaction between age and response to treatment: young couples changed more in Behavioral Marital Therapy, while older couples responded better to Communication Therapy. Results are discussed in terms of the need for developing client-tailored treatment programs.

43

A COMPARATIVE OUTCOME STUDY OF BEHAVIORAL MARITAL THERAPY AND COMMUNICATION THERAPY*

*Hillary Turkewitz and K. Daniel O'Leary***

Marital therapy has grown markedly in the last decade. This growth is reflected in increases in the number of graduate training programs devoted to marital and family therapy (Nichols, 1979) and in the percentage of psychologists, social workers, psychiatrists, and pastoral counselors whose primary professional identification is in this field (Everett, 1979). The two general approaches to marital therapy that have been most systematically evaluated are behavioral marital therapy (BMT) and communication therapy (CT).

Behavioral marital therapy is designed to increase productive problem solving and to establish pleasing interactions through reciprocal or equitable exchanges. Exemplars of BMT programs have been described by Azrin, Naster, and Jones (1973), Stuart (1976), and Weiss, Hops, and Patterson (1973). The major treatment techniques include: having spouses clearly and specifically state their desires; teaching them communication skills that are seen as prerequisites for successful negotiation; and using contingency contracting, in which explicit rewards or penalties are associated with particular behaviors designated in written agreements.

*This article is based on the first author's dissertation. An interim report of this study was presented at the Association for the Advancement of Behavior Therapy meeting, New York, 1976. We are indebted to Anne Byrnes, Bob Cohen, and Sharon Foster. We also thank Ron Prinz and Basabi Mukherji for their consultation on statistical analyses.

**The authors are co-directors of the Stony Brook Marital Therapy Program. Hillary Turkewitz, PhD, is a Research Associate and K. Daniel O'Leary, PhD, is chair of the Department of Psychology at the State University of New York at Stony Brook, Long Island, N.Y. 11794. Requests for reprints should be sent to Dr. O'Leary.

Several therapeutic approaches have been designed to enhance marital communication. The "Conjugal Relationship Enhancement" program, developed by Guerney and his associates (Ely, Guerney, & Stover, 1973), involves structured exercises to teach spouses a Rogerian, supportive communication style. A second widely-used communication therapy approach is that of Satir (1967). Drawing from a systems orientation to marital and family relationships, Satir stresses the importance of meta-communicating to clarify potential discrepancies between messages sent and received. In this approach the therapist is quite active, using role playing and feedback to prompt new communication patterns.

There have been several recent, comprehensive reviews of marital therapy outcome research (Beck, 1976; Greer & D'Zurilla, 1975; Gurman & Kniskern, 1978; Jacobson, 1978a; Jacobson & Martin, 1976). Methodologically sound studies have demonstrated the superiority of BMT to no treatment and to an attention placebo (e.g., Jacobson, 1977, 1978b). Additionally, a series of case study demonstrations and within-subject comparisons (e.g., Azrin et al., 1973; Weiss et al., 1973; Patterson, Hops, & Weiss, 1975) indicate that the behavioral approach offers promising and viable therapeutic strategies. Although communication therapy derived from systems-oriented therapeutic approaches has not undergone rigorous empirical evaluations, structured communication training has been investigated in controlled studies (e.g., Ely et al., 1973). As with BMT, it appears that CT is effective, particularly with respect to modifying verbal interaction patterns. However, it is difficult to draw definitive conclusions because of the methodological difficulties found in much of this research (O'Leary & Turkewitz, 1978a).

Only one investigation comparing the relative effectiveness of BMT and communication-oriented approaches has been conducted with couples experiencing significant marital distress (Liberman, Levine, Wheeler, Sanders, & Wallace, 1976). These authors reported no difference between the groups on self-report measures and a superiority of BMT to an "Interactional" therapy on one-third of the behavioral targets. However, methodological problems (e.g., lack of a control group, nonrandom assignment, small therapist sample) temper possible conclusions based on these data.

In the present study, major questions of interest concerned effectiveness of BMT and CT as compared to a no-treatment control; possible differential effects of the two treatment programs; stability of treatment effects; clients' evaluations of their therapists; and the demographic or dyadic interaction variables that may be predictive of response to therapy.

Method

Subjects

Thirty couples were obtained through referrals from mental health professionals (60%), newspaper announcements (37%), and previous clients (3%). Couples had to be living together, married at least 5 years, and have a mean score lower than 100 on the Locke-Wallace Marital Adjustment Test (Kimmel & Van der Veen, 1974). Couples were excluded if there was evidence of severe psychological problems, including chronic alcoholism or a history of psychiatric hospitalization within the past 2 years ($n = 3$), or if the problem appeared to be primarily a specific sexual dysfunction ($n = 1$).

Mean age of spouses involved was 35.4 years (range: 25–61 yrs.). Mean length of marriage was 12.4 years (range: 5–32 yrs.), and there was an average of two children per family. Average educational level of the spouses was 13 years. Mean family income was approximately $12,000. Twenty percent of the couples had received previous marital therapy; approximately 23% of the spouses had been in individual psychotherapy. Eight percent of the spouses had been married previously.

Therapists

Five therapists, two males and three females, participated. All had experience with marital therapy, although years of experience and theoretical and educational backgrounds varied. The therapists ranged in age from 25 to 35 years old and had from 2 to 11 years of clinical experience. There were two clinical psychologists, one social worker, and two doctoral candidates in clinical psychology. Each therapist saw four couples, two in each treatment group. Throughout the project, therapists attended weekly 2-hour group supervision meetings and followed treatment manuals which provided a session-by-session outline of each treatment program.[1]

Dependent Measures

Multiple assessment measures were administered to couples at an initial screening interview. Those who participated in the treatment programs also completed the assessment procedures immediately following termination of therapy and at 4-month follow-up interview. The couples in the Wait-List Control Group returned for their second assessment after a 10-week wait.

Locke-Wallace Marital Adjustment Test (MAT)

The MAT is a widely used self-report questionnaire that measures overall marital satisfaction. Variations of the MAT have demonstrated discriminant (Locke & Wallace, 1959) and construct validity (Murstein & Beck, 1972; Weiss *et al.*, 1973). The version used herein has demonstrated test-retest reliability and includes adjusted scoring procedures for men and women (Kimmel & Van der Veen, 1974).

Primary Communication Inventory (PCI)

The PCI (Navran, 1967) is a self-report measure of the frequency of interactions, such as talking about pleasant or unpleasant events of the day, sulking, discussing sexual matters, and understanding the spouse's tone of voice or facial expression. The PCI has demonstrated construct validity (Kahn, 1970; Navran, 1967) and test-retest reliability (Ely, *et al.*, 1973).

Positive Feelings Questionnaire (PFQ)

The PFQ is an 18-item self-report inventory developed to assess frequency of such positive feelings as looking forward to being alone with one's spouse, enjoying looking at or touching one's spouse, and feeling positive about one's spouse's personal successes. The primary reason for developing the PFQ was to test the hypothesis that the frequency of positive feelings would be predictive of success in therapy. Pilot research revealed that the PFQ correlates with the MAT ($r = .78$) and has a test-retest reliability of .93.

Personal Data Questionnaire (PDQ)

The PDQ was administered at the initial screening interview to obtain general demographic information, such as age, occupation, educational background. In addition, spouses were asked to identify major marital problems, behaviors of their partner they would most like to see change, and their major individual problems. A 7-point scale was used to rate the degree of change in these areas at posttreatment (or postwait) and at follow-up.

Behavioral Rating of Conflict Resolution

Couples engaged in tape-recorded discussions of hypothetical marital conflict situations, adapted from the Inventory of Marital Conflicts (Olson & Ryder, 1970). The procedure used to generate these discussions was a variation of Strodtbeck's (1951)

Revealed Differences Technique. Spouses read identical short vignettes describing common marital conflicts and made individual decisions regarding which spouse was responsible for each conflict. The couples were then asked to discuss those vignettes about which they disagreed for 20 minutes. Data from the first 12 minutes of the interaction were analyzed, because this was approximately the length of the majority of the discussions.

The conflict resolution discussions were rated by three undergraduates trained to use a Communication Code containing 10 categories: Agree, Meta-communication, Question, Feeling, Interruption, Positive Remark, Negative Remark, Positive Feelings, Negative Feelings, Relationship Talk.[2]

The raters recorded the occurrence of each of the 10 categories of behavior in consecutive 30-second intervals; behaviors were encoded separately for husbands and wives. The order in which the tapes were rated was randomized so that the raters were blind to both the experimental group of the couple and the date of the discussion. Reliability checks were made on a randomly selected sample of approximately 27% of the data. The Pearson product-moment correlations for the individual categories ranged from .83 to 1.0.

Procedure

Couples attended an intake interview during which the assessment materials were completed and information relevant to screening was obtained in individual interviews. Sliding scale treatment fees were set; the average per-session fee was $13. In addition, a financial deposit of $25 or 25% of the total treatment fee, whichever was higher, was secured. This deposit was to be returned at follow-up. For couples assigned to the waiting list, it was returned at the postwait interview.

Following the intakes, couples were matched on age and their mean score on the MAT and then randomly assigned to one of three experimental groups: (1) Behavioral Marital Therapy (BMT), (2) Communication Therapy (CT), or (3) Wait-List Control (WL). Treatment programs involved 10 weekly sessions; waiting-list couples were offered therapy after a 10-week wait.

Behavioral Marital Therapy

The major goal of this program was to increase the frequency of behaviors the spouses desired in one another. Therapists helped spouses construct written behavior change agreements as a means of prompting more satisfying interchanges. The agreements were similar to the "good faith" contracts of Weiss et al. (1973) in that each spouse made a commitment to follow through with the agreement. However, there were no explicit rewards or penalties. Rather, therapists stressed the positive consequences to the relationship of fulfilling agreements (e.g., increased cooperation, satisfaction, verbal support). As therapy progressed, therapists reduced their input to and direction of the process, so that couples learned to arrive at mutually satisfying change agreements on their own. This treatment program also included communication enhancement through modeling, feedback, suggestions, and some structured exercises. The major homework assignments given to couples in this treatment program involved carrying out behavior change agreements or constructing new ones.

Communication Therapy

The major goals of the communication program were to increase clear communication, decrease destructive interchanges, and increase the frequency of positive, open, supportive interactions. Primary techniques used to effect these changes were modeling, feedback, role playing, and structured exercises. Spouses were encouraged to meta-communicate, that is, ask for clarification of each other's messages and discuss the process of their communication. One of the major communication exercises employed was empathy training. Additionally, when appropriate, therapists provided rules of communication, such as, speak directly to a complaint or criticism rather than respond with a cross-complaint of your own; wait for your spouse to complete a thought before giving your reactions or comments; maintain eye contact while talking.

Therapists helped couples learn how to identify their own particular interactional difficulties so that they would be able to continue working on their communication after termination. Couples were given weekly assignments which involved such activities as practicing the structured exercises three times during the week, setting aside time to talk over the events of the day, following specific communication rules, or identifying problematic interchanges and discovering ways of modifying them.

The critical differences between the two treatment programs were:

1. BMT involved working on a series of behavior change agreements. Spouses specified changes they desired to see in each other and made written commitments to execute those changes. CT did not include this procedure.

2. CT involved more intensive work on clarifying and enhancing communication between the spouses and on increasing the spouses' understanding of each other's values and feelings. BMT involved some communication training, but primarily to develop skills necessary for constructing behavior change agreements.[3]

Process Analyses

There were two measures of therapist behavior: therapist self-report and ratings of the therapy tapes. The self-report data were obtained at the end of each session by having therapists estimate the percentage of time spent doing structured exercises designed to improve communication, working on behavior change agreements, and/or working on enhancing communication through feedback, modeling, and identifying problematic behavior.

The behavioral ratings of the therapy tapes were conducted by five undergraduates trained to a 75% agreement criterion on a therapist behavior code, who were unaware of the hypotheses regarding differences between the treatment groups. The following are brief descriptions of the eight categories for which data were analyzed:[4] (1) introducing or conducting a structured communication exercise; (2) working on behavior change agreements or compromises, for example, working with the spouses' lists of desired behaviors; (3) offering a concrete suggesion regarding a change in communication patterns at home; (4) giving positive feedback on communication; (5) offering a concrete suggestion about an alternative way of behavior at home; (6) giving positive feedback on a noncommunication behavior that has occurred at home; (7) reflecting, clarifying, making a summary statement of what has been said; (8) helping spouses examine and explore their own feelings and/or the feelings of their partner.

Twenty-minute samples of one-half of the therapy sessions were rated; the rating interval was 5 minutes. Thus, for each session, raters recorded whether or not a particular behavior occurred in each of four consecutive 5-minute intervals. Reliability checks were made on 26% of the tapes, although the raters did not know what the percentage was or which ratings would be checked. The percentage agreement procedure was used for calculating reliability rather than the Pearson product-moment correlation, because of the restricted range of the frequencies that could be recorded (0-4 occurrences could be scored across the 20-minute sample, as there were four 5-minute intervals). The reliabilities for each category ranged from 64% to 100%. The mean reliabilities across the eight categories for the three pairs of raters were 77%, 79%, and 75%.[5]

Postassessment and Follow-up Procedure

At postwait and posttreatment interviews, 29 of the 30 couples completed the major assessment measures. Couples who had participated in the treatment program were asked to rate their therapist's competence, empathy, likeableness, and concern.

At termination, the therapists were asked to provide change ratings for the problems the spouses identified at the pretherapy assessment on the PDQ. Nineteen of the 20 couples in treatment could be contacted at follow-up. At this time, the spouses completed the questionnaires and problem-solving discussion, rated the degree of change they had seen in their target problems since termination, and responded to several questions regarding their satisfaction with their marriage and the treatment program.

Results

Pretreatment Scores

To assess whether there were any initial differences between the three experimental groups, analyses of variance were computed on pretreatment measures, number of years married, and age. None of these analyses yielded significant F-ratios. Pretreatment scores on the MAT (X=78.6), the PCI (X=80.0), and the PFQ (X=57.7) all indicated that the couples were experiencing significant marital distress.

Differences Between Treatment Groups and the Wait-List Control

A MANOVA (P-stat version of MANOVA, Buhler & Buhler, 1978) was first conducted using the three major dependent measures (MAT, PCI, and PFQ). Subsequent MANOVAs were conducted with successive introduction of the spouses' change ratings. All of these analyses indicated significant differences among the groups; with all variables considered simultaneously, $F(14, 42)=2.72$; $p=.006$. However, the a priori contrasts on the specific measures yielded mixed results, in that difference scores on the MAT, the PFQ, and the behavioral ratings did not reflect significantly greater change in the treatment groups. The changes in MAT scores were certainly in the expected direction (CT--X=13.1; BMT--X=14.3; WL--X=6.0). However, there was a great deal of variability in response to treatment, which mitigated against obtaining significant differences. The difference scores on the PCI revealed significantly more change in the treatment groups than in the control [CT--X=6.8; BMT--X=11.9; WL--X=-.2; $t(27)=3.62$; $p<.001$]. In addition to difference score analyses, contrasts were performed on the change ratings the spouses gave at postwait or at therapy termination. With regard to marital problems, both husbands and wives in treatment reported significantly more positive change than did spouses in the control group [husbands--$t(27)=3.14$, $p<.01$; wives--$t(27)=3.41$, $p<.01$]. The husbands in treatment also reported significantly more desired change in their wives' behavior than did husbands in the control group, $t(26)=3.39$, $p<.01$. The data on wives' reports of desired changes indicated a similar trend, $t(27)=2.0$, $p<.06$. With regard to change in individual problems, the husbands in treatment did not report significantly greater change, although the wives did, $t(23)=2.91$, $p<.01$.[6] On the behavioral ratings of conflict resolution, the spouses in treatment did not demonstrate significantly more change than those in the control group on any of the categories.

Differences Between Treatment Groups and Follow-up Results

Following the MANOVA procedure, a second set of MANOVAs was conducted to assess potential differential effects of BMT and CT. The analysis involving the three major questionnaires (MAT, PCI, and PFQ) indicated a tendency, $F(3,16)=2.68$, $p<.08$, for BMT to produce more improvement than CT. However, following the introduction of the spouses' change ratings the groups were not significantly different.

Univariate analyses of data obtained at termination of therapy did not reveal any significant differences in outcome between the two treatment programs. The change ratings obtained from the therapists were consistent with those reported by the clients in that no significant differences between the treatments were revealed.[7] With regard to maintenance of gains during the follow-up period, spouses in both groups gave ratings indicating that during these four months there was no change to slight improvement in the problems they had identified; the questionnaire data indicated some deterioration during this period. Analyses of long-term therapy gains (pretreatment to follow-up) revealed one significant contrast: the frequency of wives' interruptions rated during the conflict resolution discussions decreased significantly more in BMT than CT, $t(16)=2.18$, $p<.05$. With regard to questionnaire data, there were no differences in the degree of change from pretreatment to follow-up, although t tests on dependent means revealed significant increases in scores on the MAT, $t(18)=2.76, p<.05$, and the PCI, $t(18)=2.97$, $p<.01$.

Predictors of Outcome

Correlational analyses revealed that, as expected, age and length of marriage were negatively correlated with outcome. Mean age of the couple was the stronger predictor; the correlations ranged from $-.76$ to $-.52$. The PFQ was the only self-report measure predictive of outcome; the couples' pretherapy score correlated .43 with the wives' ratings of change in their marital problems.

Age as a Predictor Variable

Due to the very strong correlations between age and outcome, the outcome data obtained from the PCI, MAT, and the behavioral ratings were reanalyzed with age as a classificatory variable. The couples in each of the three experimental groups were rank-ordered according to age and a median split was performed, creating two groups of Younger (Y) and Older (O) couples. The means for age and years married of these two groups of 15 couples were: (a)$x_Y=29.4$ years of age and 6.8 years married, and (b)$x_O=40.9$ years of age and 18 years married. Analyses of variance of pretreatment scores indicated no differences between the age groups on the MAT or the PCI.

To evaluate the effect of age upon response to treatment, 2×2 analyses of variance were conducted. Analyses of MAT and PCI data revealed a significant main effect of age [MAT: $F(1,16)=5.46$, $p<.05$; PCI: $F(1,16)=8.38$, $p<.05$], indicating that the younger couples demonstrated more change and also revealed significant age by treatment interactions [MAT: $F(1,16)=5.10$, $p<.05$; PCI: $F(1,16)=8.16$, $p-.05$]. Testing for simple main effects revealed that BMT was significantly more effective with younger couples than with the older sample in terms of changes on both the MAT, $F(1,16)=10.56, p<.01$, and the PCI, $F(1,16)=16.94, p<.01$. For younger couples BMT produced significantly more change in PCI scores than did CT, $F(1,16)=11.93, P<.01$. This significant superiority of BMT over CT for younger couples was not reflected in the analysis of the MAT scores.

Dunnett's t tests revealed that on the MAT the young BMT group demonstrated significantly more change than the young control group, $t(24)=2.27, p<.05$; the young CT group did not. Mann-Whitney U tests, used to study the older sample because of heterogeneity of variances, revealed that older couples in CT changed significantly more than older couples in the control group, $U=4, n_1, n_2=5, 5, p<.05$, although older couples in BMT did not. With regard to the PCI, the young couples in the BMT group showed significantly more change than the young couples in the control group, $t(24)=5.51, p\leq.01$; the young couples in CT did not. For older couples, again the reverse pattern was obtained: CT produced significantly more change than the control, $t(24)=2.41$, $p\leq.05$; BMT did not.

Process Analyses

Therapist self-report. The therapists' ratings of their activities were averaged across the 10 sessions for each couple. T tests performed between the groups revealed the following significant differences in the therapists' reports: (1) More time was spent conducting structured exercises in communication skills in CT than in BMT, $t(18)=2.71$, $p<.05$; (2) More time was devoted to giving feedback on specific communication behaviors in CT than BMT, $t(18)=2.72$, $p<.05$; (3) More time was spent working on behavior change agreements in BMT than CT, $t(18)=-5.56$, $p<.001$.

Ratings of therapy tapes. The eight categories of therapist behavior were analyzed via $2\times2\times5$ (2 treatment groups by 2 time periods—first and second half of therapy—by 5 therapists) analyses of variance. These analyses revealed significant differences between the treatment groups on two categories: (1) behavior change agreements, $F(1,80)=9.14$, $p<.01$, and (2) positive feedback on behavior changes not related to communication, $F(1,80)<11.69$, $p\leqslant.001$. Results indicated that therapists were following the manuals and working on behavior change agreements more in the BMT group. The analysis of the category of communication exercises indicated a nonsignificant but suggestive trend toward more of these exercises being conducted in CT, $F(1,80)=2.99$, $p<.1$. There were significant main effects for time on two categories: positive feedback on communication, $F(1,80)=8.57$, $p<.01$, and on behavior changes, $F(1,80)=5.51$, $p<.05$, indicating that the therapists became more reinforcing as therapy progressed.

Clients' reactions to the treatment programs. The clients' ratings of their therapists were very high: using a 7-point scale, wives' ratings averaged 6.83 and the husbands' mean was 6.71 across the four personal characteristics of empathy, concern, likableness, and competence. There were no significant differences between the treatment groups reflected in the wives' ratings. However, the husbands in BMT rated their therapists as significantly more competent, $t(18)=-2.55$, $p<.05$, and more empathic, $t(18)=-2.24$, $p<.05$, than did the husbands in CT. At follow-up, 76% of the spouses reported that no new problems had developed in their marriage; 71% reported they were not in need of further marital therapy. However, although 79% of the husbands reported being satisfied with the number of sessions at termination, 58% of the wives felt they would have preferred more sessions. Even with this reservation, at termination, 18 of the 20 spouses in each treatment group noted that they would recommend the program to a friend. There were no significant differences between the treatment groups with regard to any of the above input from the clients.

Discussion

Couples in both treatment programs reported significantly more therapeutic gains than those in the control group. While an initial MANOVA with the three major questionnaires indicated a nonsignificant tendency for BMT to be superior to CT, the remaining analyses did not demonstrate differential effectiveness between the two programs. One implication is that such common variables as relationship and expectation effects were operating to produce the similar changes.

A major commonality between the two treatment programs was therapist attention to communication patterns. This overlap was necessitated by the authors' feeling that improving communication is essential to any viable approach to marital therapy. It could be argued that the BMT conducted in this study is unrepresentative of general clinical practice. However, there appears to have been a trend among behavioral marital therapists to place an increasing emphasis on communication enhancement (e.g., Liberman, 1970, to Liberman *et al.*, 1976; Stuart, 1969, to Stuart, 1976; Weiss *et al.*, 1973, to Weiss, 1978). In summarizing the research on BMT, Jacobson (1978a) speculated that the most effective element in the behavioral approach may be communication training, which is the element least unique to BMT. The results of the present study can be viewed as supportive of this speculation.

Although there was a clear overlap in the treatment programs, both the process analyses and the husbands' ratings of their therapists indicate procedural differences. The higher competence ratings given by the men to therapists in BMT may have been due to the fact that the therapists were more directive, and this style more closely fits the clients' image of a professional. One interpretation of the high ratings of empathy given in BMT is that the husbands felt the therapists were not only speaking empathically, but were showing understanding and "being" empathic by helping the couple construct behavior change agreements.

Possibly one of the most important findings of this study, and another clear indication of procedural differences between the programs, is the effect of age on outcome. While BMT varied tremendously in its effectiveness across the two age groups, CT had a similar effect for the two samples. The age by treatment interactions and the comparisons with the waiting list indicated that BMT would be the treatment of choice for younger couples and CT should be used for older couples. One hypothesis regarding this differential effectiveness is that younger couples do not yet have as rigid a structure in their relationship as couples who are married longer. Therefore, they may have been more willing to adopt a structure imposed by the therapist (i.e., that of negotiated change and written agreements). It is also possible that older couples have more dysfunctional communication patterns, although the pretherapy data did not indicate this.

One nonsignificant contrast between the treatment groups and the wait-list controls was on the MAT. The analyses of age by treatment interactions indicated that the differential effectiveness across age groups was one factor that mitigated against an overall successful treatment/control comparison. That is, even with a reduction to $n=5$, when the treatments were evaluated within the age group for which each was most appropriate, a significantly greater improvement was seen in couples in therapy as compared to those on the waiting list.

The husbands in treatment did not report significantly more change in their individual problems than those in the control group, although there was a significant treatment/control difference reflected in the wives' data on individual problems. One explanation for this difference between the men and women may lie in the fact that 53% of the husbands listed occupational or financial difficulties as one of their individual problems, and these problems are not particularly amenable to marital therapy. Another hypothesis is that because 73% of the women were houswives and thus presumably very dependent upon their marital relationship as a source of gratification, an improvement in the marital relationship would in turn lead to more improvement in the wives' individual adjustment than in the husbands'.

Summary

The major conclusion that can be drawn from the present study is that both BMT and CT are promising therapeutic approaches for alleviating marital distress. Both produced positive changes in the couple's relationships that exceeded those evidenced by a wait-list control group and that were maintained during a 4-month follow-up. One interpretation of the observed similarity in outcome is that communication enhancement is the effective component of the treatment programs. Further research is necessary to identify the process of change or the aspects of CT that contribute significantly to outcome; e.g., clarifying expectations, providing emotional support, obtaining validation for one's viewpoint, or decreasing hostile interchanges. The data indicating differential effectiveness across age groups need replication but have clear implications for both the refinement of therapeutic strategies and the improvement of research methodology.

The two treatment programs investigated have clearly different theoretical underpinnings. Yet, as already noted, BMT has been modified over the past several years to include an increasing emphasis on communication. The opposite trend may be occurring with regard to CT. The Conjugal Relationship Enhancement Program which was developed from Rogers' therapeutic approach, in that spouses were exclusively taught empathic skills (Ely et al., 1973), has also been modified. A more recent description of this program includes a treatment module labeled "Communication on Problem Solving," which involves such techniques as compromise and bargaining (Rappaport, 1976). Thus, the two approaches are merging, each drawing on the techniques of the other. However, the theoretical conceptualizations remain disparate and until recently the investigators have not cited each other. Particularly in light of the present study, it would seem advisable to begin collaborative projects with the goals of synthesizing an integrated theory of marital distress and developing a multi-modal treatment program.

REFERENCES

Azrin, N. H., Naster, B. J. & Jones, R. Reciprocity counseling: A rapid learning-based procedure for marital counseling. *Behaviour Reserach and Therapy*, 1973, *11*, 365–382.

Beck, D. F. Research findings on the outcomes of marital counseling. In D. H. L. Olson (Ed.), *Treating relationships*. Lake Mills, Iowa: Graphic Publishing Co., 1976.

Buhler, S., & Buhler, R. *P-stat 78 Users Manual*. Princeton: P-Stat, Inc., 1978.

Ely, A. L., Guerny, B. G., & Stover, L. Efficacy of the training phase of conjugal therapy. *Psychotherapy: Theory, Research and Practice*, 1973, *10*, 201–207.

Everett, C. A. The Masters Degree in marriage and family therapy. *Journal of Marriage and Family Therapy*, 1979, *5*, 7–13.

Greer, S. E., & D'Zurilla, T. J. Behavioral approaches to marital discord and conflict. *Journal of Marriage and Family Counseling*, 1975, *1*, 299–315.

Gurman, A. S., & Kniskern, D. P. Research on marital and family therapy: Progress, perspective and prospect. In S. L. Garfield & A. E. Bergin (Eds.), *Handbook of psychotherapy and behavior change: An empirical analysis* (2nd ed.). New York: Wiley, 1978.

Jacobson, N. S. Problem-solving and contingency contracting in the treatment of marital discord. *Journal of Consulting and Clinical Psychology*, 1977, *45*, 92–100.

Jacobson, N. S. A review of the research on the effectiveness of marital therapy. In T. J. Paolino, Jr. & B. S. McCrady (Eds.), *Marriage and marital therapy: Psychoanalytic, behavioral and systems theory perspectives*. New York: Brunner/Mazel, 1978. (a)

Jacobson, N. S. Specific and nonspecific factors in the effectiveness of a behavioral approach to marital discord. *Journal of Consulting and Clinical Psychology*, 1978, *46*, 442–452. (b)

Jacobson, N. S., & Martin, B. Behavioral marriage therapy: Current status. *Psychological Bulletin*, 1976, *83*, 540–556.

Kahn, M. Non-verbal communication and marital satisfaction. *Family Process*, 1970, *9*, 449–456.

Kimmel, D., & Van der Veen, F. Factors of marital adjustment in Locke's Marital Adjustment Test. *Journal of Marriage and the Family*, 1974, *36*, 57–63.

Liberman, R. Behavioral approaches to family and couple therapy. *American Journal of Orthopsychiatry*, 1970, *40*, 106–118.

Liberman, R. P., Levine, J., Wheeler, E., Sanders, N., & Wallace, C. J. Marital therapy in groups. A comparative evaluation of behavioral and interactional formats. *Acta Psychiatrica Scandinavica*. Supplementum 266, 1976.

Locke, H. J., & Wallace, K. M. Short marital-adjustment and prediction tests: Their reliability and validity. *Marriage and Family Living*, 1959, *21*, 251–255.

Murstein, B. I., & Beck, G. D. Person perception, marriage adjustment, and social desirability. *Journal of Consulting and Clinical Psychology*, 1972, *39*, 396–403.

Navran, L. Communication and adjustment in marriage. *Family Process*, 1967, *6*, 173–184.

Nichols, W. C. Education of marriage and family therapists: Some trends and implications. *Journal of Marriage and Family Therapy*, 1979, *5*, 19–28.

O'Leary, K. D., & Turkewitz, H. Methodological errors in martial and child treatment research. *Journal of Consulting and Clinical Psychology*, 1978, *46*, 747–758. (a)

FAMILY STUDIES REVIEW YEARBOOK

O'Leary, K. D., & Turkewitz, H. Marital therapy from a behavioral perspective. In T. J. Paolino, Jr. &
    B. S. McCrady (Ed.s), *Marriage and marital therapy: Psychoanalytic, behavioral and systems
    theory perspectives.* New York: Brunner/Mazel, 1978. (b)
Olson, D. H., & Ryder, R. G. Inventory of Marital Conflicts (IMC): An experimental interaction
    procedure. *Journal of Marriage and the Family,* 1970, *32,* 443–448.
Patterson, G. R., Hops, H., & Weiss, R. L. Interpersonal skills training for couples in early stages of
    conflict. *Journal of Marriage and the Family,* 1975, *37,* 295–303.
Rappaport, A. F. Conjugal Relationship Enhancement Program. In D. H. L. Olson (Ed.), *Treating
    relationships.* Lake Mills: Graphic Publishing Co., 1976.
Satir, V. *Conjoint family therapy. A guide to theory and technique* (Rev. ed.). Palo Alto: Science and
    Behavior Books, Inc., 1967.
Strodtbeck, F. L. Husband-wife interaction over revealed differences. *American Sociological Review,*
    1951, *16,* 468–473.
Stuart, R. B. Operant-interpersonal treatment for marital discord. *Journal of Consulting and
    Clinical Psychology,* 1969, *33,* 675–682.
Stuart, R. B. An operant interpersonal program for couples. In D. H. L. Olson (Ed.), *Treating
    relationships.* Lake Mills: Graphic Publishing Co., 1976.
Weiss, R. L. The conceptualization of marriage from a behavioral perspective. In T. J. Paolino, Jr. &
    B. S. McCrady (Eds.), *Marriage and marital therapy: Psychoanalytic, behavioral and systems
    theory perspectives.* New York: Brunner/Mazel, 1978.
Weiss, R. L. Hops, H., & Patterson, G. R. A framework for conceptualizing marital conflict: A
    technology for altering it, some data for evaluating it. In L. A. Hamerlynck, L. C. Handy, & E. J.
    Mash (Eds.), *Behavior change: Methodology, concepts, and practice.* Champaign: Research
    Press, 1973.

NOTES

[1]The treatment manuals are available from the authors. Interested readers should send $2 to cover
the costs of printing and mailing.
[2]A copy of the communication code can be obtained from the authors.
[3]A detailed clinical discussion of the strategies and difficulties of constructing behavior change
agreements and enhancing communication may be found in O'Leary and Turkewitz (1978b).
[4]Some of the categories in the original therapist behavior code were not included in the data
analyses because of either low reliability or extremely low frequency.
[5]The procedure for selecting the therapy sessions to be rated is described in an extended manuscript,
available from the authors.
[6]Degrees of freedom vary because one husband could not identify any desired changes in his wife,
and four of the women did not report any individual problems.
[7]Analyses of additional data obtained from the therapists regarding their reaction to the clients and
the treatment program may be found in the first author's dissertation.

This report presents salient issues for therapists in understanding and treating the remarried (Rem, second, blended, reconstituted or step) family. The structure of the remarried family is differentiated from that of the intact family. Specific treatment goals for Rem families are elaborated and various treatment modalities advocated. The need to include former spouses and to consider the metafamily system are discussed. Common reactions and difficulties engendered in therapists when working with Rem systems are explicated.

44

IMPROVING FUNCTIONING OF THE REMARRIED FAMILY SYSTEM

Clifford J. Sager,* Elizabeth Walker, Hollis Steer Brown, Helen M. Crohn, and Evelyn Rodstein

In 1976 we began to be more intensely aware that the customary family and child therapy methods of our agency[2] were not adequately meeting the needs of the growing population of remarried (Rem, blended, second, reconstituted or step) families seen in our clinics. The family systems were different and more complex than those of the usual intact family or even the so-called single parent family. Old models were no longer applicable. A special service with its own staff, the Remarried Consultation Service, was established to study the phenomenon of the remarried (Rem) family in its many polymorphous states[3]. Our objective was to develop a better understanding of the structure and dynamics of Rem, and to determine improved and preventive measures.

We define the Rem family as one that is created by the marriage (or living together in one domicile) of two partners, one or both of whom have been married previously and was divorced or widowed, with or without children who visit or reside with them. The couple and the children (custodial or visiting) comprise the Rem family system. The *metafamily* system is composed of the Rem family plus former spouses, grandparents, stepgrandparents, aunts, uncles and others who may have significant input into the Rem system. The children are part of *each* of their bioparents' household systems. Because of the high divorce rate, both the Rem system and the metafamily system have now become permanent common family variations.

Visher and Visher (1979) were the first to publish a professional volume on stepfamilies, in which they emphasized a meaningful prophylactic approach. Walker, et al. (1979) recently prepared an annotated bibliography of the literature on Rem and in another article, Sager, et al. (1980) reviewed the areas of our knowledge of Rem and step families.

*Clifford J. Sager, MD, is a Clinical Professor of Psychiatry, New York Hospital—Cornell Medical College Center, Payne Whitney Clinic. He and the other authors are currently[1] (June 1980) on the staff of The Remarried Consultation Service, Jewish Board of Family and Children's Services, Inc., 120 West 57th Street, New York, N.Y. 10019

Reprinted from Volume 7, Number 1 of *Journal of Marital and Family Therapy*. Copyright © 1981 American Association for Marriage and Family Therapy. Reprinted by permission.

In this article we shall present briefly how the Rem family structure differs from the intact family, some principles of therapeutic intervention and the problems of clinicians working with Rem[4].

Structural Differences

In a *nuclear family,* the membership is well defined and the family boundaries clearly delineate "external" from "internal." There is input from significant others, but this input does not usually endanger the system's functioning. Family expectations, rules, roles, tasks and purposes are also clear. They conform with the generational boundaries and sexual taboos defined by society.

In contrast, membership in the *Rem system* is open to interpretation: some members may belong in two systems, or they may feel they do not belong at all in either parental household. The system has permeable boundaries (Messinger, 1976), and significant input from others in the metafamily. Not only former spouses, grandparents and children, but institutions can have marked impact on the Rem family's viability and functioning.

Generational and sexual boundaries are often vague and can be more easily trespassed. Expectations, rules, roles and tasks in the Rem system have remained ill defined by society. Each Rem system has to generate itself with no pattern on which to model itself. Rem marriages start with at least one spouse having suffered the ending of a primary relationship with all its attendant pain, and with continuing responsibilities and ties to children and possibly ties to a former spouse. Often they are financially encumbered. Children have suffered serious life disruption and losses. These factors affect and condition future attitudes and relationships.

When we think of the structure of Rem, we always take into account the metafamily system. Thus, we disagree with the emphasis of Ransom, et al. (1979) who only examine the type of Rem family in which a child is raised primarily in one family unit. The authors seem to deny the existence of the metafamily, and advocate "the actual reconstitution of the family" as the objective of the new marriage. That is, the stepfather plays the role of father to child, and the role of husband to wife, reconstituting a facsimile of the intact nuclear family.

We believe this "reconstituted" family model denies the realities of the existence of the metafamily system when the latter should be considered. We have observed a large number of possible Rem structures and are impressed as are Baideme, et al. (1979) with the many times *both* bioparents desire to participate in child rearing and will share responsibility.

When a divorced or separated couple has children, there is first a two *single parent phase.* "Single parent family" is an erroneous appellation except when one parent has disappeared and abdicated all responsibility, contact and support. When one parent remarries there is then a Rem household system and a single parent household system. Children are part of both of these systems, each of which is part of the metafamily system. Not to comprehend or to ignore this dual family structure makes incomprehensible much that otherwise may be readily understood on a structural, dynamic and behavioral basis.

We do agree with Ransom that the Rem family must be consolidated—but not as a replacement for the nuclear family! It will always be different. To gloss over this difference makes for a common source of trouble for the Rem family and for the work of the therapist. A guiding principle for our work flows from our recognition of the necessity to involve both bioparents and any stepparents in the treatment process when any of these have input into the system that affects the others. Using the potential of the metafamily system does make the task for families and therapist more difficult, but ultimately, more rewarding for all.

Entry to Treatment

Treatment with the clinical population of Rem families can be an effective and exciting process for family and therapist, but also a time consuming one because of the complexity of the family systems involved. Instead of having been a system that functioned well at one time and then began to malfunction, Rem families often have not been able to consolidate themselves into a viable functioning unit except perhaps for a brief "honeymoon" period. Characteristically, these families call for help when in crisis and desperate, seeing the spectre of another "failure" hanging over the adults' heads. It is not uncommon for a family to arrive at the point of having expelled a member or at the point of doing so before asking for help. The pressure on the therapist to try immediately to rectify the situation is tremendous and must be resisted.

Evaluation: Initial Phases

Therapy starts with the first phone call. When an emergency exists (that which is beyond crisis) we attend first to the emergency while simultaneously beginning the process of evaluating the metafamily system. Regardless of what else may be transacted in these early sessions, the mere seeking and ordering of information brings knowledge, intelligence and structure to the family members as it does to the therapist, when it is a shared process.

As in treatment with nuclear families, the therapist has the greatest leverage in the initial phases to involve everyone who is part of, or who affects the system. Once therapy has begun, it is often more difficult to include a former spouse because the therapist is likely to be viewed with hostility and identified as being on the Rem system's side. We do not refuse to see those members who ask for help if we cannot enlist the others at the start, but neither do we accept a simple NO—it spurs us to utilize our ingenuity. In the process that ensues the metafamily learns how interrelated they are and when and how to disengage appropriately.

Whoever calls for help, whether it be bioparent or stepparent or child, we make every effort to include both bioparents and stepparents from the outset. Frequently clients will articulate anxiety about including their former mate, or the stepparent might be anxious or jealous about being present with the former spouse due to ex-spouse hostilities or hidden collusive affection. The therapist can hear the concern and point out that since the child lives in *both* families, it is in the best interests of the child for the adults to work together; *it is the parenting and stepparenting issues, not the ex-marital hurts or financial issues that will be addressed.* The therapist is active in setting clear limits in sessions which include ex-spouses and stepparents. Only when all adults agree should one include in the therapeutic contract attempts to resolve residual pain and anger or to put residual affection and love into appropriate perspective.

Work with the metafamily requires therapeutic flexibility. It may be necessary to see each bioparent separately in order to establish a connection and promote comfort with the therapist before setting up joint meetings. If the therapist is already identified with one partner of the system, it may be necessary initially to enlist a co-therapist to make the connection to the other partner, who may have been excluded. Sometimes we employ an adaptation of McGregor's multiple impact family therapy by assigning a different therapist to each subsystem of the metafamily. However, this is a costly luxury which cannot be continued for a long period of time.

Use of the Genogram

The genogram is an effective tool which we use initially with the family to map out the metafamily, and to understand fairly quickly the complicated structure of this particular Rem family.[5] We find that the multiple changes that have occurred, and most likely the multiple losses also, are dramatically highlighted and may facilitate a delayed mourning reaction in some family members. We inquire about the children's bioparents, even if one of them isn't present, to soften any loyalty conflict a child may have between his parents and/or stepparent, and to support his needed connection to both. The therapist's implicit and explicit recognition of the other important persons in the child's life does more than any statement could. Information specific to the Rem situation can be asked for directly as well as deduced from observation and interaction, including data on:

1. *The present Rem unit:* living in, living out and visiting children; when they visit, how often, holiday schedules, who makes school visits on parent's day and other sensitive living arrangements in the household.

2. *How the present Rem unit was formed:* the background of the couple's meeting and courtship. How and if the children were prepared for the remarriage; if the former partner(s) knew, were informed and by whom. Changes in residence, financial arrangements, and other cathected parameters.

3. *The two single parent household structures:* the quality and quantity of time spent with each child by each parent; the role of grandparents, the relation between the separated spouses during this period.

4. *The original nuclear family system:* when, why and how this was dissolved; what each adult and child's understanding of that dissolution was in the past and currently. Dates of actual physical separation and of the legal divorce.

5. *The families of origin of all the adults:* both Rem spouses and former spouses, assessment of input by each significant person both current and past.

It is important to observe overt and covert alliances, power structures, levels of intimacy and bonds between members, and patterns of inclusion and exclusion in the system. However, one need not be compulsive about history taking: basic facts first, then the rest unfolds as therapy goes on.

Two other areas in Rem are crucial to learn about as rapidly as possible: mate choice and life cycles.

1. *Mate choice:* the unconscious as well as conscious factors determining mate choice for the second as well as the first marriage. Did those who are married more than once learn from past experiences; is their choice appropriate; does it reflect a positive change in their level of maturity; are there reasonable expectations and goals? Are marriage contracts of the couple concordant, complementary or in conflict (Sager, 1976, p. 164)?

2. *Life cycles:* life, marital and family cycle needs of Rem couples. Are the life cycle needs of each marital partner consistent with the other partner's and with the needs of their Rem family? To illustrate the marital cycle problem:

> An older man with adolescent children remarries a younger woman who has no children. She accepts in good faith his condition that they will not have children together. After a while her desire to have children with him becomes a pressing need. He persists in his position and wants to hold her to their "contract."

To illustrate the family cycle problem:

> A woman with elementary school age children who live with her remarries a man who knows that she expects him to be a caring stepfather. He agrees, denying his own needs to have a child-like relationship with his wife. He increasingly refuses to accept any responsibility for parenting.

Treatment Goals

Goals are not a simple matter; they reflect the multiple levels of the determinants of behavior. It is necessary for the therapist to be alert to the desires beyond awareness which put obstacles in the way of attaining expressed goals. Masochistic or self-defeating needs can be revealed during anamnestic data collection by noting self-defeating patterns and in behavior and interactions observed in the family sessions. Often such patterns can be bypassed in therapy. As change begins to occur, the therapist should expect to see resistance initiated by the obstructor, often with the unconscious collusion of other system members. *If negative goals cannot be bypassed, they must be brought into the open and dealt with more directly.* This is one of the many complexities of human system behavior that defeats attempts at cook book therapy and requires a broad spectrum of skills and knowledge.

There are immediate, intermediate and long range treatment goals. Individuals and the family as a system are helped to define achievable goals. For example, when a child says, "I want to feel like I felt when my parents were married," it is usually meant, "I want my parents reunited," a goal that cannot be the order of the day. One then tries to help the child to achieve a more reasonable goal: to accept thoroughly the loss and irretrievability of the original nuclear family, experiencing the anger and sadness which leads to acceptance.

The therapist too may have goals which must be shared with the family. Those goals that are decided upon must be agreed to by all involved. Goals and contracts are under constant evaluation and review as treatment progresses, and this work forms the essence of the therapeutic process.

Common treatment goals with Rem families include many that are premised on acceptance and enhancement of the effectiveness of the metafamily system. For example, an early goal may be to stop scapegoating a child. This might be approached by helping former spouses and their own biofamilies (grandparents, etc.) to eschew fixing blame for the termination of the former marriage. Then adult anger can be worked through or more readily bypassed for the children's needs, and guilt or retribution for past acts need not be utilized as motivation for current action, thus allowing bio and stepparents to share some responsibility for child rearing.

Some other goals frequently encountered are:

1. To consolidate the Rem couple as a unit and establish their authority in the system.
2. To consolidate the parental authority in the system among bio and stepparents with the formation of a collaborative co-parenting team.
3. As a corollary to item 2, to help children deal with and minimize the continuance and exacerbation of loyalty binds.
4. To facilitate mourning of the nuclear family, former partner, old neighborhoods, friends and way of life.
5. To be certain there is a secure place for the child's development through optimal utilization of the entire metafamily system.
6. To help family members accept and tolerate their differences from some idealized intact family model. These include differences such as: lack of complete control of money, children; differences in feelings for and of the bioparent and stepparent; differences in rules and expectations in two households; different levels of bonding in Rem household as opposed to nuclear household.

Therapy is structured to achieve goals in as orderly a progression as possible, accented by a dash of the serendipitous. Rarely have we had a treatment plan, however, that did not have to be revised (Sager, 1957). For example:

> The presenting complaint was of a child's recent poor functioning in school. Evaluation indicates the child is living in a chaotic metafamily system in which none of the adults take responsibility for setting limits with him, and that this situation began following his mother's remarriage. In the Rem family there is role confusion between mother and her spouse—each is expecting the other to parent the child. Biofather has abdicated his parental position, not only communicating hastily and uneasily with his former wife about the child but also focusing only on entertaining the child and giving him anything that he wants when they are together. Both of the Rem adults are frustrated because the

child's needs seem to interfere constantly with the fulfillment of their love needs for each other.

The immediate goal is to help all the adults: biomother, biofather and stepfather form a collaborative parenting team and begin to clarify their parenting expectations both with each other and the child. Once this is accomplished the chaos diminishes and the child's functioning in school is restored. The Rem couple then request further help in consolidating their relationship with each other, which becomes a new treatment goal. Biofather seeks help to work through his feelings about the loss of his former wife and family; which had been stirred anew by the remarriage and which he could now see had been interfering with his capacity to function optimally as a single parent.

Goals of the two bioparental systems may be mutually exclusive, as may be those of any subsystem or individual vis-a-vis another. These goal differences must be clearly delineated to determine if they are real or only apparent; if real, can they be reconciled or negotiated in some fashion? Some are so pervasive and mutually exclusive that family members and therapist may have to accept that the system is not viable.

Treatment

To achieve the immediate and long range goals, we have three general theoretical systems of psychological treatment available to us: insight methods such as the various psychoanalytic systems, Gestalt and transactional analysis; methods based on general systems theory such as Minuchin's structured therapy, or Bowen's detriangulation therapy; and those approaches derived from learning theory such as behavior modification methods. Although many of our techniques are based on treating the family and metafamily systems, we also utilize our knowledge of individual intrapsychic dynamics and couple dynamics to determine some of our interventions as well as utilizing tasks and positive reinforcement techniques. The individual should not become lost in the system; neither should the therapist lose sight of the power of the family system to shape and alter behavior.

Common Treatment Issues with Rem

We have referred previously to some Rem couples' inability to consolidate into a viable marital unit, meeting the love needs of the adults and yet allowing them to carry on with parenting and other appropriate family needs. Often there are bonds and priorities as powerful, or more powerful elsewhere, which can produce crisis, confusion and jealousy in the current couple relationship. Such factors may lead to a concomitant failure to resolve pivotal marital issues of intimacy, power, exclusion-inclusion of others, and to failure to negotiate and resolve their individual and joint marital contracts (Sager, 1976; 1979).

These failures may have come about through a variety of circumstances. Parents often experience guilt or confusion between loyalty to their children of a former spouse and to a current spouse. The parent, not the child or new spouse, must take prime responsibility for confronting and resolving this resolvable dilemma. One partner may have failed to mourn, appropriately work through and accept the loss of his/her former spouse. Other couples may be involved in a bond of either pseudomutuality or pseudohostility (Wynne, 1958). This bond inevitably intrudes destructively into the relationship. Conversely, the former spouse may have refused to accept termination of the marital relationship, and may constantly intrude him/herself into the current pairing, at times using the children for this purpose. The remarried partner may covertly condone this intrusion out of his/her own guilt over the end of one marriage. When a former spouse intrudes, the marital bond is defused.

Some parents develop an overly close bond to a child during the two single parent household phase. Later, neither the parent nor the child is able to alter the quality and intensity of this bond in order to make room for the entry/inclusion of the new marital partner into the system. It is a process that usually takes time and patience. The new marital partner may have been unable or unwilling to help his mate separate from the child and move into a closer couple pairing without arousing defensiveness and drawing hostility onto himself. *The difficulty in keeping the adult-pairing love separate from parent-child love reappears as a common problem of Rem families.*

To the child, remarriage represents finality and the loss of the dream of reinstating the "old" family. Acceptance of reality may be postponed and the child instead can enter into disruptive denial or undoing maneuvers.

Treatment Modalities

Starting with knowledge of family systems theory and a conviction regarding the correctness of the concept of multiple genetic and environmental inputs to all individuals and family systems, we approach working with the Rem family, keeping in mind family structure and individual function, values and adaptations. Some issues are specific to Rem families, some emotional and interactional family system dynamics are more generalized. Our point of view, both for evaluation and treatment, is to conceptualize the problems in terms of the metafamily system while keeping in mind the needs of the individual members and the two bioparent systems as well as the specific Rem unit. Our primary therapeutic process is to refocus and redefine the problem with the family in terms of the whole system and its subsequent needs and responsibilities. In Rem, the therapist helps the family understand the expanded system: its differences from a nuclear family, the appropriate significance and role, if any, of the metafamily non-household members and how they all may affect one another. This process facilitates de-scapegoating children, who often are blamed for the Rem family's troubles. Insight methods are utilized if and when the therapist views them as applicable. When tasks are used, we are concerned with any resistance to carry them out and the feelings evoked by them as well as the actual effects on individuals and the system of having completed the task. The reasons and feelings surfaced by an incompleted task are often of great therapeutic import. The therapist should choose tasks that are designed to produce a specifically predicted behavioral and/or attitudinal change.

Key treatment questions include whom to include, when to include them and for what purposes, and which treatment modalities to use, when and for what ends. There are no hard and fast rules, and sensitive timing is of the essence. Familiarity and ease in working with a variety of modalities is helpful. It is easier to begin immediately with everyone involved in the problem and then work down, breaking into subunits, than it is to begin with the microsystem (for instance the child), and try to include others later. If the Rem couple relationship is the presenting problem and the children are not involved, but there is clearly unfinished business with a prior partner, then a few couple sessions with the divorced pair, or individual sessions with that Rem partner may be held to further completion of the divorce, while at the same time moving into couples work with the current partners. We do not necessarily include all metafamily or Rem members in every session. However, we try to keep in mind the different subsystems and how the present parts fit into the whole dynamic mosaic. The capacity for both flexibility and activity on the part of the therapist is crucial; successful treatment depends on the therapist's comfort with moving in and out of the different parts of the system easily, and with treatment in different modalities, including family, couple, individual and child, as indicated. Since emotions in Rem families often run high, the therapist must be comfortable in being active and able to take charge of the sessions. These abilities are particularly necessary when: 1) the session includes the former spouse; 2) there is a psychotic individual; 3) members are manipulative or form an alliance to defeat the therapist, or 4) the family's underlying feelings of hopelessness and despair are rampant.

Multiple Impact Therapy With Families

At times we use a modified multiple impact therapy model (McGregor, 1964) with our metafamily systems. A different therapist is assigned to work with, support and model for separate subsystems, such as children, a former ex-spouse, or grandparents. In a large conjoint meeting the therapist may then act as supporter, interpreter, advocate, negotiator, and spokesperson as well as therapist for that part of the system. This modality is particularly helpful with extremely chaotic, polarized or conflicted systems, or when there are individuals who would be unable to enter treatment which he/she may consider as hostile territory, without the added support of his or her therapist. It is also recommended for large systems; for instance, where both of the bioparents are remarried and have several children with needs different from those of the original and the new family. It may be necessary to use this modality only initially around a crisis, and for a brief period until some resolution takes place and clear goals are agreed upon. Ongoing treatment may then proceed as usual. We try not to use co-therapists, unless absolutely necessary; for instance, when there is strong conflict between one subunit and another. Co-therapy is sometimes prohibitively expensive. A solo therapist can achieve similar results through separate appointments with different subsystems of the metafamily, for instance, with the Rem system and with the single parent system, prior to meeting with the entire system. Another excellent way is to split a session, seeing one subsystem for part of the session, the second subsystem for another part of the session, and then all together.

The Use Of Groups

Couples groups often are the treatment of choice for many Rem couples. Our experience demonstrates that this modality best addresses several important problem sources in the Rem system, notably, the lack of consolidation of the couple; ill-defined mourning of the lost relationship and spouse; and guilt and conflict about children. The group can provide a structure for the couples, separate from their children and stepchildren. It provides time and privacy to work on their mutual contracts with each other, support from others in the same situation, struggling with similar issues. At the same time they have the opportunity to be "reparented" in a corrective emotional experience with therapist and one another. Family meetings separate from the group can be held periodically, both for the purpose of helping the couple integrate their changes into the system and to facilitate the children's integration into the Rem family.

We have tried multiple family therapy groups (Lacquer, 1972) of unselected Rem families but *do not* recommend this modality for families who are very chaotic and needy. Further, MFT makes it more difficult to include former spouses and other metafamily members because to include these makes the group unwieldy and is disruptive of on-going processes as many metafamily members need be only transiently engaged in treatment. Adolescents, though, have found MFT to be beneficial. As a result we currently advocate couples groups, and separate groups for children of Rem, particularly for adolescents, who often feel like "orphans" in their Rem families, and isolated from their peers.

We are also experimenting with including the children in the couples group for some sessions, after the couples have been successful at consolidating themselves, and are then ready to address the parenting issues directly, within the supportive framework of the group. We will return to the use of MFT with better consolidated Rem couples, whose situations are not so chaotic as were those in our earlier experiences.

The Therapist

The therapist working with Rem family systems is subjected to constant confrontation with his own emotions and value systems. The first area of emotional assault on the therapist has to do with male/female relatedness and systems of loyalties and consanguinity. The therapist may have values markedly different from those that have allowed Rem adults to divorce and remarry, live with someone, or break up a marriage. Actions and feelings of various Rem family members touch off emotional reactions based on experiences the therapist has had, has feared will happen or has not dared to bring about in his or her own life because of guilt, anxiety, superego constraints or cultural considerations. True countertransferential reactions may also occur wherein patients and/or their system enmesh the therapist and he reacts the way individuals or the system unconsciously set him up to react.

The complexities of the Rem systems, the sense of despair, hopelessness and loss, and the chaos and crisis that are at work may spill over into the therapists' personal life. We found ourselves putting our personal relationships on "hold" and avoiding decisions about making or ending commitments to others. Depression and despair were common reactions without clarity about the source of these feelings, as were making moralistic judgments about clients.

These reactions can best be dealt with through the use of a trusting and supportive group of peers; our Service has provided that for the staff. Consultation, supervision, and the use of the group to help individual therapists resolve personal reactions has mitigated some of the anxiety and pain which seems built into the work with Rem systems. At the same time our team approach has facilitated consolidation of our clinic families, who felt cared about and "special" to the unit, and less isolated once they knew that there was a specialized "team" of therapists supporting them. Within the team, we have used ourselves to identify specific areas of vulnerability for therapists working with Rem systems and we will outline them briefly here.

Unrealistic Expectations: Many Rem couples marry with the hope that this marriage will right all previous relationship disappointments, including both parental and past marital "failures," and that *this* time, their marriage contract and expectations, even if unrealistic *and* magical—will be fulfilled. Other family members may also expect their unmet needs will now be gratified.

If the therapist accepts the unrealistic expectations, he too may be dragged down into feelings of hopelessness that so often characterize the clinic population of Rem. To accept the fantasies is to get enmeshed in disappointment and disillusionment and will lead to paralysis and despair.

Denial: If the adult partners are pseudomutual and deny their differences, conflicts and disappointments, they are likely to focus their problems on a child or children who are scapegoated. The therapist, sensing that certain material is forbidden, may join the denial and also displace to the child, thereby encouraging the pseudomutuality and scapegoating. Therapists may also collude with the family in their denial of the importance of their history and the metafamily as relevant to the present problem. All too often children are told by their remarrying parent that the marriage is for the child's benefit or welfare, the parent denying his/her own needs to the child. This type of denial may arouse critical feelings within the therapist that are often denied too and come out indirectly. The key is knowledge; the more the therapist knows about Rem, the less likely he is to join family members in their resistance and obfuscation.

Abandonment Fears: Loss and abandonment are prime issues for children and adults in Rem, and may trigger the therapists' own abandonment anxieties. Thus a therapist dealing with a child who has been deserted by a parent may be drawn into becoming the good parent for the child, reinforcing the child's unresolved feelings to his parent, instead of helping the child work through his feelings of loss, anger and disappointment. Similarly, children who have been abandoned often use abandonment as a threat: "If I can't have my way, I'll leave and go live with Daddy" or "I'll leave therapy." If the therapist joins with the child rather than challenging the threat and its meaning, then the therapist will become anxious and immobilized which will lead to great chaos in the system and in treatment. The child is left with the feeling that no one cares enough about him either to go after him or take him on.

Control Issues: The therapist may attempt to allay his anxiety by becoming overcontrolling, as do some harried stepparents, or by taking impulsive therapeutic action. He may rush too soon to try to impose order and consequently push the family away. He is likely to despair when the chaos does not right itself quickly in response to his interventions and may consciously or unconsciously dismiss the family. Ability to tolerate ambiguity and chaos is required along with patience and awareness of the process that needs to take place during treatment.

Summary

We have summarized a great deal in this paper, attempting to explain briefly the results of four years' work. As in all mental health areas, our prime concern must be prevention of distress and damage to people. What we have presented, although centered around theory and therapy, provides the underpinning for our prophylactic work. In our forthcoming book we will explain our therapeutic approach more comprehensively and discuss the important area of education and prevention. Working with this group of families clinically can be very rewarding. While the complexity of Rem can create problems, it also is the basis of the richness of relationships and experiences such a family can provide to the individual, satisfying a need we all have for a variety of encounters and emotions. When we work with these families we are attuned to both how they are alike and different from nuclear families. We attend to the metafamily as well as the Rem family, including all people who have an impact on the current situation. We look at the family's development over time and take an eclectic approach which emphasizes flexibility, understanding of behavioral and dynamic factors, goal directed work as well as the play of the therapists' own reactions in his or her intervention.

REFERENCES

Baideme, S. M., Hill, H. A. & Serritella, D.A. Conjoint family therapy following divorce: An alternative strategy. *International Journal of Family Counseling,* 1978, *6* (1), 55–59.

Bowen, M. *Family therapy in clinical practice,* New York: Jason Aronson, 1978.

Crohn, H. M., Sager, C. J., Rodstein, E., Brown, H. S. & Walker, E. Understanding and treating the child in the remarried family. In Abt. L. E. and Stuart, I. R., (Eds.) *Children of separation and divorce,* New York: Van Nostrand Reinhold, 1980.

Goldstein, J., Freud, A. & Solnit, A. J. *Beyond the best interest of the child.* New York: Free Press, 1973.

Guerin, P. J. & Penagast, E. G. Evaluation of family system and genogram. In Guerin, P.J. (Ed.) *Family therapy: Theory and practice,* New York: Gardner Press, 1976.

Lacquer, A. P. Mechanics of change in multiple family therapy. In Sager, C. J. and Kaplan, H. S. (Eds.). *Progress in group and family therapy.* New York: Brunner/Mazel, 1972.

MacGregor, R., Ritchie, A. M., Serrano, A. C. & Schuster, F. P. *Multiple impact therapy with families.* New York: McGraw-Hill, 1964.

Minuchin, S. *Families and family therapy.* Cambridge: Harvard University Press, 1974.

Random, J. W., Schlesinger, S. & Derdeyn, A. P. A stepfamily in formation. *American Journal of Orthopsychiatry,* 1979, *49* (1), 36–43.

Ranz, J. & Ferber A. How to succeed in family therapy. In Ferber, A., Mendelsohn, M. and Napier, A. (Eds.). *The book of family therapy.* Boston: Houghton Mifflin, 1973.

Sager, C. J. & Hunt, B. *Intimate partners—Hidden patterns in love relationships.* New York: McGraw-Hill, 1979.

Sager, C. J. The psychotherapist's continuous evaluation of his work, *The Psychoanalytic Review,* 1957, *44* (3), 298–312.

Sager, C. J. *Marriage contracts and couples therapy.* New York: Brunner/Mazel. 1976.

Sager, C. J., Brown, H. S., Crohn, H. M., Rodstein, E. & Walker, E. Remarriage revisited. *Family and Child Mental Health Journal,* 1980, *6*, 19–25.

Walker, K. N. & Messinger, L. Remarriage after divorce: Dissolution and reconstruction of family boundaries. *Family Process,* 1979, *18*, (2), 195–192.

Walker, L., Brown, H. S., Crohn, H. M., Rodstein, E., Zeisel, E. & Sager, C. J. An annotated bibliography of the remarried, the living together and their children. *Family Process,* 1979, *18*, 193–212.

Wynne, L. C., Ryckoff, I. N., Day, J. & Hirsch, S. I. Pseudomutuality in the family relations of schizophrenics. *Psychiatry,* 1958, *21*, 205–220.

Visher, Emily & Visher, John. *Stepfamilies,* New York: Brunner/Mazel, 1979.

NOTES

[1]With the exception of Elizabeth Walker, who is currently in private practice in New York City.

[2]Then, Jewish Family Service of New York City. In 1978 this agency merged with the Jewish Board of Guardians to form the Jewish Board of Family and Children's Services, Inc.

[3]Between May 1977 and April 1979, 213 Rem families were treated through this service, among them were 367 children. Data concerning these families is available in Crohn, Sager, et al. (1980).

[4]A book that will report more comprehensively on the results of our therapeutic and conceptual work with Rem families is now in preparation. It will include material about the important area of education and prevention.

[5]For a complete explanation of the genogram see Guerin (1976).

PAIR, acronym for Personal Assessment of Intimacy in Relationships, was developed as a tool for educators, researchers and therapists. PAIR provides systematic information on five types of intimacy: emotional, social, sexual, intellectual and recreational. Individuals, married or unmarried, describe their relationship in terms of how they currently perceive it (perceived) and how they would like it to be (expected). PAIR can be used with couples in marital therapy and enrichment groups.

45

ASSESSING INTIMACY
The Pair Inventory*

*Mark T. Schaefer** and David H. Olson***

Intimacy is a term widely used by marriage counselors and educators. The explosion of the marriage and family enrichment movement, precipitated by the "human potential" or "growth" movement, has developed a continually growing awareness of intimacy in relationships. It seems that highly marketable enrichment programs teach the "how to's" of being intimate. Enrichment may, in fact, casually be equated with movement toward intimacy. "Marriage Enrichment" implies change, growth, enhancement and development of already present ingredients in a relationship; and the assumed direction of this change and growth is from the non-intimate to the intimate.

Intimacy is sometimes assumed to be characteristic of the ideal type of marriage and family relationships. It is a word used casually, but few have tried to conceptualize it, operationalize it, or assess its impact on relationships. Research literature mentions the term with some frequency, but has barely paused to clearly conceptualize it, nor validate the nature of its presence in human relationships.

Our culture, unlike others, places a high value on intimacy and, although not restricted to marriage, most get married to seek and maintain it. It is considered to be the reward and benefit of friendship. Many developmental theorists include intimacy as a vital ingredient in their hierarchy of needs (Maslow, 1954; Erikson, 1950; Sullivan, 1953). Research with primates infers that without some meager degree of intimacy, humans cannot adequately develop (Harlow, 1971). The overriding predominance of intimacy as a cultural value, whether mythical or actual in occurrence, suggests the need for a clear, well-defined operational concept.

This paper explores the nature and multi-dimensional aspects of intimacy; delineates fundamental assumptions about it; demonstrates what is known about intimacy and describes a newly developed assessment measure of the concept called the *PAIR, (Personal Assessment of Intimacy in Relationships)*. Finally, it describes how the PAIR can be used in marriage counseling and enrichment programs.

*Copies of PAIR, a Counselor's Manual, Scoring Template, Answer Sheets and Profile Forms for five couples can be purchased for $20.00 by writing the second author.

**Mark T. Schaefer, PhD, Assistant Professor, Rural Physicians Associate Program, Medical School, University of Minnesota, Minneapolis, Minnesota 55455. David H. Olson, PhD, Professor, Family Social Science, University of Minnesota, St. Paul, Minnesota 55108.

Reprinted from Volume 7, Number 1 of *Journal of Marital and Family Therapy*. Copyright © 1981 American Association for Marriage and Family Therapy. Reprinted by permission.

Review of Literature

Historically, intimacy does not frequently appear in literature, but it is considered a significant dimension for some writers (Ferreira, 1964, Bowlby, 1958). Erikson (1950) includes it in his hierarchy of human development, referring to it as a critical developmental task in making the transition from adolescence to adulthood. Sullivan (1953) likewise associates "the need for intimacy" with the phases of life beginning in adolescence, describing it as the need "for collaboration with at least one other person." Angyal (1965) emphatically claims that the establishment and maintenance of a close relationship, whereby one "exists in the thought and affection of another" is the "crux of our existence from the cradle to the grave" (p. 19). He continues to outline the need to be "needed" in an intimate relationship as a fundamental precept to his theory.

Although lay persons and clinicians alike find Erikson's and Sullivan's insights to ring "true," how intimacy relates to any theory or what role it actually plays in development has proven to be difficult to define or to empirically test (Gruen, 1964). Harlow and Zimmerman (1959) have taken another track through their research on monkeys and human infants, demonstrating the need for affectionate responses with a more empirical approach.

Others include intimacy as a crucial variable in their work, but with few exceptions have not attempted to define it (Collins, 1974; Stone, 1973; Powers and Bultena, 1976; Strong, 1975). Often intimacy has been associated with dyadic patterns of conformity (Stone, 1973), the public nature of couple and parent-child relationships (Kanter, et al., 1975), or adolescent norms and peer expectations (Collins, 1974). Intimacy is often defined in terms of levels of sexual involvement, or level of courtship; that is, the greater the sexual involvement, the more intimacy.

In a social psychological vein, intimacy has been examined for its relationship to distance, eye contact, environment, and verbal behavior. Argyle and Dean (1965) assert that an equilibrium exists for any pair of individuals, and that the equilibrium point is a function of eye contact, physical proximity, discussion topic, amount of smiling, and assorted other related variables. They deduce that if one of these components of intimacy change, one or more of the others will shift in the reverse direction to maintain the equilibrium between the two individuals. Jourard and Friedman (1970) examined self-disclosure among strangers for its relationship to "distance." In one experiment they found that subjects increased disclosure time as distance decreased, and therefore concluded that the Argyle and Dean's "equilibrium" is not maintained when there is increasing trust and positive feelings toward the person that comes close (Cozby, 1973).

Intimacy has begun to gain attention in the field of aging and life-span analysis. Lowenthal and Haven (1968), in their analysis of interaction and adaptation in later stages of the lifespan, were "struck by the fact that the happiest and healthiest among them often seemed to be the people who were, or had been, involved in one or more close relationships" (p. 20). They claim that their data clearly supports the fact that there are other viable forms of intimacy which are not necessarily substitutes for, or supplements to, a stable heterosexual relationship. However, they do not attempt any alternate definitions.

While banking on some early work on friendship and aging (Rosow, 1967; Arth, 1962; Blau, 1961), they explored the depth of friendship with so-called confidants. Although the methods were crude, they found support for their assertion that the depth of intimacy is a key correlate in a person's ability to adapt over the lifespan. Lowenthal and Weiss (1976) propose that most men and women find energy and motivation to live autonomous, self-generating and satisfying lives only through the presence of one or more mutually supportive and intimate dyadic relationships.

One of the areas of research most closely related to, or confused with, intimacy is that of self-disclosure. Jourard's studies of self-disclosure (1964, 1971) revealed that "the act of revealing personal information to others" (Jourard and Jaffee, 1970) is characterized by mutual reciprocity (Jourard and Richman, 1963); that the perceived appropriateness of self-disclosure exerts a strong influence on recipients of it (Kiesler, Kiesler and Pallak, 1967); that high disclosures are characterized as having higher self-esteem than low disclosures (Shapiro, 1968); and that the most consistent intimate disclosure occurs in marital relationships (Jourard and Lasokow, 1958).

Whereas some references to self-disclosure seem to equate it with intimacy (e.g., Derlega and Chaikin, 1975), Altman and Haythorn (1965) and Gilbert (1976) distinguished the two concepts, with the latter calling for a rethinking of the current constructs of self-disclosure and intimacy. He suggests, along with Cozby (1973), that the relationship between self-disclosure and relationship satisfaction may be curvilinear, and that there may exist a point at which increased self-disclosure actually reduces satisfaction with the relationship. In vague support of this hypothesis are Chaikin and Derlega (1964) who concluded from their study that the appropriateness rather than the amount of self-disclosure is a salient variable associated with perceived adjustment of the discloser.

By intimacy Gilbert refers "to the depth of exchange, both verbally and/or non-verbally, between two persons, which implies a deep form of acceptance of the other as well as a commitment to the relationship." If relationship satisfaction is highly associated with intimacy, then self-disclosure may also have a curvilinear relationship with intimacy, or "intimacy may be a very special instance of self-disclosure." Whatever the concomitant variables, Gilbert poses several interesting conceptual links to intimacy; namely that reciprocity of disclosures is an insufficient explanation of intimacy; that acceptance and commitment of the person making the disclosure, as well as self-esteem and ability to resolve conflict, may exert a significant influence on the level of intimacy.

The most extensive and refined conceptual definitions purport intimacy to be . . . "a mutual need satisfaction" (Clinebell and Clinebell, 1970) and a closeness to another human being on a variety of levels (Dahms, 1972). Clinebell and Clinebell identify several facets of intimacy including: sexual, emotional, aesthetic, creative, recreational, work, crisis, conflict, commitment, spiritual, and communication intimacy. While their definition lacks theoretical conceptual clarity, (and it does not seem that they intended to develop such), Dahms proposes a conceptual hierarchy of three dimensions of intimacy: intellectual, physical, and emotional. Furthermore, he characterizes the concept with four inherently important qualities: mutual accessibility, naturalness, non-possessiveness, and the need to view it as a process.

Most attempts to conceptualize intimacy have not distinguished it from self-disclosure. Gilbert emphasizes that high self-disclosure may not be appropriate at times. It may not involve commitment, and most importantly, it may not take the individual's self-esteem into account. Many therapists would attest to the harsh pre-divorce period as being characterized by high self-disclosure, but the content and style of the disclosures may only prove to attack the self-esteem of the participants and not accomplish a resolution of conflict. The authenticity of a "cold truth" may serve only to separate individuals, resulting in non-intimacy.

An intact relationship may, in fact, be better off with some degree of idealization where some negative "facts" are ignored or withheld while the focus is on maintained positive images. Hall and Taylor (1976) conclude from their experiments that "marriage involves a validation and reaffirmation of a joint construct of reality, suggesting that a continued high evaluation of the other is critical, not only for survival of the marriage, but for the continuance of one's world view as well." The enhancement of the other's value through idealization and, therefore, not disclosing particular negatives, allows the spouse to continue to be a source of positive reinforcement for beliefs, attitudes, and values. Behaviorists would agree, as they have demonstrated, that the primary focus of a long-term relationship should be on the positive. The therapeutic effectiveness of Stuart's

(1976) "caring days" attests to the need of avoiding any unnecessary disclosures of negative responses during later stages of the therapeutic process while emphasizing positive actions, thereby providing for mutually reciprocated acceptance and support.

It should be emphasized, however, that conflict itself is not a block to intimacy (Clinebell and Clinebell, 1970). Rather, conflict can frequently facilitate intimacy, depending on the way in which it is resolved (Strong, 1975; Clinebell and Clinebell, 1970; Bach and Wyden, 1975). As communication theory has demonstrated, unresolved conflict can facilitate distancing the members of a dyad (Clinebell and Clinebell, 1970).

Another concept closely linked to intimacy, and also somewhat confused with it, is "cohesion." Olson, et al., (1979) extensively review the assorted concepts within family therapy, sociology, small group and social psychology literature and conclude that cohesion is a central dimension with the extremes of "separateness-togetherness." Whereas family cohesion is "the emotional bonding which members *feel* toward one another," it is a *resultant condition* of the dynamic processes within the group. Intimacy is actually part of the myriad of processes. A sharing of intimate experiences is a precondition for cohesion.

Another recently developed intimacy scale is the Waring Intimacy Questionnaire (WIQ) composed of the following eight variables: conflict resolution, affection, cohesion, sexuality, identity, compatibility, autonomy, and expressiveness. In a validity study of the WIQ and PAIR by Hanes and Waring (1979), they found these two scales were significantly related ($r = .77$; $p > .01$).

Conceptual Definition of Intimacy

Olson (1975; 1977) provides a conceptual definition of intimacy that seems to integrate the approaches currently found in the literature. He identifies seven types of intimacy by drawing mainly on the previous work of Dahms (1971) and Clinebell and Clinebell (1970). Olson focuses on the "process" aspects of intimacy by distinguishing between intimate experiences and an intimate relationship. An *intimate experience* is a feeling of closeness or sharing with another in one or more of the seven areas. It is possible to have intimate experiences with a variety of persons without having or developing an intimate relationship. An *intimate relationship* is generally one in which an individual shares intimate experiences in several areas, and there is the expectation that the experiences and relationship will persist over time.

The seven types of intimacy originally described by Olson (1975) were: (1) *emotional intimacy*—experiencing a closeness of feelings; (2) *social intimacy*—the experience of having common friends and similarities in social networks, (3) *intellectual intimacy*—the experience of sharing ideas; (4) *sexual intimacy*—the experience of sharing general affection and/or sexual activity; (5) *recreational intimacy*—shared experiences of interests in hobbies, mutual participation in sporting events; (6) *spiritual intimacy*—the experience of showing ultimate concerns, a similar sense of meaning in life, and/or religious faiths; (7) *aesthetic intimacy*—the closeness that results from the experience of sharing beauty.

Intimacy is a *process* that occurs over time and is never completed or fully accomplished. Couples may create false expectations if they assume that they have "achieved" intimacy or that they need not work at maintaining it. While intimate experiences are elusive and unpredictable phenomena that may occur spontaneously, an intimate relationship may take time, work, and effort to maintain.

Individuals desire differing degrees of each kind of intimacy. While studies have inferred that some degree of intimacy is necessary for normal human development and adaptive capability, we do not know the minimum or maximum required, nor do we know the ideal amount or degree of intimacy for any person. However, many developmental theorists (Maslow, 1970; Erikson, 1950) seem to indicate that highly developed individuals usually have several significant friendships. So, while some individuals may not be capable of sustaining an intimate relationship, and some choose reclusive, isolated lifestyles, one or more intimate dyadic relationships may be preferred by most individuals.

Operationalizing Intimacy

Past operational measures of intimacy have been either too global, such as marital satisfaction measures, or have measured closely related but dissimilar concepts, such as group cohesion or self-disclosure. Self-disclosure scales (Jourard, 1971; Taylor and Altman, 1966) tend to measure respondents' willingness to disclose intimate feelings, but do not indicate the kind, character, or frequency of intimacy experienced in the relationship. Intimacy is a *process* and an *experience* which is the outcome of the disclosure of intimate topics and sharing of intimate experiences. An inauthentic, inappropriate, or insensitive disclosure may produce conflict and anger more than a feeling of closeness.

In order to assess the degree of intimacy that an individual perceives he/she has with another, the *PAIR (Personal Assessment of Intimacy in Relationships)* Inventory was developed. This self-report inventory can be used at all levels of dyadic heterosexual relationships, from friendship to steady dating to marriage. It measures the *expected* versus *realized* degree in five areas of intimacy: *emotional intimacy, social intimacy, sexual intimacy, intellectual intimacy,* and *recreational intimacy. Spiritual* and *aesthetic* intimacy were dropped because they were conceptually and empirically unclear.

The PAIR attempts to: (1) identify the degree to which each partner presently feels intimate in the various areas of the relations (realized); (2) identify the degree to which each partner would like to be intimate (expected); and (3) is scored and plotted in such a fashion that direct feedback can be given to a therapist and the couple about their perceptions and expectations in the relationship.

The instrument does *not* assume any ideal or absolute degree of intimacy *per se,* although validity tests indicate that couples, in general, distribute themselves in a normal fashion around the mean. The scores have meaning in terms of the difference *within* each of the partner's perceived and expected degrees of intimacy and also in terms of the difference *between* the two partners.

Phase 1: Initial development of the PAIR. There were originally seven a priori conceptual dimensions of intimacy, including the five mentioned above and "aesthetic" and "spiritual" intimacy. We solicited statements from family professionals concerning the nature of intimacy in general, as well as statements about these seven dimensions in particular. Rather than presuming the nature of intimacy entirely from a professionally conceptual perspective, the first author facilitated and taped four discussions of intimacy with several different groups of lay persons who had completed marital enrichment programs. The tapes were analyzed for possible sub-dimensions of intimacy, resulting in the seven sub-dimensions mentioned.

In addition, statements about intimacy were solicited from graduate students in Family Social Science and from marriage and family therapists. Those statements, plus the analyzed tapes, were transformed into 350 potential items for the PAIR. These items were then classified by marriage and family professionals into the seven types of intimacy. Of those 350, 113 were selected that were conceptually related, clear, and appropriate to the categories.

A sample of males and females was then selected to complete the PAIR. The pilot sample (N = 85) had an age range from 18 to 61 years (median age = 29), 70 percent females, 30 percent males. Over 50 percent were married. They were selected from community enrichment groups (12 percent), one undergraduate day-class (28 percent), and several post-graduate extension classes (with spouses) at a large metropolitan university. While the pilot sample had a predominance of females and is therefore biased to some degree, the actual study sample contained an equal number of males and females and was twice as large.

Several psychometric test construction criteria were used to select ten items for each scale. *First,* those items with the frequency split closest to 50%–50% were chosen. This avoids selecting items that do not adequately discriminate between respondents because of more-than-obvious choice. *Second,* items had to correlate higher with their own a priori scale than with other scales. *Third,* the items had to have a sufficiently high factor-loading to meet the criteria prescribed. Responses were factor analyzed using varimax rotation and principal factor rotation. With a factor loading criterion level of .20, both approaches clearly delineated six major factors with nearly half the items having a factor loading of .50+. *Fourth,* each of the sub-scales needed to have an equal number of items that are positively and negatively scored to control for an acquiescent response set.

Of the seven a priori dimensions only one dimension failed to meet the criterion (aesthetic intimacy), during this phase of the development. Although aesthetic intimacy seems to be a valid conceptual sub-dimension, we could not validly assess its presence with the subjective self-report that we developed. Of the 113 items in the original factor pool, 60 were selected for the inventory with ten items representing each sub-dimension. At this point the PAIR contained 75 items: ten items for each of the six types of intimacy and 15 items for a conventionality scale (adapted from Edmonds, 1967).

The procedure for taking the PAIR was arranged as follows. Each partner independently responds to the questionnaire in two consecutive steps. In the *first step,* the partner responds to the item "as it is now" (perceived) and in the *second step* the individual responds "how he/she would like it to be" (expected). For example, when indicating agreement-disagreement (on a 5-point Likert Scale) to the item "I often feel distant from my partner," in step one, the individual responds as he/she perceives the relationship to be at present, whereas in step two the respondent indicates how he/she would like to be able to respond, given the relationship could be any way they might want. All items are completed for step one before proceeding to step two to insure independent responses.

The scored PAIR is translated from raw scores into a score similar to a percentile (actual range = 0 to 96). Edmond's Conventionality Scale is also included and scored separately in order to assess how much the individual is attempting to create a good impression.

Phase 2: Validity and Reliability Testing. Using the 75-item inventory, the PAIR was administered to 192 non-clinical couples before they began an enrichment weekend offered by a national enrichment program. Data was gathered from 12 separate enrichment weekends, each having 12 to 20 couples participating. The PAIR was one instrument among several used in an overall evaluation of the effects and outcome of this program. A battery of instruments was administered before the weekend, one month after the weekend, and then a followup six months later. Only the Pre-test data was used for this validity and reliability analysis. The other instruments used included the Locke-Wallace Marital Adjustment Scale (Locke and Wallace, 1959) an adapted version of one of Jourard's "Self-disclosure" Scales (Jourard, 1964), and "Empathy" Scale developed by Truax and Carkhoff (Truax and Carkhoff, 1967), six of the Moos' ten "Family Environment Scales" (Moos and Moos, 1976), and a background form.

The sample consisted of 192 couples who had been married between one and 37 years ($\bar{x}$ length of marriage = 11.8, SD = 8.3), ranging in age from 21 to 60-years-old ($\bar{x}$ Age = 35.3, SD = 8.6), with 9% having been formerly married, and 55% having more than a high school education ($\bar{x}$ years of education = 14.1, SD = 2.2). In finding a sample to make validity and reliability tests, we considered it essential to have a fairly representative population of married individuals who had experienced their relationship over an extended period of time and who also represented couples across a wide range of ages. The usual college dating relationship was, of course, not sufficient for meeting our criteria.

As in phase one, both an item analysis and factor analysis were conducted to test for adequacy of the items and the scales. Of the ten items in each intimacy scale and the 15 items in the conventionality scale, only those with the best factor loading in the a priori scales and those that met the item analysis criteria remained. Those items having a frequency split in responses closest to 50%–50% were considered the best discriminators. The items had to correlate higher with their own a priori scale than with other scales. The items had to have a sufficiently high factor loading.

Using the same method and criteria of factor analysis described in phase one and the information from the item analysis, six items were ultimately selected for each intimacy scale and the conventionality scale. Six items were chosen because they not only had the best results on the factor and item analysis, but also because the PAIR was intended to be as short as possible for quicker administration and scoring. Table I lists the final items with their factor loadings and distributions. All PAIR scores are generated in a "profile"

Table 1: PAIR Item and Factor Analysis By Each Subscale (N = 386)

I. Emotional Intimacy	Direction	Factor Loading	Mean	SD	Freq. Split
1. My partner listens to me when I need someone to talk to.	(a)	.48(II)	3.33	1.38	37–53
7. I can state my feelings without him/her getting defensive.	(a)	.48(II)	2.90	1.17	50–39
13. I often feel distant from my partner.	(s)	.58(II)	2.69	1.29	58–34
19. My partner can really understand my hurts and joys.	(a)	.52(II)	3.38	1.28	32–58
25. I feel neglected at times by my partner.	(s)	.46(II)	2.52	1.28	67–26
31. I sometimes feel lonely when we're together.	(s)	.41(II)	2.90	1.33	54–37
II. Social Intimacy					
2. We enjoy spending time with other couples.	(a)	.55(IV)	3.90	1.23	19–73
8. We usually "keep to ourselves."	(s)	.53(IV)	3.37	1.31	34–55
14. We have very few friends in common.	(s)	.53(IV)	3.76	1.33	25–67
20. Having time together with friends is an important part of our shared activities.	(a)	.63(IV)	3.76	1.24	23–69
26. Many of my partner's closest friends are also my closest friends.	(a)	.39(IV)	3.54	1.36	29–62
32. My partner disapproves of some of my friends.	(s)	.21(IV)	3.7	1.35	28–62
III. Sexual Intimacy					
3. I am satisfied with our sex life.	(a)	.78(III)	3.12	1.42	43–46
9. I feel our sexual activity is just routine.	(s)	.57(III)	3.19	1.37	41–47
15. I am able to tell my partner when I want sexual intercourse.	(a)	.38(III)	3.73	1.32	23–70
21. I "hold back" my sexual interest because my partner makes me feel uncomfortable.	(s)	.65(III)	3.63	1.41	30–60
27. Sexual expression is an essential part of our relationship.	(a)	.47(III)	3.52	1.26	26–60
33. My partner seems disinterested in sex.	(s)	.56(III)	3.78	1.39	25–65

	Direction	Factor Loading	Mean	SD	Freq. Split
IV. Intellectual Intimacy					
4. My partner helps me clarify my thoughts.	(a)	.32(II)	3.23	1.30	33–52
10. When it comes to having a serious discussion it seems that we have little in common.	(s)	.45(II)	3.26	1.38	40–52
16. I feel "put-down" in a serious conversation with my partner.	(s)	.65(II)	3.46	1.38	33–56
22. I feel it is useless to discuss some things with my partner.	(s)	.63(II)	2.67	1.40	60–31
28. My partner frequently tries to change my ideas.	(s)	.47(II)	3.20	1.25	37–51
34. We have an endless number of things to talk about.	(a)	.57(V)			
V. Recreational Intimacy					
5. We enjoy the same recreational activities.	(a)	.49(VII)	3.24	1.33	40–52
11. I share in very few of my partner's interests.	(s)	.40(VII)	3.17	1.29	40–40
17. We like playing together.	(a)	.34(VII)	3.78	1.13	18–68
23. We enjoy the out-of-doors together.	(a)	.56(VIII)	3.60	1.21	24–69
29. We seldom find time to do fun things together.	(s)	.28(VII).	3.06	1.40	45–48
35. I think that we share some of the same interests.	(a)	.48(VII)	3.91	1.06	14–80
VI. Conventionality Scale *					
6. My partner has all the qualities I've ever wanted in a mate.	(a)	.55(I)	3.20	1.24	38–52
12. There are times when I do not feel a great deal of love and affection for my partner.	(s)	.60(I)	2.55	1.28	67–27
18. Every new thing that I have learned about my partner has pleased me.	(a)	.60(I)	2.66	1.19	57–29
24. My partner and I understand each other completely.	(a)	.59(I)	2.38	1.20	62–26
30. I don't think anyone could possibly be happier than my partner and I when we are with one another.	(a)	.66(I)	2.70	1.25	53–33
36. I have some needs that are not being met by my relationship.	(s)	.57(I)	2.16	1.13	76–14

*An additional factor analysis was conducted for this scale, wherein the conventionality scale was included with the other PAIR scales. The other factor loadings represent a factor analysis of all PAIR scales without the conventionality scale.

format with separate scores for each specific type of intimacy. Therefore, there is no "total" score. As on similar "profile" tests (e.x. MMPI, SPI) a single "total" score is meaningless.

In addition to the validity analysis already mentioned, the PAIR was analyzed for its ability to discriminate and converge with other variables in an expected fashion. To do this, Pearson correlation coefficients were obtained to test post-hoc hypotheses. The most obvious hypothesis is that those couples who in general receive high scores on the *Locke-Wallace Marital Adjustment Scale* should also have rather high perceived scores on the PAIR, in that the tendency to describe one's relationship as presently being intimate is presumed to be associated with the tendency to be maritally adjusted. Table 2 lists the Pearson Correlation Coefficients for the Locke-Wallace with each PAIR subscale.

Except for the Spiritual subscale, all of the others positively correlate with the Locke-Wallace coefficients consistently exceeding .30. The most consistently high coefficients appear with the Emotional, Intellectual, and Recreational Intimacy.

Table 2: PAIR & Marital Adjustment, Self-Disclosure, Moos' Family Environment Scale and Reliability

PAIR Subscales

	Emotional	Social	Sexual	Intellectual	Recreational
Marital Satisfaction					
Husband	.47	.38	.34	.51	.51
Wife	.57	.44	.36	.55	.51
Couple	.62	.98	.41	.61	.59
Self Disclosure					
Couple	.27	.13*	.13*	.31	.27
Family Environment					
Scales Cohesion					
Husband	.42	.35	.25	.47	.45
Wife	.48	.30	.25	.47	.40
Couple	.53	.39	.30	.54	.49
Independence					
Husband		.15		.16	
Wife	.17		.14	.17	
Couple	.16			.20	
Expressiveness					
Husband	.29	.20	.20	.36	.30
Wife	.42	.27	.21	.46	.29
Couple	.42	.25	.24	.48	.35
Conflict					
Husband	−.35	−.17	−.15	−.31	−.33
Wife	−.30	−.14		−.31	−.28
Couple	−.39	−.18	−.13	−.35	−.36
Control					
Husband	−.15			−.22	−.20
Wife	−.20			−.23	−.20
Couple	−.22			−.26	−.23
Reliability of PAIR	.75	.71	.77	.70	.70

All correlations listed are significant at $p > .001$ except those starred (*) which are significant at $p > .01$.

The *Truax and Carkhoff Empathy Scale* did not prove to be very useful. In addition to the insignificant and low correlations with the PAIR subscales, it did not correlate at any significant level with any other single scale or subscale in the battery. In post-administration discussion with some respondents, some seemed to indicate that they "knew what the appropriate empathic response should be" to the vignette given but said they probably would not choose it in everyday life. Others were confused by the directions, not knowing how well they were to know the person in the vignette, who supposedly is sharing significant information with the respondent, and they did not understand what setting it was taking place in.

A post-hoc hypothesis concerning *self-disclosure* stemming primarily from the literature review above is that self-disclosure is a necessary ingredient in the development of intimacy, but that given the setting, too much self-disclosure can be counterproductive. The size and significance of the coefficients in Table 2 represent this positive correlation between the two concepts. Though not conducted, an analysis of curvilinearity may explain why the coefficients are not higher (e.g., nearer. 60), for curvilinearity is the conceptual presumption of self-disclosure's relationship to intimacy.

The *Moos Family Environment Scale* was used to gather data from couples regardless of their having children living at home. If they did not have children, they were asked to view themselves as a "family" in responding to the items. In essence, the Moos was not used as a "family" environment measure, but a "household" environment measure. We would expect the PAIR to positively correlate with the "Cohesion Scale," bimodally with the "Independence Scale," positively correlate with the "Expressiveness Scale," negatively correlate with the "Conflict Scale," and negatively correlate with the "Control Scale." We cannot hypothesize how the "Organization Scale" should correlate. We presume the Independence Scale to be bimodal, or more precisely, to have an inverted

Table 3: Distribution of PAIR Couple Scores; Mean, Standard Deviation, Maximum and Minimum Scores
(N=192 Couples)

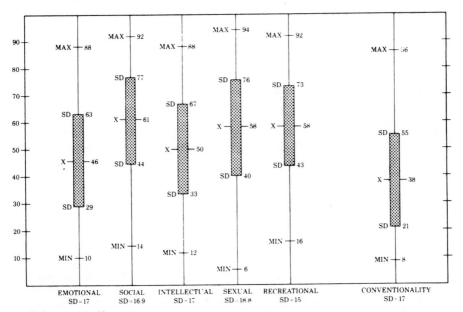

Absolute range = 0 to 96

Couple Scores = Mean score for each couple. (Husband · Wife) 5

curvilinearity in its correlation because the high extreme of the independence continuum is total separateness, or disengagement, in Minuchin terms. The other extreme would be total dependence or enmeshment. Therefore, neither extreme seems to allow for intimacy as we define it.

Every PAIR subscale correlates significantly in the positive direction with Moos' cohesion and expressiveness scale. Both the Control and Conflict Scales have significant negative correlations for the PAIR's Emotional, Intellectual, and Recreational Scale. Eighteen out of 20 PAIR-Scale-by-Moos-Scale correlations proved to be significant for the hypotheses that presumed positive and negative correlations, specifically.

Reliability testing consisted of a split-half method of analysis. No test-retest analysis had been conducted at the time of this writing. Table 5 reflects the impressively strong Cronbach's Alpha Reliability Coefficients achieved with the resulting six item scale. All of the six scales have coefficients of at least .70.

Another important finding is that most of the subscales have a fairly normal distribution. Table 3 graphically displays the distribution of each scale using its absolute range of 0 to 96 points.

The PAIR as an Assessment Measure

The PAIR was primarily developed to meet the growing demand for more specific assessment of relationships. It offers an assessment of the individual (intrapersonal system) and the relationship (interpersonal system) in terms of *perceived* and *expected* intimacy.

Marital counselors and family life educators can both use this profile: (1) to clearly articulate the various kinds of intimacy in their clients'/students' relationships, and (2) to give feedback about the levels of intimacy that they expect and experience in their relationship. The areas of intimacy that have a considerable discrepancy between what is experienced and what is expected may indicate concerns for both partners individually and conjointly, depending on how they *feel* about these discrepancies.

Clinical Use of the PAIR

The PAIR is not a global measure of a person's general attitude about marriage. It is focused specifically on the couple's relationship and is, therefore, personalized. Comparison of the partner's scores of both "perceived" and "expected" intimacy can provide a measure of their goals, needs, or perhaps, expectations in the relationship, but also the couple's perceptual agreements and disagreements. The PAIR is easy to administer because of its short length of 36 items and is hand-scorable by the counselor to provide quick and inexpensive results. We have attempted to facilitate feedback by incorporating a method of visually displaying the plotted scores.

As Figure 1 indicates, a scored profile is a graphic representation of the degree of *perceived* and *expected* intimacy in each area for the couple. For illustrative purposes, we have graphed scores from one of the couples who have used the PAIR in a clinical setting.

Couple 1

John (39) and Ann (35) presented themselves for counseling with Ann making the initial contact. They were married 12 years. She complained of "not counting" in the relationship, of "not being important to John," and her not receiving any support from him. Although John admitted to not being as involved in the relationship as he knew she wanted him to be, he did not know how to change the situation. Ann had developed physical problems that were reported to be psychosomatic by several specialists.

Figure 1: Summary of PAIR Scores for Couple #1

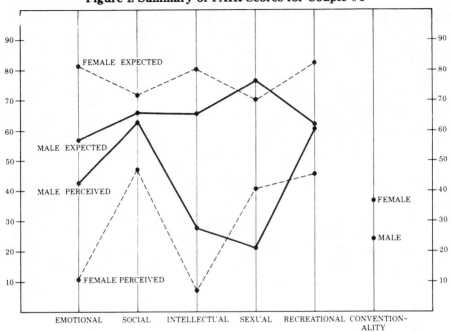

The PAIR was administered after the intake session (along with other procedures) to provide the counselor with immediate information about the couple's perceptions and expectations.

As Figure 1 indicates, Ann demonstrates a severe discrepancy between her perceived and expected scores on her Emotional, Intellectual and Sexual Intimacy scales. A clear discrepancy also exists for the remaining two scales of Social and Recreational Intimacy.

John's scales likewise demonstrate a severe "deprivation" because of the large discrepancies on his Intellectual and Sexual Intimacy scales. These two areas are conjointly viewed as being areas that they are "not receiving what they would like to receive" and, therefore, are a necessary area of focus in therapy.

Their Conventionality score indicates that the information can be trusted in that neither one is higher than one standard deviation above the mean (see Table 5).

As the example illustrates, the PAIR is primarily used as a method of information gathering for both counselor and clients. The feedback can provide a source of emphasis and reinforcement for what the couple already knows about themselves and is a source of objective information about some things not presently in their awareness. It can be used for critical examination of their unmet needs and for support of their relationship's strengths. While focusing on perceptions of the relationship at present, it also helps articulate intentions or expectations. This seems to serve as a measure of hope for the couple, for while they may not know how to create a certain level of intimacy, it is often reassuring for them to at least know that their partner wants to work at it. A pre-therapy and end-of-therapy administration would serve to demonstrate change.

Use of the PAIR in Enrichment Groups

Enrichment groups can, perhaps, be more successful if they provide couples with the opportunity to focus on specific strengths and limitations of their relationship. The PAIR allows for a clear articulation of a dimension that most enrichment programs seek to enhance: intimacy. It brings the nebulous, or perhaps magical concept of intimacy out of the clouds of romance and into the realm of realistic perception so as to assess each partner's needs and the degree to which they are being met. It provides for a specific delineation of the variety of types of intimacy. Rather than equating intimacy with only sexual sharing, it can be viewed as the experience of sharing in several different areas.

The PAIR also allows direct feedback to the participants about their specific relationship. If PAIR is administered early during the enrichment experience, the couples can use the feedback to focus on specific areas of the relationship, thereby making most efficient use of their time. The information may provide objective feedback and insight into their own unrealized perceptions and expectations.

REFERENCES

Altman, I. & Haythorn, W. W. Interpersonal exchange in isolation. *Sociometry*, 1965, *28*, 522.

Angyal, A. *Neurosis and treatment: A holistic theory.* New York: John Wiley, 1965.

Argyle, M. & Dean, J. Eye contact, distance, and affiliation. *Sociometry*, 1965, *28*,289–304.

Arth, M. American culture and the phenomena of friendship in the aged. In C. Tibbits and A. Donahue, (Eds.), *Social and Psychological Aspects of Aging,* New York: Columbia University Press, 1962, 529–534.

Blau, Z. S. Structural constraints on friendship in old age. *American Sociological Review,* 1961, *26,* 429–440.

Bach, G. & Wyden, P. *The intimate enemy.* New York: William Morrow and Co., 1969.

Bowlby, J. The nature of the child's tie to his mother. *International Journal of Psychoanalysis,* 1958, *39,* 350–372.

Carkhoff, R. R. *Helping and human relations.* Vol. I, New York: Holt, Rinehart and Winston, 1969.

Clinebell, H. J. & Clinebell, C. H. *The intimate marriage.* New York: Harper and Row, 1970.

Collins, J. K. Adolescent dating intimacy: Norms and peer expectations. *Journal of Youth and Adolescence,* 1974, *3,* 68–73.

Cozby, P. C. Self-disclosure: A literature review. *Psychological Bulletin,* 1973, *79,* 73–91.

Cromwell, R. E., Olson, D. H. & Fournier, D. G. Diagnosis evaluation in marital and family counseling. In D. H. Olson (Ed.) *Treating relationships,* Lake Mills, Iowa: Graphic Publishing, 1976, 517–562.

Dahms, A. *Emotional intimacy.* Denver, Colorado: Pruett, 1972.

Derlega, W. J. & Chaikin, A. L. *Sharing intimacy: What we reveal to others and why.* Englewood Cliffs, New Jersey: Prentice-Hall, 1975.

Edmonds, V. H. Marital conventionalization: Definition and measurement. *Journal of Marriage and the Family,* 1967, *29,* 681–688.

Erickson, E. *Childhood and Society.* New York: W. W. Norton, 1950.

Ferreira, A. J. The intimacy need in psychotherapy. *American Journal of Psychoanalysis,* 1964, *24,* 189–194.

Gilbert, S. J. Self-disclosure, intimacy and communication in family. *Family Coordinator,* 1976, *25,* 221–231.

Gruen, W. Adult personality: An empirical study of Erickson's theory of ego development. In B. L. Neugarten (Ed.) *Personality in middle and late life.* New York: Prentice Hall, 1964, 1–14.

Hall, J. A. & Taylor, S. E. When love is blind and maintaining idealized images of one's spouse. *Human Relations,* 1976, *29,* 751–762.

Hanes, J. & Waring, E. M. Marital intimacy and nonpsychotic emotional illness. Unpublished manuscript. School of medicine: University of South Carolina, 1979.

Harlow, H. F. & Zimmerman, R. R. Affectional responses in the infant monkey. *Science,* 1953, 130.

Jourard, S. M. *The transparent self.* Princeton, New Jersey: Van Nostrand Reinhold, 1964.

Jourard, S. M. *Self disclosure.* New York: Wiley, 1971.

Jourard, S. M. & Friedman, R. Experimenter-subject distance and self disclosure. *Journal of Personal and Social Psychology,* 1970, *15,* 278–282.

Jourard, S. M.& Jaffee, P.E. Influence of an interviewer's disclosure on the self-disclosing behavior of interviewers. *Journal of Counseling Psychology,* 1970, *17,* 252–257.

Jourard, S. M. & Lasokow, D. Some factors in self-disclosure. *Journal of Abnormal and Social. Psychiatry,* 1958, *56,* 91–98.

Jourard, S. M. & Richman, P. Disclosure output and input in college students. *Merrill-Palmer Quarterly,* 1963, *14,* 136–148.

Kanter, R. M., Jaffee, D. & Wersberg, D. K. Coupling, parenting, and the presence of others: Intimate relations in communal households. *The Family Coordinator,* 1975, *24,* 433–452.

Kiesler, C. A., Kiesler, S. & Pallak, K. M. Effects of commitment to future interaction on reaction to norm violations. *Journal of Personality,* 1967, *35,* 585–599.

Locke, H. J. & Wallace, K. M. Short marital adjustment and prediction tests: Their reliability and validity. *Marriage and Family Living,* 1959, *21,* 251–255.

Lowenthal, M. F. & Haven, C. Interaction and adaption: Intimacy as a critical variable. *American Sociological Review,* 1968, *33,* 20–30.

Lowenthal, M. F. & Thurner, M. & Cheseboga, D. *Four stages of life.* San Francisco, California: Jossey-Bass, 1975.

Lowenthal, M. F. & Weiss, L. Intimacy and crises in adulthood. *The Counseling Psychologist,* 1976,*6,* 88–94.

Mace, D. R. & Mace, V. C. Marriage enrichment concepts for research. *Family Coordinator,* 1975,*24,* 171–173.

Maslow, A. H. *Motivation and personality.* New York: Harper and Row, Publishers, 1970. Originally published in 1954.

Moos, R. H. & Moos, B. A typology of family social environments. *Family Process,* 1976,*15,* 357–372.

Murstein, B. *Theories of attraction and love.* New York: Springer, 1971.

Olson, D. H. *Communication and intimacy.* Unpublished monograph, 1974. University of Minnesota, 1977.

Olson, D. H. Intimacy and the aging family. *Realities of aging.* College of Home Economics, University of Minnesota, 1975.

Olson, D. H. Quest for Intimacy. Unpublished paper, University of Minnesota, 1977.

Olson, D. H. Russell, C. S. & Sprenkle, D. H. Circumplex model of marital and family systems: I, Cohesion and Adaptability dimensions, Family types and clinical applications *Family Process,* 1979, *18,*3–28.

Rosow, I. *Social integration of the aged.* Glencoe, New York: Free Press, 1967.

Shapiro, A. The relationship between self-concept and self disclosure. Dissertation Abstracts International, 1968, *39,* 1180–1181.

Stanley, J. C. Reliability. In R. L. Thorndike (Ed.), *Educational Measurement* (2nd ed.) American Council on Education, Washington, D. C., 1971.

Stone, W. F. Patterns of conformity in couples varying in intimacy. *Journal of Personality and Social Psychology,* 1973, *27,* 413–418.

Strong, J. R. A marital conflict resolution model: Redefining conflict to achieve intimacy. *Journal of Marriage and Family Counseling,* 1975, *1,* 269–276.

Stuart, R. B. An operant interpersonal program for couples. *Treating relationships.* In D. H. Olson, (Ed.) Lake Mills, Iowa: Graphic Publishing, 1976, 119–132.

Sullivan, H. S. *The interpersonal theory of psychiatry.* In H. S. Perry and M. C. Gowel (Eds.) New York: W. W. Norton, 1953.

Taylor, D. A. & Altman, I. Intimacy-scaled stimuli for use in research in interpersonal relations. *Psychological Reports,* 1966, *19,* 729–730.

Truax, C. B. and Carkhoff, R. R. *Toward effective counseling and psychotherapy: Training and practice.* Chicago: Aldine Publishing Co., 1967.

Therapists in training as marriage and family therapists often do not learn techniques for bringing about change. They also do not learn ways to conceal from colleagues and from clients the fact that they do not know how to solve the presenting problems of couples in distress. Both general and specific techniques are reviewed for concealing ignorance as well as ways to make correct excuses for failure. The presentation is designed for therapists who find themselves not knowing what to do with a couple in a particular case and for therapists who do not know what to do with any case.

46

HOW TO BE A MARRIAGE THERAPIST WITHOUT KNOWING PRACTICALLY ANYTHING

*Jay Haley**

During their professional training therapists are taught psychodynamic and other theories of abnormal psychology, learning theory, personality development and the science of diagnosis. Some even learn what medications to give troubled people that will cause the least harm. Yet a surprising number of clinicians graduate from departments of psychology, social work and psychiatry without learning how to solve the presenting problem of a client. In addition, a new generation of marriage and family therapists are appearing who do not know how to solve marriage and family problems. Young marriage therapists by the thousands are in graduate schools for members of the "fourth profession" of marriage and family therapists. They not only learn psychological theories but also systems theory, family development, divorce statistics, and what to say to pass the state licensing examinations. Yet a surprising number have not beeen taught how to change a marital problem. Not knowing ways to change anyone, they have also not been taught how to conceal that fact. This paper is designed for therapists who find themselves not knowing what to do with a couple in a particular case, as happens to all of us. However, it is primarily for a therapist who is ignorant about how to change a marriage relationship in any case and wishes to sound knowledgeable and appear to know what he, or she,[1] is doing.

The many varieties of marital problems brought to a therapist are all dilemmas to the therapist who does not know what to do to cause a change. The problem might be a husband who is insanely jealous of his wife, or a couple might be using a child to carry on a marital quarrel, or a spouse could have a symptom as part of the marriage contract. A symptomatic spouse could be one who drinks, or is depressed, or who has stomach aches, or is anxious, or has some other distressing problem that maintains the marriage and makes it unfortunate.

It does not matter what the marital problem might be when a therapist does not know how to solve *any* problem and can only diagnose, talk about defenses and anxiety, and discuss systems theory. It is incorrect for the therapist to say to a client in distress, "I don't know what on earth to do with a problem like yours." The therapist must pull up his, or her, socks and proceed as if competent enough to be worthy of a fee.

*Jay Haley, MA, is Director of the Family Therapy Institute, 4602 North Park Avenue, Chevy Chase, Maryland 20015.

Reprinted from Volume 6, Number 4 of *Journal of Marital and Family Therapy*. Copyright © 1980 American Association for Marriage and Family Therapy. Reprinted by permission.

Concealing Ignorance from Colleagues

There are two problems for the therapist who does not know how to change anyone: how to conceal that fact from colleagues, and how to conceal it from the customers. It is most simple to conceal incompetence from colleagues. Methods have been worked out by several generations of clinicians. To review a few common ones:

1. One should routinely insist on the importance of confidentiality in therapy. All doors and walls of offices should be soundproofed so that a colleague casually leaning against a door will not hear a therapist being ineffectual. If it is suggested that videotapes of interviews by made for training or research purposes, this idea should be banished with a contemptuous comment about unethical practices and a patient's right to privacy.

2. All supervision should be done without recordings or observation. If one takes notes to a supervisor, the notes can emphasize relationship issues. The fact that one floundered ineffectually in the therapy need not be known. Supervisors often prefer to discuss dynamics rather than interventions to cause change since that subject was usually neglected in their supervisory training.

3. Long term therapy should be done so that colleagues who refer people will forget who they referred. In this way people continue to refer marital problems over the years to a therapist without ever discovering that he never changed anyone.

4. At professional meetings one should emphasize the scientific nature of diagnosis, research, systems theory, and family and child development. Therapy should be referred to as a mere "how to do it" matter. When clinical work is denigrated as practical, in contrast to scientific contributions, therapy is made to seem too unimportant for the revelations of incompetence that might be made by scientific research.

5. When accrediting therapists for licensing, and in academic training, one should emphasize the importance of having the correct degree and not skill in therapy. The accredited therapist is a person who has a Ph.D., an M.S.W., an M.D., an Ed.D., an R.N., or a Master's in Marital Therapy. Basing licensing on degrees protects a therapist who does not know how to do therapy. He, or she, only needs to know how to take classes in a university for a number of years. Should there be a public clamor to base licensing on more than an academic degree because of obvious incompetence, it is possible to insist that there must also be one hundred and two hours of supervised therapy experience. This is not a problem since the therapist can see customers alone in a room and later disclose to a supervisor only what he wishes to have known (see #2 above). Attempts to accredit therapists by tests of skill or measures of successful outcome should be ridiculed as impractical. One can say, "After all, who can really define a successful marriage in this complex and changing world? Therefore, how can we say that we succeeded in improving a marriage?"

Concealing Ignorance from the Customers

Colleagues need not know what actually happens in a therapy room but clients must. The procedures for concealing from customers the fact that one does not know how to change them can be classed as general and specific.

The general procedure used by most experienced therapists who don't know how to cause change is to encourage the client to talk and talk on the gamble that this will cause improvement. When interviewing a spouse alone, the therapist can use what he learned in academia and from watching television shows and say, "Tell me more about that," and "Have you wondered why that was so important to you?" When seeing the couple together, the therapist can say, "I want you to talk to each other so I can observe your communication." Then he can be quiet and need only encourage them occasionally if their argument sags.

While encouraging clients to talk, a therapist should say as little as possible to conceal the fact that he does not know what to say. This is called "active listening." Silent behavior also introduces an air of mystery, which makes specific skills less necessary, as high priests have known for centuries. Since the client inevitably attributes significant meanings to silence, the therapist is given a reputation for eloquence when the fact of the matter is he just does not know what to say. To further encourage the couple to talk, the therapist can make occasional interpretations, pointing out that the unfortunate things the couple are saying to each other are examples of their poor interpersonal relationship. It is helpful to say "Isn't that a sexist statement?" at random moments. The couple will begin to prefer the therapist be silent, and then he can be so comfortably without feeling he, or she, should do more.

Discussing past history is always welcomed by clients who would rather avoid present issues. The review of the past might have no relation to change, but it is expected by most people. A phrase to use is, "I see this problem is very distressing to you both. Now tell me what your marriage was like before, and when you first began to notice this problem developing." Unless the clients are mute or retarded, which calls for modifications of the approach, that inquiry will release a deluge of words that can last anywhere from one interview to a whole course of therapy. Married couples enjoy arguing about the past and about who said what and when since they have experience at that. How long the talk will last depends partly upon the loquaciousness of the customers and also on how skillfully the therapist encourages them by saying, "Can you tell me more about that?" Involved in arguing about the past, the customers do not notice that the therapist does not know what to do about their present problem.

An unfortunate happening can occur when the therapist encourages a couple to talk freely, express their feelings, and to argue about who caused what in the past. That type of discussion often leads to such anger and disruption in the marriage that the couple decides to separate. The therapist can feel sad about this. However, he soon finds compensation in the fact that a separation makes it possible to do "divorce therapy." The therapist can help the couple in the difficult task of separating. In the process, the therapist can be pleasantly surprised to discover that one customer has become two customers, each paying a separate fee.

Many therapists who are not able to help couples separate can double their fees by seeing them as a couple in interviews and also placing them in a group with other couples. The therapist does not need skill when doing a couples group because the couples take over the sessions and share and talk and interpret to each other. Everyone feels something important is happening even if they are not changing, and the therapist gains a double fee while needing to know only how to remain silent.

Exploring other problems is something to do either early or late in the therapy. For example, if a couple comes in with a husband who is angry and jealous of his wife who has had an affair, the therapist who does not know what to do should take the focus off the presenting problem as quickly as possible. He can say, "After all, jealousy is just a symptom and we must talk about other matters so we can get at the roots of the symptom in the marriage relationship." Another way to put it is to appear thorough and cautious by saying, "Well now, I would like to put this jealousy problem in perspective. Could you review for me all the different problems about your marriage that have ever distressed you?" Some clients need to be encouraged to bring up other problems, but most of them can think of enough to keep the conversation going. Examples help bring out reminiscences and satisfy the curiosity of the therapist, such as, "After a group sexual orgy do you have special marital conflicts?"

Examining the consequences of the problem will provide clients with the impression that the therapist appreciates how serious it is even if nothing is being accomplished. One can ask how much time is wasted with the problem, what it prevents the couple from doing, how many inconveniences it causes, how embarrassing it is in relation to children or in-laws, and what would be done if the couple did not have the problem. Often the couple will say they had not realized how many consequences there were, and now they are determined to get over the problem. The therapist can say, "Well, you've taken the first step by coming to therapy; that is the important thing."

If the therapist likes to focus upon interpersonal relations, he can make insightful comments about the client-therapist relationship by saying, "Have you noticed that you treat me as if I am an authority figure who is supposed to solve your problem for you?" This kind of comment encourages the clients not to expect the therapist to be an expert and will also bring out reminiscenses about bosses and other authorities. The therapist can also have the spouses not only talk about the ways they relate to each other but to all their relatives and friends.

Exploring what has been tried to get over the problem includes discussing previous therapy, if any. One should always explore what advice customers were given in the past. While appearing to explore history, the therapist is actually getting ideas of what he might do with a customer. Therapists communicate about therapy techniques to one another through their clients as they learn what colleagues have done to try to solve a problem.

Before proceeding to more specific tactics, the general ones can be summarized with a case example. Choosing an arbitrary problem, let us suppose that a woman comes to a therapist and says she is failing in her marriage and her career, as well as going out of her mind, because she cannot stop compulsively counting everything she does. When she does housework, walks, plays tennis, has sex, or chairs a board meeting, she must count the numbers of times that everything happens. She reports that a crisis came about when her husband discovered she was counting how many breaths he took when they were having sexual relations. The husband threatened divorce as they entered therapy and said he now looks longingly at women who count less.

What can a therapist do with this problem when he does not know how to change it? In general, he can follow the procedures outlined here. He can keep confidential what happens in the therapy from his colleagues, he can encourage the couple to talk while he actively listens. He can have them explore their past marriage relationship, their past individual histories, and their childhood with their extended families. He can talk about philosophical issues in marriage, including tolerance for weaknesses of mates. Out of the problem he can manage months, perhaps years, of marital therapy without having any idea how to change the couple and without anyone discovering that fact. He might even be able to include the case in a paper or book on the topic of interesting problems in marriage therapy. It should be noted in passing that when a therapist wishes to conceal his, or her, incompetence he should avoid any verbatim transcripts of therapy interviews in a publication. Instead, he should offer summaries of cases. For example, a clinician can say about a woman who has the problem of compulsive counting, "The patient was encouraged to explore the origins of the counting compulsion, and the roots of psychopathology were discovered in childhood experiences." This will sound better than a verbatim transcript which might read, "Therapist: When you were a child, did you refer to different ways of going to the bathroom as number one and number two?"

Specific Tactics

Within the framework of general principles for concealing ignorance, the therapist can use specific procedures learned at workshops or in the literature. Some are passing fads while others remain classic maneuvers because they help give the customer the impression that the therapist is skillful.

Reflecting back to people whatever they say is a classic tactic which has stood the test of time and generations of inadequate therapists. The procedure conceals like a blanket the fact that the therapist does not know what to do to cause change. Most important, it impresses the customer with the idea that the therapist is empathetic and understanding. Reflecting back a person's words gives an illusion of intimacy. A spouse says, "I feel so ashamed of myself because we have this childish marital problem." The therapist replies, "M hmm, you feel so ashamed of yourself because you have this childish marital problem." As far as the couple is concerned, two minds have met and understanding has been achieved. Even a socially withdrawn therapist appears to be warm, empathetic and understanding by just thoughtfully repeating back what people say. The chief merit of the procedure is that it is easy to learn even by people with limited intelligence. Research studies have shown that six-year-old children, both male and female, can master the technique with only one 40-minute training session.

Getting in touch with feelings is another classic procedure which can be done, and always is, by novice therapists. Whatever customers say, the therapist says, "How do you feel about that?" With experience, or with the help of a particularly inspiring professor in social work school, the therapist risks more complex phrases such as, "How do you *really* feel about that," or even "I wonder if you could communicate to your husband the depths of your feelings about that." These statements encourage the expression, or the simulation, of feelings and distract the emotionally aroused customer from noticing that nothing is being done about his problem.

Interpretations which make connections between this and that are, of course, the trusted tactic of a therapist who does not know how to cause change. A customer with even a rudimentary education enjoys interpretations which connect one thing with another, and so they are easily distracted from noticing that nothing is changing. One can find a similarity between a husband and a boss, or a mother and a wife. Since people do not think randomly, there is always a connection between what a person says about something at one time and what is said at another time.

Relationship games and sensitivity procedures are a way to pass the time and give the customers the illusion that change must be happening because they get upset. One can easily learn confronting games from the group therapy literature and popular self-help books. For example, one can confront the couple with the way they are playing the game "help me." The clients are impressed with the self discovery and do not notice that the therapist does not know how to help. One can point out that the "adult" in one spouse is talking to the "child" in the other, and discuss their games of teasing and rejection, or dependency. Talking about one's own marital difficulties and divorces sometimes helps the therapist and shows that he, or she, is human and that everyone's problem is humanistic.

Another modern technique is "sculpting." One can bring action into the room by having the couple sculpt their problem instead of just talking about it. The husband can lean on his wife to show his dependence on her, and she can hover over him as he leans on her to show how she is burdened with protecting him. The therapist can say things like, "Now we're getting to the basic kinesics and not merely intellectualizing." Couples enjoy this kind of action, and the therapist can learn the technique in an afternoon workshop. Some experience in amateur theatricals helps. With a dramatic type couple one can have them do genograms of everyone in their family networks and then do simulations of their relationships with all their relatives. They might not get over their marital problem, but they benefit from therapy by having lots more to talk about with their relatives and friends.

Excusing Failure

Therapists who do not know what to do will fail, but not in all cases because of the high rate of spontaneous remission. It is spontaneous change which keeps referral sources providing clients and gives the therapist the illusion that perhaps, after all, he really knew what to do even if he did not realize it. Still, failures often occur and the therapist must be able to conceal the fact that failure happened because he did not know what to do.

There are two audiences to be concerned about when failing: fellow professionals, and the customers. Colleagues are the least problem since one can avoid observation and not be involved with outcome studies. There are various ways to avoid outcome studies ranging from the concern with confidentiality through arguments about complexity to the emphasis upon growth as not a measurable issue. One can also use the classic argument originated by Freud where he said that each case is unique and, therefore, cannot be classed with another in any percentage measurement.

Dealing with the disappointed customer is the main problem. Let us suppose that a couple says indignantly that no change has taken place. After months of therapy they are still miserable and their only marital agreement is that the therapist failed with them. There are several standard defenses to follow. (Showing one's state license, or listing one's degrees and naming the famous universities where one trained might be useful early in therapy but not at this point. The customer will not be impressed, and the *alma mater* is given a poor reputation.) The correct procedures fall into two categories: blaming the customer, and saying that more change has taken place than was realized.

Blaming the client can be done in many ways. When the couple says they are disappointed at the failure by the therapist, they can be asked whether they have noticed that there might be a life pattern here of finding helpers disappointing. This topic becomes a subject to "work on." The therapist has turned an awkward moment into a reason for continuing therapy so they can discuss their past disappointments in people back through their lifetimes.

Another way to blame the customer is more subtle. One can imply that the couple has gone about as far as they can go right now, given the material they are made of. Even with the masterful skills of the therapist nothing more can be done. The implication is that the customers have reached a plateau, not the therapist. Sometimes this can be done by suggesting that a new stage of social development needs to be achieved, like getting older, before the couple can solve the problem. A good word to use is "integrate." One can say that the couple needs to "integrate" their insight into the meaning of the emotional experiences achieved in therapy before it is possible to go further with the problem.

If the customer has not done everything asked, the therapist can imply that more cooperation would have solved the problem, and perhaps the couple isn't quite ready yet to get over it.

An amiable way to end without admitting that one did not know what to do is to say that the customer does not really know how much change has taken place. "The way you talk about your marital problems now, and the way you talked about them when you first came in—well, the change is remarkable." In the case of the woman's counting, the therapist can say, "You might not remember it now, but when you first came in you counted every word I said and every breath your husband took. Now it's only occasional." This kind of statement prepares the way for the classic ending of the incompetent therapist—the customers say they still have the problem but do not mind it so much.

The therapist can also review all the gains made in self-expression, in insight and self-understanding, in resolving problems with distant relatives, and point out that after all these are more important than the trivial presenting problem the customer once thought was so important.

This list of ways to deal with failure is not meant to be all-inclusive, and each therapist has his own favorite way. One way becoming popular recently is to refer to someone in your own group of therapists when you have failed with a couple. That colleague supports whatever you said to the clients and also proceeds just as you did so it appears that all therapists do that and what you did was correct even if it failed. (Some therapy groups of colleagues of this kind are small, and some are quite large.)

In general, dealing gracefully with failure means offering an ending that is pleasing. Termination should leave the customers feeling a bit guilty about not having done all that they should, believing they have gone as far as they are capable of progressing in their marriage at this time and no therapist could have done more, and sorry to have put the therapist to so much trouble when more severe problems are undoubtedly waiting at the door. The customer should also be pleased that the problem, even if it is still there, is really more of an irritation than the misfortune it once was. With these simple techniques a therapist can do therapy for months, even years, with customers who fail to change and they never discover that the therapist knew no more than a plumber about how to get them over the problem they presented when they came in the door.

NOTES

[1]The author uses the pronoun *he* for convenience and acknowledges the inequity of the traditional use of the masculine pronoun since ignorance about how to do therapy occurs in both sexes.

PART X

FAMILY THERAPY

This paper reviews and highlights the mushrooming growth of marital and family therapy during the 1970s. The field has gained credibility and emerged as a viable treatment approach for most mental health problems. Entering the 1980s, the field is beginning to develop integrative conceptual models, utilize clinically relevant assessment techniques, conduct systematic outcome research, and develop preventative and enrichment programs.

47

MARITAL AND FAMILY THERAPY
A Decade Review*

*David H. Olson,** Candyce S. Russell,***
and Douglas H. Sprenkle****

In the last decade, marital and family therapy has emerged as a significant and separate mental health field. Treating relationships is no longer a practice carried out in secret by a small number of practitioners as it was in the 1950s, but is now a service provided by most mental health agencies. It is becoming the treatment method of choice for problems ranging from sexual impotency to child abuse and from cases of adolescent delinquency to problems with alcoholism. Increasingly, the public has become aware of these services and they are requesting, even demanding, relationship-oriented treatment. Truly, the field of marital and family therapy reflects the *Zeitgeist*.

*The authors with to thank Alan Gurman and James Hawkins for their constructive comments on this paper. Also, we appreciated the assistance of Bradford Keeney on the theory section and the work of Raymond Atilano on the summary of outcome studies. Work on this paper was funded by the Agricultural Experiment Station, University of Minnesota in a grant to the first author.

**Family Social Science, 290 McNeal Hall, University of Minnesota, St. Paul, Minnesota 55108.

***Department of Family and Child Development, Kansas State University, Manhattan, Kansas 66502.

****Department of Child Development and Family Studies, Purdue University, Lafayette, Indiana 47907.

The mushrooming interest in marital and family therapy is reflected by a variety of indicators. First, there have been over 1,500 articles and 200 books on marital and family therapy published between 1970-1979. The number of journals on this topic has increased from two in the early 1970s to more than 10 in 1979. The American Association for Marriage and Family Therapy (AAMFT) increased its membership from about 1,000 in 1970 to almost 8,000 in 1980. Also, a second organization was formed called the American Family Therapy Association.

The rapid emergence and acceptance of marital and family therapy has had a dramatic impact on the entire mental health profession. *First,* the traditional distinctions between marriage counseling and family therapy from the 1960s has faded so that it is now more accurate to describe marital and family therapy as a unitary, but not fully unified and integrated field. It is, therefore, appropriate to talk about *the field* of marital and family therapy. *Second,* the emergence of this field has attracted professionals interested in working with persons within a relationship context and has become a "melting pot" of therapists. It has, thereby, broken down, but not destroyed, the identity of traditional professional groups, *i.e.,*

From David H. Olson, Candyce S. Russell, and Douglas H. Sprenkle, "Marital and Family Therapy: A Decade Review," *Journal of Marriage and the Family*, 1980, 42, pp. 973-993. Reprinted by permission of the publisher and authors.

psychologists, psychiatrists, and social workers. *Third,* many types of emotional and physical problems are treated within a relationship context. Increasingly, professionals are finding that treatment of most problems can be more effectively accomplished and maintained if the client's significant others are involved in the treatment process. *Fourth,* the field is increasingly focusing on all types of relationships ranging from gay and cohabiting couples to single-parent and reconstituted families. However, the majority of services are still offered to individuals in a marriage and family relationship. *Fifth,* the field is beginning to deal with individuals at all stages of a relationship ranging from those beginning their relationship (premarital counseling) to those terminating their relationship (divorce counseling) and to those forming new family structures (custody resolution counseling). *Sixth,* the type and variety of agencies and settings that offer family-oriented services have mushroomed. This trend has become so prominent that it is difficult to identify professional agencies that do not offer such services. Even medical clinics are beginning to offer family-oriented treatment, and medical schools are developing a new field called family practice.

The *hallmark* and unifying characteristic of the field of marital and family therapy is the emphasis on treating problems within a *relationship context.* This practice was reinforced theoretically in the last decade by the emergence and acceptance of family systems theory. As a result, family systems theory has seen further development and has provided a general theoretical orientation for many marital and family therapists.

Viewed from a developmental perspective, the field of marital and family therapy has emerged from its infancy in the 1950s, achieved childhood in the early 1960s, adolescence in the late 1960s, and has reached young adulthood in the 1970s.

In the decade review of the 1960s (Olson, 1970), marriage counseling and family therapy were described as young "fraternal twins" developing along parallel but surprisingly separate lines. While the benefits of interchange seemed obvious and necessary, the relative autonomy of the two fields was seen in their separate training centers, their divergent literatures, sources of theory, type of

clientele served, and professional organizations.

During the 1960s, these two youthful professions were developing with a great amount of vigor but without a sufficient amount of rigor. Not unlike youth, both fields experienced enormous growth spurts which resulted in limited conceptual or empirical grounding. Specifically, the main feature of clinical practice could best be described as therapists "doing their own thing."

However, in the decade of the 1970s, the two professions began to converge and they clearly established their presence and identity as a separate mental health field. Young adulthood was achieved through therapeutic, conceptual, and empirical developments. *Therapeutically,* schools of therapy and specific therapeutic techniques were developed for working with couples and families. *Conceptually,* therapists generated a wealth of concepts, often redundant, that related to marital and family dynamics. Increasingly, family therapy and family dynamics were understood within a family systems orientation. *Empirically,* both the quality and quantity of outcome research on the effectiveness of marital and family therapy improved.

THEORETICAL DEVELOPMENTS IN MARITAL AND FAMILY THERAPY

In his previous Decade Review article, Olson (1970:516) reported that "the search for *the* theory of marital (and family) therapy is slowly changing to a realization that there needs to be considerably more exploration of various theoretical approaches before a more integrated and comprehensive approach can be developed." This exploration is perhaps the benchmark of theory development in the decade of the seventies.

The exploration and refinement of existing ideas has characterized the decade, rather than the introduction of dramatically new theoretical approaches. Most recent family therapy literature has been devoted to either: (1) the integration and refinement of previous models (*i.e.,* Minuchin's, 1974, synthesis of family development, family systems, and structural-functionalism); (2) simplified descriptions of previous theoretical work (*i.e.,* cookbooks or working-guides of family therapy and textbooks of family therapy); or (3) extensions of existent theoretical models to specific problems like chemical addiction (Stanton, 1979; Steinglass, 1976) and aging (Herr and Weakland, 1979).

The charge that marriage and family therapy is a technique in search of *a* theory (Manus, 1966) is probably no longer applicable. In addition to refining particular theoretical approaches, steps have been taken to examine the presuppositions of the various theories (Paolino and McCrady, 1978; Ritterman, 1977; Levant, 1980) and therapists (Foley, 1974).

Classification: A First Step

The exploration of various theoretical approaches has been enhanced by several deliberate attempts at classification. In the previous decade, the only scheme cited in the literature was Beels and Ferber's (1969) classification based on the role of the therapist. In the current decade, the Group for the Advancement of Psychiatry (1970) examined the goals of treatment. Foley (1974) compared the similarities and differences among therapists on the eight dimensions of history, diagnosis, affect, learning, values, conscious versus unconscious, transference, and the therapist as model or teacher. Relying more on the theoretical orientation of the family therapists, Guerin (1976) identified two basic groups, those with a psychodynamic and those with a systems orientation. The psychodynamic group included individual, group, experiential, and Ackerman-type approaches while the system group was composed of strategic, structural, and Bowenian family therapy.

Ritterman (1977) utilized the "mechanistic" versus "organismic" views of systems to compare family therapy approaches. Structural family therapy was represented as organismic, and the Mental Research Institute communications theory was described as mechanistic. Although this analysis was criticized (Weakland, 1977), it does point to the value of examining the epistemological assumptions on which the various family theories are based. After extending and critiquing Ritterman's schema, Levant (1980) inductively developed a paradigm which described three schools of family therapy: historical approaches, structure/process approaches, and experiential approaches.

The most sophisticated critique and comparative analysis of the psychoanalytic, behavioral, and systems theory (Bowenite and communications) approaches to marital therapy was conducted by Gurman (1978). He systematically compared these theoretical orientations on the following characteristics: (1) the role of the past and the unconscious; (2) the nature and meaning of presenting problems and the role of assessment; (3) the importance of mediating goals; and (4) the importance of ultimate goals and various therapist roles.

Integration and Model Buiding

Although it is useful to classify and describe various approaches to family therapy, a critical step is to begin integrating concepts and principles and develop theoretical models. One recent attempt to develop an integrative model of the family was done by Olson, Russell, and Sprenkle in their Circumplex Model (Olson *et al.*, 1979, 1980). In developing the Circumplex Model, three dimensions emerged from the conceptual clustering of concepts from six social science fields, including family therapy. The three dimensions were: *cohesion, adaptability, and communication.*

Evidence for the salience of these three dimensions is the fact that numerous theorists and therapists have independently selected concepts related to these dimensions as critical to their work (Table 1). (See Fisher and Sprenkle, 1978 and Sprenkle and Fisher, 1980 for empirical evidence of the importance of these three dimensions.)

Family cohesion is defined as the emotional bonding that family members have toward one another (Olson *et al.*, 1979). At the extreme high end of the cohesion dimension (enmeshed systems) there is an over-identification with the family which results in an emotional, intellectual and/or physical closeness. The low extreme of cohesion (disengaged systems) results in emotional, intellectual and/or physical isolation from the family. It is hypothesized that the central area of this continuum is most viable for family functioning because individuals are able to *experience* and *balance* being independent from, as well as connected to, their families.

TABLE 1. THEORETICAL MODELS OF FAMILY SYSTEMS UTILIZING CONCEPTS RELATED TO COHESION AND ADAPTABILITY AND COMMUNICATION DIMENSIONS

	Cohesion	Adaptability	Communication	Others
Benjamin (1974 and 1977)	Affiliation	Interdependence		
Epstein, Bishop, and Levin (1978)	Affective Involvement	Behavior Control Problem Solving Roles	Communication Affective Responsiveness	
French and Guidera (1974)		Capacity to Change Power		Anxiety; Role as Symptom Carrier
Kantor and Lehr (1974)	Affect Dimension	Power Dimension		Meaning Dimension
Leary (1957) and Constantine (1977)	Affection-Hostility	Dominance-Submission		
Lewis et al. (1976) and Beavers (1977)	Closeness Autonomy Coalitions	Power Negotiation	Affect	Mythology
Parsons and Bales (1955)	Expressive Role	Instrumental Role		

Family adaptability is the second major dimension and is defined as the ability of a marital or family system to change its power structure, role relationships, and relationship rules in response to situational and developmental stress (Olson *et al.,* 1979). As with cohesion, adaptability is a continuum where the central levels of adaptability are hypothesized as more conducive to marital and family functioning than the extremes. In family theory, adaptability was originally presented as homeostasis or the ability of a system to maintain equilibrium (Haley, 1964). More recently, writers have stressed the dual concepts of morphogenesis (system altering or change) and morphostasis (system maintaining or stability) and the family's need for a dynamic balance between these two (Speer, 1970; Wertheim, 1973, 1975). Families very low on adaptability (rigid systems) are unable to change even when it appears necessary. On the other hand, families with too much adaptability (chaotic systems) also have problems dealing with stress and problems. Thus, a balance of stability and change appears most functional to individual and family development (Olson *et al.,* 1979).

By placing these two dimensions of cohesion and adaptability at right angles, Olson *et al.* (1979) have developed a Circumplex Model which delineates 16 *family types.* These authors have also developed a series of hypotheses with direct clinical utility derived from the Model, several of which have

already been tested empirically (Olson *et al.,* 1980).

The theme of cohesion is highly developed in Minuchin's work (1974; Minuchin *et al.,* 1975, 1978). He writes that the human experience of identity has two elements: a sense of belonging and a sense of separateness. A family's structure may range from the one extreme of the "enmeshed" family to the other extreme of the "disengaged" family. In the former, the quality of connectedness among members is characterized by "tight interlocking" and extraordinary resonance among members. The enmeshed family responds to any variation from the accustomed with excessive speed and intensity. In sharp contrast, individuals in disengaged families seem oblivious to the effects of their actions on each other. "Actions of its members do not lead to vivid repercussions . . . the overall impression is one of an atomistic field; family members have long moments in which they move as in isolated orbits, unrelated to each other" (Minuchin *et al.,* 1967:354).

Minuchin also devotes considerable attention to family adaptation. He stresses the importance of the family's capacity to change in the face of external or internal pressures, *i.e.,* those related to developmental changes such as the addition or loss of members or changes in life-cycle stages. Minuchin notes that many families in treatment are simply going through transitions and need help in adapting to them. "The label of pathology would be reserved for families who, in the face of stress, increase the rigidity of their transactional patterns and boundaries, and avoid or resist any exploration of alternatives" (Minuchin, 1974:60).

Carl Whitaker (1975a, 1975b, 1977; Napier and Whitaker, 1978) is probably the most influential experiential family therapist of the decade. His emphasis on therapy as a "here and now" experience, on unconscious process, "psychotherapy of the absurd," and "the therapist as artist rather than technician" ostensibly suggest that he has little in common with Minuchin. Yet, the need for balanced cohesion in families is also crucial to Whitaker's understanding of healthy family functioning and the goals of family therapy. Whitaker (1977:4) writes that a healthy family is "one that maintains a high degree of inner unity and a high degree of individuation. This includes the freedom to leave and return without family dissension and a comfort in belonging to intimate sub-groups outside the family and on occasion, including outside intimates in the family." Also, like Minuchin, Whitaker believes there should be clear boundaries surrounding the parental subsystem. Whitaker calls this the need for a "generation gap."

Whitaker also stresses several themes highly relevant to family adaptability. One of these is his emphasis on role flexibility. He thinks it important that the father can feel free to play the spoiled brat at the dinner table, the mother can be a little girl, the daughter can play mother to the father and the father can have a make-believe affair with his daughter without provoking his spouse's jealousy. The point is that no one individual gets "stuck" playing one rigid role all of the time. In addition to encouraging flexible roles, Whitaker also emphasizes the positive value of shifting alliances. For example, he thinks it is exciting and dynamic when, *temporarily,* mother and daughter team up against father, or father and daughter against mother. The formation of triangles is not inherently evil as long as they do not become rigid triangles. On the other hand, Whitaker also emphasizes that the family needs to provide its members enough stability to afford a sense of security amidst life's inherent untidiness. Another way of stating this is that the family

should fall somewhere between extreme morphogenesis and extreme morphostasis.

Family communication has been stressed by most family theorists from Ackerman to the present. It is emphasized especially by those associated with the "Palo Alto" communications group (Watzlawick *et al.,* 1967, 1974; Satir, 1972). Also, many practitioners have begun to isolate the specific components of effective marital and family communication (Miller *et al.,* 1975) and have created skill development workshops to facilitate family communication (Miller *et al.,* 1976; Guerney, 1977).

In conclusion, there appears to be considerable consensus among family therapists about the salience of the cohesion, adaptability, and communication dimensions. How these dimensions are operationalized, hypothesized to relate to each other, and utilized in therapy are still areas requiring considerable investigation.

SCHOOLS OF FAMILY THERAPY

Although a few of the pioneers of family therapy continue to influence the field, several schools of family therapy have emerged to the forefront in the decade of the 1970s.

Structural Family Therapy

This highly influential school centers around Salvadore Minuchin and the Child Guidance Center in Philadelphia. Some of Minuchin's key ideas have been described previously. The structural approach to family therapy focuses on how the myriad of subsystems which encompass and comprise families are connected. Minuchin's key notion of "boundary" refers to the degree of permeability which characterizes such systemic interfaces. By interacting with a family's various subsystems, a structural family therapist assesses its structural viability. Therapeutic interventions follow on the basis of rearranging the family's structure in a way which attempts to: (1) establish a clear generational hierarchy and (2) promote semipermeable boundaries (*i.e.,* neither enmeshed nor disengaged).

Strategic Family Therapy

1. *Haley's Approach:* Haley (1976) blends Minuchin's structural work with formal ideas of communication theory. Although he

strives for a clear generational hierarchy, he describes his diagnostic and intervention work in terms of communication rather than "structural engineering." Haley focuses on the presenting problem (*e.g.*, symptomatic behavior) and tries to see what communicative function the problem has in the sequence of family events which embody it. His task is then to change the sequence, which, if effectively done, will change the outcome (*e.g.*, alleviation of symptomatic behavior).

2. *Mental Research Institute Communicational Approach.* If one were to drop the parts of Haley's work which connect with structural family therapy, one would come close to having the MRI communication approach (Watzlawick *et al.*, 1967, 1974; Watzlawick and Weakland, 1977; Sluzki, 1978). The MRI method is not necessarily a school of family therapy, but since it was derived from a context historically associated with family therapy, it has been treated as such. The MRI group strictly attends to the chess-game-like approach to solving problems. Thus, the context of the problem is first perceived and then altered. A change is metaphorically tagged as a "second-order change" when the target of change is the system and not just the symptom. This group has given particular attention to the therapeutic paradox and the use of therapeutic language which addresses the right (nonrational) hemisphere of the brain. The work of Gregory Bateson (1972, 1979) and Milton Erickson (Haley, 1973) has had a significant impact on the MRI orientation.

3. *The Strategic Group Approach.* Selvini's strategic group model in the treatment of schizophrenic transaction is based on a blending of the work of Bateson, Haley, and Watzlawick (Selvini *et al.*, 1978, 1980). The group tends to do strategic work in the way in which Pentagon officers plan a battle. At the heart of this approach is a paradoxical relabeling maneuver called "positive connotation," in which the family's homeostatic, yet dysfunctional, organizational pattern is respected. The injunction not to change, paradoxically, gives the family freedom to change. The group also uses a wide variety of other paradoxical maneuvers, including family rituals, to achieve their ends. This strategic approach is also becoming popular in the United States and is utilized by such therapists as

Papp (1977, 1980) and Hoffman (1976) at the Ackerman Family Institue in New York. Another strategic group is located at the Menniger Foundation in Topeka and is headed by Arthur Mandelbaum (1977).

Experiential Family Therapy

The leading proponents of this school are Whitaker (1977), Napier (Napier and Whitaker, 1978) and Keith (Keith and Whitaker, 1978). A number of Whitaker's key ideas have been presented previously. The term experiential family therapy is Whitaker's label for what is essentially an existential orientation. These therapists emphasize personal and family growth through experiencing one's own irrationality and "craziness." Dysfunctional families are depicted as locked into their own rationality which must be blocked by "right brain" strategies such as use of metaphor, absurd overstatement of the clients' problem, or the therapist discussing his own "craziness."

Social Learning Approach

Another school of therapy has organized itself around the tenets of social learning theory. In an excellent review of this approach and its relationship to family intervention, Vincent (1980a and 1980b) makes it clear that social learning theory does not have a unified set of propositions. Rather the "theory" is an assembly of several models: most importantly, operant learning and social exchange theories, along with smatterings of general systems theories (Alexander and Barton, 1976) and attribution theory (Margolin and Weiss, 1978). Their emphasis on "states" versus "traits" is shared by other theoretical approaches. What distinguishes this group most markedly is its emphasis on observational assessment methods, behavioral specifics, and the interplay of data, theory, and clinical application.

Social learning theory has had a significant effect because its basic tenets are readily translatable into treatment modalities and techniques that can be tested empirically. Although social learning conceptualizations of marital and family distress vary somewhat, all of these therapists stress that intervention is most effective if it focuses on increasing positive acts and decreasing negative ones. These behavioral changes are hypothesized to produce positive changes in feelings and cognitions about relationships.

Gerald Patterson and colleagues (Patterson, 1976; Patterson *et al.*, 1975) have developed systematic social learning programs for problem children which actively involve parents and teachers as change agents. They have also completed some of the most intensive studies of behavioral change in families.

Weiss and colleagues (Weiss *et al.*, 1972; Birchler *et al.*, 1975; Weiss, 1978; Vincent, 1980a and 1980b) have done extensive studies on the use of social learning theory for understanding and changing interaction patterns in marital systems. Recently, Weiss (1978) has described how to integrate problem-solving and communication skills into behavioral marital therapy. Stuart's (1976) work with distressed couples in the early 1970s, using an "operant interpersonal approach," has served as a stimulus for more rigorous theorizing and studies.

James Alexander and his colleagues have worked extensively with families of delinquents (Alexander and Barton, 1976). Alexander's work represents an interesting synthesis of behavioral and family systems approaches. Testing system reciprocity (interdependence), these investigators have found that, in normal families, members tend to reciprocate supportive, but not defensive communication, with the reverse true in delinquent families. The group has employed social learning techniques to increase the rate and reciprocity of supportiveness in these families.

Concluding Comments

This review has suggested that the hallmark of the current decade has been less the development of dramatically new theories and more the expansion and refinement of existing ones. One might well ask whether the existence of these multiple theories of marriage and family therapy is a boon or a bane. As we attempted to demonstrate in our section on "Integration and Model Building," we believe there is considerable conceptual similarity among these divergent views and the fact that the theories were often developed independently of one another provides construct validity for the three dimensions of cohesion, adaptability, and communication.

It should also be mentioned that the various *actions* taken in therapy that flow from the divergent theories are often more similar than would be expected (Gurman, 1978). As a result, the various schools of marriage and family therapy seem to have become less dogmatic in their approach and less triumphal in their assessments of their efficacy. Perhaps there is a growing appreciation of the sentiment behind the words of Framo (1973:211) who stated: "I have been impressed with how similarly experienced family therapists function in the actual therapy situation, despite differences in theoretical persuasion."

OUTCOME RESEARCH ON THE EFFECTIVENESS OF MARITAL AND FAMILY THERAPY

During the last decade, the empirical outcome literature has improved in both quantity and quality. This progress is clearly documented by the several comprehensive reviews already available (*e.g.,* Gurman, 1973, 1975; Beck, 1976; Jacobson and Martin, 1976; Wells *et al.*, 1976; Gurman and Kniskern, 1978a, 1978b; Jacobson, 1978; Wells and Denzen, 1978; Jacobson and Margolin, 1979).

The trend in the family therapy field appears to be toward specifying which mode of therapy is most effective for which group of clients presenting which sorts of problems. This is a more effective approach to therapeutic outcome studies. As Frank (1979:312) has suggested: "Instead of continuing to pursue the therapeutic relatively unrewarding enterprise of statistically comparing the effectiveness of different therapies, we should focus on particular forms of therapy that seem to work exceptionally well with a few patients and seek to define the characteristics of both the therapy and the patients that lead to this happy result."

An alternative to focusing on presenting symptoms is to focus on the type of family system. Olson *et al.* (1980) have emphasized the importance of *system* diagnosis prior to intervention. A given "symptom" may serve multiple functions in a relationship system. Therefore, the "system diagnosis" and presenting complaint may not uniformly covary. For instance, Killorin and Olson (1980) describe the course of therapy with

TABLE 2. RELATIONSHIP-ORIENTED TREATMENT STRATEGIES YIELDING SOME DEGREE OF DOCUMENTED EFFECTIVENESS BY PRESENTING PROBLEM*

Presenting Problem	Behavioral Exchange Contracting	Conjoint Couples Group Therapy	Behavioral Family Therapy	Conjoint Interactional Family Therapy	Structural Family Therapy	Strategic Family Therapy	Zuk's Triadic Approach	Multiple Family Therapy	Drug Therapy plus Marital Therapy	Family Crisis Intervention (Langsley et al.)
Alcoholism	X	X								
Drug Abuse				X	X		X			
Juvenile Status Offense			X **	X **	X					
Adolescent Psychopathology				X			X			
Childhood Conduct Problems			X							
School and Work Phobias								X		X
Psychosomatic Symptoms						X				
Adult Depression									X	
Marital Distress	X									

*Limited primarily to outcome studies reported 1970-1979.
**Though labeled behavioral, the Alexander group at Utah actually used a mix of behavioral and communication approaches in conjoint family sessions.

four alcoholic families, each of whom operated at different (though extreme) levels of family cohesion and adaptability. There are other recent projects where the type of system is diagnosed prior to treatment, specific treatment programs are planned and outcome is assessed for a narrowly defined treatment group (e.g., Alexander and Barton, 1976; Minuchin et al., 1978; Stanton et al., 1979; Steinglass, 1979a, 1979b).

Table 2 provides a summary of relationship-oriented treatment strategies which have yielded some degree of documented effectiveness. Unfortunately, space does not allow for a detailed review of the current literature on outcome research. For a listing of selected references, the reader is referred to the auxiliary bibliography found at the end of this article. In addition, a detailed summary table of outcome studies and an expanded version of this paper may be obtained by writing the first author.

Summary of Improvement Rates by Type of Therapy

Reporting gross improvement rates across several studies by type of marital and family therapy masks important interaction effects (Bergin, 1971). However, such rates may offer a useful gross comparison with other types of psychotherapy as we look back upon the decade.

Table 3 summarizes improvement rates for four types of marital therapy and four family therapy approaches by "identified patient." Details of these studies can be obtained from Gurman and Kniskern's (1978b) recent review. Overall, it appears that marital and family therapy improvement rates are

TABLE 3. IMPROVEMENT RATES IN MARITAL AND FAMILY THERAPY

Marital Therapy	Number of Studies	Number of Patients	Improved	Outcome (%) No Change	Worse
Conjoint	8	261	70	24	1
Conjoint Group	15	397	66	30	4
Concurrent and Collaborative	6	464	63	35	2
Individual	7	406	48	45	7
Total	36	1,528	61	35	4
Family Therapy					
Child as Identified Patient	10	370	68	32	0
Adolescent as Identified Patient	9	217	75	25	0
Adult as Identified Patient	11	475	65	33	2
Mixed Identified Patient	8	467	81	17	2
Total	38	1,529	73	26	1

Abstracted with permission from A.S. Gurman and D.P. Kniskern, "Research on marital and family therapy: Progress, perspective and prospect". In *Handbook of Psychotherapy and Behavior Change*, by Garfield and Bergin (1978).

superior to those reported for individual therapies.

The following implications for practice are supported by the empirical research and overlap with the recommendations Gurman and Kniskern (1978b) make for the training of marriage and family therapists:

1. Conjoint marital therapy appears more useful than individual therapy for improving marital relationships.
2. Family therapy appears as effective as individual therapy for a wide range of presenting problems. However, for most presenting problems, it is not possible to specify the best type of family treatment.
3. No one "school" of marital or family therapy has been demonstrated to be effective with a wide range of presenting problems.
4. Therapist relationship skills are important regardless of the conceptual orientation or "school" of the family therapist.

Advances and Suggestions for Outcome Research

The decade of the 1970s has seen the following *advances* in the empirical evaluation of relationship therapy:

1. Use of multimethod assessment aimed at multiple system levels.
2. Increased use of "objective" as well as "subjective" data.
3. Inclusion of comparison and control groups.
4. Use of short-term followups.

5. Acknowledgment of deterioration.
6. Development of sequential research projects which link an understanding of relationship dynamics to intervention.

The following are *recommendations* for future outcome research based upon the progress already documented. There should be:

1. Increased assessment of outcome by practicing therapists, which will require diagnosis and followup assessment.
2. Continued use of multiple outcome measures, including combinations of "subjective," "objective," and "system-relevant" measures.
3. Greater specification of treatment procedure applied to a narrowly defined client group.
4. Continued effort to match treatment to relationship dynamics rather than to presenting complaints—*e.g.*, match treatment to "system" rather than to "symptom."
5. Investigation of the generalizability of treatment approaches to different settings.
6. Investigation of the generalization of treatment effects from the marital to parent-child subsystems and vice versa.

PROMISING TRENDS AND FUTURE DIRECTIONS

Bridging Research, Theory, and Practice

The bridging of research, theory, and practice has generally been lacking in the area of marital and family therapy (Olson, 1976; Sprenkle, 1976). Although some headway has been made in this regard during the past decade, it has primarily been because one individual utilized all three perspectives, not because of any cooperative efforts by several individuals specializing in these areas. Some of these more integrated projects have made significant contributions to the field in the last decade and are described in greater detail elsewhere (Olson, 1976).

The lack of integration of research, theory, and practice has retarded the development of each of these domains. There are many ways, however, that family researchers and family therapists can be helpful to each other (Olson, 1980). Hopefully, the next decade will bring more collaboration between these two groups, since they have each suffered conceptually and methodologically from their mutual isolation.

Treating Family Systems Versus Family Symptoms

A potentially revolutionary idea regarding treatment is to focus therapy on the *type* of marital and family *system* rather than the *presenting symptom*. Increasingly, treatment centers have emerged based on the type of presenting symptoms in one or more family member (*i.e.,* alcoholism, drug abuse, child abuse, wife abuse, juvenile runaways, incest and sexual problems). These symptom-oriented treatment centers have emerged primarily because of state and federal funding generated by public and professional concern about these issues. Since specific problems are easy to identify and rally support for, treatment programs and centers have simply taken advantage of these funding opportunities.

A major limitation with symptom-focused treatment is that family members often receive treatment from different, and often therapeutically and economically competing, programs and agencies. This is because problem families often encounter multiple symptoms which are dynamically related. Symptom-oriented treatment also focuses too much attention on the presenting complaint and, thereby, suggests more individually-oriented treatment. The reduction or elimination of a symptom in one family member does not guarantee that new symptoms may not emerge later in the same

person or in another member in the same family. In fact, family therapists have anecdotally reported that treating a symptom without changing the family system will only provide temporary symptomatic relief. Thus, there is an increasing trend for even symptom-oriented centers to treat problems within a family or relationship context.

An example of the application of a family treatment program based on the type of family system was conducted at the Family Renewal Center in Minneapolis (Killorin and Olson, 1980). Four consecutive families that came for treatment because of an alcoholic family member were diagnosed using the Circumplex Model of Marital and Family Systems (Olson *et al.,* 1980). One interesting finding was that, even though each family had the same presenting complaint (*i.e.,* an alcoholic family member), all four families had very different family systems. One family represented each of the four extreme family types on the Circumplex Model: rigidly enmeshed, rigidly disengaged, chaotically enmeshed, and chaotically disengaged. In most traditional alcohol treatment programs, these four different family systems would have received the same treatment program, since they had the same presenting symptom. However, in this project, the goals for treatment and therapeutic strategies were specifically designed for the type of family system involved. This enabled the therapist to more adequately observe the changes in the family system and assess the impact of treatment.

Pilot and case studies have indicated that family treatment can be more effective and efficient when treating the family system, rather than the presenting symptoms. Hopefully, the next decade will demonstrate, clinically and empirically, the utility of family system-based treatment. If a shift from treating symptoms to family systems seems a more viable approach, diagnostic assessment and treatment of families will need to become more system-focused. Unfortunately, the development of family system-oriented treatment has been retarded because the field has not developed effective and efficient ways of conceptually and/or empirically describing types of marital and family systems.

Typologies of Marital and Family Systems

The use of typologies of couples and families constitutes a major breakthrough for the field because they help to bridge the gap between research, theory, and practice (Olson, 1980). Typologies, whether developed empirically or intuitively (theoretically and clinically), offer numerous conceptual and methodological advantages over traditional variable analysis.

Conceptually, they bridge research and practice by focusing on actual couples and families, rather than on variables. For example, describing a family system as a "rigidly enmeshed" type provides considerable information about the family, since the typology incorporates and summarizes a cluster of variables uniquely related to each type. Typologies enable a researcher or therapist to: (1) classify and describe couples and families on a number of variables; (2) summarize numerous characteristics of all the cases of a particular type; (3) establish criteria which determine whether a couple or family fits within a particular type; and (4) distinguish and describe differences between types.

Methodologically, typologies enable an investigator to: (1) pool statistical variance across a number of variables uniquely related to each type; (2) empirically discover more stable and meaningful relationships between variables and types; and (3) translate the findings directly to couples and families rather than to variables.

In the last few years, there has been increasing interest among family scholars in identifying types of marital and family systems. For example, Cuber and Haroff (1955) developed one of the first inductively derived typologies of *marriages* based on interviews with high status couples. A typography of husbands' and wives' personality traits was derived from condensed interview reports with 200 couples (Ryder, 1970a, 1970b). Kantor and Lehr (1975) developed a typology of *families* based on the concepts of open, closed, and random systems. Constantine (1977) extended the four-player model into a more comprehensive and unified typology. A descriptive analysis of dysfunctional, mid-range, and healthy families was developed by Lewis *et al.* (1976), while Wertheim (1973) developed a typology based on three aspects of the morphogenesis-morphostatis dimension which described eight types of family systems related to the empirical types of families described by Reiss (1971). Most major typologies, however, have been developed intuitively and have suffered from one or more of the following problems: (1) criteria for classifying are not clearly specified; (2) procedures for assigning couples to types are subjective and ambiguous with unknown reliability; and (3) types are not exhaustive or mutually exclusive (Miller and Olson, 1978).

The empirical approach to developing typologies of marital and family systems is becoming more popular because of recent developments in computer programs on cluster and small-space analyses. Some of the first attempts to empirically develop "couples types" were done by Goodrich *et al.* (1968) and Ryder (1970b), using profile analysis to describe newlywed couples. Shostrum and Kavanaugh (1971) used a self-report instrument to develop types of couples based on their scores on the dimensions of anger-love and strength-weakness, and Moos and Moos (1976) developed a typology of families based on their Family Environment Scale. Similarly, using the Ravich Interpersonal Game-Test, Ravich and Wyden (1974) described eight types of marital interaction patterns.

Olson and his colleagues have been working for the past five years developing two different approaches to couple and family typologies, one empirical and the other theoretical. The empirical approach has focused on typologies of couples and families based on their verbal interaction patterns (Miller and Olson, 1978), generated by the Inventory of Marital Conflicts (Olson and Ryder, 1970) and other related inventories. The theoretical typology is the Circumplex Model of Marital and Family Systems developed by Olson *et al.* (1979).

Advances in Clinical Assessment

Although a variety of diagnostic tools have been developed which could be used by marital and family therapists (Cromwell *et al.*, 1976; Cromwell and Fournier, in progress), the statement made by Olson (1970:512) in the last decade review of the field still applies:

"Most therapists seem to make their diagnostic evaluations in rather unsystematic and subjective ways using unspecified criterion that they have found helpful in their clinical practice." However, for the field to advance it is important to learn what types of therapeutic intervention work best with specific presenting symptoms or family systems. As Broderick (1976:xv) stated: "It is a simpleminded but often overlooked concept that couples are different and require differential diagnosis procedures leading to different treatment procedures."

There are a variety of reasons why most marital and family therapists do not currently use standardized diagnostic tools for their clinical assessment. *First,* most therapists have not clearly identified the conceptual dimensions they consider important for diagnostic assessment. *Second,* there is a lack of concern with systematic diagnosis since it has often had little relationship to the therapeutic approach used. *Third,* most marital and family assessment tools do not assess clinically relevant concepts, are not designed for use in clinical settings, and do not adequately capture the complexity of marital and family systems.

There are, however, some recent attempts to base the treatment program on the diagnostic assessment. These bridging projects are different because they can be accomplished only when the conceptual, clinical, and empirical domains are integrated. Three examples of projects where this integrated approach has been attempted are the McMaster Model of Therapy by Epstein and colleagues (Epstein *et al.,* 1978; Santa-Barbara *et al.,* 1977), the Circumplex Model by Olson and colleagues (Olson *et al.,* 1979, 1980), and the Timberlawn project by Lewis and colleagues (Lewis *et al.,* 1976; Beavers, 1977). All three projects have developed clinical indicators for diagnosis, and research procedures for assessing couples and family systems. These assessment tools enable the investigators to do clinical diagnosis before treatment and postevaluation at the end of treatment.

There are also attempts to develop more clinically relevant and useful diagnostic tools for couples and families. In this regard, Cromwell and colleagues are continuing to describe the value of "systemic diagnosis" (Cromwell and Keeney, 1979; Cromwell,

in press) which integrates systems theory and a multilevel (individual, interpersonal, and total system), multitrait, and multimethod assessment. This comprehensive approach is very ambitious but reflects the type of systematic assessment that has been lacking in the field to date.

There are few therapeutic models which integrate the clinical assessment and the therapeutic approach. However, this type of integration could be accelerated if family therapists and family researchers worked together in a more collaborative manner. Numerous benefits could be accrued by both therapists and researchers if they formed a more cooperative relationship (Olson, 1980).

Sex Therapy

The publication of Masters and Johnson's *Human Sexual Inadequacy* (1970) did a great deal to establish sex therapy as a legitimate form of intervention in the decade of the seventies. It helped spur the rapid growth of a variety of sex clinics and programs (Annon, 1971, 1975; Hartman and Fithian, 1972; Kaplan, 1974, 1979; Maddock, 1976; Fisher and Gochros, 1977). The American Association of Sex Educators, Counselors, and Therapists (AASEC) also grew rapidly in size and initiated a certification program for professionals in this discipline.

Although there is considerable diversity across treatment programs, the new sex therapies share the following commonalities in that they: (1) emphasize the mutual responsibility of the couple for the sexual dysfunction; (2) stress information and education in treatment; (3) attend to attitudinal change and performance anxiety; (4) increase communication skills and effectiveness of sexual technique; (5) prescribe changes in behavior; and (6) change destructive life styles and sex roles (LoPiccolo, 1978).

There is also increasing recognition of the pervasive interaction between the sexual dysfunction and the marital relationship (Kaplan, 1974; Messersmith, 1976). There has been a trend away from the intensive and costly residential cotherapy format of Masters and Johnson to outpatient programs in the client's home community with a single therapist (Messersmith, 1976). The results of the latter approach appear as successful as the former (Kaplan, 1974,

1979). Although the emphasis has been on working with couples, groups have been formed with individuals having the same sexual complaints (Schneidman and McGuire, 1976) as well as different sexual problems (Leiblum et al., 1976).

As noted in several reviews of the efficacy of sex therapy (e.g., Sotile and Kilmann, 1977; Hogan, 1978), we do not know which components of the various sex therapy programs contribute to their success. There has, however, been a rather high success rate for some sexual dysfunctions (premature ejaculation, impotence, non-orgasmic response) across various treatment programs. Even though these empirical studies were lacking in scientific rigor (Kockott et al., 1975), "there seems to be general agreement that sex therapy works . . . but why and when are questions yet to be answered" (Kinder and Blakeney, 1976:1).

Divorce Therapy

The 1970s witnessed the emergence of a new subspecialty—divorce therapy. It was stimulated in part by the large increase in the number of divorces during the past decade (708,000 in 1970; 1,170,000 in 1979) and the growing awareness that divorcing individuals need help uncoupling and dealing with this process. While marital therapy often has operated on the implicit assumption of "saving marriages," it is perhaps a sign of the times that divorce therapy " . . .does not focus on improving the husband-wife relationship but on decreasing the function of that relationship with the goal of eventual dissolution of that relationship" (Brown, 1976:410). Even the criteria for successful marital therapy has been expanded to include helping individuals through the process of dissolving their relationship.

Although a number of helpful works have appeared on the divorce process (Levinger and Moles, 1979; Salts, 1979), its effect on children (Wallerstein and Kelly, 1980), and the process of divorce therapy (Brown, 1976), there is almost no empirical research on divorce therapy per se. Most of the relevant data come from marriage counseling cases where divorce was an unintended outcome. Sprenkle and Storm (1980a) have demonstrated how the misuse of this data has led to the untested assumption that individual, rather than conjoint, therapy is more effective for divorcing persons. These authors (1980b) have also prepared a critique of the methodology of research related to divorce therapy.

Divorce, like marriage, is a complex process that proceeds in stages and work needs to be done to determine the intervention strategies most appropriate for particular families and circumstances. At this point we know considerably more about therapist's views of divorce therapy (Kressel and Deutsch, 1977) than we have empirical evidence about the process and outcome.

Preventative and Enrichment Programs

One promising trend in the last five years has been the increasing interest on developing marital and family enrichment programs. Reviews of the historical development of the marital enrichment movement have been completed by L'Abate (1974), Mace and Mace (1976), and Otto (1976). Most marital and family therapists have been so preoccupied with treating problematic relationships that they have failed to develop or use more preventative approaches. Vincent (1967, 1977) has long been an advocate of focusing on marital health and has identified the barriers to this preventative orientation in the mental health field.

Although a general goal of enrichment programs has been prevention through the attempt to improve the quality of the marital and family relationship, there have been two basically different types of enrichment programs. While both types of enrichment approaches have primarily focused upon couples rather than families, one approach has focused on structured communication skill building programs, while the other approach (often called "marriage encounter") has been composed of more loosely focused programs.

Although marriage encounter programs were developed in the last decade, they have gained increasing acceptance as churches have begun sponsorship. The Catholic Church developed one of the earliest versions (Bosco, 1972; Koch and Koch, 1976), and now most church denominations have developed some type of marriage encounter program. David and Vera Mace (1976) have been leading advocates of marriage enrichment. They have developed an Association for Couples for Marital Enrichment (ACME) which offers weekend retreats and other programs.

Communication skill building programs have been more systematically developed and researched than marriage encounter programs and represent a significant advance in the field. Miller and associates (1976) have developed a Couples Communication Program (CCP) and recently completed a program for families entitled "Understanding Us." Guerney (1977) and colleagues have developed a Conjugal Relationship Enhancement (CRE) program (Rappaport, 1976) and a program for Parent-Adolescent Relationship Development (PARD). L'Abate (1974, 1977) and associates have developed and evaluated a variety of programs for marital and family enrichment.

In a recent review of marital enrichment programs, Gurman and Kniskern (1977) concluded that one must be cautious about the overly zealous claims about the impact of these programs—especially the marriage encounter programs. They reviewed 29 studies of marital and premarital enrichment programs and found only six had an untreated control group. Although these studies generally demonstrated positive change, the results should be tempered by the serious methodological limitations.

Another promising preventative approach is the development of premarital programs and tools for preparing couples for marriage. There is growing evidence that traditional lecture programs for premarital couples most often offered by churches are not very effective (Druckman et al., 1979; Norem et al., 1980). A recent Canadian study by Bader and associates (Microys and Bader, 1977) demonstrated that experiential programs are helpful to premarital couples. Another recent study (Druckman et al., 1979) found that a structured premarital instrument called PREPARE was more useful than traditional education programs.

SUMMARY

Marital and family therapy became a significant mental health profession during the 1970s. Conceptually, numerous family concepts and ideas were developed, and integrative models began emerging in the late 1970s. Clinically, schools of family therapy became identified with specific techniques and training centers. Empirically, more effective assessment tools were developed, and systematic outcome research was conducted.

Promising new directions for the 1980s include the development of integrative models that bridge research, theory, and practice. Theoretical and empirical typologies are being developed which facilitate the bridging process. Specialities are emerging like sex and divorce therapy, and there is increasing interest in preventative and enrichment programs for couples and families.

REFERENCES

Alexander, J. F., and C. Barton
1976   "Behavioral systems therapy with delinquent families." Pp. 167-188 in D. H. Olson (Ed.), Treating Relationships. Lake Mills, Iowa: Graphic Publishing Company.
Annon, J. S.
1971   The Behavioral Treatment of Sexual Problems, Vol. I: Brief Therapy. Honolulu: Enabling Systems.
1975   The Behavioral Treatment of Sexual Problems, Vol. II: Intensive Therapy. Honolulu: Enabling Systems.
Bateson, G.
1972   Steps to an Ecology of Mind. New York:Ballantine Books.
1979   Mind and Nature: A Necessary Unity. New York:E. P. Dutton.
Beavers, W. R.
1977   Psychotherapy and Growth: A Family Systems Perspective. New York:Brunner/Mazel.
Beck, D. F.
1976   "Research findings on the outcomes of marital counseling." Pp. 433-473 in D. H. Olson (Ed.), Treating Relationships. Lake Mills, Iowa:Graphic Publishing Company.
Beels, D. C., and A. Ferber
1969   "Family therapy: A view." Family Process 8 (September):280-318.
Bergin, A. E.
1971   "The evaluation of therapeutic outcomes." In A. E. Bergin and S. L. Garfield (Eds.), Handbook of Psychotherapy and Behavior Change. New York:John Wiley and Sons.
Birchler, G. R., R. L. Weiss, and J. P. Vincent
1975   "Multi-method analysis of social reinforcement exchange between maritally distressed and non-distressed spouse and stranger dyads." Journal of Personality and Social Psychology 31:349-360.

Bosco, A.
1972 Marriage Encounter: The Re-Discovery of Love. St. Meinard, Indiana:Abbey Press.
Broderick, C.
1976 "Foreword," Pp. xv-xvii in D. H. Olson (Ed.), Treating Relationships. Lake Mills, Iowa:Graphic Publishing Company.
Brown, E. M.
1976 "Divorce Counseling." In D. H. Olson (Ed.), Treating Relationships. Lake Mills, Iowa: Graphic Publishing Company.
Constantine, L.
1977 "A verified system theory of human process." Paper presented at Department of Family Social Science, University of Minnesota.
Cromwell, R. E.
In "A systems approach to marital and family
press diagnosis." Journal of Counseling and Psychotherapy.
Cromwell, R. E., and D. G. Fournier
In Diagnosing Relationships: Clinical Assess-
progress ment for Marriage and Family Therapists. San Francisco:Jossey-Bass.
Cromwell, R. E., and B. P. Keeney
1979 "Diagnosing marital and family systems: A training model." Family Coordinator 28:101-108.
Cromwell. R. E., D. Olson, and D. Fournier
1976 "Diagnosis and evaluation in marital and family counseling." Pp. 499-516 in D. H. Olson (Ed.), Treating Relationships. Lake Mills, Iowa:Graphic Publishing Company.
Cuber, J. F., and P. B. Haroff
1955 The Significant Americans: A Study of Sexual Behavior Among the Affluent. New York: Appleton-Century-Croft.
Druckman, J. M., D. M. Fournier, B. Robinson, and D. H. Olson
1979 "Effectiveness of five types of pre-marital preparation programs." Final Report for Education for Marriage. Grand Rapids, Michigan.
Epstein, N. B., D. S. Bishop, and S. Levin
1978 "The McMaster model of family functioning." Journal of Marriage and Family Counseling 40:19-31.
Fisher, B. L., and D. H. Sprenkle
1978 "Therapists' perceptions of healthy family functions." The International Journal of Family Counseling 6:9-18.
Fisher, J., and H. Gochros (Eds.)
1977 A Handbook of Behavior Therapy With Sexual Problems (Vols. 1 and 2). New York: Pergamon Press.
Foley, V. D.
1974 An Introduction to Family Therapy. New York:Grune and Stratton.
Framo, J.
1973 "Comments." Pp. 210-214 in Ferber, A., M. Mendelsohn, and A. Napier. The book of Family Therapy. Boston:Houghton Mifflin Company.
Frank, J. D.
1979 "The present status of outcome studies."

Journal of Consulting and Clinical Psychology 47:310-316.
Goodrich, D. W., R. G. Ryder, and H. L. Rausch
1968 "Patterns of newlywed marriage." Journal of Marriage and the Family 30:383-389.
Guerin, P. J., Jr.
1976 Family Therapy: Theory and Practice. New York:Gardner Press.
Guerney, B.
1977 Relationship Enhancement. San Francisco: Jossey-Bass.
Gurman, A. S.
1973 "The effects and effectiveness of marital therapy: A review of outcome research." Family Process 12:145-170.
1975 "The effects and effectiveness of marital therapy." Pp. 383-406 in A. S. Gurman and D. G. Rice (Eds.), Couples In Conflict. New York:Jason-Aronson.
1978 "Contemporary marital therapies: A critique comparative analysis of psychoanalytic, behavioral and systems theory approaches." Pp. 445-566 in J. Paolino, Jr. and B. S. McCrady (Eds.), Marriage and Marital Therapy. New York:Brunner/Mazel.
Gurman, A. S., and D. P. Kniskern
1977 "Enriching research on marital enrichment programs." Journal of Marriage and Family Counseling 3:3-11.
1978a "Deterioration in marital and family therapy: Empirical clinical and conceptual issues." Family Process 17:3-20.
1978b "Research on marital and family therapy: Progress, perspective, and prospect." Pp. 817-901 in S. L. Garfield and A. E. Bergin (Eds.), Handbook of Psychotherapy and Behavior Change. New York:John Wiley and Sons.
Haley, J.
1964 "Research on family patterns: An instrument measurement." Family Process 3:41-65.
1973 Uncommon Therapy. New York:W. W. Norton and Company.
1976 Problem-Solving Therapy. San Francisco:Jossey-Bass.
Hartman, W., and M. Fithian
1972 Treatment of Sexual Dysfunction. Long Beach, California:Center for Marital and Sexual Studies.
Herr, J. J., and J. H. Weakland
1979 Counseling Elders and Their Families. New York:Springer Publishing Company.
Hoffman, L.
1976 "Breaking the homeostatic cycle." Pp. 501-519 in P. Guerin (Ed.), Family Therapy: Theory and Practice. New York:Gardner Press.
Hogan, D. R.
1978 "The effectiveness of sex therapy: A review of the literature." Pp. 57-84 in LoPiccolo, J. and LoPiccolo, L. (Eds.), Handbook of Sex Therapy. New York:Plenum Press.

Jacobson, N. S.
1978   "Specific and non-specific factors in the effectiveness of a behavioral approach to marital discord." Journal of Consulting and Clinical Psychology. 46:442-452.

Jacobson, N. S., and G. Margolin
1979   Marital Therapy: Strategies Based on Social Learning and Behavior Exchange Principles. New York:Brunner/Mazel.

Jacobson, N. S., and B. Martin
1976   "Behavioral marriage therapy: Current status." Psychological Bulletin 83:540-556.

Kantor, D., and W. Lehr
1975   Inside the Family. San Francisco:Jossey-Bass.

Kaplan, H. S.
1974   The New Sex Therapy. New York:Quadrangle Books.
1979   Disorders of Sexual Desire. New York:Brunner/Mazel.

Keith, D., and C. A. Whitaker
1978   "Struggling with the impotence impasse: Absurdity and acting-in." Journal of Marriage and Family Counseling 4:69-77.

Killorin, E., and D. H. Olson
1980   "Clinical application of the circumplex model to chemically dependent families." Unpublished manuscript, University of Minnesota.

Kinder, B. H., and P. Blakeney
1976   "Treatment of sexual dysfunction: A review of outcome studies." Unpublished manuscript, University of Texas Medical Branch.

Koch, J., and L. Koch
1976   "The urgent drive to make good marriages better." Psychology Today 10:33-35.

Kockott, G., F. Ditmar, and L. Nussett
1975   "Systematic desensitization of erectile impotence: A controlled study." Archives of Sexual Behavior 4:493-500.

Kressel, K., and M. Deutsch
1977   "Divorce therapy: In depth survey of therapists views." Family Process 16:413-443.

L'Abate, L.
1974   "Family Enrichment Programs." Journal of Family Counseling 2:32-44.
1977   Enrichment: Structured Intervention With Couples, Families, and Groups. Washington, D.C.:University Press of America.

Leiblum, S. R., R. C. Rosen, and D. Pierce
1976   "Group treatment format: Mixed sexual dysfunctions." Archives of Sexual Behavior 5:313-322.

Levant, R. F.
1980   "A classification of the field of family therapy: A review of prior attempts and a new paradigmatic model." American Journal of Family Therapy 8:3-16.

Levinger, G., and O. C. Moles
1979   Divorce and Separation: Context, Causes, and Consequences. New York:Basic Books.

Lewis, J., W. R. Beavers, J. T. Gussett, and V. A. Philips
1976   No Single Thread: Psychological Health in Family Systems. New York:Brunner/Mazel.

LoPiccolo, J.
1978   "Direct treatment of sexual dysfunction." In LoPiccolo, J. and LoPiccolo, L. (Eds.), Handbook of Sex Therapy. New York:Plenum Press.

Mace, D., and V. Mace
1976   "Marriage Enrichment: A Preventative Group Approach in Couples." In D. H. Olson (Ed.) Treating Relationships. Lake Mills, Iowa: Graphic Publishing Company.

Maddock, J. W.
1976   "Sexual health: An enrichment and treatment program." Pp. 355-382 in D. H. Olson (Ed.), Treating Relationships. Lake Mills, Iowa: Graphic Publishing Company.

Mandelbaum, A.
1977   "The inhibited child: A family therapy approach." Pp. 121-130 in E. J. Anthony and D. C. Gilpin (Eds.), Three Clinical Faces of Childhood. New York:Spectrum.

Manus, G. I.
1966   "Marriage counseling: A technique in search of a theory." Journal of Marriage and the Family 28:449-453.

Margolin, G., and R. L. Weiss
1978   "Comparative evaluation of therapeutic components associated with behavioral marital treatments." Journal of Consulting and Clinical Psychology 46:1476-1486.

Masters, W. H., and V. E. Johnson
1970   Human Sexual Inadequacy. Boston:Little, Brown and Company.

Messersmith, C. E.
1976   "Sex therapy and the marital system." Pp. 339-353 in D. H. Olson (Ed.), Treating Relationships. Lake Mills, Iowa:Graphic Publishing Company.

Microys, G., and E. Bader
1977   "Do pre-marriage programs really help?" Unpublished manuscript, University of Toronto.

Miller, B. C., and D. H. Olson
1978   "Typology of marital interaction and contextual characteristics: Cluster analysis of the IMC." Unpublished manuscript, University of Minnesota.

Miller, S., R. Corrales, and D. B. Wackman
1975   "Recent progress in understanding and facilitating marital communication." The Family Coordinator 24:143-152.

Miller, S., E. W. Nunnally, and D. Wackman
1976   "Minnesota couples communication program (MCCP): Premarital and marital groups." In D. H. Olson (Ed.), Treating Relationships. Lake Mills, Iowa:Graphic Publishing Company.

Minuchin, S.
1974   Families and Family Therapy. Cambridge: Harvard University Press.

Minuchin, S., L. Baker, B. Rosman, R. Liebman, L. Milman, and T. Todd
1975   "A conceptual model of psychosomatic illness in children." Archives of General Psychiatry 32:1031-1038.

Minuchin, S., B. Montalvo, B. Guerney, Jr., B. Rosman, and F. Schumer

1967 Families of the Slums: An Exploration of Their Structure and Treatment. New York: Basic Books.

Minuchin, S., B. L. Rosman, and L. Baker
1978 Psychosomatic Families: Anorexia Nervosa in Context. Cambridge:Harvard University Press.

Moos, R., and B. Moos
1976 "Typology of family social environments." Family Process 15:357-371.

Napier, A. Y., and C. A. Whitaker
1978 The Family Crucible. New York:Harper and Row, Publishers.

Norem, R. H., M. Schaefer, J. Springer, and D. H. Olson
1980 "Effective premarital education: Outcome study and follow-up evaluation." Unpublished manuscript, University of Minnesota, St. Paul.

Olson, D. H. (Ed.)
1970 "Marital and family therapy: Integrative review and critique." Journal of Marriage and the Family 32:501-538.
1976 Treating Relationships. Lake Mills, Iowa: Graphic Publishing Company.

Olson, D. H., C. Russell, and D. H. Sprenkle
1980 "Circumplex model of marital and family systems II: Empirical studies and clinical intervention." Pp. 129-176 in J. P. Vincent (Ed.), Advances in Family Intervention, Assessment and Theory (Vol. 1). Greenwich, Connecticut:JAI Press.

Olson, D. H., and R. G. Ryder
1970 "Inventory of marital conflicts: An experimental interaction procedure." Journal of Marriage and the Family 32:443-448.

Olson, D. H., D. H. Sprenkle, and C. Russell
1979 "Circumplex model of marital and family systems: I. Cohesion and adaptability dimensions, family types, and clinical applications." Family Process 18:3-28.

Otto, H. A.
1976 Marriage and Family Enrichment: New Perspectives and Programs. Nashville:Abingdon.

Paolino, T. J., and B. S. McCrady
1978 Marriage and Marital Therapy: Psychoanalytic, Behavioral and Systems Theory Perspectives. New York:Brunner/Mazel.

Papp, P. (Ed.)
1977 Family Therapy: Full Length Case Studies. New York:Gardner Press.
1980 "The Greek chores and other techniques of family therapy." Family Process 19:45-58.

Patterson, G. R.
1976 "Parents and teachers as change agents: A social learning approach." In D. H. Olson (Ed.), Treating Relationships, Lake Mills, Iowa:Graphic Publishing Company.

Patterson, G. R., J. B. Reid, R. R. Jones, and R. E. Conger
1975 "A social learning approach to family intervention." In Families With Aggressive Children (Vol. 1). Eugene, Oregon:Castalia Publishing Company.

Rappaport, A. F.
1976 "Conjugal relationship enhancement program." In D. H. Olson (Ed.), Treating Relationships. Lake Mills, Iowa:Graphic Publishing Company.

Ravich, R., and B. Wyden
1974 Predictable Pairing. New York:Wyden Publishing.

Reiss, D.
1971 "Varieties of consensual experience: I. A theory for relating family interaction to individual thinking." Family Process 10:1-27.

Ritterman, M. K.
1977 "Paradigmatic classification of family therapy theories." Family Process 16:29-48.

Ryder, R.
1970a "A topography of early marriage." Family Process 9:385-402.
1970b "Dimensions of early marriage." Family Process 9:51-68.

Salts, C.
1979 "Divorce process: Integration of theory." Journal of Divorce 2:233-240.

Santa-Barbara, J., C. A. Woodward, S. Levin, D. Streiner, J. T. Goodman, and N. B. Epstein
1977 "Interrelationships among outcome measures in the McMaster family therapy outcome study." Goal Attainment Review 3:47-58.

Satir, V.
1972 Peoplemaking. Palo Alto, California:Science and Behavior Books.

Schneidman, B., and L. McGuire
1976 "Group therapy for nonorgasmic women: Two age levels." Archives of Sexual Behavior 5:239-248.

Selvini, M., M. S. Palazzoli, L. Boscolo, G. Cecchin, and G. Prata
1978 Paradox and Counterparadox. New York: Aronson.
1980 "Hypothesiting—Circularity—Neutrality: Three guidelines for the conductor of the session." Family Process 19:3-12.

Shostrum, E., and J. Kavanaugh
1971 Between Man and Woman. Los Angeles:Nash Publishing.

Sluzki, C. E.
1978 "Marital therapy from a systems theory perspective." Pp. 366-394 in T. J. Paolino, Jr. and B. S. McCrady (Eds.), Marriage and Marital Therapy. New York:Brunner/Mazel.

Sotile, W. M., and P. R. Kilmann
1977 "Treatment of psychogenic female sexual dysfunctions." Psychological Bulletin 84:619-633.

Speer, D. C.
1970 "Family systems: Morphostatis and morphogenesis, or is homeostasis enough?" Family Process 9:254-278.

Sprenkle, D. H.
1976 "The need for integration among theory, research and practice in the family field." The Family Coordinator 24:261-263.

Sprenkle, D. H., and B. L. Fisher
In
press   "Goals of family therapy: An empirical assessment." Journal of Marriage and Family
Therapy.
Sprenkle, D. H., and C. L. Storm
1980a   "The unit of treatment in divorce therapy." In
A. S. Gurman (Ed.), Practical Problems in
Family Therapy. New York:Brunner/Mazel.
1980b   "Divorce therapy: The first decade review of
research and implications to practice." Paper
presented at the annual meeting of the National Council on Family Relations, Portland.
Stanton, M. D.
1979   "Family treatment approaches to drug abuse
problems: A review." Family Process
18:251-280.
Stanton, M. D., T. C. Todd, F. Steier, J. M.
VanDeusen, L. R. Marder, R. J. Rosoff, S. F. Seaman,
and I. Skibinski
1979   "Family characteristics and family therapy of
heroin addicts: Final report 1974-1978."
Report prepared for the Psychosocial Branch,
Division of Research, National Institute on
Drug Abuse, Department of HEW. Washington, D.C.:U.S. Government Printing Office.
Steinglass, P.
1976   "Experimenting with family treatment. approaches to alcoholism 1950-1975: A review."
Family Process 15:97-123.
1979a   "The alcoholic family in the interaction
laboratory." The Journal of Nervous and
Mental Disease 167:428-436.
1979b   "An experimental treatment program for
alcoholic couples." Journal of Studies on
Alcohol 40:159-182.
Stuart, R. B.
1976   "An operant interpersonal program for
couples." In D. H. Olson (Ed.), Treating
Relationships. Lake Mills, Iowa:Graphic
Publishing Company.
Vincent, C. E.
1967   "Mental health and the family." Journal of
Marriage and the Family 29:18-38.
1977   "Barriers to the development of marital health
as a health field." Journal of Marriage and
Family Counseling 4:3-11.
Vincent, J. P. (Ed.)
1980a   "The empirical-clinical study of families:
Social learning theory as a point of
departure." Pp. 1-28 in J. Vincent (Ed.), Advances in Family Intervention, Assessment,
and Theory (Vol. 1). Greenwich, Connecti-
cut:JAI Press.
1980b   Advances in Family Intervention, Assessment, and Theory (Vol. 1). Greenwich, Con-
necticut:JAI Press.
Wallerstein, J. S., and J. E. Kelly
1980   Surviving the Break-Up: How Children Actually Cope With Divorce. New York:Basic
Books.
Watzlawick, P., J. H. Beavin, and D. D. Jackson
1967   Pragmatics of Human Communication. New
York:W. W. Norton and Company.
Watzlawick, P., and J. H. Weakland (Eds.)

1977   The Interactional View. New York:W. W.
Norton and Company.
Watzlawick, P., J. Weakland, and R. Fisch
1974   Change: Principles of Problem Formation and
Problem Resolution. New York:W. W. Norton and Company.
Weakland, J. H.
1977   "Comments on Ritterman's paper." Family
Process 16:46-47.
Weiss, R. L.
1978   "The conceptualization of marriage from a
behavioral perspective." Pp. 165-239 in T. J.
Paolino and B. S. McCrady (Eds.), Marriage
and Marital Therapy. New York:Brunner/
Mazel.
Wells, R. A., and A. E. Dezen
1978   "The results of family therapy revisited: The
non-behavioral methods." Family Process
17:251-274.
Wells, R. A., T. Dilkes, and T. Burckhardt
1976   "The results of family therapy: A critical
review of the literature." Pp. 499-516 in D. H.
Olson (Ed.), Treating Relationships. Lake
Mills, Iowa:Graphic Publishing Company.
Wertheim, E.
1973   "Family unit therapy and the science and
typology of family systems." Family Process
12:361-376.
1975   "The science typology of family systems. II.
Further theoretical and practical considerations." Family Process 14:285-308.
Whitaker, C. A.
1975a   "Psychotherapy of the absurd: With a special
emphasis on the psychotherapy of
aggression." Family Process 14:1-16.
1975b   "A family therapist looks at marital therapy." In A. S. Gurman, and D. G. Rice
(Eds.), Couples in Conflict: New Directions
in Marital Therapy. New York:Aronson.
1977   "Process techniques of family therapy."
Interaction I:4-19.

ADDENDA

Alcoholism

Cadogan, D.A.
1973   "Marital group therapy in the treatment of
alcoholism." Quarterly Journal of Studies on
Alcoholism 34:1187-1194.
Corder, B. F., R. F. Corder, and N. D. Laidlaw
1972   "An intensive treatment program for alcoholics and their wives." Quarterly Journal of
Studies on Alcoholism 33:1144-1146.
Davis, D., D. Berenson, P. Steinglass, and S. Davis
1974   "The adaptive consequences of drinking."
Psychiatry 37:209-215.
Ewing, J. A., V. Long, and G. G. Wenzel
1961   "Concurrent group psychotherapy of
alcoholic patients and their wives." The International Journal of Group Psychotherapy 11:
329-338.

Hedberg, A. G., and L. Campbell
1974   "A comparison of four behavioral treatments of alcoholism." Journal of Behavior Therapy and Experimental Psychiatry 5:251-256.
Kennedy, D. L.
1976   "Behavior of alcoholics and spouses in a simulation game." Journal of Nervous and Mental Disease 162:23-24.
McCrady, B. S., T. J. Paolino, R. L. Longabaugh, and J. Rossi
1977   "Effects on treatment outcome of joint admission and spouse involvement in treatment of hospitalized alcoholics reported." Pp. 120-121 in T. J. Paolino and B. S. McCrady (Eds.), The Alcoholic Marriage. New York:Grune and Stratton.
Orford, J.
1975   "Alcoholism and marriage: The argument against specialism." Journal of Studies on Alcohol 36:1537-1563.
Steinglass, P.
1979a   "The alcoholic family in the interaction laboratory." Journal of Nervous and Mental Disease 167:428-436.
1979b   "An experimental treatment program for alcoholic couples." Journal of Studies on Alcohol 40:159-182.
Steinglass, P., D. I. David, and D. Berenson
1977   "Observations of conjointly hospitalized 'alcoholic couples' during sobriety and intoxication." Family Process 16:1-16.

Drug Abuse

Alexander, B. K., and G. S. Dibb
1975   "Opiate addicts and their parents." Family Process 14:499-514.
1977   "Interpersonal perception and addict families." Family Process 16:17-28.
Harbin, H. T., and H. M. Maziar
1975   "The families of drug abusers: A literature review." Family Process 14:411-431.
Hendricks, W. J.
1971   "Use of multifamily counseling groups in treatment of male narcotic addicts." International Journal of Group Psychotherapy 21:84-90.
Noone, R. J., and R. L. Reddig
1976   "Case studies in the family treatment of drug abuse." Family Process 15:325-332.
Polakow, R. L., and R. M. Doctor
1973   "Treatment of marijuana and barbitate dependency by contingency and contracting." Journal of Behavior Therapy and Experimental Psychiatry 4:375-377.
Stanton, M. D.
1979   "Family treatment approaches to drug abuse problems: A review." Family Process 18:251-280.
Stanton, M. D., T. C. Todd, F. Steier, J. M. Van-Deusen, L. R. Marder, R. J. Rosoff, S. F. Seaman, and I. Skibinski
1979   "Family characteristics and family therapy of heroin addicts: Final report 1974-1978."

Report prepared for the Psychological Branch, Division of Research, National Institute on Drug Abuse, Department of HEW. Washington, D.C.:U.S. Government Printing Office.
Ziegler-Driscoll, G.
1977   "Family research at Eagleville Hospital and Rehabilitation Center." Family Process 16:175-189.

Juvenile Offenses

Alexander, J. F.
1973   "Defensive supportive communication in normal and deviant families." Journal of Consulting and Clinical Psychology 40:223-231.
Alexander, J. F., C. Barton, R. S. Schiavo, and B. V. Parsons
1976   "Systems-behavioral intervention with families of delinquents: Therapist characteristics, family behavior and outcome." Journal of Consulting and Clinical Psychology 44:656-664.
Alexander, J. F., and B. V. Parsons
1973   "Short-term behavioral intervention with delinquent families: Impact on family process and recidivism." Journal of Abnormal Psychology 81:219-225.
Beal, D., and P. Duckro
1977   "Family counseling as an alternative to legal action for the juvenile status offender." Journal of Marriage and Family Counseling 3:77-81.
Druckman, J. M.
1979   "The family-oriented policy and treatment program for female juvenile status offenders." Journal of Marriage and the Family 41:627-636.
Johnson, T. F.
1977   "The results of family therapy with juvenile offenders." Juvenile Justice 28:311-326.
Klein, N. C., J. F. Alexander, and B. V. Parsons
1977   "Impact of family systems intervention on recidivism and sibling delinquency: A model of primary prevention and program evaluation." Journal of Consulting and Clinical Psychology 45:469-474.
Langsley, D., F. Pittman, P. Machotka, and K. Flomenhaft
1968   "Family crisis therapy-results and implications." Family Process 7:145-158.

Adolescent Psychopathology

Evans, H., L. Chagoya, and V. Rakoff
1971   "Decision-making as to the choice of family therapy in an adolescent in-patient setting." Family Process 10:97-110.
Garrigan, J., and A. Bambrick
1977   "A family therapy for disturbed children: Some experimental results in special education." Journal of Marriage and Family Counseling 3:83-93.

Ro-Trock, G. K., D. K. Wellisch, and J. C. Schoolar
1977   "A family therapy outcome study in an inpatient setting." American Journal of Orthopsychiatry 47:514-522.

Wellisch, D., J. Vincent, and G. Ro-Trock
1976   "Family therapy versus individual therapy: A study of adolescents and their parents." Pp. 275-302 in D. H. Olson (Ed.), Treating Relationships. Lake Mills, Iowa:Graphic Publishing Company.

Childhood Conduct Problems

Karoly, P., and M. Rosenthal
1977   "Training parents in behavior modification: Effects on perceptions of family interactions and deviant child behavior." Behavior Therapy 8:406-410.

Patterson, G. R.
1974   "Intervention for boys with conduct problems: Multiple settings, treatments, and criteria." Journal of Consulting and Clinical Psychology 42:471-481.

Wiltz, N. A., and G. R. Patterson
1974   "An evaluation of parent training procedures designed to alter inappropriate aggressive behavior of boys." Behavior Therapy 5:215-221.

Work and School Phobias

Johnson, A. M., E. I. Falstein, S. A. Szurek, and M. Svendsen
1941   "School phobia." American Journal of Orthopsychiatry 11:702-711.

Pittman, F., D. Langsley, and C. DeYoung
1968   "Work and school phobias: A family approach to treatment." American Journal of Psychiatry 124:1535-1541.

Skynner, A. C.
1974   "School phobia: A reappraisal." British Journal of Medical Psychology 47:1-16.

Psychosomatic Symptoms

Alexander, R., M. D. Lucas, J. W. Duncan, and V. Piens
1976   "The treatment of anorexia nervosa." American Journal of Psychiatry 133:1034-1038.

Bruch, H.
1974   "Perils of behavior modification in treatment of anorexia nervosa." Journal of the American Medical Association 230:1419-1422.

Goetz, P. L., R. A. Succop, J. B. Reinhart, and A. Miller
1977   "Anorexia nervosa in children: A follow-up study." American Journal of Orthopsychiatry 47:597-603.

Minuchin, S., L. Baker, B. Rosman, R. Liebman, L. Milman, and T. Todd
1975   "A conceptual model of psychosomatic illness in children." Archives of General Psychiatry 32:1031-1038.

Minuchin, S., B. Rosman, and L. Baker
1978   Psychosomatic Families: Anorexia Nervosa in Context. Cambridge: Harvard University Press.

Palazzoli, M. S.
1974   Self-Starvation: From the Intrapsychic to Transpersonal Approach to Anorexia Nervosa. London:Chaucer Publishing.

Reinhart, J. B., M. D. Kenna, and R. A. Succop
1972   "Anorexia nervosa in children: Outpatient management." Journal of American Academy of Child Psychiatry 11:114-131.

Silverman, J. A.
1977   "Anorexia nervosa: Clinical and metabolic observations in a successful treatment plan." Pp. 331-339 in R. A. Vigersky (Ed.), Anorexia Nervosa. New York:Raven Press.

Adult Depression

Friedman, A. S.
1973   "Drug therapy and marital therapy in outpatient depressives." Psychopharmacology Bulletin 9:55-57.

1975   "Interaction of drug therapy with marital therapy in depressive patients." Archives of General Psychiatry 32:619-637.

Janowsky, D. W., M. Leff, and R. S. Epstein
1970   "Playing the manic game." Archives of General Psychiatry 22:252-261.

McLean, P. D., K. Ogston, and L. Grauer
1973   "Behavioral approach to the treatment of depression." Journal of Behavior Therapy and Experimental Psychiatry 4:323-330.

Marital Distress

Azrin, N. H., B. J. Naster, and R. Jones
1973   "Reciprocity counseling: A rapid learning-based procedure for marital counseling." Behavior Research and Therapy 11:365-382.

Gurman, A. S., and R. M. Knudson
1978   "Behavioral marriage therapy: I. A psychodynamic-systems critique and reconsideration." Family Process 17:121-138.

Gurman, A. S., R. M. Knudson, and D. P. Kniskern
1978   "Behavioral marriage therapy: IV. Take two aspirin and call us in the morning." Family Process 17:165-180.

Jacobson, N. S.
1977   "Problem-solving and contingency contracting in the treatment of marital discord." Journal of Consulting and Clinical Psychology 45:92-100.

1978   "A review of the research on the effectiveness of marital therapy." In T. J. Paolino and B. S. McCrady (Eds.), Marriage and Marital Therapy: Psychoanalytic, Behavior and Systems Theory Perspectives. New York:Brunner/Mazel.

1979   "Increasing positive behavior in severely distressed marital relationships: The effects of problem-solving training." Behavior Therapy 10:311-326.

O'Leary, K. D., and H. Turkewitz
  1978 Marital therapy from a behavioral perspective." Pp. 240-297 in T. J. Paolino and B. S. McCrady (Eds.), Marriage and Marital Therapy: Psychoanalytic, Behavior and Systems Theory Perspectives. New York: Brunner/Mazel.

Patterson, G. R., H. Hops, and R. L. Weiss
  1975 "Interpersonal skills training for couples in early stages of conflict." Journal of Marriage and the Family 37:295-303.

Stuart, R. B.
  1969 "Operant-interpersonal treatment for marital discord." Journal of Consulting and Clinical Psychology 33:675-682.

While the structural and strategic family approaches have many similarities, their espoused differences have sometimes left therapists in a position of having to choose between them. However, they may be more compatible than has commonly been believed. This paper reviews their basic concepts and operations and presents a model for integrating both approaches in a concurrent and contrapuntal fashion, drawing on the best and most appropriate features of each. Case examples are used to clarify points. Special attention is given to the technique of "strategic disengagement." A set of rules is provided for decision-making as to when one approach or the other might be applied.

48

AN INTEGRATED STRUCTURAL/STRATEGIC APPROACH TO FAMILY THERAPY

*M. Duncan Stanton**

Two of the predominant modes within what have been termed "systems," or, perhaps more accurately, "communication" approaches (Madanes and Haley, 1977) to family therapy are the "structural" and "strategic" types. Frequently there has been confusion as to how these two general approaches overlap and how they differ. More to the point, many family therapists and trainees are often unsure as to whether they might be able to utilize both in therapeutic practice. They sense the similarities and wonder whether "purity" must be maintained or whether the two can be applied interchangeably or in combination, perhaps according to certain rules.[1]

Certainly there are differences between the two approaches, especially at the theoretical level. For instance, no existent theory entirely encompasses both modes adequately.[2] In particular, the temporal (behavioral sequences over time) emphasis of the strategic, versus the spacial-hierarchical emphasis of the structural, is difficult to resolve (Keeney, 1979). However, the clinician cannot always wait for the emergence of theoretical harmony in order to do his job and must proceed as best he can with the tools available.[3] In other words, this may be an instance—common within the family therapy field—where theory must catch up with practice.

Given the present theoretical inadequacies, the thesis of this paper is that these two schools are in many ways compatible on an operational level.[4] It is possible to construct a paradigm which comfortably allows utilization of both structural and strategic techniques, drawing upon the strengths and particular applications of each.

The overall format will be to present the basic principles and practices of both approaches, followed by a set of rules for their use, and ending with case examples. The details of this paradigm as it pertains specifically to marital therapy have been presented elsewhere (Stanton, 1981a), so the ensuing discussion will place primary emphasis on work with whole families.

*M. Duncan Stanton, PhD, is Director, Addicts and Families Program, and senior psychologist, Philadelphia Child Guidance Clinic; Associate Professor of Psychology in Psychiatry, University of Pennsylvania School of Medicine; Director of Family Therapy, Drug Dependence Treatment Center, Philadelphia VA Hospital.

Reprinted from Volume 6, Number 2 of *Journal of Marital and Family Therapy*. Copyright © 1981 American Association for Marriage and Family Therapy. Reprinted by permission.

Before dealing with them separately, it seems appropriate to note some of the common threads between structural and strategic therapy. As a rule, both schools subscribe to the following ideas or methods of treatment:

A. *View of the Family or Couple*
   1. People are seen as interacting within a context—both affecting it and being affected by it.
   2. The family life cycle and developmental stage are important both in diagnosis and in defining therapy strategy—a problem family being seen as "stuck" at a particular stage in its development.
   3. Symptoms are both system-maintained and system-maintaining.
   4. The family or couple can change, allowing new behaviors to emerge, if the overall context is changed. Further, in order for individual change to occur, the interpersonal system itself must change. This would permit different aspects of such family members' (potential) "character" to come to the fore.

B. *Therapy and the Therapist*
   1. Treatment is viewed pragmatically, with an eye toward what "works."
   2. Emphasis is on the present rather than the past.
   3. Repetitive behavioral sequences are to be changed.
   4. While structural therapists may not be as symptom-focused as strategic therapists, both are much more symptom-oriented than psychodynamic therapists.
   5. Process is emphasized much more than content. This includes interventions which are nonverbal and noncognitive—in a sense, "doing away with words."
   6. The therapist should direct the therapy and take responsibility for change.
   7. Diagnosis is obtained through hypothesizing, *intervening* and examining feedback.
   8. Therapeutic contracts are negotiated with clients revolving around the problem and the goals of change.
   9. Interpretation is usually employed to "relabel" or "reframe" rather than to produce "insight."
   10. Behavioral tasks are assigned.
   11. Considerable effort may go into "joining" the family positively and reducing apparent "guilt" or defensiveness. This is more than simply "establishing rapport," as it is often done selectively and in regard to what the therapist deems is necessary for system change.
   12. Therapy cannot usually progress from the initial dysfunctional stage to a "cure" stage without one or more intermediate stages which, on the surface, may appear dysfunctional also. For instance, a therapist may have to take sides with a spouse, thereby "unbalancing" the couple in an opposite way from which it entered treatment, in order to restabilize at a point of parity.
   13. Therapy tends to be brief and often does not exceed six months.

It may be apparent that some of the above points are shared by other, more active interpersonal therapies also, such as the behavioral and "communications training" approaches. However, many of them are distinctive of structural and strategic therapy.

Structural Therapy

The structural approach to family therapy is most closely identified with Salvador Minuchin, Braulio Montalvo, and associates. Its literature has been covered in at least two reviews (Aponte & Van Deusen, 1981; Stanton, 1980) and the principles and techniques appear in two books (Minuchin, 1974; Minuchin, Rosman & Baker, 1978). The coverage herein will necessarily be brief. However, while there are specific features of structural therapy which distinguish it from other modalities, it is important to note that a structural aspect of treatment applies to all therapies and to therapists of all persuasions, as follows: *Any therapeutic intervention made by any therapist necessarily includes a structural component.* For example, by choosing to talk to or interact with one family member or another, or with two parents together, the therapist makes a structural decision, whether or not he is aware of it; not to do so would mean that the therapist acts at random with the participants. In focusing his attention on, or making a statement about, a given member (or subsystem) at a particular point, he is, by nature of the power and status vested in him as a therapist, elevating that person and separating him from the other(s). He shares his power by his attention, so that, as Haley (1976) states, "a comment by the therapist is not merely a comment but also a coalition with one spouse in relation to the other or with the unit against a larger group" (p. 160). The therapist cannot (and probably should not) avoid doing this in most treatment contexts, so the important point is whether he does it with some plan in mind and remains consistent with his plan. In other words, does his (structural) intervention lead the family toward the change that he would like to implement? Ignoring this notion handicaps the therapist and can even prove detrimental to treatment.

Some Basic Structural Therapy Concepts
    In this therapy *the focus is less on theory of change than on theory of family* (Stanton, 1980). The model is not particularly complex, theoretically. Some of the primary concepts are:
    1. Attention is paid to *proximity and distance* between family members and subsystems and these are defined through *boundaries,* that is, the rules which determine "who participates and how" in the family (Minuchin, 1974, p. 53).
    2. The extremes of the proximity and distance continuum are *enmeshment* and *disengagement,* with most (e.g., "normal") families and subsystems lying at intermediate points between the two poles.
    3. A family is described or schematized spatially in terms of its hierarchies and its alliances or coalitions.
    4. Problems result from a rigid, dysfunctional family structure.

Structural Techniques
    1. The basic goal is to induce a "more adequate family organization" of the sort that will maximize growth and potential in each of its members (Minuchin, 1974).
    2. The thrust of the therapy is toward "restructuring" the system, such as establishing or loosening boundaries, differentiating enmeshed members and increasing the involvement of disengaged members.
    3. The therapeutic plan is gauged against knowledge of what is "normal" for a family at a given stage in its development, with due consideration of its cultural and socioeconomic context.
    4. The desired interactional change must take place *within the actual session* (enactment), with the family sitting in the room (Hoffman, 1976).
    5. Techniques such as *unbalancing* a system and *intensifying* an interaction are part of the therapy.
    6. The therapist "joins" and accommodates to the system in a sort of blending experience, but retains enough independence both to resist the family's pull and to challenge (restructure) it at various points. He thus *actively uses himself* as a boundary-maker, intensifier and general change agent in the session.

7. Treatment is usually limited to include those members of a family who live within a household or have regular contact with the immediate family. However, this might involve grandparents living nearby, or even an employer, if the problem is work-related.

8. The practice is to bring a family to a level of "health" or "complexity" and then stand ready to be called in the future, if necessary. Such a model is seen to combine the advantages of short and long-term therapy.

Strategic Therapy

Haley (1973) has defined strategic therapy as that in which the clinician initiates what happens during treatment and designs a particular approach for each problem. Strategic therapists take responsibility for directly influencing people. They want to at least temporarily enhance their influence over the interpersonal system at hand in order to bring about beneficial change. In fact, they are *not as concerned about family theory as they are with the theory and means for inducing change.*

A number of people and groups are considered representative of this school, such as Milton Erickson, Jay Haley, the Mental Research Institute (MRI) group (including Don Jackson, John Weakland, Paul Watzlawick, Richard Fisch, Arthur Bodin and Carlos Sluzki), Gerald Zuk, the Institute for Family Study group in Milan (including Mara Palazzoli-Selvini, Luigi Boscolo, Gianfranco Cecchin and Giuliana Prata), Lynn Hoffman, Richard Rabkin, Peggy Papp, and Olga Silverstein. These therapists do not all operate in exactly the same way, but rather than devote inordinate space to their individual contributions, styles, and differences, the approach here will be more superficial—presenting the principles and practices which apply to most of them. The reader interested in greater detail is referred to their various published works or to several synopses which have emerged in the literature (Madanes and Haley, 1977; Stanton, 1980, 1981b).

Some Basic Strategic Therapy Concepts

Strategic therapists see symptoms as the resultants or concomitants of misguided attempts at changing an existing difficulty (Watzlawick, Weakland and Fisch, 1974). However, such symptoms usually succeed only in making things worse, while attempts by the family to alleviate the problem often exacerbate it. A symptom is regarded as a communicative act, with message qualities, which serves as a sort of contract between two or more members and has a function within the interpersonal network (Watzlawick, Beavin & Jackson, 1967). It is a label for a nonlinear or "recursive" *sequence of behaviors* within a social organization (Haley, 1976). A symptom usually appears when a person is "in an impossible situation and is trying to break out of it" (Haley, 1973, p. 44). He is locked into a sequence or pattern with his significant other(s) and cannot see a way to alter it through non-symptomatic means. The symptom is thus a homeostatic mechanism regulating marital or family transactions (Jackson, 1957).

Strategic Techniques

A basic tenet of strategic therapy is that therapeutic change comes about through the "interactional processes set off when a therapist intervenes actively and directively in particular ways" in a family or marital system (Haley, 1971, p. 7). The therapist works to substitute new behavior patterns or sequences for the vicious, positive feedback circles already existing (Weakland, Fisch, Watzlawick & Bodin, 1974). In other words, his goal is to change the dysfunctional *sequence* of behaviors shown by the family appearing for treatment. Some primary techniques are:

1. The utilization of *tasks and directives*. In fact, this emphasis on directives is the cornerstone of the approach.
2. The problem must be put in solvable form. It should be something that can be objectively agreed upon, e.g., counted, observed or measured, so that one can assess if it has actually been influenced.
3. Considerable emphasis is placed on *extra-session change*—altering the processes occurring outside of the session.
4. Power struggles with the family are generally avoided, the tendency being to take the path of least resistance and use implicit or indirect ways of turning the family's investment to positive use (Weakland, *et al.*, 1974).
5. "Positive interpretation" (Soper & L'Abate, 1977) to the family of its symptom(s), motives, and homeostatic tendencies is readily employed.
6. "Paradoxical" interventions are common and may be directed toward the whole family or to certain members. This category encompasses more than simply "prescribing the symptom," and may also include strategies outlined by Rohrbaugh and associates (in Stanton, 1981b) such as "restraining" (discouraging or denying the possibility of change), and "positioning" (e.g., exaggerating a family's position, for instance by becoming more pessimistic than they are). In a sense, the therapist becomes more homeostatic than the family and thereby "turns their resistance back on itself" (Stanton, 1981b, 1982).

The Interplay Between Structural and Strategic Approaches

Within the systems or communication approaches presented here it is possible to apply either a structural or strategic tack separately, or to use the two both concurrently and contrapuntally. Three general rules and three specific situations apply.

General Rule No. 1

The first rule being proposed is to *initially deal with a family through a structural approach*—joining, accommodating, testing boundaries, and restructuring. Under this rule the therapist begins by essentially assuming a direct posture toward the family. The major rationale for beginning treatment in this fashion is because the structural approach: (a) is more straightforward or direct and therefore more parsimonious (it seems wisest not to complicate matters when a simpler mode will suffice); (b) is more comprehensible, especially for the less experienced therapist, because the reactions of the family to interventions are immediate and easy to observe, not requiring guesswork as to what will happen outside and after the session; interventions directed toward extra-session behavior often demand a good deal of therapeutic experience and without this the therapist is "flying blind"; (c) is easier, in my experience, for therapists who are learning to do family therapy to understand than certain facets of strategic therapy— especially paradoxical techniques—so that with such therapists it seems reasonable to begin this way; (d) has demonstrated its utility and efficacy with many different kinds of symptoms and problem groups (Gurman and Kniskern, 1978; Olson, *et al.*, 1980; Stanton, 1980).

General Rule No. 2

The second general rule is to *switch to a predominantly strategic approach when "structural" techniques either are not succeeding or are unlikely to succeed*. The rationale here is that many of the strategic techniques were developed from treating excessively homeostatic families (e.g., those of schizophrenics) and are more effective for dealing with extreme "resistance." Such techniques include the heavy use of positive interpretation, the introduction of paradoxical instructions, or the use of "strategic disengagement" (discussed below). There are at least three situations which might dictate such a switch, as follows:

1. *Switching from a structural to strategic approach*. In this kind of situation the therapist works within a structural framework and finds that resistance mounts progressively in the family, or simply that no change is occurring. It is not uncommon to encounter certain families in which the somewhat confrontational structural approach only leads to escalation in defensiveness by the members. The therapist finds himself beset by a group of people working overtime to bring him around to their respective points of view. An example is the "warring" couple, with the partners engaging in an ongoing battle involving matters both large and small. Any attempt by the therapist to suggest change or to attribute error to a spouse or to the couple is met by massive counter-attack; the therapist's confrontation, no matter how gentle, mobilizes all the couple's energy to resist him, thus minimizing the possibility that efforts can be rechanneled in the direction of positive change. Another situation where a switching of approach may be indicated is with families in which an extremely strong homeostatic tendency is noted. The therapist makes structural interventions which seem accurate, but nothing happens—there is no "second-order" change (Watzlawick *et al.*, 1974). Tasks are never followed or are distorted to disadvantage. The resistance is often covert, and the therapist starts to sense defeat. This kind of pattern is not atypical in families with a schizophrenic member, an addict, or in which one or more members display what historically has been termed a "personality disorder." Often such families are entwined with other systems, commonly those of the grandparents, and therapeutic leverage is slight or nonexistent.

Encountering problems such as the above requires a change in tactics. When meeting these kinds of resistances it may be helpful for the therapist to: (a) use "compression" (Stanton, 1981b, 1982) and push certain members or the whole family toward each other; or (b) switch immediately to a (strategic) technique of profuse positive interpretation. In the latter, he should take the tack that everything the family does is "wonderful," is based on noble intentions, and probably should not be changed. He notes the benefits which the symptom provides for the family. He may then direct that they continue to do things as they have in the past, since change would result in the loss of some very helpful and functional attributes.

2. *Determining strategy from prior knowledge*. This is the second situation in which a switch in tactics may be indicated. Based on what is learned before ever seeing a given case, the therapist may decide to lean toward more strategic techniques. Common examples might be when one has pre-therapy information that a family has a severely dysfunctional member, or a lengthy history of unsuccessful treatments. Such families have apparently not been as responsive to conventional structural therapy techniques (or to other psychotherapies) as they have been to strategic modes. In such situations, a model applied by Andolfi, Menghi, Nicoló and Saccu (1980) might be fitting. These therapists tend to work paradoxically from the start with such cases. They constantly take a position which is more homeostatic than that of the family, at least in the early phases of treatment. Interestingly, as a family progresses, Andolfi *et al.* tend to move toward a more structural approach (see General Rule No. 3, below). It almost seems as if such severely disturbed families need to experience a strategic intervention first, before they become individuated enough to respond to structural techniques.

A somewhat similar approach, using planned directives (but rarely paradoxical instructions) is used by Berenson (1979; also in Stanton, 1981b) in dealing with alcoholic couples. In the initial stage, emphasis is on establishing space between the partners and on building external support systems for them. In a later stage other techniques are used, many of which have a structural flavor.

3. *Confusion and loss of "understanding" by the therapist.* There are times in therapy when the therapist becomes befuddled, being unsure of what is occurring with the family and unclear as to where to go with treatment. At such times, Sluzki (1978) offers the following principle: "If you find yourself not understanding what is going on with the couple (or family), *then* cease paying attention to content, and observe verbal patterns, sequences, gestures and postures, and/or observe your own emotions, attitudes or postures" (p. 389). He notes that such occurrences usually indicate that the therapist is being pulled by a fascination for content and has probably been inducted into the system; he has thus lost control of his own behavior and needs to gain distance. At this point, it behooves him to change his behavior. Sluzki notes that simply acknowledging his confusion—stating, "I don't understand"—is one way of differentiating from the system. There are other ways, also, such as disengagement, which have a more strategic flavor to them.

Strategic Disengagement

While this is not, per se, a rule for deciding on a strategic or structural tack, it is an important option and one which can be very effective if properly applied. Thus it is given special attention here. It involves the therapist distancing himself from the family at a point of entanglement and is therefore applicable most specifically to situations No. 1 and 3 (above). It first requires that the therapist be at least minimally joined with the family, or certainly in a position where he has enough leverage to be sought or respected by them. It can be invoked when the therapist finds himself being drawn into a family's quarrels. If he is not careful, he can easily slide toward working hard with them to "patch things up," serving as a kind of matchmaker, or trying to pour oil on troubled waters. Too often this is a trap, and can lead to failure. At such points the therapist may want to disengage almost entirely, leaving the family, in a sense, alone—almost abandoning them momentarily, or at least bowing out of the battle (a technique in which Carl Whitaker, in particular, excels). When the therapist senses that a family or couple is both strongly resisting change and trying to foist responsibility on him, he might counter with a calm, withdrawing statement such as "I can see . . . you've got a problem." When they agree and then ask what to do about it, such a therapist might say "It's a tough one." If they pursue further, asking (or telling) him to help, he might respond with "I don't know what you should do," or "It beats me." This tactic shares some elements with Selvini-Palazzoli *et al.*'s (1978) declaration of "total impotence" in a case. Such a retreat, in addition to differentiating the therapist, can have at least two effects. First, it shifts the responsibility for change back onto the family; the intent is to bring them, in effect, to the conclusion, "Well, if the therapist can't do anything about this, or is not competent to help, maybe we will have to do it ourselves." Related to this, a second effect may be to unite them, possibly against the therapist, but nonetheless placing them in a position where they are no longer diverting their energies toward triangulating an outsider; they must turn to each other and perhaps try to find a common ground for cooperation, problem-solving and change.

General Rule No. 3

Following success with strategic methods, and given that a case is to continue in therapy, it may be advisable to *revert once again to a structural approach.* As noted above, this procedure has also been applied by Andolfi *et al.* (1980) in their work with families in schizophrenic transaction; it forms the final phase of their "restructuring" phase. In this phase the IP becomes less central and family members start to behave more as separate *people* rather than as a system which only reacts massively and in concert. At such a point structural techniques, such as creating boundaries and enactment, are appropriate.

Case Examples

The following two cases present somewhat different versions of the selective or sequential use of structural and strategic techniques. The first involves a number of more conventional moves, while the major intervention in the second is a bit more unusual.

Case A

This was a white, blue-collar family residing in a small city. The identified patient was an 11-year-old boy, John, who had become a behavior problem at home and school. He had been stealing money and jewelry—both from his mother and from his friends' families. At home he constantly stretched rules and aggravated his younger brother. His schoolwork was fine, but the teacher called his mother several times to complain that he was disruptive and could not "sit still" in class. The nuclear family also included John's four-year-old half-brother, Billy, who was the child of these parents. Mother had been married before, and John was the child of her previous marriage. John's biological father was rarely heard from and was essentially out of the picture, so the term "father" will henceforth refer to his step-father. Two other facts are important. First, even though he was working steadily, the father's level of social adaptation was marginal. He appeared somewhat "schizoid," showing paranoia, ambivalence, and rigidity; he had few friends and preferred to preoccupy himself with motorcycles and guns. Second, a certain amount of John's upbringing had been carried out by his maternal grandparents: They lived in town and he stayed with them several months each year and visited regularly. As treatment progressed it was learned that John was usually sent to stay with these grandparents when he got into trouble.

When this case was brought to supervision—after three or four sessions—therapy was not going well. The parents were heading toward divorce—father having moved out of the home—and John's misbehavior had not abated. From that point on therapy evolved through three stages. First, an attempt was made by the therapist (Edward Albee) to get the parents at least to cooperate in the management of their son. While father took an interest in this, mother undercut and devalued all such attempts. After two or three sessions it became clear that (a) the marriage was unsalvageable, (b) we may have been overlooking something important, and (c) a new strategy was indicated.

The second, more strategic phase of treatment began when a session was held which included the nuclear family and the maternal grandparents. In the session grandfather appeared supportive of his son-in-law, stating that he did not blame the younger man for becoming upset with his wife (grandfather's daughter) and emphasizing that she did not deserve good treatment in view of the way she was behaving. While this ostensible joining of grandfather and father might have a noble ring to it, in effect it was an insidious and subversive move by the grandfather: It conveyed the message that the younger couple's marriage had no reason to succeed, and perhaps that it *should not* succeed. The grandfather sided with his son-in-law for the purpose of subverting the marriage. It was also noted in the session that the grandmother was disgruntled by the whole exercise. She was the grandfather's second wife and it was apparent that she did not like being ensnared in her stepdaughter's problems. Another stress factor for her was that she was about to enter the hospital for surgery, and was naturally anxious about this.

From the above session an hypothesis was formed: Grandfather was overinvolved with his daughter, holding onto her while neglecting his wife. Mother used John as a substitute for herself, sending him to his grandparent's home as a way of buying at least a bit of her own freedom. John's misbehavior served as a convenient reason to send him to the grandparents, thereby keeping grandfather involved and giving him a problem to solve; he was retired and therefore was in need of such a "job."

This hypothesis was used to develop a strategic plan. It included the following steps:

(1) the therapist was to exert considerable effort in joining the grandmother, such as commiserating with her about her illness and noting how she had "enough to do" without worrying about her stepdaughter's problems; this joining was to be done by one or more visits to the hospital or home; (2) the therapist was to take sides with the grandparents against the daughter, noting how she was "conning" them into caring for John so she could "galavant around"; they were to be warned that she would do her best to pawn John off on them whenever she could, and that this did not seem fair because they had already done enough child-rearing in their lives. (This reframing was necessary in order to get the grandfather mobilized enough to distance from his daughter; his tendency had been to solicitously give in and "feel sorry" for her, rather than to establish an appropriate boundary); (3) related to this, it was to be emphasized separately (by telephone or home visit) to grandfather that his wife was about to be hospitalized and would need his close, regular care and attention; his daughter's foisting her son on him would draw him away from this important task and was a thoughtless thing for her to do at such a time of crisis; (4) it was also to be separately conveyed to daughter that her father, because he was a "good father," seemed to always be trying to "tell her how to run things," but that now, since he had to give more attention to his sick wife, maybe he could "let up"; however, she was to be careful in the near future not to allow him to involve her and John too much, even if he might try again "because of his concern."

The above plan was implemented and things started to change. After grandmother was discharged from the hospital, she and her husband stayed fairly close and started to plan a vacation trip. Mother consciously avoided seeing her parents too often or sending John to them; she only made visits on appropriate occasions, such as Christmas, and reduced her telephone calls to them to once every week or two. John became less of a problem and therapy moved to the next phase.

The third stage began following a brief hiatus around grandmother's hospitalization and involved the therapist working on parenting issues with mother and the two boys, in a straightforward structural fashion. She had tended to "give in" to them too easily and not to praise their good behavior when it occurred. These final six sessions included actually practicing new parenting methods in the therapist's office. Behavioral tasks were used liberally. Mother grew increasingly more competent in taking control of her children and the three of them also began enjoying recreational activities together. In addition, the therapist worked with mother on her own social relationships. Therapy was terminated with this phase—the total process extending over a period of 5–6 months and involving approximately 15 sessions.

A follow-up was made a year later. No problems with either child were reported, and mother was closely involved with an apparently competent man with whom both she and her sons got along well.

Discussion. It should be apparent that structural conceptualizations were used throughout this therapy, including such notions as proximity/distance, boundaries, and cross-generational coalitions. However, the operations introduced in the second stage, while still based on a structural framework, were more strategic in nature (Rule No. 2). While paradoxical techniques were not used, a clear *plan* was developed which encompassed extra-session change, some positive interpretation and, halting of behavioral sequences. In addition, grandmother's unfortunate hospitalization, an event which had the potential to exacerbate the situation, was used to advantage in the therapy—it gave grandfather a new job and permitted greater joining between him and his wife. In the final stage, the therapist moved to a more conventional structural mode (Rule No. 3), including enactment of desired changes within the session, and the maintenance of generational boundaries.

Case B

This was a self-referred black family composed of mother (age 29), mother's boyfriend (age 43), who was a municipal employee, Paul (age 9), Ellen (age 8), and Marie (age 6). Mother's boyfriend had lived in the home for three years, and the children liked him, considering him a kind of stepparent. He and mother were planning to marry. Since the children almost never saw their biological father, mother's boyfriend will henceforth be referred to as "father."

The identified patient was Ellen. She was reported by mother to be a problem at school—not paying attention, not completing her work, and subtly defying the teacher in passive-aggressive ways (although we later found that in reality the school was not having difficulty with her). She was also noted to fight frequently with her siblings and to be a behavior problem when she went to visit relatives. However, later—in the second session—the parents noted they were having problems with all the children.

The family was seen ten times over five months, with several lapses in treatment due to illness, weather and several other "reasons." The therapist was Ms. Gene Zug.[5] A multitude of structural interventions was tried, including the following:

1. Enacting an obedience task. The children's reactions to orders by either parent were examined; they responded quickly and appropriately.

2. Establishing generational boundaries, connecting parents and distributing their workloads at home. Father was to share the discipline and the parents were to be alone at a certain time once or twice a week.

3. Securing a volunteer or part-time job for mother. This was intended to direct some of her energy and interests from the children. It was discussed with, and positively entertained by, the couple.

4. Obtaining parental agreement and cooperation on discipline. The father tended to be too strict and the mother too lenient. They did agree on six of the children's behaviors as being problematic and on the appropriate punishments for these. The task was to focus on only two of these for a week, and to mete out the agreed upon punishments for these two types of behavior.

5. Developing a behavioral reward system. This was instituted around parental directives. The parents agreed to apply it three times during the week.

6. Differentiating the children and connecting father and son. The children were seen as a "three-headed-monster." A discussion was held with father (with mother present) about taking a more "gentle" stance toward Paul and spending more time with him. Father agreed, Paul was brought into the room, and the two of them talked amicably—planning an activity which they would like to do together during the week, plus listing some others for the future. Mother stayed out of the interaction.

7. Uniting parents on a rule. Without the children present, the parents discussed and agreed upon a single rule for them, including rewards and punishments. This took 30 or 40 minutes. When the children re-entered, the father presented this "mini-program" to them. Then the mother corrected him and changed the rule.

The result in nearly every one of the above interventions was that the parents would agree to a task and not carry it through. At best, they made a feeble, token effort, even though we checked up on them in subsequent sessions. Although Ellen seemed to become more outgoing as treatment progressed, the parents reported no change. They would return for a session complaining anew about the children's behavior.

Clearly, we had been working too hard. We had assumed too much responsibility, while the parents continued to subvert each other. There was need to reappraise our methods and redefine our hypotheses. The consistently resistant, homeostatic behavior of the parents indicated that they were strongly invested in keeping the children's behavior as it was. We also noted that the date the parents had told us (at the beginning of treatment) that they planned to get married was fast approaching, but there were no indications that they would actually take this step. This would be another in what we had more recently learned was a series of wedding postponements extending over several years prior to therapy. We hypothesized that the children were being used by the parents to avoid intimacy and the more complete commitment that a marriage would entail. Thus we decided to hold one more session and end with the following strategic intervention:

In the final meeting the therapist began by apologizing to the parents for misunderstanding the whole situation. She said she had been working under the assumption that the appropriate goal for treatment was for the children to improve their behavior. Now she realized that this was all wrong—that she had been "way off base." She noted that if the children improved, the parents would be alone more often in the evening and would be brought closer together. Now she saw that this was not the best thing for them—they were not ready to get that close or to get married. She apologized again and stated that it made no sense for them to waste their time coming to therapy, because if it succeeded, the couple would be put in a situation that they did not want. She also suggested that they may never want to get married. The session was ended by leaving the door open to meeting again in the future if need be, but that to continue at this time was definitely wrong.

Four months after termination the therapist received a phone call from the mother. She said that the couple had just gotten married. She also mentioned in passing that she was 3½ months pregnant. Father was reported to be very pleased about the pregnancy and at the prospect of having a child of his own. Mother said that things were "going pretty well" for her. The children were attending day camp (which was a change, because she had not permitted them such freedom in past summers). This gave her some "breathing time." She also observed that they arrived home tired, so they were less trouble in the evenings. The family was going out to parks or on picnics almost every weekend.

The mother made brief "social" contacts with the therapist at 9½ and 18 months post-treatment. Their baby had arrived, and father was "pleased as punch" with it (he had accompanied mother in the delivery room). Paul had entered a class for gifted children and the other children were doing fine. The parents had worked out a system for handling the children.

As of two years post-treatment the family was functioning well and had not felt the need for additional therapy.

Discussion. This case fairly clearly demonstrates the switch from structural to strategic techniques (Rule No. 2). Of course, the point could be made that the switch should have been made sooner, before reaching a point of near desperation. However, the therapist wanted to learn the structural approach and this may have influenced the decision to continue so far down this path.

The parting intervention is an example of strategic disengagement. We no longer agreed to play the game. We also left the couple with a thinly veiled challenge, that is, that they would not get married. We thus became more homeostatic than they, and they "rebounded", perhaps to prove us wrong. It is not clear whether the final intervention would have worked if it had not been preceded by at least a certain amount of joining and a show of commitment on the part of the therapist. This is a question open to further investigation.

Conclusion

The purpose in this paper has been to present a model for the combined or sequential use of both structural and strategic techniques. It is an attempt to incorporate the best and most appropriate features of each. The rules which are provided are designed to assist in decision-making as to when elements of one or the other approach should be applied.

REFERENCES

Aponte, H. J. & Van Deusen, J. M. Structural family therapy. In A. L. Gurman and D. P. Kniskern (Eds.), *Handbook of family therapy*. New York: Brunner/Mazel, 1981.

Andolfi, M., Menghi, P., Nicoló, A. M., & Saccu, C. Interaction in rigid systems: A model of intervention in families with a schizophrenic member. In M. Andolfi and I. Zwerling (Eds.), *Dimensions of family therapy*. New York: Guilford Press, 1980.

Berenson, D. The therapist's relationship with couples with an alcoholic member. In E. Kaufman and P. Kaufmann (Eds.), *Family therapy of drug and alcohol abuse*. New York: Gardner, 1979.

Gurman, A. S. & Kniskern, D. P. Research on marital and family therapy: Progress, perspective and prospect. In S. L. Garfield and A. E. Bergin (Eds.), *Handbook of psychotherapy and behavior change: An empirical analysis* (2nd Edition), New York: Wiley, 1978.

Haley, J. A review of the family therapy field. In J. Haley (Ed.), *Changing families*. New York: Grune & Stratton, 1971.

Haley, J. *Uncommon therapy*. New York: W. W. Norton, 1973.

Haley, J. *Problem solving therapy*. San Francisco: Jossey-Bass, 1976.

Haley, J. *Leaving home: The therapy of disturbed young people*. New York: McGraw-Hill, 1980.

Hoffman, L. Breaking the homeostatic cycle. In P. Guerin (Ed.), *Family therapy: Theory and practice*. New York: Gardner Press, 1976.

Jackson, D. D. The question of family homeostasis. *Psychiatric Quarterly Supplement*, 1957, *31*, 79–90.

Keeney, B. P. Ecosystemic epistemology: An alternate paradigm for diagnosis. *Family Process*, 1979, *18*, 117–129.

Madanes, C. & Haley, J. Dimensions of family therapy. *Journal of Nervous and Mental Disease*, 1977, *165*, 88–98.

Minuchin, S. *Families and family therapy*. Cambridge, Mass.: Harvard University Press, 1974.

Minuchin, S., Rosman, B. & Baker, L. *Psychosomatic families: Anorexia nervosa in context*. Cambridge, Mass.: Harvard University Press, 1978.

Olson, D. H., Russell, C. S. & Sprenkle, D. H. Marital and family therapy: A decade review. *Journal of Marriage and the Family*, 1980, *42*.

Palazzoli-Selvini, M., Boscolo, L., Cecchin, G. & Prata, G. *Paradox and counter-paradox: A new model in the therapy of the family in schizophrenic transaction*. New York: Jason Aronson, 1978.

Sluzki, C. E. Marital therapy from a systems theory perspective. In T. J. Paolino and B. S. McCrady (Eds.), *Marriage and marital therapy: Psychoanalytic, behavioral and systems theory perspectives*. New York: Brunner/Mazel, 1978.

Soper, P. H. & L'Abate, L. Paradox as a therapeutic technique: A review. *International Journal of Family Counseling*, 1977, *5*, 10–21.

Stanton, M. D. Family therapy: Systems approaches. In G. P. Sholevar, R. M. Benson and B. J. Blinder (Eds.), *Emotional disorders in children and adolescents: Medical and psychological approaches to treatment*. Jamaica, New York: S. P. Medical and Scientific Books (division of Spectrum Publications), 1980.

Stanton, M. D. Marital therapy from a structural/strategic viewpoint. In G. P. Sholevar (Ed.). *The handbook of marriage and marital therapy*. Jamaica, N. Y: S. P. Medical and Scientific Books (division of Spectrum Publications), 1982a.

Stanton, M. D. Strategic approaches to family therapy. In A. S. Gurman and D. P. Kniskern (Eds.), *Handbook of family therapy*. New York: Brunner/Mazel, 1981b.

Stanton, M. D. Fusion, compression, expansion and the workings of paradox: A theory of therapeutic/systemic change. Paper submitted for publication, 1982.

Watzlawick, P., Beavin, J. H. & Jackson, D. D. *Pragmatics of human communication*, New York: W. W. Norton & Company, 1967.

Watzlawick, P., Weakland, J. & Fisch, R. *Change: Principles of problem formation and problem resolution*. New York: W. W. Norton & Company, 1974.

Weakland, J., Fisch, R., Watzlawick, P. & Bodin, A. M. Brief therapy: Focused problem resolution. *Family Process*, 1974, *13*, 141–168.

NOTES

[1]Appreciation is extended to the following for helpful comments on portions of this paper: Edward C. Albee, MS; Ellen Berman, MD; H. Charles Fishman, MD; Monica McGoldrick-Orfanidis, ACSW; Thomas C. Todd, PhD; Gene Zug, MS.

[2]The author has been engaged for some time in the development of a theory which logically subsumes structural and strategic concepts and operations. This work is only now reaching fruition (e.g., Stanton, 1982) and its efficacy must await the test of time.

[3]The masculine pronoun is used here and later in the text for purposes of convenience. To paraphrase Haley (1980), therapists and clients come in both sexes, and the author acknowledges the inequity of the traditional use of the masculine pronoun.

[4]Their compatibility in many areas is not surprising, since a strategic therapist, Jay Haley, was instrumental in the development of structural family therapy. Both Haley's strategic model and the structural approach place considerable emphasis on hierarchical family organization, noting that aberrant hierarchies (such as cross-generational coalitions) are frequently diagnostic of family dysfunction.

[5]The author served as supervisor and also entered several sessions to conduct the therapy.

A review of theoretical mechanisms underlying paradoxical interventions is undertaken in an effort to classify them into three broad types: redefinition, symptom escalation and crisis induction, and redirection. A list of individual and family patient characteristics and problems particularly applicable to each type of paradoxical intervention is presented along with contraindications for use. Last, implications for training and cautions as to their use are presented.

49

TYPES OF PARADOXICAL INTERVENTION AND INDICATIONS/CONTRAINDICATIONS FOR USE IN CLINICAL PRACTICE*

Lawrence Fisher,† Ann Anderson,‡ and James E. Jones‡

THE USE of paradoxical interventions is enjoying widespread popularity in recent years as evidenced by increasing numbers of papers (13). Although a potentially powerful and influential therapeutic tool, these techniques are often inappropriately used as substitutes for an effective understanding of family dynamics or as a "quick and easy" solution to complex therapeutic problems. Yet the clinical power of these approaches, when properly used, cannot be easily dismissed.

Working in a large, inpatient-outpatient teaching hospital, we found ourselves asked to consult with therapists who had run into

therapeutic impasses with their patient families or individual patients. Working as a team, we observed and participated in several therapy sessions for each referral and then made a number of recommendations as to possible courses out of the impasse, using a paradoxical frame of reference. This experience led us to three general conclusions with respect to the use of paradoxical techniques in clinical practice.

First, it became clear that paradoxical maneuvers could be categorized into a series of well-defined, relatively circumscribed intervention strategies, each of which shared given theoretical similarities but emphasized different aspects of the paradox. Such a cohesive frame of reference proved very helpful in devising specific interventions in particular clinical situations.

Second, we developed a hesitancy to suggest paradoxical interventions to therapists working with certain types of families or families presenting with certain kinds of problems, whereas with other families these techniques seemed appropriate and productive. What developed from this experience

* Reprint requests should be addressed to Lawrence Fisher, Ph.D., U.C.S.F., Fresno-Central San Joaquin Medical Education Program, Department of Psychiatry, V.A.M.C., 2615 East Clinton Avenue, Fresno, California 93703.

† University of California, San Francisco: Fresno Central San Joaquin Valley Medical Education Program; and Veterans Administration Hospital, Fresno, Calif.

‡ Department of Psychiatry, University of Rochester Medical School, Rochester, New York.

From Lawrence Fisher, Ann Anderson, and James E. Jones, "Types of Paradoxical Intervention and Indications/Contraindications for Use in Clinical Practice," *Family Process*, 1981, 20, pp. 25-35. Reprinted by permission of the publisher and authors.

was a list of indications and contraindications for the use of these techniques in family-oriented psychotherapy.

Last, several cautions and considerations came into play in our efforts to train other professionals, whether colleagues or budding family therapists, in the use of paradoxical maneuvers. The present paper will focus on each of these three topics.

Techniques of Paradoxical Intervention

To understand the development of a classification of paradoxical techniques and its application to specific types of family problems, it is first necessary to briefly review some of the mechanisms under which therapeutic change under paradoxical intent is thought to take place. In this way some linkage between the prescription for change and the theoretical process of change can occur.

Mozdierz et al. (6) report that Adler was probably the first to write about a paradoxical strategy in psychological intervention. Adler saw the paradox as a dialectic in which the patient simultaneously wanted and did not want to give up his symptom. This dilemma escalated into a power struggle with the therapist who was seen by the patient as forcing the patient into a one-down position in an effort to rid the patient of his ambivalently held symptom. In Adlerian terms, the patient improved by an increase in self-esteem following a successful power move against the therapist who suggested that he keep the symptom.

Frankl (2, 3) emphasizes a shift from studying the symptom in phobias and obsessive-compulsive patterns to a focus on observing anticipatory anxiety surrounding the fear of the object or the thought, respectively. In sexual problems, the third symptom area addressed in his writing, the same emphasis prevails: a shift away from actual sexual performance to the role of spectator.

This shift of emphasis, in a sense an alteration of perspective from the symptom

to the rules that govern its maintenance, has been the subject of more recent work by Watzlawick and his colleagues (12) and still more recent by Selvini Palazzoli and her colleagues (9). Watzlawick is quite explicit in terms of defining a mechanism of change. He suggests that change occurs through a process of "reframing," which is defined as an alteration in "the conceptual and/or emotional setting or viewpoint in relation to which a situation is experienced and to place it in another frame which fits the facts of the same concrete situation equally well or even better, thereby changing its entire meaning" (12, p. 95). In other words, the meaning attributed to the situation is altered or redefined and therefore its consequences change as well.

Selvini Palazzoli et al. (10), whose theoretical position tends to be based on Watzlawick's pioneering work, extends these underlying premises to suggest that the mechanism of change resides with the therapist's positive connotation of all behavior. In this way the family is thrown into a bind by being asked to accept the positive qualities of the symptom they ambivalently ask to be rid of.

The notion of the double bind brings to mind the early work of the Palo Alto group and Haley's relatively recent writings continue in that tradition. Haley (4) suggests that all communication occurs at both overt and covert, or metacommunicative levels. The latter message informs or interprets the former. He suggests that the therapeutic paradox clarifies the contradictory messages often posed by overt and metacommunications by making them both public in an understandable manner. More recently, however, Haley (5) has emphasized the use of analogy and metaphor. By clarifying these messages, often symbolically, the therapist can overtly accept the presenting and covert symptoms and literally suggest their repeated, perhaps accelerated occurrence, once a trusting relationship has been established. In this sense, the ambivalence expressed by the symptom's presence is taken by the therapist as reality, not as symbol. Interestingly, Haley emphasizes a component of therapy that many others often omit; the effect of giving up a symptom on the family system and the necessity for incorporating family issues in the paradoxical therapy of individual patients.

Papp (7), in a recent paper on the work of the Ackerman group, describes the mechanism of change as a redefinition of the problem. Whereas the family enters treatment with the "problem" being their inability to remove the presenting symptom, the therapist paradoxically ties the elimination of the symptom to a change in the family system itself; one cannot occur without the other. The issue is no longer how to change the symptom but what will happen to the family if it is changed.

Raskin and Klein (8) state three fundamental mechanisms of change following paradoxical intent—(a) it attacks the patient's power over therapy by undercutting the patient's control of symptom display; (b) it utilizes principles of human learning to extinguish, satiate, or aversively reduce the presentation of the symptom; and (c) it redefines the symptom within another frame of reference.

This review, admittedly brief and not exhaustive, has served to point up some of the similarities and differences with respect to mechanisms of change postulated by various authors within the rubric of a paradoxical frame of reference. After reviewing these theorists as well as pooling our clinical experience with similar techniques, it became apparent that interventions based upon the paradox were those in which the therapist rechanneled the energy the family generated in an effort to maintain the symptom by: (a) redefining it by giving the behavior another meaning; (b) escalating it by promoting a crisis or increasing the frequency of its expression; or (c) redirecting it by changing an aspect of the symptom. It also became apparent that (a) insight was not required, although it often occurred as a spontaneous result of the technique; (b)

symptom removal was not the initial goal because of the desire not to challenge the family's resistance; and (c) the therapist's behavior was often unexpected and could not fit into the patient's existing cognitive or emotional structure.

These three strategies—redefinition, escalation and crisis induction, and redirection—plus the above three criteria were used as a theoretical formulation and as a map for therapeutic intervention. It became clear that our paradoxical stance would be maintained if we met the three criteria and utilized some form of one of the three strategies, given a particular therapeutic impasse in a particular family.

It should be kept in mind, however, that these strategies need to be viewed within the context of family dynamics and not as external "techniques" to be rigidly applied in the presence or absence of given criteria. These strategies can be helpful in thinking through a particular therapeutic impasse but only after a thorough knowledge of the family's dynamics has been obtained. More on this in a later section of this paper.

The classification of these strategies does not preclude a degree of playfulness or humor in their initiation or application. Often an idea for a paradoxical intervention seemed to emerge from the therapist as a kind of playful or even comic maneuver. A categorization of approaches, such as the one presented above, does not preclude such modes or styles of treatment; rather in our view it guides and channels them, assuring careful consideration of the dynamic picture presented by the family.

Also, it was recognized that often more than one of the three strategies might be used at the same time and that in some ways one therapeutic intervention contained aspects of more than one approach. Hence, these were seen only as rough guidelines, a kind of broadly based check sheet to assist in thinking through and deciding upon an approach to a given clinical situation. What follows is a definition of each strategy, a description of the kinds of presenting family characteristics particularly applicable to each approach (see Table I). and a brief clinical example.

Redefinition

Redefinition is an attempt to alter the apparent meaning or interpretation the family places on the symptomatic behavior. For example, in a simple case a child's negative provocativeness can be seen as a temper tantrum, but in a particular kind of family setting it may also serve the purpose of uniting drifting parents. When such a redefinition of the "negative" behavior is identified and made public, its repeated occurrence is often made unnecessary. In this case, the symptom is then dropped by the "helpful" child.

This technique seems most appropriate with families possessing some capacity for reflection and insight, as opposed to action-oriented families. Suitable families need to have the capacity to handle frustration for reasonable periods without acting out or without impulsive displays. Such families may present with repeated moderate family crises but without the kinds of problems requiring immediate and direct action. Often these families have relatively rigid structures, and their resistance to change is judged as moderate without the occurrence of overt, hostile, oppositional behavior. In essence, families that seem most open to reframing techniques are those that can, at the minimum, reflect upon the therapist's attempts to redefine the symptom, and whose problems permit some time for the process to occur. Also, their resistance and view of the therapist are such that power struggles between patients and therapist and other forms of oppositional behavior do not dominate the situation.

An example of the use of redefinition occurred in the G family. This family was referred by a local pediatrician and came with the chief complaint that the oldest

TABLE I

Patient Characteristics Applicable to Three Types of Paradoxical Interventions

Reframing	Escalation or Crisis Induction	Redirection
Moderate resistance	Vague style	Individual Settings
Non-oppositional	Super-verbal manipulation	Presenting problem with young child
Not short term	Oppositional	
Ability to reflect	Power Struggle	Specific symptoms
Non-action-oriented	Marked resistance	Repetitive symptoms
Can handle frustration & uncertainty	Need to move quickly	Educational & guidance setting
Little or no severe impulsive or acting-out behavior	Potential for acting out	Family can respond to direction without undue sabotage
	Excessively rigid	
No pressing external problems	Blocked with no area of compromise	Non-oppositional
Rigid family structure	Adults competitive with therapist	Overly compliant
Repeated crises—not severe		

child's seizure disorder was causing family problems. Living in the house at the time were mother, father, identified patient Paula (age 11), sister (age 9), brother (age 5), and father's mother, who had come to live with them following her husband's death. In the sessions, there was little discussion of mother's family, who lived in California. Mother was one of two children; her brother, two years older than she, was living in California near their parents. It was as if Mrs. G had been absorbed into Mr. G's family when they were married and had no further contact with her own family.

Mr. G was a successful business executive who worked long hours and traveled to some extent. Mrs. G did not work outside the home. She spent a great portion of her time involved with Paula's problem, chauffeuring the children, and carrying out many of the tasks expected of her as the wife of a successful business executive.

Paula, the identified patient, looked younger than her stated age, had short hair, and was dressed in jeans and a tee shirt. She was described by parents as having a very complex and at times medically uncontrolled seizure disorder and was also intellectually retarded. At the initial session, her sister, younger by two years, looked older than her stated age, sat with her parents, listened to the conversation, combed her hair, and in general was quite preoccupied with her appearance. Paula, on the other hand, played with her 5-year-old brother.

In the first interview the discussion centered around Paula and her grand mal seizures, which were occurring at a rate of about one or two per week and seemed in many ways correlated with the level of tension in the home. Most of the family's time was spent either in responding to the seizure itself or in seeking professional help around the problem. The family had already had a great deal of professional help around the physical problem and were now seeking help around the resultant family problem. Gradually the discussion left the children and the seizure disorder and fo-

cused on the parents, with grandmother correctly perceiving that there were conflicts between husband and wife around the management of the home in general. Grandmother's self-defined position was to side with the wife as she felt her role in the family was to keep the wife's spirits up in light of Mr. G's critical attitudes.

In this, as in all families, it was quite important to discover the homeostatic rules of the family: the rules necessary for the system to maintain its equilibrium. In this case it appeared that the women, mother and grandmother, were responsible for maintaining a "well-run house." Father was excused from this because of the demands of filling an upper management job; the expectation was that the house should be quiet and comfortable when he returned home. He was not called in until things were out of control, usually related to Paula's behavior, and then was criticized by the family for being too harsh in his interventions. One method of intervention chosen by the therapists was redefinition. In this way, the system by which the family functioned was able to be maintained, although redefined in a more positive light. Father was defined and overtly labeled the "real manager" of the house (as he was in his business) and was given the job of directing how things should be done at home, as it was evident that he had very clear ideas of how the house should be managed in order to provide him with peace and quiet. The women could still maintain their control over running the house by carrying out father's directions. Rather than devaluing father for being too harsh, he was vigorously applauded for his managerial service to the family, which took a great deal of responsibility off the women's shoulders and also kept the system functioning. "Unfortunately," this relabeling brought to light the real underlying family structure, and although father liked the control he held as manager, he was not sure he could handle the responsibility.

As with the other examples that will be

presented, redefinition was only one part of the therapy with this family. There were other tasks related to increasing the closeness between the couple and tasks related to altering family responses to Paula's seizure activity. But redefinition of the problem from the family's responses to Paula's seizures to a problem of family management under the direction of an unwilling executive "expert" presented the family with a task couched in different terms from their original conception. As can be seen in this example, the redefinition was incorporated into a knowledge of the family's dynamics and explained in terms of the family's idiosyncratic language, e.g., the business manager and the family manager.

Escalation

Two broad types of symptom escalation methods have been used. The first is similar in practice to early techniques based on the learning theory principle of massed practice. For example, facial tics can be placed under voluntary control in given settings by prescribing their massed occurrence several times a day. This approach takes the response out of the realm of unconscious control.

A couple in their late fifties came for treatment because the husband was ruminating about his physical ills and was depressed. His "illness" threatened to call a halt to a long-planned trip to Florida, and his wife was both concerned and disappointed. These symptoms came during the first year of his retirement from an active, successful career in insurance. His adjustment to retirement had been difficult because of the couple's lack of friends and interests outside the family. His favorite daughter, who was currently experiencing marital problems, was extremely concerned about her father's health; she visited daily and telephoned several times each day to learn of his condition. Attempts at gaining a better understanding of the dynamics of the symptom through other methods failed,

and it was difficult getting the topic of conversation away from the husband's aches and pains and his dramatic requests for a cure. After several sessions, it became clear that the symptom served the function for both husband and wife of maintaining a rather enmeshed and family-based way of life. The husband's retirement caused a removal of the major extrafamilial activity for both spouses. The symptom filled the void by channeling the family's (including daughter's) energies toward "family" matters and prevented the couple from developing new, extrafamilial contacts, which the Florida trip would certainly entail.

With all of this in mind, the husband was instructed to spend the next two days in one room dressed in pajamas and bathrobe preparing a log of his every thought and physical problem. He was also to record his blood pressure and heart rate at 15-minute intervals and to report to the "doctor" twice daily. This was to "increase" his depression so as to enable us to study it as well as to gather more data in an effort to understand his physical problems more clearly. Mother and daughter were to help in this two-day effort by not allowing him to talk with them, by leaving him isolated in the bedroom, and by setting a tray with his meals outside his door without conversation so that "he could concentrate more effectively." Although this task was difficult, all parties succeeded. The technique here was to escalate the symptom as well as to redefine an aspect of the symptom by legitimizing it for purposes of the "doctor's cure." Needless to say, the husband became "sick" of his task and went to Florida instead. Again, the prescription for change was seen within the dynamics of the family and not as an isolated technique to be used regardless of setting.

The second type of symptom escalation aims at increasing in intensity or frequency certain aspects of a clinical situation by provoking a crisis. At times the patient or family is forced to deal with the feared situation, but in all cases the crisis undermines a rigid family defense and forces a decision or some kind of action.

An illustrative family in which this technique was used included a 42-year-old successful father who was a member of a suburban school board and active in the local Catholic church, a 40-year-old mother who managed the home and worked part-time in a retail children's clothing store, and four children: a boy age 18; Betty the identified patient, age 16; and a girl and boy, ages 14 and 11, respectively. Betty was referred because management problems both at home and at school had escalated to the point that the school threatened suspension because of skipping classes and parental attempts at discipline were failing.

Betty had become pregnant 16 months previously and had given the baby up for adoption because of parental pressure. Although from time to time Betty agreed that this decision was wise, she claimed she really had no say in the matter, and both she and her mother were having difficulty working through the loss. The other family members, however, described the family as happy and congenial except for the tension caused by Betty's flagrant violation of parental demands.

Father, a successful corporation executive, was used to having his way, although his wife frequently stood up to him precipitating a full-scale battle whenever she pushed an issue. With Betty, however, he felt threatened and was enraged at her lack of compliance, threatening her possible removal from the home if her behavior did not improve. Mother reluctantly agreed. The therapists believed that mother was covertly encouraging Betty's negative behavior because of her own unresolved and unexpressed anger at her husband regarding the decision to give the baby up for adoption. Somehow she believed father was to blame for the entire episode.

In treatment, all efforts at sidetracking, redefining, supporting, and interpreting failed, and Betty's negative behavior increased with mother's subtle encouragement. The therapists, feeling somewhat paralyzed by father's attacking style and by their reluctance to take sides, decided to provoke a crisis by permitting the negative behavior to escalate to some crucial event and then to suggest that father was right all along, that the situation was untenable, and that perhaps Betty should be removed from the home. When Betty stayed out all night with a "friend" without her parents knowing her whereabouts, the therapists decided the time was ripe and the crisis was provoked. The family was covertly shocked but overtly in agreement, and they were sent home with lists of foster placements, residential schools, etc. Needless to say, they returned a week later reporting literally hours of family discussions, a markedly reduced level of family tension, and a decision to keep the family intact. In this example, the locked battle between father and mother on the one hand and Betty and father on the other was undermined by provoking a family crisis in order to force a realignment of positions and permit options for action within the family.

These techniques seem most applicable when family resistance is extreme, some form of oppositional behavior is present, and the family has successfully walled off all areas of compromise and problem-solving. By admitting defeat or escalating to the point of crisis, the therapist gains an upper hand in short-circuiting vague complaints, circumventing paralyzing resistance, or outmaneuvering the superverbal and overly logical family. This "end-running" tactic is often sucessful with excessively rigid, domineering, or autocratic families in which battles for control potentially undermine successful outcome.

Of particular concern, however, is the issue of timing. Crisis induction, in particular, requires careful planning as well as a series of frustrating sessions in which every attempt is made to use other, less stressful techniques. If the technique is applied too early, it will fail because of a lack of sufficient tension built up from previous failures at change. If applied too late, the family may have left treatment or given up, or an external crisis of more serious magnitude may have developed. In general, then, this technique seems most applicable with families that are excessively rigid, resistant, and highly skilled at being vague or overly explanatory in an effort to prevent change.

Redirection

This technique is similar in some ways to symptom escalation, in that both attempt to place the symptom under voluntary control. Whereas in escalation the symptom is removed by satiation under massed display or by provoking a crisis, in redirection the circumstances under which the symptom is to occur are prescribed, although the frequency is not necessarily altered. Redirection, like the other techniques, is applicable in both individual and family treatment, provided that knowledge of the family system is integrated into the conceptualization of the symptom.

A form of redirection was helpful in working with a hospitalized 45-year-old woman of Dutch origin with numerous physical complaints bordering on somatic delusions—e.g., "I feel as if there is a hole in my esophagus through which food escapes into my insides." She had had five hospitalizations over the previous nine years, each time carrying the diagnosis of schizophrenia. Her 19-year-old son was currently being prosecuted for check forgery following a six-year history of continual scrapes with the law. Her 21-year-old daughter, a well-functioning woman who was her father's pride, had just married two months earlier. The identified patient's husband, a competent supervisor of highly skilled mechanics, was finding it increasingly difficult to ignore his wife's continuous physical complaints. In family sessions it became apparent that she began ruminating about her body whenever angry exchanges be-

tween family members threatened to break out. Her husband had longstanding resentments about the restrictions on their social lives caused by her physical problems. The wife had major unexpressed disappointments with her husband going back to, among other things, his unresponsiveness eleven years earlier when she miscarried an intensely anticipated baby. It seemed that anger between them over these disappointments threatened the only emotionally supportive relationship for each of these two middle-aged people who were isolated from their families of origin in Holland. On the inpatient unit the woman quickly established a pattern of complaining to staff about her symptoms.

Redirection was used with the intent to clear the field for the very difficult marital and life problems to be approached. On the unit, staff were instructed to listen to her talk about symptoms for only ten minutes every evening at 10:00 P.M., and she was instructed to approach staff at that time even if she felt no urge.

In the family sessions, symptom talk was deferred until the last five minutes, and the family negotiated together a time for symptom talk during her visits home. Simultaneously, the family sessions supported the very difficult work of their hearing each other's anger and disappointment. As expected, the intensity of her symptoms subsided, both in terms of amount of talk and of her subjective experience of the symptoms.

Clearly, in this case, the paradoxical maneuver was only one part of what can be seen as the difficult treatment of a severe marital problem. In addition, this particular kind of intervention required, in part, the family's willingness to comply with the therapists' directives for symptom talk both during the sessions and at home.

This technique is appropriate when resistance is low, when little oppositional behavior exists, and when the family can follow through on directives without undue sabotage.

Contraindications

Paradoxical techniques, while powerful in many settings, can be equally harmful if misapplied. These techniques deal directly with other fundamental family defenses and when ineptly applied can lead to a flight from treatment or to more severe crises. In fact, we suggest that of all the therapeutic interventions we have tried in clinical or consulting settings, paradoxical interventions constitute the highest risk for subsequent no-show appointments and premature terminations. This demonstrates their power, but it also indicates the need to apply these interventions carefully, in a skillful and well-timed manner, with families, couples, and individuals with whom the risk of negative outcome is small.

There are several kinds of families with which the use of paradoxical techniques as a major therapeutic modality is ill advised. Paradoxical techniques seem least applicable in *chaotic families* (1), with loose and variable structures. In such families, it is often difficult to gain hold of a concrete issue to work on, and the aim of therapy may be the establishment of some kind of internal cohesion and stability rather than on eliminating particularly troublesome behaviors. Often paradoxical ploys are used to undermine powerful family coalitions aimed at resisting change. In chaotic and poorly organized families, however, there are insufficient positive and negative collusions and alliances to begin with, making these techniques inappropriate. The use of the paradox may be appropriate at later stages of intervention when some semblance of internal structure becomes stabilized and the focus shifts to other directions.

Similarly, paradoxical maneuvers are not appropriate with *childlike families* (1), in which all members, including adults, tend to function on an immature level seeking parenting from the therapist. Such systems are again too loose and lack sufficient cohesiveness and unity of purpose for a paradoxical ploy to be effective. Often such families see the intervention as another rejection from a parental figure, and their need for parenting either leads to a search for a new mother or father or to an unproductive rebellion against the therapist, thereby compounding the problem.

Some kinds of *impulsive families* (1), families with members who overtly express conflict in the community or at home in a socially undesirable or potentially harmful manner, are also inappropriate for paradoxical intervention. In this case, careful consideration of such techniques as escalation needs to occur in order to prevent potential harm. For example, depressive or aggressive symptoms should not be exaggerated in families in which the risk of suicide or physical harm to self or others is a real possibility. Yet in other families in which the same style is present but the degree of symptom expression is less, these techniques may be highly appropriate to force the family into action. Again, careful clinical judgment should prevail.

Insight-oriented, structural, or other kinds of interpretive techniques may be more helpful in stimulating growth than paradoxical techniques in families that are already demonstrating solid therapeutic movement. Paradoxical ploys are also inappropriate in families seeking therapy to resolve specific developmental or situational crises in which support, information, or guidance seem more appropriate. These are families that have the resources to manage the presenting difficulty but need a setting in which to work issues through or professional support and direction in solving their own problems.

Last, these techniques seem little suited to families that accept responsibility for their own behavior, in which therapeutic interventions are accepted at face value with minimal oppositional or negative behaviors, or in which control of therapy in terms of course and direction are well agreed upon and remain an unconflicted area of interaction. In general then, paradoxical procedures are contraindicated when marked resistance, power struggles, and oppositional behavior are minimally present, when family structure is so disorganized that family solidarity is minimal, or when a potential for sharp escalation of symptoms or other severe forms of acting-out behavior with strongly negative consequences is possible.

Conclusions

Other than their use by well-known (11) and often charismatic figures, little has been written about the planning and implementation of paradoxical procedures in everyday clinical practice. In our view, this has led to frequent misuse of these potentially powerful procedures, which often are employed as excuses for lack of skill or insufficient diagnostic study. What is clearly needed, given this situation, is more detailed study of the kinds of clinical situations that are most open to their use as well as to potential negative effects.

In our experience, the failure of a paradoxical intervention is most usually due to a lack of understanding of the dynamics of the family. Frequently, a therapist will come up with a spur-of-the-moment ploy, an off-hand idea based upon limited data. Although even the most bizarre of ideas often have merit in their absurdity, we found it necessary to set up two primary cautions about our interventions in order to reduce the chance of failure or a more serious outcome, premature termination. First, we agreed that all paradoxical interventions should be discussed with the consulting group prior to initiation. Such a consultation insured a carefully thought-through intervention by opening the case up to group scrutiny. In addition, the group was able to assist in maintaining a paradoxical set by assuring that systems dynamics were being properly considered, and by preventing regression to more linear modes of thinking, as often happens in solo practice.

Second, paradoxical interventions require a clear understanding of the family's symptom and the role the symptom plays in the life of the family. Each family member's stake in the maintenance of the symptom needs to be understood in detail from an individual as well as from a systems perspective. As such, our team agreed upon the necessity of a complete family evaluation prior to initiation of the intervention. Such an agreement reduced the chances of impulsive and therapeutic ploys that have little chance of success, not because they spontaneously arise from the clinical situation, but because often they are not carefully thought through. We learned again and again that the effective use of a paradoxical intervention requires a thorough knowledge of the family as a dynamic system.

Unlike many other types of therapeutic interventions, the approaches under discussion here require a change of set, an ability to look at what is clinically presented with a new pair of glasses, and an ability to deal effectively with the absurd, often with humor. It is quite apparent that not every therapist is suited to this kind of work in terms of style and general personality. Of all the methods of intervention we have utilized in the course of clinical experience and training, we have found no other in which such stylistic issues play such a powerful role. For example, there are some trainees who simply cannot carry off the interventions in a meaningful and convincing manner. Their physical presence, appearance, and way of relating preclude an effective intervention and sharply reduce their ability as clinical change agents using this technique. While of concern in other modalities of therapy as well, this issue appears crucial in paradoxical work. Therefore, we have found it necessary to thoroughly think through whether or not a recommendation for the use of a paradoxical technique will be productive given the personality and style of the therapist, whether trainee or staff. There is little question that therapist variables play a powerful role in the success or failure of these techniques.

As a side note in this regard, we have found a particular lack of success in teaching paradoxical techniques to very young or inexperienced therapists. Somehow they have noticeable difficulty in carrying off the intervention, even with group consultation and support. Two reasons come to mind for our first-year trainees' singular lack of success in this area. First, as mentioned above, these techniques require a finely tuned sense of timing as well as a degree of patience. New and inexperienced therapists often need continual exposure to patients over time to develop this skill; consequently, training in paradoxical formats may be best postponed to later in their training. Second, paradoxical strategies often deal with rigid family defenses that frequently lead to therapeutic impasses and binds. We have found that novice therapists do not have the first-hand experience of wrestling with the impasse, of experiencing the paralysis of a resistive family, and of developing a gut reaction to the family's desire to entrap the change agent and render him powerless. Such experience takes time to develop, and pushing young therapists into the use of paradoxical strategies in our experience often leads to the use of "cookbook" modes of intervention without the conceptual and experiential understanding of the therapeutic wrestling match.

Our experience with paradoxical techniques has in general been positive and successful when incorporated both in broad clinical practice and in training activities in which a number of approaches were utilized, depending upon the problem at hand. Although the paradoxical bandwagon has many "avant-garde" therapists jumping aboard, our experience indicates that the techniques are effective when, like all intervention strategies, they are well thought through and appropriately applied.

REFERENCES

1. Fisher, L., "On the Classification of Families: A Progress Report," *Arch. Gen. Psychiat.* 34: 424–433, 1977.

2. Frankl, V. E., *The Doctor and the Soul: An Introduction to Logotherapy*, New York, Alfred Knopf, 1957.

3. _____, "Paradoxical Intention and Dereflection: Two Logotherapeutic Techniques," in S. Arietz and G. Chrzamowski (eds.), *New Dimensions in Psychiatry: A World View*, New York, John Wiley, 1975.

4. Haley, J., "Paradoxes in Play, Fantasy, and Psychotherapy," *Psychiat. Res. Rep.* 2: 52–58, 1975.

5. _____, *Problem-Solving Therapy*, San Francisco, Jossey-Bass, 1976.

6. Mozdierz, G.; Maccitelli, F.; and Lisiecki, J., "The Paradox in Psychotherapy: An Adlerian Perspective," *J. Individ. Psychol.* 32: 169–184, 1976.

7. Papp, P., "The Greek Chorus and Other Techniques of Paradoxical Therapy," *Fam. Proc.* 19: 45–58, 1980.

8. Raskin, D. E. and Klein, Z. E., "Losing a Symptom Through Keeping It: A Review of Paradoxical Treatment Techniques and Rationale, *Arch. Gen. Psychiat.* 33: 548–555, 1976.

9. Selvini Palazzoli, M.; Boscolo, L.; Cecchin, G. F.; and Prata, G., "The Treatment of Children Through Brief Therapy of Their Parents," *Fam. Proc.* 13: 429–442, 1974.

10. Selvini Palazzoli, M.; Cecchin, G. F.; Prata, G., and Boscolo, L. S., *Paradox and Counterparadox; A New Model in the Therapy of the Family in Schizophrenic Transaction*, New York, Jason Aronson, 1978.

11. Selvini Palazzoli, M.; Boscolo, L.; Cecchin, G.; and Prata, G., "Hypothesizing-Circularity-Neutrality: Three Guidelines for the Conductor of the Session," *Fam. Proc.* 19: 3–12, 1980.

12. Watzlawick, P.; Weakland, J.; and Fisch, R., *Change: Principles of Problem Formation and Problem Resolution*, New York, W. W. Norton, 1974.

13. Weeks, G.; and L'Abate, L., "A Bibliography of Paradoxical Methods in Psychotherapy of Family Symptoms," *Fam. Proc.* 12: 95–98, 1978.

This paper proposes that psychopathology in children can be the result of an incongruity in the hierarchical organization of the family. The parents are in a superior position to the child by the fact of being parents, and yet the problem child assumes a superior position to the parents by protecting them through symptomatic behavior that often expresses metaphorically the parents' difficulties. The paper describes three paradoxical strategies for arranging that the parents solve the presenting problem of the child and the incongruity in the family hierarchy. The therapeutic techniques described are characterized by the use of communication modalities, such as dramatizations, pretending, and make-believe, that are appropriate to children.

50

PROTECTION, PARADOX, AND PRETENDING

Cloe Madanes†

W HEN A CHILD exhibits problem behavior, he is singled out in the family as a special source of concern for the parents who are involved in a struggle to change him. A child might have any of a variety of symptoms, such as night terrors, headaches, setting fires, or wetting the bed, but whatever the difficulties of the child, the disturbed behavior keeps the parents involved in attempting to help him and to change his behavior. If the parents fail to solve the problem, they turn to an expert. When the expert consulted has a family orientation, he will typically think of the child as involved in a conflict within the family. That is, the child will be thought of as involved in a coalition with one parent against the other parent, or with a grandparent or relative against a parent, or as involved in a conflict between the parents by providing the bond that holds the conflicting parents together (3). In these approaches the child is seen as a participant taking sides in a conflict between other family members. Typically, the child is said

† Family Therapy Institute of Washington, D.C.

to be used by the parents in a conflict between them. This conflict is said to detour through the child, so that, for example, the mother encourages the daughter to disobey the father, who attacks the daughter when he is angry at the mother (4). The child's involvement in a family conflict might also be seen as the replication of family issues in a previous generation (1).

PROTECTION

This paper offers a different view. The child is seen as a concerned benefactor or protector of others in his family. A parent might have trouble at work, difficulties with relatives, concern about the threatened separation of a spouse, but the parent will set aside his own problems, at least temporarily, to focus on the child, to help him or control him and to attempt to change his behavior. The parent will try to overcome his own deficiencies and hold himself together in order to help the child. In this sense, the child's disturbed behavior is protective of his parents. It provides a respite from the parent's own troubles and a reason to overcome their own difficulties. Typi-

From Cloe Madanes, "Protection, Paradox, and Pretending," *Family Process*, 1980, 9, pp. 73-85. Reprinted by permission of the publisher and author.

cally, the disturbed behavior of the child elicits attempts from the parents to help the child and to change his behavior. Whether the child's behavior provokes helpful, protective, or punitive acts from the parents, it focuses the parents' concern on him and makes the parents see themselves as parents to a child who needs them rather than individuals overwhelmed by personal, economic, or social difficulties.

Problem behavior in children can be helpful to parents in quite specific ways. For example, a child might develop a problem that will keep his mother at home to take care of him, and in this way the mother will not have to face the issue of looking for a job. The child's problem provides a convenient excuse to the parent to avoid unpleasant situations. If a father comes home from work upset and worried and a child misbehaves, the father can then feel angry at the child instead of feeling worried about his work. In this sense, the child's misbehavior is protective of his father. Also, by making the father angry at him, he saves the mother from having to help her husband by sympathizing with him or quarreling with him. In this way, the child is protecting both parents.

HIERARCHY

In any organization there is hierarchy in the sense that one person has more power and responsibility to determine what happens than another person. In a family organization the parents are higher in the hierarchy than the children. When a child's disturbed behavior is protective of the parents, there is an incongruous hierarchical organization in the family. That is, the parents, by the fact of being parents, are in a superior position in the hierarchy with respect to the child for whom they have legal responsibility, for whom they provide, and for whom they care. But the child, with his disturbed behavior, protects the parents by helping them to avoid their own difficulties

and overcome their own deficiencies. In this sense the child is in a superior position to the parents by the fact of helping them. If the child behaves normally, he loses the power that his disturbed behavior gives him over his parents and, therefore, the possibility of protecting them. To be successful in changing the child's behavior, the parents must deal with their own difficulties in such a way that the child's protectiveness is no longer necessary. The more the parents attempt to change the child's behavior, the more the function of the child's protectiveness is maintained. But this protectiveness of his parents by the child, although helpful in aiding them temporarily to avoid their problems, does not help them to face and resolve the issues that concern them and can even prevent their resolution.

The therapist's problem is how to get the child to give up the disturbed behavior that is the basis of his power. This cannot be done directly by the therapist. The child's power is over his parents, and it is the parents who must take it away from him. In order to solve the child's problem, the therapist must arrange that the parents be able to dispense with the child's protection; that the child's disturbed behavior no longer serve the purpose of protecting the parents but that it actually serve the opposite purpose and have unfortunate consequences for the parents; or that the child can be helpful in a different, more appropriate way.

To achieve the goal of the therapy, the therapist must restore the family to a single hierarchical organization with the parents in a superior position to the child, that is, an organization in which the parents protect and help the child and in which the child does not protect them. In order to restore the family hierarchy to one in which the parents are in a superior position to the child, it is the parents who must solve the child's problem. The parents, and not the therapist alone, must be involved in changing the child's behavior.

THE THERAPY

In the therapeutic approaches described here the therapist plans a strategy for solving the client's problem. The goal is always clearly set and consists of solving the presenting problem.

1. The therapist must assume that a symptom, analogically or metaphorically, expresses a problem and is also a solution, although usually an unsatisfactory one for the people involved. For example, when a child is talking about his headaches, he is talking about more than one kind of pain. That is, behavior is always a communication on many levels. The message, "I have a headache," is a report on an internal state, but it might also be a way of declining to do the chores or of getting the father to help with the homework.

2. The therapist must first decide who is the focus of the child's concern—who is being protected by the child and in what way. Next, he must decide on an intervention that will change the family organization to one in which there is a single hierarchy, with the parents in a superior position. The therapist's intervention usually takes the form of a directive about something that the family is to do both in and out of the interview. Directives may be straightforward or paradoxical and may involve one or two people or the whole family. These directives have the purpose of changing the interaction of family members with each other and with the therapist.

3. There is not an emphasis on being aware of how communication takes place; if a problem can be solved without the family knowing how or why, that is satisfactory.

4. The therapy is planned in stages, and it is assumed that usually the presenting problem cannot be solved in one step. Relationships in each family are unique and may require different therapeutic plans, even when the presenting problems are similar.

To restore the family to a single hierarchical organization with the parents in a superior position to the child, the therapist must arrange that the parents solve the child's problem. Some paradoxical techniques for doing this will be presented here with case examples.[1]

Approach No. 1: The Parent Requests That the Child Have the Problem

Sometimes a child's symptom expresses the problem of a parent metaphorically. For example, if the father is worried about his job, the child might have headaches. The child's symptom expresses the parent's problem and is also an attempt to solve it— i.e., the father forgets his own "headaches" while trying to help the child with his. The more the parents are focused on trying to change the child, the more the function of the symptom is maintained. The relationship between parent and child is based on benevolent helpfulness in which the child helps the parent with his symptom and the parent helps the child unsuccessfully to try to overcome the symptom. One way to solve the problem is to arrange that the parent encourage the child to have the symptom. In this way both the child's and the parent's helpfulness will be blocked. The symptom will no longer have the function of helping the parents and of eliciting helpfulness from them and it will be dropped.

As an example, a 12-year-old boy was brought to therapy because he wet the bed almost every night. The mother had been hospitalized at one time for depression. The father worked long hours, and the mother complained about his lack of interest in her and his attraction to other women. It was hypothesized that the bed-wetting was both a metaphorical expression of the father's improper behavior in bed and an attempt to help the parents by eliciting their con-

---

[1] All cases were conducted under my live supervision. The therapists were Michael Fox, M.D., Tobias Lopez, M.D., Virginia Lopez. Family Counselor, and Thomas C. Todd, Ph.D.

cern and distracting them from their other problems. Because of the boy's symptom, the mother could focus on his problems rather than on her own depression, and she could nag the father to spend more time with the son and to help him rather than nag him to spend more time with her and to help her. The father could discuss with the mother the boy's bed-wetting rather than his own improper behavior in bed and the couple's marital difficulties. Mother and father could judge what each was thinking about the other by discussing the boy, and, in this way, the child was helping both parents.

The therapy started with several routine ways to have the father solve the son's problem. If the son wet the bed, the father—not the mother—was to wash the sheets. The son's bed-wetting would be an inconvenience to the father rather than to the mother. The father also had to buy an alarm clock for the son so he could wake up in the middle of the night and go to the bathroom, and he was to reward the son if he did not wet the bed. The father never did what was requested of him, although he excused himself and always promised that he would do it the next week.

After several weeks, the therapist told the father that because he had not done what he promised, he would now have to carry out a more difficult task but one that would assure the cure for the son's symptom. However, the therapist would not reveal what the "cure" was until he had the father's commitment that he would follow the therapist's instructions. The father agreed, and the therapist told him that every evening he had to give his son a large glass of water, take him up to his room, and then demand that the son urinate on the bed on purpose and go to sleep on the wet bed. He was to stay with the son in the bedroom until the son wet the bed and went to sleep in it. This was to be done every evening for one week. The strategy was based on a procedure of Milton Erickson (2).

The family came back after one week, and the father reported that he had gone through torture with the dilemma of whether to impose this ordeal on his son. He said he felt like Abraham when God wanted him to sacrifice his son. He had not enforced the ordeal, although he had attempted to do it a couple of times and the boy had cried and begged him not to make him wet the bed. The father said he now understood that the therapist had not really wanted him to carry out the task. The therapist, he said, had only wanted to bring him to his senses and show him that he had to do his part or else the situation would not change. He had spent a great deal of time that week talking to his son and had even missed work one day. The boy had not wet the bed during the last four nights and as a reward was allowed to be absent from the family session and participate in a sports event at school instead. The father said he wanted to help his son in his own way by spending more time talking to him. Since the boy had improved, the therapist agreed.

The therapist's paradoxical instructions created a situation in which the son was no longer helpful to his father through his symptomatic behavior, since it now resulted in great anxiety for the father. The father took charge of the relationship with the son and spent time talking to him and advising him. A single hierarchy was defined with the father in a superior position and the son no longer protecting the father through his symptoms.

The son did not wet the bed again, and the couple spent a few sessions discussing their marriage. The father explained that he had been irresponsible and compulsive in his relations with other women; he called himself "a cat on a hot tin roof." The parents began to have sexual relations regularly and were pleased about it; the father had not been sexually interested in his wife for a year and a half. The therapy ended with a better relationship between husband and wife. During the course of the therapy, the mother had also quit smoking and the son had been taken off Ritalin with which he had been medicated for many years for his hyperactivity. His behavior improved, and the parents no longer considered him hyperactive.

Approach No. 2: The Parent Requests That the Child Pretend to Have The Problem

Rather than encourage the symptom, a therapist can encourage the child to *pretend* to have the symptom. The parent can also be encouraged to pretend to help the child when the child is pretending to have the problem. In this situation, the child no longer needs actually to have the symptom to protect the parent; pretending to have it is enough to become the focus of concern of the parent. But the parent's concern will also be a pretense, and the situation will have changed to a game—to make-believe and play. Two examples will clarify this approach.

Case No. 1: Stomach-Aches

A boy was referred to therapy because of recurrent stomach-aches for which a medical cause could not be found. He lived with his brother and their elderly grandmother. The therapist asked the grandmother what she did every time that the boy had stomach-aches. She explained that she took him in her arms and cuddled and comforted him; she took out her rosary to pray; and she helped him by putting oil drops inside his nose. The pediatrician had told her not to use the oil drops because of the danger of choking the child, but she had heard Christ's voice telling her to do this so she continued to do it.

It was hypothesized that the stomach-aches provided the opportunity for grandmother and child to express affection for each other and also introduced some drama in an otherwise dreary, limited existence. The therapist's goal was to have the expression of affection and the drama take place without the symptomatic behavior.

The child was asked to pretend to have a stomach-ache in the session, like the ones he had at home, and his brother and grandmother were to pretend to do exactly what they did at home in those cases. The boy pretended to have a stomach-ache and the grandmother cuddled him and did all the things she had described but in a make-believe way. The brother helped by handing to grandmother the pretend rosary and oil drops. The therapist asked the family to pretend in the same way every evening at home for a week. They set aside a particular time every evening when the boy would pretend to have a stomach-ache and the grandmother would pretend to help him in the way she had done in the session. The real stomach-aches were no longer necessary. The child was still helping his old grandmother by providing some drama to her life, but he now did it in a playful way, without symptomatic behavior. The family discontinued the pretend procedure, and the stomach-aches no longer occurred.

Case No. 2: Epileptic Seizures

A 15-year-old girl was referred to therapy because she had frequent epileptic seizures and did not respond to medication. She usually had the seizures during the night and her moaning woke up the family, who gathered around her in great concern trying to help her. Sometimes she had the seizures during the day, and the family was terrified of the harm that could come to her. She was hospitalized, and a doctor witnessed a seizure during the night so there was no question that these were documented grand mal seizures with the usual postictal phenomena. She was released from the hospital and referred to therapy by her pediatrician.

In the first session, the parents appeared very concerned and upset about the girl. They described her symptoms and her history with a wealth of detail, and the father seemed particularly involved and concerned about her. The siblings were also interested and involved and volunteered information while the girl was mostly silent and shy. It was assumed that the girl's symptoms had a protective function in the family, but there was no indication of what their function was except that this mysterious illness gave a certain excitement to their lives.

The therapist asked the girl, in the first session, to try to have a seizure right there in the therapy room and the family (mother, father and several siblings) to do what they usually did at home on those occasions. The girl lay down on the floor, surrounded by the family, and began to make noises and shake trying to have a seizure. The family hovered over her, particularly the concerned father, encouraging her and giving her directions. She did not succeed, however, in having a seizure, and the therapist asked her then to pretend to have one and the family to pretend to do what they usually did in those circumstances. The girl began to shake with a little more enthusiasm, and the family hovered around her even more, especially the father, touching her and holding her.

These directives were given to the family with the rationale that if the girl could first control having the seizures voluntarily, she could then control *not* having them voluntarily. Because she was not able to produce a seizure voluntarily, the next best thing was to pretend to have one. This would give her the practice she needed in controlling them. The family had to help her by instructing and directing her so that the seizure would be as authentic as possible.

The parents were told to do this dramatization at home every evening with the whole family. If the girl had a seizure during the night, after she had the "real" seizure, the parents were to wake up the other children and the girl was to pretend to have a seizure. They would do this no matter what time of night it was or how tired they were. This ordeal was designed to encourage the family members to change the way in which they were protecting each other.

After the first interview, the seizures disappeared. The girl, who had previously been docile and timid, began to go out two

weeks later without permission and to misbehave in various ways. The parents were asked to make specific rules and to specify consequences if she disobeyed the rules. She began to be treated in the same manner as the other children in her family.

The therapist went away on vacation for a week and, on his return, found the family in the middle of a crisis. The girl had had an hallucination one night about a blond, green-eyed man who she said had attacked her and killed her brother and sister. She began to run around the house out of control, and the father had to hold her down. Her behavior had a similar quality to the way she behaved when she had a seizure, and the parental response was also similar. The parents took her to the emergency room where a resident did not label her schizophrenic, although he thought she was, and referred her back to the therapist.

In the following days, the girl continued to talk about her fear of this blond, green-eyed man who she said had tried to rape her and who was after her. For a few days the family had the whole neighborhood looking for this man whom the girl said she saw repeatedly. Because the neighborhood was all black and the man would have been easily spotted, the parents concluded that the girl was lying. She would suddenly act terrified about this blond man and would run away from the family, out of control. These episodes were like tantrums and occurred when she did not want to do something that the parents wanted her to do.

The therapist had the family reenact the night when she said that the siblings had been killed by this blond man and the father had had to hold her down. The therapist asked the family to replay the events of that dramatic night once a day at home on the same schedule they had had for the seizures. If the girl woke up during the night, they were all to get up and pretend again.

The therapist reformulated the girl's conduct as misbehavior and rebelliousness and encouraged the parents to set strict rules and to be in charge of the girl. It was decided that if she ran off, she had to stay home the entire next day. In a few days, the episodes disappeared and the misbehavior subsided as the girl became more mature and responsible.

During this time the therapist had to give special support to the father, who had been very attached to the girl and helpful in her distress and who became upset, depressed, and quarreled with his wife as the girl improved and began to go out more.

A few months later the parents called to say that the girl had again had seizures during the night. A family session was held, and the dramatization was repeated. The family was instructed in the same procedure as previously— the girl dramatizing a seizure in the session and the family to repeat the dramatization at home. At the end of the session the parents asked the therapist for a letter stating that the girl's delicate condition was made worse because of the family's living conditions and requesting the housing authorities to transfer the family to a better housing project. The therapist agreed to do this (although in the letter he referred to the nervousness and fears of all the children). Up to that time, it had been assumed that the girl's symptom had a protective function in the family, but there was no indication of what this function was except for the fact that this mysterious illness gave a certain glamour and excitement to their lives, and brought father and daughter closer together. Now it was clear that the family could gain from the girl's illness. The therapist told the girl, the parents, and the siblings that in the future he would be happy to be of help to them in any way he could whether the girl had seizures or not. In that way, the daughter did not need to have seizures to obtain help for the family. A year later the girl had not had seizures or behaved bizarrely.

Approach No. 3: The Parent Requests That the Child Pretend to Help the Parent

When a child protects the parents through symptomatic behavior, he is help-

ing them in a covert way. The symptomatic behavior is no longer necessary if the situation is made explicit, and it is arranged that the child overtly protect the parents. Typically, when a child presents a problem, the parents are overtly in a superior position in the hierarchy in relation to the child, but covertly they are in an inferior position in relation to him. If the therapist encourages the parents to be overtly in an inferior position to the child, both parents and child will resist the inappropriateness of this hierarchical organization, and the family will reorganize with the parents in a superior position.

A similar approach is to encourage the parents to *pretend* to be in an inferior position, to pretend to need the child's help and protection, rather than to actually be in this position. The child can then be encouraged to pretend to help the parents when the parents are pretending to need his help. In order to protect the parents, the child will no longer need to behave in symptomatic ways since the parents will explicitly ask for help and the child will overtly help them. But the parents' need for help will be a pretense, and so will the child's helpfulness. In a pretend framework, parents and child will be involved with each other in a playful way. One aspect of the incongruous hierarchy, the one in which the child is in a superior position to the parents, will be in play; it will be make-believe, and the incongruity will be resolved. Some examples will clarify this approach.

Case No. 1: Night Terrors

A mother sought therapy because her 10-year-old son had night terrors. There were two older daughters in the family and a baby brother. The family was Puerto Rican, and the mother spoke little English. The three older children were the product of a first marriage that ended in divorce. The mother had a second husband who died, and there had obviously been a third man since the baby was only a few months old. However, the mother denied at the beginning of therapy that there was a man living with the family. It was later found that she was afraid of losing her welfare benefits if she admitted that a man was contributing to her support.

The son appeared taciturn and preoccupied. Although it was not expressed, it was suspected that he was concerned about his mother who had lost two husbands, was poor, did not speak English, and was involved with a man in a relationship that had to be kept secret even though he was the father of her child.

Since the boy had night terrors, the therapist asked each member of the family about his dreams. Only the mother and the son had nightmares. The mother often dreamed that somebody was breaking into the house, and the boy described a recurrent nightmare in which he was attacked by a witch. The therapist asked what happened when the boy had nightmares. The mother explained that she took him to her bed and told him to think about God and to pray. She made the sign of the cross on his forehead to protect him from the devil. She explained that she thought that the boy's problem was due to the influence of the devil.

It was hypothesized that the boy's night terrors were both a metaphorical expression of the mother's fears and an attempt to help her. If the boy was the one who was afraid, then the mother had to be strong and pull herself together to reassure him and protect him; therefore, she could not be afraid herself. But when she protected him, she frightened him more, by talking about God and the devil. Mother and son were caught in a situation in which they were helping each other in unfortunate ways.

In the first session the family was asked to pretend they were at home and that the mother was very frightened because she heard noises as of someone breaking into the house. One of the sisters played the role of the thief who was trying to enter the house, and the son was asked to protect his mother. In this way the mother was requested to pretend to need the child's help rather than actually to need it. The child was encouraged to pretend to help the mother by attacking the make-believe thief. The mother's need for help was now in play and so was the son's helpfulness.

The family had difficulty with the dramatization because the mother would attack the make-believe thief before the son could help her. The therapist had to ask them repeatedly to try again. The message that resulted from this failure to act out the scene correctly was that the mother was a capable person who would defend herself; she did not need the son's protection.

When the dramatization was performed correctly and the son attacked the thief, everybody sat down to discuss the performance. The therapist criticized the mother for her difficulty in expressing fear and in restraining herself so that the son would have a chance to attack the thief. The mother responded to this criticism by talking about how she was a competent person who could defend herself well and that was why it was so difficult for her to play this part. This was a spontaneous message from the mother to the son that she did not need his protection.

The family was asked to get together every evening at home during the following week and repeat the dramatization. If, during the night, the mother heard that the son was screaming in his sleep, she was to get up, wake him, and wake the sisters, and they would all perform the same dramatization. They would do this no matter what time of night it was or how tired they were. This ordeal was designed to encourage mother and son to change the unfortunate way in which they were protecting each other.

The son did not have night terrors again. The family continued to be seen in therapy for several weeks, and other issues were resolved in different ways. The therapist helped mother and son to deal with the school, and the boy's behavior and grades improved. The father of the baby came to a session and was encouraged, without much success, to become more involved with the boy. The mother arranged for the son to participate in activities with peers—a rock band and a soccer team. The therapist encouraged the mother in her work as a dance teacher and supported her in her difficulties with the father of the baby.

In follow-up a year later, the boy's grades in school were so good that, as a reward, the mother had bought him a bicycle. She had become a community worker in a mental health center.

There were two stages in this therapy. In the first, the unfortunate ways in which mother and son protected each other were blocked through a paradoxical intervention. In the second stage, the mother was encouraged to be in charge of her son in relation to school and peer group activities and to take charge of herself in terms of her work and the organization of her family.

Case No. 2: Head-Aches

A family requested a consultation because their 7-year-old son had frequent headaches. There were two parents and a 5 year old sister. The parents described the boy's problem so vaguely that it was impossible to determine how frequent the headaches were or whether they had recently become worse or better. Behavior problems at school were also mentioned, although it was not clear what these were, and apparently they had been solved by changing schools. It was implied by the mother that the son was jealous of the sister because she was brighter, and the father agreed. Several times mother and father talked about the son in a way that made it difficult for the therapist to determine whether they were referring to the son or to the father.

The vagueness and confusion in the way the problem was presented, the parents' choice of words that were more appropriate for describing an adult than a child, and the difficulty in distinguishing whether the parents were talking about the son or the father led to the hypothesis that the father had problems that were painful for the couple to discuss and that the parents had established a pattern of talking about the son's difficulties as a way of metaphorically discussing father's troubles. It was later confirmed that the father did have serious problems. He was recovering from alcoholism, there was a possibility that he would lose his job, and he had written a novel that he could not get published. The goal of the therapy was to free the child from being a metaphor that the parents could use to discuss father's problems.

Ordinarily the son would develop a headache when he came home from school and the father came home from work feeling miserable. In the first session, the family was asked to act out a scene in which the father was to pretend that he was coming home in the evening with a terrible headache. The son was directed to try to cheer him up by playing games with him. He was also to try to find out if the father had a real headache by asking him about how he was feeling and what his day had been like at work. The father was to talk about make-believe problems at work. While father and son were involved this way in the interview, mother and daughter were pretending to prepare dinner.

The parents were asked to perform this scene at home every evening for one week. Father would come home pretending to have a headache, son would cheer him up, father would not say whether his headache was real. In the meantime, mother and daughter would be preparing dinner.

The family followed the directive and reported the following week that the son was much improved. They continued to perform the same scene for three more weeks, and the headaches disappeared.

The hypothesis behind the intervention was that the son was protecting the father by having a symptom that elicited concern from the father and therefore helped him to pull himself together to help the son instead of feeling devastated by his own problems. Also, the boy provided a metaphor that the parents could use to discuss father's problems and in this way saved them from talking directly about issues that were too painful to discuss explicitly.

By asking the father to pretend every day to have a headache and to justify it by talking about make-believe problems at work, a situation was created in which the son no longer knew whether the father was really upset or not and therefore could not help him in his usual way. A different way of protecting the father was arranged—the son had to play games and talk with him. The child no longer needed to have headaches to help the father. The father's make-believe headaches became a metaphor for his real problems and were discussed in a playful way by the family. The son was no longer used as a metaphor.

The problem of the headaches had been solved, but the mother complained that the son teased and bothered his sister. The little girl would come "screeching" to the mother who had constantly to reprimand the son. The therapist asked the mother to pretend that she was the daughter and the son to tease her as he usually did his sister. The mother was then to run screeching to the little girl, who would play the role of the mother and who would say, "Don't bother me; that is your problem, not mine." This scene was rehearsed several times in the session to the great enjoyment of the family. They were also instructed that every time the son felt like teasing or bothering his sister, he was to bother his mother instead. The mother would then run screeching to the little girl, who would dismiss her saying that she could handle the problem with her brother. Mother and children carried out these instructions at home for two weeks, and the relationship between brother and sister improved to the point that the mother did not consider it a problem any longer. The son, who was to initiate the sequence, did so several times during the first week but seldom after that. With

this sequence, the therapist had prescribed one aspect of the incongruous hierarchy, the one in which the children were in a superior position to the mother. This was a paradoxical directive designed to provoke the mother to respond by behaving in a more competent way and drawing a generational line between herself and the children. The therapist was also taking power away from the son by taking over the control of the symptom and instructing the child as to how and whom he should tease. The family responded to the directive and reversed their hierarchical order, so that brother and sister were no longer harassing mother with their quarrels and mother was no longer complaining that she was incompetent to handle the difficulties between her children.

The family came to a termination session just before they were leaving on vacation. The father, who was often depressed, seemed particularly sad, and the therapist decided to change the father's mood to relieve him of his depression and to have the family leave in a more cheerful spirit. The father was asked to pretend that he was very depressed, that he was a failure in life, and to tell his family so. He had to give good reasons, however, to justify his feelings. As soon as the father started to do this, the therapist began to criticize him for not pretending well enough to be depressed; particularly the reasons he was giving for his depression were not good, they were not authentic, they had to do with matters that were out of his control and therefore not really his fault, etc. As the therapist continued to criticize the husband, the wife began to support him by saying how difficult it was for him to be depressed. Finally, the therapist accepted as a valid depression the father's feelings about his failure to fix the sink at his house properly. At the end of the session, the father was talking about how difficult it is to pretend to be depressed when one is really in such good spirits.

Husband and wife were moved to change their usual interaction in which husband was depressed and wife attempted to cheer him up. When the husband had to pretend to be depressed and was criticized by the therapist for not doing it well, the wife supported him because he could *not* be depressed, rather than supporting him, as usual, because he *was* depressed. A new sequence of interaction was elicited between husband and wife in a playful, make-believe way.

When the family originally came to therapy, the son was a metaphor for the father's difficulties, and his symptoms were protective of the father. The quarrels between brother and sister were a metaphor for the difficulties between the parents, the implicit message being that the husband was jealous of the wife's intelligence. The wife had, in fact, abandoned her career and devoted herself to supporting him in his depression. By the end of the therapy, the children were no longer protecting the parents, the symptoms had disappeared, the parents were discussing the issues between them more openly and finding solutions.

Months after the therapy ended, the husband wrote to the therapist that they were all doing well. The son was behaving properly, doing well in school, and involved in activities with peers. The mother had gone back to school for an advanced degree, and things were better for the father. The little girl continued to do well as usual.

Case No. 3: The Fire-Setter

A mother consulted a therapist because her 10-year-old son was setting fires. He was a twin and the oldest of five children. The family had many other serious problems. The father had just left them and moved to another city. The mother was not receiving any financial support from him. She was Puerto Rican, did not speak English, and did not know how to go about obtaining the help she needed. The mother would not leave the boy alone for a minute for fear that he would set the house on fire.

In the first interview, the therapist gave the boy some matches and told him to light

one and asked the mother to do whatever she usually did at home when she caught him lighting a match. The therapist then left the room to observe from behind the one-way mirror. The boy reluctantly lit a match, and the mother took it and burned him with it.

By providing a focus for her anger, the boy was helping his mother. He was someone that she could punish and blame. He made her feel angry instead of depressed and in this way helped her to pull herself together in spite of all her troubles.

The therapist told the child that she was going to teach him how to light matches properly. She then showed him how one closes the matchbox before lighting the match and how after the match burns, one carefully puts it in the ashtray. She then asked the mother to light a fire with some papers in an ashtray and to pretend to burn herself. The son had to help her by putting out the fire with some water that the therapist had brought into the office for this purpose. The boy had to show his mother that he knew how to put out fires correctly. As all this was going on, the other children were allowed to look but not to participate in any way. After the fire was put out, the therapist talked with the boy about how he now knew how to light fires and put them out correctly. She emphasized to the mother that now she could trust him because he knew about fires. The therapist then asked the mother to set aside a time every evening for a week when she would get together with the boy and she would light a fire and pretend to burn herself and he would help her to put it out. The other children were not allowed to participate.

The interaction between mother and son was changed so that instead of helping his mother by providing a focus for her anger, the son was helping her in a playful way when she pretended to burn herself. Before, the boy was helping the mother by threatening her with fires. Now he was helping her because he was an expert on fires. Before the therapy the child was special in the family because he was setting fires. After the therapeutic intervention, he was special because he was an expert on fires. When the boy was unpredictably lighting fires, he was in a superior position to the mother. When he set fires under direction, he was beneath her in the hierarchy.

When the family came back a week later, the boy had not set fires. They went through the same procedure of lighting a fire and putting it out, but this time it was a bigger fire in a trash can. The therapist talked to the boy about different ways of putting out a fire. She then told the mother that because her son had now become an expert on fires, he should be allowed a privilege that the other children did not have, such as lighting the stove at home. The mother agreed to this and said that she felt confident that the boy was not going to set fires any more. The therapist then proceeded for the next two months to help the mother with her other problems. The son did not set fires again. By helping the mother with her many other difficulties, the therapist arranged to protect the mother herself and, therefore, the son no longer needed to do so.

CONCLUSION

It has been proposed here that psychiatric problems in children are the result of an incongruity in the hierarchical organization of the family. The parents are in a superior position to the child by the fact of being parents, and yet the child is in a superior position to the parents by protecting them through symptomatic behavior that often metaphorically expresses the parents' difficulties. Three strategies were presented for arranging that the parents solve the presenting problem in the child while resolving the incongruity in the family hierarchy.

The advantage that the child derives from his symptomatic behavior is to protect the parents by providing a focus of concern that helps them to avoid their own difficul-

ties and to overcome their own deficiencies. This advantage is the interpersonal gain that the child derives from the symptom—similar to secondary gain in psychoanalytic theory. In the three therapeutic strategies presented here, the interpersonal gain for the child is maintained while the symptom disappears. That is, in the case examples presented, it was arranged that the child maintain the interpersonal gain by organizing a different way in which he could protect the parents or by arranging other solutions for the parents' difficulties, or both.

The therapist must follow certain steps to carry out this therapy:

1. The problem should be defined clearly and specific goals set.
2. The therapist should conceptualize the problem (to himself only) as one in which the child is protecting one or both parents or a relative through his symptoms.
3. The therapist must plan an intervention in the form of a directive that the parents will give to the child. Other family members can participate in auxiliary ways. The directive must include a prescription
    (a) to have the problem; or
    (b) to pretend to have the problem; or
    (c) to pretend to help the parents.
4. It is often best to have the directive first practiced in the session and then carried out at home.
5. In the next session, a report on the performance of the directive must be obtained, and the therapist must continue to prescribe the same directive.
6. As change occurs and the problem behavior disappears, the therapist must drop the issue of the symptom and begin to deal with other problems in the same or in different ways or terminate the therapy, taking care always to give credit to the parents for the improvement of the child.

The therapeutic techniques that were described are characterized by the use of communication modalities that are appropriate to children, such as dramatizations, pretending, and make-believe. These techniques are most effective when the relationship between parent and child is basically loving and helpful. They should be used with caution when violence and abuse are involved, since play can easily become an ordeal or a punishment.

The techniques presented here represent one segment of a range of possible therapeutic techniques. The problems of each family are unique, and the best strategies for solving them are those designed specifically for each particular family.

REFERENCES

1. BOWEN, M., "Family Therapy After Twenty Years," in S. Arieti (Ed.), *American Handbook of Psychiatry*, vol. IV, pp. 367–392, Basic Books, New York, 1975.
2. ERICKSON, M., "Indirect Hypnotic Therapy of an Enuretic Couple," in J. Haley, (Ed.), *Advanced Techniques of Hypnosis and Therapy*, New York, Grune & Strattton, 1976.
3. HALEY, J., *Problem-Solving Therapy*, New York, Harper & Row, 1976.
4. Minuchin, S., *Families and Family Therapy*, Cambridge Mass., Harvard University Press, 1974.

Reprint requests should be addressed to Cloe Madanes, Family Therapy Institute, 4602 North Park Avenue, Chevy Chase, Maryland 20015.

Thirty-three families experiencing parent-adolescent conflict received problem-solving communication training, alternative family therapy, or a wait-list condition. Problem-solving communication training consisted of training in skills for negotiating solutions to specific disputes, remediation of negative communication patterns, cognitive restructuring of inappropriate attitudes, and practice in applying negotiation-communication skills at home. Alternative family therapy consisted of a heterogeneous blend of dynamic, family systems, and eclectic family therapy practiced at the clinic where the study took place. Both treatments resulted in significant reductions in self-reported disputes and conflictual communication at home; however, only problem-solving communication training resulted in significant improvements in problem-solving communication behavior objectively coded during family discussions. Most of the significant treatment effects were maintained at a 10-week follow-up. The results support the effectiveness of problem-solving communication training in ameliorating parent-adolescent conflict.

51

A CONTROLLED EVALUATION OF PROBLEM-SOLVING COMMUNICATION TRAINING WITH PARENT-ADOLESCENT CONFLICT

Arthur L. Robin

Adolescence is a period in which many parent-child conflicts arise as teenagers increasingly assert their independence from their families. From a social learning perspective, parent-adolescent conflict can be viewed as the result of skill deficits and inappropriate attitudinal responses leading to reciprocally punishing transactions (Alexander, 1973; Prinz, Rosenblum, & O'Leary, 1978; Robin, 1980). Behaviorally oriented clinicians and researchers have developed and also begun to evaluate the

This project was partially funded by Public Health Service Grant R03-31,000, awarded to the author while he was a member of the faculty at the University of Maryland Baltimore County. The opinions expressed herein, however, do not necessarily represent the views of the granting agency. The author gratefully acknowledges the assistance of Mary Fox, administrative assistant; Ray Callegary, Stephanie Donahoe, Phyllis MacKay, and Teresa Vorce, coders; and the Family Life Center of Howard County, Columbia, MD. Reprints can be obtained from Dr. Arthur Robin, Psychiatry/Psychology Division, Children's Hospital of Michigan, 3901 Beaubien, Detroit, MI 48201.

From Arthur L. Robin, "A Controlled Evaluation of Problem-Solving Communication Training with Parent-Adolescent Conflict," *Behavior Therapy*, 1981, 12, pp. 593-609. Reprinted by permission of the publisher and author.

TABLE 1
DEMOGRAPHIC INFORMATION FOR FAMILIES

Variable	PSCT[a]	AFT[a]	WL[a]
Mean age of adolescent	13.8	13.8	14.4
Mean age of mother	38.7	39.5	38.1
Mean age of father	40.5	40.6	40.5
Mean SES[b]	1.81	1.73	1.73
Mean school grade of adolescent	8.2	8.2	8.4
Number of triads	5	9	7
Number of dyads	6	2	4
Number of female adolescents	7	6	7
Number of male adolescents	4	5	4
Number of intact marriages	11	9	10
Number of eldest children	8	8	6
Number of middle children	3	3	2
Number of youngest children	0	0	3

[a] PSCT = Problem-solving communication training. AFT = Alternative family therapy. WL = Wait-list control.
[b] Hollingshead (Note 2) Scale.

effectiveness of several innovative approaches to the treatment of parent-adolescent conflict. These treatment programs have shared a common emphasis on teaching problem solving, communication, and cognitive restructuring, and analyzing the functions of behavior within family relationships (Alexander & Parsons, 1973; Barton & Alexander, 1981; Ginsberg, 1977).

Robin (Robin, 1979; Robin, Kent, O'Leary, Foster, & Prinz, 1977) developed a problem-solving communication training program. Based upon a cognitive-behavioral analysis of problem-solving deficits (D'Zurilla & Goldfried, 1971; Little & Kendall, 1979; Spivack, Platt, & Shure, 1976), this intervention trains parents and adolescents in the democratic resolution of specific disputes. Because negative communication habits interfere with effective problem solving (Alexander, 1973; Gordon, 1970; Robin & Weiss, 1980), family members are taught appropriate receptive and expressive communication skills. A cognitive restructuring component is also integrated into the intervention to counter faulty cognitive processes which may mediate rigid, emotionally charged responses to disagreements (Beck, 1967, 1976; Ellis & Harper, 1975).

Two previous studies have evaluated problem-solving communication training. Robin et al. (1977) found that problem-solving communication training produced significantly greater improvements in verbal problem-solving skills than a wait-list control. Despite these improvements, there was less than optimal amelioration of communication-conflict behavior at home. Foster, Prinz, and O'Leary (Note 1) evaluated the skill training package with and without the use of a generalization programming component involving homework designed to foster application of the skills in the natural environment. The problem-solving communication training groups were superior to a wait-list condition, but the generalization component did not appear to contribute clearly to the outcome.

In the present study, the effectiveness of problem-solving communication training was again evaluated using Prinz, Foster, Kent, and O'Leary's (1979) dependent measures and Foster et al.'s (Note 1) generalization programming techniques. The maintenance of treatment gains was assessed by including a follow-up. In addition, the importance of the structured components of problem-solving communication training was evaluated by including a group that was designed to control for nonspecific factors in the treatment situation. Since it was considered unethical and impractical to expose clinically distressed families to an attention-placebo condition, a "best alternative treatment" contrast group was used (O'Leary & Borkovec, 1978). Families receiving problem-solving communication training were contrasted to families receiving the heterogeneous blend of alternative family therapy typically offered at the clinic where the study was conducted.

METHOD

Participants

Thirty-three families with adolescents aged 11 to 16 were selected to meet the following criteria: (a) reports of disagreements concerning rules, responsibilities, and values, (b) willingness of at least one parent and one adolescent to attend sessions together, (c) agreement to the constraints of the research design (random assignment to conditions, audiotaping of therapy sessions, completion of questionnaires, and submission of a $10 deposit to be returned upon completion of the program), and (d) absence of retardation, psychosis, or known organic brain damage in either the parents or teenagers. Families were recruited through announcements placed in newspapers, and schools, churches, and mental health clinics. While the specific referral problems varied, the general themes (e.g., incorrigibility) did not.

Families were matched on the number of participating parents, the sex of the adolescent, and the severity of negative communication reported by parents on the Conflict Behavior Questionnaire (Prinz, 1977). Families were then randomly assigned to one of three conditions: problem-solving communication training (PSCT), alternative family therapy (AFT), or wait-list control (WL). Comparative demographic information for the three groups is presented in Table 1. Chi-square analyses and one way analyses of variance revealed no significant differences across groups. Within each group, families were assigned to therapists solely on the basis of scheduling convenience.

Therapists

One doctoral and three Masters-level psychologists served as the PSCT therapists. Training included didactic instruction, exposure to tapes of previous therapy cases, and cotherapy experience. Two hours of group supervision were held weekly throughout the study. One psychiatrist and four Masters-level mental health professionals served as AFT therapists. These therapists explicitly indicated that they used forms of short term family therapy other than problem-solving communication training and agreed that the design of the study and the dependent measures would provide a fair test of their therapeutic procedures. Although similar in terms of formal training, the alternative family therapists averaged 5.7 years of prior experience while the problem-solving communication training therapists averaged 1.8 years of prior experience.

Procedure

In a brief preliminary interview, an assessor determined whether the family met the criteria for inclusion in the program. A preassessment was conducted consisting of administration of the Issues Checklist, Conflict Behavior Questionnaire, Demographic Data Questionnaire, and the audiotaping of two family discussions. Each family was then given copies of the Home Report to complete at home and return by mail. Families were informed that when the Home Reports had been received, they would be contacted, informed of their group assignment and therapist, and the first session would be scheduled. After the treatment sessions had been completed, a postassessment occurred. This consisted of the administration of the Issues Checklist, Conflict Behavior Questionnaire, Home Report, an attitude survey for the treated groups, and the audiotaping of two family discussions. Ten weeks after the postassessment, treated families completed the Issues Checklist and Conflict Behavior Questionnaire by mail. Families in the treatment groups met with their therapists for seven 1-hour weekly sessions. A 2-month interval intervened between pre- and postassessment for the wait-list group. Treatment was offered to the wait-list families after the postassessment.

Problem-solving communication training.[1] Family members were taught a four-step model of problem solving: (a) define the problem concisely and without accusations, (b) brainstorm alternative solutions, (c) decide upon a mutually satisfactory solution by projecting positive and negative consequences, assigning solutions positive or negative ratings, adopting one or more solutions rated positively by everyone, (d) specify the details for implementing the agreement.

Communication training involved feedback, modeling, and behavior rehearsal to correct negative habits such as accusations, interruptions, lectures, put-downs, and inattentive postures. These were replaced with positive habits such as verification of meaning, active listening, I-messages, appropriate eye contact, and appropriate nonverbal postures.

Cognitive restructuring was tailored to the cognitive distortions exhibited by each family. When unreasonable beliefs interfered with the res-

, [1] A detailed manual describing problem-solving communication training is available (Robin, 1980). Copies of the dependent measures can be obtained from the author for a fee of $7.00.

olution of specific disputes, the therapist followed four steps: (a) the "underlying" cognitive distortion was made explicit, (b) the logical premises of the distortion were challenged through the use of direct feedback, exaggeration and humor, or reframing techniques, (c) an alternative, more flexible belief was suggested; and (d) the family was asked to "experiment" by implementing a solution to the dispute consistent with the more flexible belief and determining whether the solution was successful.

Generalization programming consisted of homework: (a) implementation of solutions negotiated during therapy sessions, (b) discussion of additional problems at home, and (c) application of component problem-solving communication skills in daily interchanges.

At the beginning of the first session, the rationale for problem solving was presented, outlines of the four-step model were distributed, and a topic was selected for initial discussion. The therapist modeled each step of problem solving and then asked the family members to imitate him or her. Instructions, prompts, behavior rehearsal, and feedback were used to correct inappropriate verbalizations. An additional topic was problem solved at each session, with the therapist gradually increasing the subtlety of the corrections for deficient behaviors. At the start of each session, the therapist announced the negative communication habits to be corrected and modeled positive, alternative responses. Then the therapist intervened whenever the targeted negative response occurred. During the last two sessions, the therapist faded out the prompts for correcting negative responses, encouraged family members to progress naturally from step to step, and helped them to recognize when they were getting bogged down and to move forward.

Alternative family therapy. The five therapists in this group were instructed to conduct seven sessions of family therapy in accordance with their respective theoretical orientations, previous experience, and training. They were permitted to structure therapy as they wished, with the restrictions that parents and adolescents attend sessions together and that the problem-solving communication training model not be employed. In essence, this condition represented a diversified cross-section of family therapy and was a representative sample of the predominant modality of therapy received by families seeking help at the clinic prior to the onset of this study. Specifically, two therapists described their orientations as "family systems," two as "eclectic," and one as "psychodynamic."

Assessment

A comprehensive battery of measures for the assessment of parent-adolescent conflict has also been shown to have discriminant validity (Prinz et al., 1979; Robin & Weiss, 1980). The assessment measures tap parental control and decision making, specific disputes, communication-conflict behavior, and problem-solving skills.

Parents and adolescents independently completed four questionnaires. When both parents were participating in treatment, separate forms of the measures were used for mothers and fathers, and the adolescent com-

726

FAMILY STUDIES REVIEW YEARBOOK

pleted separate versions of the questionnaires for relations with mother and father.

Issues checklist. The Issues Checklist (IC) required parents and adolescents to recall disagreements about 44 specific issues such as curfew, dating, chores, smoking, and drugs. For each topic, the respondent indicated whether or not the issue had been discussed during the past 2 weeks. For each topic that was endorsed positively, the respondent rated the degree of negative affect of the discussions on a five-point scale ranging from calm to angry, and estimated how often the topic had been broached. The IC yielded three scores for each family member: (a) the quantity of issues discussed, (b) the mean anger-intensity level of the endorsed issues, (c) the weighted average of the frequency and anger-intensity level of the endorsed issues. High anger-intensity and weighted frequency by anger-intensity scores are indicative of angry arguments while low scores are indicative of calm discussions. The quantity of issues was included for descriptive purposes; it cannot necessarily be assumed that high scores correspond to conflictual situations since improved communication may result in an increased rate of discussions.

Conflict behavior questionnaire. The Conflict Behavior Questionnaire (CBQ) consisted of 75 dichotomous (yes-no) items, assessing communication-conflict behavior. Each item was endorsed "yes" or "no" depending upon whether the individual judged it to be mostly true or mostly false. The CBQ yielded scores tapping each family member's (a) appraisal of the other member's behavior and (b) appraisal of the dyadic interactions between the two members. High scores indicated negative communication, and low scores indicated positive communication.

Home report. The Home Report (HR) (10 yes-no items and one five-point rating scale), assessed the degree of daily conflict at home. Each family member filled out and mailed one Home Report per evening for 7 days. Two scores were obtained for each family member by averaging across the 7 days: (a) daily conflict and (b) argument ratio.

The three self-report measures used were selected because of their reliability and discriminant validity (Prinz et al., 1979; Robin & Weiss, 1980).

Attitude survey. At postassessment, treated families completed an attitude survey, which measured satisfaction with treatment. The attitude survey consisted of nine-point Likert-scale items (16 for parents, 13 for adolescents).

Parent-adolescent interaction coding system. A sample of each family's problem-solving communication behavior was collected by asking the family to discuss and attempt to resolve two problems for 10 min apiece. The problems were based on responses to the IC. The topics with the highest weighted frequency by anger-intensity scores on the parents' and adolescents' checklists were used. Discussions were audiotaped and later coded by four trained raters, who were blind to the existence of the treatment study, using the Parent-Adolescent Interaction Coding System (PAICS) (Robin & Fox, Note 3). With the PAICS, which is based upon the Marital Interaction Coding System (Weiss, Hops, & Patterson, 1973), each verbal behavior emitted by either a parent or adolescent is classified into one of 15 categories. A "verbal behavior" is defined to be a statement by one family member which is homogeneous in content and affect and bounded by the statements of other family members. Thus, one family member's statement may be classified sequentially (but not simultaneously) into more than a single category if the content or affect change in accordance with the coding rules before another member begins to speak.

There are seven positive problem-solving communication categories (agree-assent, appraisal, consequential statements, facilitation, humor, problem solution, and specification of the problem), five negative problem-solving communication categories (command, complain, defensive behavior, interrupt, and put-down), and three neutral problem-solving communication categories (no response, problem description, and talk). Categories were classified as positive, negative, or neutral on the basis of an empirical analysis of an earlier version of the present coding system with distressed and nondistressed families (Robin & Weiss, 1980). The proportions of positive and negative problem-solving communication behavior were computed for each family member by summing the frequencies of the appropriate categories across the two discussions and dividing the sums by the total number of behaviors in all of the categories. Neutral behavior was not analyzed in this study.

Reliability was computed on a representative sample (9.3%) of the discussions. Each of four raters coded the reliability discussions unaware of the fact that a particular discussion was serving as a reliability check. Session reliability was assessed by computing the average product-moment correlation for the six pairings of the four coders on the total frequencies of positive and negative parent and adolescent behavior. Session reliability averaged $r(9) = +.85$, $p < .01$, with the following means for the four summary scores: positive parent behavior $r(9) = +.92$, $p < .01$; negative parent behavior $r(9) = +.73$, $p < .01$; positive adolescent behavior $r(9) = +.88$, $p < .01$; and negative adolescent behavior $r(9) = +.87$, $p < .01$. Trial reliability was computed by randomly designating one of the coders as the master coder. The coding sheets of the master coder and the other three coders were compared, and the number of behaviors on which they agreed in content and order was noted. Each behavior that the master coder had registered had to have been recorded by the second coder or a disagreement was marked. Overall reliability was computed by dividing the number of agreements between each coder and the master coder by the total number of codes recorded by the master coder, and then multiplying by 100. Trial reliability averaged 64% (range: 51% to 81%).

Expectation questionnaire. Expectations for therapeutic change were assessed through the use of a three-item scale distributed to each family member at the end of the first treatment session. Family members completed the questionnaire at home and mailed it to the research staff. The three items assessed appraisal of the logic of the treatment procedures, confidence in treatment, and confidence in recommending treatment to a friend.

RESULTS

Pre-Post Analyses

Postassessment scores on the IC, CBQ, and PAICS were submitted to a two-factor multivariate analysis of covariance, with the preassessment scores as covariates, using the Miami MANOVA computer program (Landrum, Ajiri, & Biasatti, 1978). With this program, the multivariate tests of significance are conducted according to the Wilk's Lameda criterion employing Rao's approximate F values. The factors were group (PSCT, AFT, and WL) and agent (parent and adolescent). Omnibus F tests were conducted for the main effect of agent and for the group by agent interaction. Two a priori contrasts (PSCT and AFT versus WL; PSCT versus AFT) were conducted for groups. Scores were averaged across mothers and fathers since unequal numbers of triads and dyads participated in each treatment condition. Examination of the intercorrelation matrix of the IC, CBQ, and PAICS suggested that the following five variables would be least redundant for inclusion in the analysis.

From the IC, the quantity of issues, and the weighted average of frequency and anger-intensity of issues were selected; the anger-intensity of issues, which correlated highly $r(29) = +.82, p < .01$ with the weighted average of frequency and anger-intensity, was excluded to avoid redundancy. From the CBQ, the appraisal of the other's behavior and the appraisal of the dyadic relationship were selected. On the PAICS, the proportions of positive and negative problem-solving communication behavior were significantly correlated $r(29) = -.53, p < .01$; to minimize redundancy, a single, composite score was computed for analysis by subtracting the proportion of negative from the proportion of positive behavior for parents and for adolescents.

In order to enter these five scores into the analyses, the data from two families who had not completed all of the measures at postassessment had to be dropped, one apiece from each of the treatment groups. Since a substantially lower percentage of the families completed the HR, this measure was analyzed individually.

For the comparison of the two treatments versus the control groups, there was a significant overall multivariate difference, $F(5,47) = 2.53$, $p < .05$. Subsequent univariate analyses revealed significant differences between the treatment and control groups on the weighted average of frequency and anger-intensity of issues, $F(1,51) = 6.79, p < .02$, the appraisal of the dyadic relationship, $F(1,51) = 7.17, p < .01$, and the composite proportion of PAICS behavior, $F(1,51) = 7.78, p < .007$. Examination of the mean scores indicated that families in both treatment groups improved from pre- to postassessment while control families did not (See Table 2). There were also improvements on the appraisal of the other person's behavior in the two treatment groups, but the high degree of variability rendered these improvements nonsignificant.

A significant multivariate difference was also obtained between the two treatment conditions, $F(5,47) = 5.71, p < .001$. The pattern of difference across groups was apparently most strongly influenced by one measure, the composite proportion of behavior on the PAICS. This was the only measure which showed a significant group difference in subsequent univariate analysis, $F(1,51) = 25.46, p < .001$. Inspection of mean scores for this measure indicated that PSCT families improved considerably while AFT families either worsened slightly or stayed the same from pre- to postassessment.

There was no significant main effect of agent and no significant interaction of groups by agent. Although none of the univariate tests for the group by agent interaction achieved significance, a single univariate test was significant for the main effect of agent: the composite proportion of behavior on the PAICS, $F(1,51) = 4.98, p < .03$. Parents emitted a greater composite proportion of behavior on the PAICS than adolescents both before and after treatment, regardless of group assignment.

The Daily Conflict Scores and Argument Ratio from the Home Report were submitted to a two-factor multivariate analysis of covariance comparable to the analysis conducted with the other measures. There were no significant outcomes with these measures. Examinations of the mean scores suggested that all of the three groups improved slightly from pre- to postassessment.

Component Analysis of the PAICS

In order to disentangle the incremental effects of treatment on problem-solving and communication behavior, two composite scores were computed by summing the proportions of behavior across the following categories of the PAICS: (a) problem solving: appraisal, consequential statements, problem solution, and specification of the problem, (b) communication: assent/agree, facilitation, and humor. Each postassessment composite score was submitted to a two-factor univariate analysis of covariance, with the preassessment scores as covariates. The factors were group (PSCT, AFT, and WL) and agent (parent and adolescent). As with the multivariate analysis, omnibus F tests were computed for the main effect of agent and for the groups by agent interaction, while two a priori contrasts were computed for groups (PSCT and AFT versus WL, and PSCT versus AFT).

Inspection of the mean scores in Table 3 reveals that the PSCT group improved on both problem-solving and communication behavior while the AFT group improved slightly on communication behavior. At postassessment PSCT was superior to AFT on problem solving, $F(1,55) = 21.22, p < .001$, and communication behavior, $F(1,55) = 10.50, p < .002$. The WL group either worsened or remained unchanged on these two variables. The combined treatment groups were superior to the WL

TABLE 2

UNADJUSTED MEAN SCORES AND STANDARD DEVIATIONS ON THE ISSUES CHECKLIST,
CONFLICT BEHAVIOR QUESTIONNAIRE, HOME REPORT, AND PARENT-ADOLESCENT
INTERACTION CODING SYSTEM

		Issues checklist	
		Pre	*Post*
Quantity of issues			
Parents	PSCT[a]	22.8 (6.9)[b]	17.0 (8.4)
	AFT	19.7 (5.5)	18.4 (6.5)
	WL	22.3 (7.1)	17.8 (5.9)
Adolescents	PSCT	17.7 (7.5)	11.9 (6.3)
	AFT	17.6 (6.1)	13.5 (8.2)
	WL	18.0 (6.3)	15.4 (7.1)
Weighted average of intensity × frequency of conflict			
Parents	PSCT	2.72 (0.54)	2.03 (0.63)
	AFT	2.46 (0.66)	2.24 (0.55)
	WL	2.57 (0.53)	2.74 (0.72)
Adolescents	PSCT	2.85 (0.86)	2.22 (0.83)
	AFT	2.73 (0.82)	2.04 (0.78)
	WL	2.76 (0.77)	2.57 (0.76)

		Conflict behavior questionnaire	
Appraisal of the other's behavior			
Parents	PSCT	28.5 (7.1)	17.8 (7.1)
	AFT	22.6 (8.6)	17.8 (8.4)
	WL	26.4 (5.7)	24.7 (7.3)
Adolescents	PSCT	17.1 (9.0)	14.7 (11.9)
	AFT	20.3 (7.6)	15.8 (8.5)
	WL	15.4 (9.7)	14.0 (9.8)
Appraisal of dyad			
Parents	PSCT	11.3 (4.2)	5.8 (2.4)
	AFT	8.4 (4.2)	6.2 (4.7)
	WL	10.9 (2.9)	9.7 (4.0)
Adolescents	PSCT	10.1 (5.3)	7.9 (5.6)
	AFT	10.6 (4.6)	6.7 (3.8)
	WL	7.9 (4.9)	7.4 (3.6)

		Parent-adolescent interaction coding system	
Proportion of composite positive minus negative behavior			
Parents	PSCT	.187 (.166)	.382 (.084)
	AFT	.142 (.124)	.137 (.128)
	WL	.192 (.134)	.167 (.087)

TABLE 2
CONTINUED

		Pre	Post
Parent-adolescent interaction coding system			
Adolescents	PSCT	.015 (.213)	.181 (.219)
	AFT	−.077 (.210)	−.058 (.192)
	WL	.053 (.174)	−.027 (.215)
Home report			
Daily conflict			
Parents	PSCT[c]	3.04 (.76)	2.69 (.77)
	AFT	2.94 (1.33)	2.48 (.54)
	WL	2.73 (.84)	2.87 (1.08)
Adolescents	PSCT	3.45 (1.30)	2.78 (1.47)
	AFT	3.70 (.97)	2.20 (1.41)
	WL	2.58 (1.04)	2.34 (.98)
Argument ratio			
Parents	PSCT	1.89 (.44)	1.60 (.41)
	AFT	1.63 (.60)	1.58 (.35)
	WL	1.75 (.33)	1.56 (.44)
Adolescents	PSCT	2.28 (.73)	1.86 (.60)
	AFT	2.18 (.57)	1.58 (.49)
	WL	1.74 (.60)	1.54 (.41)

[a] PSCT = Problem-Solving Communication Training (N = 10). AFT = Alternative Family Therapy (N = 10). WL = Wait-List Control (N = 11).

[b] Standard deviations are in parentheses.

[c] N for Home Report: PSCT = 7, AFT = 8, WL = 8.

group on communication, $F(1,55) = 14.94$, $p < .001$, but not problem-solving behavior.

While parents emitted higher proportions of problem-solving behavior than adolescents, $F(1,55) = 13.19$, $p < .001$, family members emitted comparable proportions of communication behavior. There were no significant group by agent interactions.

This component analysis suggests that PSCT resulted in increments in both positive problem-solving and communication behavior while AFT had minimal impact on either behavior. In general, families tended to emit slightly higher proportions of communication than problem-solving behavior (grand means = .17 versus .11 per 20-min discussions).

Follow-Up Analyses

Six of the eleven PSCT families and eight of the AFT families returned completed sets of follow-up questionnaires. To test for improvement at

TABLE 3

UNADJUSTED MEAN PROPORTIONS OF PROBLEM-SOLVING AND COMMUNICATION
BEHAVIORS FROM THE PAICS

		Problem-solving behavior	
		Pre	*Post*
Parents	PSCT	.143 (.054)[1]	.192 (.044)
	AFT	.108 (.056)	.100 (.061)
	WL	.143 (.061)	.150 (.053)
Adolescents	PSCT	.075 (.044)	.118 (.065)
	AFT	.074 (.046)	.060 (.039)
	WL	.091 (.049)	.068 (.028)
		Communication behavior	
Parents	PSCT	.168 (.080)	.263 (.079)
	AFT	.163 (.042)	.171 (.058)
	WL	.178 (.077)	.136 (.030)
Adolescents	PSCT	.170 (.118)	.205 (.103)
	AFT	.100 (.069)	.137 (.046)
	WL	.171 (.127)	.148 (.091)

[1] Standard deviations are in parentheses.

follow-up with the reduced sample, three-factor, mixed multivariate analysis of variance were conducted comparing (a) preassessment with postassessment scores and (b) preassessment with follow-up scores. The between-subject factors in each analysis were group (PSCT versus AFT) and agent (parent versus adolescent) while the repeated-measures factor was time. Four scores were entered into the analyses as dependent measures: the quantity of issues, the weighted average of the frequency by anger-intensity of issues, the appraisal of the other person's behavior, and the appraisal of the dyadic relationship.

There were significant multivariate main effects of time in both the preassessment to follow-up, $F(4,21) = 23.73$, $p < .001$, and pre- to postassessment analyses, $F(4,21) = 6.61$, $p < .001$. Subsequent univariate analyses revealed preassessment to follow-up main effects of time for three of the four variables: the quantity of issues, $F(1,24) = 47.39$, $p < .001$, the appraisal of the other person's behavior, $F(1,24) = 30.45$, $p < .001$, and the appraisal of the dyadic relationship, $F(1,24) = 26.77$, $p < .001$. Pre- to postassessment main effects of time were significant for each of the four variables: the quantity of issues, $F(1,24) = 8.59$, $p < .007$; the weighted average of frequency by anger-intensity of issues, $F(1,24) = 11.36$, $p < .003$; the appraisal of the other person's behavior, $F(1,24) = 11.00$, $p < .003$; and the appraisal of the dyadic relationship, $F(1,24) = 24.06$, $p < .001$. Examination of the pattern of mean scores (see Table 4) reveals that in most cases, both treatment groups improved from pre- to postassessment and either remained stable or continued to improve

TABLE 4
UNADJUSTED MEAN SCORES AND STANDARD DEVIATIONS ON THE IC AND CBQ FOR
REDUCED FOLLOW-UP SAMPLE OF FAMILIES

		Issues checklist		
		Pre	*Post*	*Follow-Up*
Quantity of issues				
Parents	PSCT[a]	20.1 (8.5)[b]	13.2 (7.4)	13.1 (6.6)
	AFT	19.0 (5.8)	18.0 (7.1)	13.6 (6.8)
Adolescents	PSCT	15.8 (8.1)	13.0 (6.7)	10.7 (5.0)
	AFT	17.5 (6.8)	13.9 (9.3)	9.3 (6.9)
Weighted average of intensity × frequency of conflict				
Parents	PSCT	2.71 (.50)	1.64 (.60)	2.18 (.46)
	AFT	2.50 (.69)	2.23 (.62)	2.18 (.48)
Adolescents	PSCT	2.61 (.68)	2.30 (.68)	2.47 (.48)
	AFT	2.92 (.81)	2.17 (.83)	2.69 (2.61)
		Conflict behavior questionnaire		
Appraisal of the other's behavior				
Parents	PSCT	27.3 (6.2)	15.7 (7.5)	14.0 (9.1)
	AFT	23.3 (8.6)	17.1 (9.3)	14.8 (6.2)
Adolescents	PSCT	18.1 (10.9)	17.6 (16.2)	16.8 (16.9)
	AFT	21.0 (6.7)	17.3 (8.9)	9.5 (8.1)
Appraisal of dyad				
Parents	PSCT	11.8 (4.0)	5.2 (1.9)	5.8 (3.3)
	AFT	9.3 (4.2)	6.8 (5.1)	7.0 (5.1)
Adolescents	PSCT	10.7 (4.3)	9.2 (5.4)	7.3 (6.3)
	AFT	11.7 (3.9)	8.0 (2.9)	5.9 (2.4)

[a] PSCT = Problem-Solving Communication Training ($N = 6$). AFT = Alternative Family Therapy ($N = 8$).
[b] Standard deviations are in parentheses.

from postassessment to follow-up. The exception to this pattern occurred for the measure of weighted frequency by anger-intensity of issues; on that variable, the treatment groups improved from pre- to postassessment but deteriorated from postassessment to follow-up.

None of the remaining multivariate effects reached significance in the preassessment to follow-up analysis, although the main effect of agent was significant in the pre- to postassessment analysis, $F(4,21) = 3.75$, $p < .02$. Subsequent univariate analyses of each measure revealed no significant main effects of agent, and an examination of the four marginal mean scores for agent revealed no consistent pattern of differences between parents and adolescents.

Taken together, the analyses of the follow-up data suggested that for the reduced sample in both the PSCT and AFT groups, self-reported parent-adolescent conflict was significantly lower 3 months following the termination of treatment than prior to the beginning of treatment.

Attitude Survey

Ratings on the attitude survey were generally positive. Ninety-one percent of the mean scores on individual items were above five, the midpoint of the scale. The PSCT and AFT groups were compared on individual items of the attitude survey using two-tailed t tests for independent groups. Parents were generally more satisfied with PSCT than with AFT. Adolescents were equally satisfied with both types of therapy. Specifically, parents reported significantly more positive attitudes towards PSCT than AFT on the following items: (a) improvement in communication with their adolescent, $t(20) = 2.49$, $p < .05$, (b) the amount of this improvement due to the program, $t(20) = 6.95$, $p < .05$, (c) the amount of improvement in their adolescent's behavior at home due to the program, $t(20) = 6.64$, $p < .05$, (d) improvement in their adolescent's relationship with them, $t(20) = 7.09$, $p < .05$, (e) improvement in discussion of problems at home, $t(20) = 4.54$, $p < .05$, and (f) the extent to which the program lived up to their expectations, $t(20) = 2.61$, $p < .05$. Parents in both groups rated their liking for their therapist and their perception of the fairness of their therapist equally positively, suggesting that the differences on the earlier items were due to program characteristics rather than therapist variables. Adolescents displayed equally positive attitudes towards the two treatment conditions, with one exception: adolescents in the AFT condition reported significantly greater improvement in their parents' behavior at home than did adolescents in the PSCT condition, $t(19) = 2.25$, $p < .05$.

Expectation Questionnaire

Comparisons between PSCT and AFT were conducted for parental and adolescent expectation ratings using t tests. There were no significant differences between groups for either parents or adolescents on any expectation ratings.

DISCUSSION

The results confirmed the effectiveness of PSCT for ameliorating parent-adolescent conflict. Families who received PSCT improved significantly more than a wait-list control group on both behavioral measures of problem-solving communication skills and on self-report measures of the level of negative affect associated with specific disputes and communication-conflict behavior at home. PSCT produced comparable gains to a heterogeneous blend of non-problem-solving oriented family therapy on the measures of communication and conflict at home; in addition, PSCT was clearly superior to AFT on the observational measure of interactional behavior. The comparability of the two treatment groups on expectations for therapeutic change suggests that any differences between them are unlikely to have been a function of differential cognitive sets at the outset of treatment. The pattern of results therefore suggests that the specific skill training components of PSCT contributed to the gains on the PAICS; the lack of differences between the two treatment groups on the IC and CBQ leaves unanswered the question of the extent to which explicitly programmed skill training is necessary to produce generalized improvement in family relations at home.

The analyses of the follow-up data suggested that most of the gains on the questionnaire measures were maintained 3 months after the termination of treatment with either PSCT or AFT. Brief family therapy produced lasting amelioration in self-reported levels of parent-adolescent conflict. Because of the attrition of families returning the follow-up questionnaires, however, these results should be viewed with caution pending replication. It is possible that the families who benefited most from the program returned the follow-up questionnaires, positively skewing the results.

In addition to the treatment gains, there was evidence of consumer satisfaction with the outcome of the interventions. Parents and adolescents rated the outcome of therapy and their therapists positively on the attitude survey. They perceived most of the improvement in their relationships to be due to treatment. Parents were generally more satisfied with problem-solving communication training than with the alternative, less structured form of family therapy while adolescents were equally satisfied with both forms of brief family intervention.

Several methodological limitations of the present investigation may restrict the external validity of the results. First, the AFT therapists averaged 5.7 years of previous experience while the PSCT therapists averaged 1.8 years of previous experience. While this differential would typically be taken as a conservative test of PSCT, it might be argued that less experienced therapists are more likely to be enthusiastic and pay attention to supervisory directions than experienced therapists. The PSCT therapists were provided with supervision to compensate for their lack of experience; unfortunately, it was not feasible to provide supervision to the experienced therapists. The supervision provided to the PSCT therapists may have confounded the results by enhancing their motivation and further increasing their attention to structuring variables. Second, hierarchical nesting of families within therapists and therapists within treatment conditions may have created greater statistical dependency between the families seen by each therapist than between families seen by all of the therapists within each treatment condition, possibly violating independence assumptions of factorial analyses.

Third, the inclusion of both triads and dyads made it difficult to analyze separately the results for fathers and mothers. However, a visual inspection suggested that there were few clear-cut differences in the pattern of results obtained from these two sources.

The results of the present study replicate and extend previous evaluations of problem-solving communication training (Foster et al., Note 1; Robin et al., 1977) and related approaches to behavioral family therapy (Alexander & Barton, 1976; Blechman & Olson, 1976; Ginsberg, 1977). There is now a need for parametric, dismantling investigations to determine the active ingredients of PSCT, the appropriate prognostic criteria for deciding which families will benefit most from this form of treatment, and the type of alternative treatments needed for families who do not benefit from PSCT.

REFERENCE NOTES

1. Foster, S. L., Prinz, R. J., & O'Leary, K. D. *Impact of problem-solving communication training and generalization procedures on family conflict.* Manuscript submitted for publication, 1980.
2. Hollingshead, A. B. *Two-factor index of social position.* Unpublished manuscript, Yale University, 1957.
3. Robin, A. L., & Fox, M. *The parent-adolescent interaction coding system: coding manual.* Unpublished manuscript, University of Maryland Baltimore County, January, 1979.

REFERENCES

Alexander, J. F. Defensive and supportive communication in normal and deviant families. *Journal of Consulting and Clinical Psychology,* 1973, **40**, 223–231.
Alexander, J. F., & Barton, C. Behavioral systems therapy with delinquent families. In D. H. L. Olson (Ed.), *Treating relationships.* Lake Mills, IA: Graphic Publishing, 1976.
Alexander, J. F., & Parsons, D. V. Short-term behavioral intervention with delinquent families: Impact on family process and recidivism. *Journal of Abnormal Psychology,* 1973, **81**, 219–225.
Barton, C., & Alexander, J. F. Functional family therapy. In A. S. Gurman & D. P. Kniskern (Eds.), *Handbook of family therapy.* New York: Brunner/Mazel, 1981.
Beck, A. T. *Depression: Clinical, experimental, and theoretical aspects.* New York: Harper & Row, 1967.
Beck, A. T. *Cognitive theory and the emotional disorders.* New York: International Universities Press, 1976.
Blechman, E. A., & Olson, D. H. L. The family contract game: Description and effectiveness. In D. H. L. Olson (Ed.), *Treating relationships.* Lake Mills, IA: Graphic Publishing, 1976.
D'Zurilla, T. J., & Goldfried, M. R. Problem-solving and behavior modification. *Journal of Abnormal Psychology,* 1971, **78**, 107–126.
Ellis, A., & Harper, R. A. *A new guide to rational living.* Hollywood, CA: Wilshire Books, 1975.
Ginsberg, B. G. Parent-adolescent relationship development program. In B. G. Guerney (Ed.), *Relationship enhancement.* San Francisco: Jossey-Bass, 1977.
Gordon, T. *Parent effectiveness training.* New York: Wyden, 1970.
Landrum, W. L., Ajiri, E., & Biasatti, L. *Miami multivariate analysis of variance or covariance.* Detroit: Wayne State University Computing Services Center, 1978.

Little, V. L., & Kendall, P. C.   Cognitive-behavioral interventions with delinquents: Problem-solving, role-taking, and self-control. In P. C. Kendall & S. D. Hollon (Eds.), *Cognitive-behavioral interventions: Theory, research, and procedures.* New York: Academic Press, 1979.

O'Leary, K. D., & Borkovec, T. D.   Conceptual, methodological, and ethical problems of placebo groups in psychotherapy research. *American Psychologist,* 1978, **33,** 821–830.

Prinz, R. J.   The assessment of parent-adolescent relations: Discriminating distressed and nondistressed dyads. (Doctoral dissertation, State University of New York at Stony Brook, 1976). *Dissertation Abstracts International,* 1977, **37,** 5370B. (University Microfilms No. 77-7774).

Prinz, R. J., Foster, S., Kent, R. N., & O'Leary, K. D.   Multivariate assessment of conflict in distressed and nondistressed mother-adolescent dyads. *Journal of Applied Behavior Analysis,* 1979, **12,** 691–700.

Prinz, R. J., Rosenblum, R. S., & O'Leary, K. D.   Affective communication differences between distressed and nondistressed mother-adolescent dyads. *Journal of Abnormal Child Psychology,* 1978, **6,** 373–383.

Robin, A. L.   Problem-solving communication training: A behavioral approach to the treatment of parent-adolescent conflict. *The American Journal of Family Therapy,* 1979, **7,** 69–82.

Robin, A. L.   Parent-adolescent conflict: A skill training approach. In D. P. Rathjen & J. P. Foreyt (Eds.), *Social competence: Interventions for children and adults.* Elmsford, NY: Pergamon, 1980.

Robin, A. L., Kent, R. N., O'Leary, K. D., Foster, S., & Prinz, R. J.   An approach to teaching parents and adolescents problem-solving communication skills: A preliminary report. *Behavior Therapy,* 1977, **8,** 639–643.

Robin, A. L., & Weiss, J. G.   The criterion-related validity of observational and self-report measures of problem-solving communication skills in distressed and nondistressed parent-adolescent dyads. *Behavioral Assessment,* 1980, **2,** 339–352.

Spivack, G., Platt, J. J., & Shure, M. B.   *The problem-solving approach to adjustment.* San Francisco: Jossey-Bass, 1976.

Weiss, R. L., Hops, H., & Patterson, G. R.   A framework for conceptualizing marital conflict, a technology for altering it, and some data for evaluating it. In A. Hamerlynck, L. C. Handy, & E. J. Mash (Eds.), *Behavior change: Methology, concepts, and practice.* Champaign, IL: Research Press, 1973.

RECEIVED: July 16, 1980
FINAL ACCEPTANCE: June 24, 1981

Six months after termination, mothers and daughters in a traditional, discussion-oriented treatment showed no greater gains over pretreatment in specific communication skills, general communication patterns, or the general quality of their relationship than those receiving no treatment. Participants in PARD, a Relationship Enhancement therapy/enrichment program, showed significantly greater gains in all these areas relative to both the other groups, demonstrating not only that the method is superior to the type of traditional treatment studied, but that a significant portion of such gains are treatment-specific. A booster program enhanced maintenance of gains, but significant gains were also maintained by those not assigned to it. The participants (low in socioeconomic status) had been assigned to treatments and the booster condition randomly. Very few were lost. The treatments were closely matched on all but their essential features. Variables were measured by self-report, behavioral, and/or quasi-behavioral instruments. Mothers and daughters generally did not differ from one another in the gains they achieved as a result of exposure or nonexposure to any of the treatments or to the booster program. Limitations and strengths of the study were discussed in terms of their generalizability and suggestions for needed further research.

52

RELATIONSHIP ENHANCEMENT VERSUS A TRADITIONAL TREATMENT

Follow-Up and Booster Effects

*Bernard G. Guerney, Jr., Edward Vogelsong,
and Jeannette Coufal*

Relationship Enhancement, or RE (Guerney, 1977; Guerney and Vogelsong, 1980), is a method designed to help an individual client, a couple, or a family improve relationships with intimates. RE is appropriate for therapy, prevention, and enrichment. Its major use to date has been with family members seen together, as is also the case in the present study. Large-scale controlled experiments have demonstrated the effectiveness of RE with premarital couples (D'Augelli et al., 1974; Ginsberg and Vogelsong, 1977), married couples (Collins, 1977; Ely et al., 1973; Rappaport, 1976), and fathers and sons (Ginsberg, 1977; Grando and Ginsberg, 1976).

AUTHORS' NOTE: This research was supported by grant 1 RO1 MH 22807 from the National Institute of Mental Health and is based in part on the Ph.D. dissertations of the junior authors under the chairmanship of the senior author. The authors are grateful for the assistance of Louise Guerney, Ted Huston, Richard Lundy, Carl Ridley, and Rex Warland, who served on their doctoral committees.

The present study is a follow-up to an experiment with mothers and their adolescent daughters (Guerney et al., forthcoming). That study demonstrated that traditional, discussion-based treatment was superior to no treatment in improving the general quality of the relationship. It further showed that a format of Relationship Enhancement called PARD (Parent Adolescent Relationship Development), in addition to being superior to no treatment, was superior to traditional treatment with respect to: (1) the specific, behaviorally assessed communication skills which were studied—namely, empathic skills and expressive skills; (2) general patterns of communication in such areas as selecting items to communicate, the frequency of communication, providing appropriate feedback, and feeling understood; and (3) the general quality of the relationship, as measured by a questionnaire, in terms of trust, empathy, genuineness, intimacy, openness and harmony, general satisfaction with the relations, and the ability to solve family problems. The traditional treatment was designed to be the equal of the RE treatment in every respect, including credibility, and since the clients perceived the leaders of the two treatments as equal with respect to all pertinent therapeutic qualities studied—confidence, enthusiasm, empathy, competence, and genuineness—the study showed that the effectiveness of RE should not be attributed to suggestions, attention, thank-you, or other nonspecific treatment effects, but to its specific characteristics.

The purpose of the present six-month follow-up of the earlier study just described was to ascertain: (1) the durability of the effects of traditional and Relationship Enhancement treatments in comparison with a no-treatment control group, and (2) whether a booster program would contribute to the durability of effects.

METHOD

The Independent Variables

As in the initial study, three conditions were compared: (1) no-treatment, (2) Relationship Enhancement (PARD), and (3) traditional treatment. The *no-treatment* group received no attention other than that required to secure their cooperation in gathering data. The two treatment groups were systematically equated as follows. The two leaders participated equally in conducting each treatment, and in both endeavored to produce the most positive changes possible and to convey to clients the highest levels of genuineness, empathy, warmth, competence, and enthusiasm. The subgroups of parents and adolescents in each treatment were of the same size—two to four pairs. In both treatments, the format was the same—once each week for two hours for about three months. Mothers and daughters in both treatments participated jointly and used the same vehicle, a Relationship Questionnaire (Guerney, 1977), to choose topics meaningful to their relationship. Both groups had the same amount of home assignments (one hour) to complete each week.

The Parent Adolescent Relationship Development (PARD) treatment is a format of family RE wherein the major focus is on one parent and one adolescent from the same family. RE programs in general and PARD in particular have been described in detail elsewhere (Guerney, 1977) and hence will be described here only in general terms. RE seeks the same objectives as psychodynamic and humanistic forms of therapy. The major difference is that in striving for such objectives, RE uses an educational, skill-training model (Authier et al., 1975; Guerney et al., 1971/1972). Through demonstration, modeling, behavioral rehearsal, social reinforcement, and other instructional techniques, clients are taught six sets of skills. The first set of principles and skills, called the *expressive* mode, promotes clients' awareness of their own emotions and interpersonal needs and their ability to express them promptly, honestly, and constructively. The second set, called the *empathic* mode, is designed to help clients convey genuine, appreciative acceptance and thus decrease the use of psychological defense mechanisms and hostility in others and to increase their openness and cooperativeness. The third set, *mode switching,* teaches clients how to steer away from vicious cycles of hostility and/or withdrawal and toward deeper understanding of personal and interpersonal needs and dynamics through the proper employment of the expressive and empathic modes. The fourth set, *facilitation,* teaches the client to influence and teach others to use RE skills as a means of promoting mutual self-esteem and psychosocial growth. The fifth set, *problem-solving,* teaches clients to obtain more creative, satisfying, and durable resolutions to interpersonal problems and conflicts. The sixth set, *generalization,* is designed to promote and maintain over time the day-to-day use of RE skills in situations where they are helpful in promoting and maintaining personal and interpersonal growth. Under the close supervision of the leader/therapist, clients use the skills to work through personal and, especially, family problems, as well as to enhance their relationships. The therapist's role is limited to helping clients learn and use their skills. All traditional therapist responses dealing with problem *content*—such as questions, encouragement, reassurance, suggestions, advice, persuasion, information-giving, and interpretation—are proscribed except under clearly defined, rare circumstances.

The *traditional* treatment has been outlined in detail elsewhere (Coufal, 1975) and will be described here only in general terms. The objectives are identical with those of PARD: to promote skillful communication, improve general communication patterns, resolve problems, and maximize the long-range growth of personal and family relationships. The essential difference is that here the leader/therapist is free to use any of the traditional responses he or she considers appropriate. The therapist is also free to model, that is, to use RE skills, but not to systematically instruct clients in their use. The general orientation is eclectic, with a client-centered emphasis. Psychodynamic probing, interpretation, or direct advice-giving are rarely used. Rather, as in most types of traditional group therapy, client gains are expected to emerge primarily from the therapist's modeling of appropriate behavior, the general promotion of openness, genuineness, warmth, and positive regard between the pairs, and the orchestration of constructive interaction, support, feedback, and advice from the group members to one another. This includes pointing out the importance, in addition to discussing problems, of expressing *positive* reactions and feelings to one another, as well as the value of mutual social reinforcement as opposed to put-downs or reprimands. The therapist also reinforces participants for open expression of their views and for listening attentively to others. The therapist attempts to keep the conversation focused on issues important to the relationship of the mother-daughter pair and also attempts to keep all group members participating actively, drawing out the quiet members and diplomatically keeping the most uninhibited members from dominating the group's process. In contrast to PARD, the traditional treatment leader is free to ask questions or present information about the content of what is being discussed. Each week, participants in the study were asked to read a chapter from *Children and Their Parents* (Fremon, 1968) and to discuss it at home together. In addition to providing information, stimulation, and helpful ideas for ensuing group sessions, the assignment provided a match for the home assignments in the PARD treatment.

Booster and No-Booster Groups

Just before the last meeting, half of the groups in each of the two treatment conditions were assigned by a coin toss to either the booster or no-booster condition. Participants in *both* conditions were encouraged to continue to set aside time each week to discuss issues at home that were pertinent to their relationships. (Those in the PARD group were told to use their skills during the discussions.) During the last regular group session, each mother-daughter pair was given six logs on which to report the results of their *first six* weekly discussions. These were to be mailed back to the therapist in prestamped, preaddressed envelopes. The *booster* participants were informed, in addition, that the therapist would like to meet with them four more times at six-week intervals and would keep in touch with them.

A week later, all booster participants were called and asked whether they had held their home discussion and were asked to send in their logs. All were called again at the end of the second week to reinforce them for sending in the logs or to encourage them to meet and to send them in. A call was made at the end of the fourth week for similar purposes and to arrange the first booster group meeting. During the second six-week posttreatment period, booster participants were called every two weeks. During the next six weeks of the follow-up period they were called once, in the fourth week. During the last six weeks of the follow-up period, no calls were made. The booster meetings were held during the 6th, 12th, 18th, and 24th weeks of the follow-up period. At each of these two-hour meetings, participants discussed any difficulties in their relationships (using their skills in the PARD group) and any problems they had encountered concerning their weekly discussions. They were also encouraged to continue those discussions at home and were provided with additional logs and envelopes. Mother-daughter pairs in the *no-booster* condition received no such phone calls and did not meet as a group during the follow-up period. They were provided with six logs and envelopes at the last regular meeting and were sent additional logs and envelopes as needed.

Subjects, Recruitment, and Assignment

Mother and daughter pairs were used in the present study in order to determine whether RE would yield with them the positive results that had earlier been obtained with fathers and sons (Ginsberg, 1977; Grando and Ginsberg, 1976). By offering the possibility of a free program to help improve their relationship, such pairs were recruited through encouraging therapy referrals from clergymen, guidance counselors, and mental health professionals, as well as by means of newspaper notices, letters, articles, and presentations in school classrooms. Few who came to the intake considered themselves to have serious problems.

At intake, the two treatment programs were explained by means of a single generic description, and client pairs were informed that they had a two-in-three chance of being randomly assigned to such a program. If they were not, they would instead each be given $10 at each of the three times they would be asked to complete research measures. After the explanations, participants decided whether or not they wished to commit themselves to the project under those conditions. Those who did then opened an envelope which showed the pair's assignment to one of the three conditions. (A table of random numbers had been used to make the assignment.) The intake worker then explained more about the nature of the specific treatment to which they had been assigned. Thus, clients had no knowledge that two different treatments were being compared. Also, the intake worker did not know which condition was in store for them until after clients had committed themselves to the project.

No subjects backed out upon learning the nature of their assignment. All subjects were, of course, free to seek additional help if they wished. Although no formal data were collected, there was sufficient communication with the treatment clients to indicate that few, if any, sought additional help during either the primary study or the follow-up. (Any help obtained by no-treatment participants would have worked against confirmation of the hypotheses.) After random assignment to treatment, the subgroups of clients were arranged in accord with scheduling convenience and in such a way as to place daughters of similar ages together (11-14 versus 15-18 years).

Of the 77 pairs who had attended the intake session, 61 pairs agreed to participate. Subject loss before project completion was as follows: on PARD pair moved away; one traditional treatment pair terminated because of change in work status of the mother, and one traditional treatment pair was a drop-out; three other traditional treatment pairs completed the program but would not complete posttesting despite repeated requests; and one no-treatment pair failed to complete testing. The final sample, therefore, was 108 clients: 36 in traditional treatment, 38 in PARD, and 34 in no-treatment.

To check on whether random assignment was successful in equating subjects in the three conditions on demographic variables, one-way analyses of variance were conducted. There were no significant differences among them on mother's age, daughter's age, years married, number of children in the family, socioeconomic status on Hollingshead's (1957) Index of Social Position, or mother's educational level.

The typical mother in the study was a 40-year-old white Protestant who frequently attended church, had never attended college, and was still married, after 17 years and three or four children, to her first husband. The family social position (Hollingshead, 1957) was quite low: 3.5, with 5 being the lowest point in the scale. The age of the typical participating daughter was 13 years, 4 months.

Testing and Treatment Procedures

Pretesting was at intake or within the next few days. Clients participating in treatments began to meet within the next few weeks in groups of two or three pairs for two hours once each week with one therapist. Posttesting was conducted for all three conditions within a few days of the final session; follow-up testing was six months after that.

The therapists were graduate students, one male and one female. Prior to this study, they had co-led one group of each type to standardize procedures. The male had led four PARD and three traditional treatment groups, and the female had led four groups of each type.

To determine whether any biases might have influenced their group leadership, especially since they were part of the investigative team, and to assess the credibility of the treatments, the clients' perceptions of the leaders' performance were investigated. At the time of posttesting, a summary rating of each leader was made by all of the clients in treatment. Ratings were done anonymously and with the assurance that the leader would neither see nor in any way be affected by the ratings. Ratings were done on a Group Leader Rating Form assessing five variables chosen because of their widely acknowledged importance to the therapeutic process: confidence, enthusiasm, empathy, competence, and genuineness.

The mean ratings of the same leader in one treatment compared to the other never differed significantly and in fact were always extremely close to one another. The ratings also revealed that the quality of leadership as perceived by the clients and, by inference, the credibility of both treatments were extremely high: Means on each of the five variables in each treatment were never lower than 3.5 and reached as high as 3.9, with 4 being the highest possible.

Dependent Variables

Some of the measures used involved the coding of taped interactions. To neutralize any possible coder bias predictions, all coders of taped interactions were naive as to the hypotheses being investigated, time of testing, and treatment conditions. To eliminate any possible effects of individual differences between coders, each coder was given the same number of tapes to code from each testing time and each of the experimental conditions. All of the measures used have been shown to have sufficient reliability and construct validity for a study such as this (Coufal, 1975; Guerney, 1977).

Specific Communications Skills. These were of two types: *empathic* and *expressive*. Each of the two types was measured in two ways, behaviorally and quasi-behaviorally. *Behavioral* data were obtained through the Verbal Interaction Task (Guerney, 1977), in which each mother-daughter pair engaged in four, four-minute audio-recorded discussions. In two, the daughter was asked to express her feelings openly about: (1) "something I would like to see changed in myself"; and (2) "something I would like to see changed in you." The mother's instruction during each discussion was to help her daughter express her feelings about the issue. In the other two discussions, the mother spoke about each of the two topics while the daughter was to help her express her feelings. After giving each of the participants a card with the appropriate instructions written on it, they were left alone to carry on the discussion. The *quasi-behavioral* data were obtained from a Situations Questionnaire consisting of 16 frequently encountered mother-daughter problem situations (Coufal, 1975). A short paragraph describes the situation, and the respondent then writes in the exact words she (a) *should* say and then (b) *would* say in that situation.

Expressive skills were measured in the Verbal Interaction Task by means of the Self/Feeling Awareness Scale (Guerney, 1977), which is designed to assess the degree to which a speaker's statements acknowledge his or her own feelings, values, and phenomenology as opposed to statements of "the" truth, "the" norm, or "the" correct values or outright vituperation. On the Situation Questionnaire, expressive skills were also measured by ratings on the Self/Feeling Awareness Scale and by judging whether each appropriate item contained a Direct Expression of Feelings response (Ely et al., 1973).

General Communication Patterns were measured by Beaubien's (1970) Adolescent-Parent Communication Checklist, which assesses communication style and satisfaction. The original items assess adequacy of content selection and transmission in communication by adolescents, adequacy of parental feedback to the adolescent, and adolescent satisfaction with communication. The present study employed additional items developed by Ginsberg (1971) which tapped adequacy of content selection and transmission by the parent, adequacy of adolescent feedback to the parent, and parental satisfaction with communication. The additional items are virtually identical to the original ones except for appropriate substitutions of "mother" for "daughter" (or vice versa) in the items.

General Quality of the Relationship was assessed with the following measures: (1) the Family Life Questionnaire (Guerney, 1977), designed to measure family harmony and satisfaction with family life; (2) the Dyadic Relationship Questionnaire, adapted from the Truax and Carkhuff (1967) Relationship Questionnaire, used to assess empathy and genuineness in the mother-daughter relationship; (3) the Relationship Change Scale (Guerney, 1977), measuring client perception of change in the quality of a relationship with respect to intimacy, trust, openness, and understanding; (4) the Handling Problems Change Scale (Guerney, 1977), assessing client perception of change in ability to resolve problems; and (5) the Satisfaction Change Scale (Guerney, 1977), assessing client perception of change in satisfaction with the relationship.

As would be expected, there are correlations among the measures of the dependent variables. The highest correlations were between the questionnaire measures. The Family Life Questionnaire, the Dyadic Relationship Questionnaire, and the Adolescent-Parent Communication Questionnaire correlated in the .80s with one another (Coufal, 1975). Correlations on the three "should say" measures from the Mother-Daughter Situations Questionnaire ranged from .58 through .71. None of the other correlations among the measures was as high as .50. This means, as was anticipated, that the hypotheses should not be considered as fully independent of one another. On the other hand, the correlations were not so high as to make separate analyses for each measure so redundant as to be unnecessary.

RESULTS

Treatment Comparisons

It was hypothesized that six months after treatment, in each of the three general areas being investigated (specific communication skills, general communication patterns, and the quality of the relationship): (1) the traditional treatment would be superior to no treatment; (2) the PARD group would be superior to the no-treatment group; and (3) the PARD treatment would be superior to the traditional treatment.

To get the broadest overview with respect to the comparisons of traditional, PARD, and no-treatment conditions, a 3 (treatments) × 2 (mother-daughter) × 3 (pre-, post-, follow-up) analysis of variance of repeated measures was conducted for each of the subvariables in each of the three general areas. To test the specific hypotheses comparing these treatments, a series of 2 (treatments) × 2 (pre- and follow-up) analyses of variance were then conducted for each of the subvariables. This, in turn, was followed by a series of preplanned t-tests comparing the treatments with one another at pre and at follow-up and assessing the gain from pretreatment to follow-up within each group.

Table 1 presents the following information: (1) the treatments × testing time interaction F ratios; (2) the mean scores for mothers and daughters (combined) in each of the three conditions at pre and at follow-up testing; (3) whether participants in each of the three conditions differed from one another at pretreatment and at follow-up; and (4) whether participants in each of the conditions showed significant changes from pretreatment to follow-up. To read Table 1, first note the F ratio, which shows whether any of the treatments gained

TABLE 1   Discriminant Function for Predictions of Balanced
and Imbalanced Family Groups

	F df:2, 102	Pretreatment versus Means			Follow-Up Means		
		No-Tr.	Trad.	PARD	No-Tr.	Trad.	PARD
Specific Skills: Empathic							
Behavioral Acceptance of Other	78^a	3.37	3.33	3.50	3.30^a	3.38^a	5.45^A
Quasi-Behavioral Acceptance of Other							
Should Say	31^a	2.94	3.18	3.33	3.05^a	3.04^a	5.76^A
Would Say	19^a	2.86	2.88	2.73	2.86^a	2.88^a	4.71^A
Restatement of Content–Should							
Say	20^a	.03	.14	.21	$.03^a$	$.17^a$	2.68^A
Would Say	8.2^a	.03	.03	.03	$.00^a$	$.17^a$	1.47^A
Feeling Clarification							
Should Say	24^a	.06	.22	.55	$.09^a$	$.28^a$	3.82^A
Would Say	8.5^a	.09	.03	.18	$.03^a$	$.33^a$	2.03^A
Specific Skills: Expressive							
Behavioral Self/Feeling Awareness	13^a	4.87^a	4.92^a	5.32	4.93^a	5.03^a	6.05^A
Quasi-Behavioral Self/Feeling Awareness							
Should Say	16^a	4.46	4.59	4.87	$4.70^{c*,a}$	4.20^a	6.68^A
Would Say	13^a	4.02	4.15	4.25	4.36^a	3.98^a	6.00^A
Direct Expression of Feeling							
Should Say	12^a	1.77	1.42	2.08	1.97^a	1.64^a	5.26^A
Would Say	5.3^a	1.68	1.11^c	2.05	1.68^a	1.83^a	4.50^A
General Communication Patterns							
Adolescent-Parent Check List	5.9^a	166	159	165	163^a	161^a	180^A

(continued)

TABLE 1 (Continued)

	F df:2, 102	Pretreatment versus Means			Follow-Up Means		
		No-Tr.	Trad.	PARD	No-Tr.	Trad.	PARD
		General Quality of Relationship					
Family Life Questionnaire	2.8^c	73.3	70.9	72.8	72.6^c	72.4^c	79.3^A
Dyadic Relat. Questionnaire	5.8^a	118	111	118	116^a	117^{aC}	130^A
Relationship Change	9.0^a	86.6	86.4	87.7	87.9^a	89.1^c	96.2^A
Satisfaction	2.9	.15	.31	.21	.24	.42	.08
Handling Problems	1.7	.21	.28	.16	.15	.44	.26

NOTES: Mean within each half of the table differ when they do not share an underline. Comparisons between treatments at pretreatment versus follow-up: a = p $<$ .005; b = p $<$ .01; c = p $<$ .05. A: (When there are two lowercase superscripts together, the second superscript indicates a difference with the mean to the far right.) Comparisons between preatment and follow-up within each treatment condition: A = p $<$ .005; B = p $<$ .01; C = p $<$ .05. B: Asterisk indicates a difference opposite from that expected.

more than any of the others over time. The superscripts denote the chance probability levels of each change. Second, consider each half (pretest and follow-up) of the table *independently* of the other half. The left half shows which treatments, if any, differed from the others; means that share an underline do not differ. The levels of probability are denoted by lowercase superscripts. Third, consider the two halves of the table *in relationship to one another*. This comparison reveals whether there was a significant improvement from pre to follow-up testing within a single treatment condition. The significance level for this comparison is denoted by uppercase superscripts in the right half of the table.

SPECIFIC COMMUNICATION SKILLS

Empathic skills did not differ among participants in the three conditions before treatment began. There were differential changes among the groups between then and follow-up. Neither the no-treatment participants nor the participants in the traditional treatment showed significant improvement. Nor did the participants in the no-treatment condition differ from the participants in the traditional condition at the time of follow-up. However, participants in the PARD treatment did show significant improvement in their empathic skill. Also, at follow-up they had a higher degree of empathic skills than those who had received no treatment or a traditional treatment.

All of the above-mentioned comparisons apply to each of the subvariables of empathic skills studied: (1) showing acceptance of their partner, as measured by

(a) ratings of actual discussions about important interpersonal topics, and (b) written responses to hypothetical common mother-daughter problem-situations; and (2) the use of statements reflecting (a) the views and (b) the feelings of the other, as measured by their written responses. In the variables involving written responses, the pattern of findings cited held both with respect to what the respondents reported they thought they should say and to their report of what they actually would say. (No significant tests were run, but in assessing the meaning of the self-report of responses to hypothetical situations, it seems worth mentioning that there were consistent notable differences between the mean "should say" and "would say" responses. The differences always favored the "should say" category, suggesting that there was an attempt at least to be honest and realistic in answering the questionnaire.)

Expressive skills did not differ at pretreatment among participants in the three conditions except that (a) relative to both groups, PARD participants showed higher self/feeling awareness in their discussions, and (b) relative to the participants assigned to the traditional treatment, PARD participants indicated that they would say things that contained more Direct Expression of Feeling. There were differential changes among the three groups from pretesting to follow-up. Neither the no-treatment clients nor the traditional treatment clients changed from pretesting to follow-up. Clients in no-treatment and traditional treatment did not differ from each other either at follow-up, except on one subvariable: Contrary to expectations, the participants in traditional treatment had lower Self/Feeling Awareness ("should say") at follow-up than did control clients. In contrast, participants in the PARD treatment showed significant improvement in expressive skill from pretreatment to follow-up. Also, PARD participants showed a significantly greater degree of expressive skill at the time of follow-up than those in no-treatment or traditional treatment. The findings just mentioned apply to all measures of expressive skills: (1) Self/Feeling Awareness as displayed in (a) actual discussions of significant topics and (b) written responses to hypothetical mother-daughter situations; and (2) Direct Expression of Feeling as measured by written responses. In the variables that assessed what they thought they *should* say and what they actually *would* say, the above-mentioned pattern of findings was found in both.

GENERAL COMMUNICATION PATTERNS

At pretreatment, participants in the three conditions did not differ in the quality of their general communication patterns as measured by the Parent-Adolescent Communication Checklist. There were differential changes among the groups. Neither the no-treatment nor the traditional treatment participants showed significant improvement from pretesting to follow-up, nor did they differ from each other at follow-up. However, the participants in the PARD treatment did show significant improvement in their general communication patterns. Also, at the time of follow-up the mothers and daughters in the PARD treatment showed better communication with each other than did the mothers and daughters in no-treatment or in traditional treatment.

GENERAL QUALITY OF THE RELATIONSHIP

At pretreatment, participants in the three groups did not differ from one another in the general quality of their relationships. There were differential changes among the conditions from pretesting to follow-up. Participants in traditional treatment showed a significant gain on one of the measures, the Dyadic Relationship Questionnaire. The gain, however, was not so large as to result in a significant difference from the no-treatment group at follow-up. It is worth noting, however, that although not reaching statistical significance, the mean gains of participants in traditional treatment were superior to the mean gains of the no-treatment pairs on every one of the five measures. Mothers and daughters in the PARD treatment showed significant improvement in the general quality of their relationship at follow-up, in comparison to pretreatment. Also, at follow-up these mothers and daughters had significantly better relationships with one another than did their counterparts in no-treatment or traditional treatment. These findings apply to the following subvariables: (1) family harmony and satisfaction as measured by the Family Life Questionnaire; (2) empathy and genuineness as measured by the Dyadic Relationship Questionnaire; and (3) changes in intimacy, trust, openness, and understanding between the mothers and daughters as measured by the Relationship Change Scale. The finding cited above did not pertain to two subvariables: (a) personal satisfaction derived from the relationship as measured by the Satisfaction Change Scale or (b) ability to deal effectively with their relationship problems as measured by the Handling Problems Change Scale. As measures, these two instruments appear to be weaker than the others. (The score of each is simply the difference between only two items.) Hence, the lack of significance on these two subvariables is not viewed as detracting a great deal from the overall findings of the superiority of the PARD program in improving the general quality of the relationship.

RESPONSIVENESS OF MOTHERS VERSUS DAUGHTERS

There were no significant differences in the changes of mothers versus daughters from pretest to follow-up except on two measures (restatement of content and clarification of feelings) where mothers showed greater gains than daughters with respect to what they should say. The relative superiority of the mothers was over and above the already significant gains shown by their daughters.

Booster Versus No-Booster Comparisons

It will be recalled that immediately following treatment, half of the participants in each of the two treatments were assigned to a booster condition and that the other half comprised a no-booster condition. It was hypothesized that participants in the booster program would show greater relative gain (more improvement or less decline) than participants not in such a program. To assess this, a 2 (booster, no-booster) × 2 (mothers, daughters) × 2 (posttreatment, follow-up) analysis of variance of repeated measures was first conducted for each measure. The treatment × time interaction of this analysis reveals whether there were relative differences in gain (or loss) between the two conditions. Where such differences were found, t-tests revealed whether (1) the booster and no-booster groups differed significantly from each other at the time of (a) posttesting and (b) follow-up, and (2) whether there were absolute changes in either of these groups from posttesting to follow-up. Next, to determine whether any changes attributable to being in a booster group could be more attributed to participants who had earlier been in one of the two treatments as compared to the other, the booster condition was broken down into two parts. Participants who earlier had been in the traditional condition were compared to those who earlier had been in the PARD condition. This was done by means of a 2 × 2 Analysis of Variance of Repeated Measures, with the treatment × time interaction F ratio revealing whether one type of booster participant changed more from posttesting to follow-up than the other type.

SPECIFIC COMMUNICATION SKILLS

Empathic Skills. Clients in the booster and no-booster condition did not differ significantly from one another in any of the empathic skills, either at posttreatment or at follow-up. This does not mean, however, that one of the groups might not have changed significantly from posttreatment to follow-up, nor does it mean that one group did not improve more or decline less than the other during that interval. Such significant changes could occur, and yet the groups remain insignificantly different, wherever one group of clients started out higher than the other and ended up lower. In fact, such significant differences did occur. There were such significant differences in relative change during the six-month follow-up period on four of the seven empathic skill subvariables. In their response to hypothetical mother-daughter problem situations, booster participants showed greater relative improvement on the subvariables: Acceptance of Other—Would Say ($F = 4.09$; $df = 1,70$; $p < .05$); Restatement of Content—Would Say ($F = 5.12$; $df = 1,70$; $p < .05$); Clarification of Feeling—Should Say ($F = 4.23$; $df = 1,70$; $p < .05$); and Clarification of Feeling—Would Say ($F = 17.49$; $df = 1,70$; $p < .05$). In each of these instances, the scores of the booster participants rose, while the scores of those in the no-booster condition fell. For the no-booster group, none of the declines was significant, but the gains from the posttreatment to follow-up for booster participants were significant for three of the four variables just mentioned. These were Acceptance of Other—Would Say ($t = 2.10$; $p = < .05$); Clarification of Feeling—Should Say ($t = 2.16$; $p = < .05$); and Clarification of Feeling—Would Say ($t = 2.06$; $p = < .05$).

Expressive Skills. The same pattern prevailed here. There were no significant differences between the booster and no-booster groups at posttesting or follow-up. However, the booster group showed greater relative improvement on two of the five subvariables: Self/Feeling Awareness—Should Say ($F = 4.29$; $df = 1,70$; $p < .05$) and Direct Expression of Feeling—Should Say ($F = 4.10$; $df = 1,70$; $p < .05$). The mean scores of the booster group rose on Self/Feeling Awareness—Should Say, showing a trend toward significance ($t = 1,88$; $p = .10$), and rose significantly on Direct Expression of Feeling—Should Say (t = 2.32; p < .05), while the scores of the no-booster group fell (insignificantly) on both these variables.

GENERAL COMMUNICATION PATTERNS

In this area, measured by the Parent-Adolescent Communication Checklist, there were no significant differences between the booster and no-booster group at the beginning or at the end of the follow-up period. Again, there was a rise in mean score for the booster group and a very slight fall in mean score for the no-booster group, but neither of these changes, nor the relatively greater gain of the booster group, approached statistical significance.

QUALITY OF THE RELATIONSHIP

Again, there were no significant differences at posttesting or at follow-up. Relatively greater improvement was shown by the booster group on two of the subvariables: The Family Life Questionnaire (F= 5.95; df = 1,70; p < .05) and the Dyadic Relationship Questionnaire (F = 4.56; df = 1,70; p < .05). The booster group showed a rise, not approaching significance, on the Family Life Questionnaire, while the no-booster group fell with a trend toward significance (t = 1,86; p < .10). The booster group also rose, insignificantly, on the Dyadic Relationship Questionnaire, while the no-booster group fell significantly (t = 2.32; p < .05). Unlike the other areas, in this area, while the booster group did show a gain, the difference in change between the two groups is attributable more to the decline in the no-booster group than it is to the gain in the booster group.

PARD VS. TRADITIONAL BOOSTER PARTICIPANTS

It was known from the preceding study (Guerney et al., forthcoming) that the traditional groups had shown significant gains from pre- to posttreatment in only one area—the general quality of their relationship. Thus, although there was the possibility of delayed effects, it was not surprising, in the present study, to find that for subjects who formerly had been in the traditional program, there were no significant differences or trends approaching significance (p = < .15) between booster and no-booster conditions. Since there was little in the way of gains to begin with, the booster program had little to "boost." On the other hand, with subjects who formerly were in the PARD program, a significant difference, or a trend toward a significant difference, was found for each of the variables cited in an earlier section of these results as showing a booster effect: Acceptance of Other Scale—Would Say (F = 4.01; df = 1,32; p = .05); Restatement of Content—Would Say (F = 4.38; df = 1,32; p < .05); Clarification of Feeling—Should Say (F = 4.95; df = 1,32; p < .05); Clarification of Feeling—Would Say (F = 7.54, df = 1,32; p < .05); Self/Feeling Awareness—Should Say (F = 3.20; df = 1,32; p = .08); Direct Expression of Feeling—Should Say (F = 9.48; df = 1,32; p < .005); Family Life Questionnaire (F = 3.42; df = 1,32; p = .07); Relationship Questionnaire (F = 2.41, df = 1,32; p = .13).

MAINTENANCE OF GAINS WITHOUT BOOSTER

The finding that the booster program offered some significant advantages to PARD participants in maintaining gains led to the question: "Do PARD participants who do not participate in a booster program nevertheless show lasting gains?" To answer this question, t-tests comparing pretreatment with follow-up scores for no-booster PARD participants were run on every variable which showed a significant booster effect. Despite the small N, the no-booster group was shown to maintain a significant level of gain in all instances (p values ranged from $< .05$ to $< .001$).

Differences in Responses of Mothers vs. Daughters

RESPONSIVENESS TO TREATMENT CONDITIONS

It will be recalled that with the exception of the traditional group's change on the Dyadic Relationship Scale, there were no pretreatment to follow-up changes in any of the three conditions except for the PARD condition. Thus, it is not surprising that the only condition in which mothers and daughters showed different degrees of change during that time was the PARD condition. Such change was found on only 2 of the 18 measures. Both of them were in the area of empathic skill and on quasi-behavioral measures: Restatement of Content— Should Say and Clarification of Feeling. The mothers gained more than the daughters on both measures. The daughters themselves had gained significantly from pre- to follow-up on both measures. It was just that the mothers' gains were even greater. Since one significant difference in 20 could be expected by chance, and both showed positive gains even where there was such a difference, it may be concluded that, when viewed from a follow-up perspective, mothers and daughters respond very similarly to the treatments in general and the PARD program in particular.

RESPONSIVENESS TO BOOSTER VS. NO-BOOSTER

Mothers and daughters responded differently to the two posttreatment conditions on two measures, both quasi-behavioral measures. The measures were Clarification of Feeling—Should Say and Direct Expression of Feeling— Would Say. Mothers tended to gain more than daughters in the booster condition on the former variable and more than daughters in the no-booster condition on the latter variable. The fact that differences in reaction occurred on only 2 of the 18 variables and that the changes there were in contradictory directions leads us to conclude that in fact, mothers and daughters react very similarly to a booster program.

DISCUSSION AND CONCLUSIONS

Naturally, the results of the present study should not be generalized to populations that may differ significantly from it in terms of such variables as socioeconomic status, ethnic and religious background, and degree of pathology. Within such limits, however, the results of the present study should be considered quite generalizable for the following reasons: The sample solicited was everyone who could be secured through professional referrals for therapy, public presentations, and mass media; no volunteers were screened out; the sample was composed mainly of lower-socioeconomic class individuals (higher levels seem unlikely to fare worse); participants were assigned to conditions in accord with strict random procedures; few subjects were lost in the earlier treatment-phase study, and none between posttreatment and follow-up. Also, because of the close similarity of the results obtained here with those obtained with marital couples and with fathers and sons in the studies cited in the introduction, and because of the paucity of age differences, we consider the pattern of results obtained here from the mother-daughter pairs as probably generalizable to family members in general (except for children younger than 11 or 12 years). That is, we think the burden of proof is now on those who would maintain that the results would differ significantly depending on specific family role positions. The following discussion and conclusions should be considered in light of both the limitations and the positive factors just cited.

With respect to (a) *specific communication skills* and (b) *general communication patterns,* in the earlier companion study neither the no-treatment group nor the participants in traditional treatment had shown any gains from pre- to posttreatment. Nor did one of these groups show superiority over the other at posttreatment. In the present study, six months after posttreatment the results were similar: Neither the no-treatment nor traditional treatment participants showed significant change relative to their pretreatment status, and there were no significant change differences between them at follow-up. With respect to the *quality of the general relationship,* in the earlier companion study, significant gains from pre- to posttreatment were found on some measures. Only on one of these, the Relationship Change measure, were the gains large enough to bring the traditionally treated group to a level significantly higher at posttesting than the participants who did not receive any treatment. In the present study, six months later, participants in traditional treatment scored higher than their initial scores on only one of these measures, the Dyadic Relationship Questionnaire. Because this significant gain reflected their lower initial scores rather than higher posttreatment scores, the participants in traditional treatment were not superior on this variable at posttreatment to mothers and daughters who had had no treatment. Nor were they superior at posttreatment on any of the other general relationship measures. Therefore, it seems reasonable to draw the conclusion that traditional treatment of the type studied here, even when executed with high levels of enthusiasm, competence, confidence, empathy, and genuineness in the eyes of clients, does not result in lasting improvement in clients' use of *empathic* or *expressive communication skills.* Possibly, however, this type of traditional treatment does lead to some lasting improvement in the *general quality of the clients' relationships.* However, even the isolated gain found in this area may well be attributable not to the specific nature of this traditional treatment, but rather to artifacts such as the attention the participants received, their desire to justify the time expended, their desire to please the researchers, and so forth.

In contrast, it can be concluded that RE treatment, executed with high levels of enthusiasm, competence, confidence, empathy, and genuineness in the eyes of clients, does result in lasting improvement among family members. Lasting improvement is found in *empathic and expressive communication skills, general communication patterns,* and the *general quality of the relationship.*

The lasting improvement found in specific communication skills means that clients retain the desire and knowledge necessary to make use of empathic and expressive skills in emotionally significant dialogs. The improvement in empathic skills means that clients retain the ability and inclination to replace argumentativeness with compassionate understanding of their partner's values and feelings in some emotionally significant dialogs. The improvement in expressive skills means that family members have the ability in some emotionally significant dialogs to present their beliefs, perceptions, values, and emotions to others openly and yet in a way which acknowledges their subjective, idiosyncratic nature. Both of these skills are believed to induce better conflict/problem resolution and to enhance relationships.

The last improvement in general communication patterns means that as they see it, clients maintain greater proficiency in such areas as selecting appropriate things to communicate, communicating more frequently, providing appropriate feedback to others, and feeling that they have been understood when they communicate.

The lasting improvement in the quality of the relationship means that clients retain their perceptions of greater trust, empathy, genuineness, intimacy, openness, and satisfaction in their relationships.

The fact that the RE treatment was superior in these respects to the traditional treatment is of paramount importance. It is this finding which makes both the generally negative findings for the traditional treatment and the positive findings of the RE treatment very meaningful. It makes the negative results for the traditional treatment much more meaningful than is usually the case with negative results, because positive results were simultaneously found for another treatment under comparable research conditions. Because of that comparability, the negative findings here cannot, as usually is the case, be dismissed as very likely resulting from lack of research-potency because of an inadequate number of subjects, unreliability or invalidity of measures, procedural deficiencies, and the like. More importantly, it means that the positive results obtained for the RE treatment, although they may be *enhanced* to some degree by such nonspecific treatment factors as experimenter-demand, placebo effects, and the like, cannot be *explained* in terms of such factors. Rather, they can be attributed to specific treatment factors, namely, skill-training in one or more of the types of skills taught in RE.

Lasting gains are found for PARD participants who do not participate in a booster program. However, when clients are exposed to such a program, one where they continue, at predetermined increasingly spaced intervals, to be prompted—via phone calls and group meetings—to continue to use their skills, they maintain their gains even better. This booster effect was found for some of the measures used to assess: (a) empathic and expressive communication skills and (b) the general quality of the relationship, but not on measures of general communication patterns.

On the variables studied here, mothers and daughters do not differ substantially from each other in their long-term response to: (a) the absence of treatment, (b) traditional treatment, and (c) RE. Also, mothers and daughters respond similarly one to the other when exposed to a booster program.

Future research to overcome the limited scope of the present study might profitably be directed toward: (a) comparing RE with other, less eclectic types of traditional treatments, especially ones which emphasize highly directive and interpretive techniques; (b) establishing whether the present findngs may be generalized to other types of populations, especially more deeply disturbed ones; (c) determining whether other types of RE formats are equally beneficial—for example, the dyadic format, wherein pairs are seen alone rather than in groups, or the "unilateral" format, in which only one member of a family is trained; (d) isolating the effects of the specific methodological ingredients comprising the RE approach, or comparing these with other skill training approaches, such as those which use more tangible reinforcements and/or ones in which clients more systematically tabulate data on their own performance; (e) determining whether positive results also would be obtained on the variables studied here if different measures of those variables were used—for example, with measures assessing resolution of specific presenting problems; (f) determining whether positive would be found using the same behavioral measures in different settings—for example, within the home setting; and (g) assessing entirely different issues pertinent to treatment outcome, such as whether skill use and relationship improvement generalize to nonparticipating family members and/or to persons outside the family.

REFERENCES

AUTHIER, J., K. GUSTAFSON, B. G. GUERNEY, Jr., and J. A. KASDORF (1975) "The psychological practitioner as a teacher: a theoretical-historical practical review." Counseling Psychologist 5: 31-50.

BEAUBIEN, C. O. (1970) "Adolescent-parent communication styles." Ph.D. dissertation, Pennsylvania State University.

COLLINS, J. (1977) "Experimental evaluation of a six-month conjugal therapy and relationship enhancement program," in B. G. Guerney, Jr. (ed.) Relationship Enhancement: Skill-Training Programs for Therapy, Problem Prevention, and Enrichment. San Francisco: Jossey-Bass.

COUFAL, J. D. (1975) "Preventive-therapeutic programs for mothers and adolescent daughters: relationship enhancement versus discussion methods." Ph.D. dissertation, Pennsylvania State University.

D'AUGELLI, A. R., C. S. DEYSS, B. G. GUERNEY, Jr., B. HESHENBERG, and S. SPOROF-
    SKY (1974) "Interpersonal skill training for dating couples: an evaluation of an educational
    mental health service." J. of Counseling Psychology 21: 385-389.
ELY, A., B. G. GUERNEY, Jr., and L. STOVER (1973) "Efficacy of the training phase of conjugal
    therapy." Pyschotherapy: Theory, Research, and Practice 10: 201-207.
FREMON, S. S. (1968) Children and Their Parents: Toward Maturity. New York: Harper & Row.
GINSBERG, B. (1977) "Parent-adolescent relationship development program," in B. G. Guerney,
    Jr. (ed.) Relationship Enhancement: Skill-Training Programs for Therapy, Problem Prevention,
    and Enrichment. San Francisco: Jossey-Bass.
——— (1971) "Parent-adolescent relationship development: a therapeutic and preventive mental
    health program." Ph.D. dissertation, Pennsylvania State University.
——— and E. VOGELSON (1977) "Premarital relationship improvement by maximizing empathy
    and self-discolusure: the PRIMES program," in B. G. Guerney, Jr. (ed.) Relationship Enhance-
    ment: Skill-Training Programs for Therapy, Problem Prevention, and Enrichment. San Fran-
    cisco: Jossey-Bass.
GRANDO, R. and B. G. GINSBERG (1976) "Communication in the father-son relationship: the
    parent adolescent development program (PARD)." Family Coordinator 4: 465-473.
GUERNEY, B. G., Jr. (1977) Relationship Enhancement: Skill-Training Programs for Therapy,
    Problem Prevention, and Enrichment. San Francisco: Jossey-Bass.
——— and E. L. VOGELSONG (1980) "Relationship enhancement therapy," in R. Herin (ed.)
    Psychotherapy Handbook. New York: New American Library.
GUERNEY, B. G., Jr., J. COUFAL, and E. VOGELSONG (forthcoming) "Relationship enhance-
    ment versus a traditional approach to therapeutic/preventative/enrichment parent-adolescent
    programs."
GUERNEY, B. G., Jr., L. GUERNEY, and G. STOLLAK (1971/1972) "The potential advantages
    of changing from a medical to an educational model in practicing psychology." Interpersonal
    Development 2: 238-245.
HOLLINGSHEAD, I. B. (1957) Two Factor Index of Social Position. New Haven, CT: A. B.
    Hollingshead. (mimeo)
RAPPOPORT, A. F. (1976) "Conjugal relationship enhancement program," in D.H.L. Olson (ed.)
    Treating Relationships. Lake Mills, IA: Graphic.
TRUAX, C. B. and R. R. CARKHUFF (1967) Toward Effective Counseling and Psychotherapy:
    Training and Practice. Chicago: Aldine.
VOGELSONG, E. L. (1975) "Homework exercises for relationship enhancement programs." Un-
    published.

Scatter, an index of variability of daily written classwork around the child's baseline accuracy mean, was used to identify the most inconsistent and the most stable performance among students in 13 classrooms (grades 2-5). At baseline, inconsistent students differed significantly from stable students on prior identification as educationally handicapped, math and reading classwork consistency and accuracy, and 5 self-, peer-, and teacher-rating variables. Inconsistent students were randomly assigned within classes to experimental (20) and control (20) conditions. Families of the former children wrote and carried out contracts specifying rewards for teacher-notification of a daily mean which equaled or exceeded the child's baseline mean. Intervention brought significant reductions in scatter in the target academic subject and borderline increases in accuracy and self-ratings of academic success compared to the control condition. After intervention, only math and reading accuracy and teacher identification of underachievers discriminated between the stable and experimental groups. Consensus between teachers indicated clinically significant improvement in 75% of children in the experimental condition.

53

FAMILIES AND SCHOOLS TOGETHER

Early Behavioral Intervention with High Risk Children

Elaine A. Blechman, Nancy L. Kotanchik, and Cynthia J. Taylor

Children who perform poorly at school are logical targets for early intervention (Kessler & Albee, 1975). They constitute about 75% of childhood clinical referrals (Eme, 1979). School achievement correlates with most childhood measures of adjustment and with almost every form of adult maladjustment except suicide and neurosis (Kohlberg, LaCrosse, & Ricks, 1970; Roff, Knight, & Wertheim, 1976). In the quantitative

Portions of this paper were presented at the Association for Behavior Analysis, Michigan, June 1979. NIMH Grant 31403 to the first author partly supported the study's execution. Data analysis was facilitated by cooperation of the Wesleyan Computing Center. The research was conducted with the cooperation of the Middletown, Connecticut Public Schools and the help of J. Colonghi, E. DeToro, J. Downey, P. Joyce, H. Kaplan, W. Kensel, K. Rodriguez, C. Salamone, S. Scott, L. Shearer, S. Schmutzler, M. Snyder, V. Swanton, K. Thody, N. Woodmore, and in particular N. Bischoff. Reprints may be obtained from the first author, Department of Psychology, Wesleyan University, Middletown, CT 06457.

model for classification of behavior disorders, statistical deviation from the norm is an index of risk status (Lefkowitz, 1980). The present study used scatter in children's daily math and reading classwork to identify children who often performed at school below the potential they had demonstrated, to set intervention criteria geared to children's own recent accomplishments, and to assess the effects of a collaborative home-school intervention.

Since the family accounts for much more of the variance in children's educational success than the school (Coleman, Campbell, Hobson, McPartland, Mood, Weinfeld, & York, 1966; Jencks, 1972; Mosteller & Moynihan, 1972), early intervention aiming to improve academic perfor-mance might benefit from family cooperation. Parents have often been trained as change agents for children with academic problems (Atkeson & Forehand, 1979) but home-based reinforcement has not been tested as a means of early intervention. Moreover, Atkeson and Forehand found methodological deficiencies in evaluations of home-based reinforcement: small samples, reliance on single subject rather than control group de-signs, and an absence of multiple outcome measures. The present study tested the effects of a home-based intervention system as a method of early intervention with inconsistent math and reading students.

Contingency contracting between parents and children has not always proved successful, possibly because the contracts are often written for the family by outsiders who make incorrect assumptions about what con-sequences will prove reinforcing (Blechman, 1977). A board game, *Fam-ily Contract,* has been used to help families in conflict write their own contingency contracts and to reduce reliance upon nonspecific therapist relationship skills (Blechman, in press a, b; Blechman, Olson, Schorna-gel, Halsdorf, & Turner, 1976). A game called *Solutions* guided families in the experimental condition in the present study when they negotiated their contracts.[1]

METHODS

Subjects, staff, and setting. The classes of 13 volunteer teachers (1 second, 3 third, 6 fourth, 3 fifth grades) in two public elementary schools in a city of 40,000 and a university clinic were the study's sites. The study was implemented by two special-education teachers, two class-room-behavior observers, and 14 scorers of daily classwork who were blind to the study's procedures and to children's experimental assign-ments.

Experimental design. The study had a two-way repeated measures design: Condition (Experimental, Control) × Phase (Baseline, Interven-tion). Because it was impractical to begin intervention with all children at once, teachers were randomly assigned to Baseline 1 (2 months), Base-line 2 (4 months), or Baseline 3 (5 months). The six most inconsistent children in each class were randomly assigned within class, four to the experimental, and two to the control condition. A comparison group of stable students included the three in each class with the least scatter. Random assignment within class eliminated teachers as a design factor and insured that teachers worked with only two children in the experimental condition. Twice as many children were assigned to the experimental as to the control condition because some families were expected to refuse intervention. During the first week of school a letter informed parents that if they consented, throughout the year data concerning their children would be collected. Because the classwork of all children (except for one whose parent declined) was collected throughout the year, the progress of children in the control and stable comparison conditions could be followed without revealing their identities as could the progress of children whose families declined intervention. The identities of inconsistent children in the control condition were not revealed to teachers or parents to prevent negative expectancies that might have artificially inflated the superiority of the experimental condition, and to avoid endangering children by alarming their parents but providing them with no guidance.

Identification of students. From October through May, math and reading classwork was collected daily, scored, and returned to teachers the next day. Except for classwork that could not be objectively scored (e.g., creative writing), the number of correct answers to each assignment was divided by the total number of tasks. Scores on individual assignments were averaged daily. The sum of a child's daily scores was divided by the number of days in baseline when the child attended school and was assigned classwork, yielding the child's baseline mean. Interscorer reliability was periodically and unobtrusively calculated by assigning the same classwork to two different scorers. A scatter index[2] consisting of the number of daily scores falling at least 12.5% below the child's baseline mean was calculated and used to rank children within each class. The six children with most baseline math and reading scatter were designated inconsistent; the three with least scatter were designated stable; the remainder were intermediate. Three weeks before intervention, inconsistent students in each class were randomly assigned to experimental and control conditions at a ratio of 2:1. Children assigned to the experimental condition were discussed by project and classroom teachers. Two identified children were excluded because of teacher objections.

Dependent measures. During baseline, 19 dependent variables were scored for each child of which 4 were background variables (sex, grade in school, number of parents, identification by the school as a special

---

[2] The scatter index is related to the standard deviation of daily scores since it is based on the distance of daily scores from the baseline mean. It has advantages for teachers who in dissemination of intervention procedures will be change agents, as it is easily calculated by hand from a graph of daily scores and explained to parents and children. The cut-off of 12.5% was chosen after review of the preceding year's data.

education or handicapped student). Of the 15 repeated dependent variables, 7 were objective measures of academic work and behavior. A scatter index, a mean classwork accuracy score, and a total number of daily scores were calculated for math and for reading for the entire baseline and intervention periods. Intervention was designed to increase children's daily attainment of their goals, thereby reducing scatter scores, the primary dependent variable. If children worked just hard enough to achieve (but not exceed) their goals, accuracy would not increase significantly. Therefore changes in accuracy were also measured. Total number of daily scores was calculated to determine if performance changes would be accompanied by less work assigned or less days of school attendance. On-task behavior during math class was scored to determine if inconsistent children were more off-task during baseline than classmates and to determine if behavior would spontaneously improve during intervention. During three baseline and three intervention math classes, coders rated how often each child was on-task (attended, complied with directions, asked questions, volunteered information, worked quietly). The on-task score was the number of 30-sec intervals at the end of which a child was on-task divided by the number of intervals in a session.

Eight other dependent variables collected once before intervention and once at its end, measured attitudes and perceptions. They were designed to determine whether identified children differed at baseline from classmates on nonacademic variables, and to probe during intervention for unexpected negative side-effects (Rogers-Warren & Warren, 1977). Teachers rated "how happy the child is today" on a 0 to 100 (not at all to very happy) scale. Teachers stated whether the children were underachievers based on the information used for formal identification of inconsistent students, namely, "Does this child in math and in reading often perform less well than his/her average daily performance suggests he/she can?" The children answered questions ("How happy are you today?", "How nervous are you before tests?", "How good a student are you?", "How much do you like school?", "How well do you get along with other students in your class?") by coloring in 0 to 100 (not at all to very much) thermometer-shaped scales. They did this after demonstrating correspondence between verbal responses and ratings with unrelated questions. The children nominated their three best friends in class and each child was assigned a sociometric choice score: the number of times chosen first, second, and third, weighted by rank, and divided by number of children choosing (Lindzey & Byrne, 1968).

Intervention. Families who accepted intervention came individually to the clinic for a one-hour appointment the week before the note system began. They met a project teacher, learned about intervention, and saw their children's baseline data. They spent as much as 15 minutes playing the Solutions board game, which guided them through the writing of a contingency contract and decisions about the reward for a "good news note" (when it would be given, how often, and by whom). The contract target would be the academic subject (math or reading) in which the child was most inconsistent throughout baseline, the goal would be performance at or above the child's baseline mean. After this meeting, the project teacher talked weekly by telephone to parents and children about their contract. Once the families had written their contracts, teachers began scoring children's work and calculating daily means using the method employed by project scorers. Teachers scored children's work so that a note could be sent home on the same day it was earned, and because future applications of intervention would require teachers to score papers. Each day project scorers collected all children's classwork including work of children in the experimental condition already scored by teachers. When children achieved their goals, the teachers were to fill in note forms so that they read, for example, "Good News! John's reading work was 85% correct today." When children did not achieve their goals, no notes were to go home. When teachers assigned no work, no-work-assigned-today notes were to go home. Teachers were to explain to children how they earned each note by referring to the day's work. Parents were to provide the promised reward when the note came home but to say nothing when no note came home. Throughout intervention, staff checked whether teachers sent home notes when merited by the work, and whether parents rewarded children as agreed.

RESULTS

Reliability. Inter-scorer reliability for math and reading classwork was calculated for 58 classwork samples with the formula: total agreements between raters divided by total agreements and disagreements. Inter-scorer reliability ranged from .36 to 1.00 with a mean of .94. Inter-rater reliability was calculated on 19 of 77 occasions when behavior was rated (it was economically impossible to overlap raters more often) using the formula: number of intervals in which raters 1 and 2 agreed about the occurrence or the nonoccurrence of on-task behavior divided by total intervals for the session. Inter-rater reliability ranged from .70 to 1.00 with a mean of .91. During intervention, teachers' reliability at giving notes when earned (calculated by: $A/A + B + C$, with A = number of days when notes went home and the child achieved the goal; B = number of days when no notes went home although the child achieved the goal; C = number of days when notes went home although the child didn't achieve the goal) ranged from .13 to 1.00 with a mean of .49. Teachers' reliability at withholding notes when not earned (calculated by: $D/D + B + C$, with D = number of days when no notes went home and the child did not achieve the goal) ranged from .05 to 1.00 with a mean of .33.[3] At the end of intervention, teachers guessed which children were in

[3] Estimates of teachers' reliability at giving notes, suggesting that teachers were moderately reliable, are probably overly conservative. Some teachers gave notes contingently but a day later than the papers were produced. Given their large classes, imperfect reliability is understandable and would be expected in popular application of this study's procedures; it may have engendered intermittent schedules of reinforcement slowing initial change but enhancing maintenance.

TABLE 1
SIGNIFICANT CORRELATIONS[a] BETWEEN SCATTER AND OTHER BASELINE MEASURES

	Reading	Scatter	Math	Scatter
Reading accuracy	−.72	***	−.35	***
Math accuracy	−.39	***	−.76	***
Math scatter	+.31	***		
Teacher ratings	−.25	***		
Of Child happiness				
On-task behavior	−.21	**		
Identification	+.21	**		
As underachiever				
Self-rating	−.16	*		
"Get along w. others"				
Self-rating	−.16	*		
"Likes school"				
Sociometric choice	−.15	*	−.17	*
Male	+.15	*		
# Math scores			−.25	***
# Reading scores			−.24	***

[a] Pearson's r, $n = 199$.
* $p < .05$, ** $p < .01$, *** $p < .001$.

the control condition; 28% of their guesses were correct. During intervention the staff teacher spoke weekly to each parent and child in the experimental condition. Judging by children's and parents' reports (there was no feasible way to objectively verify family compliance) parents regularly provided the rewards stipulated by their contracts.[4]

Inconsistent, intermediate, and stable students. In the 13 classrooms, 71 children were tentatively identified as inconsistent; no occupants of sixth-place tied ranks were identified, accounting for a total of 71 (not 78) identified inconsistent children. Since the performance of 10 of these children became more consistent in the last 3 weeks of baseline, only 61 children were included in the inconsistent group. There were 33 children in the stable comparison group, 105 children in the intermediate group, 38 children who were not included in this study because they left school during the year, yielding 199 children involved in data analysis. Inconsistent students were targets for early intervention on the assumption that scatter in academic performance is associated with social and behavioral as well as academic dysfunction. Pearson's r ($n = 199$) tested this assumption. As Table 1 shows, high scatter scores in reading were signif-

---

[4] For measures of teachers' and children's attitudes, no reliability information was gathered because there is no implication of an objective continuum to which these subjective ratings conform (Bereiter, 1967).

TABLE 2
BASELINE DIFFERENCES BETWEEN GROUPS

Stable vs. Intermediate vs. Inconsistent[a]

	df	F	p
Reading scatter	(2,179)	42.55	$p < .001$
Math scatter	(2,188)	49.32	$p < .001$
Reading accuracy	(2,179)	38.46	$p < .001$
Math accuracy	(2,188)	31.57	$p < .001$
Teacher choice of	(2,190)	14.72	$p < .001$

Child as underachiever

Stable vs. (intermediate and inconsistent)[b]

	df	F	p
Teacher happiness ratings	(2,189)	5.25	$p < .01$
Educationally handicapped	(2,192)	3.85	$p < .05$
Self-rating "happy"	(2,190)	3.65	$p < .05$
Self-rating "Get along w. others"	(2,190)	2.80	$p < .06$
Sociometric choice	(2,190)	2.85	$p < .06$

[a] Planned contrasts were significant, $p < .001$.

[b] Planned contrasts were significant, $p < .05$.

icantly associated with low: mean accuracy in reading and math, teacher ratings of child happiness, on-task behavior, self-ratings of "gets along with others," "likes school," and sociometric choice; and with high: math scatter, probability of being a boy, and probability of being nominated by the teacher as an underachiever. High math scatter was significantly associated with low: mean accuracy in math and reading, number of math and reading scores, and sociometric choice.

Scatter was used to identify students (regardless of level of mastery) who frequently dropped below their own high levels of performance (i.e., underachievers). Had accuracy been the criterion, students who had never mastered their classwork would have been chosen (i.e., low achievers). Teachers generally group children within a classroom in respect to their math and reading performance and assign work which is moderately difficult to each subgroup. An inspection of these groupings suggests that scatter did detect underachievers. The inconsistent students in this class came from low (15), average (19), and high (15) reading groups, and from low (6), average (37), and high (6) math groups. The stable students came from average (28), and low (5) reading groups, and from average (17) and high (16) math groups. (Teachers did not place all children in subgroups.) Of the inconsistent children, 9 had been legally identified by the school as educationally handicapped and 1 was deaf; no stable student carried such labels.

One-way ANOVAs on baseline scores and significant planned contrasts ($p < .001$) summarized in Table 2, indicate that each of the three groups differed significantly from the other two on reading scatter, math scatter, reading accuracy, math accuracy, and teacher choice of the child as an underachiever. Group means were ordered so that the identified group looked worst and the stable group looked best. The stable group had the lowest reading and math scatter, the highest reading and math accuracy, and no underachievers identified by the teacher. Moreover, as Table 2 shows, the stable differed significantly from both intermediate and identified groups on teacher happiness ratings of children, number of children identified by the school as special-education or handicapped, children's self-ratings of "happy" and of "gets along with others," and sociometric choice. Compared to children in the intermediate and identified groups, children in the stable group were rated happier by teachers, never identified as special-education or handicapped, rated themselves happier and getting along better with others, and were more often chosen as best friends by classmates. In sum, there were baseline between-groups differences on 1 of 4 background variables, 4 of 7 academic variables, and 5 of 8 attitudinal variables.

Of the 61 inconsistent students, 41 were randomly assigned to the experimental and 20 to the control conditions; 2 of the former were excluded because of teacher disagreement, yielding 39 families invited to participate in intervention. Of the 39, 20 accepted and completed intervention, 15 did not respond to the letter inviting participation, 2 accepted and dropped out of the study, and 2 accepted and moved out of town. One-way ANOVAs comparing baseline scores in the experimental (20) and experimental/declined (15) conditions found no significant differences on any of the 19 dependent measures.

Effects of intervention. Although there were no differences at baseline between the experimental and experimental/declined conditions, the latter was included in the analysis of treatment effects. Teachers and parents were told these children needed help, when parents declined intervention their children might have suffered. To test the effects of intervention, 3×2 repeated-measures ANOVAs[5] were used; Condition (Experimental, Experimental/Declined, Control) $\times$ Period (Baseline, Intervention). Figs. 1 and 2 illustrate baseline to intervention changes in scatter and accuracy. The analysis of scatter scores in the target academic subject yielded a significant Condition $\times$ Period interaction, $F(2,52) = 6.62$, $p < .01$. A subsequent test of the simple main effect of Period at each level of Condition showed that only children in the experimental condition reduced their scatter scores in the target academic subject from baseline to intervention, $F(1,19) = 14.05$, $p < .001$. The analysis of accuracy in the target academic subject yielded a significant Condition $\times$ Period interaction, $F(2,52) = 3.68$, $p < .05$. A subsequent test showed

[5] Univariate data analysis was used because the experimental hypothesis (that intervention would reduce classwork scatter) was univariate not multivariate (Cooley & Lohnes, 1971). Given evidence that intervention had its intended effects, specific questions were entertained about the side effects of intervention. Univariate tests reduced the chance of erroneous failure to reject the null hypothesis in the presence of a small number of true negative side effects (Type II error).

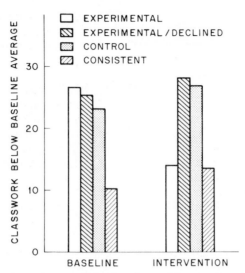

FIG. 1. Classwork consistency during baseline and intervention of children in the experimental, experimental/declined, control, and stable conditions.

that children in the experimental condition made borderline significant improvement in accuracy in the target academic subject, ($p < .06$). Children's self-ratings as students yielded a borderline interaction between Condition and Period, ($p < .07$); the means suggest that the experimental condition rated themselves better students during intervention than baseline, the experimental/declined condition did not change their ratings, and the control condition rated themselves poorer students. All conditions reported less liking for school later in the year, $F(1,52) = 5.42$, $p < .05$; and less nervousness before tests later in the year ($p < .06$).

There were significant baseline differences between children in the identified, intermediate, and stable conditions on four academic and five attitudinal repeated variables. Since intervention brought improvement in the experimental but not in the experimental/declined or control conditions (thereby ruling out regression as a competing explanation), one-way ANOVAs were used to determine what differences remained after intervention between children in the experimental and stable groups. During intervention there no longer were significant differences between the experimental and stable groups on math and reading scatter. The stable group still had significantly higher reading, $F(1,49) = 18.04$, $p < .001$, and math accuracy, $F(1,51) = 12.19$, $p < .001$. At the end of intervention teachers still chose significantly more underachievers from the experimental than from the stable group, $F(1,51) = 10.95$, $p < .01$. There was no longer a significant difference between groups in teachers' ratings of children's happiness. There was a borderline difference between groups on children's self-ratings of happiness ($p < .08$); this reversed the base-

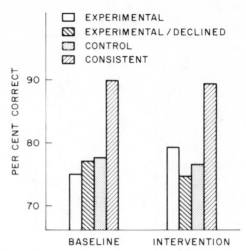

F<small>IG</small>. 2.   Classwork accuracy during baseline and intervention of children in the experimental, experimental/declined, control, and stable conditions.

line difference between groups since the happiness mean of children in the experimental condition (79.45) was higher than the mean of the stable condition (65.31). There were no longer any significant differences between experimental and stable groups on self-ratings of "gets along with others" or on sociogram scores. In sum, only 2 of 4 significant baseline differences on classwork variables, and 1 of 5 significant baseline differences on attitudinal variables distinguished the experimental and stable groups after intervention.

The classroom and the project teachers independently rated each child's improvement on 0–100 scales. Perfect agreement between these ratings indicated improvement of 50% or more in 15 of the 20 children in the experimental condition. To determine if children were more likely to benefit from intervention when teachers had nominated them as underachievers during baseline, children nominated by teachers and identified by their classwork scores were compared with children who were not nominated but were identified. The two groups did not differ; teachers agreed that ten of thirteen in the former group and five of seven in the latter improved during intervention. Families in the experimental condition were briefly interviewed during their visit before intervention ($n = 20$) and during a visit at the end of the school year ($n = 14$). According to these consumer reactions to intervention (Wolf, 1978), all families reported an improvement in children's schoolwork and liking for school. Families of children judged improved by teachers (11 of the 14 interviewed twice) were distinguished by the breadth of improvements they reported in the child (e.g., "gets along with others at home,") and in the family (e.g., "has fun together").

DISCUSSION

Students whose baseline classwork performance was stable differed on social, emotional, as well as academic measures from peers whose classwork was inconsistent. Compared to inconsistent students, stable students seem far less vulnerable to the life problems that accompany poor academic progress (Kohlberg et al., 1970). Several features recommend classwork scatter as a risk index: it is criterion referenced, it permits repeated measurement of intervention's process and outcome, it detects children whose academic performance deviates from their demonstrated potential rather than children whose unruly behavior annoys adults, or whose family origins are culturally deviant.

Inconsistent students, involved in a collaborative home-school treatment, became more consistent in their classwork performance, achieving the primary aim of intervention. Even though they would have been reinforced if they just achieved their daily goals, they often did better work than was required. This improved their classwork accuracy and was acknowledged by the children in better ratings of themselves as students. Improvement apparently was caused by the contingent reinforcement of classwork performance rather than by maturation or by some nonspecific by-product of intervention. Pointing to such a conclusion are these findings: improvement did not generalize to nontarget academic subjects, teachers' global opinions about underachievers did not change, and children in the control condition did not improve. The validity of scatter as a risk index is corroborated by the failure of inconsistent children to spontaneously improve with age. Intervention also narrowed the gap between high risk and competent children, with no evidence of undesirable side effects. Stable students were academically proficient, well regarded by peers, teachers, and themselves. After intervention only three of nine baseline differences between the experimental and stable groups remained significant.

Unlike earlier research (Atkeson & Forehand, 1979), this study used home-based reinforcement for early intervention in the regular classroom and assessed results with multiple outcome measures in a group design. Candidates for early intervention were selected by an objective measure. Internal validity was established by a comparison of inconsistent children randomly assigned to experimental and control conditions. External validity was heightened by the involvement of change agents who are found in all schools and children from all elementary school grades. The social value of change in the experimental condition was assessed by comparing progress in the experimental condition with the performance of competent children. Finally, the family was actively involved in contingency contracting. Research in progress inquires whether the last feature enhances the generality of results of home-based reinforcement.

REFERENCES

Atkeson, B. M., & Forehand, R.   Home-based reinforcement programs designed to modify classroom behaviors: A review and methodological evaluation. *Psychological Bulletin,* 1979, **86,** 1298–1308.

Bereiter, C.   Some persisting dilemmas in the measurement of change. In C. W. Harris (Ed.), *Problems in measuring change.* Madison: The University of Wisconsin Press, 1967.

Blechman, E. A.   Objectives and procedures believed necessary for the success of a contractual approach to family intervention. *Behavior Therapy,* 1977, **8,** 275–277.

Blechman, E. A.   On the road to comprehensive behavioral family intervention: An algorithm for matching families and interventions. *Behavior Modification,* in press. (a)

Blechman, E. A.   Family problem-solving training. *American Journal of Family Therapy,* in press. (b)

Blechman, E. A., Olson, D. H. L., Schornagel, C. Y., Halsdorf, M. J., & Turner, A. J.   The family contract game: Technique and case study. *Journal of Consulting and Clinical Psychology,* 1976, **44,** 449–455.

Coleman, J. S., Campbell, E. Q., Hobson, C. J., McPartland, J., Mood, A. M., Weinfeld, F. D., & York, R. L.   *Equality of educational opportunity.* Washington, DC: U.S. Office of Education, 1966.

Cooley, W. W., & Lohnes, P. R.   *Multivariate data analysis.* New York: Wiley, 1971.

Eme, R. F.   Sex differences in psychopathology: A review. *Psychological Bulletin.* 1979, **86,** 574–595.

Jencks, C.   *Inequality.* New York: Basic Books, 1972.

Kessler, M. & Albee, G. W.   *Primary prevention.* In M. R. Rosenzweig & L. W. Porter (Eds.), *Annual review of psychology, Vol. 26.* Palo Alto: Annual Reviews, 1975.

Kohlberg, L., LaCrosse, J., & Ricks, D.   The predictability of adult mental health from childhood behavior. In B. B. Wolman (Ed.), *Handbook of child psychopathology.* New York: McGraw-Hill, 1970.

Lefkowitz, M. M.   Childhood depression: A reply to Costello. *Psychological Bulletin,* 1980, **87,** 191–194.

Lindzey, G., & Byrne, D.   Measurement of social choice and interpersonal attractiveness. In G. Lindzey & E. Aronson (Eds.), *The handbook of social psychology, Vol. 2.* Reading, MA: Addison-Wesley, 1968.

Mosteller, F., & Moynihan, D. P. (Eds.), *On equality of educational opportunity: Papers deriving from the Harvard University Faculty Seminar on the Coleman Report.* New York: Vintage, 1972.

Roff, J. D., Knight, R., & Wertheim, E.   A factor-analytic study of childhood symptoms antecedent to schizophrenia. *Journal of Abnormal Psychology,* 1976, **85,** 543–549.

Rogers-Warren, A., & Warren, S. F.   *Ecological perspectives in behavior analysis.* Baltimore: University Park Press. 1977.

Wolf, M. M.   Social validity: The case for subjective measurement *or* How applied behavior analysis is finding its heart. *Journal of Applied Behavior Analysis,* 1978, **11,** 203–214.